# MATERIALS ON
# ENVIRONMENTAL LAW

By

## John-Mark Stensvaag
*Professor of Law*
*University of Iowa*
*College of Law*

**AMERICAN CASEBOOK SERIES®**

**WEST GROUP**

ST. PAUL, MINN., 1999

**ISBN** 0–314–21147–0

TEXT IS PRINTED ON 10% POST
CONSUMER RECYCLED PAPER

*To*
*Nancy*

# Preface

No matter where you are studying or who your professor may be, you will probably confront the following paradox in your environmental law course. While you are taking the course, you may be stunned by the density and volume of materials. Yet, if you enter the world of environmental law practice, you may be stunned by how much was omitted from your introductory course.

Given that inescapable paradox, this book has one overarching goal. The goal is not to help you master the field of environmental law or any portion of it in a comprehensive way. That aim would be futile. The goal is not to provide a truly up-to-date reference work on the present state of environmental law or any corner of it. Such a challenge would be impossible to meet.

It sounds trite, but it is true. The single goal of this book is to help you learn to think like an environmental lawyer. That goal is meritorious and attainable in an introductory course. How does an environmental lawyer think? It is impossible to tell you. The only way to answer this question is to show you. Welcome to the daunting, intimidating, exhilarating world of environmental law.

JOHN-MARK STENSVAAG

August, 1999

# Acknowledgments

I am indebted to the copyright holders identified below for permission to reprint excerpts from the following copyrighted materials (listed in the order they appear in the book). Every effort has been made to trace all the copyright holders but if any have been inadvertently overlooked I will be pleased to make the necessary arrangements at the first opportunity. Except for granting me permission to reprint in this book, the following copyright holders have retained all rights:

Zupko & Laures, Straws In The Wind: Medieval Urban Environmental Law (1996), copyright © 1996, by Westview Press, Inc. Reprinted by permission of Westview Press, a member of Perseus Books, L.L.C.

Anderson, The Meaning of Environmental Practice (1981), copyright © 1981, by William A. Anderson II. Reprinted by permission of William A. Anderson II.

Stensvaag, The Not So Fine Print of Environmental Law, copyright © 1994, by the Loyola of Los Angeles Law Review. Reprinted courtesy of Loyola of Los Angeles Law Review. This article originally appeared at Vol. 27:1093, April 1994.

Elliott, The Last Great Clean Air Act Book? 5 Envtl. Lawyer 321 (1998), copyright © 1998 by the American Bar Association; E. Donald Elliott. Reprinted by permission of the American Bar Association and E. Donald Elliott.

Rodgers, Defeating Environmental Law: The Geology of Legal Advantage, 15 Pace Envtl. L. Rev. 1 (1997), copyright © 1997, by Pace University School of Law. Reprinted by permission of Pace University School of Law.

Farber, Is the Supreme Court Irrelevant? Reflections on the Judicial Role in Environmental Law, 81 Minn.L.Rev. 547 (1997), copyright © 1997, by the Minnesota Law Review Foundation. Reprinted by permission of the Minnesota Law Review Foundation.

Fritsch, Friend Or Foe? Nature Groups Say Names Lie, N.Y. Times (Mar. 25, 1996) at A1, col. 5, copyright © 1996, by The New York Times. Reprinted by permission.

THE FAR SIDE, by Gary Larson, copyright © 1984 FARWORKS, INC. Used by permission. All rights reserved.

Commoner, The Closing Circle (1971), copyright © 1971, by Barry Commoner. Reprinted by permission of Alfred A. Knopf Inc.

Ehrlich & Holdren, Review: The Closing Circle, 14 Environment 24 (Apr. 1972). Reprinted with permission of the Helen Dwight Reid Educational Foundation. Published by Heldref Publications, 1319

Eighteenth Street N.W., Washington, D.C. 20036-1802. Copyright ©
1972.

The Worldwatch Institute, The Global Environment and Basic Human
Needs (1978). Reprinted by permission.

World Dynamics, 25 Bulletin of the American Academy of Arts and Sciences (1972), copyright © 1972, by Jay W. Forrester. Reprinted by
permission of Jay W. Forrester. Material based on "World Dynamics" by Jay W. Forrester, now available from Pegasus Communications, Waltham, MA.

Meadows, Meadows & Randers, Beyond The Limits (1992), copyright ©
1992, by Donella H. Meadows, Dennis L. Meadows & Jørgen
Randers. Reprinted from *Beyond the Limits* copyright © 1992, by
Meadows, Meadows & Randers. With permission from Chelsea
Green Publishing Co., White River Junction, Vermont.

Kaysen, The Computer that Printed Out W*O*L*F*, 50 Foreign Affairs
660 (July 1972). Reprinted by permission of Foreign Affairs, July
1972. Copyright © 1972 by the Council on Foreign Relations, Inc.

Starr, The Growth Of Limits, Saturday Review 30 (Nov. 24, 1979). Reprinted by permission of The Saturday Review, © 1979, General
Media International, Inc.

Simon, Resources, Population, Environment: An Oversupply of False
Bad News, 208 Science 1431 (1980). Excerpted with permission
from Simon, Resources, Population, Environment: An Oversupply of
False Bad News, 208 Science 1431 (1980). Copyright © 1980 American Association for the Advancement of Science.

Julian Simon, 65, Optimistic Economist, Dies, N.Y. Times, Feb. 12,
1998, at B11, col. 1, copyright © 1998, by The New York Times. Reprinted by permission.

Hardin, The Tragedy Of The Commons, 162 Science 1243 (Dec. 13,
1968). Reprinted with permission from Hardin, The Tragedy Of The
Commons, 162 Science 1243 (1968). Copyright © 1968 American
Association for the Advancement of Science.

How Poverty Breeds Overpopulation (And Not the Other Way Around),
in Bread for the World, The Challenge of World Hunger 25A-26A
(1980), copyright © 1980 by Bread for the World. Reprinted by permission of Bread for the World.

Hardin, The Survival of Nations and Civilizations, 172 *Science* 1297
(1971). Excerpted with permission from Hardin, The Survival of
Nations and Civilizations, 172 Science 1297 (1971). Copyright ©
1971 by The American Association for the Advancement of Science.

Ophuls & Boyan, Ecology and the Politics of Scarcity Revisited (1992),
copyright © 1992, by W.H. Freeman and Company. Reprinted by
permission of A. Stephen Boyan, Jr.

Richard A. Posner, The Economics of Justice 76 (1981). Reprinted by permission of the publisher from THE ECONOMICS OF JUSTICE by Richard Posner, Cambridge, Mass.: Harvard University Press, Copyright © 1981 by the President and Fellows of Harvard College.

Cline, Gingrich: Speaker, Author—But King of the Jungle?, N.Y. Times (July 13, 1995) at A17, col. 1, copyright © 1995, by The New York Times. Reprinted by permission.

Calabresi & Melamed, Property Rules, Liability Rules, and Inalienability: One View of the Cathedral, 85 Harv. L. Rev. 1089 (1972), copyright © 1972 by the Harvard Law Review Association. Reprinted by permission of the Harvard Law Review Association.

Restatement (Second) of Torts (1977), copyright © 1977 by The American Law Institute. Reprinted by permission of The American Law Institute.

Pierce, Encouraging Safety: The Limits of Tort Law and Government Regulation, 33 Vand. L. Rev. 1281 (1980), copyright © 1980 by the Vanderbilt Law Review. Reprinted by permission of the Vanderbilt Law Review.

Meckler, School Bus Handrails Deadly—Problem Still Not Fixed, Despite Deaths, Recall, Rocky Mountain News, Apr. 5, 1997, at 2A, copyright © 1997 by the Associated Press. Reprinted by permission of the Associated Press.

Driscoll, Wieners or Losers; Chicago Sausage Maker Says Either It or Big Residential Proposal Must Go, Chicago Tribune, Mar. 3, 1996, at C3, copyright © 1996 by the Associated Press. Reprinted by permission of the Associated Press.

Page, A Generic View of Toxic Chemicals and Similar Risks, 7 Ecol. L.Q. 207 (1978), copyright © 1978 by the Ecology Law Quarterly. Reprinted by permission of the Ecology Law Quarterly.

Krier, Environmental Litigation and the Burden of Proof, in Law and the Environment 105 (Malcolm F. Baldwin & James K. Page eds. 1970), copyright © 1970 by The Conservation Foundation. Reprinted by permission of The Conservation Foundation.

Ruckelshaus, Risk in a Free Society, 14 Envtl. L. Rep. 10190 (1984), copyright © 1984 by the Environmental Law Institute®. Reprinted by permission from the *Environmental Law Reporter®*. All rights reserved.

Rosenthal, Gray & Graham, Legislating Acceptable Cancer Risk from Exposure to Toxic Chemicals, 19 Ecol. L.Q. 269 (1992), copyright © 1992 the Ecology Law Quarterly. Reprinted by permission of the Ecology Law Quarterly.

Stensvaag, Regulating Radioactive Air Emissions from Nuclear Generating Plants: A Primer for Attorneys, Decisionmakers, and Intervenors, 78 N.W.U. L. Rev. 1 (1983), copyright © 1983 by the Northwestern University School of Law. Reprinted by permission of the Northwestern University School of Law.

Atcheson, The Department of Risk Reduction or Risky Business, 21 Envtl.L. 1375 (1991), copyright © 1991 by Environmental Law. Reprinted by permission of Environmental Law.

Shere, The Myth of Meaningful Environmental Risk Assessment, 19 Harv. Envtl. L. Rev. 409 (1995), copyright © by the Harvard Environmental Law Review. Reprinted by permission of the Harvard Environmental Law Review.

DILBERT (Apr. 27, 1999), copyright © 1998 by United Feature Syndicate, Inc. Reprinted by permission of United Feature Syndicate, Inc.

Hudson, Sierra Club v. Department of Interior: The Fight to Preserve The Redwood National Park, 7 Ecol. L. Q. 781 (1978), copyright © 1978 by the Ecology Law Quarterly. Reprinted by permission of the Ecology Law Quarterly.

Swanlund, Redwood Creek Photograph #4638 (1977). Reprinted by permission of Save-the-Redwoods League.

Araiza, Democracy, Distrust, and the Public Trust: Process-Based Constitutional Theory, the Public Trust Doctrine, and the Search for a Substantive Environmental Value, 45 U.C.L.A. L. Rev. 385 (1997). Originally published in 45 UCLA L. Rev. 385. Copyright © 1997, The Regents of the University of California. Reprinted by permission of The Regents of the University of California. All Rights Reserved.

Huffman, A Fish Out Of Water: The Public Trust Doctrine in a Constitutional Democracy, 19 Envtl. L. 527 (1989). Copyright © 1989 by Environmental Law 1989. Reprinted by permission of Environmental Law.

Egan, Unlikely Alliances Attack Property Rights Measures, N.Y. Times (May 15, 1995) at A1, col. 4, copyright © 1995 by The New York Times. Reprinted by permission.

Buccino, Turmoil Over "Takings": How H.R. 1534 Turns Local Land Use Disputes into Federal Cases, 28 Envtl. L. Rep. 10083 (1998), copyright © 1998 Environmental Law Institute®. Reprinted by permission from the *Environmental Law Reporter*®. All rights reserved.

Sugameli, Takings Bills Would Harm People and Property, 5 Envtl. Law at Maryland 4 (Winter 1997), copyright © 1997 by Environmental Law at Maryland. Reprinted by permission of Environmental Law at Maryland.

Cushman, Senate Halts Property Bill Backed by G.O.P., N.Y. Times (Jul. 14, 1998) at A13, col. 4, copyright © 1998 by The New York Times. Reprinted by permission.

Verhovek, Texas Joins Parade of States Colliding with Clean Air Act, N.Y. Times, Feb. 14, 1995 at A1 col. 1, copyright © 1995 by The New York Times. Reprinted by permission.

Johannes, New EPA Flexibility on Emissions Puts Texas Officials in a Costly Bind, Wall St. J., Dec. 14, 1994, at T1. Reprinted by permission of Dow Jones, Inc. via Copyright Clearance Center, Inc. © 1994 by Dow Jones and Company, Inc. All Rights Reserved Worldwide.

Aeppel, Not in My Garage: Clean Air Act Triggers Backlash as Its Focus Shifts to Driving Habits, Wall St. J., Jan. 25, 1995 at A1. Reprinted by permission of Dow Jones, Inc. via Copyright Clearance Center, Inc. © 1995 by Dow Jones and Company, Inc. All Rights Reserved Worldwide.

Dwyer, The Practice of Federalism Under the Clean Air Act, 54 Md. L. Rev. 1183 (1995), copyright © 1995 by the Maryland Law Review. Reprinted by permission of the Maryland Law Review.

Recent Legislation: Unfunded Mandates Reform Act of 1995, 109 Harv. L. Rev. 1469 (1996), copyright © 1996 by The Harvard Law Review Association. Reprinted by permission of The Harvard Law Review Association.

Jaber, Comment, Unfunded Federal Mandates: An Issue of Federalism or a "Brilliant Sound Bite"?, 45 Emory L.J. 281 (1996), copyright © 1996 by the Emory Law Journal. Reprinted by permission of the Emory Law Journal.

Illinois Suspends Trip Reduction Program, 25 [Curr. Dev.] Env. Rep. (BNA) 2301 (1995). Reprinted with permission from *Environment Reporter*, Vol. 25, excerpts from pages 2301-03 (Copyright © 1985) by The Bureau of National Affairs, Inc. (800-372-1033) <http://www.bna.com>

Rodgers, Environmental Law: Air and Water (1986), copyright © 1986 by West Group. Reprinted by permission.

Hines, A Decade of Nondegradation Policy in Congress and the Courts: The Erratic Pursuit of Clean Air and Clean Water, 62 Iowa L. Rev. 643 (1977), copyright © 1977 by the Iowa Law Review. Reprinted with permission.

Quarles, Federal Regulation of New Industrial Plants, Env. Rep. (BNA) Monograph No. 28 (1979). Reprinted with permission from Environment Reporter, Monograph No. 28, excerpts from pages 7-15 (Nov. 21, 1980). Copyright © 1980 by The Bureau of National Affairs, Inc. (800-372-1033) <http://www.bna.com>

Raffle, Prevention of Significant Deterioration and Nonattainment Under the Clean Air Act—A Comprehensive Review, Env. Rep. (BNA) Monograph No. 27 (1979). Reprinted with permission from Environment Reporter, Monograph No. 27, excerpts from pages 3-7 (May 4, 1979). Copyright © 1979 by The Bureau of National Affairs, Inc. (800-372-1033) <http://www.bna.com>

D.C. Circuit Upholds EPA Rules on Air Act Non-Compliance Penalties, 13 [Curr. Dev.] Env. Rep. (BNA) 1571 (1983). Reprinted with permission from Environment Reporter, Vol. 13, excerpts from page 1571. Copyright © 1983 by The Bureau of National Affairs, Inc. (800-372-1033) <http://www.bna.com>

Reitze, A Century of Air Pollution Control Law: What's Worked; What's Failed; What Might Work, 21 Envtl. L. 1549 (1991), copyright © 1991 by Environmental Law. Reprinted by permission of Environmental Law.

Axline, Environmental Citizen Suits (1992), copyright © 1991, Lexis Law Publishing. Reprinted with permission from *Environmental Citizen Suits* by Michael D. Axline. Lexis Law Publishing Charlottesville, VA (800)446-3410. All Rights Reserved.

Cline, Clean Air Act Citizen Suits on Rise, Precautions Needed, Attorney Warns, 29 [Curr. Dev.] Env. Rep. (BNA) 452 (1998). Reprinted with permission from Environment Reporter, Vol. 29, excerpts from page 452. Copyright © 1998 by The Bureau of National Affairs, Inc. (800-372-1033) <http://www.bna.com>

Martel, Clean Air Violations May Become Easier to Prove (Mar. 1, 1996), copyright © 1996 by Arnold & Porter. Reprinted by permission of Arnold & Porter.

Glaberson, Novel Antipollution Tool is Being Upset by Courts, N.Y. Times, Jun. 5, 1999, at A1, col. 1, copyright © 1999 by The New York Times. Reprinted by permission.

Cushman, EPA and States Found to be Lax on Pollution Law, N.Y. Times, Jun. 7, 1998, at 1 col. 1, copyright © 1998 by The New York Times. Reprinted by permission.

Wald, U.S. Agencies Use Negotiations to Preempt Lawsuits Over Rules, N.Y. Times, Sep. 23, 1991 at A1, col. 1, copyright © 1991 by The New York Times. Reprinted by permission.

Rechtschaffen, Deterrence vs. Cooperation and the Evolving Theory of Environmental Enforcement, 71 So. Cal. L. Rev. 1181 (1998), copyright © 1998 by the Southern California Law Review. Reprinted by permission of the Southern California Law Review.

Ruff, Price Pollution Out of Existence, L.A. Times, Dec. 7, 1969, at G7, copyright © 1969 by the Los Angeles Times. Reprinted by permission of the Los Angeles Times.

The Brookings Institution, Setting National Priorities: The 1973 Budget (1972), copyright © 1972 by The Brookings Institution. Reprinted by permission of The Brookings Institution.

Hoppe, A License to Steal, S.F. Chronicle, Feb. 8, 1971, at 39, copyright © 1971 by the San Francisco Chronicle. Reprinted by permission of the San Francisco Chronicle.

Houck, Ending the War: A Strategy to Save America's Coastal Zone, 47 Md. L. Rev. 358 (1988), copyright © 1988 by Oliver A. Houck. Reprinted by permission of Oliver A. Houck.

Houck, TMDLs: The Resurrection of Water Quality Standards-Based Regulation Under the Clean Water Act, 27 Envtl. L. Rep. 10329 (1997), copyright © 1997 by the Environmental Law Institute®. Reprinted by permission from the Environmental Law Reporter®. All rights reserved.

Houck, TMDLs, Are We There Yet? The Long Road Toward Water Quality-Based Regulation Under the Clean Water Act, 27 Envtl. L. Rep. 10391 (1997), copyright © 1997 by the Environmental Law Institute®. Reprinted by permission from the Environmental Law Reporter®. All rights reserved.

Stever, Waste Load Allocation, in 2 Law of Environmental Protection (Sheldon M. Novick, ed. 1998), copyright © 1998 by the Environmental Law Institute®. Reprinted by permission of the Environmental Law Institute®. All rights reserved.

Houck, The Regulation of Toxic Pollutants Under the Clean Water Act, 21 Envtl. L. Rep. 10528 (1991), copyright © 1991 by the Environmental Law Institute®. Reprinted by permission from the Environmental Law Reporter®. All rights reserved.

Dernbach, The Unfocused Regulation of Toxic and Hazardous Pollutants, 21 Harv. Envtl. L. Rev. 1 (1997), copyright © 1997 by the President and Fellows of Harvard College. Reprinted by permission of the President and Fellows of Harvard College and the Harvard Environmental Law Review.

Worobec, An Analysis of the Resource Conservation and Recovery Act, 11 [Curr. Dev.] Env. Rep. (BNA) 634 (1980), Reprinted with permission from Environment Reporter, Vol. 11, excerpts from page 634-40. Copyright © 1980 by The Bureau of National Affairs, Inc. (800-372-1033) <http://www.bna.com>

EPA Issues RCRA's "Cradle-to-Grave" Hazardous Waste Rules 10 Envtl. L. Rep. 10130 (1980), copyright © 1980 by the Environmental Law Institute®. Reprinted by permission from the Environmental Law Reporter®. All rights reserved.

Stensvaag, Hazardous Waste Law and Practice (1995), copyright © by 1995 by John Wiley & Sons. Reprinted by permission of Aspen Publishers, Inc.

Stensvaag, Hazardous Waste Law: An Essential Introduction for the Non-Specialist, 17 Vanderbilt Lawyer 16 (1987), copyright © 1987 by John-Mark Stensvaag. All rights reserved.

Novick & Stever, The Regulation of Hazardous Waste, in 3 Law of Environmental Protection (Sheldon M. Novick, ed. 1998), copyright © 1998 by the Environmental Law Institute®. Reprinted by permission of the Environmental Law Institute®. All rights reserved.

Mandelker, NEPA Law and Litigation (2d ed. 1998), copyright © 1998 by West Group.

Serpe, Reviewability of Environmental Impact Statements on Legislative Proposals after *Franklin v. Massachusetts*, 80 Cornell L. Rev. 413 (1995), copyright © 1995 by the Cornell Law Review. Reprinted by permission of the Cornell Law Review.

Senators, Witness Disagree on Effect of NEPA on Statutory Role of Agencies, 2 [Curr. Dev.] Env. Rep. (BNA) 1354 (1972). Reprinted with permission from Environment Reporter, Vol. 2, excerpts from page 1354. Copyright © 1972 by The Bureau of National Affairs, Inc. (800-372-1033) <http://www.bna.com>

Sax, The (Unhappy) Truth About NEPA, 26 Okla. L. Rev. 239 (1973), copyright © 1973 by the Oklahoma Law Review. Reprinted by permission of the Oklahoma Law Review.

Lundberg, E-mail Message (Jul. 28, 1995), copyright © 1995 by Constance K. Lundberg. Reprinted by permission of Constance K. Lundberg.

Sax, *Environmental Law: More Than Just a Passing Fad*, 19 U. Mich. J.L. Ref. 797 (1986), copyright © 1986 by the University of Michigan Law School. Reprinted by permission of the University of Michigan Journal of Law Reform.

Pollack, Reimagining NEPA: Choices For Environmentalists, 9 Harv. Envtl. L. Rev. 359 (1985), copyright © 1985 by the President and Fellows of Harvard College. Reprinted by permission of the President and Fellows of Harvard College and the Harvard Environmental Law Review.

I am also grateful to the following research assistants: Bruce Alford, Deborah Birgen, Carmen Chittick, Chris Douglass, David Tweeten, and Chris Walker.

# Summary of Contents

## PART THREE. ENVIRONMENTAL
## LEGISLATION

# Table of Contents

## PART THREE.  ENVIRONMENTAL LEGISLATION

# Table of Cases

The principal cases are in bold type. Cases cited
or discussed in the text are roman type.
References are to pages.

xlv

# Table of Statutes and Regulations

# MATERIALS ON
# ENVIRONMENTAL LAW

*

# Part One

## PERSPECTIVES

# Chapter One

# INTRODUCTION

---

## A. ENVIRONMENTAL LAW ORIGINS

In 1969—the year that humans first set foot on the moon—a law school course in the subject of environmental law would have been most unusual. Scarcely anyone perceived that a separate body of law even existed. But two events in early 1970 marked the beginning of an extraordinary surge of activity in this previously unrecognized field: (1) the National Environmental Policy Act (NEPA) was signed into law on January 1, 1970; and (2) the first Earth Day was held later that spring. Environmental law—as we now know it—first took shape in those opening months of 1970. In the intervening decades, the field has exploded in scope and importance.

Nevertheless, modern environmental law was not created out of nothing. Indeed, its origins long precede the founding of America.

## RONALD E. ZUPKO & ROBERT A. LAURES, STRAWS IN THE WIND: MEDIEVAL URBAN ENVIRONMENTAL LAW

### 1, 5, 33, 35, 37, 85, 111 (1996)

Environmental awareness is portrayed as a thoroughly modern movement, arising out of the tumult of a half-century of war and depression * * * .

[W]e present evidence that human beings have been interested in the quality of the environment for almost as long as there are written records available. Men and women have long deemed it their responsibility to tend to the environment and the world about them. * * *

Environmental law in its most rudimentary forms can be detected in Italian municipal law codes as early as the eleventh and twelfth centuries. * * * [T]he town elites realized early on that their visions of their towns and their aspirations for a particular quality of life would never be implemented without the force of law. * * *

Recent scholarship has demonstrated that medieval people were driven to create an environment as clean and healthy as their technology, priorities, and civilization permitted. * * *

[L]aws were enacted to control the economic behavior of various classes of tradesmen. * * * One approach employed by the local elites to limit pollution within the city was the restriction of the number of places where butcher shops might be located. * * *

Limiting the number of butcher shops had the practical effect of reducing the volume of the waste products dumped within the town's environment. Butcher shops in each town slaughtered and sold thousands of animals annually; the inevitable result of this activity was thousands of pounds of blood, entrails, and other waste products. * * * In Bologna, Bassano, and Verona * * * butchers were explicitly told to take the waste products out of the city. * * *

[T]he Veronese code * * * [provided]: "No one should throw or cause anything to be thrown into the River Adige, or into its streams, narrows, banks, or into any sewers during the day." * * *

To maintain a constant supply of fish, legislation was enacted mandating that fishnets were to have meshes "two fingers" wide, multihooked lines were not to be used, and no one was permitted to fish throughout the month of February. * * *

[Piran] recognized that there was a conflict of interest between its butchers and bakers. Meat was, and still is, a rather inefficient means of providing adequate protein in the diet of a population; that is, it takes a disproportionate amount of pastureland to produce one pound of meat. Consequently, meat was expensive and was eaten primarily by the well-to-do classes. Bread products were produced more efficiently (that is, with a greater yield of food per acre) than meat and were therefore cheaper and more readily available to the poorer classes. The statute makers recognized this problem and limited the amount of precious arable land that could be used to pasture animals. For instance, in 1307, the Piranese statute makers declared that "no one can enter or keep more than ten * * * [parcels] of the land belonging to the communes or to anyone else to pasture their animals. And they are obligated to pasture their animals on those lands for no more than four years." * * *

The efforts of northern Italian medieval cities to control and improve their environments were like "straws in the wind," in the sense that the phrase carries with it the notion of an event that acts as * * * the harbinger of a future trend. The medieval tradition of environmental legislation did not represent a thoroughly integrated movement for the protection of the environment * * *. Rather, it represented the efforts, often incomplete, sporadic, and sometimes misguided, of a class of literate, concerned political leaders at the local level attempting to provide for a respectable quality of life for the citizens of their community. They realized that their physical environment was a fragile, frequently damaged, but ultimately repairable milieu over which they exercised dominion, for better or for worse.

## B. DEFINING ENVIRONMENTAL LAW

What is environmental law? What would a fully comprehensive course in this subject encompass? Someone has suggested that the environment is the house created on earth for living things. Environmental law, then, is "the law of planetary housekeeping." As appealing as that definition may be, it does little good in trying to explain what is within and without the scope of this discipline. Alternatively, one could argue that this legal field should be as all-embracing as the cosmology of Carl Sagan; after all, the environment can be defined as "the universe and all that surrounds it." But most environmental lawyers are more modest than that and try to place limits on their claimed expertise. Those limits are unclear and evolving.

Fortunately, no real-world consequences hinge on the correct characterization of an issue as one of environmental law. For now, the following description may suffice: environmental law seeks to control the impacts of human beings and their activities on the natural environment and on natural resources, recognizing that these impacts may also harm human beings.

## C. ENVIRONMENTAL PRACTICE

What does an environmental lawyer do? In the following memorandum to summer associates, a senior partner now in the Washington, D.C., law firm of Winston & Strawn summarizes the practice of environmental lawyers. The memo is as useful today as when it was first written.

## WILLIAM A. ANDERSON II, THE MEANING OF ENVIRONMENTAL PRACTICE

1-3, 7-9, 6, 9-10 (1981)

Environmental law, perhaps because of its sometime Alice-in-Wonderland quality, enjoys a mystique that often obscures its pervasive reach. Riding the wave of environmentalism for the past decade, the federal and state legislatures have passed laws to regulate an astonishing array of activities, from major new enterprises to common everyday conduct. Virtually any activity that poses the potential for some environmental impact is apt to be subject to some form of regulation. * * *

Environmental law is, for the most part, a statutory creature: a gangly dragon designed by a zealous committee. Its legislative roots mean that it often reaches farther and applies more broadly than necessary for valid legislative purposes; that it tends to embrace extreme solutions; that it has less flexibility than the common law to adjust for peculiar circumstances; and that it often leaves controversial policy questions unanswered. This latter characteristic means the agencies, and sometimes the courts, are left to grope for the answers to major social and economic policy questions. * * *

The uninitiated might think the federal constellation of laws enough to fill the galaxy. But one of the perplexing features of environmental law is that any given statutory scheme is likely to be two-tiered: federal statutes are replicated, with differing variations, in state laws. Whether the problem is one of air, water, solid waste or some other brand, neither the federal nor the state law alone will yield a complete answer. Both must be consulted. And often the two will yield conflicting answers * * * .

The lawyer's role in the environmental dragon's thicket is similar to his or her role in other substantive areas. Clients expect the attorney to be shaman, interpreter, intermediary, advocate, and defender. Functionally, an environmental lawyer serves the client in the six principal ways discussed below.

### LEGISLATIVE ASSISTANCE

Most environmental law is born in the federal and state legislatures. Here lawyers can be instrumental in lobbying activities designed to protect their clients' interests. Successful lobbying requires a close working relationship with key committee staffers, a reputation for honesty and integrity, a combination of substantive knowledge and legal craftsmanship and more than a modicum of "Hill Savvy." * * *

### REPRESENTATION IN AGENCY RULEMAKING PROCEEDINGS

In the environmental area, Congress relies heavily on administrative agencies to implement statutes through rulemaking proceedings. In these rulemakings, whether involving simple notice-and-comment procedures or more elaborate hearings, the lawyer's role is multifaceted. As in other areas of administrative practice, he or she must first assure that the procedures afford ample opportunity for the expression of the client's views. Next, the attorney must see that those views are properly presented and substantiated, where appropriate, by relevant data. In short, he or she must try to shape the rule to the client's advantage and make a record for judicial review if the effort fails.

### APPEAL OF REGULATIONS

Almost all federal environmental statutes contain exclusive (and preclusive) judicial review procedures. Judicial review must be sought, if at all, in a prescribed fashion and within a set time. Thereafter, the rules are insulated from collateral attack in civil or criminal enforcement proceedings. It has therefore become customary, almost necessary, for parties aggrieved by new environmental regulations to seek prompt judicial review * * * . The lawyer's role at this juncture is, of course, to scour the rulemaking record, to prepare the briefs and other pleadings, and to argue the case, normally before a United States Court of Appeals.

## COMPLIANCE COUNSELING

Once the statutes are passed, regulations adopted, and appeals exhausted, affected parties need to know whether they are in compliance with applicable requirements. This is where the lawyer becomes sentry, interpreter, shaman, and sometimes intermediary. There is a vast disparity in companies' awareness of environmental requirements. Some know enough to seek a lawyer's advice; others do not. At one extreme, the lawyer must either be vigilant and aggressive to alert the clients, or must be content to have them call when only a magician can help. At the other, the lawyer can comfortably rely on the client's awareness and judgment.

Many companies are now beginning to conduct regular environmental compliance audits with help from in-house or outside counsel. The audit team looks to the lawyer to identify applicable regulations, divine their meaning, and advise company personnel on whether the company's operations are in compliance with those regulations. As often as not, an audited facility will prove to be in violation. The company then typically turns to the lawyer for advice on how best to attain compliance or to change the rule. * * *

In the business and financial realm, mergers, acquisitions, loans, and SEC filings are all occasions for examination of environmental compliance. Under federal law, for instance, there are restrictions on the transferability of permits. These restrictions must be satisfied in any acquisition or merger that entails the transfer of title to permitted property. Perhaps more importantly, without careful attention to environmental matters, the acquiring company may find that it has "bought" unexpected problems. Lending institutions are also increasingly sensitive to the potential for environmental laws to stymie or disrupt projects. They frequently insist on an opinion of counsel regarding environmental compliance before they will issue a commitment letter for a loan. And the SEC has begun to demand registrants to include statements of corporate environmental policy and compliance status in filings before the Commission. * * *

## ASSISTANCE IN OBTAINING LICENSES AND PERMITS

Environmental permits are rapidly becoming the *sine qua non* for both new and existing business enterprises. Ideally, an environmental permits lawyer will be involved in the permit process from project conception until receipt of all final permits. In the early stages, the environmental lawyer helps by defining legal requirements; reviewing environmental study proposals and results; and assuring the completeness of permit application materials. Once the application is completed, one must typically negotiate permit terms and conditions. This too is lawyer's work. Contested permit proceedings normally mean hearings, in which the lawyer will prepare or review expert testimony, conduct direct examination of the applicant's witnesses, cross-examine others, and otherwise represent the applicant. At the conclusion of the hearing, the lawyer normally takes on proposed findings of fact and conclusions of law, often submitted in the form of briefs. Occasionally, the decision of the hearing officer will lead to administrative or judicial appeals, in which the lawyer assumes the traditional role of appellate advocate.

### DEFENSE IN ENFORCEMENT ACTIONS

Environmental law is endowed with an impressive arsenal of enforcement weapons, ranging from notices of violation and administrative penalties to staggering civil fines and criminal penalties. The typical federal statute provides for civil penalties of up to $25,000 per day per violation. These penalties can be visited on "any person," including responsible corporate officers as well as the corporation. Criminal penalties of a similar amount can be coupled with imprisonment of up to one year per day of violation. Although liability for criminal penalties normally depends upon the violation's being "willful," liability for the civil penalties can accrue without regard to knowledge or intent. Add to these penalty provisions potential exposure of up to $50 million for clean-up costs under some statutes, and it is apparent that an unwitting violator can quickly be exposed to staggering liability. The dragon's bite can be as severe as its bark.

The lawyer's role in this context is that of defense counsel. He or she must review the client's conduct, assess the government's case, devise a defense strategy, and advise the client on settlement prospects. Three features differentiate environmental enforcement actions from other enforcement cases. First, the tight self-monitoring and self-reporting requirements make it easy for the government to prove its case and difficult to set up a successful defense. Failure to report a violation is itself a violation. Second, technology-forcing standards and impossible deadlines mean no one can comply; the system is sustained by the generous exercise of prosecutorial discretion. Then, when the government assumes an enforcement posture, vengeance supplants generosity. The often continuing nature of any violation is the third distinguishing feature. It can expose defense counsel to potential prosecution on various conspiracy or aiding and abetting theories. It can also present difficult ethical questions.

## D. SOME PECULIAR ATTRIBUTES OF ENVIRONMENTAL LAW

All fields of law exhibit unique attributes. Environmental law is no exception. The following readings alert you to some of the oddities of American environmental law.

## JOHN-MARK STENSVAAG, THE NOT SO FINE PRINT OF ENVIRONMENTAL LAW

27 Loy. L.A. L. Rev. 1093, 1093-94, 1102-03 (1994)

In the [past] twenty-five years * * * one development [is] more significant than any other: environmental law has been transformed from a discipline of broad phrases into a realm dominated by fine print. * * * [S]uch vague concepts as "reasonable man," "prudent and feasible alternative," "abnormally dangerous activity," "suitability to the locality," "intentional invasion," "reasonable use," "gravity of harm," and "utility of conduct" * * * were the hallmark of the first Earth Day's environmental law.

Today, * * * a regime of broad phrases fails adequately to address modern environmental problems. The solution, as everyone knows, has been fine print—particularized wording crafted by legislatures and administrative agencies. * * * [T]he quantity of minutely detailed language in modern environmental law beggars description. The Clean Air Act's comparison to the tax code is legendary. And the federal hazardous waste regulations defy the comprehension of any one person.

In some ways, the increasingly detailed codification of environmental law is a healthy and a natural development. As polluters find ways to wiggle out of existing obligations, regulators find it necessary to tighten the screws with ever more detailed directives. And as footdragging bureaucrats fail to carry out the broadly-worded mandates of the legislatures, legislators find it necessary to hem the agencies in with ever more specific instructions. Much modern environmental law is comprised of fine (meaning excellent) print.

Unfortunately, however, much environmental law today is "fine print" in the pejorative sense. The dictionary defines "fine print" as "something * * * presented in a deliberately ambiguous or cryptic manner." But the phrase conjures up more than this definition would suggest. To the layperson, "fine print" has three attributes: (1) it is hidden and difficult to detect; (2) it has been crafted by someone who seeks to use it to his or her advantage; and (3) it leads to unexpected outcomes. * * * [M]uch modern environmental law consists of this not so fine print. * * *

[A] new age of * * * "micro-environmental law" is upon us—an age in which the minutiae of environmental statutes and regulations have become extraordinarily important. * * * Moreover, only a dreamer of the tax simplification variety would suggest that this field will become a less complex and more broadly demarcated discipline in the coming decades. The fine print is here to stay. As a result, modern environmental law is seldom what it appears to be.

The rise of micro-environmental law has profound ramifications for persons who study, practice, and implement this law, as well as those who seek to shape and reform its content. Students must be forced to confront the likelihood that their initial understanding of each environmental control scheme is misleading, because the scheme will be shown to be vastly different once the fine print has been explored. Practitioners must likewise shed their simplistic first impressions. Those representing regulated entities will doubtless search for and exploit the fine print; after all, that is why the print was created in the first place. Others, representing regulators and environmental advocacy groups, must attack the regulations with the tenaciousness of gardeners, seeking and rooting out whatever weeds lie within their reach.

Ultimately, however, the task of clarifying micro-environmental law will fall disproportionately on the shoulders of the academy. Environmental law scholars must continue to bring all of their analytic powers to bear on what has become a truly frightening tangle of materials, illuminating the fine print and flushing it out for public scrutiny. What is needed is the patient and thoughtful exposure of more minutiae, not less. In the end, there is no other way. If we fail to plumb the fine print, we deceive ourselves, and the real environmental law will surge along, hidden behind the facade that we all too simplistically embrace.

## E. DONALD ELLIOTT, THE LAST GREAT CLEAN AIR ACT BOOK?

5 Envtl. Lawyer 321, 321-22, 326-27, 329-30 (1998)

[E]very practicing environmental lawyer knows that "the devil is in the details." For every statutory section, the administrative rules and regulations are at least an order of magnitude more complex than the statute itself; beneath the rules lie numerous interpretations, caveats, exceptions, guidance documents, regulatory preambles, agency manuals, letter rulings, policies, precedents, and manifold other administrative utterances. These administrative constructions and interpretations add at least another hundredfold to a thousandfold of additional detail. Together the multiple levels of administrative lawmaking form a vast interpretative pyramid of stunning detail and complexity that translates "law at the wholesale level" (the goal proclaimed in the statute) into "law at the retail level" (the specific, enforceable dictates to a regulated entity).

The reality of environmental law practice today takes place deep down in the interpretative pyramid, not in the statutes and regulations at its apex. * * * [N]o competent environmental lawyer would dare to advise a client based upon the wording of the statute alone. * * * [T]he issue in advising a client is no longer what the words of the statute seem to say, but what the agency has said that they say, and whether that administrative construction is within the broad parameters of agency discretion * * * .

Perhaps the central defining feature of environmental law in the United States is its mind-numbing complexity and detail. A decade ago

I used to argue with my tax colleagues about whether tax law or environmental law was more complicated. They gave up long ago; we won— or lost! Today there is no serious question that environmental law is the most complicated and detailed body of law the world has ever known; we have won the (dubious) distinction of representing the "state of the art" in legal complexity and detail. * * *

The complexity and detail typical of late 20th century environmental law in the United States far surpasses the limits of the individual human mind. * * * [N]o one is really an "environmental lawyer" any more; we are air lawyers, or water lawyers, or Superfund lawyers. The field has simply gotten too large and complex for anyone to master it all.

Nowhere is this trend toward subspecialization within environmental law more evident than in the Office of General Counsel (OGC) at EPA. No one understands the details of a particular little corner of environmental law better than an EPA/OGC attorney * * * . This was first brought home to me soon after I became EPA General Counsel in 1989. Four EPA/OGC attorneys were briefing me about new proposals implementing section 304(*l*) of the Clean Water Act. As an academic * * * I quite naturally asked if what they were telling me about section 304(*l*) fit together with what I had heard the day before about section 304(m). There was a momentary hesitation followed by an uneasy silence in the room as they looked from one to another. Finally, one of them said, we're the section 304(*l*) team; if you want to know about section 304(m) you'll have to call in another lawyer in the office. * * *

Another major source of complexity in U.S. environmental law is the search for political acceptability. In my experience, many, if not most, complex distinctions in environmental rules are the fossilized evidence of a past political deal. Typically, one interested stakeholder group gets the result it wanted most in a certain area, and another stakeholder group gets the result it wanted in another area, even if the two results are logically inconsistent (thus provoking the term "unholy compromise"). These stakeholder groups are not necessarily external to EPA, but often consist of offices, or even informal groups within offices, that attach a high degree of importance to a particular policy in a particular area.

One of the great strategic insights of all time was Baron von Clausewitz's theory that a numerically inferior force could defeat a numerically superior force by concentrating its efforts in a particular area of the line to create local superiority. In the same way, interest groups that lack sufficient force to globally prevail in efforts to get an entire rule rewritten to their liking can often can prevail by confining their demands to the narrow issues that they care most about. As the process of public participation and input from interested groups takes place, EPA rules and interpretations typically become more and more complex; one group after another gets a little something here and a little something there, each winning small battles on issues that it cares about more than the other groups care to oppose. The optimal EPA rule from the standpoint of political acceptability is one in which there is a little something for everyone, not a simple, clear-cut victory on every issue for any one interest group or constituency.

In a sense, the complex lawmaking [embodied in the Clean Air Act] is the residue from thousands of ad hoc political compromises struck over the years. * * *

# WILLIAM H. RODGERS, JR.,
# DEFEATING ENVIRONMENTAL LAW:
# THE GEOLOGY OF LEGAL ADVANTAGE

15 Pace Envtl. L. Rev. 1, 1-8, 11, 13-15, 18-20, 31 (1997)

Complexity is the first word students and practitioners of environmental law learn. The primary reason for this is that environmental law is the result of an additive process where layer upon layer is added to the preexisting strata as if guided by the laws of geology. There are occasional reductions in this cumulative mass * * * but they are far outnumbered by the additions, accretions, faults, folds, and fractures that mar the surface and shape the deep content of this legal world. * * *

Nobody enjoys the complexity of environmental laws, but many gain from it.

It is not difficult to discern the primary beneficiaries of this mass of complexity called environmental law. They are the lawyers who use their guile to trace a satisfactory path down the seam of Law A to its intersection with Law B, just below the surface of Law C. They are the judges who impart their wisdom to discern when Law 26 is impliedly repealed by Law 49. They are the lawmakers who reap the benefits of cleaning up a river not once, not twice, but three times with three different laws, and who later reap the benefits of fashioning exemptions that permit escape from the collective repression they created. * * *

These fine lawyers can sneer at the ambiguities while they seek to widen them, and these wise judges can condemn the complexity while they add yet another layer to it.

Lawyers thrive on the complexity they pretend to despise because complexity multiplies opportunities for legal objection and contention. It creates niches of advantage where unwelcome laws can be ambushed, stifled, and avoided. It creates cracks and seams into which fine legal differences can flow. The environmental laws have been damaged gravely by these predations. * * *

## NEGLECT: LAW AS JOKE

Environmental literature is filled with references to legal directions not taken, legal opportunities not exploited, and legal commitments not remembered. Agencies, for example, are empowered to choose the laws they will enforce. They can chart their own course through the jumbled legal geologies erected in their paths. But the power to choose also includes the discretion to disregard. In the environmental law field, this body of disregarded law is so conspicuous that it has been given a name—"sleeper"—meaning a law or rule that is forgotten, buried, or ignored. A conspicuous reason for sleepers is that the responsible agency puts them to bed as unworthy of attention. Sleepers are forever in danger of slipping beneath the radar because there is little in them that promises administrative advantage, and there is much in them that creates discomfort. * * *

## DIVERSION: LAW AS SPECIALTY

The cracks and fissures of environmental laws enable law managers to use their specialty and exploit the fissures to defeat otherwise good intentions. * * *

Polluted soils and groundwater at [the] Hanford [Nuclear Reservation] are measured in cubic miles. * * * [T]his reservoir of pollution from the bomb making years * * * is without planetary precedent. * * *

The diversion point that consigns challenges to the Hanford cleanup to some legally distant Pluto is Section 113(h) of the Superfund law. Section 113(h) declares that lawsuits that deal with disputes over cleanups must await completion of construction activities. In the case of Hanford, this eagerly anticipated date, barring extensions, might be: 2018, when some units are supposed to be cleaned up; 2055, when reactor cores are supposed to be removed; or it might be 2118, 121 years from the present, when unrestricted use of land and groundwater is to be achieved. * * *

One finds little difference between civilized law of this sort and pure farce. * * *

## ABANDONMENT: LAW AS LIABILITY

It is intuitively difficult to explain why an agency might opt for trading or abandoning a powerful law while cherishing or honoring a weak one. But one reason why this abandonment occurs is that enforcing powerful laws * * * can inspire resistance and backlash. * * *

Regulation never works in the face of massive resistance. Those who are called upon to do the job will abandon the effort when the pain becomes too great, leaving a law that is false and hollow.

## PROCESS TRANSFORMATION: LAW AS ATTRITION

The National Environmental Policy Act (NEPA) is commonly regarded as the most significant environmental law on the planet. It has been copied worldwide, and its inspiration is said to extend to the laws of 150 nations. * * *

In a series of twelve decisions in the 1970s and '80s, the high court slowly squeezed the life out of this law. These decisions covered twenty-two separate legal issues. * * *

The cases brought to the Supreme Court were tactically and serially aligned to produce a law that became all process and no substance. * * *

[T]he process is so thoroughly neutral and so completely oblivious to result that those who resort to its use are not the protectors of [the environment] but * * * despoilers who say their rights were insufficiently weighed.

### PRETENSE: LAW AS PONTIFICATION AND MYTHOLOGY

Environmental laws are filled with empty threats. Some of these are designed to be mere postulations. Others had emptiness thrust upon them. Law serves nicely as a source of moral pronouncement. It serves, too, as the resting place for the self-deceptions and hopes that accumulate in this written record of social ambition. * * *

[T]he [Clean Water Act (CWA)] declares that the discharge of pollutants from sewage treatment plants shall achieve secondary treatment by July 1, 1977. But raw sewage overflows make regular appearances without legal consequence if (as they frequently are) combined with stormwater. These are called combined stormwater overflow (CSO) events. * * * It is not possible to have a CSO event without violating the water quality standard for fecal coliform. But to the rescue came the judges * * * who announced that citizens could not enforce this obligation because it was a "water quality standard" and not an "effluent limitation." This small product of judicial sabotage * * * is * * * the product of a point of view that sheds no tears over empty law * * * [and is] of no discernible benefit to the fish or to * * * people * * * .

Reading the geology of environmental law is not an easy task. Truths can be hidden, buried, accreted over, and twisted under. Illusions can be pushed to the surface, strengthened by transformation, and revealed by accident, but the process is run by lawyers. * * *

## DANIEL A. FARBER, IS THE SUPREME COURT IRRELEVANT? REFLECTIONS ON THE JUDICIAL ROLE IN ENVIRONMENTAL LAW

81 Minn. L. Rev. 547, 547-50 (1997)

Federal environmental law is over a quarter century old * * * . Since [1970], the Supreme Court has decided roughly two or three environmental law cases per year—or somewhere between fifty and one hundred cases altogether. To assess the Court's relevance, imagine that all those cases were wiped off the books. If the Court had never granted certiorari in a single environmental case, would the Environmental Protection Agency (EPA) or other federal agencies operate any differently? Would firms be subject to different federal regulations? In short, how different would environmental protection be today?

The answer, according to my thesis, is "not much." During the past twenty years, the Court's decisions have not substantially affected environmental regulation. In the first few years of the environmental era, the Court did hand down some significant decisions. Since the late 1970s, however, the Court has been largely irrelevant. * * *

[C]onsider a thought experiment. Suppose the Supreme Court were to embark on a campaign to minimize its own influence on the development of environmental law and policy, while still continuing to hear environmental cases. What strategies would it use to do so? The following seems a plausible list of strategies:

- Hear a lot of cases with unique or atypical facts, so the holdings will be irrelevant or difficult to apply in more typical cases.

- Refuse to hear cases in some vital areas of environmental law.

- Shunt as many issues as possible away from the judiciary entirely.

- Adopt a strong policy of deferring to administrative agencies on environmental issues.

- When a decision on the legal merits cannot be avoided, base it on an extremely narrow, technical ground having little general significance.

To a remarkable extent, the Supreme Court's actual performance in environmental law since the mid-1970s mirrors these hypothetical strategies. * * * [T]he Court behaves almost as if it had deliberately undertaken to minimize its own influence on environmental law. * * *

The Supreme Court has limited time and many issues to consider outside of environmental law. Yet, it tends to fritter away docket space on oddball environmental cases with little precedential value. In the meantime, large, important areas of environmental law have escaped its attention. * * *

## E. WE ARE ALL ENVIRONMENTALISTS NOW

### JANE FRITSCH, FRIEND OR FOE? NATURE GROUPS SAY NAMES LIE

N.Y. Times (Mar. 25, 1996) at A1, col. 5

Northwesterners for More Fish. The words conjure up visions of earth-shoed activists and leaping trout joined in battle against the greedy pillagers of the land.

That is just the kind of image a group of Washington consultants had in mind when they named this "grassroots coalition" for their new clients: big utilities and other companies in the Northwest under attack by environmental groups for depleting the fish population.

To environmentalists, Northwesterners for More Fish is just the latest example of "greenscamming," the increasingly common practice of giving environmentally friendly names to groups whose agendas have little to do with the welfare of the environment.

Examples of such groups abound. In Riverside County, Calif., a public relations firm organized Friends of Eagle Mountain on behalf of a mining company that wants to create the world's largest landfill in an abandoned iron ore pit. The National Wetlands Coalition was formed to fight the Endangered Species Act.

And a measure on the California ballot this Tuesday pits the Californians for Balanced Wildlife Management against the California Wildlife Protection Coalition over the hunting of mountain lions. The first group wants to kill them and the second wants to save them.

Even as the public has become disillusioned with large corporations, government and other American institutions, the environmental movement has remained widely popular. The widespread use of environmentally friendly names is industry's grudging tribute to the environmental movement.

A Gallup Poll last year showed that 63 percent of Americans considered themselves "environmentalists," while 34 percent did not. Sixty-two percent said they would give priority to the environment over economic growth while 32 percent said they would give economic growth priority over the environment.

"No one wants to dance with the devil, so they try to come up with a name that's not too devilish," said Bennett Beach, a spokesman for the Wilderness Society. "I suspect that as the country's becoming more and more environmentally sensitive, it's more difficult to be burdened with a name that speaks the truth about your intentions."

One nemesis of the Wilderness Society is the National Wilderness Institute, a group formed in recent years to roll back wetlands regulation in the Endangered Species Act. Though groups like this one assert that environmental regulations are overly burdensome and unnecessary, they recognize the value of an environmentally friendly name.

Other groups that environmentalists consider foes are the Wilderness Impact Research Foundation, a Nevada organization that represents logging, ranching and related interests; the American Environmental Foundation, a Florida property-rights group; the Abundant Wildlife Society of North America, which advocates for hunters, loggers and miners, and the Global Climate Coalition, an association of corporations concerned about regulations to control global warming.

"People sometimes create groups that try to fudge a little bit about what their goals are," said Hal Dash, the president of Cerrell Associates, a public relations firm in Los Angeles that has represented clients with environmental problems. "They want to create a patina of good guy-ness."

Mr. Dash, who represents the American Automobile Manufacturers Association, said he "fiddled with a lot of names" that he might have used for his client in a California campaign regarding requirements for electric cars.

"But we decided in our case it was silly, and the best thing to do was be the American Automobile Manufacturers Association," he said. "The press has spent less time worrying about a front group and more focusing on the issue."

In the case of Northwesterners for More Fish, the organization is barely three months old, and environmentalists are trying to "out" it. * * *

[The organization's] aim is to defeat environmentalists who say that utilities, aluminum companies and the timber industry are destroying fish habitats on the Columbia and other rivers. Chief among the environmental groups is Trout Unlimited, perhaps the inspiration for the new group's name.

Northwesterners for More Fish has a budget of $2.6 million for the next year to pay for the costs of establishing itself "as a credible group supporting positive solutions to enhancing fish populations," according to the memorandum. The group aims to limit Federal efforts to protect endangered fish species if the efforts might interfere with industries that rely on the river. * * *

The Washington Water and Power Company [paid] * * * for an organizing meeting of Northwesterners for More Fish * * *. It could not be learned who attended the session, but the list of invitees included mostly representatives of aluminum, chemical, mining, oil, power and timber companies.

"They don't give a damn about fish," said Glen Spain, the Northwest regional director of the Pacific Coast Federation of Fishermen's Associations. "This is an ersatz organization. It's like a Styrofoam dummy; it has no relationship to anything but the industries and their vested Federal coffer porkbarrel products."

### Notes and Questions

1.  How should greenscamming be handled? Should there be a law against it? If you were to write a statute forbidding it, what would such a statute say?

2.  According to the Lewiston Morning Tribune, Northwesterners for More Fish "sank like a rock after the fakery of its name was exposed. * * * [P]eople tend to resent an organization calling itself one thing when it is

really the opposite." Jim Fisher, *If These Folks are Green, That Grass Must be Brown*, Lewiston Morning Tribune, Jul. 20, 1998, at 8A.

# Chapter Two

# ENVIRONMENTAL DEGRADATION

This chapter is designed to acquaint you with the problems of environmental degradation that have spawned a vast outpouring of laws. The readings can do little more than whet your appetite for the rich literature in ecology and environmental policy. For these and all excerpts in this book, please construe the masculine gender in the generic sense, to include women as well as men.

## A. ECOLOGY, THE ENVIRONMENT, AND HUMAN ACTIVITY

## U.S. COUNCIL ON ENVIRONMENTAL QUALITY, ENVIRONMENTAL QUALITY: FIRST ANNUAL REPORT

### 6-11, 16-17 (1970)

*Ecology* is the science of the intricate web of relationships between living organisms and their living and nonliving surroundings. These interdependent living and nonliving parts make up *ecosystems*. Forests, lakes, and estuaries are examples. Larger ecosystems or combinations of ecosystems, which occur in similar climates and share a similar character and arrangement of vegetation, are *biomes*. The Arctic tundra, prairie grasslands, and the desert are examples. The earth, its surrounding envelope of life-giving water and air, and all its living things comprise the *biosphere*. Finally, man's total *environmental system* includes not only the biosphere but also his interactions with his natural and manmade surroundings.

Changes in ecosystems occur continuously. Myriad interactions take place at every moment of the day as plants and animals respond to variations in their surroundings and to each other. Evolution has produced for each species, including man, a genetic composition that limits how far that species can go in adjusting to sudden changes in its surroundings. But within these limits the several thousand species in an ecosystem, or for that matter, the millions in the biosphere, continuously adjust to outside stimuli. Since interactions are so numerous, they form long chains of reactions. Thus small changes in one part of an ecosystem are likely to be felt and compensated for eventually throughout the system. * * *

The stability of a particular ecosystem depends on its diversity. The more interdependencies in an ecosystem, the greater the chances that it will be able to compensate for changes imposed upon it. A complex tropical forest with a rich mosaic of interdependencies possesses much more stability than the limited plant and animal life found on the Arctic tundra, where instability triggers frequent, violent fluctuations in some animal populations, such as lemmings and foxes. The least stable systems are the single crops—called monocultures—created by man. A cornfield or lawn has little natural stability. If they are not constantly and carefully cultivated, they will not remain cornfields or lawns but will soon be overgrown with a wide variety of hardier plants constituting a more stable ecosystem. * * *

### HUMAN IMPACTS ON ECOSYSTEMS

Dramatic examples of change can be seen where man has altered the course of nature. It is vividly evident in his well-intentioned but poorly thought out tampering with river and lake ecosystems. The Aswan Dam was primarily built to generate electric power. It produced power, but it also reduced the fish population in the Mediterranean, increased the numbers of disease-bearing aquatic snails, and markedly lowered the fertility of the Nile Valley. * * *

[Similarly], a proposed jetport west of Miami and north of the Everglade National Park * * * imperiled a unique ecological preserve. Planners for the jetport had considered density of population, regional transportation needs, and a host of other related variables. But they gave slight consideration to the wildlife and recreational resources of the Everglades. The jetport could have spawned a booming residential, commercial, and industrial complex which would have diminished water quality and without question drastically altered the natural water cycle of Southern Florida. This in turn would have endangered all aquatic species and wildlife within the park and beyond. * * *

### POLLUTION

Although pollution may be the most prominent and immediately pressing environmental concern, it is only one facet of the many-sided environmental problem. It is a highly visible, sometimes dangerous sign of environmental deterioration. Pollution occurs when materials accumulate where they are not wanted. Overburdened natural processes cannot quickly adjust to the heavy load of materials which man, or sometimes nature, adds to them. Pollution * * * often represents valuable resources out of place. * * *

Most pollutants eventually decompose and diffuse throughout the environment. When organic substances are discarded, they are attacked by bacteria and decompose through oxidation. They simply rot.

However, some synthetic products of our advanced technology resist natural decomposition. Plastics, some cans and bottles, and various persistent pesticides fall into this category. Many of these materials are toxic, posing a serious health danger.

Some pollutants, which may be thinly spread throughout the environment, tend to reconcentrate in natural food chains. Pesticides tend to diffuse in ocean water. The physical effects of 1 pound of a well-mixed pesticide in 10 billion pounds of water may seem negligible. But many sea animals filter out particular kinds of chemical compounds * * * and collect them in certain parts of their bodies at concentrations far higher than in the water in which they live. * * * A well-known example of * * * accumulation occurred in 1957 at Clear Lake, [California]. DDD (similar to DDT) was diffused through the water in a concentration of only 0.02 parts per million. The lake's plant and animal organisms, however, had stored residues of DDD at 5 parts per million—250 times greater than the concentration in the water itself. Fish, which consumed large quantities of these small organisms, accumulated DDD concentrations in their body tissues of over 2,000 parts per million. And there was heavy mortality among grebes which fed on the fish. * * *

## U.S. COUNCIL ON ENVIRONMENTAL QUALITY, ENVIRONMENTAL QUALITY ELEVENTH ANNUAL REPORT

### 31-32 (1980)

Some biologists estimate that one to three extinctions are now occurring daily and that the rate will increase to one per hour by the late 1980s. * * * [A]t least one million [species] are likely to be lost within our lifetimes. Rapid species loss on such a scale would be unprecedented in the last 65 million years or, conceivably, since the beginning of life on this planet.

In a world filled with pressing problems, one may ask why the loss of a million species should be considered an unparalleled tragedy. Surely there is enough human misery to occupy a legion of Albert Schweitzers; why should not all efforts focus on our own species? A basic answer is that by reducing biological diversity, humanity is squandering its greatest natural resource, on which we depend for food, oxygen, clean water, energy, building materials, clothes, medicines, psychological well-being, and countless other benefits.

The recent discovery of a tall, undistinguished-looking plant illustrates just how valuable some species are. *Zea diploperennis*, one of several Mexican grasses called teosinte, is very closely related to corn, *Z. mays*, and can be crossbred with it. But corn is an annual that must be replanted after every harvest, whereas *Z. diploperennis* is a perennial that grows from rhizomes (underground stems). If perennial corn varieties could be developed, they might greatly reduce the major corn production costs of plowing under stubble and sowing seed one or more times per year. This and other traits, such as virus resistance or ability to grow in wet soils, could increase the value of corn gene pools by billions of dollars. Yet *Z. diploperennis* might easily have become extinct before it was discovered. Only a few thousand of these plants exist, occupying three minute sites in an isolated mountain range now being developed. A bulldozer could have destroyed them all in an hour. It will never be known how many other multibillion dollar plants will be clear cut, paved over, plowed under, nibbled by goats, or poisoned into extinction before their value is recognized. * * *

## BARRY COMMONER, THE CLOSING CIRCLE

### 39-41 (1971)

#### THE SECOND LAW OF ECOLOGY: EVERYTHING MUST GO SOMEWHERE

This is, of course, simply a somewhat informal restatement of a basic law of physics—that matter is indestructible. Applied to ecology, the law emphasizes that in nature there is no such thing as "waste." In every natural system, what is excreted by one organism as waste is taken up by another as food. Animals release carbon dioxide as a respiratory waste; this is an essential nutrient for green plants. Plants excrete oxygen, which is used by animals. Animal organic wastes nourish the bacteria of decay. Their wastes, inorganic materials such as nitrate, phosphate, and carbon dioxide, become algal nutrients.

A persistent effort to answer the question "Where does it go?" can yield a surprising amount of valuable information about an ecosystem. Consider, for example, the fate of a household item which contains mercury—a substance with serious environmental effects * * * . A dry-cell battery containing mercury is purchased, used to the point of exhaustion, and then "thrown out." But where does it really go? First it is placed in a container of rubbish; this is collected and taken to an incinerator. Here the mercury is heated; this produces mercury vapor which is emitted by the incinerator stack, and mercury *vapor* is toxic. Mercury vapor is carried by the wind, eventually brought to earth in rain or snow. Entering a mountain lake, let us say, the mercury condenses and sinks to the bottom. Here it is acted on by bacteria which convert it to methyl mercury. This is soluble and taken up by fish; since it is not metabolized, the mercury accumulates in the organs and flesh of the fish. The fish is caught and eaten by a man and the mercury becomes deposited in his organs, where it might be harmful. And so on. * * *

Nothing "goes away"; it is simply transferred from place to place, converted from one molecular form to another, acting on the life processes of any organism in which it becomes, for a time, lodged. One of the chief reasons for the present environmental crisis is that great amounts of materials have been extracted from the earth, converted into new forms, and discharged into the environment without taking into account that "everything has to go somewhere." The result, too often, is the accumulation of harmful amounts of material in places where, in nature, they do not belong.

## PAUL R. EHRLICH & JOHN P. HOLDREN, REVIEW: THE CLOSING CIRCLE

14 Environment 24 (Apr. 1972)

[Human] ecological transformation of the planet * * * has long been recognized. The earth has been badly scarred by the results of ecocatastrophes which predated by centuries the faulty technologies that have attracted Commoner's attention. Perhaps the most frequently cited is the conversion to desert, or desertification, of the lush Tigris and Euphrates valleys, a process that started more than two millennia before Christ and was completed before Columbus sailed. The destruction of that rich, ancient granary was a direct result of problems with irrigation, a difficult and ecologically risky operation even under the best of conditions. Often irrigation involves a constant battle against silting and salinization (the accumulation of salts in the soil as water evaporates—a problem not present when the water is "distilled" as it is in normal rainfall). The battle was lost in Mesopotamia, and silting and salinization are growing problems today as population growth forces mankind to bring more and more land under irrigation. These difficulties are not confined to underdeveloped countries, as abandonment of large salinized areas in California's rich Imperial Valley clearly shows.

## B. THE GLOBAL PERSPECTIVE

## THE WORLDWATCH INSTITUTE, THE GLOBAL ENVIRONMENT AND BASIC HUMAN NEEDS

Prepared for the U.S. Council on Environmental Quality
1-4, 10-11, 15-16, 24, 26, 29-32 (1978)

Today, enmeshed as we are in sometimes raucous debates over the dilemmas of environmental protection, grasping the magnitude of recent changes in public perceptions of the world environmental problem is difficult. * * *

Before the [1972] Stockholm Conference, many people throughout the world thought of environmental quality primarily in terms of the needs to control pollution and protect natural beauty—and primarily as an esthetic question at that. Poor-country spokesmen sometimes attacked what they viewed as efforts by the rich to force irrelevant or unaffordable environmental concerns upon the destitute. * * *

[S]ince the Stockholm Conference, however, perceptions about the meaning of environmental quality have almost universally grown more sophisticated. Awareness has spread that many of the world's most life-endangering environmental threats stem not from industrialization but from unrelieved poverty, that failure to initiate appropriate forms of development in many of the poorest countries is undermining the productivity of the agricultural systems on which life depends, and that biological contamination of the water drunk by the poor causes more misery and fatalities than any other form of pollution.

People everywhere are beginning to understand that recklessly used technologies and polluting industries can do more than spoil beautiful landscapes, that they can also—whether by aiding the spread of parasites or by unleashing carcinogens—shorten the lives of rich and poor alike. The international community is beginning to recognize that along with whales and tigers, unique ecosystems populated by thousands of unrecorded plant and animal species face rapid destruction—irreversible genetic losses that will profoundly alter the course of evolution. * * *

Over the long term, efforts to safeguard the global environment do not compete with efforts to raise people's incomes and social opportunities. Economically and socially sound development will also be ecologically sound, or it will be neither sustainable nor socially beneficial over time. Concern for the environmental ramifications of development policies—in countries at all income levels and of all political hues—is not a luxury. The skill with which we manage and protect the earth's natural systems and resources will help determine the quality of our lives and the timing and nature of our deaths. * * *

### DEFORESTING THE EARTH

The accelerated deforestation now experienced in many regions is * * * undermin[ing] the productivity of agricultural systems. Denudation of watersheds often promotes soil erosion and landslides. It also increases the frequency of flooding and the degree of siltation of streams, reservoirs, and irrigation systems downstream. The loss of trees in semi-arid regions encourages wind erosion and furthers the creation of desert-like conditions. Because rain falling on bare ground tends to run off rather than soak in, wells and springs sometimes dry up when the surrounding area has been stripped of vegetation.

Apart from such negative ecological consequences, the loss of trees poses significant economic and social problems in its own right. All societies depend on forests for timber and paper. Shortages of either product can cripple economic development efforts. Moreover, for more than one-third of humanity, wood or charcoal is the sole source of fuel for cooking and heating; thus, as obtaining firewood becomes more difficult, the poor are saddled with a heavy economic burden. * * *

### POVERTY'S TOLL

The environment influences the health of both the poor and the rich, but the nature of the effects varies considerably according to income levels. Because they lack access to pure water and safe waste disposal facilities and because of their often extreme economic deprivation, the world's poor are ravaged by the infectious diseases and undernutrition that similarly ravaged North Americans and Europeans less than a century ago. Childhood deaths remain tragically commonplace; an estimated 35,000 children under the age of 5 die *every day*, in almost all cases of simple infectious diseases, often combined with undernutrition. Poor sanitation gives rise to frequent infection, especially among children; poor nutrition gives rise to high mortality from intestinal and respiratory diseases that are regarded as merely routine aspects of childhood among the affluent. In large measure because so many infants and children die in the poorer countries, average life expectancy at birth ranges between about 40 and 65 years.

Judged in terms of the human suffering and death that it causes, the poor sanitation faced daily by nearly one-third of humanity is by far the world's most critical environmental problem. Good health requires access to water that is not only reasonably germ free but is also abundant enough so that it can be used to keep the body and the household clean. Safe waste disposal facilities are essential to the prevention of the contamination from the dangerous bacteria and parasites transmitted by human excrement.

Although the proportion of the world's population living in proximity to safe and plentiful water has risen steadily over the last quarter century, vast numbers of people are still deprived of a healthy water supply. As of 1975, according to the World Health Organization (WHO), 62 percent of the residents of the developing countries (excluding China)—1.2 billion people—did not have reasonable access to safe water supplies. * * *

Safe waste disposal facilities are even scarcer than safe water supplies. Two-thirds of the developing country population, 1.4 billion people, lived without safe latrines or sewage systems in 1975. * * * [E]nvironmental pollution by untreated human waste exacts a disease and death toll that dwarfs the known toll of industrial pollutants. * * *

### GENETIC IMPOVERISHMENT: THE COST TO HUMANITY

The accelerated extermination of species does not pose the obvious immediate threat to human well-being that trends such as desertification or the spread of environmentally induced diseases do. Yet a decline in the diversity of life forms is of grave concern to all people for a wide range of reasons. * * *

[P]erhaps the greatest industrial, agricultural, and medical costs of species reduction will stem from future opportunities unknowingly lost. Only about 5 percent of the world's plant species have yet been screened for pharmacologically active ingredients. Ninety percent of the food that humans eat comes from just 12 crops, but scores of thousands of plants are edible, and some will undoubtedly prove useful in meeting human food needs. It is a statistical certainty that socially significant uses will be discovered for many tropical plants as more are studied. * * *

## WHO PAYS THE COSTS OF PROTECTION?

Because so much of the responsibility for preserving the earth's genetic heritage falls to poorer countries, the possibility of distributing the costs of conservation among nations has naturally arisen. Those concerned about the depletion of species are, in effect, asking tropical countries to leave untapped the economic potentials of sizable areas and to pass up certain possible development projects—for example, a dam that would destroy a unique habitat but would produce needed power and food. In the United States, * * * halting construction of a dam that threatened a rare fish species engendered widespread resentment and political opposition. Can it be surprising, then, if people living at subsistence level in, say, Malaysia or Zaire refuse to forsake the benefits of a new dam or road simply because some obscure plant or animal species may perish? This predicament might be at least partially untangled through global sharing of the costs of habitat protection, by which wealthier nations contribute to conservation-related expenses incurred by poorer countries. If the world's extant species and gene pools are the priceless heritage of all humanity, then people everywhere may need to share the burdens of conservation according to their ability to do so.

## THE FIREWOOD CRISIS

The firewood crisis of the poor has been largely neglected by analysts of world energy problems and even by many governments of countries where the problem is acute. Many developing country governments have devoted considerable resources to procuring fossil fuels for industries and urban elites and in some cases to developing nuclear power plants while giving scant attention to the worsening energy situation faced by the poor majority of their populations. More than 90 percent of the residents of many less developed countries depend on wood, charcoal, plant residues, or dried dung to meet their basic energy needs. So long as trees are plentiful, this system is workable. But in many areas—particularly South Asia, the Middle East, Central America, northwestern South America, and the drier regions of Africa—the growth of the human population has far outpaced that of new trees. As a result, obtaining wood becomes increasingly time consuming and expensive. The poor must hunt for wood, sometimes spending entire days gathering just enough wood for one person to carry. Those with more money pay soaring prices for wood or charcoal brought in on animals or trucks. Charcoal prices in the central Sudanian town of Bara, for example, have tripled in the last decade while charcoal prices in larger Sudanian cities have multiplied by an even higher factor. Families in some West African cities now spend one-fourth of their income on fuel wood. * * *

The negative social and economic consequences of firewood scarcity are paralleled by negative ecological consequences. The bulk of the world's fuel wood is cut—legally or illegally—either throughout rural countrysides or from designated forest areas. Only rarely is woodcutting matched by the commensurate replanting of trees. Thus, firewood gatherers and charcoal merchants are contributing to the spread of desert-like conditions in semi-arid zones and to rampant soil erosion, silting, and flooding in and below denuded mountain zones. Still more agricultural costs are exacted when wood scarcity becomes so acute that villagers turn to dried dung for fuel, as they have throughout much of the Indian subcontinent and in scattered spots elsewhere. The diversion of precious dung from agricultural soils denies them both the nutrients and the organic matter contained in animal manures. * * *

### Notes and Questions

1. Because the foregoing reading was published in 1978, its many figures are not up to date. More timely figures for many variables may be found in two annual publications of The Worldwatch Institute: *The State of the World*, and *Vital Signs*. Although these reports do not always provide comparable figures, they suggest that the relative magnitudes of the global environmental problems catalogued in 1978 remain essentially unchanged.

For example, the Institute reports that "[b]etween 1991 and 1995, the world lost an average of 11.3 million hectares of net forest annually—an area roughly the size of Honduras." The Worldwatch Institute, Vital Signs 1997 at 96 (1997). Moreover, "[a]t least 200 million hectares of forest were lost between 1980 and 1995 alone—an area larger than Mexico or Indonesia, or three times the state of Texas." The Worldwatch Institute, Vital Signs 1998 at 124 (1998). "In India, the demand for fuelwood is now six times the sustainable yield of its remaining forests, forcing the burning of cow dung and crop residues for cooking, thus depriving the soil of nutrients and organic matter. Satellite photographs of India show forests receding from virtually every city in the country." The Worldwatch Institute, State of the World 1998 at 10 (1998).

Similarly, figures in a more recent Institute publication suggest that approximately 35,000 children under the age of 5 still die every day. *See* The Worldwatch Institute, State of the World 1996 at 126 (1996) (noting that diarrhea "kills nearly 3 million children under age 5 every year and accounts for one fourth of the deaths in this age group").

More recent figures continue to suggest—as the Institute concluded in 1978—that "the poor sanitation faced daily by nearly one-third of humanity is by far the world's most critical environmental problem." More than one billion people in developing countries lacked clean drinking water in 1990, and more than 1.7 billion people "threw their sewage out untreated." *Id.*

Finally, it seems as true as ever that "many of the world's most life-endangering environmental threats stem not from industrialization but from unrelieved poverty," as the Institute concluded in 1978. "[T]he gap between the rich and the poor is growing: in 1960, the richest 20 percent of the world earned 30 times as much income as the poorest 20 percent; by 1991, the richest fifth was appropriating 61 times as much wealth as the poorest." The Worldwatch Institute, State of the World 1995 at 176 (1995).

2.   What might it mean to adopt a "global perspective" when evaluating the significance and worth of the environmental policies that have been or may be adopted in the United States? Assume that, at this very moment, one billion people lack clean drinking water. Does this global problem make it inappropriate to pour American money and effort into relocating grizzly bears in our national parks or reducing smog in Cincinnati?

3.   In assessing the significance and worth of American environmental policies, should we seek ever more recent figures to assure that our picture of the global environment is fully up to date? Would your judgment about the relative significance of American and global environmental problems be affected if you discovered that only 21,000 (rather than 35,000) children under the age of 5 die every day of disease and malnutrition, or that only one-fifth (rather than one-third) of humanity faces a firewood crisis?

## C. EARTH IN THE BALANCE?

The remainder of Chapter 2 examines the uncertain magnitude of our environmental problems. We begin by contrasting gloomy and optimistic projections of the world's future. We then briefly consider the contributions that individuals and governments can make in remedying environmental disruption, including the claims of some writers that individuals and governments can and will do little to avert impending catastrophe. Finally, we consider calls for fundamental changes in our perceptions and behavior.

### 1.   SOBER FORECASTS

We begin with a summary and excerpts from one of the most famous of the pessimistic publications: D.H. Meadows, D.L. Meadows, J. Randers & W. Behrens III, *The Limits to Growth* (1972), as updated by D.H. Meadows, D.L. Meadows, & J. Randers in *Beyond the Limits* (1992). *The Limits to Growth* was a study conducted at the Massachusetts Institute of Technology (MIT) under the auspices of the Club of Rome (a private international group of business persons, officials, and academics). Accordingly, it is often referred to as the "Club of Rome Report." The Club of Rome Report and its 1992 update were prepared using a computer model, "World3," initially developed by Jay W. Forrester, Professor of Management at MIT.

## WORLD DYNAMICS

25 Bull. Am. Acad. Arts & Sciences 5-10 (1972)

Mr. Forrester pointed out that the behavior of even the most complex social systems can now be interpreted through methods developed over the last several decades. This new approach, known as "system dynamics," has made it possible to construct realistic laboratory models of social systems. * * *

With the aid of a simple diagram [**Figure 2-1**], [Mr. Forrester] explained that all systems which change through time are composed of two kinds of variables: levels and rates. The levels are the accumulations or integrations within the system, while the rates are the flows that cause the levels to change. These two types of variables are both necessary and sufficient for representing the dynamics of any system. * * *

All our social systems belong to a class known as multi-loop nonlinear feedback systems. In this kind of system, the action is circular, that is, it takes place within a closed path known as a feedback loop. As indicated in the diagram, this path connects an action to its effect on the surrounding conditions; the resulting conditions, in turn, come back as "information" to influence further action. The levels and rates are an integral part of the feedback loops. Changes in levels are brought about only by rates of flow, while the rates are controlled only by one or more of the system levels through the information link shown by the dashed line. (The irregular cloud symbol in the diagram is a source for the flow and lies outside the system.)

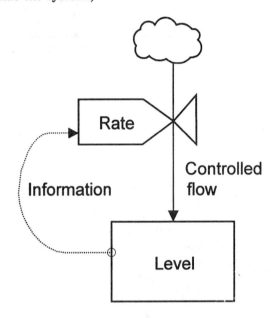

**Figure 2-1**

The fact that all action takes place within the feedback loops is * * * the most important concept in establishing the structure of a system. It is significant precisely because it contradicts the generally accepted way of thinking about cause and effect. In the human mind, cause and effect flows in only one direction. We tend to say that action A will produce result B without carrying the thought process a step further to determine how result B can change the future influences that affect the action at A. To illustrate this closed loop structure, Mr. Forrester described the simple process of filling a water glass. Most people would say that the flow of water from the faucet fills the glass, and there the description would end. To make the perception complete, we would have to add that the water in the glass shuts off the faucet. In other words, we turn on the faucet, watch the water filling the glass, and respond to the rising water level by turning off the facet; the flow of water fills the glass, but the water in the glass controls the faucet. Within this circular process, there is no uni-directional cause and effect; instead the actions and consequences close back on themselves. * * *

[T]he [World3] dynamic model, as thus far developed, shows several different alternative futures depending on whether population growth is eventually suppressed by shortage of natural resources, by pollution, by crowding and consequent social strife, or by insufficient food. It is certain that these pressures or some other equally powerful force will ultimately limit population and industrialization even if persuasion and psychological factors do not. * * *

## DONELLA H. MEADOWS, DENNIS L. MEADOWS & JØRGEN RANDERS, BEYOND THE LIMITS

### 1-2, 104-06, 109-18, 130-31, 119, 133, 179 (1992)

To overshoot means to go beyond limits inadvertently, without meaning to do so. Daily life is full of small and not-so-small overshoots. A car on an icy road can slide past a stop sign. * * * On a larger scale a fishing fleet can become so large and efficient that it depletes the fish population upon which it depends. * * *

This book is about overshoot on a much larger scale, namely the scale at which the human population and economy extract resources from the earth and emit pollution and wastes to the environment. Many of these rates of extraction and emission have grown to be unsupportable. The environment cannot sustain them. Human society has overshot its limits, for the same reasons that other overshoots occur. Changes are too fast. Signals are late, incomplete, distorted, ignored, or denied. Momentum is great. Responses are slow. * * *

Powerful trends are running counter to each other. To put them together and glimpse their combined implications, we need a model more complex than the ones in our heads. * * *

World3 is not a difficult [computer] model to understand. It keeps track of stocks such as "population" and "industrial capital" and "pollution" and "cultivated land." These stocks change through flows such as "births" and "deaths" (in the case of population), "investment" and "depreciation" (in the case of capital), and "pollution generation" and "pollution assimilation" (in the case of pollution). Land cultivated multiplied by average land yield gives total food production. Food production divided by population gives food per capita. The amount of food per capita influences the death rate. Nothing remarkable here. The components of World3 are quite ordinary. But they are put together in a way that is dynamically complex. * * *

The purpose—the *only* purpose—of World3 is to understand the possible modes of approach of the human economy to the carrying capacity of the planet. * * *

[I]f you throw a ball straight up in the air, you know enough to forecast what its general behavior will be. It will rise with decreasing velocity, then reverse direction and fall with increasing velocity until it hits the ground. You know it will not continue rising forever, nor begin to orbit the earth, nor loop three times before landing.

If you wanted to predict exactly how high the ball will rise or precisely where and when it will hit the ground, you would need precise information about the ball, the altitude, the wind, the force of the initial throw. Similarly, if we wanted to predict the exact size of the world population in 2026, or when world oil production will peak, or which limit will affect a specific nation first, we would need a very complicated model—in fact an impossible one. * * *

It is possible, however, and critically important, to understand the broad behavioral possibilities of the system, especially since collapse is one of them. Therefore we put into World3 the kinds of information one uses to understand the generic behavior of thrown balls, not the kinds of information one would need to describe the exact trajectory of one particular throw of one specific ball. * * *

World3 contains just four kinds of physical and biological limits. All of them can be raised or lowered by actions, changes, and choices within the world model. These limits are:

*Cultivable land,* which can be increased up to a limit of 3.2 billion hectares by investment in land development. The cost of developing new land is assumed to rise as the most accessible and favorable land is developed first. Land can also be removed from production by erosion and urbanization.

*The yield achievable on each unit of land,* which can be raised by inputs like fertilizer. These inputs have diminishing returns; each additional kilogram of fertilizer produces less additional yields than the kilogram before. We assume that the upper yield limit is a worldwide average of 6500 kilograms of grain per hectare, equivalent to the highest yields obtained by single countries today. World3 also assumes that land yield can be reduced by pollution.

*Nonrenewable resources* like minerals and fossil fuels. We assume there are enough of these resources to supply 200 years worth of extraction at 1990 extraction rates. The capital cost of finding and developing nonrenewable resources is assumed to rise, as the richest and most convenient deposits are exploited first.

*The ability of the earth to absorb pollution,* which is assumed to erode as pollution accumulates, and which can regenerate itself if the pollution load decreases. Quantitatively this is the least known limit of all.

We assume that if pollution rises to 10 times its 1990 global level, it would reduce human lifetime by only 3% and accelerate the degradation of land fertility by 30% (and then we test other estimates in the model to see what their effects would be). * * *

What if we're wrong, say, about the amount of resources still to be discovered? What if the actual number is only half of what we've assumed, or double, or 10 times more? What if the earth's "real" ability to absorb pollution without harm to the human population is not 10 times the 1990 rate of emission, but 50 times or 500 times? (Or 0.5 times?)

A computer model is a device for making tests, and all those "what ifs" are testable. * * *

In the simulated world of World3 the industrial ethic is one of continuous economic growth. The World3 population will stop growing only when it is rich enough. Its resource base is limited and erodable. * * * It should come as no surprise that the most common mode of behavior of the model is overshoot and collapse. * * *

[The authors explain various "scenarios" in which different combinations of assumptions are fed into the World3 model.]

When the new numbers [for each scenario] are entered, we use World3 to calculate the interactions among 225 variables. The computer calculates a new value for each variable every six months in simulated time from the year 1900 to the year 2100. The model thus produces more than 90,000 numbers for each scenario. We can't possibly picture all this information; we have to consolidate and simplify it to understand it ourselves and to convey it to you. * * *

One lesson from these runs is that in a complex, finite world if you remove or raise one limit and go on growing, you encounter another limit. Especially if the growth is exponential, the next limit will show up surprisingly soon. * * *

We would expect different parts of the "real world," if they keep on growing, to run into different limits in a different order at different times. But the experience of successive and multiple limits in any one place, we think, would unfold much the way it does in World3. * * *

A second lesson is that the more successfully society puts off its limits through economic and technical adaptations, the more likely it is in the future to run into several of them at the same time. In most World3 runs * * * the world system does not run out of land or food or resources or pollution absorption capability, it *runs out of the ability to cope.*

### Editor's Note

The outcomes for each scenario are depicted by the authors of *Beyond the Limits* in two graphs: (1) a "state of the world" graph displaying population, nonrenewable resources, industrial output, pollution, and food; and (2) a "material standard of living" graph displaying life expectancy, and food, consumer goods, and services per person. Scenario 1, for example, assumes that society will continue on its present course. The graphs depicting the consequences of such a course of action are set forth as **Figure 2-2**, taken from *Beyond the Limits* at 133.

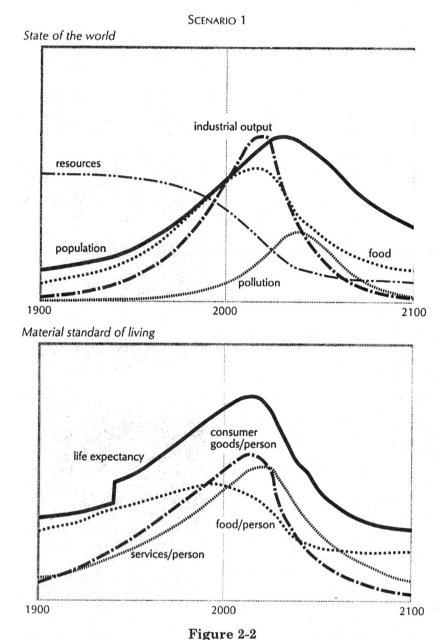

SCENARIO 1

*State of the world*

*Material standard of living*

**Figure 2-2**

The textual discussion of the various scenarios in *Beyond the Limits* is too long to reproduce here. In Scenarios 1 through 9, world population and life expectancy generally increase until life expectancy encounters (usually massive) declines at various points between the years 2000 and 2100. A tenth scenario achieves near global equilibrium—a situation in which population levels, life expectancy, and all other variables are held essentially constant, notwithstanding inflows and outflows. These ten scenarios and their consequences are summarized in **Table 2-1**, culled from the text of *Beyond the Limits*.

**Table 2-1.** Scenarios (Adapted from *Beyond the Limits*)

| | Assumptions | Consequences |
|---|---|---|
| 1 | No policy change from present practices. Nonrenewable resources assumed to last 100 years at 1990 consumption rates. | Pollution degrades land fertility. Land erosion increases. Food production falls. Economy shifts to agriculture and pursuit of nonrenewable resources. Industrial capital falls, taking with it agricultural and service sectors. Death rate driven up by lack of food and health services. |
| 2 | Nonrenewable resources assumed to last 200 years at 1990 consumption rates ("double resources"). | Increased pollution from greater industrial production degrades land fertility, triggering remainder of Scenario 1 consequences. |
| 3 | Double resources. Pollution is cut, over time, to 1975 levels ("1975 pollution levels"). | Reduced pollution nevertheless eventually degrades land fertility, triggering remainder of Scenario 1 consequences. |
| 4 | Double resources. 1975 pollution levels. Agricultural yields are increased fourfold by 2100 ("quadruple yields"). | Galloping land erosion from ever intensive agriculture on less and less suitable land triggers Scenario 1 results. |
| 5 | Double resources. 1975 pollution levels. Quadruple yields. Land erosion is reduced by factor of 3 starting in 1995 ("erosion control"). | Costs of all technologies and of obtaining diminishing resources outstrip the economy, leading to drop in life expectancy. |
| 6 | Double resources. 1975 pollution rates. Quadruple yields. Erosion control. Resource use per unit of production is reduced by 3% annually until 1975 resource use levels are reached ("1975 resource use levels"). | Life expectancy nevertheless falls because declining economy cannot maintain high levels of health services. |
| 7 | Double resources. 1975 pollution rates. Quadruple yields. Erosion control. 1975 resource use levels. Timetable for all accomplishments is accelerated. | Crisis is postponed, but cost of holding off all limits with growing population eventually halts and depresses industrial growth and life expectancy. |

**Table 2-1.** Scenarios (Adapted from *Beyond the Limits*)

| | Assumptions | Consequences |
|---|---|---|
| 8 | Double resources. All couples limit family size to two surviving children, starting in 1995 ("zero population growth"), but Scenario 3 through 7 technologies are not used. | Standard of living rises, but increasing pollution and depletion of resources lead to catastrophic decline in life expectancy. |
| 9 | Double resources. Zero population growth. World-wide acceptance of "enough" material goods, curbing average industrial output per capita to $350 per person per year ("intentionally reduced material standard of living"), but Scenario 3 through 7 technologies are not used. $350 per person is approximately the equivalent of South Korea, or about twice the level of Brazil in 1990. | Pollution rises steadily, degrading food production. Industrial sector eventually collapses as ever more money is needed for agriculture and scarcer resources. |
| 10 | Double resources. Zero population growth. Intentionally reduced material standard of living. 1975 pollution rates. Quadruple yields. Erosion control. 1975 resource use levels. Accelerated timetable for all accomplishments. | Desired material standard of living maintained for almost a century. Life expectancy levels off at 80 years, with sufficient food for all. Pollution peaks and falls. Nonrenewable resources deplete so slowly that one-half of original endowment remains in 2100. |

The outputs of World3 are so numerous that it is helpful to focus on a single variable: life expectancy. **Figure 2-3** displays the essential shapes and locations of the life expectancy curves for Scenarios 1 through 10, culled from ten graphs in *Beyond the Limits*.

## 2. CHEERFUL ASSURANCES

The methods and conclusions of the original 1972 Club of Rome Report (published as *The Limits to Growth*) were heavily criticized as simplistic and unsupportable. Dennis Meadows reports that the 1992 update, *Beyond the Limits*, has not generated such a rich response, at least in the English-speaking world. Nevertheless, says Meadows, because the 1992 text conveys the same arguments as the original Club of Rome Report, criticisms of the 1972 Report apply just as well to the newer text. The following readings represent a sampling of these criticisms.

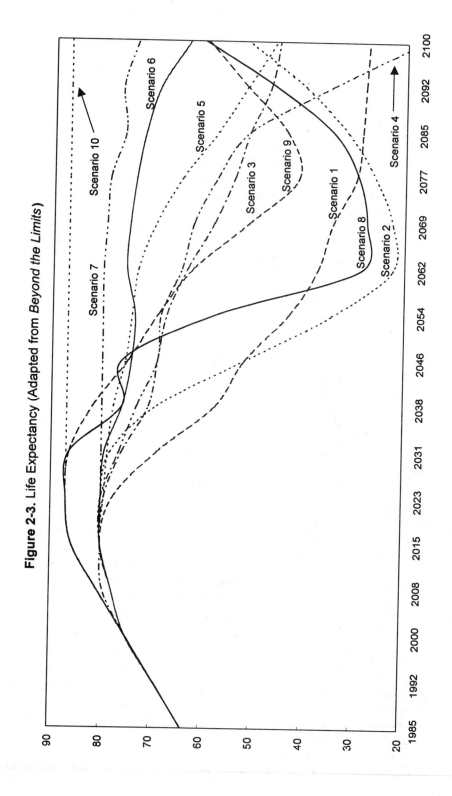

Figure 2-3. Life Expectancy (Adapted from *Beyond the Limits*)

# CARL KAYSEN, THE COMPUTER
## THAT PRINTED OUT W*O*L*F*

50 Foreign Aff. 660-68 (July 1972)

"The Limits to Growth" is a brief, forceful, easily read polemic which has already generated many times its own weight in enthusiastic encomia and equally strong condemnations. It advances a familiar, indeed fashionable, thesis. The goals and institutions of our present world society stimulate population growth and production increase at a rate that cannot be sustained. Further, and perhaps less familiarly, we are now about a generation from the point of no return, after which the world must suffer a catastrophic drop in numbers and wealth, no matter what is then done to restrain further growth. The argument is presented with a sufficient panoply of graphs, flow diagrams, references to the World Model and the new discipline of System Dynamics, and invocations of the computer to produce an aura of scientific authority for the conclusions. * * *

It is my contention that the authors' analysis is gravely deficient and many of their strongest and most striking conclusions unwarranted. * * *

The most important question concerns the nature of the limits that enforce the growth ceiling in the model. Basically, there are two: arable land and the supply of exhaustible minerals. The first operates primarily on population, the second on industrial production. In order to demonstrate the ineluctability of the limits, and unimportance of the precise magnitudes assigned to them, the authors show that doubling the productivity of agricultural land, or doubling the reserves of natural resources, leads to no qualitative change in the behavior of the system, and only a relatively brief postponement of the moment of catastrophe. Pollution operates as a limit too, but somewhat more indirectly, through its effect on length of life and thus on population. Making pollution control more effective is seen as possible only with sharply increasing costs; thus an economic limit is built into the model in respect to pollution control that functions in the same way as the physical limits on agricultural land and mineral resources. The various alternative assumptions the authors work into the model always rely on one or more of these limits to bring about the characteristic crisis of the system. * * *

The notion that such limits must exist gains plausibility from the use of physical terms to indicate the relevant quantities—acres of arable land, tons of chrome ore reserves—implicitly invoking the physical finiteness of the earth as the ultimate bound. But this is fundamentally misleading. Resources are properly measured in economic, not physical, terms. New land can be created by new investment, as when arid lands are irrigated, swamps drained, forests cleared. Similarly, new mineral resources can be created by investment in exploration and discovery.

These processes of adding to the supplies of "fixed" resources have been going on steadily throughout human history. * * *

[O]nce the problem is recognized as one of cost limits, not physical limits, it appears in a different light. The force of rising costs as mines go deeper or exploit thinner veins, or as drier and more distant lands need more water brought from farther sources and the like, meets the force of advancing technology, which brings down the costs of using existing resources and literally creates new resources by bringing within the bounds of cost feasibility materials or methods which formerly lay outside it. Thus, for example, the Hall process for reducing aluminum oxide by bringing the costs of the metal down to a level that made it an industrially usable material rather than a jeweller's curiosity, literally added hundreds of millions of tons to our reserves of metal ores. New ways of locating oil pools and new ways of exploiting them have combined to keep oil reserves * * * about constant over the past generation, though the actual rate of consumption has been growing exponentially. In general, the relative prices of mineral raw materials and agricultural products have not been rising * * * .[4]

[T]echnical progress over the life of a generation has made it possible for our children to get twice as much output from the same bundle of inputs as their parents. * * *

Once an exponentially improving technology is admitted into the model, along with exponentially growing population and production, the nature of its outcomes changes sharply. The inevitability of crisis when a limit is reached disappears, since the "limits" themselves are no longer fixed but grow exponentially too. * * *

[A] second major flaw in the authors' analysis lies in the total absence of adjustment mechanisms of any kind in the model. * * * Especially in the workings of the economy, adjustment mechanisms play a crucial role. The most important of these is price: as a resource becomes scarce, the consequent rise in price leads to savings in use, to efforts to increase supply, and to technical innovations to offset the scarcity. * * *

So much for the analysis. Can the major conclusion stand alone * * * ? Is there merit in the proposition that we must seek now to move as rapidly as possible to the state of "global equilibrium" defined by stability of both population and capital, and that failure to do so in-

---

[4] At this point, the reader probably feels uneasily that there must be some flaw in the argument. Surely the earth is finite, and even the wonders of technology must have some limit. The earth is finite, to be sure, and without broaching the larger question of whether the universe is or is not, it can be shown that the finiteness of the earth does not in itself set limits to what technology might accomplish that are relevant to the time horizons of the kind of argument with which we are concerned. I owe to Professor Robert Socolow of Princeton University a calculation that shows that in terms of physical limits alone, i.e., available matter and energy, the earth could support a population at least 1,000 times the present one at the current U.S. per capita income level.

vites catastrophe? * * * Briefly, and simply, the answer is "No." There are no credible reasons for believing that the world as a whole cannot maintain a fairly high rate of economic growth (though not necessarily the present one) over a long period of time into the future. Further, if it becomes necessary, for whatever reason, to slow down the growth rate, a relatively smooth transition from higher to lower rates will be perfectly possible, and not achievable only through the mechanism of catastrophe. * * *

In the legend, there were in the end, real wolves. * * * Two of the authors' three central concerns, population growth and pollution, do indeed present genuinely urgent and difficult problems. A third equally important and difficult one, mentioned in "Limits," but only in passing, is the assessment of the indirect consequences of technical change, the unanticipated "side effects" that can sometimes outweigh the benefits. * * *

Determined effort to deal with these problems is important. Failure to pay proper attention to them might well result in serious troubles, though they are unlikely to be of a kind which can properly be termed catastrophic. * * *

Finally, therefore, how much does "crying Wolf" help to direct social energies toward improving our responses to these problems? In principle, it is not only useful, but indispensable. The social mechanism is made up of human beings moved by passion far more than by reason. The mobilization of feeling that is the necessary prelude to all but the most routine social action requires some stimulus stronger than a sound argument. But to be effective, the cry must be well directed: the wolves must be imminent and they must indeed be wolves. On this score we can give only a moderate grade to "Limits" * * * . The problems [it calls] us to attend are real and pressing. But none are of the degree of immediacy that can rightly command the urgency they feel. Indeed, at least two problems of worldwide consequence outside the scope of this work seem to be more urgent than any it deals with: the creation of an international order stable enough to remove the threat of nuclear war, and the diminution of the staggering inequalities in the international distribution of wealth. A good sentry does not cry up tomorrow's wolves and ignore today's tigers.

## CHAUNCEY STARR, THE GROWTH OF LIMITS

Saturday Rev. 30 (Nov. 24, 1979)

[S]cience and technology historically have opened new frontiers * * * stimulating the "growth of limits." I do not accept the premise that constraints on such growth are in view or that our long-range planning should be determined by today's perceptions of existing limits. * * * The real question we face is: do we want to accept the idea of limits as a guide to human expectations and societal planning, or do we want to keep alive the idea of expanding expectations and new horizons? * * *

For proponents of [the "limits to growth"] theme, the obvious course would be to limit the personal economic expectations of those now alive and to limit sharply the growth in the world's population. This is a seductive dogma, because if it were socially and politically feasible to accept such limitations, and thus reduce the worldwide demand for goods and services, we would simultaneously reduce the stress on our natural environment, on our political and social institutions and on our problem-solving and decision-making mechanisms. But is such a prescription acceptable from a social and political standpoint? Perhaps it is for the comparatively wealthy, but what about the poor people of the world? For them, limits to growth would mean lives of hopelessness.

## JULIAN L. SIMON, RESOURCES, POPULATION, ENVIRONMENT: AN OVERSUPPLY OF FALSE BAD NEWS[a]

208 Science 1431, 1435-36 (1980)

Incredible as it may seem at first, the term "finite" is not only inappropriate but is downright misleading in the context of natural resources, from both the practical and the philosophical points of view. * * * [T]he future quantities of a natural resource such as copper cannot be calculated even in principle, because of new lodes, new methods of mining copper, and variations in grades of copper lodes; because copper can be made from other metals; and because of the vagueness of the boundaries within which copper might be found—including the sea, and other planets. Even less possible is a reasonable calculation of the amount of future services of the sort we are now accustomed to get from copper, because of recycling and because of the substitution of other materials for copper * * * .

Even the total weight of the earth is not a theoretical limit to the amount of copper that might be available to earthlings in the future. Only the total weight of the universe—if that term has a useful meaning here—would be such a theoretical limit, and I don't think anyone would like to argue the meaningfulness of "finite" in that context. * * *

[T]he ultimate constraint upon our capacity to enjoy unlimited raw materials at acceptable prices is knowledge. And the source of knowledge is the human mind. Ultimately, then, the key constraint is human imagination and the exercise of educated skills. Hence an increase of human beings constitutes an addition to the crucial stock of resources, along with causing additional consumption of resources.

---

[a] Excerpted with permission from Simon, Resources, Population, Environment: An Oversupply of False Bad News, 208 Science 1431 (1980). Copyright © 1980 American Association for the Advancement of Science.

### *Notes and Questions*

1. Kaysen, Starr, and Simon are optimistic about our global future, in large part because of the wonders of technology. In effect, they predict that increases in human knowledge will stave off ecological disasters. How reliable are predictions based on assumed advances in human knowledge? Is the future growth of human knowledge so unpredictable that no assumptions should be made about such growth? Would it make sense to assume that human knowledge has reached its limits? Should we just defer to Yogi Berra, who allegedly said "making predictions is difficult, especially about the future"?

2. Recall the suggestion in *Beyond the Limits* that systems are prone to overshoot. Might soothing words about human cleverness be as disturbing to global passengers as assurances by a speeding driver on an icy road that, "after all, the car has brakes"? Then again, how do we know that the road is icy?

3. Recall Kaysen's declaration at page 36, *supra*, that "[n]ew land can be created by new investment, as when arid lands are irrigated, swamps drained, forests cleared. * * * These processes of adding to the supplies of 'fixed' resources have been going on steadily throughout human history." Do you find this claim persuasive? May efforts to bring about the "growth of limits" entail negative side effects?

4. The New York Times ran an obituary on the death of Julian Simon in 1998. The article stated in part:

> Mr. Simon's sunny view of the future became the basis for a highly publicized bet in 1980 with Paul R. Ehrlich, the Stanford University ecologist whose 1968 book, "The Population Bomb," predicted that one-fifth of humanity would starve to death by 1985.

> Mr. Ehrlich and two colleagues * * * responded to a challenge by Mr. Simon * * * that the price of any natural resource would be lower by a mutually agreed-upon date, not higher.

> Mr. Ehrlich and his colleagues took the bet on the belief that rising demand for raw materials by an exploding global populace would pare supplies of nonrenewable resources, driving up prices. * * *

> The Ehrlich group bet $1,000 on five metals—chrome, copper, nickel, tin and tungsten—in quantities that each cost $200 in October 1980, when the bet was made. Mr. Simon agreed that he would sell the agreed-upon metals to the Ehrlich group 10 years later at 1980 prices. If the combined prices of acquiring the metals in 1990 turned out to be higher than $1,000, Mr. Simon would pay the difference in cash. If prices fell, the Ehrlich group would pay him.

> During the decade, the world's population grew by more than 800 million, the greatest increase in history, and the store of metals did not get any larger. Yet in the fall of 1990, with the prices of the metals down sharply, Mr. Ehrlich mailed Mr. Simon a check for $576.07.

> Mr. Simon wrote back a thank you note, along with a challenge to raise the wager to as much as $20,000, tied to any other resource and to any

other year in the future. Mr. Ehrlich declined to take him up on the offer.

*Julian Simon, 65, Optimistic Economist Dies*, N.Y. Times, Feb. 12, 1998, at B11, col. 1. *See also* Peter Passell, *Economic Scene: Knowing When and How to Protect the Planet*, N.Y. Times, Jan. 1, 1998, at D2, col. 1 (arguing that the 1972 Club of Rome Report failed to correctly predict the 25-year period 1972-1998, because "the computer experts who simulated resource use failed to incorporate market forces in their models").

## 3.  THE COLLECTIVE ACTION IMPERATIVE

We will shortly consider some questions about the debate between the pessimists and the optimists. Before doing so, we consider the roles that individuals and governments might play in coping with problems of scarcity. Garrett Hardin argues that individuals can do little—perhaps nothing—to change the fate of the world; he asserts that the only solution is "mutual coercion, mutually agreed upon"—a phrase suggesting government intervention. William Ophuls and A. Stephen Boyan, Jr. explain why they believe government action may be futile. Bear in mind that Hardin, Ophuls, and Boyan operate under the shared assumption that we are constrained by limits to growth.

## GARRETT HARDIN, THE TRAGEDY OF THE COMMONS[b]

### 162 Science 1243-48 (1968)

The tragedy of the commons develops in this way. Picture a pasture open to all. It is to be expected that each herdsman will try to keep as many cattle as possible on the commons. Such an arrangement may work reasonably satisfactorily for centuries because tribal wars, poaching, and disease keep the numbers of both man and beast well below the carrying capacity of the land. Finally, however, comes the day of reckoning, that is, the day when the long-desired goal of social stability becomes a reality. At this point, the inherent logic of the commons remorselessly generates tragedy.

As a rational being, each herdsman seeks to maximize his gain. Explicitly or implicitly, more or less consciously, he asks, "What is the utility to *me* of adding one more animal to my herd?" This utility has one negative and one positive component.

1)  The positive component is a function of the increment of one animal. Since the herdsman receives all the proceeds from the sale of the additional animal, the positive utility is nearly +1.

---

[b] Reprinted with permission from Hardin, The Tragedy of The Commons, 162 Science 1243 (1968). Copyright © 1968 American Association for the Advancement of Science.

2) The negative component is a function of the additional over-grazing created by one more animal. Since, however, the effects of overgrazing are shared by all the herdsmen, the negative utility for any particular decision-making herdsman is only a fraction of -1.

Adding together the component partial utilities, the rational herdsman concludes that the only sensible course for him to pursue is to add another animal to his herd. And another; and another. * * * But this is the conclusion reached by each and every rational herdsman sharing a commons. Therein is the tragedy. Each man is locked into a system that compels him to increase his herd without limit—in a world that is limited. * * * Freedom in a commons brings ruin to all. * * *

The National Parks present [an] instance of the working out of the tragedy of the commons. At present, they are open to all, without limit. The parks themselves are limited in extent—there is only one Yosemite Valley—whereas population seems to grow without limit. The values that visitors seek in the parks are steadily eroded. Plainly, we must soon cease to treat the parks as commons or they will be of no value to anyone.

What shall we do? We have several options. We might sell them off as private property. We might keep them as public property, but allocate the right to enter them. The allocation might be on the basis of wealth, by the use of an auction system. It might be on the basis of merit, as defined by some agreed-upon standards. It might be by lottery. Or it might be on a first-come, first-served basis, administered to long queues. These, I think, are all the reasonable possibilities. They are all objectionable. But we must choose—or acquiesce in the destruction of the commons that we call our National Parks.

## POLLUTION

In a reverse way, the tragedy of the commons reappears in problems of pollution. Here it is not a question of taking something out of the commons, but of putting something in * * * . The calculations of utility are much the same as before. The rational man finds that his share of the cost of the wastes he discharges into the commons is less than the cost of purifying his wastes before releasing them. Since this is true for everyone, we are locked into a system of "fouling our own nest," so long as we behave only as independent, rational, free-enterprisers.

The tragedy of the commons as a food basket is averted by private property, or something formally like it. But the air and waters surrounding us cannot readily be fenced, and so the tragedy of the commons as a cesspool must be prevented by different means, by coercive laws or taxing devices that make it cheaper for the polluter to treat his pollutants than to discharge them untreated. * * *

### FREEDOM TO BREED IS INTOLERABLE

In a welfare state, how shall we deal with the family, the religion, the race, or the class (or indeed any distinguishable and cohesive group) that adopts overbreeding as a policy to secure its own aggrandizement * * * ? To couple the concept of freedom to breed with the belief that everyone born has an equal right to the commons is to lock the world into a tragic course of action. * * *

### CONSCIENCE IS SELF-ELIMINATING

It is a mistake to think that we can control the breeding of mankind in the long run by an appeal to conscience. * * * The argument is straightforward and Darwinian.

People vary. Confronted with appeals to limit breeding, some people will undoubtedly respond to the plea more than others. Those who have more children will produce a larger fraction of the next generation than those with more susceptible consciences. The difference will be accentuated, generation by generation. * * *

The argument has here been stated in the context of the population problem, but it applies equally well to any instance in which society appeals to an individual exploiting a commons to restrain himself for the general good—by means of his conscience. To make such an appeal is to set up a selective system that works toward the elimination of conscience from the race. * * *

### MUTUAL COERCION MUTUALLY AGREED UPON

The social arrangements that produce responsibility are arrangements that create coercion, of some sort. Consider bank robbing. The man who takes money from a bank acts as if the bank were a commons. How do we prevent such action? Certainly not by trying to control his behavior solely by a verbal appeal to his sense of responsibility. Rather than rely on propaganda we * * * insist that a bank is not a commons * * * . That we thereby infringe on the freedom of would-be robbers we neither deny nor regret. * * *

To many, the word coercion implies arbitrary decisions of distant and irresponsible bureaucrats; but this is not a necessary part of its meaning. The only kind of coercion I recommend is mutual coercion, mutually agreed upon by the majority of the people affected.

To say that we mutually agree to coercion is not to say that we are required to enjoy it, or even to pretend we enjoy it. Who enjoys taxes? We all grumble about them. But we accept compulsory taxes because we recognize that voluntary taxes would favor the conscienceless. * * *

### RECOGNITION OF NECESSITY

[T]he commons, if justifiable at all, is justifiable only under conditions of low-population density. As the human population has increased, the commons has had to be abandoned in one aspect after another. * * *

Every new enclosure of the commons involves the infringement of somebody's personal liberty. * * * But what does "freedom" mean? When men mutually agreed to pass laws against robbing, mankind became more free, not less so. Individuals locked into the logic of the commons are free only to bring on universal ruin * * * .

## 4. THE LIFEBOAT ETHIC

Garrett Hardin, author of *The Tragedy of the Commons*, has advocated a "lifeboat ethic" to solve the problem of overpopulation: restricting immigration in wealthier nations (the "lifeboats") and ending food subsidies to the starving people of developing countries. *See* Garrett Hardin, "Living on a Lifeboat," 24 *Bioscience* 561 (1974); Garrett Hardin, "Lifeboat Ethics: The Case Against Helping the Poor," 8 *Psychology Today* 38 (Sep. 1974). Hardin summarized his lifeboat ethic in a paper presented to the 1974 annual meeting of the American Association for the Advancement of Science:

> So long as nations multiply at different rates, survival requires that we adopt the ethic of the lifeboat. A lifeboat can hold only so many people. There are more than two billion wretched people in the world—ten times as many as in the United States. It is literally beyond our ability to save them all. * * * . Both international granaries and lax immigration policies must be rejected if we are to save something for our grandchildren.

Barry Commoner, "How Poverty Breeds Overpopulation (And Not the Other Way Around)" in *Bread for the World, The Challenge of World Hunger* 25A-26A (1980). Hardin further asserted in an earlier work:

> Every day we [i.e., Americans] are a smaller minority. We are increasing at only one percent a year; the rest of the world increases twice as fast. By the year 2000, one person in 24 will be an American; in one hundred years only one in 46 * * * . If the world is one great commons, in which all food is shared equally, then we are lost. Those who breed faster will replace the rest * * * . In the absence of breeding control a policy of "one mouth one meal" ultimately produces one totally miserable world. In a less than perfect world, the allocation of rights based on territory must be defended if a ruinous breeding race is to be avoided. It is unlikely that civilization and dignity can survive everywhere; but better in a few places than in none. Fortunate minorities must act as the trustees of a civilization that is threatened by uninformed good intentions.

Garrett Hardin, "The Survival of Nations and Civilizations," 172 *Science* 1297 (1971).[c] For a collection of essays on the lifeboat ethic and the duty of wealthy nations to assist poorer countries, see William Aiken & Hugh LaFollette, eds., *World Hunger and Morality* (2d ed. 1996).

---

[c] Excerpted with permission from Hardin, The Survival of Nations and Civilizations, 172 Science 1297 (1971). Copyright © 1971 by The American Association for the Advancement of Science.

## 5. PROSPECTS FOR COLLECTIVE ACTION

### WILLIAM OPHULS & A. STEPHEN BOYAN, JR., ECOLOGY AND THE POLITICS OF SCARCITY REVISITED

189-92, 202-03, 237-42, 244-46, 251-52 (1992)

#### THE POLITICAL EVILS OF SCARCITY

[S]carcity is the source of original political sin: Resources that are scantier than human wants have to be allocated by governments, for naked conflict would result otherwise. * * * [T]here must be a civil authority capable of keeping the peace by regulating property and other scarce goods. Scarcity thus makes politics inescapable. * * *

Presumably, the establishment of a truly just civil authority would eliminate all the political problems that arise from scarcity. * * * Unfortunately, this has never happened. * * * [C]ivilized polities have always institutionalized a large measure of inequality, oppression, and conflict. Thus, in addition to being the source of original political sin, scarcity is also the root of political evil.

The reason is quite simple. For most of recorded history societies have existed at the ecological margin or very close to it. An equal division of income and wealth, therefore, would condemn all to a life of shared poverty. Not unnaturally, the tendency has been for political institutions to further impoverish the masses by a fractional amount in order to create the surplus that enables a small elite to enjoy more than its share of the fruits of civilized life. * * * Except for a few relatively brief periods when for some reason the burden of scarcity was temporarily lifted, inequality, oppression, and conflict have been very prominent features of political life, merely waxing and waning slightly in response to the character of the rulers and other ephemeral factors.

Our own era has been the longest and certainly the most important exception. During roughly the last 450 years, the carrying capacity of the globe (and especially of the highly developed nations) has been markedly expanded, and several centuries of relative abundance have completely transformed the face of the earth and made our societies and our civilization what they are today—relatively open, egalitarian, libertarian, and conflict-free.

#### THE GREAT FRONTIER

The causes of the four-century-long economic boom we have enjoyed are readily apparent: the European discovery and exploitation of the New World, Oceania, and other founts of virgin resources (for example, Persian Gulf oil); the take-off and rapid-growth phases of science-based, energy-intensive technology; and the existence of vast reservoirs of "free" ecological goods such as air and water to absorb the consequences of our exploiting the new resources with the new technology. However, the first cause is clearly the most important.

Before the discovery of the New World, the population of Europe pressed hard on its means of subsistence, and as a result, European societies were politically, economically, and socially closed. But with the opening up of a "Great Frontier" in the New World * * * [a] bonanza of found wealth lifted the yoke of ecological scarcity and, coincidentally, created all the peculiar institutions and values characteristic of modern civilization—democracy, freedom, and individualism. * * *

But the boom is now over. The found wealth of the Great Frontier has been all but exhausted. And technology is no real substitute, for it is merely a means of manipulating *what is already there* rather than a way of creating genuinely new resources on the scale of the Great Frontier. * * * Thus a scarcity at least as intense as that prevailing in the premodern era, however different it may be in important respects, is about to replace abundance, and this will necessarily undercut the material conditions that have created and sustained current ideas, institutions, and practices. Once relative abundance and wealth of opportunity are no longer available to mitigate the harsh political dynamics of scarcity, the pressures favoring greater inequality, oppression, and conflict will build up, so that the return of scarcity portends the revival of age-old political evils, for our descendants if not for ourselves. In short, the golden age of individualism, liberty, and democracy (as those terms are currently understood) is all but over. * * *

### The Political Functions of Economic Growth

From our earliest colonial beginnings, rising expectations have been a fundamental part of the American credo, each generation expecting to become richer than the previous one. Thanks to this expectation of growth, the class conflict and social discontent typical of early nineteenth-century Europe were all but absent in America; politics was accordingly undemanding, pragmatic, and laissez-faire. * * *

Growth is still central to American politics. * * * The pursuit of happiness has come to be defined almost exclusively in material terms, and the entire society—individuals, enterprises, the government itself—has an enormous vested interest in the continuation of growth.

### Ecological Scarcity versus Economic Justice

To state the problem succinctly, growth and economic opportunity have been substitutes for equality of income and wealth. We have justified large differences in income and wealth on the grounds that they promote growth and that all members of society would receive future advantage from current inequality as the benefits of development "trickled down" to the poor. * * * But * * * with a cessation of growth, [the rationale for differential rewards] virtually disappears. * * * Because people's demands for economic betterment are not likely to disappear, once the pie stops growing fast enough to accommodate their needs, they will begin making demands for redistribution.

Even more serious than the frustration of rising expectations is the prospect of actual deprivation as substantial numbers of people get worse off in terms of real income as a result of scarcity-induced inflation and the internalization of environmental costs. Indeed, the eventual consequence of ecological scarcity is a lower standard of living, as we currently define it, for almost all members of society. One does not need a gloomy view of human nature to realize that this will create enormous political and social tension. It is, in fact, the classic prescription for revolution. At the very least, we can expect that our politics will come to be dominated by resentment and envy * * * .

To make the revolutionary potential of the politics of emulation more concrete, let us imagine that the current trend toward making automobile ownership and operation more expensive continues to the point where the car becomes once again a luxury item, available only to "the carriage trade." How will the average person, once an economic aristocrat with his or her own private carriage but now demoted to a scooter or a bicycle, react to this deprivation, especially in view of the fact that the remaining aristocrats will presumably continue to enjoy their private carriages? * * *

The political stage is set, therefore, for a showdown between the claims of ecological scarcity on the one hand and socioeconomic justice on the other. * * *

### THE NON-POLITICS OF DUE PROCESS

In many areas, the American government will be obliged to have genuine policies—that is, specific measures or programs designed to further some particular conception of the public interest. This will require radical changes, because in our laissez-faire political system, ends are subordinated to political means. In other words, we practice "process" politics as opposed to "systems" politics * * * . [P]rocess politics emphasizes the adequacy and fairness of the rules governing the process of politics. If the process is fair, then, as in a trial conducted according to due process, the outcome is assumed to be just—or at least the best that the system can achieve. * * *

The process model has many virtues. Keeping the question of ends out of politics greatly diminishes the intensity of social conflict. People debate the fairness of the rules, a matter about which they find it relatively easy to agree, and they do not confront each other with value demands, which may not be susceptible to compromise. However, by some standards, the process model hardly deserves the name of politics, for it evades the whole issue of the common interest simply by declaring that the "will of all" and the "general will" are identical. The common interest is thus, by definition, whatever the political system's invisible hand cranks out, for good or ill. * * *

Coping with the consequences of ecological scarcity will require explicit, outcome-oriented political decisions taken in the name of some conception of an ecological, if not a political and social, common interest. What likelihood is there of this happening? * * *

### THE ECOLOGICAL VICES OF MUDDLING THROUGH

The logic of the commons is enshrined in a system of process politics * * * . The ecological vices of this system are further intensified by the decision-making style characteristic of all our institutions—disjointed incrementalism or, to use the more honest and descriptive colloquial term, "muddling through."

Incremental decision making largely ignores long-term goals; it focuses on the problem immediately at hand and tries to find the solution that is most congruent with the status quo. It is thus characterized by comparison and evaluation of marginal changes (increments) in current policies, not radical departures from them; by consideration of only a restricted number of policy alternatives * * * ; and by a remedial orientation in which policies are designed to cure obvious immediate ills rather than to bring about some desired future state. Moreover, analysis of policy alternatives is not disinterested, for it is carried out largely by partisan actors who are trying to improve their bargaining position with other partisan actors.

Muddling through is therefore a highly economic style of decision making that is well adapted to a pragmatic, laissez-faire system of politics. Moreover, it has considerable virtues. * * * Disjointed incrementalism is * * * conservative in a good sense: It does not slight traditional values, it encourages appreciation of the costs of change, and it prevents overly hasty action on complex issues. It may also avoid serious or irreversible mistakes, for an incremental measure that turns out to be mistaken can usually be corrected before major harm has been done. Under ideal circumstances, disjointed incrementalism therefore produces a succession of policy measures that take the system step by step toward the policy outcome that best reflects the interests of the participants in the political market.

Unfortunately, muddling through has some equally large vices. For example, it does not guarantee that all relevant values will be taken into account, and it is likely to overlook excellent policies not suggested by past experience. In addition, disjointed incrementalism is not well adapted to handling profound value conflicts, revolutions, crises, grand opportunities, and the like—in other words, any situation in which simple continuation of past policies is not an appropriate response. Most important, because decisions are made on the basis of immediate self-interest, muddling through is almost guaranteed to produce policies that will generate the tragedy of the commons. * * * [T]he short-term adjustment and stability achieved by muddling through is likely to be achieved at the expense of long-term stability and welfare.

A perfect illustration of the potential dangers of muddling through is our approach to global warming. As a result of millions of separate decisions made by industry and individuals, 6 billion tons of carbon dioxide are emitted into the atmosphere each year, and emissions are increasing by 3% annually. Yet no real congressional debate has occurred on whether to control these private decisions in order to reduce carbon emissions. * * * As a result, we go on unwittingly pursuing business as usual, making short-term calculations of costs and benefits, and bring upon ourselves the greenhouse effect almost by default. * * *

As we have seen, the basic institutional structure and modus operandi of the American political system are primarily responsible for this. Nevertheless, the lack of courage and vision displayed by the current set of political actors should not escape notice. Neither Congress nor the executive branch has provided real leadership or faced up to crucial issues. * * * [I]t is hard to conclude that our political leaders are doing the job they were elected to do. But of course, the inability or reluctance of our political officials to act simply reflects the desires of the majority of the American people, who have so far evinced only modest willingness to make minor sacrifices (for example, to support and engage in recycling) for the sake of environmental goals, but no willingness to accept fundamental changes in their way of life (for example, to restrict development to areas where public transit is available or to support and use public transit and drive less).

Our public officials can hardly be expected to commit political suicide by forcing unpopular environmental measures on us. Until the will of the people ordains otherwise or fundamental changes are quite literally forced on us, the best we can expect is piecemeal, patchwork, ineffective reform that lags ever farther behind onrushing events.

### Questions

1. Who do you think is right on the issue of the limits to growth—the authors of *Beyond the Limits*, at pages 29-36, *supra*, or Kaysen, Starr, and Simon, at pages 36-39, *supra*? Why?

2. If we cannot tell who is right, who should we *assume* is right for the purposes of selecting governmental policies? Why?

3. Reexamine carefully the excerpt from *Beyond the Limits* and the summary of its findings. What specific actions do the authors advocate?

4. Assume that the authors of *Beyond the Limits* are correct and that their prescribed actions are urgently needed. What are the chances—according to Ophuls and Boyan—of effectively implementing those steps in the United States? Do you agree with Ophuls and Boyan? Why or why not?

## D. ENVIRONMENTAL QUALITY AND THE GOOD LIFE

## BILL MCKIBBEN, NOT SO FAST

N.Y. Times (July 23, 1995) at 6:24, col. 2

Here's a short chemistry lesson. Grasp it and you will grasp the reason the environmental era has barely begun; perhaps you will grasp the history of the next 50 years.

Put a gallon of gasoline in the tank of your car and go out for a drive. Assuming your engine's well tuned, burning that gallon of petroleum should put about half a pound of carbon in the form of carbon monoxide—CO—into the air. A generation ago that number was closer to one pound; by decade's end, as new technologies clean the exhaust, it should drop to barely a tenth of a pound. The steady decrease in CO emissions, as well as in those of nitrous oxide and particulates, is the reason the air is clearer and safer now in Los Angeles than it was a generation ago.

On the same drive, however, that gallon of gas will transmute itself into almost five and a half pounds of carbon in the form of carbon dioxide. Long considered proof that gas was burning cleanly, invisible and odorless $CO_2$ is the inevitable byproduct of fossil fuel consumption. It doesn't matter if your car's old or new; there's no filter you can stick on the exhaust to reduce $CO_2$ production. And if the wide international consensus of scientists is correct, this carbon dioxide is now warming the planet more quickly and to higher temperatures than ever in human history.

CO versus $CO_2$. One damn oxygen atom, and all the difference in the world.

If you focus on carbon monoxide, then you can count yourself among the currently fashionable environmental optimists. Pollution, from their perspective, is an unfortunate byproduct of an essentially sound system. Since smog and its many analogues (river pollution, acid rain, crowded landfills) are precisely the sorts of things that can be tamed with filters and scrubbers, or with small changes in human behavior like recycling, the optimists are in some ways right. Though * * * there are plenty of poor and minority communities that never began to get cleaned in the first place, the technology exists to diminish smog, to purify drinking water. It's merely a matter of finding the will to pay for it—there's no reason for rivers to catch fire. * * * So if CO turns out to be the real issue, then it's just a systems problem. Environmentalism is a success story, and the world we die in will resemble the one we were born into, albeit with more computers.

That's the conventional wisdom of the moment, best expressed by Gregg Easterbrook in his recent book, *A Moment on the Earth*. And yet there are those of us who are not soothed—who grow more worried with each passing month * * * . Those in this second camp tend to be focused on problems like widespread extinction, growing populations, dying fisheries and dwindling wilderness—signals, like the ever-expanding cloud of $CO_2$, indicating that our societies and their appetites have simply grown too large. Signals still all but ignored.

Since the environmental movement began, all these crises have been lumped together. The same people who worried about clean air worried about recycling and species extinction, about dirty rivers and the press of population. All these causes are important * * * but acting as if they were all essentially the same crisis carries risks as well as benefits. While it's certainly easier to focus on things like smog, which people see around them every day, the logic of focusing on the most visible pollution cuts both ways. Such a narrowly pragmatic vision is potentially paralyzing precisely because you can clean urban air, you can return fish to the Great Lakes, you can recycle enough to keep landfills from overflowing.

Unfortunately, you can do all these quite vital things without having any real effect on the more systematic troubles. The progress we've made in solving environmental problems is deceptive: we're making no progress at all on the deeper problems, because they do not spring from the same sources. One set stems from a defect in the car; the other set comes from the very existence of the car. And in an odd way, solving the first kind of problem makes the deeper ones ever more intractable—if visible air pollution starts to decline, then the push for better mass transit dwindles, and with it the chances of cutting the invisible $CO_2$ .

The environmental movement, in other words, has reached a diagnostic crisis.

To use a medical analogy: The world has presented itself, complaining of chest pains. After three decades of examination, there are still those who insist it's indigestion and want to prescribe some Bromo. Others say arteriosclerosis, which means our most basic behaviors must change. Most people—not just C.E.O.'s—badly want to find out that our problems are not related to our life styles. Change frightens us: we've come to believe, for instance, that our well-being is lashed to constant economic growth. "It's the economy, stupid."

And yet the basic laws of chemistry may soon demand that we give up such fixations. The Intergovernmental Panel on Climate Change, a group of scientists assembled by the United Nations, has calculated that an immediate 60 percent reduction in fossil fuel use is necessary to stabilize global climate. This could not happen in a world that closely resembles ours. Addicted to growth, busily spreading our vision of the good life around the globe, we are sprinting in the opposite direction. The growth in our economies and populations wipes out our incremental gains in energy efficiency: from 1983 to 1993, despite a tremendous push toward efficiency by power companies, Americans increased their per capita power usage by more than 22 percent. Electric utilities offered rebates for installing compact fluorescent bulbs, and, indeed, between 1986 and 1991 the typical household added one such light. But * * * the typical household also added more than seven incandescent lamps.

Since the greenhouse effect and other consequences of our civilization's basic momentum have yet to hit us full-on, no mass movement has developed to challenge that momentum. * * *

But this state of affairs may not last. According to the most accurate computer models of global climate, for instance, increased global temperatures may be obvious to the man in the street by decade's end. * * * [I]t will take only a hot summer or two, a string of crop failures or some similar catastrophe to bring these issues center stage once more. A spate of recent studies has begun to make clear that an average temperature increase of only a few degrees hides tremendous heat waves, droughts and storms; the insurance industry has actually begun to worry publicly about the greenhouse effect and the losses it will cause.

If and when such stresses really show themselves, though, we will need an environmental movement that understands what is happening—that understands that more recycling is not the main answer, that is willing to advocate the unpopular and the disturbing. Partly this means a stepped-up political campaign—continual pressure on governments around the world to sign and fulfill treaties, share renewable technologies and pass steep new taxes on the use of fossil fuels and other polluters. Already a small segment of the environmental movement has begun to focus on such issues.

But remember the numbers. A 60 percent reduction in fossil fuel use? Even under the most hopeful technological scenarios, it won't happen if we're simultaneously doubling or tripling our economies. More money makes reducing smog easier, because you can afford to build better cars; more money makes dealing with the greenhouse effect harder, because you can afford to buy more cars. So the sweet dream that we'll all grow rich enough to turn green is simply that—a dream, and one that will turn into a nightmare if we try to follow it.

# KENNETH E. BOULDING,
## THE ECONOMICS OF THE
## COMING SPACESHIP EARTH

in Environmental Quality in a Growing Economy
3, 5-6, 9-12 (H. Jarrett ed. 1966)

We are now in the middle of a long process of transition in the nature of the image which man has of himself and his environment. * * * [M]en of the early civilizations imagined themselves to be living on a virtually illimitable plane. * * * [T]here has been something like a frontier—some place else to go when things got too difficult, either by reason of the deterioration of the natural environment or a deterioration of the social structure in places where people happened to live. * * *

Gradually, however, man has been accustoming himself to the notion of the spherical earth and a closed sphere of human activity. * * *

The closed earth of the future requires economic principles which are somewhat different from those of the open earth of the past. * * * I am tempted to call the open economy the "cowboy economy," the cowboy being symbolic of the illimitable plains and also associated with reckless, exploitative, romantic, and violent behavior, which is characteristic of open societies. The closed economy of the future might similarly be called the "spaceman" economy, in which the earth has become a single spaceship, without unlimited reservoirs of anything, either for extraction or for pollution * * * . The difference between the two types of economy becomes most apparent in the attitude towards consumption. In the cowboy economy, consumption is regarded as a good thing and production likewise; and the success of the economy is measure by the amount of the throughput * * * . If there are infinite reservoirs from which material can be obtained and into which effluvia can be deposited, then the throughput is at least a plausible measure of the success of the economy. The gross national product is a rough measure of this total throughput. * * *

By contrast, in the spaceman economy, throughput is by no means a desideratum, and is indeed to be regarded as something to be minimized rather than maximized. The essential measure of success of the economy is not production and consumption at all, but the nature, extent, quality, and complexity of the total capital stock, including in this the state of the human bodies and minds included in the system. In the spaceman economy, what we are primarily concerned with is stock maintenance, and any technological change which results in the maintenance of a given total stock with a lessened throughput (that is, less production and consumption) is clearly a gain. This idea that both production and consumption are bad things rather than good things is very strange to economists, who have been obsessed with the income-flow concepts to the exclusion, almost, of capital-stock concepts.

There are actually some very tricky and unsolved problems involved in the questions as to whether human welfare or well-being is to be regarded as a stock or a flow. * * * Is it, for instance, eating that is a good thing, or is it being well fed? Does economic welfare involve having nice clothes, fine houses, good equipment, and so on, or is it to be measured by the depreciation and the wearing out of these things? I am inclined myself to regard the stock concept as most fundamental, that is, to think of being well fed as more important than eating, and to think even of so-called services as essentially involving the restoration of a depleting psychic capital. Thus I have argued that we go to a concert in order to restore a psychic condition which might be called "just having gone to a concert," which, once established, tends to depreciate. When it depreciates beyond a certain point, we go to another concert in order to restore it. If it depreciates rapidly, we go to a lot of concerts; if it depreciates slowly, we go to few. On this view, similarly, we eat primarily to restore bodily homeostasis, that is, to maintain a condition of being well fed, and so on. * * * [T]here is nothing desirable in consumption at all. The less consumption we can maintain a given state with, the better off we are. If we had clothes that did not wear out, houses that did not depreciate, and even if we could maintain our bodily condition without eating, we would clearly be much better off.

It is this last consideration, perhaps, which makes one pause. Would we, for instance, really want an operation that would enable us to restore all our bodily tissues by intravenous feeding while we slept? Is there not, that is to say, a certain virtue in throughput itself, in activity itself, in production and consumption itself, in raising food and in eating it? It would certainly be rash to exclude this possibility. Further interesting problems are raised by the demand for variety. We certainly do not want a constant state to be maintained; we want fluctuations in the state. Otherwise there would be no demand for variety in food, for variety in scene, as in travel, for variety in social contact, and so on. The demand for variety can, of course, be costly, and sometimes it seems to be too costly to be tolerated or at least legitimated, as in the case of marital partners, where the maintenance of [the] state [of] the family is usually regarded as much more desirable than the variety and excessive throughput of the libertine. There are problems here which the economics profession has neglected with astonishing singlemindedness. * * * [E]conomists continue to think and act as if production, consumption, throughput, and the GNP were the sufficient and adequate measure of economic success.

It may be said, of course, why worry about all this when the spaceman economy is still a good way off (at least beyond the lifetimes of any now living), so let us eat, drink, spend, extract and pollute, and be as merry as we can, and let posterity worry about the spaceship earth. * * *

There has always been something rather refreshing in the view that we should live like the birds, and perhaps posterity is for the birds in more senses than one; so perhaps we should all call it a day and go out and pollute something cheerfully. As an old taker of thought for the morrow, however, I cannot quite accept this solution; and I would argue, furthermore, that tomorrow is not only very close, but in many respects it is already here. The shadow of the future spaceship, indeed, is already falling over our spendthrift merriment. * * *

# Chapter Three

# ENVIRONMENTAL ECONOMICS

## A. INTRODUCTION

Environmental lawyers and policymakers cannot avoid the discipline of economics. Recognizing that law students bring different backgrounds to the subject—ranging from utter ignorance to Ph.Ds.—this chapter explores a limited number of core economics concepts essential to the practice of environmental law. Bear in mind the observation of one wit that "[t]he purpose of studying economics is * * * to learn how to avoid being deceived by economists." John K. Galbraith, *Economics and the Public Purpose* (1973) (quoting Joan Robinson).

The initial readings introduce the goal of *economic efficiency*—a situation characterized by the absence of "waste" (or "misallocation" of resources)—and the role of the market in achieving efficiency. The first reading explains the concept of *Pareto Optimality*—a purely theoretical criterion that is closely related to the applied criterion of economic efficiency. Do not get hung up on the theoretical details of Pareto Optimality (although you will need a vague idea of what the term means to cope with later readings); the purpose of this excerpt is to introduce the basic notion of maximizing human satisfactions by relying on the marketplace, rather than by using other devices—such as a central economic planning committee that might dictate the production of goods and services in specified quantities.

## B. PARETO OPTIMALITY

### OTTO A. DAVIS & MORTON I. KAMIEN, EXTERNALITIES AND THE QUALITY OF AIR AND WATER

in Economics of Air and Water Pollution 12-16
(William R. Walker, ed. 1969)

Every economic system, be it of the free enterprise variety such as ours or of the mixed government directed and free-enterprise type found in Great Britain and the Scandinavian countries, or of the completely government controlled variety as in the Soviet Union, is confronted with the question of how to "best" allocate resources—raw materials, land, and labor. Because resources are ordinarily available only in limited amounts their diversion into the production of a certain class of goods and/or services results in a diminution in the production of other goods and/or services. This basic insight leads immediately to the concept of opportunity or real cost. The real cost of producing a given item is the sacrifice of another good or service that might have been produced with the resources employed. The reason for emphasizing the term real cost is to draw attention to the fact that the nominal or money cost of an item does not always reflect the opportunity cost * * * .

Knowledge that allocation of resources to the production of automobiles precludes the use of the same resources to produce, say, washing machines does not in itself reveal how the resources should be used. The determination of the quantities of automobiles and washing machines to be produced can be accomplished by the assignment of relative values to the two items and the maximization of the total value of their production. Notice that maximization of the total value of the two items means that the total value of the relevant resources is maximized and that resources withdrawn from the production of automobiles must be used to produce the largest number of washing machines possible. * * * To put it another way, production must be efficient—the sacrifice of other goods and services entailed in the production must be as small as possible under existing technology. * * *

There are many alternative ways of assigning relative values to all the potentially producible commodities. At one end of the spectrum of possibilities is the assignment of values by a committee or even a single individual on behalf of all the members of the society. At the other end of this spectrum is the assignment by each individual or family group [of] relative values to all commodities and the aggregation of these valuations via some mechanism. Our present form of economic organization is closer to the latter end of the spectrum than the former. We believe in consumer sovereignty—the right for each individual to place his own valuations on all commodities—and we might add in producer sovereignty—the right for each producer to produce whatever he wishes. There are of course various laws and regulations that circumscribe these rights, yet by and large, the individual in his capacity either as a consumer or a producer has considerable freedom of choice. Tacitly, we suppose in adhering to consumer sovereignty that individuals act in their own best interest and that they have the necessary information and mental capacity of doing so. Even if these assumptions are somewhat heroic, we are even more reluctant to accept the proposition that any single individual or committee is better able to determine what is in the best interest of other people.

Our assertion that each individual is capable of placing his own valuation on each and every good poses difficulties when it comes to aggregating the valuations of many individuals. The essential difficulty arises because even if individuals express their valuations of the various commodities in terms of numbers the scales they use may be different. Consequently it is meaningless to add the numbers together. For example, it makes no sense to add centimeters and inches directly to determine the length of some object. However, with the use of transformation [1 inch equals 2.54 centimeters] the two units of length can be made conformable for addition. Unfortunately we have no way of transforming one individual's valuation of the commodity. The upshot of all this is that we cannot determine what commodities should be produced and thereby how the available resources should be allocated by maximizing the simple sum of individual valuations. Because of this economists have substituted another criterion for the determination of how resources should be allocated. This criterion is called Pareto Optimality and asserts that an allocation of resources is optimal if no reallocation could make some members of society better off without making others worse off. Thus, if the constellation of commodities produced is such that any change designed to increase the well being of one individual must be detrimental to the well being of another individual, then the original constellation of goods and the underlying allocation of resources is Pareto Optimal. On the other hand, if it is possible by reallocating resources to make some individual better off without affecting the well being of others then the original allocation of resources is not Pareto Optimal.

It should be noticed that the Pareto Optimality criterion allows for many alternative allocation[s] of resources, or what is the same thing, commodity production configurations. For it is possible that departure from a commodity constellation consisting of many colored television sets and few bath tubs will make some people better off only at the expense of others being made worse off. Likewise, a constellation of commodities in which the proportion of colored televisions and bath tubs is reversed may also be Pareto Optimal. The upshot of all this is that Pareto Optimality is an efficiency criterion which in itself does not tell us which commodities should be produced. It does tell us however, that any resource allocation that does not meet this criterion can be improved upon. In other words, Pareto Optimality requires that there be no waste in the utilization of resources and the distribution of commodities among individuals. * * *

The device we use for allocating resources that is compatible with consumer sovereignty is the market mechanism. We allow individuals to express their relative valuations among different commodities by purchasing those they desire more and declining to buy those they like less. We rely on [producer's] motivation for high profits for the production of those goods presently most preferred by the public and a change in the mixture of commodities produced as consumer's tastes or incomes change. It is evident that the real market place does not always operate so smoothly. If a firm is isolated from competitive pressures it tends to become less responsive to consumer needs. Also, firms attempt to alter consumer taste via advertising. In short, in reality the market place has many shortcomings. The government tries via anti-trust legislation, truth in advertising bills, and the dissemination of information to mention only a few methods, to counteract these faults. The important point to note in connection with some of these maladies is that they are shortcomings of the market place in practice but not in principle. We shall not be concerned with them here, though they may be responsible for a substantial misallocation of resources. Instead, our major concern will be with failures of the market place which may be thought of as being more fundamental.

Under ideal conditions a competitive market structure would result in a Pareto Optimal allocation of resources. This statement may be regarded as the fundamental theorem of modern welfare economics. * * *

## C. EFFICIENCY AND MARKET FAILURE

Changes that will make some individuals better off without making others worse off are uncommon; accordingly, the theoretical criterion of Pareto Optimality is of little practical use and must give way to the applied criterion of *economic efficiency*. Economists assume that the value of all commodities can be quantitatively measured and compared by using a money price, reflecting the willingness of individuals to pay for various quantities of the commodities. The goal of economic analysis then becomes the maximization of society's total value of production: economic efficiency. If all things of value were measurable commodities and if the market price system included all relevant commodities, the signals given to producers by the market would ensure an economically efficient society—one in which the correct quantities of each commodity were produced.

The foregoing assumptions are frequently contradicted in the realm of natural resources. Indeed, Paul Hawken, in *The Ecology of Commerce* (1993), declares that "[w]ithout a doubt, the single most damaging aspect of the present economic system is that the expense of destroying the earth is largely absent from the prices set in the marketplace." *Id.* at 13. The discipline of economics tells us, therefore, that excessive levels of pollution are a result of market failures.

## ROYAL COMMISSION ON ENVIRONMENTAL POLLUTION, FIRST REPORT

Cmnd. No. 4585, pp. 4-6 (1971)

It may well be asked why it is that there should be a growing conflict between economic and technological advance on the one hand, and the quality of the environment on the other. There are two main reasons. One is rooted in a basic law of nature: it is impossible to add to the material resources with which the world is endowed and impracticable to dispose of waste materials outside the world and its envelope of air. * * * The second reason for the growing conflict is largely economic. Little can be done about the first reason, for even the most powerful legislatures cannot change the laws of nature; but many things can be done about the second. Governments can protect the environment through legal and institutional arrangements.

The economic reason why society may not strike the right balance between economic output and the quality of the environment is that the costs of many kinds of pollution are borne not by the polluters, but by somebody else. As a result these "external" costs will not, in general, be taken fully into account by firms, individuals or other bodies who cause pollution. The other side of the coin is that those who spend money on reducing pollution may not always be the people who gain from the resulting improvement in the environment. This applies both to "tangible" pollution, such as the poisoning of fish in polluted waters, and to "intangible" pollution, such as unpleasant smells or ugly landscapes.

This characteristic of pollution has three main consequences:

(a) Output of goods and services which give rise to pollution tends to be pushed beyond the socially optimum point. Also, expenditure to reduce pollution will often be inadequate. This is true not only for private firms or individuals: it is true also for public authorities. For example, it is hardly surprising that a large proportion of the many sewage works in this country are inadequate, since it may well be that the benefits from better installations—in the form of cleaner effluent and hence cleaner rivers—would be enjoyed only by communities living further downstream. In such cases all the benefits are external to the sewage authority, which therefore has little inducement to improve its plant.

(b) There is generally not enough incentive to reduce the amount of pollution per unit of output of the goods and services responsible, so that not enough resources and effort are devoted to this objective. For example, if it becomes cheaper to distribute milk in plastic containers instead of glass bottles, this will be done whether or not the production and disposal of plastic containers impose higher pollution costs per unit of milk consumed than does the use of glass bottles. * * * [W]e cannot rely on technological innovation automatically to reduce environmental pollution.

(c) Insofar as pollution costs are not borne by those who cause pollution or by the purchasers of their products, but by people who happen to be the victims of the pollution, some of the total welfare resulting from the economic activity of the community is being redistributed away from the victims of pollution in favour of other groups in the community. Manufacturers whose production gives rise to pollution make greater profits than they would if they were obliged to bear the full social costs of their production, and purchasers of their goods buy them at a lower price than they would if the price had to cover the full social costs involved. * * *

# D. PIGOU'S SOLUTION: COST-INTERNALIZATION

The preceding readings are important because of what they suggest about the proper assignment of legal rights and liabilities between two entities or groups of entities that will occupy our attention during much of this book: polluters and receptors. The concept of *negative externalities* or *external costs*—with its associated notion that unacceptable levels of pollution result from a divergence between private and social costs of an activity—has led many economists to conclude that excessive pollution can be most readily abated by forcing polluters to *internalize* the external costs of their pollution. Indeed, Ronald Coase, in the next reading, asserted in 1960 that most economists had reached that conclusion. Cost internalization might be achieved in a variety of ways by the legal system. For example, polluters might be held strictly liable under the common law or by statute for all harms caused to receptors by their pollution; alternatively, the government might impose a tax on pollution equal to the harm imposed by emissions. These techniques (and various others that we will explore in this book) would force polluters to confront the social costs of their pollution, internalizing social costs into their profit and loss calculations.

For convenience, we will refer to this cost-internalization solution as the "neoclassical economics viewpoint." *See* David M. Driesen, *The Societal Cost of Environmental Regulation: Beyond Administrative Cost-Benefit Analysis*, 24 Ecology L.Q. 545, 553 (1997). Because this approach was suggested by the famous welfare economist Arthur Cecil Pigou, we will sometimes use Pigou's name as a convenient label when referring to the cost-internalization theory. *See* Hawken, *The Ecology of Commerce* 82-83 (1993); A.C. Pigou, *The Economics of Welfare* (1920).

# E. THE COASE THEOREM

In the following path-breaking essay, Ronald Coase, winner of the 1991 Nobel prize in economics, takes issue with the neoclassical economics approach of Pigou, making some startling suggestions about the nature of pollution and about the government's proper role in assigning legal rights and liabilities between polluters and receptors. The Coase analysis is fundamental to an understanding of modern environmental law.

# RONALD H. COASE, THE
# PROBLEM OF SOCIAL COST

3 J. Law & Econ. 1-8, 11-13, 15-16, 19, 23-24, 26-28, 42-44 (1960)

## THE PROBLEM TO BE EXAMINED

This paper is concerned with those actions of business firms which have harmful effects on others. The standard example is that of a factory, the smoke from which has harmful effects on those occupying neighbouring properties. The economic analysis of such a situation has usually proceeded in terms of a divergence between the private and social product of the factory, in which economists have largely followed the treatment of Pigou in *The Economics of Welfare*. The conclusion to which this kind of analysis seems to have led most economists is that it would be desirable to make the owner of the factory liable for the damage caused to those injured by the smoke, or alternatively, to place a tax on the factory owner varying with the amount of smoke produced and equivalent in money terms to the damage it would cause, or finally, to exclude the factory from residential districts (and presumably from other areas in which the emission of smoke would have harmful effects on others). It is my contention that the suggested courses of action are inappropriate, in that they lead to results which are not necessarily, or even usually, desirable.

## THE RECIPROCAL NATURE OF THE PROBLEM

The traditional approach has tended to obscure the nature of the choice that has to be made. The question is commonly thought of as one in which A inflicts harm on B and what has to be decided is: how should we restrain A? But this is wrong. We are dealing with a problem of a reciprocal nature. To avoid the harm to B would inflict harm on A. The real question that has to be decided is: should A be allowed to harm B or should B be allowed to harm A? The problem is to avoid the more serious harm. I instanced in my previous article the case of a confectioner the noise and vibrations from whose machinery disturbed a doctor in his work. To avoid harming the doctor would inflict harm on the confectioner. The problem posed by this case was essentially whether it was worth while, as a result of restricting the methods of production which could be used by the confectioner, to secure more doctoring at the cost of a reduced supply of confectionery products. * * * What answer should be given is, of course, not clear unless we know the value of what is obtained as well as the value of what is sacrificed to obtain it. * * * It goes almost without saying that this problem has to be looked at in total *and* at the margin.

## THE PRICING SYSTEM WITH LIABILITY FOR DAMAGE

I propose to start my analysis by examining a case in which most economists would presumably agree that the problem would be solved in a completely satisfactory manner: when the damaging business has to pay for all damage caused[a] *and* the pricing system works smoothly (strictly this means that the operation of a pricing system is without cost).

A good example of the problem under discussion is afforded by the case of straying cattle which destroy crops growing on neighbouring land. Let us suppose that a farmer and a cattle-raiser are operating on neighbouring properties. Let us further suppose that, without any fencing between the properties, an increase in the size of the cattle-raiser's herd increases the total damage to the farmer's crops. What happens to the marginal damage as the size of the herd increases is another matter. This depends on whether the cattle tend to follow one another or to roam side by side, on whether they tend to be more or less restless as the size of the herd increases and on other similar factors. For my immediate purpose, it is immaterial what assumption is made about marginal damage as the size of the herd increases.

To simplify the argument, I propose to use an arithmetical example. I shall assume that the annual cost of fencing the farmer's property is $9 and that the price of the crop is $1 per ton. Also, I assume that the relation between the number of cattle in the herd and the annual crop loss is as follows:

| Number in Herd (Steers) | Annual Crop Loss (Tons) | Crop Loss per Additional Steer (Tons) |
|---|---|---|
| 1 | 1 | 1 |
| 2 | 3 | 2 |
| 3 | 6 | 3 |
| 4 | 10 | 4 |

Given that the cattle-raiser is liable for the damage caused, the additional annual cost imposed on the cattle-raiser if he increased his herd from, say, 2 to 3 steers is $3 and in deciding on the size of the herd, he will take this into account along with his other costs. That is, he will not increase the size of the herd unless the value of the additional meat produced * * * is greater than the additional costs that this will entail, including the value of the additional crops destroyed. * * * Given that the annual cost of fencing is $9, the cattle-raiser who wished to have a herd with 4 steers or more would pay for fencing to be erected and maintained * * * . When the fence is erected, the marginal cost due to the liability for damage becomes zero * * * . But, of course, it may be cheaper for the cattle-raiser not to fence and to pay for the damaged crops, as in my arithmetical example, with 3 or fewer steers. * * *

[F]or any given tract of land, if the value of the crop damaged is so great that the receipts from the sale of the undamaged crop are less than the total costs of cultivating that tract of land, it will be profitable for the farmer and the cattle-raiser to make a bargain whereby that

---

[a] *Ed.*—We will call this strict liability principle *Rule B.*

tract of land is left uncultivated. This can be made clear by means of an arithmetical example. Assume initially that the value of the crop obtained from cultivating a given tract of land is $12 and that the cost incurred in cultivating this tract of land is $10, the net gain from cultivating the land being $2. * * * Now assume that the cattle-raiser starts operations on the neighbouring property and that the value of the crops damaged is $1. In this case $11 is obtained by the farmer from sale on the market and $1 is obtained from the cattle-raiser for damage suffered and the net gain remains $2. Now suppose that the cattle-raiser finds it profitable to increase the size of his herd, even though the amount of damage rises to $3 * * * . [T]he total payment for damage is now $3. The net gain to the farmer from cultivating the land is still $2. The cattle-raiser would be better off if the farmer would agree not to cultivate his land for any payment less than $3. The farmer would be agreeable to not cultivating the land for any payment greater than $2. There is clearly room for a mutually satisfactory bargain which would lead to the abandonment of cultivation. * * *

What payment would in fact be made would depend on the shrewdness of the farmer and the cattle-raiser as bargainers. But * * * such an agreement would not affect the allocation of resources but would merely alter the distribution of income and wealth as between the cattle-raiser and the farmer. * * *

THE PRICING SYSTEM WITH NO LIABILITY FOR DAMAGE

I now turn to the case in which, although the pricing system is assumed to work smoothly (that is, costlessly), the damaging business is not liable for any of the damage which it causes.[b] This business does not have to make a payment to those damaged by its actions. I propose to show that the allocation of resources will be the same in this case as it was when the damaging business was liable for damage caused. * * *

Suppose that the size of the cattle-raiser's herd is 3 steers * * * . Then the farmer would be willing to pay up to $3 if the cattle-raiser would reduce his herd to 2 steers, up to $5 if the herd were reduced to 1 steer and would pay up to $6 if cattle-raising was abandoned. The cattle-raiser would therefore receive $3 from the farmer if he kept 2 steers instead of 3. This $3 foregone is therefore part of the cost incurred in keeping the third steer. Whether the $3 is a payment which the cattle-raiser has to make if he adds the third steer to his herd (which it would be if the cattle-raiser was liable to the farmer for damage caused to the crop [**Rule B**]) or whether it is a sum of money which he would have received if he did not keep a third steer (which it would be if the cattle-raiser was not liable to the farmer for damage caused to the crop [**Rule A**]) does not affect the final result. In both cases $3 is part of the cost of adding a third steer, to be included along with the other costs. If the increase in the value of production in cattle-raising through increasing the size of the herd from 2 to 3 is greater than the additional costs that

---

[b] *Ed.*—We will call this non-liability principle **Rule A**.

have to be incurred (including the $3 damage to crops), the size of the herd will be increased. Otherwise, it will not. The size of the herd will be the same whether the cattle-raiser is liable for damage caused to the crop or not.[c] * * * [A] receipt foregone of a given amount is the equivalent of a payment of the same amount. * * * [T]he long-run equilibrium position * * * is the same whether or not the cattle-raiser is held responsible for the crop damage brought about by his cattle.

It is necessary to know whether the damaging business is liable or not for damage caused since without the establishment of this initial delimitation of rights there can be no market transactions to transfer and recombine them. But the ultimate result (which maximises the value of production) is independent of the legal position if the pricing system is assumed to work without cost. * * *

### THE PROBLEM ILLUSTRATED ANEW

The problem of straying cattle and damaging of crops * * * [is] but one example of a problem which arises in many different guises. * * *

*Bryant v. Lefever* [4 C.P.D. 172 (1878-1879)] raised the problem of the smoke nuisance in a novel form. The plaintiff and defendants were occupiers of adjoining houses, which were of about the same height.

Before 1876 the plaintiff was able to light a fire in any room of his house without the chimneys smoking; the two houses had remained in the same condition for some thirty or forty years. In 1876 the defendants took down their house, and began to rebuild it. They carried up a wall by the side of the plaintiff's chimneys much beyond its original height, and stacked timber on the roof of their house, and thereby caused the plaintiff's chimneys to smoke whenever he lighted fires.

The reason, of course, why the chimneys smoked was that the erection of the wall and the stacking of the timber prevented the free circulation of air. In a trial before a jury, the plaintiff was awarded damages of £40. The case then went to the Court of Appeals where the judgment was reversed. Bramwell, L.J., argued:

> It is the plaintiff who causes the nuisance by lighting a coal fire in a place the chimney of which is placed so near the defendants' wall, that the smoke does not escape, but comes into the house. Let the plaintiff cease to light his fire, let him move his chimney, let him carry it higher, and there would be no nuisance. * * *

And Cotton, L.J., said:

> The plaintiff creates the smoke, which interferes with his comfort. * * * It is as if a man tried to get rid of liquid filth arising on his own land by a drain into his neighbour's land. * * * [T]he neighbour might stop the drain without incurring liability by so doing. No doubt great inconvenience would be caused to the owner of the property on which the liquid filth arises. But the act of his neighbour would be a

---

[c] *Ed.*—We will call this principle the *invariance thesis*.

lawful act, and he would not be liable for the consequences attributable to the fact that the man had accumulated filth without providing any effectual means of getting rid of it. * * *

Who caused the smoke nuisance? The answer seems fairly clear. The smoke nuisance was caused both by the man who built the wall *and* by the man who lit the fires. Given the fires, there would have been no smoke nuisance without the wall; given the wall, there would have been no smoke nuisance without the fires. Eliminate the wall *or* the fires and the smoke nuisance would disappear. On the marginal principle it is clear that *both* were responsible and *both* should be forced to include the loss of amenity due to the smoke as a cost of deciding whether to continue the activity which gives rise to the smoke. And given the possibility of market transactions, this is what would in fact happen. Although the wall-builder was not liable legally for the nuisance, as the man with the smoking chimneys would presumably be willing to pay a sum equal to the monetary worth to him of eliminating the smoke, this sum would therefore become for the wall-builder, a cost of continuing to have the high wall with the timber stacked on the roof.

The judges' contention that it was the man who lit the fires who alone caused the smoke nuisance is true only if we assume that the wall is the given factor. This is what the judges did by deciding that the man who erected the higher wall had a legal right to do so. * * *

Judges have to decide on legal liability but this should not confuse economists about the nature of the economic problem involved. In the case of the cattle and the crops, it is true that there would be no crop damage without the cattle. It is equally true that there would be no crop damage without the crops. * * * If we are to discuss the problem in terms of causation, both parties cause the damage.[d] If we are to attain an optimum allocation of resources, it is therefore desirable that both parties should take the harmful effect (the nuisance) into account in deciding on their course of action. * * *

The reasoning employed by the courts in determining legal rights will often seem strange to an economist because many of the factors on which the decision turns are, to an economist, irrelevant. Because of this, situations which are, from an economic point of view, identical will be treated quite differently by the courts. * * * [T]he immediate question faced by the courts is not what shall be done by whom but who has the legal right to do what. It is always possible to modify by transactions on the market the initial legal delimitation of rights. And, of course, if such market transactions are costless, such a rearrangement of rights will always take place if it would lead to an increase in the value of production.

---

[d] *Ed.*—We will call this assertion that pollution is caused jointly by the actions of the polluter and receptor the **reciprocal harm thesis**.

### THE COST OF MARKET TRANSACTIONS TAKEN INTO ACCOUNT

The argument has proceeded up to this point on the assumption * * * that there were no costs involved in carrying out market transactions. This is, of course, a very unrealistic assumption. In order to carry out a market transaction it is necessary to discover who it is that one wishes to deal with, to inform people that one wishes to deal and on what terms, to conduct negotiations leading up to a bargain, to draw up the contract, to undertake the inspection needed to make sure that the terms of the contract are being observed, and so on. These operations are often extremely costly, sufficiently costly at any rate to prevent many transactions that would be carried out in a world in which the pricing system worked without cost. * * *

Once the costs of carrying out market transactions are taken into account it is clear that * * * rearrangement of rights will only be undertaken when the increase in the value of production consequent upon the rearrangement is greater than the costs which would be involved in bringing it about. When it is less, * * * the initial delimitation of legal rights does have an effect on the efficiency with which the economic system operates. One arrangement of rights may bring about a greater value of production than any other. But unless this is the arrangement of rights established by the legal system, the costs of reaching the same result by altering and combining rights through the market may be so great that this optimal arrangement of rights * * * may never be achieved. * * *

### THE LEGAL DELIMITATION OF RIGHTS
### AND THE ECONOMIC PROBLEM

[I]f market transactions were costless, all that matters (questions of equity apart) is that the rights of the various parties should be well-defined and the results of legal actions easy to forecast. But as we have seen, the situation is quite different when market transactions are so costly as to make it difficult to change the arrangements of rights established by the law. In such cases, the courts directly influence economic activity. It would therefore seem desirable that the courts should understand the economic consequences of their decisions and should, insofar as this is possible without creating too much uncertainty about the legal position itself, take these consequences into account when making their decisions. Even when it is possible to change the legal delimitation of rights through market transactions, it is obviously desirable to reduce the need for such transactions and thus reduce the employment of resources in carrying them out. * * *

## 1. DIAGRAMMING THE COASE ANALYSIS

The following reading makes the transition from cows and crops to the pollution control problems to be examined in this book. Our analysis of the Coase theorem will focus extensively on the diagram set forth in **Figure 3-1**. You should carefully study that diagram and struggle to understand what it represents.

# RICHARD B. STEWART & JAMES E. KRIER, ENVIRONMENTAL LAW AND POLICY

133-36 (2nd ed. 1978)

### THE COASE ANALYSIS IN THE ABSENCE OF TRANSACTION COSTS

Coase essentially argues that in a world without transaction costs in which cost-free bargaining could occur, an economically efficient allocation of resources would always be reached. Moreover, this efficient allocation would occur regardless of how the courts define the rights and duties of the relevant parties. In such an ideal, frictionless world, the "problem" of pollution, viewed either as a collective good problem or an external cost problem, would disappear * * *.

Coase's thesis may be illustrated diagrammatically as follows. [*See* **Figure 3-1**] Assume a pollution source P emitting 100 tons of pollution per day, and a receptor R whose well being (personal, commercial, etc.) is impaired by the pollution or would be enhanced by cleaner air.

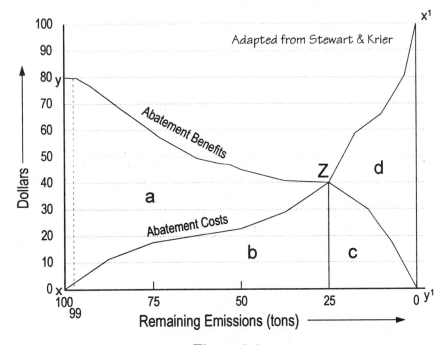

**Figure 3-1**

The horizontal axis represents P's emissions, with uncontrolled emissions of 100 at the extreme left-hand side, and complete control (zero emissions) at the extreme right. The vertical axis measures the costs and benefits of pollution control in dollars.

The curve of $yy^1$ represents the *marginal* value to R of reducing emissions. On the diagram, it would be worth about $80 to R to reduce emissions from 100 to 99, about $79 to reduce emissions from 99 to 98, and so on. For purposes of the diagram we have assumed that the value to R of reducing pollution declines with each successive reduction in control, but this would not always be the case. The exact shape of the curve would depend on the adverse effects of various pollution levels and the value to R of avoiding them. The total value of eliminating all emissions is represented by the sum of the areas a, b and c.

The curve $xx^1$ represents the *marginal* resource costs of reducing pollution. It shows that to reduce emissions by one ton would cost about $1, to reduce an additional ton would cost about $1.50, and so on. The curve as drawn shows the cost of additional control continuing to increase, becoming extremely high when the last few tons are eliminated. It is characteristic of most forms of pollution control that the costs of eliminating the last bit of pollution rise very sharply, but the precise shape of the curve would vary widely depending on the nature of the source and the control technology available. The total costs of eliminating all emissions are represented by the areas b, c and d.

Under Coase's assumptions of no transaction costs, 75 tons of emissions will be eliminated regardless of what tort or property rules apply. Assume P is not liable in any way to R for the damage caused by P's emissions. It will be in R's best interests to pay P to reduce emissions to 25 and no further. Why? Conversely, assume P must compensate R for the damage caused. It will be in P's best interests to reduce emissions to 25 and no further. Why? Finally, assume that R can enjoin P from emitting any pollutants at all. It will be in the best interests of P and R for P to pay R in exchange for R's permitting P to emit 25 tons of emissions. Why?

The point Z at which the curves $yy^1$ and $xx^1$ intersect represents the most economically efficient level of control. At any point to the left of Z, the curve $yy^1$ is above the curve $xx^1$, indicating that the benefits to society of removing an additional ton of emissions exceed the costs to society of such removal. At any point to the right of Z, curve $xx^1$ is above the curve $yy^1$, indicating that the marginal costs to society of removing an additional ton of emissions exceeds the marginal benefit. The point Z, where the marginal benefits of additional control just equal the marginal cost, accordingly represents the optimal point of control.

### Notes and Questions

1.  Assume a single Polluter and a single Receptor having the abatement cost and abatement benefit curves depicted in **Figure 3-1**. Assume also a society governed by what we will call *Rule A*—Polluter is not liable in any way to Receptor for the damage caused by Polluter's emissions. What does Coase say will happen, given this initial assignment of legal rights?

2.   Still assuming a single Polluter and a single Receptor having the abatement cost and abatement benefit curves depicted in **Figure 3-1**, assume that society is governed by *Rule B*—Receptor may recover damages from Polluter. What will happen, according to Coase?

3.   Continuing to assume a single Polluter and a single Receptor having the abatement cost and abatement benefits curves depicted in **Figure 3-1**, assume that society is governed by *Rule C*—Receptor has an automatic right to an injunction against Polluter to cease all discharge. What will happen, according to Coase?

4.   Two aspects of Coasian analysis are vital to our study of environmental law. First, Coase asserts that *all* problems of pollution are reciprocal, with the Polluter and the Receptor jointly causing the harm. We refer to this assertion as the *reciprocal harm thesis*. Second, Coase asserts that, in a perfectly functioning market (involving no transaction costs) the initial assignment of legal rights between the Polluter and Receptor is of no consequence: the parties will, through bargaining, arrive at a single optimal level of pollution control. We refer to this assertion as the *invariance thesis*. Given the numerous transaction costs that prevent perfect bargaining in the real world, Coase then suggests that the task of courts and regulators should be to mandate the single optimal level of pollution control that would be achieved by the operation of a perfect market.

5.   Do you agree that all problems of pollution are reciprocal? If not, how would you articulate the distinction between reciprocal and non-reciprocal pollution problems?

6.   Do you accept the invariance thesis? Might changes in the assignment of legal rights alter the optimal level of pollution control in a perfectly costless market?

## 2.   TESTING THE INVARIANCE THESIS IN A HYPOTHETICAL COSTLESS MARKET

The next three readings and the problem following those readings are designed to probe the validity of the invariance thesis, assuming a perfectly functioning (costless) market.

## RICHARD B. STEWART & JAMES E. KRIER, ENVIRONMENTAL LAW AND POLICY

### 137 & n.43 (2nd ed. 1978)

By affecting the relative financial position of the parties, may not the assignment of legal rights and liabilities affect the allocation of resources? Suppose, for example, the court decides that P is not liable in any way to R, and R doesn't have enough money to bribe P to remove 75 tons of pollutants? Suppose P is held liable in damages to R and P can't afford to remove 75 tons of pollutants, compensate R, and still make a profit? More generally, the allocation of legal rights and liabilities will always affect the distribution of wealth, which will in turn affect the allocation of resources because it will alter the purchasing power of consumers with differing tastes, and may affect the survival of polluting enterprises. In the absence of transaction costs, the parties will always reach *an* economically efficient resource allocation, but the *particular* allocation attained will depend upon the initial allocation of rights and duties.

The allocation of legal rights will, in theory, affect the location of the economically efficient point in almost every case. If P is held not liable to R, then R will have to pay P to obtain clean air. The curve $yy^1$ [in **Figure 3-1** at page 67, *supra*] will represent R's *willingness to pay for clean air*. If P is held liable to R, then P must pay R in order to take away clean air from R. In that event, curve $yy^1$ will represent R's *demand for compensation for deprivation of clean air*. R's valuation will always be greater in the latter case, because valuation is in part a function of wealth or income, and R's total wealth or income (nonmonetary as well as monetary) is greater when he has the right to enjoy clean air than when he does not. By changing R's wealth or income, the allocation of legal rights therefore changes R's valuation of clean air, which means that the location of curve $yy^1$ will also shift, altering in most cases the location of the economically efficient point Z. This is simply an illustration of the general point * * * that the distribution of income will affect willingness to pay for various commodities and will therefore affect the economically efficient allocation of resources. Diagrammatically, the argument can be represented in this fashion [*See* **Figure 3-2**]:

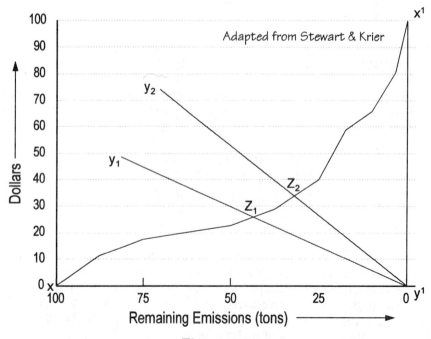

Figure 3-2

Let $y_1y^1$ represent R's willingness to pay for clean air when P is not liable to R, and let $y_2y^1$ represent R's willingness to accept compensation for loss of clean air when P is held liable to R; $y_2y^1$ will always be above and to the right of $y_1y^1$ because it represents a situation in which R's total wealth is greater. The determination of the point Z will shift accordingly. * * *

---

The next reading is taken from a mathematical examination of the invariance thesis by Professor E.J. Mishan. The excerpt includes some of his more important conclusions expressed in non-mathematical language. What Professor Mishan refers to as the *welfare effect* is sometimes called the *income effect*—"the change in the quantity of a good or service demanded by an individual resulting exclusively from a change in the individual's real income, all prices * * * being held constant." E. Hanks, A.D. Tarlock & J. Hanks, Environmental Law and Policy 738 (1974). It is widely recognized that an increase in an individual's real income results in an increased demand (and a greater willingness to pay) for many goods; the individual's demand for "inferior goods" (such as macaroni, Spam, and Hamburger Helper) would ordinarily decrease with increasing income. *Id.*

# E.J. MISHAN, PARETO
# OPTIMALITY AND THE LAW

19 Oxford Economic Papers
(New Series) 255-56, 272 n.2, 279 n.2 (1967)

Over the past few years it has been generally recognized that the nature of any optimal solution depends * * * on the existing distribution of income. Inasmuch as the distribution of income is itself influenced by legislation—through taxes and subsidies, through price regulation and controls, and through a vast and growing public expenditure on goods and services—the optimal solutions attainable must depend also upon the laws of a country. * * * In cases of conflicting interest, according as the law, deliberately or by default, places the burden of reaching optimal arrangements on one party or group rather than on the other, both the characteristics of the optimal outcome and the costs of its attainment are altered. * * *

This paper * * * is concerned primarily with demonstrating (1) that the characteristics of an optimal solution are not uniquely specified but depend, in general, on the existing law * * * .

A "normal" welfare effect, implying that an improvement in the individual's welfare raises his demand for the good, also implies that the maximum sum he will pay for a given amount of it (or, alternatively, the minimum sum he will accept to forgo a given amount of it) will arise with an increase in his welfare. It has the further implication that the maximum he will pay for a [good] thing is less than the minimum sum he will accept to forgo it. * * *

On issues that make a significant difference to the individual's welfare the difference between the maximum sum he would pay to avoid a certain fate (his view being permanently obscured, or his peace being shattered over a long period) and the minimum sum he would accept for submitting to that fate is likely to be far greater than is habitually suggested by our notions of difference in welfare effect, so frequently assumed negligible in order to reach elegant theoretical results. The current and prospective income and assets of a person form a limit to the maximum he can afford to pay and remain alive, while no such limit restricts the minimum sum he would consent to receive. A man dying of thirst in the middle of the Sahara could offer, for a bucket of water that would save his life, no more than his prospective earnings (above some subsistence level). And this sum would be infinitesimal compared with the sum of money needed to induce him to forgo the bucket of water and fatally reduce his chance of survival. * * *

[T]he question of who, under the circumstances, ought to pay compensation, must also be referred to ethical considerations, distinct from and possibly in conflict with those invoked in discussing the distribution of welfare. If my neighbour's weeding machine is eccentric enough to blow his weeds into my garden, I should not like to think that the question of who compensates whom is to be decided by reference to our relative incomes.

## HERBERT J. HOVENKAMP, LEGAL POLICY AND THE ENDOWMENT EFFECT

20 Journal of Legal Studies 225-28 (1991)

The "endowment effect" arises because the price many people are willing to pay for a particular entitlement may be significantly less than the price they are willing to accept in order to give up the same entitlement. * * *

Welfare economists have generally assumed that the maximum price a person is willing to pay for some entitlement ($WP$) and the minimum price that a person who already had this entitlement would be willing to accept in exchange ($WA$) are approximately equal, with $WP$ being only slightly less than $WA$. The small difference was believed to result from the income effects that a change of position might have on one's preferences. * * *

[T]he assumption that $WP = WA$ drives most forms of cost-benefit analysis, which equates value with willingness to pay, and generally disregards willingness to accept. * * *

[I]ndeed, the endowment effect appears to be much greater than once thought. In fact, $WA$ may be many times larger than $WP$ for certain kinds of entitlements. Some tests conducted in experimental markets, with relatively small sums of money, have found that *WA* can exceed *WP* by a factor of three or more. In a recent study, two sets of subjects were presented with a harmless but foul-tasting fluid. One group was told that the fluid would be placed in their mouths for twenty seconds unless they bid successfully for an entitlement not to be subjected to the fluid. A second group was told that they would receive a certain amount of money for being subjected to the fluid, provided that they were the low bidder. The bidding showed consistently that willingness to pay was much lower than willingness to accept. In some tests willingness to pay to avoid the fluid averaged under $3, while willingness to accept the fluid required average payments higher than $10.

Other tests, using larger amounts of money, but in hypothetical markets, have produced similar results. When the entitlements at issue are public goods that are not commonly traded on markets—such as rights to clean air—the disparities between *WA* and *WP* are much larger than they are for market goods. In some cases involving environmental entitlements, differences between willingness to pay and willingness to accept ranged from factors of four to sixteen. * * *

---

Professor Kelman illustrates the potential difference between willingness to pay (*WP*) and willingness to accept (*WA*) by imagining a person who has paid $5 for a bottle of wine now worth $100. Such a person might rationally refuse an offer to sell the bottle for $100, even though she would never pay $100 for a bottle of wine. *See* Mark Kelman, *Consumption Theory, Production Theory, and Ideology in the Coase Theorem*, 52 S. Cal. L. Rev. 669, 678-79 (1979).

### Problem

Imagine a single farmer who lives with her family on a large farm. She has a great deal of farming equipment and supplies, but it is all mortgaged to the hilt; her farm is also heavily mortgaged. She has no money in the bank. Adjacent to this farmer's land is a manufacturing plant which produces DDT. The plant emits significant quantities of DDT which settle on the farmer's land, poisoning her crops and dairy products and making her family chronically ill. Assume that there are no impediments to bargaining between these two parties; the market is the costless one first addressed by Coase. The farmer and the manufacturer are now about to bargain to reach Coase's optimal pollution control point.

Coase tells us that there must be at least *some* initial assignment of legal rights by society, or the farmer and manufacturer will not know where they stand. But his invariance thesis asserts that the actual assignment of legal rights will in no way affect the ultimate level of pollution control, assuming our costless market. For the moment, we will consider three possible legal rules which might control the initial assignment of rights between the parties:

**Rule A**: The Polluter (manufacturer) is not liable in any way to the Receptor (farmer).

**Rule B**: The Polluter must pay *damages* to the Receptor for any injuries.

**Rule C**: The Receptor has an automatic right to obtain an *injunction* against any DDT discharges from the Polluter's operations.

1. Assume that **Rule A** is in force. Consider **Figure 3-1** (at page 67, *supra*).

   (a) What will curve $yy^1$ represent as the farmer and manufacturer approach the bargaining table?

   (b) What will be the likely shape and location of curve $yy^1$?

   (c) Considering the point at which curve $yy^1$ is likely to intersect curve $xx^1$, what is likely to be the optimal level of pollution control (point Z)?

2. Assume that **Rule B** is in force. Consider again, **Figure 3-1**.

   (a) What will curve $yy^1$ now represent as the farmer and manufacturer approach the bargaining table?

   (b) What will be the likely shape and location of the curve $yy^1$? This may require speculation.

   (c) Is the optimal level of pollution control (point Z) likely to be the same as under legal Rule A? If not, will the optimal level of pollution be greater or less than under Rule A?

3. Assume that **Rule C** is in force. Consider, once more, **Figure 3-1**.

   (a) What will curve $yy^1$ represent in the bargaining process?

   (b) What will be the likely shape and location of the curve $yy^1$? Let your imagination soar.

   (c) Is the optimal level of pollution control (point Z) likely to be the same as under either Rule A or Rule B? If not, will the optimal level of pollution be greater or less than under Rules A or B?

4. You are a judge. Your bedtime reading of Coasian analysis has convinced you that pollution is a reciprocal problem. The farmer and manufacturer are now before you and you have a clean slate with no pre-existing assignment of legal rights. You wish to mandate by decree that the optimal level of pollution control be reached by the manufacturer. By going through the foregoing exercise, however, you believe that there may be several optimal levels of control to choose from, depending on the selection of the governing legal rule. Does anything in Coasian analysis tell you how to select among these alternative levels of control? Why or why not?

## 3. REAL-WORLD TRANSACTION COSTS

In the preceding readings we have considered what Coasian analysis has to say about the problem of pollution, assuming a perfectly functioning ("costless") market. We now abandon that unrealistic assumption, confronting the relevance of economics to a world in which bargains can rarely be accomplished without *transaction costs*. To whom should courts and legislatures assign legal rights and liabilities in the real world?

The next reading addresses the implications of transaction costs. Before doing so, it adds two new concepts to our understanding of the pollution problem: (1) the role that *incentives* may play in altering control costs (and in altering "optimal" pollution levels); and (2) the possibility that *avoidance* measures by Receptors might reduce the harmful effects of pollution.

### RICHARD B. STEWART & JAMES E. KRIER, ENVIRONMENTAL LAW AND POLICY

139-42 & n.44 (2nd ed. 1978)

Thus far we have considered the problem of assigning legal rights purely from a *static* analysis of efficient resource allocation: given existing resources (including technology), how can they be deployed in order to maximize the present value of production? But now suppose that we take into account the dynamic considerations involved in change over time. Wouldn't it be appropriate to give P an incentive to develop or seek out new and cheaper ways of pollution control in order to lower control costs and increase the society's *future* production of goods and services? How would the various liability rules that we have examined affect P's incentives in this regard?

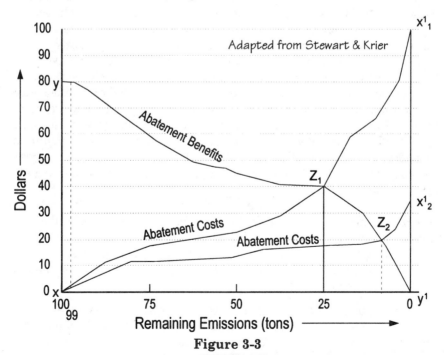

Figure 3-3

Diagrammatically, let $xx^1_1$ represent the present costs of controlling pollution and $xx^1_2$ the costs of control at some future time with improved technology. [*See* **Figure 3-3**] The lowering of control costs from $xx^1_1$ to $xx^1_2$ will shift the efficient control downwards and to the right, reducing the total social costs associated with the use of the air resource and thereby increasing the net benefits to society of such use. * * *

Until now our analysis has assumed that the only way of preventing the adverse effects of pollution is to install controls or change P's production in some way so as to reduce the discharge of pollutants to the atmosphere. But suppose R can take steps to avoid the adverse effects of pollution. Assume a simplified model in which the only alternatives open to P are to emit 100 tons per day or eliminate pollution entirely by expending $5,000, but that R (a recluse who lives entirely indoors) can avoid all of the adverse effects caused by 100 tons of emissions per day by installing an air conditioning system at a cost of $1,000. What is the economically efficient solution in that case? Will the parties reach the economically efficient solution regardless of what liability or property rules are imposed? * * *

### THE COASE ANALYSIS IN THE
### PRESENCE OF TRANSACTION COSTS

In the real world, as Coase admits, bargaining is not costless. Time and other resources are required to acquire, evaluate, and exchange information and engage in bargaining. In a developed economy characterized by a complex division of labor and numerous externalities caused by spillovers among individuals, these obstacles to exchange are as, or more, formidable an obstacle to increasing production as the existence of friction or the resistance of material to malleability. These transaction costs mount when numerous individuals are involved in a potential bargaining situation, a circumstance which is characteristic of most environmental problems. Even where there is only a single source of pollution, such as a power plant, many persons are likely to be affected. More often there will be many sources of pollution and masses of individuals will be affected by the combined impacts of such pollution. Consider, for example, the air pollution problem in a major air basin such as Los Angeles. If we assumed no transaction costs, Coase's analysis would apply to Los Angeles * * * . All the affected individuals would, through a series of bargains, arrive at an economically efficient allocation of resources, and this would occur regardless of the initial allocation of legal rights and duties. But what would be the real world obstacles to such bargaining successfully occurring? In light of such obstacles, what impact will the assignment of legal rights and responsibilities have on resource allocations?

Assume one pollution source, P, and 1,000 Rs, persons adversely affected. Assume further that the costs and benefits of pollution control are the same as depicted in [**Figure 3-1**, at page 67, *supra*], except that the curve $yy^1$ represents the cumulative sum of the willingness to pay with respect to clean air of each of the one thousand Rs. Assume, for example, that each of the Rs would pay \$.08 to have P's emissions reduced from 100 to 99 tons; the cumulative willingness to pay for such a reduction is \$80. (In practice, of course, the willingness of various Rs to make such payments will vary because of differences in taste and income.)

In the absence of transaction costs, P and the 1,000 Rs would still bargain to the efficient point Z regardless of the initial assignment of legal rights and duties. But what would happen in the real world?

Suppose the court holds that P is not liable [**Rule A**]. It would be in the interests of the Rs collectively to bribe P to control pollution to the efficient point Z, each R contributing his or her appropriate share of the bribe. But why in the real world is this unlikely to occur? * * * If the bribe does not occur, will resources be efficiently allocated?

Suppose the court holds that P may be enjoined at the instance of any affected R from emitting any pollutants at all [**Rule C**]. It would be in P's interest to bribe the various Rs to forego their right to a prohibitory injunction and permit P to operate at the efficient point Z. But why in the real world might this not occur? If P is unable to bribe all of the Rs, will resources be efficiently allocated?

Now assume that the court holds that P is liable in damages to the various affected Rs [**Rule B**]. Will transaction costs preclude the efficient point Z from being reached? Consider that real world transaction costs include the costs of hiring a lawyer and trying a lawsuit in order to vindicate one's legal rights, and that it is the general rule in the United States that a successful litigant is not entitled to recover his or her litigation expenses from the losing party. Consider also that in many instances environmental harms are long run in character, uncertain in severity, and consist of stresses on natural ecosystems that cannot be readily linked to demonstrable harm to a given individual.

Which legal rule should the court adopt—no liability, damages, or injunction? How would the efficient choice of legal rules be affected by the possibility that R could take steps (such as the installation of air conditioners) to avoid part or all of the adverse effects of pollution? What incentives would alternative rules provide for decisions by Ps and Rs as to where to locate their activities? For the future development by P or R of new technologies that would more cheaply eliminate or avoid environmental damage? What sort of information would a court need in order to select the most economically efficient rule, and how likely is the court to acquire the necessary information? To what extent do alternative legal rules facilitate or preclude subsequent bargaining among Ps and Rs if the rule chosen by the court leads to an inefficient resource allocation that would be improved by mutual agreement of the affected parties? * * *

In these circumstances, what general approach should we take towards framing legal rules and other governmental measures with respect to pollution and other forms of environmental degradation? Should we attempt to determine on a case-by-case basis which result [is] likely to achieve efficient resource allocation? Should we devise rigid general rules, knowing that they will lead to resource misallocations in some applications but hoping that on balance they will result in a more efficient resource allocation overall, especially when information and administrative costs are involved?

---

Many of the foregoing questions are addressed in the following essay by a distinguished federal court of appeals judge, formerly Dean of the Yale Law School.

## GUIDO CALABRESI, TRANSACTION COSTS, RESOURCE ALLOCATION AND LIABILITY RULES—A COMMENT

### 11 J. Law & Econ. 67, 69-71, 73 (1968)

[P]roblems of misallocation of resources and externalities are not theoretical but empirical ones. The resource allocation aim is to approximate, both closely and cheaply, the result the market would bring about if bargaining actually were costless. The question then becomes: Is this accomplished most accurately and most cheaply by structural rules (like anti-trust laws), by liability rules, by taxation and governmental spending, by letting the market have free play or by some combination of these? This question depends in large part on the relative *cost* of reaching the correct result by each of these means (an empirical problem which probably could be resolved, at least approximately, in most instances), and the relative *chances* of reaching a widely *wrong* result depending on the method used (also an empirical problem but one as to which it is hard to get other than "guess" type data). The resolution of these two problems and their interplay is *the* problem of accomplishing optimal resource allocations.

Two points are implied in the foregoing discussion. The first is that since transactions do cost money, and since substitutes for transactions, be they taxation, liability rules, or structural rules, are also not costless, the "optimal" result is not necessarily the same as if transactions were costless. Whatever device is used, the question must be asked: Are its costs worth the benefits in better resource allocations it brings about or have we instead approached a false optimum by a series of games which are not worth the candles used? This does not mean, though, that the actual optimum is necessarily the one an unaided market would reach. Further market improvements may well be prohibitive at a stage where laws and their enforcement are still a relatively cheap way of getting nearer the goal.

The second point is that both the unreachable goal of "that point which would be reached if transactions were costless," and the gains which reaching nearer the goal would bring are not usually subject to precise definition or quantification. They are, in fact, largely defined by guesses. As a result, the question of whether a given law is worth its costs (in terms of better resource allocation) is rarely susceptible to empirical proof. This does not mean, of course, that the best we can do is adopt a laissez faire policy and let the market do the best it can. It is precisely the province of good government to make guesses as to what laws are likely to be worth their costs. Hopefully, it will use what empirical information is available and seek to develop empirical information which is not currently available (how much information is worth *its* costs is also a question, however). But there is no reason to assume that in the absence of conclusive information no government action is better than some action. This is especially so if the guesses made take into account two factors. The first is: Action in an uncertain case is more likely to be justified if the market can correct an error resulting from the proposed action more cheaply than it could an error resulting from inaction. The second is: Action in an uncertain case is more likely to be justified if goals *other* than resource allocation (like proper income distribution) are served by the action. In effect the first factor says, in uncertainty increase the chances of correcting an error, while the second says, the achievement of other goals is accomplished very cheaply where the most that can be said about the resource allocation effect of a move is that we cannot be *sure* that it will be favorable. * * *

Coase's analysis * * * gives us an admirable tool for suggesting what kind of empirical data would be useful in making resource allocation decisions, and for indicating what kinds of guesses are likely to be justifiably made in the absence of convincing data. Some may take Coase's analysis to suggest that little or no government intervention is usually the best rule. My own conclusions are quite different. His analysis, combined with common intuitions or guesses as to the relative costs of transactions, taxation, structural rules and liability rules, can go far to explain various types of heretofore inadequately justified governmental actions. This is especially so if one considers the relevance of goals other than resource allocations to those situations where inadequate data makes resource allocations an unsatisfactory guide. Perhaps more precise data will some day prove some of these interventions to be improper from the standpoint of resource allocation. Then we shall have to choose, as we often do, between the bigger pie and other aims. Coase's analysis certainly suggests situations where this has been done. Its principal importance lies, however, in helping to delineate those areas of uncertainty where more facts would help us make better resource allocation judgments, and where, at least in the absence of more facts, the lawyer must be guided by guess work as to what the facts are and by goals other than resource allocations in suggesting workable solutions for problems which cannot wait till all the facts are in.

*Notes and Questions*

1. One of the most striking things about the foregoing reading is that Calabresi assumes the correctness of Coase's invariance thesis: "The resource allocation aim is to approximate, both closely and cheaply, *the* result the market would bring about if bargaining actually were costless." (emphasis added) Notwithstanding Calabresi's references to uncertainty and the need for "guess work," he assumes throughout his analysis that a perfectly functioning (costless) market would yield a single optimal result.

2. Assume that "the facts are in," removing the uncertainties of which Calabresi speaks. If the invariance thesis is false, is Calabresi encouraging decisionmakers in such circumstances to advance toward of an endlessly moving target—a target that changes location with each decision? Reconsider your analysis of the Problem at page 73, *supra*. Might the "optimal" allocation of resources differ so significantly—depending on the selection of legal rules—that Calabresi's articulation of the resource allocation aim is unworkable? Professor Kelman has reached that conclusion:

> Available evidence suggests that most people would insist on being paid far more to assent to the worsening of their situation than they would be willing to pay to improve their situation. * * * But this creates a circularity problem for any attempt to use cost-benefit analysis to determine *whether* to assign to, say, the homeowner the right to an unobstructed mountain view. For willingness to pay will be different depending on whether the right is assigned initially or not. The value judgment about whether to assign the right must thus be made first.

Steven Kelman, *Cost-Benefit Analysis: An Ethical Critique*, 5 Regulation 33, 37-38 (Jan./Feb. 1981).

———

In the following reading, Professors Stewart and Krier further explore Calabresi's approach to achieving economic efficiency through decisionmaking.

# RICHARD B. STEWART & JAMES E. KRIER, ENVIRONMENTAL LAW AND POLICY

### 145-46 (2nd ed. 1978)

Note Professor Calabresi's statement that in the real world of transaction costs the "resource allocation aim is to approximate, both closely and cheaply, the result the market would bring about if bargaining actually were costless." Is this correct? If substantial transaction costs are inevitable, why should we aim at a resource allocation that would occur in a hypothetical world where they are absent? Shouldn't transaction costs be given explicit recognition in the definition of the "resource allocation aim"?

One can distinguish four different types of costs associated with the use of a natural resource such as air:

(a) *Damage costs* occurring as a result of pollution or other forms of environmental degradation;

(b) *Abatement costs* incurred in reducing pollution or other environmental degradation;

(c) *Avoidance costs* incurred in preventing or minimizing the adverse effects of pollution once it has occurred;

(d) *Transaction costs* involved in deciding upon resource allocations, including the costs of selecting and applying liability rules and other governmental measures that bear upon resource allocation.

From the viewpoint of economic efficiency, shouldn't our aim be to minimize the sum of these various costs? * * * If we focused on less than all of these costs, what we gained in reducing them might be more than offset by increases in costs that we had not considered. Moreover, the dynamic relation among these various costs may be far from obvious and even counterintuitive, suggesting the desirability of a "systems" approach * * * . Such a systems approach to legal rules relating to accidents is developed by Professor Calabresi in his book *The Costs of Accidents* (1970). For an illuminating evaluation of Professor Calabresi's approach and its implications for environmental law, *see* Michelman, *Pollution as a Tort*, 80 Yale L.J. 647 (1971). Professor Michelman notes two points in the Calabresi argument that have special importance here.

First, in cases where substantial harm occurs to one or a few persons, the total social cost of such harm can be reduced if the economic burden of harm is spread among many persons, a conclusion that is confirmed by the willingness of firms and individuals to pay for insurance. Insurance could therefore be an important technique for reducing damage costs caused by certain forms of pollution. * * * Note that there is a danger that the availability of such insurance may lessen the incentive for undertaking possibly more cost-effective steps to avoid damage, such as refraining from moving into a polluted area. For example, federal flood insurance may actually have increased the total social costs associated with flooding by encouraging people to live in flood plains.

A second pertinent point in Calabresi's and Michelman's analyses * * * is that an evaluation of cost-minimizing alternatives on a case-by-case basis may overlook more basic and general alternatives that would be the most cost-effective. Calabresi gives the example of focusing on which driver is at fault in a given accident, which may ignore highway and automobile design changes that could be a cheaper way of preventing accidents than imposing liability based on fault. * * *

The fact that information is costly to acquire means that decisions about appropriate liability rules and other possible governmental measures must be made without complete information under conditions of uncertainty. Accordingly, these decisions will be shaped by our attitudes toward risk and uncertainty. * * * For example, should we aim for the best possible resource allocation, when to do so will involve a substantial chance of being wrong and ending up with a quite inefficient resource allocation? Or should we aim in the first instance at a somewhat less than optimal allocation where our chances of achieving it are extremely high?

## F. ECONOMICS TEST CASES

We have now examined the economic criterion of efficiency and addressed how that criterion might be achieved in the real world. We now turn to two judicial opinions that struggle with resource allocation issues. Examine these two opinions critically. Try to articulate the arguments that economists might make for and against the outcomes of the two cases in light of the efficiency criterion.

## VERSAILLES BOROUGH v. McKEESPORT COAL & COKE CO.

83 Pittsburgh Legal Journal 379 (July 22, 1935)

Before MOORE, GARDNER and MUSMANNO, JJ.

MUSMANNO, J.

The borough of Versailles, city of McKeesport and thirteen private plaintiffs have filed a bill in equity seeking an injunction against the defendant, McKeesport Coal & Coke Company * * * .

Upon conclusion of the trial, which consumed an entire month, in which 51 witnesses were heard on behalf of plaintiffs and 71 on behalf of the defense, the chancellor filed findings of fact and conclusions of law and entered a decree *nisi* in which he dismissed the bill and the case is now before us upon exceptions filed by plaintiffs.

Defendant is the owner of 2500 acres of coal of the upper Freeport vein, located in the borough of Versailles, near the southern boundary of the city of McKeesport, where, in December 1923, it erected a modern tipple and has since been engaged in the operation of a large mine.

In the process of mining, certain impurities are found in the coal veins. These impurities, known to the industry as gob * * * consist of slate and coal—the coal being deposited in quarter-inch layers between laminations of slate of similar thickness. Because of these laminations of slate, the coal found in this gob is unmerchantable * * * .

It was established at the trial that wherever coal is mined, large quantities of gob are encountered, and that for every 100 tons of merchantable coal produced, 20 tons of gob are found and must be disposed of; that it is the general practice in the industry—a practice followed by defendant, to dispose of as much of its gob as possible in the underground workings of the mine, in the so-called "rooms", after the coal has been removed, and to bring the remainder to the surface. * * * [I]n the operation of its mine defendant has driven through the coal seam 62 miles of entries or main haulage ways. All of the gob encountered in these entries must be brought to the surface as there is no place inside the mine where it may be stored. Thus about half of the gob produced in a mine or the equivalent by weight, of ten per cent of the coal produced, must be brought to the surface. Brought to the surface it is piled at some point near the tipple. This is the general practice, (in fact the only method known to the industry for the disposal of this refuse), and was followed by defendant.

During the years which have intervened since it opened its mine, defendant has deposited gob on a 20 acre tract of surface, located 230 feet from its tipple. On November 3, 1933, the gob pile caught fire. At a preliminary hearing on June 11, 1934, a temporary injunction issued, enjoining the defendant from the piling of gob on the burning heap.

Immediately following the granting of the temporary injunction, the defendant started a new gob pile, adjacent to the old (the burning one). It is now depositing its mine refuse on a new heap. At the final hearing of the bill in equity, the plaintiffs asked for an injunction against the defendant from depositing gob on the new pile, or any place near to it, claiming that such act constituted a nuisance under the law * * * .

The defendant denied that the piling of gob at any place on its property in reasonable proximity to its tipple constituted a nuisance.

Plaintiffs do not dispute * * * that gob is a necessary incident to coal mining; that it is something which cannot be avoided if coal is to be mined at all; that a large part of it cannot be left in the mine, but must be brought to the surface, and that in bringing it to the surface and depositing it on a gob pile close to its tipple, defendant has followed the most approved method of gob disposal—the method followed by all the large and best managed mines. The uncontroverted testimony is that there is no feasible method of operating a coal mine without a gob pile on the surface, as no use has ever been found for this troublesome by-product of mining; that every large coal mine has a large gob pile close to its tipple; that sooner or later these piles all ignite through spontaneous combustion; that practically every large mine in Western Pennsylvania has a burning gob pile, and that there is no known means of averting such a fire.

If we accept the uncontroverted testimony as fact, and in the absence of denial we must so accept it, then it must follow that if we enjoin the deposit of gob and the erection of gob piles, we perforce enjoin the mining of coal, for without gob and gob piles coal mines cannot be operated, since the one is a necessary and unavoidable result of the other. * * *

That the plaintiffs are subjected to annoyance, personal inconvenience and aesthetic damage by the burning of the gob pile, is not seriously disputed. * * * If by decree we prohibit the defendant from mining coal, and thereby relieve the plaintiffs from all the vexation of smoke, dust and odors that come from a burning gob pile, we must consider what harm, if any, comes to those who are interested in the continued operation of the coal mine. * * *

The uncontradicted testimony discloses that upon an investment of $2,561,000.00 made eleven years before this trial, not a dollar has ever been paid by defendant in dividends; no year's operation has shown a profit and the result for the entire period shows a net loss in excess of $500,000.00. Since this has been the financial experience of defendant with its gob pile located but 230 feet from its tipple, for us to decree that it must desist from further dumping near its present pile—for us to decree that it must bear the expense of purchasing additional large surface acreage at locations distant from the tipple, would be equivalent to ordering the closing down of the mine. Defendant is engaged in a lawful business. Its stockholders are entitled to a fair and reasonable return on their investments as this gob pile ignited through causes over which defendant had no control.

Four hundred and thirteen men were employed at this mine at the time of the trial. These men and their families—about two thousand people in all, are economically dependent upon this mine for subsistence. When in full operation defendant's payroll disbursement exceeds $10,000.00 per week, and although the stockholders have received no dividends, the defendant company disbursed as wages to its employees $2,801,000 during the eleven years prior to the trial. Neither directly nor indirectly will we destroy a legitimate business without cogent and adequate reason. Under testimony adduced in this case, we cannot and will not jeopardize the employment of these miners. To do so would be to cause a far greater injury than that we are asked to enjoin. Of course, if the continued operation of this mine were a serious menace to the health or lives of those who reside in its vicinity, there would be another question before us, but there is no evidence in this case to warrant the assumption that the health of anyone is being imperiled.

The only things emanating from a coal or gob fire that might be injurious to health, are the gases arising therefrom—sulphur dioxide, hydrogen sulphide and carbon monoxide. Expert witnesses testifying for both the plaintiffs and the defendant were agreed at the trial that only negligible quantities of hydrogen sulphide and carbon monoxide were present in and about the gob fire. So that the only factor to consider, so far as injurious gas is concerned, is sulphur dioxide. Mr. Holden, a witness for the plaintiffs, testified that his tests (of which he made eighty-eight) revealed an average concentration of .67 of one part per million, and a maximum concentration of 3 parts per million. The treatise of Henderson and Haggard on noxious gases was accepted by both sides, at the trial, as a recognized authority on the effect of irritant gases. That authority states that the physiological response to various concentrations of sulphur dioxide is as follows: [*See* **Table 3-1**]

It is to be observed here that the least amount causing immediate irritation to the throat is 8 to 12 ppm., and that, without prolonged exposure, no harm is possible until the concentration reaches a density of 10 ppm., or a concentration over three times as strong as that discovered by Mr. Holden in eighty-eight tests.

### Table 3-1

| | |
|---|---|
| Least detectable odor of sulphur dioxide | 3 to 5 ppm. |
| Least amount causing irritation to the eyes | 20 ppm. |
| Least amount causing immediate irritation to the throat | 8 to 12 ppm. |
| Least amount causing coughing | 20 ppm. |
| Maximum concentration allowable for prolonged exposure | 10 ppm. |
| Maximum concentration allowable for short exposure (½ to 1 hour) | 50 to 100 ppm. |
| Dangerous for even a short period | 400 to 500 ppm. |

A number of witnesses called by the plaintiffs, testified to complaints of irritated throats, hay fever, asthma, coughs, headaches, eye and nose irritations, all caused by the noxious effects of the smoke, dust and odors emanating from the gob pile. Some of these witnesses stated that they were under the care of physicians, but it is extraordinary that not one of these physicians was called to testify that his patient's malady was directly traceable to residential proximity to the gob pile. It is also remarkable that the head of the bureau of health of the city of McKeesport was not subpoenaed to testify to the deleterious effect of the gob fire on the health of the people in that vicinity.

An equal if not greater number of witnesses called by the defendant testified that they lived close to and adjacent to the gob fire, yet they suffered no injurious effects because of that proximity. Four men, ranging in age between twenty-two and forty-six, testified that they actually lived in shacks, on the gob pile, while it was on fire, and they declared in court that while they did not enjoy the odors and the excessive heat, yet they suffered no cough, throat or eye irritation, headache or any other ill effect. While we would hesitate to recommend the gob pile as a suitable place for a dwelling, yet, lacking evidence that these four men were salamanders, we cannot declare that the gases thrown off by this fire are sufficient in volume or density to bring about the dire results intimated by plaintiffs' witnesses and contended for by plaintiffs' counsel.

On the other hand, we cannot believe that one's health would improve by living close to the gob fire, and we cannot believe, despite testimony advanced by defendant's witnesses to the contrary, that there is no physical discomfort or annoyance caused to residents of that vicinity, by the burning mountain. In fact, our decision in this case is not based on the assumption that the people living close to the gob fire suffer no annoyance, but that the annoyance which is theirs is trivial in comparison to the positive harm and damage that would be done to the community, were the injunction asked for granted.

Much of our economic distress is due to the fact that there is not enough smoke in Pittsburgh and the Pittsburgh district. The metropolis that earned the sobriquet of the "smoky city" has not been living up to those vaporous laurels. The economic activity of the city that was known as "the workshop of the world" has decreased in proportion as its skies cleared of smoke. While smoke *per se* is objectionable and adds nothing to the outer aesthetics of any community, it is not without its connotational beauty as it rises in clouds from smoke stacks of furnaces and ovens (and even gob fires) telling the world that the fires of prosperity are burning,—the fires that assure economic security to the workingman, as well as establish profitable returns on capital legitimately invested.

If the coal mine of the defendant had been sunk in the midst of a residential district, utterly free of factories and mills, and devoid of all of those transportational facilities which create smoke, dust, dirt and grime, the complaint of the plaintiffs might have some force and effect, but the defendant's property is in the very heart of one of the most industrialized districts of Allegheny county. Within one hundred feet of the defendant's tipple, is located the galvanizing works of the National Tube company, a plant three thousand feet in length. The Columbia foundry is close by, as is also the rubbish dump of the city of McKeesport. A garbage dump, 100 feet by 60 feet in dimensions, is located in the immediate vicinity of the gob pile. The main line of the Baltimore and Ohio railroad is but three hundred and seventy-six feet away; this is a four-track system, and over it pass approximately forty-five trains daily,—all users of bituminous coal, and all throwing off black smoke. To the north of the gob pile, within a distance ranging between three-tenths of a mile and two and six-tenths miles, there are factories and tin plate mills; the Christy Park works of the National Tube company; the national works of the National Tube company, and many other industries, with hundreds of stacks which emit black and grey smoke from the coal consumed.

The inhabitants of this district were cognizant of the industrialization of the community when they moved into it. They voluntarily took up abode in this territory, and can scarcely with consistency now be heard to voice a protest about the smoky atmosphere. One who voluntarily goes to war should not complain about cannon smoke. * * *

Mrs. Knox, [one] of plaintiffs' witnesses * * * [conceded] "I don't think there is any place in the McKeesport district that is clean." She stated further that * * * she had great difficulty keeping her porches clean before the gob fire started. * * *

The plaintiffs are subject to an annoyance * * * but it is an annoyance they have freely assumed. Because they desired and needed a residential proximity to their places of employment, they chose to found their abode here. * * *

Without smoke, Pittsburgh would have remained a very pretty *village*. * * *

Sitting in equity we are compelled here to consider whether an injunction in this case might not work a greater mischief, and far greater injury, than the wrong we are asked to redress. To enjoin the piling of gob would, of course, prevent a gob fire, and the resulting smoke and dust so destructive to the aesthetic values of the community; but the philosophy of the beautiful must give way to the realities of a bread and butter existence. Furthermore, if there were no gob fire, the plaintiffs would not be free of the disturbance of smoke; they would still have the factories, mills, garbage dumps, incinerators and railroads to contend with. * * *

There is no testimony on the part of the plaintiffs that the defendant is mining its coal in an unordinary way. On the contrary, all the evidence in the case is to the effect that the methods of mining and disposing of gob employed by the defendant are the methods used in practically all mines. Every mine has its gob pile, and it was testified that practically one hundred percent of these gob piles catch fire. It was established further that at practically every mine, the rule is to pile the gob somewhere adjacent to the hole in the earth from which it is lifted to the surface. If we enjoin the defendant company from piling its gob at that point and in that manner, we inferentially declare that all the mines in the state, at any rate in this county, must not dispose of their gob in that manner, and, since no other practical method has been recommended, (we discuss this point later) we declare by implication that all coal mines must cease operating which, of course is absurd.

It was not established, nor charged at the trial, that the defendant operated its mine in a negligent or inefficient manner. * * *

To haul away the gob from the district by rail, would be an exorbitant expense, and would naturally result in an increased cost of coal. Furthermore, where would the gob be hauled to? and wouldn't it catch fire at that point? and wouldn't the defendant then be liable for any damage suffered by third parties, on account of that distant gob fire? A gob pile near the tipple of the mine is a natural use of the land, but there would be no legal defense to a gob fire away from the mine property. * * *

Counsel for the plaintiffs are working on a *theory*, but we have a condition here to face. * * *

We repeat that it is established that the plaintiffs are subjected to an annoyance, and the court sympathizes with them in the violence which is done to the aesthetic unities of the community. Were it not for the greater violence (by granting the injunction) which would be done to the all-too-vital necessity of living, we would gladly exercise the power that is lodged in our office to decree the banishment of those factors that are so inimical to the sensitive application of the harmonious and beautiful. But we cannot give Mediterranean skies to the plaintiffs, when by doing so, we may send the workers and bread-winners of the community involved to the Black Sea of destitution.

Pennsylvania is the great industrial state of the Union. Its prosperity and leadership are entirely dependent upon its smoke producing industries. If the necessary and unavoidable smoke produced by these industries were to be enjoined, the plants could not operate, many millions of dollars in invested capital would be destroyed and many thousands of persons thrown out of gainful employment. * * *

[T]he bill is dismissed at the costs of the plaintiffs.

## U.S. DEPARTMENT OF HEALTH, EDUCATION, AND WELFARE, PUBLIC HEALTH SERVICE, AIR QUALITY CRITERIA FOR SULFUR OXIDES

### 153, 161-62 (1969)

This document presents criteria of air quality in terms of the effects empirically obtained and published for various concentrations of one family of pollutants, the sulfur oxides, their acids, and acid salts. These effects do not, for the most part, derive solely from the presence of sulfur oxides in the atmosphere. They are the effects that have been observed when various concentrations of sulfur oxides, along with other pollutants, have been present in the atmosphere. Many of these effects are produced by a combination of sulfur oxides pollution and undifferentiated particulate matter; the contributions of each class are difficult to distinguish. Moreover, laboratory studies have shown that a combination of sulfur oxides and particulates may produce an effect that is greater than the sum of the effects caused by these pollutant classes individually. * * *

Analyses of * * * epidemiological studies clearly indicate an association between air pollution, as measured by sulfur dioxide, accompanied by particulate matter, and health effects of varying severity. * * *

[T]he following conclusions are listed in order of reliability, with the more reliable conclusions first. * * *

At concentrations of about 1500 $\mu g/m^3$ [*micrograms per cubic meter*] (0.52 ppm) of sulfur dioxide (24-hour average), and suspended particulate matter measured as a soiling index of 6 cohs or greater, *increased mortality* may occur. * * *

At concentrations of about 715 $\mu g/m^3$ (0.25 ppm) of sulfur dioxide and higher (24-hour mean), accompanied by smoke at a concentration of 750 $\mu g/m^3$, *increased daily death rate* may occur. * * *

At concentrations of about 500 $\mu g/m^3$ (0.19 ppm) of sulfur dioxide (24-hour mean), with low particulate levels, *increased mortality rates* may occur. * * *

At concentrations ranging from 300 $\mu g/m^3$ to 500 $\mu g/m^3$ (0.11 ppm to 0.19 ppm) of sulfur dioxide (24-hour mean), with low particulate levels, *increased hospital admissions* of older persons for respiratory disease may occur; absenteeism from work, particularly with older persons, may also occur. * * *

At concentrations of about 715 $\mu g/m^3$ (0.25 ppm) of sulfur dioxide (24-hour mean), accompanied by particulate matter, a sharp rise in illness rates for patients over age 54 with severe bronchitis may occur. * * *

At concentrations of about 600 $\mu g/m^3$ (about 0.21 ppm) of sulfur dioxide (24-hour mean), with smoke concentrations of about 300 $\mu g/m^3$, patients with chronic lung disease may experience *accentuation of symptoms.* * * *

At concentrations ranging from 105 $\mu g/m^3$ to 265 $\mu g/m^3$ (0.037 ppm to 0.092 ppm) of sulfur dioxide (annual mean), accompanied by smoke concentrations of about 185 $\mu g/m^3$, *increased frequency of respiratory symptoms and lung disease* may occur. * * *

At concentrations of about 120 $\mu g/m^3$ (about 0.046 ppm) of sulfur dioxide (annual mean), accompanied by smoke concentrations of about 100 $\mu g/m^3$, *increased frequency and severity of respiratory diseases* in schoolchildren may occur. * * *

At concentrations of about 115 $\mu g/m^3$ (about 0.040 ppm) of sulfur dioxide (annual mean), accompanied by smoke concentrations of about 160 $\mu g/m^3$, *increased mortality* from bronchitis and from lung cancer may occur.

### *Notes and Questions*

1.  The *Versailles* court finds that the burning gob piles are an annoyance to nearby residents. How would neoclassical economists, such as Pigou, describe this annoyance in economic terms? What economic harms did Pigou see in this structure, and what solution did he advocate?

2.  Suppose McKeesport Coal & Coke were ordered to pay damages to compensate the plaintiffs for the annoyance. What would probably happen to the company? Would that be a good or a bad thing, from Pigou's point of view?

3.  The *Versailles* court declared: "If we enjoin the defendant company from piling its gob at that point and in that manner, we inferentially declare * * * by implication that all coal mines must cease operating which, of course is absurd." *See* page 87, *supra*. Is this statement—that an injunction against McKeesport's deposit of gob near its mine would shut down all Pennsylvania coal mines—necessarily true, even assuming that all Pennsylvania courts would follow the *Versailles* precedent? Why or why not?

4.  Reconsider **Figure 3-1**, at page 67, *supra*. How would you chart the location of the $xx^1$ and $yy^1$ curves in the *Versailles* case, based on Judge Musmanno's opinion?

5.   The *Versailles* court relied on a treatise to determine what was known about the harmful health effects of sulfur dioxide gas in 1935. *See* pages 84-85 and **Table 3-1** *supra*. Yet the HEW document excerpted in pages 88-89, *supra*, reaches quite different conclusions about SO₂ in the presence of particulates, which are presumably associated with a burning gob pile. How can the court say that the benefits of abatement would be meager, when the HEW document suggests that the abatement benefits might be profound?

# WASCHAK v. MOFFAT

### 379 Pa. 441, 109 A.2d 310 (1954)

Before STERN, C. J., and STEARNE, JONES, BELL, CHIDSEY and MUSMANNO, JJ.

ALLEN M. STEARNE, Justice.

The appeal is from a judgment of the Superior Court refusing to enter judgment *non obstante veredicto* for defendants in an action in trespass and affirming the judgment of the Court of Common Pleas of Lackawanna County in favor of plaintiffs.

Gas or fumes from culm banks, the refuse of a coal breaker, damaged the paint on plaintiffs' dwelling. In this action for damages the applicable legal principles are technical and controversial. Considerable confusion appears in the many cases. * * *

Plaintiffs are owners of a dwelling in the Borough of Taylor which is in the center of Pennsylvania's anthracite coal lands. An action in trespass was instituted against two partners, operators of a coal breaker in that Borough. Without fault on the part of defendants, gas known as *hydrogen sulfide* was emitted from two of defendants' culm banks. This caused discoloration of the white paint (with lead base) which had been used in painting plaintiffs' dwelling. The painted surface became dark or black. The sole proven damage was the cost of restoring the surface with a white paint, having a titanium and zinc base, which will not discolor. There was no other injury either to the building or occupants. The verdict was for $1,250.

While the verdict is in a relatively modest amount, the principles of law involved, and their application, are extremely important and far reaching. Twenty-five other cases are at issue awaiting the decision in this case. The impact of this decision will affect the entire coal interests—anthracite and bituminous—as well as other industries. Application of appropriate legal principles is of vital concern to coal miners and to other labor.

The pivotal facts are undisputed. To mine anthracite coal, either by deep or strip mining, requires processing in a coal breaker before marketing. Usable coal, broken to various sizes, must first be separated from its by-products of minerals, rock, etc. The by-products are deposited in piles known as culm banks, portions of which may be reclaimed, while other parts are presently regarded as waste. The mining and processing in the present case are conceded to have been conducted by defendants without fault. Fires frequently appear in the culm banks long after the accumulation. Defendants neither committed any negligent act nor omitted any known method to prevent combustion, fires or the emission of gases. In addition to *hydrogen sulfide* two other gases, *carbon monoxide* and *sulfur dioxide* were shown to have also been emitted, but it is not contended that either of these two gases affected the paint in question. *Hydrogen sulfide* was conceded to have been the gas which caused the damage. The emission of this gas is not ordinarily found in the operation of coal mining and processing. *Defendants did not know and had no reason to anticipate the emission of this gas and the results which might follow.* Of the five culm banks only two of them, the Washington Street bank and the settling basin were shown to have emitted *hydrogen sulfide.*

In the court below the case was tried on the theory of *absolute liability* for the maintenance of a nuisance. The jury was instructed that it should determine, as a *matter of fact,* whether or not what the defendants did and the conditions resulting therefrom constituted a "reasonable and natural use" of defendants' land. * * *

The Rule of the Restatement [of Torts] * * * which unquestionably is accurate and most comprehensive, is as follows:

"Section 822. GENERAL RULE.

The actor is liable in an action for damages for a non-trespassory invasion of another's interest in the private use and enjoyment of land if,

(a) the other has property rights and privileges in respect to the use or enjoyment interfered with; and

(b) the invasion is substantial; and

(c) the actor's conduct is a legal cause of the invasion; and

(d) the invasion is either

    (i) intentional and unreasonable; or

    (ii) unintentional and otherwise actionable under the rules governing liability for negligent, reckless or ultrahazardous conduct."

This rule we adopt. We agree that the adoption will obviate the difficulty and confusion in attempting to reconcile or distinguish the great mass of cases. * * *

Prior to the year 1934 the Glen Alden Coal Company, owners, had ceased to mine coal in this area. The colliery in question was idle, the breaker was dismantled and minors [sic] in Taylor Borough were out of work. A committee of citizens of the Borough called upon the Glen Alden Coal Company requesting that the mines be reopened in order to aid the citizens. The Glen Alden Company agreed to this and leased coal lands comprising a continuous area of coal veins running from

Taylor to Dickson City. When the defendants, in 1934, first began to operate the breaker a large culm bank close to the breaker was in existence and was then burning. In 1937 a new culm bank was started because of the fire in the old one and a conveyor was used to carry the culm to the new location. This was the Main Street bank and was used from 1937 to 1944. A new bank was then started known as the Washington Street bank, which was used from 1944 until October 1948. This bank was the same distance from the breaker as the Main Street bank, but in the opposite direction. In 1948 defendants commenced the construction of a settling basin in compliance with the State law concerning pollution of streams. During the construction the State inspectors approved. In 1949, six months after the Washington Street culm bank was discontinued, fire was discovered and defendants ceased using this breaker material for the settling basin. In the spring of 1949 walls in the settling basin ignited.

It is significant that plaintiffs purchased their home on June 23, 1948. It was close to the breaker, near the Washington Street bank.

Of the various gases emitted from the five culm banks, *hydrogen sulfide* was the gas which caused the damage. The record shows that this was emitted only from the Washington Street bank and the settling basin and from no others. Defendants did not know, and had no reason to be aware, that this particular gas would be so emitted and would have the effect upon the painted house. The record shows that the defendants were guilty of no negligence and used every known means to prevent damage or injury to adjoining properties.

Even if the reasonableness of the defendants' use of their property had been the *sole* consideration, there could be no recovery here. * * *

The dwelling in question had been formerly used by a mine inspector who doubtless desired to be close to the breaker. When plaintiffs purchased the dwelling they were fully aware of the surrounding situation.

In *Versailles Borough v. McKeesport Coal & Coke Co.* * * * Mr. Justice Musmanno, when a county judge, accurately encompassed the problem when he said:

"The plaintiffs are subject to an annoyance. This we accept, but it is an annoyance they have freely assumed. Because they desired and needed a residential proximity to their places of employment, they chose to found their abode here. It is not for them to repine; and it is probable that upon reflection they will, in spite of the annoyance which they suffer, still conclude that, after all, one's bread is more important than landscape or clear skies.

"Without smoke, Pittsburgh would have remained a very pretty *village.* * * *"

In applying the rule of the Restatement, Torts, Sec. 822(d), it is evident the invasion of plaintiffs' land was clearly *not intentional*. And even if it were, for the reasons above stated, it was not unreasonable.

On the contrary, since the emission of gases was not caused by any act of defendants and arose merely from the normal and customary use of their land without negligence, recklessness or ultrahazardous conduct, it was wholly *unintentional*, and no liability may therefore be imposed upon defendants.

The judgment is reversed and is here entered in favor of defendants *non obstante veredicto*. * * *

MUSMANNO, Justice (dissenting).

The plaintiffs in this case, Joseph J. Waschak and Agnes Waschak, brother and sister, own a modest home in Taylor, Pennsylvania, a town of 7,000 inhabitants in the anthracite region of the northeastern part of the State. * * *

In 1948 the plaintiffs painted their house with a white paint. Some time later the paint began to turn to a light colored brown, then it changed to a grayish tint, once it burst into a silvery sheen, and then, as if this were its last dying gasp, the house suddenly assumed a blackish cast, the blackness deepened and intensified until now it is a "scorched black." The plaintiffs attribute this chameleon performance of their house to the hydrogen sulfide emanating from the defendants' culm deposits in the town—all in residential areas. The hydrogen sulfide, according to the plaintiffs, not only assaults the paint of the house but it snipes at the silverware, bath tub fixtures and the bronze handles of the doors, forcing them, respectively, into black, yellowish-brown and "tarnished-looking" tints. * * *

The jury by verdict decided that the defendants did not make a reasonable, lawful and natural use of their land. Reading the record in the case, I am satisfied that the jury was amply justified in their conclusion and I see no warrant for disturbing that verdict. When a property owner so uses his land that it injures his neighbor's the burden is on him to show that he did use his land naturally, reasonably and legally. The defendants in this case failed to meet the burden put on them by the law. * * *

The evidence here does not show any *necessity* on the part of the defendants to locate the culm banks in the very midst of the residential areas of Taylor. * * *

The poisonous gases lifting from the defendants' culm banks were destructive of property, detrimental to health and disruptive of the social life of the town.

There was evidence that the poisonous hydrogen sulfide was of such intensity that the inhabitants compelled to breathe it suffered from headaches, throat irritation, inability to sleep, coughing, lightheadedness, nausea and stomach ailments. These grave effects of the escaping gas reached such proportions that the citizens of Taylor held protest meetings and demanded that the municipal authorities take positive action to curb the gaseous invasion.

Did the release of the gases from the defendants' culm banks constitute under the law a nuisance? Nearly every witness testifying for the plaintiff as to the nature of the gas rising from the culm banks declared that it had the odor of rotten eggs. Otto John Zang, the town druggist, testified that the gas was like a nocturnal prowler that would come to his window while he was sleeping and wake him up in the middle of the night * * *

Several of the witnesses testified that because of the rotten egg smell which entered their parlors and sitting rooms, it was difficult to entertain visitors. This statement could well qualify as the prize understatement of the case.

It must always be kept in mind that these culm banks were not mole hills. The Main Street dump measured 1,100 feet in length, 650 feet in width and 40 feet in height. If these dimensions were applied to a ship, one can visualize the size of the vessel and what would be the state of its odoriferousness if it was loaded stem to stern with rotten eggs. And that is only one of the dumps. There is another dump at Washington Street and, consequently, another ship of rotten eggs. Its dimensions are 800 feet by 750 feet by 50 feet. A third dump measures 500 feet by 500 feet by 40 feet. Then the defendants constructed a silt dam with the same rotten-egg-smelling materials.

I do not think that there can be any doubt that the constant smell of rotten eggs constitutes a nuisance. If such a condition is not recognized by the law, then the law is the only body that does not so recognize it.

Although the defendants sought to belittle the testimony adduced by the plaintiffs with regard to the intolerable conditions in Taylor caused by the defendants' gaseous banks, it is interesting to note that defendant Robert Y. Moffatt [sic] found it convenient and desirable to live outside the Borough of Taylor and, in all the years that he has been operating the coal business which is the subject of this litigation, he never found it profitable to spend a single night in Taylor. Even so, neither he nor his partner can successfully argue that they were unaware of the deleterious fumes rising from the coal refuse which they distributed through the town. * * *

Whether the facts in the case at bar constitute an actionable nuisance is not a question of law. It is one of fact for a jury to determine. * * *

There is a golden rule in law as well as in morals and it reads: "Sic utere tuo ut alienum non laedas." The defendants oppose this maxim with the one that every person has the right to a lawful, reasonable and natural use of his land. But it is entirely possible and in fact desirable that these two maxims live together in peace and harmony. The plaintiffs in this case do not question that the defendants have the right to mine coal and process it, but is it a natural and reasonable use of land to deposit poisonous refuse in residential areas when it can be deposited elsewhere? Certainly the defendants may lawfully operate a breaker in Taylor, and whatever noises, dust and commotion result from the breaker operation are inconveniences which the plaintiff and other Taylor inhabitants must accept as part of the life of a mining community. But the disposition of the poisonous refuse of a mining operation does not fall within the definition of lawful and normal use of land. * * *

The Majority states that the "emission of offensive odors, noises, fumes, violations, etc., must be weighed against the utility of the operation." In this respect, the Majority Opinion does me the honor of quoting from an Opinion I wrote when I was a member of the distinguished Court of Common Pleas of Allegheny County: *Versailles Borough v. McKeesport Coal & Coke Co.* * * * . That was an equity case where the plaintiffs sought an injunction against the defendant coal company for maintaining a burning gob pile which emitted smoke. The coal mine was located in the very heart of an industrialized area which contained factories, mills, garbage dumps, incinerators and railroads, all producing their own individualized smoke and vapors so that it could not be said that the discomforts of the inhabitants were due exclusively to the operation of the coal mine. Furthermore, after hearings lasting one month I found that the operation of the mine in no way jeopardized the health of the inhabitants:

> Of course, if the continued operation of this mine were a serious menace to the health or lives of those who reside in its vicinity, there would be another question before us, but there is no evidence in this case to warrant the assumption that the health of anyone is being imperiled.

In the instant case the exact contrary is true. The health of the town of Taylor is being imperiled. And then also, as well stated by the lower court in the present litigation, "Many factors may lead a chancellor to grant or deny injunctive relief which are not properly involved in an action brought to recompense one for injury to his land * * * A denial of relief by a court of equity is not always precedent for denying redress by way of damages."

Even so, there is a vast difference between smoke which beclouds the skies and gas which is so strong that it peels the paint from houses. I did say in the *Versailles* case, "One's bread is more important than landscape or clear skies." But in the preservation of human life, even bread is preceded by water, and even water must give way to breathable air. Experimentation and observation reveal that one can live as long as 60 or 70 days without food; one can keep the lamp of life burning 3 or 4 days without water, but the wick is snuffed out in a minute or two in the absence of breathable air. For decades Pittsburgh was known as the "Smoky City" and without that smoke in its early days Pittsburgh indeed would have remained a "pretty village." But with scientific progress in the development of smoke-consuming devices, added to the use of smokeless fuel, Pittsburgh's skies have cleared, its progress has been phenomenal and the bread of its workers is whiter, cleaner, and sweeter. * * *

Even if the rights of the plaintiffs were to be considered by Restatement rules they would still be entitled to recover under the proposition that the defendants were so well informed of the probable harmful effects of their operation that their actions could only be regarded as an intentional invasion of the rights of the plaintiff. Section 825 of the Restatement, Torts declares:

> An invasion of another's interest in the use and enjoyment of land is intentional when the actor
>
> (a) acts for the purpose of causing it; or
>
> (b) knows that it is resulting or is substantially certain to result from his conduct.

The record amply proves that the defendants were at least "substantially certain" that their burning culm deposits would invade the plaintiffs' interest in the use and enjoyment of their land.

If there were *no* other way of disposing of the coal refuse, a different question might have been presented here, but the defendants produced no evidence that they could not have deposited the debris in places removed from the residential districts in Taylor. Certainly, many of the strip-mining craters which uglify the countryside in the areas close to Taylor could have been utilized by the defendants. They chose, however, to use the residential sections of Taylor because it was cheaper to pile the culm there than to haul it away into less populous territory.

This was certainly an unreasonable and selfish act in no way indispensably associated with the operation of the breaker. It brought greater profits to the defendants but at the expense of the health and the comfort of the other landowners in the town who are also entitled to the pursuit of happiness. * * *

No one will deny that the defendants are entitled to earn profits in the operation of their breaker, but is it reasonable that they shall so conduct that business as to poison the very lifestream of existence? Is it not reasonable to suppose that if hydrogen sulfide emanating from culm banks can strip paint from wood and steel that it will also deleteriously affect the delicate membranes of the throat and lungs?

The defendants have made much of the case of *Pennsylvania Coal Company v. Sanderson*, 113 Pa. 126, [6 A. 453, 459], where this Court did say that: "To encourage the development of the great natural resources of a country trifling inconveniences to particular persons must sometimes give way to the necessities of a great community." But here we are not dealing with trifling inconveniences. We are dealing with a situation where in effect the inhabitant of Taylor, Pennsylvania, awakens each morning with a basket of rotten eggs on his doorstep, and then, on his way to work finds that some of those eggs have been put into his pocket. No matter how often he may remove them, an invisible hand replaces them. This can scarcely be placed in the category of "trifling inconveniences."

The decision of the Superior Court in this case is logical, fair and in keeping with the philosophy and the pragmatics of the law. It does no violence to the precedents. It applies them in the light of the facts so clearly established in the 600 printed pages of testimony.

I would affirm the decision of the Superior Court.

### *Notes and Questions*

1. Suppose the *Waschak* dispute had been brought to an economist to resolve, instead of a judge. How do you suppose the economist would rule, and what reasons would she give for her ruling?

2. Reconsider **Figure 3-1**, at page 67, *supra*. How would you chart the location of the $xx^1$ and $yy^1$ curves in the *Waschak* case, based on Judge Musmanno's opinion?

3. The *Waschak* majority says that the plaintiffs came to the nuisance at a time when the culm banks were already burning, implying that the plaintiffs were "fully aware" of the hydrogen sulfide. Do the facts as set forth in the majority opinion support this implication?

4. Judge Musmanno enumerates several ways in which the *Waschak* case is distinguishable from *Versailles*, explaining what might otherwise seem to be his inconsistent positions on the fires of prosperity. Do you find any of these distinctions to be convincing? Why or why not? Given what you may know about the law of evidence and your understanding of the plaintiffs' claims in *Waschak*, do any of Judge Musmanno's arguments surprise you?

# G. THE LIMITATIONS
# OF ECONOMIC ANALYSIS

Like any decisionmaking tool, economic analysis has its limits. The following readings are designed to explore some of them.

## STEVEN KELMAN, COST-BENEFIT
## ANALYSIS: AN ETHICAL CRITIQUE

### 5 Regulation 33 (Jan./Feb. 1981)

At the broadest and vaguest level, cost-benefit analysis may be regarded simply as systematic thinking about decision-making. Who can oppose, economists sometimes ask, efforts to think in a systematic way about the consequences of different courses of action? The alternative, it would appear, is unexamined decision-making. But defining cost-benefit analysis so simply leaves it with few implications for actual regulatory decision-making. Presumably, therefore, those who urge regulators to make greater use of the technique have a more extensive prescription in mind. I assume here that their prescription includes the following views:

1. There exists a strong presumption that an act should not be undertaken unless its benefits outweigh its costs.

2. In order to determine whether benefits outweigh costs, it is desirable to attempt to express all benefits and costs in a common scale or denominator, so that they can be compared with each other, even when some benefits and costs are not traded on markets and hence have no established dollar values.

3. Getting decision-makers to make more use of cost-benefit techniques is important enough to warrant both the expense required to gather the data for improved cost-benefit estimation and the political efforts needed to give the activity higher priority compared to other activities, also valuable in and of themselves.

My focus is on cost-benefit as applied to environmental, safety, and health regulation. In that context, I examine each of the above propositions from the perspective of formal ethical theory, that is, the study of what actions it is morally right to undertake. My conclusions are:

1. In areas of environmental, safety, and health regulation, there may be many instances where a certain decision might be right even though its benefits do not outweigh its costs.

2. There are good reasons to oppose efforts to put dollar values on non-marketed benefits and costs.

3. Given the relative frequency of occasions in the areas of environmental, safety, and health regulation where one would not wish to use a benefits-outweigh-costs test as a decision rule, and given the reasons to oppose the monetizing of non-marketed benefits or costs that is a prerequisite for cost-benefit analysis, it is not justifiable to devote major resources to the generation of data for cost-benefit calculations or to undertake efforts to "spread the gospel" of cost-benefit analysis further.

How do we decide whether a given action is morally right or wrong and hence, assuming the desire to act morally, why it should be undertaken or refrained from? * * * [E]conomists who advocate use of cost-benefit analysis for public decisions are philosophers without knowing it: the answer given by cost-benefit analysis, that actions should be taken so as to maximize net benefits, represents one of the classic answers given by moral philosophers—that given by utilitarians. To determine whether an action is right or wrong, utilitarians tote up all the positive consequences of an action in terms of human satisfaction. The act that maximizes attainment of satisfaction under the circumstances is the right act. * * *

Utilitarianism is an important and powerful moral doctrine. But it is probably a minority position among contemporary moral philosophers. It is amazing that economists can proceed in unanimous endorsement of cost-benefit analysis as if unaware that their conceptual framework is highly controversial in the discipline from which it arose—moral philosophy.

Let us explore the critique of utilitarianism. * * *

[T]wo very close friends are on an Arctic expedition together. One of them falls very sick in the snow and bitter cold, and sinks quickly before anything can be done to help him. As he is dying, he asks his friend one thing, "Please make me a solemn promise that ten years from today you will come back to this spot and place a lighted candle here to remember me." The friend solemnly promises to do so, but does not tell a soul. Now, ten years later, the friend must decide whether to keep his promise. It would be inconvenient for him to make the long trip. Since he told nobody, his failure to go will not affect the general social faith in promise-keeping. And the incident was unique enough so that it is safe to assume that his failure to go will not encourage him to break other promises. * * * [T]he costs of the act outweigh the benefits. A utilitarian would need to believe that it would be *morally wrong* to travel to the Arctic to light the candle. * * *

To those who believe that it would not be morally wrong * * * for the explorer to return to the Arctic to light a candle for his deceased friend * * * utilitarianism is insufficient as a moral view. We believe that some acts whose costs are greater than their benefits may be morally right and, contrariwise, some acts whose benefits are greater than their costs may be morally wrong.

This does not mean that the question whether benefits are greater than costs is morally irrelevant. Few would claim such. Indeed, for a broad range of individual and social decisions, whether an act's benefits outweigh its costs is a sufficient question to ask. But not for all such decisions. These may involve situations where certain duties—duties not to lie, break promises, or kill, for example—make a moral act wrong, even if it would result in an excess of benefits over costs. Or they may involve instances where people's rights are at stake. * * * We do not do cost-benefit analyses of freedom of speech or trial by jury. * * *

In order for cost-benefit calculations to be performed the way they are supposed to be, all costs and benefits must be expressed in a common measure, typically dollars, including things not normally bought and sold on markets, and to which dollar prices are therefore not attached. The most dramatic example of such things is human life itself; but many of the other benefits achieved or preserved by environmental policy—such as peace and quiet, fresh-smelling air, swimmable rivers, spectacular vistas—are not traded on markets either.

Economists who do cost-benefit analysis regard the quest after dollar values for non-market things as a difficult challenge—but one to be met with relish. They have tried to develop methods for imputing a person's "willingness to pay" for such things, their approach generally involving a search for bundled goods that *are* traded on markets and that vary as to whether they include a feature that is, *by itself*, not marketed. Thus, fresh air is not marketed, but houses in different parts of Los Angeles that are similar except for the degree of smog are. Peace and quiet is not marketed, but similar houses inside and outside airport flight paths are. The risk of death is not marketed, but similar jobs that have different levels of risk are. Economists have produced many often ingenious efforts to impute dollar prices to non-marketed things by observing the premiums accorded homes in clean air areas over similar homes in dirty areas or the premiums paid for risky jobs over similar nonrisky jobs.

These ingenious efforts are subject to criticism on a number of technical grounds. It may be difficult to control for all the dimensions of quality other than the presence or absence of the non-marketed thing. More important, in a world where people have different preferences and are subject to different constraints as they make their choices, the dollar value imputed to non-market things that most people would seek to avoid will be lower than otherwise, because people with unusually weak aversion to those things or unusually strong constraints on their choices will be willing to take the bundled good in question at less of a discount than the average person. Thus, to use the property value discount of homes near airports as a measure of people's willingness to pay for quiet means to accept as a proxy for the rest of us the behavior of those least sensitive to noise * * * or of others who are susceptible to an agent's assurances that "it's not so bad." To use the wage premiums accorded hazardous work as a measure of the value of life means to accept as proxies for the rest of us the choices of people who do not have many choices or who are exceptional risk-seekers. * * *

[O]ne may oppose the effort to place prices on a non-market thing and hence in effect incorporate it into the market system out of a fear that the very act of doing so will reduce the thing's perceived value. Cost-benefit analysis thus may be like the thermometer that, when placed in a liquid to be measured, itself changes the liquid's temperature. * * *

A true anecdote is told of an economist who retired to another university community and complained that he was having difficulty making friends. The laconic response of a critical colleague—"If you want a friend why don't you buy yourself one"—illustrates in a pithy way the intuition that, for some things, the very act of placing a price on them reduces their perceived value. * * *

Economists tend to scoff at talk of pricelessness. For them, saying that something is priceless is to state a willingness to trade off an infinite quantity of all other goods for one unit of the priceless good, a situation that empirically appears highly unlikely. For most people, however, the word priceless is pregnant with meaning. Its value-affirming and value-protecting functions cannot be bestowed on expressions that merely denote a determinate, albeit high, valuation. John Kennedy in his inaugural address proclaimed that the nation was ready to "pay any price [and] bear any burden * * * to assure the survival and the success of liberty." Had he said instead that we were willing to "pay a high price" or "bear a large burden" for liberty, the statement would have rung hollow. * * *

My own judgment is that modest efforts to assess levels of benefits and costs are justified, although I do not believe that government agencies ought to sponsor efforts to put dollar prices on non-market things. I also do not believe that the cry for more cost-benefit analysis in regulation is, on the whole, justified. If regulatory officials were so insensitive about regulatory costs that they did not provide acceptable raw materials for deliberative judgments * * * my conclusion might be different. But a good deal of research into costs and benefits already occurs—actually, far more in the U.S. regulatory process than in that of any other industrial society. The danger now would seem to come more from the other side.

# MARK SAGOFF, ECONOMIC THEORY AND ENVIRONMENTAL LAW

79 Mich. L. Rev. 1393-94, 1396-1405, 1410-13, 1415-19
& nn.26, 50, 51, 84, 87 & 111 (1981)[e]

Many economists take the view that environmental problems are economic problems. * * * Although this economic approach purports to allow us to choose the best among available policies, in fact it makes economic efficiency our only goal. * * *

Anyone who believes that government ought to be primarily interested in correcting market failure must find puzzling much of our environmental legislation. * * * These laws attempt to correct perceived environmental rather than economic, problems. Congress did not limit itself to providing economically optimal solutions.

Consider, for example, the 1977 Clean Air Act Amendments, which designated all national parks and wilderness areas as Class I lands to protect them from significant deterioration of air quality. This insistence upon preserving air quality in pristine areas does not rest upon an economic calculation. It is justified, rather, by a national sense of responsibility. What kind of nation would turn magnificent wilderness areas into polluted fens in order to make energy cheaper and therefore easier to waste? Questions like this have led many Americans to believe that the preservation of wilderness from pollution is what national dignity and self-respect minimally require. This belief has little to do with economic "common sense." Those of us who approve of the amended Clean Air Act are not necessarily likely to use the wilderness areas that these laws protect. We are more likely to consume the energy that would be produced by polluting these lands. Cost-benefit analysis, insofar as it reflects what consumers buy rather than what citizens respect, would lead to a policy directly opposed to the Act. * * *

---

[e] *Ed.*—To facilitate reading, footnotes have been blended into the text.

A few acres near Los Angeles, known as the Antioch dunes, are the habitat of several species of butterflies, including the endangered and beautiful Lange's metalmark, whose range has otherwise been replaced by golf courses, outdoor cinemas, and highways. * * * The dunes are also a place where people can go on a Saturday afternoon to tear around on their dune buggies or dirt bikes. The economic "common sense" way to handle this situation would be to ask whether bikers will pay more to use the dunes than butterfly fanciers will pay to preserve them. The Endangered Species Act, however, prevented the Fish and Wildlife Service from asking any such question. * * * The Service simply acquired the dunes to protect the metalmark. * * *

The Endangered Species Act remains popular, even though people must recognize that the benefits of preserving Lange's metalmark, the snail darter, or the furbish lousewort may not equal the costs. We choose to save the metalmark to prove to ourselves that we are not motivated solely by economic self-interest. Rather, we act upon moral values and a sense of national responsibility to the land that we inhabit.

Our environmental laws illustrate that we are governed by legislatures, not by markets. * * * Industry argues that regulations imposing costs far in excess of their benefits are unreasonable, and that courts interpreting [such] regulations should consider economic factors. That benefits exceed costs, however, is not a constitutional requirement for congressional regulation of commerce. A legislative majority voted for the Clean Water and Clean Air Acts, the Endangered Species Act, and other environmental legislation. Courts should enforce regulations that conform to the statutes, even if consumers as a result have to pay more than they receive in benefits. * * *

[W]e may, as citizens, believe that certain public values or collective goals (e.g., that an innocent person not be convicted) supersede the values that we pursue as self-seeking individuals (e.g., security from crime). Moreover, we might decide to sacrifice economic optimality for cleaner air and water. Once legislatures, responding to political pressure, have made this choice, is it defensible for economists to insist that our policymaking process include the very consumer values that we have decided to sacrifice? Shall economic analysts, rather than legislatures, determine the balance to be struck between our preferences as consumers and our opinions as citizens? * * *

An individual may buy a vacation home even if he or she disapproves of the vacation home industry because it destroys wilderness. What we do as consumers—the choices that we make and may feel constrained to make within markets—may dismay us as citizens. * * *

Economic methods cannot supply the information necessary to justify public policy. Economics can measure the intensity with which we hold our beliefs; it cannot evaluate those beliefs on their merits. Yet such evaluation is essential to political decision making. This is my greatest single criticism of cost-benefit analysis. The many problems involved in applying the concept of shadow pricing are secondary, because the concept itself rests on a mistake.

To recognize this mistake, we must first understand what it is that economists attempt to measure. * * * They believe that they can account for citizen-preferences as well as consumer-preferences by determining their dollar value. They do this, for example, by asking citizens what they would pay for a certain level of environmental protection. But this attempt to measure the convictions or values of citizens by pricing them as market externalities confuses what the individual wants as an individual and what he or she, as a citizen, believes is best for the community.

This confusion involves what logicians call a category-mistake. One makes a category-mistake by treating facts or concepts as if they belong to one logical type or category, when they actually belong to another. Several examples are illustrative. It is logically correct to predicate whiteness of snow or even of coal. (It may not be true, but it is intelligible.) To say that the square root of four is white, however, makes no sense because it is impossible meaningfully to predicate color of a number. When two concepts are in different categories, one cannot measure the first by methods that are appropriate only to the second. * * * A person who inquires about the address of the average American family asks an absurd question, and commits a category-mistake.

Private and public preferences also belong to different logical categories. Public "preferences" do not involve desires or wants, but opinions or beliefs. They state what a person believes is best or right for the community or group as a whole. These opinions or beliefs may be true or false, and we may meaningfully ask the individual for the reasons that he or she holds them. But an economist who asks how much citizens would pay for opinions that they advocate through political association commits a category-mistake. The economist asks of objective beliefs a question that is appropriate only to subjective wants.

When an environmentalist argues that we ought to preserve wilderness areas because of their cultural importance and symbolic meaning, he or she states a *conviction* and not a *desire*. When an economist asserts that we ought to attain efficient levels of pollution, he or she, too, states a belief. Both beliefs are to be supported by arguments, not by money. * * *

The issue is no longer to measure the stake that the individual has in his proposal; indeed, the larger the individual's private stake, the more suspect is his public pretension. What matters is whether the argument that he or she offers is sound. * * *

For example, when Professor Friedman advocated a voucher system in education * * * no one asked him how much he would pay to see that policy implemented. The question would have been inappropriate because he was not expressing a consumer preference; a voucher system would probably not affect his children. Rather, he was proposing what he thought would be good for society. He was presenting an idea, to be judged on its merits, concerning what we should do about public education. It is my thesis that cost-benefit analysis has no plausible way of assessing ideas of this kind or taking them into account. * * *

[W]hy should we think economic efficiency is an important goal? Why should we take wants or preferences more seriously than beliefs and opinions? Why should we base public policy on the model of a market transaction rather than the model of a political debate? * * *

If we were to pursue efficiency as our goal in environmental policy, I believe that we would quickly turn all of our natural beauty into commercial blight. This is what happens when self-fueling and irreversible consumer markets have their way. To forestall this result by "pricing" beliefs, values, and ideals as if they were consumer benefits * * * is to commit a category-mistake. Cost-benefit analysis, at that point, disintegrates into storytelling; it becomes a bad exercise in *ad hoc* justification.

I do not pretend to assess the merits of the argument that I have made here. I only want to point out that it *is* an attempt at argument. I did not treat the position that economists defend as if it were merely their private preference. I did not survey economists to find out how much they were willing to pay to have their views implemented. Why, then, do economists survey environmentalists to find out how much they would pay to keep a vista clear or a river pure? Why do economists believe that opinions that oppose theirs deserve a price and not a reply?

The environmental legislation of the last twenty years has consistently indicated our preference for national policies that respond to concerns other than economic efficiency. This legislation rejects markets as the indicator of the national will. There is nothing in this legislation or in the public debate on environmental protection that remotely suggests that most people regard pollution as a problem only because pollution is inefficient. Rather, we regard it as a problem because it is efficient. * * *

To notice that the Endangered Species Act is not cost-beneficial is to recognize the obvious. That is the *point* of the Act, and of much of our environmental legislation. * * *

### Notes and Questions

1.  Might economic analysis be subject to cynical manipulation by self-interested actors? Professors Stewart and Krier say:

> [E]conomic analysis will rarely point to a single choice of legal rules or governmental policies as clearly correct. More frequently, there will be respectable economic arguments for a number of different alternatives.

> At best, decision makers attempting to utilize economic analysis for environmental decision making will be left with a considerable residuum of discretionary choice, exercised on the basis of intuition, political

pressure, or whatever. At worst, economic apparatus will be utilized to rationalize decisions or advocacy positions reached on other grounds.

Richard B. Stewart & James E. Krier, Environmental Law and Policy 164 (2nd ed. 1978).

2. In a subsequent publication, Professor Sagoff is even more blunt:

[W]hen cost-benefit analysis attempts to do the work of ethical and political judgment, it loses whatever objectivity it might have had and becomes a tool of partisan politics * * * . [W]hen cost-benefit analysis assigns "shadow" prices to * * * citizen beliefs and values, theoretical "breakthroughs" replace sound judgment and common sense. At that point, economic analysis deteriorates into storytelling and hand-waving likely to convince no one except those partisans who agree with—and possibly have paid for—its results.

Mark Sagoff, The Economy of the Earth 39 (1988).

# H. THE TRIUMPH OF EFFICIENCY? H.R. 9 AND S. 343

Should society pursue environmental policy goals *other* than economic efficiency? One of the two major American political parties has insisted in recent years that the answer should be "no." Republican legislators swept into Congress following the 1994 elections, promising to forge a new *Contract with America*. On March 3, 1995, the House of Representatives passed by a 271-141 vote margin the proposed Job Creation and Wage and Enhancement Act of 1995, including within it a proposed Risk Assessment and Cost-Benefit Act of 1995. H.R. 9, Title II Division D, 104th Cong. (1995); 141 Cong. Rec. D282 (1995). The bill ("H.R. 9"), if agreed to by the Senate and enacted over President Clinton's threatened veto, would have provided that:

1. All "major" health, safety, and environmental protection rules (those involving annual costs of $25 million of more) must be preceded by a formal analysis determining whether the identifiable "benefits" would exceed the "costs." H.R. 9 § 421(a)(4). The term "benefit" was defined as the "reasonably identifiable *significant* * * * benefits" that are expected to result directly or indirectly from the rule. *Id.* § 405(2) (emphasis added). The term "costs" was defined to include *all* direct and indirect costs to government entities, the private sector, wage earners, consumers, and the economy, of complying with the rule. *Id.* § 405(1) (emphasis added).

2. No such final rule may be promulgated unless the agency certifies that "the * * * benefits of any strategy chosen will be likely to justify, and be reasonably related to, the * * * costs incurred by State, local, and tribal governments, the Federal Government, and other public and private entities." H.R. 9 § 422(a)(2).

3. The foregoing criteria "shall supplement and, to the extent there is a conflict, supersede the decision criteria for rulemaking otherwise

applicable under the statute pursuant to which the rule is promulgated." H.R. 9 § 422(b).

4. Compliance with the criteria must be supported by "substantial evidence." H.R. 9 § 422(b).

5. A court on judicial review "shall consider the agency action unlawful" if the agency's analyses and determinations do not comply with the foregoing requirements. H.R. 9 § 441.

The Senate counterpart to H.R. 9 (S. 343) would have flatly prohibited regulation absent a finding that benefits outweigh costs. S. 343 § 623(a)(1). Then-Senator Robert Dole (the Republican Party's 1996 nominee for President) sought to bring S. 343 to a floor vote on three occasions in a single week in July, 1995, each time failing to get the 60 votes necessary to cut off debate. *See* John H. Cushman, Jr., *Democrats Block Vote on Anti-Regulation Measures*, N.Y. Times, July 21, 1995, at A16. On the last occasion, he fell two votes short in his effort to force a final vote that he was "sure to win." *Id.*

Senator Dole further urged that the cost-benefit analysis requirement of S. 343 and its accompanying judicial review procedure should be extended to all *existing* environmental regulations, allowing industry to petition federal agencies to overturn existing rules failing to meet the cost-benefit test, and automatically repealing rules if not promptly reviewed. *See* John H. Cushman, Jr., *Senators Seek Different Way of Regulating*, N.Y. Times, Jul. 10, 1995, at A1.

### Notes and Questions

1. Assume that the Food and Drug Administration (FDA) has decided that it is no longer adequate to inspect beef and poultry by eyeballing it for gross contamination, such as animal feces. The FDA wishes to promulgate a regulation requiring slaughterhouses to use modern laboratory tests in a quality assurance program to confirm the absence of the types of bacterial contamination that may cause illness or death in consumers. The agency anticipates the usual tussling about how many lab tests will be needed, how often they must be conducted, and so forth, but these battles between industry and regulators have been routine. Assume further that H.R. 9 has been enacted. What must the FDA do before promulgating the rule? What will happen if the FDA fails to comply with one or more of H.R. 9's directives? What if the Food and Drug Act—the statute originally establishing the agency—provides that the FDA must act to prohibit any food contamination that might lead to human sickness or death, and the agency has substantial evidence that some people will die unless the new regulation is adopted? If the agency is unable to marshal substantial evidence that the quantified "significant benefits" of the proposed regulation justify and are reasonably related to all quantified costs, may the agency follow the command of the Food and Drug Act and promulgate the rule? Why or why not?

2. Assume that federal Occupational Safety and Health regulations currently prohibit the operation of bread and deli meat slicing machines by employees younger than 18 years of age. Assume also that Senator Dole's

variation on S. 343 has been enacted. If the deli industry petitions the Occupational Safety and Health Administration (OSHA) to overturn this regulation based on industry's assertion that the benefits do not exceed the costs, what will happen if OSHA fails to act on the petition within the statutory deadline (e.g., 90 days)? Would you anticipate many or few industry petitions challenging the validity of existing health, safety, and environmental laws under the Dole statute?

4.   Assume that the U.S. Forest Service and Department of Interior propose to spend $50 million to create new roads in Alaska wilderness areas, so that private logging companies may clear cut vast expanses of virgin timber and private oil companies may explore for and extract large petroleum deposits. Assume, again, that H.R. 9 has been enacted. Would the statute have any application to the proposed actions of the Forest Service and Interior Department? Why or why not?

5.   Would H.R. 9 apply to the following actions: (1) tripling the size of the Atlanta airport with federal funds; (2) imposing a 100% import tariff on Lexus automobiles, in an effort to force Japan to allow greater imports of American cars; (3) the purchase by the Defense Department of $4 billion of defective airplanes?

6.   Should government *spending* be subjected to rigorous cost-benefit analysis, or should we subject only environmental, health, and safety *regulations* to such scrutiny? Are there principled grounds for limiting H.R. 9's approach to the latter category of governmental activities?

7.   Reconsider **Figure 3-1** at page 67, *supra*. Recall that economic efficiency is achieved if and only if pollution controls are imposed to point Z. Accordingly, for any given combination of costs and benefits, a pollution control regime may be inefficient in either of two ways. First, if Polluter is directed to reduce emissions anywhere to the *right* of optimal point Z (for example, to 10 tons of remaining emissions), the situation is one of "overcontrol," in which too much money is being spent on pollution reduction. H.R. 9 and S. 343 are plainly designed to preclude this possibility. Second, if Polluter is directed to reduce emissions anywhere to the *left* of optimal point Z (for example, to 50 tons of remaining emissions), the situation is one of "undercontrol," in which insufficient money is being spent on pollution reduction. Do H.R. 9 and S. 343 preclude this second type of inefficiency? Given the great effort and cost associated with the preparation of a formal cost-benefit analysis, do not H.R. 9 and S. 343 guarantee the persistence of this second type of inefficiency in all those cases in which the regulator lacks the resources, information, or ability to complete a cost-benefit analysis sufficient to withstand judicial scrutiny?

8.   In analyzing H.R. 9 and S. 343, Professor Driesen asks: "Does it advance * * * efficiency to adhere to a rule that harms should continue unless their economic value outweighs the polluter's prevention costs?" David M. Driesen, *The Societal Cost of Environmental Regulation: Beyond Administrative Cost-Benefit Analysis*, 24 Ecol. L.Q. 545, 582 (1997). He concludes: "the only justification for a rule that allows 'underregulation' while forbidding 'overregulation' relative to an optimum is a political preference for polluter interests over other interests." *Id.* at 583. Driesen notes further:

[M]ost of the critics who claim that society spends too much on trivial harms also assert that it spends too little on serious harms. [Cost-benefit analysis] will likely exacerbate this problem by tying up enormous resources * * * .

In order to predict that [cost-benefit analysis] will be * * * efficient, one must show that transaction costs are unimportant. In fact, [cost-benefit analysis] requires an extremely comprehensive and difficult analytical effort that takes enormous resources and saps agencies' abilities to comprehensively address environmental problems, which stem from numerous sources, including cumulatively significant, but small and difficult to regulate sources. During the analytical phase, judicial review of [cost-benefit analysis], and remand of unsatisfactory analysis (which may be very common, because non-arbitrary [cost-benefit analysis] is so difficult), pollution continues unabated.

*Id.* at 565, 601-02.

## SCOTT ADAMS, DILBERT

Sep. 6, 1998
Reprinted by permission of
United Feature Syndicate, Inc.

# Chapter Four

## NONECONOMIC GOALS

### A. INTRODUCTION

Reasonable people—and reasonable societies—may choose to pursue one or more goals *other* than economic efficiency when formulating environmental policies, even though economists might lament the resulting policies as wasteful. Chapter 4 contains excerpts from a small fraction of the rich and provocative literature on this subject.

Professor Sagoff's essay, at pages 101-04 *supra*, is critical of economists and others who refuse to accept the *legislature's* judgment that other values are sometimes more important than the goal of economic efficiency. Indeed, in a more recent publication, Sagoff has declared:

> The Reagan administration reasoned correctly that hundreds of economists happily whacking away at their cost-benefit analyses would constitute a layer of bureaucracy impervious to any efforts line agencies might make to fulfill their legislative mandates. This is generally how things worked out.

Mark Sagoff, The Economy of the Earth 22 (1988).

To be sure, if Congress *itself* makes efficiency the only goal—as proposed in H.R. 9 and S. 343, discussed at pages 105-08, *supra*—the legislative mandates of agencies like the Environmental Protection Agency will have changed overnight: it may then become unlawful to consider noneconomic values and many more hundreds of economists will happily whack away at the cost-benefit analyses of fewer and fewer rules. Moreover, Congress will have served notice that it does not intend to consider other goals in establishing environmental policy.

Nevertheless, many people believe that there should be more to environmental policy than maximizing human appetites. We will explore in the remainder of Chapter 4 a number of goals that might augment or supplant the economic goal of efficient resource allocation. For these and all excerpts in this book, please construe the masculine gender in the generic sense, to include women as well as men.

# B. ENVIRONMENTAL JUSTICE

We begin with a recognition that environmental policy decisions—like all resource allocation decisions—may have profound impacts on the *distribution* of wealth. In keeping with the opening phrase of the Declaration of Independence, one of the most important values in American society has been the notion of equality—the idea that rights, privileges, and opportunities should be equally available to all. Although we are not committed to a total equality of wealth in our society, American policymakers by and large give lip service to the belief that gross disparities in wealth threaten the ideal of equal opportunity, and that government policies should ordinarily not exacerbate inequality of wealth without compelling justification. Moreover, many lawmakers support proposals by claiming that implementation of their policies will help bring about a more "proper" distribution of wealth. However ephemeral the goal of "proper" distribution may be, it is a value separate and distinct from the goal of economic efficiency—a value frequently not enhanced by the pursuit of efficiency.

The discipline of economics cannot provide any assistance in resolving disputes about "appropriate" wealth rearrangement:

> Economic analysis is unable to deal with distributional considerations, both because there is no economic criterion for "correct" wealth distribution and because "there is no objective basis for balancing * * * distributive benefits against allocative costs." Often it is simply assumed that the initial distribution of income is optimal and that any changes in distribution occasioned by the attainment of economic efficiency will be costlessly corrected by other means, such as transfer payments authorized by the legislature, or that, given a series of administrative decisions, such changes will tend to cancel out.

> These assumptions may be highly unrealistic.

Richard B. Stewart & James E. Krier, Environmental Law and Policy 168 (2d ed. 1978). Professors Stewart and Krier further note:

> Many environmental programs benefit the wealthy disproportionately. This is most obviously true of wilderness preservation, clean-up of fishing streams, and the creation of other amenities that can only be enjoyed by those with the wealth to visit and utilize them and/or the experience and education to appreciate them. The opportunity to backpack in the Rockies is of little value to a poor resident of New York City who lacks both the air fare and the know-how to take advantage of it. J. K. Galbraith has sardonically defined a conservationist as "a man who concerns himself with the beauties of nature in roughly inverse proportion to the number of people who can enjoy them."

*Id.* at 171.

The following readings recognize the inability of economic analysis to cope adequately with distributional concerns, and explore whether government policies should be shaped by a desire to pursue a goal of environmental justice.

# RICHARD J. LAZARUS, PURSUING "ENVIRONMENTAL JUSTICE": THE DISTRIBUTIONAL EFFECTS OF ENVIRONMENTAL PROTECTION

87 Nw.U.L.Rev. 787-90, 792-94, 796, 812-14, 816-20, 856-57 (1993)

Environmental protection policy has been almost exclusively concerned with two basic issues during the last several decades: (1) what is an acceptable level of pollution; and (2) what kinds of legal rules would be best suited for reducing pollution to that level. By contrast, policymakers have paid much less attention to the distributional effects, including the potential for distributional inequities, of environmental protection generally.

To be sure, scholars have engaged in considerable discussion of how the costs of environmental controls affect particular industries, and how these costs place a disproportionate burden on new versus existing, and large versus small, industrial sources of pollution. But there has been at best only an ad hoc accounting of how the benefits of environmental protection are spread among groups of persons. And, when the costs of pollution control have been considered, such discussions have been narrowly confined to the economic costs. There has been virtually no accounting of how pollution controls redistribute environmental risks among groups of persons, thereby imposing a cost on some for the benefit of others.

The 1970s marked the heyday of the modern environmental era. Earth Day in 1970 caught the imagination of a nation * * * . Largely ignored in the celebration * * * were those distinct voices within minority communities that questioned the value of environmentalism to their communities. * * * Some minority leaders described environmentalism as "irrelevant" at best and, at worst, "a deliberate attempt by a bigoted and selfish white middle-class society to perpetuate its own values and protect its own life style at the expense of the poor and the underprivileged." Environmentalists were seen as ignoring both the "urban environment" and the needs of the poor * * * . As one commentator described, environmentalists "would prefer more wilderness * * * for a more secure enclave in nature from * * * the demands of the poor." * * *

Neither the United States Environmental Protection Agency (EPA) nor the mainstream environmental groups appear to have paid attention to these charges. Quite possibly, this was because such claims were so unsettling and potentially divisive, particularly to the extent that they implicated the welfare of racial minorities. The environmental movement of the 1970s finds much of its structural roots and moral inspiration in the civil rights movement that preceded it. Hence, for many in the environmental community, the notion that the two social movements could be at odds was very likely too personally obnoxious to be believed or even tolerated.

More recently, however, the number of those suggesting that there may be serious distributional problems in environmental protection policy has significantly increased, and the character of their claims has shifted. Prominent voices in racial minority communities across the country are now forcefully contending that existing environmental protection laws do not adequately reflect minority interests and, in some instances, even perpetuate racially discriminatory policies. * * * [T]he potential for a regressive distribution of the economic costs associated with pollution control is * * * not the principal focus of their concerns. Rather, it is the prevalence of hazardous pollutants in the communities where they live and work that draws the brunt of their attention. One shorthand expression for such claims is "environmental racism," but "environmental justice" (or "equity") appears to have emerged as the more politically attractive expression, presumably because its connotation is more positive and, at the same time, less divisive. * * *

### THE POTENTIAL FOR DISTRIBUTIONAL INEQUITY

Environmental protection confers benefits and imposes burdens in several ways. To the extent that the recipients of related benefits and burdens are identical, no problem of discrimination is presented * * * . But identical recipients are rarely, if ever, the result. * * * Virtually all laws have distributional consequences, including those laws designed to further a particular conception of the public interest. Problems of discrimination, therefore, may arise in the disparities between the distribution of benefits and their related burdens.

The benefits of environmental protection are obvious and significant. * * * The burdens of environmental protection range from the obvious to the more subtle. They include the economic costs borne by both the producer and the consumer of goods and services that become more expensive as a result of environmental legislation. For consumers, product and service prices may increase; some may become unavailable because the costs of environmental compliance renders their production unprofitable; while other goods and services may be specifically banned because of their adverse impact on the natural environment. For those persons who produce goods and services made more costly by environmental laws, personal income may decrease, employment opportunities may be reduced or displaced, and certain employment opportunities may be eliminated altogether. Finally, environmental protection requires governmental expenditures * * * . These expenditures necessarily decrease public monies available for other social welfare programs.

The burdens of environmental protection, however, also include the redistribution of the risks that invariably occur with pollution control techniques that treat pollution following its production. For instance, air pollution scrubbers and municipal wastewater treatment facilities reduce air and water pollution, but only by creating a sludge that, when disposed, will likely impose risks on a segment of the population different than the segment which would have been exposed to the initial pollution in the air or water. * * * Just transporting solid and hazardous wastes from one geographic area to another for treatment or storage results in a major redistribution of the risks associated with environmental protection. * * *

### EVIDENCE OF ENVIRONMENTAL INEQUITY

To date, there has been relatively little systematic empirical investigation concerning the extent of inequity in the distribution of the benefits and burdens of environmental protection. The evidence that is available, however, "lends support to the view that, on balance, programs for environmental improvement promote the interests of higher-income groups more than those of the poor; they may well increase the degree of inequality in the distribution of real income." * * *

[T]he available evidence is not immune from challenge. But * * * it seems enough to suggest the strong possibility that virtually all of the theoretical distributional inequities outlined earlier in this Article are in fact occurring. * * *

### THE STRUCTURE OF ENVIRONMENTAL INEQUITY

Minority interests have traditionally had little voice in the various points of influence that strike the distributional balances necessary to get environmental protection laws enacted, regulations promulgated, and enforcement actions initiated. * * *

Much of environmental protection lawmaking has * * * been highly centralized, with the geographic focus in Washington, D.C. The enactment of environmental statutes within that geopolitical setting has required the expenditure of considerable political resources. * * * [I]t is no easy task to obtain the attention of the numerous congressional committees, and to form the coalitions between competing interest groups, so necessary to secure a bill's passage.

Environmental legislation has ultimately been produced through intense and lengthy horse-trading among interest groups * * * . This process has often depended upon the forging of alliances between diverse interests both within the environmental public interest community and within government bureaucracy. * * *

It is not surprising, therefore, that those environmental laws enacted by Congress typically address some, but hardly all, environmental pollution problems. And, even with regard to those problems that are explicitly addressed, there are usually discrepancies and gaps within the statutory scheme. Which problems are confronted, and where the discrepancies and gaps occur, is quite naturally an expression of the priorities of those participants who wield the greatest influence and resources in the political process.

For this reason, much environmental legislation may not have focused on those pollution problems that are of greatest concern to many minority communities. For instance, air pollution control efforts typically have [focused] on general ambient air quality concerns for an entire metropolitan region rather than on toxic hot spots in any one particular area. * * *

The absence of any systematic consideration of minority interests in environmental protection has also likely affected the implementation of environmental protection laws. The siting of hazardous waste treatment, storage, and disposal facilities is a prime example. * * *

Similar considerations are also likely to affect the development and implementation of environmental enforcement priorities, including the allocation of resources necessary for inspections of polluting facilities and other factfinding investigations. * * *

[S]ubstantial resources are generally required to discover a violation of a prescribed environmental quality standard, to bring an enforcement action against the violator, and to monitor for future violations. * * *

Some evidence supports the claim that, because of inequities in the distribution of enforcement resources, environmental quality is actually less in minority than in nonminority areas. * * *

In all events, racial minorities have had little influence on either the lawmaking or priority-setting processes at any of the legislative, regulatory, or local enforcement levels. * * * Their voices have not been heard. * * *

### CONCLUSION

The last two decades have witnessed a radical rewriting of the nation's laws in an effort to promote environmental protection concerns. These laws have been widely viewed as progressive in their thrust, and even excessively idealistic in their stated goals. It is enormously unsettling that such laws could themselves be riddled with distributional inequities, especially when the nation's modern environmental movement * * * was largely inspired by the civil rights movement * * * .

A full redressing of those distributional inequities * * * in environmental protection will * * * occur only with a change in present attitudes, including those rooted in racial stereotypes.

## R. GREGORY ROBERTS, ENVIRONMENTAL JUSTICE AND COMMUNITY EMPOWERMENT

48 Am. U. L. Rev. 229, 233-39, 242-42 (1998)

[T]he environmental justice movement is more than an environmental movement. In fact, environmentalism, as most Americans have come to describe it, is near the bottom of the environmental justice movement's priorities. * * *

In its quest for social justice, the environmental justice movement must overcome the same fundamental obstacle faced by the Civil Rights Movement: powerlessness of poor and minority communities, both economic and political. This powerlessness is the underlying cause of environmental injustice, manifesting itself in (1) the disproportionate siting of undesirable land uses in poor and minority communities, and (2) the inequitable enforcement of environmental laws in these communities.

To date, three primary means have been used to pursue environmental justice: litigation, legislation, and environmental justice strategies developed by executive branch agencies pursuant to Executive Order 12,898. * * *

[E]nvironmental justice litigation strategies have focused on the Equal Protection Clause of the Fourteenth Amendment and more recently, Title VI of the Civil Rights Act. * * *

### EQUAL PROTECTION

[T]he Equal Protection Clause has proven [ineffective] * * * primarily due to * * * *Washington v. Davis*, [426 U.S. 229 (1976)] * * * [holding] that a showing of discriminatory intent [is] necessary to prevail on equal protection grounds. * * * This burden has proven insurmountable for environmental justice plaintiffs. * * * [T]here have been several fully litigated cases in which plaintiffs sought to use the Equal Protection Clause to block an environmental siting decision. In each case, plaintiffs were able to show that a particular decision would adversely and disproportionately affect their community, but were unable to show that the decisions at issue constituted intentional discrimination. * * *

### TITLE VI

The difficulties of proving discriminatory intent forced environmental justice advocates to seek alternative avenues * * * . One strategy that may hold some promise of success is Title VI of the Civil Rights Act. * * *

Section 601 * * * of Title VI * * * provides that "no person in the United States shall, on the ground of race, color, or national origin, be excluded from participation in, be denied the benefits of, or be subjected to discrimination under any program or activity receiving Federal financial assistance." The Supreme Court has held * * * that section 601 only prohibits instances of *intentional* discrimination. [*Alexander v. Choate*, 469 U.S. 287, 293 (1985)]

Section 602 [of Title VI] requires federal agencies to promulgate rules and regulations to implement section 601. In developing these regulations, the Supreme Court * * * held [in *Alexander*] that agencies may prohibit certain disparate impacts as a condition for receipt of federal assistance. * * * [T]he EPA has adopted a disparate impact standard in its Title VI regulations. [40 C.F.R. § 7.35(b)] * * *

There are, however, at least three limitations to Title VI. First, it applies only to actions receiving federal funds. * * * Second, in the absence of a showing of discriminatory intent, it may only be possible to obtain declaratory or injunctive relief. Third, and perhaps most important, * * * it is uncertain whether a private right of action exists * * * that will enable private citizens to enforce the EPA's discriminatory effects regulations. * * *

PROPOSED LEGISLATION AND EXECUTIVE ORDER 12,898

[E]nvironmental justice proposals now appear regularly on the congressional agenda. * * * Unfortunately, Congress has not passed any environmental justice legislation. * * *

[T]he environmental justice movement received its biggest boost on February 11, 1994, when President Clinton issued Executive Order 12,898 * * * . The Executive Order requires each federal agency to develop strategies to achieve environmental justice by "identifying and addressing * * * disproportionately high and adverse human health or environmental effects of its programs, policies and activities on minority populations and low-income populations." * * *

Although the Executive Order represents a significant achievement for the environmental justice movement, its efficacy is still to be determined. In fact, since none of its provisions allows for judicial review, it ultimately risks failure.

# IN THE MATTER OF LOUISIANA ENERGY SERVICES, L.P. (CLAIBORNE ENRICHMENT CENTER)

No. LBP-97-8 (NRC Atomic Safety & Licensing Board 1997)

*In 1989, Louisiana Energy Services sought a license from the Nuclear Regulatory Commission (NRC) to build a nuclear fuel production facility, the Claiborne Enrichment Center (CEC). The Applicant's chosen site lay between the unincorporated communities of Forest Grove (population 150) and Center Springs (population 100). The two communities are in one of the poorest regions of the United States, and have populations that are 97 percent African-American. Citizens Against Nuclear Trash (CANT) intervened in the proceeding. The NRC's Atomic Safety and Licensing Board (ASLB) concluded that the proposed facility met all applicable licensing requirements, but then addressed CANT's environmental justice claims in the following ruling.*

THOMAS S. MOORE, CHAIRMAN, RICHARD F. COLE, AND FREDERICK J. SHON

It is the NRC's position that, as an independent regulatory agency, the NRC is not mandatorily subject to Executive Order 12898. Nevertheless, on March 31, 1994, the then Chairman of the Commission wrote the President stating that the NRC would carry out the measures in the Executive Order. * * * By voluntarily agreeing to implement the President's environmental justice directive, the Commission has made it fully applicable to the agency and, until that commitment is revoked, the President's order * * * applies to the NRC to the same extent as if it were an executive agency. * * *

### RACIAL DISCRIMINATION IN SITE SELECTION

Executive Order 12898 requires that the NRC conduct its licensing activities in a manner that "ensures" those activities do not have the effect of subjecting any persons or populations to discrimination because of their race or color. * * *

In the circumstances presented in this licensing action, * * * by limiting its consideration to a facial review of the information in the Applicant's [environmental report], the [NRC] Staff has failed to comply with the President's directive. * * * [A] thorough Staff investigation is needed not only to comply with Executive Order 12898, but to avoid the constitutional ramifications of the agency becoming a participant in any discriminatory conduct through its grant of a license.

Racial discrimination in the facility site selection process cannot be uncovered with only a cursory review of the description of that process appearing in an Applicant's environmental report. If it were so easily detected, racial discrimination would not be such a persistent and enduring problem in American society. Racial discrimination is rarely, if ever, admitted. Instead, it is often rationalized under some other seemingly racially neutral guise, making it difficult to ferret out. Moreover, direct evidence of racial discrimination is seldom found. Therefore, * * * if the President's nondiscrimination directive is to have any meaning a much more thorough investigation must be conducted by the Staff to determine whether racial discrimination played a role in the CEC site selection process. * * * [T]he Staff must lift some rocks and look under them. * * *

Substantial evidence presented by the Intervenor * * * demonstrates why it is imperative that the Staff conduct such a thorough investigation. * * * [T]he Intervenor's evidence * * * is more than sufficient to raise a reasonable inference that racial considerations played some part in the site selection process * * * . A finding that the selection process was tainted by racial bias is far too serious a determination, with potentially long lasting consequences, to render without the benefit of a thorough and professional Staff investigation aided by whatever outside experts as may be necessary. * * *

Intervenor's statistical evidence presented by Dr. Bullard * * * shows that as the site selection process progressed and the focus of the search narrowed, the level of minority representation in the population rose dramatically. * * * Of the [initial] 78 proposed sites * * * the aggregate average percentage of black population within a 1-mile radius of each of sites * * * is 28.35%. After the initial site cuts reduced the list to 37 sites * * * the aggregate percentage of black population rose to 36.78%. * * * Ultimately, the process culminated in a chosen site with a black population of 97.1% within a 1-mile radius * * * which is the site with the highest percent black population of all 78 examined sites. This statistical evidence very strongly suggests that racial considerations played a part in the site selection process. * * * Certainly, the possibility that racial considerations played a part in the site selection cannot be passed off as mere coincidence. * * *

### DISPROPORTIONAL IMPACTS

[In addition to racial discrimination], Executive Order 12898 is concerned with * * * disparate impacts * * * [and] instructs the [NRC] * * * to * * * [identify] and [address] disproportionately high and adverse human health and environmental effects on minority and low income populations as part of its licensing activities. * * *

Intervenor * * * asserts that the [NRC Staff analysis] is deficient because it fails to address the impacts of closing Parish Road 39, which currently bisects [the proposed CEC site] and joins the communities of Forest Grove and Center Springs. * * * According to Dr. Bullard, it is apparent that the Staff did not even consult with any of the residents of Forest Grove and Center Springs * * * for if it had, the Staff would have found that Forest Grove Road is a vital and frequently used link between the two communities, with regular pedestrian traffic. * * *

Staff witnesses * * * asserted that the relocation of Parish Road 39 should not affect * * * residents who attend church services * * * although driving distances will be slightly increased, * * * [suggesting] that the road relocation may require residents of the communities to adjust carpools. * * * The Staff * * * does not discuss Forest Grove Road's status as a pedestrian link between Forest Grove and Center Springs and the impacts of relocation on those who must walk the distance between the communities on this road. * * * [T]he Staff calculates how much additional gasoline it will take to drive between the communities when the road is relocated and the added travel time the road relocation will cause for various trips. * * *

[A] significant number of the residents of these communities have no motor vehicles and often must walk. Adding 0.38 mile to the distance between the Forest Grove and Center Springs communities may be a mere "inconvenience" to those who drive, as the Staff suggests. Yet, permanently adding that distance to the 1- or 2-mile walk between these communities for those who must regularly make the trip on foot may be more than a "very small" impact, especially if they are old, ill or otherwise infirm. * * *

### CONCLUSION

[W]e conclude that a thorough Staff investigation of the CEC site selection process is essential to determine whether racial discrimination played a role in that process * * * . Additionally, * * * we conclude that the Staff's treatment * * * of the impacts of relocating Parish Road 39 on the communities of Forest Grove and Center Springs is inadequate * * * .

[T]he Applicant's requested authorization for a * * * license is hereby denied.

### Notes and Questions

1.   The uranium enrichment facility at stake in the *Louisiana Energy Services* proceeding was projected to cost $855 million when initially proposed in 1989. Isn't it obvious that the potential harms complained of by the Intervenors—whatever their dollar value might be—could not possibly exceed the benefits sought by the license Applicant? Given the undeniable economic efficiency of the proposed project, why should anything else matter?

2.   The full Nuclear Regulatory Commission affirmed the portion of the ASLB ruling in *Louisiana Energy Services* directing the NRC staff to reexamine—in light of Executive Order 12898—the disparate impacts on pedestrians. *See In the Matter of Louisiana Energy Services, L.P. (Claiborne Enrichment Center)*, 47 N.R.C. 77 (April 3, 1998) at Slip Op. 73-77. However, the Commission reversed the Board's directive that the NRC staff engage in a thorough analysis of racial discrimination in the site selection process:

> What the Board in this case seems to envision is a free-ranging NRC Staff inquiry into the motives of [Louisiana Energy Services] (and perhaps state and local) decisionmakers, with only the broad instruction that the Staff should "lift some rocks and look under them." With no clear legal basis or clearly discernible objective, the Board's approach cannot in our view be sustained, notwithstanding the worthy intentions that motivated it. * * *

> [T]he Board's effort to enforce what it saw as a "nondiscrimination directive" in the Executive Order was misplaced. The Executive Order, by its own terms, established no new rights or remedies. Its purpose was merely to "*underscore* certain provision[s] of *existing* law that can help ensure that all communities and persons across this Nation live in a safe and healthful environment" (emphasis added).[19]

> The only "existing law" conceivably pertinent here is NEPA, a statute that centers on environmental impacts. The Board's proposed racial discrimination inquiry goes well beyond what NEPA has traditionally been interpreted to require. Despite nearly 30 years of extensive NEPA litigation on countless putative impacts and effects of federal actions we are unaware of a single judicial or agency decision that has invoked NEPA to consider a claim of racial discrimination. * * *

*In the Matter of Louisiana Energy Services, L.P. (Claiborne Enrichment Center)*, 47 N.R.C. 77 (April 3, 1998) at Slip Op. 58-65 (citations omitted).

3.   It might seem that Louisiana Energy Services won on the key issues in the Commission's decision. Nevertheless, the company ended the long and bitter fight over its proposed facility by withdrawing its application for a federal license:

> "After seven years, it still seemed like there was no end in sight," said company President Roland Jensen, estimating that [the company] had

---

[19] The Environmental Protection Agency (EPA) agrees with the view we express today that the Executive Order establishes no new legal rights or remedies. The EPA has held in a series of cases that the Executive Order grants the agency no independent authority to act, but is to be implemented within the constraints of EPA's existing enabling statutes and associated regulations. * * *

sunk $34 million into the struggle * * * . "We had just reached the point where we could no longer continue the process," he said.

Chris Gray, *Uranium Project is Scrapped*, The Times-Picayune C1 (Apr. 23, 1998).[a]

# CHESTER RESIDENTS CONCERNED FOR QUALITY LIVING v. SEIF

### 944 F. Supp. 413 (E.D. Pa. 1996)

*The Pennsylvania Department of Environmental Protection granted Soil Remediation Services a permit to open a waste facility in Chester, a predominantly African-American community. Residents sued the Department and various officials therein.*

DALZELL, DISTRICT JUDGE.

The Chester Residents allege violations of Title VI[b] * * * and the EPA's regulations adopted pursuant thereto. * * * [They] essentially argue that the process defendants use to determine whether to grant a waste facility permit has the effect of discriminating against them by concentrating the burden of pollution and the negative health effects it causes, within the African-American community in Chester while leaving the white residents of Delaware County essentially free of the pollution their waste caused. In this regard, the [EPA] has noted that:

> The City of Chester has among the highest concentration of industrial facilities in Pennsylvania. Chester hosts a number of waste processing plants * * * and at least 85% of raw sewage and associated sludge is treated there. A large infectious medical waste facility was also recently sited in Chester. Many of the plants are located in close proximity to low income, minority residential neighborhoods. In fact, a clustering of waste treatment facilities have been permitted within 100 feet of over 200 Chester homes. * * *

Defendants move for dismissal, arguing * * * that (1) plaintiffs have failed to state a claim under Title VI because they did not allege discriminatory intent, and (2) plaintiffs have failed to state a claim under the EPA regulations because there is no private right of action under them. * * *

[B]y alleging only discriminatory effect rather than discriminatory intent, plaintiffs failed in their complaint to allege a violation of Title VI. We shall therefore grant defendants' motion to dismiss Claim I of plaintiffs' complaint, but we shall do so without prejudice to plaintiffs' right to amend their complaint to satisfy their pleading burden [to show discriminatory intent] under Title VI * * * .

---

[a] Copyright © 1998 by The Times-Picayune. Reprinted by permission of The Times-Picayune.

[b] The text of Title VI, Section 601, 42 U.S.C. § 2000d, is set forth at page 115, *supra*.

The EPA has promulgated civil rights regulations pursuant to § 602 of Title VI * * * . [The EPA regulation] provides:

> A recipient [of federal financial assistance] shall not use criteria or methods of administering its program which have the *effect* of subjecting individuals to discrimination because of their race, color, national origin, or sex, or have the *effect* of defeating or substantially impairing accomplishment of the objectives of the program with respect to individuals of a particular race, color, national origin, or sex.

40 C.F.R. § 7.35(b) [emphasis added]. * * *

We * * * find that there is no private cause of action under the EPA civil rights regulations promulgated pursuant to § 602 of Title VI. Defendants are therefore entitled to dismissal of Claims II and III of plaintiffs' complaint with prejudice. * * *

### Notes and Questions

1.　The lower court opinion in *Chester Residents* was reversed in part by the Third Circuit. *Chester Residents Concerned for Quality Living v. Self*, 132 F.3d 925 (3d Cir. 1997). The appellate court held that a private cause of action is implied in the EPA regulations and noted further that an action may be maintained under the regulations without alleging discriminatory intent. *Id.* at 927. The United States Supreme Court granted certiorari, but subsequently vacated and remanded the case with directions to dismiss it as moot, 67 U.S.L.W. 3155 (U.S. 1998), after Soil Remediation Services abandoned its plans to locate its facility in the area and the State of Pennsylvania revoked the underlying permit. *See* 29 Env. Rep. (Curr. Dev.) 849 (1998). Even though the EPA requested that the Third Circuit's ruling be left intact, the Supreme Court followed conventional practice and required the court below to dismiss the action, reopening the private cause of action issue. *See* Marc R. Poirier, *Facing the Passaic*, 29 Seton Hall L. Rev. 1, 11 (1998).

2.　If you were a poor, African-American resident of Forest Grove, Louisiana (or Chester, Pennsylvania), would you conclude that you had found environmental justice in the legal system? Or would you conclude that the NRC (or the Supreme Court) had given you the run around?

3.　Despite the plaintiffs' legal setbacks, the *Louisiana Energy Services* and *Chester Residents* cases are success stories. In each case, the proposed project was abandoned. It would be misleading, however, to convey the impression that environmental justice claimants have been generally successful. Moreover, even the few success stories invariably involve *siting* decisions, in which local citizens have rallied to oppose specific projects.

4.　Recall that the broader issue of environmental justice discussed by Professor Lazarus at pages 111-114, *supra*, involves far more than siting decisions. Which environmental laws should be enacted? Which pollutants should be curtailed? Which violations should be met with vigorous and effective enforcement? Where should society spend its limited environmental protection resources: on wilderness preservation or on the removal of lead paint from inner city dwellings? Decisions on these and countless other questions may be attacked as unjust, because each decision has distributional consequences. Which distributional consequences are "just," and worthy of pursuit? Which are "unjust"? What remedies might the legal system provide for unjust decisions, and what types of proof should be necessary to earn such remedies? Perhaps these questions are so difficult that their resolution must be left to the political process. But if, through the political process, legislators determine in duly enacted statutes that certain policies—even inefficient ones—should be pursued precisely because those policies are just and appropriate, should the courts, executive branch, and administrative agencies implement and enforce such decisions? Or should these actors decline to implement and enforce inefficient commands?

5. Suppose our elected representatives declared, in duly enacted statutes, that government decisions must be guided solely by the criterion of economic efficiency? *See* pages 105-08, *supra*, discussing H.R. 9 and S. 343. It is plain that such a directive could not trump constitutional rights. But the Constitution protects us only from those decisions that violate certain narrowly prescribed rights—not from all decisions that might otherwise be called "unjust." Presumably, therefore, we would be bound by the legislative enactment of H.R. 9 or S. 343 until we elected a legislature with a contrary viewpoint.

## C. JUSTICE BETWEEN GENERATIONS

Closely related to the value of "proper" wealth distribution is the problem of justice between generations. This problem concerns the appropriate distribution of wealth along temporal lines: between ancestors and descendants. The next set of readings explores the obligations of environmental policymakers to consider the ramifications of today's policies for future generations.

Professor John Rawls' discussion of intergenerational obligations is part of a much broader discussion of justice. To place this discussion in context, the following reading also includes brief excerpts from earlier portions of his work, in which he sets forth: (1) the theoretical model of the "original position"—a provocative recasting of the social contract theory of government; and (2) his two principles of justice.

## JOHN RAWLS, A THEORY OF JUSTICE

12, 60, 284, 287-93 (1971) (emphasis added)

In justice as fairness the original position of equality corresponds to the state of nature in the traditional theory of the social contract. This original position is not, of course, thought of as an actual historical state of affairs * * * . It is understood as a purely hypothetical situation characterized so as to lead to a certain conception of justice. Among the essential features of this situation is that no one knows his place in society, his class position or social status, nor does any one know his fortune in the distribution of natural assets and abilities, his intelligence, strength, and the like. * * * The principles of justice are chosen behind a veil of ignorance. This ensures that no one is advantaged or disadvantaged in the choice of principles by the outcome of natural chance or the contingency of social circumstances. Since all are similarly situated and no one is able to design principles to favor his particular condition, the principles of justice are the result of a fair agreement or bargain. * * *

[The principles of justice are] * * * First: each person is to have an equal right to the most extensive basic liberty compatible with a similar liberty for others. Second: social and economic inequalities are to be arranged so that they are both (a) reasonably expected to be to everyone's advantage, and (b) attached to positions and offices open to all. * * *

We must now consider the question of justice between generations. There is no need to stress the difficulties that this problem raises. It subjects any ethical theory to severe if not impossible tests. Nevertheless, the account of justice as fairness would be incomplete without some discussion of this important matter. * * *

Now the contract doctrine looks at the problem from the standpoint of the original position. The parties do not know to which generation they belong or, what comes to the same thing, the stage of civilization of their society. They have no way of telling whether it is poor or relatively wealthy, largely agricultural or already industrialized, and so on. The veil of ignorance is complete in these respects. Thus the persons in the original position are to ask themselves how much they would be willing to save at each stage of advance on the assumption that all other generations are to save at the same rates. * * * In effect, then, they must choose a just savings principle that assigns an appropriate rate of accumulation to each level of advance. Presumably this rate changes depending upon the state of society. When people are poor and saving is difficult, a lower rate of saving should be required; whereas in a wealthier society greater savings may reasonably be expected since the real burden is less. Eventually once just institutions are firmly established, the net accumulation required falls to zero. At this point a society meets its duty of justice by maintaining just institutions and preserving their material base. Of course, the just savings principle applies to what a society is to save as a matter of justice. If its citizens wish to save for various grand projects, that is another matter. * * *

Since no one knows to which generation he belongs, the question is viewed from the standpoint of each and a fair accommodation is expressed by the principle adopted. * * * Moreover, it is immediately obvious that every generation, except possibly the first, gains when a reasonable rate of saving is maintained. The process of accumulation, once it is begun and carried through, is to the good of all subsequent generations. Each passes on to the next a fair equivalent in real capital as defined by a just savings principle. (It should be kept in mind here that capital is not only factories and machines, and so on, but also the knowledge and culture, as well as the techniques and skills, that make possible just institutions and the fair value of liberty.) This equivalent is in return for what is received from previous generations that enables

the later ones to enjoy a better life in a more just society. Only those in
the first generation do not benefit, let us say, for while they begin the
whole process, they do not share in the fruits of their provision. Nevertheless, since it is assumed that a generation cares for its immediate
descendants, as fathers say care for their sons, a just savings principle,
or more accurately, certain limits on such principles, would be acknowledged.

It is also a characteristic of the contract doctrine to define a just
state of society at which the entire course of accumulation aims. * * *
[W]e are not bound to go on maximizing indefinitely. * * * [A]ll generations are to do their part in reaching the just state of things beyond
which no further net saving is required * * * . In attempting to estimate
the fair rate of saving the persons in the original position ask what is
reasonable for members of adjacent generations to expect of one another at each level of advance. They try to piece together a just savings
schedule by balancing how much at each stage they would be willing to
save for their immediate descendants against what they would feel entitled to claim of their immediate predecessors. Thus imagining themselves to be fathers, say, they are to ascertain how much they should
set aside for their sons by noting what they would believe themselves
entitled to claim of their fathers. * * * [O]nce this is done for all stages,
we have defined the just saving principle. When this principle is followed, adjacent generations cannot complain of one another; and in fact
no generation can find fault with any other no matter how far removed
in time.

The last stage at which saving is required is not one of great abundance. This consideration deserves perhaps some emphasis. * * *
[A]verage income may not, in absolute terms, be very high. Justice does
not require that early generations save so that later ones are simply
more wealthy. Savings is demanded as a condition of bringing about the
full realization of just institutions and the fair value of liberty. If additional accumulation is to be undertaken, it is for other reasons. It is a
mistake to believe that a just and good society must wait upon a high
material standard of life. What men want is meaningful work in free
association with others, these associations regulating their relations to
one another within a framework of just basic institutions. To achieve
this state of things great wealth is not necessary. * * *

We should now observe that there is a peculiar feature of the reci-
procity principle in the case of just savings. Normally this principle applies when there is an exchange of advantages and each party gives
something as a fair return to the other. *But in the course of history no
generation gives to the preceding generations, the benefits of whose saving it has received.* In following the savings principle, each generation
makes a contribution to later generations and receives from its predecessors. The first generations may benefit hardly at all, whereas *the
last generations*, those living when no further saving is enjoined, *gain
the most and give the least*. Now this may appear unjust. Herzen re-

marks that human development is a kind of chronological unfairness, since those who live later profit from the labor of their predecessors without paying the same price. And Kant thought it disconcerting that earlier generations should carry their burdens only for the sake of the later ones and that only the last should have the good fortune to dwell in the completed building. These feelings while entirely natural are misplaced. * * *

It is a natural fact that generations are spread out in time and actual exchanges between them take place only in one direction. *We can do something for posterity but it can do nothing for us.* This situation is unalterable and so the question of justice does not arise. * * *

### Notes and Questions

1. Reread the last two paragraphs of the Rawls' excerpt. Do you agree with those portions of his analysis to which emphasis has been added—particularly the statement: "We can do something for posterity but it can do nothing for us"? Why or why not?

2. Edith Brown Weiss proposes three possible approaches to an asserted environmental obligation to future generations:

> the "opulent" model, which denies any such obligation and permits present extravagance and waste; the "preservationist" model at the other extreme, which requires the present generation to make substantial sacrifices of denial so as to enhance the environmental legacy; and the "equality" model—favored by Professor Weiss—which says we owe to future generations a global environment in no worse condition than the one we enjoy.

Anthony D'Amato, *Do We Owe a Duty to Future Generations to Preserve the Global Environment?* 84 Am. J. Intl. L. 190 (1990), summarizing Edith Brown Weiss, On Fairness to Future Generations: International Law, Common Patrimony and Intergenerational Equity (1989). Which model is most consistent with the views of John Rawls?

3. Professor Weiss has also proposed three basic principles of intergenerational equity:

> First, each generation should be required to conserve the diversity of the natural and cultural resource base, so that it does not unduly restrict the options available to future generations in solving their problems and satisfying their own values, and should also be entitled to diversity comparable to that enjoyed by previous generations. This principle is called "conservation of options." Second, each generation should be required to maintain the quality of the planet so that it is passed on in no worse condition than that in which it was received, and should also be entitled to planetary quality comparable to that enjoyed by previous generations. This is the principle of "conservation of quality." Third, each generation should provide its members with equitable rights of access to the legacy of past generations and should conserve this access for future generations. This is the principle of "conservation of access."

Edith Brown Weiss, *Our Rights and Obligations to Future Generations for the Environment*, 84 Am. J. Intl. L. 198, 201-02 (1990). Are these principles consistent with the Rawls analysis? Could any reasonable person oppose them?

## TOLES

Apr. 21, 1987

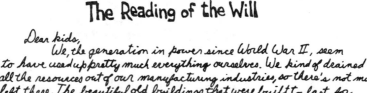

## JOHN PASSMORE, MAN'S RESPONSIBILITY FOR NATURE

78-80, 87-88 (1974)

[I]f all that can be predicted—the hypothesis I have for the moment adopted—is a very long-term exhaustion of resources, no *immediate* action on our part seems to be called for. Anything we can do would, over millions of years, be infinitesimal in its effects; not even by reducing our consumption of petrol to a thimbleful apiece could we ensure the availability of a similar quantity to our remotest descendants.

If the exhaustion of resources is really, as the more optimistic scientists assert, a problem only for a future so distant as to be scarcely imaginable, then I do not think there is any good reason for our troubling our heads about it.

Should we, then, move to the opposite extreme and leave the future to look after itself, concentrating all our efforts on making the best we can of today? Then it would not matter whether the scientists are right or wrong in predicting an early exhaustion of resources. For the future would be none of our business. * * * Nor is it by any means a preposterous attitude. We are confronted, in the present, by evils of every kind: in some of the developing countries by precisely the starvation, the illiteracy, the abysmal housing, the filth and disease which we fear for posterity; in many of our own cities by urban decay, impoverished schools, rising tides of crime and violence. It might well seem odd that the conservationist * * * is so confident that he knows how to save posterity when he cannot even save his own contemporaries. Over a large part of the globe, too, the "needs of posterity" are already being used to justify not only tyranny but a conspicuous failure to meet the needs of the present. One can easily be led to the conclusion that it would be better to let the morrow look after itself and to concentrate, as more than sufficient, upon the evils of our own time. * * *

Men are now being called upon, entirely without help, to save the future. * * * No previous generation has thought of itself as being confronted by so Herculean a task. * * *

*Passmore then discusses the Club of Rome report, see pp. 27-35, supra, and questions whether that Report's recommendations can be implemented "without social and political disruption, including the risk of civil and nuclear war." He then considers the approach of John Rawls.*

Each generation, Rawls is suggesting, should decide what it ought to save for posterity by answering in particular terms a general question: what is it reasonable for a society to expect, at the stage of development it has reached, from its predecessor? * * * [E]ach generation is concerned * * * only with the next succeeding generation, not with some remote posterity. * * *

Rawls's theory * * * leaves no room for the heroic sacrifice. Yet if the conservationists are right it is precisely such a heroic sacrifice we are now called upon to make, a sacrifice far beyond anything our ancestors had to make. * * *

# IN THE MATTER OF DUKE POWER COMPANY (PERKINS NUCLEAR STATION, UNITS 1, 2, AND 3)

2 CCH: Nuc. Reg. Rep. ¶ 30,312
(NRC Atomic Safety & Licensing Board 1978)

*The preparation of fuel for a commercial nuclear power plant requires the mining and milling of uranium. In the milling process, approximately one to five pounds of uranium is extracted from each 2,000 pounds of ore, leaving large quantities of sandy waste called "tailings." The tailings contain substantial amounts of thorium-230 and radium-226, two radioactive solids that naturally decay to form radon-222, an inert radioactive gas which may cause cancer and genetic mutations. Historically, these waste tailings have been discarded in enormous storage piles. By 1978, approximately 140 million tons of tailings had accumulated at active and inactive sites. Occasionally, tailings had been used as "fill" underneath homes or to make cinder blocks for the construction of homes and other buildings and perhaps—according to some news reports—to fill sandboxes for children. Congressional concern over the health hazards posed by uranium mill tailings led to enactment of the Uranium Mill Tailings Radiation Control Act of 1978, Pub. L. No. 95-604. See 6 U.S. Code Cong. & Adm. News 7433 (1978).*

*Beginning in 1972, the Nuclear Regulatory Commission [NRC] (formerly the Atomic Energy Commission) struggled to quantify the environmental effects of the "nuclear fuel cycle," including mining, milling, power generation, and nuclear waste disposal. In a so-called "Table S-3," set forth in 10 C.F.R. § 51.20 (1974), the Commission purported to quantify all adverse environmental effects associated with each "annual fuel requirement" (AFR) for each standard commercial nuclear power plant. The conclusion of Table S-3 was that total adverse environmental effects were "insignificant." Table S-3 was designed to preclude the raising of nuclear fuel cycle issues in licensing proceedings for individual plants. See Vermont Yankee Nuclear Power Corp. v. Natural Resources Defense Council, Inc., 98 S. Ct. 1197 (1978).*

*In 1977, Dr. Walter H. Jordan, a physicist member of an NRC Atomic Safety and Licensing Board (ASLB) panel, concluded in a report to the Commission that there was a serious error in Table S-3, resulting in a staggering understatement of the amount of radon emitted by uranium mill tailing piles. The Commission, in adopting the table, had calculated only the radon emitted during the period 1975 to 2000. Because radon will continue to be emitted for thousands of years, Dr. Jordan concluded that Table S-3 understated radon emissions by approximately 100,000 times. His report stated that "[d]eaths to future generations due to cancer and genetic effects resulting from the radon from the uranium required to fuel a single reactor for one year can run into the hundreds." 8 [Curr. Dev.] BNA Env. Rep. (Curr. Dev.) 1139 (1977).*

*The Commission responded by deleting from Table S-3 all reference to the impacts of uranium mining and milling. This made it possible for intervenors in ongoing licensing proceedings to reassert the issue of environmental impacts from such sources. The lead case within the Commission's adjudicatory system eventually became Duke Power Company's application for a permit for the Perkins Nuclear Station. The following is a brief excerpt from the Partial Initial Decision of the ASLB in the Perkins case, a decision which is only one of many on the radon issue. Dr. Jordan was one of the three members on the panel issuing the decision.*

FREDERIC J. COUFAL, CHAIRMAN, DR. WALTER H. JORDAN, AND DR. DONALD P. DE SYLVA

Radon-222 is one of the natural products of the decay of uranium-238 which has a half-life 4.5 billion years. The precursors of radon are all solids, two of them of long half-life, thorium-230 with 80,000 years and radium-226 with 1600 years. Radon is a gas having a half life of 3.8 days and readily diffuses through the soil or ore body; the amount reaching the atmosphere depends on the length of the path (and hence the lapse of time) between the origin of the radon (the ore body) and the air interface. Typically 2 feet of soil will hold up the radon long enough to permit about 25% of the radon to decay, allowing 75% to escape. If a body of uranium ore is exposed to the air, radon gas will escape into the air. * * * Since most of the thorium and radium remain in the ore after the uranium has been removed, radon will continue to be released from the * * * tailings piles * * * for billions of years. * * *

The total amount of radon emitted per AFR depends entirely on the assumptions that are made concerning the stabilization of the tailings piles after they dry out. If the piles remain uncovered, or are protected only by a foot or two of soil, as has been the practice in the past, the radon will continue to be emitted at a rate of 100 Ci/yr/AFR [curies per year per annual fuel requirement] for tens of thousands of years. The total to infinite time would be about 11 million curies per AFR or nearly 1.3 billion curies for the 100 AFRs required to fuel the Perkins Nuclear Station for 40 years. * * *

The Board agrees with the Intervenors that the amount of radon that would be emitted from unstabilized tailings piles when integrated far into the future will be very large. * * *

Neither the Intervenors nor the [NRC] Staff have argued that stabilized piles are a menace. The intervenors argue that we cannot guarantee that they will be stabilized for all future times. [Staff witness] Gotchy conservatively assumed that after 100 years the soil coverings will be eroded to the point that the radon release rate will be 10 Ci/AFR and that after 500 years it will be 100 Ci/AFR. He also assumes that the population of the U.S. will remain stable at 300 million.

It appears to us that Dr. Gotchy is being excessively conservative. It is not apparent that piles that meet present NRC standards will be eroded in a matter of a few hundred or a few thousand years. Furthermore if there are people around to breathe the radon, those people can readily repair any damage to the piles. We see no reason for piling uncertainty on top of uncertainty. There may be another period of glaciation within the next 10,000 years, but we do not have to assume it to project radon emissions into the future. If all the stabilization is destroyed by some catastrophic event, then radon will be a minor problem.

The Intervenors argue that even if stabilization could be assured for the next few thousand years, it surely could not be guaranteed for millions of years. Most of the impact that they project occurs after the first thousand or 10 thousand years. That impact is cancer deaths to future generations. * * *

There is good evidence that miners who in the past breathed air containing a large concentration of radon gas (over 100 pCi/liter [pico-curies per liter]) for extended periods were much more likely to die of cancer than were members of the public who breathed air containing only the normal background concentration of radon (about 0.1 pCi/liter). * * *

Using the foregoing risk conversion factor and his estimates of radon release from mining and milling, Dr. Gotchy calculates the total deaths during the 1000 year period following the mining of 1 AFR to be 1.2 additional deaths * * * . This number should be multiplied by 110 AFRs to get the total impact of the Perkins plant or approximately 130 deaths in 1000 years.

Dr. Gotchy's testimony discusses at length the reasons for his conclusion that he cannot predict specific health effects into the future beyond 1000 years. * * *

In contrast to Dr. Gotchy, Dr. Kepford [Intervenor's witness] continues his computations of health effects on the same basis for periods to millions and billions of years. On that basis, of course, although the annual increment is small, the total period of time is so enormous that the total number of deaths summed over this period of time, as computed by Dr. Kepford, is very large, e.g., the impact accumulated for 10,000 years is 4800 computed deaths, for a billion years it is 230 million computed deaths * * * . It is this impact that Dr. Kepford urges us to debit nuclear power when assessing nuclear power vs. an impact associated with coal * * * .

The Board has weighed carefully the views of the Staff, Applicant and Intervenors. They do not differ greatly on factual evidence but they do differ on the proper treatment of projections of potential effects into a distant future. We believe that we have an obligation to assess the effects of today's actions on future generations. We certainly must consider any known effects on our immediate successors as of importance comparable to effects on those now living. When it comes to balancing adverse impacts to those descendants who may follow a million years from now against the benefits to the present generation, we would weight benefits to the present population. The benefits are certain—the impacts hypothetical.

The action presently proposed is not one that presents a serious risk to any future generation. Even if Dr. Kepford's projections were to come about, Perkins would result in, at most, 500 deaths per millennium at any time in the future. We believe those estimates are inflated. A possible half a death per year in a population of 300 million people is a minimal impact. Under the NRC stabilization procedures and reasonable regulations on open pit reclamation, the impact will be 100 times less.

### Questions

1. Consider the foregoing *Perkins* excerpt in light of Rawls' theory of justice, Weiss' three principles of intergenerational equity, and Passmore's

comments about intergenerational obligations. Bear in mind the following factors:

(a) The *Perkins* decision is addressed to the long-term impacts of a single nuclear plant. At the time of the *Perkins* decision, the federal government envisioned as many as 1,000 such plants within the next few decades. Presumably, Dr. Kepford's projection could be extrapolated to predict 500,000 deaths per millennium under such a scenario.

(b) The *Perkins* decision makes certain assumptions about the mechanical responsibilities of future generations to keep the tailings covered: "if there are people around to breathe the radon, those people can readily repair any damage to the piles." These activities would presumably be undertaken at a cost for which those generations would receive no direct benefit.

2. Consider critically the "certain" benefits to the present generation relied on by the ASLB panel. What, specifically, are those benefits? Would the present generation have to make "heroic sacrifices" (Passmore's phrase) to forego those benefits?

## D. PREFERENCE SHAPING

Thus far, we have examined two goals that might be selected instead of, or in addition to, the economic goal of efficient resource allocation: (1) securing a more acceptable distribution of goods and services ("environmental justice"); and (2) fulfilling obligations to our descendants. The next set of readings addresses a possible third goal: preserving present beliefs (or attempting to change beliefs) about what things *will* maximize human satisfactions—beliefs about what things are good, desirable, and beautiful. Professor Stewart refers to this as the "preference-shaping problem."

## RICHARD B. STEWART, THE REFORMATION OF AMERICAN ADMINISTRATIVE LAW

### 88 Harv. L. Rev. 1667, 1704-06 (1975)

Economic analysis normally assumes that choices among alternatives are to be made by reference to the population's existing preferences for goods and services. These preferences are normally assumed to be fixed; however, our present choices among goods and services will affect our future preferences because tastes and values are shaped by experience. * * *

[This poses] serious problems for proposals that agency policies be selected through economic analysis. Uncertainty is created as to whether the choices should be based on existing preferences or the alternative sets of future preferences that would be generated by other policies that might be chosen. Because policy choice may affect preferences, administrators must at least address the question of whether policy choices should be based on individuals' actual preferences at any given time, or whether such preferences should be discounted, in order to give weight either to the preferences individuals might develop if they were well-informed, or to normative judgments that certain preferences should be encouraged or discouraged. * * *

[I]t is hardly self-evident that only existing preferences should "count." Economic analysis cannot ultimately resolve the question of which preferences to encourage or discourage, ignore or implement; but issues of just this sort are at the heart of many governmental choices.

## MARK SAGOFF, THE ECONOMY OF THE EARTH

### 63-64 (1988)

Our decisions concerning the environment will * * * determine, to a large extent, what future people are like and what their preferences and tastes will be.

If we leave them an environment that is fit for pigs, they will be like pigs; their tastes will adapt to their conditions * * * . Suppose we destroyed all of our literary, artistic, and musical heritage; suppose we left to future generations only potboiler romances, fluorescent velvet paintings, and disco songs. We would then ensure a race of uncultured near illiterates. Now, suppose we leave an environment dominated by dumps, strip mines, and highways. Again, we will ensure that future individuals will be illiterate, although in another way. Surely, we should strive to make the human race better, not even worse than it already is. Surely, it is morally bad for us to deteriorate into a pack of yahoos who have lost both knowledge of and taste for the things that give value and meaning to life.

Future generations might not complain: A pack of yahoos will *like* a junkyard environment. That is the problem. That kind of future is efficient. It may well be equitable. But it is tragic all the same.

Our obligation to provide future individuals with an environment consistent with ideals we know to be good is an obligation not necessarily to those individuals but to the ideals themselves. * * * These ideals * * * have to do not with the utility but with the meaning of things, not with what things are used for but what they express. * * *

We cannot avoid paternalism with respect to future generations. * * * Yet this paternalism, if that is what it is, is of a peculiar kind. It is not paternalism about the welfare of future generations; for, as I have argued, whatever policy we choose is likely to be optimal for the individuals and interests it helps to create. Rather, it is a paternalism about the character of future individuals, their environment, and their values. In short, it is a concern about the character of the future itself. We want individuals to be happier, but we also want them to have surroundings to be happier about. We want them to have what is *worthy of happiness.*

## SOLOMON FABRICANT, ECONOMIC GROWTH AND THE PROBLEM OF ENVIRONMENTAL POLLUTION

in Kenneth E. Boulding, et al., Economics of Pollution 137, 148-49 (1971)

The political problem, which I can only mention, is very difficult. * * * We are not all of one mind; not everyone agrees on the relative values of what everyone agrees is "good." This means that we must learn to settle our differences—we must be prepared, having urged our case as strongly as we can, for compromise. To you and to me, who value highly the silence of the forest's glade at noon, and the song of the bird at dusk, the prospect of what we shall have to settle for can be anything but pleasant.

Nor can we take pleasure in knowing that, from our point of view, tastes are bound to deteriorate further in the long years ahead. For the values of future generations will be molded by the world into which they are born, and this world will be very different from ours because of the continued process of economic growth. * * * Our descendants will set environmental standards that we would view as intolerable. * * *

We are confronted by a problem broad enough, and permanent enough, to draw us into the realm of science-fiction. If pollution is permitted to worsen over the centuries and the eons, we can nevertheless suppose that life will somehow adapt itself. "Living systems are systems that reproduce," yes: but as the biologists define them, they are also systems "that mutate, and that reproduce their mutations." That is why living things "are endowed with a seemingly infinite capacity to adapt themselves to the exigencies of existence"— even in a cesspool.

But we cannot be certain that it is *human* life that would adapt and survive.

## GEORGE F. WILL, VALUE-FIXING

Wash. Post (Jan. 18, 1981) at C7

*George F. Will is a distinguished conservative columnist. Although environmental activism has recently been associated with political liberalism, and the Republican Party's 1994* Contract with America *was a supposedly conservative document, Will's remarks about the preference-shaping problem remind us that, in previous generations, "environmentalists" were known as "conservationists"—a word sharing a common root with the word "conservative."*

Today's turn toward more hard-edged economic calculation in public policy is called for by common sense, and the electorate. But it is producing a cold climate for environmentalists, and may leave environmentalism intellectually disarmed, to the long-term detriment of American life. * * *

It is, perhaps, odd that it would require a surgical operation to get into the heads of some people who fancy themselves conservative an idea sympathetic to conservation and other environmental values. But there are many such people.

So, environmentalists need a new, or at least enriched, vocabulary of values * * * that can tap * * * the best impulses of today's conservatism. They should begin with basics, insisting that what is at stake in defining a basic attitude toward environmental questions is not what you think about redwoods or ducks, but what you think about man. Father Richard McCormick, S.J., of Georgetown University identifies, for example, two sharply contrasting images of man and his relation to nature * * * .

One image is the "power-plastic" model. According to it, "nature is alien, independent of man, possessing no inherent value. It is capable of being used, dominated, and shaped by man. * * * In contrast, there is the "social-symbiotic" model. * * * Man is not the master, he is the steward, and nature is a trust. * * *

What will be the irrecoverable cost to precious intangibles—our capacity for awe; our moral imagination; our sense of nature, including human nature as a realm of values—when we regard the world around and within us just as raw material in the service of our (by then necessarily) vagrant passions and imperious appetites?

## E. DUTIES OWED TO NATURE

We have now examined three possible goals for environmental policy that might augment or supplant the economic goal of efficient resource allocation: (1) securing a more acceptable distribution of goods and services ("environmental justice"); (2) fulfilling obligations to our descendants; and (3) preserving present beliefs (or seeking to change beliefs) about what things will maximize human satisfactions ("preference shaping"). The next set of readings addresses a possible fourth goal: fulfilling obligations owed to nature.

## CARL SAGAN, COSMOS

### 271-73 (1980)

The sea is murky. Sight and smell, which work well for mammals on the land, are not of much use in the depths of the ocean. Those ancestors of the whales who relied on these senses to locate a mate * * * did not leave many offspring. So another method was perfected by evolution; it works superbly well and is central to any understanding of the whales: the sense of sound. * * * The finbacks, for example, emit extremely loud * * * low-frequency sounds [that] are scarcely absorbed in the ocean. * * * [U]sing the deep ocean sound channel, two whales could communicate with each other at twenty Hertz essentially anywhere in the world. One might be off the Ross Ice Shelf in Antarctica and communicate with another in the Aleutians. * * *

For tens of millions of years these enormous, intelligent, communicative creatures evolved with essentially no natural enemies. Then the development of the steamship in the nineteenth century introduced an ominous source of noise pollution. As commercial and military vessels became more abundant, the noise background in the oceans, especially at a frequency of twenty Hertz, became noticeable. * * * Two hundred years ago, a typical distance across which finbacks could communicate was perhaps 10,000 kilometers. Today, the corresponding number is perhaps a few hundred kilometers. * * * We have cut the whales off from themselves. Creatures that communicated for tens of millions of years have now effectively been silenced.

### Notes and Questions

1. Should the noise pollution problem articulated by Sagan be analyzed on a cost-benefit basis? Is it possible to define, in monetary terms, the benefits to be gained by abating ocean noise pollution (the $yy^1$ curve in **Figure 3-1** at page 67, *supra*)? Should we do so by attempting to ascertain the degree to which noise interferes with the harvesting of whales by humans? (Perhaps there is no interference, making the benefits of noise abatement equal to zero.) Does such analysis make any sense? On the other hand, are the benefits of ocean silence so priceless from a philosophical point of view that rigorous noise abatement should be mandated regardless of cost? If economic analysis (comparing costs and benefits) cannot assist us with this problem, how can we attempt to ascertain an answer by referring to other values?

2. Judge Richard Posner would apparently have no difficulty in concluding that the value of noise abatement in the oceans—at least for the purpose of enhancing the communication ability of whales—is zero. He states:

> Animals count, but only insofar as they enhance wealth. The optimal population of sheep is determined not by speculation on their capacity for contentment relative to people, but by the intersection of the marginal product and marginal cost of keeping sheep.

Richard A. Posner, The Economics of Justice 76 (1981). Compare the United Methodist Church's Book of Discipline: "Water, air, soil, minerals, energy resources, plants, animal life and space are to be valued and conserved because they are God's creation and not solely because they are useful to human beings," *quoted in An Environmental Agenda for the World's Faiths*, N.Y. Times, Oct. 24, 1998, at A15, col. 3.

3. Would George F. Will accept Posner's analysis as the final word on environmental matters? Would former House Speaker Newt Gingrich—once one of America's most powerful political conservatives—agree with Posner? Consider the following reading.

## FRANCIS X. CLINE, GINGRICH: SPEAKER, AUTHOR—BUT KING OF THE JUNGLE?

N.Y. Times (Jul. 14, 1995) at A17, col. 1

At the seventh hour, the Speaker came forth to protect the rhinoceros and the tiger and the elephant.

The Interior Department budget was being slashed through the day by multimillion-dollar bites in a long, often dreary session when a buzz suddenly shook the House floor. Speaker Newt Gingrich had indeed emerged from the inner sanctum of leadership, where the budget-cutting plan was being kept on schedule, to make a rare floor appearance and speak up for some exotic animals, asking the members to spare one of the tinier budget items tagged for extinction.

Scores of millions of dollars worth of programs had already been voted cut back with no comment from the Speaker's office. But it was the threat to a mere $800,000 appropriation supporting the efforts of African and Asian nations to preserve the three species that, it turned out, lured Mr. Gingrich forth with characteristic enthusiasm.

"We don't have to cut mindlessly just because we want to get to a balanced budget," Mr. Gingrich declared as members listened reverently and with considerable surprise.

The House was only half way through a long session scheduled to enact a total of $1.56 billion in cuts in funding and services. These included many millions of dollars targeted to be taken from arts, humanities, education and park services touching a wide swath of the nation's flora and fauna. In this context, the Speaker's special pleading seemed almost a *non sequitur*, a countervailing asterisk in the heavy budget-slashing day.

The sponsors of the floor amendment to eliminate the preservation aid for tigers, elephants and rhinoceroses thought they had an easy additional mark for cutting as the Republican majority controlled by Mr. Gingrich held the line. There was some easy laughter as Representative Mark W. Neumann, Republican of Wisconsin, made the case that three foreign animals should not be spared the scythe-like cuts affecting life so much closer to home.

But then Mr. Gingrich made an unscheduled appearance and asked for the floor. He warned that the animal amendment would send the wrong message to foreign nations struggling to fight poachers and preserve "some of the most magnificent animals of the modern era."

The House, unruly so often during the day, sat up and listened as the leader spoke of his favorite creatures. His appearance interrupted a week-long skein of sloggingly deep cuts, with votes already taken for significant foreign aid reductions as well as for $9.3 billion in labor, education and health cuts in domestic human welfare programs.

"This amendment means well but does wrong," he said.

Any Republican has a soft feeling toward elephants, he admitted, beginning on a light note. "But as a person I have a particular affection for rhinos," he continued, noting he had helped the Atlanta zoo obtain two of the creatures and looked forward to helping them survive well into the future.

"Join together in sending a signal to these poor countries in Africa and Asia that this is a project they ought to have the courage to stay with," he said, clearly serious in his rare personal mission, however impetuous it seemed to House members.

"This is a very tiny and very good series of programs," he said of the anti-poaching aid which, he noted, had already been cut by 50 percent to the remaining $800,000 that was now at stake.

"Don't allow them to disappear and join the dinosaur skull in my office and be extinct," he cautioned firmly.

The House heard the Speaker and quickly pronounced his message good, by a vote of 289 to 132. By then, Mr. Gingrich was gone from the floor, out of sight, with members wondering what other budgetary sparrows his eye might fall upon.

### Notes and Questions

1.  The official text of Speaker Gingrich's remarks includes the following:

    I think that for this tiny amount of money, we are helping maintain an effort on behalf of some large mammals, all of which are severely threatened and all of which could disappear, literally be gone, unable to ever again find them in the wild. Frankly, we are learning more and more about just how difficult it is to reintroduce large animals, because they do not learn the habits in zoos of being capable of survival. * * *

    I will tell all of the Members, when we look at some of these countries that are very poor, and they have suppressed poaching, and they have suppressed that, if you look at the value of a rhinoceros horn and you are a poor villager in southern Africa, look at the value of an elephant tusk, look at the value of a tiger skin, and look at countries which have voluntarily imposed on their own local people economic deprivation in order to sustain these species so that our children and our grandchildren can have a chance to see some of the most magnificent animals in the modern era; and then to say that we are going to allow them to disappear * * *

    [T]hen some day, 20 or 30 years from now, if the rhinoceros still survives in the wild and the tiger still survives in the wild and the elephant still survives in the wild, you can feel like, hey, this was a nice thing to do for the human race.

141 Cong. Rec. H6979 (Jul. 13, 1995).

2.  Compare the Speaker's remarks—particularly his praise for the imposition by African and Asian nations of "economic deprivation" on "their own local people" in order "to sustain these species"—with H.R. 9 and S. 343, discussed at pages 105-08, *supra*. Wasn't the whole point of H.R. 9 and S.

343 to *forbid* any economic deprivation of our "own local people" in the United States that cannot be shown to be efficient? Can the Speaker's remarks be harmonized with his sponsorship of H.R. 9? If not, does that mean that his remarks are wrong?

## F. PROCESS VALUES

We have now examined four possible goals for environmental policy that might augment or supplant the economic goal of efficient resource allocation: (1) securing a more acceptable distribution of goods and services ("environmental justice"); (2) fulfilling obligations to our descendants; (3) preserving present beliefs (or seeking to change beliefs) about what things will maximize human satisfactions ("preference shaping"); and (4) fulfilling obligations owed to nature. A final noneconomic goal suggested by some authors is the pursuit of process values.

Perhaps the *way* in which decisions are made may be more important than the ultimate policies adopted through decisionmaking procedures. As long as everyone is provided an opportunity to be heard, and as long as all significant ramifications of various policy choices are fully confronted, the substantive content of the resulting decisions may be acceptable. This argument is fleshed out more fully in Richard B. Stewart & James E. Krier, Environmental Law and Policy 196 (2d ed. 1978).

It is true that we Americans are big on process. In creating the United States system of government, for example, Articles I, II, and III of the Constitution fashion processes whereby the Congress, President, and Judiciary are selected and check each others' powers.

You may recall, however, that Ophuls and Boyan argue at pages 45-49, *supra*, that the American fixation on "due process" causes long-term environmental solutions to be lost in a flurry of short-term incremental adjustments. Decrying "the ecological vices of muddling through," these authors warn that "the American government will be obliged to have *genuine policies*" in the face of ecological scarcity. Moreover, the cost-benefit provisions of H.R. 9 and S. 343 have been characterized by opponents as the cynical creation of allegedly neutral processes actually designed to derail environmental regulation.

We will reserve discussion of this issue until Chapter 13, when we examine the National Environmental Policy Act and its requirement of environmental impact statements.

# Part Two

ENVIRONMENTAL LAW
IN THE COURTS

# Chapter Five

## COMMON LAW
## REMEDIES

---

### A. INTRODUCTION

Much modern environmental law consists of statutes enacted by legislatures and regulations promulgated by administrative agencies. Prior to the late 1960s, however, there were relatively few environmental law statutes in America and even fewer regulations. Environmental problems were addressed primarily by courts, exercising their common law powers to decide controversies in litigated cases. In Chapter 5, we examine the common law principles that still govern disputes not controlled by statutes or regulations.

Our first reading provides a theoretical explanation for how governments allocate rights between polluters and receptors.

### GUIDO CALABRESI & A. DOUGLAS MELAMED, PROPERTY RULES, LIABILITY RULES, AND INALIENABILITY: ONE VIEW OF THE CATHEDRAL

85 Harv. L. Rev. 1089, 1090, 1092-93 (1972)

The first issue which must be faced by any legal system is one we call the problem of "entitlement." Whenever a state is presented with the conflicting interests of two or more people, or two or more groups of people, it must decide which side to favor. Absent such a decision, access to goods, services, and life itself will be decided on the basis of "might makes right"—whoever is stronger or shrewder will win. Hence the fundamental thing that law does is to decide which of the conflicting parties will be entitled to prevail. The entitlement to make noise versus the entitlement to have silence, the entitlement to pollute versus the entitlement to breathe clean air, the entitlement to have children versus the entitlement to forbid them—these are the first order of legal decisions.

Having made its initial choice, society must enforce that choice. Simply setting the entitlement does not avoid the problem of "might

140

makes right"; a minimum of state intervention is always necessary. * * *

The state not only has to decide whom to entitle, but it must also simultaneously make a series of equally difficult second order decisions. These decisions go to the manner in which the entitlements are protected and to whether an individual is allowed to sell or trade the entitlement. In any given dispute, for example, the state must decide not only which side wins but also the kind of protection to grant. It is with the latter decisions, decisions which shape the subsequent relationship between the winner and the loser, that this article is primarily concerned. We shall consider three types of entitlements—entitlements protected by property rules, entitlements protected by liability rules, and inalienable entitlements. The categories are not, of course, absolutely distinct; but the categorization is useful since it reveals some of the reasons which lead us to protect certain entitlements in certain ways.

An entitlement is protected by a property rule to the extent that someone who wishes to remove the entitlement from its holder must buy it from him in a voluntary transaction in which the value of the entitlement is agreed upon by the seller. It is the form of entitlement which gives rise to the least amount of state intervention: once the original entitlement is decided upon, the state does not try to decide its value.[7] It lets each of the parties say how much the entitlement is worth to him, and gives the seller a veto if the buyer does not offer enough. Property rules involve a collective decision as to who is to be given an initial entitlement but not as to the value of the entitlement.

Whenever someone may destroy the initial entitlement if he is willing to pay an objectively determined value for it, an entitlement is protected by a liability rule. This value may be what it is thought the original holder of the entitlement would have sold it for. But the holder's complaint that he would have demanded more will not avail him once the objectively determined value is set. Obviously, liability rules involve an additional stage of state intervention: not only are entitlements protected, but their transfer or destruction is allowed on the basis of a value determined by some organ of the state rather than by the parties themselves.

An entitlement is inalienable to the extent that its transfer is not permitted between a willing buyer and a willing seller. The state intervenes not only to determine who is initially entitled and to determine

---

[7] A property rule requires less state intervention only in the sense that intervention is needed to decide upon and enforce the initial entitlement but not for the separate problem of determining the value of the entitlement. Thus, if a particular property entitlement is especially difficult to enforce—for example, the right to personal security in urban areas—the actual amount of state intervention can be very high and could, perhaps, exceed that needed for some entitlements protected by easily administered liability rules.

the compensation that must be paid if the entitlement is taken or destroyed, but also to forbid its sale under some or all circumstances. Inalienability rules are thus quite different from property and liability rules. Unlike those rules, rules of inalienability not only "protect" the entitlement; they may also be viewed as limiting or regulating the grant of the entitlement itself.

It should be clear that most entitlements to most goods are mixed. Taney's house may be protected by a property rule in situations where Marshall wishes to purchase it, by a liability rule where the government decides to take it by eminent domain, and by a rule of inalienability in situations where Taney is drunk or incompetent. This article will explore two primary questions: (1) In what circumstances should we grant a particular entitlement? and (2) In what circumstances should we decide to protect that entitlement by using a property, liability, or inalienability rule?

## B. AWARDING THE ENTITLEMENT

The "first order of legal decision" discussed by Calabresi and Melamed—who shall be given the "entitlement"?—has traditionally been addressed in the pollution context by means of common law tort principles. Prior to recent statutory developments, a receptor would typically seek redress from a court by bringing an action against the polluter in trespass or in nuisance. The court's decision about where to award the "entitlement" was controlled by well-established common law doctrines. Even in the present regulatory era, recovery may still be sought for trespass or nuisance unless the specific regulatory scheme is found to "preempt" or displace traditional tort law.

You have probably already taken courses in torts and property, in which you may have studied trespass and nuisance. The following sections from the Restatement (Second) of Torts (1977) summarize the common law doctrines. *Reynolds Metals Co. v. Yturbide*, the subsequent reading, is a classic example of a common law nuisance opinion.

## RESTATEMENT (SECOND) OF TORTS

§§ 158, 162-163, 165, 821F-822, 825-828, 519-520 (1977)

### TRESPASS ON LAND

#### Section 158. Liability for Intentional Intrusions on Land

One is subject to liability to another for trespass, irrespective of whether he thereby causes harm to any legally protected interest of the other, if he intentionally

(a) enters land in the possession of the other, or causes a thing or a third person to do so, or

(b) remains on the land, or

(c) fails to remove from the land a thing which he is under a duty to remove.

### Section 162. Extent of Trespasser's Liability for Harm

A trespass on land subjects the trespasser to liability for physical harm to the possessor of the land at the time of the trespass, or to the land or to his things, or to members of his household or to their things, caused by any act done, activity carried on, or condition created by the trespasser, irrespective of whether his conduct is such as would subject him to liability were he not a trespasser.

### Section 163. Intended Intrusions Causing No Harm

One who intentionally enters land in the possession of another is subject to liability to the possessor for a trespass, although his presence on the land causes no harm to the land, its possessor, or to any thing or person in whose security the possessor has a legally protected interest.

### Section 165. Liability for Intrusions Resulting From Reckless or Negligent Conduct and Abnormally Dangerous Activities

One who recklessly or negligently, or as a result of an abnormally dangerous activity, enters land in the possession of another or causes a thing or third person so to enter is subject to liability to the possessor if, but only if, his presence or the presence of the thing or the third person upon the land causes harm to the land, to the possessor, or to a thing or a third person in whose security the possessor has a legally protected interest.

## PRIVATE NUISANCE

### Section 821F. Significant Harm

There is liability for a nuisance only to those to whom it causes significant harm, of a kind that would be suffered by a normal person in the community or by property in normal condition and used for a normal purpose.

*[handwritten margin notes: Nuisance — rules out the "eggshell" plaintiff, hyper-sensitive people]*

### Section 822. General Rule

One is subject to liability for a private nuisance if, but only if, his conduct is a legal cause of an invasion of another's interest in the private use and enjoyment of land, and the invasion is either

*[handwritten margin notes: aka. forseable; → maybe commercial or private use]*

    (a)   intentional and unreasonable, or

    (b)   unintentional and otherwise actionable under the rules controlling liability for negligent or reckless conduct, or for abnormally dangerous conditions or activities.

### Section 825. Intentional Invasion—What Constitutes

An invasion of another's interest in the use and enjoyment of land or an interference with the public right, is intentional if the actor

    (a)   acts for the purpose of causing it, or

    (b)   knows that it is resulting or is substantially certain to result from his conduct.

### Section 826. Unreasonableness of Intentional Invasion

An intentional invasion of another's interest in the use and enjoyment of land is unreasonable if

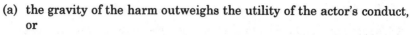
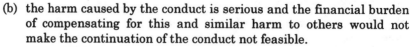

(a) the gravity of the harm outweighs the utility of the actor's conduct, or

(b) the harm caused by the conduct is serious and the financial burden of compensating for this and similar harm to others would not make the continuation of the conduct not feasible.

### Section 827. Gravity of Harm—Factors Involved

In determining the gravity of the harm from an intentional invasion of another's interest in the use and enjoyment of land, the following factors are important:

(a) The extent of the harm involved;

(b) the character of the harm involved;

(c) the social value that the law attaches to the type of use or enjoyment invaded;

(d) the suitability of the particular use or enjoyment invaded to the character of the locality; and

(e) the burden on the person harmed of avoiding the harm.

### Section 828. Utility of Conduct—Factors Involved

In determining the utility of conduct that causes an intentional invasion of another's interest in the use and enjoyment of land, the following factors are important:

(a) the social value that the law attaches to the primary purpose of the conduct;

(b) the suitability of the conduct to the character of the locality; and

(c) the impracticability of preventing or avoiding the invasion.

### ABNORMALLY DANGEROUS ACTIVITIES

### Section 519. General Principle

(1) One who carries on an abnormally dangerous activity is subject to liability for harm to the person, land or chattels of another resulting from the activity, although he has exercised the utmost care to prevent the harm.

(2) This strict liability is limited to the kind of harm, the possibility of which makes the activity abnormally dangerous.

### Section 520. Abnormally Dangerous Activities

In determining whether an activity is abnormally dangerous, the following factors are to be considered:

(a) existence of a high degree of risk of some harm to the person, land or chattels of others;

(b) likelihood that the harm that results from it will be great;

(c) inability to eliminate the risk by the exercise of reasonable care;

(d) extent to which the activity is not a matter of common usage;

(e) inappropriateness of the activity to the place where it is carried on; and

(f) extent to which its value to the community is outweighed by its dangerous attributes.

# REYNOLDS METALS COMPANY v. YTURBIDE

*Nuisance*

258 F.2d 321 (9th Cir.), *cert. denied*, 358 U.S. 840 (1958)

POPE, CIRCUIT JUDGE.

In July, 1946, Reynolds Metals Company, a Delaware corporation, acquired through lease, an aluminum plant belonging to the Government and located at Troutdale, Oregon. It commenced operation of its first potline for the production of aluminum in September of that year. In the operation of the plant chemical compounds containing aluminum were collected in the reduction cells of the so-called "pots" and were reduced or separated by the process of electrolysis or passage of current through the cell. In the process, temperatures up to 1775 degrees F. were developed. As the compounds with which the cells were charged, (cryolite or sodium fluoride or calcium fluoride and aluminum fluoride) contain large percentages of fluorine ranging around 50 percent, a considerable portion of fluoride material was volatilized in the process and reached the atmosphere.

Shortly after the operation of the [plant] began, and in December, 1946, the appellees in these three appeals, Paul Martin, his wife, Verla Martin, and his daughter, Paula Martin (now Mrs. Yturbide), moved to their cattle farm or ranch near Troutdale located about a mile to a mile and one-half from the aluminum plant, and they resided there until November, 1950. The law suits out of which these appeals grew were based upon claims that during the period of their residence on the farm they were poisoned by fluorides which originated at the appellant's plant and were borne on the air to the farm where they breathed these fluoride effluents claimed to be highly toxic and also ate vegetables growing in their garden which also had been absorbing the same toxic elements.

The principal question presented here is whether the evidence adduced at the trial below, (the three cases were tried together and upon the same evidence) was sufficient to permit the case to go to the jury. Upon the part of the appellant it is contended, (1) that there was insufficient proof to demonstrate that the damage to the persons of the plaintiffs, of which they complain, was caused by the fluorides escaping from defendant's plant; and (2), that there was no evidence of any negligence, or any other breach of duty, on the part of the defendant.

With respect to the question of causation—whether the escaping fluorides did in fact cause plaintiffs' injuries—the evidence was sufficient to warrant the jury's conclusion that the escaping fluorides were the cause of the injuries. It was not disputed, in fact it was stipulated, that "fluorides in some quantities and forms, did escape, when the pot-lines of said plant were operating, from defendant's plant." The pre-trial stipulation, after stating the specific fluoride combinations which did escape in the form of gases, liquids and solids, and which became air-borne, recited that "portions thereof have settled at various times upon the lands" of the Martins.

A horticulturist from the Oregon State College, in the years 1948, 1949 and 1950 made test samples of plants grown on selected plots in the vicinity of the Martin property, for the purpose of determining the fluorine content of such plants. Some of the test plots used were on the Martin property and as close as 1.1 miles from the aluminum plant. Others located in the same direction from the plant were farther away. Those plants tested on plots nearest the aluminum plant showed substantial amounts of fluorine content. The plants tested on plots which were farther away from the plant showed a substantially decreasing fluorine content, thus indicating that relatively speaking the nearer the aluminum plant the greater the concentration of the gases, fumes and particulates, (i.e. fine solids). In making such test, plants which readily absorbed fluorine compounds such as buckwheat and gladioli were used so as to facilitate the testing. The results therefore did not indicate the quantities of fluorine which would likely be found in garden vegetables such as those the Martins grew in their garden plot for their domestic use.

In general there was an absence of proof as to just what quantities of fluorides contained in these gases, fumes, and particulates, passed over the Martin land or were inhaled by them or ingested from the garden vegetables eaten by them. There was, however, proof that these fluorides were toxic. One of the chemists who testified stated without challenge that hydrofluoride acid or hydrogen fluoride, one of the effluents from the plant, was "quite toxic" and that "the books on chemistry warned against inhaling it." Appellant concedes that such fluorides "are poisonous in excessive amounts."

That very large quantities of these gases, fumes, and particulates, did leave the plant and were diffused into the air, was unquestioned. Appellant's own exhibits disclose that with the equipment which was used to control the escape of gases during the period that the Martins lived on their farm, hundreds of pounds of these effluents escaped each day. Thus in the year 1947, the amount of fluorine alone escaping per day from the plant averaged 2845 pounds. Comparable amounts escaped in the years 1948-1949 and throughout the first half of 1950, after which time the appellant began the installation of a new control system which was much more efficient in arresting the escape and fall-out.

There is no showing as to where these large quantities of effluents finally settled. The experiments mentioned above would indicate that the greater portion settled on those areas nearest the plant, and those areas included the Martin farm. That the effluents did have some degree of toxic or harmful effect was indicated by proof that cattle upon the Martin place showed damage from fluorosis. Generally with respect to cattle it does not appear to have been controverted that cattle damage from an aluminum plant is a fairly common phenomenon.

Of course it does not follow from mere proof of some damage to cattle on the Martin place that the plaintiffs' physical injuries were due to excessive amounts of fluorides from the plant. Cattle get their whole food from grass and ingest large quantities. A human diet contains a relatively small proportion of vegetables. * * *

A significant bit of testimony adduced was proof that glass in the Martin home became etched by acid, probably hydrofluoric acid which was one of the effluents from the aluminum plant. One of the expert witnesses, [a] British doctor who had some prior experience with similar etching of glass located near industrial plants abroad, testified that the glass from the Martin window which he was shown during the testimony was an indication of excessive quantities of fluoride contamination in the atmosphere.

Although the cases of the Martins are unique in that they were unable to produce either from medical literature or expert witnesses histories of persons situated as they were, namely, persons not working in the plant but simply living outside and near the plant, who developed symptoms similar to theirs in consequence of the fall-out of emanations from an aluminum plant * * * nevertheless they did produce substantial medical testimony which did connect their disabilities and physical injuries with the fluorides escaping from the plant. Of course there was also testimony to the contrary, but the evidence adduced on their behalf, principally from the British medical expert * * * and from a Dr. Capps, a Chicago specialist on diseases of the liver, was substantial, and in our view, fully worthy of credit. * * * Their qualifications to testify [were] not only adequate but their experience with the subject upon which they testified was outstanding. For the purposes of this opinion it is sufficient to say that the evidence clearly warranted the jury in accepting the testimony and conclusions of these doctors. Hence there is no point in undertaking to detail their testimony at length.[6]

---

[6] Dr. Capps described Paul Martin's symptoms as follows: "In the first place, he developed diarrhea, indigestion, and heartburn, and bloating, particularly after meals. Those symptoms all were referable to the intestinal tract. And, secondly, he developed symptoms which we might refer to as skeletal symptoms: pain, particularly in his back, occasionally down the leg sufficiently severe so that he was unable to bend over and tie his shoes, for example, or even put his shoes on, as a matter of fact. These pains were aggravated by lifting and by various types of exertions. The third group of symptoms had to do with the respiratory tract, the lungs. He developed a dry cough and shortness of breath particularly on exertion. And, finally he developed frequency of urination particularly at night, to such an extent that—seven or eight times at night, and he was unable to sleep. * * * In view, then, of this potential history of the exposure and in view of the fact that we were advised—that we were faced with a rather bizarre group of symptoms—here is an involvement of a

The medical witnesses expressed confidence in their conclusions because of the fact that they found substantially the same symptoms in the three individuals, thus lessening the possibility that the symptoms were attributable to individual idiosyncracies. Neither one was able to testify as to the degree of concentration—how many parts per million of fluorides—would be required to bring about the injuries found, but both attached some significance to the fact that the window in the house was etched by acid. As stated by Dr. Capps, "I think that if there is enough fluorine to etch a window, it should be able to etch a lung."

Dr. Hunter related his own experience in finding in England a family with the same symptoms as the Martins who lived in a house near an industrial plant whose windows were similarly etched and said that the etching he observed in the glass taken from the Martin home was an indication of excessive quantities of fluorine in the atmosphere. He referred to studies made in 1946 warning the industrial world "against throwing into the atmosphere an effluent which would etch glass."

A further circumstance which the medical witnesses emphasized was that in the case of the Martins their abnormal symptoms were reduced and lessened after they had moved away from the vicinity of the plant. We are thus led to the conclusion that the jury was warranted in finding, as they did, that physical injuries to the Martins were caused by the fluoride emanations from the plant which found their way to the Martin place.

On behalf of the defendant evidence was adduced to show that only a very small concentration of fluorides could have reached the Martin home. We think the jury were warranted in accepting plaintiffs' testimony, and the inferences therefrom, that excessive amounts of fluorides reached them, for they actually suffered fluoride poisoning.

There was no proof on the part of plaintiffs as to what particular percentage or concentration of fluorides was necessary to produce such results. Plaintiffs were obliged to accept in that respect the concession made by the defendant to the effect that such fluorides are "poisonous in excessive amounts." The only possible conclusion is that because the damage was actually caused by the fluorides, they somehow managed to get there in excessive quantities. We think we must accept this as a permissible finding of the jury.

The important question is whether there was proof of any negligence or other breach of duty on the part of the defendant which brought about these injuries as its proximate result. * * * [A discussion of the applicability of the doctrine of strict liability] is unnecessary to a

---

number of the symptoms in the body which was unusual and definitely bizarre, and it corresponds exactly to the description of published cases of fluorosis; furthermore, there is no other explanation. One cannot make another single diagnosis that would cover all of these symptoms. One could make four or five diagnoses, but, of course, that is always obviously a very poor thing to do. This is the picture of fluorosis. * * * [Y]ou are forced to make the diagnosis of poisoning with fluorine."

decision of this case. Furthermore, this case was not submitted to the jury which heard it upon any such theory.[8]

Appellant argues that there is a complete absence of proof of any want of care on its part in the operation of the aluminum plant. In this respect its contention is that before the plant was put in operation it equipped it with facilities for minimizing the amount of effluents that escaped from the plant. Each potroom building was equipped with a ventilator extending the full length of the building at the roof or ceiling. Air was supplied to the room through louvre doors at the base and the heated air carrying the escaping gas, fumes and particulates moved upward to the ventilators. At the ventilators a washing system was installed which consisted of a series of sprays running the full length of the building so that any air that left the building had to pass through these sprays.

After the spray system was first started, baffles were inserted to intercept and condense the moisture which came from the spray into the escaping air; in other words, to take "mist" out of the air. The result of this spray system was that it removed some 60 percent of the fluorides from the air coming through the roof so that only 40 percent of these compounds actually escaped from the plant.

Defendant's Assistant Vice-President testified that during this period from 1946 to 1950, when the spray system of fluorides elimination was in use, the company was carrying on experiments to devise and find better ways of making a more efficient capture of the effluents. In 1948, a pilot plant was designed for the purpose of trying out an improved system of elimination, and as a result of the experiments with that pilot plant, it was arranged about May, 1949, to change over to a new system. The installation of that was completed in November, 1950. The new system involved the placing of hoods over each pot and the installation of fans which sucked the air coming from the pots upward and forcing it through sprays and washtowers. The result of the use of this improved system was to eliminate 90 percent of the fluoride compounds from the air which escaped from the plant. While, as we previously indicated, the average pounds of fluorine escaping per day during 1947 were 2845 and in the month of March, 1950, they were as high as 3988 pounds, yet beginning in July, 1950, when the new system began to be used, there was a sharp reduction so that in November and December, 1950, after the completion of the improved system, the average daily flow of fluorine escaping was reduced to 643 pounds. In short, by this improved method, the portion of the emanating fluorides which

---

[8] * * * The able trial judge, expressing doubt that the doctrine of *Fletcher v. Rylands* would be applied by the Oregon court to a case of this kind, held that the case should go to the jury upon the issue of negligence. Although in appropriate cases a judgment may be affirmed upon grounds other than those adopted in the court below, we think it questionable that such rule is applicable where the judgment is based upon the verdict of a jury acting upon instructions not comprehending the new grounds urged.

reached the air was 10 percent of the total as against 40 percent under the earlier system.

In determining the duty of care the law imposed upon the defendant, it is to be borne in mind that the ordinary care which the law requires of such a defendant is measured in part by the defendant's knowledge of potential dangers. Thus a seller of fur coats who actually knows that some few persons are especially susceptible to poisoning by a particular fur dye must take precautions accordingly, and greater precautions than would be required if he were ignorant of this particular susceptibility. * * *

The record here amply demonstrates that the defendant was fully aware of the potential dangers in the escape of fluorides. It is not questioned that numerous claims of injury to cattle from the operation of such plants had been presented to this and other manufacturers. The defendant's senior chemist at the Troutdale laboratory testified that he was familiar with the literature upon the toxic qualities of these fluorides; that he knew that in quantities they were toxic; that some of these were heavier than air and would reach the earth after being airborne; that quantities of them would drift in the direction of the Martin land and that there were publications which dealt with dangers to human beings from fluorides.

The question is whether in view of the knowledge which the company was reasonably required to have as a manufacturer in this field, and the knowledge which it actually did have of the potential dangers of these escaping fluorides there was evidence of a failure to use reasonable care for the protection of persons in the situation of the Martins.

On behalf of the defendant it was testified that at all these times defendant was utilizing and had installed the latest and best known means of protecting against the escape of the fluorides; that the company, continually studying the problem, installed an experimental pilot plant to develop a new process and then changed over to the improved process as soon as its feasibility was developed.

On behalf of plaintiffs it was urged that the evidence warranted a conclusion that the company did not exercise the care in this direction which it might have done in that it allowed the plant to be operated with the less efficient elimination system from 1946 until 1950 whereas proper care required an earlier use of the better devices.

The only bit of evidence which was taken to sustain such a contention is found in the testimony of Dr. Hunter who testified as follows: "Q. (By Mr. Mead): Doctor, are you familiar with an induced air system of dust control or fume control? A. Naturally, I haven't been trained as a ventilating engineer. But since I first studied industrial hygiene in the Harvard School of Public Health with the famous Phillip Drinker—he is a ventilating engineer—and because of the work which I have to do and so teach, which is industrial medicine, I am, naturally, interested in systems of ventilation. And in all of the chapters of that book there is an exact description of systems of ventilation which are used in various parts of the world. And in 1946 it was well-known to all industrialists the world over that exhaust ventilation could be effectively applied to remove these effluents."

Possibly we can assume that the question relating to an "induced air system" referred to the sort of system established by the company in 1950. Testimony that such a system was well known in 1946 would permit an inference that failure to use that better system at that time constituted negligence. We believe it is unnecessary in reaching our ultimate conclusion here to draw such inference from this single answer in this long record for we are of the opinion that the trial court properly submitted to the jury the question of negligence on the part of the defendant on the theory that this was a case correctly permitting the application of the doctrine of res ipsa loquitur.

The court instructed the jury as follows: "Under the law and the facts of these actions, the defendant was the sole operator and in exclusive possession and direct control of the aluminum plant involved during the time involved, namely, between on or about September 23, 1946, and November 30, 1950. Further, that under the ordinary course of events, it is unexpected that persons being in the vicinity of such a plant would be injured or harmed by fluorine compounds emanating therefrom, and that such a mishap would not occur." The statement in the first of these two sentences is unquestionable; the second sentence is in conformity with defendant's theory and much of the evidence adduced by it at the trial. The instruction was consistent with the testimony that the plant as equipped and operated, would not cause fluorosis to persons who had not been employed in the plant itself. The court noted that there was no evidence as to the amount or concentration of fluorides that would bring about fluorosis in the case of such persons. While during the critical period here 40 percent of the gases, fumes and particulates got by the sprinkler system and escaped into the air, the fluorine contents aggregating hundreds of pounds all told, the tests made at various localities near the plant and on every side thereof, according to defendant's witnesses, produced no significant concentration of fluorides at the time the tests were made. Hence, the court, accepting this proof, told the jury that, "under the ordinary course of events, it is unexpected that persons being in the vicinity of such a plant would be injured or harmed by fluorine compounds emanating therefrom."

In so ruling the court in effect determined that the accident was of a kind which ordinarily does not occur in the absence of someone's negligence. That is a prime condition for the application of the so-called rule of res ipsa loquitur. Said the court: "Here was an instrumentality that was in the exclusive possession and control of the defendant. Something that ordinarily we would not expect to happen did happen and damage resulted. This is the pure and simple test as the Court sees it, of res ipsa loquitur." The court was using language similar to that of *Ritchie* *v. Thomas*, 190 Or. 95, 224 P.2d 543, 551: "An inference of negligence may arise only when injury is caused by an instrumentality which is under the control and management of the defendant, and when the accident is such as, in the ordinary course of events does not happen, if those who have the management use ordinary care." Such is the test generally approved in such cases. * * * Of course the inference of negligence * * * is merely a permissible one * * * but it carries the case to the jury.

Viewing plaintiffs' case in the most favorable light, as we are required to do, we have the following: (1), Damage to persons in the position of the Martins was possible from "excessive amounts" of fluorides; (2), the Martins were poisoned and from this plant and by these fluorides; (3), from this it is permissible to infer that "excessive amounts" reached them—that there were such excessive amounts; (4), the emission of excessive amounts from the plant was circumstantial evidence of negligence. Res ipsa loquitur. * * *

In the present case the jury might have accepted defendant's proof and explanation but obviously it did not. It was not obliged to do so. The procedural problem which faces any defendant such as this, as it has developed in the cases, is discussed at some length by both Prosser and Harper & James. The latter say, (§ 19.12):[10] "Defendant in a res ipsa case may show by evidence how the accident happened, but ordinarily this does not entitle him to a directed verdict. The jury may still reject the evidence or find that the explanation does not preclude the likelihood of negligence. * * * In most res ipsa loquitur cases defendant cannot definitely explain the accident. His usual defense consists of proof of the precautions he did take in constructing, maintaining, and operating the injuring instrumentality. Once in a great while such proof may conclusively show that the accident did not in fact happen, or that it was not caused by defendant. But this is seldom the outcome. And where it is not, defendant is in this dilemma: the less effective his precautions to prevent the occurrence the more apt they are to appear negligent; the more effective the precautions testified to, the less likely they are to have [been] taken in this case since the accident *did happen*." * * *

When res ipsa loquitur is applied the facts of the occurrence warrant the inference of negligence. They furnish substantial evidence of

---

[10] * * * Prosser discusses the same matter (pp. 216-217) as follows: "But if the defendant merely offers evidence of his own acts and precautions amounting to reasonable care, it is seldom that a verdict can be directed in his favor. The inference from the circumstances remains in the case to contradict the evidence. If he testifies that he used proper care to insulate his wires, to inspect his chandelier, to drive his bus, or to keep defunct mice and wandering insect life out of his bottled beverage, the fact that electricity escaped from the wires, that the chandelier fell, that the bus went into the ditch and the bug was in the bottle, with the background of common experience that such things do not usually happen if proper care is used, may permit reasonable men to find that his witnesses are not to be believed, that the precautions described were not sufficient to conform to the standard required or were not faithfully carried out, and that the whole truth has not been told. * * *"

negligence where the direct evidence of it may be lacking, but they make a case to be decided by the jury. In finding itself in the dilemma mentioned by Harper & James in the language quoted above, appellant is in no different situation than any other defendant who finds itself in a res ipsa case and before a jury. It is not, as appellant asserts, the victim of the application of a rule of absolute liability. * * *

The judgments are affirmed.

### *Notes and Questions*

1. The facts in *Reynolds* seem to show that the defendant's conduct has interfered with one or more of the plaintiffs' exclusive possessory interest in land. Why, do you suppose, the plaintiffs' attorney failed to bring this lawsuit as a trespass action?

2. Assume that the *Reynolds* case had been brought as an *unintentional* trespass action. What must the plaintiffs show to prevail under the Restatement (Second) of Torts? Would there be any advantage to suing in unintentional trespass, rather than nuisance?

3. Assume that the *Reynolds* plaintiffs could demonstrate that the defendant's interference with their interests was *intentional*, within the meaning of the Restatement. Would there be any advantage in suing for intentional trespass, rather than nuisance?

4. The *Reynolds* case was actually brought as a private nuisance action. Notice that the Restatement envisions a series of forks in the road for anyone seeking to establish a right to recover for private nuisance, depending on whether the defendant's invasion of the plaintiffs' rights is intentional or unintentional. Diagram the optional methods for establishing a right to recovery in private nuisance. Trace through that diagram the path taken by the *Reynolds* court in awarding relief to the plaintiffs.

## C. RESTATEMENT § 826(b)

Restatement (Second) of Torts § 826(b) was added in 1970 after a vigorous debate among American Law Institute participants. Some scholars advocated retention of § 826(a) as the *sole* principle for awarding the entitlement when one actor intentionally invades another's interest in the use and enjoyment of land. Others supported the addition of § 826(b), providing an alternative basis for awarding the entitlement to the plaintiff. The following case continues the debate.

## CARPENTER v. DOUBLE R CATTLE CO.

108 Idaho 602, 701 P.2d 222 (1985)

BAKES, JUSTICE.

Plaintiffs appealed a district court judgment based upon a court and jury finding that defendant's feedlot did not constitute a nuisance. The Court of Appeals, 105 Idaho 320, 669 P.2d 643, reversed and remanded for a new trial. On petition for review, we vacate the decision of the Court of Appeals and affirm the judgment of the district court.

Plaintiff appellants are homeowners who live near a cattle feedlot owned and operated by respondents. Appellants filed a complaint in March, 1978, alleging that the feedlot had been expanded in 1977 to accommodate the feeding of approximately 9,000 cattle. Appellants further alleged that "the spread and accumulation of manure, pollution of river and ground water, odor, insect infestation, increased concentration of birds * * * dust and noise" allegedly caused by the feedlot constituted a nuisance. After a trial on the merits a jury found that the feedlot did not constitute a nuisance. The trial court then also made findings and conclusions that the feedlot did not constitute a nuisance.

Appellants assigned as error the jury instructions which instructed the jury that in the determination of whether a nuisance exists consideration should be given to such factors as community interest, utility of conduct, business standards and practices, gravity of harm caused, and the circumstances surrounding the parties' movement to their locations. On appeal, appellants chose not to provide an evidentiary record, but merely claimed that the instructions misstated the law in Idaho.

The case was assigned to the Court of Appeals which reversed and remanded for a new trial. The basis for this reversal was that the trial court did not give a jury instruction based upon subsection (b) of Section 826 of the Restatement (Second) of Torts. That subsection allows for a finding of a nuisance even though the gravity of harm is outweighed by the utility of the conduct if the harm is "serious" and the payment of damages is "feasible" without forcing the business to discontinue.

This Court granted defendant's petition for review. We hold that the instructions which the trial court gave were not erroneous, being consistent with our prior case law and other persuasive authority. We further hold that the trial court did not err in not giving an instruction based on subsection (b) of Section 826 of the Second Restatement, which does not represent the law in the State of Idaho * * * . Accordingly, the decision of the Court of Appeals is vacated, and the judgment of the district court is affirmed. * * *

Not only did the appellants not request an instruction based on subsection (b) of Section 826, Restatement (Second), appellants objected to the court giving any instructions based upon the Restatement. Additionally, the appellants did not assign as error on appeal the trial court's failure to give such an instruction based on subsection 826(b) of the Restatement (Second). Nevertheless, the Court of Appeals, apparently sua sponte, reversed for failure to give such an instruction. In so doing, the Court of Appeals erred. * * *

The Court of Appeals adopted subsection (b) of Section 826 of the Restatement Second, that a defendant can be held liable for a nuisance regardless of the utility of the conduct if the harm is "serious" and the payment of damages is "feasible" without jeopardizing the continuance of the conduct. We disagree that this is the law in Idaho.

At the outset, it is important to again note that appellants neither requested such an instruction nor assigned as error the failure of the trial court to give an instruction consistent with the new rule stated above. In fact, the appellants initially argued both at trial and on appeal that the Second Restatement should not apply and objected to giving any instructions based on the Restatement. It is therefore not surprising that the trial court did not give an instruction on the new rule in Section 826(b), Restatement (Second). Further, the instructions given were consistent with both the First Restatement and Section 826(a) of the Second Restatement, and also our [prior] decisions * * * .

The State of Idaho is sparsely populated and its economy depends largely upon the benefits of agriculture, lumber, mining and industrial development. To eliminate the utility of conduct and other factors listed by the trial court from the criteria to be considered in determining whether a nuisance exists, as the appellant has argued throughout this appeal, would place an unreasonable burden upon these industries. We see no policy reasons which should compel this Court to accept appellants' argument and depart from our present law. Accordingly, the judgment of the district court is affirmed and the Court of Appeals decision is set aside.

BISTLINE, JUSTICE, DISSENTING.

I applaud the efforts of the Court of Appeals to modernize the law of nuisance in this state. I am not in the least persuaded to join the majority with its narrow view of nuisance law as expressed in the majority opinion.

The majority today continues to adhere to ideas on the law of nuisance that should have gone out with the use of buffalo chips as fuel. We have before us today homeowners complaining of a nearby feedlot—not a small operation, but rather a feedlot which accommodates 9,000 cattle. The homeowners advanced the theory that after the expansion of the feedlot in 1977, the odor, manure, dust, insect infestation and increased concentration of birds which accompanied all of the foregoing, constituted a nuisance. If the odoriferous quagmire created by 9,000 head of cattle is not a nuisance, it is difficult for me to imagine what is. However, the real question for us today is the legal basis on which a finding of nuisance can be made.

The Court of Appeals adopted subsection (b) of § 826 of the Restatement (Second) of Torts. The majority today rejects this Restatement section * * * . Instead, the majority holds that the 1953 case of *McNichols v. J.R. Simplot Co.* * * * espoused the correct rule of law for Idaho: in a nuisance action seeking damages, the interests of the community, which includes the utility of the conduct, should be considered in determining the existence of a nuisance. I find nothing immediately wrong with this statement of the law and agree wholeheartedly that the interests of the community should be considered in determining the existence of a nuisance. However, where this primitive rule of law fails is in recognizing that in our society, while it may be desirable to have a serious nuisance continue because the utility of the operation causing the nuisance is great, at the same time, those directly impacted by the serious nuisance deserve some compensation for the invasion they suffer as a result of the continuation of the nuisance. This is exactly what the more progressive provisions of § 826(b) of the Restatement (Second) of Torts addresses. Clearly, § 826(b) recognizes that the continuation of the serious harm must remain feasible. * * * What § 826(b) adds is a method of compensating those who must suffer the invasion without putting out of business the source or cause of the invasion. This does not strike me as a particularly adventuresome or far-reaching rule of law. In fact, the fairness of it is overwhelming.

The majority's rule today overlooks the option of compensating those who suffer a nuisance because the interests of the community outweigh the interests of those afflicted by the nuisance. This unsophisticated balancing overlooks the possibility that it is not necessary that one interest be ignored when the community interest is strong. We should not be adopting a rule of preference which suggests that if the community interest is preferred any other interest must be disregarded. Instead, § 826(b) accommodates adverse interests by contemplating continuation of the facility which creates the nuisance while compensating those who suffer the direct impact of the nuisance—in the instant case the homeowners who live in the vicinity of the feedlot.

The majority's rule today suggests that part of the cost of industry, agriculture or development must be borne by those unfortunate few who have the fortuitous luck to live in the immediate vicinity of a nuisance producing facility. Frankly, I think this naive economic view is ridiculous in both its simplicity and its outdated view of modern economic society. The "cost" of a product includes not only the amount it takes to produce such a product but also includes the external costs: the damage done to the environment through pollution of air or water is an example of an external cost. In the instant case, the nuisance suffered by the homeowners should be considered an external cost of operating a feedlot and producing beef for public consumption. I do not believe that a few should be required to pay this extra cost of doing business by going uncompensated for a nuisance of this sort. If a feedlot wants to continue, I say fine, providing compensation is paid for the serious invasion (the odors, flies, dust, etc.) of the homeowner's interest. My only qualification is that the financial burden of compensating for this harm should not be such as to force the feedlot (or any other industry) out of business. The true cost can then be shifted to the consumer who rightfully should pay for the entire cost of producing the product he desires to obtain.

The majority today blithely suggests that because the State of Idaho is sparsely populated and because our economy is largely dependent on agriculture, lumber, mining and industrial development, we should forego compensating those who suffer a serious invasion. If humans are such a rare item in this state, maybe there is all the more reason to protect them from the discharge of industry. At a minimum, we should compensate those who suffer a nuisance at the hands of industry and agriculture. What the majority overlooks is that the cost of development should not be absorbed by few, but rather should be spread out and paid by all. I am not convinced that agriculture or industry will be put out of business by requiring compensation for the nuisance they generate. Let us look at the case before us. The owners of the feedlot will not find themselves looking for new jobs if they are required to compensate the homeowners for the stench and dust and flies attendant with 9,000 head of cattle. Rather, meat prices at the grocery store will undoubtedly go up. But, in my view it is far better that the cost of the nuisance be carried by the consumer of a product than by the unfortunate homeowners currently suffering under adverse conditions. Some compensation should be paid the homeowners for suffering the burden from which we all benefit. * * *

### Notes and Questions

1. For a case applying the principle of Restatement (Second) of Torts § 826(b), *see Crest Cheverolet-Oldsmobile-Cadillac v. Willemsen*, 129 Wis.2d 129, 140, 384 N.W.2d 692, 696 (1986) (defendant's intentional invasion is unreasonable if the conditions of Restatement § 826(b) are established, and social utility of defendant's conduct is irrelevant under § 826(b) analysis).

2. The dissenting opinion of Justice Bistline in the *Carpenter* case is an excellent articulation of the arguments favoring Restatement § 826(b). Recall the earlier readings at pages 60-78, *supra*, setting forth the economic theories of A.C. Pigou and Ronald Coase. To whose economic viewpoint does Justice Bistline evidently subscribe: Pigou or Coase?

4. Suppose you represent an aluminum company, as in *Reynolds*—or a cattle operation, as in *Carpenter*—but the courts in your jurisdiction have adopted Restatement § 826(b). Can you imagine advising your aluminum company or cattle operation client to take some rather unusual and counter-intuitive steps to avoid liability? Does your answer suggest a weakness in § 826(b)?

## D. CHARACTERIZING THE ENTITLEMENT

Recall the reading from Calabresi and Melamed at page 140, *supra*, in which the authors describe the first and second orders of legal decision. To explore the first order question—to whom will the entitlement be assigned?—we looked at the *Reynolds* and *Carpenter* cases and their application of the common law of nuisance. We now turn to what Calabresi and Melamed call the second order of legal decision: determining how we will protect the entitlement that has been awarded, particularly what rules shall govern the purchase and sale of the entitlement. The authors assert that entitlements can be of three types: inalienable entitlements; entitlements protected by a property rule; and entitlements protected by a liability rule. The possible combinations of first and second order legal decisions are depicted in **Figure 5–1**.

## Entitlement

|  | Polluter | Receptor |
|---|---|---|
| **Inalienable** | | |
| **Property Rule** | | |
| **Liability Rule** | | |

*Protection*

**Figure 5–1**

As you read (and recall) the judicial opinions in Chapter 5, consider two questions for each case: (1) in which of the **Figure 5–1** boxes has the court placed the entitlement; and (2) why has the court chosen to assign it to that location?

## 1. NO LIABILITY

### *Notes and Questions*

1. You have already read several cases concluding that the polluter was not liable and denying all relief to the plaintiffs. Thumb through the earlier portions of the text to find them. Where should each of those cases be plotted in **Figure 5–1**? Why? Why did the court in each case place the outcome in that **Figure 5–1** location?

2. What are the rules about the future purchase and sale of the entitlement awarded in each of the cases involving a finding of nonliability? May the entitlement in each case be bought and sold? At what price? May either party veto the sale?

## 2. INJUNCTIVE RELIEF

## RENKEN v. HARVEY ALUMINUM

226 F. Supp. 169 (D. Ore. 1963)

KILKENNY, DISTRICT JUDGE.

Each of the plaintiffs, since 1958, and in many instances prior to that year, has been in continuous possession of land in Wasco County,

Oregon, which land was and is used principally for agricultural and horticultural purposes, in growing and production, for home and commercial purposes, of certain fruit consisting of cherries, prunes, peaches and apricots.

Plaintiffs seek to enjoin the defendant from operating its plant in such a manner as to permit the escape therefrom of excessive quantities of the element, fluorine, which is carried by air currents to plaintiffs' lands. * * *

Defendant's plant was constructed, and is being operated, pursuant to the Defense Production Act of 1950, as amended. Its original cost, and subsequent additions, is in excess of $40,000,000.00. The plant annually produces approximately 80,000 tons of aluminum, which is used by the defendant, and others, throughout the United States for industrial and National Defense purposes. Approximately 550 persons, living in the area of The Dalles, are employed in said plant. It has a gross annual payroll of $3,500,000.00.

The plant produces primary aluminum, by the use of what is known as the vertical stud soderberg electrolytic cells. At present 300 cells are in operation. The basic process employed at the plant is the same as that employed the world over in making aluminum, the process being precisely described by Judge East in his opinion in *Fairview Farms, Inc. v. Reynolds Metals Company*, 176 F.Supp. 178 (D.C.Or.1959). The vertical stud soderberg cells employed by Harvey were not used in the Reynolds plant. The essential difference between the cells, or pots, used in the Reynolds plant is, insofar as the escape of particulates and gasses is concerned, that Reynolds uses a hood, with a controlling air system, which captures most of the stray gasses, affluents [sic] and particulates which might escape into the open area around the pots. The vertical type, employed by Harvey, has an apron which collects approximately 80% of these gasses and particulates, but the remaining 20% escapes from the area where the hoods would be located, mixes with other air in the building and then drifts upward into the water spray controls in the roof. It is conceded that in the production of aluminum there is inevitably a release, from the cells, of some gasses and particulates, including fluorides.

The initial fume control apparatus at the Harvey plant consisted of a cast iron skirt surrounding the anode, which collected a portion of the fumes at the source and directed them to burners mounted at both ends of each anode. To these burners were connected fume exhaust ducts which lead the fumes to a main collector pipe carrying them to the dust collector and a fan. The fan created a suction which pulled the fumes from the cells and the burners, through the ducts. From the fans the fumes are directed to a humidifying and bubbling chamber before entering the scrubber tower. The fumes are washed in the tower by multiple layers of water sprayers placed 10 feet apart. At the top of the towers is a mist eliminator.

Tests made, from time to time, indicate that the fume control system, thus described, operated at 95% efficiency, or better, during the test periods on the portion of the fumes caught and delivered to the system. The amount of equivalent fluoride ion leaving the scrubbing towers into the atmosphere from this control apparatus is calculated at 300 pounds per day. This system treats approximately 80% of the fumes released from the cells. The remaining 20% of the fumes escape into the open building, and rise to the top where they pass into roof monitors located at the top of each of the buildings housing the cells. In the spring of 1962, a system of sprayers and screens were installed in the roof monitor and this system has been operating at full capacity since the beginning of 1963. These sprayers and screens collect a portion of the fluorides reaching the roof monitor. Since this latest installation the roof monitor sprays and screens have been between 67 and 70% effective in collecting the fluorides reaching the roof monitors. The amount of equivalent fluoride ion leaving the roof monitors into the atmosphere is calculated at 1,000 pounds per day. Overall, the combination of the original fume control system, as it has been added to and improved from time to time, and the roof monitor sprays and screens has achieved approximately 90% effectiveness with respect to collecting the fluorides released from the aluminum cells.

The record is undisputed that approximately 1,300 pounds of fluoride ion escape from the roof monitors and scrubbing towers into the atmosphere each day. Although the prevailing wind is southwesterly, the record clearly shows that on numerous days each month and on many hours of each day, the area is without measurable wind. At such times, a blanket of smoke from defendant's plant, covers the area, including plaintiffs' lands and orchards. This blanket was observed by the Court, not only on the day of inspection of the plant, but also on many occasions since that time. There is no doubt in my mind but that better controls can be exercised over the escape of the material in question. No sound reason has been advanced by defendant why hoods, similar to those employed by Reynolds, should not be installed. While it is true that a substantial portion of the gasses and particulates escape at the time when the new aluminum ore is being introduced into the pot or the liquid metal is removed, I am convinced that such an escape could be prevented by a properly designed hood over the open area. I agree with the expert, that after the installation of the hood, the small amount of gasses which might escape on the introduction of ore or the removal of liquid metal would be inconsequential.

Likewise, the record convinces me of the [feasibility] of the introduction of electrostatic precipitators for the removal of the minute or small particulates which are not removed by the other processes. The multi-cyclone dust collector now used in the plant at The Dalles is efficient in collecting the large or heavy particulates, but is of little value in removing the smaller variety. All of the experts agree that this is the field in which the electrostatic precipitators are at their best. The great weight of the evidence points to the conclusion that the installation of the cell hoods and the employment of electrostatic precipitators would greatly reduce, if not entirely eliminate, the escape of the excessive material now damaging the orchards of the plaintiffs.

While the cost of the installations of these additional controls will be a substantial sum, the fact remains that effective controls must be exercised over the escape of these noxious fumes. Such expenditures would not be so great as to substantially deprive defendant of the use of its property. While we are not dealing with the public as such, we must recognize that air pollution is one of the great problems now facing the American public. If necessary, the cost of installing adequate controls must be passed on to the ultimate consumer. The heavy cost of corrective devices is no reason why plaintiffs should stand by and suffer substantial damage.

### DAMAGES TO PLAINTIFFS

It is my considered opinion that the evidence on damage to cherries is so conflicting and controversial it would be difficult to hold that the cherry crops were severely damaged by the gasses or particulates emitted from defendant's plant. The evidence clearly shows that the year 1960, the one in which plaintiffs claim their principal cherry damage, was an exceptionally light cherry crop, not only in Wasco County, but throughout the States of Oregon and Washington. I am convinced that the light cherry crop in 1960 was due to factors other than the fluorides escaping from the plant of the defendant. However, the evidence is convincing that the deposit of this material on the trees at blossom time creates damage.

On the other hand, I find that the evidence is clear and convincing that peaches and apricots and peach and apricot trees were damaged by the escape of the fluorine and fluorides from defendant's plant, and, that each plaintiff owning a peach or apricot orchard, sustained a substantial damage from said source to his crops and trees during each year since 1958. This fact is not seriously contested by the defendant. * * *

### REMEDY

Defendant concedes that plaintiffs repeatedly warned it of the emissions, damages to and alleged trespasses on plaintiffs' property. The evidence supports, and I find, that the emissions from defendant's plant continued to settle on plaintiffs' land and orchards to and including the time of the trial. That the continued settling of the fluorides from defendant's plant on plaintiffs' property constituted a continuing trespass, as a matter of law, is beyond question. * * *

That equity will intervene to prevent a continuing trespass is well recognized. * * *

[Defendants] rely on *Fairview Farms, Inc. v. Reynolds Metals Co.,* supra, and in particular on that portion of the opinion in which it is indicated that an award of compensatory damages for past trespasses and future trespasses would adequately compensate the plaintiffs. The basic reason the Court did not grant an injunction in the Fairview case was that there was no evidence the acts or conduct of Reynolds were reasonably certain to be repeated in the future. Here, of course, the evidence is entirely to the contrary. Here, Harvey has taken the position that it has done everything possible to eliminate the problem, and that it must continue to operate with its present control system. * * *

I find that the injury in this case is irreparable to each of said plaintiffs and that they would be relegated to pursuing a judicial merry-go-round in actions at law, if they were required to seek a remedy in a Court of law.

## BURDEN OF PROOF

Throughout, I have taken the position that the burden of proof was on the plaintiffs on all issues. I find they have sustained that burden. I am now convinced that once the plaintiffs established that fluorides were deposited on their lands from the plant of the defendant, the burden of going forward with the evidence was on the defendant to show that the use of its property, which caused the injury, was unavoidable or that it could not be prevented except by the expenditure of such vast sums of money as would substantially deprive it of the use of its property. This seems to be the general rule. * * * [The] defendant made no attempt to carry the burden of going forward with the evidence. On the other hand, the plaintiffs called experts, whose testimony was clear and convincing to the effect that the amount of the emitted material could be substantially reduced, or almost eliminated, without an expenditure which would substantially deprive defendant of the use of its property. Frankly stated, there is no good reason why the defendant company, like other companies similarly situated, should not make a reasonable expenditure in the erection of hoods, or like devices, over or around its pots or cells. To require less would be placing a premium on air pollution. What's good for Reynolds should be good for Harvey, even though the cost of the new system might exceed $2,000,000.00, as it did in the case of Reynolds. * * *

The defendant will be required to install proper hoods around the cells and electrostatic precipitators in usual, advantageous and proper places in the plant, within one year of the date of the decree. Otherwise, an injunction will issue as prayed for by plaintiffs.

There is no room for application of the doctrine of balancing of the equities at this time. The required improvements should entirely eliminate the problem. * * *

### Notes and Questions

1.   The court in *Renken* ordered injunctive relief. Which box in **Figure 5-1** at page 158, *supra*, represents the court's remedy? Why? What are the rules about the future purchase and sale of the entitlement awarded by the

*Renken* court? May the entitlement be bought and sold? At what price? May either party veto the sale?

2. Why did the *Renken* court conclude that the injunctive remedy was required? Do you agree with the court's analysis?

3. The injunctive relief in *Renken* required the installation within one year of a specific control technology (albeit one that is somewhat vaguely articulated by the court): "proper hoods around the cells and electrostatic precipitators in usual, advantageous and proper places in the plant." Rules requiring polluters to employ specific control devices are called *specification standards*. By contrast, rules requiring polluters to achieve a certain level of emissions are called *performance standards*. This distinction is so central to environmental law that you must learn to recognize it.

4. In what ways might specification standards (ordering a polluter to use specific controls) be a poor way to frame relief, so that performance standards (ordering a polluter to achieve a certain level of emissions) are preferable? In what ways might specification standards be a good way to frame relief, so that they should be the preferred approach?

## 3. DAMAGES

### BOOMER v. ATLANTIC CEMENT CO.

*Nuisance*

26 N.Y.2d 219, 257 N.E.2d 870, 309 N.Y.S.2d 312 (1970)

*In the early 1960s, the Burwill Realty Company, formed in 1959, quietly purchased more than 1500 acres in a rural area of New York State that was just beginning to become suburban. In early 1961, the company changed its name to Atlantic Cement Company and began construction of a $40 million facility (including a massive quarry), which commenced operations in September 1961. The effect of the cement plant on its neighbors was profound. The blasting at the quarry caused large cracks in the walls, ceiling, and exterior of plaintiffs' homes, and fine dust emanating from the plant coated everything with a "plastic-like" coating, which the plaintiffs were unable to remove. Because more than half of the assessed value of the township involved the cement company's property, closing the plant would have drastically reduced the tax revenues of the local government and school board. See Farber, Reassessing Boomer: Justice, Efficiency, and Nuisance Law, in Essays on the Law of Property and Legal Education, in Honor of John E. Cribbet (M. Hoeflich & P. Hay 1988).*

BERGAN, J.

Defendant operates a large cement plant near Albany. These are actions for injunction and damages by neighboring land owners alleging injury to property from dirt, smoke and vibration emanating from the plant. A nuisance has been found after trial, temporary damages have been allowed; but an injunction has been denied. * * *

The cement making operations of defendant have been found by the court of Special Term to have damaged the nearby properties of plaintiffs in these two actions. That court * * * accordingly found defendant maintained a nuisance and this has been affirmed at the Appellate Division. The total damage to plaintiffs' properties is, however, relatively small in comparison with the value of defendant's operation and with the consequences of the injunction which plaintiffs seek.

The ground for the denial of injunction, notwithstanding the finding both that there is a nuisance and that plaintiffs have been damaged substantially, is the large disparity in economic consequences of the nuisance and of the injunction. This theory cannot, however, be sustained without overruling a doctrine which has been consistently reaffirmed in several leading cases in this court and which has never been disavowed here, namely that where a nuisance has been found and where there has been any substantial damage shown by the party complaining an injunction will be granted. The rule in New York has been that such a nuisance will be enjoined although marked disparity be shown in economic consequence between the effect of the injunction and the effect of the nuisance.

The problem of disparity in economic consequence was sharply in focus in *Whalen v. Union Bag & Paper Co.* (208 N. Y. 1). A pulp mill entailing an investment of more than a million dollars polluted a stream in which plaintiff, who owned a farm, was "a lower riparian owner." The economic loss to plaintiff from this pollution was small. This court, reversing the Appellate Division, reinstated the injunction granted by the Special Term against the argument of the mill owner that in view of "the slight advantage to plaintiff and the great loss that will be inflicted on defendant" an injunction should not be granted * * * . "Such a balancing of injuries cannot be justified by the circumstances of this case," Judge Werner noted * * * . He continued: "Although the damage to the plaintiff may be slight as compared with the defendant's expense of abating the condition, that is not a good reason for refusing an injunction" * * * .

Thus [an] unconditional injunction * * * was reinstated. The rule laid down in that case, then, is that whenever the damage resulting from a nuisance is found not "unsubstantial," viz., $100 a year, injunction would follow. This states a rule that had been followed in this court with marked consistency * * * . Thus if * * * the damage to plaintiffs in these present cases from defendant's cement plant is "not unsubstantial," an injunction should follow.

Although the court at Special Term and the Appellate Division held that injunction should be denied, it was found that plaintiffs had been damaged in various specific amounts up to the time of the trial and damages to the respective plaintiffs were awarded for those amounts. The effect of this was, injunction having been denied, plaintiffs could maintain successive actions at law for damages thereafter as further damage was incurred.

The court at Special Term also found the amount of permanent damage attributable to each plaintiff, for the guidance of the parties in the event both sides stipulated to the payment and acceptance of such permanent damage as a settlement of all the controversies among the parties. The total of permanent damages to all plaintiffs thus found was $185,000. * * *

This result at Special Term and at the Appellate Division is a departure from a rule that has become settled; but to follow the rule literally in these cases would be to close down the plant at once. This court is fully agreed to avoid that immediately drastic remedy; the difference in view is how best to avoid it.*

One alternative is to grant the injunction but postpone its effect to a specified future date to give opportunity for technical advances to permit defendant to eliminate the nuisance; another is to grant the injunction conditioned on the payment of permanent damages to plaintiffs which would compensate them for the total economic loss to their property present and future caused by defendant's operations. * * * [T]he court chooses the latter alternative.

If the injunction were to be granted unless within a short period— e.g., 18 months—the nuisance be abated by improved methods, there would be no assurance that any significant technical improvement would occur. * * *

[T]echniques to eliminate dust and other annoying by-products of cement making are unlikely to be developed by any research the defendant can undertake within any short period, but will depend on the total resources of the cement industry nationwide and throughout the world. The problem is universal wherever cement is made.

For obvious reasons the rate of the research is beyond control of defendant. If at the end of 18 months the whole industry has not found a technical solution a court would be hard put to close down this one cement plant if due regard be given to equitable principles.

On the other hand, to grant the injunction unless defendant pays plaintiffs such permanent damages as may be fixed by the court seems to do justice between the contending parties. All of the attributions of economic loss to the properties on which plaintiffs' complaints are based will have been redressed.

The nuisance complained of by these plaintiffs may have other public or private consequences, but these particular parties are the only ones who have sought remedies and the judgment proposed will fully redress them. The limitation of relief granted is a limitation only within the four corners of these actions and does not foreclose public health or other public agencies from seeking proper relief in a proper court.

It seems reasonable to think that the risk of being required to pay permanent damages to injured property owners by cement plant own-

---

* Respondent's investment in the plant is in excess of $45,000,000. There are over 300 people employed there.

ers would itself be a reasonably effective spur to research for improved techniques to minimize nuisance.

The orders should be reversed, without costs, and the cases remitted to Supreme Court, Albany County to grant an injunction which shall be vacated upon payment by defendant of such amounts of permanent damage to the respective plaintiffs as shall for this purpose be determined by the court.

JASEN, J. (DISSENTING).

I agree with the majority that a reversal is required here, but I do not subscribe to the newly enunciated doctrine of assessment of permanent damages, in lieu of an injunction, where substantial property rights have been impaired by the creation of a nuisance.

It has long been the rule in this State, as the majority acknowledges, that a nuisance which results in substantial continuing damage to neighbors must be enjoined. * * * To now change the rule to permit the cement company to continue polluting the air indefinitely upon the payment of permanent damages is, in my opinion, compounding the magnitude of a very serious problem in our State and Nation today. * * *

I see grave dangers in overruling our long-established rule of granting an injunction where a nuisance results in substantial continuing damage. In permitting the injunction to become inoperative upon the payment of permanent damages, the majority is, in effect, licensing a continuing wrong. It is the same as saying to the cement company, you may continue to do harm to your neighbors so long as you pay a fee for it. Furthermore, once such permanent damages are assessed and paid, the incentive to alleviate the wrong would be eliminated, thereby continuing air pollution of an area without abatement.

It is true that some courts have sanctioned the remedy here proposed by the majority in a number of cases, but none of the authorities relied upon by the majority are analogous to the situation before us. In those cases, the courts, in denying an injunction and awarding money damages, grounded their decision on a showing that the use to which the property was intended to be put was primarily for the public benefit. Here, on the other hand, it is clearly established that the cement company is creating a continuing air pollution nuisance primarily for its own private interest with no public benefit. * * *

I would enjoin the defendant cement company from continuing the discharge of dust particles upon its neighbors' properties unless, within 18 months, the cement company abated this nuisance.

I am aware that the trial court found that the most modern dust control devices available have been installed in defendant's plant, but, I submit, this does not mean that *better* and more effective dust control devices could not be developed within the time allowed to abate the pollution. * * * I believe it is incumbent upon the defendant to develop such devices, since the cement company, at the time the plant commenced production (1962), was well aware of the plaintiffs' presence in the area, as well as the probable consequences of its contemplated operation. Yet, it still chose to build and operate the plant at this site. * * *

### *Notes and Questions*

1. The majority in *Boomer* denied injunctive relief but effectively ordered a one-time grant of permanent damages. Which box in **Figure 5-1** at page 158, *supra*, represents the court's remedy? Why? What are the rules about the future purchase and sale of the entitlement awarded by the *Boomer* court? May the entitlement be bought and sold? At what price? May either party veto the sale?

2. Why did the *Boomer* majority conclude that an injunctive remedy was inappropriate? Do you agree with the majority's analysis? Are there sufficient distinctions between *Boomer* and the *Renken* case at page 158, *supra*, to justify the difference in result?

3. The dissenting judge in *Boomer* would have preferred a delayed injunction, giving the defendant 18 months to develop and install control measures. In environmental law, such a delayed sanction is sometimes called a "hammer" or a "delayed hammer," particularly when the legislature orders that certain consequences will flow automatically from the failure of an administrative agency to comply with a statutory deadline. Why did the dissenting judge prefer this approach? Do you agree with his analysis?

3. The approach preferred by dissenting Judge Jasen might also be called "technology-forcing"—a concept that you will encounter often in environmental law. Do you believe that the specific technology-forcing approach preferred by Judge Jasen would have worked to resolve the *Boomer* dispute? Why or why not?

4. Can you imagine an approach that might have furthered the goals of both the majority and the dissenting judges in *Boomer*? Why wasn't the remedy ordered by the Appellate Division the perfect compromise? Under what circumstances might the Appellate Division's remedy turn out to have been more advantageous to the cement company defendant?

## 4. CALCULATING DAMAGES

Regardless of the *standard* for awarding damages (negligence, strict liability, or what have you) the judicial system must take a further step and calculate the *amount* of damages to be awarded. Recent writings suggest that we have overlooked serious deficiencies in the manner in which damages are calculated and that it is time to reconsider the odd "signals" which these damage awards may give to the market. Although the following two excerpts address the issue of safety, the examples are equally relevant to the problem of pollution.

# RICHARD J. PIERCE, JR., ENCOURAGING SAFETY: THE LIMITS OF TORT LAW AND GOVERNMENT REGULATION

33 Vand. L. Rev. 1281-82, 1289-90. 1293-94 (1980)

[S]afety can be increased without an increase in safety-related spending. * * * [S]ociety spends more on safety in some areas than others relative to the potential for reduction of accident costs in each area. For example, if some of the money now spent on airline safety were shifted to school bus safety, more lives would be saved without increasing total safety spending. * * *

Some of the irrationalities inherent in tort calculations emerge from an analysis of the manner in which damages are determined, but the true anomalies become starkly apparent when the results of that process are analyzed. Consider the wrongful death of a child. While the adult wage earner's life is assigned a relatively high value in most cases, the life of a child is given little value in tort law. The general approach to determining damages for wrongful death should actually yield a negative value for the life of a child, but judges and juries usually "cheat" in this area and find some basis to assign a positive value to the life of a child. Still, the results of the process imply a very low value for the life of a child. The average award for wrongful death of a child was determined in a recent study to be $28,355. Thus, the signal given a firm is that it should spend up to, but no more than, $28,355 on safety per child's life saved by its expenditures. It is inconceivable that society actually desires to establish a market in safety that assigns such an absurdly low value to the life of a child. This valuation also is absurd relative to other implicit valuations in tort law. Indeed, the average damage award in a personal injury case is $181,401, and the average damage award for wrongful death of an adult male is $240,228. It is unlikely that society really wants to encourage firms to spend six times as much to avoid personal injury to an adult and ten times as much to avoid the death of an adult male as it spends to avoid the death of a child. Nevertheless, by merging the compensation decision with the liability decision, and then selecting compensation as the more important goal, the tort system has precisely this effect.

The argument might be made that the anomalous relative values placed on life versus serious injury, life of a child versus life of an adult wage earner, etc. are of no great importance in determining whether tort law creates a rational and effective market for safety because firms have very limited ability to make decisions on safety that reflect fine distinctions among the potential consequences of accidents. In other words, it is practically impossible for a firm to take measures that avoid serious injury or death to wage earners without also protecting children. If this view is correct, it follows that irrational differences in the valuation of particular consequences of accidents do not create functional aberrations in the market for safety as long as the aggregate valuation of the consequences of accidents is rational.

There are two reasons why this defense of current tort law cannot be accepted. First, there are many circumstances in which firms can determine their optimum level of spending on safety based upon the specific type of individual whose safety is at stake or the particular type of injury affected by a safety decision. A clear example is the manufacture of children's clothing. The rational children's clothing manufacturer can ignore the tort law signals concerning the relatively high value attached to serious injuries or death of an adult wage earner and base its decisions on expenditures for features such as resistance to fire entirely upon the $28,355 value tort law places on the life of a child. For instance, a toy manufacturer might spend money to redesign a toy so that its edges cannot cut a child, but decline to analyze the toxicity of a toy part that is small enough to ingest. The tort system's relative valuations of injury versus loss of life of a child make this decision rational. Indeed, there are many broad areas in which tort law's bizarre relative valuations of accident costs have a material effect upon safety spending decisions. * * * For instance, manufacturers of airplanes, intercity buses, and school buses confront very different tort-derived incentives to spend on safety because of the wide disparities in the average earning capacities and dependency status of their respective passengers.

## LAURA MECKLER, SCHOOL BUS HANDRAILS DEADLY—PROBLEM STILL NOT FIXED, DESPITE DEATHS, RECALL

### Rocky Mountain News, Apr. 5, 1997, at 2A

Twelve-year-old Carey Chipps hopped off her school bus one April afternoon and was almost immediately yanked from her feet. The drawstring of her jacket had caught in the handrail, and the departing bus dragged her 40 feet until the string snapped. Carey, thrown under the bus, was crushed by its rear wheels.

Today, six years after Carey died and four years after a safety recall, handrails on nearly 200,000 buses—almost half of those recalled—still have not been fixed, according to an Associated Press analysis of the most recent government statistics. That includes thousands with handrails made improperly after the recalls began. "That is higher than it should be, no question about it," said Bill Paul, editor and publisher of School Transportation News. "That should be unacceptable."

Fixing the problem—a narrow V-shaped space where the handrail tapers to meet the bus wall—costs less than $10 and takes less than 10 minutes. Depending on bus model, it's as simple as inserting a wedge in the space. Yet, at least six more children have been killed and 15 injured in drawstring snaggings since Carey died in 1991. "Carey was alive when I got to her," said her mother, Jane Chipps, who still lives in

Beckley, W.Va. "I said, 'Oh, Carey, I love you so much,' and she said, 'I love you too, Mommy.'"

The most recent parents to grieve are in Georgetown, Ky., where 7-year-old Brittany Nichole Marcum became victim No. 7 when she stepped off a bus in December. Federal officials are investigating a January death in Dalton, Ga., to determine whether an 8-year-old's coat was caught on the handrail or the door.

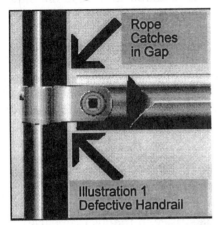 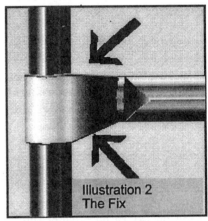

**Figure 5-2[a]**

Under recall rules, bus makers are required only to notify bus owners—usually school districts, states or leasing firms—and the owners are responsible for making repairs. Nationally, about 385,000 school buses had the handrails with a gap that could snag a drawstring and needed to be modified with a safer design, according to the National Highway Traffic Safety Administration, which orders and monitors manufacturers' compliance with safety recalls.

But just 50.2 percent have been fixed, according to the agency's reports from manufacturers through 1996. That leaves 191,858 buses in which deadly handrails may still be in place. A 100 percent compliance rate is unrealistic for a recall involving older buses, experts say, noting that some buses have been junked, shipped overseas or sold to unknown owners. But such recalls usually have rates approaching 80 percent.

Transportation officials believe many school districts are fixing their handrails without telling manufacturers. The agency is conducting audits to get a better count. Still, they admit, finding and fixing the buses has been tough. Difficulties include resistance by bus makers and owners, identifying problem buses and devising successful modifications.

---

[a] **Figure 5-2** is adapted from National Highway Transportation Safety Administration, This Could Save Your Child's Life: A School Bus Handrail Handbook 3-4 (Sep. 1996).

Bus makers resisted the recall from the start, asserting the problem was not handrails that had been safe for decades, but instead new kids' fashions featuring dangling drawstrings. "We kind of cajoled manufacturers to do something," said Jonathan White, chief of NHTSA's recall analysis division. The Consumer Product Safety Commission, in turn, has since persuaded clothing makers to make sure drawstrings at the waist don't extend more than 3 inches. Manufacturers insist they have worked hard to find problems and solutions. "I know everybody in our industry wants them fixed because we're very concerned about safety," said John Thomas III, president of Thomas Built Buses, one of the largest makers.

Charlie Gauthier, who worked on the case at NHTSA and now directs a group of school transportation directors, said regulators wouldn't have had enough evidence to force a recall if bus makers hadn't agreed to one voluntarily. In two years, 1991 and 1992, kids got off buses 20 billion times: two were killed in drawstring accidents, Gauthier said. "I don't know of anybody that would say that's an unreasonable risk."

Ultimately, bus makers did agree to a voluntary recall, but they had little enthusiasm and completion rates were low, White said. In fact, five manufacturers—including the nation's three largest—ordered remedies that didn't work. For instance, AmTran Corp. told bus owners to insert a spacer made of plastic foam between the handrail and the wall, but later found it collapsed over time. In all, 50,884 buses that were "fixed" had to be fixed again. In 1995, NHTSA called for a new round of recalls ordering a new, improved set of repairs. But in the meantime, companies had produced thousands of new buses, meaning they had to be fixed, too.

As more children died and publicity spread, federal officials added more bus models to the recall list, thanks to schools and parents who checked buses, found problems and reported to NHTSA. And the agency added recalls to fix handrails on the left side exiting the bus. Initially, officials thought only handrails on the right caused problems.

In the end, a solution involves more than recalling handrails, said Sen. Mike DeWine, a Republican from southwestern Ohio, where Brandi Browder's head was crushed after her jacket string snagged and she was thrown to the ground. DeWine has written to states asking they include handrails in annual bus inspections. "If you rely on the recall process, you're going to have huge numbers that are never going to get fixed," DeWine said. "With the amount of paperwork a school district may get, that piece of paper may not make it to the right person." Forty-nine of 50 states told DeWine's office they inspect buses for handrail defects. But not all pull buses off road if they fail. Making sure drivers are well-trained is also crucial, DeWine said.

Meanwhile, buses are still added to the recall list as new models are found with unsafe rails. Just this February, NHTSA said 26,000 more buses should be checked. "It really doesn't surprise me anymore," said Bill Brucken of Ashtabula, Ohio, whose 11-year-old daughter almost died in 1994 after her drawstring caught in a bus. At the last moment, lying on the ground with tires coming toward her, Briana turned her head. The wheels went over her shoulder, not her skull, and she survived. Says her father: "It's just not high on anyone's priority list."

## 5.  THE "REVERSE" LIABILITY RULE

# SPUR INDUSTRIES, INC. v. DEL
# E. WEBB DEVELOPMENT CO.

108 Ariz. 178, 494 P.2d 700 (1972)

CAMERON, VICE CHIEF JUSTICE.

From a judgment permanently enjoining the defendant, Spur Industries, Inc., from operating a cattle feedlot near the plaintiff Del E. Webb Development Company's Sun City, Spur appeals. Webb cross-appeals. Although numerous issues are raised, we feel that it is necessary to answer only two questions. They are:

1.  Where the operation of a business, such as a cattle feedlot is lawful in the first instance, but becomes a nuisance by reason of a nearby residential area, may the feedlot operation be enjoined in an action brought by the developer of the residential area?

2.  Assuming that the nuisance may be enjoined, may the developer of a completely new town or urban area in a previously agricultural area be required to indemnify the operator of the feedlot who must move or cease operation because of the presence of the residential area created by the developer?

The facts necessary for a determination of this matter on appeal are as follows. The area in question is located in Maricopa County, Arizona, some 14 to 15 miles west of the urban area of Phoenix, on the Phoenix-Wickenburg Highway, also known as Grand Avenue. About two miles south of Grand Avenue is Olive Avenue which runs east and west. 111th Avenue runs north and south as does the Agua Fria River immediately to the west. * * *

Farming started in this area about 1911. In 1929, with the completion of the Carl Pleasant Dam, gravity flow water became available to the property located to the west of the Agua Fria River, though land to the east remained dependent upon well water for irrigation. By 1950, the only urban areas in the vicinity were the agriculturally related communities of Peoria, El Mirage, and Surprise located along Grand Avenue. Along 111th Avenue, approximately one mile south of Grand Avenue and 1 1/2 miles north of Olive Avenue, the community of Youngtown was commenced in 1954. Youngtown is a retirement community appealing primarily to senior citizens.

In 1956, Spur's predecessors in interest, H. Marion Welborn and the Northside Hay Mill and Trading Company, developed feed-lots, about 1/2 mile south of Olive Avenue, in an area between the confluence of the usually dry Agua Fria and New Rivers. The area is well suited for cattle feeding and in 1959, there were 25 cattle feeding pens or dairy operations within a 7 mile radius of the location developed by Spur's predecessors. In April and May of 1959, the Northside Hay Mill was feeding between 6,000 and 7,000 head of cattle and Welborn approximately 1,500 head on a combined area of 35 acres.

In May of 1959, Del Webb began to plan the development of an urban area to be known as Sun City. For this purpose, the Marinette and the Santa Fe Ranches, some 20,000 acres of farmland, were purchased for $15,000,000 or $750.00 per acre. This price was considerably less than the price of land located near the urban area of Phoenix, and along with the success of Youngtown was a factor influencing the decision to purchase the property in question.

By September 1959, Del Webb had started construction of a golf course south of Grand Avenue and Spur's predecessors had started to level ground for more feedlot area. In 1960, Spur purchased the property in question and began a rebuilding and expansion program extending both to the north and south of the original facilities. By 1962, Spur's expansion program was completed and had expanded from approximately 35 acres to 114 acres. * * *

Accompanied by an extensive advertising campaign, homes were first offered by Del Webb in January 1960 and the first unit to be completed was south of Grand Avenue and approximately 2 1/2 miles north of Spur. By 2 May 1960, there were 450 to 500 houses completed or under construction. At this time, Del Webb did not consider odors from the Spur feed pens a problem and Del Webb continued to develop in a southerly direction, until sales resistance became so great that the parcels were difficult if not impossible to sell. * * *

By December 1967, Del Webb's property had extended south to Olive Avenue and Spur was within 500 feet of Olive Avenue to the north. * * * Del Webb filed its original complaint alleging that in excess of 1,300 lots in the southwest portion were unfit for development for sale as residential lots because of the operation of the Spur feedlot.

Del Webb's suit complained that the Spur feeding operation was a public nuisance because of the flies and the odor which were drifting or being blown by the prevailing south to north wind over the southern portion of Sun City. At the time of the suit, Spur was feeding between 20,000 and 30,000 head of cattle, and the facts amply support the finding of the trial court that the feed pens had become a nuisance to the people who resided in the southern part of Del Webb's development. The testimony indicated that cattle in a commercial feedlot will produce 35 to 40 pounds of wet manure per day, per head, or over a million pounds of wet manure per day for 30,000 head of cattle, and that despite the admittedly good feedlot management and good housekeeping practices by Spur, the resulting odor and flies produced an annoying if not unhealthy situation as far as the senior citizens of southern Sun City were concerned. There is no doubt that some of the citizens of Sun City were unable to enjoy the outdoor living which Del Webb had advertised and that Del Webb was faced with sales resistance from prospective purchasers as well as strong and persistent complaints from the people who had purchased homes in that area. * * *

It is noted, however, that neither the citizens of Sun City nor Youngtown are represented in this lawsuit and the suit is solely between Del Webb * * * and Spur Industries * * * .

### MAY SPUR BE ENJOINED?

We have no difficulty * * * in agreeing with the conclusion of the trial court that Spur's operation was an enjoinable public nuisance as far as the people in the southern portion of Del Webb's Sun City were concerned. * * *

It is clear that as to the citizens of Sun City, the operation of Spur's feedlot was both a public and a private nuisance. They could have successfully maintained an action to abate the nuisance. Del Webb, having shown a special injury in the loss of sales, had a standing to bring suit to enjoin the nuisance. * * * The judgment of the trial court permanently enjoining the operation of the feedlot is affirmed. * * *

### MUST DEL WEBB INDEMNIFY SPUR?

In the so-called "coming to the nuisance" cases, the courts have held that the residential landowner may not have relief if he knowingly came into a neighborhood reserved for industrial or agricultural endeavors and has been damaged thereby * * * .

Were Webb the only party injured, we would feel justified in holding that the doctrine of "coming to the nuisance" would have been a bar to the relief asked by Webb, and, on the other hand, had Spur located the feedlot near the outskirts of a city and had the city grown toward the feedlot, Spur would have to suffer the cost of abating the nuisance as to those people locating within the growth pattern of the expanding city * * * .

There was no indication in the instant case at the time Spur and its predecessors located in western Maricopa County that a new city would spring up, full-blown, alongside the feeding operation and that the developer of that city would ask the court to order Spur to move because of the new city. Spur is required to move not because of any wrongdoing on the part of Spur, but because of a proper and legitimate regard of the courts for the rights and interests of the public.

Del Webb, on the other hand, is entitled to the relief prayed for (a permanent injunction), not because Webb is blameless, but because of the damage to the people who have been encouraged to purchase homes in Sun City. It does not equitably or legally follow, however, that Webb, being entitled to the injunction, is then free of any liability to Spur if Webb has in fact been the cause of the damage Spur has sustained. It does not seem harsh to require a developer, who has taken advantage of the lesser land values in a rural area as well as the availability of large tracts of land on which to build and develop a new town or city in the area, to indemnify those who are forced to leave as a result.

Having brought people to the nuisance to the foreseeable detriment of Spur, Webb must indemnify Spur for a reasonable amount of the cost of moving or shutting down. It should be noted that this relief to Spur is limited to a case wherein a developer has, with foreseeability, brought into a previously agricultural or industrial area the population which makes necessary the granting of an injunction against a lawful business and for which the business has no adequate relief.

It is therefore the decision of this court that the matter be remanded to the trial court for a hearing upon the damages sustained by the defendant Spur as a reasonable and direct result of the granting of the permanent injunction. Since the result of the appeal may appear novel and both sides have obtained a measure of relief, it is ordered that each side will bear its own costs. * * *

### Notes and Questions

1. Calabresi and Melamed, authors of the essay excerpted at pages 140-142, *supra*, anticipated the principle of the *Spur Industries* case, calling it the "fourth rule." *See* Guido Calabresi & Douglas A. Melamed, *Property Rules, Liability Rules, and Inalienability: One View of the Cathedral*, 85 Harv. L. Rev. 1089, 1116-17 (1972). Their "fourth rule" is "now commonly referred to as the 'reverse' liability rule, under which the victim has the right to prevent harm, but must pay the injurer his cost of doing so." Louis Kaplow & Steven Shavell, *Property Rules Versus Liability Rules: An Economic Analysis*, 109 Harv. L. Rev. 713, 724 (1996).

2. Which box in **Figure 5-1** at page 158, *supra*, represents the court's remedy in *Spur Industries*? Why? What are the rules about the future purchase and sale of the entitlement awarded by the *Spur Industries* court? May the entitlement be bought and sold? At what price? May either party veto the sale?

3. Assume that the developer had been the only injured receptor in *Spur Industries*. Do you suppose the court would have granted relief requiring the feedlot to move? Why or why not?

4. Assume that the homeowners had been the plaintiffs—rather than the developer—in *Spur Industries*. Do you suppose the court would have made the homeowners pay for the defendant's costs of moving or shutting down? Why or why not?

5. If you were the developer's attorney, what might you argue on remand to avoid paying the full amount of the feedlot's moving or shut down costs? To how large a nuisance did the developer actually come?

The "reverse" liability rule of *Spur Industries* has apparently been widely ignored by the court system. Consider its potential application in the following zoning battle.

## PAUL A. DRISCOLL,
## WIENERS OR LOSERS

Chicago Tribune, Mar. 3, 1996, at C3

Ultimately, Chicago is going to have to choose—sausage makers or Yuppies. A developer wants to turn an industrial plot along the river into an upscale island of townhouses, residential lofts and single-family homes. But the owner of the Vienna Sausage Co. fears that once the well-to-do catch a whiff of his wiener factory, Vienna's days in Chicago will be numbered. "At some point it will become so difficult we'll have to pack our bags and leave," James Bodman said. And if Vienna Sausage leaves the city, so will its 500 jobs and $18 million annual payroll.

The issue is familiar for many cities: fleeing industries, the decline of skilled and semi-skilled jobs, displaced blue-collar workers, gentrification of working-class neighborhoods. "A lot of passion has been stirred up on both sides, but particularly among people backing Vienna," said Matt Smith, spokesman for the city Department of Planning and Development. "This is a tremendously big issue."

Chicago likes sausages the way Brooklyn loves bagels. Ads for hot dogs are everywhere, and hot dog stands are emblazoned with the name Vienna Sausage, the nation's oldest producer of processed meat. Vienna Sausage was founded in 1893 and has been cranking out meat in its current plant for a quarter-century. The plant four miles north of the Loop produces most of the $100 million worth of sausages, hot dogs and other products Vienna ships nationwide.

Across the Chicago River, however, is a 20-acre parcel that has residential developers salivating. It is now home to shuttered warehouses and other industrial buildings. Sold as industrial property, the land is worth about $4 million; with a zoning change, it could be closer to $17 million. Developer Ron Shipka wants to put up 525 residential units. Total cost: $125 million. "As soon as the city commits itself to this project is the day we start making plans to move out," Bodman said. "It might take us five or 10 years, but we're convinced that if they build residential, that will be the death knell for our ability to stay in Chicago."

Bodman and Shipka, both highly successful entrepreneurs, don't come close to talking the same language. "It's terribly important for the city to try to keep its industry," Bodman said. "We don't need any more homes. We need jobs." "As a Chicagoan," Shipka said, "I want him to stay in Chicago. Cohabitation of manufacturing and residential is Chicago. That's what a city is all about." Besides, Shipka said, his survey of businesses in the area turned up not one objection to odors or noise from Vienna.

Try standing 180 feet downwind from the plant some summer day when it's 95 degrees—right where the development would be—and inhale the fatty, rancid odor, Bodman said. Homes could also wind up with grease on their windows. "I'd bitch about it if I lived there," he said. City officials have said they want to preserve an industrial corridor along the river that for generations has provided thousands of factory and warehouse jobs. But huge chunks already have given way to restaurants, bars, boutiques and loft residences. The zoning ordinance is Shipka's only obstacle to continuing this trend.

---

Vienna Sausage prevailed when Mayor Daley pronounced that he would not support the zoning change necessary for the residential development project. *See* John H. White, *Spoiler Role for Hot Dogs; City Picks Jobs Over Homes*, Chicago Sun-Times, Mar. 8, 1996 at 3.

## 6.  COMING TO THE NUISANCE

The "coming to the nuisance" defense raises some thorny questions about the propriety of having a polluter take by "private condemnation" something that it would otherwise be required to pay for. The following brief excerpt from a relatively recent federal court case summarizes what it asserts to be the majority view on the subject.

## PATRICK v. SHARON STEEL CORP.

### 549 F.Supp. 1259 (N.D. W.Va. 1982)

HADEN, CHIEF JUDGE.

This action was commenced by fifteen individual Plaintiffs to recover for damages they claim resulted from Sharon Steel Corporation's (Sharon) operation of its Fairmont Coke Works in Fairmont, West Virginia. Plaintiffs allege that Sharon "willfully emitted into the ambient air large quantities of gaseous and solid pollutants which are both harmful and noxious." Plaintiffs further assert that these pollutants had deleterious effects on Plaintiffs' health, and their real and personal property. The complaint also states that Sharon maintained refuse "ponds or dumps into which were discharged manufacturing byproducts or refuse including, but not limited to, cyanide and other noxious and toxic compounds" which have drained into the local water table and streams. * * *

Sharon argues that the doctrine of "coming to the nuisance" bars any recovery by Plaintiffs. * * * This assertion is premised on the fact that the coke works was in operation when Plaintiffs moved into their residences near the coke works and, therefore, Plaintiffs assumed the risk of living near the nuisance.

This argument is untenable. Sharon relies upon an outdated doctrine that has never been recognized in West Virginia and which has been rejected by the majority of jurisdictions in which it had been previously adopted. * * * See Restatement 2d Torts § 840(d); Prosser, Law of Torts, § 91 (4th Ed. 1971). As the Supreme Court of Florida stated in *Lawrence v. Eastern Airlines, Inc.*, 81 So.2d 632, 634 (Fla.1955):

> The majority view rejects the doctrine of coming to the nuisance as an absolute defense to a nuisance action. Support for the majority view is found in the argument that the doctrine is out of place in modern society where people often have no real choices as to whether or not they will reside in an area adulterated by air pollution. In addition, the doctrine is contrary to public policy in the sense that it permits a defendant to condemn surrounding land to endure a perpetual nuisance simply because he was in the area first. Another reason given for rejecting the doctrine is that the owner of land subject to a nuisance will either have to bring suit before selling his land in order to attempt to receive the full value of the land or reconcile himself to accepting a depreciated price for the land since no purchaser would be willing to pay full value for land subject to a nuisance against which he is barred from bringing an action.

Jurisdictions as near to West Virginia as Kentucky and as distant as the United Kingdom have rejected the doctrine of coming to the nuisance as a defense. Considering the ample authority on this point, the Court believes West Virginia would follow the majority view * * * in disallowing this anachronistic doctrine to serve as a defense in nuisance cases.

## 7. SELF-HELP

# RICHARD B. STEWART & JAMES E. KRIER, ENVIRONMENTAL LAW AND POLICY

### 253-55 (2nd ed. 1978)

We have thus far identified four basic legal rules for dealing with environmental degradation, but there is a further possibility: one or both of the parties may be permitted to engage in self-help. Thus a complete listing of potential common law rules for dealing with environmental resource use [is] as follows:

(1) Polluter subject to injunction for interfering with receptor's use of air resource.

(2) Polluter liable in damages for interfering with receptor's use of air resource.

(3) No liability on either party; either may engage in self-help without liability.

(4) Receptor liable in damage (*Spur* rule: receptor, either through self-help or court action, can interfere with polluter's use of the air resource, but must compensate polluter).

(5) Polluter not liable; receptor subject to injunction (receptor may not through self-help interfere with polluter's use of air resource).

If both polluter and receptor are allowed to engage in unlimited self-help, they are left, in effect, in a state of nature. Pollution may be viewed as a form of self-help by polluters, since it appropriates use of the air resource to the polluter at receptor's expense.

Sometimes receptors seek to abate a nuisance on their own—by "self-help"—without seeking judicial recourse. Consider the case of "The Fox," a "sort of antipollution Zorro, who has been harassing various companies" in the Chicago area to make them cut down on polluting activities. "The Fox" has been doing such things as plugging up the draining systems and sealing the chimneys of polluting factories. "'Nothing seemed to make them stop. So I decided that even if I was only one man, I'd do something. I don't believe in hurting people or in destroying things, but I do believe in stopping things that are hurting our environment,'" "The Fox" has said. *See* Royko, *"The Fox" Stalks the Polluters* * * * *and Strikes*, Los Angeles Times, Sept. 23, 1970, § 1 at 1, 7. *See also* "The Fox," Newsweek, Oct. 5, 1970, at 90; and the account of "The Billboard Bandit" devoted to beautifying Michigan roadsides in Time, March 22, 1971, a 48 ("In two weeks the Bandit's roaring chain saw * * * toppled 35 offensive billboards * * *"). More recently, billboard interests have retaliated by cutting down trees obstructing motorists' view of the billboards. * * * *Cf. 2 Men, Facing Trial for Releasing Dolphins, Say They Are Too Intelligent to Be Captive*, N.Y. Times, July 5, 1977, p. A23, col. 1.

Might such acts be legally justifiable? *See* Cal. Civ. Code §§ 3495, 3502 (West 1970), which provide respectively as follows:

> Any person may abate a public nuisance which is specially injurious to him by removing, or, if necessary, destroying the thing which constitutes the same * * * .

> A person injured by a private nuisance may abate it by removing, or, if necessary, destroying the thing which constitutes the nuisance, without committing a breach of the peace, or doing unnecessary injury.

*See generally*, W. Prosser, Torts 605-06 (4th ed. 1971).

## 8. AWARDING MIXED ENTITLEMENTS

### SMITH v. STASO MILLING CO.

18 F.2d 736 (2d Cir. 1927)

The plaintiff is the owner of a summer residence in the town of Castleton, Vermont, something less than a mile distant from the defendant's crushing mill. This residence he occupied in substantially unchanged form at the time the defendant bought its land and before it put up its mill. The defendant blasts slate rock upon its premises, which it crushes, and makes from the product ground slate roofing material. The grinding creates clouds of dust, part of which, when the wind is in the right direction, is carried over to the plaintiff's premises, which it covers with pulverized dust. This is one grievance.

In the defendant's process of manufacture there are waste products which it puts upon a dump by a belt conveyor. Through the conveyor streams of water are run from driven wells, and the thin, muddy or plastic mass flows out into the first of three settling ponds, the overflow from which passes into a second, and so to a third, the three being together designed to retain all the waste. During heavy rains these ponds become filled with water and carry off through the sluices quantities of the sludge or mud, which the defendant has deposited in them. The last of these empties into a brook which runs through the premises of both parties, and on such occasions quantities of the muddy slate reach the plaintiff's land and leave a sediment upon it. He uses the brook for part of his domestic water supply, and the sludge or silt fills his reservoirs and otherwise interferes with his enjoyment of the premises. This is another and more important grievance.

The third is the defendant's heavy blasting in the course of its work, which at times has been violent enough to break the plaintiff's windows, and at others to shake the whole house. This was more serious three years before the trial, when it occurred not only during the day, but at night.

After the defendant had purchased the land, but before it had put up the plant, the plaintiff wrote, calling attention to the brook which flowed through both premises, advising it that it[s] continued purity was a valuable asset to him, and protesting against any pollution or interference with its flow. The defendant's superintendent called upon him, assured him that there was no danger, because the proposed system of filters and settling basins would prevent any such possibility. The assurance was several times repeated. After the erection of the mill the defendant again assured the plaintiff more than once that the trouble had been in management of the settling ponds.

The defendant has installed dust arresters which are rated to stop 99 per cent. of the dust which is produced. It has invested about $1,000,000 altogether in the plant, employs between 125 and 200 men, and its monthly pay roll [is] between $25,000 and $40,000.

The plaintiff valued his premises at $40,000, though it cost in all less than $30,000, but the defendant's witnesses put its value at between $10,000 and $15,000. * * *

The District Judge on conflicting evidence found for the plaintiff on all the questions of fact involved, and absolutely enjoined the activities complained of. He fixed the damages from the first operation of the mill in 1917 until February, 1924, at $10,000, for which he allowed judgment. The defendant appealed.

L. HAND, CIRCUIT JUDGE (after stating the facts as above).

The defendant, not arguing that the facts justify no relief, insists that no injunction should go, because of the disastrous effect upon his crushing mill, which must stop its operation if enjoined. * * *

[S]o far as concerns the pollution of the stream, we think that the injury is so substantial and the wrong so deliberate, that we ought to impose upon the defendant the peril of any failure successfully to avoid it. * * * [N]ot only did the defendant have the most explicit warning from the plaintiff, but it gave an equally explicit assurance that it could avoid defiling the brook. It has several times repeated that assurance after occasional overflows. If the plaintiff had filed his bill before the mill was built, the balance of convenience would have been different, and we should not have hesitated to stop what as yet remained only a project. Whether the assurances in fact determined his inaction we need not say; he has shown himself pertinacious, though forbearing, and the chances are that they did. Even if not, these preliminary negotiations seem to us enough absolutely to impose upon the defendant the execution of what it promised. As respects the pollution of the stream, we therefore think that the injunction should remain absolute, and that the defendant must find some way to avoid further injury, or make its peace with the plaintiff as best it can.

As regards the dust the facts are different. True, it is equally a tort so to defile the air. * * * But the injury is less oppressive, and neither the plaintiff's original protest, nor the defendant's promise, covered it. We are not prepared in such a situation to say that, if the defendant cannot by the best known methods arrest all the dust which it emits, it must shut down its mill. The record shows that it has installed arresters which are designed to stop all but one per cent. of the dust, and apparently do so. Yet that which escapes is still enough to affect the plaintiff's enjoyment, and the record does not show beyond question that the defendant cannot prevent it. The best disposition of the case is to affirm the injunction as it stands, but to give leave to the defendant to apply at the foot of the decree for relief upon showing there are no better arresters extant, that it operates those it has at maximum efficiency, that it is [therefore] impossible further to reduce the dust, and that if the injunction continues it has no alternative but to stop operation. If that be proved to the satisfaction of the District Judge the injunction should be modified so as merely to limit the dust to that which will escape the arresters now in use. * * *

There remains only the question of damages. We cannot accept the estimate of the District Judge as to the value of the plaintiff's premises, which rests only upon his own appraisal, contradicted by the defendant's witnesses, who were surely in a more impartial position. A country residence, on which so much is spent to suit the owner's fancy, cannot be said to have a value equal to its cost. Nor is it fair to take the price which it might bring from a purchaser whom it might chance to please. Its value is what it will fetch, and, while any appraisal is at best scarcely more than a guess, we think that $15,000 is upon this record the most that we can give it. The damages are even more troublesome to fix than the value. We must take it that the operation of the mill has prevented the plaintiff from leasing the property as a residence, and converted its value into merely agricultural land, but we have no right to say that he would have been able to lease it, had the mill been absent. On the other hand the injury went on for seven years * * * . It appears to us that an award of five hundred dollars a year is as much as the evidence will warrant. The damages are therefore fixed at thirty-five hundred dollars.

### Notes and Questions

1.  Why does Judge Hand specify that the air pollution decree should require no more than the application of available technology, while the water pollution decree must remain absolute? Is the distinction based on tort law? Environmental law? Some other field of law?

2.  Why does Judge Hand seem unconcerned about the possibility that the water pollution injunction might theoretically lead to a shut down of defendant's extremely costly facility?

3.  Which box in **Figure 5-1** at page 158, *supra*, represents Judge Hand's remedy for the water pollution in *Staso Milling*? Which location effectively represents his remedy for the air pollution, if the defendant succeeds in demonstrating on remand that further controls are impossible?

# Chapter Six

# UNCERTAINTY AND
# RISK ANALYSIS

## A. INTRODUCTION

Chapter 6 focuses on two problems that permeate modern environmental law: uncertainty and risk analysis. A road map may be helpful. First, we will look at excerpts from an article identifying a unique category of environmental problems—"environmental risk"—and suggesting ways to think about such problems. Second, we will explore how courts and administrative agencies have struggled to resolve three questions typically arising in connection with "environmental risk" pollutants: (1) does the pollutant pose any risk of harm at all? (2) does the pollutant pose a significant risk of harm at existing exposure levels? and (3) can a court (or administrative agency) justify the establishment of an abatement standard? These three questions are not always neatly sorted out in the readings, but you would do well to keep them separate in your mind.

## B. ENVIRONMENTAL RISK

## TALBOT PAGE, A GENERIC VIEW OF TOXIC CHEMICALS AND SIMILAR RISKS

7 Ecol. L.Q. 207 (1978)[a]

A new type of environmental problem * * * differs in nature from the more familiar pollution and resource depletion problems. This * * * may be called *environmental risk* * * * . One of the main obstacles to satisfactory management of environmental risks is that concepts and institutions which developed in response to classical problems have been applied indiscriminately to environmental risks. * * *

Environmental risk problems are exemplified by: the risk of leakage and contamination in the disposal of nuclear wastes; * * * the risk of [stratospheric] ozone depletion [from the use of freon propellants in

---

[a] *Ed.*—To facilitate reading, footnotes have been blended into the text and several paragraphs have been resequenced.

aerosol cans]; and the danger presented by recombinant DNA of the creation and escape of a new disease against which mankind has no natural defense. * * *

An environmental risk gamble may be thought of as a seesaw with the potential costs on one side of the pivot and the potential benefits on the other. The distances from the pivot represent the relative magnitudes of benefits and costs. [**Figure 6-1**] illustrates the freon propellant example. The distance from zero to B represents the benefit of the convenience of using propellants. Foregoing this convenience is the cost of opting out of the gamble. The distance from zero to C-B represents the net cost of taking the gamble and losing. The net cost is the potential, relatively large "catastrophic" cost reduced by the comparatively small benefit of using propellants that will accrue even if propellants do deplete the ozone.

**Net Costs and Benefits Associated with Two Hypotheses**

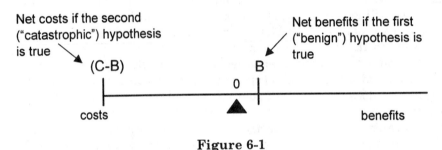

Figure 6-1

In [**Figure 6-1**] the potential costs, due to their greater magnitude, are considerably farther from the pivot than the modest benefits. If both hypotheses were of equal weight the seesaw would tip toward the potentially great loss. Common sense then suggests that the gamble is too risky to undertake.

However, there is a dilemma. There often are reasons to believe that the probabilities of the safe and catastrophic hypotheses are not equal and that the catastrophic outcome is considerably less likely than the favorable outcome. For many potentially toxic chemicals, and for nuclear power, ozone depletion, and recombinant DNA, what little is known about mechanism suggests that the probability of the catastrophic outcome is low, much lower than the probability of the favorable outcome. Just how low is impossible to say with confidence, because of the incomplete knowledge of mechanism. * * *

[T]he probabilities of the benign and catastrophic hypotheses can be thought of as weights placed upon the seesaw at distances from the pivot equal to the magnitude of the respective potential costs and benefits. A heavy weight close to the pivot can more than balance a light weight farther from the pivot. * * *

Whether the greater likelihood of the favorable outcome compensates for its smaller relative size is a fundamental question of environmental risk management. In the extreme case, the problem is called a "zero-infinity dilemma": a virtually zero probability of a virtually infinite catastrophe. * * *

The various uncertainties surrounding the quantification of costs, benefits, and probabilities are illustrated in [**Figure 6-2**]. The range of uncertainty associated with benefits, represented by *a*, is the uncertainty of *efficacy*. In the freon propellant example, it is not clear how well freon works as a propellant. The corresponding range of uncertainty associated with *costs*, represented by *b*, is typically much larger than the uncertainty of efficacy. In addition, there is uncertainty as to the *likelihood* of each hypothesis (*c* and *d*). * * *

Costs and Benefits Weighted by Probability

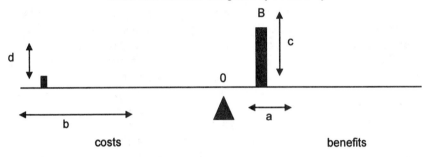

**Figure 6-2**

FALSE NEGATIVES AND FALSE POSITIVES

The concept of false negatives and false positives helps to illustrate [the challenge of environmental risk management] * * * . In criminal law, two basic kinds of mistakes can occur: the jury (or judge) can find a guilty man innocent or an innocent man guilty. Testing chemicals for toxicity presents the same problem. Test results may indicate that a toxic chemical is not toxic or that a non-toxic chemical is toxic. The former type of error is called a false negative and the latter a false positive. In environmental risk assessment, the latter type of error is labeled a false alarm, but (perhaps significantly) there is no common name for the former error. * * *

Although there are several approaches for defining acceptable risk, there is little agreement on what is the best approach. * * * A few of the approaches are discussed below.

LIMITING FALSE POSITIVES

This approach * * * starts with the assumption that there is no risk and requires that a hazard be proved beyond some standard. * * * [I]f the standard of proof is not met, then the risk is acceptable. The burden of proof is placed on those seeking precautionary action. * * * In its extreme, the approach of limiting false positives requires positive evidence of "dead bodies" before acting. * * * An example of this perspective is a comment by the Water Commissioner of Philadelphia: "If future research proves a true link between water-borne organics and cancer in humans, Philadelphia will spend whatever is necessary to cope with the problem." Initially, this perspective appears reasonable, * * * [in that open-ended expenditures for control will not be spent unnecessarily. However, the approach of limiting false positives * * * has questionable value for the management of environmental risk. * * *

The distinction between the failure to find an effect and the conclusion that there is no effect is not trivial. This distinction is so important * * * that its blurring can be given the name *fallacy of false negative*. The fallacy is to believe that a decision procedure designed to limit false positives necessarily yields *any* conclusion about the nonexistence of an effect when there is a negative finding.

A simple illustration is helpful. A pail contains tennis balls, all white except for the possibility of a single yellow ball. The problem is to determine whether the pail contains the yellow ball. In the decision procedure an observer is allowed to look only at the top layer. Under the procedure, the test scores positive if the observer sees a yellow ball in the top layer; the test scores negative if the observer does not see a yellow ball in the top layer. In this simple procedure the probability of a false positive is limited to zero. If there is no yellow ball in the pail, the observer will not see one in the top layer; there is no way for the test erroneously to find an effect when it does not exist. However, the probability of a false negative, a conclusion that the ball is not present when it actually is, can vary all the way from zero to one, from never to always, depending on the number of layers of balls.

If the pail is only one layer deep, the probability of a false negative is zero. In this situation, if the observer does not see the yellow ball, it is not in the pail. In this extreme case, there is no distinction between the failure to see the yellow ball and the finding that there is no yellow ball in the pail. However, if the pail is several layers deep, the distinction becomes important. There exists the possibility of not seeing the yellow ball even though it is present. If the pail is several hundred layers deep, the chance of a false negative, not seeing the ball even though it is in the pail, is nearly 100 percent.

Thus, as the depth of the pail is varied from a single to an infinite number of layers, the probability of a false negative varies from zero to one, even though the chance of a false positive is always held to the same limit, zero. As can be seen by this illustration, limiting the chance of a false positive does not by itself yield any conclusion regarding the chance of an effect not being present upon a negative finding.

This does not mean that decision makers can never draw negative conclusions from negative findings. However, in order to do so the structure of the problem must be investigated directly. * * * In the illustration, the important structure is the depth of the pail or the ratio of the balls that can be seen to those that cannot. If the observer is allowed to see nine-tenths of the balls and still does not see the yellow ball, he can conclude, with only a ten percent chance of a false negative, that the yellow ball is not present. Thus, a negative conclusion has been established from a negative finding.

In many decision problems the pail may be shallow, so a negative finding will impart a good deal of information about the nonexistence of effect. But in environmental risk, with long latencies and diffusion of effects, effects are well hidden. For these risks, the pail is deep and careful investigation is required to support a negative conclusion drawn from a negative finding. * * *

The attuned reader will find the fallacy of the false negative ubiquitous in legal, regulatory, and statistical reasoning. When the press reports that saccharin has been in use for 70 years without a single human cancer death proven as a result of its use, the suggested inference is that this is evidence of saccharin's non-carcinogenicity to humans. Before drawing this inference, regulatory institutions and other decision makers should investigate the likelihood of detecting saccharin [carcinogenicity] even if, for example, it should contribute 700 to 1,000 extra cancer deaths a year. * * * For a meaningful interpretation of a negative finding, there must first be an explicit investigation of the power of the statistical or other decision procedure to detect hidden effects.

### LIMITING FALSE NEGATIVES

Limiting false positives is the guiding principle of criminal law. The objective is to limit the chance of a false conviction. The common-sense justification for this objective is that it is better to free a hundred guilty men than to convict one innocent man. * * * A principal reason for this is that liberty is a primary good, *i.e.*, a good for the deprivation of which there is no adequate compensation. The asymmetrical results achieved by the criminal justice system are intentional and follow from the exceptional value placed on liberty.

A comparison of criminal law with environmental risk, however, suggests an important difference. The costs of false negatives and false positives are asymmetric for environmental risk as well, but the asymmetry is in reverse order. For environmental risk, the asymmetrically high cost arises from a false negative; in criminal law from a false positive. * * * The analogy between criminal law and environmental risk requires that the roles of negatives and positives be reversed. If the emphasis on limiting false positives for criminal law is sensible * * * then the implication is that a decision procedure based upon limiting false negatives is more appropriate for environmental risk than one based upon limiting false positives. * * *

### BALANCING FALSE POSITIVES AND FALSE NEGATIVES

[M]anaging environmental risk need not be restricted to choosing between limiting either false positives or false negatives. Instead, it can seek to weigh the risk of one wrong decision against another. The most frequently proposed means to accomplish this is to make the decision to regulate or not to regulate an environmental risk by comparing the cost of a false negative weighted by its probability with the cost of a false positive weighted by its probability, and choosing the alternative with the lower weighted costs. * * * Application of this approach requires four pieces of information: the cost of a false negative; the cost of a false positive; and the probability of each. * * *

### POTENCY

Concentrations of environmental risk pollutants are typically much lower than concentrations of classical pollutants. Classical pollutants often are measured in parts-per-million (ppm), while environmental risk candidates often appear at the parts-per-billion (ppb) level. Experts in the management of traditional pollutants occasionally have dismissed environmental risk problems simply on the basis of their low concentrations. * * * [For example] * * * [when] chloroethyl-ether was present in Philadelphia water in concentrations of 0.5 ppb * * * [the] Philadelphia Water Commissioner [declared that] such a "minute quantity" is "like making a martini with one ounce of vermouth to 156 railroad tank cars of gin, * * * like the width of your fingers compared to the distance from Philadelphia to San Francisco." * * * A part-per-billion is clearly a very small number, but it still means roughly 100 million trillion molecules of the carcinogen per liter of water. * * * Some carcinogens are potent at extremely low concentrations. Aflatoxin, for example, is carcinogenic at the 100 parts-per-trillion level. * * *

# C. THE RESERVE MINING LITIGATION

# RESERVE MINING CO. v. UNITED STATES

498 F.2d 1073 (8th Cir. 1974)

Before BRIGHT, ROSS and WEBSTER, CIRCUIT JUDGES.

BRIGHT, CIRCUIT JUDGE.

Reserve Mining Company * * * mines low-grade iron ore, called "taconite," near Babbitt, Minnesota. The taconite is shipped by rail to Reserve's "beneficiating" plant at Silver Bay, Minnesota, on the north shore of Lake Superior, where it is concentrated into [iron ore] "pellets" * * * . The process involves crushing the taconite into fine granules, separating out the metallic iron with huge magnets, and flushing the residue into Lake Superior. Approximately 67,000 tons of this waste product, known as "tailings," are daily discharged into the lake.

The use of Lake Superior for this purpose was originally authorized by the State of Minnesota in 1947 * * * . In granting this permit to Reserve, the State of Minnesota accepted Reserve's theory that the weight and velocity of the discharge would insure that the tailings would be deposited at a depth of approximately 900 feet in the "great trough" area of the lake, located offshore from Reserve's facility. * * *

[T]he United States Government—joined eventually by the States of Minnesota, Wisconsin, and Michigan and by various environmental groups—filed a complaint alleging that Reserve's discharge of tailings into Lake Superior violated Section 13 of the 1899 Refuse Act, Section 10 of the Federal Water Pollution Control Act, and the federal common law of public nuisance. * * *

[A]fter 139 days of trial * * * [involving] more than 100 witnesses and * * * over 1,600 exhibits, Judge Miles Lord of the United States District Court for the District of Minnesota entered an order closing Reserve's Silver Bay facility. * * * Judge Lord held that Reserve's water discharge violated federal water pollution laws, that its air emissions violated state air pollution regulations, and that both were common law nuisances. * * *

Reserve * * * noticed [its] appeal to this court and * * * applied to us for a stay. * * * We grant the stay subject to certain conditions and limitations as stated herein.

Although there is no dispute that significant amounts of waste tailings are discharged into the water and dust is discharged into the air by Reserve, the parties vigorously contest the precise nature of the discharge, its biological effects, and, particularly with respect to the waters of Lake Superior, its ultimate destination. Plaintiffs contend that the mineral cummingtonite-grunerite, which Reserve admits to be a major component of its taconite wastes, * * * is substantially identical in morphology (or shape and form) and similar in chemistry to amosite asbestos, a fibrous mineral which has been found, in certain occupational settings, to be carcinogenic. The plaintiffs further argue that the mineral fibers discharged represent a serious health threat, since they are present in the air of Silver Bay and surrounding communities and, by way of dispersion throughout Lake Superior, in the drinking water of Duluth and other communities drawing water from the lake.

Reserve has maintained throughout this litigation that its cummingtonite-grunerite does not have a fibrous form and is otherwise distinguishable from amosite asbestos. Reserve further maintains the tailings cannot be said to pose any health hazard and, in any event, with respect to its discharge into water, the tailings largely settle to the bottom of the lake in the "great trough" area within close range of the plant.

The evidence presented on these points was extensive and complex. * * * The district court found, as plaintiffs contended, that Reserve discharged particles identical to and similar to amosite asbestos, and that the particles discharged into Lake Superior were dispersed widely.

The suggestion that particles of the cummingtonite-grunerite in Reserve's discharges are the equivalent of amosite asbestos raised an immediate health issue, since inhalation of amosite asbestos at occupational levels of exposure is a demonstrated health hazard resulting in asbestosis and various forms of cancer. * * * [T]he rather drastic rem-

edy ordered by the district court—the immediate closing of the plant—
was a response to the finding of a substantial danger to the public
health. * * *

Given the concededly enormous economic impact that an immediate
plant closure would have upon Reserve, given the personal impact on
its approximately 3,000 employees and their families, and given the social and economic impact upon the communities in which the employees
live, we think that our preliminary resolution of the health hazard
question should control * * * whether to grant or deny a stay. * * *

We have reviewed the testimony on the health issue, giving careful
and particular attention and weight * * * to the testimony of the impartial court witnesses and that of plaintiffs' chief medical witness, Dr.
Irving Selikoff, Director of the Environmental Sciences Laboratory of
Mt. Sinai School of Medicine. * * * [O]ur review suggests that this evidence does not support a finding of substantial danger and that, indeed * * * such a finding should not be made. * * * [W]e conclude that
Reserve appears likely to succeed on the merits of its appeal on the
health issue. * * *

### Two Key Unknowns

The theory by which plaintiffs argue that the discharges present a
substantial danger is founded largely upon epidemiological studies of
asbestos workers occupationally exposed to and inhaling high levels of
asbestos dust. * * * [These] studies * * * leave no doubt that asbestos, at
sufficiently high dosages, is injurious to health. * * *

[E]nvironmental exposure from Reserve's discharges into air and
water is simply not comparable to that typical of occupational settings.
The occupational studies involve direct exposure to and inhalation of
asbestos dust in high concentrations and in confined spaces. This pattern of exposure cannot be equated with the discharge into the outside
air of relatively low levels of asbestos fibers. * * * Nor can the occupational pattern of exposure be equated with the exposure resulting from
the ingestion of fibers via the Duluth drinking water. * * * Thus, it cannot be said that either the discharge into the water or the discharge
into the air results in circumstances of exposure comparable to those in
an occupational context.

If this is true, no conclusions about health hazards in occupational
settings may be utilized in the present situation except on the ground
that certain principles of asbestos-disease pathology may be extrapolated from relevant medical knowledge and applied in altered circumstances. In order to make a prediction * * * at least two key findings
must be made. First, an attempt must be made to determine * * * what
that lower level of exposure is. Second * * * it must be determined
whether the level of exposure is safe or unsafe.

Unfortunately, the testimony of Dr. Arnold Brown[8] indicates that neither of these key determinations can be made. Dr. Brown testified that, with respect to both air and water, the level of fibers is not readily susceptible of measurement. This results from the relatively imprecise state of counting techniques and the wide margins of error which necessarily result, and is reflected in the widely divergent sample counts received by the court. * * * [His] testimony indicates that little more can be said about the level of fibers present in air or water other than that some fibers are present.

Even assuming that one could avoid imprecision and uncertainty in measuring the number of fibers at low levels, there remains vast uncertainty as to the medical consequences of low levels of exposure to asbestos fibers. In order to predict the likelihood and magnitude of disease resulting from exposure, one must have some idea of the relevant threshold value and dose-response relationships.[9] Although there seems to be agreement that threshold values and dose-response relationships are observable with respect to cancer generally, the particular values and relationships associated with asbestos-induced cancer appear to be unknown. * * *

## THE TISSUE STUDY

In the face of these two key unknowns * * * a tissue study [was] conducted * * * to measure the hazard * * * of ingesting fiber-contaminated water. This study was prompted by an almost complete lack of knowledge with respect to the human ingestion of asbestos fibers, since previous experiments had dealt largely with the effects of fiber inhalation, where interaction by asbestos with the respiratory tract was established. Any theory attempting to deal with the effects of ingestion of asbestos in liquid had to bridge the gap between the ingestion of fibers and the interaction by those fibers with the body tissues. If the fibers do not interact with the tissues but simply are eliminated by the body as wastes, presumably no disease will result. Accordingly, the court-appointed experts formulated a "protocol" or study plan designed to test whether people who drink Lake Superior waters accumulate asbestos-like fibers in body tissues from taconite.

This protocol involved analysis by electron microscope of the tissues of recently deceased Duluth residents who had ingested Duluth water for at least 15 years * * * . Those results * * * indicated that the tissues of Duluth residents were virtually free of any fibers which could be attributed to the Reserve discharge. * * *

Plaintiffs * * * [argue] that the specimens of tissue from body organs surveyed were too minute, and thus fibers that were present may

---

[8] Dr. Brown, a research pathologist associated with the Mayo Clinic * * * served the court * * * [as] an impartial witness.

[9] A threshold value is that level of exposure below which no adverse health effects occur, while the dose-response relationship quantifies the association between disease-producing levels of exposure and the incidence of disease.

have been overlooked. However, this judgment must be balanced by * * * [Dr. Selikoff's statement] that the design of the protocol was sound and would yield significant information. * * *

Although * * * we agree with Dr. Brown's statement that the ingestion of asbestos fibers cannot be exonerated as a hazard, we feel that, on any fair reading of the circumstances of the protocol, the results of the tissue study must weigh heavily against the assessment of any demonstrated hazard to health. * * * [T]he tissue study raises a major obstacle to the proof that ingestion of Duluth water is hazardous. * * *

### EVALUATION OF TESTIMONY

[T]he discharges by Reserve can be characterized only as presenting an unquantifiable risk * * * . [I]t is not known what the level of fiber exposure is, other than that it is relatively low, and it is not known what level of exposure is safe or unsafe. * * * Finally, no basis exists, save a theoretical one, for assuming that drinking water, otherwise pure but containing asbestos-like particles, is dangerous to health. * * *

We do not think that a bare risk of the unknown can amount to proof in this case. Plaintiffs have failed to prove that a demonstrable health hazard exists. This failure, we hasten to add, is not reflective of any weakness which it is within their power to cure, but rather, given the current state of medical and scientific knowledge, plaintiffs' case is based only on medical hypothesis and is simply beyond proof.

We believe that Judge Lord carried his analysis one step beyond the evidence. * * * [T]he district court's determination to resolve all doubts in favor of health safety represents a legislative policy judgment, not a judicial one. * * *

We emphasize that our evaluation rests not on any view that the discharge exposes North Shore residents to no risk, but rather on the view that, given the evidence, no substantial danger has been, or could be proven. * * * [W]e are a court of law, governed by rules of proof, and unknowns may not be substituted for proof of a demonstrable hazard to the public health. * * *

### *Notes and Questions*

1.   The Eighth Circuit concluded that evidence of asbestos-induced disease in occupational settings was of little value, because the exposure of people to Reserve's fibers in air and water was not "comparable" to occupational exposure, in which workers were directly exposed to and inhaled asbestos dust "in high concentrations and in confined spaces." This accurate observation led Reserve to argue in subsequent court submissions that there was no risk to the public, because *environmental* exposure levels resulting from Reserve's operations were less than *occupational* exposure *standards* that had been set for the asbestos industry. Variations on this argument occur frequently in environmental law. For example, if an occupational standard permits 5 asbestos fibers per cubic centimeter in the workplace, then an environmental exposure of 3 fibers per cubic centimeter is said to be obviously "safe." Is this conclusion appropriate? Why or why not?

2.   The tissue study failed to discover significant contamination by Reserve's fibers in the tissues of deceased Duluth residents. Does this mean that the ingestion of Reserve's fibers is harmless? Why or why not?

3.   Talbot Page, in the reading beginning at page 184, *supra*, discusses two approaches to environmental risk: limiting false negatives and limiting false positives. Which label best describes the approach of the Eighth Circuit's 1974 *Reserve Mining* opinion? Why?

4.   Page suggests at pages 187-188, *supra*, that a decisionmaker might seek to *balance* the risks of false positives and false negatives, if four pieces of information are known: "the cost of a false negative; the cost of a false positive; and the probability of each." For which of these items do you suppose the court had sufficient information to engage in such balancing?

5.   The Eighth Circuit concluded that the trial court's decision to resolve all doubts in favor of health safety represented "a legislative policy judgment, not a judicial one." Doesn't this make sense? Given the extraordinary uncertainties of a case like *Reserve Mining*, shouldn't elected representatives, rather than federal judges, choose the "appropriate" attitude toward risk? Suppose the issue of Reserve Mining's fiber discharges were brought to the Minnesota state legislature for resolution. How do you suppose this issue would be handled? Does your conclusion give you pause about the proper forum for choosing society's attitude toward risk?

## JAMES E. KRIER, ENVIRONMENTAL LITIGATION AND THE BURDEN OF PROOF

in Law and the Environment 105, 107 (Malcolm F.
Baldwin & James K. Page eds. 1970)

[B]urden of proof rules at present have an inevitable bias against protection of the environment and preservation of natural resources. This is the case for the following reasons. Essentially two classes of demands can be made on such resources as air, land, water, wildlife and so on: (1) demands which consume or deteriorate those resources (water pollution, the slaughter of wildlife, the harvesting of forests); (2) demands which *do not* consume or deteriorate them (swimming, birdwatching, hiking and camping). In a world without laws, those who wish to use resources for consumptive or deteriorating ends will *always* prevail over those who wish to use them for nonconsumptive or nondeteriorating ends. This is simply because consuming users, by exercising their demands, can foreclose nonconsuming users from exercising theirs, while the contrary cannot hold true. In short, the polluter's use can stop the swimmer from using and enjoying a lake, but the swimmer's use *cannot* stop the polluter from polluting the lake.

Of course, we live in a system with laws, but it is a loaded system. And it is loaded precisely because of the point I have just made. For even in a world with rules against resource consumption (against, for example, pollution), the leverage inherent in resource consumers means that they can continue their conduct until sued. In short, they will almost inevitably be *defendants*, and those whose uses preserve rather than deteriorate will ineluctably be *plaintiffs*. And it is one of the simple facts of our present system that (for a host of reasons) plaintiffs most generally carry the major burden of [proving] most of the basic issues in a lawsuit. The result is striking: Even with a system of substantive rules *against* resource consumption, our present rules ensure that in cases of doubt about any facet of those rules, resource consumption will prevail. * * *

# RESERVE MINING CO. v.
# ENVIRONMENTAL PROTECTION AGENCY

### 514 F.2d 492 (8th Cir. 1975)

Before LAY, BRIGHT, ROSS, STEPHENSON and WEBSTER, CIRCUIT JUDGES, EN BANC.

BRIGHT, CIRCUIT JUDGE.

* * * We think it significant that Dr. Brown, an impartial witness whose court-appointed task was to address the health issue in its entirety, joined with plaintiffs' witnesses in viewing as reasonable the hypothesis that Reserve's discharges present a threat to public health. Although, as we noted in our stay opinion, Dr. Brown found the evidence insufficient to make a scientific probability statement as to whether adverse health consequences would in fact ensue, he expressed a public health concern over the continued long-term emission of fibers into the air. We quote his testimony * * * .

[Dr. Brown]. Based on the scientific evidence, I would be unable to predict that * * * cancer would be found in Silver Bay.

Now, going beyond that, it seems to me that, * * * where it has been shown that a known human carcinogen * * * is in the air of any community, and if it could be lowered I would say, as a physician that, yes, it should be lowered. And if it could be taken out of the air completely, I would be even more happy. * * *

If I knew more about that human carcinogen, if I knew what a safe level was in the air, if I knew what a safe level was in the water, then I could draw some firm conclusions and advise you in precise terms. That information is not available to me [or] * * * to anyone else. * * *

In assessing probabilities in this case, it cannot be said that the probability of harm is more likely than not. * * * On this record it cannot be forecast that the rates of cancer will increase from drinking Lake Superior water or breathing Silver Bay air. The best that can be said is that the existence of this asbestos contaminant in air and water gives rise to a reasonable medical concern for the public health. The public's exposure to asbestos fibers in air and water creates some health risk. * * *

[T]he existence of this risk to the public justifies an injunction requiring abatement of the health hazard on reasonable terms as a precautionary and preventive measure to protect the public health. * * *

*The court then found that: (1) Reserve's air emissions violated Minnesota air pollution control regulations but—given the lack of evidence on interstate effects—did not constitute a violation of the federal common law of nuisance; (2) Reserve's water discharges into Lake Superior violated Minnesota's water quality standards, the federal Refuse Act (forbidding discharges into navigable waters without a permit), and the federal Water Pollution Control Act (prohibiting certain discharges "endangering the health or welfare of persons").*

Reserve directs our attention to the benefits arising from its operations, as found by a Minnesota state district court, as follows:

In reliance upon the State and Federal permits * * * [Reserve] constructed its plant * * * [and] developed the Villages of Babbitt and Silver Bay and their schools and other necessary facilities where many of [Reserve's] employees live with their families, as do the merchants, doctors, teachers and so forth who serve them. [Reserve's] capital investment exceeds $350 million. As of June 30, 1970 [Reserve] had 3,367 employees. * * *

With respect to the water, [the] probabilities [of harm] must be deemed low for they do not rest on a history of past health harm attributable to ingestion but on a medical theory implicating the ingestion of asbestos fibers as a causative factor in increasing the rates of gastrointestinal cancer among asbestos workers. With respect to air, the assessment of the risk of harm rests on a higher degree of proof, a correlation between inhalation of asbestos dust and subsequent illness. But here, too, the hazard cannot be measured in terms of predictability, but the assessment must be made without direct proof. * * *

A court is not powerless to act in these circumstances. But an immediate injunction cannot be justified in striking a balance between unpredictable health effects and the clearly predictable social and economic consequences that would follow the plant closing. * * *

At oral argument, Reserve advised us of a willingness to spend 243 million dollars in plant alterations and construction to halt its pollution of air and water. Reserve's offer * * * weighs heavily against a ruling which closes Reserve's plant immediately.

Indeed, the intervening union argues, with some persuasiveness, that ill health effects resulting from the prolonged unemployment of the head of the family on a closing of the Reserve facility may be more certain than the harm from drinking Lake Superior water or breathing Silver Bay air. * * *

We believe that on this record the district court abused its discretion by immediately closing this major industrial plant. In this case, the risk of harm to the public is potential, not imminent or certain * * * . Reserve must be given a reasonable opportunity and a reasonable time to construct facilities to accomplish an abatement of its pollution * * * . Accordingly, we direct that the injunction order be modified as follows.

THE DISCHARGE INTO WATER

Reserve shall be given a reasonable time to stop discharging its wastes into Lake Superior. A reasonable time includes the time necessary for Minnesota to act on Reserve's present application to dispose of its tailings at [the] Milepost 7 [site] * * * or to come to agreement on some other site acceptable to both Reserve and the state. * * * We suggest * * * that * * * a final administrative decision should be reached within one year after a final appellate decision in this case. * * *

Should Minnesota and Reserve be unable to agree on an on-land disposal site within this reasonable time period, Reserve * * * must be given a reasonable period of time thereafter to phase out the Silver Bay facility. * * * [T]his additional period of time is set at one year after Minnesota's final administrative determination that it will offer Reserve no site acceptable to Reserve for on-land disposal of tailings. * * *

AIR EMISSIONS

Pending final action by Minnesota on the present permit application, Reserve must promptly take all steps necessary to comply with Minnesota law applicable to its air emissions * * * .

Reserve, at a minimum, must comply with APC 1 and 5 [state regulations setting forth ambient air standards and design standards for particulate emissions]. Furthermore, Reserve must use such available technology as will reduce the asbestos fiber count in the ambient air at Silver Bay below a medically significant level. According to the record in this case, controls may be deemed adequate which will reduce the fiber count to the level ordinarily found in the ambient air of a control city such as St. Paul.[85] * * * [W]e view the air emission as presenting a hazard of greater significance than the water discharge. * * *

### Notes and Questions

1.  The Eighth Circuit's 1974 opinion concluded at page 190, *supra*, that Reserve was likely to succeed on the merits of the health question. Yet, in the 1975, the plaintiffs—not Reserve—prevailed. What changed in the interim leading to the 1975 en banc opinion? The 1974 opinion stated that the plaintiffs were unlikely to prevail on the health issue, because they had not demonstrated a health hazard. Did the 1975 opinion find adverse health effects to be more probable than not?

2.  Talbot Page, in the reading beginning at page 184, *supra*, discusses two approaches to environmental risk: limiting false negatives and limiting false positives. Which label best describes the approach of the Eighth Circuit's 1975 opinion? Why?

3.  If the Eighth Circuit had been an administrative agency, like the Environmental Protection Agency, and if H.R. 9 or S. 343—described at pages

---

[85] We here order Reserve to meet a court-fashioned standard which may exceed the standards of existing * * * regulations * * * . The broad remedial policy behind Minnesota's pollution control laws authorizes injunctive relief of this scope.

105-08, *supra*—had been adopted, would the decisionmaker have been free to do anything to halt or curtail Reserve's pollution? Why or why not?

4.   The sentence in the Eighth Circuit's 1975 opinion to which footnote 85 is appended promulgated a "control city standard" for Reserve's air emissions. Is the control city standard a specification standard or a performance standard? *See* page 163, *supra*. If you were Reserve's attorney, would you conclude that the control city standard is good or bad for your client? Why?

# SUBSEQUENT HISTORY OF
# THE RESERVE MINING LITIGATION

After the Eighth Circuit's 1975 decision, Reserve sought permits from two Minnesota state agencies for an on-land disposal facility at the company's preferred site (Mile Post 7), located close to the Silver Bay taconite processing plant. The massive engineering plan proposed gradual construction of four dams (using taconite tailings as the building material) to form a basin of six square miles. The biggest dam—almost three miles long and 180 feet high—would eventually rank as one of the largest 30 dams in the world.

In ruling on the permit applications, the state agencies were required to follow the Minnesota Environmental Policy Act, which provides, in relevant part:

No * * * permit for natural resources management and development [shall] be granted, where such * * * permit * * * is likely to cause pollution, impairment, or destruction of the * * * natural resources [of] the state, so long as there is a feasible and prudent alternative consistent with the reasonable requirements of the public health, safety, and welfare and the state's paramount concern for the protection of its * * * natural resources * * * . Economic considerations alone shall not justify such conduct.

Minn. Stat. Ann. sec. 116D.04 Subd. 6. This statute was modeled after the Michigan Environmental Protection Act. *See* page 224, *infra*.

After more than one year of hearings, a Hearing Officer appointed by the two agencies recommended that applications for the Mile Post 7 permits be rejected, because a potential site located considerably further from Silver Bay (the Midway site) represented a "prudent and feasible alternative," even though the company insisted that the costs of the Midway site were so prohibitive that the company would terminate its operations if the Mile Post 7 permits were denied. Among the reasons given for this recommendation were the following:

Construction and operation of the proposed * * * system would result in the distribution of air borne dust containing asbestiform fibers * * * generated by construction activity, transporting and movement of * * * tailings, and wind action on exposed areas. * * * Dust emissions from Mile Post 7 would cause substantial numbers of potentially hazardous fibers to reach Silver Bay, at least partially negating the effect of planned emission controls at the processing plant. The level of fibers present in Silver Bay resulting from Mile Post 7 implementation would be at least comparable to the level which the courts have determined to be now in existence and which the courts have determined to be a potential health hazard. * * *

Prudence dictates that the best site is the one which offers the least exposure. * * * Fugitive dust and fiber concentration at Silver Bay resulting from tailings disposal at Midway would be substantially lower than for Mile Post 7 because of its greater distance.

Hearing Officer's Report at 18-23, 49-50.

Relying on the Hearing Officer's recommendation, the agencies denied the Mile Post 7 permit applications. The company promptly filed an appeal in the Minnesota courts, in accordance with the state administrative procedure act. Pointing to extensive evidence in the record about its proposed fugitive dust mitigation procedures, the company argued: "Reserve's Mile Post 7 plan *will* meet, in addition to all applicable air quality standards, the court ordered [control city] standard articulated by the Eighth Circuit Court of Appeals."

The Minnesota Supreme Court reversed the agencies' determinations, directing them to issue permits for the Mile Post 7 facility. *Reserve Mining Co. v. Herbst*, 256 N.W.2d 808 (1977). With respect to the air pollution issue, the Court said:

We cannot accept the proposition, * * * implicit in the position of the state, that the emission of fibers dangerous to public health at [Midway] renders it a feasible and prudent alternative site. * * * [T]hose who reside closer to [Midway] [are] entitled to the same protection as the residents of Silver Bay * * * . [W]e are confident the mitigation efforts * * * will be entirely adequate * * * .

The standards, among others, to which Reserve shall adhere are set forth by the Federal court as * * * achieving a level of asbestos fibers in the ambient air at Silver Bay below * * * the level ordinarily found in the ambient air of the city of St. Paul * * * .

In accordance with the Minnesota Supreme Court's mandate, the stage agencies issued permits for the construction of the Mile Post 7 facility. Each permit contained the following condition:

The air quality standards at or beyond the property line of the disposal system to which the Permittees shall adhere * * * are, among others, as follows: * * * the ambient air shall contain no more fibers than that level ordinarily found in the ambient air of the City of St. Paul * * * .

The company promptly filed another round of state court appeals, arguing that the control city standard was "unworkable," that the company could not possibly comply with the standard, that the agencies were well aware of that impossibility, and that the permit condition would force the company to cease operations. The Minnesota state district court accepted the company's contentions, ordering the agencies to alter the permits to provide the following amended standard:

a fiber level no greater than that level ordinarily found in the ambient air of a control city such as the City of St. Paul, provided that a fiber level exceeding the level in any control city shall not be non-compliance with this permit unless such level is in excess of a medically significant level.

The agencies appealed, arguing that the control city standard * * * had been promulgated by the Eighth Circuit, and that the Minnesota courts were powerless to change it. The Minnesota Supreme Court agreed with the agencies and upheld all contested permit provisions. *Reserve Mining Co. v. Minnesota Pollution Control Agency*, 267 N.W.2d 720 (1978). Notwithstanding its shutdown threat, the company accepted the permits and commenced construction of the Mile Post 7 facility. In the spring of 1980, the company's discharge of taconite tailings into Lake Superior came to an end.

### Notes and Questions

1.    Reexamine the amended "control city standard" permit language ordered by the Minnesota state district court. Who do you suppose drafted this condition? Why? Talbot Page, in the reading beginning at page 184, *supra*, discusses two approaches to environmental risk: limiting false negatives and limiting false positives. Which label best describes the approach of the amended permit condition? Why?

2.    The agencies argued on appeal that the Minnesota Supreme Court was powerless to change the control city standard promulgated by the Eighth Circuit. Were the plaintiffs correct in this assertion? Why or why not?

## D. QUANTITATIVE RISK ASSESSMENT

At its core, the *Reserve Mining* case represents one type of uncertainty—corresponding to the first of the three uncertainty questions articulated at page 183, *supra*—an inability to know whether a given substance is harmful at all to human receptors. Many pollutants, however, are known to be harmful and present a different kind of uncertainty: how harmful are they at various levels of exposure? This uncertainty calls into play the second and third questions, having to do with the "safety" of current exposure levels and the appropriateness of specific exposure standards. In dealing with these issues, regulatory agencies such as the EPA have increasingly turned to a technique called *quantitative risk assessment* or QRA. The following readings introduce the topic of QRAs and their various limitations. The first author, William Ruckelshaus, was Administrator of the EPA in 1984.

## WILLIAM D. RUCKELSHAUS, RISK IN A FREE SOCIETY

14 Envtl. L. Rep. 10190-94 (1984)

Risk assessment is the use of a base of scientific research to define the probability of some harm coming to an individual or a population as a result of exposure to a substance or situation. Risk management, in contrast, is the public process of deciding what to do where risk has been determined to exist. * * *

The [National Academy of Sciences has] proposed that these two functions be formally separated within regulatory agencies. I said that this appeared to be a workable idea and that we would try to make it happen at EPA. This notion was attractive because the statutes administered by many federal regulatory agencies typically force some action when scientific inquiry establishes the presence of a risk * * * .

When the action so forced has dire economic or social consequences, the person who must make the decision may be sorely tempted to ask for a "reinterpretation" of the data. We should remember that risk assessment data can be like a captured spy: if you torture it long enough, it will tell you anything you want to know. So it is good public policy to so structure an agency that such temptation is avoided.

But we have found that separating the assessment of risk from its management is rather more difficult to accomplish in practice. In [the] first place, values, which are supposed to be safely sequestered in risk management, also appear as important influences on the outcome of risk assessments. For example, let us suppose that a chemical in common use is tested on laboratory animals with the object of determining whether it can cause cancer. At the end of the test a proportion of the animals that have been exposed to the substance show evidence of tumor formation.

Now the problems begin. First, in tests like these, the doses given are extremely high, often close to the level the animal can tolerate for a lifetime without dying from toxic non-cancer effects. Environmental exposures are typically much lower, so in order to determine what the risk of cancer is at such lower exposures—that is, to determine the curve that relates a certain dose to a certain response—we must extrapolate down from the high-dose laboratory data. There are a number of statistical models for doing this, all of which fit the data, and all of which are open to debate. We simply do not *know* what the shape of the dose-response curve is at low doses, in the sense that we know, let us say, what the orbit of a satellite will be when we shoot it off.

Next, we must deal with the uncertainty of extrapolating cancer data from animals to man, for example, determining which of the many different kinds of lesions that may appear in animals is actually indicative of a probability that the substance in question may be a human carcinogen. Cancer is cancer to the public, but not to the pathologist.

Finally, we must deal with uncertainty about exposure. We have to determine, usually on the basis of scant data and elaborate mathematical models, how much of the stuff is being produced; how it is being dispersed, changed, or destroyed by natural processes; and how the actual dose that people get is changed by behavioral or population characteristics.

These uncertainties inherent in risk assessment combine to produce an enormously wide range of risk estimates in most cases. For example, the National Academy of Sciences report on saccharin concluded that over the next 70 years the expected number of cases of human bladder cancer resulting from daily exposure to 120 milligrams of saccharin might range from 0.22 to 1,144,000. * * *

Historically at EPA it has been thought prudent to make what have been called conservative assumptions; that is, in a situation of unavoidable uncertainty, *our* values lead us to couch our conclusions in terms of a plausible upper bound. As a result, when we generate a number that expresses the potency of some substance in causing disease, we can state that it is unlikely that the risk projected is any greater.

This conservative approach is fine when the risks projected are vanishingly small; it is always nice to learn that some chemical is *not* a national crisis. But when the risks estimated through such assessments are substantial, so that some action may be in the offing, the stacking of conservative assumptions one on top of another becomes a problem for the policymaker. If I am going to propose controls that may have serious economic and social effects, I need to have some idea how much confidence to place in the estimates of risk that prompted those controls. I need to know how likely *real* damage is to occur in the uncontrolled and partially controlled and fully controlled cases. * * * This, of course, tends to insert the policymaker back into the guts of risk assessment, which we had concluded is less than wise.

This is a real quandary. I now believe that the main road out of it lies through a marked improvement in the way we communicate the realities of risk analysis to the public. * * * [A] great part of the answer is to bring about a major improvement in the quality of public debate on environmental risk.

This will not be easy. Risk assessment is a probabilistic calculation * * * . Most people are not comfortable with mathematical probability as a guide to living and the risk assessment lingo we throw at them does not increase their comfort. Tell someone that their risk of cancer from a 70-year exposure to a carcinogen at ambient levels ranges between $10^{-5}$ and $10^{-7}$, and they are likely to come back at you with, "Yes, but will I get cancer if I drink the water?" * * *

We have research that points out that people tend to overestimate the probability of unfamiliar, catastrophic and well-publicized events and underestimate the probability of unspectacular or familiar events that claim one victim at a time. Many people are afraid to fly commercial airlines, but practically nobody is afraid of driving in cars, a victory of subjectivity over actuarial statistics. * * *

The way risks and options are presented also influences perceptions. You might be worried if you heard that occupational exposure at your job doubled your risk of some serious disease; you might be less worried if you heard that it had increased from one-in-a-million to two-in-a-million. * * *

Many people interested in environmental protection, having observed this mess, conclude that considerations of risk lead to nothing useful. After all, if the numbers are no good and the whole issue is so confusing, why not just eliminate all exposure to toxics to the extent that technology allows? The problem with such thinking is that * * * risk estimates are the only way we have of directing the attention of risk management agencies toward significant problems.

There are thousands of substances in the environment that show toxicity in animals; we cannot work on all of them at once, even with an EPA 10 times its current size. More important, technology does not make the bad stuff "go away"; in most cases it just changes its form and location. We have to start keeping track of the flow of toxics through the environment, to what happens *after* they are "controlled." Risk management is the only way I know to do this. * * *

## ALON ROSENTHAL, GEORGE M. GRAY & JOHN D. GRAHAM, LEGISLATING ACCEPTABLE CANCER RISK FROM EXPOSURE TO TOXIC CHEMICALS

19 Ecol. L.Q. 269, 278-279 (1992)

As currently practiced, risk assessment of a carcinogen takes place in four steps: hazard identification, dose-response evaluation, exposure assessment, and risk characterization.

The first step, hazard identification, is the process of determining whether an "agent" * * * increases a person's risk of developing cancer. The second step, dose-response evaluation, reveals how the likelihood of cancer changes with the level of exposure. * * * The third step, exposure assessment, quantifies the amount, or dose, of the carcinogen to which people may be exposed. * * *

After these quantitative inputs to a risk assessment have been determined, the numbers are combined to yield an overall estimate of risk, the basic component of the final step, risk characterization. A risk characterization is usually expressed numerically as the incremental lifetime risk of cancer due to a particular agent at a particular level of exposure (also referred to as an incremental risk). This is the number that a risk manager might compare to a legislated bright line. Good risk characterizations contain not only a final risk number but also a discussion of the uncertainties in and the assumptions behind the assessment, but unfortunately this step is rarely taken. * * *

In evaluating the seriousness of incremental cancer risks, it is useful to have a sense of perspective about the frequency of cancer. At current U.S. mortality rates, a baby born today has about a one-in-four, or 0.25, chance of contracting fatal cancer in his or her lifetime. This is the average American's baseline cancer risk from all causes. An incremental risk of one in a million, or $10^{-6}$, the most frequently proposed bright line risk standard, is equivalent to a change in lifetime cancer risk from 0.25 to 0.250001.

## E. RISK ASSESSMENT BLUES[b]

The use of formalized quantitative risk assessments sounds pretty cool, and also sounds like "good science." What could be better than to make pollution control decisions on the basis of good science—the use of the well-accepted "scientific method" to produce reliable results? Ruckelshaus tells us that it is impossible to keep values out of the supposedly scientific enterprise of risk assessment. But even apart from the intrusion of values, do we need to worry about "bad science" or mistaken science, or science that proceeds in the face of numerous unknowns to produce numbers that are then *treated* as if they are as reliable as the orbit of a satellite?

Probably no pollutants have been more subject to quantitative risk assessment methodology than the ionizing radiations. Millions of dollars have been spent in efforts to determine whether there are "safe" thresholds of exposure to radiation, and to ascertain the relationship between specific radiation doses and adverse health effects. Yet, uncertainty about the effects of radiation at low levels of exposure is remarkably persistent. It may even be due, in part, to poor science.

The essay by Rosenthal, Gray, and Graham at page 202, *supra*, notes that risk assessment involves four steps. The core problem for radiation risk assessment lies in the second step—dose-response evaluation. The key question is simply this: how may one validly extrapolate from the *measured* effects of high doses to the *most probable* effects of low doses? **Figure 6-3** depicts the uncertainty.

At certain high dose levels, enough is known so that effects may be correlated with dose. At such levels (labeled "known response" on **Figure 6-3**), the shape and location of the dose-response curve are known. Uncertainty arises, however, for lower dose levels; for the portion of the graph labeled "area of uncertainty" on **Figure 6-3**, the curve can only be extrapolated. Scientists have suggested four basic shapes for the dose-response curve in this dose range, based on mathematical properties. Although these alternative curves are labeled on **Figure 6-3**, it is not necessary to understand the meaning of all the labels.

Two examples will suffice. If the curve is *linear*, each unit of dose causes precisely the same effect as the preceding and succeeding unit. To use a simplistic example, if one rem of dose to one million individuals causes one cancer, two rems of dose to the same one million indi-

---

[b] The opening reading in this section is based on John-Mark Stensvaag, *Regulating Radioactive Air Emissions from Nuclear Generating Plants: A Primer for Attorneys, Decisionmakers, and Intervenors*, 78 N.W.U. L. Rev. 1, 81-86, 90-99 (1983).

viduals would cause two cancers, and so on. In that event, the dose-response curve would be a straight line proceeding from the intersection of the vertical and horizontal axes. Line *a* on **Figure 6-3** represents such a linear curve. Alternatively, if the dose-response curve is *quadratic*, the effects incurred depend on the square of the dose. To return to our simplistic example, if one million person-rems cause one cancer, two million person-rems would cause four cancers. Each succeeding unit of radiation thus causes far more effects than the preceding one. Line *b* on **Figure 6-3** depicts one possible quadratic curve, assuming a threshold dose below which radiation causes no harm.

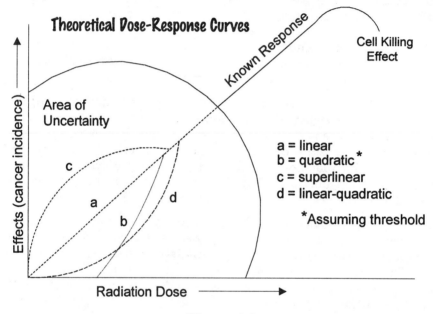

**Figure 6-3**

The significant thing for our purposes is that low doses of radiation cause a great deal more damage if theory *a* is correct than under theory *b*, and even more damage if theory *c* is correct. How do scientists determine *which* theory for extrapolating the effects of low doses is the most valid?

Epidemiological studies of human populations are one tool that scientists use to search for a workable dose-response curve. To conduct an epidemiological study of radiation damage, one must know two things with as much accuracy as possible: the doses incurred by each member of the sample and the cancer incidence within the sample. The single epidemiological study most relied on by the scientists who recommend radiation safety standards has been the study of the incidence of leukemia in atomic bomb survivors at Hiroshima and Nagasaki. At both cities, researchers have spent millions of dollars to calculate doses and incidence, because the unique ranges of dose, the unbiased selection and large size of the sample, and the considerable length of time since exposure make this data probably the most valuable in the field. The dose information for each irradiated individual used in these epidemiological studies was prepared in 1965; this "tentative dose estimate, 1965" (T65D) has served as the equivalent to the "Rosetta stone" in determining the significance of observed cancer incidence.

In 1981, two revelations about T65D stunned the scientific community. One, the recognition by scientists that they had incorrectly calculated the amount of various types of radiation emitted by the Hiroshima and Nagasaki bombs, is too complex to explore here. The other revelation, however, is comprehensible even to lay people. Some methodical scientist noticed in 1981 that the 1965 dose data included many inaccurate assumptions about shielding. For example, when the 1965 researchers were unable to pinpoint the location of each of the many workers within a Mitsubishi steel factory in Nagasaki, they arbitrarily assumed that each worker was irradiated while standing outside. By ignoring the substantial shielding provided by the concrete and steel building, the 1965 dose figures resulted in a much higher than accurate estimate of radiation dose. The people suffering from leukemia had actually been exposed to far less radiation than previously thought.

Because of these discoveries, previous estimates of the dose response curve for low level radiation were blown out of the water. It took considerable time for these revelations to play out in the appropriate scientific circles, but the National Research Council eventually concluded—based primarily on changes in the Hiroshima and Nagasaki exposure data—that "[t]he risk of getting cancer from low levels of radiation appears to be four times as high as previously estimated." Philip J. Hilts, *Higher Cancer Risk Found in Radiation*, N.Y. Times (Dec. 20, 1989) at A22, col. 4. Also in reaction to the atomic bomb study errors, the International Commission on Radiological Protection issued new recommendations for radiation protection limits for workers, suggesting that the dose limit from occupational exposure should be more than halved. *See New Limits Recommended by ICRP*, Nuclear News 89 (Aug. 1990).

### Notes and Questions

1.   Did your eyes glaze over when you read the foregoing materials about radiation dose-response curves, quadratic curves and the like? This type of guesstimate by extrapolation lies at the heart of a great many current environmental standards. Do you think you will be a better environmental attorney if you roll up your sleeves and struggle to understand what is going on here? Or would you rather accept on faith environmental standards established by unexamined actors? How do you suppose your clients would like you to answer these questions?

2.   Somewhere in approximately 1980, a cautious scientist noticed a simple but obscure fact about the work of other scientists in 1965: "For heaven's sake! We've been assuming that all those Mitsubishi workers exposed to the Nagasaki atomic bomb blast were standing out in the open air!" At approximately the same time, another cautious scientist poured

over newly obtained, highly technical information about the specific radiations emitted by the Hiroshima and Nagasaki blasts, discovering that earlier assumptions were erroneous. These two events led to a radical revision of occupational radiation exposure standards, rendering them much more stringent. Do you find it jarring that profound defects in our assessment of the dose-response curve were cured only because of these two "Eureka" moments? Do you suppose that other environmental standards might be similarly flawed? Might existing standards—flawed by defective science—be too lenient *or* too stringent?

## JOHN ATCHESON, THE DEPARTMENT OF RISK REDUCTION OR RISKY BUSINESS

21 Envtl. L. 1375, 1389-90 (1991)

Risk, by its nature is reactive. It must be actively applied to a problem: therefore, one must know a problem exists. * * * In short, we must anticipate a problem in order to decide whether we want to assess it. This presents a kind of ecological Catch-22. Clearly, the range of human activities is too broad, and the sensitivity of our biological and ecological systems too acute to allow a realistic identification of those activities that will prove to be dangerous. * * *

Risk works best when telling us where we ought not to have gone and it can tell us only a little about where we ought not go. It does nothing to inform us as to where we should be heading and what we should be doing.

## MARK ELIOT SHERE, THE MYTH OF MEANINGFUL ENVIRONMENTAL RISK ASSESSMENT

19 Harv. Envtl. L. Rev. 409, 413-17 (1995)

[E]nvironmental risk assessment as currently practiced is anything but scientific, objective, and credible. A typical risk assessment consists of about fifty separate assumptions and extrapolations, each of which may skew the analysis by a factor of ten or more. Taken together, these assumptions and extrapolations can alter the final numeric estimate of risk by a multiple of billions, and this result * * * is unverifiable. As one scholar suggests, it is as if you had no idea whether your wallet contained enough money to pay for a cup of coffee or to pay for the national debt, and no way of finding out. The hard fact is that quantitative risk assessment generates numbers that are meaningless.

The unreliability of risk assessment is an open secret. Commentators have described risk assessment as being "fraught with gaps in knowledge that are filled with guesses and assumptions." Because of these guesses and assumptions, "[w]hile EPA cancer risk estimates appear precise, the final numbers conceal profound scientific uncertainties." Indeed, the "outstanding characteristic" of risk assessment "is chronic and pervasive uncertainty." In this context, the National Academy of Sciences has similarly observed that "[c]onclusions based on a large number of sequential, discretionary choices necessarily entail a large, cumulative uncertainty."

This open secret about risk assessment has not, however, reached the administrative agencies or the courts, which continue to speak in precise terms about the number of lives purportedly "saved" by various regulations. Academic observers and practitioners often make the same mistake, treating risk assessments as if they provide an accurate count of lives at risk. Even when uncertainty is acknowledged, it is almost always treated as a limited, manageable problem that can be resolved through refinements in the risk assessment process. * * *

The implicit premise in these and similar proposals is that risk assessment provides a solid core of information that can be reached if only the surrounding uncertainty were stripped away. This premise is incorrect. As currently practiced, risk assessment is no more than the elaborate quantification of long chains of controversial assumptions. The quantification process could be refined endlessly, and it would not make the starting assumptions any more certain or valid. * * *

[T]he issues concerning risk assessment cut across ideological lines. Indeed, one of the main reasons that risk assessment has become so widely advocated and used is that it potentially offers all things to all people. Depending on the day and the issue, risk assessment has been advocated by liberals or conservatives, environmentalists or industry, and courts or regulators. All of these groups should agree, however, that rational regulation requires tools that provide meaningful information. Quantitative risk assessment is not such a tool.

## SCOTT ADAMS, DILBERT

Apr. 27, 1999
Reprinted by permission of
United Feature Syndicate, Inc.

# Chapter Seven

# PUBLIC TRUST DOCTRINE

## A. INTRODUCTION

The readings in Chapter 7 comprise a series of grand variations on the public trust theme. The first reading is the most significant articulation of the public trust doctrine by the United States Supreme Court.

## B. RESTRAINTS ON ALIENATION

## ILLINOIS CENTRAL RAILROAD CO. v. ILLINOIS

### 146 U.S. 387 (1892)

MR. JUSTICE FIELD delivered the opinion of court.

This suit was commenced on the 1st of March, 1883, in a circuit court of Illinois, by * * * the attorney general of the State, in the name of its people, against the Illinois Central Railroad Company * * * and against the City of Chicago. * * *

The object of the suit is to obtain a judicial determination of the title of certain lands on the * * * lake front of the City of Chicago, * * * which have been reclaimed from the waters of the lake, and are occupied by the tracks, depots, warehouses, piers and other structures used by the railroad company in its business; and also of the title claimed by the company to the submerged lands, constituting the bed of the lake * * * . The determination of the title of the company will involve a consideration of its right to construct, for its own business, as well as for public convenience, wharves, piers, and docks in the harbor. * * *

The case proceeds upon the theory and allegation that the defendant the Illinois Central Railroad Company has, without lawful authority, encroached, and continues to encroach, upon the domain of the State, and its original ownership and control of the waters of the harbor and of the lands thereunder * * * .

The State prays a decree establishing and confirming its title to the bed of Lake Michigan, and exclusive right to develop and improve the harbor of Chicago, * * * against the claim of the railroad company that it has an absolute title to such submerged lands by the Act of 1869, and the right * * * to fill all the bed of the lake * * * for the purpose of its business, and the right, by the construction and maintenance of wharves, docks and piers, to improve the shore of the lake for the promotion generally of commerce and navigation. And the State, insisting that the company has, without right, erected, and proposes to continue to erect, wharves and piers upon its domain, asks that such alleged unlawful structures may be ordered to be removed, and the company be enjoined from erecting further structures of any kind. * * *

[T]he Act [of 1869] declares that all the right and title of the State in and to the submerged lands, constituting the bed of Lake Michigan, and lying east of the tracks and breakwater of the company for the distance of one mile * * * "are granted in fee to the railroad company, its successors and assigns." The grant is accompanied with a proviso that the fee of the lands shall be held by the company in perpetuity, and that it shall not have the power to grant, sell, or convey the fee thereof. * * *

The act, if valid and operative to the extent claimed, placed under the control of the railroad company nearly the whole of the submerged lands of the harbor, subject only to the limitations that it should not authorize obstructions to the harbor, or impair the public right of navigation * * * .

The question, therefore, to be considered, is whether the legislature was competent to thus deprive the State of its ownership of the submerged lands in the harbor of Chicago, and of the consequent control of its waters; or, in other words, whether the railroad corporation can hold the lands and control the waters by the grant, against any future exercise of power over them by the State.

That the State holds the title to the lands under the navigable waters of Lake Michigan, within its limits, in the same manner that the State holds title to soils under tide water, by the common law, we have already shown * * * . But it is a title different in character from that which the State holds in lands intended for sale. * * * It is a title held in trust for the people of the State, that they may enjoy the navigation of the waters, carry on commerce over them, and have liberty of fishing therein, freed from the obstruction or interference of private parties. The interest of the people in the navigation of the waters and in commerce over them may be improved in many instances by the erection of wharves, docks, and piers therein, for which purpose the State may grant parcels of the submerged lands; and, so long as their disposition is made for such purpose, no valid objections can be made to the grants. * * * But that is a very different doctrine from the one which would sanction the abdication of the general control of the State over lands under the navigable waters of an entire harbor or bay, or of a sea or lake. Such abdication is not consistent with the exercise of that trust which requires the government of the State to preserve such waters for the use of the public. * * *

The control of the State for the purposes of the trust can never be lost, except as to such parcels as are used in promoting the interests of the public therein, or can be disposed of without any substantial impairment of the public interest in the lands and waters remaining. It is only by observing the distinction between a grant of such parcels for the improvement of the public interest, or which when occupied do not substantially impair the public interest in the lands and waters remaining, and a grant of the whole property in which the public is interested, that the language of the adjudged cases can be reconciled. * * *

A grant of all the lands under the navigable waters of a State has never been adjudged to be within the legislative power; and any attempted grant of the kind would be held, if not absolutely void on its face, as subject to revocation. The State can no more abdicate its trust over property in which the whole people are interested, like navigable waters and soil under them, so as to leave them entirely under the use and control of private parties, * * * than it can abdicate its police powers in the administration of government and the preservation of the peace. In the administration of government the use of such powers may for a limited period be delegated to a municipality or other body, but there always remains with the State the right to revoke those powers and exercise them in a more direct manner, and one more conformable to its wishes. * * * [Such trusts] cannot be placed entirely beyond the direction and control of the State.

The harbor of Chicago is of immense value to the people of the State of Illinois, * * * and the idea that its legislature can deprive the State of control over its bed and waters, and place the same in the hands of a private corporation, created for a different purpose—one limited to transportation of passengers and freight between distant points and the city—is a proposition that cannot be defended.

The area of the submerged lands proposed to be ceded by the Act in question to the railroad company embraces something more than 1,000 acres * * * . It is as large as that embraced by all the merchandise docks along the Thames at London; is much larger than that included in the famous docks and basins at Liverpool; is twice that of the port of Marseilles, and nearly if not quite equal to the pier area along the water front of the City of New York. And the arrivals and clearings of vessels at the port exceed in number those of New York, and are equal to those of New York and Boston combined. * * * It is hardly conceivable that the legislature can divest the State of the control and management of this harbor, and vest it absolutely in a private corporation. Surely an act of the legislature transferring the title to its submerged lands and the power claimed by the railroad company to a foreign state or nation would be repudiated, without hesitation, as a gross perversion of the trust over the property under which it is held. So would a similar transfer to a corporation of another State. It would not be listened to that the control and management of the harbor of that great city—a subject of concern to the whole people of the State—should thus be placed elsewhere than in the State itself. All the objections which can be urged to such attempted transfer may be urged to a transfer to a private corporation like the railroad company in this case.

Any grant of the kind is necessarily revocable, and the exercise of the trust by which the property was held by the State can be resumed at any time. Undoubtedly there may be expenses incurred in improvements made under such a grant which the State ought to pay; but, be that as it may, the power to resume the trust whenever the State judges best is, we think, incontrovertible. The position advanced by the railroad * * * would place every harbor in the country at the mercy of a majority of the legislature of the State in which the harbor is situated.

### Notes and Questions

1. What does the United States Supreme Court say about the 1869 Illinois statute, which had conveyed property to the railroad? Why?

2. Why does the court refer to the State's relationship to the disputed land as a "trust"? What is that supposed to mean?

3. Does the Supreme Court say that the State's grant of property to the railroad was void? Or does the Court say that the grant was voidable by a subsequent State legislature? Is there a difference?

# C. BASIS FOR
# GOVERNMENT REGULATION

## JUST v. MARINETTE COUNTY

56 Wis.2d 7, 201 N.W.2d 761 (1972)

HALLOWS, CHIEF JUSTICE.

Marinette county's Shoreland Zoning Ordinance, * * * effective October 9, 1967, * * * follows a model ordinance published by the Wisconsin Department of Resource Development * * * . The ordinance was designed to meet standards and criteria for shoreland regulation which the legislature required to be promulgated by the Department * * * . The legislation * * * authorizing the ordinance was enacted as a part of the [Wisconsin] Water Quality Act of 1965 * * * .

Shorelands for the purpose of ordinances are defined * * * as lands within 1,000 feet of the normal high-water elevation of navigable lakes, ponds, or flowages * * * . All county shoreland zoning ordinances must be approved by the Department * * * prior to their becoming effective. * * * If a county does not enact a shoreland zoning ordinance which complies with the state's standards, the Department * * * may enact such an ordinance for the county. * * *

There can be no disagreement over the public purpose sought to be obtained by the ordinance. Its basic purpose is to protect navigable waters and the public rights therein from the degradation and deterioration which results from uncontrolled use and [development] of shorelands. In the [Wisconsin statute], the purpose of the state's shoreland regulation program is stated as being to "aid in the fulfillment of the state's role as trustee of its navigable waters and to promote public health, safety, convenience and general welfare." * * *

The shoreland zoning ordinance divides the shorelands of Marinette county into general purpose districts, general recreation districts, and conservancy districts. A "conservancy" district * * * is defined in * * * the ordinance to include "all shorelands designated as swamps or marshes on the United States Geological Survey maps * * * ." The ordinance provides for permitted uses and conditional uses. One of the conditional uses requiring a permit * * * is the filling, drainage or dredging of wetlands * * * .

In April of 1961, several years prior to the passage of this ordinance, the Justs purchased 36.4 acres of land in the town of Lake along the south shore of Lake Noquebay, a navigable lake in Marinette county. This land had a frontage of 1,266.7 feet on the lake and was purchased partially for personal use and partially for resale. During the years 1964, 1966, and 1967, the Justs made five sales of parcels having frontage and extending back from the lake some 600 feet, leaving the property involved in these suits. * * *

The land owned by the Justs is designated as swamps or marshes on the United States Geological Survey Map and is located within 1,000 feet of the normal high-water elevation of the lake. Thus, the property is included in a conservancy district and * * * classified as "wetlands." Consequently, in order to place more than 500 square feet of fill on this property, the Justs were required to obtain a conditional-use permit from the zoning administrator of the county and pay a fee of $20 or incur a forfeiture of $10 to $200 for each day of violation.

In February and March of 1968, six months after the ordinance became effective, Ronald Just, without securing a conditional-use permit, hauled 1,040 square yards of sand onto this property and filled an area * * * . More than 500 square feet of this fill was upon wetlands located contiguous to the water and which had surface drainage toward the lake. * * * [T]he trial court correctly found a violation [of the ordinance].

The real issue is whether the conservancy district provisions and the wetlands-filling restrictions are unconstitutional because they amount to a constructive taking of the Justs' land without compensation. Marinette county and the state of Wisconsin argue the restrictions of the conservancy district and wetlands provisions constitute a proper exercise of the police power of the state and do not so severely limit the use or depreciate the value of the land as to constitute a taking without compensation.

To state the issue in more meaningful terms, it is a conflict between the public interest in stopping the despoilation of natural resources * * * and an owner's asserted right to use his property as he wishes. The protection of public rights may be accomplished by the exercise of the police power unless the damage to the property owner is too great and amounts to a confiscation. The securing or taking of a benefit not presently enjoyed by the public for its use is obtained by the government through its power of eminent domain. The distinction between the exercise of the police power and condemnation has been said to be a matter of degree of damage to the property owner. * * *

Many years ago, Professor Freund stated in his work on The Police Power, * * * "It may be said that the state takes property by eminent domain because it is useful to the public and under the police power because it is harmful * * * . From this results the difference between the power of eminent domain and the police power, that the former recognizes a right to compensation, while the latter on principle does not." Thus the necessity for monetary compensation for loss suffered to an owner by police power restriction arises when restrictions are placed on property in order to create a public benefit rather than to prevent a public harm. * * *

This case causes us to reexamine the concepts of public benefit in contrast to public harm and the scope of an owner's right to use of his property. In the instant case we have a restriction on the use of a citizens' property, not to secure a benefit for the public, but to prevent a harm from the change in the natural character of the citizens' property. We start with the premise that lakes and rivers in their natural state are unpolluted and the pollution which now exists is man made. The state of Wisconsin under the trust doctrine has a duty to eradicate the present pollution and to prevent further pollution in its navigable waters. This is not, in a legal sense, a gain or a securing of a benefit by the maintaining of the natural *status quo* of the environment. What makes this case different from most condemnation or police power zoning cases is the interrelationship of the wetlands, the swamps and the natural environment of shorelands to the purity of the water and to such natural resources as navigation, fishing, and scenic beauty. Swamps and wetlands were once considered wasteland, undesirable, and not picturesque. But as the people became more sophisticated, an appreciation was acquired that swamps and wetlands serve a vital role in nature, are part of the balance of nature and are essential to the purity of the water in our lakes and streams. * * *

This is not a case where an owner is prevented from using his land for natural and indigenous uses. * * * The shoreland zoning ordinance prevents to some extent the changing of the natural character of the land within 1,000 feet of a navigable lake and 300 feet of a navigable river because of such land's interrelation to the contiguous water. The changing of wetlands and swamps to the damage of the general public by upsetting the natural environment and the natural relationship is not a reasonable use of that land which is protected from police power regulation. * * *

The Justs argue their property has been severely depreciated in value. But this depreciation of value is not based on the use of the land in its natural state but on what the land would be worth if it could be filled and used for the location of a dwelling. * * *

The ordinance does not create or improve the public condition but only preserves nature from the despoilage and harm resulting from the unrestricted activities of humans. * * *

The Judgment * * * dismissing the Justs' action, is modified to set forth declaratory adjudication that the shoreland zoning ordinance of respondent Marinette County is constitutional; that the Justs' property constitutes wetlands and that particularly the prohibition in the ordinance against the filling of wetlands is constitutional; and the judgment, as so modified, is affirmed. * * *

### Notes and Questions

1.  What does the public trust doctrine have to do with *Just v. Marinette County*? Where is the asset protected by the trust? Does the court hold that the wetlands—the land owned by the Justs—are themselves public trust assets?

2.  If the county had passed an ordinance forbidding the direct deposit of garbage in Lake Noquebay, surely that would be upheld as a valid enactment. Is the public trust holding in *Just v. Marinette County* more significant than such a ruling on a garbage ordinance? Why or why not?

## D. CALIFORNIA REDWOODS

In 1968, Congress enacted the Redwood National Park Act, currently codified at 16 U.S.C. §§ 79a-79q. The resulting park in California includes a peculiar "worm-shaped" area extending eight miles south from the main body of the park in a half-mile wide corridor. The purpose of this unusual corridor is to preserve the "Tall Trees Grove," a stand of redwoods including the world's tallest, third tallest, and sixth tallest known surviving trees.

In an excellent article on the California Redwoods controversy, Dale A. Hudson, Sierra Club v. Department of Interior: *The Fight To Preserve The Redwood National Park*, 7 Ecol. L. Q. 781 (1978), the author argues persuasively that the conservation of natural resources such as stands of Redwood trees must be undertaken in terms of whole ecological units. To preserve merely a part of a watershed is essentially futile, because inevitable erosion and flooding will destroy that which has been "preserved."

Redwood Creek in 1975. The Tall Trees Grove is located on the "peninsula" jutting out in the foreground. The land in the foreground had been logged over prior to park establishment. The area in the background had been clear cut since park establishment. Photograph by David Swanlund, 1977. Reprinted by permission of Save-the-Redwoods League.

### Figure 7-1

Figure 7-1, taken from page 806 of the Hudson article, reproduces a photograph of the plight of the world's tallest trees in 1975. The trees were almost surrounded by areas that had been clear-cut. The article does not indicate how old these trees are, but does indicate that Coastal Redwoods commonly reach 700 to 800 years of age and have been known to reach 2,200 years.

### *Problems*

1.   Assume that: (a) the State of California still owns the Tall Trees Grove; (b) the State once owned the adjacent land and timber but conveyed them to private companies; and (c) the adjacent timber has not yet been cut. Could the State invoke the public trust doctrine to preclude the harvesting of adjacent timber? What remedies might the State seek and might a court provide under that doctrine?

2.   Suppose instead that the State of California fails to act under the conditions described in Problem 1. Assuming standing, could a non-governmental plaintiff, such as the Save-the-Redwoods League, invoke the public trust doctrine to minimize the disruption caused by the proposed timber

harvesting? What remedies might the plaintiff seek and might a court provide under that doctrine?

According to the Save-the-Redwoods League, all land in the 1975 photograph has been the subject of an ambitious restoration project. A League representative reported in 1999:

> The Tall Trees Grove, unfortunately, is now so exposed to wind and receives so much debris from erosion upstream that the tops of the trees are almost all dead. In fact, there is a new tallest measured tree, whose location has not yet been made public, because the Libby Tree (the tree in the Tall Trees Grove measured as the tallest tree in 1964) is shorter from the ground to top than it was when first measured.[a]

# E. CUSTOM

## STATE EX REL. THORNTON v. HAY

### 462 P.2d 671 (Oregon 1969)

GOODWIN, JUSTICE.

William and Georgianna Hay, the owners of a tourist facility at Cannon Beach, appeal from a decree which enjoins them from constructing fences or other improvements in the dry-sand area between the sixteen-foot elevation contour line and the ordinary high-tide line of the Pacific Ocean. The issue is whether the state has the power to prevent the defendant landowners from enclosing the dry-sand area contained within the legal description of their ocean-front property. * * *

The land area in dispute will be called the dry-sand area. This will be assumed to be the land lying between the line of mean high tide and the visible line of vegetation. * * * Below, or seaward of, the mean high-tide line, is the state-owned foreshore, or wet-sand area, in which the landowners in this case concede the public's paramount right, and concerning which there is no justiciable controversy. * * *

The trial court found that the public had acquired, over the years, an easement * * * . Because we hold that the trial court correctly found in favor of the state on the rights of the public in the dry-sand area, it follows that the state has an equitable right to protect the public in the enjoyment of those rights by causing the removal of fences and other obstacles. * * *

The dry-sand area in Oregon has been enjoyed by the general public as a recreational adjunct of the wet-sand or foreshore area since the beginning of the state's political history. The first European settlers on these shores found the aboriginal inhabitants using the foreshore for clam-digging and the dry-sand area for their cooking fires. The newcomers continued these customs after statehood. Thus, from the time of

---

[a] Email correspondence from Martha Benioff (Jun. 3, 1999).

the earliest settlement to the present day, the general public has assumed that the dry-sand area was a part of the public beach, and the public has used the dry-sand area for picnics, gathering wood, building warming fires, and generally as a headquarters from which to supervise children or to range out over the foreshore as the tides advance and recede. In the Cannon Beach vicinity, state and local officers have policed the dry sand, and municipal sanitary crews have attempted to keep the area reasonably free from man-made litter.

Perhaps one explanation for the evolution of the custom of the public to use the dry-sand area for recreational purposes is that the area could not be used conveniently by its owners for any other purpose. The dry-sand area is unstable in its seaward boundaries, unsafe during winter storms, and for the most part unfit for the construction of permanent structures. While the vegetation line remains relatively fixed, the western edge of the dry-sand area is subject to dramatic moves eastward or westward in response to erosion and accretion. For example, evidence in the trial below indicated that between April 1966 and August 1967 the seaward edge of the dry-sand area involved in this litigation moved westward 180 feet. * * *

Until very recently, no question concerning the right of the public to enjoy the dry-sand area appears to have been brought before the courts of this state. The public's assumption that the dry-sand as well as the foreshore was "public property" had been reinforced by early judicial decisions. *See Shively v. Bowlby*, 152 U.S. 1 (1894), which affirmed *Bowlby v. Shively*, 22 Or. 410, 30 P.154 (1892). These cases held that landowners claiming under federal patents owned seaward only to the "high-water" line, a line that was then assumed to be the vegetation line.

In 1935, the United States Supreme Court held that a federal patent conveyed title to land farther seaward, to the mean high-tide line. *Borax Consolidated, Ltd. v. Los Angeles*, 296 U.S. 10 (1935). While this decision may have expanded seaward the record ownership of upland landowners, it was apparently little noticed by Oregonians. In any event, the *Borax* decision had no discernible effect on the actual practices of Oregon beachgoers and upland property owners.

Recently, however, the scarcity of ocean-front building sites has attracted substantial private investments in resort facilities. Resort owners like these defendants now desire to reserve for their paying guests the recreational advantages that accrue to the dry-sand portions of their deeded property. * * *

Because many elements of prescription are present in this case, the state has relied upon the doctrine in support of the decree below. We believe, however, that there is a better legal basis for affirming the decree: * * * the English doctrine of custom. Strictly construed, prescription applies only to the specific tract of land before the court, and doubtful prescription cases could fill the courts for years with tract-by-tract litigation. An established custom, on the other hand, can be proven with reference to a larger region. Ocean-front lands from the northern to the southern border of the state ought to be treated uniformly. * * *

Blackstone set out the requisites of a particular custom. * * * [T]he first requirement of a custom * * * is that it must be ancient. It must have been used so long "that the memory of man runneth not to the contrary." * * * [T]he record in the case at bar satisfies the requirement of antiquity. So long as there has been an institutionalized system of land tenure in Oregon, the public has freely exercised the right to use the dry-sand area up and down the Oregon coast * * * .

The second requirement is that the right be exercised without interruption. * * * [T]here was evidence that the public's use and enjoyment of the dry-sand area had never been interrupted by private landowners. Blackstone's third requirement, that the customary use be peaceable and free from dispute, is satisfied by the evidence which related to the second requirement. The fourth requirement, that of reasonableness, is satisfied by the evidence that the public has always made use of the land in a manner appropriate to the land and to the usages of the community. * * * [W]hen inappropriate uses have been detected, municipal police officers have intervened to preserve order. * * *

Finally, a custom must not be repugnant, or inconsistent, with other customs or with other law. The custom under consideration violates no law, and is not repugnant. * * * The custom of the people of Oregon to use the dry-sand area of the beaches for public recreational purposes meets every one of Blackstone's requisites. * * *

[T]he record shows that the custom of the inhabitants of Oregon and of visitors in the state to use the dry-sand as a public recreation area is so notorious that notice of the custom on the part of persons buying land along the shore must be presumed. In the case at bar, the landowners conceded their actual knowledge of the public's long-standing use of the dry-sand area * * * .

Because so much of our law is the product of legislation, we sometimes lose sight of the importance of custom as a source of law in our society. * * * The rule in this case * * * takes from no man anything which he has had a legitimate reason to regard as exclusively his.

## STEVENS v. CITY OF CANNON BEACH

### 114 S.Ct. 1332 (1994)

On Petition For Writ of Certiorari to The Supreme Court of Oregon. The petition for a writ of certiorari is denied.

JUSTICE SCALIA, with whom JUSTICE O'CONNOR joins, dissenting.

This is a suit by owners of a parcel of beachfront property against the City of Cannon Beach and the State of Oregon. Petitioners purchased the property in 1957. In 1989, they sought a building permit for construction of a seawall on the dry-sand portion of the property. When the permit was denied, they brought this inverse condemnation action * * * alleging a taking in violation of the Fifth and Fourteenth Amendments. That court dismissed the complaint for failure to state a claim * * * on the ground that under *State ex rel. Thornton v. Hay* * * * petitioners never possessed the right to obstruct public access to the dry-sand portion of the property. * * * The * * * Supreme Court of Oregon, * * * relying on *Thornton*, affirmed. * * *

The [Oregon Supreme] court * * * framed the issue as the continuing validity of *Thornton* in light of *Lucas v. South Carolina Coastal Council*, 112 S.Ct. 2886 (1992). The court quoted our opinion in *Lucas*: "Any limitation so severe [as to prohibit all economically beneficial use of land] cannot be newly legislated or decreed (without compensation), but *must inhere in the title itself*, in the restrictions that background principles of the State's law of property and nuisance already placed upon land ownership" (emphasis added). * * * The court held that the doctrine of custom was just such a background principle of Oregon property law * * * .

As a general matter, the Constitution leaves the law of real property to the States. But * * * a State may not deny rights protected under the Federal Constitution * * * by invoking nonexistent rules of state substantive law. Our opinion in *Lucas* * * * would be a nullity if anything that a State court chooses to denominate "background law" * * * could eliminate property rights. "[A] State cannot be permitted to defeat the constitutional prohibition against taking property without due process of law by the simple device of asserting retroactively that the property it has taken never existed at all." *Hughes v. Washington*, 389 U.S. 290, 296-297 (1967) (Stewart, J., concurring). * * *

To say that this case raises a serious Fifth Amendment takings issue is an understatement. The issue is serious in the sense that it involves a holding of questionable constitutionality; and it is serious in the sense that the land-grab (if there is one) may run the entire length of the Oregon coast. It is by no means clear that the facts * * * meet the requirements for the English doctrine of custom. * * * Particularly in light of the utter absence of record support for the crucial factual determinations in [*Thornton*], * * * petitioners must be afforded an opportunity to make out their constitutional claim by demonstrating that the asserted custom is pretextual. If we were to find for petitioners on this point, we would not only set right a procedural injustice, but would hasten the clarification of Oregon substantive law that casts a shifting shadow upon federal constitutional rights the length of the State.

## F. TAKINGS

There is a limit to the usefulness of the public trust doctrine as a vehicle for controlling private actors. That limit is enshrined in the "Takings Clause" of the Constitution: "* * * nor shall private property be taken for public use, without just compensation." Amendment V. The *Hay* opinion effectively concluded that the landowners had no property right to be "taken." The *Just* opinion concluded that compensation was unnecessary, because the state was exercising its police power rather than the power of eminent domain; this approach of demarcating a line between the police and eminent domain powers is a central component of land use planning law.

It would be misleading to leave you with the impression that the public trust doctrine provides a magical tool for evading the Takings Clause. Justice Scalia's dissent from the denial of *certiorari* in *Stevens v. City of Cannon Beach* is an ominous indication to the beachcombers of Oregon that the breathtaking sweep of the *Hay* opinion may be vulnerable to the takings argument. Moreover, other Supreme Court pronouncements on the subject, including *Nollan v. California Coastal Commission*, 107 S.Ct. 3141 (1987), and *Dolan v. City of Tigard*, 114 S.Ct. 2309 (1994), are much more protective of landowners' rights than the *Just* and *Hay* opinions.

Distinctions between the exercise of the police power and the exercise of the eminent domain power are surprisingly elusive. Whole books have been written on the subject. One is reminded of ancient world maps; at the point where the world had not yet been charted, such maps might say something like "Here there be monsters." So it is here. We cannot deal effectively with the Takings Clause in this course, but be forewarned that the public trust doctrine is eventually constrained by constitutional principles that are constantly undergoing change.

## G. RECONSIDERING THE PUBLIC TRUST

## WILLIAM D. ARAIZA, DEMOCRACY, DISTRUST, AND THE PUBLIC TRUST

45 U.C.L.A. L. Rev. 385 (1997)

The modern public trust doctrine traces its origins to Byzantine law—specifically, the Justinian Code's statement that "By natural law, these things are common property of all: air, running water, the sea, and with it the shores of the sea." * * * [T]he principle eventually found its way into the codified or customary law of most medieval European legal systems, including England's.

From England, the public trust principle became part of American common law. * * * [T]he unquestionable fountainhead of the American public trust doctrine was the Supreme Court's 1892 decision in *Illinois Central Railroad Co. v. Illinois*. * * * The doctrinal basis for this conclusion is unclear, as the Court's opinion cited no authority for its conclusion. Decades later, the Court described the case as involving merely a matter of Illinois law * * * . [*See Appleby v. City of New York*, 271 U.S. 364, 395 (1926).]

Despite the vagueness of the support for the Court's holding, the *Illinois Central* decision became the basis for state court decisions employing the public trust doctrine. In the decades following *Illinois Central*, a number of courts, especially in Wisconsin and Florida, held that the public enjoyed rights in various types of waterways, which served to limit the legislature's ability to alienate those resources. * * *

The last twenty-five years have witnessed a remarkable renaissance of the public trust doctrine * * * directly attributable to the publication of Joseph Sax's seminal 1970 article[b] calling attention to the doctrine, finding it already reflected in contemporary American law, and lauding its use as a tool for judicial supervision of resource-allocation decisions made by government. Since the publication of Sax's article, many courts have relied on the doctrine to impose limits both on the government's ability to alienate natural resources, and on the government's and private owners' ability to use such resources in ways deemed incompatible with the public trust with which the resource was found to be impressed. * * *

The doctrine, at least in its modern incarnation * * * is designed to respond to the problem of resource-allocation decision making skewed by * * * "perceived imperfections in the legislative and administrative process." * * * Sax identifies two sources of such "imperfect" decisions and suggests carefully tailored judicial remedies. The first * * * is decision making at an inappropriate level of government, resulting in a lack of consideration of important resource-conservation interests. Sax * * * considers the problem to be decision making at too local a level, with the result that the more broadly distributed benefits of conserving a public use of the resource are undervalued relative to the (usually economic) benefits of alienating the resource. A classic example is a local government's decision to allow the development of a wetland that provides benefits (such as flood control and wildlife habitat) for a much broader population. In response to this problem, Sax cites and applauds a line of Wisconsin cases requiring that decisions adversely affecting public trust interests be made at a larger governmental level—for instance, by the state instead of a county or city.

The second process defect Sax discusses is the phenomenon of allocation decisions he characterizes as "low-visibility," such as those made by an administrative agency or by means of a governmental grant of a land title to a private party. According to Sax, the relative invisibility of such decisions means that they do not attract the notoriety necessary to inform and energize the general public, whose interests these decisions may harm. To illustrate the point, Sax relies primarily on a series of Massachusetts cases dealing with decisions by state agencies to transfer control of a public trust resource to either a private party or another governmental agency desiring the resource for a non-public trust use.

---

[b] Joseph L. Sax, *The Public Trust Doctrine in Natural Resource Law: Effective Judicial Intervention*, 68 Mich. L. Rev. 471 (1970).

As with the Wisconsin cases, the Massachusetts courts did not flatly prohibit the proposed action; instead, they required explicit legislative authorization for the agency to make the transfer. Sax explains these cases in process terms, arguing that the requirement of express legislative authorization would put the people's representatives on notice of the public trust implications of such a transfer, with the result that the beneficiaries of the trust—the people—could exert political pressure to safeguard the resource. * * *

There is no question but that the public trust doctrine has blossomed into an important doctrine in natural resource law. Since 1970, courts from at least twenty-five American jurisdictions have embraced some form of the doctrine. Paralleling this widespread recognition has been a broadening of the doctrine to include resources not previously within its scope. The original Byzantine version of the doctrine concerned mainly water-based resources, although it also included air as a common property. Since 1970, however, the doctrine has been invoked to support claims for preservation of any number of natural areas and man-made items, including parks, historical areas, cemeteries, archeological sites and remains, and works of art. While not all of these claims have been accepted, courts are clearly receptive to requests to extend the doctrine beyond its traditional water-related focus. * * *

[T]hree issues [are] prominent in discussions of the public trust doctrine: first, can the doctrine be justified against the charge that it constitutes antidemocratic judicial interference in matters properly left to the political branches of government?; second, can coherent rules be developed regarding the scope of the resources protected by the doctrine?; and third, how should the doctrine be affected by the unquestioned increase in governmental concern for the environment? * * *

## JAMES L. HUFFMAN, A FISH OUT OF WATER: THE PUBLIC TRUST DOCTRINE IN A CONSTITUTIONAL DEMOCRACY

19 Envtl. L. 527 (1989)

### ANTIDEMOCRATIC RESTRAINTS ON ALIENATION

In a democracy, the correct outcome is that which properly functioning democratic institutions prescribe. Unless there is unanimity in a decision, some members of the community will disagree with the substantive outcome, and they may well argue that it is ill-advised and even stupid, but they have no basis to claim that it is incorrect or wrong. It can be incorrect only if the democracy is functioning so that a minority is in control. * * *

It is self-serving to claim that public decisions about resources are particularly important and thus require the courts to impose higher standards on legislators and administrators. Every political interest group can make this claim about the public decisions about which it is concerned. There is no persuasive reason why the conservationists and environmentalists should be able to take a simple doctrine of property law and turn it into a justification for broad-ranging judicial review of legislative and administrative actions. * * * [T]he [public trust] doctrine often permits nondemocratic courts to overrule the decisions of theoretically democratic legislatures. * * *

UNCONSTITUTIONAL BASIS FOR GOVERNMENT
REGULATION WITHOUT COMPENSATION

Perhaps the greatest distortion of the historical purposes of the public trust doctrine is that the doctrine is a source of authority for state regulation. * * * [T]he result is a police power * * * effectively unlimited by ordinary constitutional constraints. * * * The state can * * * evade the due process and takings limits on the police power by extending the reach of the public trust doctrine. * * * The * * * potential for state intrusion upon the private rights of individuals is limited only by the vision of those who would extend the reach of the public trust doctrine. * * *

Professor [Michael] Blumm says that there is no instance in which a state court public trust decision has been held to violate the takings clause. Indeed there are no such decisions, and this is not surprising given the nature of the public trust claim. The wonder of the public trust doctrine is that it evades the takings issue by insisting that the public rights in question predate all private rights. If we call it a public trust right, there can be no claim of superior private rights. That is why the modern expansions of the doctrine are so pernicious. * * *

In the final analysis, Professor Blumm and the many others who would rely exclusively on central planning to allocate scarce natural resources persist in evading and avoiding a basic question that can be asked in every case of impact on private property rights. Why not pay? If property rights are being changed, as Blumm admits they are, and if there is no indirect compensation, as often there is not, the only explanation is that it is expensive to pay and we would rather get our public benefits for nothing. But that is not consistent with the basic premise of constitutional democracy, which is limited democracy. Compensation of frustrated property owners is a small price to pay for the preservation of the liberties that our Constitution is supposed to protect. * * *

## H. CODIFICATION OF THE PUBLIC TRUST

Much public trust law has been hammered out in court opinions. As of 1986, according to Professor Lazarus, "approximately one hundred cases [had] been reported involving the public trust doctrine." Richard J. Lazarus, *Changing Conceptions of Property and Sovereignty in Natural Resources: Questioning the Public Trust Doctrine*, 71 Iowa L. Rev. 631, 644 (1986). Nevertheless, a significant variation on the public trust theme is the trend toward *codification*. Professor Lazarus points out that the modern revival of the trust doctrine "spawned legislation in

Michigan * * * [and] likely influenced the adoption of trust language in several state constitutions." *Id.* at 644 n.77 (1986) (referring to the constitutions of Pennsylvania, Massachusetts and Rhode Island).

# NOTE ON THE MICHIGAN ENVIRONMENTAL PROTECTION ACT

The Michigan Environmental Protection Act of 1970 (MEPA), drafted in large part by Professor Joseph Sax, is a leading example of public trust codification. MEPA was designed to provide a comprehensive cause of action to challenge environmental degradation resulting from both private activities and decisions by government administrators. The key provisions are as follows:

## § 324.1701

(1) The attorney general or any person may maintain an action * * * for declaratory and equitable relief against any person for the protection of the air, water, and other natural resources and the public trust in these resources from pollution, impairment or destruction.

(2) In granting relief provided by subsection (1), if there is a standard for pollution or for an antipollution device or procedure, fixed by rule or otherwise, by the state or an instrumentality, agency, or subdivision of the state, the court may:

(a) Determine the validity, applicability and reasonableness of the standard.

(b) If a court finds a standard to be deficient, direct the adoption of a standard approved and specified by the court.

## § 324.1703

(1) When the plaintiff in the action has made a prima facie showing that the conduct of the defendant has polluted, impaired, or destroyed or is likely to pollute, impair or destroy the air, water or other natural resources or the public trust in these resources, the defendant may rebut the prima facie showing by the submission of evidence to the contrary. The defendant may also show, by way of an affirmative defense, that there is no feasible and prudent alternative to defendant's conduct and that his or her conduct is consistent with the promotion of the public health, safety and welfare in light of the state's paramount concern for the protection of its natural resources from pollution, impairment, or destruction. * * *

## § 324.1704

(1) The court may grant temporary and permanent equitable relief or may impose conditions on the defendant that are required to protect the air, water, and other natural resources or the public trust in these resources from pollution, impairment, or destruction. * * *

## § 324.1705

* * *

(2) In administrative, licensing, or other proceedings, and in any judicial review of such a proceeding, the alleged pollution, impairment, or de-

struction of the air, water, or other natural resources, or the public trust in these resources, shall be determined, and conduct shall not be authorized or approved that has or is likely to have such an if there is a feasible and prudent alternative consistent with the reasonable requirements of the public health, safety, and welfare. * * *

### *Notes and Questions*

1. Is the Michigan Environmental Protection Act open to Huffman's criticism at page 223, *supra*, that the public trust doctrine is antidemocratic? Why or why not?

2. Assume the following facts. The Tanya Tanning Co. has purchased a plot of undeveloped land along the Hidden River in the State of Michigan. It intends to construct a leather tannery at that location. The plant will have capacity to process 1,000 hides per day. The blueprints for the plant are complete and the company plans to break ground within a matter of days. Various pollution control devices have been designed and will be included in the tannery. Nevertheless, it will discharge significant processing wastes to the Hidden River; in addition, it will emit various substances to the air resulting in an unpleasant odor in the immediate vicinity. The "Friends of the Hidden River" is an environmental organization consisting primarily of college students attending school 200 miles away from the proposed plant site. It brings suit under the Michigan Environmental Protection Act to enjoin construction of the tannery.

     a. What must the plaintiff plead in its complaint and show at trial to demonstrate an initial right to an injunction?

     b. What must the defendant tannery show to prevent the issuance of an injunction, once the plaintiff has made out a prima facie case?

     c. What alternatives should the court consider under the statute? Assume that you represent the plaintiff. What alternatives would you insist must be explored by the defendant's evidence?

     d. What relief may the court order under the statute?

3. If you were representing a receptor or potential receptor, which would you prefer: a lawsuit in nuisance or a lawsuit under the Michigan Environmental Protection Act? Why?

## I. PROPERTY RIGHTS BACKLASH

## TIMOTHY EGAN, UNLIKELY ALLIANCES ATTACK PROPERTY RIGHTS MEASURES

### N.Y. Times (May 15, 1995) at A1, col. 4

Rarely does an issue unite an anti-pornography preacher in Mississippi, the cultural elite in New York City and families living in the cozy towns of the Cascade foothills. But the nationwide campaign to expand private property rights, which has been embraced by the new Congress and is under consideration in more than half the state's legislatures, has managed to do just that, creating the most unlikely of allies to oppose the enactment of laws that seemed a sure bet in the opinion polls last fall.

Taken together, a House-passed bill that was a barely noticed provision of the Republicans' Contract With America and an even broader measure that has been proposed in the Senate would require taxpayers to compensate property owners whenever the Government did something that reduced the value of the owners' holdings. Whatever law emerges would arguably affect more people than anything else considered by Congress this session.

The Fifth Amendment to the Constitution already requires "just compensation" for land that is "taken" for public use. But the new proposals would carry the concept of compensation to a level rarely approved by the courts * * * . The move in Congress is aimed largely at environmental laws that restrict development of wetlands or land that is home to endangered species. * * * Representative Tom DeLay of Texas, the Republican whip, calls the bills "an answer to a growing movement of property owners at the grass-roots level who believe their rights are being infringed upon."

But opponents maintain that some of the language in the bills, and [similar] proposals in at least 30 states, is so broad that it amounts to an attempt to rewrite the Fifth Amendment and therefore amend the Constitution on the sly.

The House bill would compensate property owners only for a loss of value resulting from environmental regulation. The Senate bill, and one just passed here in Washington State, would apply to virtually any government regulation and, like the House measure, even to enforcement of regulations already adopted. The Interior Department estimates that the cost resulting from surface-mining regulation alone would be $27 billion.

Opponents everywhere along the political spectrum say these bills could dramatically change American life for the worse. They raise a number of questions: What if a government entity decided that a topless bar could not open next to a church, or that an open-pit mine was not appropriate on farmland with shallow wells, or that the flight path of incoming jets had to be changed? Would acts of government even as routine as these require taxpayers to pay the owners of property that declined in value as a result? Is a commercial seller of assault weapons entitled to payment when Congress bans them, as one gun dealer in California has claimed? Would a motel owner be entitled to compensation if he could prove that complying with the public accommodations provisions of Federal civil rights law had reduced the value of his business, as an owner in Georgia has asserted? * * *

Rev. Donald E. Wildmon, president of the conservative American Family Association in Tupelo, Miss., calls a property rights bill proposed in his state "the porn owners' relief measure." * * * [I]n New Orleans, some people wonder what the French Quarter would look like without property regulation. "These kinds of proposals are terribly dangerous," said Christina Ford, the planning director of the City of New Orleans. "Our powers are mostly persuasive. We try to prevent a city from looking like a fence on a windswept prairie that has collected all the debris thrown at it."

Billed as a boon for small landowners, the property rights movement has stirred even some of them against it. Five years ago, when Steve Mansky found his dream home here in Granite Falls, a small town about 35 miles northeast of Seattle, he thought he was buying himself a respite from the noisy clutter of urban America. Then came a proposal to build the state's largest gravel and sand quarry just a stone's throw from Mr. Mansky's home. If the project is approved, as many as 600 trucks a day will rumble down the valley's narrow main road and around its blind curves. The road, designated a National Scenic Byway, is heavily traveled by tourists venturing into the North Cascades. * * * Should Snohomish County, where Mr. Mansky lives, choose not to change zoning regulations to allow an industrial use like a quarry in Granite Falls, its decision could be viewed by the owners of the property where the quarry would be located as a government taking that required full compensation, Mr. Mansky said.

### Note on H.R. 925 and S. 605

The House of Representatives overwhelmingly passed H.R. 925, a proposed "Private Property Protection Act," on March 3, 1995, in connection with its approval of H.R. 9, discussed at pages 105-08, *supra*. The bill would have provided that the federal government must compensate "an owner of property whose use of *any portion* of that property has been limited by an agency action * * * that diminishes the fair market value *of that portion* by 20 percent or more." H.R. 925 § 3(a) (emphasis added). Its Senate counterpart—S. 605, introduced by former Senate Majority Leader Robert Dole—never made it to a floor vote:

> S. 605 * * * was even more extreme than the takings language passed by the House * * * . Dole's bill would have required taxpayers to compensate business for lost profits, as well as land restrictions, resulting from health and safety regulations. * * * [It would have required] the government to pay companies to obey health and safety laws.

Sharon Buccino, *Turmoil Over "Takings: How H.R. 1534 Turns Local Land Use Disputes into Federal Cases,"* 28 Envtl. L. Rep. 10083 (1998).

H.R. 925 and S. 605 were crafted to overturn Supreme Court precedent on the takings issue:

> The House and Senate takings bills would have required payments when there is: (1) a specific diminution in the value of (2) any affected portion of property. Yale Law Professor Carol Rose testified that by focusing only on the "affected portion" of the property "any diminution can be manipulated to become a 100% diminution. This effectively means that virtually any regulation with *any* adverse impact on an owner's parcel could become an occasion for compensation, without re-

gard to the owner's expectations and whether they were reasonable." * * *

In 1993, the Supreme Court unanimously reaffirmed the Court's longstanding rejection of these two major premises of the House and Senate bills:

> [Y]ears ago * * * we held that a claimant's parcel of property could not first be divided into what was taken and what was left for the purpose of demonstrating the taking of the former to be complete and hence compensable. * * * [O]ur cases have long established that mere diminution in the value of property, however serious, is insufficient to demonstrate a taking.

*Concrete Pipe & Products v. Construction Laborers Pension Trust*, 113 S.Ct. 2264, 2290-91 (1993). As more than 370 law professors wrote in a May 2, 1996 letter to Congress regarding the takings bills: "Not only has the [Supreme] Court never adopted that radical view of the Fifth Amendment; no single past or present Justice on the Court has."

Glenn P. Sugameli, *Takings Bills Would Harm People and Property*, 5 Envtl. Law at Maryland 4 (Winter 1997).

Sponsors of federal takings legislation have remained persistent, as indicated by the following article.

## JOHN H. CUSHMAN, JR., SENATE HALTS PROPERTY BILL BACKED BY G.O.P.

N.Y. Times (Jul. 14, 1998) at A13, col. 4

Blocking a conservative drive to make it easier for developers to challenge zoning and environmental laws in Federal courts, the Senate today effectively killed a property rights bill supported by Republican leaders. By a vote of 52 to 42, with the leadership falling well short of the 60 needed to prevent a filibuster, the Senate refused to limit debate on the measure, and signaled that the legislation could probably not survive this Congress. Similar legislation passed the House last year by a wide margin, but even if the Senate had concurred, the proposal faced a Presidential veto. * * *

The bill, favored by home builders and agricultural groups but opposed by environmental advocates and local governments, would broaden the powers of two specialized courts, the Court of Federal Claims and the Court of Appeals for the Federal Circuit in Washington, to review Federal, state and local restrictions on how property may be used. * * * The bill would allow developers to move swiftly to challenge state and local zoning rules in the Federal courts, overturning a legal doctrine that allows Federal courts to defer to state courts on many such issues and making Federal claims ripe for review even before local challenges are exhausted. While conservatives in Congress have offered property rights proposals before, this attempt was unusual because it would have affected state and local regulations as well as Federal rules.

The legislation has been opposed by the national organizations that represent state governors, state legislators, mayors and county officials.

Senator John H. Chafee of Rhode Island, a leading Republican environmentalist, called it "strange to me that this is being brought up by Republicans, who are always concerned about activist Federal judges. This puts everything in the lap of activist Federal judges."

But supporters argued that the constitutional rights of property owners were at stake. "We all know that every day in America, private property is being taken without just compensation," said Senator Phil Gramm, a Republican of Texas. "We all know in the name of endangered species, in the name of wetlands, in the name of numerous other public purposes, that private property is being trampled on."

Kathryn Hohmann, a lobbyist for the Sierra Club, who was working the phones right up to the vote, said: "This is a very difficult vote for moderate Republicans. These are the wedge issues in America, the giant hog farms, the incinerators in local communities. I don't understand why [Senate Majority Leader] Trent Lott is making moderate Republicans walk that plank."

---

Property rights advocates have been active on both federal and state levels. The following reading summarizes state developments through 1996.

### SHARON BUCCINO, TURMOIL OVER "TAKINGS": HOW H.R. 1534 TURNS LOCAL LAND USE DISPUTES INTO FEDERAL CASES

28 Envtl. L. Rep. 10083, 10086-87 (1998)

Several states * * * have approved new laws giving residents greater opportunities for compensation under state law than is available under federal law. As of 1996, 20 states had enacted takings legislation in the previous five years. Some are compensation bills * * * that require taxpayer funded payments to those who claim that certain laws restrict their property use. Others are assessment bills that generally require local governments to conduct complex and expensive studies to predetermine how their programs might affect property owners throughout the state.

State laws that provide expanded rights to compensation will have a more dramatic effect on environmental protection than assessment statutes. These statutes define what constitutes a taking generally by identifying a percentage decrease in property value that triggers compensation. While the Supreme Court has traditionally required the loss of all economically viable use, legislation has been introduced in several states that requires compensation when government action results in any diminished value.[47] None of these extreme bills has been enacted into law.

Nevertheless, as of last year, four states [Florida, Louisiana, Mississippi, and Texas] have enacted some kind of compensation bill. These statutes would find a taking for diminution in property value ranging from 20 percent to 40 percent. The most rigorous takings bill to date was enacted by Texas in 1995. That law provides that a taking occurs when government action reduces the value of property by 25 percent or more. The statute applies to government action that affects private property "in whole or in part or temporarily or permanently." It also requires state agencies to write "taking impact assessments" for almost any rule that might affect property interests.

## J. LEGISLATIVE TAKING BY SHIELDING POLLUTERS

The "property rights movement" seeks to define many environmental, safety, and health regulations as "takings," requiring just compensation. Is there a mirror image to this movement? Might a government's *failure* to regulate or condemn polluting behavior sometimes rise to the level of a taking?

In 1982, the Iowa legislature enacted a statute designed to further agricultural development by shielding certain agricultural activities from nuisance suits. The statute was especially helpful to the newly emerging technology of massive hog factories, which give off such powerful odors that even life-long farmers assert that the factories make them ill. *See* Frank Santiago, *Hog Lots Lose Lawsuit Protection*, Des Moines Register (Sep. 24, 1998) at 1. The Iowa Supreme Court addressed a novel challenge to the statute in the following case.

## BORMANN v. BOARD OF SUPERVISORS

584 N.W.2d 309 (Iowa 1998) (en banc)

LAVORATO, JUSTICE.

In this appeal we are asked to decide whether a statutory immunity from nuisance suits results in a taking of private property for public use without just compensation in violation of federal and Iowa constitutional provisions. We think it does. We therefore reverse a district court ruling holding otherwise and remand. * * *

In September 1994, Gerald and Joan Girres applied to the Kossuth County Board of Supervisors for establishment of an "agricultural area" that would include land they owned as well as property owned by [several neighbors] * * * . *See* Iowa Code § 352.6 (1993). The real property involved consisted of 960 acres. * * * The Board [eventually] approved

---

[47] The Washington state legislature, for example, passed a bill that required payment for any diminution in value. * * * This bill was subsequently rejected by popular statewide referendum.

the agricultural area designation by a 3-2 vote * * * . In April 1995, several neighbors of the new agricultural area filed [an] * * * action in district court. * * *

The Board's approval of the agricultural area here triggered the provisions of Iowa Code section 352.11(1)(a). More specifically, the approval gave the applicants immunity from nuisance suits. The neighbors contend that the approval with the attendant nuisance immunity results in a taking of private property without the payment of just compensation in violation of federal and state constitutional provisions.

The neighbors concede, as they must, that their challenge to section 352.11(1)(a) is a facial one because the neighbors have presented neither allegations nor proof of nuisance. * * *

Iowa Code section 352.11(1)(a) provides the immunity from nuisance suits:

> A farm or farm operation located in an agricultural area shall not be found to be a nuisance regardless of the established date of operation or expansion of the agricultural activities of the farm or farm operation. * * *

The immunity does not apply to a nuisance resulting from a violation of a federal statute, regulation, state statute, or rule. Iowa Code § 352.11(1)(b). Nor does the immunity apply to a nuisance resulting from the negligent operation of the farm or farm operation. *Id.* * * *

[T]he federal and state constitutional provisions * * * provide the following framework for a "takings" analysis: (1) Is there a constitutionally protected private property interest at stake? (2) Has this private property interest been "taken" by the government for public use? and (3) If the protected property interest has been taken, has just compensation been paid to the owner? * * *

State law determines what constitutes a property right. * * * Thus, in this case, Iowa law defines what is property. The property interest at stake here is that of an easement, which is an interest in land. Over one hundred years ago, this court held that the right to maintain a nuisance is an easement. * * *

[T]he nuisance immunity provision in section 352.11(1)(a) creates an easement in the property affected by the nuisance * * * in favor of the applicants' land * * * . This is because the immunity allows the applicants to do acts on their own land which, were it not for the easement, would constitute a nuisance. For example, in their farming operations the applicants would be allowed to generate "offensive smells" on their property which without the easement would permit affected property owners to sue the applicants for nuisances. * * * Easements are property interests subject to the just compensation requirements of the Fifth Amendment to the Federal Constitution * * * [and] of our own Constitution. * * *

[T]he state cannot regulate property so as to insulate the users from potential private nuisance claims without providing just compensation to persons injured by the nuisance. * * * In enacting section 352.11(1)(a), the legislature has exceeded its authority * * * by authorizing the use of property in such a way as to infringe on the rights of others by allowing the creation of a nuisance without the payment of just compensation. * * *

Here the neighbors seek no compensation. Rather, they seek only invalidation of that portion of section 352.11(1)(a) that provides immunity against nuisance suits. We therefore need not concern ourselves with damages for any temporary taking. Accordingly, we hold unconstitutional and invalidate that portion of section 352.11(1)(a) that provides for immunity against nuisance suits. * * *

We reverse and remand for an order declaring that portion of Iowa Code section 352.11(1)(a) that provides for immunity against nuisances unconstitutional and without any force or effect.

We reach this holding with a full recognition of the deference we owe to the General Assembly. * * * [W]ith all respect, this is not a close case. When all the varnish is removed, the challenged statutory scheme amounts to a commandeering of valuable property rights without compensating the owners, and sacrificing those rights for the economic advantage of a few. In short, it appropriates valuable private property interests and awards them to strangers. * * *

We recognize that political and economic fallout from our holding will be substantial. But we are convinced our responsibility is clear because the challenged scheme is plainly—we think flagrantly—unconstitutional.

### Question

Assume that Polluter has been subject—for the past fifteen years—to a particulate emission standard of 30 pounds per hour, under a lawful regulation promulgated pursuant to a state statute. Polluter has consistently complied with this law. After intense lobbying by Polluter, the state legislature enacts a statute specifying that Polluter may emit 90 pounds of particulates per hour. Receptor, who lives nearby, is now subject to much more obnoxious air pollution. Has the legislature engaged in a taking without compensation of the Receptor's right to be protected by the former 30 pound per hour limit? Why or why not?

# Part Three

## ENVIRONMENTAL LEGISLATION

# Chapter Eight

## STANDARD SETTING: A CASE STUDY

### A. INTRODUCTION

We are now ready to move beyond the role of the courts to an analysis of modern pollution control legislation and its implementation by administrative agencies. In doing so, we will focus primarily on the Clean Air Act.

Before turning to that statute, however, Chapter 8 provides an important detour into the topic of standard setting. The detour is valuable for two reasons. First, standard setting lies at the core of much modern environmental law and is especially central to most pollution control regimes. A lawyer who understands the policy choices inherent in the standard setting process will not be afraid to participate in that process, will not be cowed by scientific experts and engineers, and will not shrink from probing into the true significance of a given standard. An attorney who has not struggled with these issues may incorrectly accept a defective or questionable standard as inevitable and unassailable.

Second, the Chapter 8 standard setting detour provides a vital opportunity to provide a coherent overview of a single pollution problem. Readings in most environmental law casebooks—including this one—typically hop from pollutant (e.g., fluorides) to pollutant (e.g., hydrogen sulfide) and from source (e.g., coal mining gob piles) to source (e.g., cement plants). This disjointedness is unfortunate, because students are robbed of fundamental insights that can be developed only by exploring one pollution problem in depth.

Chapter 8 presents a case study in standard setting for a single category of emission sources (nuclear generating plants) and a single class of pollutants (radioactive air emissions).[1] "Case study" means an intensive, thorough examination of: (1) the technical nature of the pollution problem; (2) the technological options for its control; (3) the policy choices to be made in establishing standards; (4) the content and mean-

---

[1] The Chapter 8 case study has been adapted from John-Mark Stensvaag, *Regulating Radioactive Air Emissions from Nuclear Generating Plants: A Primer for Attorneys, Decisionmakers, and Intervenors*, 78 Nw.U.L.Rev. 1 (1983).

ing of specific standards; and (5) prospects for measuring compliance with specific standards. Such intensive scrutiny draws on many extra-legal disciplines.

Do not be intimidated by the readings. Even highly technical scientific matters can be understood by lay persons if broken down into their constituent parts and explained in plain language. If you wish to master environmental law, you must confront complexity.

Although our case study is directed to a single problem, you will miss the point if you focus solely on the intricate details of the radioactive air emission standards. Instead, you should reflect on the aspects of this study that are transferrable to all types of standard setting. Most importantly, your eyes should be opened to the staggering range of choices available to pollution decisionmakers.

## B. SETTING FOR THE CASE STUDY

Nuclear generating plants were first authorized by the 1954 Atomic Energy Act, a statute that said nothing about pollution control. Starting in the 1960s, state and local governments sought to regulate radioactive pollution from such facilities, only to be rebuffed by Supreme Court rulings that the federal government had preempted the field.

In 1977, the federal Clean Air Act was amended to authorize state and local regulation of radioactive air pollution from nuclear generating plants. Imagine that you are a lawyer on the Attorney General's staff of a state in which there are two nuclear generating plants. The time is 1982, because that is when the research underlying this case study was compiled into a law review article. The Attorney General has asked you to examine the problem of routine radioactive air emissions at these facilities, to consider the adequacy of federal standards, and to fashion your recommendations for state pollution control standards.

This is a daunting challenge. You've met with experts at the state's pollution control agency, and you've read a lot of materials. The following pages summarize what you've learned so far.

## C. TECHNICAL BACKGROUND

The contamination of the environment by radioactive air pollutants at nuclear generating plants involves a complex chain of events: (1) the creation of radioactive substances within the reactor; (2) the movement of those substances from the reactor to other areas of the generating plant; (3) the treatment, if any, of the substances within the plant; (4) their release to the atmosphere; (5) the atmospheric, environmental, and metabolic transport of the substances; and (6) their eventual impacts on human beings.

At first, you hoped to gloss over these technical details. But this would amount to surrender before you even started the project. You are now convinced that a rudimentary grasp of the life cycle of radioactive pollution is essential to understanding the options for standard setting.

## 1. BASIC SCIENTIFIC CONCEPTS

When you were a law student, you asked your teacher, "how much science does an environmental lawyer need to know"? The answer was something like "the more the better." You now believe that you are a good lawyer, in part, because you recognize what you do and do not know, relying on experts to educate you and bring you up to speed. Even once you have been educated, you continue to consult with experts whenever you are out of your depth—which is often. Here's what your notes say about the basic science of radiation physics.

### ATOMS

The nucleus of every atom contains one or more positively charged protons and (with the exception of the ordinary hydrogen atom) one or more neutrons, which bear no electrical charge. The number of protons in a given atom is called its *atomic number*; each atomic number denotes a different *element* in the periodic table. For example, hydrogen, with an atomic number of one, has one proton; carbon, with an atomic number of six, has six protons; and uranium, with an atomic number of 92, has 92 protons. When scientists talk about specific atoms they frequently call them *nuclides*.

### INSTABILITY

Instability in an atom is a key to radioactivity. An index of an atom's stability may be found in the number of neutrons in its nucleus. The sum of the protons and neutrons in any given atom yields its mass number or *atomic weight*. For example, most naturally occurring hydrogen has an atomic weight of one, denoting a nucleus consisting of one proton and no neutrons; similarly, most naturally occurring carbon has an atomic weight of 12, with a nucleus consisting of six protons and six neutrons. These familiar elements are stable nuclei: their atomic structure does not spontaneously change over time.

Even such common, relatively light elements as hydrogen and carbon, however, can have different *isotopes*—atoms with the same number of protons but with different numbers of neutrons. One isotope of carbon, for example, has seven neutrons instead of the usual six, yielding an atomic weight of 13. The common practice is to identify the isotope of an element by declaring both the name of the element and its atomic weight: for example, "carbon-13."

Approximately 279 nuclides are known to be stable. However, there are some 5,000 nuclides with neutron/proton ratios—either too low or too high—that are unable to assure stability in the nucleus. These atoms are radioactive and will eventually go through a spontaneous change, or disintegration, to move toward a more stable state, giving off radiation in the process. At the lower end of the periodic table, a neutron/proton ratio of 1:1 brings stability. As one moves up the periodic table to the heavier elements, however, more and more neutrons are necessary to form a stable nucleus, eventually representing a neutron/proton ratio of 16:1.

When one reaches the massive elements at the higher end of the periodic table, all elements in their natural state are unstable and, therefore, radioactive. The uranium-235 atoms used in nuclear reactor fuel in the United States have massive nuclei which are so unstable that they are "fissile": they will break apart ("fission") into fragments when bombarded with neutrons under the proper conditions.

## RADIOACTIVITY

To say that an atom is radioactive—a *radio*nuclide or a *radio*isotope of a given element—is to describe a condition of instability that will eventually lead to a spontaneous change in the structure of the nucleus (disintegration) and an emission of radiation in the form of subatomic particles or electromagnetic energy. Such an atom is stabilizing. When disintegration occurs, the radiation emitted by the parent atom may be of three types: an alpha particle, a beta particle, or a gamma ray.

## RADIATION

An *alpha particle* is an ordinary helium atom stripped of its orbital electrons—a bare nucleus of two protons and two neutrons. It is a massive, positively-charged particle, readily stopped by a few sheets of paper. It shouldn't take much to shield someone from alpha particles. But if such particles were emitted in your body (for example, in your lungs) that would be very bad news.

A *beta particle* has a very light mass and a negative charge, each of which is equal in magnitude to that of an electron. The energy of beta particles and their penetrating power, varies from nuclide to nuclide.

*Gamma rays* are not particles but rather are electromagnetic energy being transferred through space; they have wave properties similar to those of visible light or ultraviolet radiation, yet they have sufficient energy to initiate ionization of atoms in their paths. These highly penetrating rays are essentially identical to X rays.

Each type of radiation emissions generates unsettling effects on atoms and molecules that it encounters. Because you are trying to organize your notes according to the chronological life cycle of radioactive air pollutants, your notes about radiation's effects are set forth later in this summary.

## DECAY SEQUENCES

Some radionuclides decay directly into stable nuclides (for example, carbon-14 to nitrogen-14). Others go through a predictable decay chain or radioactive series of successive radioactive daughter products before finally reaching a stable end product (for example, radium-226 goes through ten successive daughter products, ending in stable lead-206). Accordingly, the radionuclide composition of various mixtures of radioactive substances (for example, in the reactor core or in the environment) changes dramatically with the passage of time.

This is a strange but important aspect of radioactive material. For example, if you measure a container of polluted air at one time, you will find certain amounts of radionuclide A, certain amounts of B, and so forth. But if you measure exactly the same container at a later time, it will have different amounts of each radionuclide and will even have some new ones, all because of radioactive decay. This phenomenon will complicate standard setting.

### MEASURING RADIOACTIVITY

The *curie* is a measure of the quantity of radioactivity present in a material. This quantity is measured, not by the number of radioactive nuclei contained therein, but by the number of nuclei which disintegrate in unit time. One curie of radioactivity is an amount of any radioactive material that produces 37 billion disintegrations per second (an arbitrary number based on the approximate rate of decay of one gram of radium). The curie is such a large amount of radioactivity that fractions of the unit are necessary. Standard prefixes are used to denote such fractions: milli- (one one-thousandth); micro- (one one-millionth); nano- (one one-billionth); and pico- (one one-trillionth). One pico-curie is any quantity of radioactive material undergoing 2.22 disintegrations per minute.

### HALF-LIVES

Different radionuclides decay at vastly different, predictable, rates. These rates are expressed in terms of half-lives. A half-life is the time it takes for one-half of the atoms in a given quantity of the substance to decay. For example, the half-life of iodine-131 is roughly eight days. A mass of material containing one curie of iodine-131 would contain only one-half curie of iodine-131 after eight days, one-fourth curie after 16 days, and so on. By contrast, because carbon-14 has a half-life of approximately 5,730 years, a mass of material containing one curie of carbon-14 today will still contain almost one curie of that radionuclide 100 years from now. The radioactive elements in reactor cores have half-lives ranging from fractions of a second to millions of years and more.

## 2. RADIOACTIVE WASTE GENERATION

If you're going to propose meaningful radioactive air emission standards, you should understand how the radionuclides that are escaping into the environment were first created at the nuclear generating plant. After all, the easiest way to control a pollutant is often to avoid creating it in the first place. Here are your notes on that topic.

### NUCLEAR FUEL

The fuel in a commercial nuclear generating plant typically consists of millions of cylindrical ceramic pellets of molded uranium oxide, each approximately one inch long and less than one-half inch in diameter.

You could hold them between your thumb and index finger. The pellets are stacked end on end and enclosed inside fuel rods, which are thin metal tubes approximately twelve feet long. The metal fuel rod shell, called the cladding, is usually a zirconium alloy. Large numbers of fuel rods are bundled together by hardware to form fuel assemblies, in a configuration that allows cooling water to flow between the rods. **Figure 8-1** depicts a typical fuel rod and fuel assembly. Several hundred fuel assemblies, weighing more than 100 tons, are placed together inside a reactor vessel to form the reactor core.

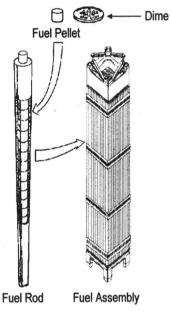

**Figure 8-1[2]**

### FISSION

In an operating reactor, a carefully controlled fission chain reaction is allowed to take place. Uranium-235 oxide atoms are bombarded with neutrons and split, or fissioned, into two—or, very rarely, three—atoms, or fission fragments, giving off two to three new neutrons in the process to sustain the reaction. The sum of the masses of the resulting fission fragments and free neutrons is less than the mass of the original uranium atom; the difference in mass is released as energy—primarily heat. This heat is removed by a cooling medium (water) and eventually harnessed to turn a turbine attached to an electric generator.

### FISSION PRODUCTS AND TRANSURANICS

During this fission process, hundreds of radioactive nuclides are produced within the fuel rods, many of them with the potential to become radioactive air emissions. By far the largest quantities of radio-

---

[2] Joseph Gonyeau P.E., Virtual Nuclear Tourist (1999).

active substances produced are the *fission products*—the fragments of the original uranium-235 atoms and the radioactive decay products of those fragments. More than 200 isotopes of nearly thirty-five elements result from the fission process, and almost all of them are radioactive. Because of the various decay sequences, more than 300 different radionuclides are present in the fission products after a short time.

The most significant fission products for purposes of radioactive air emission controls are tritium (a radioactive isotope of hydrogen); radioactive isotopes of xenon, argon, and krypton (called noble gases because of their chemical inertness); bromine and iodine (both of which are halogens on the periodic table); and cesium, strontium, ruthenium, tellurium, technetium, and barium. Virtually all, if not all, fission fragments are characterized by beta decay; a large proportion of the fission products also emit gamma radiation.

In addition to these fission products, *transuranic* radionuclides are formed when nonfissile uranium-238 in the fuel rods captures neutrons without fissioning, creating plutonium-239 and even heavier elements, such as neptunium, americium, and curium. They are called transuranics because they have higher atomic numbers on the period table than uranium. Virtually all transuranics are alpha particle emitters.

In addition to the fission products and the transuranics, the fission process also produces something called "activation products," but these materials are dealt with later in this summary of your notes.

## 3.   MIGRATION OF WASTES WITHIN THE FACILITY

Your expert has convinced you that you'll never be able to figure out where and how to regulate radioactive air emissions until you understand how the radioactive materials at nuclear generating plants end up getting into the environment. That makes sense to you, so you've taken notes on that topic.

### ESCAPE TO THE COOLANT

The largest quantities of fission products and transuranic element wastes are contained within the fuel rods. One purpose of the fuel rod cladding is to retain these radioactive substances and prevent their release into the environment. If the cladding worked perfectly, so that none of these radionuclides escaped from the fuel rods, there would be virtually no fission products or transuranic elements released to the environment from the nuclear generating plant. Under these circumstances, the only time when these radionuclides could be released would be at the point of ultimate disposal of the "spent" fuel

The cladding does not perform perfectly. Despite precautions, small numbers of fuel rods develop tiny pinhole leaks or hairline cracks. Some fission products and transuranic elements escape through the cladding, migrating to the "primary coolant"—the cooling water that comes into direct contact with the fuel rods. The contamination of the cooling water by the fission products and transuranic elements is the first step in their release to the environment and by far the most significant event in the transport of these nuclides from the core to the atmosphere.

### TRAMP URANIUM AND ACTIVATION PRODUCTS

Even if the cladding did retain perfectly all of the fission products and transuranic elements generated within the fuel rods, two phenomena guarantee that potential radioactive air emissions from nuclear generating plants would still exist. First, tiny specks of uranium dust adhere to the outside of the cladding during fuel fabrication and may remain on the cladding if improperly cleaned. Once these "tramp" uranium particles are transformed into fission products and transuranic elements, they float freely in the cooling water.

Second, the fission process creates an additional type of radionuclides—*activation products*—many of which, unlike fission products and transuranic elements, do not originate within the fuel rods. In activation, a neutron is captured by a nucleus, creating a (frequently unstable) compound nucleus that is an isotope of the original atom. Radioactive activation products may be generated in the fuel cladding and related hardware, in the ambient air in the immediate vicinity of the reactor, in the cooling water, and in chemical additives and corrosion products in the cooling water. No matter how effective the cladding, these activation products will inevitably build up in the primary coolant.

The various structural materials in the primary loop—pumps, valves, piping, the reactor vessel, and the like—corrode and erode under operating conditions, creating fine particulates, known as "crud." From 40 to 200 pounds of crud must be removed from the coolant system annually and much of it has become radioactive through the process of activation.

Variations in reactor design, structural components, chemical additives, and operating procedures may significantly affect the types and quantities of crud and the types and quantities of activation products produced at a nuclear generating plant. In particular, scrupulous adherence to good housekeeping practices in maintaining the purity of the coolant may reduce substantially the creation of these radionuclides.

At this point in your notes, you have developed one of your first insights into the whole problem of radioactive air pollution from nuclear generating plants. Here it is. Two factors seem critical in determining the total quantity of radioactivity that a nuclear generating plant's pollution control system must treat: (1) the integrity of the fuel cladding; and (2) the purity of the reactor cooling water.

### CHEMISTRY

After struggling with physics, it turns out that you need more science: chemistry. Up to this point in your analysis, you've been concerned only with the *nuclear* properties of radionuclides—that is, with the structure and behavior of their nuclei. When you examine the transport of radionuclides from one location to another, however—migration within a nuclear generating plant, in the environment, or in the human body—you must deal with characteristics that are controlled by *chemical* properties of the nuclides.

Chemical properties—the properties that determine how atoms relate to other atoms—are governed by the extra-nuclear electron fields of each atom, rather than by their nuclear composition. The orbits of extra-nuclear electrons are arranged in shells. The outermost shell, which is frequently incomplete, holds the "valence" electrons and determines the chemical properties of the atom. The shell structure also accounts for the periodic regularity of chemical properties depicted by the periodic table of the elements. For example, the noble gases share a common chemical property of relative inertness because the outermost electron shell for each of these elements is complete.

Although chemical behavior is a function of extra-nuclear atomic structure, one aspect of nuclear composition—the number of protons in the nucleus—is a talisman of chemical behavior. Because an atom in its normal state is electrically neutral, which means that it has the same number of electrons as protons, the atomic number (or the number of protons) tells us the number of electrons in the atom. It follows that, because the atomic number of all isotopes of a single element is identical, the electron fields and chemical properties of such isotopes are also identical. Thus, despite their different atomic weights, all isotopes of a single element (for example, carbon-12, carbon-13, and carbon-14) are chemically indistinguishable. In other words, each behaves in the same manner as the other isotopes in its interactions with other atoms. For purposes of modeling the transport of fission products and transuranic elements, we have, then, an enormously simplifying factor: even though we must deal with more than 300 different isotopes, we need confront the chemical behavior of only a few dozen elements.

### THE IMPORTANCE OF MOLECULAR FORM

Unfortunately, this simplifying aspect is more than outweighed by a complicating factor: the aggregation of individual atoms into a wide variety of molecular compounds. Through interactions between their valence electrons, groups of atoms join together to form molecules with totally new chemical properties, submerging the chemical characteristics of the individual atoms. To use a familiar example, the molecular compound $H_2O$ (water) has chemical properties entirely different from either of its individual elements and, indeed, different from the chemical behavior of any element on the periodic table. Literally billions of different kinds of molecules can exist at the temperatures typical of our planet's surface. This is an enormously confounding variable for one who attempts to trace the movement of radionuclides within the facility, in the environment, and within the human body.

Fission products, transuranic elements, and activation products may join with various other elements in the reactor core, in cooling water, and in the environment to create a wide array of molecular compounds. Some of the radioactive fission products and transuranic elements that escape to the coolant are in solid molecular form; they tend to stay in the water, from which they eventually are removed by demineralizers. Other escaping radionuclides are more volatile, tending to diffuse into the atmosphere. Escape or removal of these more volatile radionuclides from the primary coolant occurs in various ways, depending on the type of reactor involved, but such escape or removal is inevitable.

### ESCAPE OR REMOVAL FROM THE COOLANT

The gases and corrosion products that build up within the primary coolant must be removed periodically or the system will not operate properly. The process of removing gases and crud sends the more volatile radionuclides into various airstreams within the plant. The mechanisms by which this transfer occurs differ, depending on whether the reactor is a boiling water reactor (BWR) or a pressurized water reactor (PWR). Approximately two-thirds of the nation's commercial generating plants are PWRs; the rest are BWRs.

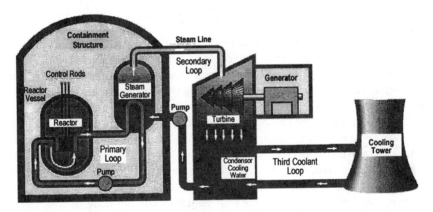

Figure 8-2[3]

Your expert tells you that all nuclear generating plants in your state have the PWR design, so you won't have to learn about BWRs. It does seem clear, though, that you won't be able to make intelligent recommendations about pollution control standards unless you understand enough about PWR design so that you can grasp how these radionuclides are getting into the atmosphere.

### PWR DESIGN

**Figure 8-2** is a diagram of a typical PWR. In a PWR, the primary coolant is contained in a sealed system somewhat like an air conditioning refrigerant, under pressures of up to 2,250 pounds per square inch (psi). Although the water is heated to approximately 325° F, the tremendous pressure of the primary loop keeps it from boiling. From

---

[3] Source: http://www.tva.gov/orgs/nuclear/wbndiag.htm (Nov. 1998).

the reactor, the superheated primary coolant is carried by piping to one of three or four steam generators, which are massive tube-in-shell heat exchangers measuring more than 65 feet tall and 14 feet in diameter. Within the steam generators, the primary coolant flows through thousands of inverted U-shaped thin-walled tubes that bring the primary coolant directly adjacent to an entirely separate secondary loop of cooler water. Each of the 2,000 to 15,000 steam generator tubes in a single steam generator is approximately the diameter of a quarter and is from 57 to 62 feet long. The secondary coolant, on the shell side of the steam generator configuration, picks up the heat, converts to steam, and is then sent to the turbine at a temperature of approximately 555° F and under a pressure of 1,100 psi. After expanding to turn the turbine, the secondary coolant is finally condensed with the aid of a third coolant loop passing through the condenser and returned to the steam generator for recycling. Meanwhile, the primary coolant, still under pressure, has been recycled to the reactor core to be reheated. The PWR is therefore designed so that radioactive contaminants in the primary coolant will ideally never reach the turbine or the condenser.

### PRIMARY COOLANT LOOP

An examination of the points within a PWR facility at which radionuclides are stripped from the coolant and become airborne is complicated because the PWR has two loops that become contaminated. The primary coolant, which is in direct contact with the core and more contaminated, is stripped of volatile radionuclides in two ways. First, a portion of the primary coolant is continuously sent through the chemical volume and control system, a complex grouping of subsystems designed to maintain proper purity, volume, and chemical balance; radionuclides are transferred to airstreams at a number of points in this system. Second, whenever the reactor is brought to a cold shutdown condition for refueling or repair that requires the opening of the reactor vessel, the primary coolant undergoes complete degasification. The radioactive airstreams resulting from these two processes are sent to the primary waste gas processing system.

### SECONDARY COOLANT LOOP

Because the radioactive gases and other contaminants in the primary coolant of a PWR are isolated from the secondary (steam) loop, gaseous streams emanating from the secondary loop should ideally be clean and could be ignored. Indeed, the assumption underlying the design of PWRs is that there will be little or no radioactivity in the secondary loop. In fact, however, there may be as many as forty miles of thin-walled tubes in a single steam generator, and there is an enormous pressure differential between the primary coolant and the secondary (shell) side of the steam generators, so that leakage from the primary to the secondary loops is inevitable. Small holes develop in the miles of tubing, and contaminated primary coolant leaks into the clean steam. Although the industry anticipated small amounts of leakage, performance has been much worse than expected, and high failure rates for steam generator tubes present ongoing problems at PWR facilities. Accordingly, the gases stripped from the secondary loop at a PWR are a significant source of the plant's radioactive air emissions.

There are four major release points at which gaseous and volatile radionuclides are removed from the secondary coolant at PWRs. At most operating PWRs, the airstreams resulting from these release points are not sent to the primary waste gas processing system; instead, they are released to the environment with minimal or no treatment.

### OTHER ROUTINE RELEASES

In the foregoing ways, radioactive gases and aerosols that develop in or migrate to the primary coolant will eventually be released within the plant as an intentional side effect of routine operating procedures. These are not the only ways in which radionuclides escape the coolant and become airborne. In all plants, coolant and steam may leak through valve stems, pump shaft seals, and other equipment, escaping into various buildings. A portion of the leaked material evaporates, becoming diluted by the large volumes of air in the building atmospheres. Unless these radionuclides decay or are removed from those atmospheres, sooner or later they are released into the general environment.

### TREATMENT SYSTEMS

The major routine sources of radioactive air emissions from the primary coolant encounter one final barrier before release to the environment: the plant's treatment systems. The design of air cleaning systems differs from plant to plant, especially between old and new plants and between BWRs and PWRs. Your expert tells you, however, that three basic methods of treatment are now used by the nuclear generating plants in your state: (1) high efficiency particulate air (HEPA) filters, which are employed universally in the industry to capture particulate radionuclides; (2) storage tanks, used to detain emissions allowing for greater decay of the shorter-lived radionuclides within the plant; and (3) charcoal adsorber beds, used to capture radioiodines and to delay noble gas releases until further decay.

These treatment methods have a dramatic effect on the level of emissions for the shorter-lived radionuclides, the particulates, and the radioiodines. Some radionuclides, however, receive no treatment other than delay. Three of these radionuclides have such long half lives—krypton-85 (10.57 years), tritium (12.3 years), and carbon-14 (5,730 years)—that holdup times on the order of days or months do not meaningfully reduce their radioactivity.

## 4. RELEASE TO THE ENVIRONMENT

When a nuclear generating plant operator decides that treatment is at an end, or when airborne radionuclides bypass treatment systems, the radionuclides become *environmental* contaminants. The total quantities and chemical forms of radionuclides released into the atmosphere over a given period of time are called the "source term," apparently because they are the source or initial numbers used in calculating the environmental impact of releases.

## MONITORING

Your expert tells you that the monitoring of releases at a nuclear generating plant is a complex undertaking, requiring different sampling methods for different radionuclides. Moreover, sampling methods apparently differ from plant to plant. You may need to learn more about monitoring methods in the future, but it all seemed too technical to summarize in your notes.

You did get the impression, however, that there are three ways in which monitoring may be imperfect. First, there may be release points to the environment that are not monitored at all. Second, there may be no attempt to monitor some radionuclides such as carbon-14. Third, monitoring may be defective if the sampling devices fail to obtain a representative sample of the emissions.

Your expert says that monitoring of routine releases is imperfect, but is thought to be relatively reliable. Monitoring during accident conditions has been famously poor. At Three Mile Island, for example, some monitors were scaled to such low ranges that indicators quickly went off scale, leaving plant operators to guess at the magnitude of the releases. Some release points were apparently not monitored at all.

## 5. ATMOSPHERIC AND ENVIRONMENTAL TRANSPORT

At this point in pollutant life cycle analysis, the radionuclides are at large in the atmosphere. Whether and how they affect human receptors depend on the mechanisms of atmospheric, environmental, and metabolic transport. Each radionuclide—indeed, each separate molecular form of a given radionuclide—behaves differently in the environment. Accordingly, radionuclides reach human receptors through a variety of different pathways. Moreover, impacts on human beings—called radiation doses—may be delivered through different modes. These modes include external radiation to the whole body from the plume or radionuclides deposited on the ground, and internal radiation delivered to the whole body or specific body organs from radionuclides inhaled, transpired through the skin, or ingested in foodstuffs or drinking water.

**Figure 8-3** portrays the many pathways and exposure modes whereby radionuclides may affect human beings. The nature of a given radionuclide's journey from source to receptor and its exposure mode or modes depend on its propensity to follow the various pathways. Usually, each radionuclide (and molecular form of such nuclide) has no more than one or two critical pathways and exposure modes dominating all others in the movement of the nuclide toward human beings.

### Atmospheric Transport

The atmosphere does five things to emissions. First, it *transports* the plume as a whole in certain directions at certain speeds. Wind speed and direction obviously determine this transport. Knowledge of transport conditions is necessary to ascertain both the locations of potential receptors and the length of time during which the plume dwells in such locations.

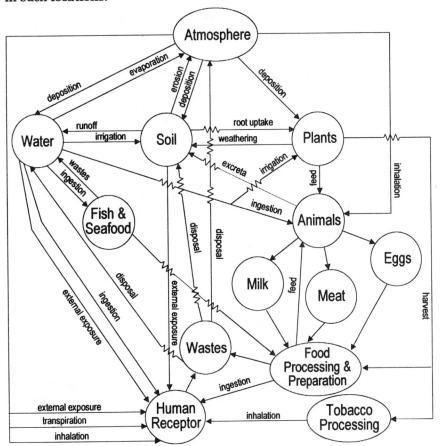

**Figure 8-3.** Pathways and exposure modes for airborne radionuclides affecting human receptors

Second, the atmosphere *disperses*, or diffuses, the individual contaminants, diluting them with various volumes of air. The extent of turbulence in the atmosphere determines the dispersal of the contaminants. "Atmospheric stability" is an index used to judge the extent of this turbulence and, hence, the extent of dilution undergone by contaminants in the plume. Knowledge of atmospheric dispersion is necessary to ascertain the *concentrations* of contaminants at various downwind distances in the plume.

Third, the atmosphere *mixes* contaminants in highly complex ways and thus constitutes a medium in which the molecular forms of various radionuclides undergo change. Gaseous radionuclides interact with particles and aerosols, creating radioactive particulates and droplets. Particulates undergo growth processes or disintegrate into finer pieces. Alterations in temperature and pressure may cause radionuclides to go through the gaseous, liquid, and solid phases. Finally, radioactive decay may turn gaseous radionuclides into solid radioactive decay products and solid radionuclides into gaseous decay products. Atmospheric transport thus does not consist of the movement of pollutants whose size, shape, phase, and molecular form remain constant throughout the dispersion process. Instead, strange things are happening.

Fourth, the atmosphere *deposits* many of the radioactive contaminants on the surfaces of vegetation, human-made structures, and the ground. The deposit of radionuclides occurs through gravitational settling, through surface impaction, electrostatic attraction, adsorption, and chemical interaction (dry deposition), and through precipitation.

Finally, the atmosphere *resuspends* previously deposited radioactive materials. Material originally too coarse to present an inhalation risk may disintegrate to a size that can be inhaled.

For any given nuclear generating plant, the consequences of atmospheric transport, dispersion, mixing, deposition, and resuspension depend on a large number of site-specific variables. The height of the release, the momentum and buoyancy of the emitted plume, the locations and configurations of adjacent structures, the terrain, the presence of various effluent removal surfaces in the environment, and the extent of precipitation all influence the atmosphere's role in the transport of radioactive air pollutants.

## ENVIRONMENTAL TRANSPORT

For radionuclides delivering their impacts exclusively through external radiation, a regulator is concerned only with transport and dispersion through the atmosphere to the receptor's location. Moreover, for radionuclides inhaled or transpired through the skin, the regulator need only add consideration of metabolic transport in order to complete the picture of nuclide movement. For the many radionuclides that reach receptors through the food chain, however, a vital additional series of movements—environmental transport—must be considered.

Environmental transport, or the movement of radionuclides to human beings through biota and other environmental media, reverses the dilution process of atmospheric dispersion, reconcentrating nuclides in food products and bringing them to receptors. Plants are frequently intermediaries in environmental transport.

## ATMOSPHERIC CONTAMINATION OF PLANTS

Airborne radionuclides may contaminate plants in three basic ways: by atmospheric deposition onto plant surfaces, by root uptake from contaminated soil, and through transpiration (as when carbon-14 is taken up by leaves during photosynthesis).

Radioactive isotopes of strontium, cesium, and iodine are chemically similar to elements ordinarily taken up by plants in large quantities—calcium, potassium, and bromine/chlorine, respectively. Because their uptake will be influenced by a given plant's need for these elements, root uptake varies widely between plant type and species.

Other factors affecting root uptake rates include attributes of the soil in which the plants grow. An especially important variable is the amount of certain stable (nonradioactive) elements present in the soil. Whenever radionuclides encounter living organisms, they "compete" with sister elements having similar metabolic properties and with stable isotopes having identical properties. For example, because calcium and strontium have similar metabolic properties, these sister elements compete for uptake by root structures.

Agricultural practices may significantly alter many important soil attributes. For example, the addition of lime to acidic soils raises the pH and dilutes strontium-90 with stable calcium; potassium fertilizing may decrease greatly plant uptake of cesium. Your expert agrees that simple changes in farming practices might benefit people who get their food from the farms most heavily affected by nuclear facility plumes.

### FOODSTUFFS

Animal products—meat, milk, and eggs—are a valuable part of the human diet and are often consumed in large quantities. Because of the sheer bulk of animal diet, radionuclides that are taken up in feed become concentrated in animal products. Milk is a particularly important pathway because it is moved quickly from dairy farm to consumer and is a major source of nutrients for young children.

The transfer of radionuclides from vegetation to humans through animals depends, in the first instance, on animal feeding practices. The types of feed ingested, the quantities consumed (including the mix of various feeds), the feed storage methods used, and the amounts of certain stable elements in the animal's diet all affect the initial animal uptake of radionuclides. Once domestic animals ingest radionuclides, the amounts of those substances in meat, milk, and eggs depend on metabolism within the organism. Animal metabolic rates vary considerably based on physiological characteristics, including breed. For some metabolic pathways within animals, transport rates may vary significantly with the animal's age. Secretion of radioiodines into milk varies with milk production rates and may vary significantly with ambient temperature.

The movement of radionuclides to humans through all foodstuffs, including meat, milk, eggs, and food crops, may be affected dramatically by food processing and kitchen preparation practices. The time required for processing foodstuffs and for distributing and marketing the goods to consumers may allow considerable decay of the shorter-lived radionuclides. For example, the iodine-131 half-life is sufficiently short (approximately eight days) that conversion of contaminated milk into butter or cheese for delayed consumption may effectively eliminate the radionuclide's adverse impacts on humans.

Food processing may remove contaminated portions of foodstuffs and may remove or add stable metabolic competitors. For example, because strontium-90 contaminates wheat through floral deposits and is not transported to internal plant tissues, white bread, made of thoroughly milled grain containing no bran, contains significantly less strontium-90 than does whole meal bread. Moreover, white flour also contains mineral calcium, a metabolic competitor of strontium often lacking in whole wheat bread. Thus, consuming whole wheat bread may have the double effect of increasing strontium-90 intake and reducing that of calcium. This one choice alone may alter the strontium-90/calcium ratio in the total diet by as much as 100 percent, even though whole wheat bread is widely understood to be healthier than white bread.

## 6. METABOLIC TRANSPORT

The end of atmospheric/environmental transport and the beginning of metabolic transport occur when humans inhale or ingest contaminated air, water, or foodstuffs. The mode of entry may be highly significant. Certain radionuclides that may pass straight through the gastrointestinal (G.I.) tract if ingested, may become lodged in or absorbed through the lungs if inhaled. For example, the conventional wisdom is that plutonium-239 is very poorly absorbed by the G.I. tract but extremely dangerous if inhaled.

### INTAKE RATES AND DIET

Intake rates for ingestion of foodstuffs depend, of course, on highly subjective choices as to diet. Two humans of similar age and size may ingest considerably different amounts and mixtures of water, dairy products, meat, eggs, vegetables, fruits, nuts, and grains; the radionuclides ingested will show similar variation.

This business of foodstuffs struck you at first as rather dull, but you are starting to see some interesting twists. You already know, for example, from notes summarized later in this document, that the NRC has effectively said that nuclear generating plants must not deliver more than certain radiation doses to the "maximum exposed individual." But who is the maximum exposed individual? Might that be, for example, a person who eats unusual amounts of whole wheat and no milk?

Some receptors must limit their intakes of certain metabolic competitor elements for medical reasons; their bodies may take up a higher proportion of certain radionuclides than do the bodies of receptors who do not restrict intake of these elements. For example, persons who rigidly adhere to low iodine diets—selecting, for example, noniodized salt—may take up greater quantities of iodine-131 than persons who pay no attention to such dietary items, because the thyroids of the latter group may already be full of non-radioactive iodine from their salt intake, causing the radioactive iodine-131 to simply cruise in and out of their system before causing significant damage.

There is even a pill that people can take to temporarily block the uptake to their thyroids of radioactive iodine-131. Potassium iodide—a form of nonradioactive iodine that can saturate the thyroid—costs approximately 7 cents a pill and can be sold over the counter, but is not available at pharmacies because it serves no other medical purpose. A 130-milligram dose can protect the thyroid for several days if taken within a few hours of exposure to radiation.[4]

### METABOLISM

Once a radionuclide has been inhaled or ingested, it is metabolized according to the chemical properties of the element and compound in which it is contained. Where a given radionuclide ends up in the body may make a great difference in whether it will cause significant adverse health effects. Many radionuclides are metabolized in ways that deliver them to so-called "critical organs." For example, the radioisotopes of iodine concentrate in the thyroid gland and strontium isotopes concentrate in the bones, making the thyroid and the skeleton, respectively, the critical organs for these radionuclides.

Up to this point, your notes address only the *locations* of radionuclides and their movements through various transport mechanisms from the reactor core to the receptor. You have focused on the chemical behavior of nuclides, but have not paid attention to their radiological properties, with the exception of their half-lives. The radionuclides have now arrived, through atmospheric, environmental, and metabolic transport, at the locations from which they expose the receptor to radiation. Some float in a passing cloud, others rest on terrestrial surfaces, and still others reside in or flow through various body tissues. Their significance as air pollutants now depends on the doses that they deliver and the biological effects of such doses. To examine these doses and effects, it is necessary to consider the nature of radiation and what it does to materials in its path.

## 7. BIOLOGICAL EFFECTS OF IONIZING RADIATION

Radionuclides undergoing nuclear disintegration emit, in general, three types of radiation: alpha particles, beta particles, and gamma photons. The energy of the radiation emitted by a single disintegrating nucleus varies, depending on the identity of the source atom and the

---

[4] You would not know this at the time of this case study (1982), but potassium iodide pills were distributed to approximately 10 million people in Poland immediately after the 1986 Chernobyl accident, leading to profoundly lower incidences of thyroid cancer than in neighboring Ukraine, where people did not receive the pills. Accordingly, the NRC dropped its longstanding opposition to making such pills available to public health agencies. *See* Jonathan Rabinovitz, *States Will Receive Drug for Public Use In Nuclear Mishaps*, N.Y. Times, Aug. 22, 1998, at A1, col. 6.

type of radiation emitted. When a beam of radiation encounters material, all or a portion of its energy may be transferred to and absorbed by the material. This energy is initially absorbed at the atomic and molecular level, where the effects of the energy transfer are reasonably well understood. When radiation encounters a living organism, however, biological processes may magnify the initial effects through changes at progressively broader levels—macromolecules, cells, tissues, and organs—eventually leading to biological damage to the organism.

## IONIZATION AND EXCITATION

The initial effects of alpha, beta, and gamma radiation at the atomic and molecular level are *ionization* and *excitation*. Although ionization is a complex process, it may be envisioned as the tearing away of orbital electrons from atoms and molecules through electrostatic attraction to, and repulsion from, charged particles passing in the radiation beam. Each ionized atom yields an electron-ion pair—a negatively charged free electron and a positively charged residue atom, each of which is called an *ion*. Excitation occurs when the energy imparted by the radiation is insufficient to tear an electron away from its atom or molecule but is sufficient to raise the electron to a higher, more excited energy level than its normal or ground state.

## CHEMICAL CHAOS

Ionization and excitation are merely the first steps in a chain of events set in motion by radiation bombardment. The electrically charged ions—fragments of dissociated atoms or molecules—are chemically reactive. Most of them will eventually reunite to form electrically neutral atoms or molecules. Unfortunately, however, they may recombine in new ways to form undesirable compounds. These foreign compounds, in turn, may interact in new ways with surrounding atoms and molecules. Meanwhile, excited atoms and molecules, in shedding excess energy to return to their ground states, may give off secondary ionizing radiation. In short, the atoms and molecule in the wake of an alpha, beta, or gamma radiation beam undergo chemical chaos.

This chaos has adverse effects when it takes place within living cells. Indeed, health physicists assume that biological effects will follow irradiation, however small its amount. The ultimate effects of radiation on the organism may be *somatic*—manifested in the exposed individual—or *genetic*—manifested in descendants of the exposed individual. The effects are well known. At sufficiently high doses, irradiated organisms will promptly die. At much lower doses, radiation may unquestionably lead to cancer, genetic damage to offspring, and developmental abnormalities.

The critical question is obvious: what effects result from the doses delivered by nuclear generating plant releases? You cannot answer this question without knowing what those doses are. That knowledge, in turn, requires a rudimentary understanding of the ways in which radiation doses are measured.

## 8.  UNITS OF RADIATION DOSE

The ideal unit of dose for purposes of radiation protection analysis would be a unit that would produce the same biological effect regardless of type and energy of the radiation: a true common denominator. Due to the complexity of radiation-induced damage in living organisms, such a unit may not exist. Health physicists have pursued that goal, however, and their historical struggle complicates matters for the lay person. Units have come and gone, and the subject is a little confused. To make matters worse, existing radiation *standards* are expressed in different units. Therefore, it is essential to understand what each unit represents and how the units relate to one another.

The unit devised to denote the quantity of energy that ionizing radiation deposits in a specified amount of material (or that is absorbed by the material) is called the *rad*—an acronym for "radiation absorbed dose." This unit is expressed in terms of the quantity of energy deposited *per unit of mass* of irradiated material; thus, no description of dose is complete unless it tells the amount of material or portion of the body involved. For example, a whole-body dose of one rad represents a much greater total quantity of radiation absorbed than a dose of one rad to a leg or foot.

With the development of the rad came the first true dose unit. Early biological experiments showed, however, that equal absorbed doses of different types of radiation did not produce the same biological response. For example, 10,000 rads of X-radiation might be required to kill a microorganism, while a mere 1,000 rads of alpha radiation might accomplish the same effect. Rad units were not truly comparable and could not simply be added together to yield biological effect.

Persistent researchers eventually concluded that the differences in biological effects were related, in part, to the microdistribution in tissues of the radiation energy—more specifically, to the density of ionizations produced by the tracks of individual alpha and beta particles and gamma rays. The differences can be substantial. An alpha particle, for example, might have a very short path in tissue (it can be stopped by a few sheets of paper), yet produce an extraordinary 7,600 ion-pairs in every micron of that path; some gamma rays with a much longer path might produce only 10 ion-pairs in each micron of path.

Accordingly, it was decided that dose measurements should be converted to a common scale of "dose equivalent" measurements by multiplying the dose, in rads, by a value reflecting this difference in effect. The new unit resulting from this adjustment process was the *rem*—an acronym for "radiation equivalent in man [sic]." The rem is intended to be the common unit for expressing biological effects so that assessment of the effects of ionization caused by different types of radiation can be compared and summed.

Today, many radiation protection standards are expressed in terms of rems, including fractions and multiples of those units. Because the rem is an inconveniently large unit for many purposes, doses often are expressed in millirems (mrem) or thousandths of a rem. When reference is made to the collective dose received by large numbers of people, the dose is expressed in terms of "person-rems," a figure calculated by multiplying the total number of exposed persons by their average individual dose in rems. Thus, for example, one million person-rems is the dose received collectively by two million people, each exposed to an average of 500 millirems, *or* by one million people each exposed to one rem, *or* by 500,000 people each exposed to two rems.

To put these radiation dose units in perspective, it is usually said that the average American individual is exposed to approximately 125 millirems to the whole body each year from natural sources such as radionuclides in the earth's crust, cosmic rays from outer space, naturally occurring radionuclides that have been ingested and inhaled, and radionuclides that appear in building materials.

## 9.  INITIAL THOUGHTS ON HOW TO FASHION STANDARDS

The preceding pages summarize your notes on the technical aspects of radioactive air emissions from nuclear generating plants. As you sit at your desk, preparing to put the first draft of your recommendations on paper, you have decided to operate on the following assumptions: (1) the health effects are not yet quantifiable; (2) there are no demonstrably safe dose threshold levels; and (3) the guiding principle for federal standard setting has been to keep doses "as low as reasonably achievable," a concept referred to as ALARA.

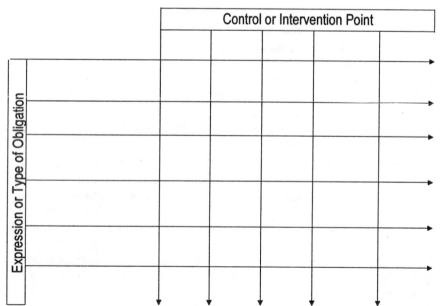

Figure 8-4

You intend to take a hard look at the federal standards governing nuclear generating plants, but want to put some of your initial thoughts on paper before your imagination is crushed by the choices of other regulators. It is true that you do not have information that would enable you to make intelligent judgments about acceptable *levels* of radionuclide pollution and radiation dose; your notes do not yet address levels at all. You do, however, have sufficient information to consider two more fundamental questions: (1) *where* (in each radionuclide's life cycle) could standards or requirements be applied to minimize the health effects of nuclear generating plant emissions and (2) how might such standards or requirements be *expressed*?

You've started to doodle on a legal pad, and are beginning to think in terms of the open-ended grid depicted in **Figure 8-4**. The grid is a way of sketching out your tentative answers to these two fundamental questions. Across the top of the grid, you are starting to fill in *locations* where the state might interpose obligations: things like "release point" (where the radionuclides hit the atmosphere). Down along the left-hand side of the grid, you are starting to fill in different types of obligations, like "design standards," and "release limits."

### Problem

Review the preceding materials in this Chapter 8 and compile a detailed list of regulatory options. For each option: (1) list the point in the pollutant's life cycle at which a standard or requirement could be applied; (2) give an example of how such a standard or requirement might be expressed; (3) think about the strengths and weaknesses of the option; and (4) consider whether it might make sense for a *state* (as opposed to the federal government) to adopt each option. Try to be imaginative and creative.

To prime the pump, here are a few examples of "standards"—requirements that might be expressed in a *quantified* way. [1] Facility operators might be told that they cannot release any more than a specified quantity of radioactivity to the atmosphere (expressed as pico-curies per second). [2] Facility operators might be told that they cannot release radionuclides at levels that would result in more than a specified dose equivalent (expressed in millirems) to the thyroid of any individual receptor. [3] Baking companies might be told that they cannot sell bread containing more than a specified level of radioactivity (expressed in pico-curies).

Here are a few examples of other types of regulatory requirements—the kind that might be less easy to quantify, but might still be of great value. [1] To maximize dispersal of airborne emissions, facility operators could be required to use tall stacks, or to employ fans, furnaces, or other devices to increase the buoyancy of the plume. [2] To minimize uptake of cesium by agricultural crops, farmers in the vicinity of nuclear generating facilities might be required to use potassium fertilizers. [3] To minimize uptake of carbon-14 by vegetation, facility operators might be required to limit carbon-14 releases to night time hours during which photosynthesis is not occurring.

# D. FEDERAL STANDARDS

## 1. INTRODUCTION

Having assembled and studied the foregoing notes, you now have a reasonably thorough technical background on radioactive air emissions from nuclear generating plants. You even have some tentative thoughts about how your state might begin to regulate such emissions. But it seems pointless to suggest state regulation, if the federal government is already doing an ample job. The Attorney General will need to know what the existing federal standards are and whether you and your experts think they are adequate.

You've gone to the Commerce Clearing House publication, Nuclear Regulation Reporter, and have also spent some time pouring over the Code of Federal Regulations. Here is what your notes say about the existing federal regulations.

## 2. THREE OVERLAPPING FEDERAL REGULATIONS

You've discovered that a nuclear power plant operator ("licensee") is governed by three overlapping sets of radioactive air emission standards established by the federal government. These three sets of standards are commonly referred to as Part 20, Appendix I, and Part 190, because of their locations in the Code of Federal Regulations. The Nuclear Regulatory Commission (NRC) and its predecessor, the Atomic Energy Commission (AEC), developed Part 20 and Appendix I. The Environmental Protection Agency (EPA) promulgated Part 190.

The study of these three regulatory schemes and how they mesh is not a task for the faint hearted. Your expert helped sort things out by explaining that there are various ways in which radioactive air emission standards might be established for nuclear generating plants. Such standards can be *expressed* in a large number of ways. Moreover, they can be designed to pursue quite different *approaches*.

## 3. MODES OF EXPRESSION AND APPROACHES

Consider, first, the bewildering variety of ways in which radioactive air emission standards could be expressed. Bearing in mind the chronological chain from the creation of radionuclides in the reactor to their eventual health effects, regulators could express standards in terms of: (1) inventory limits, (2) design standards, (3) release limits, (4) dispersion and reconcentration limits for air, water, and foodstuffs, (5) intake limits, (6) dose limits, or (7) health effects limits. Moreover, numerous approaches to standard setting are possible within each of these categories. One reason the federal standards are so confusing is that federal agencies have expressed radioactive air emission standards in a wide variety of ways, sometimes even using several of these categories within a single regulation.

Regardless of the manner in which the regulator chooses to express radioactive air emission standards, the regulator must have a guiding approach for setting the actual numbers for those standards. The federal government has used two approaches since embarking on the comprehensive regulation of environmental contaminants in the early 1970s. One approach is to set standards that require every polluter in a given source category to reduce emissions as much as possible, given existing pollution control technology and taking into account some notion of cost ("technology-based standards"). The other approach is to set standards that limit adverse effects to an acceptable level, considering the specific mechanisms whereby a given pollutant may harm the environment or receptors ("effects-based standards").

Lawmakers and regulators have been reluctant to ignore either of these approaches. In fact, much modern pollution control legislation tries to combine the two. To make matters even more complicated, the choice between these two approaches does not necessarily preordain the way in which standards will be expressed, although it may influence that secondary choice.

The federal agencies involved in setting radioactive air emission standards have had enormous discretion in establishing approaches. The NRC has consistently claimed that the primary purpose of its regulations has been to prevent adverse human health effects. In particular, the federal agencies have focused on the eventual radiation doses delivered by radioactive air emissions. Because it would be impossible actually to measure doses delivered by nuclear generating plant emissions, however, the agencies have expressed many dose-related standards in other ways. They have most frequently started with "acceptable" dose limits and worked back through dosimetric and transport models to establish *derived* limits, which are then applied to operating reactors. Recognition of this basic technique helps to make the regulatory schemes somewhat more intelligible.

## 4. PART 20

Of the three federal regulations controlling nuclear generating plant emissions, the one with the longest history and, therefore, the one that influenced the design of the oldest operating reactors in your state, is Part 20. Technically, Part 20 applies not just to nuclear generating plants ("utilization facilities"), but to all actors licensed by the NRC to handle so-called special nuclear material. The heart of Part 20 is the following command:

(a) A licensee shall not * * * use * * * licensed material [nuclear fuel] so as to release to an unrestricted area radioactive material in concentrations which exceed the limits specified in Appendix B, Table II of this part except as authorized pursuant to * * * paragraph (b) of this section. * * * For purposes of this section concentrations may be averaged over a period not greater than one year.

(b) An application for a license or amendment may include proposed limits higher than those specified in paragraph (a) of this section. The Commission will approve the proposed limits if the applicant demonstrates:

    (1) That the applicant has made a reasonable effort to minimize the radioactivity contained in effluents to unrestricted areas; and

    (2) That it is not likely that radioactive material discharged in the effluent would result in the exposure of an individual to concentrations of radioactive material in air or water exceeding the limits specified in Appendix B, Table II of this part. * * *

(d) For the purposes of this section the concentration limits in Appendix B, Table II of this part shall apply at the boundary of the restricted area. * * * [If] radioactive material [is] discharged through a stack, pipe or similar conduit * * * within the restricted area, the concentration at the boundary may be determined by applying appropriate factors for dilution, dispersion, or decay between the point of discharge and the boundary.

10 C.F.R. § 20.106 (1982). Section 20.1(c) also contains a general command that radioactive emissions be kept "as low as reasonably achievable" (ALARA), but this language has no meaning apart from Appendix I—the second of the three sets of federal standards.

You've checked further, and an "unrestricted area" is defined by 10 C.F.R. § 20.3(a)(17) (1982) as essentially any area to which access cannot be controlled by the licensee.

Appendix B is called "Concentrations in Air and Water Above Natural Background," and sets forth limits for approximately 250 radionuclides. You hardly know what to make of it, but you do jot in your notes the Table II numbers for two pollutants. The number for iodine-131 is $1 \times 10^{-10}$ microcuries per milliliter, and the one for strontium-90 is $3 \times 10^{-11}$ microcuries per milliliter.

You go to your expert for help in figuring this all out, and she turns the tables on you. "I can tell you where to go to find out what all these numbers are supposed to mean, but first let me ask you some questions to see if you've read the regulation carefully. After all, you're supposed to be the lawyer."

### Questions

1. Suppose you wanted to test whether a nuclear generating plant is in compliance with Part 20. Where would you measure, and what would you measure? Do you see any problems in setting up your measurement stations?

2. Suppose you and your qualified expert went out today and took the measurements that you have articulated in answer to the preceding ques-

tion. Will it be possible for you to show today that the nuclear generating plant is in violation of Part 20? Why or why not?

3. Does Part 20 impose a limit on the total *quantities* of radionuclides that a nuclear generating plant may emit? Why or why not?

4. If you were a nuclear generating plant operator, and it turned out that you were exceeding the Part 20 standard, what might be the cheapest way for you to bring yourself into compliance? Why?

## 5. THE NUMBERS IN APPENDIX B, TABLE II

After testing your understanding of Part 20's language with these questions, your expert gives you some documents to read about the Appendix B, Table II numbers. Here are your notes on those documents.

Although it is rather confusing, the concentration limits for the 250 or so radionuclides listed in Part 20 are *alternatives*: a facility may emit the maximum allowed for any one radionuclide only by avoiding emissions of any other radionuclides. Something called the "rule of mixtures" is used to assess compliance with this feature of the regulation. For example, if the known concentrations of radionuclides A, B, and C in the gaseous emissions are $C_A$, $C_B$, $C_C$, and the maximum permissible concentrations for those radionuclides in Table II are $MPC_A$, $MPC_B$, $MPC_C$, then the concentrations of each radionuclide in the mixture must be limited so that the *sum* of

$$\frac{C_A}{MPC_A} + \frac{C_B}{MPC_B} + \frac{C_C}{MPC_C}$$

is less than or equal to one.

The "concentration guides" that form the backbone of Part 20 (including the rule of mixtures feature) were chosen in an effort to assure that no individual received from sources other than natural background and medical radiation any more than certain doses deemed to be acceptable in 1955—the year when Part 20 was adopted. In other words, the Appendix B, Table II concentration values are mathematically *derived* release concentration limits whose real purpose is to assure compliance with dose limits. The concentration guides were based on assumptions about standardized intake rates by human beings for air, water, and foodstuffs, taking into account the effects of radionuclide concentration in the food chain and accumulation in the body.

Among the "acceptable" *dose* values standing mathematically behind the Appendix B, Table II *concentration* values are 500 millirems to the whole body or 1,500 millirems to the thyroid. You flip back through your notes and see that the 500 millirem whole body limit for the maximum exposed individual exceeds average natural background radiation by approximately a factor of four. You also discover from the various publications provided by your expert that the scientific community has overwhelmingly concluded in the years since 1955 that the maximum permissible doses underlying Part 20 are unnecessarily high.

As if this weren't enough to indicate that the Part 20 values are too lenient, the operating *performance* of nuclear generating plants has strongly suggested that something is mighty wrong with the Part 20 numbers. Indiana Point Unit 1, for example, with reported actual average annual releases of 28 curies, is legally free under Part 20 to emit 16,000,000 curies per year in the vicinity of New York City.

Something else has caught your eye. Appendix B, Table II refers cryptically to maximum permissible concentrations in air "above natural background." That phrase is not defined in the regulations, but the NRC ruled in a formal 1974 licensing proceeding that doses incurred from reactors on any site other than the site undergoing compliance review must be considered as part of the "background" exposure to any person incurring a cumulative dose. This ruling interprets Part 20 to allow *each* of several reactors on separate sites to contribute an incremental radiation concentration to the air in the Appendix B, Table II, amounts, even though the resulting dose to individual receptors may be higher than the drafters of Part 20 intended.

You are starting to think that existing federal standards may be inadequate, but you've still only looked at the first regulation: Part 20.

## 6. APPENDIX I

The second of the three federal regulations controlling nuclear plant emissions is contained in 10 C.F.R. Part 50 and the accompanying Appendix I, conventionally referred to together as "Appendix I."

### NUMERICAL GUIDES

Unlike Part 20, which applies to all NRC licensees, Part 50 and Appendix I apply only to light-water-cooled nuclear power reactors (including the PWRs in your state). The "Appendix I" part of the regulation sets forth "Numerical Guides for Design Objectives and Limiting Conditions for Operation" to meet the general command of 10 C.F.R. § 20.1(c) that radioactive emissions be kept "as low as reasonably achievable" (ALARA). Section II of Appendix I provides:

> The applicant shall provide reasonable assurance that the following design objectives will be met. * * *
>
> B.1. The calculated annual total quantity of all radioactive material above background[1] to be released from each light-water-cooled nuclear power reactor to the atmosphere will not result in an estimated annual air dose from gaseous effluents at any location near ground level which could be occupied by individuals in unrestricted areas in excess of 10 millirads for gamma radiation or 20 millirads for beta radiation. * * *
>
> C. The calculated annual total quantity of all radioactive iodine and radioactive material in particulate form above background to be

released from each light-water-cooled nuclear power reactor in effluents to the atmosphere will not result in an estimated annual dose or dose commitment from such radioactive iodine and radioactive material in particulate form for any individual in an unrestricted area from all pathways of exposure in excess of 15 millirems to any organ. * * *

[1] Here and elsewhere in this appendix background means radioactive materials in the environment and in the effluents from light-water-cooled power reactors not generated in, or attributable to, the reactors of which specific account is required in determining design objectives.

10 C.F.R. Part 50, Appendix I § II (1982).

To focus your energies on the foregoing language, your expert urges you to address the following questions.

### *Questions*

1.  You've learned from various sources that radioiodines may appear in both the gaseous and solid (particulate) "phases," depending on molecular structure, temperature, and other variables. Paragraph C is designed to limit radioiodines whether gaseous or particulate. Other radioactive gases (such as krypton-85) may be inhaled by human receptors and may also enter the food chain. Carbon-14, for example, is taken up by plants during photosynthesis. Putting aside the radioiodines—addressed in paragraph C—do the foregoing numerical guides provide limits for inhaled gaseous radionuclides or from gaseous radionuclides that enter the food chain? Where?

2.  Given economies of scale, many nuclear generating sites contain multiple reactors, with some having as many as four. Assuming a four-reactor site, what calculated air doses and organ doses would comply with the Appendix I guidelines for the site as a whole. Why?

3.  The Appendix I language quoted above refers to the "applicant," and directs the "applicant" to do something. Who do you suppose the applicant is? What is the applicant required to do by the language of Appendix I? When? How often?

## 7. DESIGN OBJECTIVES AND TECHNICAL SPECIFICATIONS

In addition to the numerical guides of Appendix I, 10 C.F.R. Part 50 sets forth two sections telling nuclear generating plant operators what they are supposed to do with the guides.

### DESIGN OBJECTIVES

First, the regulation provides:

(a) An application for a permit to construct a nuclear power reactor shall include a description of the preliminary design of equipment to be installed to maintain control over radioactive materials in * * * effluents produced during normal reactor operations * * * .

[T]he application shall also identify the design objectives, and the means to be employed, for keeping levels of radioactive material in effluents to unrestricted areas as low as is reasonably achievable [ALARA]. * * * The guides set out in Appendix I to this part provide numerical guidance on design objectives * * * to meet the [ALARA] requirements * * * . These numerical guides for design objectives and limiting conditions for operation are not to be construed as radiation protection standards. * * *

10 C.F.R. § 50.34a (1982).

This provision is obscure but, as far as you can tell, the "design objectives" are the quantities of the principal radionuclides that the applicant expects to release on an annual basis when the equipment is installed and operated. If modeling demonstrates that the applicant will not exceed the maximum dose levels set forth in Appendix I, the applicant has made a conclusive showing that releases will comply with ALARA, and the equipment and operating procedures will be approved.

TECHNICAL SPECIFICATIONS

Second, another portion of the regulation provides

(a) In order to keep releases of radioactive materials to unrestricted areas during normal reactor operations * * * [ALARA], each license authorizing operation of a nuclear power reactor will include technical specifications that, in addition to requiring compliance with applicable provisions of § 20.106 of this chapter, require:

   (1) That operating procedures developed pursuant to § 50.34a * * * for the control of effluents be established and followed and that equipment installed in the radioactive waste system, pursuant to § 50.34a be maintained and used.

   (2) The submission of a report * * * within sixty (60) days after January 1 and July 1 of each year specifying the quantity of each of the principal radionuclides released to unrestricted areas in liquid and in gaseous effluents during the previous six (6) months of operation, and such other information as may be required by the Commission to estimate maximum potential annual radiation doses to the public resulting from effluent releases. * * *

10 C.F.R. § 50.36a (1982).

At this point, your expert has further questions for you.

### Questions

1.   10 C.F.R. § 50.36a (1982) provides that each nuclear generating plant license will contain "technical specifications" ordering the license holder to do certain things. In other words, these will be conditions written into each operator's license. What things must the technical specifications require the operator to do?

2.   Suppose the semi-annual reports required by a nuclear generating plant's license show that the facility has delivered doses to individuals in

excess of the Appendix I values. Will the operator be in violation of its license? Will it be in violation of 10 C.F.R. Part 50 or Appendix I? Will *any* releases—no matter how large the quantity—be unlawful? Why or why not?

---

You've now reviewed your notes on Part 20 and Appendix I. You are starting to wonder whether state regulation might be a good thing after all. But you still have one more federal regulation to examine.

## 8. PART 190

The third and final federal regulation governing radioactive air emissions from nuclear generating plants is 40 C.F.R. Part 190. This regulation was promulgated by the EPA in 1976.

Part 190 contains two complementary substantive provisions. First, the regulation sets forth maximum cumulative radiation doses for individual members of the general public. Second, it sets forth maximum quantities of a few long-lived radionuclides that may be released to the general environment. The overriding command of Part 190 is that facilities within the nuclear fuel cycle must be operated in such a manner as to provide reasonable assurance that these two substantive provisions are met.

Unlike Appendix I, which applies solely to light-water-cooled nuclear power reactors, Part 190 applies to the "uranium fuel cycle." The uranium fuel cycle is broadly defined to include all aspects of nuclear power generation, from the milling of uranium ore to reprocessing of spent fuel, but excluding nuclear waste disposal. The key section declares:

Operations covered by this subpart shall be conducted in such a manner as to provide reasonable assurance that:

(a) The annual dose equivalent does not exceed 25 millirems to the whole body, 75 millirems to the thyroid, and 25 millirems to any other organ of any member of the public as the result of exposures to planned discharges of radioactive materials, radon and its daughters excepted, to the general environment from uranium fuel cycle operations and to radiation from these operations.

(b) The total quantity of radioactive materials entering the general environment from the entire uranium fuel cycle, per gigawatt-year of electrical energy produced by the fuel cycle, contains less than 50,000 curies of krypton-85, 5 millicuries of iodine-129, and 0.5 millicuries combined of plutonium-239 and other alpha-emitting transuranic radionuclides with half-lives greater than one year.

40 C.F.R. 190.10 (1982).

Your expert has provided you with further questions to test your understanding of Part 190.

### *Questions*

1. What does Part 190 require of nuclear generating plant operators? Under what circumstances will a nuclear generating plant be in violation of the regulation?

2. Does Part 190 put any limits on the number of people who may lawfully receive the doses enumerated in § 190.10(a)? Does it matter whether there are such limitations?

3. What limits do Part 190 put on nuclear generating plant releases of tritium (12.3-year half-life) and carbon-14 (5,730-year half-life)?

4. How do you suppose the EPA, the NRC, and nuclear generating plant operators are measuring compliance with Part 190's cumulative dose and long-lived radionuclide limitations? What information would be required to get a handle on whether the regulation is being violated? Do you have any idea how such information could be developed?

## 9.  IMPLEMENTATION OF PART 190

Your expert has provided you with a number of additional EPA and NRC documents, explaining how those agencies have implemented Part 190. Here are your notes.

The EPA concluded in promulgating Part 190 that only minor adjustments would be necessary to deal with nuclear power reactor sites within ten miles of one another and that cumulative contributions to dose from more widely spaced sites should be ignored. Moreover, in a series of publications, the EPA and NRC concluded that, if a multiple-reactor site containing as many as five or six reactors complied with Appendix I, the agencies would *presume* compliance with Part 190 dose limits, and no cumulative dose analysis need be undertaken.

Accordingly, the license for a four-reactor site in your state provides that the operator can ignore the Part 190 dose limits completely unless and until the reactors' emissions exceed Appendix I doses by more than a factor of two.

### ENFORCEMENT

In the event that a facility's emissions exceed Appendix I doses by more than a factor of two, the operator is told by an EPA publication (and in the 4-reactor plant license in your state) that it must prepare a "Special Report" analyzing the potential cumulative doses. The NRC provides instructions about how to carry out this Part 190 analysis. First, the licensee is told to ignore the liquid release pathway because "doses via liquid release are very conservatively evaluated [so] there is reasonable assurance that no real individual will receive a significant dose." Accordingly, "only doses to individuals via airborne pathways and doses resulting from direct radiation need to be considered in determining potential compliance with * * * Part 190." Second, the licensee is told that it should "reevaluate" the exceeded Appendix I dose limit, "using 'more realistic assumptions'."

If the Special Report demonstrates compliance problems, operators are told that they must seek a variance, if necessary. The NRC declares that the mere submission of the Special Report will be considered to be "a timely request [for a variance] and a variance [will be automatically] granted until staff action on the request [is] complete."

### Questions

1.   What is the maximum dose of millirems to an organ of the maximum exposed individual that the four-reactor site in your state may deliver before it is required by its license to pay attention to the Part 190 standards? Does this strike you as unusual? Why or why not?

2.   What is the purpose of the Part 190 "Special Report"? To determine ways to reduce excessive emissions? To achieve some other objective?

3.   A variance from compliance with Part 190 is automatic whenever a Special Report is filed. Why do you suppose the NRC has taken this approach?

4.   Why don't the NRC and the EPA simply express radiation standards as *consequence* limits? For example, "thou shalt not emit radionuclides in amounts sufficient to cause any receptor to contract cancer." Or "thou shalt not emit radionuclides in amounts sufficient to cause any birth defects." Wouldn't that be a straightforward way to get to the heart of the matter, which is to prevent adverse health effects? Do you think that regulating nuclear generating plants in such a manner would be a good or a bad thing? Why?

5.   Surely, the NRC has a good idea of the "best" pollution control technology available for reducing radioactive air emissions at a nuclear generating plant. Why doesn't the NRC simply order nuclear generating plants to install and use that technology? Would reliance on such *specification* standards be a good or a bad thing? Why?

6.   Surely the NRC also has a good handle on the levels of radioactive air emissions that would be emitted from a nuclear generating plant that had installed and implemented the best available control technology. Why doesn't the NRC order nuclear generating plants to limit their emissions to those levels? Would reliance on such *performance* standards be a good or a bad thing? Why?

7.   Suppose the NRC did decide to promulgate performance standards based on the capabilities of the best available control technology. It could express those standards as:

   a.   *Concentration* limits applied at the point of release (for example, "thou shalt emit no more than 1 pico-curie of iodine-131 per cubic meter of air");

   b.   *Quantity* limits applied *at the point of release* (for example, "thou shalt emit no more than 10 curies of iodine-131 per year");

c. *Percentage reduction* requirements (for example, "thou shalt remove 99.99% of all iodine-131 particulates by HEPA filtration");

d. *Concentration* limits applied *somewhere out in the environment* (for example, "thou shalt reduce emissions of iodine-131 so that the ambient air at the property line does not exceed concentrations of 1 pico-curie of iodine-131 per cubic meter of air");

What are the strengths and weaknesses of each approach? Do some modes of expression pose greater problems in spotting noncompliance? Do any of these modes provide adequate assurance that the public health is being protected?

8.    Dose limits seem like a cool idea. For example, "thou shalt deliver no more than 75 millirems to the thyroid of the maximum exposed individual." Appendix I provided the illusion of dose limits, but it was only an illusion. Part 190 set forth dose limits, but the NRC and EPA agreed that compliance would simply be assumed at nuclear generating plants—even those plants that reported violations. Suppose the NRC took dose limits seriously. Do you see problems with a directive that a nuclear generating plant deliver no more than 75 millirems to the thyroid of the maximum exposed individual? How could we measure compliance or noncompliance?

## 10. GOVERNMENT DECEPTION IN RADIATION MATTERS

Before proceeding with additional aspects of the case study, it is useful to take a break and come up for air. Why is the public so distrustful of nuclear power generation and the way in which the federal government regulates it? A partial answer is evident from the preceding pages setting forth the federal government's impenetrable radioactive air emission standards. But the public distrust is hardly attributable to this esoteric minutiae; no more than a few hundred people know what you've now seen about the federal standards.

A simpler explanation may be that the public has been misled about radiation releases too frequently and for too long. This does not mean that nuclear power is unsafe or a bad thing. It does not mean that the doses being delivered by nuclear generating plants are unacceptable. It does mean, however, that public suspicions about this technology are inevitable.

The federal government's willingness to overlook excessive radioactive air emissions and its attempts to hide such emissions from the public are legendary. On July 11, 1990, Department of Energy (DOE) Secretary James Watkins conceded, on behalf of the United States government, that residents in the vicinity of the Hanford nuclear facility in Washington state had been deceived for more than forty years about massive radioactive air emissions from that facility. *See* Keith Schneider, *U.S. Admits Peril of 40's Emissions at A-Bomb Plant*, N.Y. Times Jul. 12, 1990, at A1, col. 6. A report issued by DOE demonstrated that hundreds of thousands of Washington, Oregon and Idaho residents had been continually and secretly exposed to large quantities of radiation from Hanford in air, drinking water and food for a quarter of a century. *See* Keith Schneider, *Radiation Peril at Hanford is Detailed*, N.Y. Times, Jul. 13, 1990, at A8, col. 4. "'The fact they've been hiding the data for 2½ decades is inexcusable,' said Thomas Cochran, a scientist at the Natural Resources Defense Council in Washington. 'They should have been monitoring these people' to see whether they needed to have their thyroids removed." Larry Tyle, *U.S. Makes Chernobyl Comparison in Dealing 1940s Nuclear Leak*, Boston Globe, Jul. 13, 1990, at 1.

Not only did the government repeatedly deceive people about the Hanford facility, but it also exposed millions of Americans to large amounts of radioactive iodine in fallout from Nevada nuclear bomb tests from 1951 to 1962. *See* Matthew L. Wald, *U.S. Atomic Tests in 50's Exposed Millions to Risk*, N.Y. Times, Jul. 29, 1997, at A8 col. 1. The National Cancer Institute concluded in 1997 that fallout during the 1950s atmospheric tests had probably caused 10,000 to 75,000 extra thyroid cancers. *See* Matthew L. Wald, *U.S. Alerted Photo Film Makers, Not Public, About Bomb Fallout*, N.Y. Times, Sep. 30, 1997, at A18, col. 1. Radioiodine releases from the atmospheric tests were at least ten times larger than those caused by the 1986 explosion at Chernobyl. To add insult to injury, the Atomic Energy Commission regularly warned the Eastman Kodak Company and other film manufacturers during the 1950s about fallout that might damage film wrapped in contaminated corn husks, even while it was assuring the public that there was no health risk. *See id.*

# E. ECOSYSTEMS MODELING

In the preceding pages, you have examined the federal standards governing radioactive air emissions at nuclear generating plants. Virtually all of these requirements are either expressed as dose standards (Appendix I and Part 190) or were originally derived through dose calculations (Part 20). Accordingly, their efficacy is heavily dependent on the validity of the underlying transport and dosimetric models. With the help of your expert, you have obtained a stack of books, articles, and other documents on modeling.

## 1. THE ROLE OF MODELS IN FEDERAL STANDARDS

Readily available techniques can measure compliance with the *concentration* limits set forth in Appendix B, Table II of Part 20. Therefore, even though models initially played a major role in the establishment of the Part 20 concentration values, reliance on models is not necessary to determine compliance with Part 20. But Appendix I and Part 190 purport to limit *doses* to individual receptors. How can compliance with such standards be determined?

The best way to determine compliance with those dose standards would be to measure the doses each individual receives. Some doses, however, are extremely difficult to measure for any given individual. Even for those doses that can be measured, it would be utterly impracticable to measure every individual in a large population. The alternative of directly measuring doses received by only a few "representative" individuals or locations provides no assurance that doses to other individuals or at other locations are not higher than those measured. For all of these reasons, dose determinations must be based primarily on effluent measurements that are then extrapolated through mathematical models.

## 2. INTRODUCTION TO ECOSYSTEMS MODELING

### STATE VARIABLES

Ecosystems modeling simulates the dynamic behavior of radionuclides in the environment by means of a system of compartments through which radionuclides move. Consider, for example, the ways in which a single radionuclide, iodine-131, may journey from a nuclear generating plant to a single organ, the thyroid. This real world system might be shown in a crude compartment model or box-and-arrow diagram like that depicted in **Figure 8-5**. The compartments in the diagram represent the source of the iodine-131 and the various environmental media that the iodine-131 contaminates, up to and including the critical organ of the receptor. In this particular model, we are concerned about the quantities or concentrations of iodine-131 in the compartments. These contents, or entities within the compartments, are called the "state variables" of the system—"state," because they define the condition or state of the contents of each compartment, and "variable," because they change with time. The symbol $Q$ represents a state variable, and the subscript following the symbol identifies which state variable is being discussed.

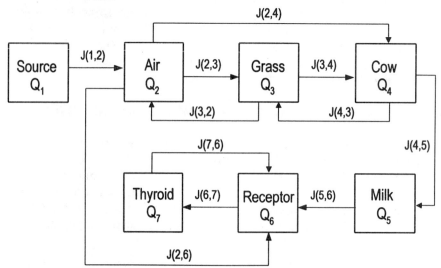

**Figure 8-5.** Ecosystems modeling

The model is designed to explain the real world system by greatly simplifying it. The real world contains billions of air parcels, dozens of varieties (not to mention blades) of grass, thousands of cows (as well as goats), dairy products other than milk, and thousands of receptors; moreover, the compartments for cow and receptor could be broken down further into the G.I. tract, blood, and various organs. While one could imagine a hypothetical "true" or "base" model as complex as the world itself, such a model would be impossible to construct or use. Most importantly, it would defeat the purpose of modeling: to simplify.

### SELECTING AND AGGREGATING STATE VARIABLES

The first step in the modeling process is to lump large numbers of real world entities into a small number of compartments. This simplifying step, called "aggregation," is crucial to constructing a model. The model depicted in **Figure 8-5**, for example, could be aggregated further by establishing only three compartments: source, air, and thyroid. It could be disaggregated by establishing separate compartments for each variety of grass or for each breed of cow. The *appropriate* degree of aggregation depends on the goals of the modeler and the information available to her.

The structure of the model also depends on the point within the chain of environmental transport at which monitoring is being conducted. The model depicted in **Figure 8-5** assumes that we know only the quantities of iodine-131 released to the air by the source; therefore, the required length of the modeling chain is quite long. If one routinely measured radioiodine concentrations in milk, one might need a model consisting of no more than the last three compartments.

### FLOWS

The next step in structuring an ecosystems model is to consider the inputs to and outputs from each compartment. The movements of materials between the entities described by the state variables are called flows, and the rates of those movements are called flow rates. The symbol J represents flows; the parenthetical information following that symbol denotes the two compartments involved and the direction of flow. For example, $J(1,2)$ denotes the flow rate from state variable $Q_1$ to state variable $Q_2$. Factors not described by the state variables may also influence flow rates; such influences from outside the system are called "exogenous variables" and may be denoted by the symbol X. In **Figure 8-5**, for example, one exogenous variable might be temperature; empirical studies have shown that variations in ambient temperature influence secretion of iodine-131 into cow's milk.

### SELECTING AND AGGREGATING FLOWS

If the real world system under study is rather complex, the modeler will probably not include all flows and exogenous variables within the model. The modeler may consider some flows between state variables so insignificant to the question being asked (what will be the iodine-131 concentration in the thyroid?) that she will leave them out of the model. For example, even though **Figure 8-5** includes the flow of iodine-131 from cows to grass via excretion—J(4,3)—this pathway may be so trivial that a modeler would omit it. A modeler may also leave out some of the exogenous variables that only slightly influence flow rates. An example, again, might be ambient temperature, insofar as it affects grass to milk iodine-131 transfer; a modeler might ignore such exogenous variables because they are minor or because their effects are poorly understood.

These decisions to include or exclude variables from the model are an essential part of the process of model construction. When flows are included, the modeler may lump together, or aggregate, some of them. For example, in a model of the food chain pathway for radionuclides taken up by edible plants, a modeler might lump together the varied processes whereby different vegetables are harvested, transported, and prepared for consumption.

### Establishing Transfer Coefficients

Once the modeler has constructed the model, she is ready to define mathematically the functional relationships between the state and exogenous variables. To ascertain flow rates for each of the flows depicted on the model, she conducts experiments or consults experiments conducted by others. For most transfer processes in radionuclide transport models, it is believed that flow rates are functions of inputs and are essentially linear: an increase in input to a compartment results in a proportional increase in output from that compartment. The empirically-derived values for these flow rates, therefore, are transformed into linear "transfer coefficients," or mathematical multipliers, that may be applied to the quantity or concentration of the nuclide entering a donor compartment in order to predict the flow of the nuclide out of the donor to a recipient compartment. These coefficients are also called "constants."

For example, experimental studies may indicate that each unit of iodine-131 in a cow's feed results (on average) in 0.01 units of iodine-131 in the cow's milk. If so, the transfer coefficient in the mathematical form of the model would be 0.01. Most radionuclide transport models consist of a series of transfer coefficients, each of which has been given its own symbol. For example, the transfer coefficient for feed to milk, represented in **Figure 8-5** by the flow J(4,5), usually is referred to by the symbol $F_m$. The equations used in modeling are beyond the comprehension of most laypersons. Nonetheless, the basic modeling technique—a series of multiplications based on empirically-derived transfer factors that shows the movement of radionuclides from compartment to compartment—is comprehensible.

The iodine-131 ecosystems model crudely depicted in **Figure 8-5** represents only one of the many nuclides and two of the many pathways (breathing and milk ingestion) associated with nuclear generating plant emissions. There are hundreds of nuclides and numerous complex pathways whereby those nuclides may reach humans. An evaluation of all radionuclides and all pathways would be essentially an impossible task. Moreover, even if it were pursued relentlessly, the resulting dose estimates would differ little from the estimates resulting from a careful evaluation of a few critical nuclides and pathways. Therefore, radionuclide transport modeling customarily gives primary emphasis to a half dozen radionuclides moving through three or four pathways.

### THREE TRANSPORT PROCESSES

Models used in radioactive air emission controls correspond to the three transport processes addressed earlier: atmospheric transport models, environmental transport models, and metabolic/dosimetric models. You have organized your notes on these topics by first addressing the general features of each type of model and then describing the specific models used by the NRC.

## 3. MODELING ATMOSPHERIC TRANSPORT

### GENERAL PRINCIPLES

You recorded earlier in your notes that the atmosphere transports, disperses, mixes, deposits, and resuspends radionuclides in complex ways. Despite this complexity, atmospheric transport models are often rather simple. While it is true that the short-term behavior of plumes may be erratic, the significant danger created by low-level continuous releases of radionuclides is not acute exposure during a few minutes or hours, but rather the doses incurred by the maximum exposed individual and by population groups over such extended periods as a full year. The movement of plumes over time spans as long as a year may be projected by using only a handful of meteorological inputs.

### AIR QUALITY MODELING GRIDS

The goal of atmospheric transport modeling is to make accurate projections of ambient air concentrations of pollutants at selected ground level locations away from the source. These locations might be called "receptor sites." A typical air quality model begins by defining these locations. As depicted in **Figure 8-6**, concentric circles are drawn around a point at the center of the diagram; the point represents the facility. The circles form annuli, which are the areas between the concentric rings. The annuli are then subdivided into 16 equal pie shaped wedges. The wedges are formed by segmenting the concentric circles along the compass sectors at angles of 22.5 degrees. The resulting grid contains numerous locational compartments. For example, if 3 radial distances are used, as in **Figure 8-6**, there will be 48 compartments; if 20 radial distances are used, there will be 320 compartments. The state variables represented by each compartment are the ambient air concentrations of radionuclides at ground level for specific locations. The output of the model provides estimates of those state variable concentrations. This information is vital for ascertaining the locations of maximum exposed individuals. It may be used to calculate external doses and to begin the modeling of environmental transport for internally deposited radionuclides.

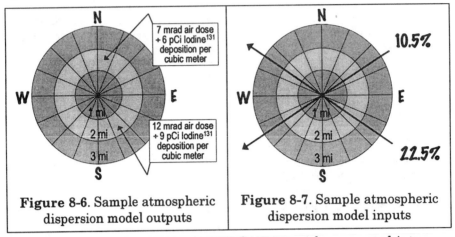

**Figure 8-6.** Sample atmospheric dispersion model outputs

**Figure 8-7.** Sample atmospheric dispersion model inputs

The resulting dose concentration figures may be converted into another helpful form known as isodose curves; the result is a map of dose levels consisting of nonuniform, irregularly shaped rings (isopleths) of progressively decreasing doses as one moves away from a facility. You haven't been able to get a good copy of a figure of an isodose curve map for your notes, but you are able to use your imagination to "see" what it might look like. Such a map would resembles a topographic map as the elevation falls off away from a mountain; irregular rings are labeled for the different elevations: 12,500 feet, 12,000 feet, and so forth.

Similar maps of dose patterns could be constructed for doses delivered through the food chain. Such maps might provide an ideal mechanism for ascertaining compliance with Part 190's cumulative dose limits; by superimposing the isodose curves of two neighboring facilities, additive effects could be modeled rather simply.

### MODELED BEHAVIORS

To provide the desired output—ambient concentrations at specified locations—air quality models typically consider three aspects of atmospheric activity: transport, dispersion, and deposition (if appropriate for the radionuclide being modeled). The models used by NRC licensees do not address mixing. This means that changes in molecular associations, size, shape, and phase (solid, liquid, and gaseous) of the radionuclides are ignored. Nor do NRC licensee models address resuspension.

### ATMOSPHERIC TRANSPORT

Consider, first, transport. To know *which* locational compartments the plume encounters and how long it *remains* in any given compartment, one must ascertain the direction of the plume's path and its speed. Wind speed and direction at specific locations may be easily measured by standard meteorological devices. But how does one ascertain wind speeds and directions—and hence the transport of radionuclides—over a large three dimensional area?

Two basic types of models can be used to ascertain these values. The first type—the "constant mean wind direction model"—assumes that during its entire passage through the modeled area, the plume continues to follow the mean wind direction of airflow at the point of release. Such "straight-line trajectory models" often assume further that the plume continues to move at a constant speed, determined at the point of release, as it passes through all model compartments. Because the measured wind speed and direction at a single point determine the speed and direction of the plume throughout the entire straight-line trajectory model, the selection of the measuring location is of utmost importance. This is especially true of elevated releases, because wind speeds and directions may vary at different elevations.

The second type of model, the "variable trajectory model," takes into account the fact that wind speeds and directions vary spatially and temporally. Such models require regional data for wind speeds and directions at numerous locations. Obviously, the former type of transport model is much less complex than the latter and requires input data that is significantly easier to acquire. The NRC will accept, but does not require, the use of variable trajectory models.

### ATMOSPHERIC DISPERSION

The second aspect of atmospheric activity that must be modeled to obtain ambient air concentrations is dispersion. You cannot determine ambient concentrations until you know the extent to which the contaminants have been diffused and diluted with noncontaminated air. Most atmospheric dispersion models are based on statistical theory and are variations of the Gaussian plume dispersion model. In this model, a mathematical equation simulates dispersion. The output of the equation is the center-line concentration in the plume at ground level.

Two of the three meteorological inputs for the standard Gaussian plume model—wind speed and direction—will already have been determined in calculating the transport of the plume as a whole. The third input, however, is unique to the dispersion portion of the model. This is called the "atmospheric stability" variable and is denoted by reference to a standard index of "atmospheric stability categories," ranging from A (extremely unstable) to G (extremely stable), and first introduced by Pasquill.

Many models assume that atmospheric stability is a constant throughout the entire region being modeled and, therefore, determine it only at the release point. Unlike wind speed and direction, however, stability categories cannot be measured directly. Instead, the model user must extrapolate stability categories from measurements of one of several possible substitute phenomena. The choice of the phenomenon to be measured is an important step in the process of dispersion modeling because it may have a profound effect on the determination of stability category.

## DEPOSITION

The third aspect of atmospheric activity that must be modeled to obtain ambient air concentrations is deposition. Deposition is obviously important to ambient air quality assessments because of the associated depletion of plume concentrations; contaminants deposited on the ground can no longer contribute to ambient levels unless resuspended. Deposition is also important as a first step in ascertaining external doses from ground deposits and internal doses from radionuclides taken up into the food chain.

Models of the dry deposition process are typically based on a transfer coefficient known as deposition velocity. When multiplied times the air concentration, this coefficient yields the deposition rate. Values for the coefficient must be derived by experimental measurements; because deposition behavior differs from nuclide to nuclide and from compound to compound, no single deposition velocity will be accurate for all contaminants.

## ASCERTAINING LONG-TERM AVERAGE VALUES

The foregoing description of the various components of air quality models addresses only temporary plumes for which associated meteorological inputs can be measured. The goal of air quality modeling for radionuclide releases, however, is almost always to obtain long-term—for example, annual average—concentration values for each locational compartment. The model is used to calculate such long-term concentrations in two steps. First, the annual emissions for each possible combination of the three meteorological inputs are run through the model. One such combination might be wind from the NNW, wind speed of 5 meters per second, and stability category C. The results are the concentrations that would have appeared in each compartment had these weather conditions prevailed throughout the entire year. Next, each of these sets of results is multiplied by the percentage of time during the year that the three meteorological input values coexisted—their so-called "joint frequency." The results achieved through this series of calculations yield the average annual concentration for each compartment.

To obtain annual average concentration figures, therefore, the model user must provide "joint frequency" distributions for the meteorological inputs of wind speed, wind direction, and stability category. These crucial meteorological inputs may be obtained from measurements made during the time period of the release, in which case the model output will reflect "real time meteorology." Alternatively, the input data may be taken from meteorological measurements made at a time preceding the period of release, in which case the model output reflects not "real time" meteorological conditions but historical ones. **Figure 8-7** at page 272, *supra*, for example, illustrates how historical measurements might be plotted on the atmospheric transport grid to reflect the percentage of time during which specific wind *directions* are experienced in the course of a sampled year. Regardless of the source of the meteorological data, that pile of articles and books on your desk indicates that this input data is often the most vulnerable aspect of the air quality dispersion model.

### *Questions*

1.   Does it make a difference, do you suppose, if a nuclear generating plant uses historical average meteorological data, rather than "real time" measurements, when tracking the atmospheric transport and dispersion of its radionuclide emissions? Why or why not?

2.   Under what circumstances might outputs resulting from the use of historical average meteorological data be positively misleading? Why?

---

### ACCURACY OF AIR QUALITY MODELS

How accurate is air quality modeling? A group of experts who met in 1977 concluded that "application of models to relatively flat terrain using accurate meteorological input data could yield calculated air concentrations within a factor of 4 of measured concentrations out to distances as great as 100 km." Yet other experts at the meeting "felt that a factor of 10 was more realistic." For the shorter distances associated with maximum doses, the group concluded for flat terrain that center line, ground level concentrations within ten kilometers of a continuous release point could be modeled to within approximately twenty percent of actual concentrations. For more complex terrains, however, they concluded that the uncertainties were "unquantifiable." Because the terrain, wind patterns, and climatic conditions of nearly every facility are unique, the calculation of air concentrations is an extremely complicated task with great potential for error. If errors do creep in, they will ripple throughout all subsequent environmental transport and dose calculations.

### CALCULATING EXTERNAL DOSES FROM AIR QUALITY MODEL OUTPUTS

Once the outputs of the air quality model are obtained, very little further modeling is necessary to compute the external doses delivered by the plume and by ground shine to human receptors. Annual average concentrations in air and on the ground surface can be converted to dose rates, based on known radiological properties for each radionuclide. Only the occupancy time by receptors for a given location must be considered in order to calculate whole-body and skin doses from such external sources. By finding the locational grid compartment with the highest combination of dose rate and occupancy time for a single receptor, one can readily ascertain the *location* of the maximum exposed individual as well as the *dose* incurred by that individual. Population exposures can be calculated by multiplying the total annual dose for each grid by the number of persons in that grid on an annual average.

## 5. NRC ATMOSPHERIC TRANSPORT MODELS

The NRC's "Regulatory Guides" have specified the models that are acceptable to the Commission. These publications do not contain regulations, but rather "regulatory positions" held by the NRC staff, accompanied by narrative discussions. The NRC declares that compliance with the Regulatory Guides is not required. Models "differing from those set out in the guides are acceptable if they provide a basis for the findings requisite to the issuance or continuance of a * * * license."

The flexibility inherent in this approach is commendable. However, it contributes to the lack of uniform license conditions and uniform reporting of emissions and doses. Because of the freedom given each licensee to devise its own models in an Offsite Dose Calculation Manual (ODCM), it is impossible to compare reported doses without going through the tedious process of comparing the ODCMs used by each licensee to discover how the models differ. For example, the Sequoyah nuclear generating plant ODCM sets forth a relatively disaggregated model, using real time meteorology and shifting locations for maximum receptors, but the Prairie Island nuclear generating plant's manual sets forth an extremely aggregated model, using historical average meteorology, with fixed maximum receptor locations.

Regulatory Guide 1.111 describes the types of air quality models and input data that the NRC staff will accept for projecting annual doses and determining compliance with Appendix I. It lists several dispersion models in order of decreasing model complexity, declining to specify a single model and declaring simply that "the preferred model is that which best simulates atmospheric transport and diffusion in the region of interest."

### Questions

1. The NRC's atmospheric dispersion models give nuclear generating plants a number of options. Straight-line trajectory models or variable trajectory models. Real-time or historical average meteorological inputs. Stability categories determined by using vertical temperature measurements or "other well-documented parameters." Suppose you are a nuclear generating plant environmental compliance engineer. Which of these various options are you likely to pick? Why?

2. Here are some possible answers to the preceding question:

   a. The options that are most suitable to our site, because we want to assure the most accurate possible dose calculation outputs.

   b. The options that are the cheapest and simplest to implement, because we want to minimize costs.

   c. None of the above, because we are driven by a different motivation.

Which of the foregoing answers seems the most realistic. Why?

## 6. MODELING ENVIRONMENTAL TRANSPORT

### GENERAL PRINCIPLES

In the modeling process, environmental transport models begin where atmospheric transport models end. Accordingly, the models must "interface" properly; the atmospheric transport model outputs must be *inputs* for the environmental transport model. For this reason, environmental transport models for radionuclides typically commence with two inputs: (1) ambient air radionuclide concentrations, and (2) quantities of radionuclides deposited on terrestrial surfaces.

A thorough environmental transport model would contain at least as many compartments as the diagram depicted in **Figure 8-3**, set forth at page 247, *supra*. A less aggregated model would have separate compartments for the different plant and animal species; the compartments representing species might then have subcompartments representing metabolic properties within organisms. A thorough model would also contain transfer factors (for dozens of different radionuclides) for each of the transfer activities depicted in **Figure 8-3**, as well as for the many exogenous variables (for example, soil acidity and ambient temperatures) that may affect transfer rates. Finally, a thorough model would include geographic elements. Specific crops and farm animals—perhaps even acreages or numbers for each—would be associated with each locational compartment. Movements of animal feeds and human foodstuffs between compartments would be depicted through additional transfer activities and coefficients.

Models of such complexity, even though they simplify the real world considerably, are rarely used to determine the environmental transport of radionuclides. Typical models ignore nuclides and pathways that are not "critical." Whether a given pathway is critical depends in part on the dietary habits and agricultural practices in a given location. Critical foods vary throughout the world, including—at different locations—caribou meat, fish, milk, cereals, and fruit, with each foodstuff involving a different radionuclide.

Typical models also ignore dozens of exogenous variables. Some may even be so aggregated that they consist of a mere two compartments. Despite the need to simplify environmental transport modeling, however, many presently used models are wondrously complex.

## 7. NRC ENVIRONMENTAL TRANSPORT MODELS

Regulatory Guide 1.109 sets forth the environmental transport models favored by the NRC. The Guide is intended to play the central role in the NRC's proposed scheme for enforcing Appendix I through ODCMs drafted by individual licensees, as well as for assessing compliance with Part 190. In comparison with the breadth of the environmental transport process depicted in **Figure 8-3**, the NRC model has a relatively narrow coverage. Moreover, because the Regulatory Guide is not binding, licensees are free to use much simpler models. In fact, some licensees use extraordinarily simplistic models.

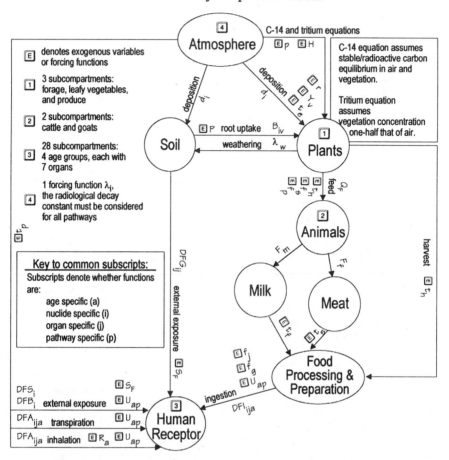

**Figure 8-8** NRC Environmental Transport Model

The NRC model can be understood best by carefully studying **Figure 8-8** and the accompanying definitions in **Table 8-1** and **Table 8-2**. **Figure 8-8** depicts the state variables, the transfer functions, and the forcing functions addressed in Regulatory guide 1.109 for modeling the environmental transport of radioactive air emissions. The definitions for the transfer and forcing functions are set forth in **Table 8-1** and **Table 8-2**.

In the NRC model, the human receptor state variable is broken down into four subcompartments, based on age: infants (0 to 1 year), children (1 to 11 years), teenagers (11 to 17 years), and adults (17 years and older). Each of these receptor compartments is then further subdivided into seven organs for modeling internal doses: bone, liver, total body, thyroid, kidney, lung, and G.I. tract/lower intestine. The output of the model consists of doses to the whole body and to various organs for maximum exposed individuals and for population groups.

**Table 8-1.** Transfer functions and generic default values.

| Symbol | Definition | Generic Default Value |
|---|---|---|
| $B_{iv}$ | concentration factor for uptake of radio-nuclide i from soil by edible parts of crops, in pCi/kg (wet weight) per pCi/kg dry soil | single transfer functions (regardless of plant species) are provided for each of 31 stable elements |
| $D_i$ | deposition rate of nuclide i, in $pCi/m^2$ per hr | curves are set forth for deposition at various downwind distances for different release heights and stability classes |
| $DFA_{ija}$ | inhalation dose factor for radionuclide i, organ j, and age group a, in mrem/pCi | factors are set forth for 73 radionuclides, 7 body organs, and 4 age groups |
| $DFB_i$ | total body gamma dose factor for a semi-infinite cloud of radionuclide i (including the attenuation of 5 $g/cm^2$ of tissue) in mrem—$m^3$/pCi—yr | factors are set forth for 15 noble gases |
| $DFG_{ij}$ | open field ground plane external dose conversion factor for organ j from radio-nuclide i, in mrem—$m^2$/pCi—hr | factors are set forth for total body and for skin for 72 radionuclides |
| $DFI_{ija}$ | dose conversion factor for the ingestion of nuclide, i, organ j, and age group a, in mrem/pCi | factors are set forth for 73 radionuclides, 7 body organs, and 4 age groups |
| $DFS_i$ | beta skin dose factor for a semi-infinite cloud of radionuclide i, in mrem—$m^3$/pCi—yr | factors are set forth for 15 noble gases |
| $F_f$ | fraction of the animal's daily intake of nuclide i that appears in each kilogram of flesh, in days/kg | transfer functions are provided for each of 31 stable elements |
| $F_m$ | average fraction of the animal's daily intake of radionuclide i that appears in each liter of milk, in days/liter | transfer functions are provided for each of 31 stable elements for cows |
| $Q_F$ | amount of feed consumed by the animal per day, in kg/day (wet weight) | 50 kg/day (wet weight) for dairy and beef cattle |
| $\lambda_w$ | removal rate constant for physical loss by weathering | 0.0021 $hr^{-1}$ (corresponds to a 14 day half-life), regardless of plant species or geographical location |

**Table 8-2.** Forcing functions and generic default values.

| Symbol | Definition | Generic Default Value |
|---|---|---|
| $f_g$ | respective fraction of the ingestion rate of produce that is produced in the garden of interest | 0.76 |
| $f_l$ | respective fraction of the ingestion rate of leafy vegetables that is produced in the garden of interest | 1.0 |
| $f_p$ | fraction of the year that animals graze on pasture | 1.0 |

| Symbol | Definition | Generic Default Value |
|---|---|---|
| | **Table 8-2.** Forcing functions and generic default values. | |
| $f_s$ | fraction of daily feed that is pasture grass when the animal grazes on pasture | 1.0 |
| $H$ | absolute humidity of the atmosphere at the modeled location in $g/m^3$ | $8.0 \ g/m^3$ |
| $P$ | effective "surface density" for soil, in kg (dry soil)/$m^2$ | $240 \ kg/m^2$ |
| $p$ | ratio of the total annual release time for carbon-14 to the total annual time during which photosynthesis occurs | 1.0 (continuous releases) |
| $r$ | fraction of deposited activity retained on crops, dimensionless | 1.0 (iodines), 0.2 (other particulates) |
| $R_a$ | annual air intake for individuals in the age group a, in $m^3/yr$ | values are provided for individuals in each of four age categories |
| $S_F$ | shielding factor accounting for dose reduction due to shielding provided by residential structures during occupancy, dimensionless | 0.7 (maximum exposed individual), 0.5 (general population) |
| $t_e$ | time period that crops are exposed to contamination during the growing season, in hours | 30 days (grass-cow-milk pathway), 60 days (crop-vegetation-person pathway) |
| $t_f$ | average transport time of the activity from the feed into the milk and to the receptor | 2 days (maximum exposed individual), 4 days (general population) |
| $t_h$ | holdup time representing time interval between harvest and consumption of food, in hours | zero (pasture grass), 90 days (stored cattle feed), 1 day (leafy vegetables to maximum exposed individual), 60 days (produce to maximum exposed individual), 14 days (general population) |
| $t_p$ | average transit time required for nuclides to reach the point of exposure | determined by the atmospheric transport model; default value might be zero |
| $t_s$ | average time from slaughter to consumption | 20 days |
| $U_{ap}$ | usage factor that specifies the exposure time or intake rate for an individual of age group a associated with pathway p, in hr/yr, liters/yr, or kg/yr | values are provided for average and maximum exposed individuals in each of four age categories for produce, milk, meat, and leafy vegetables |
| $Y_v$ | agricultural productivity (yield), in kg (wet weight)/$m^2$ | $0.72 \ kg/m^2$ (grass-cow-milk pathway), $2.0 \ kg/m^2$ (crop-vegetation-person pathway) |
| $\lambda_I$ | Radiological decay constant of nuclide i, in $sec^{-1}$, $hours^{-1}$, $days^{-1}$, or $yr^{-1}$ | |

GENERIC DEFAULT VALUES

Besides providing acceptable model structure, Regulatory Guide 1.109 also provides "generic default values" for virtually all of the transfer and forcing functions—values that the staff would use and licensees could use in lieu of site-specific information. These generic default values are summarized in **Table 8-1** and **Table 8-2**. The NRC and the EPA encourage the use of site-specific information, but nothing in the Regulatory Guide or in other NRC publications require the licensee to generate such data where it does not exist.

Although Regulatory Guide 1.109 cites numerous references, the NRC staff has not disclosed the process or the principles by which it selected these default values from wide ranges of values that appear in the literature. For a number of functions, the staff states that it has assigned values despite the lack of any empirical bases for such assignments.

### Questions

1.　The NRC invites but does not require the use of site-specific information for the various environmental transport model state variables, transfer functions, and forcing (exogenous) functions. Does this strike you as a good thing or a bad thing? Why? How do you think nuclear generating plants will respond to this invitation? Why?

2.　Values for the transfer and forcing functions can be either "conservative" (tending to overstate ultimate radiation doses by representing the "high end" of a range of possible values) or "non-conservative" (tending to understate ultimate radiation doses by representing the "low end" of a range of possible values). For example, a conservative value for $t_S$ (average time from slaughter to consumption) might be zero days—an approach for this function which would result in the maximum possible receptor dose from radionuclides in the meat pathway, because it would remove any opportunity for radioactive decay prior to consumption. Which of the generic default values in **Table 8-1** and **Table 8-2** seem to you to be conservative? Which seem to be non-conservative? Which are impossible for you to allocate to the conservative or non-conservative categories? Why?

## F.　ADEQUACY OF FEDERAL STANDARDS

### 1.　THREE OVERARCHING QUESTIONS

The adequacy of federal nuclear generating plant air emissions standards can be broken down into three overarching questions. First, is the *form* of the federal standards adequate? This question has to do with how the standards are *worded*. As you glance through your notes on Part 20, Appendix I, and Part 190, you are pleased to discover that you have an informed opinion on this question. Indeed, you have informed opinions on many closely related subquestions that flow from the matter of form. Are the standards comprehensible and enforceable?

Do the standards mesh effectively? Are they crawling with "fine print" so that the standards don't really say what at first they seem to say? Are they being implemented at operating reactors in a consistent and uniform fashion, leading to comparable pollution control measurements and comparable monitoring reports? You will have worthwhile and intelligent things to say in this part of your memo to the Attorney General, based solely on what you've learned from your notes in the preceding pages.

The second overarching issue might be called the "health question": do the federal standards guarantee radiation exposures sufficiently low to assure that the public health is being protected? This question makes you feel more uneasy, because it comes down to the doses being reported by nuclear generating plant licensees. Those doses, in turn, are no better than the licensees' monitoring of radionuclide releases and the models being used to crank out the dose numbers.

The final overarching issue might be called the "hardware question": do the federal standards demand as much as they reasonably should from control technology? This question, too, makes you somewhat uneasy, because you are ignorant about almost all aspects of radionuclide emission control possibilities.

## 2. THE HEALTH QUESTION

Turning, first, to the health question, it seems virtually indisputable that, *if* the monitoring of releases and the pathway and dosimetric models are accurate, the average annual doses incurred from routine releases of nuclear generating plants are extremely low—so low, in fact, that it might be a waste of time for your state to seek further decreases in actual emissions from the two nuclear generating plants. The standard practice of comparing such reported doses to natural background radiation and to radiation from other sources indicates that the annual dose to the *average* population from nuclear generating plant emissions is truly minuscule. This is especially obvious when one compares such exposure to the doses incurred by the American public from medical uses of radiation. Moreover, increasing our knowledge of the dose-response curve, discussed at pages 203-06, *supra*, will not change this conclusion. Average annual doses calculated by NRC models and reported by nuclear generating plants for their routine releases simply do not pose a health hazard for the general population.

This does not necessarily lead to the conclusion that federal standards governing radioactive air emissions from nuclear generating plants are adequate to protect the public health. At least three aspects of the federal regulatory scheme preclude that conclusion:

(1) Maximum individual exposures may be considerably higher than average population exposures.

(2) Federal standards governing the release of radioactive air emissions from nuclear generating plants are so much higher than actual release levels that they provided little guarantee that such low levels of routine releases will continue.

(3) There may be defects in pathway and dosimetric modeling, leading to underestimations—perhaps even rather large underestimations—of doses, so that the reported values are simply wrong.

Based on your previous notes, you are reasonably well equipped to deal with the issues raised by the first two items on this list of possible inadequacies in the federal standards. The final item, however—the possibility of modeling error—is so complex and central to the adequacy of the federal regulatory scheme that it requires much more extended research.

## 3. STRUCTURAL DEFECTS

In their efforts to simulate accurately the complex interactions of real world systems, modelers strive to minimize two major sources of error in model outputs: structural defects in model design and erroneous assignment of parameter values. Although the two aspects are closely related, it is helpful to address them separately.

Consider, first, structural defects. Two steps in model construction—the aggregation of entities and processes into state variables and functions, and the exclusion of other entities and processes—inevitably reduce the accuracy of the model.

## 4. AGGREGATION ERROR

To model complex ecosystems, one must lump together large numbers of components into a few variables. This process is called *aggregation*. Consider, for example, **Figure 8-3**, set forth at page 247, *supra*. With the exception of the receptor, every living thing is lumped into three compartments: plant, animal, and fish and seafood.

Aggregation has unfortunate side effects. Each time two entities or processes in the real world are lumped into a single compartment or function in the model, error occurs, regardless of how that aggregate was created. Moreover, lumping several elements together into a single variable involves additive error. To minimize aggregation error, therefore, the best models involve a high degree of resolution—i.e., more boxes or compartments.

Paradoxically, the attempt to minimize the inherent error of aggregation by increasing the degree of resolution creates more opportunities for potential errors in quantification. At the very least, an increase in resolving power requires greater investments of time and effort in quantifying the extra variables—investments that may not be worth the slight increase in accuracy. Even worse, an increase in complexity may result in a less accurate model; the model variables may be so poorly known that parameter uncertainty error more than outweighs the benefits of disaggregation. For these reasons, the modeler must strive to achieve an *optimal* level of aggregation.

There are two primary methods by which the modeler can seek the optimal level of aggregation. First, the modeler may follow some simple rules for minimizing aggregation error. Two standard rules are: (1) lump only components with nearly identical turnover rates, and (2) lump rare species with common ones. It follows from these principles that aggregation error will tend to be large if the components tend to be equally abundant or differ greatly in turnover rates. A second way to minimize aggregation error is to build different levels of aggregation into different models of the same system and see if the outputs of the models are different with respect to the question being asked.

Every state variable, transfer function, and forcing function depicted in **Figure 8-8**, at page 278, *supra*, and defined in the accompanying **Table 8-1** and **Table 8-2** involves the inevitable error of the aggregation process. Using the principles for minimizing aggregation error and the test procedure of running models with varying levels of aggregation to compare outcomes, a decisionmaker committed to reducing aggregation error might wish to scrutinize the lumped state variables in the NRC models.

### *Questions*

1. Which lumped variables in **Figure 8-8** suggest the possibility of serious aggregation error, significantly affecting model outputs? Why?

2. The NRC environmental transport model in **Figure 8-8** simulates radionuclide delivery to four age groups: infants (0 to 1 year), children (1 to 11 years), teenagers (11 to 17 years), and adults (17 years and older). The NRC then uses something called a "standard man" to model the metabolic transport of radionuclides *within* the bodies of human receptors to such organs as the thyroid and lungs. The standard men used to model metabolic transport are a newborn, a four-year-old, a 14-year-old, and a 17-year-old. Is it likely that the metabolic transport model is subject to aggregation error with respect to age? Why or why not?

3. Analysis has shown that six-year-olds receive the highest dose to the lungs from radon daughters. Is the NRC model optimally aggregated to calculate doses to six-year-olds? Why or why not?

4. Do you suppose the standard man infant in the NRC model consumes fruits, vegetables, grains, leafy vegetables, meat, or poultry? Would it surprise you that the answer is "no"? Remember that the "standard man" infant is supposed to represent a receptor for the full year of reactor emissions for which it serves as the model. Does any state variable in the model accurately represent the combined consumption habits and organ shapes and sizes of a one-year-old?

5. Which "standard man" represents you in this model? Is it likely, do you suppose, that this surrogate adequately represents you?

## 5. EXCLUSION BIAS

One major technique of model building is aggregation. A second technique might be called *exclusion*: the omission of information from the model. Sometimes state variables and functions are deliberately omitted to avoid trivializing the model. Other exclusions occur because the modeler, due to ignorance, may not be able to identify all the subsystems which make up the system. Regardless of the reasons for these exclusions, they will result in biased model outputs.

Exclusions from the model may be of many types. First, certain nuclides may be ignored; for instance, the NRC models consider only seventy-three nuclides for internal radiation. Second, pathways may be overlooked by excluding from the model's state variables and transport processes entities (the NRC models omit tobacco) and phenomena (the NRC models omit resuspension of deposited radionuclides and inhalation of radionuclides by farm animals). Third, exogenous variables that play vital roles in transfer rates may be ignored.

One special instance of pathway omission involves the exclusion of feedback loops: the model builder assumes that the fraction of radionuclides or radiation failing to move to the next sequential compartment leaves the system forever. Here are some examples in the NRC models: gamma rays are modeled for only one geographic sector or organ; radionuclides removed from plant surfaces by weathering or by grain milling processes seem to have disappeared; animal and human excreta seem to have exited the biosphere; and airborne radionuclides passing the fifty-mile radius seem to have vanished. For short-lived radionuclides in some contexts, this assumption makes sense. For example, the short half-life of iodine-131 (8 days) makes recycling of this nuclide through cow dung or plant weathering pathways trivial. In other contexts, such exclusions should perhaps be analyzed more carefully.

### *Notes and Questions*

1. Articles reporting the results of empirical studies show that agricultural practices may greatly affect the uptake rate of specific radionuclides by various crops. For example, the addition of lime to acidic soils raises the pH and dilutes strontium-90 with stable calcium; potassium fertilizing may decrease greatly plant uptake of radioactive cesium. These are classic examples of exogenous variables (sometimes called forcing functions). What function in the NRC model (**Figure 8-8** and **Tables 8-1** and **8-2**, set forth at page 278, *supra*) is used to calculate movement of radionuclides from soil to plants? How are the exogenous variables of lime addition and potassium fertilizing represented in the NRC model?

2. One published empirical study concludes that radioiodine metabolism by lactating animals is so heavily influenced by temperature that it may be necessary to develop a series of transfer figures or equations to cover seasonal and geographical temperature ranges. What function in the NRC model (**Figure 8-8** and **Tables 8-1** and **8-2**) is used to calculate movement of radionuclides from dairy cow to milk? How is the exogenous variable of

temperature, insofar as it affects cow to milk transfer, represented in the NRC model?

3. Does the omission of significant exogenous variables complicate the modeler's search for the *value* to be used for such functions as $B_{iv}$ and $F_m$? If $F_m$ is one number when the temperature is 80° F but a very different number when the temperature is 10° F, how does the modeler select *which* value to use in the model? Do you suppose that there is a principled way to select the "appropriate" $F_m$ number for a given model? What might be some principles for selecting specific values for the various model functions?

## 6. PARAMETER UNCERTAINTY

You now have a pretty solid understanding of the potential *structural* inadequacies of the NRC models, including aggregation error and exclusion bias. To be thorough, however, you intend to explore a second potential vulnerability in the NRC's models: the selection of parameter values.

The errors introduced into the model in the process of selecting parameter values may be of two basic types: technical and philosophical. Many technical errors are possible. The empirical data consulted in the parameter selection process inevitably contains measurement error and sampling bias. Researchers have repeatedly stated that there is simply not enough empirical data about many NRC model parameters to form reliable judgments as to representative values. For other parameters, data has been poorly documented. The NRC has misapplied empirical studies, leading to the establishment of unsupported values. In other instances, the NRC has selected pairs of obviously interdependent default values that are logically inconsistent. All of these conclusions are supported by various health physics articles in your pile of research materials. For example, the NRC uses one set of curves to depict plume depletion (radionuclides dropping out of the plume) and another set of curves to depict deposition (radionuclides landing on terrestrial surfaces). The curves should be measuring a single phenomenon, but are so inconsistent that researchers have concluded that the NRC models may significantly underestimate the actual deposition occurring outside plant boundaries.

The main weakness of the NRC default values, however, is more philosophical than technical. The selection of generic default values to represent wide ranges of empirical measurements ("model fitting") demands the exercise of principled judgment, including a deliberate commitment to a preferred type of bias. Without such a commitment, the model will be made up of such a hodge-podge of default values that it cannot be use with confidence. A number of researchers assert that this has happened to the NRC models.

The NRC has claimed in the past that its generic default values are selected to be "conservative"—to overestimate actual doses. You struggled with whether and how the NRC has really been conservative in its environmental transport models, as you answered the questions at page 281, *supra*. It is unquestionably true that some of the default values are conservative. For example, the NRC model assumes that all deposited radionuclides reach edible parts in all plants, and that no nuclides are removed by washing foodstuffs. Portions of the iodine-milk pathway model are so cautious that they properly may serve as a showcase of conservatism. But the conservative philosophy is not followed in other pathways. Moreover, conservatism is a tricky thing in modeling; the assumption, for example, that all radioiodines are in elemental form with an r value of 1.0 is conservative for the milk pathway but inevitably causes a lower prediction of radioiodine inhalation.

### Notes and Questions

1. In 1979, researchers at the University of Heidelberg issued the "Heidelberg Report." In this document, researchers used the NRC's environmental and metabolic transport models, but substituted for the NRC's generic default values significantly higher numbers gleaned from the empirical literature. The Heidelberg Report projected annual nuclear generating plant doses to an adult of 940 millirems to the whole body, 12,300 millirems to the kidney, and 5,803 millirems to the bone.

2. In selecting parameter values from a wide range of numbers reported in empirical literature, should the standard setter use the highest reported measurements for *each* parameter, as done in the Heidelberg Report? Wouldn't that give confidence that no maximum exposed individual could ever incur the dose calculated by the model? Would such an approach be sensible? Should you recommend it to the Attorney General?

## 7. SITE-SPECIFIC PARAMETER VALUES

If at least some of the NRC's generic default values deficient, as suggested by some scientists, maybe the best way to minimize the effects of parameter uncertainty would be to require the licensee to generate and use site-specific data. Intuitively, this would seem to reduce the bias of the model.

Ironically, however, the use of site-specific data for some pathways may result in a considerable reduction in the conservatism of the NRC models, making dose underestimation more likely. This points out a danger in the structure of the NRC models: by inviting but not requiring the licensee to use site specific data, the NRC has made it possible for the user to *manipulate* the model outputs. The rational licensee may select favorable site-specific values while ignoring those that would lead to higher dose calculations; in fact, the licensee might refuse to even learn anything about parameters for which site-specific values might result in higher doses. The NRC staff could disapprove of such manipulation, but the absence of any coherent NRC philosophy concerning appropriate parameter values makes such rejection unlikely.

This possibility of manipulation is present whenever the NRC gives the licensee an option to select its own parameter values or model inputs—for example, when the licensee is given the freedom to determine atmospheric stability class on the basis of alternative measurements. The inherent biases of models are exacerbated when users are invited to tinker with them. Moreover, such tinkering further confounds the noncomparability of the doses reported by each generating plant.

## 8. THE HARDWARE QUESTION

Before writing your memorandum to the Attorney General, you sense that you should take at least a tentative whack at the hardware question: do the federal radioactive air emission standards require as much from control technology as they may reasonably demand?

If the extremely low doses reported by nuclear generating plants based on their use of the NRC models were unassailable, the hardware question might be unimportant. You believe, however, that the question of hardware is important because the uncertainties associated with model outputs cast considerable doubt on the reliability of the reported doses calculations.

You have stated the hardware question as one of reasonableness: do the federal radioactive air emission standards require as much from control technology as they may reasonably demand? Cost-benefit analysis cannot provide the answer to the question of reasonableness because of the imprecision of dose projections, coupled with uncertainty about the dose-response curve. Moreover, because the extent of required controls differs considerably from plant to plant, your state regulatory agency can answer the question only by examining the performance of specific facilities. In doing so, your state might consider five facets of plant design and operation.

First, treatment devices may be unnecessarily primitive. Holdup times at the older nuclear generating plants may be surprisingly short, and older plants may lack recombiners or charcoal adsorbers. Even plants with such devices may have systems that could be improved significantly. All plants could install advanced systems for capture and storage of krypton-85, carbon-14, and tritium. An additional "treatment" system for radioiodines might involve the deliberate use within the plant of materials and surface coatings designed to attract and retain fugitive iodine emissions.

You are confident, based on your research, that no plant is using the best *possible* treatment system, and you doubt that plant operators will dispute that conclusion. Whether it would be *reasonable* to require nuclear generating plants to augment their treatment systems is, of course, a matter of judgment.

Second, all plants have contaminated airstreams that are not treated. Frequently, such airstreams are not even monitored. As control devices become more sophisticated, these untreated airstreams assume greater relative significance.

Third, facilities can be designed to minimize the generation of some of the more troublesome radionuclides. Tritium production can be lowered by reducing primary coolant volume and by replacing boron and lithium with substitute materials. Carbon-14 generation might be lessened by reducing the amounts of nitrogen and oxygen moving through the core. Crud generation might be reduced by selection of different alloys, more efficient continuous purification of primary coolant, and better pH control.

Fourth, many nuclear generating plants could improve the overall quality of their monitoring activities and operating procedures. No matter how inclusive and modern the control components may be, radioactive waste management *practices* will play a vital role in determining the level of emissions. Operating procedures could be established and painstakingly implemented to minimize incidence of tramp uranium activation, fuel leakage, crud generation, air inleakage, filter malfunction, charcoal adsorber breakdowns, and leakage from valves, pipes, and purge lines. Without incentives to be vigilant about these matters, performance may be substandard.

Finally, when the foregoing aspects of plant design and operation have been optimized a number of creative steps might be available to minimize the doses delivered by emissions. Batch releases might be held until favorable meteorological conditions exist. Carbon-14 might be released in agricultural areas only at night, when photosynthesis has ceased. Metabolic competitors of the most significant radionuclides might be made available to the public, as potassium iodide tablets were distributed in Poland. One prominent health physicist, Dr. Karl Morgan, has advocated installation and continuous operation of equipment to deliberately and automatically release into the atmosphere at all radioactive iodine-131 discharge points enough stable (nonradioactive) iodine to thwart radioiodine uptake in the food chain. Such a control scheme of chemical prophylaxis would deliver stable metabolic competitors to receptors no matter how meteorological conditions varied.

Your state might endeavor to control agricultural locations and practices—for example, requiring mandatory sheltering of livestock feed and water supplies. Or your state might aggressively regulate the marketing of foodstuffs contaminated by radioactivity—for example, by requiring that milk obtained from nearby dairy farms be converted into powdered and evaporated milk, butter, and cheese, so that they could be withheld from the market until their radioactive contaminants had decayed. These last suggestions should not be overlooked even though they involve control of the environment, rather than radionuclide *emissions*; after all, if the goal is to protect the public health, public officials should be creative in pursuing that goal.

### Questions

1. Various publications demonstrate that nuclear generating plants can be *designed* to minimize the generation of some of the more troublesome

radionuclides, by reducing primary coolant volume, replacing boron and lithium with substitute materials, by reducing the amounts of nitrogen and oxygen moving through the core, and by the selection of different alloys in structural components of the facility. Do you see any drawbacks to a regulatory regime in which your state may impose such design requirements on nuclear generating plants? Why or why not?

2.   Are some of the options in the preceding three pages more suitable for state (as opposed to federal) implementation than others? Why or why not?

3.   What do you think of Dr. Karl Morgan's proposal for the deliberate and continuous injection of stable iodine into the atmosphere at all iodine-131 release points? Do you suppose that would that be a good thing? Might there be persons who must restrict their iodine intake for health reasons? Are they being clobbered by radioactive iodine-131 in any event, so that they would be no worse off under the Morgan scheme? *Cf. Minnesota State Board of Health v. City of Brainerd*, 308 Minn. 24, 241 N.W.2d 624 (1976) (mandatory fluoridation litigation).

# Chapter Nine

# CLEAN AIR ACT

## A. AIR POLLUTANTS

We now begin our in-depth examination of one federal statutory scheme: the Clean Air Act. We start with a background reading on the general nature of the air pollution problem.

### AIR CONSERVATION COMMISSION OF THE AMERICAN ASSOCIATION FOR THE ADVANCEMENT OF SCIENCE, AIR CONSERVATION

#### 26-32, 35-39 (1965)

The sources * * * of air pollutants are anywhere that energy is converted under human direction. From the smallest hearth fire to the largest factory, all contribute their share. The pollutants are even greater in number than the sources. However, a small number of groups of substances comprise the vast bulk of human emissions to the atmosphere.

#### WATER

The greatest single product of the energy conversion processes is of least concern here—water. Only in very rare instances can it qualify as a pollutant. Occasionally, the vapor from the stack of a large factory may reduce visibility on a nearby highway. But normally, water vapor does not represent an air pollution problem.

#### CARBON DIOXIDE

Carbon dioxide is next in quantity of the waste products produced by our use of organic fuels. It is naturally abundant in the atmosphere, and [humans are] well adapted to living with widely varying levels of it. However, while water vapor precipitates out of the atmosphere to join the oceans, carbon dioxide normally remains in a gaseous state for a long time. The liberation of this gas has been so great that we have already increased the global concentration by a substantial figure—around 5 percent; the exact figure is still in dispute. This increase has had no effect on any known living organism.

However, carbon dioxide is intimately involved in the mechanism that maintains the overall temperature of the earth. Although so many factors are involved in this overall atmospheric heat balance that it is impossible to evaluate the effect of any given increase in atmospheric carbon dioxide, a continued increase over a long period could possibly change the global climate. And, if such a change were to involve an increase of the earth's temperature, thereby causing a large portion of the global ice caps to melt and the oceans to rise, available land area would be reduced at precisely the time when more land is needed for an increasing population. In the light of this possibility, the use of fossil fuels as the principal source of our energy should be continually evaluated.

## CARBON MONOXIDE

The complete combustion of carbonaceous fuels produces carbon *dioxide*; the incomplete combustion, characteristic of many processes involving the conversion of energy, yields carbon *monoxide*. In American cities, the primary source of this gas is the automobile. Carbon monoxide begins to be hazardous to most human beings at concentrations of about 100 parts per million (ppm) if experienced over a period of several hours. Particularly susceptible individuals may be affected at lower levels. Although the toxic level seems very high when compared with other pollutant gases, this level has actually been reached occasionally in areas where traffic is heavy; more frequent occurrences may be expected unless automotive emissions can be effectively controlled.

## SULFUR DIOXIDE AND SULFURIC ACID

In addition to substances emitted in massive amounts, there are a variety of materials that normally occur in much lower concentrations. However, these materials are much more toxic. Sulfur dioxide and the sulfuric acid that forms when the gas comes in contact with air and water seldom reach levels above a few parts per million. However, the present consensus is that these two substances have been principal factors in all the air pollution disasters of recent history, including the London smog of 1952 in which some 4000 persons died. (There are many scientists who believe that factors as yet undiscovered contributed materially to these deaths, but most of them would identify sulfur dioxide and sulfuric acid as the major causative agents, perhaps combined with soot or other particles.) Sulfur dioxide results primarily from the combustion of coal or oil, both of which contain substantial percentages of sulfur in various chemical forms. To some extent in the combustion itself, and to a greater extent in the external atmosphere, sulfur dioxide is converted by the action of atmospheric oxygen and water to sulfuric acid. Sulfur dioxide by itself is extremely irritating to the upper respiratory tract in concentrations of a few parts per million. Sulfuric acid appears as a fine mist that can be carried deep into the lungs to attack sensitive tissues. In addition, droplets of sulfuric acid carry absorbed sulfur dioxide far deeper into the system than the free gas alone could penetrate, thus spreading the effect of this irritant over the entire respiratory tract. On the other hand, because of the ease with which sulfur dioxide is converted into sulfuric acid and sulfates, its lifetime in the atmosphere is seldom more than a few days. Consequently, it would not be expected to accumulate in the atmosphere.

## HYDROGEN SULFIDE

Hydrogen sulfide can result from a variety of industrial and other processes, but it usually enters the atmosphere as a result of the accumulation of industrial wastes in stagnant waters. Here bacterial action reduces the sulfur-containing compounds to hydrogen sulfide, which is relatively insoluble in water. It has the well-known odor of rotten eggs and it is highly objectionable. In high concentrations, it is also rapidly lethal. There are only a few cases in which concentrations of hydrogen sulfide in the open atmosphere exceeded the level of mere nuisance. (In one such case, a score of deaths resulted from an accidental release from a refinery in Poza Rica, Mexico.) The bacterial processes described constantly occur in nature, and by far the bulk of the total sulfur found in the atmosphere comes from natural causes. However, concentrations at any one place are usually not sufficient to be detected by the senses, or, in fact, by any but the most delicate measuring devices.

## OXIDES OF NITROGEN

There are six known oxides of nitrogen, and there is presumptive evidence for a seventh. However, only two are normally considered as pollutants: nitric oxide and nitrogen dioxide. These are what might be called "status symbol" pollutants. Only a highly mechanized and motorized community is likely to suffer serious pollution from them. *Nitric oxide*, the primary product, is formed when combustion takes place at a sufficiently high temperature to cause reactions between the nitrogen and oxygen of the air. Such temperatures are reached only in highly efficient combustion processes or when combustion takes place at high pressure. A great deal of nitrogen is fixed in the latter way in automobile cylinders. Electrical power plants and other very large energy-conversion processes will also fix nitrogen in this fashion. However, in most cities, automobiles are the largest single source.

Nitric oxide is generally emitted as such into the atmosphere. However, a complex of processes, some of them photochemical in nature, may convert a substantial portion of the nitric oxide to *nitrogen dioxide*, a considerably more toxic gas and the only important and widespread pollutant that is colored. As a result, nitrogen dioxide can significantly affect visibility. Nitrogen oxides are also liberated from a variety of chemical processes, such as in the manufacture of guncotton and nitric acid. In large-scale pollution, these sources are usually less significant than the broad area source represented by vehicular traffic.

## OZONE

There is little or no ozone emitted as such into the atmosphere. However, this gas, which is extremely toxic, is formed in the atmosphere on sunny days as a result of the interaction of nitrogen oxides with certain organic compounds.

## HYDROGEN FLUORIDE

In addition to the inorganic gases just mentioned, nearly any other objectionable inorganic gaseous material that is used in industry can become a pollutant if it escapes into the atmosphere. However, these are not the general emissions of what might be called the metabolic processes of civilization and they are likely to be restricted to a few locations. Consequently, only one of them, hydrogen fluoride, deserves separate attention. Because of its extreme toxicity for some living organisms, it is likely to be an acute problem wherever materials containing fluorides are processed. Hydrogen fluoride is apparently taken up from the air by nearly all plants, and certain species are damaged by concentrations as low as 1 part per billion. Furthermore, since vegetation tends to concentrate the fluoride that it receives, continuing low atmospheric levels of fluoride can produce toxic levels in forage and probably in some leafy vegetables as well. The manufacture of phosphate fertilizer, the smelting of certain iron ores, and the manufacture of aluminum are all sources of hydrogen fluoride gas as well as of some particulate fluoride.

## ORGANIC GASES

The organic gases are very numerous. The chemical process industries inevitably release into the atmosphere some of almost everything they manufacture. However, only a few general classes need separate consideration since a number of the organic materials that can be identified in the atmosphere appear to have no adverse effects.

## ETHYLENE

Probably the simplest organic substance significant to air pollution is ethylene. Aside from its participation in the "smog" reaction, it is a potent phytotoxicant (plant damaging agent) in its own right. Concentrations of a few parts per billion, for example, are extremely damaging to orchids, and only slightly higher concentrations adversely affect the growth of tomatoes. Ethylene, like the bulk of other simple hydrocarbons, emanates in part from industrial sources, but is primarily a product of automotive exhaust.

## OLEFINS

The higher members of the series to which ethylene belongs, the olefins, appear to have no direct effect upon vegetation or animal life. However, when they (together with several other classes of organics) are exposed to sunlight in the presence of nitrogen dioxide or nitric oxide, an extremely complex reaction sequence ensues. The end products appear to be ozone, aldehydes, and a variety of organic compounds that contain nitrogen. In adequate concentrations, this mixture injures plants and irritates the eyes and mucous membranes in human beings. There is some indication that animals are also affected. This reaction was first noticed in Los Angeles, and is therefore popularly referred to as the "Los Angeles smog reaction." The substances needed for this reaction can be produced by the right combination of industries, but they are present in almost ideal concentrations in automotive exhaust. Consequently, the presence of this type of pollution is characteristic of areas having a high density of automobile traffic.

### ALDEHYDES

Some of the aldehydes characteristic of the Los Angeles smog can also arise from other sources. Formaldehyde and acrolein, which are particularly irritating to the eyes and nose, are found in the smoke of poorly operating incinerators and also in stockyards and a number of other sources.

### MERCAPTANS

Mercaptans, which are organic substances related to hydrogen sulfide, are among the most odorous materials known. Aside from chemical processes that directly employ or produce these compounds, they are undesired by-products of Kraft paper mills and of some petroleum refineries.

### SOLVENTS

Finally, there is a large class of organic vapors generally referred to as "solvents." They escape from such processes as dry cleaning and painting. They are very diverse chemically, and some of them can probably participate in the smog reaction. Others have objectionable odors. Most of them are toxic to some degree, although it would be difficult to produce toxic concentrations over any period of time in the open air.

### PARTICULATES: DUST

Aside from these gases and vapors, large quantities of more or less finely divided particulate matter are put into the air or are formed there as a result of human activities. The largest single [type of] particle in nearly all urban atmospheres is dust. This word is used here to denote soil from areas denuded of vegetation, whipped up by natural wind, by the passage of vehicular traffic, or by agricultural activities. For the most part it is without physiological effect, but it is a very substantial nuisance. The particle sizes are usually large, so that, under most circumstances, such dust will not travel great distances. Obvious exceptions occur during times of high winds, as was demonstrated in the dust storms of the middle 1930's.

### SOOT

In many cities, the next most prevalent substance among the airborne particles is soot. Soot is very finely divided carbon clumped together into long chains and networks. Because the individual particles are so fine, they present an enormous surface per unit weight. This surface is extremely active, and it can absorb a large variety of substances from its environment. Soot generally carries with it a substantial load of heavy hydrocarbons that are formed simultaneously with it in smoky flames. These hydrocarbons include organics that are either known or are suspected causes of environmental cancer on sufficiently prolonged contact. Soot can also act under some circumstances in the same manner as sulfuric acid mist; that is, it can absorb vapors that would normally be removed in the upper respiratory tract and carry them deep into the lungs. In addition to all the known or suspected physiological effects, soot is a nuisance because it obscures visibility and soils buildings and clothing. The fall of combined soot, dust, and other particulate materials on a single square foot of horizontal surface in a city may easily exceed a pound per year.

### SMOG PARTICULATES

Another variety of fine particles is one of the end results of the photochemical smog reaction. The nature of the particulate matter formed is not understood, but it is oily, not easily wetted, and of a size that is highly effective in obscuring visibility.

### OTHER PARTICULATES

The typical urban atmosphere also contains particles caused by practically every process carried on within the city. There are lead salts from the combustion of leaded gasoline and particles of airborne ash from all the solid and liquid fuels burned in the area. The metallurgical industries, the manufacture of fertilizer, the storing of grain, and the milling of flour all add particles that are characteristic of their own processes.

### RESUSPENDED MATTER

Finally, there is a quantity of material generally referred to as "resuspended matter," refuse dropped into the streets or onto the ground, there to be slowly pulverized and blown into the air. Bits of newspaper, residue of plant matter, particles of glass and tire rubber, all go to make up the complex found suspended in the atmosphere of a typical city.

### ECONOMIC POISONS

There are two additional classes of particulate matter which, while not of peculiarly urban origin, have had a substantial impact on human well-being and have received a great deal of attention recently. The first of these are the economic poisons. They include insecticides, herbicides, and other chemicals used by [humans]. A number of them are normally disseminated through the air, and some portion may well find its way substantial distances from the intended site of application. While many of them are toxic to [humans], they can also harm other forms of life not intended as their targets.

### RADIONUCLIDES

The second category is radioactive material. There are three major sources of radioactive gases and particles. The first is research, which is generally not an important source of contamination except in the case of a major accident. The second is nuclear power plants, which almost continuously give off some gaseous materials. * * * The final source is, of course, nuclear weapons. They belong in a special category, not because of any chemical or physiological difference in the compounds involved or in their effects, but because the political and economic considerations that govern their use are so special. * * *

### THE FATE OF POLLUTANTS

For virtually every known pollutant, there are natural processes that tend to remove it from the atmosphere, thus preventing [humans] from smothering in [their] own by-products. * * *

[P]articulate pollutants [have a tendency] to coagulate, to increase in size, and to fall. Rain and snow carry large amounts of both particulate and gaseous pollutants out of the atmosphere and into the soil and the water of the earth. Trees and grasses act like the fibers of an enormous filter mat to collect particulates and some gases.

The oxygen of the air combines with many pollutants, either directly or indirectly, gradually changing them into forms that are more readily removed. In many cases, sunlight plays a role in this reaction, and frequently particulate matter is formed from gases. These particulates can then enter the cycle of filtration, aggregation, and washout, and can thus be removed from the atmosphere. It is worth noting that the droplets of sulfuric acid that have been implicated by many as contributing to the death toll in London, and the photochemical smog that is characteristic of the West Coast, are actually steps in the atmosphere's own process of self-purification. The misfortune is that these intermediate products are physiologically active and that they frequently form in heavily inhabited areas.

A few miscellaneous substances do not participate rapidly enough in the reactions of photochemical oxidation to be removed by that process. The outstanding examples are methane and a few of its relatives and carbon monoxide. They are ultimately destroyed by oxidation, entirely in the gas phase, and become carbon dioxide, although the rate of destruction is not known. Carbon dioxide appears to be removed effectively by direct solution in the ocean, the disposal point for most of the soluble inorganic substances. The capacity of the ocean to ultimately consume such materials by dilution is enormous. However, our rapid production of carbon dioxide seems to be outstripping the ocean's ability to remove it from the atmosphere. It appears that roughly one-third of the carbon dioxide put into the air by combustion remains there and, as noted earlier, it may have an effect on the world's weather.

Thus, the atmosphere has tremendous powers to dilute, disperse, and destroy a large variety of substances that [humans], for one reason or another, [elect] to discharge into it. Pollution occurs when these processes cannot keep up with the rate of discharge, and when this happens, only one more factor is needed to constitute pollution—a susceptible receptor, such as [human beings].

[Human beings remove] some of the pollutants from the air, for if they did not, the pollutants would not affect [them]. (The only exception is when pollution is manifested by loss of visibility. This can have economic repercussions in delaying aircraft schedules, in increasing automobile accidents, and in making a location less favorable to paying tourists, or its effect may be purely aesthetic.)

Pollutants collect on, and may affect, buildings, plants, and animals, including [humans]. They enter the lungs of creatures that breathe the air. With the pollution density of the atmosphere increasing rapidly, the possibility of any pollutant leaving the atmosphere without contacting [humans], [their] property, plants, or animals is becoming increasingly small. Although it is certainly necessary to use the atmosphere as one of the places to dispose of our wastes, it is going to become more and more difficult to find a parcel of air that can be used for waste disposal and that can adequately detoxify its load of pollutants before it is needed again.

CONTROL

The first and most obvious solution, historically, to the problem of a "dirty" industry is to move it out of town. This has also been, historically, a quite unsatisfactory solution; the town has often promptly grown out until it encompassed the industry. Attempts have been made to segregate industry in areas generally downwind of the residential portion of the city. This has at least two weaknesses. The first arises from the problem of transporting workers to these segregated sites, and sometimes the pollution from the workers' automobiles has added as much pollution as the industry would have had it been close to the population center. The other weakness arises from the facts of meteorology. The wind simply does not blow from the prevailing direction at all times. Consequently, this particular approach can succeed only where it is possible for industry to suspend emissions during periods of adverse wind.

Another widely used technique, particularly in the power industry, is the erection of extremely tall stacks, which usually also have very high air velocities in them. As a result, pollutants are discharged into the atmosphere at high levels, and their vertical velocity tends to carry them still higher. It is thus hoped that the dispersive processes in the atmosphere will have diluted the effluents below the level of physiological significance before they reach the ground. This technique has considerable merit, but it is not a complete guarantee against an occasional very high concentration reaching the ground. * * * [D]uring periods of high wind, the turbulent processes of the atmosphere can bring clouds of undiluted effluent into inhabited areas.

In most industries, it is at least theoretically possible, and in many cases it is economically feasible, to remove the bulk of the pollutants from the effluent stream before it is discharged into the atmosphere. There are devices for removing nearly all particulate pollutants and the bulk of the gases if they are in sufficiently high concentrations. However, some industries are characterized by an enormous total volume of effluent that contains impurities at rather low concentrations. The actual discharge in terms of tons per hour may be quite large, but the concentration in the effluent air stream can be so low that efficient removal of the pollutants is extremely expensive.

Another very general problem with techniques for cleaning the air is the disposal of the collected material. It is generally unacceptable to solve an air pollution problem by generating a water pollution problem. In some industries the recovered material may have substantial economic value. In other cases, extensive research may be necessary to find uses for these materials. Economics may become extremely important in the problem; for example, the potentially recoverable by-product sulfur from all present emissions into the atmosphere considerably exceeds the entire primary production of sulfur in the United States. The sudden entrance of this recovered sulfur into the market could be disruptive.

In some cases, it is possible to avoid emissions into the atmosphere by simply modifying the process being used. The main obstacle frequently is tradition. Certainly those cities that have changed from heating homes by coal to gas have greatly cut down on their concentrations of soot and sulfur compounds in the atmosphere. Tradition is partly to blame for the air pollution problems of English cities, since central heating, even by coal, is considerably cleaner than the traditional coal fire in every room. But it is also true that the first cost of conversion to central heating is also a deterring factor. Sometimes a troublesome emission of solvents into the atmosphere can be averted by changing to a less volatile solvent. The advent of latex-based paints has decreased the amount of turpentine given off in painting homes. These last examples are perhaps trivial, but they illustrate in familiar terms the potential of modifying a process.

A final and little-explored approach is simply better collaboration with nature. It was noted earlier that air pollution is the result of [human] conversion of energy * * * to oppose or to overcome nature—to create heat when it is cold, to create light when it is dark, and to substitute the strength of machines for the weakness of the human frame. This opposition to nature has become so much a part of [people] that [they] now sometimes choose the more difficult way simply because it is more in opposition to nature. Thus, [they] build houses in hot climates without the large roof overhang that would decrease the necessary air conditioning load and build houses in cold areas with enormous windows, and thereby increase the amount of fuel burned.

There is, of course, no panacea for air pollution. The intelligent location of sources of pollution is an important first step. Discharge of pollutants high in the air will compensate to some degree for the inevitable eventual crowding together of activities in the horizontal plane. Proper choice of fuels and raw materials will decrease process effluents.

The removal of some of these effluents before they are emitted into the atmosphere will further decrease the burden that the atmosphere is called upon to destroy. Finally, an intelligent program of general conservation—the use of energies available in nature, the avoidance of certain frills that produce pollution out of balance with the benefits they create, and the selection of alternatives to highly polluting activities—will decrease the incidence of high levels of pollution. None of these taken alone can solve any substantial portion of the problems that face [us] in [our] attempt to conserve [the] atmosphere.

# B. CLEAN AIR ACT OVERVIEW

Table 9-1. National Ambient Air Quality Standards for the Criteria Pollutants

| Pollutant | Primary (Health Related) | | Secondary (Welfare Related) | |
|---|---|---|---|---|
| | Type of Average | Standard Level Concentration | Type of Average | Standard Level Concentration |
| CO | 8-hour | 9 ppm (10 mg/m³) | No Secondary Standard | |
| | 1-hour | 35 ppm (40 mg/m³) | No Secondary Standard | |
| Pb | Maximum Quarterly Average | 1.5 µg/m³ | Same as Primary Standard | |
| NO$_2$ | Annual Arithmetic Mean | 0.053 ppm (100 µg/m³) | Same as Primary Standard | |
| O$_3$ | Maximum Daily 1-hour Average | 0.12 ppm (235 µg/m³) | Same as Primary Standard | |
| | Maximum Daily 8-hour Average | 0.08 ppm | Same as Primary Standard | |
| PM$_{10}$ | Annual Arithmetic Mean | 50 µg/m³ | Same as Primary Standard | |
| | 24-hour | 150 µg/m³) | Same as Primary Standard | |
| PM$_{2.5}$ | Annual Arithmetic Mean | 15 µg/m³ | Same as Primary Standard | |
| | 24-hour | 65 µg/m³) | Same as Primary Standard | |
| SO$_2$ | Annual Arithmetic Mean | 0.03 ppm (80 µg/m³) | 3-hour | 0.50 ppm (1,300 µg/m³) |
| | 24-hour | 0.14 ppm (365 µg/m³) | | |

Note: Compliance with the standards is measured in different, complicated ways. The CO standards and the 24-hour and 3-hour SO$_2$ standards are not to be exceeded more than once per year. The 1-hour O$_3$ standard is attained when the expected number of days per calendar year with maximum hourly average concentrations above 0.12 ppm is equal to or less than one. The 8-hour O$_3$ standard is met when the average of the annual fourth-highest daily maximum 8-hour average ozone concentration is less than or equal to 0.08 ppm. Compliance with the PM$_{2.5}$ standards is based on the 98th percentile of measurements over 3 years.

The text of the Clean Air Act (CAA) is set forth in the statutory pamphlet: *Selected Environmental Law Statutes* (West Group). Environmental attorneys usually cite to the "session law" section numbers (for example: "Clean Air Act § 112"), rather than to the U.S. Code numbers (for example: "42 U.S.C. § 7412"). These parallel citation forms are shown in the running headers of the statutory pamphlet.

The first federal statute to bear the title "Clean Air Act" was enacted in 1963. However, the present statutory scheme commenced with the 1970 Clean Air Act amendments, a thorough overhaul of the prior legislation. The statute was extensively modified thereafter on two occasions: first in the 1977 amendments and then in the monumental 1990 amendments. We begin our analysis with the seeds first planted in 1970.

*history of CAA*

**Table 9-1** sets forth all "criteria pollutants" under Clean Air Act § 108, for which national ambient air quality standards (NAAQS) have been set pursuant to § 109 of the Act. This compilation has been gleaned from 40 C.F.R. §§ 50.4-.12 (1998), and U.S. EPA, 1996 National Air Quality and Emissions Trends Report 7 (1997).

Prior to 1987, particulates were measured as "total suspended particulate matter" or TSP, by a method which collected particulates up to a nominal size of 25 to 45 microns. Since 1987, EPA has measured only "coarse" particles with an aerodynamic diameter less than or equal to a nominal 10 microns ($PM_{10}$). On September 16, 1997, new $PM_{2.5}$ standards, measuring "fine" particles—those less than 2.5 micrometers in diameter—became effective. New 8-hour $O_3$ standards also became effective on that date. The 8-hour $O_3$ standards will eventually *replace* the 1-hour standards, on a location by location basis, when the EPA determines that a given area has met the 1-hour standards.

The 1997 $PM_{2.5}$ and $O_3$ standards were remanded by the D.C. Circuit on May 14, 1999, in *American Trucking Associations v. U.S. Environmental Protection Agency*, 175 F.3d 1027 (D.C. Cir. 1999), a case excerpted at page 322, *infra*.

## 1. CRITERIA POLLUTANT LISTING

---

Read the following sections of the Clean Air Act

☐ § 108(a)        ☐ § 108(b)(1)        ☐ § 108(d)

---

"Criteria" pollutants are those which have been listed by the EPA Administrator under CAA § 108. The following case addresses the listing process.

# NATURAL RESOURCES
# DEFENSE COUNCIL v. TRAIN

545 F.2d 320 (2d Cir. 1976)

Before SMITH, OAKES and MESKILL, Circuit Judges.

SMITH, Circuit Judge:

The Environmental Protection Agency, ("EPA"), and its Administrator, Russell Train, appeal from an order of the United States District Court for the Southern District of New York * * * requiring the Administrator of the EPA, within thirty days, to place lead on a list of air pollutants under § 108(a)(1) of the Clean Air Act * * * . We affirm the order of the district court.

The 1970 Clean Air Act Amendments provide two different approaches for controlling pollutants in the air. One approach, incorporated in §§ 108-110, provides for the publication of a list of pollutants adverse to public health or welfare, derived from "numerous or diverse" sources, the promulgation of national ambient air quality standards for listed pollutants, and subsequent implementation of these standards by the states. The second approach of the Act provides for control of certain pollutants at the source, pursuant to §§ 111, 112, 202, 211 and 231. * * *

Once a pollutant has been listed under § 108(a)(1), §§ 109 and 110 of the Act are automatically invoked. These sections require that for any pollutant for which air quality criteria are issued under § 108(a)(1) (C) after the date of enactment of the Clean Air Amendments of 1970, the Administrator must simultaneously issue air quality standards. Within nine months of the promulgation of such standards, states are required to submit implementation plans to the Administrator. The Administrator must approve or disapprove a state plan within four months. If a state fails to submit an acceptable plan, the Administrator is required to prepare and publish such a plan himself. State implementation plans must provide for the attainment of primary ambient air quality standards no later than three years from the date of approval of a plan. Extension of the three-year period for attaining the primary standard may be granted by the Administrator only in very limited circumstances, and in no case for more than two years.

The EPA concedes that lead meets the conditions of §§ 108(a)(1)(A) and (B) that it has an adverse effect on public health and welfare, and that the presence of lead in the ambient air results from numerous or diverse mobile or stationary sources. The EPA maintains, however, that under § 108(a)(1)(C) of the Act, the Administrator retains discretion whether to list a pollutant, even though the pollutant meets the criteria of §§ 108(a)(1)(A) and (B). The EPA regards the listing of lead under § 108(a)(1) and the issuance of ambient air quality standards as one of numerous alternative control strategies for lead available to it. Listing of substances is mandatory, the EPA argues, only for those pollutants for which the Administrator "plans to issue air quality criteria." He may, it is contended, choose not to issue, i. e., not "plan to issue" such criteria, and decide to control lead solely by regulating emission at the source, regardless of the total concentration of lead in the ambient air. The Administrator argues that if he chooses to control lead (or other pollutants) under § 211, he is not required to list the pollutant under § 108(a)(1) or to set air quality standards.

The EPA advances three reasons for the position that the Administrator has discretion whether to list a pollutant even when the conditions of § 108(a)(1)(A) and (B) have been met: the plain meaning of § 108(a)(1)(C); the structure of the Clean Air Act as a whole; and the legislative history of the Act.

The issue is one of statutory construction. We agree with the district court and with appellees, National Resources Defense Council, Inc., et al., that the interpretation of the Clean Air Act advanced by the EPA is contrary to the structure of the Act as a whole, and that if accepted, it would vitiate the public policy underlying the enactment of the 1970 Amendments as set forth in the Act and in its legislative history. * * *

Section 108(a)(1) contains mandatory language. It provides that "the Administrator *shall* * * * publish * * * a list * * * ." (Emphasis added.) If the EPA interpretation were accepted and listing were mandatory only for substances "for which (the Administrator) plans to issue air quality criteria * * *", then the mandatory language of § 108(a)(1)(A) would become mere surplusage. The determination to list a pollutant and to issue air quality criteria would remain discretionary with the Administrator, and the rigid deadlines of § 108(a)(2), § 109, and § 110 for attaining air quality standards could be bypassed by him at will. If Congress had enacted § 211 as an alternative to, rather than as a supplement to, §§ 108-110, then one would expect a similar fixed timetable for implementation of the fuel control section. The absence of such a timetable for the enforcement of § 211 lends support to the view that fuel controls were intended by Congress as a means for attaining primary air quality standards rather than as an alternative to the promulgation of such standards. * * *

The EPA contention that the language of § 108(a)(1)(c) "for which (the Administrator) plans to issue air quality criteria" is a separate and third criterion to be met before § 108 requires listing lead and issuing air quality standards, thereby leaving the decision to list lead within the discretion of the Administrator, finds no support in the legislative history of the 1970 Amendments to the Act. The summary of the provisions of the conference agreement furnished the Senate by Senator Muskie contain the following language:

> The agreement requires issuance of remaining air quality criteria for major pollutants within 13 months of date of enactment. * * *

Within the 13-month deadline, the Congress expects criteria to be issued for nitrogen oxides, fluorides, lead, polynuclear organic matter, and odors, though others may be necessary. * * *

Language relating to the issuance of new source performance standards makes it clear that the Senate intended these standards to be supplementary to, not in lieu of, ambient air quality standards * * * .

While the literal language of § 108(a)(1)(C) is somewhat ambiguous, this ambiguity is resolved when this section is placed in the context of the Act as a whole and in its legislative history. The deliberate inclusion of a specific timetable for the attainment of ambient air quality standards incorporated by Congress in §§ 108-110 would become an exercise in futility if the Administrator could avoid listing pollutants simply by choosing not to issue air quality criteria. The discretion given to the Administrator under the Act pertains to the review of state implementation plans under § 110, and to § 211 which authorizes but does not mandate the regulation of fuel or fuel additives. It does not extend to the issuance of air quality standards for substances derived from specified sources which the Administrator had already adjudged injurious to health.

The structure of the Clean Air Act as amended in 1970, its legislative history, and the judicial gloss placed upon the Act leave no room for an interpretation which makes the issuance of air quality standards for lead under § 108 discretionary. The Congress sought to eliminate, not perpetuate, opportunity for administrative foot-dragging. Once the conditions of §§ 108(a)(1)(A) and (B) have been met, the listing of lead and the issuance of air quality standards for lead become mandatory.

The order of the district court is affirmed.

### *Notes and Questions*

1.  Suppose you wanted to convince the EPA Administrator today to add a new substance to the list of criteria pollutants. What would you have to demonstrate to the Administrator? Does this standard seem particularly difficult to meet?

2.  Why do you suppose that no new criteria pollutants—other than lead—have been listed since 1971? Wouldn't you imagine that there are dozens of substances meeting the listing touchstones of CAA § 108(a)(1)? Doesn't the *NRDC v. Train* opinion provide that the EPA Administrator *must* list each of these pollutants?

3.  According to the legislative history quoted in the *NRDC* opinion, the Conference Committee putting together the final version of the 1970 Clean Air Act amendments assumed that criteria documents would be issued for fluorides, polynuclear organic matter, and odors (as well as for lead and nitrogen oxides). We will see at page 372, *infra*, that fluorides are now regulated as "designated pollutants at designated facilities" under the New Source Performance Standards of CAA § 111. The conventional wisdom is that odor problems in and of themselves are *not* addressed by the Clean Air Act. *But see* the discussion of *Save Our Health Organization v. Recomp of*

*Minnesota*, 37 F.3d 1334 (8th Cir. 1994), at page 489, *infra*. Under the Clean Air Act, each NAAQS must be met in every location in the country. Can you imagine how difficult it would be to establish a single odor standard to be met throughout the United States? Would that even make sense?

## 2. NATIONAL AMBIENT AIR QUALITY STANDARDS

Read the following sections of the Clean Air Act

☐ § 109(a)       ☐ § 109(b)       ☐ § 109(d)

---

### LEAD INDUSTRIES ASSOCIATION, INC. v. EPA

647 F.2d 1130 (D.C. Cir. 1980), *cert. denied*, 449 U.S. 1042 (1981)

Before WRIGHT, Chief Judge, and ROBINSON and MACKINNON, Circuit Judges.

WRIGHT, Chief Judge:

This is the third occasion on which this court has been asked to review Environmental Protection Agency (EPA or Agency) regulations promulgated under authority of the Clean Air Act * * * and specifically designed to deal with the health problems associated with lead in the ambient air. In *Amoco Oil Co. v. EPA*, 501 F.2d 722 (D.C. Cir. 1974), we upheld regulations prohibiting the sale of leaded gasoline for use in automobiles equipped with "catalytic converter" devices for controlling exhaust emissions and requiring widespread retail marketing of at least one grade of unleaded gasoline. And in *Ethyl Corp. v. EPA*, 541 F.2d 1 (D.C. Cir.) (*en banc*), *cert. denied*, 426 U.S. 941 (1976), we affirmed an EPA order requiring annual reductions in the lead content of leaded gasoline. In the present consolidated cases we are asked to review EPA regulations establishing national ambient air quality standards for lead. These air quality standards prescribe the maximum concentrations of lead that will be permitted in the air of our country. We must decide whether EPA's Administrator acted within the scope of his statutory authority in promulgating these regulations and, if so, whether the evidence adduced at the rulemaking proceeding supports his final determinations. In addition, we must examine the petitioners' claims that infirmities in the procedures employed by EPA in this rulemaking warrant remand of the regulations to the Agency. Petitioners are the Lead Industry Association, Inc. (LIA), a nonprofit trade association whose 78 members include most of the country's producers and commercial consumers of lead (No. 78—2201), and St. Joe Minerals Corporation (St. Joe) (No. 78—2220). * * *

Acting pursuant to authority conferred on it by Congress in the Clean Air Act * * * EPA has been involved in regulation of lead emissions almost since the Agency's inception. Its initial approach to controlling the amount of lead in the ambient air was to limit lead emissions from automobiles by restricting the amount of lead in gasoline. To this end it promulgated the regulations which we upheld in *Amoco Oil Corp. v. EPA, supra,* and *Ethyl Corp. v. EPA, supra.* However, in 1975 the Natural Resources Defense Council, Inc. (NRDC), and others brought suit against EPA claiming that the Agency was required by Section 108 of the Clean Air Act to list lead as a pollutant for which an air quality criteria document would be prepared, and for which national ambient air quality standards should be promulgated under section 109 of the Act. The District Court agreed with NRDC and directed the administrator to list lead as a pollutant under section 108 of the Act, by March 31, 1976. *Natural Resources Defense Council, Inc. v. Train,* 411 F.Supp. 864 (S.D. N.Y. 1976). The Second Circuit affirmed, 545 F.2d 320 (1976), and EPA initiated the proceedings outlined in the statute which are under review here.

The first step toward establishing national ambient air quality standards for a particular pollutant is its addition to a list, compiled by EPA's Administrator, of pollutants that cause or contribute to air pollution "which may reasonably be anticipated to endanger public health or welfare[.]" Section 108(a)(1). Within twelve months of the listing of a pollutant under Section 108(a) the Administrator must issue "air quality criteria" for the pollutant. Section 108 makes it clear that the term "air quality criteria" means something different from the conventional meaning of "criterion"; such "criteria" do not constitute "standards" or "guidelines," but rather refer to a document to be prepared by EPA which is to provide the scientific basis for promulgation of air quality standards for the pollutant. This criteria document must "accurately reflect the latest scientific knowledge useful in indicating the kind and extent of all identifiable effects on public health or welfare which may be expected from the presence of such pollutant in the ambient air, in varying quantities." Section 108(a)(2).

At the same time as he issues air quality criteria for a pollutant, the Administrator must also publish proposed national primary and secondary air quality standards for the pollutant. Section 109(a)(2). National primary ambient air quality standards are standards "the attainment and maintenance of which in the judgment of the Administrator, based on such criteria and allowing an adequate margin of safety, are requisite to protect the public health." Section 109(b)(1). Secondary air quality standards "specify a level of air quality the attainment and maintenance of which in the judgment of the Administrator, based on such criteria, is requisite to protect the public welfare from any known or anticipated adverse effects associated with the presence of such air pollutant in the ambient air." Section 109(b)(2). Effects on the "the public welfare" include "effects on soils, water, crops, vegetation, manmade materials, animals, wildlife, weather, visibility, and climate, damage to and deterioration of property, and hazards to transportation, as well as effects on economic values and on personal comfort and well-being." Section 302(h). The Administrator is required to submit the proposed air quality standards for public comment in a rulemaking proceeding, the procedure for which is prescribed by Section 307(d) of the Act.

Within six months of publication of the proposed standards the Administrator must promulgate final primary and secondary ambient air quality standards for the pollutant. Section 307(d)(10). Once EPA has promulgated national ambient air quality standards, responsibility under the act shifts from the federal government to the states. Within nine months of promulgation of the standards each state must prepare and submit to EPA for approval a state implementation plan. Section 110(a)(1). These state implementation plans must contain emission limitations and all other measures necessary to attain the primary standards "as expeditiously as practicable," but no later than three years after EPA approval of the plan, and to attain the secondary standards within a reasonable period of time. Section 110(a)(2)(A) & (B). The Administrator is authorized to extend the deadline for attainment of the primary air quality standards by two years, but thereafter it must be met. Section 110(e).

As required by statute, EPA's first step toward promulgating air quality standards for lead was to prepare a criteria document. The Lead Criteria Document was the culmination of a process of rigorous scientific and public review, and thus is a comprehensive and thoughtful analysis of the most current scientific information on the subject. The Lead Criteria Document went through three major drafts, and three separate reviews, including public meetings by the Subcommittee on Scientific Criteria for Environmental Lead of EPA's Science Advisory Board (SAB Lead Subcommittee). The Agency reviewed over 280 public comments, most of a sophisticated scientific nature, before it issued the final Criteria Document. Members of the public, industry (including the petitioners in these cases), environmental groups, the scientific community, and state and federal government agencies actively participated in the review of the drafts. Notice of the meetings of the SAB Lead Subcommittee was published in the *Federal Register*, and the drafts of the Criteria Document which were to be reviewed were available before the meetings. A formal record and a transcript of the proceedings were kept, and a review of the transcript shows that scientists with differing views could—and did—exchange ideas with each other as well as agency staff, and that all were questioned by the members of the Subcommittee. * * *

Simultaneously with the publication of the Lead Criteria Document on December 14, 1977, the Administrator proposed a national primary ambient air quality standard for lead of 1.5 $\mu$g Pb/m$^3$ [micrograms of lead per cubic meter] monthly average. * * * He also proposed that the secondary air quality standard be set at the same level as the primary standard because the welfare effects associated with lead exposure did not warrant imposition of a stricter standard. * * *

The petitioners' first claim is that the Administrator exceeded his authority under the statute by promulgating a primary air quality standard for lead which is more stringent than is necessary to protect the public health because it is designed to protect the public against "subclinical" effects which are not harmful to health. According to petitioners, Congress only authorized the Administrator to set primary air quality standards that are aimed at protecting the public against health effects which are known to be *clearly harmful*. They argue that Congress so limited the Administrator's authority because it was concerned that excessively stringent air quality standards could cause massive economic dislocation.

In developing this argument St. Joe contends that EPA erred by refusing to consider the issues of economic and technological feasibility in setting the air quality standards for lead. St. Joe's claim that the Administrator should have considered these issues is based on the statutory provision directing him to allow an "adequate margin of safety" in setting primary air quality standards. In St. Joe's view, the Administrator must consider the economic impact of the proposed standard on industry and the technological feasibility of compliance by emission sources in determining the appropriate allowance for a margin of safety. St. Joe argues that the Administrator abused his discretion by refusing to consider these factors in determining the appropriate margin of safety for the lead standards, and maintains that the lead air quality standards will have a disastrous economic impact on industrial sources of lead emissions.

This argument is totally without merit. St. Joe is unable to point to anything in either the language of the Act or its legislative history that offers any support for its claim that Congress, by specifying that the Administrator is to allow an "adequate margin of safety" in setting primary air quality standards, thereby required the Administrator to consider economic or technological feasibility. To the contrary, the statute and its legislative history make clear that economic considerations play no part in the promulgation of ambient air quality standards under Section 109.

Where Congress intended the Administrator to be concerned about economic and technological feasibility, it expressly so provided. For example, Section 111 of the Act directs the Administrator to consider economic and technological feasibility in establishing standards of performance for new stationary sources of air pollution based on the best available control technology. * * * In contrast, Section 109(b) speaks only of protecting the public health and welfare. Nothing in its language suggests that the Administrator is to consider economic or technological feasibility in setting ambient air quality standards.

The legislative history of the Act also shows the Administrator may not consider economic and technological feasibility in setting air quality standards; the absence of any provision requiring consideration of these factors was no accident; it was the result of a deliberate decision by Congress to subordinate such concerns to the achievement of health goals. Exasperated by the lack of significant progress toward dealing with the problem of air pollution under the Air Quality Act of 1967, 81 Stat. 485, and prior legislation, Congress abandoned the approach of offering suggestions and setting goals in favor of "taking a stick to the States in the form of the Clean Air Amendments of 1970 * * * ." *Train v. Natural Resources Defense Council, Inc., supra,* 421 U.S. at 64; *see Union Electric Co. v. EPA,* 427 U.S. 246, 256-257 (1976). Congress was well aware that, together with Sections 108 and 110, Section 109 imposes requirements of a "technology-forcing" character. *Id.* at 257 * * * . The Senate Report on the 1970 Amendments declared:

> The protection of public health—as required by the national ambient air quality standards * * *—will require major action throughout the Nation. Many facilities will require major investments in new technology and new processes. Some facilities will need altered operating procedures * * * . Some may be closed. * * *

> In the Committee discussion, considerable concern was expressed regarding the use of the concept of technical feasibility as the basis of ambient air standards. The Committee determined that (1) the health of people is more important than the question of whether the early achievement of ambient air quality standards protective of health is technically feasible; and, 2) the growth of pollution load in many areas, even with application of available technology, would still be deleterious to public health.

The Report concluded:

> Therefore, the Committee determined that existing sources of pollutants either should meet the standard of the law or be closed down, and in addition that new sources should be controlled to the maximum extent possible to prevent atmospheric emissions.

S. Rep. No. 91-1196, *supra,* at 2-3. It is difficult to reconcile these statements of legislative intent with St. Joe's claim that Congress wanted the Administrator to consider economic and technological feasibility in setting air quality standards. The "technology-forcing" requirements of the Act "are expressly designed to force regulated sources to develop pollution control devices that might at the time appear to be economically or technologically infeasible." *Union Electric Co.* * * * at 257.

Furthermore, St. Joe's attempt to find a mandate for the Administrator to consider economic or technological feasibility in the Act's "adequate margin of safety" requirement is to no avail. The Senate Report explained the purpose of the margin of safety requirement:

> Margins of safety are essential to any health-related environmental standards if a reasonable degree of protection is to be provided against hazards which research has not yet identified.

S. Rep. No. 91-1196, *supra,* at 10. We are unable to discern here any congressional intent to require, or even permit, the Administrator to consider economic or technological factors in promulgating air quality standards. And when Congress directs an agency to consider only certain factors in reaching an administrative decision, the agency is not free to trespass beyond the bounds of its statutory authority by taking other factors into account. * * *

Section 109(b) does not specify precisely what Congress had in mind when it directed the Administrator to prescribe air quality standards that are "requisite to protect the public health." The legislative history of the Act does, however, provide some guidance. The Senate Report explains that the goal of the air quality standards must be to ensure that the public is protected from "adverse health effects." S. Rep. No. 91-1196, *supra*, at 10. And the report is particularly careful to note that especially sensitive persons such as asthmatics and emphysematics are included within the group that must be protected. It is on the interpretation of the phrase "adverse health effects" that the disagreement between LIA and EPA about the limits of the Administrator's statutory authority appears to be based. LIA argues that the legislative history of the Act indicates that Congress only intended to protect the public against effects which are known to be *clearly harmful* to health, maintaining that this limitation on the Administrator's statutory authority is necessary to ensure that the standards are not set at a level which is more stringent than Congress contemplated. The Administrator, on the other hand, agrees that primary air quality standards must be based on protecting the public from "adverse health effects," but argues that the meaning LIA assigns to that phrase is too limited. In particular, the Administrator contends that LIA's interpretation is inconsistent with the precautionary nature of the statute, and will frustrate Congress' intent in requiring promulgation of air quality standards.

The Administrator begins by pointing out that the Act's stated goal is "to protect and enhance the quality of the Nation's air resources so as to promote the public health and welfare and the productive capacity of its population[.]" Section 101(b)(1). This goal was reaffirmed in the 1977 Amendments. For example, the House Report accompanying the Amendments states that one of its purposes is "[t]o emphasize the preventive or precautionary nature of the act, i.e., to assure that regulatory action can effectively prevent harm before it occurs; to emphasize the predominant value of protection of public health[.]" H.R. Rep. No. 95-294, 95th Cong., 1st Sess. 49 (1977). The Administrator notes that protecting the public from harmful effects requires decisions about exactly what these harms are, a task Congress left to his judgment. He notes that the task of making these decisions is complicated by the absence of any clear thresholds above which there are adverse effects and below which there are none. Rather, as scientific knowledge expands and analytical techniques are improved, new information is uncovered which indicates that pollution levels that were once considered harmless are not in fact harmless. Congress, the Administrator argues, was conscious of this problem, and left these decisions to his judgment partly for this reason. In such situations the perspective that is brought to bear on the problem plays a crucial role in determining what decisions are made. Because it realized this, Congress, the Administrator maintains, directed him to err on the side of caution in making these judgments. First, Congress made it abundantly clear that consideration of economic or technological feasibility are to be subordinated to the goal of protecting the public health by prohibiting any consideration of such factors. Second, it specified that the air quality standards must also protect individuals who are particularly sensitive to the effects of pollution. Third, it required that the standards be set at a level at which there is "an absence of adverse effect" on these sensitive individuals. Finally, it specifically directed the Administrator to allow an adequate margin of safety in setting primary air quality standards in order to provide some protection against effects that research has not yet uncovered. The Administrator contends that these indicia of congressional intent, the precautionary nature of the statutory mandate to protect the public health, the broad discretion Congress gave him to decide what effects to protect against, and the uncertainty that must be part of any attempt to determine the health effects of air pollution, are all extremely difficult to reconcile with LIA's suggestion that he can only set standards which are designed to protect against effects which are *known to be clearly harmful to health.*

We agree that LIA's interpretation of the statute is at odds with Congress' directives to the Administrator. As a preliminary matter, though it denies this, LIA does at times seem to be arguing, along with St. Joe, that the Administrator should have considered economic and technological feasibility in setting the standards, a claim that must be rejected for reasons we have already stated. Be that as it may, it is not immediately clear why LIA expects this court to impose limits on the Administrator's authority which, so far as we can tell, Congress did not. The Senate Report explains that the Administrator is to set standards which ensure that there is "an absence of adverse effects." The Administrator maintains that the lead standards are designed to do just that, a claim we will examine in due course. But LIA would require a further showing—that the effects on which the standards were based are *clearly* harmful or *clearly* adverse. We cannot, however, find the source of this further restriction that LIA would impose on the Administrator's authority. It may be that it reflects LIA's view that the Administrator must show that there is a "medical consensus that [the effects on which the standards were based] are harmful * * * ." If so, LIA is seriously mistaken. This court has previously noted that some uncertainty about the health effects of air pollution is inevitable. And we pointed out that "[a]waiting certainty will often allow for only reactive, not preventive regulat[ory action]." *Ethyl Corp. v. EPA, supra,* 541 F.2d at 25. Congress apparently shares this view; it specifically directed the Administrator to allow an adequate margin of safety to protect against effects which have not yet been uncovered by research and effects whose medical significance is a matter of disagreement. * * *

Furthermore, we agree with the Administrator that requiring EPA to wait until it can conclusively demonstrate that a particular effect is adverse to health before it acts is inconsistent with both the Act's precautionary and preventive orientation and the nature of the Administrator's statutory responsibilities. Congress provided that the Administrator is to use his judgment in setting air quality standards precisely to permit him to act in the face of uncertainty. And as we read the statutory provisions and the legislative history, Congress directed the Administrator to err on the side of caution in making the necessary decisions. We see no reason why this court should put a gloss on Congress' scheme by requiring the Administrator to show that there is a medical consensus that the effects on which the lead standards were based are *"clearly harmful to health."* All that is required by the statutory scheme is evidence in the record which substantiates his conclusions about the health effects on which the standards were based. Accordingly, we reject LIA's claim that the Administrator exceeded his statutory authority and turn to LIA's challenge to the evidentiary basis for the Administrator's decision. * * *

*The court then concluded, after a lengthy discussion of the health evidence in the criteria document, that the evidence supported the ambient standards selected by the Administrator.*

The national ambient air quality standards for lead were the culmination of a process of rigorous scientific and public review which permitted a thorough ventilation of the complex scientific and technical issues presented by this rulemaking proceeding. Interested parties were allowed a number of opportunities to participate in exploration and resolution of the issues raised by the standard setting exercise. EPA, and ultimately the public whose health these air quality standards protect, have benefitted from their contribution. To be sure, even the experts did not always agree about the answers to the questions that were raised. Indeed, they did not always agree on what the relevant questions were. These disagreements underscore the novelty and complexity of the issues that had to be resolved, and both the EPA and the participants in the rulemaking proceeding deserve to be commended for the diligence with which they approached the task of coming to grips with these difficult issues.

We have accorded these cases the most careful consideration, combining as we must careful scrutiny of the evidence in the record with deference to the Administration's judgments. We conclude that in this rulemaking proceeding the Administrator complied with the substantive and procedural requirements of the Act, and that his decisions are both adequately explained and amply supported by evidence in the record. Accordingly, we reject petitioners' claims of error. The regulations under review herein are *Affirmed.*

### Notes and Questions

1.   Within 30 days after enactment of the 1970 Clean Air Act Amendments on December 31, 1970, the EPA Administrator was required to publish *pro-*

*posed* regulations establishing primary and secondary national ambient air quality standards (NAAQS) for all pollutants for which a criteria document had already been prepared. *See* CAA § 109(a)(1)(A). There were five such pollutants on December 31, 1970: $SO_2$, particulates, CO, hydrocarbons (HC) (dropped from the criteria pollutant list in 1983), and photochemical oxidants (now regulated as $O_3$). Not later than 90 days after such initial publication of the proposed standards, the Administrator was required to publish *final* NAAQS for these same pollutants. *See* § 109(a)(1)(B). Why do you suppose Congress provided such a short time deadline for finalizing the proposed NAAQS? What kind of public input did Congress envision?

2.　The EPA Administrator is directed by CAA § 109(d) to periodically review the criteria documents with the help of a Scientific Advisory Committee, revising them as necessary and proposing revised NAAQS simultaneously with the publication of any new criteria document. *See* § 109(a)(2). The statute seems to impose a 90-day deadline for finalizing revised NAAQS, *see* § 109(a)(1)(B), but § 307(d) provides a somewhat more elaborate opportunity for public comment on proposed revisions, and § 307(d)(10) authorizes extending the deadline to six months after the date of proposal.

3.　In proposing and finalizing the initial or revised NAAQS, what record or information base may the Administrator consider? *See* CAA §§ 109(b)(1) & (b)(2). Does your answer surprise you?

4.　The criteria documents are obviously crucial to the Administrator's establishment of the NAAQS. What are the criteria documents supposed to contain? *See* CAA § 108(a)(2). The summary portion of the initial criteria document for $SO_2$ is set forth at pages 88-89, *supra*. Turn to that summary and glance through it. Do you assume that all scientists in the relevant field agreed with the information set forth in that brief summary at the time of its promulgation in 1969? Why or why not?

5.　How is the EPA Administrator supposed to pluck a primary NAAQS standard for each of the criteria pollutants out of the criteria document? What has Congress told her to do in § 109(b)(1)? Should the Administrator consider "super sensitive" receptors, such as children with asthma or elderly people with heart conditions? What does the *Lead Industries* decision say?

6.　In establishing the *primary* NAAQS, may the EPA Administrator take into account the costs of achieving compliance with the standard? Why or why not? May the Administrator take costs into account when promulgating the *secondary* NAAQS? Why or why not? Do the answers to these questions make any sense? Paul R. Portney, president of Resources for the Future, thinks not: "Laws that say you can't look at both sides of the equation, to me, are a recipe for stupid rulemaking." Alec Zacaroli, *Economist Blasts EPA Cost-Benefit Report for Clean Air Act*, 29 [Curr. Dev.] Env. Rep. (BNA) 1629 (1998). Why might Congress have created such a recipe?

7.　**Table 9-1**, at page 300, *supra*, sets forth the NAAQS for the six criteria pollutants. The brevity of the table is deceptive. The EPA regulations setting forth the standards are accompanied by "reference methods," specifying how compliance with the standards must be measured. As we will see in later readings, the consequences of noncompliance with one or more NAAQS may be profound. Accordingly, the measurement techniques for determining compliance are extraordinarily important. In the BNA's *Environment Reporter*,[a] the NAAQS themselves—the standards—occupy approximately two and one-half pages; the all important reference methods explaining how compliance with these standards is to be measured occupy more than one hundred additional pages. *See* 2 [Federal Regulations] Env. Rep. (BNA) 120:0101 (1999).

# RICHARD B. STEWART & JAMES E. KRIER, ENVIRONMENTAL LAW AND POLICY

### 339-40, 350-51, 361-63 & n.20 (2nd ed. 1978)

At this point, you should develop your own preliminary views on * * * issues of federalism in the context of environmental policy.

First, to what extent is environmental quality an appropriate concern of the federal government? Given our traditions in favor of decentralized decision making, there must be substantial, affirmative justification for intervention by the federal government in an area of domestic policy. The existence of substantial environmental spillovers from one state to another provides strong justification for national intervention because the originating state is likely to treat the adverse effects on the receiving state as an "external cost," and give inadequate regard to the welfare of the latter state. * * * Suppose, however, that the effects of pollution are confined to the state generating them. What special reason is there for federal intervention in order, for example, to force California to have cleaner air than it wishes? Why isn't California competent to trade off the costs and benefits of intrastate pollution control? Indeed, aren't California officials far more competent than federal officials to make such tradeoffs because they are closer to California citizens and more responsive to their preferences for environmental quality? Nonetheless, might the competition among states for industry and economic development give rise to a "commons" dilemma that prevents individual states from fully implementing their environmental preferences and justifies federal intervention? Are there other reasons why industry, developers, and unions might be systematically "overrepresented" in state decision making and environmental interests systematically "underrepresented"? * * * If so, would federal intervention be justified to "correct" this disparity? Is there a stronger case for federal intervention where serious adverse health effects or irreversible environmental degradation is threatened?

Second, to the extent you believe national direction of environmental policy to be appropriate, to what extent should the federal gov-

---

[a] The most definitive, reliable copy of federal and state environmental regulations may be found in the Bureau of National Affairs' multi-volume subscription service—the *Environment Reporter*—updated weekly—or on Westlaw™. The *Code of Federal Regulations*, printed by the Government Printing Office, is always out of date in the dynamic field of environmental law, and should be consulted only for historical purposes.

ernment rely upon state and local governments to implement national policies? On the one hand are the dangers of overcentralization, with accompanying disregard of important local variations and circumstances; the limited extent of federal enforcement resources and Congress' reluctance to create a national police force; and the interrelation of pollution control measures and land use planning, traffic control, and other subjects of state and local control. On the other hand, state and local governments may lack the capability or political incentive to take effective implementation measures. * * *

On the face of it, wouldn't the statutory requirements for setting * * * ambient [NAAQS] standards appear completely irrational to the economist? She would certainly maintain that standards should be based on an assessment of the costs and benefits of various control measures; more specifically, standards should be set at the point where the marginal benefit (in terms of reduced mortality, illness, materials damage, etc.) from somewhat more stringent standards just equals the marginal costs to society of achieving those standards. Yet the statute rather clearly seems to exclude cost considerations in setting the primary standards, and also appears to exclude them in setting secondary standards. Moreover, the statute seems to contemplate that the [NAAQS] standards should be *geographically uniform* throughout the nation. Yet the welfare benefits from achieving a given concentration of pollutants would vary geographically depending on the size of the population exposed to it, the nature of local vegetation, and so on. The costs of achieving a given concentration would also vary, depending on the number and size of air pollution sources in the area, the availability and cost of means for reducing pollution from those sources, local meteorological conditions, and so on. Economics thus suggests the desirability of local or regional variations in standards based on an assessment of costs and benefits in each locality and region.

What sort of data would be relevant in setting standards in order to maximize economic efficiency? * * * [I]n order to set efficient standards, one must have information on the *marginal* costs of damage, avoidance, abatement and transaction costs, in order to determine the economically optimum standard. * * * Ideally, one would require data on the marginal benefits and costs in each *locality*. How much would it cost to acquire all of the relevant information to set optimally efficient standards? Acquisition of such information represents a transaction cost that should be included in the relevant costs to be considered in efficient resource allocation. Accordingly, the decision maker must carefully consider the marginal extent to which it is economically worthwhile to expend resources to develop information and eliminate uncertainty in order to reduce other costs. This is simply another reflection of Calabresi's point that efficient resource allocation will depend on a number of contingent, empirically-based judgments and can never be a wholly mechanical exercise.

Transaction costs also raise difficult questions as to the extent to which it is efficient to introduce *geographical variations* in environmental standards. * * * One of the recurrent problems that we will encounter in assessing various types of governmental measures to deal with environmental degradation—judicial liability rules, regulatory controls, emission fees—is to determine the extent to which the benefits in terms of efficient resource allocation of increasing "fine tuning" such measures to localized costs and benefits begin to be outweighed by increasing information and administrative costs. The existence of such costs means that environmental measures must necessarily be somewhat crude. The objective is to determine the optimum degree of crudity in such measures.

Geographic variations are not the only type of variations that influence environmental costs and benefits and that must accordingly be taken into account in designing governmental measures. The concentrations of an air pollutant in a given locality will vary over *time*. Monitoring devices could be utilized to measure concentrations of a pollutant either at intermittent intervals or on a continuous basis. Reliable continuous monitoring equipment is expensive, and the degree of reliability that can be achieved is often poor. The emission of pollutants may be intermittent. For example, a factory may be operated only during the daytime, or may produce emissions only at certain noncontinuous stages of the production process. Emissions from automobiles in a given location will be greater during rush hour periods. Moreover, meteorological conditions—wind speed and direction, temperature and barometric variations—will produce temporal variations in pollutant concentrations at a given spot even if emissions are constant. In the case of *water* pollution, seasonal and annual variations in a river's annual flow will cause wide variations in the amount of ecological harm a given pollutant discharge will cause.

These variations have significance both for the measurement of environmental quality and for control strategies. *Temporal* variations raise the problem of expressing the variation in statistical terms. Measurement of average air quality over a given period—such as a year, a month, a day, or even an hour—may conceal wide variations between the maximum and minimum concentrations during that period.

As respects control strategies, do we aim for some given *average* of air quality throughout a region or over time, or do we seek to prevent concentrations of a pollutant from exceeding a given *maximum* at any time and in any part of the region? The answer must rest on a variety of considerations, including the nature of the damage caused by pollutant concentrations (whether, for example, damage to health is a function of short "peaks" of high concentration or sustained exposure to a lower concentration of pollution over an extended period of time), the costs of controlling emissions in order to achieve a given air quality goal (given extreme meteorological conditions it may be very difficult, short of the very costly goal of prohibiting emissions entirely, to ensure that moderate concentration levels are not exceeded at some location at some time in a given region), and our value judgments about the appropriate social goals in controlling pollution. * * *

Thus an average 24-hour concentration of sulfur dioxide of .10 parts per million may represent either a continuous .10 concentration throughout the time period or a concentration of zero for 80 percent of the day and of .50 parts per million during 20 percent of the day. If adverse health effects occur whenever concentrations exceed .20 parts per million for an hour, a 24-hour .10 p.p.m. average air quality standard would be adequate to prevent adverse health effects in the former case but not in the latter.

The problem of *geographical* variation poses similar difficulties. With limited funds, one cannot have sophisticated monitoring equipment at every street corner. One must attempt to local monitors at sites that are representative of air quality in a broader region, recognizing that it is not feasible to provide an accurate record of the full extent of variations within a region. * * *

Note too that all of these questions of measurement and control strategies are complicated by the fact that the impact of air pollutants is sometimes synergistic—that two pollutants in combination may cause far more damage than either alone.

Does the preceding discussion persuade you that economic analysis does not represent a very useful approach to setting environmental quality standards? If so, what alternative criteria for choosing standards would you offer? It may be that such choices inevitably involve a number of unruly and incompatible factors, including protection of human health, economic efficiency, avoidance of potentially irreversible ecological impacts, avoiding abrupt disruption of settled expectations, other political constraints, and the like. If so, there may be no authoritative and consistent set of criteria for standard setting.

## 3. THE 1997 $O_3$ AND $PM_{2.5}$ STANDARDS

### LUCINDA MINTON LANGWORTHY, EPA'S NEW AIR QUALITY STANDARDS FOR PARTICULATE MATTER AND OZONE

28 Envtl. L. Rep. 10502 (1998)

In 1997, after a contentious debate, the EPA issued new NAAQS for PM and ozone. * * * The Agency admits that implementation of these standards, which it claims will provide significant health benefits, will cost billions of dollars each year. Moreover, the new NAAQS raise complicated questions of how the states will implement them and on what schedule. Indeed, EPA is unable to identify technology capable of producing compliance with these standards in many parts of the country.

EPA's long-standing interpretation of the CAA is that the feasibility and cost of controls needed to attain NAAQS, including possible adverse impacts on health resulting from measures necessary to attain the standards, are not considered when the Agency establishes the standards. The Agency believes that these factors are relevant only to the choice of measures used to attain and maintain the standards. This view has received support from the D.C. Circuit. *See, e.g., Natural Resources Defense Council, Inc. v. U.S. EPA*, 902 F.2d 962, 973 (D.C. Cir. 1990).

The CAA establishes an independent scientific advisory body to assist EPA in reviewing the science and developing appropriate NAAQS. This Clean Air Scientific Advisory Committee (CASAC) consists, pursuant to the CAA, of seven members, including at least one member of the National Academy of Sciences, one physician, and one person from a state air pollution control agency. * * *

EPA's obligations * * * do not end with the promulgation of NAAQS and the approval of states' plans to implement them. The Agency must review both the standards themselves and the criteria on which they are based at least every five years. At the end of such a review, the Agency revises the standards as appropriate. The new 1997 PM and ozone NAAQS followed such a review.

EPA has long regulated both PM and ozone through its NAAQS program. The initial PM standards, limiting levels of total suspended particles (TSP), were established in 1971. * * *

In 1987, in recognition of significant limitations of the TSP indicator and questions concerning its relevance to health effects related to inhalation of PM, EPA replaced the TSP standards with standards for PM nominally 10 micrometers and less in diameter ($PM_{10}$), a measure that focused on a subset of TSP that was small enough to enter human lungs. The Agency reasoned that $PM_{10}$ was a better indicator of ambient particles that could cause problems if inhaled and was superior to TSP as a measure of PM associated with welfare effects such as soiling of household and other surfaces. * * *

Despite its legal obligation to review each NAAQS every five years, EPA took no action to reevaluate its 1987 PM NAAQS until the Agency was sued over its inaction, a lawsuit it lost in 1994. *American Lung Ass'n v. Browner*, 884 F. Supp. 345 (D. Ariz. 1994). The review of the $PM_{10}$ standards triggered by the lawsuit led, for the first time, to regulations that addressed two types of PM separately: "coarse" PM and "fine" PM. The Agency reasoned that coarse and fine PM constituted different pollutants based on their size and their formation mechanism. Thus, EPA established annual primary and secondary standards for fine PM—PM smaller than 2.5 micrometers in diameter ($PM_{2.5}$) * * * annual standards for coarse PM (measured as $PM_{10}$) * * * and daily $PM_{10}$ standards * * * . In essence, then, the new coarse PM standards varied little from the previous, more generic $PM_{10}$ standards. The new

$PM_{2.5}$ standards, on the other hand, focused on a specific subset of the material that had previously been regulated as $PM_{10}$.

The new standards were based primarily upon concerns that air pollution was associated with an increased risk of mortality. Premature mortality is obviously a very serious health concern. Others, including EPA's own scientific advisors, however, have pointed out the "many unanswered questions and uncertainties associated with establishing causality of the association between $PM_{2.5}$ and mortality."

The history of EPA's NAAQS for ozone is somewhat more complicated. In 1971, the Agency established the NAAQS for photochemical oxidants. These standards essentially regulated ozone, the most significant component of the photochemical oxidants. The primary and secondary standards were identical: a 1-hour standard of 0.08 parts per million (ppm).

The first true ozone NAAQS were promulgated in 1979. EPA replaced both the primary and secondary photochemical oxidant standards with standards that established a maximum permissible ozone concentration of 0.12 ppm, on a one-hour basis. This revision, in effect, constituted a relaxation of the NAAQS.

In 1997, EPA reversed this relaxation. The Agency purportedly replaced the one-hour 0.12 ppm primary and secondary NAAQS with eight-hour 0.08 ppm standards. Even with the longer eight-hour averaging time, the new standards are more stringent than the previous standards for most parts of the country. In fact, given the way the Agency has chosen to make the transition from the one-hour to the new eight-hour standards, each part of the country will be required to attain both standards because the existing one-hour standards will have to be attained in each area before they are revoked.

EPA explained that the new standards protect against changes in lung function and respiratory changes as well as the risk of increased hospital admissions and other less certain or less clearly important effects. The question, however, was less whether some of these effects resulted from ozone exposure, but whether the new standards provided a meaningful improvement in public health protection beyond that provided by the one-hour standard. Again, EPA scientific advisors were not clear that a more stringent standard was needed. * * *

Development of plans for bringing nonattainment areas into attainment of the new NAAQS has not yet formally begun. EPA has determined that specific additional information is necessary before states can even designate areas as nonattainment for the new NAAQS. For ozone, EPA has indicated that states will require information on how nonattainment area boundaries should be drawn. For $PM_{2.5}$, the Agency has determined that three years of ambient $PM_{2.5}$ monitoring data of violations of the standards is needed. * * *

EPA's own documents provide evidence of the massive impact that these standards will have. In documents submitted to the House Commerce Committee, EPA estimated that 546 counties will not meet the new ozone rules and that 283 counties will violate the $PM_{2.5}$ rules. In contrast, there were 59 nonattainment areas for the one-hour ozone NAAQS and 79 nonattainment areas for the previous $PM_{10}$ standards at the time the new standards became effective. In other words, hundreds of new areas will be added to the list of those already struggling to attain the nation's air quality standards. Not surprisingly, the cost of bringing these hundreds of areas into attainment of the NAAQS will be high. The regulatory impact analyses that EPA prepared for these standards illustrates how costly and difficult it will be to attain these standards. Using an attainment date of 2010, * * * EPA estimates an annual direct cost of $9.6 billion for ozone attainment and $37 billion for $PM_{2.5}$ attainment in addition to the cost of meeting the prior standards. Others have calculated the cost of attaining these standards to be as much as $90 to $150 billion annually.

Not only will attaining these standards be costly, it will be technically challenging, if not infeasible. According to EPA's regulatory impact analyses, 17 areas would still not attain the ozone standard even after applying all reasonably available control technologies costing less than $10,000 per ton. * * *

The financial impact of the requirements for attaining these standards is widespread. * * * Of course, not all industry will bear the burden equally. Many of the business types that are most significantly impacted in terms of the ratio of control costs to sales (e.g., both residential and nonresidential construction) are predominantly small businesses. * * *

The impact of complying with these new air quality standards will not be limited to the cost to industry of adding control equipment or changing production methods. The impact of implementing these standards will be felt by all of us through decreases in employment and disposable income. In fact, EPA acknowledges that jobs will be lost at electric generation units, coal mines, and coal transportation facilities as a result of the compliance activities required of electric power plants. Although EPA does not report the total impact of the new standards on employment generally, a study by the Reason Public Policy Institute estimates that the number of lost jobs will reach at least 147,000 by 2010 (the date of EPA's projections) and will level off at no less than 200,000 lost jobs by 2014 and beyond. This study also predicts that the bulk of these job losses will occur within lower income ranges and small businesses. Finally, this study explains that per capita disposable income is likely to fall by $250 to $440 per year during the same period as a result of the new NAAQS.

EPA argues, however, that these estimates of the adverse impacts of the new NAAQS are too high. EPA claims that costs can be reduced through technological innovation and creative approaches to implementation. It is true that these impact estimates consider only available technology. Nevertheless, it is speculative to assume that technology will advance sufficiently not only to find ways to achieve reductions for which no demonstrated technology presently exists, but also to achieve those reductions at lower costs than the reductions we currently have the technology to achieve. * * *

If the consequences of implementing these standards are unacceptable, as some in Congress have suggested, there appear to be two ways to make the ambient standards program more acceptable. First, it may be appropriate for EPA to reconsider whether the CAA precludes consideration of all factors except the possible risk of health effects from air pollution in specifying a NAAQS. Second, if the Act cannot be interpreted in a manner that produces results that are acceptable to the American public, it may be appropriate to consider revising the Act.

## DATA ADEQUATE FOR EPA TO PUSH AHEAD WITH FINE PM STANDARD, BROWNER SAYS

28 [Curr. Dev.] Env. Rep. (BNA) 184 (1997)

It would not be appropriate for the Environmental Protection Agency to delay making a decision on whether to set a new fine particulate matter standard until more information on the pollutant is available, * * * EPA Administrator Carol M. Browner said May 21. * * * Browner made her comments before the House Science Subcommittee on Energy and Environment. The hearing was the third the panel has held on EPA's proposals to revise the existing ozone and PM rules.

"I don't believe the law allows me to ignore the science that is available today," Browner said in response to a question by Rep. Vern Ehlers (R-Mich) on whether the agency should delay the $PM_{2.5}$ standard. Ehlers said he was concerned that EPA does not have an adequate scientific basis to justify the new standard, adding that the agency would be "well advised" to spend the next five years gathering additional data.

Browner said in her testimony, however, that EPA officials believe they have adequate data. She said the proposal is based on results from 87 studies that show considerable health risks associated with fine PM, including one that took seven years and involved collecting health diaries from more than 300,000 residents in 50 cities. * * *

"This is not a rush to judgment," Browner said of both the ozone and PM proposals. She pointed to the size of the criteria documents upon which EPA relied—1,500 pages for ozone and 2,400 pages for PM—as evidence of the magnitude of study done by the agency. In comparison, she said, the agency's first review of these ambient air quality standards produced documents for each pollutant that were just 200 pages long.

# AMERICAN TRUCKING
# ASSOCIATIONS v. EPA

175 F.3d 1027 (D.C. Cir. 1999)

BEFORE WILLIAMS, GINSBURG AND TATEL, CIRCUIT JUDGES.

PER CURIAM.

In July 1997 EPA issued final rules revising the primary and secondary NAAQS for particulate matter ("PM") and ozone. * * * Numerous petitions for review have been filed for each rule.

[W]e find that the construction of the Clean Air Act on which EPA relied in promulgating the NAAQS at issue here effects an unconstitutional delegation of legislative power. See U.S. Const. art. I, § 1 ("All legislative powers herein granted shall be vested in a Congress of the United States."). We remand the cases for EPA to develop a construction of the act that satisfies this constitutional requirement. * * *

[Other] remaining issues cannot be resolved until such time as EPA may develop a constitutional construction of the act (and, if appropriate, modify the disputed NAAQS in accordance with that construction). * * *

## I. DELEGATION

Certain "Small Business Petitioners" argue in each case that EPA has construed §§ 108 & 109 of the Clean Air Act so loosely as to render them unconstitutional delegations of legislative power. We agree. Although the factors EPA uses in determining the degree of public health concern associated with different levels of ozone and PM are reasonable, EPA appears to have articulated no "intelligible principle" to channel its application of these factors; nor is one apparent from the statute. The nondelegation doctrine requires such a principle. *See J.W. Hampton, Jr. & Co. v. United States*, 276 U.S. 394, 409, 48 S.Ct. 348, 72 L.Ed. 624 (1928). Here it is as though Congress commanded EPA to select "big guys," and EPA announced that it would evaluate candidates based on height and weight, but revealed no cut-off point. The announcement, though sensible in what it does say, is fatally incomplete. The reasonable person responds, "How tall? How heavy?"

EPA regards ozone definitely, and PM likely, as non-threshold pollutants, i.e., ones that have some possibility of some adverse health impact (however slight) at any exposure level above zero. * * * For convenience, we refer to both as non-threshold pollutants; the indeterminacy of PM's status does not affect EPA's analysis, or ours.

Thus the only concentration for ozone and PM that is utterly risk-free, in the sense of direct health impacts, is zero. Section 109(b)(1) says that EPA must set each standard at the level "requisite to protect the public health" with an "adequate margin of safety." These are also the criteria by which EPA must determine whether a revision to existing NAAQS is appropriate. * * * The factors that EPA has elected to examine for this purpose in themselves pose no inherent nondelegation problem. But what EPA lacks is any determinate criterion for drawing lines. It has failed to state intelligibly how much is too much.

We begin with the criteria EPA has announced for assessing health effects in setting the NAAQS for non-threshold pollutants. * * * EPA basically considers severity of effect, certainty of effect, and size of population affected. These criteria, long ago approved by the judiciary, see *Lead Industries Ass'n v. EPA*, 647 F.2d 1130, 1161 (D.C.Cir.1980) ("*Lead Industries*"), do not themselves speak to the issue of degree.

Read in light of these factors, EPA's explanations for its decisions amount to assertions that a less stringent standard would allow the relevant pollutant to inflict a greater quantum of harm on public health, and that a more stringent standard would result in less harm. Such arguments only support the intuitive proposition that more pollution will not benefit public health, not that keeping pollution at or below any particular level is "requisite" or not requisite to "protect the public health" with an "adequate margin of safety," the formula set out by § 109(b)(1).

Consider EPA's defense of the 0.08 ppm level of the ozone NAAQS. EPA explains that its choice is superior to retaining the existing level, 0.09 ppm, because more people are exposed to more serious effects at 0.09 than at 0.08. * * * In defending the decision not to go down to 0.07, EPA never contradicts the intuitive proposition, confirmed by data in its Staff Paper, that reducing the standard to that level would bring about comparable changes. * * * Instead, [EPA asserts that] * * * effects are less certain and less severe at lower levels of exposure. This seems to be nothing more than a statement that lower exposure levels are associated with lower risk to public health. * * *

In addition to the assertion quoted above, EPA cited the consensus of the Clean Air Scientific Advisory Committee ("CASAC") that the standard should not be set below 0.08. That body gave no specific reasons for its recommendations, so the appeal to its authority * * * adds no enlightenment. The dissent stresses the undisputed eminence of CASAC's members, * * * but the question whether EPA acted pursuant to lawfully delegated authority is not a scientific one. Nothing in what CASAC says helps us discern an intelligible principle derived by EPA from the Clean Air Act. * * *

EPA frequently defends a decision not to set a standard at a lower level on the basis that there is greater uncertainty that health effects exist at lower levels than the level of the standard. * * * But the increasing-uncertainty argument is helpful only if some principle reveals how much uncertainty is too much. None does. * * * The principle EPA invokes for each increment in stringency—that it is "possible, but not certain" that health effects exist at that level—could as easily, for any nonthreshold pollutant, justify a standard of zero. The same indeterminacy prevails in EPA's decisions not to pick a still more stringent level.

For example, EPA's reasons for not lowering the ozone standard from 0.08 to 0.07 ppm—that "the more serious effects ... are less certain" at the lower levels and that the lower levels are "closer to peak background levels," * * * could also be employed to justify a refusal to reduce levels below those associated with London's "Killer Fog" of 1952. In that calamity, very high PM levels (up to 2,500 μg/m3) are believed to have led to 4,000 excess deaths in a week. Thus, the agency rightly recognizes that the question is one of degree, but offers no intelligible principle by which to identify a stopping point.

The latitude EPA claims here seems even broader than that OSHA asserted in *International Union, UAW v. OSHA* ("Lockout/Tagout I"), 938 F.2d 1310, 1317 (D.C.Cir.1991), which was to set a standard that would reduce a substantial risk and that was not infeasible. In that case, OSHA thought itself free either to "do nothing at all" or to "require precautions that take the industry to the brink of ruin," with "all positions in between * * * evidently equally valid." *Id.* Here, EPA's freedom of movement between the poles is equally unconstrained, but the poles are even farther apart—the maximum stringency would send industry not just to the brink of ruin but hurtling over it, while the minimum stringency may be close to doing nothing at all. * * *

EPA cites prior decisions of this Court holding that when there is uncertainty about the health effects of concentrations of a particular pollutant within a particular range, EPA may use its discretion to make the "policy judgment" to set the standards at one point within the relevant range rather than another. * * * *Lead Industries*, 647 F.2d at 1161 (D.C.Cir.1980). We agree. But none of those panels addressed the claim of undue delegation that we face here, and accordingly had no occasion to ask EPA for coherence (for a "principle," to use the classic term) in making its "policy judgment." The latter phrase is not, after all, a self-sufficient justification for every refusal to define limits. * * *

[H]ere EPA's formulation of its policy judgment leaves it free to pick any point between zero and a hair below the concentrations yielding London's Killer Fog. * * *

Where (as here) statutory language and an existing agency interpretation involve an unconstitutional delegation of power, but an interpretation without the constitutional weakness is or may be available, our response is not to strike down the statute but to give the agency an opportunity to extract a determinate standard on its own. * * * Doing so serves at least two of three basic rationales for the nondelegation doctrine. If the agency develops determinate, binding standards for itself, it is less likely to exercise the delegated authority arbitrarily. * * * And such standards enhance the likelihood that meaningful judicial review will prove feasible. * * * A remand of this sort of course does not serve the third key function of non-delegation doctrine, to "ensure[ ] to the extent consistent with orderly governmental administration that important choices of social policy are made by Congress, the branch of our

Government most responsive to the popular will" * * * . The agency will make the fundamental policy choices. But the remand does ensure that the courts not hold unconstitutional a statute that an agency, with the application of its special expertise, could salvage. In any event, we do not read current Supreme Court cases as applying the strong form of the nondelegation doctrine voiced in Justice Rehnquist's concurrence. *See Mistretta v. United States*, 488 U.S. 361, 377-79, 109 S.Ct. 647, 102 L.Ed.2d 714 (1989).

What sorts of "intelligible principles" might EPA adopt? Cost-benefit analysis * * * is not available under decisions of this court. Our cases read § 109(b)(1) as barring EPA from considering any factor other than "health effects relating to pollutants in the air." * * * *Lead Industries*, 647 F.2d at 1148 * * * .

In theory, EPA could make its criterion the eradication of any hint of direct health risk. This approach is certainly determinate enough, but it appears that it would require the agency to set the permissible levels of both pollutants here at zero. No party here appears to advocate this solution, and EPA appears to show no inclination to adopt it.

EPA's past behavior suggests some readiness to adopt standards that leave non-zero residual risk. For example, it has employed commonly used clinical criteria to determine what qualifies as an adverse health effect. * * * On the issue of likelihood, for some purposes it might be appropriate to use standards drawn from other areas of the law, such as the familiar "more probable than not" criterion.

Of course a one-size-fits-all criterion of probability would make little sense. There is no reason why the same probability should govern assessments of a risk of thousands of deaths as against risks of a handful of people suffering momentary shortness of breath. More generally, all the relevant variables seem to range continuously from high to low: the possible effects of pollutants vary from death to trivialities, and the size of the affected population, the probability of an effect, and the associated uncertainty range from "large" numbers of persons with point estimates of high probability, to small numbers and vague ranges of probability. This does not seem insurmountable. Everyday life compels us all to make decisions balancing remote but severe harms against a probability distribution of benefits; people decide whether to proceed with an operation that carries a 1/1000 possibility of death, and (simplifying) a 90% chance of cure and a 10% chance of no effect, and a certainty of some short-term pain and nuisance. To be sure, all that requires is a go/no-go decision, while a serious effort at coherence under § 109(b)(1) would need to be more comprehensive. For example, a range of ailments short of death might need to be assigned weights. Nonetheless, an agency wielding the power over American life possessed by EPA should be capable of developing the rough equivalent of a generic unit of harm that takes into account population affected, severity and probability. Possible building blocks for such a principled structure might be found in the approach Oregon used in devising its health plan for the poor. In determining what conditions would be eligible for treatment under its version of Medicaid, Oregon ranked treatments by the amount of improvement in "Quality-Adjusted Life Years" provided by each treatment, divided by the cost of the treatment. Here, of course, EPA may not consider cost, and indeed may well find a completely different method for securing reasonable coherence. Alternatively, if EPA concludes that there is no principle available, it can so report to the Congress, along with such rationales as it has for the levels it chose, and seek legislation ratifying its choice. * * *

We remand the cases to EPA for further consideration of all standards at issue. * * *

Because of the substantial investment of time this matter has required and the many unresolved issues bearing on application of whatever standards may emerge, this panel will in the interest of judicial economy retain jurisdiction over the cases following remand. * * *

TATEL, CIRCUIT JUDGE, dissenting from Part I:

The Clean Air Act has been on the books for decades, has been amended by Congress numerous times, and has been the subject of regular congressional oversight hearings. The Act has been parsed by this circuit no fewer than ten times in published opinions delineating EPA authority in the NAAQS setting process. Yet this court now threatens to strike down section 109 of the Act as an unconstitutional delegation of congressional authority unless EPA can articulate an intelligible principle cabining its discretion. In doing so, the court ignores the last half-century of Supreme Court nondelegation jurisprudence, apparently viewing these permissive precedents as mere exceptions to the rule laid down 64 years ago in *A.L.A. Schechter Poultry Corp. v. United States*, 295 U.S. 495, 55 S.Ct. 837, 79 L.Ed. 1570 (1935). Because section 109's delegation of authority is narrower and more principled than delegations the Supreme Court and this court have upheld since *Schechter Poultry*, and because the record in this case demonstrates that EPA's discretion was in fact cabined by section 109, I respectfully dissent.

Section 109 requires EPA to publish air quality standards "the attainment and maintenance of which in the judgment of the Administrator, based on such criteria and allowing an adequate margin of safety, are requisite to protect the public health." * * * Compare section 109 to the language of section 303 of the Communications Act of 1934, which gave the FCC authority to regulate broadcast licensing in the "public interest," and which the Supreme Court sustained in *National Broadcasting Co. v. United States*, 319 U.S. 190, 225-26, 63 S.Ct. 997, 87 L.Ed. 1344 (1943). The FCC's general authority to issue regulations "as public convenience, interest, or necessity requires" was sustained in *United States v. Southwestern Cable Co.*, 392 U.S. 157, 178, 88 S.Ct. 1994, 20 L.Ed.2d 1001 (1968). The Supreme Court has sustained equally broad delegations to other agencies, including the Price Administrator's authority to fix "fair and equitable" commodities prices, *Yakus v. United States*, 321 U.S. 414, 426-27, 64 S.Ct. 660 (1944), the Federal Power Commission's authority to determine "just and reasonable" rates, *FPC v. Hope Natural Gas Co.*, 320 U.S. 591, 600, 64 S.Ct. 281 (1944), the War Department's authority to recover "excessive profits" earned on military contracts, *Lichter v. United States*, 334 U.S. 742, 778-786, 68 S.Ct. 1294 (1948), and the Attorney General's authority to regulate new drugs that pose an "imminent hazard to public safety," *Touby v. United States*, 500 U.S. 160, 165, 111 S.Ct. 1752 (1991). * * *

Given this extensive Supreme Court precedent sustaining general congressional delegations, no wonder the First Circuit rejected a similar nondelegation challenge to the Clean Air Act's "requisite to protect the public health" language:

> The power granted to EPA is not "unconfined and vagrant." * * * The Agency has been given a well defined task by Congress—to reduce pollution to levels "requisite to protect the public health," in the case of primary standards. * * * [T]here are many benchmarks to guide the Agency and the courts in determining whether or not EPA is exceeding its powers, not the least of which is that the rationality of the means can be tested against goals capable of fairly precise definition in the language of science.
>
> Administrative agencies are created by Congress because it is impossible for the Legislature to acquire sufficient information to manage each detail in the long process of extirpating the abuses identified by the legislation; the Agency must have flexibility to implement the congressional mandate. Therefore, although the delegation to EPA was a broad one, * * * we have little difficulty concluding that the delegation was not excessive.

*South Terminal Corp. v. EPA*, 504 F.2d 646, 677 (1st Cir.1974).

### Notes and Questions

1. Congress could, of course, select the NAAQS values itself by legislative enactment. For example, it might amend the CAA to provide that the primary NAAQS for ozone is 0.11 ppm maximum daily one-hour average. The advantages of such an approach are obvious: an essentially political decision involving difficult value judgments is made by elected representatives and would presumably be unassailable in court. Congress could alternatively enact such detailed directions for standard setting that the agency's task is essentially mechanical. The directions in CAA § 112(d)(2) for establishment of maximum achievable control technology (MACT) standards for hazardous air pollutants are an example of such an approach. *See* page 337 note 2, *infra*. Did the *American Trucking* court conclude that the Constitution requires one or the other of these approaches? If so, wasn't the court required to find CAA § 109 itself unconstitutional? If not, how can the *delegation*—an activity undertaken by Congress—be unconstitutional?

2. The *American Trucking* court declined to vacate the new $O_3$ and $PM_{2.5}$ standards. Accordingly, the standards have been placed in limbo until such

time as the agency responds to the court's invitation to "develop a constitutional *construction* of the act (and, if appropriate, modify the disputed NAAQS in accordance with that construction)" (emphasis added). Can you articulate a construction of CAA § 109 that the D.C. Circuit panel would find to be constitutional? What would that construction provide?

3.   What does the court mean by the following statement: "*EPA's* formulation of its policy judgment leaves it free to pick any point between zero and a hair below the concentrations yielding London's Killer Fog" (emphasis added)? How could such a policy comply with the statutory directive to establish standards "requisite to protect the public health" with "an adequate margin of safety?" Is it the *EPA's* formulation of its policy judgment that leads to such an absurd conclusion, or is it the *court's* formulation?

4.   Suppose the EPA invents a guiding "principle" to somehow flesh out the meaning of the statutory words. Let's consider two such principles:

(a)   we will set the ozone NAAQS at the level at which it is more probable than not that 2% of the affected population will experience impaired breathing for a period greater than 30 minutes; or

(b)   we have assigned weights to all sorts of ailments short of death, and will set the ozone NAAQS at the level where the computed value of the weighted ailments equals or exceeds 3.14159.

How does either "principle" solve the nondelegation problem? Hasn't the agency simply invented its own constraint? Does an unconstitutional delegation of legislative power somehow become constitutional when an *agency* invents a "principle" to which a reviewing *court* will give two out of three thumbs up?

5.   Do the wordings of principles (a) and (b) in the preceding paragraph suggest that the *range* of potentially available principles is essentially infinite? *Cf.* Dilbert, page 207, *supra.* By what principle does a *court* determine that one selected principle—out of an infinite universe of options—is constitutional and another selected principle is not? Isn't the court's directive on remand "fatally incomplete," inducing a reasonable person to respond, "How are *you* going to measure the adequacy of any principle the agency invents?" Sooner or later, aren't we going to have to hit the red reset button with this kind of analysis?

7.   Suppose the agency invents a principle which is unable to withstand judicial scrutiny. The agency then invents a second principle, which also flunks judicial review. Has the court effectively adopted a legal rule committing the nation to avoiding false positives in ozone and particulate regulation until such time as Congress drafts the pertinent standards? *See* pages 185-87, *supra.* Does CAA § 109 indicate that Congress wished to pursue a commitment to limiting false positives?

8.   Is the court requiring—under the guise of constitutional analysis— *quantified* risk assessment? *See* pages 199-207, *supra.* Does it seem likely that Congress, when it enacted CAA § 109, wished the agency to engage in a numerical weighting of ailments and an arithmetical toting of quantified harms, especially when it forbid the consideration of costs?

9.   The Atomic Energy Act did not expressly grant power to establish radiation protection standards. Nevertheless, an early case held that an implied power to enact such standards was discretionary, *see Blaber v. U.S.*, 212 F. Supp. 95, 98 (E.D. N.Y. 1962), *aff'd*, 332 F.2d 629 (2d Cir. 1964), and the EPA and NRC standards have been promulgated under this implied authority. The absence of any express statutory grant of rulemaking authority means that the NRC and EPA have not had to conform their regulations to any statutory standard. *See* Stensvaag, *Regulating Radioactive Air Emissions from Nuclear Generating Plants*, 71 Nw. U. L. Rev. 1, 103 n.596 (1983). Does this mean that the federal radioactive air emission standards explored at pages 256-66, *supra*, are the result of an unconstitutional delegation of congressional power? Are these standards vulnerable to judicial attack under the nondelegation doctrine twenty or thirty years after their adoption? How about all other environmental and occupational standards administratively adopted to control nonthreshold pollutants?

## 4.  SIPS: A PRELIMINARY LOOK

Section 110 of the Clean Air Act is one of the most monstrous provisions ever created by the Congress. Its basic thrust is to set forth the contents that must be present in an acceptable "state implementation plan" (SIP). By the time you have completed your study of the Clean Air Act, you will have read almost all of this section, but it would be hopelessly confusing to try to absorb it all in one sitting. In this first assignment, the goal is to acquaint you with the most elementary, skeletal contents of a SIP. Therefore, you are told to read only specific sub-parts of this section (along with a brief portion of § 302) at this time.

In reading the specific sub-parts, bear in mind the basic structure of the Clean Air Act. The Administrator promulgates *ambient* air quality standards for all "criteria" pollutants; it is the job of the state authorities, in the SIP-creation process, to translate these ambient air quality requirements into specific *emission limitations* to be applied to particular sources of pollution. States have done this in a wide variety of ways. For example, it is not unusual for state regulations to provide that only so many tons of $SO_2$ may be emitted by a coal fired plant for each million BTU of heat input per hour. One key feature of the Clean Air Act scheme is that the SIP for each state may look quite different from the SIPs of other states.

Section 110(h)(1) of the Clean Air Act directs the EPA Administrator to publish a comprehensive document setting forth the SIP for each state on a regular basis. These SIPs—which are really the sum total of all state regulations on air pollution—are published piecemeal in the Federal Register and compiled in the Bureau of National Affairs' *Environment Reporter*; they occupy several volumes in the multi-volume set entitled "State Air Laws."

If you get the chance, you should find your state's implementation plan in the Environment Reporter, glancing through it to get the feel of its bulk and complexity. Pretending that you operate a factory that emits particulates and $SO_2$, see if you can find your state's emission limitations for those pollutants.

---

Read the following sections of the Clean Air Act

☐ § 110(a)(1)          ☐ § 110(a)(2)(A)          ☐ § 110(a)(2)(B)

☐ § 110(a)(2)(E)          ☐ § 110(a)(2)(H)          ☐ § 110(c)(1)

☐ § 110(h)(1)          ☐ § 110(k)(1)(A)          ☐ § 110(k)(3)

☐ § 110(k)(5)          ☐ § 110(*l*)          ☐ § 302(q)

---

### Questions

1.  Assume that you are an employee of your state's pollution control agency. The time is 1971, and the EPA has just promulgated the initial primary NAAQS for $SO_2$: 0.03 ppm (80 $\mu g/m^3$) measured as the annual arithmetic mean. You are charged with the task of drafting an implementation plan to achieve compliance with this NAAQS in your state. What steps must you go through to accomplish this task?

2.  Assume that your state has adopted an implementation plan providing for the attainment of the $SO_2$ standard. The plan must be submitted to the EPA Administrator for her approval. If the Administrator concludes that the plan is inadequate, what is supposed to happen?

## RICHARD B. STEWART & JAMES E. KRIER, ENVIRONMENTAL LAW AND POLICY

### 366-67 (2nd ed. 1978)

Under the Clean Air Act, the states have basic responsibility for imposing limits on emissions of air pollutants in order to achieve and maintain the federal ambient standards. Such emission limitations must be included in the states' implementation plans, and may consist of prohibitions on emissions in excess of given limits by given sources, or measures, such as requiring the use of low sulfur coal, restriction on automobile use, or land use planning to disperse emissions, that will indirectly assure compliance with the ambient standards. The degree to which controls must be imposed (which will obviously vary by location, depending upon existing emissions and ambient concentrations) is generally determined by atmospheric modeling techniques that relate changes in emissions to changes in ambient concentrations. One simple model is the "straight rollback" model, which assumes that a given percentage reduction in total emissions * * * will produce an equivalent percentage reduction in ambient concentrations. Unfortunately, this equivalency is seldom obtained under real-world conditions because emission sources vary in size and are not uniformly distributed; processes of atmospheric chemistry are frequently nonlinear; and topographical variations (such as mountains and lakes) introduce further complications. More sophisticated models are costly to develop and apply. Disputes about the validity of such models are a fruitful source of litigation. *See Texas v. EPA*, 499 F.2d 289 (5th Cir. 1974) (upholding EPA's crude "straight rollback" model). Also, models are no better than the data fed into them, and there are typically serious shortcomings in the extent and quality of ambient and emissions data needed to validate and apply diffusion models. \* \* \*

Once the degree of emissions reduction necessary to achieve the federal ambient standards is determined (often a lengthy and controversial process) a state enjoys discretion \* \* \* to decide how the burden of abatement should be allocated among the various contributing sources within a region.

## 5.  UNIFORM FEDERAL EMISSION STANDARDS

## RICHARD B. STEWART & JAMES E. KRIER, ENVIRONMENTAL LAW AND POLICY

### 367-71 (2nd ed. 1978)

[T]he Clean Air Act superimposes three sets of geographically uniform emission limitations established by the federal government: those for new stationary sources (§ 111); especially hazardous pollutants not covered by federal ambient standards (§ 112); and new motor vehicle emissions (§ 202). The states are precluded from establishing more stringent emissions limitations for new automobiles. We are interested in two principal questions: Why should emission limitations be set by the federal government? Why should such limitations be geographically uniform?

The imposition of emission limitations by the federal government for new stationary sources and motor vehicles appears inconsistent with the Act's basic policy of reserving to the states decisions about the appropriate allocation of abatement burdens among various sources. Moreover, in some areas, such limitations would impose emission reductions even though the area was already in compliance with the federal ambient standards. On the other hand, in areas with high concentrations of automotive-type pollutants (oxides of nitrogen, hydrocarbons, carbon monoxide, and photochemical oxidants), the Clean Air Act's preemption of more stringent state controls on new automobile emissions may prevent states from imposing emission limitations required in order to meet the federal ambient standards.

There are, however, countervailing considerations that might justify determination of emission limitations by the federal government. The extent to which it is feasible for various types of sources to control emissions turns on complex technological and economic issues that might more cheaply and competently be explored and resolved by the federal government than on a multiple basis by the states. * * *

Nationally uniform emission limitations would appear to be a highly irrational approach to achieving geographically uniform ambient standards, because the degree of emission limitation required to achieve a given concentration of pollutants would vary geographically depending upon existing emissions, local meteorology and topography, and the like. Requiring all new power plants or coke ovens or automobiles throughout the nation to control emissions to the identical extent is likely to involve too much control (from the perspective of meeting ambient standards) in "clean" areas of the nation, and inadequate control in "dirty" areas. * * *

Even if economic analysis is of little assistance in deciding which environmental quality standards to adopt, there is a compelling societal interest in achieving whatever standards are adopted at least resource cost. * * * [T]he criterion of least cost abatement requires a greater measure of control by those sources that can reduce emissions more cheaply, and a lesser degree of control by sources with high abatement costs. Insofar as the Act reserves discretion in the states to decide upon the appropriate distribution of abatement burdens, the Act permits (although it does not compel) the adoption of a least cost abatement strategy. However, the Act prevents least cost achievement of ambient standards by imposing geographically uniform federal emission limitations for important categories of sources when a least cost strategy in a given local area might dictate a different level of control for such sources. * * *

Does the previous discussion nonetheless provide sufficient justifications for imposing uniform federal emission limitations on some types of sources, while relegating control of other sources to the states? Is the Act an illogical and unworkable hodge-podge of differing and fundamentally incompatible approaches? Or does it represent a reasonable compromise among relevant goals and considerations?

## 6.  HAZARDOUS AIR POLLUTANTS

Although the central thrust of the Clean Air Act prior to the 1990 amendments was to confront the six criteria pollutants through national ambient air quality standards, state implementation plans, new source performance standards, and mobile source controls, the pre-1990 version of the statute further provided for the regulation of "hazardous air pollutants" (HAPs) through the federal promulgation of nationally uniform emission standards (NESHAPS), applied to new and existing air pollution sources. The NESHAPS were to be established by the Administrator "at the level which in his [or her] judgment provide[d] an ample margin of safety to protect public health from such hazardous air pollutant." Once a NESHAPS became effective, no person could construct a new source or modify an existing source emitting a regulated hazardous air pollutant unless the Administrator found that such source if properly operated would not cause emissions in violation of such standard, and no air pollutant to which such standard applied could be emitted from any stationary source in violation of such standard, subject to limited exceptions.

Congress concluded in 1990 that the EPA's implementation of the NESHAPS program was unacceptable. Accordingly, the 1990 Clean Air Act Amendments set in motion a massive revision of the statute's approach to hazardous air pollutants.

# H.R. REP. NO. 490

101st Cong., 2d Sess. 315, 317-20, 322-23 (1990)

Hazardous air pollutants are air pollutants that can cause serious illnesses, such as cancer, or death. In theory, they were to be stringently controlled under the existing Clean Air Act section 112. However, only seven of the hundreds of potentially hazardous air pollutants have been regulated by EPA since section 112 was enacted in 1970.

The Clean Air Act distinguishes between two categories of pollutants: hazardous air pollutants and criteria or conventional air pollutants. Criteria * * * pollutants tend to be more pervasive, but less potent, than hazardous air pollutants. * * *

Hazardous air pollutants are pollutants that pose especially serious health risks. Under existing law, they are pollutants that "cause or contribute to an increase in mortality or an increase in serious irreversible, or incapacitating reversible, illness." They may reasonably be anticipated to cause cancer, neurological disorders, reproductive dysfunctions, other chronic health effects, or adverse acute human health effects. * * *

A study by Tulane University reported that the lung cancer rate for residents living within a mile of major chemical plants is four times the national average. A similar study by the West Virginia Department of Health found cancer rates twice the national average in neighborhoods near chemical plants.

EPA has made preliminary estimates of the cancer risks created by individual plants, called the "ATERIS" report. Although these estimates were made for the purpose of comparing relative risks (not determining precise facility-specific risks), they represent a reasonable available approach to estimating the magnitude of risks posed by industrial facilities. As revised in January 1990, the EPA estimates found 149 facilities to be associated with lifetime cancer risks to the most exposed individual of greater than 1 in 10,000, including 52 plants with cancer risks greater than 1 in 1,000, seven plants associated with cancer risks greater than 1 in 100, and one plant associated with a cancer risk greater than 1 in 10. In each case, the analyses assumed a 70-year, constant exposure to the maximum long-term ambient concentration of the air toxic [produced] by the plant.

The EPA estimates evaluated the risks caused by emissions of a single toxic air pollutant from each plant. But many facilities emit numerous toxic pollutants. The agency's risk assessments did not consider the combined or synergistic effects of exposure to multiple toxics, or the effect of exposure through indirect pathways (such as eating vegetables on which air toxics have been deposited). The analyses also did not evaluate the cancer risks created by industrial sources of some important carcinogenic emissions, including benzene and coke-oven emissions.

In a separate study of risks associated with coke oven emissions, EPA identified an additional 20 facilities associated with a lifetime cancer risk of greater than 1 in 1000 to the most exposed individual, including six facilities associated with a greater than 1 in 100 cancer risk. * * *

There have been no quantitative assessments of the noncancer risks created by toxic emissions although it is believed that toxic emissions can cause [an] array of serious illnesses besides cancer. These include birth defects, damage to the brain or other parts of the nervous system, reproductive disorders, and genetic mutations. In the case of emissions of some neurotoxins, even small doses can be lethal. * * *

Toxics can cause adverse impacts to the environment as well as to human health. The Great Lakes in particular have been adversely affected, because their [huge] surface area acts as a sink for toxics that may come from air sources, some of which may be from hundreds of miles away. This problem was discovered when researchers found significant levels of PCBs and pesticides on remote Isle Royale National Park, a wilderness island in the middle of Lake Superior.

Many Great Lakes fish species are no longer considered edible because of toxic contamination. * * * Atmospheric deposition contributes more than 50 percent of PCB loading in the upper Great Lakes and a significant, but [undetermined], portion of the mercury loading. * * *

Since 1970, EPA has listed only eight substances as hazardous air pollutants (beryllium, mercury, vinyl chloride, asbestos, benzene, radionuclides, arsenic, and coke oven emissions) and has promulgated emission standards for seven of them (no standard for coke oven emissions has been issued). These regulations sometimes apply only to limited sources of the relevant pollutant. For example, the original benzene standard covered just one category of sources (equipment leaks). Of the 50 toxic substances emitted by industry in the greatest volume in 1987, only one—benzene—has been regulated even partially by EPA. * * *

However, some of [EPA's] actions under other provisions of the Act have coincidentally helped lower toxic emissions. Many toxic emissions are types of VOCs [volatile organic compounds]. Thus, in nonattainment areas, these emissions have been reduced as a result of VOC controls required to combat smog formation and should continue to be reduced as a result of [the nonattainment amendments in] this bill. Similarly, emissions of metals like mercury or chromium, which are often emitted in particulate form, have been controlled by particulate controls. EPA has estimated that cancer cases have been reduced by roughly 50 percent since 1970 as a result of VOC and particulate controls. This is important and significant.

Despite these successes under other provisions of the Act, some EPA actions under the Clean Air Act have inadvertently boosted toxic emissions. The phase-out of leaded gasoline reduced gasoline octane levels. In seeking alternatives to regain these levels for performance of vehicles, refiners increased benzene, toluene, and xylene levels in gasoline—all of which have high octane levels, but are also suspected toxic substances.

---

Read the following sections of the Clean Air Act

☐ § 112(a)(1)     ☐ § 112(a)(2)     ☐ § 112(b)(1)     ☐ § 112(b)(2)

☐ § 112(c)(1)     ☐ § 112(c)(2)     ☐ § 112(d)(1)     ☐ § 112(d)(2)

☐ § 112(d)(3)     ☐ § 112(e)(1)     ☐ § 112(f)(1)     ☐ § 112(f)(2)(A)

☐ § 112(i)(1)     ☐ § 112(i)(3)(A)

---

## PHILLIP D. REED, FEDERAL EMISSION LIMITATIONS

in 2 Law of Environmental Protection
11-112 to 11-119 (Sheldon M. Novick, ed. 1998).

The new section 112 completely revamps its predecessor * * * . The handful of hazardous air pollutant regulations promulgated under the old provision remain in effect, until modified under the new approach. In addition, certain of the most stringent provisions of the old section have been given the unequivocal approval of Congress. * * *

The Amendments redefine the term "hazardous air pollutant" to mean any pollutant listed under new section 112. Congress started EPA off with a list of 189 hazardous air pollutants. Included on the list are all thirteen substances that EPA had listed or announced its intent to list under the old provision, as well as most of the substances EPA had specifically decided not to regulate under section 112 or not to regulate at present due to lack of information.

The Act requires EPA to review the list periodically and to add substances (other than criteria pollutants) * * * . As a practical matter,

EPA will be so busy regulating the 189 listed substances that it will be some time before it is likely to add significantly to the list * * * .

The definition of "hazardous air pollutant" greatly expands the scope of regulation in two directions. First, EPA must address pollutants that are harmful to the environment, but not to health. Second, EPA must address pollutants that cause harm when not airborne, that is, after being deposited onto the ground or a body of water.

The Act authorizes EPA to remove substances from the list, but this authority will not be easy to use. Removal must be based on an affirmative finding that there is adequate data available to demonstrate that the substance "may not reasonably be anticipated to cause *any adverse* effects to human health or adverse environmental effects." CAA § 112(b)(3)(C) (emphasis added). * * *

As required by the 1990 Amendments, for the hazardous pollutants listed in section 112(b), EPA has published a list of all categories and subcategories of major sources (including a number of significant area source categories). A major source is "any stationary source or group of stationary sources located within a contiguous area and under common control that emits or has the potential to emit considering controls, in the aggregate, 10 tons per year or more of any hazardous air pollutant or 25 tons per year or more of any combination of hazardous air pollutants." § 112(a)(1). An area source is any other [stationary] source * * * .

The Act requires EPA to list all categories and subcategories of area sources that EPA determines constitute health or environmental threats "warranting action" under section 112. § 112(c)(3). While EPA thus has some discretion in listing area source categories, the Amendments also require the Agency to list within five years categories of area sources accounting for 90 percent of the urban area emissions of the thirty listed substances that create the greatest risk to health in the largest number of such urban areas. *Id.* In addition, EPA must list enough major and area source categories of alkylated lead compounds, polycyclic organic matter, hexachlorobenzene, mercury, polychlorinated biphenyls, furans and dioxins within five years of enactment to account for 90 percent of emissions of those substances. * * *

[T]he initial list [issued by EPA in 1992] includes only eight area source categories.

In developing emission limitations for categories of major sources, EPA is to refer to a new, variable formulation for technology-based standards: "maximum achievable control technology" (MACT). The definition of MACT [is set forth in § 112(d)(2)] * * * . The standards give EPA remarkably broad power over American industry, since they may be based on process changes, materials substitutions, enclosure of processes, collection, capture and treatment of stack or fugitive emissions or design, equipment, work practice or operational standards or a combination of measures. §112(n)(3). * * * For area sources, EPA may choose to base standards on "generally available control technology" [GACT] instead of MACT.

The core of MACT analysis (as with other technology-based standards under the Act) is a review of the emission control achievements of other sources. For new sources, the reference point is the best-controlled source that EPA determines is similar. For existing sources in categories with more than thirty sources, the reference point is the average emission reduction achieved by the best 12 percent of the sources * * * . (EPA has delineated a controversial modeling method to define the average emission reductions by the best 12 percent of existing sources. It is explained [at] 59 Fed. Reg. 19,401, 19,414-17 (1994).) For sources in categories with less than thirty sources, EPA is to base the standard on the average emission reduction achieved by the five best-performing sources in the category. * * *

The Amendments set forth a schedule for promulgating hazardous air pollutant standards that is leisurely compared to the superseded requirements. § 112(e)(5) * * * (EPA announced its schedule for the promulgation of MACT rules [at] * * * 58 Fed. Reg. 63,941 (1993) (covering 166 major sources and eight area sources).) * * *

The order in which EPA is to address various listed categories is to be determined on the basis of the potential harmfulness of the pollutants involved, the volume of emissions in proximity to vulnerable human or environmental receptors characteristic of each category, and regulatory efficiency. § 112(e)(3). * * *

Congress did not require any consideration of health effects in setting MACT standards, but made it likely that a second tier of risk-based regulation will be added for major sources. Unless EPA can persuade Congress that residual risk regulation is not warranted, EPA will have to develop standards to provide an ample margin of safety to protect public health * * * .

By November 15, 1996, EPA must provide a comprehensive report to Congress on the residual risk to health caused by emissions from sources in compliance with MACT standards and recommend amendments to address such risk as EPA believes exists. If Congress does not act, EPA must promulgate residual risk standards to protect public health with an ample margin of safety and prevent adverse environmental effects. § 112(f)(2).

### Notes and Questions

1.   Section 112(a)(1), defining "major source," for purposes of the hazardous air pollutant program, contains clumsy language about a "group of stationary sources located within a contiguous area and under common control." Why is this language necessary?

2.   Examine the general MACT definition in § 112(d)(2). Notice that this is technology-based. Moreover, Congress is relatively rigid in specifying the meaning of MACT. For example, for existing sources, Congress specifies

that MACT must be the average emission limitation being achieved by the best performing 12 percent in an industry category containing 30 or more sources. § 112(d)(3)(A). Is this a technology-forcing provision? Why or why not?

3.   Nothing in the pre-1990 Act required emission reductions for the vast majority of the 189 newly listed hazardous air pollutants. Assume that air emissions of chloroprene, for example, have never been regulated before the 1990 Clean Air Act Amendments. Does the MACT definition for existing sources of chloroprene strike you as rather odd? Why or why not?

4.   Suppose that the EPA publishes a report pursuant to § 112(f)(1), concluding that hazardous air pollutant emissions from sources complying with MACT standards pose a residual risk to human health or the environment, and recommending legislation to address the remaining risk. Congress is so busy not legislating on other matters that it ignores the EPA's report. What must the EPA do under such circumstances? Why?

5.   Assume that the EPA must publish residual risk standards. What is the statutory standard specifying how the EPA is supposed to carry out this obligation? Can you find the text of that standard in the Clean Air Act? Why or why not?

# U.S. EPA, OFFICE OF AIR & RADIATION, 1996 NATIONAL AIR QUALITY: STATUS AND TRENDS

### August 1998

EPA's program to control toxics, ozone, and PM complement each other. Many toxic air pollutants are emitted in the form of particulates or as VOC [volatile organic compounds]. For example, EPA's final toxic air pollutant regulation for organic chemical manufacturing is not only expected to reduce benzene and other toxics, but also VOC emissions by an amount equivalent to removing millions of cars from the road. * * *

EPA is using the National Toxics Inventory (NTI) to track nationwide emissions trends for toxic air pollutants listed in the Clean Air Act. The NTI includes emissions information for 188 hazardous air pollutants from more than 900 stationary sources. There are approximately 3.7 million tons of air toxics released to the air each year according to NTI. * * * NTI includes emissions from large industrial or "point" sources, smaller stationary sources called "area" sources, and mobile sources. The NTI estimates of the area source and mobile source contributions to the national emissions of toxic air pollutants are approximately 35 and 41 percent, respectively.

Data from the Toxic Release Inventory (TRI), a product of the Community Right-to-Know Act of 1986, were used as the foundation of NTI. The TRI data alone represent less than half of the total emissions from the point source category, with no data for mobile and area sources. Therefore, the NTI has incorporated other emissions data to create a more complete inventory.

As of January 1998, EPA has issued 23 air toxics standards under the Clean Air Act. These standards affect 48 categories of major industrial sources, such as chemical plants, oil refineries, aerospace manufacturers, and steel mills, as well as eight categories of smaller sources, such as dry cleaners, commercial sterilizers, secondary lead smelters, and chromium electroplating facilities. EPA has also issued two standards to control emissions from solid waste combustion facilities. Together these standards reduce emissions of over 100 different air toxics. When fully implemented, these standards will reduce air toxics emissions by about 1 million tons per year—almost ten times the reductions achieved prior to 1990. By the year 2005, EPA projects that the toxic air pollutant program will reduce toxic emissions by 75 percent. Because controls for toxic air pollutants also reduce VOC and PM emissions the program should realize reductions in VOC and PM emissions of more than 4 billion pounds per year, over the next ten years.

## 7. ACID RAIN

### S. REP. NO. 228

101st Cong., 1st Sess. 261-63, 272-73, 275, 279, 282-83, 289, 301 (1989)

Acid rain is created when oxides of sulfur and nitrogen are emitted—most often from electric utilities—and then transformed in the atmosphere or on surfaces into sulfuric and nitric acids. * * *

Sulfur (S) is contained in almost all fossil fuels, but especially coal. When burned, the sulfur combines with the oxygen in the air to create sulfur dioxide ($SO_2$). * * *

$SO_2$ is a colorless gas, so it cannot be seen with the naked eye. It is, nevertheless, a powerful lung irritant which can cause lung seizures in asthmatics and other sensitive groups. When $SO_2$ is transformed into sulfate—a process which begins almost immediately—it escapes regulation under the Clean Air Act. $SO_2$ emitted by power plants and other industrial sources combines with oxygen in the atmosphere to form sulfate ($SO_4$).

Sulfate ($SO_4$) is an extremely fine particle, capable of reaching the deepest recesses of the lung. Coincidentally, the sulfate particle is also perfectly sized for reducing visibility. This is one reason that airport visibility measurements are sometimes used as a surrogate for sulfate concentrations. When sulfate settles out of the air onto leaves, buildings or other surfaces it attracts water, which converts it into sulfuric acid ($H_2SO_4$). If inhaled, the lung's own moisture supports the conversion. And, if the $SO_4$ is washed out [of] the air by fog, clouds, mist or rain, it has become "acid" rain, as it is popularly called.

Sulfuric acid ($H_2SO_4$) is powerfully corrosive and can therefore directly damage tissues and materials. But it can also start a chemical reaction of its own, with effects that ripple through an ecosystem. When common dirt is washed in acid, heavy metals that were tightly bound to the soil particles—aluminum, lead, and mercury are three examples—are dissolved, entering the water runoff in massive quantities. Aluminum, for example, increases 1000 percent for every 100 percent increase in rainfall acidity. Thus if the acidity of rain increases 10-fold—which almost all agree is a fair definition of how "acid" today's acid rain is—the aluminum content of rainwater runoff increases 10,000 percent.

Exactly what damages can be fairly attributed to aluminum and other heavy metals freed by acid rain has not been sorted out completely. It is well established that the aluminum is extremely toxic to fish if it reaches lakes and streams. Many scientists believe that it is aluminum which is primarily responsible for the losses of lakes throughout Scandinavia, Canada and New England, rather than the sulfuric acid itself. It is equally clear that some of the other heavy metals—especially lead, cadmium and mercury—can pose a serious threat to human health as drinking water contaminants. * * *

Nitrogen undergoes a fairly similar process of conversion: nitrogen ($N_2$) combines with oxygen ($O_2$) to form several different oxides ($N_2O_2$, $N_2O$, $NO_2$, etc.). These, in turn, form nitrates which, when exposed to water convert to nitric acid. There are, however, some important differences.

Oxides of nitrogen ($N_2O_2$, $N_2O$, $NO_2$) can be created because nitrogen is found both in fuels and in the air. Roughly 80 percent of the air is nitrogen, and almost all fuels other than natural gas also contain it. But the oxides are not formed until the heat and pressure of the combustion process are brought to bear. The combustion may take place in the cylinder of a car or the furnace of a giant coal-fired power plant. But in either case, the combustion temperature and pressure are determinants of how much nitrogen is converted to oxides of nitrogen.

These oxides, like $SO_2$, are irritants which are regulated under the Clean Air Act. And, again like $SO_2$, they escape its coverage when they combine with oxygen to form nitrates ($NO_3$). Nitrates ($NO_3$), like sulfates, are fine particles which can reach the cellular levels of the lung. Unlike sulfates, nitrates and other nitrogen-based compounds are considered beneficial to vegetation because they are plant nutrients. For this reason, some scientists and policy makers have tended to minimize the role which oxides of nitrogen, nitrates and nitric acid have played in the damage caused by acid rain and [in] plans for its control.

Within the past several years, however, as scientists have searched for plausible explanations for the forest damages found throughout much of Europe and Eastern North America, they have begun to question whether one answer might be an "over fertilizing" effect of nitrogen compounds. There have also been suggestions that nitric acid could free heavy metals before being taken up by vegetation.

Nitric acid ($HNO_3$) thus may or may not be the equal of sulfuric acid in terms of the damages caused by acid rain. But the bill, including this title, imposes additional controls on nitrogen for reasons in addition to concerns over acid rain; namely, the role which it plays in the formation of ozone.

Ozone $(O_3)$, better known as an ingredient in "smog," is the indicator for a variety of chemicals which are formed when the combination of nitrogen and organic chemicals (e.g., gasoline) are exposed to sunlight. Ozone is a powerful bleach, so effective at destroying organic matter that it is used by some cities to disinfect their drinking water supplies.

Although the chain of chemical reactions which leads to the formation of ozone and other oxidants is not completely understood, there is no disagreement that there are three essential ingredients. Without all three, ozone is not formed in substantial quantities. These are hydrocarbons, oxides of nitrogen, and sunlight. Historically, the Federal government has relied on a strategy of controlling ozone by controlling [hydrocarbon] emissions. This has achieved mixed results, leading some States to begin implementing a strategy based on controlling oxides of nitrogen. California has been the leading advocate of this approach and, according to State officials, has enjoyed considerable success. * * *

Because lakes with very low acid neutralizing capacity are especially vulnerable to acid deposition, the OTA [Office of Technology Assessment] has estimated that in the Eastern United States, approximately 3,000 lakes and 23,000 miles of streams have already become acidified or have virtually no acid neutralizing capacity left. In Canada, the Ontario Ministry of the Environment has estimated that 10,000 lakes in the eastern part of the country are currently acid altered.

Without further controls, much more extensive damage is possible. Based on the observation that 25 percent of the land in the Eastern United States is not sufficiently buffered to prevent acidity from being transported to bodies of water, OTA estimates that 117,000 lakes and 112,000 miles of streams are vulnerable to damage by acid rain. * * *

Recently, several cases of unexplained regional scale forest decline have been observed throughout the United States. * * * Although the greatest amount of current attention centers on ozone's role in forest decline, the effects of increased acidity of rain and increased levels of sulfur dioxide are also thought to contribute to forest decline. * * *

Acid rain is known to cause materials damage. Among the materials affected are building stone, rubber, zinc, steel, leather, paint, and textile. Acid rain is thought to accelerate rust by as much as 30 percent. Acid rain contributes to premature soiling of paint and other materials. * * *

There is no disagreement among medical researchers that precursors of acid rain are a serious health threat. Collectively, the pollutants which form acid rain pose a threat to human health so severe that one leading researcher and pediatrician from the Mt. Sinai Medical Center in New York described them as the third leading cause of lung disease in the United States, trailing only active and passive cigarette smoking. In testimony before the Subcommittee * * * Dr. Philip Landrigan stated:

> There is a limit to what you, as Senators, can do about people's desire to smoke. With regard to occupational exposure, you have good laws on the books, but you have the problem of having to enforce those laws through hundreds of thousands of workers across the country. That is obviously a mind boggling task even if OSHA were up to it.

> But in the case of acid rain, there is really a finite number of major sources of acid air pollutants. They can be targeted with relative ease. In fact, they have been pretty well targeted already by the EPA. A few swift and sure legislative strokes could deal with these sources. * * *

According to the National Acid Precipitation Assessment Program, 23.1 million tons of sulfur dioxide and 20.5 million tons of nitrogen oxides were emitted from anthropogenic sources in 1985. Major sources of $SO_2$ released in 1985 were electric utilities (16.1 million tons), industrial combustion (2.8 million tons), industrial processes (2.8 million tons), and transportation (0.9 million tons). Major sources of $NO_x$ released in the same year were electric utilities (6.7 million tons), industrial combustion (3.3 million tons), industrial processes (0.8 million tons), and transportation (8.8 million tons). * * *

Electric utilities have become a major source of sulfur dioxide and nitrogen oxides emissions * * * . Today, sources of sulfur dioxide are generally large and centralized and emit from fairly high stacks at high temperature and exit velocities. More than 90 percent of the sulfur dioxide emitted from powerplants comes from older facilities, which are generally regulated less stringently than plants under the Act's new source performance standards. * * *

The Act was written at a time when the inter-state transport of air pollution was not widely acknowledged. Indeed, it was the implementation of the Clean Air Act which created a substantial number of the interstate pollution problems. Rather than reducing their emissions of sulfur dioxide, electric utilities proposed the use of "tall stacks" to inject pollution into the upper atmosphere where it could be diluted and transported over long distances. Although illegal, this policy was expressly approved by the first Administrator of the [EPA], William D. Ruckelshaus, and quickly lead to the widespread use of super-tall smokestacks.

Although the Congress enacted curbs on the use of tall stacks in the 1977 amendments, * * * the regulations were not issued until 1987 and, even now, are tied up in litigation. In addition, the Congress enacted a new section 126 expressly to control interstate air pollution. But this too has largely failed * * * [to control] interstate air pollution. Thus, the law remains today largely what it was when written in 1970, keyed almost entirely to achieving local ambient air quality standards. * * *

Countless reports of acid rain-related damage make clear that the country incurs real costs unless acid rain controls are implemented without delay.

---

Read the following sections of the Clean Air Act

☐ § 403(f)      ☐ § 404(a)(1)      ☐ § 404 Table A   ☐ § 411(a)

☐ § 411(b)      ☐ § 411(c)

---

## PHILLIP D. REED, STATE IMPLEMENTATION PLANS

in 2 Law of Environmental Protection
11-86 to 11-92 (Sheldon M. Novick, ed. 1998).

The 1990 Amendments' new acid rain program is the culmination of a fierce political battle that raged for over a decade. The program mandates the elimination of 10 million tons of $SO_2$ emissions and 2 million tons of $NO_x$ emissions from oil- and coal-fired utility power plants by 2000. The cuts are to be achieved across the country, with the greatest burden falling on the Midwest. Congress set a cap on $SO_2$ emissions that will be enforced through a complex marketable "allowance" system that is designed to make the necessary emission reductions cost effective and to spread the cost among regions of the country.

The primary target of the acid rain program is "affected units," fossil fuel fired combustion devices (i.e., boilers) located in utility power plants that produce electricity for sale. The program does not apply to several types of small power plants * * * .

Initially, the program does not apply to industrial sources, but EPA must inventory and project such emissions each year and, if the inventory or projection indicates that industrial $SO_2$ emissions will exceed 5.6 million tons per year, EPA is empowered to limit such emissions through new NSPS [new source performance] standards. Power plants that are exempted from the program and industrial sources of $SO_2$ emissions may "opt-in" to the program so as to be able to take advantage of the allowance market.

The heart of the acid rain program is its allowance system. A single allowance is the authority to emit one ton per year of $SO_2$. As of 2000, there will be 8.9 million allowances for all "affected units" (plus a relatively small amounts of bonus allowances). Phase I of the program, which takes effect on January 1, 1995, imposes allowances on 110 specific large power plants, which are set at levels approximately twice as high as the long-term Phase II allowances. Phase II allowances for all affected units (located at approximately 800 power plants) take effect in 2000. When an allowance takes effect, it functions as an emission limitation. Allowances will be issued by EPA at no charge to existing affected units and thereafter may be used, saved for use in a future year, sold, or traded. The amount of each affected unit's allowance is based on one of several complicated formulas that scale back emissions from heavy emitters and allow clean sources to increase emissions slightly from baseline years. The program allows the award of bonus allowances for early emission reductions, innovative control strategies and a variety of other reasons. A utility wishing to build a new fossil-fuel-fired power plant must buy into the allowance market. If aggregate emissions from affected units exceed 8.9 million tons per year after 2000, EPA is empowered to reduce the allowances pro rata.

The allowance market is a high-risk experiment. EPA must develop regulations providing for an allowance tracking system * * * . There are early signs that an allowance market is developing. * * * If a real market does develop, it will create powerful economic incentives for utilities to over-control $SO_2$ emissions and sell the extra allowances. There is no guarantee that the market will function, however. * * *

The enforcement of acid rain control requirements could be draconian. * * * Affected units must install continuous emission monitors or equivalent systems and are presumed to be emitting uncontrolled if such systems are not in place on schedule. Units that emit in excess of their allowances are subject to automatic emission penalties of $2,000 per ton that are payable without demand and do not preclude other enforcement action. CAA § 411(a). In addition, the excess emissions must be offset in future years. § 411(b).

### Notes and Questions

1. The initial Phase I acid rain allowances are set forth in CAA § 404 Table A. Find the Burlington, Iowa, coal-fired power plant. How many tons of $SO_2$ may this facility emit under the Phase I allowances?

2. Suppose the Burlington, Iowa, facility emits 1,000 tons more than permitted by its Phase I allowances over the course of a year. What is supposed to happen? *See* CAA §§ 411(a) and 411(b).

3. Is there any way that the Burlington, Iowa, facility can avoid the sanctions of §§ 411(a) and 411(b), knowing that its allowances will be exceeded by 1,000 tons of emissions?

4. If a coal-fired power plant buys a bushel full of allowances from other facilities, may it emit $SO_2$ in amounts exceeding limitations set forth in the state's implementation plan? Why or why not?

5. Coal-fired power plants have typically sought to meet $SO_2$ emission in either of two ways: (a) by using high-sulfur coal combined with "scrubbing" technology to remove sulfur from the exhaust gases; or (2) by using low-sulfur coal without scrubbing. Under the acid rain control program, what is the complete menu of options confronting each coal-fired power plant operator with respect to $SO_2$ emissions?

6. The acid rain program is apparently a qualified success. The EPA reports that the affected utilities have shown 100 percent compliance with Ti-

tle IV in 1995, 1996, and 1997—a rare accomplishment under any pollution control law. *See* Alec Zacaroli, *Utilities Subject to Title IV Program Show 100 Percent Compliance in 1997, EPA Says*, 29 [Curr. Dev.] Env. Rep. (BNA) 912 (1998). Moreover, at least one study finds a noticeable drop in sulfur deposition in the northeast, although nitrogen oxide deposition continue to be a problem and lakes in the Adirondacks continue to acidify. *See* Alec Zacaroli, *Major Study Finds Acid Rain Program Cutting Sulfur Deposition in Northeast*, 29 [Curr. Dev.] Env. Rep. (BNA) 912 (1998). *See also* Dallas Burtraw & Byron Swift, *A New Standard of Performance: An Analysis of the Clean Air Act's Acid Rain Program*, 26 Envtl. L. Rep. 10411 (1996) (calling the Title IV acid rain program "the most successful environmental programs of the past decade"). Burtraw and Swift found that "utilities have overcomplied by emitting 40 percent less $SO_2$ than the program's emission cap allows * * * [and] achieved these reductions at about one-half the cost they would have incurred through a more conventional approach." *Id.*

6.　In August 1998, the EPA reported on acid rain control attainments:

> [T]he 263 core Phase I utility units continued to emit well below the allowable emission levels required by the Clean Air Act. In total, the 431 Phase I units emitted 5.4 million tons. These emissions were 35 percent below the 1996 allowable emissions level of 8.3 million tons, and about 50 percent below 1980 levels.

> According to a study released by the U.S. Geological Survey, reductions in $SO_2$ emissions resulted in * * * a 10 to 25 percent drop in wet deposition sulfate concentration and rainfall acidity, particularly at some sites located in the Midwest, Northeast, and Mid-Atlantic Regions. These areas are some of the most acid-sensitive regions of the country.

U.S. EPA Office of Air and Radiation, 1996 National Air Quality: Status and Trends (1998).

# C. NEW SOURCE PERFORMANCE STANDARDS

## 1. OVERVIEW

### PHILLIP D. REED, FEDERAL EMISSION LIMITATIONS

in 2 Law of Environmental Protection
11-92.3 to 11-106 (Sheldon M. Novick, ed. 1998).

The 1970 Clean Air Act gave the federal government the job of setting performance standards for new stationary sources of air pollution. The states could regulate existing sources however they saw fit, so long as their implementation plans satisfied EPA that the air quality standards would be met. New sources, on the other hand, were to march to a different drummer, stringent national standards reflecting the best technology that an industry could afford. The focus of the NSPS is on industries, not pollutants. All sources in a listed industry category are covered, unless they were already under construction when the standards were proposed. All harmful pollutants are regulated, regardless of whether other Clean Air Act standards apply.

The * * * NSPS were intended to serve a variety of functions in the Clean Air Act scheme. Congress expected the NSPS to carry much of the burden of attaining and maintaining the NAAQS. Every time a dirty old factory was replaced with a new one equipped with NSPS controls, emissions would be reduced dramatically. Plants built in areas not violating the NAAQS would not degrade air quality much, helping to maintain the standards. * * * By imposing the same requirements on new sources of a given type from coast to coast, the NSPS would eliminate the powerful incentive for states to weaken their SIPs so as to attract new industry. * * * The division of labor between federal new source standards and state SIPs was expected to be more cost effective overall. The builders of new sources, with the advantage of knowing the NSPS in advance, could tailor plants to the standards, saving considerably over the cost of retrofitting a similar existing plant with advanced control technology. The SIP scheme, on the other hand, left the states flexibility to take the technological (and financial) problems facing each existing source into account. The states could also use the NSPS in their implementation plans, where necessary to control major pollution problems, without having to duplicate the sophisticated and costly technological and economic analysis EPA would perform. Finally, NSPS also provide a vehicle for regulating non-criteria pollutants. With so many jobs to perform, [NSPS] are vital to the Clean Air Act scheme.

The role of the NSPS was somewhat diminished by the 1977 Amendments, which set separate control requirements for major new sources. The 1970 Act required new source review for areas cleaner and dirtier than the air quality standards. In theory, the new source review programs established in 1977 for prevention of significant deterioration (PSD) and nonattainment areas could have made the NSPS virtually obsolete. Each program had its own technology standards that had to be at least as stringent as any applicable NSPS. Since all the country is either a PSD or nonattainment area, the NSPS could have been reduced to minor source standards. In fact, for years the standards imposed on many major sources built since the 1977 Amendments were the NSPS. Because of their strong analytical base, these standards were easier for understaffed state agencies and EPA regional offices to impose than more stringent case-by-case standards.

The Clean Air Act gives EPA a general blueprint to follow in developing NSPS and, as with the SIP requirements, the blueprint became more specific and complicated in 1977. Section 111 * * * authorizes EPA to establish technology- and cost-based "standards of performance" for categories of new and modified stationary sources that significantly contribute to health- or welfare-threatening air pollution. * * *

The NSPS process begins when EPA lists a category of stationary sources as one which "causes or contributes significantly to air pollution which may reasonably be anticipated to endanger public health or welfare." * * *

EPA has broad discretion in deciding to list categories, but is subject to statutory pressure to expand the list. The 1977 Amendments required EPA to identify all categories of major sources, those emitting more than 100 tons per year of a pollutant, and to list and regulate all the categories in three stages within four years of identification. EPA identified some eighty categories, but fell behind schedule in regulating them. The 1990 Amendments require EPA to propose standards by November 15, 1996, for all categories of major stationary sources listed prior to the Amendments. Standards for new categories must be proposed within one year after the category is listed, and promulgated within one year of proposal. EPA must review the standards every eight years, unless readily available information indicates review is not necessary. * * *

The NSPS set uniform emission limitations for industrial categories or subcategories of sources. The standards generally must be stated in terms of maximum amount of emissions, but for categories with substantial fugitive emissions that cannot practicably be quantified, EPA may specify work practice standards. The standards are supposed to apply to all pollutants emitted by the source category, but for most categories EPA has generally only regulated criteria pollutants and their precursors. * * *

Setting the NSPS is a complex analytical process. For each industry category, EPA must: (1) identify available technologies that control emissions from the types of sources found in that category; (2) determine what * * * emission rates can be achieved in practice with those technologies; while (3) simultaneously assessing the financial and other costs associated with satisfying the possible standards. An added element of uncertainty is that the standards will apply to facilities not yet in existence. * * *

The selection of the control technology on which to base the NSPS is a process not easily defined with precision. EPA must search for the "best" technology, which could lead into the realm of experimental, if not the theoretical. However, the search is constrained because the technology must be adequately demonstrated and the Agency must take into account the cost of compliance, the energy needed, and the environmental side effects of compliance. In practice, the Agency surveys air pollution control technologies in use in the industry category, sometimes both here and abroad, in search of the most efficient controls that really work. * * * EPA is not limited to technology in routine use. While it may consider technology that will only become available in the future, it is constrained by the fact that the NSPS take effect on promulgation. In sum, EPA may base NSPS on the most advanced control technologies it can reasonably expect will work in the industry to be regulated.

Once it has identified one or more applicable technologies, EPA must calculate the * * * emission limits the technologies can achieve in practice. * * * The standards must be achieved continuously, although EPA can write the standards so they do not apply to periods of time where emissions are unavoidably high, as when many industrial processes are started up. * * * While the standards specify performance, not technology, the extensive analysis of alternative technologies performed in setting the standards focuses the attention of industry and regulators alike on a narrow range of control options.

The cost analysis required by section 111 is really an assessment of economic impact on the industry. * * * EPA essentially sets the standard at the level dictated by the most advanced technology that satisfied whatever test the statute prescribes, unless the cost of compliance will cause serious economic disruption in the industry. * * *

Section 111 requires new sources to comply with the NSPS. The applicability of the standards thus turns on what is new and what is a source. Since the NSPS add considerably to the cost and cleanliness of a new facility, there has been much interest in the answers to these questions.

Congress defined "new source" broadly. The term includes not only newly constructed factories or furnaces, but also any modification of an existing source, including any physical alteration and certain changes in the way the source is operated, that increases emissions or adds a new pollutant to emissions. Generally, a change in fuels * * * is a covered change in operation, but a mere increase in the level of operation, e.g., a change from two to three shifts, is not. * * *

A source is subject to the NSPS if construction or modification was "commenced" after the publication of proposed NSPS that will be applicable. The proposal date applies even if the standard is not finalized for years. * * *

The NSPS are to be kept up to date, but doing so is no easy matter. * * * EPA may revise the standards "from time to time." With the Agency far behind schedule in writing the initial NSPS, the revisions do not receive much attention, except for small changes in measurement or monitoring requirements. EPA rarely has tightened standards to reflect new technologies. * * *

Section 111's effectiveness at forcing technology is open to question. To the extent that section 111 has forced technology, it has been in the spreading use of technologies already in existence. * * *

The coal-fired power plant NSPS did help force the development of scrubbing technology, which was more effective than any other flue gas desulfurization technology in existence before the 1970 Act * * * . Perhaps this is because the source category is an enormous source of criteria pollutant emissions and received direct congressional attention in addition to Agency and public scrutiny. In other categories, the NSPS often settled for second- or third-best technologies, because of the restraint built into the process by the need to demonstrate achievability [and] the slow pace of revisions * * * . *reality*

Although the NSPS are federal standards, EPA may delegate enforcement authority to the states. In the 1980s, authority for implementing the NSPS flooded out to the states. As of mid-1989, all * * * states and territories had some NSPS authority.

After delegation, the standards (like SIPs) continue to be federally enforceable. EPA enforcement policy gives high priority to NSPS violations.

---

Read the following sections of the Clean Air Act

☐ § 111(a)(1)     ☐ § 111(a)(2)     ☐ § 111(a)(3)     ☐ § 111(a)(4)

☐ § 111(b)(1)(A)     ☐ § 111(b)(1)(B)     ☐ § 111(b)(2)     ☐ § 111(b)(5)

☐ § 111(d)     ☐ § 111(e)

---

### Notes and Questions

1. The basic scheme of the Clean Air Act is national ambient standards to be pursued by locally devised emission controls promulgated through state implementation plans. The NSPS under CAA § 111 deviate from this basic scheme by imposing emission limitations uniformly on certain categories of sources throughout the country. Why might this be a non-sensible way to proceed? Despite the objections that you have articulated, why might Congress nevertheless have preferred the § 111 geographically uniform approach to new sources?

2. Review carefully the assigned statutory sections. Does § 111 call for the establishment of *performance* standards or *specification* standards? Could the EPA Administrator promulgate specification standards under § 111 if she wanted to? Why or why not?

## DAVID P. CURRIE, DIRECT FEDERAL REGULATION OF STATIONARY SOURCES UNDER THE CLEAN AIR ACT

128 U. Pa. L. Rev. 1389, 1407-09 (1980)

The basic statutory program for controlling existing sources of air pollution, contained in section 110, is based upon the degree of control necessary to provide ambient levels that will not harm health or welfare. New-source performance standards, however, are based on the contrasting philosophy of requiring as much control as can be provided within certain bounds of cost. * * *

[U]niform technological requirements will result in diverse ambient pollution levels because of geographical variations in such factors as meteorological conditions, topography, and the number and size of emission sources. Thus, technology-based standards are likely to be more stringent in some places and less stringent in others than is necessary to achieve compliance with ambient standards. The House Report in 1977 nonetheless provided an extensive list of arguments for imposing technological standards. Uniform national standards help "to avoid situations in which industries could be lured to one state by relaxing emissions standards. Since ambient standards made the air "a finite resource," a requirement of best technology would ration that resource so that "more new sources could locate in any given area." Third, "[b]uilding control technology into new plants at time of construction will plainly be less costly [than] requiring retrofit when pollution ceilings are reached." Technological standards were also "intended to create incentives for improved technology, which could achieve greater or equivalent emission reduction at equivalent or lower cost." Elsewhere the Report indicated doubt as to whether ambient standards had been or could be set at levels that really prevented all injury. Like the provisions preventing significant deterioration of clean areas, standards requiring best efforts to control emissions reflect "a policy of maximum practicable protection of health."

## 2. CEMENT PLANTS

In *Boomer v. Atlantic Cement*, page 163, *supra*, we saw how the common law dealt with the problem of fine particulate dust from cement plants. The following opinions show how this pollution problem is being addressed by the § 111 new source performance standards of the Clean Air Act.

# PORTLAND CEMENT
# ASSOCIATION v. RUCKELSHAUS

486 F.2d 375 (D.C. Cir. 1973), *cert. denied* 417 U.S. 921 (1974)

LEVENTHAL, Circuit Judge.

Portland Cement Association seeks review of the action of the [EPA] Administrator * * * in promulgating stationary source standards for new or modified portland[b] cement plants, pursuant to the provisions of Section 111 of the Clean Air Act. * * *

After designating portland cement plants as a stationary source of air pollution which may "contribute significantly to air pollution which causes or contributes to the endangerment of public health or welfare," under Section 111(b)(1)(A) of the Act, the Administrator published a proposed regulation establishing standards of performance for portland

---

[b] *Ed.*—"Portland" refers to a type of cement product, rather than a geographic location.

cement plants. The proposed regulation was accompanied by a document entitled "Background Information For Proposed New-Source Performance Standards," which set forth the justification. Interested parties were afforded an opportunity to participate in the rule making by submitting comments, and more than 200 interested parties did so. The "standards of performance" were adopted by a regulation, issued December 16, 1971, which requires, inter alia, that particulate matter emitted from portland cement plants shall not be:

(1) In excess of 0.30 lb. per ton of feed to the kiln (0.15 Kg. per metric ton), maximum 2-hour average.

(2) Greater than 10% opacity, except that where the presence of uncombined water is the only reason for failure to meet the requirements for this subparagraph, such failure shall not be a violation of this section.

The standards were justified by the EPA as follows:

The standards of performance are based on stationary source testing conducted by the Environmental Protection Agency and/or contractors and on data derived from various other sources, including the available technical literature. In the comments of the proposed standards, many questions were raised as to costs and demonstrated capability of control systems to meet the standards. These comments have been evaluated and investigated, and it is the Administrator's judgment that emission control systems capable of meeting the standards have been adequately demonstrated and that the standards promulgated herein are achievable at reasonable costs.

On March 21, 1972, EPA published a "Supplemental Statement in Connection With Final Promulgation," amplifying the justification for its standards * * * . This statement relied principally on EPA tests on existing portland cement plants to demonstrate that the promulgated standards were achievable.

The action of the Administrator has been challenged on the following grounds: (1) the Administrator did not comply with the National Environmental Policy Act of 1969 (NEPA); (2) economic costs were not adequately taken into account and the standards unfairly discriminate against portland cement plants, in comparison with standards promulgated for power plants and incinerators; and (3) the achievability of the standards was not adequately demonstrated.

## COMPLIANCE WITH NEPA

Petitioners argue that EPA acted contrary to the requirements of the National Environmental Policy Act of 1969, in failing to file a "NEPA" [environmental impact] statement ["EIS"] in conjunction with the promulgation of the stationary standards. * * *

Petitioners, in effect, predicate an EPA obligation to file an impact statement on this simple syllogism: (1) All federal agencies must file an impact statement; (2) EPA is a federal agency; (3) EPA must file an impact statement. * * * If the premises be accepted, the logic is clear. But the argument is more simplistic than simple, for the premises require a more precise determination of legislative intent. * * *

The impact statement issue requires us to consider not only NEPA, but also the Clean Air Act and particularly the statutory scheme by which new stationary source standards are promulgated.

Section 111 of the Clean Air Act establishes precise time schedules for the promulgation of new source standards. The Administrator was required to publish, 90 days after December 31, 1970, a list of categories of stationary sources which "contribute significantly to air pollution which causes or contributes to the endangerment of public health or welfare." Within 120 days of the inclusion of a category, the Administrator is required to propose standards, and 90 days thereafter the standards are to go into effect. Obviously, a strong argument can be made that the Clean Air Act, and the provisions for unusual expedition in disposing of the complex environmental and other problems faced by the agency, assumed that the agency would not be subject to the additional time required to prepare a "detailed" proposal of an impact statement, circulate the statement to the agencies for comment and assess the comments made. * * *

[T]here is a serious question whether NEPA is applicable to environmentally protective regulatory agencies. * * *

The policy thrust toward exemption of the environmental agency is discernible from these factors, taken in combination * * * . An exemption from NEPA is supportable on the basis that this best serves the objective of protecting the environment which is the purpose of NEPA. * * * The need in those areas for unusually expeditious decision would be thwarted by a NEPA impact statement requirement. An impact statement requirement presents the danger that opponents of environmental protection would use the issue of compliance with any impact statement requirement as a tactic of litigation and delay.

The policies against a NEPA exemption embrace the endemic question of "Who shall police the police"? * * * "It cannot be assumed that EPA will always be the good guy." Concern was also voiced by petitioners in this case that EPA might wear blinders when promulgating standards protecting one resource as to effects on other resources, as is asserted in this case, that air standards may increase water pollution. * * *

Our consideration of the complex questions raised by a broad exemption claim, reinforce our conclusion that these should not be decided in the present case, which may appropriately be determined upon the logic of a narrow exemption from NEPA applicable to determinations under section 111 of the Clean Air Act. What is decisive, ultimately, is the reality that, section 111 of the Clean Air Act, properly construed, requires the functional equivalent of a NEPA impact statement. Thus * * * we refrain from a determination of any broader claim of NEPA exemption.

Enlarging on our conclusion as to a narrower exemption, we note that section 111 of the Clean Air Act requires a "standard of performance" which reflects "the best system of emission reduction," and requires the Administrator to take "into account the cost of achieving such reduction." These criteria require the Administrator to take into account counter-productive environmental effects of a proposed standard, as well as economic costs to the industry. The Act thus requires that the Administrator accompany a proposed standard with a statement of reasons that sets forth the environmental considerations, pro and con, which have been taken into account as required by the Act, and fulfillment of this requirement is reviewable directly by this Court.

Although the rule-making process may not import the complete advantages of the structured determinations of NEPA into the decision making of EPA, it does, in our view strike a workable balance between some of the advantages and disadvantages of full application of NEPA. Without the problems of a NEPA delay conflicting with the constraints of the Clean Air Act, the ability of other agencies to make submissions to EPA concerning proposed rules, provides a channel for informed decisionmaking. These comments will be part of the record in the rule-making proceeding that EPA must take into account. * * *

To the extent that EPA is aware of significant adverse environmental consequences of its proposal, good faith requires appropriate reference in its reasons for the proposal and its underlying balancing analysis. * * *

As to the standard here at issue, petitioners raise possible adverse environmental impact questions in their briefs.[45] But they have not indicated that these problems were brought to the attention of the agency. Since we are remanding the case for other reasons subsequently discussed, EPA should respond to these questions on remand. * * * [Therefore,] we establish a narrow exemption from NEPA, for EPA determinations under section 111 of the Clean Air Act. * * *

### ECONOMIC COSTS

The objecting companies contend that the Administrator has not complied with the mandate of § 111 of the Act, which requires him to "[take] into account the costs" of achieving the emission reductions he prescribes, a statutory provision that clearly refers to the possible economic impact of the promulgated standards. * * *

The Administrator found in the Background Document that, for a new wetprocess plant with a capacity of 2.5 million barrels per year, the total investment for all installed air pollution control equipment will represent approximately 12 percent of the investment for the total fa-

---

[45] Petitioner Portland Cement Association asserts * * *: "Increased electricity needed to operate precipitators with greater collection capacity can create increased air pollution by the source of the electricity. Also, stricter standards will result in the collection of more particulates. These must be disposed of somehow. * * *"

cility. He also found that "[a]nnual operating costs for the control equipment will be approximately 7 percent of the total plant operating costs if a baghouse is used for the kiln, and 5 percent if an electrostatic precipitator is used."

Petitioners argue that this analysis is not enough—that the Administrator is required to prepare a quantified cost-benefit analysis, showing the benefit to ambient air conditions as measured against the cost of the pollution devices. However desirable in the abstract, such a requirement would conflict with the specific time constraints imposed on the administrator. The difficulty, if not impossibility, of quantifying the benefit to ambient air conditions, further militates against the imposition of such an imperative on the agency. Such studies should be considered by the Administrator, if adduced in comments, but we do not inject them as a necessary condition of action.

The EPA contention that economic costs to the industry have been taken into account, derives substantial support from a study prepared for EPA, which was made part of the rule-making record and referred to in the Background Document, entitled "The Financial Impact of Air Pollution Control Upon the Cement Industry". It concluded that the additional costs of control equipment could be passed on without substantially affecting competition with construction substitutes such as steel, asphalt and aluminum, because "[d]emand for cement, derived for the most part from demand for public and private construction, is not highly elastic with regard to price and would not be very sensitive to small price changes." The study did note that individual mills may be closed in the years ahead, but observed that these plants were obsolete both from a cost and pollution point of view. Petitioners have not challenged these findings here. The Administrator has obviously given some consideration to economic costs. * * *

Petitioners also challenge the cement standards as unfair in light of lower standards mandated for fossil fuel-fired steam generating power plants and incinerators. They claim that while the cement standard, as expressed in grains of particulates allowed per standard cubic foot of gas (g/scf), requires a reduction to .03, power plants are permitted to reach .12 and incinerators to be at .10. Also opacity standards differ, with no opacity standard set for incinerators, and with a 20% requirement for power plants (with 40% opacity permitted for not more than 2 minutes in any hour). * * *

EPA, in response to comments from petitioners on this issue of discrepancy, stated in its supplemental statement in March 1972: "The difference between the particulate standard for cement plants and those for steam generators and incinerators is attributable to the superior technology available therefor (that is, fabric filter technology has not been applied to coal-fired steam generators or incinerators)." * * *

The core of our response to petitioners is that the Administrator is not required to present affirmative justifications for different standards in different industries. Inter-industry comparisons of this kind are not generally required, or even productive; and they were not contemplated by Congress in this Act. The essential question is whether the mandated standards can be met by a particular industry for which they are set, and this can typically be decided on the basis of information concerning that industry alone. This is not to say that evidence collected about the functioning of emission devices in one industry may not have implications for another. Certainly such information may bear on technological capability. But there is no requirement of uniformity of specific standards for all industries. The Administrator applied the same general approach, of ascertaining for each industry what was feasible in that industry. It would be unmanageable if, in reviewing the cement standards, the court should have to consider whether or not there was a mistake in the incinerator standard, with all the differences in parties, practice, industry procedures, and record for decision. Of course, the standard for another industry can be attacked, as too generous, and hence arbitrary or unsupported on the record, by those concerned with excessive pollution by that industry. There is, therefore, an avenue of judicial review and correction if the agency does not proceed in good faith to implement its general approach. But this is different from the supposition that a claim to the same specific treatment can be advanced by one who is in neither the same nor a competitive industry. * * *

### ACHIEVABILITY OF EMISSION STANDARD

Section 111 of the Act requires "the degree of emission limitation achievable [which] * * * the Administrator determines has been adequately demonstrated." Petitioners contend that the promulgated standard for new stationary sources has not been "adequately demonstrated" * * * .

It is the ability of control devices such as precipitators and bags to separate out a sufficient amount of particulate from the exhaust—in accord with the proposed standards—which is under challenge by the manufacturers. * * *

We begin by rejecting the suggestion of the cement manufacturers that the Act's requirement that emission limitations be "adequately demonstrated" necessarily implies that any cement plant now in existence be able to meet the proposed standards. Section 111 looks toward what may fairly be projected for the regulated future, rather than the state of the art at present, since it is addressed to standards for new plants—old stationary source pollution being controlled through other regulatory authority. * * *

The Senate Report made clear that it did not intend that the technology "must be in actual routine use somewhere." The essential question was rather whether the technology would be available for installation in new plants. * * *

The Administrator may make a projection based on existing technology, though that projection is subject to the restraints of reasonableness and cannot be based on "crystal ball" inquiry. * * * [T]he question of availability is partially dependent on "lead time," the time in which the technology will have to be available. Since the standards here put into effect will control new plants immediately, as opposed to one or two years in the future, the latitude of projection is correspondingly narrowed. If actual tests are not relied on, but instead a prediction is made, "its validity as applied to this case rests on the reliability of [the] prediction and the nature of [the] assumptions." * * *

We find a critical defect in the decision-making process in arriving at the standard under review in the initial inability of petitioners to obtain—in timely fashion—the test results and procedures used on existing plants which formed a partial basis for the emission control level adopted, and in the subsequent seeming refusal of the agency to respond to what seem to be legitimate problems with the methodology of these tests. * * *

The regulations under review were first proposed on August 3, 1971 and then adopted on December 16, 1971. Both the proposed and adopted rule cited certain portland cement testing as forming a basis for the standards. * * *

[T]he proposed standard was accompanied by a Background Document which disclosed some information about the tests, but did not identify the location or methodology used in the one successful test conducted on a dry-process kiln. * * *

[T]he details, aside from a summary of test results, were not made available to petitioners until mid-April 1972. At that time, it was revealed that the first set of tests was conducted April 29-30, 1971, by a contractor for EPA, at the Dragon Cement Plant, a dry process plant in Northampton, Pennsylvania, and that the second set was performed at the Oregon Portland Cement plant, at Lake Oswego, Oregon, a wet process plant, on October 7 and 8, 1971. The full disclosure of the methodology followed in these tests raised certain problems, in the view of petitioners, on which they had not yet had the opportunity to comment. Their original comments in the period between the proposal and promulgation of the regulation could only respond to the brief summary of the results of the tests that had been disclosed at that time.

After intervenor Northwestern States Portland Cement Company received the detailed test information in mid-April 1972, it submitted the test data, for analysis of reliability and accuracy, to Ralph H. Striker, an engineer experienced in the design of emission control systems for portland cement plants. He concluded that the first series of tests run at the Dragon Cement Company were "grossly erroneous" due to inaccurate sampling techniques to measure particulate matter. Northwestern States then moved this Court to remand the record to EPA so that the agency might consider the additional comments on the tests. This motion was granted on October 31, 1972. * * * We considered this opportunity to make further comments necessary to sound execution of our judicial review function. * * *

In this case, EPA made no written submission as to the additional comments made by petitioners. * * * All that EPA did was to comply with the mandate that the analysis of Mr. Striker be added to the certified record. It may be that EPA considers Mr. Striker's analysis invalid—but we have no way of knowing this. As the record stands, all we have is Mr. Striker's repudiation of the test data, without response. The purpose of our prior remand cannot be realized unless we hear EPA's response to his comments, and the record must be remanded again, for that purpose.

We are not establishing any broad principle that EPA must respond to every comment made by manufacturers on the validity of its standards or the methodology and scientific basis for their formulation. In the case of the Striker presentation, however, our prior remand reflects this court's view of the significance, or at least potential significance, of this presentation. * * *

A troublesome aspect of this case is the identification of what, in fact, formed the basis for the standards promulgated by EPA—a question that must be probed prior to consideration of whether the basis or bases for the standards is reliable. Nominally, there would seem to be three major bases for the rule and its standards: (1) the tests run on the dry-process Dragon Cement Plant, (2) the tests run on the wet-process Oregon Cement Plant, and (3) literature sources. * * *

In the briefs to this Court, EPA counsel disclaim reliance on these three sources, despite statements directly to the contrary accompanying the proposed and promulgated rule * * * .

Counsel on appeal cannot substitute new reasons for those offered by the agency. Certainly, counsel cannot disclaim reliance on reasons offered by the agency in its statement of reasons, except in the sense that errors may be asserted to fall within the limited "harmless error" doctrine applicable to administrative agencies.

We turn now to the specific technical problems raised by the cement manufacturers. * * *

The first point raised by petitioner * * * was that a single test offered a weak basis for inferring that all new cement plants would be able to meet the proposed standards. * * *

A second objection is to the techniques used by the EPA to measure emissions from the Dragon plant. These "sampling" techniques assume particular importance if they deviate from procedures, outlined by regulation, for ascertaining compliance with prescribed standards. * * * [A] significant difference between techniques used by the agency in arriving at standards, and requirements presently prescribed for determining compliance with standards, raises serious questions about the validity of the standard.

The cement manufacturers point, in this regard, to the absence of continuous sampling in the EPA data, since the "longest elapsed time of any sampling episode was 30 minutes," whereas under the regulations promulgated, conformity is to be measured on the basis of maximum 2-hour averages. It is incumbent on the Administrator to explain the discrepancy.

The second point raises the question, on the basis of a handwritten note made by the EPA contractor, as to whether the tested plant was operating at maximum performance during testing. The contractor had noted, "Baghouse is undersize and production is held back due to this." Compliance tests under the regulation require, however, that "All performance tests shall be conducted while the affected facility is operating at or above the maximum production rate. * * *"

Thirdly, petitioner contends that mistakes made in the measurement process prevented the test from using observed, measured values. As previously noted, encrusted solids can collect in the bag, and must be constantly cleaned out if the baghouses are to operate with efficiency. In one of the runs conducted, the presence of the solids in a duct leading to the stack were thought to cause a high reading so lower readings from other test runs were substituted. On another run, the liquid, which was to be the basis for a measurement of particulate concentration, was erroneously poured into a beaker from a previous run. * * *

Finally, engineer Striker claims significant errors of measurement were made * * * [stating] "It is my personal opinion that the particulate matter emissions of .202 pounds in test 1 per ton of kiln feed reported * * * is grossly erroneous and that the correct emission of particulate matter is in the neighborhood of .404 pounds per ton of kiln feed." We are not competent to decide if Mr. Striker's methodology and conclusions are correct. We can note, however, that he claims that as a matter of "basic chemistry" two test values, for feed and gas volume, cannot coexist. This is certainly the type of criticism EPA should be required to discuss on remand. * * *

[Another] serious matter is presented by intervenor Northwestern, which points to the fact that the EPA contractor's report indicates that sampling was not conducted when "process operation was interrupted" and that sampling was only conducted during the periods of "normal operation". The report states: Several conditions contributing to these interruptions were: (1) excessive pressure drop across bag house, (2) visible emissions from leaking bags, and (3) breakdown of dust removal equipment. * * * The concern of the manufacturers is that "start-up" and "upset" conditions, due to plant or emission device malfunction, is an inescapable aspect of industrial life, and that allowance must be made for such factors in the standards that are promulgated. * * *

EPA admitted in its introduction to the proposed regulation that the standards here under review did not take into account this problem.

EPA attempted to obviate the implicit criticism by stating in its proposal: "Such occurrences generally are dealt with by the exercise of discretion in the Agency's enforcement activities." The exercise of this discretion would have been accomplished by means of an informal process, in which, before the Agency took enforcement action, sources that had exceeded the standards would have attempted to demonstrate to the Agency that such excess emissions had been unavoidable. Broadly read, however, this view of enforcement discretion would defer the question of "available" technology to the enforcement stage, an approach not contemplated by section 111. Companies must be on notice as to what will constitute a violation. * * *

### OPACITY STANDARD

Apart from the standard directly regulating particulate concentration, EPA has adopted an opacity standard * * * .

It may be, as EPA argues, that the opacity test is an important enforcement tool, and that the results of an opacity test, which is normally performed at some distance from the plant by trained observers, offers a cheaper and faster method of determining compliance than enforcement of the particulate concentration standard. However, it is one thing to use a method of testing to observe possible violations of a standard; it is another to constitute that method as the standard itself. If the opacity test is to be a standard, and if violations can result in enforcement actions without further testing, the standard must be consistent with the statute and congressional intent.

The thrust of the manufacturers' comments to EPA, and repeated here, is that the opacity test is arbitrary—that inspectors will be unable within any reasonable degree of accuracy to determine whether permitted opacity is 10%.

The critical question is how accurate can opacity observations be. On this point we essentially have before us only the contentions of the parties. The manufacturers do point to a test conducted for the National Center for Air Pollution Control [HEW] * * * where six trained smoke inspectors evaluated a white training plume known to have 0% opacity. All six inspectors rated the plume at more than 0% opacity and 3 evaluated it at more than 20%. A plume known to be at 20% opacity was rated higher than 20% by 5 of the 6 inspectors (one rated it lower) and 2 of them rated it at almost 40%. Problems may also be posed for deciding when opacity is due to water content and when it is not. * * *

We think the HEW test adduced by petitioners, though not decisive, suffices to require further consideration and explanation by EPA on remand, and a showing on the record that 10% opacity measurements can be made within reasonable accuracy.

### CONCLUSIONS

We are quite aware that the standards promulgated and here under review are to be applied to new stationary sources. It would have been entirely appropriate if the Administrator had justified the standards, not on the basis of tests on existing sources or old test data in the literature, but on extrapolations from this data, on a reasoned basis responsive to comments, and on testimony from experts and vendors made part of the record. This course was not followed here. Instead, the Administrator in his statement of reasons relied on tests on existing plants and the literature, which EPA counsel now discounts without reference to other record support to take its place.

The Administrator's objectives are laudable, but the statute expressly requires, for the standards he promulgates, that technology be achievable. This record reveals a lack of an adequate opportunity of the manufacturers to comment on the proposed standards, due to the absence of disclosure of the detailed findings and procedures of the tests. This was not cured following our previous October 1972 remand to the agency.

We have identified a number of matters that require consideration and clarification on remand. While we remain diffident in approaching problems of this technical complexity, * * * the necessity to review agency decisions, if it is to be more than a meaningless exercise, requires enough steeping in technical matters to determine whether the agency "has exercised a reasoned discretion." * * * We cannot substitute our judgment for that of the agency, but it is our duty to consider whether "the decision was based on a consideration of the relevant factors and whether there has been a clear error of judgment." * * * Ultimately, we believe that the cause of a clean environment is best served by reasoned decision-making. The record is remanded for further proceedings not inconsistent with this opinion.

# PORTLAND CEMENT
# ASSOCIATION v. TRAIN

513 F.2d 506 (D.C. Cir.), *cert. denied* 423 U.S. 1025 (1975)

Before FAHY, Senior Circuit Judge, and LEVENTHAL and ROBB, Circuit Judges.

PER CURIAM. LEVENTHAL, Circuit Judge did not participate.

The court remanded to the Administrator of the Environmental Protection Agency, respondent, the case then before us involving the validity of the stationary source standards he had promulgated under section 111 of the Clean Air Act for new or modified portland cement plants. * * * These matters have now been reconsidered and clarified in the Administrator's Response to the Remand Order, formulated after his draft of such Response had been the subject of comments by the Association and others. The Association has again petitioned this court, to decide whether the Administrator has complied with the remand order and whether the standards should be affirmed or set aside.

At argument petitioner's counsel relied upon a formulation of positions which he handed to the court and which reads as follows:

1. Do established constitutional guarantees against statutory discrimination apply to environmental regulations?

2. If so, may the victim of a discriminatory regulation have it set aside through direct judicial review?

3. Under what, if any, circumstances could economic considerations produce a standard lower than the highest technologically achievable?

4. How does a standard prohibiting momentary excessive emissions conform to a statute whose purpose is curbing the total volume of pollution?

5. How can plume opacity be [a] valid standard when pollution and plume opacity can not be reliably correlated and evaluations of the same plume by several qualified observers will vary substantially?

The issues raised in these questions are more limited than those presented by petitioner in its brief. Therefore, although the questions will form the frame of reference for this opinion, other issues will be touched upon as well.

Questions 1 and 2 are directed to petitioner's contention that the emission standard for cement plants is more stringent than those for incinerators and coal-fired power plants, and, also, for plants of the competing asphalt industry, as to which, however, no question had been raised at the agency level.

Petitioner's contention is weakened by its admission, made in its comments on the Administrator's draft response to the remand, that the standard for the portland cement industry is achievable by that industry. Moreover, our remanding opinion indicated our disagreement with petitioner on the subject of different emission standards for different industries. * * * Amplifying upon what we there said, we find no reasonable basis for invalidating as discriminatory the achievable emission standard for cement plants. Proof of unreasonableness in the diversity of the standards referred to is lacking. No doubt the Administrator will be influenced by accumulating experience should it give rise to reasons for modification of the range now existing between the prescribed standards.

Petitioner's question No. 3 is very generally phrased. Neither the terms of our remand nor the proceedings now before us require an answer by the court. * * * The industry has not shown inability to adjust itself in a healthy economic fashion to the end sought by the Act as represented by the standards prescribed.[4]

Question No. 4 was not at issue on the remand and we accordingly do not feel called upon to deal with it.

---

[4] The Administrator in his Response to the Remand Order has fully considered and rationally rejected the cost-benefit analysis which was submitted by petitioner.

As to question No. 5, we have considered the detailed analysis by the Administrator of numerous factors involved in the use of plume opacity to determine whether or not a portland cement plant achieves a prescribed standard of pollution control. We are not warranted on the basis of his analysis to find that plume opacity is too unreliable to be used either as a measure of pollution or as an aid in controlling emissions. * * *

Finally, we note the Administrator's response to the court's direction that the bases for the emission standard should be further identified. At the time of our remand tests on only two cement plants had been conducted. Since then the Administrator has tested five more plants. Although petitioner had an opportunity to comment on the results of only two of these, all seven tests have shown that the emission standard is achievable. The Administrator has in this as in other respects adequately responded to our remand.

The consequence is that we hold the standards prescribed to be valid. The action of the Administrator in promulgating them is, accordingly, *Affirmed*.

### *Notes and Questions*

1.   The cement industry's woes began with the EPA Administrator's decision to *list* portland cement plants as a category for which NSPS would be promulgated. Did § 111 compel the Administrator to list this industry category, or did he have discretion? Do you think that polluters will ever be successful in challenging the EPA's decision to list them in an industry category triggering § 111 NSPS? Under what circumstances could the Administrator's decision be overturned?

2.   The portland cement association made an argument with respect to cost that would strike right at the heart of NSPS setting. What was that argument? How did the court deal with the association's interpretation of the statute on this issue? Do you find its ruling to have significant practical consequences, or is the court merely engaging in hair splitting?

3.   The court cited with approval an EPA study concluding that the additional costs of control equipment could be passed on without substantially affecting competition with construction substitutes such as steel, asphalt and aluminum, because "[d]emand for cement, derived for the most part from demand for public and private construction, is not highly elastic with regard to price and would not be very sensitive to small price changes." Was the EPA study even relevant? Why should EPA or the court care whether cement could continue to compete with substitutes if the cement industry were forced to bear the control costs associated with the NSPS? Does it make sense to assume that the present market shares of cements vs. steel vs. glass vs. wood should somehow remain constant—or nearly so—after imposition of § 111 environmental controls? Why or why not?

4.   The EPA's justifications for the portland cement standards were—let's speak plainly—pretty terrible. The agency fiddled with tests and adjusted results. It failed to use continuous monitoring in its tests, even though the

NSPS promulgated pursuant to those tests required continuous monitoring. Why, do you suppose, the EPA did such a poor job? Were its staff members lazy, corrupt, inept, or what?

## 3. COAL-FIRED POWER PLANTS

The NSPS for coal-fired power plants involve one of the most plowed, re-plowed, and plowed again portions of the Clean Air Act's regulatory scheme. The standards governing $SO_2$ emissions from coal-fired power plants today are the end result of years of fiddling and revision. In the next set of readings, you will examine the history of these standards.

## DAVID P. CURRIE, DIRECT FEDERAL REGULATION OF STATIONARY SOURCES UNDER THE CLEAN AIR ACT

128 U. Pa. L. Rev. 1389, 1409-12, 1414-17, 1425-31 (1980)

The first requirement of a [NSPS] under § 111 is that the technology needed to achieve it "has been adequately demonstrated." Some of the practical, legal, and policy difficulties of administering this provision can be illustrated by a detailed examination of the problem of sulfur dioxide emissions from power plants.

"[T]he combustion of sulfur-bearing fuels," particularly of coal, the EPA's predecessor reported in 1969, was the principal source of sulfur-oxide pollution in the United States; a large percentage of that combustion was for the purpose of generating electricity. The sulfur content of fuels is highly variable, resulting in uncontrolled power-plant sulfur dioxide ($SO_2$) emissions ranging "from 1 to 7 pounds per million Btu." Consequently "[o]ne of the best existing methods for reducing sulfur oxide emissions from fuel combustion sources is the use of low-sulfur fuels." This indeed was the option chosen by many plant operators, such as Chicago's Commonwealth Edison, despite a variety of difficulties, including transportation costs that in some cases actually doubled the fuel bill. Unfortunately the EPA found in 1974 that "low-sulfur fuel supplies are now and will continue to be inadequate to provide the sole means of complying with $SO_x$ [sulfur oxide] emission limitations." This meant that "flue gas desulfurization (FGD) technology [such as scrubbing] must be installed on a large number of power plants if sulfur oxide * * * emission requirements adopted pursuant to the Clean Air Act are to be met in the 1970's."

Flue-gas desulfurization involves the removal of sulfur oxides from exhaust gases after the fuel is burned. The chemical reactions by which this end might be accomplished were well understood in 1969: for example, "limestone injected into the furnace reacts with the sulfur oxides to form calcium sulfate, a solid, which is removed by standard dust-collecting equipment." The critical question was whether the technology was well enough developed—"adequately demonstrated," in section 111's terms—to justify the adoption of emission standards that would effectively require its employment.

The federal government conceded in 1969 that "[n]o flue gas desulfurization processes are presently in widespread use." * * *

Two years later, in 1971, the EPA published its *proposed* standard of 1.2 pounds per million Btu for large new coal-burning power plants under section 111. * * *

Late in 1974 the EPA reported that there were nineteen FGD systems operating in the United States, including two over-100 megawatt coal units that had operated for eight or nine months with eighty-four percent and ninety percent reliability. By this time industry voices were heard cautiously endorsing FGD technology. * * *

Today, then, there seems to be little doubt that FGD technology is "adequately demonstrated" for purposes of section 111. * * *

So far we have considered the question of adequate demonstration as the EPA and the courts seem to have dealt with it, as a black-or-white proposition: either the technology is ready for nationwide installation today, or no regulation should be adopted at all. The contemporaneous experience of the Illinois Pollution Control Board in wrestling with the same problem illustrates that, at least on the policy level, there are intermediate shades of gray.

Surely the all-or-nothing approach is unattractive. On the one hand, to have invested millions of dollars in 1971 lemons would have been a debacle of the first magnitude. On the other, to have done nothing would have postponed indefinitely the hope of relief for people in highly polluted areas where sulfur dioxide was a serious menace to public health. Illinois took a middle course. On much the same evidence that was the basis of the 1971 federal regulation, it adopted a standard requiring significant reductions of sulfur-oxide emissions only in certain metropolitan areas with acute ambient problems, and it set a compliance date distant enough "to permit nearly a year of additional information to be accumulated before commitments must be made."

Could the EPA have taken such a middle course? One of the policy decisions essential to the Illinois position was that the standard should create an incentive for the development of better technology. This was one of the stated objectives of section 111, but the statutory requirement that the technology be "adequately demonstrated" gets in the way. The determination whether technology meets this standard is to be made when the standard is adopted; arguably it means that the control devices may have to be ready for commercial use at that time. * * *

Furthermore, the second basic premise of the Illinois decision was that the acceptable degree of risk of technology failure was directly proportional to the severity of the particular pollution problem. Section 111, however, says nothing about balancing risks against need; it is susceptible to the interpretation that nothing may be required anywhere until the technology is sufficiently advanced to justify imposing it on new sources throughout the nation. Indeed, another explicit purpose of the section was to remove competitive geographic advantages, which suggests the intent to impose nationally uniform standards. * * *

The 1970 Senate Report emphasized that flexibility in the means of compliance was intended by the choice of the term "standards of performance": "The Secretary should not make a technical judgment as to how the standard should be implemented. He should determine the achievable limits and let the owner or operator determine the most economic, acceptable technique to apply." In full accord with this congressional emphasis on the result rather than the method, the EPA adopted [in 1971] a single nationwide standard for the emission of sulfur oxides from coal-fired power plants [1.2 pounds of $SO_2$ per million Btu of input heat], anticipating that individual operators would decide whether to comply by stack-gas cleaning or by using low-sulfur fuels.

Affected citizens, however, promptly sued the EPA, seeking to have the standard revised so as to require the use of stack-gas scrubbers even when low-sulfur fuel was used. Before the matter could be administratively resolved, Congress amended the statute [in 1977] to require the requested revision. [Amended] Section 111(a)(1) [required] that performance standards reflect the best *technological system* of emission reduction, and a technological system [was] defined in section 111(a)(7) as

> (A) a technological process for production or operation by any source which is inherently low-polluting or nonpolluting, or
>
> (B) a technological system for * * * reduction of the pollution generated by a source before such pollution is emitted into the ambient air, including precombustion cleaning or treatment of fuels. * * *

The central purpose of the provision [was] made clear: "[a] major new stationary source may no longer meet NSPS requirements merely by use of untreated oil or coal." This [was] re-emphasized by the new requirement in section 111(a)(1)(A) that standards for "fossil fuel fired stationary sources" not only establish "emission limitations" in such terms as pounds per million Btu but also require "a percentage reduction in the emissions * * * which would have resulted from the use of fuels which are not subject to treatment prior to combustion." * * *

[This] congressional restriction of the permissible means of meeting performance standards may stifle innovation. A comparable requirement for vehicle emissions, for example, could put an end to industry efforts to find a fuel with less potential for pollution. Moreover, the use of clean fuels has decided advantages over add-on control technology, for it simplifies enforcement and avoids risks of malfunction. In principle, indeed, it is hard to see why Congress drew the line where it did. The same policy of maximum control that justifies requiring those who use naturally clean fuels to install stack-cleaning technology would support extending that requirement to those who clean the fuel before burning it, and to those who employ a "low-polluting" process such as fluidized-bed combustion. As a general policy matter, therefore a principle of refusing credit for clean fuels [seemed] to be a questionable basis for formulating technology-based standards, whether or not it [could] be justified, in the case of low-sulfur fuels, by the need for additional reductions or by extraneous considerations of energy policy.

The language of the amendment, moreover, [created] a number of difficulties, the most important of which [was] whether uniform percentage reductions [were] required for all sources. The EPA * * * concluded they [were] not. While it initially proposed to require eighty-five percent reduction of sulfur oxides from most new power plants regardless of the composition of their fuel, its final regulations [required] a smaller percentage reduction for plants using low-sulfur fuel. The basic standard [limited] emissions to 1.2 pounds per million Btu and [prescribed] a ninety percent reduction, but only seventy percent reduction [was] required for plants emitting less than 0.6 pounds per million Btu.

*The D.C. Circuit eventually upheld the "sliding-scale" coal-fired power plant NSPS described by Professor Currie. See Sierra Club v. Costle, 657 F.2d 298 (D.C. Cir. 1981). At the conclusion of its 253-page opinion, the court declared that it had "taken a long while to come to a short conclusion: the rule is reasonable."*

At first glance the EPA's approach [seemed] squarely contrary to Congress's decision: the "technological" requirement was based upon a policy against allowances for the use of clean fuel. Yet the statutory language [was] not air-tight. While it [required] use of technological controls, it [did] not explicitly say that the same degree of technological control [was] the "best" everywhere; while it [required] a percentage reduction for fuel-burning sources, it [did] not explicitly say that the same percentage must be applied to every plant. Even the House Report expressed the statutory purpose in terms that are less than absolute: it said that the amendment was designed to prevent compliance "*merely by use of untreated oil or coal*," not that it was meant to forbid *any* credit for clean fuel. If this were the whole story, a uniform percentage reduction should [have been] required; minor cracks in the phraseology would not obscure the overwhelming congressional objection to reliance on low-sulfur fuel. The Conference Report, however, radically [altered] the picture:

> [I]n establishing a national percent reduction for new fossil fuel-fired sources, the Conferees agreed that the Administrator may, in his discretion, set a range of pollutant reduction that reflects varying fuel characteristics * * * [upon] a finding that such a departure does not undermine the basic purposes of the House provision and other provisions of the act, such as maximizing the use of locally available fuels.

Even the Conference report, however, [did] not appear capable of avoiding the excessive rigidity of the statutory requirements in other cases. For example, finding that desulfurization of the exhaust from stationary gas turbines would triple or quadruple their cost, the Administrator sensibly proposed to declare clean fuel their best practicable means of control. Similarly, on the basis of cost-benefit comparisons the final regulations [imposed] limitations only in terms of pounds per million Btu upon plants burning anthracite, or located in Hawaii or on certain other islands, or burning liquid or gaseous fuel so clean as to emit less than 0.2 pounds per million Btu without controls. Quite apart from the perplexing question whether the definition of a "standard of performance" as one reflecting "the best technological system" [allowed] the Administrator to require nontechnological controls when technology [was] impracticable, all of these efforts [seemed] squarely contrary to the independent requirement of a percentage reduction from uncontrolled emissions. The Agency once argued that compliance with a 0.2 limit for very clean fuels "would constitute compliance with the percentage reduction requirement." It would do nothing of the sort, for by hypothesis the 0.2 level [could] be met in such a case without any reduction in uncontrolled emissions. To allow the percentage reduction to be set at zero [was] to expunge the requirement from the statute. * * *

In short, Congress [seemed] to have purchased trouble by the terminology it used to express its simple command that plants burning low-sulfur fuel should also employ flue-gas desulfurization. * * *

Additionally, the flat requirement of a percentage reduction, while responsive to the felt need to require scrubbing despite use of low-sulfur coal, was obtusely insensitive to the likelihood of special situations in which the costs of scrubbing are quite unreasonable. Congress might at least have prescribed that percentage reduction was unnecessary if a specified insignificant emission level, such as 0.2 pounds per million Btu, could be achieved without it.

### Notes and Questions

1. The EPA's 1971 NSPS for new coal-burning power plants decreed that no such plants should emit more than 1.2 pounds of $SO_2$ per million Btu of input heat, measured on an annual basis. Assume that your power plant is subject to this standard, that it is nearing the end of November, and that your facility has emitted only 0.9 pounds of $SO_2$ per million Btu over the past eleven months, because you have burned low sulfur coal. You have immediately available to you a large quantity of high sulfur coal, which may be purchased at a much lower price. What might you do in December? How much $SO_2$ per million Btu could you theoretically emit in December and still comply with the 1971 NSPS? Does this example suggest a weakness in how the 1971 NSPS was articulated?

2. Two groups formed an alliance to attack the 1971 NSPS of 1.2 pounds of $SO_2$ per million Btu: environmental groups and high-sulfur coal mining companies in the east and midwest. Why would environmentalists attack the 1971 NSPS? Why would the eastern and midwestern coal mining companies attack the NSPS?

3. Following congressional amendment of the Clean Air Act in 1977, the EPA correctly recognized that it had been ordered by newly worded § 111(a)(1)(A) to promulgate NSPS containing two elements: (a) allowable

emission *limitations* (e.g., 1.2 pounds per million Btu), *and* (b) required *percentage reductions* in emissions (e.g., a 90% cutback in the emissions of $SO_2$ which would occur if there were no controls). At first, the EPA proposed the following NSPS for coal-fired power plants: no more than 1.2 pounds of $SO_2$ per million Btu (absolute maximum) *plus* a reduction in emissions of 85%. Two other groups—Carter administration economists and western (low-sulfur) coal mining companies—blasted this proposal. Why would administration economists be unhappy with the proposed NSPS? Why would western coal mining companies attack the proposal?

4. Do your answers to the foregoing questions help to explain the eventual choice by the EPA of the peculiar "sliding-scale" NSPS, described by Professor Currie at page 366, *supra*? Are the peculiarities of the sliding-scale NSPS attributable to science? Technology? Something else?

5. Economists were caustic in their criticism of the 1977 statutory amendments altering the coal-fired power plant NSPS:

> Just in time for the debate this year about renewal of the Clean Air Act, a Yale Law School professor and a recent graduate have documented one of the classic horror stories of 1970s-style environmental rule-making. In "Clean Coal/Dirty Air" (Yale University Press * * *), Bruce A. Ackerman and William T. Hassler show, as part of their subtitle puts it, "how the Clean Air Act became a multibillion-dollar bailout for high-sulfur coal producers."
>
> Their book is a case study of how the Environmental Protection Agency and Congress decided that all coal utility plants built after 1979 had to be equipped with sulfur-scrubbing equipment whether or not it is necessary to meet federal pollution standards. The decision means that billions will have to be spent on scrubbing technology that is still not very certain, even though emission from these plants may not be as free from sulfur as they would have been without scrubbing. * * *
>
> The results are going to be extraordinary. Billions of dollars will be spent in the West on useless scrubbers cleaning coal that is already low in sulfur. The scrubbers, in fact, require minimal amounts of sulfur to function properly, and in many cases sulfur will have to be added to coal to keep the scrubbers working. In addition, scrubbers use large amounts of water and create enormous amounts of waste. One large valley in Western Pennsylvania is already being filled with the useless sulfurous sludge produced from only one plant that has been scrubbing for about four years. Once again, the problem has simply been moved outside the regulatory guidelines.

William Tucker, *The Mess Made by the Clean Air Act Alliance*, Wall St. J., May 7, 1981, at 26 col. 3.

6. Is it possible that Ackerman and Hassler overreacted? Or were the 1977 statutory amendments so bad that attacking them was like shooting fish in a barrel? Presumably, the academic world is chock full of tenure pieces bearing variations on the title "Congress Does Something Stupid," "Congress Does Something Stupid, Part II," and so forth. Critics who set out to lambast those legislative choices that fail the criterion of economic efficiency will never lack for work. But should we be surprised when Congress makes political decisions based on political consequences?

7. Consider the conclusions of Professor Howard Latin on the separate but somewhat related issue of uniform federal standards:

> [T]he academic literature on "regulatory reform" reflects an excessive preoccupation with theoretical efficiency, while it places inadequate emphasis on actual decisionmaking costs and implementation constraints. Any system for environmental regulation must function despite the presence of pervasive uncertainty, high decisionmaking costs, and manipulative strategic behavior resulting from conflicting private and public interests. Under these conditions, the indisputable fact that uniform standards are inefficient does not prove that any other approach would necessarily perform better. In a "second-best" world, the critical issue is not which regulatory system aspires to ideal "efficiency" but which is most likely to prove effective.

Howard Latin, *Ideal Versus Real Regulatory Efficiency: Implementation of Uniform Standards and "Fine-Tuning" Regulatory Reforms*, 37 Stan. L. Rev. 1267, 1270-71 (1985).

8. The 1990 Clean Air Act Amendments repealed the § 111(a)(1)(A) percentage reduction requirement in connection with establishment of the acid rain control program. The EPA thereafter amended the NSPS to require simply that emissions be limited to 1.2 pounds of $SO_2$ per million Btu—effectively restoring the standard to its 1971 version. The result has been the economic distress described in the next reading. Congress sought to soften the blow by establishing "employment transition assistance" in Title XI of the 1990 Amendments, authorizing adjustment assistance benefits and needs-related payments for workers terminated or laid off "as a consequence of compliance with the Clean Air Act." 29 U.S.C. § 1662e(a)(1). We have seen at page 344, *supra*, that the acid rain program has saved billions of dollars in pollution control costs. Were the 1990 Amendments motivated by the economic criterion of efficiency chased by legislators who had seen the light? Or did high-sulfur coal state legislators fail to salvage the interests of their coal mining constituents in a bare knuckled political fight? Or did a wise Congress effectively decide that the time had come to jettison the awkward political compromise of 1977?

## PETER T. KILBORN, EAST'S COAL TOWNS WITHER IN THE NAME OF CLEANER AIR

N.Y. Times, Feb. 15, 1996, at A1 col. 1

Charles Riley weaves his pickup through snow-coated hills spotted with the small farms and scattered homes of his fellow coal miners. He points to the mountainous gob heap of castaway shale and rock, to the tall concrete portals in the flanks of hills, to the five-story superstructure of the new, 320-foot elevator shaft.

Far beneath these roads lies the dank and eerie subterranean city that is the Tygart River Mine. The state of the art in coal mining, it spreads over more than 20 square miles with a grid of numbered streets and avenues, trolley tracks, pipes to drain off the sulfur- and acid-laced water and cables for running machines and computers.

"Last summer, management said there was another 15 or 20 years of coal in here," said Mr. Riley, 49, a son and grandson of miners, a high school graduate who put his three children through four years of college. "Everyone went and bought new homes, new cars. I bought a new Jeep Cherokee."

But the Peabody Holding Company, the nation's largest coal producer, shut down the Tygart River Mine and dismissed all 368 workers last December, making it one of hundreds of mines to close in a landscape altered by a single provision of the Clean Air Act of 1990. Tygart was the biggest operation in once-mine-pocked Marion County * * * .

Conditions across most of the Eastern coal country are the bleakest since the Great Depression, largely because the coal here is too high in sulfur to easily meet the clean air requirements. Mines are thriving in the West and in eastern Kentucky and southern West Virginia, all producers of low-sulfur coal. But they are closing through most of Appalachia and in other coal-mining areas east of the Mississippi, and their loss is leaving huge gaps in the surrounding communities. It is the anguished human face of policies that even miners acknowledge have purified the air they breathe and the streams they fish in. * * *

The mines in the high-sulfur areas are shutting because when the coal they yield is burned, the sulfur produces sulfur dioxide, a cause of acid rain. Under the Clean Air Act, power plants were required to reduce sulfur dioxide emissions by half as of January 1995, and they must cut them further by 2000.

Utilities can install scrubbers to filter their smoke, but the scrubbers cost $100 million or more, so few have. Often at less cost, they can meet the air standards by blending high-sulfur coal with low-sulfur coal from Wyoming and Montana or from eastern Kentucky and southern West Virginia. Either way, the Clean Air Act has cut demand for high-sulfur coal and driven down prices to a point where many mine operators say they cannot make profits. * * *

What hurts the miners hurts the local economy in proportions far exceeding the effect of other jobs. * * * With the loss of the mines and of several factories as well, he said, Marion County has lost nearly 400 retail jobs in the first half of the 1990's and 27 of its 355 stores. * * * "It hurts," said Charles Reese, president of the Marion County Chamber of Commerce. * * * Mr. Reese said the county's 9 percent unemployment rate, compared with the national rate of 5.6 percent, was actually higher because many workers had stopped looking for jobs and were not counted. * * *

"All of us grew up in coal camps and lived within walking distance of the mines," said Gary Pastorial, 46, who was laid off from Tygart. "Everyone burned coal in their homes, and when you went out in the evening, you couldn't see the air. One of my chores was to scrub the front porch with a mop every day because it was black." Today Mr. Pastorial lives in a spotless ranch house he just built in an upper-income subdivision, and he looks upon a horizon of pristine air. "The West Fork River was dead," he said. "Now people fish in it."

Congress is helping to soften the blow of layoffs attributed to the Clean Air Act. Like most people who lose their jobs, the miners receive unemployment compensation for six months. But the Government also pays for them to go to school for up to two years to learn new skills and keeps paying them their unemployment benefit, typically $290 a week, for the duration.

But no training is likely to yield jobs like the ones these men have lost. Many are taking courses in the construction trades, which pay a little more than a third of the $17 an hour they typically earned in the mines. But a state analysis of the county economy says that in 1994 and 1995, there were 456 applicants for 21 construction jobs. "If they don't go to school, they're going to be lucky to get $5 an hour," said Cathy Tarley, manager of Marion County office of the state job service. "If they do go to school for two years, they might get $8 to $10." * * *

John Beveridge spent 22 years in the mines, the last 13 at the Peabody mine. He is a roof bolter, a highly skilled worker who bores six-foot-long rods into the roofs of mines to keep them from falling. It is treacherous work; the driller must learn to read sounds and vibrations to know when a roof might crash. * * * As a youth, he completed three years of college, majoring in psychology. He also boxed professionally for 15 years as a hobby. But nothing paid like mining. "You could work seven days a week if you wanted to," Mr. Beveridge said. He made $48,000 last year in the mine before he was let go in early October. "I'm scared to death," he said. "I'm 44 years old. I'd like to live another 50 years. What am I going to do?"

## 4. DESIGNATED POLLUTANTS AT DESIGNATED FACILITIES

The NSPS are probably best understood as one component of the Clean Air Act's overall program to curb emissions of the six criteria pollutants so that the national ambient air standards may ultimately be achieved throughout the nation. Indeed, the vast majority of NSPS are directed at the criteria pollutants. Nevertheless, the EPA is not limited to the criteria pollutants when issuing NSPS for industry categories and subcategories, and occasionally the agency chooses to promulgate standards for non-criteria pollutants. For example, the NSPS for the aluminum manufacturing category include standards for fluorides. The agency's power to promulgate NSPS for non-criteria pollutants is strongly implied by the text of Clean Air Act § 111(d)(1).

The EPA calls such pollutants "designated pollutants from designated facilities," *see* 40 C.F.R. Part 62, because the pollutants are specifically enumerated in the process of promulgating NSPS and the pollutants are regulated *only* at the categories and subcategories to which the NSPS applies. Moreover, the pollutants are controlled by the federally-promulgated NSPS only at *new* sources.

It is somewhat daunting to spot all designated pollutants at designated facilities, because it requires a search through hundreds of pages of new source performance standards addressed to several dozen industry categories and subcategories. The designated pollutants at designated facilities list apparently includes: (1) fluorides at aluminum plants and phosphate fertilizer plants; (2) acid mist at sulfuric acid plants; (3) volatile organic compounds (VOCs) at petroleum storage vessels and approximately 18 additional source categories and subcategories; and (4) total reduced sulfur at Kraft paper mills.

Consider how odd it would be if the EPA concluded that certain pollutants—for example fluorides—are so significant that they should be regulated by NSPS at new aluminum facilities, while the Clean Air Act ignored the emission of the very same pollutants at existing facilities in the same industry category. This is where Clean Air Act § 111(d) comes in. That section effectively provides that *States* must promulgate standards for "designated pollutants" at *existing* "designated facilities" using a procedure "similar to" the SIP process. No one seems to use this terminology, but these standards might well be called "existing source performance standards" or "ESPS." Thus, for example, because the EPA has promulgated NSPS for fluorides at new aluminum manufacturing plants, States having existing aluminum manufacturing plants are responsible for establishing fluoride standards to govern emissions at those facilities. Recognizing that it is harder to retrofit an existing plant than properly outfit a new one, the statute provides that a State may "take into consideration, among other factors, the remaining useful life of the existing source to which such standard applies." § 111(d)(1).

State *plans* establishing the "ESPS" for existing designated facilities emitting designated pollutants are collated and approved in 40 C.F.R. Part 62. Many of the entries say little more than: "Alaska has no sulfuric acid plants." *See* 40 C.F.R. § 62.353. Nevertheless, some states have promulgated "ESPS" for designated pollutants at existing designated facilities. *See, e.g.,* 40 C.F.R. § 62.4620 (Louisiana).

## D. IMPLEMENTATION PLANS

### 1. OVERVIEW

## PHILLIP D. REED, STATE IMPLEMENTATION PLANS

in 2 Law of Environmental Protection
11-14.6 to 11-30.1 (Sheldon M. Novick, ed. 1998)

The Clean Air Act provides two basic mechanisms for attaining and maintaining the air quality standards. One is uniform national emission limitations, based on advanced pollution control technologies, for new stationary and mobile sources of criteria pollutants. Every time an old car is junked and a new one leaves the showroom and every time an old factory is replaced by a new one, there will be less pollution emitted and in the air. The engine of economic growth is hitched to the pollution control program. * * * The second mechanism for achieving the air quality standards is the state implementation plan or SIP. The SIP is an elaborate analytical and legal construct whose primary function is to prescribe emission standards for pre-1970 stationary sources and controls on the use of cars and trucks that are necessary to attain and maintain the NAAQS. The SIPs take into account applicable new source standards and incorporate new source review programs required by the Act, but their stationary source and transportation control requirements are key elements, because cutting pollution from older factories and modifying the traffic patterns that produce heavy smog in most American cities has proven critical to achieving the air quality standards.

State implementation plans are devised in an analytically and institutionally complex process. The country is divided into air quality control regions and each region must have a plan for each criteria pollutant. The Act prescribes different criteria for each region or portion of a region depending on whether or not the air quality standards have been attained and the extent of the pollution in each nonattainment area. For example, in areas not in attainment of the NAAQS for a pollutant, the Act requires the plan to impose "reasonably available control technology ("RACT")" on existing sources of the pollutant, while in attainment areas, the plan need not require any controls on pre-1970 sources. * * * It falls to the states to devise the plans, as the name indicates, but they must follow statutory and EPA criteria, which have become more extensive and precise over the years, and have their work approved by EPA. Once approved, the SIP is enforceable by EPA and if the state does not produce an adequate plan, EPA is supposed to step in and write a plan itself. In all, the state implementation plan is as complex a regulatory mechanism as the human mind can devise.

The SIP requirements of the Clean Air Act have reached their present state in three stages. The 1967 Air Quality Act established the concept of implementation plans for heavily polluted "air quality control regions" (AQCRs) but left the job entirely to the states. In 1970, Congress amended the Clean Air Act to make state participation as close to mandatory as it could be in our federal system and to incorporate engineering and legal principles into the process so that SIPs would have quantified and enforceable emission standards for individual sources. The SIPs were to attain the NAAQS by not later than 1977. They failed. The 1977 Clean Air Act Amendments took the SIP several steps further, extending the attainment deadlines to 1982 or 1987, mandating special SIP revisions for nonattainment areas, and tightening the screws on states unwilling to carry the load. The 1970 provisions governing SIPs stayed in force, [and] the new provisions were simply woven into the existing legal tapestry, sometimes without attention to the smooth meshing of old and new. Although there has been significant progress, many SIPs again have failed to meet Congress' deadlines. In the 1990 Amendments, Congress again gave the states more time, but at the price of more stringent control requirements that appear to deprive the states of most of their remaining discretion regarding regulation of existing sources and require especially tough new source review and mobile source controls. * * *

## THE 1967 AIR QUALITY ACT: THE FIRST SMALL STEP TOWARD FEDERALIZATION

The main contribution of the 1967 Act was the establishment of air quality control regions. The starting point for cleaning up air pollution (or any other kind for that matter) is figuring out where the pollution originates. This may not be an easy task, because the air pollution monitored at any point on any day may come from many sources, large and small, located at various distances from the monitor. Moreover, the sources responsible for the smog or smudge will change from day to day, depending on the weather and the prevailing winds. Despite these complications, it is possible to map out regions including both heavily polluted air and most of the sources typically causing it. When Congress first became serious about air pollution control in 1970 it mandated the identification of AQCRs, areas combining heavy pollution and concentrations of the sources of that pollution, as the focal points of abatement efforts. * * *

## THE 1970 CAA AMENDMENTS

The foundation of the 1970 Clean Air Act's new approach was built of three principles: nationalization, quantification, and accountability. The amendments nationalized the institutional machinery for regulating air pollution to make certain the national air quality goals would be met across the country despite regional differences in industry, meteorology, topography, automobile use, and economics. The new system is often referred to as a federal-state "partnership." If that is what it is, the federal government clearly is the senior partner, with control over the agenda and the purse strings. The 1970 Act also quantified the regulatory scheme in terms of air quality objectives, allowable emissions from individual polluters, and the time for compliance with both. The existence of quantified goals for individual and collective pollution control and finite deadlines for attaining them meant that the key players in the system, EPA, the states, and industry, could be held accountable. Accountable they were, with each subject to potentially severe sanctions for failure to comply. While any rational observer can see in the Act clear evidence that Congress did not expect nationalization, quantification, and accountability to be carried to their logical extremes, it is also clear that Congress expected these three principles to be rigorously applied.

The SIP provisions of the Clean Air Act play two critical roles. First, they bridge a gap between air quality standards and enforcement. Clean air would become not just a goal, but an enforceable mandate. Second, the SIP process created new state-federal machinery; the cumbersome, but powerful "partnership" held together with shared responsibilities and resources, and motivated by statutory deadlines and public accountability. The federal partner had leverage to ensure the job was done and in accord with national priorities; the state partners had the resources to get the job done at the local level.

The SIP was the missing link in air quality enforcement. Prior to 1970 the standard approach in federal pollution control law was to directly enforce environmental quality standards. That approach failed because enforcement must be source-specific, but environmental quality standards register aggregate pollution. Wherever more than one source contributes to the pollution of a river or air basin, it is difficult to translate environmental quality goals into control requirements for individual sources through enforcement. Where tens, or hundreds, or thousands of sources contribute, it becomes impossible. The 1970 Clean Air Act took the specification of standards for individual polluters out of the enforcement process and put it into a new state planning process.

After EPA promulgates or revises an NAAQS, each state has limited time in which to prepare a SIP or revisions to the existing plan, which explains how the state will go about attaining the standard and maintaining it thereafter. There must be a separate plan for each criteria pollutant, and a separate plan for attainment and maintenance in each AQCR. The states may factor into their calculations the emission reductions that are likely to result from implementation of federal standards of performance for new "stationary" sources (e.g., factories) and emission control requirements for new motor vehicles, but must add any necessary emission controls for stationary sources already in operation, preconstruction review for new factories, and limits on automobile use. This system was to take the guesswork out of pollution control decision making and enforcement. Quantitative air quality standards would be translated into quantitative emission limitations for individual sources.

The SIP requirements of the 1970 Amendments not only filled a gap in the enforcement process, they created a new institutional model, locking the states and federal government into a partnership that would get the clean air job done and with a degree of consistency across the land. Every step in the SIP process was governed by a deadline, culminating in deadlines for attainment of the NAAQS. To make sure the state programs lived up to these exacting standards, the Act required EPA oversight and approval of all key activities. To make the states jump through all these hoops, Congress provided program money and threatened federal takeover of air pollution control planning and enforcement. The 1970 Amendments were intended to force the states to control air pollution. The Supreme Court described the program as

Congress "taking a stick to the states." Federal control had replaced federal assistance. * * *

### AIR QUALITY CONTROL REGIONS

The 1970 Clean Air Act Amendments kept the 1967 Act's AQCR scheme, but revised its role and focus. The Amendments made three changes. First, they required that the rural areas not included in the 1967 regions be designated as AQCRs as well. The new Clean Air Act machinery had to be in place in all regions of the country if it was to see to the attainment and maintenance of the new national ambient air quality standards. Second, the Amendments eliminated a provision for modifying AQCR boundaries, because cleanup efforts had been diverted by political efforts to gerrymander the boundaries of AQCRs to spare specific sources. Third, the Amendments directed EPA to designate such interstate and major intrastate AQCRs as it deemed necessary or appropriate for attainment and maintenance of air quality standards, thus giving the federal government its first authority directly to define AQCRs. The AQCRs were important for functional reasons: they were to be the focus of state implementation plans. Where the boundaries were located would determine where the tough state programs needed to clean up NAAQS violations would take effect. The Act itself, however, did not prescribe any special programs for nonattainment AQCRs.

### THE SCOPE AND SUBSTANCE OF A SIP

Under the 1970 Act, SIPs were required for all areas. EPA initially focused its attention on areas violating the NAAQS, but was forced to provide detailed guidance for clean areas as well. The thrust of section 110, the basic SIP provision, was on cleaning up areas with more pollution than allowed by the primary NAAQS. All the SIPs had to do for clean areas, EPA concluded, was to keep air quality from dropping below the secondary standards. Environmentalists sued and the Supreme Court eventually allowed to stand a district court ruling that the Act's purpose to "protect and enhance" air quality obligated EPA to do more in attainment areas, even though all of the substantive provisions of the Act were directed toward enhancement. In response, EPA promulgated prevention of significant deterioration (PSD) rules limiting new sources, which formed the basis of a more complex PSD program established in the 1977 Amendments and, subsequently, in a new set of PSD rules * * * . Despite these considerations, most SIP attention focused on nonattainment areas. * * *

Section 110 sets out a list of substantive and procedural requirements for SIPs. As enacted in 1970, the Act envisioned that states would rely on emission limitations for stationary sources, transportation control plans to cut pollution from cars and trucks, and land use control plans to ensure that the siting of new facilities did not jeopardize attainment. The Act gives the states some flexibility, allowing "other measures" as necessary. EPA has interpreted this language to allow a number of alternatives, including economic incentives. The SIP must also provide for necessary source and ambient monitoring, enforcement, and staffing. Under the 1970 Amendments, putting these pieces together for a SIP was a three-step process.

### 1. DEFINING THE PROBLEM

The first step, defining the air quality problem, was begun by determining how much more pollution was in the air than the standards allow. The state also had to project growth over the next ten years and identify areas projected to exceed the NAAQS in the future as a result. This exercise, performed by checking air quality monitoring data or using models to estimate air quality, told the state how big a job awaited.

The state next had to figure out where the excessive pollution came from. To do so, it made an "inventory" of sources by counting the big ones, such as power plants or smelters, and counting or estimating the number of little ones, like boilers in apartment buildings. Next, the state estimated the amount of emissions from all these sources, using any monitoring data that might be available and estimating the rest with various engineering calculations and rules of thumb.

### 2. EMISSION LIMITATIONS

Once the pollutants and sources of concern were identified, the states next were to develop control strategies. * * * [C]ontrol strategies fall into three categories: emission limits for stationary sources, transportation control plans for motor vehicles, and new source review.

Although states are not limited to this strategy, emission limitations were the basic building block of stationary source control strategies in the first twenty years of implementation. Emission limits typically are set for broad categories of sources. In theory, a state regulatory agency could tailor a package of emission limits for each criteria pollutant and each AQCR, designing the rules just to attain the NAAQS at the lowest aggregate cost. The Agency would have to have reams of data on the cost and feasibility of control at each of the hundreds or thousands of individual sources, however, and that data is not readily available. The search for an administratively feasible method of setting emission limits usually led to uniform standards for broad categories of sources, based on general notions of what is feasible technologically for those sources and not too costly. The broader the category, the easier the process, which could follow either of two tracks.

The state might take an aggressive approach, setting the categorical standard at a level associated with highly efficient controls. Flexibility could be built into such a system by allowing the regulated community to make a case for lower standards for subcategories with special technological or economic difficulties during the standard-setting process or by allowing variances for hard-hit individual sources.

An alternative to the aggressive SIP approach was to set the categorical standard at the level of the least common denominator to ensure that it was "reasonable" across the board. So long as the emission reductions resulting from imposition of the standard would produce attainment of the NAAQS, the Act did not dictate either approach. The SIP also could vary the categorical standards from one AQCR to the next, imposing tighter standards where pollution is heaviest.

The 1970 Act could have been interpreted to allow individual source variances from categorical SIP standards only under the exacting standards of section 110(f). EPA, however, read section 110(a)(3) as requiring it to approve any SIP revision, whether for an individual source or an entire category, so long as the change would not cause a violation of the NAAQS. Section 110(f) was, in EPA's view, limited to variances extending beyond the attainment deadline. In one of the pivotal early Clean Air Act cases, the Supreme Court agreed with EPA. * * *

The 1970 Act has been referred to as "technology-forcing." As to existing stationary sources, however, whether and how much force to apply was left largely up to the states. EPA invited a degree of consistency by publishing information on "reasonably available" control technologies for criteria pollutants, but states were free to use other standards. The result of the process was development of a bewildering variety of stationary source SIP provisions.

Inherent in the concept of an emission limitation is the notion that the amount of pollutants emitted will be limited. Large emission sources cannot avoid violations of the air quality standards by cutting emissions only when meteorological conditions likely will direct the pollution toward air quality monitors or concentrate it under a temperature inversion. Nor may such sources rely on tall stacks * * * .

EPA came to this interpretation slowly. Initially, it deemed tall stacks and intermittent control strategies (ICS) acceptable as emission limitations. While that interpretation was in force (and in the years leading up to the 1970 Amendments) hundreds of powerplants and smelters had been equipped with very tall smokestacks to avoid the high cost of removing sulfur from their flue gas. After having its policy rejected by the courts in 1974, EPA adopted the principle that sources with post-1970 stacks taller than "good engineering practice" would normally dictate must be regulated as though they had shorter stacks, unless tall stacks were the best available technology or where alternative controls (i.e., scrubbers) were "economically unreasonable or technologically unsound." In 1977 Congress tightened the ban on tall stacks further, but the stack height issue was not put to rest.

### 3. MODELING

The last step in the SIP process is to use air quality models to demonstrate that the emission reduction produced by the control strategies will attain and maintain the air quality standards in each AQCR. The analysis also must demonstrate that projected growth will not cause the region to slip out of attainment. Air quality models perform this function. The simplest—the "roll-back" model—assumes a linear relationship between emission volume and air quality. In simplified form, 10 percent reduction in aggregate emissions in the AQCR will wipe out a 10 percent violation of the NAAQS. Computerized diffusion models are a more complex alternative. These complicated mathematical models can take into account the relative locations of air quality monitors and major sources, as well as prevailing weather conditions, to provide more precise estimates of the air quality impacts of the control strategies.

If emission limitations, transportation controls, and new source review are SIP building blocks, then air quality modeling is the engineering science that explains how to put them together into a viable structure. Some might argue, however, that modeling is more sorcery than science. Computer modeling is an extremely complex and imprecise tool whose accuracy diminishes with the number of sources, the distance between source and monitor, and variation in the terrain. The use of modeling in designing and evaluating SIPs is an inviting target for criticism because of its unavoidable imprecision, but the courts generally have recognized that modeling is the only tool EPA and the states have to carry out the air quality analyses required by the Act and have deferred to the agencies' technical expertise on these issues.

The "scientific" approach for translating a general air quality standard into enforceable, source-specific emission limitations is riddled with imprecision. Each calculation requires major assumptions and can be well off the mark. Errors at different stages might cancel each other out, but also could be additive. Moreover, the system is so complex that it is easy to manipulate pieces of it to come up with any desired result. To make it work, EPA had to develop detailed planing and modeling guidance, whose own complexity is a bar to understanding the process and a barrier to innovation.

In addition to the control strategies and attainment demonstrations themselves, SIPs had to identify legal mechanisms to impose the emissions limits on individual sources. These might be regulations, permits, orders, or some combination of these measures. * * *

### THE "DOUBLE KEY"

The dual state-federal adoption of every SIP and every SIP revision is extremely cumbersome. Each must go through the full panoply of rulemaking. The SIP process has come to be known as a "double-key" system and each key can take months or years to turn. The federal system is complex, but many state systems are even more complicated; for example, some states' rules require legislative approval. This procedural duplication, intended to safeguard the Act's national goals from too much federalist diversity, sometimes afflicted the SIP process with procedural rigidity bordering on rigor mortis.

### Notes and Questions

1.   In drafting and promulgating their SIPs, how are state officials supposed to decide whose emissions must be cut by what amount? For exam-

ple, should coal-fired power plants be required to cut back their sulfur oxide emissions by 30 percent, while smelters are required to curb their emissions by 70 percent? Should the percentages be switched? Should each type of facility be required to meet a 50 percent reduction? Does the Clean Air Act have anything to say about this core issue of allocating emission limitations between various types of sources?

2. Professors Stewart and Krier suggest at page 332, *supra*, that rule makers, such as SIP drafters, might be guided by the criterion of least cost abatement, requiring "a greater measure of control by those sources that can reduce emissions more cheaply, and a lesser degree of control by sources with high abatement costs." How would this approach be implemented? What would be its virtues? Would such an approach be practicable? Would it be equitable?

## 2. ECONOMIC AND TECHNOLOGICAL INFEASIBILITY

### UNION ELECTRIC COMPANY v. EPA

427 U.S. 246 (1976)

MR. JUSTICE MARSHALL delivered the opinion of the Court.

After the Administrator of the EPA approves a state implementation plan, the plan may be challenged in a court of appeals within 30 days,[c] or after 30 days have run if newly discovered or available information justifies subsequent review. We must decide whether the operator of a regulated emission source, in a petition for review of an EPA-approved state plan filed after the original 30-day appeal period, can raise the claim that it is economically or technologically infeasible to comply with the plan.

Petitioner is an electric utility company servicing the St. Louis metropolitan area, large portions of Missouri, and parts of Illinois and Iowa. Its three coal-fired generating plants in the metropolitan St. Louis area are subject to the sulfur dioxide restrictions in the Missouri implementation plan. Petitioner did not seek review of the Administrator's approval of the plan within 30 days, as it was entitled to do under § 307(b)(1) of the Act, * * * but rather applied to the appropriate state and county agencies for variances from the emission limitations affecting its three plants. Petitioner received one-year variances, which could be extended upon reapplication. The variances on two of petitioner's three plants had expired and petitioner was applying for extensions when, on May 31, 1974, the Administrator notified petitioner that sulfur dioxide emissions from its plants violated the emission limitations contained in the Missouri plan. *See* 40 Fed. Reg. 3566 (1975). Shortly thereafter petitioner filed a petition in the Court of Appeals for the Eighth Circuit for review of the Administrator's 1972 approval of the Missouri implementation plan. * * *

---

[c] *Ed.*—The deadline is now 60 days.

*Petitioner alleged that: (1) compliance with the SIP requirements was not technologically or economically feasible; and (2) the federal ambient standards could be met within the statutory deadlines through control requirements less stringent than those contained in the SIP. The court of appeals ruled that the petition was not timely and that technological or economic infeasibility were not grounds for challenging the Administrator's approval of a SIP.*

The Administrator's position is that he has no power whatsoever to reject a state implementation plan on the ground that it is economically or technologically infeasible \* \* \* . After surveying the relevant provisions of the Clean Air Amendments of 1970 and their legislative history, we agree that Congress intended claims of economic and technological infeasibility to be wholly foreign to the Administrator's consideration of a state implementation plan. \* \* \*

[T]he 1970 Amendments to the Clean Air Act were a drastic remedy to what was perceived as a serious and otherwise uncheckable problem of air pollution. The Amendments place the primary responsibility for formulating pollution control strategies on the States, but nonetheless subject the States to strict minimum compliance requirements. These requirements are of a "technology-forcing character," *Train v. NRDC,* [421] U.S. at 91, and are expressly designed to force regulated sources to develop pollution control devices that might at the time appear to be economically or technologically infeasible.

This approach is apparent on the face of § 110(a)(2). The provision sets out eight criteria that an implementation plan must satisfy, and provides that if these criteria are met and if the plan was adopted after reasonable notice and hearing, the Administrator "shall approve" the proposed plan. The mandatory "shall" makes it quite clear that the Administrator is not to be concerned with factors other than those specified \* \* \* and none of the eight factors appears to permit consideration of technological or economic infeasibility. \* \* \* [I]f a basis is to be found for allowing the Administrator to consider such claims, it must be among the eight criteria, \* \* \* so it is here that the argument is focused.

It is suggested that consideration of claims of technological and economic infeasibility is required by the first criterion—that the primary air quality standards be met "as expeditiously as practicable but \* \* \* in no case later than three years \* \* \*" and that the secondary air quality standards be met within a "reasonable time." § 110(a)(2)(A). The argument is that what is "practicable" or "reasonable" cannot be determined without assessing whether what is proposed is possible. This argument does not survive analysis.

Section 110(a)(2)(A)'s three-year deadline for achieving primary air quality standards is central to the Amendments' regulatory scheme and, as both the language and the legislative history of the requirement make clear, it leaves no room for claims of technological or economic infeasibility. \* \* \*

As Senator Muskie, manager of the Senate bill, explained to his chamber:

"The first responsibility of Congress is not the making of technological or economic judgments—or even to be limited by what is or appears to be technologically or economically feasible. Our responsibility is to establish what the public interest requires to protect the health of persons. This may mean that people and industries will be asked to do what seems to be impossible at the present time." 116 Cong. Rec. 32901-32902 (1970). * * *

This position reflected that of the Senate committee:

"In the Committee discussions, considerable concern was expressed regarding the use of the concept of technical feasibility as the basis of ambient air standards. The Committee determined that 1) the health of people is more important than the question of whether the early achievement of ambient air quality standards protective of health is technically feasible; and 2) the growth of pollution load in many areas, even with application of available technology, would still be deleterious to public health.

"Therefore, the Committee determined that existing sources of pollutants either should meet the standard of the law or be closed down * * * ." S. Rep. No. 91-1196, pp. 2-3 (1970).

The Conference Committee and, ultimately, the entire Congress accepted the Senate's three-year mandate for the achievement of primary air quality standards, and the clear import of that decision is that the Administrator must approve a plan that provides for attainment of the primary standards in three years even if attainment does not appear feasible. * * * The Conference Committee made clear that the States could not procrastinate until the deadline approached. Rather, the primary standards had to be met in less than three years if possible; they had to be met "as expeditiously as practicable." § 110(a)(2)(A). Whatever room there is for considering claims of infeasibility in the attainment of primary standards must lie in this phrase, which is, of course, relevant only in evaluating those implementation plans that attempt to achieve the primary standard in less than three years.

It is argued that when such a state plan calls for proceeding more rapidly than economics and the available technology appear to allow, the plan must be rejected as not "practicable." Whether this is a correct reading of § 110(a)(2)(A) depends on how that section's "as expeditiously as practicable" phrase is characterized. The Administrator's position is that § 110(a)(2)(A) sets only a minimum standard that the States may exceed in their discretion, so that he has no power to reject an infeasible state plan that surpasses the minimum federal requirements—a plan that reflects a state decision to engage in technology forcing on its own and to proceed more expeditiously than is practicable. On the other hand, petitioner and *Amici* supporting its position argue that §110(a)(2)(A) sets a mandatory standard that the States must meet precisely, and conclude that the Administrator may reject a plan for being too strict as well as for being too lax. * * *

Section 116 of the Clean Air Act * * * provides that the States may adopt emission standards stricter than the national standards. *Amici* argue that such standards must be adopted and enforced independently of the EPA-approved state implementation plan. This construction of §§ 110 and 116, however, would not only require the Administrator to expend considerable time and energy determining whether a state plan was precisely tailored to meet the federal standards, but would simultaneously require States desiring stricter standards to enact and enforce two sets of emission standards, one federally approved plan and one stricter state plan. We find no basis in the Amendments for visiting such wasteful burdens upon the States and the Administrator, and so we reject the argument of *Amici.*

We read the "as may be necessary" requirement of § 110(a)(2)(B) to demand only that the implementation plan submitted by the State meet the "minimum conditions" of the Amendments. * * * Beyond that if a State makes the legislative determination that it desires a particular air quality by a certain date and that it is willing to force technology to attain it—or lose a certain industry if attainment is not possible—such a determination is fully consistent with the structure and purpose of the Amendments, and § 110(a)(2)(B) provides no basis for the EPA Administrator to object to the determination on the ground of infeasibility. * * *

In sum, we have concluded that claims of economic or technological infeasibility may not be considered by the Administrator in evaluating a state requirement that primary ambient air quality standards be met in the mandatory three years. And, since we further conclude that the States may submit implementation plans more stringent than federal law requires and that the Administrator must approve such plans if they meet the minimum requirements of § 110(a)(2), it follows that the language of § 110(a)(2)(B) provides no basis for the Administrator ever to reject a state implementation plan on the ground that it is economically or technologically infeasible. Accordingly, a court of appeals reviewing an approved plan under § 307(b)(1) cannot set it aside on those grounds, no matter when they are raised. * * *

Perhaps the most important forum for consideration of claims of economic and technological infeasibility is before the state agency formulating the implementation plan. So long as the national standards are met, the State may select whatever mix of control devices it desires * * * and industries with particular economic or technological problems may seek special treatment in the plan itself. * * * Moreover, if the industry is not exempted from, or accommodated by, the original plan, it may obtain a variance, as petitioner did in this case; and the variance, if granted after notice and a hearing, may be submitted to the EPA as a revision of the plan. § 110(a)(3)(A) * * * . Lastly, an industry denied an exemption from the implementation plan, or denied a subsequent variance, may be able to take its claims of economic or technological infeasibility to the state courts. * * *

Even if the State does not intervene on behalf of an emission source, technological and economic factors may be considered in at least one other circumstance. When a source is found to be in violation of the state implementation plan, the Administrator may, after a conference with the operator, issue a compliance order rather than seek civil or criminal enforcement. Such an order must specify a "reasonable" time for compliance with the relevant standard, taking into account the seriousness of the violation and "any good faith efforts to comply with applicable requirements." §113(a)(4) * * * . Claims of technological or economic infeasibility, the Administrator agrees, are relevant to fashioning an appropriate compliance order under § 113(a)(4). Brief for Respondent EPA 36 n. 34.[18]

In short, the Amendments offer ample opportunity for consideration of claims of technological and economic infeasibility. Always, however, care is taken that consideration of such claims will not interfere substantially with the primary goal of prompt attainment of the national standards. Allowing such claims to be raised by appealing the Administrator's approval of an implementation plan, as petitioner suggests, would frustrate congressional intent. It would permit a proposed plan to be struck down as infeasible before it is given a chance to work, even though Congress clearly contemplated that some plans would be infeasible when proposed. And it would permit the Administrator or a federal court to reject a State's legislative choices in regulating air pollution, even though Congress plainly left with the States, so long as the national standards were met, the power to determine which sources would be burdened by regulation and to what extent. Technology forcing is a concept somewhat new to our national experience and it necessarily entails certain risks. But Congress considered those risks in passing the 1970 Amendments and decided that the dangers posed by uncontrolled air pollution made them worth taking. Petitioner's theory would render that considered legislative judgment a nullity, and that is a result we refuse to reach. *Affirmed.*

MR. JUSTICE POWELL, with whom THE CHIEF JUSTICE joins, concurring.

I join the opinion of the Court because the statutory scheme and the legislative history, thoroughly described in the Court's opinion, demonstrate irrefutably that Congress did not intend to permit the Administrator of the Environmental Protection Agency to reject a proposed state implementation plan on the grounds of economic or technological infeasibility. Congress adopted this position despite its apparent

---

[18] * * * Some courts have suggested that in criminal or civil enforcement proceedings the violator may in certain circumstances raise a defense of economic or technological infeasibility. * * * We do not address this question here.

awareness that in some cases existing sources that cannot meet the standard of the law must be closed down.[1]

The desire to impose strong incentives on industry to encourage the rapid development and adoption of pollution control devices is understandable. But it is difficult to believe that Congress would adhere to its absolute position if faced with the potentially devastating consequences to the public that this case vividly demonstrates.

Petitioner is an electric utility supplying power demands in the St. Louis metropolitan area, a large part of Missouri, and parts of Illinois and Iowa. It alleges that it cannot continue to operate if forced to comply with the sulfur dioxide restrictions contained in the Missouri implementation plan approved by the Administrator. Specifically, petitioner alleges that since the Administrator's approval of the plan, low-sulfur coal has become too scarce and expensive to obtain; reliable and satisfactory sulfur dioxide removal equipment that would enable it to comply with the plan's requirements simply has not been devised; the installation of the unsatisfactory equipment that is available would cost over $ 500 million, a sum impossible to obtain by bonds that are contingent on approval by regulatory bodies and public acceptance; and, even if the financing could be obtained, the carrying, operating, and maintenance costs of over $ 120 million a year would be prohibitive.[2] Petitioner further alleges that recent evidence has disclosed that sulfur dioxide in the ambient air is not the hazard to public health that it was once thought to be, and that compliance with the sulfur regulation in the Missouri plan is not necessary to the attainment of national primary and secondary ambient air standards in the St. Louis area.

At the risk of civil and criminal penalties enforceable by both the State and Federal Governments, as well as possible citizens' suits, * * * petitioner is being required either to embark upon the task of installing allegedly unreliable and prohibitively expensive equipment or to shut

---

[1] The record is clear beyond question that at least the sponsors and floor leaders of the Clean Air Act intended that industries unable to comply with approved state implementation plans, whether because of economic or technological infeasibility, would be "closed down." This is explicit in the Senate Report. S. Rep. No. 91-1196, p. 3 (1970). It is repeated quite candidly in the statements of various members of the Senate and is described in detail in the EPA's brief in this case. Brief for Respondent EPA 20-32. Indeed, remarkable as it may seem, it is clear from the legislative history that even total technological infeasibility is "irrelevant." See id., at 16, 18-23.

What this means in this case, if the allegations of Union Electric Co. prove to be correct, is that—in the interest of public health—the utility will be ordered to discontinue electric service to the public. As one cannot believe this would be allowed, I suppose that the State or Federal Government would find some basis for continuing to operate the company's facilities to serve the public despite noncompliance. But no such contingency program or authority therefor is found in the statute, and we must decide the case on the record before us.

[2] The burden of these extraordinary capital and operating costs, even if the technological infeasibility problems could be solved, would fall necessarily on the consumers of electric power.

down. Yet the present Act permits neither the Administrator, in approving the state plan, nor the courts, in reviewing that approval under § 307 of the Act * * * even to consider petitioner's allegations of infeasibility.

Environmental concerns, long neglected, merit high priority, and Congress properly has made protection of the public health its paramount consideration. See S. Rep. No. 91-1196, pp. 2-3 (1970). But the shutdown of an urban area's electrical service could have an even more serious impact on the health of the public than that created by a decline in ambient air quality. The result apparently required by this legislation in its present form could sacrifice the well-being of a large metropolitan area through the imposition of inflexible demands that may be technologically impossible to meet and indeed may no longer even be necessary to the attainment of the goal of clean air.

I believe that Congress, if fully aware of this Draconian possibility, would strike a different balance.

---

Read the following sections of the Clean Air Act

☐ § 110(f)(1)      ☐ § 110(f)(2)      ☐ § 110(f)(3)      ☐ § 113(a)(1)

☐ § 113(a)(4)      ☐ § 116

---

### Notes and Questions

1. Would the Supreme Court's ruling in *Union Electric* have been different if the *EPA* had drafted a *federal* implementation plan [FIP] in response to an inadequate SIP, pursuant to § 110(c)(1), so that it was a FIP that was being reviewed by the courts?

2. After the Supreme Court's decision, could Union Electric have used § 110(f) to gain extra time for compliance? If it had been able to gain relief through § 110(f), would such relief have been significant?

3. If Union Electric had been able to convince the state to *revise* the SIP to eliminate the strict emission limitation, would that have provided meaningful relief to the company? Would it have made any difference whether the new SIP would have assured attainment of ambient standards? *See* §§ 110(k)(3) and 110(*l*).

4. The Missouri state agencies did not seem to be interested in helping out Union Electric by amending the SIP. What if Union Electric had gone to the Missouri state courts and had succeeded in having the emission limitation struck down as unlawful under *state* law? Would such a state court ruling have relieved Union Electric from compliance?

5. How did the Supreme Court handle Union Electric's argument that EPA's approval of the Missouri SIP was unlawful because the emission limitations were excessively stringent—that more lenient limitations would

have sufficed to achieve compliance with the SO$_2$ NAAQS? Do you agree with the Court's reasoning?

6.   How did the Supreme Court deal with the *Amici* ("friend of the court") argument that EPA could only *enforce* the Missouri SIP's emission limitations insofar as they were necessary to achieve compliance with the SO$_2$ NAAQS—that the more stringent state limitations were somehow "outside the SIP" and could be enforced only by the state? What were the *Amici* attorneys seeking to accomplish with their "outside the SIP" argument?

## 3.  THE DOUBLE KEY AND JUDICIAL REVIEW

Here's a puzzler. Once the EPA has reviewed and approved a state's implementation plan in whole or in part, all approved portions of the SIP become federally enforceable. *See* CAA § 302(q) (defining "applicable implementation plan") and § 113(a) (federal enforcement provisions). In that event, each of the "double keys" has been effectively turned to the "on" position. But what happens if one of the two keys is subsequently reset to the "off" position?

If a SIP provision is vacated by a federal court on federal constitutional grounds, presumably the provision is enforceable by no one. If a SIP provision is vacated by a federal court on federal grounds other than the Constitution, the provision is presumably not enforceable by the EPA, but arguably may still be enforced by the state under its § 116 power to impose more stringent emissions limitations than required by federal law. What should be done, however, if a federally-approved SIP is vacated by a state court on state law grounds? This question has led to some fascinating caselaw.

## ILLINOIS v. COMMONWEALTH EDISON CO.

### 490 F. Supp. 1145 (N.D. Ill. 1980)

Defendant claims that plaintiff is barred from attempting to enforce Rule 203(g) of the Illinois Pollution Control Board Rules and Regulations because that Rule was vacated by an Illinois Appellate Court in *Ashland Chemical Co. v. Pollution Control Board*, 64 Ill. App. 3d 169, 381 N.E. 2d 56 (3d Dist. 1978), * * * and that a decision of a state court invalidating an emission limitation on state law grounds effectively bars its enforcement, at least until a replacement can be promulgated. * * *

The current enforceability of Rule 203(g) can perhaps best be understood by an examination of its procedural history. Rule 203(g)(1) provides a numerical limit on the emission of particulate matter from sources such as defendant's Kincaid and Waukegan stations. In 1972, the Illinois Pollution Control Board adopted Rule 203 pursuant to the Illinois Environmental Protection Act of 1970, Ill. Rev. Stat. ch. 111 1/2 § 1001, *et seq.* Rule 203(g) was submitted to the Administrator on January 31, 1972 as part of the Illinois State Implementation Plan. On May 31, 1972, pursuant to section 110(a)(2) of the Clean Air Act and 40

C.F.R. Part 51, the Administrator substantially approved this submission. The validity of Rule 203(g)(1) was challenged in 1974 in *Commonwealth Edison Co. v. Pollution Control Board*, 25 Ill. App.3d 271, 323 N.E. 2d 84 (1974) on the ground that the Board had not followed the correct procedures in promulgating it. The Illinois Supreme Court affirmed the Appellate Court's decision, reversing the Board's adoption of Rule 203(g)(1) and remanding the cause with instructions to the Board to validate Rule 203(g)(1) according to Section 27 of the Illinois Environmental Protection Act or to prepare a proper rule as a substitute. *Commonwealth Edison Co. v. Pollution Control Bd.*, 62 Ill.2d 494, 343 N.E.2d 459 (1976).

On August 2, 1976, pursuant to Sections 110(a)(2)(H) and 110(c) of the Clean Air Act, the E.P.A. Regional Administrator issued a Notice of Deficiency requesting that a revision of the Illinois State Implementation Plan be developed or that appropriate action be taken to correct the deficiency noted by the Illinois courts. In the Notice of Deficiency the Regional Administrator expressly stated that "[a]ll of the current applicable implementation plan remains in effect until the plan revision is submitted by the State to EPA and is approved by EPA or until EPA promulgates substitutes or additional regulations." 41 Fed. Reg. 32304 (August 2, 1976). On July 7, 1977, the Illinois Pollution Control Board issued an order revalidating Rule 203(g)(1), subject to a public comment period running 45 days from the date of the order. On September 27, 1978, Rule 203(g)(1) was again challenged in *Ashland Chemical Co. v. Pollution Control Bd., supra*. The Illinois Appellate Court held that the Board did not follow the Illinois Supreme Court's directions for validating Rule 203(g)(1) in *Commonwealth Edison Co., supra*, since it did not consider intermittent control systems, did not have an economic study prepared, nor did it provide an opportunity for Ashland or others to respond to the Marder Report, a study which the Board had commissioned. The court vacated Rule 203(g)(1) and remanded it to the Board for Proceedings consistent with the Illinois Supreme Court's directions in *Commonwealth Edison Co., supra*.

On July 12, 1979, the E.P.A. Regional Administrator again issued a Notice of Deficiency requesting that a revision of the Illinois plan be developed or other appropriate action taken to validate Rule 203(g)(1) in accordance with the instructions of the Illinois Supreme Court in *Commonwealth Edison Co., supra*. 44 Fed. Reg. 40724 (July 12, 1979).

Plaintiff maintains that because Rule 203(g)(1) was originally adopted as part of the Illinois Implementation Plan, and the Administrator's approval of the plan was subsequently sustained by the Seventh Circuit Court of Appeals in *Indiana & Michigan Electric Co. v. Environmental Protection Agency*, 509 F.2d 839 (7th Cir. 1975), it is enforceable against defendant in a federal forum notwithstanding its invalidation by the Illinois courts. Specifically, plaintiff asserts that once the Administrator approved Rule 203(g)(1) as part of the Illinois Plan pursuant to the provision of Section 110(a) of the Clean Air Act, the controlling law with respect to its implementation, enforcement and maintenance in Illinois under the federal enactment became fixed; and that, thereafter, it could only be revised, suspended, modified or postponed in accordance with the strict requirements of Section 110(i). Therefore, plaintiff argues that the unilateral action of the state in vacating Rule 203(g)(1) has no effect on its enforceability.

Section 110(i) provides:

Except for a primary nonferrous smelter order under section 119, a suspension under section 110(f) or (g) (relating to emergency suspensions), an exemption under section 118 (relating to certain Federal facilities), an order under section 113(d) (relating to compliance orders), a plan promulgation under section 110(c) or a plan revision under section110(a)(3), *no order, suspension, plan revision, or other action modifying any requirement of an applicable implementation plan may be taken with respect to any stationary source by the State or by the Administrator.* (emphasis supplied)

The court finds this provision controlling in this instance. As the Second Circuit observed in *Friends of the Earth v. Carey*, 535 F.2d 165, 169 (1976):

Since abatement and control of air pollution through systematic and timely attainment of the air quality standards is Congress' overriding objective, a plan, once adopted by a state and approved by the EPA, becomes controlling and must be carried out by the state. Modifications are permitted by the Act only cautiously and grudgingly. The EPA is authorized to approve revisions of the original plan, § 110(f), provided "it can satisfy the stringent conditions" imposed by the provision. * * * In all other cases full compliance with the plan is mandated. * * *

It should be noted, however, that defendant asserts the unenforceability of the claim in 79 C 311 which plaintiff bases on alleged violations of Rule 203(g)(1)(B) as applied to its Kincaid station because a variance from the Rule was granted in *Commonwealth Edison Co. v. Environmental Protection Agency.* Pollution Control Board Docket 77-316 (July 20, 1978). * * *

Plaintiff, on the other hand, urges the court to find that the variance granted by the Board does not bar enforcement of Rule 203(b) against defendant's Kincaid station because the variance was not approved by the Administrator of the United States E.P.A. Plaintiff asserts, and the court agrees, that the only procedural routes available to modify a federally approved implementation plan are a revision pursuant to Section 110(a)(3) of the Clean Air Act, or a postponement pursuant to Section 110(f) of the Act, both of which expressly require the Administrator's approval. * * *

The rationale for requiring strict compliance with the revision procedures of the Clean Air Act was articulated in *Metropolitan Washington Coalition for Clean Air v. District of Columbia*, 511 F.2d 809 [7 ERC 1811] (D.C. Cir. 1975), a case factually similar to the one at bar. In holding that revisions are not to be considered a part of a state implementation plan until approved by the Administrator, the court reasoned: "If unilateral state action served to relax its implementation schedule pending E.P.A. approval, any state could sidestep the crucial limitations on the revision procedure and undermine the national program of air quality improvement." *Id.* at 813.

Thus, while the Board's order granting a variance to defendant's Kincaid station was based on a finding that application of the Rule would be arbitrary and unreasonable, "the ultimate arbiter of the propriety of any particular variance is and must be the [Administrator of the] E.P.A." *Natural Resources Defense Council v. United States EPA,* 507 F.2d 905, 914 (9th Cir. 1974). * * *

It, therefore, appears well established that until a variance is sanctioned by the Administrator, any source operating in contravention of a federally approved implementation plan under the Clean Air Act is subject to an enforcement proceeding. *Natural Resources Defense Council, Inc. v. EPA,* 478 F.2d 875, 886-88 (1st Cir. 1973). Accordingly, defendant's motion to dismiss the claims based upon Rule 203(g) and 202 is denied. So ordered.

# PEOPLE v. CELOTEX CORP.

516 F.Supp. 716 (C.D. Ill. 1981)

ROBERT D. MORGAN, Chief Judge.

This is a civil suit seeking enforcement of several provisions of the Federal Clean Air Act of 1977 and the Illinois state implementation plan (SIP) which was submitted under the Act. Plaintiff State of Illinois sued under 42 U.S.C. § 7604 (State complaint) seeking enforcement in a citizen suit. Plaintiff United States of America sued under 42 U.S.C. § 7413 (Federal complaint), the federal enforcement mechanism. This court consolidated the two cases * * * .

*For the history of the Illinois SIP,* see *page 387,* supra.

Plaintiffs in this action seek to enforce portions of the Illinois SIP as part of the federal law, and the State also includes claims under the Illinois Environmental Protection Act, Ill. Rev. Stat. ch. 111 1/2 , § 1001 et seq. Both plaintiffs argue that Rules 203(g)(1)(B) and 204(c)(1)(A), while unenforceable in state courts as state law, are still enforceable in federal courts as part of the federal Clean Air Act. Basically, plaintiffs argue that the state court action was a modification of the SIP that is forbidden by 42 U.S.C. § 7410(i), thus leaving the prior regulations in place until a modification is approved by US EPA. Plaintiffs have cited in support *Illinois v. Commonwealth Edison Co.,* 490 F.Supp. 1145 (N.D. Ill. 1980), wherein the District Court allowed federal enforcement of the invalid state rules. This court has carefully considered the Northern District case but finds it cannot concur.

When the Seventh Circuit upheld USEPA's approval of the Illinois SIP, the court specifically recognized the petitioner's right to challenge the regulations in the state courts, based on procedural errors in the state administrative proceedings. This finding formed part of the basis for the court's denial of petitioner's due process claim, *Indiana & Michigan*, [509 F.2d 839, 847 (7th Cir. 1975)]. Several industries followed the cue and pursued judicial review in the state courts, with the result being that Regulations 203(g)(1)(B) and 204(c)(1)(A) were found to be invalid for the same reasons the Seventh Circuit had declined to review, i. e., technological feasibility and economic reasonableness.

It would be an anomaly, if not a denial of defendant's due process rights, to allow, at this point, full enforcement of those invalid regulations, especially by the State of Illinois, which is totally barred in its own courts. Plaintiffs have argued that unless the regulations can be enforced in federal court, polluters are totally free to continue to pollute, and the enforcers have no protection until the State of Illinois acts to repromulgate the rules. It is apparently not true, however, that a suit of this kind is the only alternative open to plaintiffs. Pursuant to 42 U.S.C. § 7410(c)(1), the Administrator of USEPA is authorized to prepare and publish regulations if a state plan is deficient and if the state fails to act to correct the deficiency. The USEPA has twice issued to Illinois notices of deficiency because of the state court decisions, 41 Fed. Reg. 32302 (August 2, 1976) and 44 Fed. Reg. 40723 (July 12, 1979), requesting the State to bring the SIP into compliance with State law. Apparently there has been no official submission by the State in response to the 1979 notice. If the USEPA Administrator has not carried out his statutory obligations, there is a method to compel his action * * * . 42 U.S.C. § 7604(a)(2).

# SIERRA CLUB v. INDIANA-
# KENTUCKY ELECTRIC CORP.

716 F.2d 1145 (7th Cir. 1983)

ROSZKOWSKI, District Judge [sitting by designation]

This consolidated appeal arises under the Clean Air Act Amendments of 1970. The issue is whether a federal court may enforce an implementation plan provision which was adopted by the state to meet federal air quality standards, subsequently was approved by the Environmental Protection Agency, but thereafter was invalidated by a court of the adopting state on state law procedural grounds. The district courts below held that such a provision is not enforceable. For the reasons herein stated, this court affirms those decisions. * * *

On April 11, 1972, the State of Indiana submitted to EPA an implementation plan that included provision APC-13, which was designed to regulate sulfur dioxide emissions. On May 31, 1972, EPA approved APC-13 in part and rejected APC-13 in part. The State of Indiana revised APC-13 to conform to EPA's objections and submitted the revised version to the EPA on September 15, 1972. The EPA accepted the revised APC-13 and revoked its prior disapproval.

A group of Indiana utilities, including one of the appellees now before us, chose to challenge APC-13 in both the federal and state courts.

The federal court challenge reached this court in 1975. In *Indiana & Michigan Electric Co. v. EPA*, 509 F.2d 839 (1975), the utilities unsuccessfully challenged the EPA Administrator's approval of the Indiana implementation plan. Among the challenges raised was a due process objection. In rejecting the claim, this court held that the procedural scheme prescribed by the Act provided "adequate opportunity for the submission of views and for judicial appeal." * * * We observed that the utilities had "a right to challenge the reasonableness of state plans in state courts, and if part of a state implementation plan is held invalid by a state court, the state would have to revise that part." * * * It was further noted, that "should the state fail [to revise the invalidated provision] * * * the Administrator must propose and promulgate a revision." * * *

As was suggested in *Indiana & Michigan Electric Co. v. EPA*, the utilities proceeded with their procedural challenges to APC-13 in state court. On November 10, 1975, the Circuit Court for Marion County held APC-13 invalid. Four years later [sic] the Indiana Court of Appeals for the Second District affirmed the Circuit Court's invalidation on the procedural ground that the state officer who presided over the hearing had failed to submit written findings to the Indiana Environmental Management Board. * * *

Despite the state court ruling, the Sierra Club brought suits to enforce APC-13 against alleged polluters * * * .

In both [of two] cases, the defendant moved to dismiss the complaints. The courts below granted the motions, essentially ruling * * * that the action[s] "seek to enforce invalid regulations."

Plaintiff, Sierra Club, now appeals the two orders of dismissal. Appellant contends that APC-13, once approved by the EPA, becomes enforceable federal law which a subsequent state court ruling may not disturb. Sierra Club essentially argues that APC-13 should continue to be enforceable until a new state implementation plan is established in its place. Otherwise, Sierra Club argues, a major loophole in the Act would open.

The appellees claim that a plan (or plan provision) invalidated in state court is unenforceable under the Act in either federal or state court. They contend that a state cannot be deemed to have submitted a plan provision when that state's own court has held that the provision was not adopted in accordance with state law. The appropriate recourse under the Act, appellees argue, is for the EPA to formulate immediately a replacement provision. * * *

The record clearly establishes that Indiana's proposed submission for the control of sulfur dioxide emissions, APC-13, was promulgated without adherence to Indiana procedural law. Because administrative actions taken without substantial compliance with applicable procedures are invalid, it is as if Indiana never submitted APC-13. Since a valid APC-13 was never submitted, EPA's adoption of APC-13 cannot be given effect since EPA approved a provision which was invalid when submitted to the agency. * * *

Federal decisions construing the Act have encouraged litigants to pursue their procedural challenges in the state courts. If it were now held that a state court ruling has no effect under the Act, the method of review held out in previous decisions would be rendered utterly meaningless. * * *

The Fourth Circuit, in *Appalachian Power Co. v. EPA*, 579 F.2d 846 (4th Cir. 1978), upheld West Virginia's revised state implementation plan over procedural objections. The Court acknowledged that "before approving a state plan, the EPA must determine that the state plan was adopted at the state level 'after reasonable notice and public hearing.'" * * * The Court held that the notice and hearing requirement was satisfied because the procedure followed "was in accordance with West Virginia law." * * * [T]he Fourth Circuit was * * * critical of the objector's failure to pursue its procedural challenges in state court, and even went so far as to suggest, in *dicta*, that the failure to pursue a state court challenge could mean the party has no standing to raise the challenge in federal court, * * * [saying] "We find persuasive the reasoning that the petitioners, by bypassing the state remedy for correction of any defect in the state proceeding, lack standing to challenge any alleged errors in those State Agency proceedings later before the EPA or this Court." * * *

If the state court procedural review afforded under the Act is to have meaning, the rulings of the state courts must be given effect. * * *

If we were to find that implementation plan provisions were enforceable despite state court invalidation of them, the state court review would be meaningless. Those who followed our pronouncements concerning the availability of state court review would find their efforts have been for naught; and the Clean Air Act would be construed to reach the inconsistent result that an implementation plan, the product of a joint federal and state effort under the same Act, would be enforceable in the courts of one level of government but not the other. * * *

We note here that Sierra Club also advances a number of other statutory arguments to establish the federal enforceability of APC-13. None of these arguments [has] merit.

Sierra Club argues that, once the EPA adopts a state implementation plan, that plan becomes federal law and only the federal government may alter that law. Sierra Club points out that [section 307(b)(1)] provides that an approved plan may be invalidated only in the appropriate federal court of appeals. This assumes, however, that the plan is adopted initially in accordance with the Act. The state-federal partnership fashioned under the Act gave a place to the states and their reviewing courts in the initial plan formulation. The state governmental bodies are entitled to review the procedures employed to adopt a state implementation plan. Once a plan is adopted by the state and it *withstands any subsequent procedural challenge*, then [section 307(b)(1)] provides that invalidation may occur only in the federal appellate courts. Any other interpretation would destroy the meaningfulness of the review this circuit and others have held would be available in the state courts.

Sierra Club next contends that the ruling in the Indiana Appellate Court amounted to a plan revision or modification by the State. Appellant correctly observes that modifications or revisions must be approved by the EPA to become effective. *See* [section 110(a)(3)(A)]. * * *

The proceeding before the Indiana courts was not a revision or a modification of a plan. Modification or revision assumes the existence of a valid plan in the first place. The Indiana Court ruled that a valid plan never existed, for there were procedural defects which invalidated the plan at its inception. The state court proceedings therefore are not modifications or revisions.

This Circuit has expressly held that state court invalidation of an original plan provision for procedural defects does not constitute a revision of the plan. * * *

In some ways, Sierra Club tacitly acknowledges that the state court ruling serves to invalidate APC-13. * * * [It] chose to spend a great deal of its time on the alternative argument that this court should at least construe the Act to allow the APC-13 to continue in effect until an alternative provision is devised. * * *

Sierra Club argues that if a state court invalidation of a plan provision is given immediate effect, then the EPA will never be entirely sure that a plan drafted at the state level is firmly in place until all state level challenges have been pursued to their bitter and protracted end.

Our examination shows that Congress * * * was aware of the risk that some states, for any number of reasons, might fail to promulgate an implementation plan which was proper in all respects. The remedy Congress built into the Act in the event of a state level failure is for the EPA to demand an immediate state replacement or to promulgate its own implementation plan (or appropriate provision) for the state. This is the remedy Congress foresaw for state inaction or ineffectiveness. The Sierra Club's proposed solution, that the invalid provision be deemed enforceable until a new plan is established, finds no support in the Act's terms or legislative history. * * *

Thus, while Congress did not explicitly foresee the possibility of a successful state court challenge *after* an implementation plan was approved by EPA, it did rather clearly embrace the general proposition that federal action was intended to remedy *any* problem with a state implementation plan. * * *

While the court acknowledges that its ruling is in some ways a set-back to environmental protection, it does not agree that years will pass before Indiana has an acceptable and workable implementation plan. * * * The EPA may submit APC-13 in its current form for proper notice and hearing and comment in Indiana, if it so desires.[11] The same basic framework may be appropriate once proper administrative proceedings have been held.

For these reasons, the district courts are *affirmed.*

## UNITED STATES v. FORD MOTOR CO.

814 F.2d 1099 (6th Cir.), *cert. denied,* 484 U.S. 822 (1987)

EDWARDS, Senior Circuit Judge

In this case Ford Motor Company and the United States are litigating a question fundamental to the authority of the federal government to control the emission of air pollutants within the boundaries of a particular state.

The pollutants at issue are volatile organic compounds which are the principal contributors to ambient ozone. The site of this dispute is a Fort Motor Company plant located in Mount Clemens, Michigan. This factory coats vinyl products with solvent-based coating and emits ambient ozone from eight production lines. * * *

The origin of this dispute is dated a decade ago. In February 1979 the EPA promulgated a combined primary and secondary national ambient air quality standard for ozone. * * * Michigan promulgated a State Implementation Plan * * * and EPA approved the SIP in 1980. Two separate legal proceedings followed. On September 26, 1984, the United States initiated the first action under section 113(b) of the Clean Air Act * * * to enforce the EPA-approved SIP. A month later, the Ford Motor Company filed suit in a Michigan state court against the Michigan Air Pollution Commission * * * [and other state agencies]. Ford sought to enjoin the state defendants from enforcing the SIP concerning which the United States had filed the first action. EPA was not a party to the state action nor was it notified of its pendency.

Ford and the state defendants * * * then negotiated a consent judgment which was entered March 18, 1985. Ford then filed a motion for summary judgment in the federal proceeding contending that the EPA-approved SIP could not be enforced because the state court consent judgment had invalidated it. * * * [T]he United States District Court * * * granted the Ford Motor Company's motion and dismissed the federal government's action. * * *

As we see the question posed by this case, it is as follows: whether a state court consent order which was entered in an action brought by the defendant (Ford) against state air pollution regulatory authorities but

---

[11] In fact, this could have been done long ago, when it first became apparent the promulgation of APC-13 may suffer from procedural defects.

not the United States or any of its agencies, and which purportedly vacated a SIP adopted under the Clean Air Act and approved by EPA, precludes federal enforcement of the previously federally-approved plan?

We believe that under the United States Clean Air Act and settled case law, the answer to this question must be "no." * * * In *Train v. NRDC*, 421 U.S. 60, 64 (1975) * * * Justice Rehnquist * * * writing for a nearly unanimous Supreme Court held:

> [A] polluter is subject to existing requirements until such time as he obtains a variance, and variances are not available under the revision authority until they have been approved by both the State and the EPA. Should either entity determine that granting the variance would prevent attainment or maintenance of national air standards, the polluter is presumably within his rights in seeking judicial review. This litigation, however, is carried out on the polluter's time, not the public's, for during its pendency the original regulations remain in effect, and the polluter's failure to comply may subject him to a variety of enforcement procedures.

The Supreme Court's conclusion in *Train* is based upon the language of the Clean Air Act, which requires revisions of SIPs to be approved by EPA before such revisions are effective. *See* [section 110(a)(3)(A) & (i)]. * * *

In the face of overwhelming authority declaring that revisions of SIPs are ineffective until approved by EPA, Ford relies principally on a Seventh Circuit decision, *Sierra Club v. Indiana-Kentucky Electric Corp.* * * * The Seventh Circuit held that federal enforcement was barred because the SIP provision was not adopted in accordance with applicable state procedures, and therefore, was an invalid plan submission to EPA. The SIP, thus, was never valid. * * *

The present suit, unlike *Sierra Club*, concerns invalidation of a SIP on technical grounds by a state court. Thus, even under the language of *Sierra Club*, such invalidation cannot be given effect, because invalidation of an EPA-approved SIP may only occur in the federal appellate courts on direct appeal from the Administrator's decision under [section 307(b)(1)], and revisions and variances of properly promulgated SIPs require EPA approval. This case, in short, does not concern a SIP found invalid on state procedural grounds by a state court, as was the case in *Sierra Club*.[1] Nor does the fact that the consent decree in this case purported to vacate and modify the SIP as of its compliance date render it void *ab initio* in the sense described in *Sierra Club*. The mere fact that state authorities, through the discovery of subsequent technical data, or otherwise, change their views on the technological or economic feasibil-

---

[1] The government indicated at oral argument that it may take the position in future litigation that *Sierra Club* was wrongly decided. Because we find *Sierra Club* readily distinguishable, we neither approve nor disapprove its conclusion that state courts may invalidate EPA-approved SIPs on state procedural grounds.

ity of a properly adopted emission limit cannot in itself render the original emission limit unenforceable. As this court has stated, "the Act clearly envisions the possibility of continuous adjustments in the basic plan by the State and the EPA. If a plan became unenforceable every time such a revision became a possibility, the entire enforcement procedure of the Clean Air Act would be crippled." * * * Instead, the original emission limit remains fully enforceable until a revision or variance is approved by both the State and EPA. * * *

State courts * * * lack the authority to invalidate EPA-approved SIPs on infeasibility grounds. * * * The Clean Air Act thus modifies the operation of the Federal Full Faith and Credit Statute, 28 U.S.C. § 1738, and determines the permissible effect of the state court judgment at issue. * * *

Ford argues that refusal to give effect to the Michigan Circuit Court judgment would violate Ford's Fifth Amendment due process rights. Ford notes that state court is the only forum available for challenging the technological and economic feasibility of SIP provisions. Ford argues that the failure to give binding effect to the feasibility determination made by the only available forum deprives it of property without a meaningful right to be heard.

Ford's contention can best be answered by noting that the Clean Air Act envisions situations where standards currently economically or technologically infeasible will nonetheless be enforced. * * * In addition, we note that meaningful opportunities for raising claims of technological and economical infeasibility have been provided by the Act. * * * While the attainment of national standards remains paramount, * * * emission sources such as Ford are offered the opportunity to have significant input on the setting of emission limits through the appropriate voicing of feasibility concerns. Ford, for example, participated in the state's promulgation of the SIP in 1979 and in EPA's approval of the SIP in 1980.

Ford's subsequent challenge to the SIP on feasibility grounds in the state court has resulted in the state proposing a revision of the SIP to EPA for approval. Thus the state court judgment, while not binding on EPA, is significant, because it has effected the first step in the revision process: the proposal of a revision to EPA by the state.

Furthermore, technical infeasibility coupled with good faith efforts can be considered by the district court as a factor mitigating against the imposition of monetary penalties in the enforcement action. * * *

The judgment of the District Court is reversed * * * .

### Notes and Questions

1. Can *Commonwealth Edison* and *Ford Motor* be harmonized with the *Sierra Club* and *Celotex* cases? Why or why not?

2.   State courts may vacate a federally-approved SIP on several state law grounds. Perhaps the most common situation is one in which the state agency responsible for drafting and promulgating the SIP is alleged to have violated state procedural requirements. In the *Sierra Club* case, for example, the state and federal courts effectively concluded that a procedural defect left Indiana without a crucial component of its SIP (APC-13) for more eleven years. What was that procedural defect? Does it make sense to conclude that this flaw left Indiana without an $SO_2$ standard for more than a decade?

3.   Can successful state court challenges to federally-approved SIPs delay enforcement forever? Does the language of CAA § 110(c)(1)—mandating EPA promulgation of a FIP—adequately reach the facts of cases in which the state's "key" has been turned to the off position by a state reviewing court? Does the language of § 110(k)(5) provide a better fit?

4.   A vital feature of the Clean Air Act is that state officials cannot grant variances from federally-approved SIP requirements. We explored this feature in the Questions following the *Union Electric* opinion, at page 386, *supra*. Do the facts of the *Ford Motor* case suggest an alternative ploy that could be used by cooperative state officials to get around this prohibition? Suppose state officials encourage an industry suit challenging a SIP on procedural grounds, and then default in the lawsuit (or enter into a consent decree conceding the SIPs invalidity). Should this method of turning off the state's "key" preclude SIP enforcement by the federal government? Does CAA § 110(c)(1) provide an effective remedy for such a situation? Why or why not?

5.   We have seen that federally-approved SIPs may be struck down in state court on procedural grounds. In some states, SIPs are also vulnerable to the claim that the SIP-drafting agency has violated substantive limits on its powers. The most intriguing substantive limits prohibit the promulgation of state environmental standards more stringent than those specified or required by federal law. Since 1987, 19 states have enacted at least one statute constraining the authority of state agencies in this manner. *See* Jerome M. Organ, *Limitations on State Agency Authority to Adopt Environmental Standards More Stringent than Federal Standards: Policy Considerations and Interpretive Problems*, 54 Md. L. Rev. 1373, 1376 n. 13 (1995). For example, a South Dakota statute prohibits promulgation of an environmental regulation "more stringent than any corresponding federal law, rule, or regulation governing an essentially similar subject or issue." S.D. Codified Laws Ann. § 1-40-4.1 (1998). Do you foresee any difficulties in applying the language of the South Dakota statute to the judicial review of specific SIP provisions? Why or why not? How do such statutes relate to the "outside-the-SIP" argument made by the *Amici* in the *Union Electric* case, discussed at page 387, *supra*?

## 4.  COMPLIANCE ORDERS

So far, all of the solutions that we have examined to Union Electric's problem require the cooperation of state authorities—the state agencies, the Governor, or its courts. One remaining solution could be invoked by the EPA acting alone: issuance of a "compliance order" under § 113. Prior to the 1977 amendments, the EPA had developed a practice of issuing compliance orders under § 113(a) that extended the final deadline for compliance far out into the future. These orders became an escape valve in the SIP system, and environmental groups lost no time in branding them as lawless variances.

In 1977, Congress added a new § 113(d), legitimizing "Delayed Compliance Orders" (DCOs), but heavily circumscribing their use. Most significant was the condition set forth in § 113(d)(1)(E): the addressee of a DCO (if it is a "major" stationary source) must pay a "noncompliance penalty" under § 120. We will examine § 120 later, but it amounts to a civil penalty for any period of noncompliance and is designed to make the stationary source wish that it had installed controls. The idea is that the source will pay in penalties the money saved by delaying installation of controls.

The DCO provision of § 113(d) was repealed by the 1990 amendments, but § 113(a) continues to authorize compliance orders, which may now forgive noncompliance for no more than one year. See § 113(a)(4). The mandatory application of § 120 noncompliance penalties has been deleted.

## 5. INFEASIBILITY: A SECOND LOOK

# DEPARTMENT OF ENVIRONMENTAL RESOURCES v. PENNSYLVANIA POWER CO.

### 490 Pa. 399, 416 A.2d 995 (1980)

The Pennsylvania Power Company (PPC), appellee herein, generates and distributes electricity in the western portion of this Commonwealth. The PPC was originally ordered by the Pennsylvania Department of Health, predecessor in interest to the Department of Environmental Resources (DER), to limit its emission of particulate matter from its electrical generating station in Lawrence County, Pennsylvania, in order to comply with the particulate collection efficiency established by Regulation V. The pollutants were emitted from the five coal powered boilers which supplied the power for the generators. That Order was affirmed on appeal by the Pennsylvania Air Pollution Commission on January 11, 1971.

The PPC, however, failed to comply and the DER, on January 12, 1972, filed a complaint in equity in the Common Pleas Court of Lawrence County, seeking judicial enforcement of the January 1971 Order. On January 27, 1972, more stringent particulate matter regulations and new controls were placed on sulfur dioxide ($SO_2$) emissions. Cognizant of these changes, the Lawrence County Court ordered the PPC to file a new plan for compliance with the new standards. No appeal from this [September 1972] order was taken * * * .

After a full hearing, the lower court found that the PPC was not in contempt of the September 1972 Order in that it was "technically impossible" to limit its SO$_2$ emissions. This finding was upheld on appeal to the Commonwealth Court, 12 Pa. Commw. Ct. 212, 316 A.2d 96 (1974) and affirmed by this Court, 461 Pa. 675, 337 A.2d 823 (1975).

The DER then pursued the civil penalty petition pending before the EHB [Environmental Hearing Board]. After a full evidentiary hearing, the EHB assessed civil penalties against the PPC for violations of the regulations. * * *

The question to be addressed is whether Section 9.1 of APCA, 35 P.S. § 4009.1, is unconstitutional to the extent that it authorized the EHB, pursuant to a DER request, to assess civil penalties for the violation of an air pollution regulation with which present technology renders compliance impossible. Prior to arriving at an answer as to the constitutionality of the civil penalty provision, it is necessary to determine whether the statute confers the authority upon the DER to set air quality standards which are "technologically impossible" at the time of the promulgation of the standard. * * *

In the instances specified, whether technological impossibility will be recognized as a defense or the SIP air quality standards steadfastly adhered to, appears to be a matter Congress left solely to the State's discretion so long as the regional ambient air quality standards are met. * * *

Prior decisions in this jurisdiction evidence a very limited acceptance of the impossibility defense. In this Court's previous encounter with this case, the claim of technological impossibility was recognized as a defense. 461 Pa. 675, 337 A.2d 823 (1975). That holding, however, is properly limited to contempt proceedings. * * * The fact that technological impossibility provides insulation to a polluter in an action for contempt, does not prevent the Commonwealth from devising means to force technological advancements to eliminate the pollution, if the activity is to be permitted to continue. The imposition of the civil penalties, with which we are here concerned, was not imposed as punishment for a willful disregard of an agency or court order, but rather as an incentive to urge the development of procedures that will eventually eliminate the pollutant. * * *

Proceeding from the premise that the state may force the termination of an industrial activity for noncompliance with technologically impossible standards, we now consider the judgment of the Commonwealth Court that the imposition of civil penalties for such conduct is unconstitutional. * * *

In *Bortz* [*Coal Co. v. Commonwealth*, 2 Pa. Commw. Ct. 441, 279 A.2d 388 (1971)], the court indicated that the coke producing company's claim that there was no practical method for compliance with the Department of Health's particulate matter emission standards and that, therefore, the industry would be forced out of business, was inconse-

quential if the evidence proved a violation. * * * On appeal after the remand * * * the court affirmed the Order of the Board requiring the
company to operate its coke ovens in accordance with the air quality
standards or close down. * * *

Thus Pennsylvania has recognized that technological impossibility
will not provide a license to continue in an industrial activity which
falls below the designated air quality standards. This judgment is con-
summate with the clearly expressed congressional intent, and its constitutional propriety has been recognized by the U.S. Supreme Court.
*Union Electric Co. v. EPA, supra.* * * *

Certainly, the establishment of sulfur dioxide emission levels, by
seeking to reduce air pollution, serves the legitimate state interest of
maintaining the health of the citizenry of this Commonwealth.

As we have stated, in order to achieve that end, the state could
have ordered closure of any facility that fails to comply with the promulgated emissions standards. By adopting a lesser sanction, imposition
of civil penalties, the state allows the facility, PPC, to continue in business, giving it an opportunity to devise new technologies to reduce the
sulfur dioxide emissions, spurred on by the desire to avoid the continued payment of fines. In this way, the assessment of civil penalties is
not only an amicable accommodation, striking a proper balance between the extremes of permitting unbridled pollution and a complete
shutdown of the polluter industry, but it provides the spark to ignite
the engine for technological change in the industry. Further, the monies collected are not merely utilized to operate the DER, but rather are
funneled directly into the Commonwealth Clean Air Fund which is specifically earmarked for the "elimination of air pollution." 35 P.S.
§ 4009.2, see 25 Pa Code § 143.1 "Technology Forcing," by the imposition of civil penalties, in this instance is reasonably related to the reduction of pollution in this state and, therefore, cannot be said to violate the constitutional protection of the PPC's property interests. * * *

## E. NEW VEHICLES

## 1. INTRODUCTION TO MOBILE SOURCE POLLUTION

Up to this point, we have studied almost exclusively those portions
of the Clean Air Act that are designed to control the emission of a handful of pollutants from *stationary* sources. We now turn our attention to
the portions of the Clean Air Act scheme that are addressed to *mobile*
sources. The mobile source provisions can be further subdivided into
four components: (1) emission limitations for *new* internal combustion
vehicles; (2) efforts to curb emissions from internal combustion vehicles
while *in use*; (3) provisions requiring alteration of fuel formulations;
and (4) strategies to spur the development and adoption of radically
new technologies such as "clean fuel vehicles" running on natural gas,
electricity, and the like. The first two components have dominated

Clean Air Act efforts to date. The 1990 amendments bring about a new focus on components three and four.

The American love affair with the automobile is legendary. Paul Hawken, in *The Ecology of Commerce* (1994), notes a paradox in the apparent cheapness of our favorite consumer good:

> Author Ivan Illich has pointed out that the average American is involved with his or her automobile—working in order to buy it, actually driving it, getting it repaired, and so on—for sixteen hundred hours a year. This means when all car mileage in a given year is divided by the time spent supporting the car, the average car owner is traveling at an average speed of five miles per hour. To attain the speed of a bicycle, we are devastating our cities, air, lungs, and lives, while bringing on the threat of global warming.

*Id.* at 13-14.

We begin our analysis of mobile source pollution by briefly considering the nature of the problem.

## H.R. REP. NO. 490
### 101st Cong., 2d Sess. 198-99, 202-03, 274, 277-81 (1990)

Ozone ($O_3$) is a photochemical oxidant and a highly reactive gas that is one of the primary constituents of smog. Chemically, ozone is a form of oxygen composed of three atoms, as compared to oxygen gas which has two atoms. The three atom arrangement is by nature unstable. In a process known as "oxidation," the extra oxygen atom * * * has an aggressive tendency to react with an extremely wide variety of substances.

The oxidation reaction is extremely corrosive. This reaction causes metals to rust; it also cracks and fades paints, dyes and rubber products. * * *

Ninety percent of the ozone breathed into the lung is never exhaled. Instead, the ozone molecules react with sensitive lung tissues, irritating and inflaming the lungs. This can cause a host of negative health consequences * * * .

These negative effects have been observed in healthy, exercising individuals at concentrations below the leve[l] of the Federal health standard. * * * Vigorous exercise, which leads to heavier breathing, is likely to increase the health impacts of exposure to ozone. The problem is exacerbated because the warm sunny conditions most conducive to ozone formation are also most attractive for outdoor activity.

Some scientific evidence indicates that over the long term, repeated exposure to ozone pollution may scar lung tissues permanently * * * in effect, prematurely aging the respiratory system. * * *

Ozone is not emitted directly from smokestacks, tailpipes, or other pollution sources. Instead, it is a "secondary pollutant," formed from a large group of hydrocarbon pollutants called "VOCs" [volatile organic compounds][d] in conjunction with $NO_x$ [oxides of nitrogen] emissions. These compounds are released into the air by motor vehicles, factories, and numerous smaller sources. The pollutant mix cooks in the sun, producing ozone through a complex chain of reactions. The hotter the temperatures, the greater the formation of ozone. * * *

The two major sources of the ozone precursors (VOCs and $NO_x$) are motor vehicles and industry. OTA [the Office of Technology Assessment] has estimated that in 1985 the most important sources of VOC emissions were "mobile sources" ( * * * which release about 50 percent of national VOC emissions), organic solvent evaporation from stationary sources such as dry cleaners, printers, and paint shops (30 percent), and home fuel combustion (12 percent). (Home fuel combustion, however, tends to take place in cold weather, and not during ozone season.)

In many urban areas, transportation sources actually account for a larger percentage of the VOC emissions, over 50 percent, because of the high concentration of motor vehicles in city centers, and the relative absence of heavy industry. OTA also states * * *

> VOC emissions from highway vehicles are projected to decline by about 25 percent between 1985 and 1999. Stationary source emissions, on the other hand, are forecast to increase steadily between 1985 and 2004, showing a 10-percent increase by 1994 and a 23-percent increase by 2004, over 1985 levels. Growth of small (less than 50 ton-per-year) stationary VOC source emissions is one of the most important reasons why overall VOC emissions are not expected to decline more rapidly in the earlier years and why total emissions may show a net *increase* after 1999. This source category effectively offsets much of the emissions reductions realized from highway vehicles.

Thus, OTA has concluded that all of the different types of sources of VOC pollution must be controlled if America's cities are to achieve the ozone standard. The Committee agrees.

The other major ozone precursor is [nitric] oxides ($NO_x$), which are also a major contributor to acid rain. $NO_x$ is produced in all fossil fuel combustion reactions. The principal sources of $NO_x$ emissions are mobile sources, which, according to OTA, account for about 35 percent of the $NO_x$ inventory, electric utilities burning fossil fuels (35 percent), and industrial fuel consumption (12 percent). $NO_x$ emissions from natural sources are "negligible."

Control of $NO_x$ is important to the effort to reduce levels in Southern California, where VOC-only emission reduction strategies failed to lower ozone levels, while a combined program of VOC and $NO_x$ reductions has provided significant gains. * * *

Nationally, mobile sources, including older vehicles are * * * responsible for roughly 40-45 percent of all VOC [volatile organic com-

---

[d] *Ed.*—Volatile organic compounds are *defined by listing* in 40 C.F.R. § 51.100(s) (1999).

pound] emissions and 45 percent of NO$_x$ [oxides of nitrogen] emissions. They are responsible for approximately two-thirds of CO [carbon monoxide] pollution * * * .

Although cars and trucks are best know[n] for their VOC, NO$_x$, and CO emissions, there are other compounds emitted through the combustion of fuels and some are toxic. * * *

There are four principal toxic emissions from motor vehicles that stem from diesel and gasoline fuel. They are: polycyclic organic matter (POM), including exhaust particulates, 1,3-butadiene, benzene, and formaldehyde.

Diesel particulates form from incomplete combustion of diesel fuel. The particulates have a carbon core with hundreds of absorbed organic compounds onto which bits of fuel, lubricants, and combustion products are absorbed. The particles' small diameters (90 percent are less than 1 micron) mean that they can be inhaled and deposited deep within the lungs.

Although gasoline powered vehicles emit far less particulate matter than diesel powered vehicles on a grams per mile basis (30 to 100 times less), in the aggregate they may pose toxicity problems similar to diesel particulates.

Next to emissions of diesel and gasoline particulates, emissions of 1,3-butadiene from mobile sources cause the greatest aggregate health threat * * * . Butadiene is one of the most potent organic carcinogens— and mobile sources are by far the greatest single source of the pollutant. * * *

Motor vehicles, through the combustion of fuels, are also the major source of benzene emissions nationally, emitting 85 percent of the national inventory. * * * Benzene emissions from vehicles cause leukemia and other forms of cancer—up to 10 percent of the motor vehicle cancer cases each year * * * .

Formaldehyde is directly emitted in the exhaust of both gasoline and diesel vehicles. It also forms in the atmosphere as a result of photochemical reactions involving other motor vehicle exhaust or evaporative emissions. Direct formaldehyde emissions from motor vehicles amount to approximately 35 percent of the national inventory, although in some regions the motor vehicle contribution can be much greater (60 percent in California, for example). Formaldehyde exhaust emissions can cause cancer, as well as acute adverse health effects, including eye, nose, and skin irritation, headaches, and nausea.

Motor vehicles also emit from exhausts and brakes, other toxic substances, including acetaldehyde, asbestos, cadmium, and ethylene dibromide. Collectively, these other toxic emissions may account for 5 percent of the total motor vehicle cancers * * * . Some of these, like asbestos, are being phased out. * * *

In the absence of new standards, the turnover of the existing fleet of vehicles will reduce emissions from highway vehicles because cleaner new vehicles will replace older vehicles. However, * * * emissions will still increase * * * .

The best estimates are that in comparison to today's levels—and in the absence of any new standards—VOC exhaust emissions from highway vehicles * * * will drop about 30 percent by the late 1990s and then turn upwards. The level of future emission increases will ultimately depend on overall growth in vehicle miles traveled (VMT) because the Act's emission standards are set on the basis of grams per mile. The more miles the public travels * * * the more grams in total are emitted nationwide. * * *

$NO_x$ and CO exhaust will follow a similar pattern without new controls, but with fewer emission reductions. By the late 1990s, for example, $NO_x$ emissions from highway vehicles should drop about 15 percent and then turn upwards. At VMT growth of 2.5 percent $NO_x$ emissions would exceed today's levels shortly after 2005. * * *

In general, EPA has not regulated emission of toxic substances by motor vehicles or fuels directly, but * * * many of the toxics are reduced principally as a direct consequence of the HC standard. For example, benzene, butadiene, and formaldehyde are types of hydrocarbons. As a result, they are controlled, at least in part, by tailpipe standards limiting exhaust emissions of hydrocarbons.

In some instances, however, controls on criteria pollutants (HC, CO, $NO_2$ [nitrogen dioxide], TSP [total suspended particulates], PM-10 [particles less than 10 microns in diameter]) have aggravated problems of toxic emissions. For instance, the rules phasing down the lead content in gasoline resulted in increases in other ingredients, such as benzene, to achieve the same octane performance level.

There is no single approach that can eliminate the pollution from the broad range of mobile sources. Rather, achieving significant reductions in VOC, $NO_x$, CO, and toxic emissions requires using a host of measures, including tighter tailpipe standards, enhanced I/M [inspection and maintenance] programs, increasing anti-tampering measures, controls on fuel volatility, encouragement of oxygenated fuels, controls on evaporative emissions and running losses, and controls of nonroad vehicles and engines.

In the long run, widespread use of clean-burning alternative fuels will be necessary to clean up the most polluted cities. * * *

## 2. NEW VEHICLE EMISSION LIMITATIONS

Since 1970, the Clean Air Act has contained extensive provisions addressing the emission of various pollutants from mobile sources—primarily "light-duty vehicles" (passenger cars), "heavy-duty vehicles" (trucks and buses), motorcycles, and aircraft. The basic theme of the

1970 amendments was that, for passenger cars, emissions of hydrocarbons (HC) and carbon monoxide (CO) were to be reduced by at least 90 percent from 1970 levels by 1975, and that similar reductions must be achieved for nitrogen oxide (NOx) emissions by 1976. Senator Muskie acknowledged that the 90 percent reduction requirements were imposed by the 1970 amendments even though: (1) technology was not available to meet the requirements; (2) lawmakers did not know whether such technology could be developed by the deadlines (or ever); and (3) no one could predict the costs of such technology. *See* 116 Cong. Rec. 32902, 32905-06 (1970).

From 1970 to 1990, the original standards and deadlines were the subject of repeated administrative and legislative postponements and modifications. The deadlines were statutorily extended by the 1977 amendments to 1980 (hydrocarbons and carbon monoxide) and 1981 (NOx), and the NOx emission standard was simultaneously relaxed to permit emissions significantly in excess of what would have been accomplished by a true 90 percent reduction.

The passenger car emission standards, expressed as grams per mile, are depicted in Table 9-2.[1] Diesel passenger cars must also meet particulate standards of 0.6 grams per mile for 1982-1986 model years and 0.2 grams per mile for 1987 and subsequent model years.

**Table 9-2**
Light Duty Vehicle Emission Standards
(grams per mile)

| Model Year | HC | CO | NO$_x$ |
|---|---|---|---|
| 1970-1971 | 4.0 | 34 | 3.4 |
| 1972 | 3.0 | 30 | 3.4 |
| 1973-1974 | 3.0 | 30 | 3.1 |
| 1975 | 1.4 | 15 | 3.1 |
| 1976-1979 | 1.4 | 15 | 2.0 |
| 1980 | .41 | 7.0 | 2.0 |
| 1981 | .41 | 3.4 | 2.0 |
| 1982-94 | .41 | 3.4 | 1.0 |
| 1994- (short useful life) | .25 | 3.4 | 0.4 |
| 1994- (long useful life) | .31 | 4.2 | 0.6 |

Section 116 provides that nothing in the Clean Air Act shall preclude each state from enforcing its own, more stringent standards. For obvious reasons, however, Congress concluded that auto manufacturers could not reasonably be required to comply with varying new car emission standards. Accordingly, the federal new motor vehicle emission

---

[1] Pre-1994 values have been adapted from 1 William H. Rodgers, Environmental Law: Air and Water § 3.26 at 407-08 nn.37-39 (1986). Values for 1994 and subsequent model years are taken from John-Mark Stensvaag & Craig N. Oren, Clean Air Act: Law and Practice § 8.5, Table 8.1 (1995).

standards are accompanied by a preemption provision. The Administrator may waive preemption for California. *See* CAA § 209(b). Moreover, any state may adopt approved California standards if necessary to achieve compliance with the national ambient air quality standards.

The basic enforcement mechanism standing behind the motor vehicle emission standards is the engine certification program. The statute prohibits the sale by any manufacturer (or importation by anyone) of any new motor vehicle or engine which is not covered by a "certificate of conformity." A certificate may be issued by the Administrator if she determines, following tests on engine prototypes, that the vehicle or engine "conforms with" the emission standards and implementing regulations. The statute further authorizes assembly-line testing to assure that production vehicles also conform to the emission standards. If the Administrator discovers that vehicles covered by a certificate of conformity do not, in fact, conform to the emission standards, he or she may revoke the certificate in whole or in part.

The sale by a manufacturer (or importation by anyone else) of a vehicle or engine *not* covered by a certificate of conformity is a violation of the Clean Air Act, subject to a civil penalty of not more than $25,000 per vehicle. Moreover, if the Administrator discovers that "a substantial number of any class or category of vehicles or engines, although properly maintained and used, do not conform" to the emission standards once they have been placed into actual use and during their "useful life," she must order a recall by issuing a formal notice to the manufacturer that it must remedy the nonconformity at its own expense.

Any driver recognizes that emission control systems may interfere with performance and fuel economy; accordingly, the temptation to sabotage emission controls is apparently irresistible. Prior to 1990, therefore, the statute made it unlawful for: (1) "any person to remove or render inoperative" emission control devices *prior* to sale and delivery; (2) "any manufacturer or dealer *knowingly* to remove or render inoperative such device" *after* sale to the ultimate purchaser; and (3) "any person engaged in the business of repairing, servicing, selling, leasing, or trading motor vehicles or * * * engines, or who operates a fleet of motor vehicles, *knowingly* to remove or render inoperative any [emission control] device * * * ." Scholars noted that these anti-tampering provisions contained significant gaps. Accordingly, § 203(a)(3)(A), added by the 1990 Amendments, now makes it unlawful for "*any* person knowingly to remove or render inoperative any [pollution control] device or element of design after * * * sale and delivery to the ultimate purchaser." Subsection (B) of the new provision also makes it unlawful for any person to manufacture, sell, offer to sell, or install so-called "defeat devices"—parts or components designed to bypass, defeat, or render inoperative pollution control features that have been included in the vehicle to comply with the Clean Air Act.

As a final spur to assure that a given vehicle actually conforms during its "useful life," the statute provides that the manufacturer must issue two warranties in connection with the emission control system. First, the manufacturer must warrant that the vehicle or engine is "designed, built, and equipped so as to conform" with the emission standards and "free from defects * * * which [might] cause such vehicle or engine to fail to conform * * * for its useful life." CAA § 207(a)(1). This design and construction warranty makes no promises about actual emission levels. Second, the statute directs the EPA to issue regulations effectively requiring manufacturers to warrant that the emission control system will not fail to conform to the emission *standards* during its useful life, as long as the vehicle or engine is maintained and operated properly. CAA § 207(b)(2). This provision contemplates a performance warranty. If the vehicle's owner or operator must "bear any penalty or other sanction" due to nonconformity, under state or federal law, the manufacturer must remedy the nonconformity at its expense.

The contents of fuels and fuel additives obviously play an important role in the creation of motor vehicle air pollutants. Accordingly, the Act has long provided that the Administrator may regulate fuels and additives. *See* CAA § 211. The regulatory power is based on two concerns: (1) protection of public health and welfare; and (2) preserving the integrity and performance of pollution control devices. The Administrator may "control or prohibit the manufacture, introduction into commerce, offering for sale, or sale of any fuel or fuel additive for use in a motor vehicle or * * * engine" to further either of these purposes. CAA § 211(c)(1). The EPA has regulated the lead content of gasoline for the purpose of protecting catalytic converters.

If the Administrator "designates" a fuel or additive, no manufacturer or processor may sell or introduce it into commerce unless the Administrator has "registered" the fuel or additive. Prior to registering fuels and additives, the EPA must obtain from the manufacturer information about the chemical composition and concentration in the fuel of any additive, and may require testing to determine any public health effects of using such fuel or additive as well as the furnishing of additional information. Registration is thus dependent solely upon submission of information, not upon any demonstration that use of the fuel or additive is compatible with public health and welfare.

Somewhat predictably, the congressional attempt to force the creation of new technology under the threat of shutting down the auto industry led to a long-running game of "chicken," in which American auto manufacturers repeatedly petitioned for postponements of the statutory deadlines (pleading that they could not meet the requirements) and the EPA Administrator, reviewing courts, and Congress attempted to assess whether the manufacturers were bluffing. Invariably, the federal government backed down and provided further time to the industry. A brief history of these developments is set forth in *Chrysler Corp. v. EPA*, at page 415, *infra*.

Delays on the technology-forcing front represent only one developmental aspect of the new automobile provisions. Many other components of the program, such as testing protocols, warranty provisions, and enforcement sanctions, have assumed greater importance as the deadline issue has receded.

## 3. ENFORCEMENT MECHANISMS

### ROBERT A. WEISSMAN, MATTHEW A. LOW & NORMAN D. SHUTLER, REGULATION OF MOTOR VEHICLES AND FUELS

in 2 Law of Environmental Protection § 11.07 (Sheldon M. Novick, ed. 1998)

In addition to the standard setting process, Title II establishes a number of enforcement mechanisms by which the Administrator * * * can assure compliance with emission standards * * * . The statutory scheme empowers the Administrator to review the emissions performance of vehicles at various stages: prototype, assembly line, and in-use. The major enforcement mechanisms are prototype certification under § 206(a), assembly line testing under § 206(b), and recall under § 207(c). Other mechanisms are warranty enforcement under §§ 207(a) and 207(b), and enforcement of the prohibited acts provision of § 203. * * *

#### CERTIFICATION OF PROTOTYPES

Section 206(a) directs EPA to require manufacturers to certify their vehicles. * * * EPA has created an extensive program through promulgation of regulations and issuance of manufacturer's advisory circulars. * * *

For light-duty vehicles, a manufacturer is required to subject a prototype representing an "engine family" to a mileage accumulation of 50,000 miles in accordance with an approved mileage accumulation procedure. At each 5,000 mile interval, the vehicle is tested in accordance with the Federal Test Procedure (FTP). These tests are relied upon to establish an emissions deterioration factor for the engine family. Production prototypes of differing configurations, but within the same family, are then tested at 4,000 miles and emission deterioration factors are applied to these results. If the production prototype emissions, with the deterioration factor applied, are under the standards at 50,000 miles, the Agency issues a certificate of conformity. * * * For parts which reasonably could be expected to affect emission controls, use of parts different from those specified in the application (a "misbuild") is sufficient to support a finding that a vehicle is not covered by the certificate. This is true whether or not the emission performance of the vehicle *actually* is affected. * * *

While certification is the predominant enforcement mechanism relied upon in the early 1970s, it became evident that certification of prototype designs was not necessarily a good barometer of the emissions performance of in-use production vehicles. The conditions of certification mileage accumulation involve use of standard fuels, trained drivers, and expert maintenance, and fail to reflect the effects of time, weather, and in-use road conditions. Thus * * * the Agency shifted emphasis to assembling line and in-use enforcement programs in the late 1970s.

### Production Line Testing

Section 206(b) expressly authorizes EPA to test actual production vehicles on the assembly line to determine whether they are conforming to the standards. If a prescribed percentage of vehicles do not conform to standards, EPA may revoke or suspend the certificate, thereby prohibiting the manufacturer from introducing the line off vehicles into commerce. * * *

Known as the Selective Enforcement Auditing (SEA) program, EPA typically issues under it a test order to a manufacturer. EPA inspectors then visit the manufacturer's assembling line and test facility to observe the selection of vehicles and the conduct of the tests. Vehicles are selected and tested according to a statistical scheme to determine, with a prescribed degree of confidence, whether EPA's assembly line criteria are met.

Section 206(b) does not specify the percentage of vehicles exceeding emissions or the average emissions level which will give rise to a suspension or revocation order. After significant debate, EPA adopted a 40 percent Acceptable Quality Level (AQL); unless the Agency has a high degree of confidence that the failure rate of any class is greater than 40 percent, the class "passes" the assembly line test. Given statistical variability, a 40 percent AQL approximates a requirement that the average vehicle meets standards. In adoption this requirement, however, the Agency expressly stated that it was not adopting "averaging" for purposes of assessing in-use compliance. * * *

### In-Use Vehicle Compliance

Perhaps the most visible EPA Title II enforcement program is the recall program. Section 207(c) empowers the Administrator to order recall of any class of vehicles if a determination is made that a substantial number, although properly maintained and used, do not conform with standards when in use throughout their useful life. * * *

[EPA] has put in place comprehensive surveillance and confirmatory testing programs designed to detect emission problems. Typically, EPA will target a class of vehicles for surveillance testing. The Agency will procure a sample of five or ten vehicles, adjust the vehicles to the manufacturer's recommended specifications and conduct FTP tests. If the surveillance testing reveals a high noncompliance rate for any of the standards, EPA will notify the manufacturer of the results and schedule the class for confirmatory testing. In the confirmatory testing program, the Agency implements a rigorous vehicle selection process designed to produce a random, unbiased sample of properly maintained vehicles which will support statistical inferences regarding emission levels. This testing then becomes the basis for an Agency determination that the class is in nonconformity and that an order be issued to the manufacturer to submit a plan to remedy the nonconformity.

# MATTHEW L. WALD, PUTTING CAR-EXHAUST TESTS ON THE ROAD TO REALITY

### N.Y. Times, Jan. 26, 1994, at D1 col.3

The way the Environmental Protection Agency tests the emissions of a car looks a lot more like a game in a video arcade than actual driving. The driver sits behind the wheel of a car on a treadmill and, using only the accelerator and the brake pedal, tries to keep the car on a course that scrolls by on a computer screen outside the driver's side window.

Pressing the accelerator moves a dot on the screen toward the right edge; the brake moves the line to the left. If the driver keeps the dot in the lines for the whole four-minute test, then the car has gone through a standard course and its emissions can be compared with the emissions from other vehicles and with the Federal standard.

But the 20-year-old test bears about as much similarity to the real world of driving a car as the computer game "Flight Simulator" bears to flying an airplane. Which may be why air quality has improved only slowly since the 1970's—even though auto makers boast that EPA tests show that tailpipe emissions of hydrocarbons and carbon monoxide are down more than 90 percent since then and nitrogen oxides are down more than 75 percent.

### MISSING DEADLINES

The Clean Air Act of 1990 instructed the EPA to devise a better test. After one extension, the agency had a deadline of the end of March to comply, but it says it cannot meet that either and is seeking another extension.

The EPA acknowledges that it needs to find a better way to test emissions of new engines. "The old procedure assumes the world is flat," said John M. German, an engineer at the EPA's National Vehicle and Fuel Emissions Laboratory here, who is helping design a new test.

Not only is the EPA's world flat, but it is traversed only by automobiles that never exceed 57 miles an hour and carry precisely 300 pounds worth of passengers to destinations exactly 7.5 miles away. And when the engine is shut off, it is either left off for 10 minutes—no more, no less—or is allowed to cool overnight before restarting.

All of this idealized motoring is done on a dynamometer, a treadmill that is connected to an electric generator, with the electricity output directly proportional to the effort made by the wheels. Engineers also put a fan in front of the car's radiator, to prevent overheating. The tailpipe emissions are captured in plastic bags for later analysis.

Engineers have long suspected that the tests are not realistic, missing such nuances as sharp accelerations and decelerations and frequent cold starts for around-town errands and the like. On shorter trips, the catalytic converter and the engine do not get properly warmed up, and the engine does not have time to suck in and burn all the fumes that collect in the charcoal canister that captures evaporation when the car is not running.

But only recently, EPA officials say, has computer technology improved their ability to measure real-world conditions to the point that the problems with the official test have become glaringly apparent. In addition, as standards have become progressively tighter, Mr. German said, "what isn't on the test becomes relatively more important."

And the margin of error is not consistent. Running sample cars through a more realistic test shows that some kinds of engines emit huge amounts of pollution that go undetected at the EPA lab. But other engines show only modestly higher pollution levels. In both cases, engineers are still puzzling out why.

One thing is clear: Cars now on the road have been designed around the existing test. "The rules are: pass the test in the cheapest way possible," said Charles L. Gray Jr., director of regulatory programs and technology at the EPA.

### BEATING THE TEST

There is nothing sinister about this, agency officials say. But the result is a little like a high school student who cannot use a single four-syllable word in a sentence but knows 2,000 of them for the college entrance examination.

Auto makers avoid criticizing the EPA the way high school students are circumspect about the shortcomings of their principals. But Dennis R. Minano, vice president of General Motors for energy and environment, acknowledged that the industry designs cars to beat the test, with such cars known as "cycle beaters."

The industry is hesitant to do better voluntarily, Mr. Minano said. If the Government requires that emissions of a pollutant be reduced to, say, one gram per mile, a car maker might aim for emissions of nine-tenths gram per mile, to make sure that the cars pass. But then the regulators will turn around and say, "Aha! You can do better," Mr. Minano said, and will impose still stricter rules.

As the EPA moves toward improving its test drive, others are rushing to embrace it; beginning in 1995, several densely populated states will beef up their emissions inspections by putting ordinary cars through the test. New York, New Jersey and Connecticut will eventually use the test. Despite its shortcomings, it is far superior to current tests in which a car idles and a machine samples for hydrocarbons and carbon monoxide, but not nitrogen oxides. That will be an improvement for testing cars in use on the streets, but for testing prototypes, Mr. German said, "we need to expand the boundaries of the test, to capture more of what's going on."

Among the real-world conditions the new EPA test must provide for is the fact that today's cars have a built-in safety mechanism to prevent the catalytic converter from burning out under stress conditions, such as driving up a steep grade. The safety mechanism involves pumping extra fuel through the engine, which cools the converter—but also raises hydrocarbon emissions by a factor of 40, and carbon monoxide emissions by a factor of more than 2,000. The current EPA procedures do not test emissions under these conditions.

At present, using its much-criticized system, the EPA's Ann Arbor lab is testing the auto industry's 1996 models. For each engine type—a certain displacement, cylinder design and configuration—the fee is $24,000. * * *

## NOTE ON TEST CHEATING

In 1998, the EPA alleged that diesel truck engine manufacturers had tinkered with fuel injection computer control chips so that the systems would give abnormally low emission readings during testing procedures. *See* John H. Cushman, Jr., *Makers of Diesel Truck Engines are Under Pollution Inquiry*, N.Y. Times, Feb. 11, 1998, at A16, col. 1. On October 22, 1998, EPA announced a $1 billion settlement with seven diesel truck manufacturers. *See* 29 [Curr. Dev.] Env. Rep. (BNA) 1285 (1998). Noting that the companies had rigged engines with computerized devices designed to curb emissions during laboratory tests while significantly increasing emissions on the open road, EPA Administrator Carol Browner said: "They were cheating. It's just that simple." *Id.* Under the settlement agreement, the computer devices must be removed from trucks coming in for planned overhauls in the next several years. *See id.* The diesel engine controversy paralleled a 1995 dispute in which General Motors agreed to recall half a million cars and pay fines and costs of $45 million, in response to government charges that the company had produced Cadillacs designed to pass emission tests but violate pollution standards on the road. *See* N.Y. Times, Feb. 11, 1998, at A16, col. 1.

---

### Read the following sections of the Clean Air Act

☐ § 203(a)(1)     ☐ § 205(a)     ☐ § 206(b)(2)(A)(i)

☐ § 206(g)     ☐ § 207(a)(1)     ☐ § 207(b)     ☐ § 207(c)(1)

---

### Question

Assume that assembly line testing indicates that thousands of new, *unsold* cars have flunked the emission standards. What is supposed to happen when the EPA receives these test results? *See* CAA § 206(b)(2)(A)(i). Consider the following news item.

## FORD HALTS MICHIGAN PLANT PRODUCTION AFTER 1980 BRONCOS FAIL EPA AUDIT

11 [Curr. Dev.] Env. Rep. (BNA) 52 (1980)

The [EPA] suspended the certificate of conformity April 16 for vehicles built at the Ford Motor Company's Michigan truck plant after 1980 model Broncos failed an emissions audit.

Under the selective enforcement auditing program, EPA issued an order March 14 requiring Ford to test 1980 models of the 5.0 NA engine family, 4,500 pound weight class manufactured at the Wayne, Mich., facility. The suspension affects F-150 trucks as well, although only Broncos were actually tested.

When the Broncos failed to meet Clean Air Act emissions criteria, Ford voluntarily ceased production March 24. Ford has 45 days from the suspension date to submit a plan for remedying the nonconformity. EPA wants this plan to emphasize the recall of the 7,000 Broncos and 3,000 F-150s that left the plant prior to the audit.

Ford has determined that a design defect caused the emission problem. According to EPA a "design fix" has been put into effect involving three mechanical system modifications, and the suspension will be lifted when all of the vehicles are brought into emission standard compliance.

### Notes and Questions

1.   Assume that Ford has at its manufacturing plant 100 Broncos which it had manufactured prior to the EPA action. May it go ahead and ship those 100 vehicles to distributors for resale? *See* section 203(a)(1).

2.   Assume that Ford does, in fact, ship 100 previously manufactured Broncos to its distributors, notwithstanding the EPA action. What is the statutory sanction for this conduct? *See* section 205(a). Compute the total civil penalty. Do you believe that a court will order Ford to pay that sum?

3.   Does the statutory scheme for regulating new light duty vehicle emissions contain any mechanism for forgiving "minor" violations of the standards?

4.   In 1977, Congress ordered that new *heavy* duty motor vehicles also conform to national emission standards. The statutory provision for ensuring compliance with those standards, section 206(g), is radically different from the statutory scheme for light duty vehicles, explored in the foregoing questions. Which approach to enforcing compliance make more sense? Why?

## 4. WARRANTY AND RECALL

### *Questions*

1. Assume that you have purchased a new motor vehicle from Ford Motor Company. Assume further that the EPA Administrator has established warranty regulations pursuant to section 207(b). Within one month after purchasing the vehicle, you have the emissions tested by a competent mechanic. The emissions flunk the national emission standards by a wide margin and the mechanic informs you that only a replacement of the catalytic converter would lead to compliance with the standards. You want to do your thing to clean up the air. Assuming that you have not failed to carry out any necessary maintenance, may you *force* Ford under the warranty to replace the converter? If your answer was yes, read carefully CAA § 207(b)(2)(C). Why do you suppose § 207(b)(2)(C) contains this unusual "fine print"?

2. Do you suppose that manufacturers such as Ford will seek to hide behind the technical language of § 207(b)(2)(C) in denying warranty coverage? Why or why not?

---

In addition to revoking or suspending the certificate of conformance, the EPA Administrator may require the manufacturer to "submit a plan for remedying the nonconformity of vehicles or engines" if a substantial number of the vehicles covered by the certificate do not conform to standards (despite proper maintenance and use by their owners) "when in actual use throughout their useful life." CAA § 207(c)(1). This provision is the seed from which the "recall authority" of the EPA has blossomed. Unquestionably, many late model cars are presently violating emission standards because of improper use and maintenance by their owners. How much maintenance may the manufacturer reasonably expect from the owner? Consider the following case.

## CHRYSLER CORP. v. EPA

631 F.2d 865 (D.C. Cir.), *cert. denied*, 449 U.S. 1021 (1980)

WRIGHT, Chief Judge.

Chrysler Corporation has petitioned for review of a final order of the Administrator of the Environmental Protection Agency (EPA), issued on November 20, 1978, directing Chrysler to recall all 1975 vehicles equipped with 360 and 400 cubic inch displacement (CID) engines having two-barrel carburetors and catalytic converters. The Administrator determined that a substantial number of the vehicles in the recall class fail to conform to the applicable carbon monoxide emission standards when in actual use, even though they have been "properly maintained and used." Having found this violation of Section 207(c)(1) of the Clean Air Act, * * * the Administrator ordered Chrysler to submit a plan for remedying the nonconformity. Jurisdiction of this court is pursuant to Section 307(b) of the Act. * * *

Chrysler has sold approximately 208,000 vehicles in the recall class, all equipped with catalytic converters designed to reduce carbon monoxide emissions to within federal standards. Not long after these vehicles had been sold, however, EPA discovered that many of them were failing to meet the standards. After extensive tests EPA determined that excessive emissions were primarily caused by misadjustment of the carburetor idle mixture of the vehicles. The Agency gathered evidence that the misadjustments were the inevitable result of certain defects in the design of the emission control system of the recall class, and later initiated an administrative proceeding to require Chrysler to recall the vehicles and correct this design. An initial hearing before an Administrative Law Judge (ALJ) resulted in a recall order against Chrysler, which the company appealed to the Administrator. The Administrator determined, first, that as a matter of law a manufacturer must be held responsible in a recall action for nonconformities primarily caused by design defects, provided the manufacturer foresaw or should have foreseen the consequences of the defects but failed to take available steps to obviate them, and second, on the evidence, that Chrysler's recall class must be recalled under this standard. Chrysler disputes both of these positions. On the legal issue Chrysler argues that since the nonconforming vehicles in the recall class were misadjusted, they were not "properly maintained" within the meaning of the Act and thus should not be recalled. On the factual issue Chrysler asserts that the Administrator's conclusions were not supported by substantial evidence in the record. Because we agree with the Administrator's interpretation of Section 207(c)(1) and determine that there was substantial evidence to support his findings of a violation, we affirm.

In 1970 Congress passed the Clean Air Amendments of 1970, Pub. L. No. 91-604, 84 Stat. 1676, which required auto manufacturers to reduce carbon monoxide emissions by 1975 to one-tenth of former levels; to 3.4 grams per mile. *See* 36 Fed. Reg. 12657 (1971). The Administrator may, however, postpone implementation of this statutory standard on grounds of technological feasibility or other factors. *See* Section 202(b)(5) of the Act. * * * In 1973 the Administrator postponed implementation of the 3.4 grams per mile standard and set an interim carbon monoxide emission standard of 15 grams per mile.[3] This 15 grams per mile standard was in effect during the 1975 model year, with which we are concerned.

To comply with the Act manufacturers must design, build, and equip each new vehicle to conform to emission standards at the time of sale and to be free from defects in material or workmanship that would cause the vehicle to fall below the standards within a five-year or 50,000-mile period after sale. Section 202(a)(1), (d)(1). * * * Manufacturers must provide a warranty to purchasers to this effect. *Id.*

---

[3] 38 Fed. Reg. 10317 (1973). This postponement was in response to this court's decision in *International Harvester Co. v. Ruckelshaus,* 478 F.2d 615 (D.C. Cir. 1973). It was the first of many postponements. * * *

§ 207(a)(1). * * * If the purchaser of a vehicle maintains and operates it in accordance with the written instructions of the manufacturer, *see id.* § 207(c)(3), * * * and it fails to conform to emission standards during the warranty period (thus subjecting the owner to penalty or other sanction) the manufacturer must remedy the nonconformity at its own expense. *Id.* § 207(b). * * *

To ensure compliance with the Act EPA conducts a three-stage testing process. Under authority of Section 206(a) * * * the Agency examines prototypes of new vehicles or new vehicle engines to determine whether they will conform to the emission standards and issues a "certificate of conformity" to vehicles passing this test. As a part of this examination the Agency inspects the written maintenance and use instructions provided to the purchasers. Until the 1977 amendments went into effect the Agency determined whether such instructions were "reasonable and necessary to assure the proper functioning" of the emission control system. Section 207(c)(3) * * * . The second stage of the testing process takes place after vehicles come off the assembly line. At this time the Agency examines sample vehicles to ensure that they conform to the requirements of the Act. Authority to conduct this examination derives from Section 206(b) * * * . If the Administrator determines that some or all of the vehicles off the assembly line fail to conform to the applicable regulations, he must suspend the certificates of conformity for those vehicles until the manufacturer corrects the deficiency.

The third stage of the testing process takes place while the vehicles are in actual use. EPA and related state agencies test sample vehicles to determine whether they continue to satisfy emission standards during the statutory period. If a "substantial number" of the vehicles in any class or category fail to conform to the emission standards "although properly maintained and used" by the owner, then the Administrator must notify the manufacturer and require it to submit a "plan for remedying the nonconformity" at the manufacturer's expense. Unlike the discovery and cure of nonconformity of individual vehicles under the warranty provisions, the remedy at this stage is recall of the *entire class* of vehicles in order to correct the design, material, or workmanship defect causing the nonconformity. This provision—Section 207(c)(1) of the Act—is the statutory basis for the order under review.

To reduce carbon monoxide emissions and bring its vehicles into conformity with the interim federal standards Chrysler, like the other American auto manufacturers, installed catalytic converters in its 1975 model year vehicles. A catalytic converter can reduce carbon monoxide emissions by 60-80 percent by promoting a chemical reaction among the carbon monoxide, hydrocarbons, and oxygen. This reaction produces two harmless byproducts, carbon dioxide and water.

An adequate supply of oxygen in the exhaust stream is essential to effective operation of the catalytic converter. Unless there is enough oxygen to oxidize all the emissions, the catalytic converter will begin to work poorly and at some point cease to operate altogether. There are two major methods of supplying enough oxygen: installation of an air pump to introduce additional oxygen into the system, and precise adjustment of the carburetor idle to ensure that sufficient oxygen is mixed with the fuel. The principal disadvantage of air pumps is that they increase the cost of the system by about $50 per car, they also decrease gasoline mileage and may in some cases inhibit proper oxidation of the emissions. On the other hand, Chrysler engineers recognized that air pumps generally decrease emissions more effectively than does the carburetor idle adjustment system. It was for just that reason that Chrysler used air pumps in its 1975 model year vehicles subject to the more stringent emission standards of California. Nevertheless, Chrysler did not use air pumps in the recall class vehicles it sold in other states, because Chrysler engineers thought them unnecessary to achieving compliance with federal standards. Instead, Chrysler decided to rely on the carburetor adjustment method to ensure an adequate supply of oxygen to the catalytic converter.

The company instructed owners to take their vehicles to a mechanic for servicing at intervals of 15,000 miles or whenever they detected a malfunction. If all went well, the mechanic would adjust the carburetor precisely in accord with Chrysler's instructions, as detailed in the service manual and summarized on a permanent label affixed to the underside of the engine hood. * * * When the carburetor idle is set to Chrysler's specifications, most of the vehicles pass the carbon monoxide emission standards; when the idle mixture is adjusted to "richer" levels, most of the vehicles fail the standards.

Unfortunately, the idle adjustment method has apparently not worked as well in practice as in theory. EPA researchers have linked the poor emission control performance of the recall class in actual use to certain characteristics of the carburetor idle adjustment process that make precise adjustment difficult and undesirable to owners and mechanics. * * *

The adjustment process is cumbersome and time-consuming, taking the mechanic approximately 30 to 40 minutes, according to an EPA investigation. * * *

The complex and time-consuming nature of the adjustment procedure is significant because the manufacturer did not allow enough time in its reimbursement schedules for dealership mechanics to make carburetor adjustments, according to a survey of Chrysler mechanics. This meant that many mechanics had to complete the specified adjustment without full compensation for their time. Moreover, Chrysler did not reimburse mechanics for a second adjustment in the event a customer was dissatisfied with the results of the first, as frequently happened when the idle was set to so "lean" a mixture. * * *

Several specific factors make the required procedures more difficult to perform. First, the Administrator found that precisely calibrated and fully operating infrared analyzers are often unavailable, and that most dealers were not attaching the analyzers to the upstream tap, as specified by Chrysler. * * *

A second special problem with the emission control system adopted by Chrysler is that the carburetor adjustment screws are so sensitive that tiny rotations of the screws will grossly affect the idle fuel-air mixture. A mere 1/20 of a turn of the mixture screws above Chrysler's specified adjustment range will cause a substantial increase in idle carbon monoxide. * * *

Chrysler attempted to alleviate the adjustment problem by installing plastic limiter caps on the idle adjustment screws. Ideally, such caps would prevent the mechanic from turning the screws to a mixture "richer" than specification. But the limiter caps are easily removed or damaged; indeed, the mechanic must remove the caps in order to make certain repairs. Moreover, Chrysler's limiter caps were such that even when in place they permitted adjustment of the idle mixture to levels many times "richer" than Chrysler's specifications.

Most important, the Chrysler procedure often disrupts the vehicles' smooth operation. Generally speaking, a vehicle drives more smoothly and has a smoother idle with a relatively "rich" fuel-to-air mixture. "Lean" settings such as those specified by Chrysler often generate "driveability" problems and hence customer dissatisfaction. * * * A large majority of dealership mechanics surveyed by EPA stated that it is not possible to achieve "acceptable engine smoothness and driveability" when the idle mixture is adjusted to Chrysler's specifications. The mechanics also said that customers complain of rough idle, hesitation, poor performance, or surge when the idle mixture is properly set. A significant majority admitted that they do not use the specified Chrysler procedure for adjusting the idle mixture. More than two-thirds of the mechanics said that they "often" or "always" remove the carburetor limiter caps in order to make a good idle adjustment, thereby indicating that they must set the idle mixture far "richer" than operation of the emission control system would permit. * * *

In comparison, most Ford vehicles in the 1975 model year were equipped with air pumps, which obviate the need for precise carburetor adjustments to extremely "lean" idle mixtures. Since air pumps provide sufficient oxygen to the catalytic converter, the idle can be set at a "richer" mixture, as driveability seems to require, without disabling the emission control system. * * *

Russell E. Train issued a letter on December 8, 1976, instructing Chrysler to submit a plan for remedying the nonconformity of the recall class. The Administrator said that the test results showed "that a substantial number of vehicles in the [recall class] are exceeding the 1975 Federal carbon monoxide standard in actual use," and that "carburetor idle CO misadjustment is the primary cause of the nonconformity of these vehicles." * * * He noted that misadjustment of the vehicles might be taken as proof that they had not been "properly maintained" under the statute, but he stated that Chrysler must nevertheless be considered liable to a recall action. He reasoned:

> Chrysler is responsible for these misadjustments because Chrysler as an automobile manufacturer should have foreseen that its carburetor design and adjustment procedures would cause widespread misadjustments and because of the agency relationship which exists between Chrysler and its authorized dealerships. * * *

The Administrator acknowledged that the key issue in the proceeding was whether the vehicles in the recall class were "properly maintained" within the meaning of Section 207(c)(1). He reviewed the interpretations of "properly maintained" urged by EPA and Chrysler, and also that adopted by the ALJ, but he found that "[t]he problem with all of these interpretations of the 'properly maintained' criterion is that they place undue emphasis on the text of the words 'properly maintained' without examining the purpose of function of the 'properly maintained' criterion in the overall statutory scheme." He reasoned that the purpose of the "properly maintained" criterion of Section 207(c)(1) was "to allocate responsibility for emission nonconformities among the manufacturer, the vehicle owner and the mechanic." * * * The manufacturer should not have to bear the expense of a recall if the fault properly lies with the vehicle operator; on the other hand, if it is principally responsible for the nonconformity the manufacturer should be held accountable, even if the nonconformity relates to maintenance of the vehicle. Otherwise, the manufacturer would be able to avoid its duty to make vehicles that would conform to the emission standards during their useful life, and could frustrate the purpose of the Act. Thus the Administrator interpreted Section 207(c)(1) as imposing recall liability on the manufacturer for maintenance-related nonconformities only if EPA could establish that the vehicles would have been maintained properly *"but for the actions of the manufacturer."* * * *

This case is the first contested recall action under § 207(c)(1) to reach the courts. * * * Chrysler's contention—that manufacturers have no responsibility for nonconformities if the owners failed to attain maintenance in accordance with the manufacturer's precise written specifications—would far exceed the purpose of the "properly maintained" criterion and would undermine the broad objectives of the Act. Such an interpretation would strip the manufacturers of a large part of the incentive to design emission systems that would operate effectively while in actual use. The manufacturer could prescribe maintenance that is difficult to perform or incompatible with smooth operation of the vehicle, but bear no responsibility for the natural consequence of such design—so long as the vehicles passed the initial certification tests. We could expect little or no progress in development of better, more maintenance-free emission controls.

The Administrator's construction—making the manufacturer responsible for nonconformities primarily attributable to design defects knowingly produced by the manufacturer—would better serve to promote the purposes of the Act. At the same time it would retain protection for those manufacturers striving, within the limits of technology, to produce effective emission controls. We agree with the Administrator that if a manufacturer knowingly used an emission control system resulting in large numbers of misadjustments, instead of a less sensitive and more durable system available to it, it should be held responsible under the Act for the consequences and be subject to a recall.

We reject Chrysler's suggestion that the responsibility of the manufacturer must be judged by maintenance performed in a laboratory setting, rather than by that typical of a mechanic's shop or a dealership. It does the public little good to pay higher costs for cleaner automobiles, only to find that they fail emission standards except when specially adjusted by trained mechanics operating under laboratory conditions. If design defects make "proper maintenance" so difficult that even Chrysler dealers do not perform it, then such "proper maintenance" is beyond the reach of the average car owner. Use of a laboratory-pure standard of "proper maintenance" is contrary to the "actual use" standard of the Act.

Although we admit that the language of Section 207(c)(1) is open to more than one interpretation, we conclude that the legislative history and the purpose of the "properly maintained" criterion require that we affirm the interpretation adopted by the Administrator. * * *

In sum, we agree with the Administrator's interpretation of Section 207(c)(1) of the Clean Air Act * * * that a manufacturer may be held responsible in a recall action for nonconformities resulting from misadjustments, if such misadjustments were principally caused by the design of the emission control system and maintenance procedures, and if the manufacturer foresaw or should have foreseen the problem and failed to take available steps to obviate it. We find substantial evidence in the record to support the Administrator's conclusion that Chrysler vehicles in the recall class fail to conform to federal carbon monoxide emission standards when in actual use, although properly maintained and used, and thus that Chrysler must submit a plan for remedying the nonconformity, in accordance with the Act. The Decision and Order is *Affirmed.*

## 5. EVADING RECALL

### GM TO TIGHTEN 1982 FLEET EMISSIONS TO AVOID RECALLING DEFECTIVE 1979 CARS

13 [Curr. Dev.] Env. Rep. (BNA) 472 (1982)

General Motors Corp. has agreed to build 2.3 million 1982 and later model year vehicles to comply with a tighter limit on nitrogen oxides emissions than required by law, to avoid recalling 695,000 cars made in

1979 which do not comply with the statutory limit, the Environmental Protection Agency announced July 29.

According to EPA, the agency ordered GM to recall the vehicles, which are equipped with Pontiac engines, to correct the problem. However, EPA continued, neither the agency nor the automaker has been able to figure out "the exact reason for the excessive pollution." EPA said the only repair which would remedy the excessive emissions of nitrogen oxides from the 1979 cars also would reduce fuel economy.

Under the agreement, GM will produce 2.3 million vehicles in 1982, 1983, and later model years if needed, which will comply with a nitrogen oxides emissions limit of 0.9 grams per mile. The statutory limit on those emissions for those years now stands at 1.0 gpm. According to EPA, the 0.9 gpm limit "has been calculated to 'offset' the excessive pollution of the 1979 models."

Kathleen M. Bennett, EPA assistant administrator for air, noise, and radiation, told reporters Aug. 4 that forcing GM to recall the impaired 1979 vehicles "would weaken" the agency's recall program because of the impression people would get from a recall where "the fix reduces fuel economy."

An EPA press spokesman told BNA Aug. 4 that, considering the age of the affected vehicles, the agency estimates no more than 60 percent of the vehicles actually would be repaired if a recall were ordered. Bennett said the plan agreed to by GM will reduce nitrogen oxide emissions about 12,700 more tons than called for by the standard. According to EPA, if a recall were required, the emissions reduction only would be about 5,700 tons.

The press spokesman said this is the first situation of its kind to arise, where no cause can be identified for the problem. The offset "won't be established [agency] policy," the spokesman added, although EPA will consider such situations on a case-by-case basis in the future.

## GM ORDERED TO RECALL 600,000 CARS; AUTOMAKER INTERVENES IN OFFSET SUIT

13 [Curr. Dev.] Env. Rep. (BNA) 886 (1982)

On Oct. 14, the U.S. Court of Appeals for the District of Columbia Circuit granted General Motors the right to intervene in one of two lawsuits filed against EPA for allowing the automaker not to recall 695,000 1979 model-year cars * * * exceeding the nitrogen oxides standard.

In July, EPA announced it would allow GM to build 2.3 million 1982 and later model-year vehicles to comply with a standard tighter than the statutory limit, in order to offset the excessive emissions from the 1979 model-year cars * * * .

At the time, EPA said it was allowing GM to offset current excessive emissions with future reductions because the automaker was unable to identify any "field fix" to the problem that did not result in reductions in fuel economy. The agency said it did not believe motorists would respond to a recall that resulted in lessened fuel economy.

In response to EPA's action, two lawsuits were filed against the agency by the Center for Auto Safety, the Natural Resources Defense Council, Public Citizen Inc., a consumer litigation organization, Rep. Toby Moffett (D-Conn), chairman of the House Government Operations Sub-Committee on Energy, Environment, and Natural Resources, and Dr. Sidney Wold, a public health expert.

The groups claimed that the Clean Air Act requires the agency to order General Motors to recall the problem vehicles and that the EPA administrator had no authority under the Act to allow the offset.

The attorney said the groups will argue in briefs due in the appellate court in mid-November that EPA Administrator Anne M. Gorsuch did not have the discretionary authority to grant the offset to GM, and that, even if she did, she exceeded her discretion in this case.

Townsend said the appellate court has ruled in *Chrysler v. EPA* that the recall is required, and that the precedent in that case is applicable in this instance. He asserted that GM's problems with excessive emissions appear to stem from the manufacturer's practice of certifying new automobiles "very close to standard."

Other manufacturers, especially foreign automakers, certify new cars "way below" the federal automobile emissions standards, Townsend said, so that if a problem develops later, they have a margin of safety. With GM products, he said, the margin is so slight, that when problems arise, any increase in vehicular emissions carries them over the allowable limits.

---

Robert Everett, GM's assistant director of emission controls, declared that the offset concept for new car emission standards "probably is legally weak, but it makes a lot of sense." 13 [Curr. Dev.] Env. Rep. (BNA) 1489 (1982). In late 1984, the D.C. Circuit struck down the agency's approval of the GM plan. The following excerpt captures the gist of the opinion.

## CENTER FOR AUTO SAFETY
## v. RUCKELSHAUS

747 F.2d 1 (D.C. Cir. 1984)

SCALIA, Circuit Judge.

We conclude * * * that section 207(c) requires recall and repair as the only statutory remedy for nonconformity. Since that is so, the EPA acted unlawfully in proceeding under section 207(c) to accept GM's offset plan as a remedy for the nonconformity—just as it would have acted unlawfully to require it. We emphasize that this is the only issue presented and decided. Specifically, we do not consider the agency's ability to take account of an offset commitment in the exercise of its enforcement discretion, should it decide in a particular case that such a course is "best calculated to achieve the ends contemplated by Congress and to allocate its available funds and personnel in such a way as to execute its policy efficiently and economically." * * * That is not what has occurred here, but rather a misinterpretation of the statute which would permit systematic substitution of offsets for recalls. That may well be a more effective means of reducing automotive air pollution; but it was not the means envisioned by the Clean Air Act.

The agency's approval of the GM plan, being not in accordance with law * * * is set aside. * * * *Petition granted.*

---

The auto industry has continued to argue that the federal government should replace the recall procedure with more flexible (and allegedly more effective) alternatives. The following reading involves one variation on the "offset" theme.

## GM CHIEF CALLS FOR EMISSION CREDITS, TRADING BETWEEN STATIONARY, MOBILE POLLUTION SOURCES

16 [Curr. Dev.] Env. Rep. (BNA) 307-08 (1985)

The current system for recalling vehicles that do not meet emission standards under the Clean Air Act is "incredibly wasteful" and should be replaced by a system that would give automobile manufacturers credit for addressing other environmental problems instead, General Motors Corp. President F. James McDonald said June 17.

Recalls of some automobiles that nearly achieve the federal standard for hydrocarbon emissions "are costing on the order of $20,000 per ton of hydrocarbons removed," according to the GM chief, who said that is more than 10 times the average cost of control for stationary sources.

Instead of recalling vehicles, McDonald suggested that automobile manufacturers be required to make financial contributions to an independent group for the amount of a penalty that would have been imposed by EPA "that could be used better someplace else to help the environment." For instance, the funds could be used more efficiently to bring some stationary sources into compliance with the 1987 deadline for ozone under the Air Act, he said.

The potential for non-compliance with the 1987 ozone deadline in some areas "is beginning to create severe restrictions on growth and on jobs for American workers," according to McDonald.

Betsy Ancker-Johnson, GM vice-president for environmental activities, told BNA June 18 that instead of paying for recalls of engines that miss the hydrocarbon standard by 20 percent or less, the company would like to contribute the funds it would spend on the recall to a state or local pollution control agency or research organization that is "responsible to the public" and could use the funds more efficiently to clean up air pollution.

When an engine fails to attain a standard by 10 or 20 percent, which she called "de minimis" failure, a recall is not cost-effective and results in an automobile that performs less efficiently, according to Ancker-Johnson. When hydrocarbon adjustments are made to an engine model as the result of a recall, engine timing is adjusted to reduce emissions in a way that reduces fuel efficiency, she said.

Under General Motors' plan, the company would get emission credits for donating funds to an independent third party, similar to the credits stationary sources buy, sell, and trade under EPA's "bubble" emission trading policy, she said. The GM vice president said the company has discussed the matter with EPA officials and "they seem favorably disposed toward the idea."

### Notes and Questions

1. Assume that the recall of a specific nonconforming vehicle class would cost General Motors $50 million. Why would the company prefer to send that $50 million to a pollution control agency or research organization, rather than recall and repair the vehicles? After all, $50 million is $50 million, isn't it? If your answer is: "because such an approach will represent a more efficient expenditure of the $50 million and will result in cleaner air," reflect a bit longer on GM's motives (and stay away from individuals selling bridges).

2. Given your answer to the previous question, which approach to nonconforming vehicles would best further the cost internalization goals of a neoclassical economist: the statutory recall requirement or GM's substitute of a donation to the environmental equivalent of the Red Cross? Why?

3. Apparently in the past, the EPA Administrator has allowed the manufacturer to *replace* the catalytic converter once during each 50,000 mile certification test. *See* Richard B. Stewart & James E. Krier, Environmental Law and Policy 439 (2d ed. 1978). Yet CAA § 202(d)(1) provides that the "useful life" of each passenger vehicle engine must be a period of five years or 50,000 miles for pre-1990 amendment requirements and 10 years or 100,000 miles for requirements imposed by the 1990 amendments. Moreover, § 202(a)(1) provides that the emission standards shall be applicable to vehicles and engines "for their useful life." Is the EPA's testing procedure consistent with the court's opinion in *Chrysler Corp. v. EPA*? Is the procedure lawful under the Act?

## 6. THE 1990 AMENDMENTS

We have seen that the prior Act's approach to mobile source pollution consists primarily of emission standards applied to new motor vehicles and engines (backed up by engine certification and warranty programs) and regulation of fuels and fuel additives. Title II of the 1990 amendments addresses mobile source pollution by building on this structure in three ways.

First, the amendments impose more stringent requirements on conventional motor vehicles, prescribing: (1) tighter tailpipe standards (including longer warranty and useful life periods) for a variety of vehicle classes; (2) requirements for onboard controls of refueling losses and running losses; (3) cold start standards for carbon monoxide emissions; (4) requirements for onboard emission control diagnostic equipment; (5) nonroad vehicle and engine control requirements; and (6) toxic air emission standards.

Second, the amendments usher in new attempts to regulate motor vehicle fuels and fuel additives, including requirements for reformulated and oxygenated gasoline. Finally, the amendments establish a new program to compel the production and use of clean-fuel vehicles and clean fuels.

## 7. SPORT UTILITY VEHICLES

One of the biggest challenges in curbing future emissions from motor vehicles is posed by the American consumers' passion for sport utility vehicles, pickup trucks, and minivans. To date, these vehicles have been classified as light trucks, allowing them to emit much more pollution than their passenger car counterparts. For example, full-size sport utility vehicles and pickup trucks are currently allowed to emit three times as much $NO_x$ per mile as cars. *See* Keith Bradsher, *Light Trucks Face Tougher Air Standards*, N.Y. Times, Nov. 3, 1998, at C1 col. 5.

The California Air Resources Board (CARB) estimates that nearly 50 percent of all vehicles sold today are pickup trucks, sport utility vehicles, or minivans that are being used as passenger cars. *See* 29 [Curr. Dev.] Env. Rep. (BNA) 1377 (1998). On November 5, 1998, by an 11-0 vote, CARB adopted an aggressive low-emission vehicle program that will hold sport utility vehicles, pickup trucks, and minivans sold in California to the same tough emission standards as passenger cars. *See id.* The standard is to be phased in over a three-year period beginning in 2004. In May, 1999, EPA announced that it would begin rulemaking proceedings to impose more stringent emission limitations on sport utility vehicles. *See* 39 [Curr. Dev.] Env. Rep. (BNA) 5 (1999).

## 8. MAGICAL TECHNOLOGIES

Occasionally, clever people invent technology that is too cool to be believed. For example, the New York Times reported in 1993 that the Ricoh Company had announced a "reverse copier"—"put in a copy and out comes a blank page." Andrew Pollack, *The Ricoh Reverse Copier; Un-Writing a New Page In the Annals of Recycling*, N.Y. Times, Aug. 21, 1993, at 37 col. 5. The device erases photocopies (and laser jet printer copies) by stripping away the toner that forms the image, allowing the paper to be used again. *Id.* A single piece of copy paper may be reused ten times before wearing out. At the time of its announcement, Ricoh conceded that its prototype could erase only three pages per minute, but expressed confidence that the speed would eventually be increased to an acceptable rate. *See id.*

Might some of our worst air pollution problems be solved by magical technologies? The Engelhard Corporation—developer of the catalytic converter—is apparently working on a plan to paint automobile radiators and air-conditioning compressors with a new catalyst that breaks down ozone into molecules of ordinary oxygen atoms. *See* Matthew L. Wald, *New Catalytic Process Would Let Cars Eat Ozone*, N.Y. Times, Apr. 6, 1995, at D4, col. 3. Because radiators and compressors interact with large volumes of air when a fan is running or a vehicle is moving, catalyst-treated vehicles could purify pollutants put into the air by other vehicles; indeed, in the most highly polluted areas of the country, automobile fans might be altered to run even while the vehicles are parked. *See id.*

# F. VEHICLES IN USE

## 1. INTRODUCTION

We have seen in the previous pages that the federal program for curbing emissions from *new* motor vehicles has been fraught with delays, marred by significant testing flaws, and impaired by exceptions for growing numbers of sport utility and other popular consumer vehicles. We now turn to the other major fork of the Clean Air Act's approach to mobile source pollutants: the attempt to curb emissions from motor vehicles *in use*.

The 1970 version of the Act contained only two provisions on this topic. First, § 110(a)(2)(B) directed that the Administrator should approve a state implementation plan (SIP) if, *inter alia,*

> it includes emission limitations, schedules, and timetables for compliance with [NAAQS], and such other measures as may be necessary to assure attainment and maintenance of such * * * standard[s], including, but not limited to, land-use and transportation controls * * * .

This language effectively required states with heavily-polluted metropolitan areas to develop *transportation control plans* or TCPs.

Second, § 110(a)(2)(G) directed that SIP approval was appropriate only if the state plan

> provides, to the extent necessary and practicable, for periodic inspection and testing of motor vehicles to enforce compliance with applicable emission standards * * * .

This language effectively directed such states to develop *inspection and maintenance* or I/M programs.

Innocent as they may seem, these two brief clauses stirred up a hornets' nest of public indignation that is greater today than at any time since their adoption almost three decades ago. The readings in the following pages are designed to explore how we have arrived at our present predicament.

# JOHN P.C. FOGARTY, JOSHUA B. EPEL, DONN L. CALKINS & JOHN STAFFORD, TRANSPORTATION CONTROLS AND MOTOR VEHICLE INSPECTION AND MAINTENANCE PROGRAMS

in 2 Law of Environmental Protection
11.08 (Sheldon M. Novick, ed. 1998)

The implementation of TCPs at first seemed straightforward. Responding to the mandate of § 110(a)(2), in April 1971, EPA promulgated the NAAQS and required states to submit SIPs by January 31, 1972. Yet in August the states were advised that their proposed TCPs to enforce the NAAQS for CO and photochemical oxidants (smog) could be deferred because neither the states nor EPA "had any practical experience that would permit the development of meaningful transportation control plans or the prediction of their impact on air quality." * * *

On May 31, 1972, EPA published the first of its notices of approval or disapproval of the state-submitted plans. Large portions of the California plan were disapproved, and EPA proposed regulations to cure its perceived deficiencies. The EPA substitute plan * * * was without transportation controls for photochemical oxidants, which were deferred in accordance with EPA's announced policy. Environmental organizations [sued] * * * and * * * EPA was ordered [in *City of Riverside v. Ruckelshaus*, 3 Envtl. L. Rep. 20043 (C.D. Cal. 1972)] to promulgate regulations to control photochemical oxidants, including all necessary transportation controls, by January 15, 1973. EPA issued the regulations, applicable to all states, but relying on the Act's provision for an extension of the attainment deadline extended the compliance time for twenty-one states by two years. * * * In *NRDC v. EPA*, 475 F.2d 968 (D.C. Cir. 1973), the [D.C. Circuit] denied EPA the authority to grant any extension of time for a state to submit a SIP. * * *

The deadlines imposed by *Riverside* and *NRDC* prompted EPA to require states to immediately submit transportation control measures for the disputed pollutants. California refused to submit a plan for Los Angeles; EPA was forced to develop its own plan to remedy the nation's worst case of photochemical oxidant pollution, and within an exceedingly short time at that. Similarly, many other states were either unwilling or unable to submit plans to EPA prior to the * * * deadline * * *. As a result, EPA had to simultaneously propose plans for numerous other, albeit less polluted, areas of the country. By necessity, the plans proposed by EPA contained some extraordinarily controversial, even radical, transportation control measures, not the least of which was a proposal to ration and reduce by over 80 percent the amount of gasoline used in Los Angeles.

At the time the Los Angeles gas rationing proposal was announced, Administrator William Ruckelshaus noted that EPA had no intention of requiring such a drastic measure; however, under the terms of the Clean Air Act, EPA could not do otherwise. * * * Nevertheless, EPA's other, less drastic control proposals, some of which included a surcharge of $3.00 per day on parking, exclusive bus and car pool lanes in approximately twenty major urban areas, and the pre-construction review of all new facilities which would contain more than a certain number of parking spaces, also generated considerable controversy. * * *

Landowners and developers, as well as commercial business establishments, particularly objected to restrictions on parking, surcharges, and gasoline rationing. These, the most despised of all control strategies, were both popularly and politically distasteful * * * .

## 2. TCP CHALLENGES ON NONCONSTITUTIONAL GROUNDS

The advent of EPA-drafted TCPs led to a spate of lawsuits, raising numerous statutory and constitutional objections. The following decision is typical of litigation raising primarily nonconstitutional issues.

## SOUTH TERMINAL CORPORATION v. EPA

504 F.2d 646 (1st Cir. 1974)

CAMPBELL, Circuit Judge.

We are asked to review the Metropolitan Boston Air Quality Transportation Control Plan (the plan). The plan is aimed at keeping two types of air-borne pollutants, photochemical oxidants and carbon monoxide, from exceeding within Greater Boston the national primary and secondary ambient air quality standards prescribed by the [EPA] * * * .[e]

The present plan (termed a "transportation" control plan because it focuses upon pollutants caused mainly by vehicles rather than by "stationary sources") * * * has been recognized from the outset to present delicate problems; inevitably it seems bound to come between the citizen and his automobile. Indeed the problems were seen to be so novel and difficult, that the EPA Administrator initially postponed compliance dates from mid-1975 to 1977; however, it was held that he lacked authority to do so. *See Natural Resources Defense Council, Inc. v. EPA*, 475 F.2d 968 (D.C. Cir. 1973).

The Administrator finally ordered Massachusetts to submit its transportation control plan by April 15, 1973. When Massachusetts did not submit an acceptable plan, the Administrator, as he is obliged to do under such circumstances, promptly proposed a plan of his own for the state, held a public hearing and, after making changes in the plan he had first proposed, promulgated regulations embodying the final plan before us.

---

[e] *Ed.*—We will examine only those portions of the opinion dealing with carbon monoxide.

The plan is designed, by May 31, 1975, to reduce the expected emission of * * * carbon monoxide in the Boston core and East Boston area of the region by about 40 percent. The Administrator has determined that reductions of this magnitude are necessary if the region's air is to conform to national standards by that date, which is the compliance date set by Congress.

At the heart of the plan is a strategy of cutting down emissions by discouraging the use of vehicles. Off-street and on-street parking spaces are to be "frozen" or cut back, and the construction of new parking facilities is regulated. There are to be special bus and car pool lanes, and a computer car pool matching system. There is also to be a program of vehicle inspection and maintenance and emission exhaust controls * * * .

The Administrator's specific *proposals* first included a ban on on-street parking in the Boston core area from 6 to 10 a.m. and 4 to 6 p.m. on weekdays, and a $5 surcharge on off-street parking from 6 to 10 a.m. in the core area and from 6 a.m. to 10 p.m. at Logan International Airport (Logan). To reduce photochemical oxidants he proposed prohibiting travel within Route 128 (an expressway circling Boston) one day out of five, by a sticker system. * * *

When the *final* plan emerged, it was, indeed, much influenced by the public hearing. The $5 surcharge and the sticker system, both of which had been sharply criticized, were dropped, as was a proposal to limit the supply of gasoline. Substituted were a much smaller surcharge and an egress toll on vehicles leaving Logan; pre-construction review of new parking facilities throughout the region; a freeze on parking spaces in selected portions of the metropolitan region; reduction in employee parking spaces; and reductions in the number of off-street parking spaces available in the Boston core during morning rush hours. The parking surcharge and egress toll were subsequently deleted. * * *

The final plan added regulations for computer car pool matching and preferential treatment throughout the region for bus/car pools. It made changes in the controls on mobile source emissions, and required vehicles to be inspected twice a year instead of once. * * *

Petitioners challenge both EPA's conclusion that emission reductions are necessary to meet national air quality standards and the magnitude of the reduction said to be required. * * *

Carbon monoxide data is attacked as unreliable. EPA determined that its national primary standard requiring the average amount of carbon monoxide in the air over an eight hour period not to exceed 9 p.p.m. is not being met in the Boston core and will not be met by mid-1975. It did this by a series of calculations which have as their essential element an ambient air quality reading obtained on one day in 1970 from a monitor at Kenmore Square. Although petitioners attack use of the rollback model itself as unsophisticated, we are mainly impressed by the contention that the crucial figure for determining required emission reduction may be unrepresentative. At the time the plan was designed the next highest reading at Kenmore Square was nearly 50 percent lower than that utilized. EPA points to readings elsewhere even higher than that used in the rollback model, recorded after the plan was announced, as evidence that it may have "underestimated the extent of the CO problem". But petitioners claim these high readings are also freak events. * * * [O]n the present record, we have no basis to say * * * that such a slender base, without further justification, is sufficient to support EPA's conclusion as to carbon monoxide in the Boston core. * * *

While * * * we are unable at this time to uphold EPA's conclusions as to * * * carbon monoxide levels in the Boston core and East Boston sectors, we do not say that they are necessarily incorrect. * * * We can only say that the objections as to data and methodology seem too serious to us simply to pass by; they demand investigation and answer. * * * [W]e think it is necessary to remand to the Agency for further proceedings with respect to these questions. * * *

Several petitioners allege that EPA is utterly without statutory authority to regulate off-street parking. The core of this argument is that the Agency was given only the authority to regulate "stationary sources" of pollution, and that *expressio unius exclusio alterius* reasoning should lead to the conclusion that "indirect sources" of pollution, such as parking lots, are outside the statutory scope.

The argument is without merit. Although the statute expressly allows EPA to regulate stationary sources,[24] there are other provisions conferring the powers in question. Under [§ 110(a)(2)(B)], Congress provided that state implementation plans shall include such measures as may be necessary to insure attainment and maintenance of the national primary ambient air quality standards, "including, but not limited to, land-use and transportation controls." And the Administrator must promulgate promptly regulations setting forth "an implementation plan for a State" should the state itself fail to propose a satisfactory one. [§ 110(c)] The statutory scheme would be unworkable were it read as giving to EPA, when promulgating an implementation plan for a state, less than those necessary measures allowed by Congress to a state to accomplish federal clean air goals. We do not adopt any such crippling interpretation. * * *

The regulation of parking is * * * supportable as a transportation control. The plentiful existence of parking facilities creates an incentive to choose motor vehicles; by destroying this incentive, EPA weights the choice more heavily in favor of less polluting transit.

Assuming the Administrator is right that * * * carbon monoxide levels must be reduced, and given his express authority to invoke land-

---

[24] We agree with several petitioners that parking structures, which themselves emit no pollutants, but instead only attract vehicles which emit pollution, are not stationary sources within the meaning of the Act.

use and transportation controls, the measures are well within his authority. * * * The "freeze" boils down to the requirement that no new parking spaces be created after October 15, 1973, in the more congested portions of Boston, Cambridge, and some other outlying areas. * * * We cannot say that such a freeze is arbitrary and capricious assuming EPA is able to support by credible data its position as to the magnitude of the need for carbon monoxide emission reductions in relevant segments of the region. * * *

In 1970 four airlines organized South Terminal in order to construct a new parking facility at Logan Airport. A contract with Massport was executed in April, 1973, at which time construction began. Both South Terminal and Massport object to the freeze, which provides that facilities in construction prior to October 15, 1973, may not be utilized to the extent that they increase existing parking facilities in specified municipalities and at Logan Airport by more than 10 percent unless any such increase is offset by retiring spaces elsewhere in the freeze zone. Each municipality and Logan constitute a separate freeze zone, for the purpose of calculating the 10 percent reduction. Thus, South Terminal may not increase spaces at Logan by more than 10 percent and it is projected to be 1,100 spaces over its limit.

The original proposal would have imposed a $5 surcharge on all persons parking at Logan. South Terminal estimated that it would have resulted in a 35 percent decrease in the utilization of its complex—more drastic, perhaps, than the final plan because South Terminal could not assure full utilization by purchasing and retiring open lot spaces. South Terminal protested that the surcharge would be ineffective and that the data did not justify the harsh treatment; it focused upon the adverse effects the plan would have on the revenue of commercial airlines, particularly the airlines which own South Terminal.

South Terminal argues that if Logan must be controlled it should not be singled out in such a fashion that it must exclusively bear the cost of any reduction. The $5 surcharge, unlike the freeze, would have affected revenues throughout the airport. We reject this argument. As we said earlier, the regulation is not aimed at South Terminal but at checking any excessive increase in the total vehicle population at this one location. Assuming EPA prevails in establishing the need for the controls, it is immaterial that they do not fall equally upon every operator; we think it rational that those seeking to build new facilities receive a lower priority than those whose facilities are already built. South Terminal had an opportunity, denied to those with completed facilities, to alter its plans and to cushion the shock of the regulations. * * *

The airport petitioners and all parking operators in the Boston core area seek to convince us that the regulations constitute a taking without just compensation. The regulations as applied to Logan exterminate some 1,100 planned-upon spaces and arguably confiscate the revenues that otherwise would have accrued from them. The 40 percent vacancy rate rule in the Boston core area compels building space to stand idle; the situation is arguably most disadvantageous to garage owners, for their space is least likely to have a reasonable alternative use. * * *

[EPA] reminds us [however] that the restriction on parking availability in the Boston core area will allow entrepreneurs to increase their prices, as is the natural consequence when supply is reduced and demand is unchanged. The Government has effectively created a parking cartel that, depending on the elasticity of demand for parking, may increase rather than decrease profits. What will happen to profits cannot be predicted, but in view of the possibility of their increase we are not impressed by the claim that the regulation is so serious, and so forecloses alternatives, that a compensable taking has occurred.

### Notes and Questions

1. Was the court in *South Terminal* reviewing an implementation plan promulgated by the state of Massachusetts (a SIP), or something else?

2. The First Circuit concluded that the EPA had been given as much power in drafting a TCP *for* a state as Congress gave to the states themselves in CAA § 110, declaring that any other interpretation would make the statutory scheme "unworkable." Does this reasoning make sense? Why or why not?

3. The South Terminal Corporation, which proposed to build a large number of new parking spaces at Logan Airport, was unhappy with either of the two approaches considered by the EPA Administrator: a freeze on parking spaces or a hefty $5 surcharge. It seems to have preferred the surcharge, because that would fall more equally on all parking facilities. Assume that you are a competitor of South Terminal and that you have a present parking lot at Logan Airport, which you have no intention of expanding. Which approach would you prefer—a freeze or a surcharge? Why?

4. Assume that the TCP in *South Terminal* is being drafted by state, rather than federal officials. The choice between a parking surcharge or a parking freeze may have profound effects on present and prospective parking lot owners—enriching some at the expense of others. Do you suppose that anything in state law constrains the ability of state bureaucrats to select between these options? Might not a cynic conclude that the extraordinary discretion granted to SIP-drafting officials presents a perfect opportunity for corruption?

### 3. CLIPPING EPA'S TCP WINGS

Public outrage against transportation control plans—particularly federally-imposed TCPs—jolted Congress to enact limitations on the EPA's TCP-drafting options in the 1977 CAA amendments. You need not read the following statutory sections with a fine-tooth comb; the purpose is to acquaint you with the flavor of the congressional response to the public's fury.

---

Read the following sections of the Clean Air Act

☐ § 110(a)(5)    ☐ § 110(c)(2)(B)    ☐ § 110(c)(2)(D)

☐ § 110(c)(2)(E)    ☐ § 110(c)(5)(A)

---

The First Circuit, in *South Terminal* declared that "[t]he statutory scheme would be unworkable were it read as giving to EPA, when promulgating an implementation plan for a state, less than those necessary measures allowed by Congress to a state to accomplish federal clean air goals." *See* page 431, *supra.* Yet, by enacting the foregoing statutory amendments, Congress created just such a regime.

The resulting discrepancy between state and EPA lawmaking powers when drafting TCPs has led to some bizarre events. A good example has been the rise and fall of "indirect source review" (ISR) programs.

## 4. INDIRECT SOURCE REVIEW

# RICHARD B. STEWART & JAMES E. KRIER, ENVIRONMENTAL LAW AND POLICY

456-57 (2nd ed. 1978)

The Court of Appeals decision in *Natural Resource Defense Council, Inc. v. EPA*, 475 F.2d 968 (D.C. Cir. 1973) [mentioned at page 428, *supra*] did not explicitly discuss the problem of post-attainment maintenance of ambient air quality standards in the face of future increases in automobile use and new land use patterns (such as shopping centers, highways, and sports complexes) that would attract heavy automobile traffic. However, Section 110(a)(2)(B) [of the 1970 Act] require[d] that SIPs include measures to *maintain* ambient standards, and the order issued by the court in *NRDC v. EPA* required EPA to review the "maintenance provisions" of SIPs. EPA was persuaded that it should take steps to ensure maintenance of ambient standards for automotive pollutants and that maintenance would require careful advance review of new land-use developments likely to attract automobile traffic. Accordingly, EPA in 1973 proposed regulations requiring states to include "indirect source" review [ISR] provisions in SIPs.

The [proposed] regulations defined the term "indirect source" as a facility, building, structure, or installation which attracts or may attract mobile source activity that results in emissions of a pollutant for which there is a national standard. Such indirect sources include, but are not limited to: highways and roads; parking facilities; retail, commercial and industrial facilities; recreation, amusement, sports and entertainment facilities; airports; office and government buildings; apartments and condominium buildings; and education facilities.

The [proposed] regulations required states to provide for *preconstruction review* of indirect sources to ensure that they would not result in concentrations of automobile traffic that would produce ambient standard violations. * * *

The proposed regulations provoked great controversy. * * * [They] were strongly opposed by developer interests and many state and local officials who claimed that the proposed regulations trenched on local planning responsibilities and represented "back door" single-purpose federal land use planning. It was also contended that the Act did not require or otherwise authorize the regulation of facilities that did not themselves cause pollution but simply attracted other sources which did pollute. Finally, there was the haunting consideration of enforcement. If state or local officials were unwilling to carry out the indirect source regulations, EPA would hardly have the resources to do so. This consideration, together with the strong political opposition to EPA indirect source regulation, persuaded EPA * * * to * * * indefinitely [suspend the ISR program]. * * *

---

In 1977, Congress brought to an abrupt halt the EPA's attempts to force ISR programs on the states through EPA-drafted TCPs. *See* § 110(a)(5)(A)(i). Ironically, however, some of the more cooperative states had "voluntarily" adopted ISR programs on their own. To be sure, some of these states were progressive and shared the EPA's belief that the programs were necessary. *See, e.g.*, Minn. Reg. APC 19 in 2 BNA Env. Rep. State Air Laws 416.0517. Other states, however, adopted ISR programs only because of the EPA's threat to impose them by force. Regardless of the impetus for these "voluntary" ISR programs, the EPA retained the power to enforce such programs, even after the 1977 amendments. See § 110(a)(5)(A)(i) (second sentence).

Recognizing that some states had been reluctantly bludgeoned into adopting ISR programs, Congress sought in the 1977 amendments to provide relief. Under § 110(a)(5)(A)(iii), states were invited to revise their SIPs to suspend or revoke ISR programs. Like unringing a bell, this did not turn out to be an easy matter, as Connecticut discovered in the following case.

## MANCHESTER ENVIRONMENTAL COALITION v. EPA

### 612 F.2d 56 (2d Cir. 1979)

TIMBERS, Circuit Judge.

On this petition to review the final order of the EPA filed January 22, 1979, which approved the application of the State of Connecticut to revise its state implementation plan, we find the chief issue is whether the EPA erred in construing [§ 110(a)(5)(A)(iii)] to require the Administrator to approve a state's request to revoke its indirect source review program without considering whether such revocation would render the state's plan inadequate to attain and maintain the national ambient air quality standards. We hold that the EPA's construction of this provision is in conflict with the statutory language. Accordingly, we vacate and remand. * * *

In 1973 the Administrator determined that the adoption of an ISR was mandatory if the SIPs were to comply with the standard set forth by the District of Columbia Court of Appeals in *Natural Resource Defense Council, Inc. v. EPA*, 475 F.2d 968 (D.C. Cir. 1973) * * * .

The court required the Administrator to promulgate implementation plans for those states who failed to do so. *Id.* at 971. Since only Florida and Guam had adopted ISRs by the date established by the court, the Administrator was forced to promulgate ISRs for the remaining states in order to comply.

The ISRs promulgated by the EPA, however, drew heavy criticism because they represented a significant federal intrusion into the traditionally local domain of land use control. * * * Congress responded to this criticism by restricting the EPA's funding of the administration of programs designed to tax or limit parking facilities. Pub. L. 95-245, 87 Stat. 1977 (1974). The EPA thus was forced to suspend all federally promulgated ISRs insofar as they pertained to parking facilities, and eventually, in 1976, to suspend the indirect source regulations indefinitely. * * *

In the meantime, however, certain states, including Connecticut, had promulgated their own ISRs. This created an anomalous situation; federally promulgated ISRs were suspended, while those states which had complied voluntarily with the EPA's requirement to establish an ISR could abolish their ISRs only if they could show that their SIPs were still capable of achieving and maintaining the NAAQS. * * * To rectify this situation, Congress included in the 1977 amendments to the Clean Air Act a special provision severely limiting the EPA's authority over ISRs, and permitting the states to revise the SIPs "provided that such plan meets the requirements of this section." [§ 110(a)(5)(A) (iii)] * * * .

Following the enactment of the 1977 amendments and pursuant to the provision referred to above, Connecticut submitted to the Administrator a series of revisions of its ISR, including a proposal to eliminate preconstruction review of all indirect sources except highways and airports. After receiving comments on these proposed revisions, the Administrator approved them on January 26, 1979. The Administrator's approval was premised on his view the section [110(a)(5)(A)(iii)] permitted a state to revise its ISR so long as the state complied with the section's *procedural* requirements of proper notice and hearing. According to the Administrator's construction of the section it did not require the state to show that its SIP was capable of achieving and maintaining the NAAQS, despite the revocation of the ISR.

On March 15, 1979, the Manchester Environmental Coalition and Michael Dworkin filed in this Court a petition to review the Administrator's approval of Connecticut's SIP revision and thereafter presented oral argument. The State of California filed an amicus curiae brief and presented oral argument, opposing the EPA's interpretation, and indicating its interest in a similar ISR deletion request by the State of Nevada. * * *

The plain meaning of the statutory language would seem to be that a state may revoke its ISR provided that its overall SIP complies with all of the requirements of section [110]— *both procedural and substantive.* * * *

We also reject the EPA's contention that its interpretation avoids the dilemma of an internal conflict within subsection (a)(5)(A). The EPA argues that if a state rescinds its ISR without EPA approval or refuses to administer such a program, then the EPA will be required to promulgate and enforce its own ISR—an action which is specifically prohibited by section [110(a)(5)(A)(ii)]. The statue itself, however, makes clear that the Administrator's remedy would not be to promulgate his own plan, inasmuch as the EPA is limited to enforcing ISR's adopted by the states. Moreover, if a state fails to enforce an existing plan, the EPA's remedy would be to enforce the *state* ISR. * * *

Finally, the EPA argues that harsh inequities would result if states that had attempted to comply with the ISR requirement were not permitted to rescind these programs without restriction. Although the adoption of these ISRs may not have been entirely voluntary, the fact nevertheless remains that these states premised their SIPs, at least in part, on the utilization of an ISR. Indeed, it may well be that harsh inequities would result, not if ISR states cannot peremptorily delete these programs, but if other states must watch while an ISR state, the success of whose implementation effort depends on its ISR, abandons its pollution control plan.

In short, none of the arguments advanced by the EPA is sufficient to overcome the clear import of the statutory language itself. * * *

Accordingly, since we find the EPA's construction of the ISR deletion proviso untenable, the EPA order is vacated and the case is remanded to the EPA for further proceedings consistent with this opinion.

## 5. TCP CHALLENGES ON CONSTITUTIONAL GROUNDS

Thus far, we have seen that states were extremely reluctant to adopt TCPs, that the EPA was often forced to do so for them, that Congress responded to public outcry by sharply curtailing the EPA's TCP-drafting options, and that some states got clobbered for "voluntarily" adopting their own TCPs under EPA pressure. Eventually, the TCP saga erupted into high-stakes constitutionally-based challenges to federally-imposed controls. The underlying federalism issues were presented most starkly by the EPA's insistence that state officials who refused to carry out EPA-drafted TCPs could be subjected to civil and perhaps even criminal penalties under Clean Air Act § 113.

# JOHN P.C. FOGARTY, JOSHUA B. EPEL, DONN L. CALKINS & JOHN STAFFORD, TRANSPORTATION CONTROLS AND MOTOR VEHICLE INSPECTION AND MAINTENANCE PROGRAMS

in 2 Law of Environmental Protection
11.08 (Sheldon M. Novick, ed. 1998)

Pennsylvania at first appeared an unlikely SIP adversary, being one of only eight states to submit its own plan before the April 15 [1973] deadline. But following *NRDC*, the state had its transportation control extension canceled, resulting in implementation of new EPA-promulgated regulations. Pennsylvania balked and charged in *Pennsylvania v. EPA*, [500 F.2d 246 (3d. Cir. 1974)] that EPA attempts at enforcement of transportation controls breached the bounds of federalism.

Section 113 * * * facially bestowed upon EPA the power to issue compliance orders, to bring civil actions to enjoin violations, and to seek criminal sanctions against knowing violators. Pennsylvania argued that this section could not be employed to force states to construct transportation control programs; the federal commerce power did not reach this far. Only this one element of the EPA plan was challenged, but if the state argument was correct, EPA would have no power to force a state to carry out transportation controls, including I/M programs.

The Third Circuit upheld the federal enforcement scheme, thereby at least temporarily saving the EPA program. * * *

The EPA victory, however, was short-lived. The Ninth Circuit arrived at a contrary result just one year later in *Brown v. EPA* [521 F.2d 827 (9th Cir. 1975)]. In *Brown*, the court pointedly disagreed with the Third Circuit's statutory and constitutional analysis, and denied to EPA the power to enforce the program intended for California, which had included an I/M program. * * * Even if the Clean Air Act required submission [of TCPs or SIPs], it was questionable whether the federal government could, by injunction, compel a sovereign state to perform a legislative function. Specifically, the court found that, as a matter of statutory interpretation, the Clean Air Act did *not* authorize EPA to take enforcement action against a state for failure to administer *federally* promulgated controls. This conclusion directly opposed that of the Third Circuit. Instead, EPA was only empowered to take action against individual polluters; while the Agency could prohibit the polluting activities of a state, no provision of the Act enabled EPA to require *state* enforcement of *federal* regulations against "polluters, potential or actual, other than the state * * * ." [A] state could always decline to become involved in a federal program.

The decision in *Brown* meant that while the federal government could establish and enforce transportation control measures, the states could not be required to implement them in EPA's stead. This was a potentially devastating blow because, as a practical matter, EPA did not have the resources to sustain a nationwide system. *Brown* was followed in short order by *Maryland v. EPA* [530 F.2d 215 (4th Cir. 1975)] and *District of Columbia v. Train* [521 F.2d 971 (D.C. Cir. 1975)], both of which supported the result in *Brown*.

The Supreme Court granted EPA's petition for certiorari in *EPA v. Brown* to resolve the disagreement among the circuits, but then denied the petition as moot when EPA suggested that its regulations were to be revised. * * *

The issue of EPA's enforcement authority, when inducements fail, remains unresolved. The problem is that the commerce clause gives the federal government some power over state activities, presumably limited by the Tenth Amendment; but the amendment seemingly recites only the tautology that whatever power is not vested in the federal government by virtue of the Constitution remains with the states. * * *

Into the void left by the Supreme Court's non-decision stepped Congress. Mindful of the delicate federal-state issues implicated by the Clean Air Act's enforcement mechanism, as well as its "legal uncertainties," Congress supplied EPA with a different sort of stick.

Congress was committed to the system of transportation controls, particularly the I/M strategy * * * . Employing a device which a few years earlier had successfully prompted the states to establish the 55 miles-per-hour speed limit on all public highways, § 176 of the Clean Air Act was amended to make the approval of projects or award of grants by EPA or the Department of Transportation contingent on state compliance with SIP requirements. The attainment deadline for primary and secondary air quality standards would be extended until 1987, and the states would avoid funding cutoffs and bans on new sources only if they submitted and enforced adequate SIPs with all "reasonably available control measures"—defined to include I/M programs.

This new approach initially produced the same old result: litigation. * * * California was one of two states that failed to submit an acceptable I/M program proposal with their 1979 SIP revision, and EPA consequently pursued federal funding cutoffs under its new authority. * * *

In *Pacific Legal Foundation v. Costle* [14 Envtl. L. Rep. Cas. (BNA) 2121 (E.D. Cal.), *aff'd*, 627 F.2d 917 (9th Cir. 1980)], the threat of a funding cutoff was challenged as an "unconstitutional coercion of the state legislature," summoning both in spirit and in name the federalist demands of *Brown v. EPA*. Far from the "virtual assumption of state sovereignty" attempted by EPA in *Brown*, however, the spending cutoff was a "classic 'carrot and stick' spending condition [of] unquestioned constitutional validity." California, the court observed, was free to reject both the federal money and the conditions attached to it. EPA now had its enforcement mechanism [for I/M programs].

The institution of other transportation control measures did not fare so well * * * . [A]s a practical matter, any alternative controls went unused. The Los Angeles experience caused EPA to be more cautious, and the Agency essentially took the position that parking restrictions and gas rationing were not "reasonably available" controls. * * *

The system of nonattainment sanctions provided by the 1977 Amendments, which were proven effective in *Pacific Legal Foundation v. Costle*, have generally been persuasive in encouraging states to comply with I/M program requisites. [However,] the Clean Air Act's once-vast vision of a comprehensive system of automotive transportation controls * * * is now primarily limited to state I/M programs. * * *

### Notes and Questions

1. What's wrong, in theory, with forcing state and local units of government to implement and enforce such federal mandates as vehicle inspection and maintenance? Why isn't it good government?

2. The Fourth Circuit, D.C. Circuit, and Ninth Circuit, in the TCP cases cited in the preceding reading (and the petitioners in those cases) expressed their constitutional objections in a number of ways. For example, they concluded or asserted that mandatory state enforcement of federally-promulgated TCPs would undermine mechanisms of local political accountability by coercing state and local officials to impose locally unpopular measures, while deflecting accountability from the federal officials who had imposed those measures. The petitioners in *Brown* argued that the lack of synchronization between decisionmaking and political accountability violated the Constitution's guarantee of a republican form of government. The Ninth Circuit strongly suggested that EPA's attempt to force state implementation of the federally promulgated California TCP unconstitutionally severed the taxing from the spending power; accordingly, it refused to construe the Clean Air Act to authorize EPA's enforcement efforts. *See Brown v. EPA* 521 F.2d 827 (9th Cir. 1975).

3. Assume that a species of alligators unique to Florida is much beloved by countless Americans. The existence of these animals is threatened by hunters who remorselessly track them down and kill them for their commercial value. Congress enacts a statute decreeing that the killing of these alligators is prohibited. The statute further commands Florida state officials to enforce this prohibition by discovering, arresting, and fining violators, and by confiscating the fruits of any violation. No federal money is appropriated for this enforcement effort. Finally, the statute provides that Florida officials may be subject to civil penalties if they fail to implement

the law. Florida officials have calculated that meaningful enforcement efforts will cost at least $50 million annually. Is the federal statute unconstitutional? Why or why not?

# PRINTZ v. U.S.

### 521 U.S. 898 (1997)

MR. JUSTICE SCALIA delivered the opinion of the Court.

The question presented in these cases is whether certain interim provisions of the Brady Handgun Violence Prevention Act * * * commanding state and local law enforcement officers to conduct background checks on prospective handgun purchasers and to perform certain related tasks, violate the Constitution.

The Gun Control Act of 1968 (GCA) * * * establishes a detailed federal scheme governing the distribution of firearms. * * *

In 1993, Congress amended the GCA by enacting the Brady Act. * * *

Under the interim provisions, * * * [the] chief law enforcement officers (CLEOs) [in many states] * * * are required to perform certain duties. * * *

Petitioners Jay Printz and Richard Mack, the CLEOs for Ravalli County, Montana, and Graham County, Arizona, respectively, filed separate actions challenging the constitutionality of the Brady Act's interim provisions. * * *

[I]t is apparent that the Brady Act purports to direct state law enforcement officers to participate, albeit only temporarily, in the administration of a federally enacted regulatory scheme. Regulated firearms dealers are required to forward Brady Forms not to a federal officer or employee, but to the CLEOs, whose obligation to accept those forms is implicit in the duty imposed upon them to make "reasonable efforts" within five days to determine whether the sales reflected in the forms are lawful. * * *

The petitioners here object to being pressed into federal service, and contend that congressional action compelling state officers to execute federal laws is unconstitutional. * * *

Federal commandeering of state governments is such a novel phenomenon that this Court's first experience with it did not occur until the 1970's, when the Environmental Protection Agency promulgated regulations requiring States to prescribe auto emissions testing, monitoring and retrofit programs, and to designate preferential bus and carpool lanes. The Courts of Appeals for the Fourth and Ninth Circuits invalidated the regulations on statutory grounds in order to avoid what they perceived to be grave constitutional issues * * * and the District of Columbia Circuit invalidated the regulations on both constitutional and statutory grounds * * * . After we granted certiorari to review the statutory and constitutional validity of the regulations, the Government declined even to defend them, and instead rescinded some and conceded the invalidity of those that remained, leading us to vacate the opinions below and remand for consideration of mootness. * * *

[L]ater opinions of ours have made clear that the Federal Government may not compel the States to implement, by legislation or executive action, federal regulatory programs. * * *

When we were at last confronted squarely with a federal statute that unambiguously required the States to enact or administer a federal regulatory program, our decision should have come as no surprise. At issue in *New York v. United States*, 505 U.S. 144 (1992), were the so-called "take title" provisions of the Low-Level Radioactive Waste Policy Amendments Act of 1985, which required States either to enact legislation providing for the disposal of radioactive waste generated within their borders, or to take title to, and possession of the waste—effectively requiring the States either to legislate pursuant to Congress's directions, or to implement an administrative solution. * * * We concluded that Congress could constitutionally require the States to do neither. * * * "The Federal Government," we held, "may not compel the States to enact or administer a federal regulatory program." * * *

[W]hat we said [in *New York*] bears repeating:

Much of the Constitution is concerned with setting forth the form of our government, and the courts have traditionally invalidated measures deviating from that form. The result may appear 'formalistic' in a given case to partisans of the measure at issue, because such measures are typically the product of the era's perceived necessity. But the Constitution protects us from our own best intentions: It divides power among sovereigns and among branches of government precisely so that we may resist the temptation to concentrate power in one location as an expedient solution to the crisis of the day.

505 U.S. at 187.

We adhere to that principle today, and conclude categorically, as we concluded categorically in *New York*: "The Federal Government may not compel the States to enact or administer a federal regulatory program." * * * The mandatory obligation imposed on CLEOs to perform background checks on prospective handgun purchasers plainly runs afoul of that rule. * * *

We held in *New York* that Congress cannot compel the States to enact or enforce a federal regulatory program. Today we hold that Congress cannot circumvent that prohibition by conscripting the State's officers directly. The Federal Government may neither issue directives requiring the States to address particular problems, nor command the States' officers, or those of their political subdivisions, to administer or enforce a federal regulatory program. It matters not whether policymaking is involved, and no case-by-case weighing of the burdens or benefits is necessary; such commands are fundamentally incompatible with our constitutional system of dual sovereignty. * * *

*Four Justices—Stevens, Souter, Breyer, and Ginsburg—dissented. Several dissenting (and concurring) opinions are omitted.*

## 6. INSPECTION AND MAINTENANCE BLUES

By the end of the 1980s, the federal government had successfully bludgeoned the states into adopting inspection and maintenance programs by using the "carrot" rather than the arguably unconstitutional "stick." Were our problems solved? Consider the following reading.

## EPA AUDITS OF STATE I/M PROGRAMS REVEAL SERIOUS ENFORCEMENT PROBLEMS

16 [Curr. Dev.] Env. Rep. (BNA) 325 (1985)

"Serious levels of non-compliance" with motor vehicle inspection and maintenance programs, including levels as high as 60 percent, were reported in four enforcement programs audited by the Environmental Protection Agency during 1984 and 1985, according to a June 18 progress report issued by the agency.

The two areas with the "worst" problems, Georgia and Memphis, Tenn., have switched from a sticker-based program, requiring motorists to display a sticker after each emissions inspection, to a registration-based program, in which the vehicle cannot be registered until it passes the emissions check * * * .

The problems were found primarily in sticker-based, decentralized programs for which many garages are authorized to perform the emissions check, according to the report, which said there is more potential for cheating in decentralized programs than at centralized facilities operated by a small number of highly-trained people.

The problems in sticker-based enforcement "tend to be caused by an indifference of police officers to sticker violations and by the failure of police departments to devote the necessary resources" to enforcing the law * * * .

The audits led EPA to conclude that, with only a few exceptions, inspection and maintenance programs are "failing to effectively use available program data to monitor and take steps to improve program performance" and the performance of individual inspection stations. Of the programs audited, only one had such routine and timely data analyses * * * .

Another problem is that decentralized programs are reporting lower test failure rates than those for which the program was designed, indicating that some vehicles may be improperly certified by such program[s] * * * . This is caused either by pre-inspection repairs, cheating by inspectors, or a combination of the two * * * .

The agency believes a strong station surveillance program, including regular audits, spot checks with unmarked vehicles, and better data analysis, are necessary to improve performance in decentralized programs * * * .

A few programs appeared to be giving too many waivers to motorists for vehicles that do not pass the emission check * * * . Waiver rates as high as 50 percent were reported in some states * * * . Waivers are allowed in most programs when a motorist has spent about $50 or the price of a tuneup and the vehicle still fails the test * * * . In decentralized programs where service stations have the authority to grant waivers, high waiver rates tend to be caused by a lack of close scrutiny by the state or local agency * * * .

The report said problems with the quality of automobile repairs were found in every program. State and local agencies are paying "minimal attention" to assuring that failed vehicles are repaired properly * * * . The vehicles are usually adjusted to pass the I/M test rather than to manufacturer specifications, resulting in much lower emission reductions * * * .

Test failure data indicate that automobiles that fail the test once have a high probability of failing it again the next year * * * .

## 7. MOTOR VEHICLE USE PROVISIONS OF THE 1990 AMENDMENTS

The 1990 Clean Air Act amendments deleted former §§ 110(a)(2)(B) and (a)(2)(G) (requiring TCPs and I/M programs, as necessary, in *all* SIPs), relocating the TCP and I/M requirements to extensive new sections governing ozone and carbon monoxide nonattainment areas. We will analyze nonattainment beginning at page 496, *infra*, but the basic idea behind the amendments is that ozone and carbon monoxide nonattainment areas are now divided into different *classifications* ("extreme," "serious," and the like), depending on the severity of nonattainment, and that increasingly more onerous SIP requirements must be met as one moves up the scale from the less polluted to the most highly polluted classifications. *See* CAA § 181(a)(1).

The following statutory sections set forth the newest congressional attempts to get mobile source pollution under control in nonattainment areas. Two provisions, especially, have plowed up a snake, as we will see in the readings following these statutory reading assignments.

First, § 182(c)(3) mandating *enhanced* inspection and maintenance programs in "serious" (and even more polluted) ozone nonattainment areas, seeks to put teeth into I/M testing procedures and to stamp out easily-obtainable waivers for flunking vehicles.

Second, § 182(d)(1)(B), mandating new "Employee Trip Reduction" programs (sometimes called the "Employer Commute Option") in *severe* (and even more polluted) ozone nonattainment areas, sought to conscript employers into the motor vehicle pollution control battle that has now dragged on for almost three decades.

------

Read the following sections of the Clean Air Act

☐ § 182(c)(3)(A)      ☐ § 182(c)(3)(C)      ☐ § 182(d)(1)(A)

☐ § 182(d)(1)(B)      ☐ § 182(e)(4)      ☐ § 187(b)(3)(A)

------

## 8. ENHANCED INSPECTION AND MAINTENANCE BLUES

### NEW U.S. EMISSIONS TEST, DEBUTING IN MAINE, IS A FLOP

N.Y. Times, Oct. 2, 1994, at 28

The nation's first experience with a tough new program of automobile emissions testing that the Federal Government will soon require in urban areas around the country has gone so badly that Maine, the program's bellweather state, has had to suspend it.

And resentment against the program, which could prove expensive to many thousands of drivers, is such that the legislatures of at least two other states, Pennsylvania and Vermont, are now balking at speedy adoption of it even though their resistance could ultimately cost them tens of millions of dollars in Federal highway money.

The new testing began in Maine on July 1 and immediately encountered a vast array of start-up problems, intense public criticism and even a petition drive intended to repeal it, a step that would cause the state to lose $72 million a year, virtually all of what Washington provides here for highway construction and maintenance.

Only two months after the program had begun, Maine decided in the face of citizen fury to drop it until next March while efforts were made to work out the kinks.

The new testing system, developed as a way to meet the requirements of the Federal Clean Air Act, is a significant technical advance over the familiar neighborhood-garage tailpipe test, which measures hydrocarbons and carbon monoxide, two of the three major pollutants from auto exhaust.

In the new test, computers connected to a treadmill-like device that causes a vehicle to replicate its highway performance at various speeds measure not only those two pollutants but also the third, nitrogen oxide, which creates ground-level ozone. The treadmill is needed to gauge nitrogen oxide because cars tend to produce much more of this pollutant when under load than when stationary.

Although Maine was the first state to use this new equipment for the Government-required testing, others are due to follow suit soon. During the next year or so, the program is to be applied to all or parts of about 25 states, including every state in New England. In New York State, the new test will be required in the most populous regions, starting in January 1996.

But if the system is more sophisticated and useful than earlier tests, it is also more expensive. Under the program, cars and light trucks must be taken once every two years to any of several special inspection centers, where in Maine the driver pays a fee of $24. That, however, is just the start of the expense for many motorists. After repeated failure to pass the test, a vehicle can ultimately qualify for motor vehicle registration under a waiver permit, but not before the cost of repairs reaches $450.

At the Maine testing stations, operated under a seven-year, $43 million state contract with Systems Control Inc., a California company owned by the Snap-On Tools Corporation, annoyance began surfacing immediately. It started with the company's policy (since abandoned) of demanding that drivers pay the testing fee in cash. Then there were complaints of long waits at the testing centers, attendants unfamiliar with the operation of equipment, computer glitches and wild fluctuations in test results.

There was grumbling, too, that buses and heavy-duty diesel trucks were not subject to testing, even though state environmental officials estimate that these vehicles produce about a third of all the nitrogen oxide on Maine highways. On top of all that, one region of the state seemed to be pitted against another. Although Washington had required the new testing only in three heavily populated areas of southern Maine, the State Legislature, seeking a broader approach to reducing volatile organic compounds, decided in 1992 that the program would apply to a much larger section of the south: 7 of the state's 16 counties. Now Mainers there began complaining because the testing was confined to their region.

Then, about a week after the tests got under way in July, public impatience with the program turned to rage. The stimulus was an offer by Gov. John R. McKernan Jr. to support an expansion of a wood paneling plant in northern Maine's Aroostook County by granting the Louisiana Pacific Corporation air pollution credits that the state had gained from the auto testing program. Motorists forced to comply with the unpopular program in the southern section of the state were incensed that they would be subsidizing industrial pollution in a section where car owners were exempt from testing.

The situation was not helped by the disclosure in news reports that Louisiana Pacific was fined $11.1 million by the Federal Environmental

Protection Agency last year for reporting incorrect air pollution levels at 14 of its plants around the country. Furthermore, the Maine Department of Environmental Protection fined the company $350,000 in 1992 for other air pollution violations—at the very plant where expansion was now planned.

Nor did the controversy subside after Louisiana Pacific announced that it was abandoning the expansion. The focus of public anger was simply redirected at the auto testing program itself. * * *

By the end of August, the state's Department of Environmental Protection and Systems Control had agreed to suspend the program for six months. During that period, to encourage motorists to have their cars tested voluntarily, the testing fee has been lowered to $14 from $24 and the maximum liability for repairs to $125 from $450.

## MATTHEW L. WALD, EPA TO ALLOW FLEXIBILITY IN AUTO TESTING

N.Y. Times, Dec. 10, 1994, at 8

The Environmental Protection Agency, facing open revolt in New Jersey, Pennsylvania, California and elsewhere, is signaling that it will allow changes to make a new kind of auto emission inspection far less burdensome to car owners * * * .

The original EPA plan was for inspections using the same equipment used by the EPA to certify new car models—a treadmill that tests cars while they are "under load," rather than while they are idling, as familiar tailpipe tests do.

Carol M. Browner, the EPA Administrator, told Gov. Christine Todd Whitman of New Jersey and six other governors on Thursday that they would be given new flexibility in meeting the requirements on tailpipe emissions so long as overall clean-air standards were met.

The EPA had counted on enforcing the program through the sanctions specified by the Clean Air Act: cutting off highway money and other Federal aid to the states. But some state legislatures seemed willing to forgo that aid, positions "equivalent to an act of civil disobedience," said David L. Cohen, a special assistant to Ms. Browner.

That would have provoked a confrontation between the EPA and the states, probably in Congress. "I would absolutely prefer not to spend my time and energy in a debate in Congress about amending the Clean Air Act," Ms. Browner said yesterday in a telephone interview. * * *

Others said that if the EPA had adhered strictly to its original emission inspection requirements, it could have unraveled the Clean Air Act, because emission testing affects millions of voters, as opposed to a handful of big industries. "When you begin to have governors organizing against the Clean Air Act, you know you're in real trouble," said Deborah S. Shprentz of the Natural Resources Defense Council, an environmental group that has long sought tougher pollution controls. * * *

The EPA treadmill test measures emissions of carbon monoxide, which is a poison, and of hydrocarbons and nitrogen oxides, which are the main ingredients of smog. In contrast, the tests familiar to millions of car owners at neighborhood gas stations measure only carbon monoxide and hydrocarbons, and those only while the car is idling.

In addition, in most states the emission tests are done by the same neighborhood shops that do the repairs. Federal and state officials believe that many shops routinely agree to pass cars to keep the good will of customers or, in some cases, in exchange for bribes.

## SAM HOWE VERHOVEK, TEXAS JOINS PARADE OF STATES COLLIDING WITH CLEAN AIR ACT

N.Y. Times, Feb. 14, 1995 at A1 col. 1

Early last month, Texas began a program to help reduce smog by 15 percent in its biggest cities. Auto-exhaust inspections were to be required during the next two years for nearly every car and truck in the Houston and Dallas areas. If Texas did not clean up the air, it stood to lose hundreds of millions of dollars in Federal money.

The state signed a contract with a company that invested $127 million in private money to set up test stations. "The skies of Texas are upon you," proclaimed bright blue billboards, informing motorists of the new $23-a-car inspections.

Then the testing began. A revolt ensued. And now the program is on hold. It is the same firestorm that has swept through several other states in recent months as the wrath of motorists has combined with a wave of anti-Federal Government sentiment in state capitals to form a potent challenge to the Federal Clean Air Act, the most comprehensive environmental legislation ever enacted. * * *

In the most thorough tests, the ones that have been strongly preferred by the Environmental Protection Agency, cars are put on treadmill devices, dynamometers. The exhaust and fuel systems are then tested at a variety of engine speeds. When the equipment is working as designed, the test takes only a few minutes.

Although about 80 percent of all cars on the road pass—that is, meet the standards imposed for a given model year—the ones that fail can cost their owners anywhere from $50 for a tuneup to hundreds of dollars for major repairs.

In Texas, the uprising against the new inspection program was swift. Newspapers and television news programs were full of reports featuring motorists objecting to the cost or inconvenience of the tests, or both. State lawmakers said they were deluged with complaints. And many drivers said they would refuse to take the tests altogether.

Within days of the program's kickoff, the Legislature rushed to pass a three-month moratorium, which became the first measure the state's new Governor, George W. Bush, signed into law. Several legislators said they hoped the Republican-controlled Congress would amend the Clean Air Act to make the tests unnecessary or, at most, voluntary.

In Maine, intended to be a kind of pilot project for the emissions tests, the program begun last summer has collapsed. In Pennsylvania, the Legislature voted to delay its inspection program late last year, and when Gov. Robert P. Casey, a Democrat who has since left office, vetoed the measure, it promptly overrode him.

In Virginia, Gov. George F. Allen, a Republican, recently sued to block the EPA from enforcing any provisions of the Clean Air Act, including a testing program. And Gov. Pete Wilson of California, also a Republican, railed against major elements of the Clean Air Act at a Congressional hearing late last week.

"We're the ones who breathe our air," Mr. Wilson said, "not the Federal bureaucrats in Washington."

The Clean Air Act also requires reformulated gasoline, a cleaner-burning fuel blend, in most major metropolitan areas, but Pennsylvania has pulled 28 counties out of that program, and New York and Maine are considering withdrawing several counties each.

The open rebellion in Texas and elsewhere against the tests has become a major headache for the Clinton Administration, which has been under relentless pressure to grant delays in the emissions program. * * * [I]f states simply refuse to carry out the tests, the Clinton Administration could be in the awkward position of having to impose sanctions under the Clean Air Act—including withholding huge chunks of highway transportation aid—at the end of next year, around the time of the Presidential election.

On the other hand, the emissions program could get a political boost from an unexpected source. A provision of the Republicans' Contract With America calls for the Federal Government to find the most cost-effective way to carry out its programs. When it comes to cleaning up the air, there is probably no cheaper way to do it than by fixing people's cars.

Removing smog-causing pollutants from the air costs roughly $500 a ton through a vehicle-emissions program. Removing pollutants from industrial smokestacks costs anywhere from $2,000 to $10,000 a ton, according to EPA figures. * * *

The EPA has long favored centralized inspections * * * . But centralized testing centers proved irritating to motorists, especially in states like Texas, where people whose cars failed were subject to what lawmakers and bureaucrats call "the Ping-Pong effect"—having to go elsewhere for repairs and then return to inspection stations for a sticker. * * *

Proposals in other states include "cash for clunkers," in which the government would pay people to trade in old cars. But there are two problems: first, it is not clear just how many miles such cars are actually driven, and second, the programs risk being excoriated as government handouts. Still, there is logic to the approach: about 15 percent of the cars on the road cause up to 80 percent of the pollution.

The city of Sacramento, Calif., recently completed a four-month trial of a promising new technology known as remote sensing. Inspectors hold a device that resembles a radar gun to measure the exhaust of cars passing on the street. Cars that pollute excessively can be pulled over by the police, or a violation notice can be mailed to an address traced through the license-plate number.

The virtue of such a program is that it does not inconvenience the majority of drivers with cleaner cars; the drawback is that the technology is expensive and relatively untested. * * *

### LAURA JOHANNES, NEW EPA FLEXIBILITY ON EMISSIONS PUTS TEXAS OFFICIALS IN A COSTLY BIND

Wall St. J., Dec. 14, 1994, at T1

Texas could be one of the big losers—to the tune of $100 million—from a decision by federal regulators to relax a tough auto emissions testing rule.

The Environmental Protection Agency said last week that it will ease a requirement, which was to take effect next year, that states implement costly, sophisticated vehicle emissions tests at a limited number of state monitored facilities. Instead, states can allow some less stringent testing at service stations and dealerships, so long as they meet overall pollution reduction goals.

That's good news for states that hadn't acted. But it leaves Texas, which had forged ahead with a testing program, in a bind: Leave the program alone, though it's widely unpopular, or change it, though doing so may be very expensive.

Texas' federally approved testing program—one of the nation's first—is scheduled to start Jan. 2, eight days before the Legislature convenes. Under the program, five million motorists in the Houston, Dallas, Beaumont and El Paso areas must have their cars tested every other year at one of 59 big state sponsored facilities. Using expensive new equipment, the centers will thoroughly test vehicle emissions in hopes of meeting pollution reduction targets in the 1990 Clean Air Act.

Ordinarily, a relaxing of federal mandates would be good news in Texas. Independent minded, car loving Texans already resent the inspections, though they haven't even started yet. And Governor-elect George W. Bush wants the EPA to "let Texans run Texas on this issue," says his spokeswoman, Karen Hughes.

But because Texas moved so quickly to comply with the stringent rules, the EPA's new flexibility appears to have left the state with no good choices. The problem is this: If the state changes the program—as many legislators want—to let people get their cars tested at a much broader network of test and repair sites where they already go for state safety inspections, then the state must compensate the two testing companies with which it contracted two years ago to build the centers and do the centralized testing.

Those companies, Systems Control Inc. of Sunnyvale, Calif., and Marta Technologies Inc. of Nashville, Tenn., built big facilities across the state thinking they would be testing all the cars in the state and getting more than $50 million a year in revenue. Under their contracts, they can demand reparations—up to the more than $100 million they have spent so far—if the state allows testing at other sites. * * *

If it comes to that, some lawmakers say, the state shouldn't have to pay for the EPA's reversal. "The state of Texas did what we were supposed to do as mandated by the federal government," says state Rep. Mike Jackson, a Republican from La Porte, who suggests the state might even sue the EPA over the late rule changes. * * * EPA spokeswoman Martha Casey says the agency will consider giving Texas and other early compliers "extra credit" toward their pollution reduction targets. * * *

Robert Miller, chief executive of Systems Control, the larger of the two contractors, says he will "work with the [State]" on changing the program, if necessary. But, he says, "we think Texas did it right the first time, and we don't see any reason to change."

Voters might, however. Despite the potential costs, political pressure to change Texas' program is already building. Since the EPA's shift, phones all over the state Capitol have been buzzing as legislators consider ways to revamp it before it even begins. "Is it hot?" says one staffer. "It's combustible." * * *

## TIMOTHY AEPPEL, NOT IN MY GARAGE: CLEAN AIR ACT TRIGGERS BACKLASH AS ITS FOCUS SHIFTS TO DRIVING HABITS

Wall St. J., Jan. 25, 1995 at A1

PITTSBURGH—People in this once-sooty industrial city have had their fill of clean air.

Motorists balk at everything from having to use gasoline nozzles that catch excess fuel vapors to buying a new blend of gasoline that trims tailpipe emissions. They refuse to subject their cars to a new type of exhaust test, even though the testing centers have already been built. And they don't want electric cars, either.

"They're like hyperactive children," says Joseph Minott, the somewhat exasperated executive director of the Clean Air Council in Philadelphia. "They just keep shouting 'No! No! No!' no matter what's suggested."

If Pittsburgh were an isolated case, it wouldn't be a problem. But it's not. The Clean Air Act—the broad federal law that gave rise to all those things Pittsburghers hate—is under attack across the country. In Maryland, angry motorists recently marched on the statehouse, demanding a halt to that state's new emissions testing program. Drivers in the New York area can listen to radio talk show hosts gripe about how reformulated gasoline—the more expensive but cleaner burning fuel now sold in the nation's smoggiest cities may be harming their engines and is generally a dumb idea dreamed up by bureaucrats. "They make it sound pretty half baked," admits Thomas Murphy, a bond salesman who tunes in during his daily commute from New Jersey.

Why the uproar? As long as the fight for cleaner skies focused on big smokestacks, few people cared. They figured big companies could afford to make changes. But clean-air rules are now biting into everyday life because they tackle a broader range of pollution problems, environmentalists and government officials say. Many people are worried about losing their jobs, particularly in heavy industry or small businesses that release fumes, like dry cleaning and printing shops. But the most intense backlash is over intrusions on people's driving habits. "Most parts of the country have already dealt with their big, obvious polluters," says Deborah Shprentz, a clean air expert at the Natural Resources Defense Council in Washington. "Auto emissions are the only major thing left that can be cut easily and cost-effectively; it's the lowest-hanging fruit."

Try telling that to the customers of Doug Hess. As owner of a bustling Pittsburgh Exxon station, Mr. Hess has handed out glossy brochures explaining the various new car related rules and even tacked up signs announcing, "We're Helping Clear The Air." The response, he says, has been overwhelmingly negative.

Consider what happened last fall, when Mr. Hess geared up to sell a costlier blend of cleaner-burning gasoline. Under the Clean Air Act, only the smoggiest cities in the U.S. had to use the new fuel as of Jan. 1. Pittsburgh wasn't on the list. But other areas could "volunteer" for it, and Pennsylvania's former Gov. Robert P. Casey had signed up much of the state. When rumors swirled that the new fuel would cost drastically more, motorists balked. As the uproar spread, those regions of Pennsylvania that had been volunteered were withdrawn. In the end, the price of the fuel was only modestly higher than conventional gasoline, averaging about five cents a gallon more.

Then there was the flap over fuel hoses. Early last year, Mr. Hess put nozzles on his pumps with floppy rubber sleeves to catch excess fumes. Many parts of the country already use them, but his customers wanted no part. And since not all stations switched to the new system at the same time, many started flocking elsewhere to fill up. Mr. Hess finally had to switch to yet another system; it still catches fumes but looks more like the original hoses. * * *

Much of the backlash against the Clean Air Act appears to stem from the same anti-Washington mood that swept Republicans into Congress. "Cars have emerged right up there with guns as a Constitutional right," says Elizabeth Thompson, senior policy analyst at the Clean Air Council in Philadelphia. * * *

Sitting at a table in the One More Time bar in suburban Pittsburgh, Glen Cauley says that is fine with him. He thinks efforts to clean the air are out of hand. "Nobody's going to tell me I can't drive my truck," says the 31-year-old auto-bodyshop worker, thumping his beer on the table. He explains that his vintage 1961 Chevy pickup—which he spent six months restoring and painting "Porsche red"—would probably flunk the new test. Older vehicles typically produce more pollution than newer models. Mr. Cauley says he usually goes along with the program when it comes to government rules. The shop where he works, for instance, will eventually have to switch to using different types of paint because of the air rules.

But he has decided that if his truck fails, he will just keep driving it until someone catches him. "Laws like this are meant to be broken," he says. Not that he faces any immediate problem. Pennsylvania is part of a growing band of states—from Texas to Maine—where public opposition is derailing the new tailpipe tests. Pennsylvania last summer suspended the program, even though it had already built a network of testing centers and was in the midst of training hundreds of workers to run them. * * *

[F]or many drivers, the controversy boils down to a simple issue. "Who wants to go sit in a line at one of these places—then go someplace else to get your car fixed?" asks Joe Frena, a 27-year-old Pittsburgh mechanic. "Most people I know have better things to do with their time."

They also can't see how ferreting out the relatively few smoke-belching cars will save the Earth. Especially when the skies around them look pretty clean already. "You should have seen this place when the steel mills were open," says Rodney Herrmann, general manager of a Pittsburgh printing company. "A really foggy day is unusual now. It used to be that way every morning."

Many here link the decline of heavy industry in the region with the rise of environmental controls. This makes them especially suspicious about programs designed to clear the air. * * * Air quality here has soared since the local steel industry collapsed and environmental controls kicked in. But Pittsburgh shows how difficult it is to define what clean air means. Under the Clean Air Act, Pittsburgh is still considered to have moderately dirty air. While it is far better than places like Los Angeles or even Philadelphia, it is still subject to tight restrictions on things such as building new factories.

Two decades ago, residents could see the problem—dirt in the air churned out by the mills. Now it is more likely to be invisible gases, such as smog-producing ozone. This helps explain why many people here are often confused. They keep hearing about how much cleaner the air is now than in the past and can see it—and know Pittsburgh meets federal standards for clean air, except for the area around Clairton. But to get reclassified as "clean," the city must prove it can stay that way.

Which brings the story back to all those things the drivers here are screaming about. Under the Clean Air Act, states have to give the EPA detailed plans showing how they intend to meet various air goals and then keep it that way. And in the case of Pittsburgh, things like reformulated gasoline and tougher emissions tests were considered key to this.

Most analysts now believe it will be almost impossible to push through all the controls on cars. But that leaves business in an awkward position. "The air-quality improvements have to come from somewhere," says Mr. Minott, from the Clean Air Council. "And if they don't get it from cars, they'll go back to focusing on the stationary sources—and that means hitting business." * * *

Meanwhile, Quentin Haigy is pondering what clean air has done for him lately. His face smudged with soot, he is on a short lunch break from his job at the Clairton coke mill. Standing near the counter in Gary's Fast Food, just outside the plant's main gate, he says he once went searching for work in Alaska, where they have very clean air. Now, he says, he has a Cadillac and a good job that pays union wages. "These clean-air people want everything perfect," he says, "like Alaska"—where he couldn't find as good a job.

### Notes and Questions

1.  Former Governor Pete Wilson of California is quoted at page 449, *supra*, complaining: "We're the ones who breathe our air, not the Federal bureaucrats in Washington." Texas lawmakers are paraphrased at page 451, *supra*, to have said: "the state shouldn't have to pay for the EPA's reversal." Radio talk show hosts gripe, according to the article at page 452, *supra*, that reformulated gasoline "may be harming their engines and is generally a dumb idea dreamed up by bureaucrats." Who is the villain in all of this whining? Is that scapegoat really the entity that has mandated the use of reformulated gasoline, enhanced inspection and maintenance, and the like? Might the whiners have political reasons for attacking their chosen scapegoat, rather than the real culprits?

2.  Why should the federal government tell Californians and Texans what their air quality must be? If "the skies of Texas are upon" Texans, shouldn't we just let them work out their own air quality solutions?

3.　Arguments for and against state and local control on various issues are often strategic and ad hoc:

> Political actors unhesitatingly change their views about the importance of state autonomy depending on their own narrow, immediate political needs. A recent example is a proposal by Republicans in the House of Representatives—the same Republicans who have championed the elimination of unfunded mandates and who want to "return power to the states"—to enact federal legislation that would preempt state law on punitive damages and products liability (including liability for drug and medical companies).

John P. Dwyer, *The Practice of Federalism Under the Clean Air Act,* 54 Md. L. Rev. 1183, 1186 n.11 (1995). Couldn't similar allegations of inconsistency be leveled against members of the Democratic Party? Can such examples of inconsistency (by Republicans and Democrats alike) be explained by commitments to overarching values other than state and local autonomy? What might those values be?

### 9.　UNFUNDED MANDATES REFORM ACT OF 1995

The anger of state and local officials over the enhanced inspection and maintenance program requirements is just one example of the intergovernmental friction that fueled enactment of the Unfunded Mandates Reform Act of 1995, codified in scattered sections of Title 2 of the United States Code.

### RECENT LEGISLATION: UNFUNDED MANDATES REFORM ACT OF 1995

109 Harv. L. Rev. 1469, 1470-73 (1996)

The Unfunded Mandates Reform Act [UMRA] was one of only two bills in the Contract with America enacted in the first 100 days of the 104th Congress, undoubtedly because it received President Clinton's support. * * *

The UMRA requires the separate, recorded approval of a majority of both houses of Congress for any provision in a bill that imposes costs of more than $ 50 million on state and local governments. The law also largely codifies new rulemaking procedures that President Clinton adopted to require agencies to consult with state and local officials before promulgating unfunded mandates. * * *

The UMRA requires Congress to obey special procedures in order to enact new unfunded mandates. The Act defines a federal intergovernmental mandate, in part, as "any [involuntary] provision in legislation, statute, or regulation that * * * would impose an enforceable duty upon State, local, or tribal governments," or that would reduce funding for a previously imposed mandate. [2 U.S.C. § 1555] The Act exempts federal mandates that enforce constitutional rights; prohibit discrimination on account of race, color, religion, sex, national origin, age, handicap or disability; * * * impose accounting and auditing requirements for federal funds[;] * * * that are imposed as part of a disaster relief program requested by the state; that are "necessary for the national security" or to implement treaties; that the President and Congress designate as emergency legislation; or that relate to the old-age, survivors, and disability insurance program under * * * the Social Security Act. [2 U.S.C. § 1503] The Congressional Budget Office (CBO) must evaluate all bills that contain significant intergovernmental or private sector mandates to determine their costs. [2 U.S.C. § 658b] A bill's committee report must contain this cost estimate * * * . [2 U.S.C. §§ 658d] If the estimated cost of an unfunded mandate exceeds $50 million per year, the provision establishing the mandate will not be "in order," [2 U.S.C. § 1514] which means that any member may object to its passage by raising a point of order with the Chair. The mandate will be stricken from the bill unless a majority votes to waive the point of order. * * *

If a bill contains a significant intergovernmental mandate that the CBO has not evaluated and the bill somehow makes it to the floor, it too would be subject to a point of order. * * * There is no point-of-order enforcement against "private sector mandates," but the CBO must still evaluate such mandates if they exceed a $ 100 million threshold. * * *

The Act also codifies new agency rulemaking procedures that President Clinton established in response to Vice President Gore's "reinventing government" report. Agencies must identify mandates that are likely to cost governments or the private sector more than $100 million annually and provide detailed reports, including cost-benefit analyses, justifying such mandates. [2 U.S.C. § 1532] Agencies must also select the "least costly, most cost-effective or least burdensome" of "a reasonable number of regulatory alternatives" or provide a written explanation for their failure to do so. [2 U.S.C. § 1535] * * *

For structural critics, unfunded mandates stem from Congress's desire to provide government services without raising the revenue needed to pay for them. * * * The burden of unfunded mandates is a form of "hidden taxation" designed to prevent the electorate from realizing the cost of the services that interest groups support. * * * To avoid this problem, structural critics advocate substantive safeguards against unfunded mandates—such as court intervention, a constitutional amendment, or supermajority requirements. * * *

Less strident critics, such as Vice President Al Gore, view unfunded mandates not as a structural problem, but as a managerial one. * * *

Surprisingly, Vice President Gore's managerial vision, rather than the Contract with America, animates the UMRA. First, and most important, the Act merely establishes new procedures. The point of order limits unfunded mandates by making Congress more accountable, but imposes no substantive limits on Congress's enumerated powers; the point of order can be waived by a simple majority vote. Second, the Act has a list of exceptions so expansive that it may swallow up the rule. Only nine of twenty-seven mandates passed during the 1980s would have fallen under the Act. Finally, the Act provides no relief for already existing mandates, which, after all, provoked the unfunded mandates reform movement. * * *

---

As a practical matter, the UMRA will require the sponsor of any bill imposing unfunded intergovernmental mandates exceeding $50 million per year to: (1) obtain federal funding to pay for the implementation (precluding a point of order under 2 U.S.C. § 658d(a)(2)); or (2) win a majority of both houses of Congress to waive the requirement and, thus, enact the legislation without federal funding. This "ensures that a majority of Congress is either willing to underwrite the cost of the implementation of the mandate, or considers the costs of the mandate to be properly the business of state, local or tribal governments." Eileen M. Luna, *The Impact of the Unfunded Mandates Reform Act of 1995 on Tribal Governments*, 22 Am. Indian L. Rev. 445, 450 (1998). If a member of the House of Representatives raises the point of order, the statute limits debate to 10 minutes for each side of the issue. *See* 2 U.S.C. § 658e(b)(4).

One author concludes that the point of order mechanism is best understood as a tinkering with leadership powers in the Congress:

> UMRA gives the speaker of the House and, to a lesser extent, the Senate's leadership broad discretion to block consideration of a bill subject to a point of order. This is so because, at least in the House, the Speaker rarely refers points of order for a vote by the full House, but rules on them himself. And, while the Speaker's ruling is technically appealable to the full House, this type of appeal is extremely rare. * * * Even if appealed, the Speaker's ruling is likely to be upheld along partisan lines, because the vote becomes a battle over the powers of the Speaker.

Makram B. Jaber, *Comment: Unfunded Federal Mandates: An Issue of Federalism or a "Brilliant Sound Bite"?*, 45 Emory L.J. 281, 282 n.8 (1996).

In any event, because the point of order may be overridden a simple majority, "[t]he political will necessary to override the UMRA is * * * no more—and no less—than the will necessary to enact the mandate in the first place." Rena I. Steinzor, *Unfunded Environmental Mandates and the "New (New) Federalism": Devolution, Revolution, or Reform?*, 81 Minn. L. Rev. 97, 144-45 (1996).

## 10. EMPLOYEE TRIP REDUCTION PROGRAM

In addition to the enhanced inspection and maintenance requirement of the 1990 Clean Air Act Amendments, state and local officials have balked at the employee trip reduction program for severe (and more highly polluted) ozone nonattainment areas. As originally enacted in the 1990 Amendments, § 182(d)(1)(B) provided:

(B) Within 2 years after November 15, 1990, the State shall submit a revision requiring employers in such area to implement programs to reduce work-related vehicle trips and miles traveled by employees. Such revision shall be developed in accordance with guidance issued by the Administrator pursuant to section 7408(f) of this title and shall, at a minimum, require that each employer of 100 or more persons in such area increase average passenger occupancy per vehicle in commuting trips between home and the workplace during peak travel periods by not less than 25 percent above the average vehicle occupancy for all such trips in the area at the time the revision is submitted. The guidance of the Administrator may specify average vehicle occupancy rates which vary for locations within a nonattainment area (suburban, center city, business district) or among nonattainment areas reflecting existing occupancy rates and the availability of high occupancy modes. The revision shall provide that each employer subject to a vehicle occupancy requirement shall submit a compliance plan within 2 years after the date the revision is submitted which shall convincingly demonstrate compliance with the requirements of this paragraph not later than 4 years after such date.

### Notes and Questions

1.  Observe that the statute, as originally enacted by Congress, measured success by average vehicle occupancy or AVO. Specifically, each employer of 100 or more persons must increase the average passenger occupancy per vehicle during peak travel times to "not less than 25% of the average vehicle occupancy for all such trips in the area at the time the [SIP] revision is submitted."

2.  Suppose all 100 employees at a given company drive to work alone at the time when the revised SIP is submitted. What is the company's initial AVO rate?

3.  If the AVO rate for *all* trips in a severe ozone nonattainment area is 1.2, what AVO level must the company achieve under the command of § 182(d)(1)(B), as originally worded by the Congress?

4.  If all 100 employees continue to ride in automobiles, they will obviously have to carpool to achieve the target AVO. What is the maximum number of cars that these 100 employees may use, if the target AVO is to be achieved? How many cars would be taken off the road under this approach?

5.  Now suppose that 36 of the 100 employees leave their cars at home. Rather than catching rides with co-workers, however, they take public transportation, walk, bicycle, or telecommute. What would be the company's resulting AVO? Would the employer have succeeded in attaining the target AVO mandated by the original congressional enactment? Why or why not? *See* Michael Herz, *Judicial Textualism Meets Congressional Micromanagement: A Potential Collision in Clean Air Act Interpretation*, 16 Harv. Envtl. L. Rev. 175, 188-89 (1992).

# ILLINOIS SUSPENDS TRIP REDUCTION PROGRAM

25 [Curr. Dev.] Env. Rep. (BNA) 2301 (1995)

Illinois Gov. James Edgar suspended the state's commute options program under the Clean Air Act March 12. He said the trip reduction requirements under the act are burdensome, expensive, and ill-conceived.

At a press briefing in Chicago, Edgar called the trip reduction requirements a costly federal mandate that "produces little environmental benefit." He criticized the U.S. Environmental Protection Agency for failing to give states a clear understanding of how to implement the federal program. Pennsylvania, New Jersey, and Texas have also announced the suspension of their programs. In addition, Edgar said Illinois should not be obligated to proceed with the program at a time when Congress is considering a repeal of the requirements or legislative action making trip reduction voluntary.

"The U.S. Environmental Protection Agency has sent mixed signals on whether we should take the program seriously, and Congress is now considering legislation to remove the mandate," Edgar said. "So, it makes no sense for Illinois employers and state officials to proceed with this ill conceived program."

The commuter provisions of the Clean Air Act would have forced more than 6,000 employers in the Chicago metropolitan area to reduce commuter trips by their employees by 25 percent. The program was scheduled to begin on April 1 with the Illinois Department of Transportation sending notification letters to the affected employers. Edgar said California's trip reduction efforts have been "an unqualified disaster." He said there are more effective ways to improve air quality in Illinois than the trip reduction program. Edgar noted, however, that the state would support employers who wished to establish trip reduction programs on a voluntary basis.

Dick Adorjan, a spokesman for IDOT, said his agency encouraged Edgar to suspend the program. He said IDOT concluded that the program served no environmental purpose and would have cost the state and employers millions of dollars unnecessarily. "We were never particularly supportive of the program because we were never convinced it could do anything to improve the environment," Adorjan said.

## 11. FULL CONGRESSIONAL RETREAT

As illustrated in the preceding pages, two significant mobile source pollution provisions in the 1990 Clean Air Act Amendments were highly controversial. The employee trip reduction program of § 182(d)(1)(B) and the enhanced inspection and maintenance requirements of § 182(c)(3)—both applicable in the most highly polluted ozone nonattainment areas—met with overwhelming public resistance.

In late 1995, Congress responded to public pressure in two enactments. First, in Public Law 104-70, 109 Stat. 773, Congress amended § 182(d)(1)(B) to make the employee trip reduction option voluntary, rather than mandatory, and invited states to withdraw previously promulgated programs. The provision was enacted in the House during one of House Speaker Newt Gingrich's widely-advertised "Corrections Days," for amending "flawed" statutes.

Second, Congress attached a "moratorium on certain emissions testing requirements" to a highway bill, Public Law No. 104-59, 109 Stat. 617 (1995). The most significant language of the moratorium (§ 348 of the public law) is as follows:

> (a) In general.—The Administrator of the Environmental Protection Agency (hereinafter in this section referred to as the 'Administrator') shall not require adoption or implementation by a State of a test-only I/M240 enhanced vehicle inspection and maintenance program as a means of compliance with section 182 or 187 of the Clean Air Act, but the Administrator may approve such a program if a State chooses to adopt the program as a means of compliance with such section.

> (b) Limitation on plan disapproval.—The Administrator shall not disapprove or apply an automatic discount to a State implementation plan revision under section 182 or 187 of the Clean Air Act on the basis of a policy, regulation, or guidance providing for a discount of emissions credits because the inspection and maintenance program in such plan revision is decentralized or a test-and-repair program.

Further explanation of the two 1995 amendments can be found in 26 [Curr. Dev.] Env. Rep. (BNA) 1262 (1995) and 26 [Curr. Dev.] Env. Rep. (BNA) 1551 (1995).

## 12. MOBILE SOURCES: A POSTMORTEM

# WILLIAM H. RODGERS, JR., 1 ENVIRONMENTAL LAW: AIR AND WATER

### § 3.29 (1986)

The evolution of the inspection and maintenance programs in the twenty-nine states in which they are required offers a capsule summary of many of the policy imperatives that drive the Clean Air Act. The system requires that increments of pollution slipping through the manufacturing grid be recaptured later if the faith is kept about the size of the pollution pie that must be retired. Nomination of individual auto owners as the ultimate losers in this game of musical chairs has been resisted on a variety of empirical and philosophical grounds, many of them quite convincing—efficiency (HC can be controlled from stationary sources at a fraction of the cost of the I & M control programs), fairness (driver harassment would be unnecessary if the standards were not consumed annually by the waiver process), utility (the marginal improvements from the shaky I & M programs don't make a difference, swamped as they are by the larger variables of vehicle design and driver habits), and technological impossibility (satisfactory short tests were a long time arriving and have never won anything approaching a scientific seal of approval). The debate over means has been so consistently debilitating that even sympathetic observers have reargued the goal, which doesn't sound so grand when characterized as a striving to improve the air on the worst days in the most polluted parts of the country to accommodate a weak-lunged minority.

## G. CLEAN AIR ACT
## PERMIT PROGRAMS

You have now been introduced to the basic structure of the Clean Air Act program, as that statute was shaped by the 1970 amendments and subsequently tinkered with in the 1977 and 1990 amendments. Superimposed on this basic 1970 structure by the 1977 and 1990 Amendments are three permit programs that dominate today's scheme for stationary sources: (1) the Prevention of Significant Deterioration (PSD) program codified in Title I, Part C, of the Act; (2) the Nonattainment program codified in Title I, Part D; and (3) the Operating Permit program codified in Title V. Because the PSD and Nonattainment programs apply primarily to new sources (they also cover certain source modifications), the two programs are frequently lumped together under the label "new source review" or NSR.

Each of the three Clean Air Act permit programs is so complex that its implementation requires the participation of highly skilled attorneys and officials.

## H. PREVENTION OF
## SIGNIFICANT DETERIORATION

### 1. THE NONDEGRADATION PRINCIPLE

### N. WILLIAM HINES, A DECADE OF NONDEGRADATION POLICY IN CONGRESS AND THE COURTS: THE ERRATIC PURSUIT OF CLEAN AIR AND CLEAN WATER

62 Iowa L. Rev. 643 (1977)

The idea of reducing pollution by spreading out discharge sources to take fuller advantage of the assimilative capacity of existing areas of high ambient air and water quality seems eminently sensible, but it raises two fundamental issues of resource management policy that have kept the nation's pollution control programs embroiled in controversy for the past ten years. The two issues are related and involve critical pollution control concepts. One concerns the question of what is the fairest and most effective approach for society to utilize if pollution is to be cleaned up; the other involves a more abstract question about the proper relationship between humans and fragile elements of their physical environment. * * *

The essence of the first issue is captured in the slogan, "Dilution is not the solution to pollution." The basic disagreement has centered on the policy soundness and the administrative feasibility of implementing a pollution control program based on the protection of specified minimum levels of ambient resource quality. The minimum levels (called ambient standards) are determined with reference to quality characteristics required to sustain present and projected human uses of the resource. * * *

The alternative position, which seems to have gained ascendance in the United States pollution control policy, holds generally that dischargers should be treated uniformly without regard to ambient resource conditions. * * * To differentiate between dischargers on the basis of more or less favorable geographic locations for ambient resource quality is thought to be administratively infeasible and equitably undesirable. * * *

The second * * * issue * * * is whether these high quality ambient resources should be allowed to suffer any degradation. The initial policy issue raised was whether existing high quality areas should be accorded any protection or should be allowed to deteriorate to the prescribed minimum level. * * * Since 1966, except for brief periods of backsliding, federal pollution control programs have been committed publicly to a policy of nondegradation. In a nutshell, nondegradation policy requires that no significant deterioration be allowed in existing high quality air and water unless necessary to meet compelling social or economic needs. Basically, the policy is a type of broad-gauge ambient standard under which the minimum is based not on specific user needs, but rather on a historic baseline of actual resource quality. Unlike conventional ambient standards that fix specific minimum levels of ambient air or water quality that cannot be violated, nondegradation policy does not make existing resource quality an absolute minimum. Rather, the existing ambient quality is treated as a baseline that cannot be transgressed to a significant degree unless it can be shown clearly that the social value of the activity that will cause deterioration in an existing high quality resource exceeds the value associated with maintenance of the status quo. Thus, the nondegradation policy serves to create a rebuttable presumption in favor of preservation of existing high quality air and water resources, and casts on the would-be developer the burden of demonstrating either that the proposed enterprise will not significantly degrade ambient resources or, that if such degradation will occur, it is justified by the social and economic value of the activity.

While nondegradation policy theoretically could be applied to all areas in which operative pollution control standards are currently being met, in practice its impact is limited to sparsely settled areas where little or no economic development has yet occurred. Thus, it serves as the pollution control analogue to wilderness preservation in public lands management. Not surprisingly, many of the high quality airsheds and watersheds in which recognition of a nondegradation policy is most critical are in, over, or adjacent to land areas that are or could be classified as wilderness.

## 2. PSD PROGRAM OVERVIEW

### JOHN QUARLES, FEDERAL REGULATION OF NEW INDUSTRIAL PLANTS

Env. Rep. (BNA) Monograph No. 28 at 7-8 (1979)

Of all the federal laws placing environmental controls on new industrial plants, perhaps the most confusing and also most restrictive are the limits imposed by the Clean Air Act to prevent significant deterioration of air quality. These limits, commonly referred to as PSD, apply in areas of the country which are already cleaner than required to meet the ambient air quality standards.

This regulatory framework evolved out of judicial and administrative action under the 1970 Clean Air Act, and subsequently was given a full-blown statutory foundation by the 1977 Clean Air Act Amendments. It is therefore particularly useful to examine that background and the basic concepts as they evolved. As enacted in 1970, the Clean Air Act contained no provisions dealing explicitly with protection of air quality in clean air regions. The entire structure of regulatory controls established through the state implementation plans focused on reducing existing levels of pollution in areas where the air quality standards were being violated. The Act did require EPA to promulgate new source performance standards to require new plants wherever located to install the best systems of emission reduction found by the Administrator to have been adequately demonstrated. Some people feared, however, that the tight controls in the implementation plans would force new industrial growth into areas of the country where little or no previous industrialization had occurred, with a risk of downgrading the existing high air quality of such areas. This fear applied particularly to the anticipated construction of huge coal-fired powerplants in portions of the Southwest historically known for their pristine air permitting visibility for distances as high as 80 miles.

The idea of establishing some controls to prevent the deterioration of high air quality had been considered in the legislative history of the 1970 Act, and an early draft of EPA guidelines under the Act would have encouraged states to develop such controls. The regulations finally promulgated by EPA to specify required elements in the state implementation plans, however, made no mention of such controls. That omission was challenged in a lawsuit brought by the Sierra Club. The suit ultimately resulted in a decision, *Sierra Club v. Train,* by the U.S. Supreme Court, which by a four-to-four tie vote left in effect a lower court decision in favor of the Sierra Club. This required EPA to develop some form of regulatory program to prevent significant deterioration.

Having no guidance at all from either Congress or the courts as to the nature of the controls it was required to establish, EPA was obliged to come up with the program on its own. The Agency's approach reflected a judgment that the amount of deterioration of air quality which should be permitted as a consequence of industrial development should retain some flexibility to respond to judgments made through the local political process on the extent of industrial growth desired in a given region. Accordingly, EPA established an *area classification scheme* to be applied in all clean air regions. The basic idea was that a moderate amount of industrial development should be routinely permitted in all areas but that industrialization should not be allowed to degrade air quality to the point that it barely complied with air quality standards, in the absence of a conscious public decision in favor of such growth. In addition, an opportunity should be provided for states to designate certain areas where pristine air quality was especially valued and any growth generating significant emissions of pollutants should be tightly curtailed. Thus, sprang to life the system for classifying all areas as Class I, Class II, or Class III.

The *Class I* category was to include the pristine areas subject to tightest control. *Class II* covered areas of moderate growth. *Class III* was for areas of major industrialization. Under the EPA regulations, promulgated in December 1974, all areas were initially classified as Class II. States were authorized to reclassify specified areas to be either Class I or Class III.

The EPA regulations also established another critical concept known as the *increment.* This is the numerical definition of the amount of additional pollution which may be allowed through the combined effects of all new growth in a particular locality. * * *

Since the PSD scheme does contemplate that certain limitations would be placed on the amount of growth permitted in any given area, an implicit question was whether a system would be devised to select which industrial projects would be permitted to use up the available increment or whether that would simply be resolved on a first-come, first-served basis. EPA did not undertake to resolve that question. Its initial analysis indicated that the numerical limits selected would be sufficient to allow substantial industrial development in any Class II area. Hence the program would not be apt to pinch new projects, at least in its early years.

EPA did impose one major additional requirement to assure that the increments would not be used up hastily. It specified that each major new plant must install the *best available control technology* ("BACT") to limit its emissions. This reinforced the same policy underlying the new source performance standards and indeed EPA declared that where new source performance standards had been promulgated they would control determinations of BACT. Where such standards had not been promulgated, an ad hoc determination was called for in each case.

To implement these controls, EPA imposed a requirement that each new source undergo a *preconstruction review*. The regulations prohibited a company from commencing construction on a new source until the review had been completed, and they provided that as part of the review procedures public notice should be given and an opportunity provided for a public hearing on any disputed questions of fact.

A fundamental feature of the PSD regulation adopted by EPA was the limited nature of the program. It excluded the automobile pollutants (hydrocarbons, photochemical oxidants, carbon monoxide, and nitrogen oxide) from the program altogether. It also excluded numerous miscellaneous activities which might cause pollution, as well as the construction of new small sources. The new controls applied only to large new plants within 19 specific industrial categories, such as power plants, steel mills, refineries, or smelters.

---

Read the following sections of the Clean Air Act

☐ § 107(d)(1)(A)    ☐ § 107(e)(1)    ☐ § 110(a)(2)(C)    ☐ § 110(a)(2)(D)

☐ § 160    ☐ § 161    ☐ § 162    ☐ § 163(a)

☐ § 163(b)    ☐ § 164(a)    ☐ § 164(b)(1)(A)    ☐ § 164(b)(1)(C)

☐ § 164(b)(2)    ☐ § 165(a)    ☐ § 165(c)    ☐ § 165(e)

☐ § 166(a)    ☐ § 166(e)    ☐ § 167    ☐ § 169(1)

☐ § 169(2)(C)    ☐ § 169(3)    ☐ § 169(4)    ☐ § 111(a)(4)

---

### Notes and Questions

1. In which geographical locations do the PSD requirements apply? The answer to this critically important issue is surprisingly difficult to locate in the statute, but is inherent in the text of CAA §§ 161 and 167.

2. Who determines which locations in the country are attainment areas, which are nonattainment areas, and which are unclassifiable areas? How is this determination made?

3. Who determines which attainment areas in the country are allocated to Class I, Class II, and Class III? How is this determination made?

---

For ease of reference, **Table 9-3** sets forth the maximum allowable increments under the PSD program for each pollutant/class combination, as well as their primary and secondary NAAQS.

**Table 9-3**
Maximum Allowable Increment
(micrograms per cubic meter [$\mu g/m^3$])
Source: CAA § 163(b) & 40 C.F.R. §§ 50.4-.12, 52.21(c) (1998)

| | $PM_{10}$ | | $SO_2$ | | | $NO_2$ |
|---|---|---|---|---|---|---|
| | Annual Arithmetic Mean | 24-hr Max | Annual Arithmetic Mean | 24-hr Max | 3-hr Max | Annual Arithmetic Mean |
| Class I | 4 | 8 | 2 | 5 | 25 | 2.5 |
| Class II | 17 | 30 | 20 | 91 | 512 | 25 |
| Class III | 34 | 60 | 40 | 182 | 700 | 50 |

| | | | | | | |
|---|---|---|---|---|---|---|
| Primary NAAQS | 50 | 150 | 80 | 365 | | 100 |
| Secondary NAAQS | 50 | 150 | | | 1300 | 100 |

# BRADLEY I. RAFFLE, PREVENTION OF SIGNIFICANT DETERIORATION AND NONATTAINMENT UNDER THE CLEAN AIR ACT—A COMPREHENSIVE REVIEW

Env. Rep. (BNA) Monograph No. 27 at 2, 5, 50-51, 58, 67 (1979)

The Clean Air Act Amendments of 1977 made comprehensive changes in EPA's regulations for preventing significant deterioration of clean air and improving the quality of polluted air. These two programs, known respectively as PSD and nonattainment, have come to dominate the regulatory and political landscape of the Clean Air Act.

The impact of these programs on the states, EPA, and industry is profound. * * *

Appreciation of the respective roles of EPA and the states under the Clean Air Act is important to understanding PSD and nonattainment. Both are federally promulgated requirements. As such, primary enforcement authority technically rests with EPA. In practice, however, the nationwide scope of these requirements has forced EPA to delegate much of this responsibility to the states. * * *

The state implementation plan revisions called for by the Act's new PSD and nonattainment provisions are stated in a way which requires the respective boundaries of a state's PSD and nonattainment areas to be accurately defined. Section 107(d), therefore, directed each state to submit a list to EPA of the NAAQS attainment status of all state areas.

EPA promulgation of the formal list, with any necessary modifications, was required within 60 days of the submittal of the state lists. This original list was published in the Federal Register on March 3, 1978, and it has been revised several times since then. These Section 107 designations are subject to revision under Section 107(d)(5) of the Act whenever sufficient data warrant a redesignation. Both the state and EPA can initiate changes to the designations, but any state redesignations must be submitted to EPA for concurrence. Private parties must, therefore, work through the state or EPA to initiate a change in the designations.

Section 107(d) specified that designations should reflect air quality levels on the date of enactment of the amendments (August 7, 1977). * * *

As noted in the preamble to the March 3 Federal Register promulgation, the designation of an area as attainment or nonattainment must be considered only a point of departure for new source review and not as a final end in itself.

There are several reasons for this. First, the Act makes clear that the designations are to be revised to reflect more current or accurate air quality data. Second, the designations will have only limited significance for new source reviews because under both the PSD and nonattainment preconstruction review procedures, major new and modified sources must undergo a preliminary modeling analysis to determine their impact upon *all* nearby areas, not merely the area in which they will be located. Thus, a case-by-case impact analysis is required to determine the impact on all neighboring areas and to account for the possibility that an area with a particular designation may encompass "pockets" which do not fit that designation. Finally, PSD rules apply in any area where at least one NAAQS is attained. Because almost every area in the U.S. shows attainment for at least one criteria pollutant, the PSD review will be required for major new and modified sources, regardless of where they locate. * * *

Few other EPA regulations have drawn so much criticism as PSD. As with other complex and expensive environmental programs, much of the criticism is valid and much of it is not. Clearly the most serious criticism of PSD is the general charge that it may stifle or even halt industrial growth in much of the nation, while producing little benefit in terms of air quality or human health.

This charge cannot be discounted as routine industry rhetoric. Despite EPA attempts to soften the PSD preconstruction review and BACT requirements, they are certain to add substantially to the cost of building and operating new industrial facilities. More significantly, there is a very real possibility that the allowable increments will be consumed in many PSD areas in the not too distant future.

Increment consumption occurs as a result of increases in allowable emissions from major new and modified sources commencing construction after January 6, 1975 and SIP relaxations submitted after August 7, 1977. Under EPA's interpretation of the Act (an interpretation which appears consistent with the legislative history) a PSD area in which the increment is consumed becomes, for all practical purposes, a nonattainment area. For major new or modified sources to be allowed to locate in or around such areas, states will have the same basic alternatives available in nonattainment areas. These include emission offset transactions or SIP revisions which tighten emission limitations for existing sources. The difficulty with both options, however is that existing sources are generally not as plentiful in PSD areas as in typically more industrialized nonattainment areas. Thus, in many cases, there will be no existing emissions available to offset or otherwise "make room" for major new sources in PSD areas where the increment has been used up.

State plan revisions to implement the new PSD requirements must specify the measures both to protect the increments and allocate their use. To meet this objective, the state must include a program to assess periodically whether emissions from exempted or unreviewed sources are endangering an applicable increment or ambient standard. If a periodic review shows an area to be in violation of an increment, then the plan must be revised to roll back emissions from *existing* sources to a level such that the increment is no longer exceeded. This may induce the use of economic incentives such as emissions charges or the development of offset markets.

To assist the states in this effort, EPA is initiating studies to assess the feasibility of various allocation programs. As noted earlier, the agency will evaluate approaches in which economic incentives serve as a supplement to, or a replacement for, an administrative permitting procedure. * * *

The concept of air quality deterioration must obviously be related to an ambient status quo. Since air pollution existed long before the PSD regulations were promulgated, this starting point is obviously not zero. Rather, it must reflect air quality at a fixed point in time. Under the PSD regulations, deterioration may occur beyond this "baseline" air quality level until the allowable increment is consumed or the ambient ceiling is reached, whichever occurs first.

Section 169(4) of the Act defines the "baseline concentration" for a pollutant as the ambient level which exists "at the time of the first application for a permit in an area subject to [Part C of the new Act]." The section then goes on to provide that this baseline concentration shall include the contribution from all projected emissions from any major source which commenced construction prior to January 6, 1975, but which had not begun operation by the date the baseline was formally established. * * *

The new PSD requirements call for tremendous commitments of public and private resources. Yet, the PSD program, by its very terms, lacks an established relationship with the public health and welfare goals it is designed to protect. While the program does protect existing clean areas, it demands a large price to protect air which is already cleaner than required by the national primary and secondary ambient standards. Theoretically, those standards are set at levels protective of public health and welfare, with an adequate safety margin built in.

# JOHN QUARLES, FEDERAL REGULATION OF NEW INDUSTRIAL PLANTS

Env. Rep. (BNA) Monograph No. 28 at 8-11, 13-15 (1979)

The current significance of the PSD program established by EPA in 1974 is that when Congress in 1977 provided the first statutory foundation for PSD it adopted in toto the basic concepts of the EPA program. Congress made many changes in critical elements, however, and in virtually every case the effect of those changes was to broaden the program and tighten its requirements. Congress statutorily placed many areas in the pristine air Class I category, and made it quite difficult for states to redesignate areas to be Class III. It also tightened some of the increments. Congress enormously expanded the number of industrial plants subject to the PSD review. It also turned the screws tighter on the requirements of BACT. It directed EPA to extend the PSD framework to other pollutants in addition to sulfur oxides and particulates. It required more monitoring to be done and added other new data requirements. Finally, it expanded the procedures for government review and public scrutiny of PSD applications. The combined effect of all these changes converts the PSD review into a formidable regulatory obstacle course confronting new industrial projects. * * *

## AREA CLASSIFICATION AND INCREMENTS

Congress continued in effect the three-class system established by EPA, but with several changes. One change was to direct by statute that *certain areas are permanently designated Class I*. These are (1) international parks, (2) national wilderness areas and memorial parks exceeding 5,000 acres, and (3) national parks exceeding 6,000 acres. Although the nature of these areas is such that industrial projects would not be located within them, their Class I status will affect projects in neighboring areas if the winds might carry their emissions into these areas. For many projects, particularly in the West, this may be a substantial constraint.

The statute provides that, except for areas specifically placed in Class I, all other areas in the country subject to PSD shall be initially designated Class II. States are then authorized to redesignate areas either as Class I or as Class III. Before doing so, a state must hold a public hearing in the affected area and prior to the hearing must prepare a detailed analysis, similar in nature to an environmental impact statement, describing the effects of the proposed redesignation.

If the proposal is *to redesignate an area as Class III*, additional requirements apply. The redesignation must be specifically approved by the governor of the state, after consultation with the state legislature; and *general purpose units of local government representing a majority of the residents of the area must enact legislation approving the change.* In view of the procedural, as well as political, obstacles created by these requirements, it is likely that redesignations to Class III will be few and far between. None has occurred to date. The statute also states that certain areas, including wildlife refuges and scenic rivers, may never be designated Class III.

The 1977 Amendments made various changes in the numerical limitations comprising the increments of pollution increase allowed in Class II and Class III areas. The numbers for Class II were generally loosened slightly, except for the short-term sulfur dioxide limitations which were tightened. For Class III, the statute established increment limitations, instead of allowing unlimited growth subject only to compliance with the air quality standards themselves.

A critical threshold question for any company planning a new project is whether it requires preconstruction approval under PSD. It was on this item that Congress made its most profound change to expand the scope of these regulations. First, the 1977 Amendments increased from 19 to 28 the number of industrial categories specifically identified in which any new plant (with potential emissions exceeding 100 tons per year) would be covered. In addition, a new plant in any other category is also covered if its potential emissions of any pollutant would exceed 250 tons per year.

In determining whether an area is subject to PSD requirements, the individual pollutants must be considered. Since most areas of the country are in compliance with the sulfur dioxide standards (with the notable exception of major industrialized regions), most areas likewise are subject to PSD. If an *area* falls under PSD on the basis of its levels of sulfur dioxides, a *source* within that area will become subject to the PSD requirements if its emissions of any pollutant regulated by the Clean Air Act exceed the size cutoff. [Emphasis added] * * *

### BEST AVAILABLE CONTROL TECHNOLOGY (BACT)

The critical feature of BACT is that it *must be determined for each plant on a case-by-case basis.* The statute specifies that "energy, environmental, and economic impacts and other costs" must be taken into account. It also states that in no case can BACT be more lenient than any applicable new source performance standard, implying that wherever possible it will be more stringent. Although the statute provides that BACT shall be required "for each pollutant subject to regulation under this Act," the EPA regulations state that BACT need be met only for those pollutants which the particular source has the potential to emit in quantities exceeding the size cutoff levels.

It is difficult to predict how the process of determining BACT will evolve in actual practice. An obvious problem is that the staff of EPA regional offices where these determinations must be made and of the state agencies as they take over the PSD program, cannot possibly possess expertise in the varied issues of control technology which will constantly arise. This may lead to a frequent practice of falling back on any relevant new source performance standards. It doubtless will also lead in many instances to the government staff making extremely ad hoc judgments on complex technical matters. In some cases applicants may be pressed to achieve levels of control that are quite unrealistic, whereas in other instances government staff may be unaware of control technology which could be used by the applicant. The dangers of inconsistent requirements are apparent. EPA has undertaken to head off this problem by promising to establish a national clearing house for distributing BACT determinations, but its effectiveness remains to be tested.

### Extension to Other Pollutants

As stated earlier, the PSD ambient air quality increments requirements now in effect are directed exclusively at only two pollutants, particulates and sulfur dioxide. The 1977 Amendments directed EPA to conduct a study and by August 1979 promulgate regulations to extend the PSD framework to cover hydrocarbons, carbon monoxide, photochemical oxidants, and nitrogen oxides. Such regulations would become effective one year later and would call for revision of existing state implementation plans during the next subsequent year. It is a good guess that this schedule will not be met. In any event, for the next few years the PSD program will continue its current focus on particulates and sulphur dioxide. But the analysis of anticipated emissions to determine whether a new source is subject to PSD review will be made in reference to any pollutant regulated by the Act. The analysis of impacts on ambient air (and also the review of possible effects on soils, vegetation, and visibility) may extend beyond those two to any of these pollutants, as may any monitoring requirements imposed under PSD. In addition, as pointed out in the description of BACT, that level of control will be required for any regulated pollutant, at least where the quantities of potential emissions would exceed the applicable size cutoffs.

### Monitoring Requirements

The amended Clean Air Act authorizes EPA to impose two types of monitoring requirements under PSD. These apply, first, before an application for approval is submitted, and second, after construction is completed and the source begins operation. Under the statute, any application submitted one year after enactment of the Amendments (i.e., submitted after August 7, 1978) must include "continuous air quality monitoring data gathered over a period of one calendar year." The nature and extent of such data is left much in doubt by the EPA regulations, and the only safe recourse for an applicant will be to obtain advance determinations by EPA as to the data it will require in regard to any individual case. * * *

## MODELING THE THRESHOLD OF CONFUSION

The complexities of the PSD program may be perceived, at one level of understanding, by reading the statute and its legislative history, the regulations, and the EPA policy explanations. The reality of the program may be seen in a far more revealing perspective, however, as one looks beyond the concepts and focuses on the methodology through which the air quality analyses will be conducted. It is at this working level that one discovers a world of abstractions and hypothetical assumptions which resemble a realm of fancy but which must be mastered and put into practice to complete the PSD process.

To start with, it may be well to note that much of the entire air pollution control program is based on artificial computations. Actual data as to air quality throughout the country is being accumulated through an extensive monitoring network but is still quite limited. It is not a situation where [we know] what air quality is at every place at every time. Instead, we have knowledge of air quality in some of the places some of the time, provided the monitors have been accurately calibrated and their data correctly interpreted. Moreover, it is seldom known exactly what emissions are coming out of a source. Actual measurement, so common in the water pollution field, rarely takes place in the case of air emissions. Most existing sources are not equipped with in-place monitoring equipment, and it is extraordinarily time-consuming and expensive (and sometimes dangerous) to install measuring devices inside the stack itself to see what is coming out of the top. Generally, therefore, calculations are made as to how much pollution is likely to be generated by specified industrial processes, how much of that will be captured by pollution control equipment if it is operating properly, and, by subtraction, what residue of pollution presumptively is escaping into the air. Such calculations are of course clearly required in regard to a new source, since until it is actually constructed any determination of its emissions inherently must be a matter of prediction. Moreover, when fugitive emissions are pertinent, they are almost impossible to estimate.

These routine complexities are multiplied when one attempts to calculate the effect of emissions from a new source on ambient air, for at this point one encounters the intricacies of modeling. It must be noted that as a stream of air comes out of a stack it is likely to contain concentrations of pollutants far in excess of the air quality standards. This is not illegal, since compliance with the ambient air quality standards is tested not at the top of the stack but at ground level, and the actual requirement of law is that a source must not cause a concentration of pollutants exceeding the air quality standards to occur anywhere at ground level in the surrounding area. This presents the enigma of how to determine whether such a prohibited concentration will occur.

An air quality model is an analytical device to project the manner in which pollutants will disperse through the air after being emitted at a specified stack height. That projection obviously depends on the use of various working assumptions, such as the description of how the emitted pollutants will be transported and dispersed. In general, the more widely they scatter, the less likely they are to cause a violation of an ambient air quality standard at ground level where the legal requirements are applied. Even that judgment, however, may vary depending on the terrain, on other sources or conditions of air pollution, and related factors.

Intense disputes occur among experts over methodology for designing models to be used in differing circumstances. EPA has adopted certain basic modeling approaches which are set forth in its publication, *Guideline on Air Quality Models*, issued in April 1978. These normally must be followed in certain standard situations, such as an isolated plant on flat terrain, but the problem is that virtually every project involves some unique circumstances including as variables the nature of the terrain, prevailing wind patterns and climatic conditions, and interactions with pollution from other sources. Another problem is that the EPA models are claimed to be "conservative," i.e., to overpredict ground level concentrations of pollutants near the source. For these reasons, a substantial part of the battle in any contested PSD case is likely to turn on disputes over design of the model to project dispersion of the emissions. * * *

### COMPUTATIONS CONTINUED—BASELINE AND BOOKKEEPING PROBLEMS

The difficulties and artificialities inherent in the hypothetical assumptions required to construct any model are further multiplied when one considers that it is necessary not only to construct a model for the proposed new source but also to put it in a setting reflecting the world in which the new plant will be located. The concentrations of pollutants attributed to the new plant must be added to any background pollution naturally occurring as well as manmade pollution from other sources. Since the theory of PSD is to place a limit on the growth of pollution above a preexisting baseline, determinations must be made of what the baseline is and how much of the available increment has already been consumed by other new sources constructed after the PSD limits came into effect. * * *

Any applicant for a PSD permit will have to explore the history of addition and subtractions against the PSD increment in its locality to determine whether it is entitled to build. *This inquiry is likely to become increasingly confusing as time passes and an increasing number of changes must be taken into account.* Moreover, the process is enormously complicated by the fact that it does not involve additions (or subtractions) of known amounts. Any future plant built under PSD will consume varying portions of the increment at each different point within the full circumference of areas within which its emissions may disperse. If a second plant wishes to build at a location ten miles downwind, the model for the first plant must be consulted to determine how much of the increment there the first plant consumed. A third plant being built five miles farther downwind will require additional calculations. Moreover, there are questions of what is downwind. If the pattern of three plants is a triangle rather than a straight line, their emissions presumably will not impact any given point all at the same time, and therefore for purposes of compliance with a short-term standard their effects are not cumulative, whereas for purposes of an annual average the effects probably will be cumulative. The bookkeeping problems as an increasing number of plants are built may become overwhelming, and it is not hard to visualize extended litigation over the disputes that might arise.

# STEVEN A. GOLDBERG, SOURCE PLANNING UNDER THE NEW PSD REGULATIONS

Env. Rep. (BNA) Monograph No. 29 at 2-4, 6-7 (1980)

PSD applies to major new stationary sources of air pollution and to major modifications of existing major sources. A major source is one which has the potential to emit 100 tons or more per year of any regulated pollutant for certain designated source categories and 250 tons or more per year for all sources. A major modification is a physical or operational change which results in a net emissions increase of any regulated pollutant in an amount greater than certain prescribed thresholds of significance.

The criteria pollutants are not the only ones regulated under the Act. The other regulated pollutants are termed "non-criteria" pollutants. If a new source or a modification is major for any pollutant, then PSD applies to every pollutant which the new source has the potential to emit, or which the modification increases, in an amount exceeding the applicable significance threshold. Any pollutant emitted or increased in an amount below its significance threshold is considered *de minimis* and is not subject to review. * * *

PSD allows only limited degradation of air quality by new and modified sources. Specific degradation increments exist for certain pollutants and new and modified sources may not degrade air quality beyond those increments. The earlier a source applies for a PSD permit, the more the increment that will be available. This problem is of particular concern in areas with very limited increment and a source wishing to locate in such an area should act promptly.

Furthermore, a source's PSD permit, when issued, will authorize the source to emit specific amounts of various pollutants. The right to these emissions may prove to be an extremely valuable asset. While a regulatory framework has not yet been devised, it is quite possible that sources will be able to sell their right to emit, which could be extremely valuable in areas of limited increment. * * *

Prior to the Clean Air Act Amendments of 1977, Pub. Law. No. 95-95 (Aug. 7, 1977), the question arose whether a state could allow the air quality to deteriorate to the NAAQS level in an area which was cleaner than the NAAQS for a particular pollutant. Environmental groups brought suit on this issue in the United States District Court for the District of Columbia. The Court held that Congress intended to prevent significant deterioration of air that was better than the applicable NAAQS. *Sierra Club v. Ruckelshaus*, 344 F. Supp. 253 (D.C. 1972), *aff'd*, 412 U.S. 541 (1973). In response to this decision, EPA promulgated its first set of regulations for preventing significant deterioration of the air quality in clean air areas. 39 FR 42510, 42514-17 (Dec. 5, 1974) *codified at* 40 C.F.R. § 52.21 (1975).

On Aug. 7, 1977, Congress substantially amended the Clean Air Act and specifically included a PSD program in the statute. Clean Air Act, §§ 160-169, 42 U.S.C. §§ 7470-79. The 1977 amendments tracked EPA's existing program in many respects, but also differed significantly in many respects. On July 19, 1978, EPA promulgated revised PSD regulations ostensibly incorporating the changes mandated by the 1977 amendments. 43 FR 26388 (June 19, 1978), *amending* 40 C.F.R. § 52.21.

The June 19, 1978, regulations (the 1978 regulations) were challenged in a lengthy and comprehensive judicial review proceeding which produced an opinion on preliminary issues, *Citizens to Save Spencer County v. EPA*, 12 ERC 1961 (D.C. Cir. 1979), a preliminary opinion on substantive issues, *Alabama Power Co. v. Costle*, 13 ERC 1225 (D.C. Cir. June 18, 1979), and a final opinion on substantive issues, *Alabama Power Co. v. Costle*, 13 ERC 1993 (D.C. Cir. Dec. 14, 1979). The two *Alabama Power* opinions are hereinafter cited collectively as *Alabama Power* and individually as *Alabama Power I* and *Alabama Power II*.

*Alabama Power I* was a summary opinion in which the Court set forth its conclusions on most of the substantive issues so that EPA could revise its regulations accordingly. On Sept. 5, 1979, EPA proposed such revised regulations. 44 FR 51924 (Sept. 5, 1979). On Aug. 7, 1980, EPA promulgated its final PSD regulations, taking into account the final decision in *Alabama Power II* and the comments received on the proposed regulations both before and after that decision. 45 FR 52676, 52735-41 (Aug. 7, 1980), *amending* 40 C.F.R. § 52.21. The Aug. 7, 1980, regulations are the primary focus of this memorandum and are hereinafter referred to as "the final regulations." Although the final regulations are subject to judicial review, it is unlikely they will be upset in any significant respect in view of the extensive court opinions on which they are based.

## WHO IS SUBJECT TO PSD

Generally speaking, PSD review applies on a pollutant-by-pollutant basis to every major new stationary source and to every major modification to an existing major source located in an area which is clean (attainment) for at least one pollutant. In order to understand who is subject to PSD, one must understand the definition of three basic terms: (1) stationary source, (2) major source, and (3) major modification. * * *

## MAJOR SOURCE

A major source is one "which emits, or has the potential to emit," specified tonnages per year of any pollutant subject to regulation under the Act. 40 C.F.R. § 52.21, 45 FR at 52735. The specified tonnages are 100 tons or more for any of the [specifically enumerated] source categories * * * and 250 tons or more for any other source. The major source determination is straightforward where actual emissions exceed the specified tonnage. The area of flexibility and concern is "potential to emit."

Potential to emit is defined as a source's maximum capacity to emit a pollutant under its physical and operational design, as reduced by any federally enforceable limitation, including the use of pollution control equipment and restrictions on hours of operation or on the type or amount of material combusted, stored or processed. 40 C.F.R. § 52.21(b)(4), 45 FR at 52737. Generally state permits are federally enforceable through EPA's right to enforce the SIP and the simplest way to make a restriction federally enforceable is to agree to make it a permit condition.

Reducing potential to emit is perhaps the greatest single area of flexibility in avoiding PSD review. If some combination of pollution control equipment and operational restrictions can reduce the source's potential emissions below the major source threshold, the owner should give this option careful consideration. It will often be cheaper, and it will always be less time-consuming, to avoid review. * * *

## WHICH POLLUTANTS ARE SUBJECT TO PSD

The pollutants regulated under the Act fall into two categories. Pollutants for which NAAQS have been established are termed "criteria" pollutants. All other pollutants regulated under the Act are termed "non-criteria" pollutants. Both criteria and non-criteria pollutants are subject to PSD if emitted by a major new source or increased by a major modification in significant amounts.

## THE PSD REQUIREMENTS

The PSD requirements may be loosely said to fall into two groups. One group consists of requirements which are general in nature and which must be met by the source whether it is subject to PSD for one pollutant or for many. The other group consists of pollutant-specific requirements; these must be met separately for each pollutant emitted in significant amounts and therefore subject to PSD. The pollutant-specific requirements are the far more burdensome group and are treated first.

## BACT

The "best available control technology" (BACT) must be applied to control the emissions of each pollutant emitted in significant amounts. BACT may take any of several forms. For some industrial processes, EPA may require specific technology. For other processes, EPA may impose emission limitations which the source may meet by any technology capable of achieving those limitations. Generally, BACT may be negotiated between the source and EPA based on source-specific considerations. 40 C.F.R. § 52.21(b)(12), 45 FR at 52736. Source owners should be sensitive to how close the application of BACT brings them to the major source threshold. It may often save money to voluntarily undertake more stringent controls and avoid PSD; it will always save time.

## IMPACT ANALYSES

Sources subject to PSD must perform several pollutant-specific impact analyses. These can be extremely burdensome.

### NAAQS AND INCREMENT CONSUMPTION

A source subject to PSD must analyze the impact of each criteria pollutant emitted in significant amounts on the NAAQS for that pollutant in that area. 40 C.F.R. § 52.21(i)(b)(k), as amended by 45 FR at 52739 (Aug. 7, 1980). This analysis is relatively straightforward. But the source must also analyze for each such pollutant its effect on increment consumption. Increment consumption is simple in its theory, but complex in computation. There is however, a potentially valuable reward for each applicants.

Establishment of the baseline for a given pollutant in a given area occurs when the first completed PSD application is filed for a source which will locate in that area and emit that pollutant in significant amounts. The first applicant will thus have the burden of gathering the baseline data and demonstrating the baseline concentration. This applicant will also have the greatest amount of increment available since no one else will yet have used any. Once a source's PSD permit is issued, the source will have the right to emit certain amounts of various pollutants. This right to emit may prove to be very valuable because increment is a limited resource. In an area where increment is scarce, the right to emit certain levels of pollutants will be particularly valuable, and although regulations on the point have not yet been proposed, it is quite possible that sources will be authorized to sell, or otherwise convey for value, their emission rights.

In areas where air quality is much cleaner than NAAQS and ample increment exists, there is no special urgency to applying for a permit. But source owners considering construction in areas believed to have limited increment should consider acting quickly. If increment availability were anticipated or known to be modest, but not tight, it might be wisest not be the first applicant, with the responsibility for establishing the baseline, but to move quickly after the first application, in order to be sure of obtaining increment.

The increment consumption analysis is complex, however, even after the baseline is established, because the source must examine a variety of possible emission changes. For example, new non-major sources consume increment and the applicant must therefore compute their effect. In addition, changes in baseline sources after the baseline [date] consume increment and these effects must be considered. In sum, more is at stake in the increment computation than the applicant's own increases.

The Court in *Alabama Power* held that section 165(e) of the Clean Air Act * * * requires a PSD permit applicant to conduct an air quality analysis for all regulated pollutants. 45 FR at 52723. This requirement applies to each pollutant emitted regardless of whether the source is major for that pollutant (criteria and non-criteria) which a new source has the potential to emit in significant amounts and for which a modification would result in a significant net increase. 40 C.F.R. § 52.21(m)(1)(i)(1980), 45 FR at 52740.

### 3. PSD REGULATIONS

When determining whether a proposed facility or modification requires a PSD permit, an attorney must carefully study and apply the EPA's regulations, particularly the following definitional provisions.

# EPA, REQUIREMENTS FOR PREPARATION, ADOPTION, AND SUBMITTAL OF IMPLEMENTATION PLANS

40 C.F.R. Part 51 (1998)

### § 51.166 Prevention of significant deterioration of air quality.

(a) (1) Plan requirements. * * * [E]ach applicable State implementation plan shall contain emission limitations and such other measures as may be necessary to prevent significant deterioration of air quality. * * *

(b) Definitions. All State plans shall use the following definitions for the purposes of this section. Deviations from the following wording will be approved only if the State specifically demonstrates that the submitted definition is more stringent, or at least as stringent, in all respects as the corresponding definitions below:

(1)(i) "Major stationary source"[f] means:

---

[f] *Ed.*—To be consistent with CAA § 169(1), this reference should be to "major *emitting facility*." The distinction is important, because the nonattainment program uses the term "major stationary source" and defines it in a different manner.

(a) Any of the following stationary sources of air pollutants which emits, or has the potential to emit, 100 tons per year or more of any pollutant subject to regulation under the Act: [enumerating the sources listed in CAA § 169(1)] * * *

(b) Notwithstanding the stationary source size specified in paragraph (b)(1)(i)(a) of this section, any stationary source which emits, or has the potential to emit, 250 tons per year or more of any air pollutant subject to regulation under the Act * * *

(4) "Potential to emit" means the maximum capacity of a stationary source to emit a pollutant under its physical and operational design. Any physical or operational limitation on the capacity of the source to emit a pollutant, including air pollution control equipment and restrictions on hours of operation or on the type or amount of material combusted, stored, or processed, shall be treated as part of its design if the limitation or the effect it would have on emissions is federally enforceable. * * *

(13)(i) "Baseline concentration" means that ambient concentration level which exists in the baseline area at the time of the applicable minor source baseline date. A baseline concentration is determined for each pollutant for which a minor source baseline date is established and shall include:

(a) The actual emissions representative of sources in existence on the applicable minor source baseline date, except as provided in paragraph (b)(13)(ii) of this section;

(b) The allowable emissions of major stationary sources which commenced construction before the major source baseline date, but were not in operation by the applicable minor source baseline date.

(ii) The following will not be included in the baseline concentration and will affect the applicable maximum allowable increase(s):

(a) Actual emissions from any major stationary source on which construction commenced after the major source baseline date; and

(b) Actual emissions increases and decreases at any stationary source occurring after the minor source baseline date.

(14)(i) "Major source baseline date" means:

(a) In the case of particulate matter and sulfur dioxide, January 6, 1975, and

(b) In the case of nitrogen dioxide, February 8, 1988.

(ii) "Minor source baseline date" means the earliest date after the trigger date on which a major stationary source or a major modification subject to 40 CFR 52.21 or to regulations approved pursuant to 40 CFR 51.166 submits a complete application under the relevant regulations. The trigger date is:

(a) In the case of particulate matter and sulfur dioxide, August 7, 1977, and

(b) In the case of nitrogen dioxide, February 8, 1988.

(iii) The baseline date is established for each pollutant for which increments or other equivalent measures have been established if:

    (a) The area in which the proposed source or modification would construct is designated as attainment or unclassifiable under section 107(d)(i)(D) or (E) of the Act for the pollutant on the date of its complete application under 40 CFR 52.21 or under regulations approved pursuant to 40 CFR 51.166; and

    (b) In the case of a major stationary source, the pollutant would be emitted in significant amounts, or, in the case of a major modification, there would be a significant net emissions increase of the pollutant.

(15)(i) "Baseline area" means any intrastate area (and every part thereof) designated as attainment or unclassifiable under section 107(d)(1)(D) or (E) of the Act in which the major source or major modification establishing the minor source baseline date would construct or would have an air quality impact equal to or greater than 1 µg/m$^3$ (annual average) of the pollutant for which the minor source baseline date is established. * * *

(17) "Federally enforceable" means all limitations and conditions which are enforceable by the Administrator, including those requirements developed pursuant to 40 CFR Parts 60 and 61, requirements within any applicable State implementation plan, any permit requirements established pursuant to 40 CFR 52.21 or under regulations approved pursuant to 40 CFR Part 51, Subpart I, including operating permits issued under an EPA-approved program that is incorporated into the State implementation plan and expressly requires adherence to any permit issued under such program.

## 4. WHO MUST OBTAIN A PSD PERMIT?

As a matter of geography, the PSD program applies in any air quality area that is attainment or unclassifiable for at least one pollutant. An attorney can answer this geographical question without considering the nature of any given stationary source.

But to which stationary sources and activities does the PSD permit program apply? CAA § 165(a) requires a PSD permit for the "construction" of a "major emitting facility." Section 169(2)(c) provides that "construction" includes "modification," as that term is defined in § 111(a)(4). What is a "major emitting facility"? That term is defined in § 169(1).

At first glance, the statute seems quite straightforward: if a facility falls within 28 listed categories of industries and will emit 100 tons per year or more of a pollutant, it is a major emitting facility; even if the facility is not within those 28 listed categories, but will emit 250 tons or more per year of a pollutant, it is a major emitting facility. It is customary to refer to the pollutant cutoff value as 100/250 tons.

In practice, the major emitting facility definition has been complicated by two significant interpretive questions associated with calculation of the 100/250 ton cutoffs: (1) which emissions count? and (2) which pollutants count?

## 5.  WHICH EMISSIONS COUNT?

Prior to the *Alabama Power* rulings, EPA insisted that the 100/250 ton phrases in CAA § 169(1) referred to a source's *uncontrolled* emissions—what would come out of the facility if there were no pollution controls. EPA put great emphasis on the statutory language embracing stationary sources which "have the potential to emit" 100 or 250 tons. Industry petitioners in *Alabama Power* argued that this interpretation was absurd; the PSD program is concerned with actual additions of pollutants to the atmosphere, and it would be silly to trigger the need for a PSD permit based on emissions that would occur only in a fairyland in which there were no controls at all. Accordingly, industry petitioners asserted that the 100/250 ton calculations should take into account only those emissions that would be discharged by the proposed new (or modified) facility after installation and operation of control technology.

### *Questions*

1.  Whose interpretation of CAA § 169(1) makes more sense? EPA's claim that the 100/250 ton cutoffs are to be measured by examining a proposed source's *uncontrolled* emissions, or industry's claim that the cutoffs should be calculated with reference to *controlled* emissions? Why?

2.  If industry's interpretation is the correct one, for *which* technological controls should the proposed source be given credit in calculating whether it needs a PSD permit? Controls that the facility is thinking about using? Controls that the facility will be somehow legally bound to install and operate? Do you see a problem here?

---

The D.C. Circuit, in *Alabama Power II*, agreed with industry on this portion of the major emitting facility definition: the 100/250 ton cutoffs are to be calculated by reference to *controlled* emissions. *See* 636 F.2d at 352-55.

Following remand, EPA amended the regulation as directed by the D.C. Circuit, but added a new wrinkle. The amended regulation insists that no credit will be given for pollution controls unless the "limitation or the effect it would have on emissions is federally enforceable." 40 C.F.R. § 51.166(b)(4). "Federally enforceable" is defined, in turn, in 40 C.F.R. § 51.166(b)(17). These regulatory provisions are set forth at pages 479-480, *supra*.

## *Problem 9-1*

Your client, Solar Cell Co., is a new corporation which holds a patent on a revolutionary technique for manufacturing solar energy cells. It wishes to build a new industrial plant for the manufacture of this product and has purchased a plot of land for that purpose in a remote corner of the desert in the Southwestern United States. The Air Quality Control Region has been listed as an "attainment area" for all criteria pollutants. *See* CAA § 107(d)(1). For purposes of the PSD program, the area embracing the land has been categorized as Class II. *See* CAA §163(b)(2).

The plant will emit no sulfur dioxide, particulates, or oxides of nitrogen. Its backers therefore assume that the PSD program will have no application and that no permit will be required. You realize, however, that the PSD program may not be quite so simple. You discover that, if no emission control technology is used, the plant will emit 400 tons of volatile organic compounds (VOCs) per year. (For purposes of this problem, assume that VOC is a pollutant that "counts" when calculating the PSD tonnage cutoffs.) You also learn that the facility can curb its emissions to 230 tons of VOCs per year if it installs and faithfully operates new and innovative control technology.

You have searched the pertinent SIP and have found no VOC emission limitation applicable to the proposed facility. You have also found no applicable VOC emission limitation in any other regulation. Finally, there is no state or federal permit establishing a VOC emission limitation for the proposed Solar Cell facility.

Will Solar Cell's proposed new industrial plant require a PSD permit? Why or why not? If you have concluded that a permit is required under the current proposal, is there anything you can do to avoid the necessity of a PSD permit?

# GEORGE VAN CLEVE & KEITH W. HOLMAN, PROMISE AND REALITY IN THE ENFORCEMENT OF THE AMENDED CLEAN AIR ACT

27 Envt'l. L. Rep. 10151 (Apr. 1997)

Evaluating a facility's potential air emissions is the critical factor in determining whether EPA classifies the facility as a "major" source or a "minor" source. The distinction between major and minor sources is critically important, because many CAA programs, such as the Title V program, the New Source Review (NSR)/Prevention of Significant Deterioration (PSD) program, and the § 112 program for hazardous air pollutants (HAPs), apply only to major sources. Moreover, the CAA typically imposes far greater regulatory requirements on major sources than it does on minor sources. To the extent that a facility can be classified as minor, rather than major, it can avoid most of the Act's regulatory requirements, and is much less likely to become an enforcement target.

Since 1980, EPA has defined "potential to emit" (PTE) for determining major source status as: [the article here quotes the language of 40 C.F.R. § 52.21(4), which is identical to the language of 40 C.F.R. § 51.166(b)(4), set forth at page 479, *supra*.] EPA has long taken the view, at least implicitly, that restrictions on PTE must be made federally enforceable to ensure that facilities will actually comply with the restrictions. From EPA's perspective, the threat of federal enforcement (as well as citizen enforcement under CAA § 304) is necessary, over and above the state or local enforcement threat, to "hold facilities' feet to the fire" and ensure that they do not violate agreed-upon PTE restrictions.

Under EPA's PTE definition, the PTE calculation begins with an estimate of the uncontrolled maximum physical and operational capacity of a source to emit pollutants. In most cases, calculating the emissions of a facility operating 8,760 hours per year at full throttle and without emission controls yields a very high potential emissions number. That PTE number is the means for determining whether facility emissions meet or exceed established major source thresholds.

To illustrate, the Act requires a Title V permit for any facility that has potential emissions of 100 tons per year of a criteria pollutant such as particulate matter. A metal-grinding operation may have the potential to emit far more than 100 tons of particulate matter in a year, even though dust collectors and filters keep its actual yearly emissions below the Title V threshold. Under EPA's PTE definition, if the grinding operation does not have a federally enforceable requirement to operate the air-pollution control equipment or to lower emissions by limiting operating hours, throughput, raw materials, etc., the high theoretical maximum emissions must be used as its PTE, subjecting the facility to regulation as a Title V major source.

To complicate matters, in the past it was often difficult for facilities to obtain federally enforceable PTE restrictions. Since the early 1980s, EPA has taken the position that an operating restriction or requirement for [controls] is not federally enforceable unless the requirement is authorized under an EPA-approved [SIP] or is contained within a currently effective state preconstruction permit. PTE restrictions contained in state operating permits were usually considered not to be federally enforceable. Accordingly, facilities have had to either try to ensure that PTE restrictions in preconstruction permits remained valid after they subsequently received their state operating permit, or they have had to wait for EPA to approve PTE restrictions into SIPs.

Facilities often have been unable to get EPA to consider PTE restrictions in state or local permits to be federally enforceable. As a result, some companies with low actual emissions but a high PTE have found themselves designated as major sources who must comply with expensive and burdensome programs * * * . When a facility's emissions have been historically well controlled, or when operating parameters serve to keep actual emissions far below major thresholds, there is little or no environmental benefit gained by forcing the facility to comply with major-source requirements.

Although industry has long been frustrated with the federal-enforceability requirement, EPA was able to defend it until recently. Following the 1990 Amendments, the expansion of the federal-enforceability requirement to PTE calculations made under the Title V and HAP programs created a new opportunity to challenge EPA's PTE definition. In three separate cases decided between July 1995 and June 1996, the U.S. Court of Appeals for the District of Columbia Circuit held that EPA failed when promulgating its PTE definition to adequately demonstrate why limits on a facility's PTE must be federally enforceable, as opposed to being enforceable by a state or local agency alone, in order to be considered "effective" in limiting PTE.[10] In the wake of these cases, the future of the federal-enforceability requirement is in serious doubt. * * *

In the wake of the three decisions, EPA was left with the choice of (1) amending the § 112, PSD/NSR, and Title V rules to recognize state and local limits as reducing a facility's PTE, or (2) justifying to the court why federal enforceability is required to ensure that PTE limits will be effective. Unless EPA can convince the D.C. Circuit that state and local limitations on a source's potential to emit can never be effective, EPA will probably have to accept at least some restrictions contained in state or local permits or other enforceable documents as effective limits that reduce a facility's potential to emit air pollutants. * * *

At present, some factions within EPA unquestionably wish to retain the federal-enforceability requirement for PTE limits. In order to argue that retaining the federal-enforceability requirement is a reasonable interpretation of the Act, however, EPA must be able to make some demonstration that federal enforceability is necessary to ensure that state limits are practically effective. * * * Given the long history of the controversy in the D.C. Circuit, and the court's apparent impatience with EPA and dissatisfaction with EPA's rationale for preserving the federal-enforceability requirement, it seems unlikely that the court will allow it to remain an element of the PTE definition. * * *

## ALEC ZACAROLI, POLICY ON DETERMINING POTENTIAL TO EMIT EXTENDED UNTIL DECEMBER 1999, EPA SAYS

29 [Curr. Dev.] Env. Rep. (BNA) 725 (1998)

The Environmental Protection Agency has decided to extend an interim policy on how to determine a facility's potential to emit air pollu-

---

[10] National Mining Ass'n v. EPA, 59 F.3d 1351 (D.C. Cir. 1995); Chemical Mfrs. Ass'n v. EPA, No. 89-1514, 1995 U.S. App. LEXIS 31475 (D.C. Cir. Sept. 15, 1995); Clean Air Implementation Project v. EPA, No. 96-1224, 1996 U.S. App. LEXIS 18402 (D.C. Cir. June 28, 1996).

tion for enforcement purposes, after finding the agency could not complete final rules addressing the matter by a July 1998 deadline.

The policy, which gives states the option of not treating certain sources as "major" for regulatory purposes if they meet certain criteria, has been extended until Dec. 31, 1999 * * * .

EPA found itself in the position of having to develop a new rule on the matter after a series of court cases either overturned or remanded existing agency rules on potential to emit determinations. * * *

### TWO CONDITIONS

EPA's interim policy essentially sets two conditions that sources must meet to be eligible for opting out of major source status based on their potential to emit. It also leaves it up to individual states to decide whether sources can take advantage of the policy.

Under the policy, state and local regulators have the option of treating sources as nonmajor for purposes of operating permit and air toxics regulations if the sources:

- maintain adequate records that show their actual emissions are less than 50 percent of the applicable major-source threshold, and that they have operated at that level since January 1994; or

- have actual emissions between 50 percent and 100 percent of the major source threshold and are subject to state limits that are "enforceable as a practical matter."

## 6. SYNTHETIC MINOR SOURCES

The EPA has come up with a delightful label for any facility evading a PSD permit (or a nonattainment permit or Title V operating permit) by limiting its potential to emit below major source (or major emitting facility) thresholds: "synthetic minor source." *See* [Draft] EPA/State Guidance on High-Priority Clean Air Act Violations, 29 [Curr. Dev.] Env. Rep. (BNA) 1267 (1998).

Why all the hullabaloo about synthetic minor sources—facilities that have evaded the various Clean Air Act major source (or major emitting facility) permit programs, such as the PSD program? Why has EPA been struggling so tenaciously with the "potential to emit" issue? Perhaps the following news item will give the flavor of what is at stake.

## KEITH SCHNEIDER, HOLLOW NOTE HEARD IN TRUMPETED POLLUTION FINE

N.Y. Times, Jun. 3, 1993, at A12 col. 1

Trying to show a tougher approach to enforcing environmental laws, the Clinton Administration last month levied an $11.1 million penalty against a company that falsely reported how much pollution it produced. It was the largest civil fine ever obtained under the Clean Air Act.

But in the days after Janet Reno, the Attorney General, and Carol M. Browner, the Administrator of the Environmental Protection Agency, jointly proclaimed what they said was a "loud and clear message" to polluters, some members of Congress, state officials and independent environmental experts have wondered just what sort of message was being sent.

These critics said the penalty against the Louisiana-Pacific Corporation, the nation's largest manufacturer of wood-fiber construction panels, was minor compared with the enormous market advantage the company had gained by breaking environmental laws in reporting pollution from plants making waferboard. Despite what investigators said was strong evidence that company officials had deliberately submitted false information to the Government, the Administration did not bring criminal charges.

"This case is a prime example of how a company can dominate a market by avoiding the costs of complying with environmental laws," said Jonathan Turley, a law professor and director of the Environmental Crimes Project at George Washington University here.

"They have enjoyed a long period of high profits and rapid expansion because of their falsification of records and misleading of regulators," he added. "To allow Louisiana-Pacific to simply internalize those costs now and not face criminal liability sends a message to industry that environmental violations remain simply the cost of doing business."

Louisiana-Pacific, which is based in Portland, Ore., said in a statement last week that the penalty would not affect the company's earnings. Harry A. Merlo, the company's chairman and president, said he was "pleased with the settlement."

And Barry Lacter, a spokesman for the company, which had sales of $2.2 billion last year, denied that Lousiana-Pacific deliberately set out to mislead state and Federal regulators.

The company's waferboard sales last year totaled more than $500 million, Mr. Lacter said. Investment analysts say the company now controls 43 percent of the $1.2 billion waferboard market, which is one of the fastest-growing sectors of the construction materials industry.

The case involved 14 plants in 11 states but was focused mainly on the 11 new plants the company built in eight states in the 1980's to manufacture waferboard, a substitute for plywood made from wafers of wood glued and pressed together. Though waferboard can be made from less-expensive wood like aspen and scrub pine, carpenters say it is as strong and nearly as versatile as plywood.

But the process of drying the wafers in a huge oven, then gluing and pressing them into panels, produces millions of pounds of carbon monoxide and toxic air pollution, state environmental officials say. Federal authorities said in interviews that in every case, states did not discover how dirty Lousiana-Pacific's plants were until after they were operating.

The Federal Clean Air Act of 1970, which is administered by the states, requires manufacturers, when applying for construction and operating permits, to say precisely how much air pollution new plants will produce. In addition, the law requires companies operating in regions with the cleanest air, like the forested areas where Louisiana-Pacific built its waferboard plants, to undergo more stringent review and to take special precautions if their plants each year produce more than 250 tons of dust, carbon monoxide, volatile organic compounds or nitrogen oxide.

Officials in the eight states said the company had avoided the more stringent review by deliberately underestimating, often by thousands of tons a year, how much pollution the new waferboard plants would produce. The states are Georgia, Idaho, Louisiana, Maine, Michigan, Minnesota, Texas and Wisconsin.

By filing inaccurate information, the authorities said, Louisiana-Pacific consistently beat its competitors in getting new waferboard plants into operation. It was also able to avoid the multimillion-dollar expense of installing and operating pollution control equipment that was required of its competitors.

In Georgia, for example, state air pollution technicians found in 1990 that a year-old Lousiana-Pacific waferboard plant in Jackson County was pouring 1,500 tons of volatile organic chemicals into the air each year, more than six times the amount the company said it would emit.

The violation was discovered after the Georgia authorities noticed that the International Paper Company, a competitor that had applied to build a similar waferboard plant in Georgia at the same time, accurately described the amount of air pollution it would produce. Georgia fined Louisiana-Pacific $400,000 for the violation, but the company had its plant operating a year before International Paper.

In Maine, Louisiana-Pacific sought construction and environmental permits in 1981 for a plant that it said would produce 240 tons of waferboard a day. The company told the state that air pollution would be minimal at such production levels. But in a routine inspection in 1988, the Maine authorities found that the plant was producing 400 tons of waferboard a day, and that air pollution was far above the levels approved in the original permit.

Last summer, according to Kevin Macdonald, a state environmental specialist, Louisiana-Pacific paid a $350,000 penalty for that violation.

In a news conference announcing the settlement on May 24, Ms. Reno and Ms. Browner said that under a consent decree, Louisiana-Pacific agreed to install $70 million in pollution control equipment at 11 plants in nine states in 1994 and 1995. The Attorney General added that for companies that do not play by the rules, "we want them to pay something more than just what it costs."

Officials in the E.P.A.'s enforcement division said the Louisiana-Pacific case, begun in 1991 by the Bush Administration, was a marked change from its earlier approach in that it sought penalties against a company's plants in many states instead of acting against individual plants.

"It is very easy to sit back and poke at a case and say it could have been done better," said Robert Van Heuvelen, the environmental agency's director of civil [enforcement]. "This is a wonderful penalty result. It's a wonderful environmental result. To say we didn't do enough is to fail to recognize the value of what happened here."

At issue for critics, though, is whether the civil penalty fit the violations, and why criminal charges were not brought. Representative John L. Mica, a freshman Republican from Florida who is a member of the House Government Operations environment subcommittee, has called for a Congressional investigation.

Companies with criminal pollution convictions under the Clean Air Act face immediate loss of the right to sell products to be used in any Federal contract.

## 7.  WHICH POLLUTANTS COUNT?

We have now struggled with the first of the two significant interpretive questions associated with calculation of the 100/250 ton cutoffs in defining major emitting facilities under the PSD program: which *emissions* count? Accordingly, we turn to the second interpretive question: which *pollutants* count?

CAA § 169(1), in defining "major emitting facility" for PSD purposes, covers sources having the potential to emit 100 (or 250) tons "of *any air pollutant*." CAA § 302(g), in turn, contains an extraordinarily broad definition of "air pollutant": "any air pollution agent or combination of such agents, including any physical, chemical, biological, radioactive * * * substance or matter which is emitted into or otherwise enters the ambient air." Accordingly, if § 169(1) were read literally, the discharge of 100 (or 250 tons) of almost *anything*—including water vapor, carbon dioxide, and other unregulated "pollutants"—would trigger "major emitting facility" status, requiring a PSD permit.

There is language in *Alabama Power II* suggesting that the *statutory* major emitting facility definition in CAA § 169(1) should, indeed, be read this broadly:

> [T]he section 169(1) definition of "major emitting facility" * * * is not pollutant-specific, but rather identifies sources that emit more than a threshold quantity of any air pollutant. Once a source has been so identified, it may become subject to section 165's substantial administrative burdens and stringent technological control requirements for each pollutant regulated under the Act, even though *the air pollutant,* emis-

sions of which caused the source to be classified as a "major emitting facility," *may not be a pollutant for which NAAQS have been promulgated or even one that is otherwise regulated under the Act.* \* \* \* Congress's intention was to identify facilities which, due to their size, are financially able to bear the substantial regulatory costs imposed by the PSD provisions and which, as a group, are primarily responsible for emission of the deleterious pollutants that befoul our nation's air. \* \* \*

*Alabama Power v. Costle*, 636 F.2d 323, 352-53 (D.C. Cir. 1979) (emphasis added).

In promulgating its PSD regulations, however, EPA has from the beginning tempered the broad statutory PSD trigger language of § 169(1), limiting the *regulatory* major emitting facility definition to sources having the potential to emit 100 (or 250) tons per year or more "of any air pollutant *subject to regulation under the Act.*" 40 C.F.R. § 51.166(b)(1)(i)(a) & (b) (emphasis added), set forth at page 479, *supra.* The italicized clause mirrors precisely the statutory language in CAA § 165(a)(4) enumerating the pollutants subject to best available control technology or BACT.

But what is meant by "pollutant subject to regulation under the Clean Air Act?" The language is deliciously ambiguous and could mean at least two things. First, "subject to regulation" could refer to only those pollutants that the EPA *has* in fact gone after under the Clean Air Act—in other words, pollutants *currently being subjected to regulation* under the Act. Second, "subject to regulation" could mean something quite different: any air pollutant that *could be subjected* to regulation under the Act.

After all, *any* "air pollutant"—as broadly defined in § 302(g)—is *potentially* subject to regulation under the Act. Thus, for example, pig farm odors unquestionably fall within the § 302(g) definition of "air pollutant." Indeed, the Eighth Circuit has held that federal courts have subject matter jurisdiction in a Clean Air Act citizen suit alleging violations of state odor standards submitted as part of a SIP and approved by the EPA. *See Save Our Health Organization v. Recomp of Minnesota,* 37 F.3d 1334 (8th Cir. 1994). Does this mean that odors and countless other pollutants that *may* some day be controlled under the Clean Air Act are pollutants "subject to regulation under the Act?"

The D.C. Circuit and the EPA have indicated that the second reading would be too broad. Thus, in *Alabama Power Co. v. EPA*, 606 F.2d 1068, 1086 (D.C. Cir. 1979), the Court concluded that the phrase "each pollutant subject to regulation under [the] Act" in CAA § 165(a)(4) encompasses "each pollutant for which EPA *has* promulgated e.g., an NAAQS [or] a new source performance standard." (emphasis added) Similarly, the EPA has declared that the phrase—for which it uses the synonym "regulated pollutant"—includes "criteria pollutants established under § 109 [and] pollutants regulated by NSPS pursuant to § 111." 56 Fed. Reg. 5,488 (1991).

In this regard, however, the EPA has added a wicked and potentially significant twist: where NSPS emission limits have been established under § 111 for noncriteria pollutants at particular source *categories*—the so-called "designated pollutants at designated facilities" discussed at page 371, *supra*—EPA has treated such pollutants as "regulated" for purposes of the PSD program regardless of the category of the source emitting such pollutants. *See id.* Thus, for example, fluorides emitted by a widget plant—even though not subject to a NSPS—could trigger the PSD requirements if emitted in sufficient amounts, because fluorides *are* subject to NSPS at aluminum manufacturing plants and at phosphate fertilizer plants.

Under the narrow (and accepted) reading of "pollutant subject to regulation under the Act," may hazardous air pollutants serve as the trigger requiring a PSD permit? Will hazardous air pollutants be subject to the BACT requirement if emitted by a PSD permittee? Buried deep within the massive text of the 1990 amendments is a clause precluding this startling consequence.

---

Read the following section of the Clean Air Act

☐ § 112(b)(6)

---

### *Problem 9-2*

Your client, Solar Cell Co., described more fully in **Problem 9-1** at page 482, *supra*, wishes to build its new industrial plant in an area which is in attainment for all criteria pollutants, and which has been rated as a Class II area for purposes of the PSD program. The plant will emit no sulfur dioxide or particulates, but will emit 300 tons of a volatile organic compounds (VOCs) per year, even after installing and operating the latest and greatest control technology. Will the facility need a PSD permit? Why or why not?

Would your answer be different if the facility will emit no VOCs, but will emit 300 tons of formaldehyde? Why or why not?

Would your answer be different if the facility will emit no VOCs or formaldehyde, but will emit 300 tons of hydrogen sulfide? Why or why not?

Assume that a PSD permit is needed for the proposed Solar Cell facility, but that the triggering pollutant, such as VOC, will dissipate and indisputably cause no harm to the surrounding area. Must the PSD permit nevertheless contain strict emission limitations on VOC emissions? *See* § 165(a)(4).

## 8. PRECONSTRUCTION REVIEW

When the PSD "trigger" is pulled by the proposed construction of a major emitting facility in an attainment area, the Clean Air Act requires not one but two things: (1) a PSD permit, *see* CAA § 165(a)(1);

and (2) preconstruction review during a public hearing on the proposed permit, *see* CAA § 165(a)(2). In the preconstruction review process, the permit applicant must make a formal *demonstration* showing compliance with conditions enumerated in CAA § 165(a)(3)-(8).

### Problem 9–3

Assume that the Solar Cell facility described in **Problem 9-2** proposes to emit only the following pollutants, after installing controls: 300 tons of $PM_{10}$ per year and 60 tons of $SO_2$ per year. What must the permit applicant *demonstrate* to obtain a PSD permit? This question requires a sophisticated and lengthy answer.

## 9. THE MOTIVATIONS BEHIND THE PSD PROGRAM

Does it strike you as odd that the PSD program may result in the most stringent ambient air standards in locations in which there are the fewest people who might suffer ill health effects? Isn't this backwards? We saw, when we looked at the regulation of radioactive air emissions from nuclear generating plants, that doses are sometimes measured in person-rems—a figure calculated by multiplying the total number of exposed persons by their average individual dose in rems. *See* page 254, *supra*. If we used that approach, the exposure of 1,000 people to ambient air concentrations of 80 $\mu g/m^3$ of $SO_2$ in New Mexico should presumably result in much lower total adverse health effects than the exposure of 3 million people to ambient air concentrations of 60 $\mu g/m^3$ in Chicago. Yet, we seemingly insist that a remote New Mexico location should be limited to an ambient air concentration of 30 or 40 or 50 $\mu g/m^3$ of $SO_2$, while ambient concentrations of 80 $\mu g/m^3$ in Chicago's air are acceptable. What's going on here?

Professors Stewart and Menell note that the PSD program may have been supported in 1977 primarily by urban legislators, who sought to lessen the likelihood that industry would flee from Clean Air Act nonattainment areas to more pristine locations in which they would be able to avoid the hassle of pollution control regulations. They also suggest that legislators from the urban east tend to view the natural resources of the western United States as "unique unspoiled terrain that must be preserved." Peter Menell & Richard B. Stewart, Environmental Law and Policy 342 (1994).

## TIMOTHY EGAN, AS EASTERNERS TRY TO SAVE WEST, WESTERNERS BLANCH

N.Y. Times, Aug. 29, 1993 at A1 col. 5

The West is crowded with vacationing Easterners this time of year, including a small posse of senators on horseback, members of Congress wading through trout streams and earnest young political aides sampling clean air and ungarnished food.

But when Eastern politicians take their holidays to the wide open spaces, many Western politicians tend to get nervous. To hear some senators from the West tell it, a visiting representative from an eastern state is held in about the same regard as a missionary by a defiant pagan.

"They come to see the intrinsic beauty of Montana, but then they go home and want to save it all in perpetuity," said Senator Conrad Burns, Republican of Montana.

Senator Malcolm Wallop, Republican of Wyoming, said, "They tend to go to the splendid watering holes and listen to people that aren't really natives who want to close the gate now that they're in." Most Westerners, he added, do not need outside help in deciding what is best for the land—an assertion that is challenged by other residents here.

Every summer brings a fresh target. This year, the source of much Western political ridicule is Representative Carolyn B. Maloney, a first-term Democrat from Manhattan. Earlier this summer, Ms. Maloney, who visited Yellowstone National Park as a tourist, introduced a bill that would prohibit any development on 16.3 million acres of Rocky Mountain high country in five states—an area bigger than Massachusetts, New Jersey and Vermont combined.

The bill, the Northern Rockies Ecosystem Protection Act, was going to be introduced by Representative Joseph P. Kennedy 2d, Democrat of Massachusetts and a longtime back packer in the West, who says he earned his stripes there guiding hikers in the Cascade Mountains and rafting dozens of swift-flowing rivers.

But Mr. Kennedy backed off after Senator Max Baucus, Democrat of Montana, threatened to use his Senate influence to block money for cleaning up Boston Harbor. Mr. Kennedy was furious. "We learned a cold, hard lesson in special-interest politics at their very worst," he said.

This tension goes back to the days of Teddy Roosevelt, a New York City native who spent many summers in the West and devoted a great deal of his political career to protecting forests and wildlife habitat from the excesses of civilization. His legacy is all over the map of the West, from national forests to parks and wildlife refuges.

Roosevelt and his modern counterparts have long said their goal is to save for future generations land that is owned by all Americans. And indeed, most of the great natural-resources battles in the West are over Federal land. But the Western politicians said the Easterners would not apply the same standard to their own states.

"The East Coast establishment has this idea that they need to protect us from ourselves, and they feel that way because they have a guilt complex about what they did to their own land," said Lieut. Gov. Jack Coghill of Alaska. Mr. Coghill was particularly critical of Representative Gerry E. Studds, Democrat of Massachusetts, and Interior Secretary Bruce Babbitt, both of whom were in Alaska this month. And although neither man has emerged with any major policy initiatives, and despite the fact that Mr. Babbitt is a third-generation Westerner from Arizona, Mr. Coghill is leery.

"They've seen all this great beauty, and now you have to watch out for them," he said.

The Governor of Alaska, Walter J. Hickel, has sarcastically countered the well-meaning Easterners by suggesting that large sections of their territory be set aside as wilderness. "We could begin with a designation to clean up that eyesore corridor between New York City and Washington, D.C.," said Governor Hickel.

Mr. Hickel, Mr. Wallop and others paint the vacationing Easterners as out of touch with the sentiments of those most affected by conditions in the West: the people who live here. But that argument ignores the numerous allies they have living in the region.

During the 1980's, for example, Representative Robert J. Mrazek, a Democrat from Long Island, was the chief proponent of a bill to protect forests in southeastern Alaska. Mr. Mrazek left Congress last year after an unsuccessful run for the Senate, but there are still cars in Sitka, Alaska, with bumper stickers that read, "Bob Mrazek is my Congressman."

Mr. Mrazek has since founded the Alaska Conservation League, in Washington.

Although no politicians in the Rocky Mountain West have signed on in support of the bill introduced by Ms. Maloney, several hundred small businesses and interest groups in Montana, most of them tied to the outdoor recreation industry, are backing it.

But even though she has allies in the West, it is Ms. Maloney who has been the target of most of the criticism by the region's politicians. Senator Baucus said she should be more concerned about her constituents in Manhattan, N.Y., than the people of Manhattan, Mont.

Senator Wallop declared, "No set of damn fools, movie actors and representatives of silk stocking districts are going to take over the economy of the West as long as I'm around." He has suggested giving Ms. Maloney's district on the Upper East Side of Manhattan back to its original owners, the Indians.

Vacationing in Europe, Ms. Maloney was unavailable for comment. But an aide, Andrew Lowenthal, defended the right of Eastern lawmakers to protect the West. "These are Federal lands, the province of every American," he said. "A few windy press releases from Senator Wallop are not going to scare her."

He added that some of the West's most beautiful places had been set aside over objections from Western politicians. Montana's biggest outdoor playground, for example, is the Bob Marshall Wilderness, where Representative Bruce F. Vento, Democrat of Minnesota, was hiking in mid-August—a few ridges away from Senator John W. Warner, Republican of Virginia, a fisherman.

The Western politicians argue that because there are no big sections of Federal land to speak of in the East, it is a risk-free political move for the Easterners to advocate setting aside large tracts of the West.

"It's very easy to be an armchair environmentalist from the East Coast who says we have to save your state from the natives," said Mark Smith, an aide to Senator Baucus, who was touring China.

But for all his criticism of out-of-state environmental advocates, Mr. Baucus himself has come under fire for the same thing. Two years ago, he voted to set aside part of the Arctic coast in Alaska as formal wilderness, and as a result was blasted by Alaska's two Senators for meddling in their state's land affairs.

In his own territory, Senator Baucus has supported a wilderness bill, but a much smaller one. It would set aside about 1.5 million acres in Montana, less than half the area of the state called for by Ms. Maloney.

The Senator's critics in Montana question whether he can truly represent the interests of wilderness areas because of pressure from the timber and mining industries—an argument Mr. Baucus disputes.

Dan Funsch, a leader of the Alliance for the Wild Rockies based here in Missoula, said environmentalists like his group "had no choice but to find out-of-state people to back our bill."

"Some of these Western senators want the American taxpayers to subsidize logging and mining in this region but they don't want to let them participate in the discussion and decisions on what to do with these lands," Mr. Funsch said.

The big wilderness bill has attracted 24 co-sponsors—Republicans, Democrats and the House's one independent, Representative Bernard Sanders of Vermont. Many of the co-sponsors said they decided to back the bill after vacationing in the area.

So it is little wonder then, that even a seemingly innocuous visit by someone like State Senator Roy Goodman from New York, who was seen in Jackson, Wyo., this summer sporting a bolo tie and a sunburn, can arouse some suspicion.

"I'm not saying they shouldn't visit our state," said Senator Wallop. "But they should try to understand that the gene pool out here is different."

————————

Menell, Stewart, and Egan make some excellent points. But, if the PSD program was crafted by Eastern legislators to protect their working constituents or to save Western wilderness, isn't it odd that the program applies in every area which is in attainment for at least one criteria pollutant? Not even Los Angeles violates all of the NAAQS. Moreover, the NAAQS for lead is rarely violated anywhere. Thus, as a practical matter, the PSD program applies nationwide.

## 10. PARTING OBSERVATIONS ON THE PSD PROGRAM

We end our PSD exploration on an ironic note. Professor Oren's seminal article on the PSD program begins by juxtaposing two quotations about the program. He then notes that the program has remained surprisingly unscathed by the legislative amendment process.

## CRAIG N. OREN, PREVENTION OF SIGNIFICANT DETERIORATION: CONTROL COMPELLING VERSUS SITE SHIFTING

74 Iowa L. Rev. 1, 4-5 (1988)

I consider [nondegradation] "my baby," since I fought for this strategy from subcommittee [markup], to full committee [markup], to Senate floor and thus for two years in conference * * * .

For me, the nondegradation provision is the jewel that made the entire effort to pass the 1977 amendments worthwhile. The beauty of this provision is that, like a fine gem, its beauty varies with the angle from which you view it * * * .

Senator Pete V. Domenici, 1978

I had a part in drawing this statute and I am absolutely, unequivocally befuddled * * * .

I just can't believe something as complicated as this is necessary to preserve areas from deterioration.

[W]hat I see isn't what I thought we [the Conference Committee] did. * * * We went all night; maybe we wrote it when we were asleep.

Senator Pete V. Domenici, 1981

PSD ignited bitter controversy during its consideration and helped arouse a filibuster at the end of the 94th Congress in 1976 that delayed passage of amendments to the Clean Air Act until the following year. Critics have since called the program an "elaborate regulatory hocus pocus" that will lead to the "environmental movement's waterloo." Despite these attacks, Congress has failed to amend PSD, and the most prominent current Congressional proposals for amendments to the Clean Air Act almost entirely ignore PSD.

EPA as well appears to have accepted the program's existence and abandoned efforts at legislative alteration. Indeed, in formulating schemes for protection of groundwater, the agency has come remarkably close to copying PSD. There is an air of resignation even in the assaults by industry representatives upon the program.

# I.  NONATTAINMENT

## 1.  THE PROBLEM OF NONATTAINMENT

In the preceding pages, we have seen that EPA was ordered by the courts and eventually by Congress in the 1997 Clean Air Act Amendments to confront the problem of growth in areas with air quality better than that required by the national ambient air quality standards—so-called *attainment* areas. The result is the PSD program.

EPA simultaneously faced the problem of widespread *nonattainment* with the ambient air standards that were initially supposed to have been met in 1975. When Congress met to hammer out the 1977 Amendments, more than half of the country's air quality control regions were in violation of the ambient air standards for at least one pollutant. Indeed, a 1977 EPA Guidance Memorandum advised the states to presume that all urban areas with a population greater than 200,000 were nonattainment for at least one criteria pollutant and that all of the country east of the Mississippi was likewise nonattainment. *See* 8 [Curr. Dev.] Env. Rep. (BNA) 902 (1977).

The challenge was daunting. How should the EPA deal with the problem of growth in "dirty" areas? Should new sources be permitted in such areas? It seemed inappropriate to add new pollution sources to locations where the air was unacceptable; such activity would only make things worse. At the same time, however, the notion that no further industrial development would be permitted in the country's major urban areas was unthinkable. Where would all the laborers find work?

The abstract problem of blending industrial growth into nonattainment areas became concrete when the Standard Oil Company of Ohio sought to establish transfer facilities in the Los Angeles area to handle crude oil shipped from Alaska. Los Angeles was in violation of ambient standards for (what were then) two criteria pollutants: hydrocarbons and photochemical oxidants. Accordingly, the company could not construct new facilities, because they would exacerbate the violations. EPA's solution to this impasse was to create, in November of 1976, what it called the "trade-off policy," allowing new polluting sources to enter a nonattainment area as long as they secured offsetting emission reductions from existing facilities.

Many environmental attorneys were amazed. "Where in the world did *this* come from?" they wondered. "In what portion of the Clean Air Act do these EPA attorneys purport to find the extraordinary notion of *trading* rights in pollution?" The answer, of course, was that the EPA attorneys were creating the program out of thin air, all for the purpose of resolving the intractable problem of blending industrial growth into nonattainment areas—a problem that Congress had not dealt with in the Clean Air Act of 1970.

Congress did eventually confront the nonattainment problem in the 1977 Amendments, which ratified and strengthened the conditions initially established in the EPA's trade-off policy. New Part D of the statute created a massive new permit program for major stationary sources in nonattainment areas.

## 2. NONATTAINMENT PERMIT PROGRAM OVERVIEW

The primary mechanism for curbing the emission of nonattaining criteria pollutants from stationary sources has been the nonattainment permit program first added to the Clean Air Act by the 1977 Amendments.

---

Read the following sections of the Clean Air Act

☐ § 110(a)(2)(I)     ☐ § 113(a)(5)(A)     ☐ § 113(b)(3)

☐ § 171             ☐ § 172(a)(2)(A)     ☐ § 172(a)(2)(D)

☐ § 172(c)         ☐ § 173(a)         ☐ § 302(j)

---

The 1977 Amendments attacked the nonattainment problem by making drastic changes in the regulatory scheme. Based on lists submitted by state officials, EPA was required to formally "designate" air quality control regions (or portions thereof) failing to meet the NAAQS as *nonattainment areas. See* CAA § 107. Because designations of nonattainment areas must be made on a pollutant-by-pollutant basis for each criteria pollutant, many (in fact most) locations are nonattainment areas for some pollutants and attainment areas for others.

Congress provided in the 1977 amendments conditional extensions of various attainment deadlines for nonattainment areas, but the problem was sufficiently great that additional time alone could not suffice; in particular, a method was desperately needed to allow industrial growth in nonattainment areas—a development that seemed foreclosed by the statute.

Following the EPA's lead, Congress adopted in the 1977 Amendments a highly innovative program, whereby the construction and operation of new or modified major stationary sources in nonattainment areas must be accompanied by a nonattainment *permit*. The program is designed to move nonattainment areas gradually toward eventual compliance with the NAAQS, simultaneously making room for further industrial growth.

Perhaps the best way to envision nonattainment is to consider the diagram in **Figure 9-1**. If we consider the vertical axis to represent *ambient* air concentrations of a pollutant and the horizontal axis to represent the passage of time, a nonattainment area is one for which existing ambient concentration of a given criteria pollutant exceeds the relevant NAAQS at the attainment deadline. The nonattainment program is designed to systematically reduce the ambient air concentrations of the pollutant through time in order to assure eventual attainment with the NAAQS by an extended deadline.

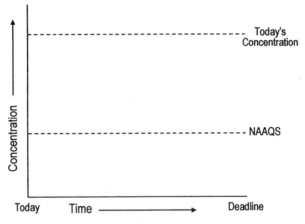

**Figure 9-1** Nonattainment

REASONABLE FURTHER PROGRESS

The 1977 amendments envisioned two ways in which such "reasonable further progress" might be assured. First, states with nonattainment areas were directed to revise their implementation plans to impose tougher, technology-based standards—known as "reasonably available control technology" (RACT)—on *existing* sources. Assuming for a moment that attainment was to be achieved solely through imposition of RACT on existing sources, the progress from nonattainment to attainment is depicted diagrammatically in **Figure 9-2**.

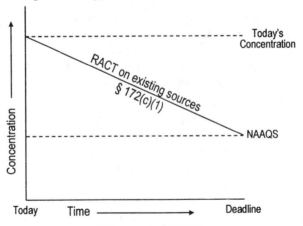

**Figure 9-2** RACT

The 1977 amendments recognized, however, that RACT requirements might be so stringent that the imposition of these controls on existing sources would create extra "room" for new sources—a windfall vaguely referred to in the statute as an "allowance" and which we might call a *growth allowance*. This possibility—that existing sources would, in effect, be ordered to "move over" to make room for new facilities—is depicted in **Figure 9-3**.

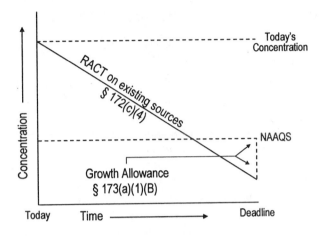

**Figure 9-3** Growth Allowance

Many nonattainment areas could not possibly find sufficient room for growth merely by imposing RACT on existing sources. Accordingly, the nonattainment provisions of the 1977 amendments authorized a second mechanism: the offset program. Pursuant to this system, a new or modified source could obtain permission to increase emissions of a nonattaining pollutant as long as it obtained sufficient emission reductions (offsets) from existing sources to assure reasonable further progress toward attainment. The basic notion is that the new facility would obtain—frequently through market transactions—and "retire" *more* existing source pollution than would be generated by its planned entry into the airshed. This possibility is depicted in **Figure 9-4**.

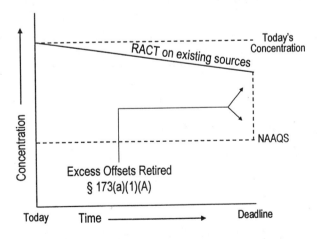

**Figure 9-4** Offsets

## 3. NONATTAINMENT PERMIT REGULATIONS

# EPA, REQUIREMENTS FOR PREPARATION, ADOPTION, AND SUBMITTAL OF IMPLEMENTATION PLANS

40 C.F.R. Part 51 (1998)

### § 51.165 Permit requirements.

(a) State Implementation Plan provisions satisfying sections 172(b)(6) and 173 of the Act shall meet the following conditions. * * *

(1) All such plans shall use the specific definitions. Deviations from the following wording will be approved only if the state specifically demonstrates that the submitted definition is more stringent, or at least as stringent, in all respects as the corresponding definition below: * * *

(xiv) "Federally enforceable" means all limitations and conditions which are enforceable by the Administrator, including those requirements developed pursuant to 40 CFR Parts 60 and 61, requirements within any applicable State implementation plan, any permit requirements established pursuant to 40 CFR 52.21 or under regulations approved pursuant to 40 CFR Part 51, Subpart I, including operating permits issued under an EPA-approved program that is incorporated into the State implementation plan and expressly requires adherence to any permit issued under such program. * * *

(2) Each plan shall adopt a preconstruction review program to satisfy the requirements of sections 172(b)(6) and 173 of the Act for any area designated nonattainment for any national ambient air quality standard under 40 CFR 81.300 et seq. Such a program shall apply to any new major stationary source or major modification that is major for the pollutant for which the area is designated nonattainment, if the stationary source or modification would locate anywhere in the designated nonattainment area.

(3)(i) Each plan shall provide that for sources and modifications subject to any preconstruction review program adopted pursuant to this subsection the *baseline* for determining credit for emissions reductions is the emissions limit under the applicable State Implementation Plan in effect at the time the application to construct is filed, except that the offset baseline shall be the actual emissions of the source from which offset credit is obtained where:

(A) The demonstration of reasonable further progress and attainment of ambient air quality standards is based upon the actual emissions of sources located within a designated nonattainment area for which the preconstruction review program was adopted; or

(B) The applicable State Implementation Plan does not contain an emissions limitation for that source or source category.

  (ii) The plan shall further provide that:

     (A) Where the emissions limit under the applicable State Implementation Plan allows greater emissions than the potential to emit of the source, emissions offset credit will be allowed only for control below this potential; * * *

     (E) All emission reductions claimed as offset credit shall be federally enforceable;

     (F) Procedures relating to the permissible location of offsetting emissions shall be followed which are at least as stringent as those set out in 40 CFR Part 51 Appendix S * * *.

# APPENDIX S TO PART 51: EMISSION OFFSET INTERPRETIVE RULING

### 40 C.F.R. Part 51, Subpart W (1998)

This appendix sets forth EPA's Interpretative Ruling on the preconstruction review requirements for stationary sources of air pollution * * *. A major new source or major modification which would locate in an area designated in 40 CFR 81.300 et seq. as nonattainment for a pollutant for which the source or modification would be major may be allowed to construct only if the stringent conditions set forth below are met. These conditions are designed to insure that the new source's emissions will be controlled to the greatest degree possible; that more than equivalent offsetting emission reductions ("emission offsets") will be obtained from existing sources; and that there will be progress toward achievement of the NAAQS. * * *

If the reviewing authority finds that the major stationary source or major modification would be constructed in an area designated in 40 CFR 81.300 et seq. as nonattainment for a pollutant for which the stationary source or modification is major, approval may be granted only if the following conditions are met:

*Condition 1.* The new source is required to meet an emission limitation which specifies the lowest achievable emission rate for such source.[5] * * *

*Condition 2.* The applicant must certify that all existing major sources owned or operated by the applicant (or any entity controlling, controlled by, or under common control with the applicant) in the same State as the proposed source are in compliance with all applicable emission limitations and standards under the Act (or are in compliance with an expeditious schedule which is Federally enforceable or contained in a court decree).

*Condition 3.* Emission reductions ("offsets") from existing sources in the area of the proposed source (whether or not under the same ownership) are required such that there will be reasonable progress toward attainment of the applicable NAAQs. * * *

---

[5] Required only for those pollutants for which the increased allowable emissions exceed 50 tons per year, 1000 pounds per day, or 100 pounds per hour, although the reviewing authority may address other pollutants if deemed appropriate. * * *

*Condition 4.* The emission offsets will provide a positive net air quality benefit in the affected area * * * .

The baseline for determining credit for emission and air quality offsets will be the SIP emission limitations in effect at the time the application to construct or modify a source is filed. Thus, credit for emission offset purposes may be allowable for existing control that goes beyond that required by the SIP. Emission offsets generally should be made on a pounds per hour basis when all facilities involved in the emission offset calculations are operating at their maximum expected or allowed production rate. * * *

Where the applicable SIP does not contain an emission limitation for a source or source category, the emission offset baseline involving such sources shall the actual emissions determined in accordance with the discussion above regarding operating conditions. * * *

*"Banking" of emission offset credit.* For new sources obtaining permits by applying offsets after January 16, 1979, the reviewing authority may allow offsets that exceed the requirements of reasonable progress toward attainment (Condition 3) to be "banked" (i.e., saved to provide offsets for a source seeking a permit in the future) for use under this Ruling. Likewise, the reviewing authority may allow the owner of an existing source that reduces its own emissions to bank any resulting reductions beyond those required by the SIP for use under this Ruling, even if none of the offsets are applied immediately to a new source permit. A reviewing authority may allow these banked offsets to be used under the preconstruction review program required by Part D, as long as these banked emissions are identified and accounted for in the SIP control strategy. A reviewing authority may not approve the construction of a source using banked offsets if the new source would interfere with the SIP control strategy or if such use would violate any other condition set forth for use of offsets. To preserve banked offsets, the reviewing authority should identify them in either a SIP revision or a permit, and establish rules as to how and when they may be used.

*Offset credit for meeting NSPS or NESHAPS.* Where a source is subject to an emission limitation established in a New Source Performance Standard (NSPS) or a National Emission Standard for Hazardous Air Pollutants (NESHAPS), (i.e., requirements under Sections 111 and 112, respectively, of the Act), and a different SIP limitation, the more stringent limitation shall be used as the baseline for determining credit for emission and air quality offsets. The difference in emissions between the SIP and the NSPS or NESHAPS, for such source may not be used as offset credit. However, if a source were not subject to an NSPS or NESHAPS, for example if its construction had commenced prior to the proposal of an NSPS or NESHAPS for that source category, offset credit can be permitted for tightening the SIP to the NSPS or NESHAPS level for such source.

*Location of offsetting emissions.* In the case of emission offsets involving volatile organic compounds (VOC), the offsets may be obtained from sources located anywhere in the broad vicinity of the proposed new source. Generally, offsets will be acceptable if obtained from within the same AQCR [Air Quality Control Region] as the new source or from other areas which may be contributing to the ozone problem at the proposed new source location. As with other pollutants, it is desirable to obtain offsets from sources located as close to the proposed new source site as possible. If the proposed offsets would be from sources located at greater distances from the new source, the reviewing authority should increase the ratio of the required offsets and require a showing that nearby offsets were investigated and reasonable alternatives were not available.

Offsets for $NO_x$ sources may also be obtained within the broad vicinity of the proposed new source. This is because areawide ozone and $NO_2$ levels are generally not as dependent on specific VOC or $NO_x$ source location as they are on overall area emissions. Since the air quality impact of $SO_2$, particulate and carbon monoxide sources is site dependent, simple areawide mass emission offsets are not appropriate. For these pollutants, the reviewing authority should consider atmospheric simulation modeling to ensure that the emission offsets provide a positive net air quality benefit. However, to avoid unnecessary consumption of limited, costly and time consuming modeling resources, in most cases it can be assumed that if the emission offsets are obtained from an existing source on the same premises or in the immediate vicinity of the new source, and the pollutants disperse from substantially the same effective stack height, the air quality test under Condition 4 * * * will be met. Thus, when stack emissions are offset against a ground level source at the same site, modeling would be required. The reviewing authority may perform this analysis or require the applicant to submit appropriate modeling results.

*Reasonable progress towards attainment.* As long as the emission offset is greater than one-for-one, and the other criteria set forth above are met, EPA does not [intend] to question a reviewing authority's judgment as to what constitutes reasonable progress towards attainment as required under Condition 3 * * * .

The necessary emission offsets may be proposed either by the owner of the proposed source or by the local community or the State. The emission reduction committed to must be enforceable by authorized State and/or local agencies and under the Clean Air Act, and must be accomplished by the new source's start-up date. * * *

A source may propose emission offsets which involve: (1) Reductions from sources controlled by the source owner (internal emission offsets); and/or (2) reductions from neighboring sources (external emission offsets). The source does not have to investigate all possible emission offsets. As long as the emission offsets obtained represent reasonable progress toward attainment, they will be acceptable. It is the reviewing authority's responsibility to assure that the emission offsets will be as effective as proposed by the source. An internal emission offset will be considered enforceable if it is made a SIP requirement by inclusion as a condition of the new source permit and the permit is forwarded to the appropriate EPA Regional Office.[10] An external emission offset will not be enforceable unless the affected source(s) providing the emission reductions is subject to a new SIP requirement to ensure that its emissions will be reduced by a specified

---

[10] The emission offset will, therefore, be enforceable by EPA under Section 113 as an applicable SIP requirement and will be enforceable by private parties under Section 304 as an emission limitation.

amount in a specified time. Thus, if the source(s) providing the emission reductions does not obtain the necessary reduction, it will be in violation of a SIP requirement and subject to enforcement action by EPA, the State and/or private parties.

The form of the SIP revision may be a State or local regulation, operating permit condition, consent or enforcement order, or any other mechanism available to the State that is enforceable under the Clean Air Act.

### *Notes and Questions*

1.  Which stationary sources must obtain nonattainment permits? *See* CAA § 172(c)(5). How does one determine whether the triggering conditions of § 172(c)(5) are met?

2.  Assume that your client wishes to build a new coal-fired power plant in an air quality control region that has been designated nonattainment for particulates but has attained the NAAQS for all other criteria pollutants. The facility will emit 40 tons per year of particulates and 110 tons per year of sulfur dioxide. Does the proposed facility need a nonattainment permit? Why or why not? Will the facility need a PSD permit? Why or why not?

3.  Assume that another one of your clients wishes to build a new cement plant in an air quality control region that has been designed nonattainment for particulates. The new facility will emit 230 tons of particulates per year. You conclude that it will need a nonattainment permit. What must you establish in the nonattainment permit hearing to obtain the necessary permit? This question requires a long and sophisticated answer.

4.  Assume that the new cement plant described in the preceding paragraph will emit 30 pounds of particulates per hour. You have found an existing manufacturing plant in the near vicinity that currently emits 35 pounds of particulates per hour. If you convince the existing facility to cease its particulate discharges, will you have obtained a sufficiently large offset to qualify for a nonattainment permit? Why or why not?

5.  Would your answer to the preceding paragraph differ if the existing manufacturing plant was subject to a SIP emission limitation of 25 pounds of particulate emissions per hour? Why or why not?

6.  Why do CAA § 173 and the EPA's nonattainment permit regulations say that any offset trade must be "federally enforceable"? What does this requirement mean?

### 4.  OFFSET PROGRAM WEAKNESSES

Obviously, the offset program can succeed in bringing about compliance by the extended attainment deadline only if the ratio of retired to newly generated emissions is sufficiently great to bring about the necessary reductions in ambient air concentration. The central importance of offset ratios to reasonable further progress may be demonstrated by a crude illustration.

Assume that the ambient air quality of an area is so much in excess of the NAAQS for a given pollutant that it is necessary to "retire" 5000 tons per year of emissions by the attainment deadline. If a new source desiring to emit 300 tons per year of the nonattaining pollutant were to obtain an offsetting emission reduction of a mere 300 tons from an existing facility, the ratio of new to old emissions would be 1:1, and there would be no progress of any kind toward attainment. On the other hand, if the new source were to obtain an offsetting emission reduction of 5300 tons per year from a single source, the ratio would be 5300:300, and attainment would be achieved through a single offset transaction, retiring the offending 5000 tons per year of excessive emissions in one fell swoop.

Defining "reasonable further progress" requires a SIP's drafters (and the EPA, when it reviews the SIP) to select a retirement ratio that falls somewhere between these extremes—great enough to assure attainment by the NAAQS deadline, but small enough to induce pollutant trading. Unfortunately, there is no way to accurately select the genuinely necessary offset ratio without knowing in advance *how many* trading transactions will occur between the present time and the compliance deadline. If only one transaction (at the illustrative size) will occur, the ratio must, indeed, be the impossible one of 5300:300. If 100 transactions of similar magnitude will take place, the ratio need only be 350:300, because each of the 100 offsets will retire 50 tons per year, resulting in a total retirement of the necessary 5000 tons. If only 50 transactions of this magnitude will occur, the ratio must be 400:300 (retiring 100 tons per transaction), and so forth.

Perhaps the greatest weakness of the nonattainment program under the Clean Air Act has been the EPA's willingness to accept any trading ratios that are greater than 1:1 as adequate to demonstrate reasonable further progress. *See* Appendix S excerpt at page 503, *supra*. Under our illustration, a feeble 1.1:1 ratio would be met by a retirement of 330 tons per year, in exchange for the new emissions of 300 tons. If attainment could not be met without retiring a total of 5000 tons, acceptance of this ratio means that more than 165 transactions of similar size must occur to achieve compliance with the NAAQS.

Moreover, because only "major stationary sources" are subject to the nonattainment program and therefore required to obtain a permit, unregulated growth from minor facilities may well eat up any reasonable further progress provided by the combined operation of the RACT emissions limitations and the offsets. Two variables are therefore essential to the success of the offset program: (1) the number of facilities escaping the requirement altogether because of the major stationary source definition; and (2) the offset trading ratio.

## 5.  OZONE NONATTAINMENT PROVISIONS OF THE 1990 AMENDMENTS

The 1977 Amendments failed to solve the problem of widespread nonattainment with the national ambient air quality standards. Many millions of people continued to be exposed to unhealthy air. Accordingly, the 1990 Amendments added numerous nonattainment provisions directed to stationary and mobile sources. To simplify our analysis of those provisions, we will confine our examination to ozone nonattainment.

### SORTING OUT THE CHANGING STANDARDS

Our analysis is complicated somewhat by the EPA's adoption of a new ozone NAAQS in 1997. *See* pages 317-29, *supra*. The 1-hour ozone standard (0.12 ppm) will eventually be replaced by the new, more stringent 8-hour standard (0.08 ppm). However, EPA will not designate areas as nonattainment for the new 8-hour ozone standard until the year 2000; this is being done to permit the Agency to collect three years of data.

The 1-hour standard was eliminated on June 5, 1998, for the almost 3,000 counties in which it had been attained; in those counties, the 8-hour standard theoretically applies. *See* 63 Fed. Reg. 31014 (1998). The new 8-hour standard was remanded, however, by the D.C. Circuit in *American Trucking Associations v. EPA*, 175 F.3d 1027 (D.C. Cir. 1999). *See* pages 322-27, *supra*.

The 1-hour standard continues to apply in any area in which it has not yet been attained. Moreover, the D.C. Circuit ruled in *American Trucking* that—even if the EPA eventually succeeds in its attempt to adopt a valid new 8-hour standard—only the older 1-hour ozone standard may be enforced through the ozone nonattainment mechanisms of the 1990 amendments (CAA §§ 181-185B). *See* 175 F.3d at 1045-50. This aspect of the *American Trucking* ruling—that EPA can make revisions but cannot enforce them—has been challenged by the agency in a motion for rehearing. *See* John H. Stam, *EPA Seeks Rehearing of Court Decision Rejecting Ozone and Particulate Standards*, 30 [Curr. Dev.] Env. Rep. (BNA) 413 (1999).

---

Read the following sections of the Clean Air Act

☐ § 181(a)(1)    ☐ § 181(b)(2)

---

### CLASSIFICATIONS AND ATTAINMENT DATES

The central feature of the 1990 Amendments is that ozone nonattainment areas are divided into five *classifications*, depending on the severity of their ozone pollution. The ever more highly polluted areas are given increasingly postponed attainment dates, but are also subjected to increasingly greater, cumulative controls mandated by the statute.

### PROGRESS TOWARD UNIVERSAL ATTAINMENT

As indicated in **Table 9-3**, the various classifications of ozone non-attainment areas are given different deadlines for ultimately achieving compliance with the ozone NAAQS. **Figure 9-5** depicts the theoretical progress toward universal attainment that is envisioned by the 1990 Amendments. The numbers in the legend represent the EPA's 1991 estimate of the nonattainment areas falling within each classification.

**Table 9-3.** Ozone Nonattainment Classifications

| Classification | Design Value (ppm) | Attainment Date |
| --- | --- | --- |
| Marginal | 0.121—0.138 | 1993 |
| Moderate | 0.138—0.160 | 1996 |
| Serious | 0.160—0.180 | 1999 |
| Severe | 0.180—0.280 | 2005 |
| Extreme | 0.280— | 2010 |

### MANDATED OZONE NONATTAINMENT SIP REQUIREMENTS

The heart of the 1990 Amendments' ozone nonattainment program is Section 182, setting forth a lengthy compilation of requirements that must be added to state implementation plans for ozone nonattainment areas. These requirements are supposed to assure that that the tidy long-range compliance picture of **Figure 9-5** will become reality.

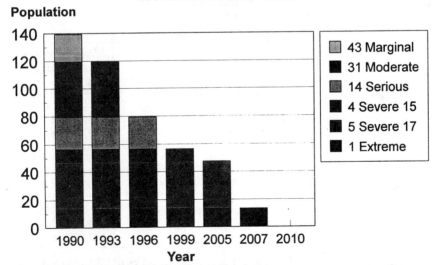

**Population Living in Ozone Nonattainment Areas**

Note: 1990 population with no growth
Source: U.S. EPA 1991 Emissions Trends Report

**Figure 9-5**

**Table 9-4.** Ozone Nonattainment
Area SIP Requirements

| Classification | NAAQS Deadline | Cumulative Requirements | Unique Provisions |
|---|---|---|---|
| **Marginal** § 182(a) | 1993 | RACT and nonattainment permit program for new sources | 1.1 to 1 offset for VOCs |
| | | Inventory VOC and NO$_X$ sources | |
| | | I/M | |
| **Moderate** § 182(b) | 1996 | Gasoline station vapor recovery systems | 1.15 to 1 offset for VOCs |
| | | RACT on all VOC stationary sources | |
| | | Reduce VOC and NO$_X$ by 15% over 6 years | |
| **Serious** § 182(c) | 1999 | Improve ambient ozone, VOC, and NO$_2$ monitoring | Major source defined as 50 tpy VOCs |
| | | Reduce VOC by 3% annually beginning 1996 | |
| | | Enhanced I/M | |
| | | Clean-fuel vehicle support program | 1.2 to 1 offset for VOCs |
| | | Triennial adjustment of TCP transportation parameter assumptions | |
| **Severe** § 182(d) | 2005 or 2007 | Employee trip reduction program (made voluntary by 1995 amendments) | Major source defined as 25 tpy VOCs |
| | | | 1.3 to 1 offset for VOCs (or 1.2 to 1 if BACT is used) |
| **Extreme** § 182(e) | 2010 | Stationary sources emitting > 25 tpy NO$_X$ must implement clean fuel requirements for primary fuels | Major source defined as 10 tpy VOCs |
| | | | 1.5 to 1 offset for VOCs (or 1.2 to 1 if BACT is used) |

The provisions of § 182 establish a graduated control program of increasingly more stringent requirements as one moves up the classification scheme. Requirements are assigned to the various severity classifications, with most requirements being *cumulative*; they must be met by all higher (more severely polluted) classifications, as well as by the classification for which they are first specified. Thus, for example, a moderate ozone nonattainment area must comply not only with the requirements specified uniquely for it, but also with all requirements set forth for the less polluted marginal areas.

It may be helpful to visualize these requirements in a table. **Table 9-4** depicts the cumulative and unique requirements essentially in the order laid out by § 182, beginning with marginal areas and moving on through extreme areas to federally imposed ozone controls.

## 6. OZONE DESIGN VALUES

EPA's national ambient air quality standard for ozone allows areas to exceed the 0.12 ppm maximum daily average one-hour value once each year without being considered in nonattainment. EPA uses a 3-year period to determine if an area is in nonattainment. If the area has 3 or less violations for the 3-year period (that is, an average of one violation or less per year), it is in attainment. *See* 57 Fed. Reg. 13,498 (1992); 40 C.F.R. 50.9 Appendix H (1998). The EPA has further explained the measurement technique and significance of the design value:

> The ozone design value is a surrogate measure of attainment status, a measure of progress, and an indicator of how much concentrations must be reduced to meet the standard. * * * The current EPA design value method is simply to select the fourth highest daily maximum 1-hour concentration as the design value during the 3-year compliance period. *The fourth highest value is the design value*, since if the fourth highest day is reduced to the level of the standard, then there will be one day per year above the level of the standard assuming three years of data.

> With passage of the Clean Air Act Amendments (CAAA) of 1990, added emphasis was placed on ozone design values. In addition to designating areas as nonattainment for ozone, the CAAA introduced a classification process to further categorize nonattainment areas according to the extent of their ozone problem. As shown in [**Table 9-3**], this area classification was based upon the ozone design value. * * * Before the 1990 CAAA, designation of nonattainment areas simply involved a yes/no determination as to whether the area met the standard. The additional classification step introduced by the 1990 CAAA placed greater emphasis on ozone concentration observations and on the methodology used to determine the design value. * * *

> As noted above, compliance with the ozone NAAQS is judged on the basis of expected exceedances, and becomes a "yes/no" decision. However, once it is established that an area exceeds the standard, the next logical question to ask is, "By how much?" The air quality design value is intended to provide a measure of how far concentrations must be reduced to achieve attainment or, equivalently, how far out of attainment

the area represented by a monitoring site is. In this respect, the design value can be viewed as an air quality indicator for a given location. * * *

U.S. EPA, Office of Air Quality Planning and Standards, *The Clean Air Act Ozone Design Value Study* (1994).

The EPA fulfilled its statutory mandate to promulgate the initial ozone nonattainment designations and classifications in 1991, resulting in 98 ozone nonattainment areas. The Agency's decision to classify areas based on the 1988-1990 period, including unusually high 1988 ozone nonattainment readings, was criticized as foolish and wasteful. Nevertheless, the EPA insisted that the statute required these calculations and that they are not as unrepresentative of ozone air quality over time as critics claim.

## 7. STATUS OF OZONE NONATTAINMENT

Since the initial 1991 ozone nonattainment designation and classification, approximately 60 areas have come into attainment, many have changed classification, and at least one has been added. **Table 9-5** sets forth the list of 38 ozone nonattainment areas as of August 10, 1998, together with their design values for the 1995-97 period, the expected number of 1-hour ozone NAAQS exceedances per year, and the total population (1990 census figures). The values in brackets represent the respective statutory cutoff numbers and attainment deadlines for each classification. Notice particularly the column headed "average expected exceedances," because that is an excellent indicator of the extent of noncompliance. In Los Angeles, for example, EPA expects 137.5 days of violation per year.

**Table 9-5.** Ozone nonattainment areas
Source: EPA Green Book
www.epa.gov/oar/oaqps/greenbk (Dec. 7, 1998)

| Nonattainment Area | 1995-97 Design Value (ppm) | Average Expected Exceed- ances | Population (1990) |
|---|---|---|---|
| **Extreme [0.280 ppm+] [2010]** | | | |
| Los Angeles South Coast Air Basin, CA | .330 | 137.5 | 13,000,000 |
| **Severe 17 [0.180-0.280 ppm] [2007]** | | | |
| Chicago-Gary-Lake County, IL-IN | .190 | 13 | 7,886,000 |
| Houston-Galveston-Brazoria, TX | .220 | 12.2 | 3,731,000 |
| Milwaukee-Racine, WI | .183 | 9.8 | 1,735,000 |
| New York-New Jersey-Long Island, NY-NJ-CT | .201 | 17.4 | 17,651,000 |

| Nonattainment Area | 1995-97 Design Value (ppm) | Average Expected Exceed-ances | Population (1990) |
|---|---|---|---|
| Southeast Desert AQMA, CA | .240 | 59.6 | 384,000 |
| **Severe 15 [0.180-0.280 ppm] [2005]** | | | |
| Baltimore, MD | .194 | 10.7 | 2,348,000 |
| Philadelphia-Wilmington-Trenton, PA-NJ-DE-MD | .187 | 8.8 | 6,010,000 |
| Sacramento Metro, CA | .160 | 15.8 | 1,639,000 |
| Ventura Co, CA | .170 | 38.8 | 669,000 |
| **Serious [0.160-0.180 ppm] [1999]** | | | |
| Atlanta, GA | .162 | 9.3 | 2,654,000 |
| Baton Rouge, LA | .164 | 4.5 | 559,000 |
| Boston-Lawrence-Worcester, MA | .165 | 10.0 | 5,505,000 |
| Dallas-Fort Worth, TX | .140 | 3.5 | 3,560,000 |
| El Paso, TX | .170 | 7.9 | 592,000 |
| Greater Connecticut, CT | .172 | 7.9 | 2,470,000 |
| Phoenix, AZ | .141 | 6.0 | 2,092,000 |
| Portsmouth-Dover-Rochester, NH | .165 | 5/3 | 183,000 |
| Providence (all of RI), RI | .162 | 6.4 | 1,003,000 |
| San Diego, CA | .185 | 12.3 | 2,498,000 |
| San Joaquin Valley, CA | .170 | 44.2 | 2,742,000 |
| Santa Barbara-Santa Maria-Lompoc, CA | .140 | 2.1 | 370,000 |
| Springfield (W. Mass), MA | .167 | 6.7 | 812,000 |
| Washington, DC-MD-VA | .165 | 5.0 | 3,924,000 |
| **Moderate [0.138-0.160 ppm] [1996]** | | | |
| Beaumont-Port Arthur, TX | .158 | 3.7 | 361,000 |
| Cincinnati-Hamilton, OH-KY | .157 | 5.4 | 1,705,000 |
| Louisville, KY-IN | .149 | 1.9 | 834,000 |
| Manitowoc Co, WI | .167 | 9.9 | 80,000 |
| Muskegon, MI | .181 | 9.4 | 159,000 |
| Pittsburgh-Beaver Valley, PA | .149 | 7.0 | 2,468,000 |
| Portland, ME | .156 | 6.1 | 441,000 |
| St. Louis, MO-IL | .156 | 6.2 | 2,390,000 |
| **Marginal [0.121-0.138 ppm] [1993]** | | | |
| Birmingham, AL | .133 | 3.0 | 751,000 |
| Door Co, WI | .126 | 1.8 | 26,000 |
| Kent & Queen Anne's Counties, MD | .131 | 1.6 | 52,000 |

| Nonattainment Area | 1995-97 Design Value (ppm) | Average Expected Exceed-ances | Population (1990) |
|---|---|---|---|
| Lancaster, PA | .125 | 1.3 | 423,000 |
| Sunland Park, NM | .136 | 2.6 | 8,000 |
| **Other (Awaiting Classification)** | | | |
| San Francisco Bay, CA | .138 | 5.7 | 5,815,000 |
| **Total** | | | 99,530,000 |

**Figure 9-6** displays the classified ozone nonattainment areas where the 1-hour standard still applies, as of September 1998.

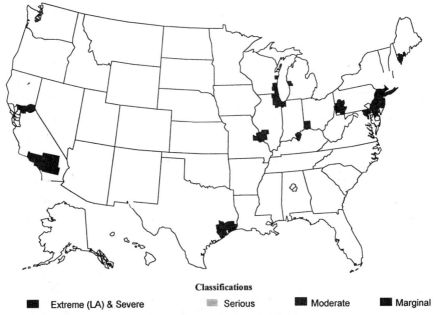

**Classifications**

■ Extreme (LA) & Severe  ▩ Serious  ■ Moderate  ■ Marginal

Note: San Francisco is Classified Other / Sec 185A & Incomplete Data Areas Not Included

**Figure 9-6.** Classified ozone nonattainment areas
where 1-hour standard still applies, Sep. 1998
Source: National Air Quality and
Emissions Trends Report, 1997, Figure 4-2

## 8. NONATTAINMENT STATUS FOR ALL CRITERIA POLLUTANTS

Each year, the EPA publishes a document called the *National Air Quality and Emissions Trends Report*. The report published in December 1998 shows that there have been dramatic reductions in the emissions of some of the six criteria pollutants (especially lead) since 1970, while the emissions of other criteria pollutants have shown a lesser decrease or even (in the case of nitrogen dioxide and particulate matter) an increase. *See* **Figure 9-7.**

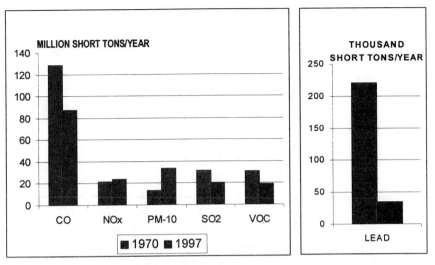

**Figure 9-7.** Comparison of 1970 and 1997 Emissions
Source: National Air Pollutant Emission Trends, 1900-1997
and ftp.pechan.com/pub/trends/tier1218.xls (Dec. 23, 1998)

According to the same report, the number of Americans living in locations with ambient air quality violating one or more of the NAAQS remains quite high. *See* **Figure 9-8.**

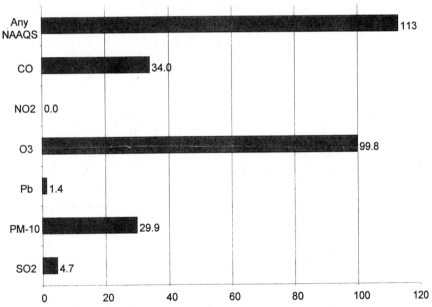

**Figure 9-8.** Number of persons (millions) living in nonattainment areas
Source: National Air Quality and Emissions Trends Report, 1997 at 67
www.epa.gov/oar/aqtrnd97/chapter4.pdf (Dec. 23, 1998)

The *Emissions Trends Report* also contains a listing of all nonattainment areas. **Table 9-6** is a depiction of the nonattainment areas for all six criteria pollutants as of September 22, 1998.

**Table 9-6**. Condensed Nonattainment Areas List
Source: U.S. EPA, National Air Quality and
Emissions Trends Report, 1997, Table A-17
www.epa.gov/oar/aqtrnd97/ (Jun. 10, 1999)

| State | Area Name | Population (1000s) | CO | SO2 | PM10 | Pb | NO2 | O3 |
|---|---|---|---|---|---|---|---|---|
| AK | Anchorage | 222 | 1 | . | 1 | . | . | . |
| AK | Fairbanks | 30 | 1 | . | . | . | . | . |
| AK | Juneau | 12 | . | . | 1 | . | . | . |
| AL | Birmingham | 751 | . | . | . | . | . | 1 |
| AZ | Ajo | 6 | . | 1 | 1 | . | . | . |
| AZ | Bullhead City | 5 | . | . | 1 | . | . | . |
| AZ | Douglas | 13 | . | 1 | 1 | . | . | . |
| AZ | Miami-Hayden | 3 | . | 2 | 1 | . | . | . |
| AZ | Morenci | 8 | . | 1 | . | . | . | . |
| AZ | Nogales | 19 | . | . | 1 | . | . | . |
| AZ | Paul Spur | 1 | . | . | 1 | . | . | . |
| AZ | Payson | 8 | . | . | 1 | . | . | . |
| AZ | Phoenix | 2122 | 1 | . | 1 | . | . | 1 |
| AZ | Rillito | 0 | . | . | 1 | . | . | . |
| AZ | San Manuel | 5 | . | 1 | . | . | . | . |
| AZ | Yuma | 54 | . | . | 1 | . | . | . |
| CA | Imperial Valley | 92 | . | . | 1 | . | . | . |
| CA | Los Angeles-South Coast Air Basin | 13000 | 1 | . | 1 | . | . | 1 |
| CA | Mono Basin (in Mono Co.) | 0 | . | . | 1 | . | . | . |
| CA | Owens Valley | 18 | . | . | 1 | . | . | . |
| CA | Sacramento Metro | 1639 | . | . | 1 | . | . | 1 |
| CA | San Diego | 2498 | . | . | . | . | . | 1 |
| CA | San Francisco-Oakland-San Jose | 5815 | . | . | . | . | . | 1 |
| CA | San Joaquin Valley | 2742 | . | . | 1 | . | . | 1 |
| CA | Santa Barbara-Santa Maria-Lompoc | 370 | . | . | . | . | . | 1 |
| CA | Searles Valley | 30 | . | . | 1 | . | . | . |
| CA | Southeast Desert Modified AQMA | 384 | . | . | 2 | . | . | 1 |
| CA | Ventura Co. | 669 | . | . | . | . | . | 1 |
| CO | Aspen | 5 | . | . | 1 | . | . | . |
| CO | Canon City | 12 | . | . | 1 | . | . | . |
| CO | Colorado Springs | 353 | 1 | . | . | . | . | . |
| CO | Denver-Boulder | 1836 | 1 | . | 1 | . | . | . |
| CO | Fort Collins | 106 | 1 | . | . | . | . | . |
| CO | Lamar | 8 | . | . | 1 | . | . | . |
| CO | Longmont | 52 | 1 | . | . | . | . | . |
| CO | Pagosa Springs | 1 | . | . | 1 | . | . | . |
| CO | Steamboat Springs | 6 | . | . | 1 | . | . | . |

| State | Area Name | Population (1000s) | CO | SO2 | PM10 | Pb | NO2 | O3 |
|---|---|---|---|---|---|---|---|---|
| CO | Telluride | 1 | | . | 1 | . | . | . |
| CT | Greater Connecticut | 2470 | . | . | 1 | . | . | 1 |
| DC-MD-VA | Washington | 3923 | . | . | . | . | . | 1 |
| GA | Atlanta | 2653 | . | . | . | . | . | 1 |
| GA | Muscogee Co. (Columbus) | 179 | . | . | . | 1 | . | . |
| GU | Piti Power Plant | 0 | . | 1 | . | . | . | . |
| GU | Tanguisson Power Plant | 0 | . | 1 | . | . | . | . |
| ID | Boise | 125 | . | . | 1 | . | . | . |
| ID | Bonner Co.(Sandpoint ) | 26 | . | . | 1 | . | . | . |
| ID | Pocatello | 46 | . | . | 1 | . | . | . |
| ID | Shoshone Co. | 13 | . | . | 2 | . | . | . |
| IL-IN | Chicago-Gary-Lake County | 7887 | . | 1 | 3 | . | . | 1 |
| IN | Marion Co. (Indianapolis) | 16 | . | . | . | 1 | . | . |
| KY | Boyd Co. (Ashland) | 51 | . | 1 | . | . | . | |
| KY | Muhlenberg Co. | 31 | . | 1 | . | . | . | . |
| KY-IN | Louisville | 834 | . | . | . | . | . | 1 |
| LA | Baton Rouge | 559 | . | . | . | . | . | 1 |
| MA | Springfield (W. Mass) | 812 | . | . | . | . | . | 1 |
| MA-NH | Boston-Lawrence-Worcester | 5507 | . | . | . | . | . | 1 |
| MD | Baltimore | 2348 | . | . | . | . | . | 1 |
| MD | Kent and Queen Anne Cos. | 52 | . | . | . | . | . | 1 |
| ME | Portland | 441 | . | . | . | . | . | 1 |
| MI | Muskegon | 159 | . | . | . | . | . | 1 |
| MN | Minneapolis-St. Paul | 2310 | 1 | . | 1 | . | . | . |
| MN | Olmsted Co. (Rochester) | 71 | . | 1 | . | . | . | . |
| MO | Dent | 2 | . | . | . | 1 | . | . |
| MO | Liberty-Arcadia | 2 | . | . | . | 1 | . | . |
| MO-IL | St. Louis | 2390 | . | . | . | 1 | . | 1 |
| MT | Butte | 33 | . | . | 1 | . | . | . |
| MT | Columbia Falls | 2 | . | . | 1 | . | . | . |
| MT | Kalispell | 11 | . | . | 1 | . | . | . |
| MT | Lame Deer | 0 | . | . | 1 | . | . | . |
| MT | Lewis & Clark (E. Helena) | 2 | . | 1 | . | 1 | . | . |
| MT | Libby | 2 | . | . | 1 | . | . | . |
| MT | Missoula | 43 | 1 | . | 1 | . | . | . |
| MT | Polson | 3 | . | . | 1 | . | . | . |
| MT | Ronan | 1 | . | . | 1 | . | . | . |
| MT | Thompson Falls | 1 | . | . | 1 | . | . | . |
| MT | Whitefish | 3 | . | . | 1 | . | . | . |
| MT | Yellowstone Co. (Laurel) | 5 | . | 1 | . | . | . | . |
| NE | Douglas Co. (Omaha) | 1 | . | . | . | 1 | . | . |
| NH | Portsmouth-Dover-Rochester | 183 | . | . | . | . | . | 1 |
| NM | Anthony | 1 | . | . | 1 | . | . | . |
| NM | Grant Co. | 27 | . | 1 | . | . | . | . |

| State | Area Name | Population (1000s) | CO | SO2 | PM10 | Pb | NO2 | O3 |
|---|---|---|---|---|---|---|---|---|
| NM | Sunland Park | 8 | . | . | . | . | . | 1 |
| NV | Central Steptoe Valley | 2 | . | 1 | . | . | . | . |
| NV | Las Vegas | 741 | 1 | . | 1 | . | . | . |
| NV | Reno | 254 | 1 | . | 1 | . | . | . |
| NY-NJ-CT | New York-N. New Jersey-Long Island | 17943 | 1 | . | 1 | . | . | 1 |
| OH | Cleveland-Akron-Lorain | 1898 | . | 3 | 1 | . | . | . |
| OH | Coshocton Co. | 35 | . | 1 | . | . | . | . |
| OH | Gallia Co. | 30 | . | 1 | . | . | . | . |
| OH | Jefferson Co. (Steubenville) | 80 | . | 1 | 1 | . | . | . |
| OH | Lucas Co. (Toledo) | 462 | . | 1 | . | . | . | . |
| OH-KY | Cincinnati-Hamilton | 1705 | . | . | . | . | . | 1 |
| OR | Grants Pass | 17 | 1 | . | 1 | . | . | . |
| OR | Klamath Falls | 18 | 1 | . | 1 | . | . | . |
| OR | LaGrande | 11 | . | . | 1 | . | . | . |
| OR | Lakeview | 2 | . | . | 1 | . | . | . |
| OR | Medford | 63 | 1 | . | 1 | . | . | . |
| OR | Oakridge | 3 | . | . | 1 | . | . | . |
| OR | Springfield-Eugene | 157 | . | . | 1 | . | . | . |
| PA | Lancaster | 423 | . | . | . | . | . | 1 |
| PA | Pittsburgh-Beaver Valley | 2468 | . | 2 | 1 | . | . | 1 |
| PA | Warren Co | 22 | . | 2 | . | . | . | . |
| PA-DE-NJ-MD | Philadelphia-Wilmington-Trenton | 6010 | . | . | . | . | . | 1 |
| PA-NJ | Allentown-Bethlehem | | . | 1 | | | | |
| PR | Guaynabo Co. | 85 | . | . | 1 | . | . | . |
| RI | Providence (all of RI) | 1003 | . | . | . | . | . | 1 |
| TN | Shelby Co. (Memphis) | 826 | . | . | . | 1 | . | . |
| TN | Nashville | 81 | . | . | . | 1 | . | . |
| TX | Beaumont-Port Arthur | 361 | . | . | . | . | . | 1 |
| TX | Dallas-Fort Worth | 3561 | . | . | . | 1 | . | 1 |
| TX | El Paso | 592 | 1 | . | 1 | . | . | 1 |
| TX | Houston-Galveston-Brazoria | 3731 | . | . | . | . | . | 1 |
| UT | Ogden | 63 | 1 | . | 1 | . | . | . |
| UT | Salt Lake City | 725 | . | 1 | 1 | . | . | . |
| UT | Tooele Co. | 26 | . | 1 | . | . | . | . |
| UT | Utah Co. (Provo) | 263 | 1 | . | 1 | . | . | . |
| WA | Olympia-Tumwater-Lacey | 63 | . | . | 1 | . | . | . |
| WA | Seattle-Tacoma | 730 | . | . | 3 | . | . | . |
| WA | Spokane | 279 | 1 | . | 1 | . | . | . |
| WA | Wallula | 47 | . | . | 1 | . | . | . |
| WA | Yakima | 54 | . | . | 1 | . | . | . |
| WI | Door Co. | 26 | . | . | . | . | . | 1 |
| WI | Manitowoc Co. | 80 | . | . | . | . | . | 1 |
| WI | Marathon Co. (Wausau) | 115 | . | 1 | . | . | . | . |

| State | Area Name | Population (1000s) | CO | SO2 | PM10 | Pb | NO2 | O3 |
|-------|-----------|-------------------|-----|-----|------|-----|-----|-----|
| WI | Milwaukee-Racine | 1735 | . | . | . | . | . | 1 |
| WI | Oneida Co. (Rhinelander) | 31 | . | 1 | . | . | . | . |
| WV | Follansbee | 3 | . | . | 1 | . | . | . |
| WV | New Manchester Gr. (in Hancock Co) | 10 | . | 1 | . | . | . | . |
| WV | Wier.-Butler-Clay (in Hancock Co) | 25 | . | 1 | 1 | . | . | . |
| WY | Sheridan | 13 | . | . | 1 | . | . | . |
| | Totals | 113001 | 20 | 34 | 77 | 10 | 0 | 38 |

Finally, **Figure 9-9** displays the location of all nonattainment areas for all criteria pollutants as of September 1998.

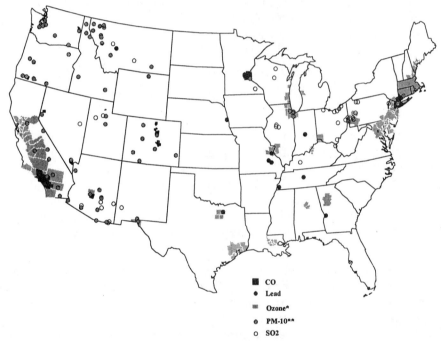

**Figure 9-9.** Location of nonattainment areas
for criteria pollutants, Sep. 1998
Source: National Air Quality and
Emissions Trends Report, 1997, Figure 4-1

### Questions

1. Assume that your client wishes to build a new industrial facility in what is known as the Anchorage, Alaska, air quality control region. Even after installing and operating federally enforceable controls, the facility will emit 115 tons of CO and 280 tons of VOCs per year. What permits will you need to commence construction under the Clean Air Act? Why? Might a PSD permit be required even though the facility will not emit $SO_2$, $NO_x$, or

$PM_{10}$, the only three pollutants for which the PSD program has established maximum allowable increments in clean air areas? Why or why not?

2.    Assume that the facts are as stated in the preceding paragraph, except that your client's proposed facility will emit 95 (rather than 115) tons of CO per year. What permits will it need under these circumstances? Why?

# J. OPERATING PERMIT PROGRAM

We have now examined the two Clean Air Act permit programs originally added by the 1977 amendments: (1) the PSD permit program for clean areas, and (2) the nonattainment permit programs for polluted areas. The last of the three permit programs is the operating permit program, added by the 1990 amendments and codified in Title V.

The operating permit program covers all "major sources." Generally, stationary sources with the potential to emit more than 100 tons per year of any regulated pollutant must obtain permits. CAA § 502(a). In nonattainment areas for which the Act now mandates lower major source thresholds, smaller sources will also be covered.

## JOHN-MARK STENSVAAG & CRAIG N. OREN, CLEAN AIR ACT: LAW AND PRACTICE

### § 14.1 (1994)

Title V requires each State to establish an operating permit program that satisfies specified requirements. Once a State obtains EPA approval for its program * * * many sources of air pollution will have to obtain permits specifying in detail the federal air pollution control requirements that apply to the source and containing measures to implement them. The issuance of such permits will be subject to EPA veto. If a State does not establish an approved program, the EPA must do so * * * .

Title V's passage marks a sea-change in the Act. * * * [T]he vast majority of air pollution sources have been regulated primarily through State Implementation Plans (SIPs). * * * A typical plan will consist of rules prescribing emission limits for sources * * * . Once approved by EPA, the limits become enforceable by the Federal Government and citizens.

This rule-based system contrasts markedly with statutes like the Clean Water Act, which requires permits for discharges into the nation's waters * * * . But the difference is not accidental. * * * The Clean Air Act * * * focuses on controlling emissions from a broad variety of sources to achieve desirable levels of environmental quality—the ambient air quality standards * * * . The decision on how and whether Source A is limited inevitably affects how and whether Source B must be limited. This is a "polycentric" problem * * * that cannot easily be addressed through individual permit adjudications, but instead requires rules. * * *   There are, though, real drawbacks to reliance on

SIPs as a means of establishing control requirements. William Pedersen, long EPA's chief lawyer on air pollution matters, was the first to describe these in detail. William Pedersen, *Why the Clean Air Act Works Badly*, 129 U. Pa. L. Rev. 1059 (1981). The SIP is not simply a compilation of a State's air pollution rules, but is a combination of the rules that the State has submitted as relevant to attainment of the ambient standards and of EPA action on those rules. Learning the status of a particular SIP provision can therefore be a considerable chore. Moreover, SIPs are frequently unwieldy. Consider the following statement by Walter Barber, then acting EPA administrator and director of the Office of Air Quality Planning and Standards:

> I don't even think I can lift this, but I will try. The box is full. The box is simply the 1979 amendment to the Illinois SIP. We couldn't bring the whole SIP. Nobody could read the whole SIP. Nobody even knows what is in one at this point.

SIPs are far too large even to be published in the Federal Register, but instead must be incorporated by reference when EPA takes action on a submittal. Worse, the SIPs are frequently disorganized. A single category of sources may be affected by overlapping or even contradictory rules. As the Senate Committee report remarked in explaining its proposed version of Title V:

> Currently, in many cases, the source's pollution control obligations— ranging from emissions controls and monitoring requirements to recordkeeping and reporting requirements—are scattered throughout numerous, often hard-to-find provisions of the SIP or other Federal regulations.

For all their volume, the SIPs, like all systems of rules, often leave unresolved crucial interstitial questions about precisely how the rules apply to individual sources. This has led to differences between EPA and the States in how to interpret a given SIP provision, thereby hampering compliance and enforcement efforts. Most States have attempted to cope with these problems by establishing operating permit programs of their own. But such programs cannot resolve interpretive disputes between EPA and the States. In addition, these programs inevitably differ from State to State, posing problems for companies with interstate operations.

Title V seeks to deal with these difficulties by ordering that all requirements that apply to a source under the Clean Air Act or a SIP—that is, in EPA's argot, all "applicable requirements"—be compiled into a single document, much like an NPDES permit under the Clean Water Act. The source, EPA, the states, and citizens will be able to look to this document to find out the source's obligations; indeed * * * compliance by the source with the permit may be a defense to enforcement actions under the Act. Sources will be obligated to submit periodic compliance reports. In this way, [Title V] is expected to make it easier to determine whether a source is in compliance, thereby improving enforcement efforts and the source's own ability to find out what requirements apply to it. * * *

Pedersen urged that a permit system should have two other features. First, he argued that States should be allowed to shield permittees from regulatory requirements established between issuance and renewal. Second, Pedersen suggested that a permit program should allow a State to alter the SIP without the formality of a SIP revision. Neither proposal * * * has survived the Congressional or regulatory process. This means a continuation of the regulatory status quo ante: sources are subject to changes by the government in control requirements, but cannot themselves easily secure alterations. This asymmetry is understandable in a statute that puts a premium on protection of public health and welfare, but it considerably limits the flexibility of sources while forcing them to run the risk that today's investments in pollution control will be rendered obsolete by tomorrow's regulatory requirements. Indeed, the creation of the permit program, by necessitating a change to the permit as well as to the SIP in order to relax a source's control requirements, potentially increases the burdens borne by sources. For this reason, efforts can be expected to provide more flexibility within SIPs to obviate the need for SIP revisions to relax control requirements. The result may be renewed debate over the fundamentals of the program. * * *

---

Issuance of the Title V operating permits has encountered delays. EPA estimated that approximately 11,000 permits should have been issued by August 1997, but only 2,075 final permits had been completed. *See* Regina P. Cline, *All Pending Title V Permits Scheduled for Completion by 2001, EPA Official Says*, 30 [Curr. Dev.] Env. Rep. (BNA) 359 (1999). Nevertheless, EPA anticipates that all permits will be issued by December 31, 2000. *Id.*

## K. ENFORCEMENT

### 1. INTRODUCTION

You have now been introduced to the elaborate regulatory structure of the Clean Air Act. The most impressive commands in the world will accomplish nothing, of course, if there is no meaningful enforcement. What are the mechanisms for assuring that the many commands of the Clean Air Act will be implemented and obeyed by the affected actors and entities? We will address some of those mechanisms in the following pages. The first reading presents an overview of the enforcement aspects of the Clean Air Act and other federal environmental statutes.

## JEFFREY G. MILLER,
## FEDERAL ENFORCEMENT

in 1 Law of Environmental Protection (Sheldon M. Novick, ed. 1998)

The environmental statutes now possess an impressive array of enforcement authorities. They most often include: notices of violation, which sometimes are jurisdictional prerequisites to other enforcement actions; administrative orders requiring compliance; administrative orders assessing civil penalties; recourse to courts for civil penalties for violations and injunctive relief to require compliance; criminal sanctions for violations; and citizen suits to enforce the statutes in the absence of effective government enforcement. Other less pervasive enforcement tools include: product recalls; stop sale orders; permit revocations; sewer connection bans; notices to affected parties; contract debarment; and protection of whistleblowing employees. * * *

While the enforcement tools * * * could be sharpened and augmented in some respects, EPA generally has sufficient enforcement authority to mount credible and effective enforcement programs if it has the will to do so. Repeated studies indicate that it sometimes lacks the will * * * .

With only a few exceptions, the statutes and EPA policy give the states the principal role in enforcing environmental protection law. * * * Almost without exception, however, the statutes give EPA residual or concurrent enforcement authority. * * *

Environmental organizations sometimes complain that EPA does not bring enforcement actions against enough violators of the environmental statutes and that, even when it does enforce, it does not seek or exact sufficient remedies and penalties. Enforcement targets complain that EPA enforces too often and seeks wholly unwarranted remedies and penalties. They also contend that EPA should enforce against other, more egregious malefactors. The common denominators between the environmental commentators and the enforcement targets are the concepts of enforcement discretion and the related questions of how it is exercised and whether it is judicially recognized.

The concept of enforcement discretion is not new and is not a creation of environmental law. It is the natural result of the fact that there are more illegal acts committed than can be identified, investigated, and prosecuted with the resources society is willing to devote to the task. * * *

Under Clean Air Act § 113 there is * * * a split of authority whether enforcement is mandatory. In *Wisconsin's Environmental Decade v. Wisconsin Power & Light Co.* [395 F. Supp. 313 (W.D. Wis. 1975)], a district court held that the issuance of a notice of violation under § 113(a)(1) was mandatory. Under that paragraph, "whenever, on the basis of any information available," EPA finds a person is in violation, it "shall" notify him of the violation and thereafter "may" issue an administrative order or "may" commence a civil action. The court found the juxtaposition of "shall" and "may" in the same paragraph persuasive in concluding that the first stage of enforcement was mandatory and the second stage was not. It also held that when presented with evidence of a violation, EPA must make a finding but that a finding of no violation may not be challenged under the citizen suit provision of the Clean Air Act. This provides EPA with such an easy out that it undercuts the main ruling. Other cases suggesting that CAA § 113 enforcement is mandatory are also less than they seem. * * *

The most interesting potential case under CAA § 113, however, has not been squarely faced. Section 113(b) deals with civil actions. Originally, like [Clean Water Act] § 309, it merely authorized EPA to bring civil actions for violation of the Act. In 1977, however, it was amended to read that EPA "shall" commence a civil action for specified violations by a major stationary source and "may" commence a civil action against another stationary source for the same violations. This appears to limit EPA's exercise of enforcement power * * * .

At the same time Congress amended CAA § 113, it also added CAA § 120, which provided that EPA "shall assess and collect" a noncompliance penalty against every person who "violates specified requirements in the Act." Here, too, the "shall" suggests a mandatory duty to enforce, although EPA does not assess section 120 penalties against all sources violating the CAA provisions specified in section 120(a)(2). Section 120 invites citizen suits to compel mandatory enforcement in the same manner as does 113(b). * * *

The federal pollution control legislation of the early 1970s was born in large measure from dissatisfaction with previous state pollution control programs and a suspicion that many states would never effectively enforce pollution control requirements. * * * The resulting statutes often call for states to develop and implement pollution control programs meeting federally established standards, but provide for their enforcement by both states and EPA. This apparent anomaly results in a very real friction between state and federal bureaucracies. * * * The peak of this friction is often found in the bitter resentment by state officials against enforcement actions taken in their backyard by EPA.

The *notice of violation* is a device intended to lessen this federalist friction. * * * The notice * * * serves two main purposes. First, it alerts states to impending federal enforcement, allowing them to perform their primary enforcement role and to limit the federal presence within their borders. Second, it alerts the violators to impending federal enforcement, allowing them to come into compliance and avoid enforcement altogether, thus achieving compliance with a minimum use of government resources.

The notice of violation is part of the CAA's enforcement scheme for violations of *state*-developed requirements, not for violations of federally developed requirements such as new source performance or hazardous emission standards * * * .

## 2.  SECTION 120 NONCOMPLIANCE PENALTIES

One of the most extraordinary enforcement mechanisms in any environmental statute is unique to the Clean Air Act: the § 120 noncompliance penalties. We examine this device in the next set of readings.

---

Read the following section of the Clean Air Act

☐ § 120

---

# EPA NONCOMPLIANCE PENALTIES SIGNED

11 [Curr. Dev.] Env. Rep. (BNA) 379 (1980)

Environmental Protection Agency Administrator Douglas M. Costle July 7 signed final noncompliance penalty regulations that, beginning January 1, 1981, will make sources pay penalties equal to the costs they would avoid by not complying with the Clean Air Act's requirements.

Section 120 of the Act mandated EPA to adopt regulations that by mid-1979 would end the incentive to pollute created by the economic savings that could be achieved by not installing the necessary pollution controls.

However, EPA will miss the Act's deadline for promulgation of the regulations by almost two and one-half years, and the regulations will not be retroactive to August 1979. The regulations were proposed by EPA March 21, 1979.

Moreover, EPA is delaying implementation of the regulations until January 1, 1981, and has set specific priorities for the types of sources that will receive non-compliance orders first—worst offenders first.

That strategy according to EPA, is needed to allow time for the agency to gear up to implement the regulations and to mesh the new administrative noncompliance penalties with EPA's current judicial enforcement program, under Section 113 of the Act.

Also, EPA says it does not have the resources to go after all of the estimated 2,000 sources that are out of compliance at once. The agency cannot meet the Act's time deadlines for administrative reviews of the penalties if it tries to handle a large number of noncompliers at the same time.

### PRIORITY SCHEME

EPA said initially it will take action against major sources that have never achieved compliance and are not complying with enforceable compliance schedules contained in either federal or EPA-approved consent decrees or administrative orders. Sources bound by such schedules and complying with them are not exempt from the regulations, but they will not be given a high priority by EPA.

Other factors to be considered in setting priorities, according to the regulations, are the amount of the economic benefit enjoyed, the nature and amount of emissions, the ability of a source to pay both the penalty and the cost of pollution control equipment without shutting down, and the likelihood that the source would qualify for an exception. * * *

EPA developed a mathematical model to be used by sources to calculate the economic benefits of noncompliance, which is the amount of their penalty. * * *

### EXEMPTIONS

As in the proposed rules, exemptions are generally limited to cases where noncompliance is due to reasons entirely beyond a source's control, and to those situations listed in Section 120 of the Act.

However, EPA did make provision for exemptions to be made on a case-by-case basis if a source was unable to raise the money to install air pollution controls due to financial market conditions and if a source acted reasonably in accordance with good engineering practices by installing equipment that should have brought it into compliance but for unforeseen reasons did not.

## FIRST NON-COMPLIANCE PENALTY NOTICES WILL BE SENT OUT BY AGENCY IN JANUARY

11 [Curr. Dev.] Env. Rep. (BNA) 1178 (1980)

The first non-compliance penalty orders will be sent out by the Environmental Protection Agency on January 2, according to an EPA enforcement branch chief.

Meetings will be held this week and next in the EPA regional offices to determine which non-complying sources will be among those receiving the first notices, according the Charles Hungerford, chief of EPA's enforcement proceedings branch.

The non-compliance penalty regulations adopted July 28 will require sources to pay penalties equal to the costs they would avoid by not complying with the Clean Air Act's requirements * * * .

In promulgating the regulations, EPA said its first priority would be to send notices to the worst offenders—sources which have never achieved compliance and are not complying with an enforceable compliance schedule derived from a consent decree or administrative order.

Hungerford said it was too early to estimate how many notices would be sent out in January.

According to EPA estimates, however, 2,000 sources are out of compliance, but the agency said it does not have the resources to go after all of them at once.

### Notes and Questions

1. The § 120 noncompliance penalty regulations—promulgated in 1980 and still codified in 40 C.F.R. Part 66—provide that the EPA will issue no-

tices of noncompliance to only *some* known violators, pursuant to a priority checklist. In 1981, although EPA knew the identities of approximately 2,000 major and non-major sources fitting the triggering definitions of §§ 120(a)(2)(A)(i) and (ii), the agency issued less than 20 noncompliance notices. Was this exercise of prosecutorial discretion lawful under the Clean Air Act? Why or why not? *See* § 120(b)(3).

2. EPA's 1981 issuance of less than 20 noncompliance notices ignored almost 2,000 violators. What difference did this make to those violators? *See* § 120(d)(3)(C)(ii). What difference did it make to the Federal Treasury Department? *See* § 120(d)(1).

3. The EPA explained its 1981 "priority enforcement policy" by referring to the lack of sufficient personnel and resources to process the volume of petitions for reconsideration which would result from the issuance of 2,000 notices of noncompliance. At the same time, Reagan administration appointees at the agency assured Congress that it was perfectly fine to slash its budget by 40 percent. Notwithstanding the election of a Democratic presidential administration in 1992, apparently no noncompliance notices have been sent since a few dozen notices were issued in the early 1980s.

4. An environmental organization might bring suit under § 304(a)(2) to require the EPA administrator to send out notices of noncompliance to all known violators. Do you believe that such a lawsuit would succeed? Why or why not?

5. Assume that you are one of the unlucky violators given top priority by the EPA and that you receive a notice of noncompliance. What are your options? *See* § 120(b)(4).

6. Assume that you decide to fight the notice of violation pursuant to § 120(b)(4)(B). Under § 120(d)(3)(B), your first payment of the noncompliance penalty is due 180 days after receipt of the notice of noncompliance. (The EPA has interpreted "date of issuance" to mean the date on which the violator receives the notice.) When the 180th day arrives, and you are still tied up in contesting the notice, may you refuse to tender payment? *See* §§ 120(d)(5) and 120(b)(7).

## P. WAKEFIELD, EPA BEGINS IMPLEMENTATION OF NONCOMPLIANCE PENALTY REGULATIONS

12 Envtl. L. Rep. 10012, 10014, 10016-18 (1982)

In January 1981 the Environmental Protection Agency (EPA) took its first steps toward enforcing the noncompliance penalty program authorized by § 120 of the Clean Air Act. * * *

In the year since the regulations became final, the Agency has made only a few attempts to assess penalties, and source operators have contested the alleged violations in several instances. Given the [Reagan] administration's desire to reduce regulatory burdens and the difficulty of implementing § 120, it seems doubtful that noncompliance penalties can live up to their original purpose as the centerpiece of EPA's enforcement program against stationary sources * * * .

Many of those who had submitted comments during the rulemaking petitioned the D.C. Circuit to review the final regulations on essentially the same grounds they had raised in opposition to the proposed regulations. The court ordered all cases consolidated and scheduled for joint briefing. Extended efforts to negotiate a settlement have not succeeded and the consolidated case, known as *Duquesne Light Co. v. EPA* has progressed slowly. * * *

While *Duquesne Light* has been pending, EPA has begun to implement the section 120 regulations. In its announcement accompanying the final regulations, EPA estimated that more than 2,000 sources were potentially subject to noncompliance penalties. Recognizing that time and resources limited its ability to apply penalties against all noncomplying sources, the Agency indicated it would establish priorities for issuing notices of noncompliance. First in priority were major sources that had neither achieved initial compliance nor negotiated a consent decree or other enforceable order establishing a schedule for achieving compliance. * * * Between January and December the Agency issued 12 notices and was processing only a few others at the end of 1981. The penalty notices, largely in regions II, IV, and V, have covered a variety of industries, from steel plants and utilities to a plastic coating business and cement plant. Most cases have been settled on the basis of the penalty formula, with final penalties ranging from 80 cents for a source that came into compliance immediately to $40,000 for a source that took longer to comply.

To date, three source owners have contested notices of noncompliance in administrative hearings. In two of the cases, they alleged that EPA did not have sufficient evidence to establish a violation and, in the alternative, that the violations were de minimis, entitling the sources to exemptions. In one of these, EPA's evidence was ruled insufficient by an administrative law judge. The second has been stayed pending a possible revision of the SIP provision on which the alleged violation was based. The opinion of the administrative law judge is pending in the third case, which presents the issues whether the source is in fact "major" and therefore subject to the penalty and whether a requested variance from the pertinent SIP provision would bring the source into compliance and render the noncompliance penalty notice moot.

Assuming somewhat freely that these cases are representative, the results indicate that the penalty program may be much more of a problem for EPA than anyone had foreseen. In some respects, the three contested penalty cases are illustrative of the difficulties EPA faces in its enforcement program generally.[66] Ironically, § 120 was intended to pro-

---

[66] For example, EPA's inability to generate sufficiently timely and accurate emissions data to take sources to court for violations and uncertainty over legal effect of pending SIP revisions on pending cases seem to hamper section 120 proceedings no less than routine enforcement efforts.

vide a streamlined system for removing the economic benefits of non-compliance without overtaxing either sources or the Agency with complex procedures. Unlike civil enforcement actions, this program was expected to be relatively free of procedural difficulty and delay.

A variety of factors have contributed to the program's failure to work as planned. An obvious difficulty is the mandatory nature of EPA's statutory duty to enforce the penalties. Although the requirement may serve as a clear message of congressional resolve to pressure all sources into compliance, it has placed the enforcement effort under great stress. EPA's original conservative estimate that proceeding against all eligible sources would be a three-year effort now seems very optimistic, and the program undoubtedly has suffered some loss of credibility. Moreover, because EPA has had to set enforcement priorities, sources not high on the list can be fairly confident that they will not face penalties for some time. * * *

EPA efforts to advance the program have been hampered because the program is administratively complex and burdensome at the federal level. * * * Penalty proceedings require resources that EPA is less able to provide each year, and it appears even less likely that states will find the resources—or the will—to assume responsibility for the program. Even taking these considerations into account, however, there is reason to believe that a factor in the slow pace of the program is a lack of interest on EPA's part to pursue noncompliance penalties at this time. Although the regulations were in place and the program was getting under way when the [Reagan] administration took office, only a dozen section 120 notices of violation have been issued over the course of the year. Even assuming the administration's commitment to the program, repeated reorganization of the Agency's enforcement office suggests uncertainty about basic enforcement policy which the Agency has only recently begun to resolve. The directions it will take with regard to section 120 are yet to be revealed * * * .

It may be expecting too much of the program to be at once streamlined and flexible yet capable of achieving the Herculean tasks with which it has been charged. If implemented conscientiously, however, the program could work well in conjunction with other enforcement tools to ensure continued progress in attaining and maintaining [air] quality standards. Whether such an effort can and will take place depends in large part on the outcome of *Duquesne Light*. That decision appears to be months away, however; in the interim, significant improvement in the pace of the program is unlikely.

## D.C. CIRCUIT UPHOLDS EPA RULES ON AIR ACT NON-COMPLIANCE PENALTIES

13 [Curr. Dev.] Env. Rep. (BNA) 1571 (1983)

Most of the Environmental Protection Agency's regulatory scheme for assessing penalties against non-complying sources of air pollution was upheld Jan. 7 by a federal appeals court. The U.S. Court of Appeals for the District of Columbia Circuit rejected industry challenges to EPA's rules implementing Section 120 of the Clean Air Act (40 CFR 66.1-67.43, 1981) [in *Duquesne Light Co. v. EPA*, 698 F.2d 456 (D.C. Cir. 1983)]. * * *

The appeals court disposed of 20 consolidated cases in which industry petitioners challenged EPA rules designed to assess penalties in amounts approximately equal to the costs owners or operators of non-complying sources would bear in coming into compliance. "In nearly all respects," Circuit Judge Abner Mikva wrote for the Court, "we find that EPA complied with the statutory mandate." The court deferred its decision on three issues still the subject of settlement negotiations.

The appeals court disagreed with the agency's interpretation of the "inability to comply" exemption to the noncompliance penalty provisions of Section 120 and also disagreed with the provisions in the rules allowing the EPA administrator to deny a hearing regardless of the issue involved. * * *

EPA administers the penalty program, the court said, even though individual states may take over responsibility for administering the program if they submit plans approved by EPA. "States have shown little interest in taking responsibility for the program," the court said. * * *

The court affirmed EPA's mathematical penalty calculation model "in all relevant respects." The industry petitioners did not disagree with the use of a model, or with the parameters used in constructing the model, the court said. The challengers did question the use of certain assumptions concerning the data to be "plugged into the model," according to the court.

## NOTE ON THE DEATH OF § 120

Following the 1983 *Duquesne Light* decision, the § 120 noncompliance penalty has fallen off the radar screen. In the only other significant reported case, the Fifth Circuit held that the EPA cannot collect a § 120 noncompliance penalty for most violations occurring after a state proposes a revised SIP that would cure the violations and before the EPA reviews and rejects the revised SIP. *See American Cyanamid Co. v. EPA*, 810 F.2d 493 (5th Cir. 1987).

Research discloses scarcely any mention of the § 120 noncompliance penalty in subsequent caselaw or scholarly writings. Apparently, the EPA occasionally throws in a request for § 120 penalties in civil lawsuits brought against Clean Air Act violators—a bizarre methodology nowhere suggested by the text of § 120.

Professor Arnold Reitze reported in 1991, five years after *Duquesne Light*:

During the first ten years of § 120, EPA concluded only 38 noncompliance penalty cases. At the same time they used § 113(b) to impose civil penalties in 342 cases. Only 24 [§ 120] cases actually resulted in the imposition of a penalty. * * * When penalties were imposed, they were low. The highest penalty was $45,528; the average was $13,526.

*Arnold W. Reitze, A Century of Air Pollution Control Law: What's Worked; What's Failed; What Might Work*, 21 Envtl. L. 1549, 1616 n.384 (1991). Professor Jeffrey Miller explains:

[S]ection 120 has been implemented "not with a bang but with a whimper." * * * The very structure of the scheme defeats its purpose. Since the penalty calculation begins when the notice of noncompliance is issued rather than when noncompliance began, the penalty will never recover the full economic benefit of noncompliance. Since EPA is not issuing notices of noncompliance and cannot subsequently recover any § 120 penalty once compliance has been achieved, congressional intent appears to be wholly frustrated. But EPA's inaction is due in large measure to the recognition that, faced with any resistance, § 120 proceedings would quickly deplete its air pollution enforcement resources. * * * It is hardly surprising the EPA has not subjected itself in any meaningful way to this procedural morass.

Jeffrey G. Miller, *Federal Enforcement* in 1 Law of Environmental Protection § 8.01 (Sheldon M. Novick ed. 1998).

Ironically, Congress may have missed the message that § 120 lacks a pulse. The 1990 Clean Air Act Amendments, actually add to the list of violations triggering the supposedly mandatory issuance of the noncompliance notice. Nevertheless, the agency has given no indication that the patient is alive. The CAA § 120 noncompliance penalty program presents a classic illustration of what Professor William Rodgers calls the neglect and abandonment of disregarded laws or "sleepers." *See* page 12, *supra*.

### Questions

1. If the impediment to implementing § 120 is that the EPA would "quickly deplete its air pollution enforcement resources," isn't the answer to beef up those resources, rather than to scrap a program that would provide an economic incentive to cease Clean Air Act violations? Could not the revenue generated through an aggressive § 120 implementation policy be used to significantly augment those resources?

2. The § 120 noncompliance penalty program was intended to be delegable to the states. Why do you suppose states have not accepted delegation, enforcing § 120 within their jurisdictions?

## 3. CITIZEN SUITS

What if other enforcers could be brought into the picture—actors other than overworked, underpaid, under appreciated government bureaucrats? What if all citizens were empowered to pursue environmental wrongdoers? The next set of readings introduces you to an extraordinary feature of most federal environmental statutes: the citizen suit provision.

## MICHAEL D. AXLINE, ENVIRONMENTAL CITIZEN SUITS

### § 1.02-1.04 (1992)

The earliest version of the modern statutory citizen suit appeared in the Michigan Environmental Protection Act of 1970. That act was drafted by Joseph Sax in 1969. The bill drafted by Professor Sax provided:

> [A] citizen of the state may maintain an action for declaratory and equitable relief in the name of the state against any person, including a governmental instrumentality or agency, for the protection of the air, water and other natural resources of the state from pollution, impairment or destruction, or for protection of the public trust in the natural resources of the state. * * *

This language next appeared, in slightly modified form, in [a draft federal Environmental Protection Act, a] * * * bill * * * [that was] never adopted. It was strongly opposed by the Nixon Administration [but eventually wound up in] * * * the Clean Air Act. * * * [T]he final version of the Act as it emerged from the conference committee contained a 60-day notice requirement and a provision barring the initiation of citizen suits if the government was "diligently prosecuting" polluters.

When Congress adopted amendments to the Clean Water Act in 1972, the amendments contained a citizen suit provision very similar to the one in the Clean Air Act. Since that time, every major federal environmental statute * * * has contained a citizen suit provision. * * *

The statutory authorization of citizen suits did not lead to significant private efforts to enforce environmental legislation until more than a decade after the first citizen suit provision was adopted. In fact, only in the last several years have citizen enforcement efforts had enough of an impact to cause regulated industries (and some scholars) to challenge the constitutional legitimacy of citizen statutes. * * * In each case, the court rejected the challenge.

Until recently it would have been difficult to identify "citizen suits" as a distinct field of law. When the first citizen suit provision was adopted in 1970, citizen enforcement of public rights was virtually nonexistent. Now it is difficult to imagine a world in which citizens do not have the right to invoke the judicial process to protect statutorily recognized public rights. * * * It is safe to say * * * that citizen enforcement of public rights now is embedded permanently in the framework of our government. * * *

The simplicity and elegance of citizen law enforcement in a participatory democracy seems irresistible. Congress now routinely includes citizen suit provisions in important social legislation and continues to refine and expand legislation authorizing citizens to enforce statutory rights. The executive branch reluctantly has accepted citizen suits as a sometimes welcome, sometimes unwelcome, adjunct to its own enforcement efforts.

In simpler times, it was each citizen's obligation to participate in enforcing the rules that governed society. We have perhaps come full circle since that time. * * * [T]he ideal of direct citizen participation in the day-to-day shepherding of society remains the same. It is an ideal worth pursuing.

---

Read the following section of the Clean Air Act

☐ § 304

---

## NOTE ON SIGNIFICANCE OF PERMITS AND DISCHARGE MONITORING REPORTS

A careful reading of a single citizen suit provision—the one set forth in Clean Air Act § 304—should convince you of the potential power of this device. Note, particularly, the provision for the award of reasonable attorneys fees and other litigation costs, authorized by § 304(d).

Suppose, however, that a group of environmental activists in a community is concerned about what it believes to be excessive pollution of the air or water by a local factory? How could the group possibly know whether the company was violating environmental laws? To bring a citizen suit without being sure of their proof might open the citizen *plaintiffs* to an order awarding attorneys fees to a victorious defendant. Even without that sober prospect, the task of assembling evidence of violations and preparing for trial is a daunting one.

One of the most important developments in empowering citizen plaintiffs has been the institution of a series of environmental discharge *permits*, coupled with an obligation on the part of the permittee to submit regular discharge monitoring reports or DMRs. Ever since its modern incarnation in 1972, the Clean Water Act's NPDES program has made permits and discharge monitoring reports the primary mechanisms of enforcement, as we will see in Chapter 11.

Members of the public must often engage in considerable effort to obtain discharge monitoring reports. Even though the information is public and must be disclosed upon demand, interested citizens must make the effort to approach the company itself (a potentially confrontational event) or to approach the appropriate central or local office of the state's pollution control agency (which may be called something like the Board of Health, Department of Environmental Protection, or so forth). Public officials are typically very nice about all of this, but the inquiring citizen should be prepared to spend long hours combing through filing cabinets of confusing materials, and standing at 1960's-vintage copying machines to obtain their own sets of the relevant documents. At the federal level, materials may be obtained under the Freedom of Information Act, in a process that may ultimately prove to be fruitful, but which is adorned by various pitfalls and potential built-in delays.

## REGINA P. CLINE, CLEAN AIR ACT CITIZEN SUITS ON RISE, PRECAUTIONS NEEDED, ATTORNEY WARNS

### 29 [Curr. Dev.] Env. Rep. (BNA) 452 (1998)

The number of citizen suits filed under the Clean Air Act is anticipated to increase, requiring facilities to take precautionary action, an environmental attorney told the annual meeting of the Air & Waste Management Association June 18.

"The days of 'I passed my stack test, so I'm OK' are over," Walter Wright, an attorney with Mitchell, Williams, Selig, Gates & Woodyard, Little Rock, Ark., told the conference.

Citizen suits are expected to increase with the advent of the new Title V operating permit program and rules on compliance assurance monitoring and credible evidence, he said.

The Title V program requires all major sources of air pollution to obtain operating permits that contain all applicable CAA requirements. This will be the first time all such information is contained in one document, which will make it easier for citizens to find instances of noncompliance, Wright said.

The compliance assurance monitoring regulations, issued Oct. 22, 1997, require major sources to monitor the operation and maintenance of their control equipment. If the equipment is not working properly, the major sources must file reports and take corrective action. Even though the CAM rule will not affect many facilities until operating permits are renewed, periodic monitoring requirements will apply.

The credible evidence rule, issued Feb. 24, 1997, provides that any credible evidence can be used to prove compliance or noncompliance with emission limits issued under the air act.

"Facilities must ensure that they can meet permit limits under all operating conditions," Wright said. Also, startup, shutdown, and malfunction plans need to be written into a permit whenever possible. Facilities also should be prepared to amend a permit as soon as possible to correct a violation, so that on the record, it is a single violation, he said. Amendments enacted in 1990 to Section 304 of the Clean Air Act allow citizens to sue with a showing of repeated past violations.

If a violation is discovered, Wright said it may be best to approach the state or EPA regional office and offer to enter into a consent decree instead of having the case settled administratively. Under the CAA, a citizen suit cannot be filed if EPA or a state has initiated and is diligently prosecuting an enforcement action, which in most cases means a binding judicial consent decree, he said.

Another way citizens could be barred from filing a lawsuit is where a facility has agreed to emission limits in its state operating permit that render it a non-major source. * * * However, if the facility violates the terms and becomes a major-emitting source, then it may be subject to a citizen suit. * * *

## JONATHAN S. MARTEL, CLEAN AIR VIOLATIONS MAY BECOME EASIER TO PROVE

### Mar. 1, 1996

The key issue in EPA's compliance assurance monitoring ("CAM") rulemaking and in a recent federal court decision, *Sierra Club v. Public Service Company of Colorado, Inc.*, 894 F. Supp. 1455 (D. Colo. 1995), is the kind of evidence that EPA and citizens may rely upon to prove violations of Clean Air Act emissions limits. Historically, air pollution regulations that set emissions limits have also specified a test method (called the "reference test method" or "compliance test method") that is to be used to determine compliance with the standard. Often, emissions tests are difficult to perform and are administered only upon start-up of the equipment and then infrequently thereafter. Although changes in operating conditions can increase emissions, industry has, until now, expected that violations could not be proven under the regulations unless a compliance test is performed during the period of increased emissions. The 1990 Clean Air Act Amendments reflect congressional recognition that reference test methods involving infrequent inspections or stack tests may not be sufficient to ensure continuous compliance with emissions limits. The 1990 Amendments increased requirements for monitoring of emissions (with devices such as continuous opacity monitors, or "COMs," and continuous emissions monitors, or "CEMs") and changed section 113 of the Act * * * to allow *any credible evidence* of the duration of violations to be considered at least in setting penalties. These 1990 Amendments * * * have led to a debate over whether evidence other than the reference test method can be used to establish initial violations of emissions limits.

*Sierra Club* involved a citizen suit against the owners and operators of a coal-fired electric utility. Sierra Club alleged violations of emissions limits under Colorado's SIP regulations. * * *

Sierra Club sought summary judgment on claims that the utility violated the 20 percent opacity limit on emissions under the Colorado SIP. Sierra Club relied on computer data from the utility's COMs that recorded opacity readings at six-minute intervals and showed exceedances of the opacity limit more than 19,000 times over five years. The Colorado SIP required the utility to operate the COMs and to submit reports of the COM data to the state. The utility responded that Colorado's SIP provides that opacity is to be measured for compliance and enforcement purposes using only EPA "Method 9," which involves visual observation by a trained inspector certified by the State, and that the COM data therefore could not be used to prove violations.

The district court rejected the utility's argument, relying heavily on the purpose of citizen enforcement to ensure continuous compliance with emissions standards, and the reliability of COM data to establish violations of those standards. The court reasoned that reading the regulations to restrict evidence of compliance to Method 9 would "gut" citizen enforcement because only state and federal officials have access to the facility to perform Method 9 observations, whereas the utility is required to disclose its COM data to the public. *Sierra Club*, 894 F. Supp. at 1460. The court rejected the utility's contention that allowing citizens to rely on COM data would constitute judicial amendment of the opacity standard, reasoning that allowing use of COM data was only evidentiary. *Id.* at 1461. * * *

### *Problem*

In early 1994, the Iowa Lumber Company (ILCO) applied for and received an Iowa state air quality permit for the construction and operation of a waferboard plant at Clinton, Iowa. Clinton is an attainment area for all six criteria pollutants. The application stated that the new facility would produce 240 tons of waferboard per day, and would emit the following pollutants in the following amounts:

Projected Emissions (tons per year)

| PM$_{10}$ | SO$_2$ | NO$_x$ | VOC | CO |
|---|---|---|---|---|
| 106.4 | 49.6 | 21.33 | 55.7 | 184 |

The state permit set forth emission limitations identical to the projected emissions. This is the only permit that ILCO has ever sought or obtained for its Clinton facility.

The facility went on line in late 1994. Stack test results submitted to the state by the company show the following emissions history:

| Year | Stack Test Measurements | | | | |
|---|---|---|---|---|---|
| | PM$_{10}$ | SO$_2$ | NO$_x$ | VOC | CO |
| 1994 | 11.60 | 0.23 | 9.45 | 36.54 | 113 |
| 1995 | 187.71 | 3.34 | 24.76 | 108.23 | 567 |
| 1996 | 193.38 | 4.61 | 35.27 | 87.42 | 625 |
| 1997 | 205.86 | 3.91 | 27.50 | 89.45 | 821 |
| 1998 | 231.92 | 5.13 | 36.19 | 90.19 | 936 |

In addition, the company has gradually increased its waferboard production rate over the years from 174 tons per day in 1994 to 431 tons per day in 1998.

May a citizen group bring an action under CAA § 304? For what violations of the Clean Air Act might such a lawsuit be brought? Who would be the defendant(s)? What relief might the citizen group seek? Do you believe that such a lawsuit would be successful? Why or why not?

# WILLIAM GLABERSON, NOVEL ANTIPOLLUTION TOOL IS BEING UPSET BY COURTS

N.Y. Times, Jun. 5, 1999, at A1, col. 1

A quarter-century after Congress gave citizens broad powers to enforce environmental laws through private lawsuits, judges across the country are cutting back on those suits so deeply that environmental groups have lost much of their power in court, legal experts on both sides of the issue say. Rulings by the Supreme Court and the lower Federal courts in recent years have sharply limited the circumstances under which citizens and their environmental organizations can sue to punish violators of pollution laws. The trend, some experts say, is one of the least noted but most profound setbacks for the environmental movement in decades.

The idea that Americans could enforce environmental laws through "citizen suits" was one of the bedrock principles of the sweeping antipollution statutes enacted in the 1970's heyday of the environmental movement. Behind that idea was a belief by its Congressional sponsors that regulators often became too close to the industries they oversaw, and therefore lacked the aggressiveness that concerned individuals would bring to court.

Since the laws were enacted, hundreds of citizen suits have been filed by environmental groups across the country, bringing millions of dollars in penalties to the Government and scores of court orders to stop pollution. Environmentalists credit the suits with helping limit air pollution in the Tennessee Valley and cleaning up waterways from Santa Monica Bay on the West Coast to Chesapeake Bay on the East. But lawyers for many businesses say the suits have given environmentalists the power to harass industry with the threat of large penalties for highly technical violations in which the plaintiff has no real stake. To the delight of these critics, an increasing number of Federal judges have begun finding constitutional problems with the private claims.

"Now, 25 years later, it is harder and harder for those citizen suits to get into court," said John D. Echeverria, director of the Environmental Policy Project at Georgetown University Law Center in Washington. "In effect, the courts are invalidating Congressional provisions granting citizens the right to enforce the environmental laws."

Unlike civil-law provisions that entitle plaintiffs to seek damages paid to them personally, the citizen-suit provisions of the Clean Water Act, the Clean Air Act and other environmental laws authorized people to be "private attorneys general" to protect the environment. In essence, the laws permitted private citizens to stand in for the Environmental Protection Agency, seeking not only injunctions to stop pollution but also penalties to be paid to the United States Treasury. Under these provisions, it did not matter whether the plaintiff himself had been physically harmed by the pollution. For years, the courts said it was enough for bird-watchers, for instance, to complain that pollution would damage wetlands they used recreationally.

But more recently judges have been far more restrictive. While neither the Supreme Court nor the lower Federal courts have invalidated the laws governing citizen suits, they have gradually raised the standard that the suits must clear, most often by citing the constitutional requirement that the courts resolve only those suits involving "cases" and "controversies." That requirement has long been interpreted by the Supreme Court as giving plaintiffs legal standing to bring suit only when they have a stake in a real dispute.

The reversal of course has drawn little public notice. It has occurred gradually, through court rulings all over the country, accelerating lately and influenced by a series of Supreme Court decisions since 1990 written by Justice Antonin Scalia. Some environmentalists now say a law review article he wrote before he was appointed to the Court in 1986 was a blueprint for erosion of the environmental laws. It called for limiting the instances in which citizen suits would be allowed.

The latest in a series of cases on the issue has now reached the Supreme Court, and some experts say this case, which began here in the Piedmont section of South Carolina, could bring the most far-reaching test of citizen suits yet when the Justices consider it in the fall. The case involves a hazardous-waste incinerator that released mercury into the North Tyger River here in Roebuck, a town of 2,500 people in western South Carolina. The incinerator was assessed a penalty of $405,800 by a Federal district judge in Columbia, but the United States Court of Appeals for the Fourth Circuit, in Richmond, overturned the ruling. The appeals court noted that the incinerator's owner, Laidlaw Environmental Services, had stopped releasing excess mercury after the suit was filed and said this meant that the plaintiffs had no claim that could be taken up by the courts under the citizen-suit laws. First, an injunction against any pollution would now serve no purpose. But beyond that, the appeals court said, penalties paid to the Government "cannot redress any injury suffered by a citizen plaintiff."

Environmentalists say such decisions give industry a license to pollute, since all that managers must do to avoid paying penalties is stop polluting after they have been caught. But Laidlaw Environmental Services says the decision exposed the absurdity of companies' spending years in court battles over technical violations that have long since ended. The incinerator here is no longer operating. "A lot of these lawsuits are brought without ascertaining whether there's a serious environmental problem, and this is a classic case," said Donald A. Cockrill, a lawyer for Laidlaw.

People who live here, however, say they worried for years about acrid or supersweet odors from the site, and chemicals in the North Tyger. Some of them say the appeals court ruling meant that ordinary Americans had lost their voice in environmental battles. "If people who live in these places cannot have a say in what's going on, then everything and everybody in this country is in trouble," said Judy Pruitt, a resident here who fought the incinerator for years.

Some conservatives say the trend toward limiting environmental suits is a needed correction after years of litigation that they describe as tantamount to blackmail. M. Reed Hopper, an environmental law specialist at the conservative Pacific Legal Foundation, said the courts had grown hostile to the "terrorism" of the citizen suits. "In some cases," Mr. Hopper said, "the citizen suits are putting a small business at risk of a multimillion-dollar judgment for a technical violation."

Beyond the cases-and-controversies issue, some judges have ruled that the citizen-suit provisions improperly expand the role of the courts. "The Federal judiciary is not a back-seat Congress nor some sort of super-agency," David B. Sentelle, a conservative judge on the United States Court of Appeals for the District of Columbia Circuit, said in a case involving wetlands pollution. In other courts, judges have held that bird-watchers, boaters, scuba divers, skiers and bicyclists failed to show that their "alleged injuries are sufficiently concrete" to justify suits, as one Federal judge put it in a 1996 suit involving a Pennsylvania landfill.

In a forthcoming academic article on the trend, Professor Echeverria and a Georgetown colleague, Jon T. Zeidler, say the erosion of the citizen suits has occurred in such "small, almost imperceptible increments" that even many environmentalists have not noticed it. The article, being published in The Environmental Law Forum this summer, argues, however, that Justice Scalia laid down what amounted to a plan for the changes in a law review article he wrote in 1983, three years before he was appointed to the Supreme Court. In that article, in The Suffolk University Law Review,[g] the author, then a Federal appellate judge in Washington, described "the judiciary's long love affair with environmental litigation," and suggested that the cases-and-controversies requirement meant that the courts should screen out more citizen suits.

In the article, Judge Scalia discussed one of the first modern environmental cases, in which a liberal judge, Skelly Wright, maintained that the goal of the new pollution suits was to assure that important Congressional intentions to reduce pollution not be "lost or misdirected in the vast hallways of the Federal bureaucracy." In his article a dozen

---

[g] Antonin Scalia, *The Doctrine of Standing as an Essential Element of the Separation of Powers*, 17 Suffolk U. L. Rev. 881 (1983).

years later, Judge Scalia asked whether his proposal meant that such goals "can be lost or misdirected." He answered his own question. "Of course it does," he wrote, "and a good thing too."

In what environmental lawyers describe as a special blow to citizen suits, the Federal appeals court that overturned the penalty in the incinerator case here also held that the law firm representing the plaintiffs could not recover any attorneys' fees from the defendant. Recovery of such fees, environmentalists say, has been a powerful weapon against polluters, since environmental law firms use them to finance later suits against other polluters.

Attorneys' fees are permitted to the winners of citizen suits under the environmental laws, but in the case here the appeals judges said the lawyers were entitled to nothing because they had not won their case. Carolyn Smith Pravlik, a Washington lawyer for the citizens' groups that sued, said the ruling reflected a trend undermining the power of citizens in environmental suits. Many Federal judges "are trying to close the courthouse doors," she said. "It means fewer and fewer cases will be brought, and you will have more and more environmental problems because the Government cannot—and in some instances will not—pick up the slack."

## 4. ENVIRONMENTAL AUDIT PRIVILEGES

Modern environmental regulation is so complicated that many regulated entities will never learn about their own noncompliance without engaging in a thorough review of (1) their activities and (2) all legal requirements governing those activities. Such a review is called an *environmental audit*. Industry representatives have expressed the fear that reports and other materials generated during good faith environmental audits may be used to clobber them in enforcement proceedings. Accordingly, they have urged the adoption of an *environmental audit privilege*, to protect the confidentiality of adverse information uncovered during an environmental audit.

The EPA, the Department of Justice, and various environmental groups have opposed creation of such a privilege, arguing that it may be used in bad faith to conceal violations that should be vigorously prosecuted. Congress failed to enact two federal environmental audit privilege bills in the 1995 legislative session, but we may expect that proponents of a federal privilege will renew their efforts on a regular basis.

Notwithstanding their setbacks at the federal level, environmental audit privilege advocates have been extraordinarily successful in state legislatures. Beginning with Oregon, at least nineteen states adopted environmental audit privilege statutes from 1993 to 1997. At least twelve states have coupled the privilege with a *voluntary disclosure immunity*, providing immunity from certain penalties in circumstances in which regulated entities have voluntarily disclosed violations of certain laws to state officials and have complied with various conditions set forth in the immunity statutes.

# OREGON ENVIRONMENTAL AUDIT PRIVILEGE STATUTE

Oregon Rev. Stat. § 468.963 (1998)

(1) In order to encourage owners and operators of facilities and persons conducting * * * activities regulated under [enumerated Oregon environmental statutes], or the federal, regional or local counterpart or extension of such statutes, both to conduct voluntary internal environmental audits of their compliance programs and management systems and to assess and improve compliance with such statutes, an environmental audit privilege is recognized to protect the confidentiality of communications relating to such voluntary internal environmental audits.

(2) An Environmental Audit Report shall be privileged and shall not be admissible as evidence in any legal action in any civil, criminal or administrative proceeding, except as provided in subsections (3) and (4) of this section.

(3) (a) The privilege * * * does not apply to the extent that it is waived expressly or by implication by the owner or operator of a facility or persons conducting an activity that prepared or caused to be prepared the Environmental Audit Report. * * *

    (b) In a civil or administrative proceeding, a court of record, after in camera review * * * shall require disclosure of material for which the privilege * * * is asserted, if such court determines that:

        (A) The privilege is asserted for a fraudulent purpose;

        (B) The material is not subject to the privilege; or

        (C) Even if subject to the privilege, the material shows evidence of noncompliance with [enumerated Oregon environmental law statutes], or with the federal, regional or local counterpart or extension of such statutes, appropriate efforts to achieve compliance with which were not promptly initiated and pursued with reasonable diligence. * * *

    (c) In a criminal proceeding, a court of record, after in camera review * * * shall require disclosure * * * if the court determines that:

        [(A)-(C) repeat the language set forth above]; or

        (D) The material contains evidence relevant to commission of * * * [a crime], the district attorney or Attorney General has a compelling need for the information, the information is not otherwise available and the district attorney or Attorney General is unable to obtain the substantial equivalent of the information by any means without incurring unreasonable cost and delay.

    (d) A party asserting the environmental audit privilege * * * has the burden of proving the privilege, including, if there is evidence of noncompliance with [enumerated Oregon environmental law statutes], or the federal, regional or local counterpart or extension of such statutes, proof that appropriate efforts to achieve compliance were promptly initiated and pursued with reasonable diligence. * * *

(e) Upon making a determination under subsection (3)(b) or (c) of this section, the court may compel the disclosure only of those portions of an Environmental Audit Report relevant to issues in dispute in the proceeding. * * *

(4) (a) A district attorney or the Attorney General, having probable cause to believe an offense has been committed * * * based upon information obtained from a source independent of an Environmental Audit Report, may obtain an Environmental Audit Report * * * pursuant to search warrant, criminal subpoena or discovery * * * . The district attorney or Attorney General shall immediately place the report under seal and shall not review or disclose its contents.

(b) Within 30 days of the district attorney's or Attorney General's obtaining an Environmental Audit Report, the owner or operator * * * may file with the appropriate court a petition requesting an in camera hearing on whether the Environmental Audit Report or portions thereof are privileged * * * . Failure by the owner or operator to file such petition shall waive the privilege. * * *

(5) The privilege described in subsection (2) of this section shall not extend to:

(a) Documents, communications, data, reports or other information required to be collected, developed, maintained, reported or otherwise made available to a regulatory agency pursuant to [enumerate Oregon environmental law statutes], or other federal, state or local law, ordinance, regulation, permit or order;

(b) Information obtained by observation, sampling or monitoring by any regulatory agency; or

(c) Information obtained from a source independent of the environmental audit.

(6) As used in this section:

(a) "Environmental audit" means a voluntary, internal and comprehensive evaluation of one or more facilities or an activity at one or more facilities regulated under [enumerated Oregon environmental law statutes], or the federal, regional or local counterpart or extension of such statutes, or of management systems related to such facility or activity, that is designed to identify and prevent noncompliance and to improve compliance with such statutes. * * *

(b) "Environmental Audit Report" means a set of documents, each labeled "Environmental Audit Report: Privileged Document" and prepared as a result of an environmental audit. * * *

(7) Nothing in this section shall limit, waive or abrogate the scope or nature of any statutory or common law privilege, including the work product doctrine and the attorney-client privilege.

*Notes and Questions*

1.   Your client, Company A, seeks to obtain a loan from Company B. Company B insists on an environmental audit of Company A's activities as a precondition to lending the money. Will the resulting report qualify for the privilege under Oregon law? Why or why not? Does the purpose of the audit matter? *See* Stensvaag, *The Fine Print of State Environmental Audit Privileges*, 16 U.C.L.A. J. Envtl. L. & Policy 69, 115-18 (1998).

2.   A supervisor at Company C orally directs an employee to "figure out what we've been doing with the contents of those drip pails, and report back to me with your findings." The employee complies with this directive and reports back to the supervisor orally. The supervisor then delivers oral instructions to the employee on how to handle the pails in the future. Does the Oregon environmental audit privilege protect these conversations? Why or why not? *See id.* at 119-20.

3.   Company D undertakes an environmental audit that unquestionably meets the definition of Or. Rev. Stat. § 468.963(6)(a). The resulting report is labeled: "Audit Report: Confidential." Is the report protected by the privilege? Why or why not? *See id.* at 127-30.

4.   Assume that certain emission monitoring reports are required by Company E's air quality permit, issued by the state's environmental protection agency. Are matters contained in those reports protected by the Oregon privilege? Why or why not?

5.   The audit privilege was, of course, created by the Oregon legislature. Does your answer to the preceding paragraph suggest a way in which the state's environmental protection agency might remove from privileged status materials that are currently protected by the privilege? *See id.* at 135-36.

6.   Company F undertakes an environmental audit that unquestionably meets the definition of Or. Rev. Stat. § 468.963(6)(a). Can the people who conducted the audit be compelled to testify about what they discovered? Why or why not?

7.   Company G undertakes an environmental audit that unquestionably meets the definition of Or. Rev. Stat. § 468.963(6)(a). The audit report discloses violations of several environmental laws. What must Company G do about those violations to avoid loss of the environmental audit privilege? Why? Must Company G cure the violations to avoid loss of the privilege? Why or why not? *See id.* at 158-60.

# NOTE ON ENVIRONMENTAL AUDIT PRIVILEGE UNCERTAINTIES

In nineteen jurisdictions, the environmental audit privilege is no longer an idea, but fully formed law, enshrined in the statute books. This move from the ideal to the real requires a new kind of scrutiny. To be sure, arguments about the abstract virtues and demerits of the privilege will continue. But from Alaska to Virginia—and in seventeen states in between—regulated entities and those seeking to obtain environmental audit materials must now grapple with the first principle of modern environmental law: *the fine print matters.*

### TEXTUAL UNCERTAINTIES

Each state's environmental audit privilege—like much modern environmental law—is seldom what it appears to be. One example is the "appropriate efforts" clause, typified by Oregon Revised Statutes § 468.963(3)(b)(C), and found in the statutes of fourteen states.

The most important consequence of an "appropriate efforts" clause may be that it profoundly undercuts the auditing incentive that the legislature sought to create—even for companies that intentionally set out to discover *and correct* all environmental law violations. This side-effect can best be understood by separating out the three incentives that must be created by an effective environmental audit privilege.

First, companies and other regulated entities must be induced to conduct environmental audits. The creation of an audit privilege—protecting the auditing entity from being hurt by its own audit report—may genuinely help to foster a climate in which companies are more willing to audit their activities. The "appropriate efforts" clause—best understood as an ongoing condition that must be met to avoid evaporation of the audit privilege—may undercut that encouragement. The auditing enterprise runs the risk that this condition may not be met. If that happens, of course, the auditing report must be disclosed and may be admitted in evidence against the company. The state legislature presumably hopes that companies will respond to the "appropriate efforts" clause by creating and implementing detailed procedures for following up on and curing violations uncovered in the auditing process. Company *policy*, therefore, may decrease the likelihood that violations will remain uncorrected and come back to haunt the company.

Second, the individual actors who conduct the environmental audit—as well as the employees whom they interview—must be encouraged to dig deeply and search without reservation for any and all environmental law violations. Because of the "appropriate efforts" condition, these auditors and their sources will know that each and every newly discovered violation must be promptly addressed by appropriate curative measures. And herein lies the difficulty. These actors may sense that, no matter how good the company's policies may look on the books, one or more violations will not be adequately addressed by the people who are charged with carrying out these policies. For some violations, therefore, the environmental audit privilege will almost certainly be "lost," resulting in court-ordered disclosure. For *which* violations and for which portions of the audit will the privilege be lost? No one can know in advance, because loss of the privilege is contingent on *future* conduct—frequently the conduct of *actors* other than the auditors and the persons whom they interview. Therefore, the auditor cannot truthfully say, "Trust me. Whatever you say here will remain privileged and will not be disclosed to the outside world." A more honest prelude to the auditing exercise would be: "The outside world will eventually know some of this stuff. Which stuff? We won't know, until we see which things get fixed in response to the audit. Now then, tell me about any noncompliance with the law that you see."

Third, the people who write the audit report must be encouraged to be as detailed and blunt in their assessments of environmental law violations as possible. Only such detail and bluntness are likely to free up the resources necessary to undertake compliance initiatives. The legislature says, "Be blunt. Be detailed. The privilege will keep your statements confidential." Company policy says: "Be blunt. Be detailed. Any violations that you uncover will be met with swift compliance initiatives." But the voice in the report writer's head may well say: "Be careful. Anything you put in writing can be used against the company. Sure, it is true that this information is privileged. But any violations that I mention will not be privileged, unless the company promptly initiates and pursues with reasonable diligence appropriate efforts to bring us into compliance. I know that this just won't happen with some fraction of the violations. How many? I don't know. Which ones? I don't know. There is no way that I can tell today, which of the things I put down on paper will eventually be blasted into the sunshine by court-ordered discovery. It all depends on what happens in this company *after* the report leaves my hands."

## NON-TEXTUAL UNCERTAINTIES

Wholly apart from issues of textual interpretation, the enactment of state environmental audit privilege statutes poses three significant real-world questions.

First, will state environmental audit privileges apply in federal proceedings? Under many circumstances, the answer is an unqualified "no." An excellent generic discussion of the applicability of state privileges to federal proceedings may be found in 2 Christopher B. Mueller & Laird C. Kirkpatrick, Federal Evidence §§ 172, 174 & 177 (2d ed. 1994). *See also* 2 Jack B. Weinstein, Margaret A. Berger & Joseph M. McLaughlin, Weinstein's Evidence ¶ 501[02], at 501-25 to -26 (1989).

Second, when the activities of a privilege holder (or disputes between litigants) involve more than one state, whose privilege law will apply? An excellent generic discussion of this issue may be found in 2 Mueller & Kirkpatrick, *supra* § 176, at 270-78.

Third, will the adoption of a state environmental audit privilege lead to the repeal of delegated state authority under various federal environmental statutes, such as the Clean Air Act, because the state no longer has sufficient enforcement authority as the federal statutes require? The EPA has repeatedly threatened to revoke delegation on this ground. Idaho allowed its environmental audit privilege law to expire at the end of 1997, in large part because the EPA had refused to grant full delegation of the Clean Air Act's Title V operating permit program. *See* 28 [Curr. Dev.] Env. Rep. (BNA) 2658 (1998).

EFFECTS OF UNCERTAINTY

Even though the typical environmental audit privilege statute is relatively brief, the implementation and consequences of each privilege will hinge on how an extraordinary thicket of complicated fine print is interpreted and applied. Each state's environmental audit privilege is accompanied by a host of intricate conditions. These conditions are so easy to flunk that we may expect many instances of "overclaiming"—persons asserting that the privilege applies when, in fact, the disputed materials are not privileged. The process of separating legitimate from illegitimate privilege claims promises to be contentious, time-consuming, and frustrating.

The Supreme Court has noted that "[a]n uncertain privilege, or one which purports to be certain but results in widely varying interpretations by the courts, is little better than no privilege at all." *Upjohn Co. v. United States*, 449 U.S. 383, 393 (1981). Given their fine print, it seems inevitable that the various state environmental audit privileges are destined to become "uncertain privilege[s], or one[s] resulting in widely varying interpretations by the courts." Such a development may prove a recipe for unhappiness on all quarters. Regulated entities may lack confidence that their auditing activities are truly privileged. Persons seeking to obtain information on environmental compliance matters may be thwarted by the convenient assertion that the materials are privileged. And judges and administrative hearing officers may find that a significant portion of their time must be spent on the inevitable bickering that fine print engenders.

In 1998, the National Conference of State Legislatures completed a survey of environmental compliance officials at 988 manufacturing facilities in more than 30 states, exploring the factors that influence the rate and quality of environmental auditing. *See* Nancy K. Stoner & Wendy J. Miller, *National Conference of State Legislatures Study Finds that State Environmental Audit Laws Have No Impact on Company Self-Auditing and Disclosure of Violations*, 29 Envtl. L. Rep. 10265, 10266 (1999). The survey found no statistically significant difference in auditing rates by companies in states having, or not having, environmental audit privileges. Relying on the study results, Stoner and Miller conclude that "enactment of an audit privilege * * * does not increase auditing rates * * * [and that] the advocated benefits of environmental audit privilege * * * laws simply do not exist." *Id.* at 10268.

## 5. ENFORCEMENT BLUES

## JOHN H. CUSHMAN, JR., EPA AND STATES FOUND TO BE LAX ON POLLUTION LAW

N.Y. Times, Jun. 7, 1998, at 1 col. 1

The inspector general of the [EPA] has documented widespread failures by Federal and local officials in several states to police even the most basic requirements of the nation's clean air and water laws. In a series of new reports, the environmental agency's independent auditing arm found waste water treatment plants operating with obsolete permits or with none at all, inspectors failing to visit and review factories, and states falling short of Federal goals.

The reports blamed both Federal and state officials for the shortcomings. Investigators found that state officials had failed to enforce the laws and to report violations to the Federal Government, but also found that Federal officials had been remiss in enforcing the law and in supervising the state authorities. * * *

In two states, Idaho and Alaska, the inspectors found that Federal authorities had not issued or renewed hundreds of permits required for factories and waste water treatment plants, often for as long as 10 years. Officials issued only a handful of permits each year as part of a deliberate policy of focusing attention on a few major sources of pollution. Very few formal enforcement actions were taken against polluters in those states when they significantly violated the terms of their outdated permits, an audit disclosed.

In New Mexico, about half the major air pollution sources as defined by the Clean Air Act were never inspected from 1990 to 1996. In 1995 and 1996, the state stopped reporting significant violations of air quality regulations to the Federal Government as the rules required. Even after the Federal agency complained and the reports resumed, the state neglected to report about a third of the violations.

In Washington, where state officials had reported that only 7 of the 178 major air pollution sources were violating permits, the auditors sampled 31 sites and found 17 in violation. The state's inspections were inadequate to meet Federal standards, the auditors found. * * *

Officials said the reports raised questions about the dedication of the states to enforcing pollution laws and the capabilities of Federal and state workers to keep up with the millions of specific pollution control requirements that are intended to govern emissions from thousands of factories and treatment plants. "Do we know what is going on out there?" one senior enforcement official at the agency asked. "And when we do, are we taking the steps to bring people into compliance? And are we setting the right priorities?"

While the pollution control authorities who were criticized in the documents generally agreed with the reports' conclusions and promised to fix many of the problems, they appeared in some cases to be slow in adopting the changes that they had promised, the inspector general's office reported. * * *

In Idaho and Alaska, the E.P.A.'s regional office in Seattle had written 33 permits in two and a half years, but there was a backlog of 1,000 permit applications. Seventy percent of the applications were at least four years old. And although the regional office has adopted an "aggressive" plan to issue new permits in the next three years, the report said, even that will provide new permits for only 4 out of 10 of the major pollution sources in the two states. * * *

Even when pollution discharges were known to violate the terms of existing permits, the regional E.P.A. office rarely took enforcement actions, the report said. The office took no action against 19 of 25 dischargers in Idaho, Alaska and Washington that were found to be in "significant noncompliance" with permits for one or more three-month periods between October 1994 and December 1996. Ten of these dischargers were out of compliance for two or more consecutive quarters, but even then officials broke agency rules and failed to explain in writing why no action was taken.

New Mexico's programs for inspecting air pollution sources and reporting violations showed problems of the kind that the E.P.A. has detected in previous audits elsewhere, officials said. The state was unaware of a requirement to inspect all major sources within a five-year period, and was using software to schedule inspections that tended to concentrate on the same places year after year. Meanwhile, inspectors left their jobs and a hiring freeze created a shortage of experienced inspectors. Finally, the person responsible for sending reports of violations to Federal authorities left the job and was not replaced.

# Chapter Ten

## SMARTER REGULATION

---

## A. INTRODUCTION

You have now struggled with the ultimate statutory beast: the Clean Air Act. We will look at several other federal environmental statutes in much less detail in succeeding chapters. For pedagogic reasons, however, this is a good time to take a break from statutory minutiae, so that we may remind ourselves of the bigger picture.

A good argument can be made that too much environmental law (and too much law) is dominated by the image of winners and losers. Many attorneys have been so steeped in the litigation regime of "us vs. them" that it is difficult to see things in any other way. Moreover, much environmental law consists of "command and control" prescriptions: "do this or else."

The purpose of this chapter is to explore other ways of looking at the problem and other ways to fashion solutions. Many of these approaches seek to harness the power of the marketplace by creating economic incentives. We begin with a reading on the benefits of an open mind and a change of attitude.

## B. COUNTER-PROPOSALS AND TRADEOFFS

During the Carter presidency, Douglas Costle (subsequently Dean of the Vermont Law School) was EPA Administrator. Under his direction, the EPA developed a large number of highly innovative ideas for coping with environmental problems. Indeed, the agency became a model emulated by other governmental agencies in their efforts to reform regulations. The following excerpts from a brochure put out by the EPA during the last days of the Carter Administration explain the regulatory philosophy leading to this reform. You will recognize that some of Costle's innovations are important components of today's Clean Air Act's nonattainment, PSD, and acid rain programs.

# EPA OFFICE OF PLANNING AND MANAGEMENT, SMARTER REGULATION

1-17 (1981)

Rules, even the best possible rules, are usually crude and wasteful. They can't do what the manager on the spot can: find the most efficient way of getting the job done. Worse, an unrelieved regime of rules destroys the manager's incentive to find new, more efficient ways of controlling pollution. In the absence of such innovation, we cannot solve the environment's core strategic dilemma: how to fit a volume of pollution that grows at a compound rate along with the economy year after year into the forever fixed carrying capacity of our air, land, and water.

Over the last several years EPA has been putting in place a new, smarter approach to regulation. If a company can find a better, more efficient, less costly way of getting the regulatory job done—which in almost every case it can—EPA will let the company do the job its way. Businesses and communities will eventually save billions of dollars a year as a result; the air and water will be as clean as before; and the public and the environment will benefit from a new flow of innovation in control technology as business puts its mind to the problem for the first time. Regardless of whether or how the Congress may modify environmental standards, this much more efficient way of implementing those standards will still have all these benefits.

This new approach promises to be the most significant innovation in *how* this country regulates since the 1930's. This simple "counterproposal" idea can be adapted and applied widely—both to most areas of environmental regulation and to a great many other regulatory fields. Business can save a great deal using these new tools right now. DuPont, for example, estimates it can cut its air pollution control bill 60 percent. However, because EPA—anxious to avoid the dangerous embarrassments associated with head-first dives—started cautiously, some of the pioneers found the going slow. Over the last several months we have removed many of the barriers that slowed them, and we're moving aggressively to further facilitate the reform. * * *

The chief objective of regulatory reformers over the last 50 years has been to get regulators to produce better rules. During these five decades these reformers have imposed on the rule-writers a complex set of procedural requirements designed to force them to work in the open and to listen to the people affected by their rules.

Reforms put in place over the last several years have further regulated the regulators by formally requiring them to take specific steps when writing rules and to document their having done so. Rule-writers now must define alternative approaches and explain why the approach they propose is preferable. They must routinely evaluate environmental, economic, energy, urban, rural, consumer, equal employment, and a steadily expanding list of other possible impacts of the actions they are considering.

These improvements are important. We are getting better rules today because they are in place. Nonetheless, there is still enormous scope for improvement. Many key techniques are just now being developed. For example, we're just beginning to learn how practically to use cost-benefit analysis. * * * However, even if we reach a state in which all our regulatory commands are the very best rules possible, we will still be dissatisfied. A rule is a rule. And a rule is unavoidably an overgeneralization and rigid. There is no escape from this fact. The more a rule-writer tries to adapt a rule to the variety of actual circumstances it must cover, the more detailed and consequently intrusive and inflexible it becomes. And vice versa.

Even a rule setting a performance standard for one process, e.g., paint spray booths, will prove a crude and wasteful generalization that cannot fit actual facts. A plant engineer who is responsible for 20 such booths knows that some are big and new while others are old and small; that several were made in Japan and have different engineering qualities than others made in Cleveland; that some are used all the time and others only for special jobs or as peak load capacity; that several will be scrapped soon. Rule-writers can never have this sort of detailed, case-by-case knowledge. If only the rule that all paint spray booths must meet a fixed standard were not in the way, the plant engineer could accomplish the same result much more efficiently by controlling big, new, easily controlled, heavily used machines more and small, old, peak load booths less.

The same principle applies across the several regulated processes in a plant. In 1977 EPA looked at a number of specific plants to get a quick sense of how serious this problem was. At the first plant it found that the cost of removing one pound of dust from the emissions of different regulated processes ranged from less than 25 cents to over one hundred dollars. Later studies—both of particular plants and of the comparative cost effectiveness of the Agency's many regulations—confirm that very wide variations between the costs of removing one pound of the same pollutant are common.

Obviously, we'd all be better off if any particular plant could control more pollution at 25 cents, or even $1, per pound, and forget about an equal number of the very expensive hundred dollar pounds. Plant managers and engineers can do just that if we let them. By altering the mix of controls and by innovating they can cut their firm's average control costs sharply.

A DuPont study of roughly fifty of its plants, for example, suggests that the company could cut its bill for controlling hydrocarbon pollution by over 60 percent, or $80 million annually, if it were allowed to make a simple switch in the mix of its controls. DuPont's actual savings will probably be much greater over time because its calculations assume no innovation and no trading across plant lines. It is easy to understand how DuPont could achieve such results after reviewing the extraordinary range of regulatory costs that industry after industry now experiences. Differences of 100:1 in the costs of removing a pound of the same pollutant are not uncommon.

Rule-writers cannot solve this problem. Although they can give priority to working on processes that are especially cost effective, they cannot possibly foresee the mix of processes found in individual plants, let alone design a rule that would command the right mix of controls for any specific plant.

Swaps across plant lines make even more sense than those within a regulated process or within a plant. The average (or median) costs experienced by industries at the high end of the range and those experienced by industries at the low end vary by roughly 100 to 1. Further, if one compares high cost tons in industries with high average costs with low cost tons in low cost industries, the gap will, of course, be even wider. If, for example, a trade could be arranged between a low cost process in the chemical industry and a high cost process in the nonferrous metals industry, the cost savings could be truly dramatic.

However, to take advantage of such possibilities is beyond the rule-writer's ken. To imagine trades across processes or plants requires broad-ranging as well as terribly specific knowledge. The rule-writer's job makes such breadth all but impossible. Rule-writers must work very hard for up to two years just to push one rule covering one process through the careful steps a half century of reform has defined for them.

Even if a rule-writer could somehow understand and account for all the regulations affecting every industry, he or she could not possibly know what opportunities are available in any particular community or air shed. A perfect trade affecting different bodies of air is no trade. Further, probably no two geographic areas have the same mix of industries; and, even if they did, the specifics of the trades would still have to be negotiated in detail, case-by-case. Machines of differing age in firms with different growth prospects and financial needs are not the same, even though they fall into the same regulatory category.

Plant engineers, managers, or environmental officers can, however, deal with this situation—if we let them—in exactly the same way firms deal with one another in every other aspect of commerce. They can negotiate and contract whatever trades prove mutually profitable. When a market that makes it easy to learn of possible trades and then to execute them begins to function, the ingenuity and initiative of thousands of plant and corporate managers will take over.

Hence, instead of traditional "command and control" regulation, EPA is moving to a fundamentally different "command, *counterproposal*, and control" approach. EPA begins, exactly as before, by writing the best set of rules it can. However, then it invites those it regulates to counterpropose smarter ways of getting the job done, in effect to trade especially expensive controls for new, cheaper alternatives. The substantial savings that are almost always available to business will create the necessary incentive to innovate and trade. Further, the Agency is working to create new market institutions to facilitate this trading.

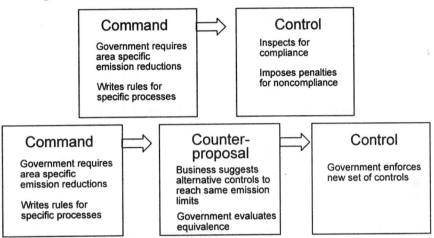

Government, as trustee for the public's interest, controls this trading to make sure each trade leaves the environment as clean as before, to ensure that each counterproposal it approves is both environmentally equivalent and equally enforceable as the set of rules the counterproposal would replace. Hence the name "controlled trading."

Controlled trading is still developing. Three key mechanisms are now in use: the bubble, offsets, and banking.

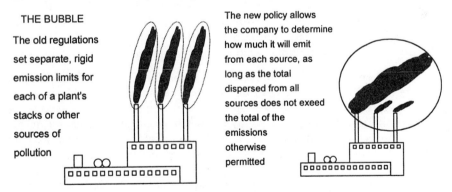

THE BUBBLE

The old regulations set separate, rigid emission limits for each of a plant's stacks or other sources of pollution

The new policy allows the company to determine how much it will emit from each source, as long as the total dispersed from all sources does not exeed the total of the emissions otherwise permitted

THE BUBBLE

The "bubble" allows managers to escape the narrow vision of existing process-by-process regulation and to look at their facilities as a whole. As they plan their counterproposal, they can imagine that their facilities are covered by an enormous plastic bubble or dome. Managers can go about controlling the several sources of pollution under the bubble in whatever way they think makes most sense as long as no more pollution escapes from the bubble than would have if the pre-existing process regulations were left unchanged. As long as air quality is protected, the bubble can stretch well beyond one plant's boundaries. It applies to all existing processes which emit the same pollutant.

Within nine months of EPA's announcing the bubble policy (December, 1979), industry had already begun developing over 70 varied bubble trades. *Those bubbles average over $2 million in compliance savings*, and many companies will save far more. * * *

As we gain more experience with this central innovation, as we work out its bugs and gain enough confidence to loosen some of its restrictions, we can expect the bubble to become more and more important. Its increased use will both improve *environmental* productivity and free scarce capital to help modernize plants and generate new jobs.

## OFFSET TRADING

It is illegal to build a new facility or expand an existing plant in an area where the air is too contaminated to meet basic health standards if doing so will aggravate the area's air quality problem. To prevent an intolerable conflict between the need for local economic growth and modernization on the one hand and this statutory public health requirement on the other, EPA developed the offset policy: the new source of pollution can meet its environmental obligation by getting another source to take additional control actions. Businesses have been using offset trades since 1977.

The offset policy requires the new facility to control its emissions as tightly as possible and then to offset what it can't control with reductions not already required by law of the same pollutants from other facilities elsewhere in the community. It was EPA's first attempt to let the market—rather than regulation-writers—find where additional reduction can be most cheaply produced. A few examples:

- When the State of Pennsylvania successfully attracted Volkswagen to a Western Pennsylvania site, one element in its package of inducements was the provision of sufficient offsetting reductions of the area's smog-causing hydrocarbon pollutants to meet this requirement. The State provided these offsets itself in large part by shifting to water-based rather than petroleum-based asphalt in its road building and repair work in 16 nearby counties. The VW plant now needs additional offsets, and it and the State are exploring several prospects at nearby steel facilities.

- Similarly, the Chamber of Commerce in Shreveport, Louisiana, and Oklahoma City, Oklahoma, made room for new GM plants in their communities by inducing local oil companies to close marginal facilities and to reduce storage tank emissions.

- General Portland Cement paid Parker Brothers $520,000 to install dust collectors on its facility in New Braunfels, Texas, so that General Portland could add a new coal-fired preheater to its plant there without pushing the area over the health standard for particulates.

During the start-up years of 1978 and 1979, business completed nearly 700 documented offset trades. The banking reform outlined below will make such trading much easier and should increase its volume substantially.

## BANKING

Swapping clean-up requirements between pollution sources is the essence of controlled trading. Where one source can provide the same pollution reduction far more cheaply than another, everyone gains. However, when the sources lie beyond one company's boundaries, trading becomes more difficult. There is inadequate information regarding both what reductions are available elsewhere and what their sales prices are. This is especially so for a firm opening a facility in an unfamiliar community. Consequently, ninety-five percent of all completed offset trades have been between different parts of one company—despite the huge price variations that exist between firms and industries.

Trading is difficult for another reason: most clean-up decisions involve capital investments that are implemented at one moment in time. Even if two decisions are highly complementary, a trade may prove impossible if they are timed differently. This is especially likely if each decision is driven by a regulatory deadline.

Following the example of most other markets, the pollution reduction market is now developing banking to deal with these problems. By August, 1980, San Francisco, Seattle, and Louisville had full-scale banks in operation and another 20 communities or states were developing them. (Even without such institutions, many companies have inventoried reductions or potential reductions both to safeguard future growth and, with the help of the bubble, to phase control investments in a more economic manner than existing regulation deadlines would allow.)

Stated most simply, a "bank" arises from a set of rules for determining *who* can get credit for extra reductions (beyond those reductions currently required by law), *what* actions will produce credits, *how much* credit can be gained, and *where* or *when* resulting Emission Reduction Credits can be used. A formal banking system creates a continuing incentive for companies to do more than required when replacing current control equipment or meeting new control requirements, since the cheap extra reductions created become valuable commodities that can be used to satisfy future control obligations, to offset their owner's expansion, or to be sold to firms seeking to locate or expand in the area. A formal banking system can create the certainty needed to encourage investment in such pollution reductions by protecting the credits against confiscation and specifying what will happen if, for example, more reductions are later needed to attain healthy air. A formal banking sys-

tem will produce a central registry of extra reductions, cut permit delays by allowing reductions to be certified in advance of their use, and
let firms treat emission reductions like any other inventory item—to be
stockpiled wherever their carrying costs are less than the expense of
producing them "as needed." In short, a formal banking system should
greatly expand the controlled trading market by letting companies
store extra reductions for future use, instead of having to create reductions at the same time as relaxations.

## Emission Banking

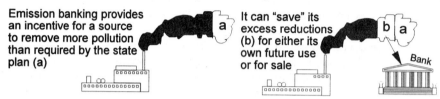

Emission banking provides an incentive for a source to remove more pollution than required by the state plan (a)

It can "save" its excess reductions (b) for either its own future use or for sale

Once it has established such a bank, a community will have a competitive advantage in attracting new industry or promoting major expansions by existing firms: it can cut their costs, regulatory uncertainty, and management frustration.

A working bank will also be valuable to established firms in a community. Before investing in new controls, a manager can quickly and efficiently determine whether or not it would be simpler or less expensive
to buy a reduction credit from the bank. * * *

### SAFEGUARDS

This new market approach to regulation could not survive laissez-
faire. If EPA or the states allowed it to become a loop-hole, it would
collapse instantly. The environmental community and the public would,
quite sensibly, reject it.

EPA has consequently taken great care to design this new approach
to be highly loophole resistant. The bubble policy, for example, incorporates a number of safeguards:

- The bubble applicant must demonstrate that its counterproposal is
  both environmentally equivalent to and equally enforceable as the
  original set of requirements it seeks to replace. This is the core test
  all trades must meet.

- Hazardous elements (e.g., benzene) of a class of pollutants (e.g.,
  hydrocarbons) can be traded only if the hazardous fraction declines. (However, the presence of trace elements cannot be used to
  block a trade.)

- It is difficult to trade road and storage pile dust with production
  process emissions, chiefly because it may be less harmful and because it is harder to measure or model. (However, one of the first
  bubbles EPA has proposed to approve was an ARMCO bubble in-

volving just this sort of trade: ARMCO actually tried its approach and demonstrated that the air was cleaner as a result.)

In addition to these substantive safeguards, the Agency has, at least initially, cautiously limited both those who can use bubbles and where they can do so.

Only those in compliance with current emission limits or on an agreed schedule to come into compliance can bubble. This provision is frankly designed to keep bad actors out of the new marketplace, especially during its start-up years. Every frontline regulatory agency I've ever served has been frustrated by—and disproportionately fixated on—a tiny handful of chronic scofflaws, firms that habitually ignore, resist, and delay.[a] If one of these firms were first in the door with a bubble application, and especially if—as is likely—the application was primarily a delaying tactic, that agency's staff would begin dealing with the bubble in such a negative, worst-case context that the reform might never recover there. EPA felt this risk was not worth running. * * *

The final safeguard of everyone's interests is, of course, the environmental agencies' final review of each counterproposal. Acting as the public's trustee, these agencies will approve a trade (or bank transaction) only if it respects their policies, and, most important, passes the cornerstone tests of environmental equivalency and equal enforceability. * * *

Until now almost all controls have been end-of-the-pipe black boxes (scrubbers, bag houses, etc.). There has been relatively little control through modification of the underlying production processes, probably a reflection of the noninvolvement of plant engineers to date. Process change is one of the most obvious areas where the innovation these new positive incentives will stimulate should take hold. * * *

Many businesses thinking about controlled trading have expressed great concern that the reduced control requirements they purchase in exchange for a greater abatement effort elsewhere may be expropriated, that they will prove an all too easy and very visible target for environmental agencies looking for new ways to offset the compounding growth of pollution. Business needs a strong guarantee against such capital expropriations if it is to enter the controlled trading market. Policy and the law must safeguard against seizures either of a banked or otherwise stored pollution reduction credit or of a relaxed permit requirement purchased with an offsetting reduction elsewhere.

That does not mean that firms who trade can be free of any future pollution reduction requirements. If they have notice that a particular trade will be at risk, e.g., because the firm was allowed, subject to such a stipulation, to bubble before its state's plan was complete, then there

---

[a] Of Connecticut's 12,000 registered sources of air pollution, for example, only 20 to 30 required serious enforcement action during the first four years of environmental regulation in that state. Only three or four of these were hard core, chronic scofflaws.

is no problem. Even without such a stipulation, all firms will have to understand that government must periodically change what it requires of an industry as environmental conditions and our scientific understanding change. They must accept their share of these adjustments. Since these periodic levies have nothing to do with the trades made by any one firm there is little risk of this process slipping into expropriation of the fruits of a trade.

Ultimately, business' chief protection is that our legislatures and courts understand how counterproductive expropriation is. If expropriation were allowed, it would wreck the market. For that reason EPA will oppose any threat of expropriation as strongly as it can. It is now working on a regulation designed to put a number of the controlled trading relationships on a more permanent footing, including this one. \* \* \*

The decades-long legacy of legal adversarial relationships continues to haunt us and is, in fact, the biggest threat to the success of this reform. The first reaction of some environmentalists is: "If it's good for business, it must be bad for the environment." Some business leaders start with a similar reaction: "If EPA is proposing it, where's the hook?"

This suspicious, zero-sum thinking is as insidious as it is irrational. It's insidious not only because it chills some people's willingness to explore controlled trading, but because it makes it hard for the parties to work together even when they've decided to give the approach a try.

It's irrational chiefly because controlled trading helps everyone importantly. It is the quintessential non-zero-sum game. It will save business (and the public) billions of dollars and return to business an important lost element of initiative. It provides the environmental movement the only serious way to offset compounding pollution and avoid a no-win choice between rapidly escalating control costs and/or deteriorating air quality.

## C. REGULATORY NEGOTIATIONS

### MATTHEW L. WALD, U.S. AGENCIES USE NEGOTIATIONS TO PREEMPT LAWSUITS OVER RULES

N.Y. Times Sep. 23, 1991 at A1, col. 1

Washington, a city of lawsuits, is embracing a new way of doing business. At stake are rules that govern everything from who may sit in the exit rows on airliners to how much a power plant can pollute. More and more, Federal agencies are collaring industries and interest groups and getting them together to decide what the new rules will say. So far the reviews are glowing. And one of the most popular elements of these negotiations is that all parties promise not to use lawsuits to upset any settlements that they reach.

Lawsuits to overturn regulations have become commonplace under the system that has been used for 45 years: an agency studies an issue, writes a rule, takes comments, issues a final version and then defends it in court against attacks by industry associations or citizens' groups. That system still predominates, but agencies are seeking negotiated settlements wherever they can.

The Environmental Protection Agency used the new system recently to develop rules to put into effect provisions of the Clean Air Act. "We had people at the table who probably wouldn't have returned each other's telephone calls," said William Rosenberg, deputy administrator for air and radiation. The environmental agency cannot hope to write all the regulations needed under the new law without similar negotiations in other fields, he said.

One of those at the table was Urvan R. Sternfels, president of the National Petroleum Refiners Association, who said he was an advocate of the new system. "It's a better situation," he said, "when people who are adversaries can sit down at the table and talk about it rather than throwing bricks at each other in courtrooms and the press." Environmental groups like the new system, too. "We'd love to see it used again and again," said Fred Krupp, president of the Environmental Defense Fund, which recently concluded a negotiation over air pollution from a power plant near the Grand Canyon. "EPA brought environmentalists and industry together to hammer out a creative, strong solution."

One such agreement was celebrated Wednesday, when President Bush and William K. Reilly, the Administrator of the Environmental Protection Agency, spoke at the Grand Canyon about an agreement to reduce the emissions of a coal-fired generating station that has been blamed for producing haze in the area. In coming months, the EPA hopes to conclude negotiations on rules governing everything from how to dispose of lead-acid batteries, which can contaminate underground water, to how to glue down wall-to-wall carpeting, which can poison indoor air. * * *

This process was formalized by Congress last year, in the Negotiated Rulemaking Act of 1990, but it has been in sporadic use on the state and Federal level for most of the last 10 years. It is being used so much by the environmental agency that it seems as if the battle lines of environmentalism are now in a conference room. This is a major advance, Mr. Reilly said, because in recent years the main battleground has been the courts. "Four of every five decisions I make are contested in court," he said in a recent telephone interview. "We spend as much time designing our rules to withstand court attack as we do getting the rules right and out in the first place."

Mr. Reilly is not the only one who wants to keep the environmental agency out of court. In the just-concluded agreement for clean fuels, oil refiners were expecting to spend billions of dollars, and wanted assurance that they would not be racing to comply with requirements that would be overturned later by a judge. As part of that negotiation, environmental groups and the oil industry promised that neither would sue to overturn the provisions of what they had agreed to. They even agreed that if a defector emerged from one side or the other—for example, an oil company that broke ranks and decided to challenge the rules, or an environmental group that took legal action to block one portion of the rules—the other oil companies or environmental groups would go to court to support the consensus.

In the negotiations over clean fuels, other participants were the states, which have the authority to issue their own rules within their borders and were believed ready to do so if they thought the Federal regulations were not strong enough. The threat that they would do so, creating a patchwork system of gasoline regulations, was another incentive for the industry to reach an agreement.

The negotiations do not set policy; that is supposed to be done by Congress. But often the law is a bare-bones structure, and the affected parties sometimes disagree over exactly what the language means. In the agreement on clean fuels, the law set certain standards for the content of gasoline, but the petroleum industry won a provision in the regulations so that the standards had to be met on average, rather than in every case. The industry believes that this interpretation will reduce its cost.

Environmentalists gained in resolving an apparent ambiguity in the legislative language. At one point, Congress appears to set an absolute limit on a parameter of gasoline called Reid vapor pressure, which measures the tendency of the fuel to evaporate. But in another section, the law appears to require a percentage reduction in Reid vapor pressure, leaving unclear whether the percentage was to be applied to the absolute limit or to the existing level.

In the Grand Canyon case, industry and environmentalists compromised on how reliable the anti-pollution equipment on the power plant would have to be, settling on a rule that requires a 90 percent reduction in emissions on an annual basis, rather than the original proposal of 70 percent in any given month. The change eliminated the need for a backup unit for reducing emissions. According to Mr. Rosenberg, the EPA air and radiation official, settling for 90 percent a year instead of 70 percent each month resulted in a 40 percent greater improvement in visibility at a 20 percent lower cost.

Experts say both those settlements are "win-win" solutions, in which both parties gain from being flexible. Finding such compromises, reducing costs and staying out of court are also goals for environmentalists, said Mr. Krupp of the Environmental Defense Fund, which had sued over the air at the Grand Canyon. If the job is done more economically, he said, that leaves more money to use elsewhere, and keeping the case out of court "can foreclose the industry from appealing the regulations and bringing the process to a stall."

While negotiations are more frequent now, they are not new. Philip J. Harter, a lawyer in Washington and professor of administrative law at American University Law School, who drafted the 1990 law, traced the origin of the technique to Washington State, where it was used in the mid-1970's to plan a route for Interstate 5 across a scenic lake near Seattle.

But negotiation is far from universally successful. Chris Kirtz, chief of the consensus and dispute resolution staff at the EPA, said his agency had tried over the years to steer 60 disputes into negotiation, but only 12 succeeded. Sometimes, he said, the dispute was too politicized, or the potential participants thought they faced a backlash. For example, he said, environmental groups declined to enter negotiations on radioactive waste regulations, fearing that whatever they agreed to would anger their constituents.

The new system will also fail in cases where the decision is "bipolar," said Mr. Harter, such as, "Are we going to locate a nuclear plant in your back yard, yes or no?" But it can settle disputes that have persisted for years. Mr. Harter cited the first Federal use of the new system, by the FAA, to revise 30-year-old rules on when pilots are required to take rest breaks.

The revision was needed because the industry had gone from DC-3's to 747's, he said, but "every time the FAA tried to revise the rules some political group had the horsepower to knock it down." As a result, Mr. Harter said, the agency kept issuing interpretations of its rule, until they had reached a total of 1,000 pages. The negotiated settlement, he said, was two pages.

### *Notes and Questions*

1. As emphasized in the foregoing readings, cooperation between regulators, regulated entities, and interest groups can be a powerful tool for designing standards that can be achieved more effectively *and* more cheaply. An additional illustration is the Michigan Source Reduction Initiative. From 1997 to 1999, the Dow Chemical facility in Midland, Michigan, engaged in an ongoing experiment in which it shared detailed information about the company's business needs and processes with environmentalists, who then set out to help the company find profitable ways to cut waste. *See* Barnaby J. Feder, *Chemistry Cleans Up a Factory*, N.Y. Times, Jul. 18, 1999, at 3-1, col. 2. The project succeeded in placing Dow on track to cut production of certain toxic chemicals by 37 percent, to reduce releases of those chemicals to air or water by 43 percent, and to save the company nearly $5.4 million per year. *Id.*

2. Can too much cooperation become counterproductive, especially if cooperation in *standard* setting spills over into cooperation in *enforcement*? In a provocative article, Professor Clifford Rechtschaffen argues that nonadversarial approaches—including greater reliance on self-enforcement and

greater willingness to waive penalties in exchange for compliance—especially when coupled with cuts to traditional enforcement activities, may result in a sorry state of affairs in which regulators "work with industry [and] don't enforce the law." Clifford Rechtschaffen, *Deterrence vs. Cooperation and the Evolving Theory of Environmental Enforcement*, 71 So. Cal. L. Rev. 1181, 1185 (1998). Professor Rechtschaffen concludes:

> [W]e should ease the rush to dismantle traditional, deterrence-based enforcement. While some of the underlying critiques of traditional enforcement have merit, they do not demonstrate that a wholesale shift to a primarily cooperative-oriented approach will improve compliance with environmental law. In fact, a deterrence-based system of enforcement contains many attributes that are equally if not more essential to achieving compliance. Rather than discarding the current enforcement approach, we should move to a system of environmental enforcement that is grounded in deterrence theory but integrates the most constructive features of a cooperative model.

*Id.* at 1186.

# D. ECONOMIC INCENTIVES: EMISSION FEES

Many analysts assert that a system of emission (air pollution) or effluent (water pollution) fees or taxes would be a more efficient and more effective way to control pollution. They point out that current regulatory regimes frequently impose inefficient, uniform pollution standards on sources whose control costs vary widely, rather than requiring greater control by those sources who could reduce pollution more cheaply.

## 1. INEFFICIENCY OF UNIFORM REGULATORY COMMANDS

The inefficiency of uniform controls can be illustrated by considering the following problem.

### *Problem*

Assume two similarly-sized coal-fired power plants, owned by Company A and Company B. Each facility uses no pollution controls whatsoever and each emits 100 tons per year of sulfur oxides. The present emissions of the two facilities combined amounts to 200 tons. If the two companies were to curb their emissions, their marginal control costs would differ considerably, as depicted in **Figure 10-1.**

Now assume further that public officials conclude that total sulfur oxide emissions in the airshed must be reduced by 100 tons to achieve national ambient standards. In other words, the present emission total must be cut in half.

1. How do you suppose a typical implementation plan under the Clean Air Act would achieve the goal of cutting 100 tons of emissions per year? In

terms of the areas marked on **Figure 10-1**, how much would it cost Company A to comply with a typical SIP? How much would it cost Company B to comply? What would be the total control costs for the two companies?

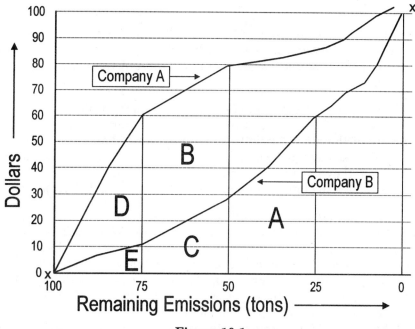

**Figure 10-1**

2.  Assume that each company does comply with the "typical SIP" commands identified in response to the previous paragraph, successfully abating combined emissions to 100 (rather than 200) tons per year. Why is this an inefficient approach for society?

3.  Alternatively, under a "least-cost abatement" approach, the regulators could insist that the marginal costs for eliminating the last ton of pollution for Company A be the same as for Company B. If that approach were adopted, what would Company A and Company B each be ordered to do? What would Company A's compliance costs be, expressed in terms of the areas marked on **Figure 10-1**? What would Company B's compliance costs be? Why would this least-cost abatement approach be more efficient than the typical SIP approach?

4.  Why don't public officials establish pollution standards on the basis of least cost? What might Company B have to say about such standards? What might such an approach mean for technological innovation?

## 2.  ADVANTAGES OF EMISSION FEES

Emission fee proponents assert that the beauties of a least-cost abatement approach can be achieved indirectly through a system of fees. They also assert that emission fees would lead to greater compliance and would create the correct incentives for technological innovation.

## LARRY E. RUFF, PRICE
## POLLUTION OUT OF EXISTENCE

L.A. Times, Dec. 7, 1969, at G7

The root cause of pollution is not selfishness, but rather the fact that the social institutions which ordinarily make self-interest coincide with the public interest do not do so for those activities which cause pollution.

In a market economy prices convey information about needs and priorities. * * * There is no way for manufacturers to know whether their use of the air is "socially more important" than other uses; and even if they strongly believe that their use of the air for waste disposal is harmful, they have no incentive to respond to the belief. There is no price to convey the information and enforce the correct behavior.

In such situations, the politicians' natural reaction is to apply direct control: require this device or forbid that action. When this is tried on any large scale, it always founders on the same problems which plague centrally directed economies. A better approach is to attack the basic cause of the problem, by providing the missing prices. Ordinary markets cannot determine these prices and force payment, so new institutions are needed. There must be an agency which sets the prices, measures the outputs of the various pollutants from each source, and collects the payments. Once such an agency is established, the same forces of self-interest which provide beefsteak and beer will provide clean air and water. * * *

When the APCB [Air Pollution Control Board] has established its measurement system, it simply announces a set of prices, with different prices for different types of pollutants, reflecting the differences in damage caused. The prices should vary according to geographical location, season of the year, even day of the week and direction of the wind, although the costs of measurement may preclude such fine distinctions. But every producer of a given type of pollution at the same time and place must pay the same price. * * * Firms and individuals are then free to adjust to the prices any way they choose. Consumers will switch from those goods which increase in price to other, less polluting and therefore less costly substitutes; there will be incentives to drive smaller cars, take the bus, or form car pools. Price differentials will encourage plants to change their products or processes, to locate where their pollution does less harm, and to produce less during the smog season, when the prices are higher. In short, pollution will be reduced by an unlimited number of subtle adjustments, so that any given reduction is obtained at the lowest possible cost to society. And if the resulting adjustment is not enough, the prices can be adjusted upward, without a lot of technical obfuscation about rapid transit systems, electrostatic collectors and Indonesian oil.

Setting up a price system is obviously no simple matter; but nobody thinks it is going to be easy to solve the pollution problem. About all that can be said in favor of this price method is that it is logical, fair, comprehensive, practical, and much better than any of its alternatives. * * * [P]robably the greatest advantage the price system has over its alternatives is the incentive it gives for technological improvements. For example, under the present system, it would be suicidal for any auto manufacturer to introduce a cleaner, but more expensive car, since no individual consumer is anxious to pay more for something which is only of the smallest direct personal benefit. However, if a cleaner car meant lower registration fees and fuel taxes for the owner, there would be strong, continuous pressure on the manufacturers to be ahead in the clean-car race. No "conspiracy" among the manufacturers to maintain the polluted status quo could last long in the face of consumer demand for clean engines; and the positive incentive of profit will bring results which can never be obtained with lawsuits or legislative bluffs. * * *

# THE BROOKINGS INSTITUTION, SETTING NATIONAL PRIORITIES: THE 1973 BUDGET

368-73 (1972)

[M]any means are available to reduce pollution, and the appropriateness of each depends on a wide variety of factors. Firms can treat the pollution they have generated to reduce its harmful effects on the quality of air or water; they can change the fuels or raw materials they use from those that pollute heavily to those that do not; they can modify their production process to generate less pollution per unit of output; they can recirculate water and thereby minimize the cost of treating waste water; they can change the kinds of products they produce from ones that cause a great deal of pollution to ones that create little. For example, the manufacture of white or pastel colored household paper products, because of the bleaching process required, causes much more water pollution than does the production of unbleached paper. * * *

Cost differences between the uniform reduction and least-cost approaches to pollution cleanup are very large. * * * A study of water pollution in the Delaware River basin estimated that current water quality standards would be roughly 50 to 100 percent more costly to achieve with uniform reductions than with a least-cost approach. * * * What is needed, therefore, is a variable standard that would concentrate the reduction in pollution where the costs of reduction are least. Different firms should cut back pollution by differing amounts, depending on the costs. Each firm should reduce pollution to the point where the cost of removing an additional unit is the same as that for every other firm. * * *

In theory, a regulatory agency could establish for each firm rules and pollution limits that meet these criteria. * * * In practice, however, this is an impossible task. There are some 40,000 individual industrial sources of water pollution alone. A regulatory agency cannot know the costs, the technological opportunities, the alternative raw materials, and the kinds of products available for every firm in every industry. Even if it could determine the appropriate reduction standards for each firm, it would have to revise them frequently to accommodate changing costs and markets, new technologies, and economic growth.

Under the alternative approach, a tax could be levied on each unit of each kind of pollutant discharged into the air or water. Faced with these taxes or "effluent charges," each firm would find it in its own interest to reduce pollution by an amount related to the cost of reduction and through the use of the least-cost means of doing so. It would compare the cost of paying the effluent charge with the cost of cleaning up pollution, and would choose to remove pollution up to the point where the additional cost of removal was greater than the effluent charge. The larger the effluent charge, the greater the percentage of pollutants a firm would find it advantageous to remove. Firms with low costs of control would remove a larger percentage than would firms with high costs—precisely the situation needed to achieve a least-cost approach to reducing pollution for the economy as a whole. The kinds of products whose manufacture generated a lot of pollution would become more expensive and would carry higher prices than those that generated less, and consumers would be induced to buy more of the latter.

The effluent charge approach has another advantage. In the case of regulations that require the removal of a specific percentage of pollutants, once a firm has achieved that point, it has no incentive to cut pollution further. Indeed, it has a positive incentive *not* to do so, since the additional reduction is costly and lowers profits. With effluent charges, however, firms are taxed for every unit of pollution they have not removed. They would have a continuing incentive to devote research and engineering talent toward finding less costly ways of achieving still further reductions. This continuing incentive is important. The quantity of air and water available to the nation is fixed, roughly speaking. But as economic activity grows over time, the volume of pollution discharged into the air and water will rise unless an ever-increasing percentage of pollutants is removed.

Objections have been raised against the effluent charge approach. Some have called effluent charges "licenses to pollute," since firms paying the charge are not subject to prosecution for causing pollution. But payment of the effluent charge is no more a license to pollute than is a permit or a pollution limit established by a regulatory agency. Effluent charges can be set high enough to reduce overall pollution by whatever degree the nation wants. A regulatory agency can similarly set pollution limits designed to achieve that goal. Under neither approach is pollution likely to be reduced to zero: the costs are too great. In a sense, the remaining pollution does result from a license to pollute. But the license will be there under either method of pollution control.

It has also been argued that large firms with substantial market power would simply pass on the effluent charge to their customers and not make the effort to clean up pollution. This might indeed occur, but there is overwhelming reason to believe that it would not be the response of the majority of firms. Effluent charges can be set high enough that the cost of removing a substantial percentage of pollution is less than the cost of paying the charge. Firms could then reduce costs by reducing pollution, just as they can now lower costs by reducing the amount of labor used per unit of output. Despite the fact that many firms do have substantial market power * * * [f]irms do not as a rule pass up opportunities to cut production costs. And with a stiff effluent charge, the reduction of pollution becomes a way to cut costs.

In the case of toxic and highly dangerous pollutants, such as mercury, effluent charges are not suitable. Even a small amount of such pollutants causes severe damage, and thus prohibition is in order. But for the vast majority of pollutants, effluent charges offer a means of harnessing self-interest and the profit motive in the direction of environmental control.

## 3.  SETTING THE FEE

There are at least two ways in which emission fees could be set. First, as suggested by Ruff, fees could be designed to compensate for the harm imposed by pollution. If this approach were adopted, the people responsible for implementing the program would determine the harm caused by each unit of pollution and establish a fee for that unit equivalent to the harm.

Second, as suggested by the Brookings Institution, emission fees could be designed to achieve a predetermined level of desired ambient environmental quality (such as a national ambient air quality standard) by inducing polluters to curb their emissions to the point where the ambient standard is attained. The basic idea is that each polluter will compare its marginal control cost curve with the emission fee schedule and will make the most economically efficient choice for each unit of pollution. For any unit where control costs are less than the fee, the rational polluter will eliminate the pollution. For any unit where control costs would exceed the fee, the rational polluter will choose to pay the fee. As numerous polluters make similar decisions in response to a single fee, the overall level of desired pollution abatement will be accomplished at the lowest possible cost.

### Questions

1.  Ruff suggests that emission fees be based on the harm caused by each unit of pollution.  Recall the discussion of cost and benefit curves in connection with **Figure 3-1**, at page 67, *supra*.  What difficulties do you anticipate for governments seeking to establish emission fees based on harm?

2.   Assume again the two similarly-sized coal-fired power plants, owned by Company A and Company B, that are described in the **Problem** at page 560, *supra*. Each facility uses no pollution controls whatsoever and each emits 100 tons per year of sulfur oxides. The present emissions of the two facilities combined amounts to 200 tons. If the two companies were to curb their emissions, their marginal control costs would differ considerably, as depicted in **Figure 10-1**. The regulatory authorities conclude that total combined emissions must be reduced from their present 200 tons to 100 tons to achieve compliance with the national ambient air quality standards. At what level should the fee be established? Why? What will each company do in response to the fee you have selected? Why?

3.   Would the outcome of the emission fee exercise in the immediately pre-ceding paragraph be more efficient than a command and control regime in which Company A and Company B were each directed to reduce an identi-cal 50 tons of pollution? Why or why not?

4.   The Brookings Institution notes that opponents criticize emission fee systems a creating a "license to pollute." In what way do emission fee sys-tems create such a license? Does the present regulatory regime of the Clean Air Act's implementation plans create a license to pollute? If so, how does that license differ from the license created by an emission fee system? Which type of "license to pollute" is preferable? Why?

5.   An emission fee system might impose a fee for *all* units of pollution, in-cluding those which the regulatory authority believes to be tolerable—for example, the 100 tons of emissions remaining after imposition of the ap-propriate fee in the example that we have been discussing. What would be the effect of a fee on the remaining emissions? Would that be a good or a bad thing? Why?

## 4.  MORALITY OF EMISSION FEES

Are there moral objections to emission fees and effluent charges? Should we allow polluters to buy their way out of noncompliance with laws that would otherwise prohibit the fouling of the air and water? Consider the following reading.

## ARTHUR HOPPE, A LICENSE TO STEAL

S.F. Chronicle, Feb. 8, 1971, at 39, col. 1

President Nixon's * * * Economic Report to Congress * * * suggests that polluters be licensed in return for a fee. * * * Now this is certainly a revolutionary concept. But why limit it to pollution? Properly expanded, it could lead to a new Federal Licensing Bureau, which might even take in enough money to balance the budget.

SCENE: The new Federal Licensing Bureau. A bored clerk is approached by a middle-age applicant who looks nervous.

Applicant: I'd like to apply for a license to emit sulphur oxides. I have this small backyard smelter and * * * .

Clerk: Okay. That'll be $10,000.

Applicant: Did you say $10,000? That's exorbitant!

Clerk: Look Mac, sulphur oxides aggravate lung diseases, dissolve nylon stockings, peel paint and create killer fogs. The right to do all that doesn't come cheap.

Applicant: I'm sorry, I didn't realize * * * .

Clerk: Remember, it's high fees that reduce damage to health and property. Now if you want something cheap I can let you have a license good for tossing three beer cans and a sandwich wrapper out your car window. That's only ten bucks.

Applicant: Littering? I don't know, there doesn't seem to be much profit in it.

Clerk: Ah, you're looking for a profit? Confidentially, I think our best buy is a Mugging License. It entitles you to hit three old ladies over the head in the park of your choice and snatch their purses. Most guys come out ahead on this one.

Applicant (surprised): Hitting old ladies over the head? That sounds anti-social somehow.

Clerk (shrugging): It's no different than a license to poison people's lungs. And it's only $100.

Applicant (indignant): That's highway robbery!

Clerk: Nope. Highway Robbery is $200. But it's a non-renewable, non-transferable, one-shot deal. * * *

Applicant (shaking his head): It seems like these days people are getting away with murder.

Clerk: Not unless they got 50,000 bucks, buddy. Remember, we got to keep the charges sufficiently high to encourage control of everyone's criminal instincts.

Applicant (appalled): What kind of concept is this? It just means the rich can get away with crimes like poisoning people's lungs that the poor can't afford to commit.

Clerk (yawning): So what else is new? Next.

## 5.  FEES R US

Up to this point, we have examined relatively modest proposals for emission fees or effluent charges—payment obligations triggered by the release of pollutants to air or water. Some proponents of the fee technique have made much more grandiose suggestions. They see the opportunity for imposing "green fees" in many corners of our daily lives, stressing the power of fees to alter human behavior.

# PAUL HAWKEN, THE
# ECOLOGY OF COMMERCE

### 161-89 (1994)

While the debate continues as to whether we have a human problem (people not willing to change their thinking and their lives) or a business problem (opportunistic companies willing and all too eager to benefit from expediency, greed, and shortsightedness), I suggest that we have a systemic problem that involves both people and commerce. What I propose does not attempt to "solve" either the human or the business problem because they are both part of evolving, complex, and dynamic systems for which there is no "solution," only change. Rather than worrying about how to save the environment, we must turn to the root cause and worry about how we can save business. Regardless of the heaps of abuse that have been and can be placed at the doorstep of commerce, the fact remains that enterprise's essential functions cannot be undertaken or better effected by any other known human institution. In studies of complex adaptive systems at the Santa Fe Institute, it has been noted that food enterprises in the city of New York, and other cities like it, manage to keep all restaurants and stores completely supplied while not retaining more than a few days' reserves on hand. Quoting John Holland, computer scientist and fellow of the Institute, "From the point of view of physics, it is a miracle that happens without any control mechanism other than sheer capitalism." * * *

In her book *Systems of Survival*, Jane Jacobs proposes that society can be viewed as encompassing two moral syndromes, the "guardian" and the "commercial." Jacobs argues that the guardian system, or governance, arose in territorial and hunting societies, cultures that guarded their boundaries, were suspicious of outsiders, and were deeply protective of their possessions. The guardian system is conservative and hierarchical, adheres to tradition, values loyalty, and shuns trading and inventiveness. The commercial system, on the other hand, is based on trading, and functions well when it is open, trusting of outsiders, innovative, positive, and forward-thinking. It values collaboration, contracts, initiative, and optimism.

Jacobs' thesis is that, ideally, society should separate these two functions as completely as possible. Trouble ensues when the two systems become confused about their roles and take on the functions—and therefore the behavioral traits—of the other. The virtues of one system become vices when exercised by the other. When the guardian syndrome—governance—intrudes with its hierarchical, bureaucratic assumptions into the realm of commerce, it founders, because it is no match for business in quickness and creativity. The S&L fiasco in this country resulted directly from business' outwitting governance. Instead of insisting that industry create its own insurance system for depositors, government guaranteed that protection directly and thereby gave private institutions every incentive to choose the riskiest investments for depositors' money. Jacobs cites the nuclear power industry in Britain as another example of failure when governance tries its hand at commerce. When the Thatcher government tried to privatize British nuclear plants, no company would buy them. No company would accept them *free*. When the cost of decommissioning and clean-up was accounted for, they were losers, and business knew it. * * *

In principle and generally in practice, business is rewarded for producing the best product demanded by the market for the lowest price. In classical economics, this free market is an efficient system because the producer has every incentive to be as thrifty and innovative as possible. The market sorts out winners and losers with democratic and sometimes draconian efficiency, relegating the ineffective producers to the economic margins, if not failure. This free-market industrial system took root in a world in which trade was expansive and global. Resources of unusual abundance were wrested away from indigenous cultures * * * by industrial nations who took what they wanted * * * .

Business did not anticipate a time when those resources would diminish or run out. It was inconceivable that the vast plains and forests of the New World could be exhausted * * * . So the system of rewarding lowest price, impelling companies to exploit the cheapest sources of labor and materials, could not anticipate a time when the lowest price would no longer actually be the lowest price, when seeking out the cheapest means to get a product to market would end up costing society in terms of pollution, loss of habitat, degradation of biological diversity, human sickness, and cultural destruction. * * *

[T]he guardian of human and natural systems must recognize its own limitations in relation to commerce. It cannot tell companies what to make and how. It does not have the ability to allocate resources in an efficient manner. It cannot set prices. But it can and must set the conditions under which commerce operates. * * *

This argument returns us to the concept of Pigovian taxes * * * . The idea of green fees or taxes is not new; an extensive and growing body of work describes how these taxes might work or have already worked. Academics, economists, utilities, and governments meet around the world to discuss how external costs of industrial production must be integrated into prices if the public is to change its habits and consumption patterns. * * *

Unfortunately, green fees are being proposed during a period in which most governments are running up large current account deficits. * * * When green fees are proposed as ways to close budget gaps and are then placed into the overall context of "more taxes," they will be justifiably unpopular among taxpayers. Anyone who argues that taxes pose no burden is either rich or doesn't pay them. * * *

The main function of green taxes is not to raise revenue for the government but to provide participants in the marketplace with accurate information about cost. They achieve both goals, of course, but their underlying purpose is to undo the distortions created by the relentless pursuit of lower prices, and to reveal true costs to purchasers. Green taxes would create, perhaps for the first time since the Industrial Age began, the closest thing approximating a truly free market, with many costs now externalized fully accounted for. To paraphrase G.K. Chesterton, there is nothing wrong with a free market; it is just that no one has tried it out yet. To assure that the public understands that the purpose of green taxes is not to raise revenue, green taxes must be explicitly revenue-neutral. Every incremental dollar collected from green fees should reduce income and payroll taxes equally, starting with the lowest income brackets and moving to the highest. * * *

The existing tax system places levies on incomes, profits, sales, payrolls, and savings. In doing so it discourages, or at least suppresses, the very elements we claim to value in a healthy economy: jobs, savings, new investment, and entrepreneurial activity. * * *

The whole key to redesigning the economy is to shift incrementally most if not all of the taxes presently derived from "goods" to "bads," from income and payroll taxes to taxes on pollution, environmental degradation, and nonrenewable energy consumption. * * * The purpose of green taxes is to give people and companies positive incentives to avoid them.

For example, if gasoline were taxed to a greater degree than it is today, we would pay more attention to a variety of alternatives, including higher mileage cars and carpooling, to bicycling, mass transit, and tele-commuting. America uses about 110 billion gallons of gasoline per year. A 50-cent tax per gallon would raise $55 billion, $1 would raise $110 billion, and $2 would raise $220, a figure that is about half of what we pay in income taxes at present. Compared to the costs borne by our competitors, even $2 per gallon would not be a severe tax. Americans pay one-eighth the taxes on gasoline that Europeans do; in Britain, France, and Germany, such taxes range from $2.21 to $2.80 per gallon. In Japan the tax runs at $1.63 per gallon. At an average of 34 cents per gallon, counting state and federal taxes, the United States has the lowest gasoline tax in the industrialized world.

Opponents of higher gasoline taxes claim that they unfairly penalize rural denizens who have to drive longer distances. * * * Yet people in rural areas are conducting economic activities such as ranching, farming, or mineral exploration. The purpose of the tax is not to punish others, but to reflect true costs in products. Thus, rural producers would raise their prices in the marketplace to reflect their energy intensity, which is the purpose of a green fee. People need to fully understand what things truly cost. * * *

There are endless debates among theoreticians as to what true external costs are. Of course there will always be such debates because the exact cost of environmental degradation cannot be calculated. * * * Properly allocated, green taxes produce adaptive economic behavior, and although jobs will be lost as certain industrial and polluting activities are reduced, far more jobs will be created as new processes and technologies are applied and invented to do what technology has always tried to do: create lower costs and more efficiency. * * *

In the OECD countries, there are already at least eighty-five levies that purport to address environmental issues. They range from charges on wastewater effluents in Germany, Holland, and France, to landing fees on aircraft that exceed certain noise levels in Switzerland, to deposits on automobiles, similar to those for soda pop bottles, that are returned when the car is scrapped, preventing indiscriminate dumping by a roadside. But in virtually all cases, the taxes are low. In Germany, the existing taxes on effluents is equal to $2 per person. Instead of reducing the amount of pollution, these taxes have become a method to finance environmental monitoring and have failed to become an alternative to regulations.

So far, significant levies on pollution and carbon have been opposed by industry because they will mean profound changes in virtually every business in the world. Substantial green fees may improve the quality of life for citizens, but they will gradually make obsolete capital investments in outdated, polluting equipment and processes. In some cases, they may completely eliminate certain businesses. Severance taxes on heavy metals would reduce the need for new mined metals, but would create in their place companies that would recapture heavy metals from industrial wastestreams (200 tons of lead, for example, are used in hair dryers every year), just as silver is recaptured in the photoprocessing industry. As we well know, there are in the world today industrial companies that destroy habitats, peoples, and health, and any worthy approach to ecological commerce must have as its agenda the replacement of these industries with endeavors and activities that have quite the opposite impact. A proposal for green taxes whose aim is merely to "clean up pollution" is essentially an agenda for the status quo. * * *

It is time that we stop pretending that industries which degrade and poison are economic or useful. The present vision that informs "economic activity" is so grossly misinformed and out of touch with ecological reality that Lawrence Summers, the chief economist of the World Bank, can issue a now widely publicized memo calling the low pollution in African countries uneconomic: "Underpopulated countries in Africa are vastly underpolluted, their air quality is probably vastly inefficiently low [in pollutants] compared to Los Angeles or Mexico City." * * *

When Chairman Rawl of Exxon warns us that if we don't open up the last and largest wildlife refuge in the United States to oil drilling and exploration, "the entire nation will forfeit * * * substantial economic benefits," we are not being schooled in classical economics, nor in neoclassical economics, but in Exxonian economics that are at the service of corporate development. The fact is that ceiling insulation and double-glazed windows can produce more oil than the Arctic National Wildlife Refuge at its most optimistic projections, at about one-twentieth the cost. * * *

Of all the possible green fees, taxing energy would be the most fruitful and beneficial, and it would provide the greatest short- and long-term benefit. A tax on the carbon content of fuels is a green tax that raises the price of energy sources proportionate to their emission of carbon, thereby providing users of those fuels with positive incentives to switch to more efficient combustion methods and, where possible, to less polluting forms of energy. * * *

Green taxes on energy will also mean higher prices for industrially produced food and thus will enfranchise the local and family farmer, a goal of every presidential administration since the beginning of this country. * * *

Consider another situation ripe for green taxes: road congestion. In the San Francisco Bay Area, after decades of building freeways and bridges, the average speed of travel is 15 miles per hour during rush hour. In southern California, it is considerably less. Hardly a person who sits in a traffic jam has not considered the costs involved in fuel, time, and stress. The World Resources Institute estimates that Americans pay an extra $300 billion per year in expenses directly related to our over-reliance on the automobile. One study estimates that by 2005 Americans will waste almost 7 billion hours a year sitting in stopped traffic, at a cost of over $75 billion. Add to that the extra fuel use of 7.3 billion gallons and wear and tear on autos, and another $40 billion is lost. * * *

Rush-hour commuters on congested highways are participating in a market system that does not fully reflect these costs. In fact, it would be hard to design a less efficient "market" than the present urban interstate system, precisely because, again, the true costs of traffic stoppages are externalized throughout society. If tolls were placed on highways to account for these costs, automobile usage would drop, traffic patterns would change, revenues would increase, and congestion would be reduced.

A variation on automotive green fees is a proposal by financial author Andrew Tobias and the National Consumer Organization for California to charge for auto insurance at the pump as a tax per gallon. The "pay at the pump" plan would charge anywhere between 30 to 50 cents additional per gallon, a fee that sounds high until you compare it to what insurance actually costs a driver in California. When the average driver divides their annual premium by the number of gallons of gasoline purchased in the year, it comes out to be 85 cents per gallon. By charging a fee at the pump, the plan would cut auto insurance costs by anywhere from 30 to 40 percent. The reductions would come in three areas. First, every driver would be insured. At present, an estimated 20 percent of California drivers are uninsured, in most cases owing to the high premiums. Second, the proposal would institute a no-fault system that would eliminate expensive litigation. Third, a 20 percent savings would be gained by eliminating the need for salesmen and advertising. * * * In 1993, in the first legislative session in which the plan was introduced, it was defeated in committee by a vote of eight to one by a group of legislators representing a variety of special interest groups, including trial lawyers and the insurance industry.

Green taxes can be applied to a wide variety of resources, products, and processes. Products that cause distinct, identifiable, and long-lasting damage should at least pay their way. These include cigarettes, guns, ammunition, and alcohol. Tobacco use alone costs society over $60 billion a year in health costs and in lost income and productivity. These are costs we are now bearing in increased medical bills, taxes, and reduced economic performance. Taxing tobacco to take on some or all of that $60 billion doesn't "cost" more, it simply shifts the costs to the marketplace, where everyone can see them, and where the person incurring the expense to society pays for his or her impact on the rest of us. When tobacco is taxed, it has second-order positive effects that are not calculated in the $60 billion costs. For example, 35 percent of all house fires are caused by cigarettes. These fires result in great losses to life and property, and they are greatly abetted by the fact that tobacco companies put chemical additives in cigarettes to prevent them from going out, making cigarettes far more dangerous than cigars or pipes.

### Questions

1.　Consider Hawken's suggestion that green taxes, if "properly allocated," will produce desirable adaptive economic behavior. Who will decide the proper allocation of green fees? Industry? If the purpose of green fees is "to give people and companies positive incentives to avoid them," industry will presumably set improperly low fees. Government? Will the guardian—which "cannot tell companies what to make and how," which "does not have the ability to allocate resources in an efficient manner," and which "cannot set prices"—be equipped to come up with proper green fees?

2.　Does Hawken propose to set the amount of green taxes based on how much harm a given product or raw material causes to human health and the environment? Does he propose to set fees based on a desire to bring about "appropriate" levels of activity? Is there a difference in these two approaches? What would the fee-setter have to know, in order to set the fee under either approach?

3.　Suppose that fees have been enacted and paid by an aluminum company that emits fluorides. Neighboring fruit orchards are devastated by the resulting emissions. Will the owners of the orchards have any remedy? Should they be able to obtain damages? Injunctive relief?

4.　What do you think of Hawken's suggestion that people should pay for their auto insurance at the pump through a tax on gasoline? Might such a suggestion leave consumers of automobile insurance unhappy with the government guardian's intrusion on commerce? Would it be good if all drivers paid the same rates for their insurance, so that the only variable affecting premiums was the amount of gasoline purchased by a given driver? Can you think of other factors that should perhaps affect auto insurance premiums?

5. Recall Hawken's assertion that the savings and loan fiasco "resulted directly from business' outwitting governance," following the government's allegedly foolish decision to guarantee banking deposits. *See* page 568, *supra*. Might the automatic car insurance technique blocked—inappropriately, according to Hawken—by California interest groups, lead to undesirable behavioral changes on the part of motorists? Is it possible that even a good idea can be pushed too far?

# E. ECONOMIC INCENTIVES: TRANSFERABLE RIGHTS

## 1. TRANSFERABLE RIGHTS PROPOSALS

We have now looked at the economic incentives provided by emissions fees. An alternative mechanism for harnessing economic incentives in the service of the environment might be to develop a system of transferable or marketable "rights" to engage in pollution. The following readings address that alternative. Although Professor Dales focuses on water pollution in the first reading, his suggestion of a transferable permit scheme could be adapted to the air pollution context.

## J. H. DALES, POLLUTION, PROPERTY AND PRICES

### 93-97 (1968)

Let us try to set up a "market" in "pollution rights." The [Water Control] Board starts the process by creating a certain number of Pollution Rights, each Right giving whoever buys it the right to discharge one equivalent ton of wastes into natural waters during the current year. Suppose that the current level of pollution is roughly satisfactory. On this assumption, if half a million tons of wastes are currently being dumped into the water system, the Board would issue half a million Rights. All waste [dischargers] would then be required to buy whatever number of Rights they need; if a factory dumps 1000 tons of waste per year it will have to buy 1000 Rights. To put the market into operation, let us say that the Board decides to withhold 5 per cent of the Rights in order to allow for the growth of production and population during the first year, and therefore offers 475,000 Rights for sale. Since the demand is for 500,000, the Rights will immediately command some positive price—say, 10 cents each.

Even at 10 cents per Right some firms will find it profitable to treat their raw wastes before they discharge them, or to dispose of them in some way other than discharging them into the water. They will thereby reduce the number of Rights they are compelled to buy, and, when the price has risen enough to reduce the demand by 25,000 Rights, the market will be in equilibrium. As time goes on, we would expect the growth of population and industry to result in an increase in the demand for Rights, and since the number of Rights issued by the Board cannot be increased the price of the Rights will move upward. As it does so, the incentive for waste dischargers to treat, or reduce, their wastes, so that they reduce the number of Rights they must buy, increases.

Once the market is in full operation, individual holders will buy and sell Rights on their own initiative, but always through the one "broker," the WCB. Firms that go out of business during the year, or that experience a slump in production, or that bring new waste disposal practices into operation, will have Rights to sell; new firms, or those that find that their production is exceeding their expectations, will appear as buyers in the market. Similarly for municipalities; those that build new or better sewage treatment plants will be sellers of Rights, while those that experience growth in their populations and do nothing to reduce their wastes will be buyers. All of these buyers and sellers, through their bids and offers, will establish the price of the Rights. The price will no doubt display minor fluctuations from time to time, like other prices; but it will probably show an upward trend over time. That makes sense; if economic growth (which causes pollution) is to continue, and yet pollution is to be checked, the cost of disposing of wastes must rise—and this increasing cost is registered in the rising price of Pollution Rights.

Like all organized markets, our Rights market must be conducted according to certain rules. As we have seen, a person who wants to sell some of his Rights (because he no longer needs them) can sell them to somebody who has a bid in for Rights; but if it happens that there is no bid at the moment, or if the bid is much below (say, more than 10 percent below) what the seller paid for his Rights, the WCB should stand ready to buy the unexpired portion of them, at, say 90 percent of their purchase price. In this way the WCB acts like a "specialist" on organized stock exchanges; as a buyer of last resort, the Board prevents any sudden fall in price that might occur, for example, if several large industries more or less simultaneously introduced waste control measures and thus temporarily flooded the market by wanting to sell large numbers of Rights. In the same way, when at the beginning of the next year old Rights are extinguished and new ones put up for sale, the Board must "rig the market" so as not to let the price fall very much; otherwise municipalities and factories that had introduced treatment procedures when the price of Rights was high might find that their investments were unprofitable at the new, lower price.

In general, though, the typical problem, if any, will be that of sharp price *rises*. The Board should try to avoid these by keeping a certain reserve of "issued but unsold" Rights on hand, and selling some of this reserve supply if demand shows a sharp rise that is expected to be only temporary. The Board should be very firm, however, in refusing to increase its authorized issue *no matter what happens.* If municipalities or factories ever got the idea that by complaining loudly enough about their inability to buy Rights ("at any price," as they will likely put it) they could get the Board to increase its issue, even "temporarily," the Board's basic pollution-control policy would be shattered; moreover, by issuing "excess" Rights the Board would be breaking faith with the owners of Rights by "diluting their equity," and preventing them from selling their Rights, if they wished to do so, at as large a profit as they otherwise could have gained.

So far we have argued as if all Rights should be for one year only. It would, in fact, be desirable to issue Rights of different terms—up to five-year Rights if the Board has announced that its present policy (the number of Rights it will issue) is to be in force for five years. Long-term Rights would no doubt command a premium over short terms—a three-year Right would cost more than three times as much as a one-year Right—since the firm (or municipality) that bought it would be secure in its discharge rights for three years rather than one year. Different dischargers will probably want to buy "security of discharge" for different lengths of time into the future, and there is no reason why they shouldn't do so.

Anyone, of course, should be allowed to buy Pollution Rights, even if they do not use them. Conservation groups might well want to buy up some Rights merely in order to prevent their being used. In this way at least part of the guerrilla warfare between conservationists and polluters could be transferred into a civilized "war with dollars"; both groups would, I think, learn something in the process. Pure speculators should also be able to buy the Rights in the expectation of being able to sell them later at a higher price—and also to sell them short if they think the price will go down in the future. Speculation is a risky business for the speculators, but it does help to "make a good market" and if enough speculators can be found to play the Rights market they will help to even out temporary price fluctuations and thus help the Board stabilize the market. As experience is gained in running the market, other rules might become desirable, just as it is often found desirable to change the rules for trading on a stock exchange. But we have perhaps established the main rules needed to get the market into operation.

How would the Government use the money the WCB took in by selling pollution rights? In any way the government [sees] fit. Let us say it goes to consolidated revenues. There is no problem in disposing of money!

Once in operation, the Pollution Rights market will, by establishing a price for Rights, relieve the Board of any necessity to *set* the proper price by trial-and-error methods. The market will also automatically solve the problem of newcomers. As population and factories grow, the price of Rights will automatically rise, and existing polluters will find it profitable to reduce their own wastes in order to sell some of their existing Rights at a profit or in order to avoid buying so many of them next year; reduced demand by existing holders will release a supply for new buyers.

At the end of the initial five-year period, the Board may wish to revise its policy about the amount of waste it will allow to be discharged into the waters of its various water control regions. Revision of policy, if any, will simply mean the authorization of different (higher or lower) maxima for the number of Rights that can be issued in each Region. At this point, all the pressures of public opinion, political considerations, and interest-group propaganda, will converge on the Board; but the Board, so long as it enjoys the confidence of the government and so long as the government enjoys the confidence of the electorate, must make its own decision. And once it decides what to do, it can [continue] to use the pollution markets to do it. * * *

# PROPOSAL FOR MARKETABLE, FIXED-TERM DISCHARGE PERMITS

in Environmental Law Institute, Effluent Charges
on Air and Water Pollution 36-38 (1973)

### THE JACOBY-SCHAUMBURG PLAN

Professors Henry D. Jacoby and Grant W. Schaumburg * * * proposed that the current allocation of discharge rights to cities and industries in a river basin, along with the effluent or treatment standards typically governing such allocations, be replaced with an administered market in fixed-term discharge permits. The market would be instituted by converting existing discharge rights with respect to BOD [biochemical oxygen demand] (and perhaps one or two additional waste parameters) into permits which could be sold to other present or prospective dischargers, or to non-dischargers who wished to enter the market for speculative or conservationist purposes. Different sets of permits might be used for summer and winter conditions in order to make more efficient use of seasonably variable assimilative capacity. Demand for these waste-disposal opportunities would then be determined by market prices. Overall stream quality would be improved and maintained by limits on the total number of permits outstanding at any time.

Under this plan, transfers of permits from one zone to another would be regulated by exchange rates so set by the issuing authority that trading could not cause water quality to fall below the stream standard at any point. For example, if discharges of BOD into stream-zone B are twice as harmful to a critical reach as identical discharges into zone A further upstream, then a permit might allow a polluter to discharge either 1 pound per day into zone B or 2 pounds per day into zone A. If a zone-B discharger wishes to increase his waste load by 100 pounds and a zone-A discharger can abate 200 pounds of his waste load at less cost [than] B would be willing to pay him for the corresponding discharge rights, A would abate accordingly and sell the necessary permits to B. New dischargers could also buy into the market in this manner. * * *

The prevailing regulatory approach, by contrast, was deemed by the plan's proponents to be insufficiently flexible to accommodate future industrial and residential growth. As new waste sources appear, treatment standards must be raised so as to require higher percentages of waste removal by all dischargers. This will necessitate revisions of individual abatement plans and deadlines, and, no doubt, some lengthy enforcement actions. The administrative cost of such measures will be high. * * * On the other hand, the market proposed by the Jacoby-Schaumburg plan would allow a smooth, continuous adjustment of discharge privileges while maintaining stream standards. It would provide continuing incentives to find improved methods of waste control, all at smaller administrative cost and greater economic efficiency. The major expense of the proposed system would be for continuous monitoring of discharges—a feature of any adequate control system.

The proponents of this plan also deemed it superior to effluent charges because, unlike the latter, it would not only rely on direct incentives to control stream quality. Charges may be set incorrectly if based on imperfect information concerning technological alternatives, abatement costs, or other factors influencing investment decisions, and political pressures may forestall upward adjustments. The need to adjust charges repeatedly in light of experience or in response to economic growth would entail heavier administrative costs than the permit market here proposed.

### Questions

1. Dales suggests that a "right" might be defined as one ton of waste discharged to water per year. Under the Clean Air Act's acid rain control program, an "allowance" (or right) is also defined as one ton per year. Assume that a government agency seeks to assure that the national ambient air quality standards for $PM_{10}$, set forth in **Table 9-1** at page 300, *supra*, are met on a consistent basis. Do you see a problem with defining marketable rights as one ton of $PM_{10}$ emissions per year? Why or why not?

2. Assume that your client presently emits 500 pounds of particulates per day. Your local pollution control agency has established a system of marketable emission rights, in which a single right authorizes the discharge of 100 pounds of particulates per day. At the initial auction for those rights, the agency is offering for sale only one-half as many rights as would be needed to authorize the total particulate emissions currently being emitted by all facilities in your airshed, because the agency has concluded that current emissions must be cut in half to achieve compliance with the national ambient quality standards for particulates. If you wish to bid intelligently on behalf of your client, what will you need to know before you head into

the auction? What will happen to the price of rights as the auction proceeds? How will this affect your own bidding?

3.   What will you do on behalf of your client if you are unable to obtain sufficient rights at the auction described in the preceding paragraph? Does the establishment of a marketable rights program remove the challenges that your client and other polluters might make under the current regulatory command and control system of the Clean Air Act? Why or why not?

## 2.  MORALITY OF TRANSFERABLE RIGHTS

### MARK SAGOFF, THE ECONOMY OF THE EARTH

205-10 (1988)

During the 1960s, some economists recommended that the government set pollution standards on political grounds, much as it sets targets for inflation and unemployment, and then use an effluent tax, an auction of rights to pollute, or some such market mechanism to reach those levels. They believed that even if an effluent tax might not be able to determine "optimal" levels of pollution, it could provide a cost-effective way of reaching the statutory targets.

Economists were not all in favor of this idea. Critics pointed out that effluents have different effects per unit even within a region; the emissions from some industries, which may be near residential or wilderness areas or the like, may be far more obnoxious than the same discharges from other industries located farther away, for example, or in the path of different wind currents. An effluent tax, however, encourages industries that can do so most cheaply—not those that cause the most harm—to make marginal investments in controlling pollution. Thus, the tax idea, though interesting, seemed too complicated and difficult to provide a cost-effective way of making progress toward the goals set by legislation.

After 1979, discussion of market incentives for abating pollution centered on EPA's Bubble Policy, which has many of the advantages without the drawbacks of an effluent tax. A "*bubble*" imagines an entire plant or even region to be surrounded by a hypothetical dome and, therefore, to have but one stack. The plant, under this legal fiction, may reduce emissions from some sources in compensation for emissions that would be more expensive to reduce from other sources—as long as a mandated overall reduction is achieved. Thus, in an area as small as a single plant, where emissions are not likely to have differential effects owing to location, EPA has allowed industries to treat different sources differently and thus to control pollution in cost-saving ways.

Under the 1982 Emissions Trading Policy, establishing an "emission reduction credit," EPA has experimented with offsets, nets, and emissions banks. *Offsets* enable new factories to enter dirty-air areas as long as they contribute no more new effluents than they offset by securing reductions from existing sources. *Netting* allows a factory to escape some regulatory review of new technology as long as net emissions do not increase. Finally, under *emissions banking*, firms can store for future use or even offer for sale credits for "extra" or nonmandated reductions.

These market-based approaches to pollution control policy have been controversial, but among the many criticisms discussed in the literature, the most interesting seems to be this: The applicable pollution control statute, let us suppose, requires plants to use the best available control technology, and it bases permissible levels on what technology can achieve. By "reducing emissions more than required by law in order to gain emission reduction credits, plants could alert control authorities to the fact that additional control was possible." These authorities, acting under the statute, should then make this better technology mandatory throughout the industry, not issue plants a "credit" to offset pollution elsewhere.

In a legal regime that allows emissions "trading," even if enforcement officials discount trading credits at, let us say, 20%, they will at best achieve a 20 percent incremental improvement over some baseline at which trading (or offsetting, or bubbling) is supposed to begin. The 20 percent improvement over a "given" baseline may not be as good as what *might* be achieved in the absence of trading schemes; it is certainly not all that the Clean Air Act literally requires. Those who defend bubbles, offsets, and so on may reply, however, that even if trading schemes relax the draconian demands of the law, they will enhance progress toward a cleaner and safer environment.

Emission trading, in theory, has two principal advantages. First, it gives polluters incentives to make all the reductions they can at the least cost, thereby saving them, consumers, and society money. Indeed, polluters can even make money by polluting less and selling the credit to neighboring industries. Second, by building in a discount or "vigorish" to reduce total pollution by a given percentage, EPA ensures that aggregate pollution will be abated by that much over what would have been achieved had polluters simply met "best available technology" requirements then in place.

Critics point out, however, that under a trading scheme, a firm may claim credits for reductions it would have made anyway—for example, because it has installed hoods that happen to exceed requirements, or introduced a cleaner way of coking—but for reasons that have nothing to do with controlling pollution. EPA cannot assess all the motivational, economic, and technological factors behind each claim; consequently, it must grant credits for many if not most of these fortuitous reductions.

The Clean Air Act, however, leaves little room either in its language or in the way the courts have interpreted it for the idea of an "extra" or a "surplus" reduction in emissions. On the contrary, the law recognizes no resting point; it requires, for example, that new sources install the "best system of emission reduction which * * * has been adequately demonstrated." This suggests that if a firm develops a new technology that does better than a previous "best," it should not be granted credit it can use to do worse than it might elsewhere. Rather, that new technology, if it works out, should become the new "best," and EPA should require it throughout the industry.

Those who defend reduction credits reply, "Beneath such arguments lies the view that more emissions reduction is always better, that each possible increment of progress must be seized because there is no 'stopping point' at which individual or cumulative reductions are truly sufficient." Advocates of emission trading urge that *even if this view is correct*—that is, even if more reduction is always better—the "better" has become a formidable enemy of the good, and it is preventing agencies and industries from doing all they can to abate pollution.

It is important to see the force of this reply. Those who offer it do not assume that there is some "optimal" level of pollution at which reductions are sufficient, for example, because the benefits of further reductions would not be worth the costs. Theirs is not that kind of argument. They may, in contrast, accept the idea that pollution is an evil that should be eliminated, not an "externality" to be priced by markets. They contend, however, that the one sure way to prevent industries from improving their performance beyond minimum requirements is to convert every additional reduction into a new minimum requirement.

If we are serious about encouraging improvements, we must recognize some as supererogatory, that is, as better than good enough, at least temporarily, and acknowledge them as such. This implies that we accept some level of accomplishment as "good enough," not on cost-benefit grounds but because we need to recognize plateaus or resting points to reward and thereby to encourage further progress.

Those who offer this reply contend, moreover, that emission-trading systems will in fact provide greater reductions than would be achieved without them, even if some reductions are credited that would have happened anyway. To suppose otherwise, according to this reply, is to commit the fallacy of disparate comparison. This is the fallacy one commits when one compares a fabulous torte shown with a complicated recipe in a gourmet magazine and a fairly good, but not great, cake actually baked and on the table.

The Clean Air Act, according to these critics, provides a fantastically complex recipe with a beautiful picture of pollution-free air. The recipe has not worked so far to produce anything like what is shown in the picture, and there are few who think that it will. Meanwhile, the results of emission trading, while not as attractive as the cake in the illustration, are still better than any we have baked—and may hope to bake—following literally the recipe provided in the Clean Air Act.

The principal environmentalist objection to "bubbles" and related methods for controlling pollution is that they assume a level of pollution that is allowed and trade within it. A market for pollution "rights," for example, may imply that certain amounts of pollution are socially acceptable at a given time, even though further reductions are technologically and economically possible. An environmentalist may prefer conventional "command and control" techniques of regulation, since they embody the uncompromising principle that "can" implies "ought"— that  polluters ought to do anything they possibly can to reduce emissions. Environmentalists may argue that industry ought to make any reductions it can, in view of the mandate of the laws.

I think that this response is mistaken. It is a commonplace of ethics that "ought" implies "can": No one has a duty to do what he or she is not able to accomplish. The converse, however, does not follow: It is not true that a person has a duty to do anything he or she can, even in a noble cause. There is some level of effort at which further attempts may become supererogatory, that is, may remain morally praiseworthy but go beyond the call of duty. I believe that environmentalists are correct in recognizing pollution as an ethical rather than primarily an economic problem. They cannot conclude from this, however, that polluters have a duty to do whatever they can to reduce their emissions.

Trading policies are most interesting, perhaps, because they highlight the line at which ethical and economic considerations meet—the line that divides what we aspire to from what we can accomplish within our means. Markets in pollution "rights," offsets, and similar schemes do not necessarily replace ethical thinking with economic thinking, moral norms with economic principles. Rather, they may help us build toward our ethical objectives from the means available to accomplish them, and this way of appraising ends and means together, to which economic theory has contributed a great deal, may be important in determining what we can do and therefore what we ought to do. At some point, we must recognize that the commitment, effort, and expense we undertake is *morally* sufficient, and that further commitment goes beyond the call of duty. This does not alter the ethical nature of our commitment. It simply distinguishes it from fanaticism.

## 3.  ACID RAIN PROGRAM

As we explored at pages 339-45, *supra*, the acid rain control program of Title IV of the Clean Air Act, added by the 1990 amendments, establishes a marketable system of rights ("allowances") to emit sulfur dioxide. Even though this marketable rights program involves a single pollutant and a few hundred sources, promulgation of the core regulations for the acid rain program, codified in 40 C.F.R. Parts 72-78, occupies more than 120 pages of small type in the *Federal Register*—rivaling or exceeding in length and complexity most of the traditional command and control regulatory schemes promulgated by EPA. *See* 58 Fed. Reg. 3590 (1993).

Operation of the allowance market can best be understood by depicting the marginal control cost curves of two affected units—Unit 1 and Unit 2. Assume, for purposes of simplicity, that each facility is presently emitting 80,000 tons of $SO_2$ annually, and that the Phase I allowance/limitation for each facility is 60,000 tons. Because operation of the market will depend on the relative control costs encountered by the owners and operators of each unit, the *marginal* control costs for each unit—the cost to remove each incremental ton of $SO_2$ emissions— are depicted in **Figure 10-2.**

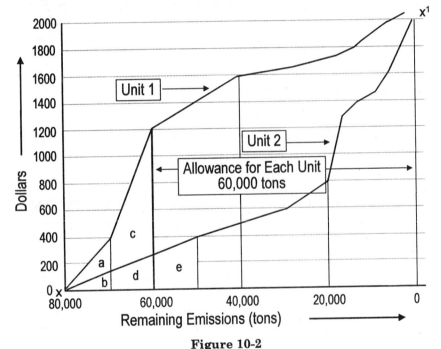

Figure 10-2

Assume, first, that each unit chooses to retain and use its own allocated allowances of 60,000 tons (and *only* those allowances). In that event, the marginal cost to Unit 1 of removing its last ton of unlawful emissions will be $1,200, and its total cost for removing the 20,000 prohibited tons will be equivalent to the sum of areas *a, b, c,* and *d* in **Figure 10-2.** By contrast, the marginal cost to Unit 2 of removing the final unlawful ton under this approach will be only $300, and its total cost for removing the 20,000 prohibited tons will be equivalent to the sum of areas *b* and *d.* Under this first approach, the total control costs to society, as represented by the areas in **Figure 10-2,** will equal *a+2b+c+2d.*

Given the relative pollution control costs encountered by the two units, however, this approach is so inefficient that it should not be pursued. Instead, Unit 2 should spend the additional sum represented by area *e* to remove an additional 10,000 tons of $SO_2$ emissions (with a marginal control cost for the final removed ton of $400), transferring its 10,000 unused allowances to Unit 1. In that event, Unit 1 need only spend control costs equivalent to the sum of areas $a$ and $b$ (with a marginal control cost for the final removed ton of $400), removing only 10,000 tons from its emissions and saving the expenditures represented by areas $c$ and $d$. Under this second approach, the total control costs to society, as represented by the areas in **Figure 10-2**, will equal $a+2b+d+e$.

The price at which the 10,000 units will be transferred from Unit 2 to Unit 1 depends on the bargaining skills of the two parties, as well as the availability of other allowances in the market, but will be a sum greater than that represented by area $e$ (the "cost" to Unit 2 of not taking advantage of the 10,000 unused allowances) but less than the total of areas $c$ plus $d$ (the "savings" to Unit 1 gained by taking advantage of Unit 2's 10,000 unused allowances).

As the foregoing illustration demonstrates, the market will only work correctly if each affected utility accurately determines its marginal pollution control costs. Only if utilities know whether they will gain from selling or buying $SO_2$ allowances will they be able to trade with confidence in the market. Utilities cannot know this without determining their options for reducing $SO_2$ emissions and the *marginal* costs for each option.

## MATTHEW L. WALD, ACID-RAIN POLLUTION CREDITS ARE NOT ENTICING UTILITIES

N.Y. Times, Jun. 5, 1995, at A11, col. 1

What do you get when you cross a free-market economist with an environmentalist? First, a Federal law that allows companies to buy and sell the right to pollute. Next, a market for the right to pollute— and a price tag on the value of that right. But in the end, maybe a lot less than was predicted.

Five years after the system was passed into law, trading in pollution rights is slow, and the price for the right to put a ton of acid-rain pollutants into the atmosphere, which had started low, has collapsed. In fact, the price is now so low—a tenth of what some utility lobbyists had predicted—that it raises questions about the assumptions that Congress used when it established the system and accompanying pollution limits. Another interpretation is that the market is simply not working. * * *

"It's one of those things that looked terrific in theory," said Peter Jump, a spokesman for the Edison Electric Institute, the Washington-based trade association for the utility industry. "But once you get into the practice of it, some things don't turn out the way you expected."

One clear difference is price. When Congress was debating the emission limits, utilities predicted that a one-ton allowance would sell for $1,000 or more; some said $1,500. The Environmental Protection Agency said $500 to $600. The price of a one-ton allowance is now less than $140. In 1992, when the first trades were made, it was about $250, and it has fallen every year. "Everybody was stunned," said Brian J. McLean, director of the Environmental Protection Agency's acid rain division. The industry estimates during debate on the bill, he said, may have involved some "gaming," meaning utility executives picked high numbers in an effort to dissuade Congress from imposing stricter standards. But no one thought the price would be so low, he said.

The economists' theory was that if the price was low, utilities whose costs were higher would rush to buy the right to pollute. But utilities appear reluctant to buy or sell, even though the GAO said earlier this year that the utilities could cut costs if they participated more. "The lesson so far is its potential has not been realized," said Peter Guerrero, an author of a December 1994 report by the accounting office on trading pollution rights. "Trading has effectively reduced the cost of compliance, but there are far greater reductions that could result."

According to the GAO, the annual cost of compliance in 2009, when the stricter pollution standards are fully phased in, will be about $2 billion, assuming heavy use of trading. In 1990, when Congress was debating the law, the environmental agency put the cost at twice that. In other words, the amount that Congress thought it was committing the power companies to spend—a cost to be picked up by electricity consumers—was fiction. The nation will achieve the pollution reduction for far less, while spending what Congress thought it was requiring would have bought far more pollution reduction. If Congress was striking a balance between environmental toughness and financial mercy, it could have required tougher standards for the amount it had agreed to make utilities spend.

And some environmentalists say that the trades have made the acid rain problem worse than it would have been with a simple order that each plant reduce its pollution. New York State tried unsuccessfully to intervene when one utility cleaned up more than required and made the excess emission credits available to utilities in the Midwest—a region whose emissions blow back into New York, aggravating the state's acid rain problem. * * *

For one thing, utilities are still choosing in-house solutions, like building scrubbers or switching to cleaner fuel, even if the cost is more than the market price of an emission credit. "You have a lot of really bright engineers who have a preference for technology over financial tools," said Christian J. Colton, a vice president of Cantor Fitzgerald, a New York firm that is a broker for emissions trades.

The engineers have been helped by a drop in the price of natural gas, which produces less sulfur dioxide than coal. Coal producers have also found lower-sulfur sources. And scrubber manufacturers have cut their prices. This is not bad, said Mr. McLean of the E.P.A. "Trading is not the bottom line," he said. "Tons coming out of stacks is the relevant piece of information. My goal was to reduce emissions at the lowest possible cost, not to see 1,000 trades occur." As far as he is concerned, the cheaper an allowance gets, the better.

But the price means little if utilities are reluctant to enter the market to buy or sell. They face two problems. One could be called the Robert Citron effect: they fear becoming like the former treasurer of Orange County, Calif., who put public money into complex financial instruments and lost it. If the utilities buy allowances now to stockpile for later use, and the price drops later, state regulators could argue that the purchases were imprudent and the financial loss should not be borne by customers, but by shareholders. Conversely, if they sell now and prices go up later, they could also look dumb. If utilities cut costs through the trading system, they could lower their rates, or raise their dividends to shareholders. But Mr. Colton said that only Connecticut has so far agreed to let any of the benefit flow back to shareholders. Faced with risking a loss to shareholders and no possibility of benefit, many have apparently decided not to bother.

Second, the industry itself is in turmoil as it moves toward open competition in electricity, where customers can leave their utilities for the lowest-priced supplier. As a result many old plants may be retired in the next few years. "They don't know if they're going to be using the plants in a year or two," said Mr. Jump of the trade group. The market could pick up in the next few years. Many utilities are believed to be stockpiling allowances for Jan. 1, 2000, when a second phase of the acid rain program takes effect and the emission limits become stricter. But some attitudes may have to change first. "Toes have got to be stuck in the water," said Mr. Jump, "and that's taking some time to do."

### Notes and Questions

1. The preceding *New York Times* article suggests that the market price of acid rain allowances is startlingly low because the EPA and Congress initially overestimated the costs of installing pollution controls to curb $SO_2$ emissions: "spending what Congress thought it was requiring would have bought far more pollution reduction." Where do you suppose Congress and the EPA got their cost estimates when enactment of the acid rain program was being debated? Might your answer explain the inflated estimates?

2. Does industry run the risk of wearing out the cost argument if this objection is used to oppose each new environmental standard? Consider the following article.

## CLAUDIA H. DEUTSCH, COOLING DOWN THE HEATED TALK

N.Y. Times, May 27, 1997 at D1

Corporate America is not a quick study. Again and again, companies have responded to proposed environmental rules by threatening bankruptcies, huge layoffs, foreign inroads into American markets, even an end to the car-based American way of life—and it has never worked. Finally, though, companies are acknowledging that the sky did not fall every time they were forced to clean up their act and their air. Now, as the Environmental Protection Agency prepares to impose yet another set of strict new air pollution controls this July,[b] they are moving their doom-and-gloom approach, if not off the stove, to the furthest back burner. "If we've learned any lesson, it's that you have to engage the debate on a different basis than costs," said John M. McManus, manager of environmental strategies for American Electric Power, a huge utility.

But without the unifying plea of untenable burdens, industry approaches the EPA's latest rules, aimed at reducing smog and soot, in disarray. Many industries are trying to cut their own deals with the agency. Others are putting pressure on mayors and governors to lobby Washington for them. Still others are attacking the science—and sometimes the scientists—on which the new rules are based. * * *

"Companies are attacking the scientific legitimacy of standards only because their cost arguments have been disproven so many times," said Daniel Rosenberg, a lawyer for the U.S. Public Interest Research Group, an environmental lobbying group. * * * [A]fter so many years of crying wolf, companies are loath to make the cost argument. Even American Electric Power, once the undisputed ringleader of the anti-Clean Air Act gang, has muted its cries. Some quick history can show why.

In the early 1970's, the utility mounted a $3.7 million advertising campaign to contend that technology did not exist to meet proposed rules on sulfur dioxide and particulates. In 1975 an equipment maker, Research Cottrell, began marketing a sulfur dioxide smokestack scrubber that proved American Electric wrong. So then the utility complained that it would cost $260 million a power plant to install enough scrubbers, leading to skyrocketing electric costs. The EPA did not budge, the cleanup tab turned out to be much lower, and electric rates went up only marginally.

Skip ahead to the late 1980's, when Congress and the EPA, worrying about acid rain—caused by sulfur-based pollution that can travel wide distances—insisted on even stricter sulfur controls. American Electric said the new standards would cost utilities more than $5 billion, raising residential electricity rates 12 percent and industrial rates as much as 39 percent. Again, Washington gave no ground. But scrubber technology improved and railroad deregulation made it cheaper to bring in low-sulfur coal. The utility industry's costs were less than half its projections. Small wonder that American Electric and its sister utilities are loath to cry economic foul this time. * * *

---

[b] The reference is to the 1997 ozone and particulate standards. *See* pages 317-29, *supra.*

All the new approaches—the begging for time, the emphasis on science, the absence of inflated cost claims—reflect industry's new relationship with investors, customers and the courts. In the 70's, while the EPA did not believe industry's threats of financial disaster, investors did—and sent Rust Belt stocks plummeting. Now utilities, heavy manufacturers and steelmakers fear that inflated cost forecasts could touch off another selling spree. "I always ask companies, 'Are you budgeted to meet new rules?' and they always answer, 'Oh, certainly,'" said Kenneth W. P. Hoffman, a steel analyst with Prudential Securities Research.

Consumers, always edgy about placing a dollar value on health, have been made more uneasy by the debate over managed health care and disclosures about the tobacco industry's suppression of data. "The public has a bad taste in its mouth about cost-benefit issues," conceded Augustine E. Moffitt Jr., vice president for safety, health and environment at Bethlehem Steel. * * *

Still, the conciliatory approach remains a rarity. * * * Some [industry organizations] are even letting histrionics—albeit not cost-related ones—creep back into the fray. Citizens for a Sound Economy, an inter-industry group, is taking out ads warning that the EPA's new rules will mean the end of backyard barbecues and fireworks—a prediction that a top EPA official termed "ridiculous." Environmentalists, not surprisingly, are fighting back. The Sierra Club and Mr. Rosenberg's group recently collected thousands of postcards from families supporting tougher rules, and orchestrated a May 9 event in which mothers and their asthmatic children delivered them to the White House.

For now, industry has forgone similar media events. But environmentalists expect that if civilized whispers and scientific studies do not derail the new smog and soot rules, industry will again make cacophony its tactic of choice. "The science argument is their lead argument inside the Beltway, but they're still running doom-and-gloom ads and Op-Eds elsewhere," Mr. Rosenberg noted. "And if the science argument doesn't work, you're going to see even more."

## F. COMPARING STANDARDS, EMISSION FEES, AND TRANSFERABLE RIGHTS

### WILLIAM J. BAUMOL & WALLACE E. OATES, THE THEORY OF ENVIRONMENTAL POLICY

171-81 (1998)

Although both effluent fees and systems of marketable permits have the capacity to achieve a set of environmental standards at least cost, they are by no means equivalent policy instruments from the viewpoint of an environmental agency. We shall consider first the grounds on which the environmental authority might prefer such permits to fees and shall then turn to the case for fees.

The first, and a major, advantage of marketable permits over fees is that permits promise to reduce the uncertainty and adjustment costs involved in attaining legally required levels of environmental quality. The environmental authority cannot be completely sure of the response of polluters to a particular magnitude of an effluent charge; in particular, if the authority inadvertently sets the fee too low, environmental standards will not be met. * * * [T]he fee may have to be raised and then altered again to generate an iterative path converging toward the target level of emissions. This means costly adjustments and readjustments by polluters in their levels of waste discharge and the associated abatement technology. The need for repeated changes in the fee is also an unattractive prospect for administrators of the program. In contrast, under a permit scheme, the environmental agency directly sets the total quantity of emissions at the allowable standard; there is, in principle, no problem in achieving the target.

Second, and closely related to the issue just discussed, are the complications that result from economic growth and price inflation. Continuing inflation will erode the real value of a fee; similarly, expanding production of both old and new firms will increase the demand for waste emissions. Both of these will require the fee to be raised periodically if environmental standards are to be maintained. The burden of initiating such corrective action under a system of fees falls necessarily upon environmental officials; they are forced to choose between unpopular fee increases or nonattainment of standards. Under a system of permits, market forces automatically accommodate themselves to inflation and growth with no increase in pollution. The rise in demand for permits, real and nominal, simply translates itself directly into a higher price.

Third, the introduction of a system of effluent fees may involve enormous increases in costs to polluters *relative* to alternative regulatory policies. This point may seem somewhat paradoxical in light of the widespread recognition that systems of pricing incentives promise large savings in aggregate abatement costs. But the two are not inconsistent. Although a system of effluent charges will reduce total abatement costs, it will impose a new financial burden, the tax bill itself, on polluting firms. Although these taxes represent a transfer payment from the viewpoint of society, they are a cost of operation for the firm. Some recent evidence on this issue suggests that the figures can be rather staggering. One such study of the use of pricing incentives to restrict emissions of certain halocarbons into the atmosphere estimates that the aggregate abatement costs under a realistic program of direct controls would total about $230 million; a system of fees or of marketable permits would reduce these costs to an estimated $110 million (a saving of roughly 50 percent). However, the cost of the fees or permits to polluters would total about $1,400 million so that, in spite of the substantial savings in abatement costs, a program of pricing incentives would, in this instance, increase the total cost to polluters by a factor of *six* relative to a program of direct controls! Some studies of other pollutants also suggest that fees can be a major source of new costs. It is true that a system of marketable permits *making use of an auction for the initial acquisition of these rights* is subject to the same problem, because sources face high prices for permits. However, there is an alternative that gets around the problem: A permit system can be initiated through a *free* initial distribution of the permits among current polluters. This version of the permit scheme effectively eliminates the added costs for existing firms without any necessarily adverse consequences for the efficiency properties of the program and with some obvious and major advantages for its political acceptability. It is interesting in this regard that existing systems of marketable permits in the United States embody a kind of "grandfathering" scheme involving an initial distribution of emission permits or "rights" among polluters based on historical levels of emissions.

Fourth, * * * there may be instances where geographical distinctions among polluters are important. In fact, for several important air and water pollutants, various studies indicate that it is imperative for the environmental authority to differentiate among polluters according to their location if environmental standards are to be realized in a cost-effective way. Sources at a highly polluted location within an airshed cannot be allowed to increase their emissions on a one-to-one basis in exchange for emissions reductions by other sources at a less-polluted point. As we have indicated, it can be administratively quite cumbersome to deal with the spatial problem under a system of effluent charges, for it will typically require the environmental agency to determine a separate emission fee for each source, depending on its location in the air shed or river basin (or alternatively, it will be necessary to introduce a system of zones with different charges). Such discrimination among sources in fee levels may either be explicitly illegal or politically infeasible. In contrast, a system of marketable permits can address these spatial dimensions of the pollution problem in a manner that is less objectionable.

Fifth, marketable permits may be the more feasible approach on grounds of familiarity. The introduction of a system of effluent fees requires the adoption of a wholly new method of controlling pollution, new both to regulators and polluters. Such sharp departures from established practice are hard to sell; moreover, some real questions have been raised about the legality of charging for pollution. In contrast, permits already exist, and it may be a less-radical step to make these permits effectively marketable.

There is thus a strong case on administrative grounds for favoring marketable permits over effluent fees. But the case is far from ironclad. Where charges are feasible, they represent a most attractive source of revenues for the public sector. Most taxes in the economy have undesired side effects: they distort economic choices in various ways. Income taxes, for example, can induce individuals to choose untaxed leisure activities rather than work; excise taxes shift peoples' purchases away from the taxed goods; and so on. Such taxes generate an "excess burden" on the economy—a cost in addition to the reduced disposal income directly attributable to the revenues. Effluent fees, in contrast, have a beneficial side effect: They tend to correct distortions in the economy while at the same time generating public revenues. Such fees can be said to impose a "negative excess burden." Fees, then, to the extent they are feasible, are a very desirable source of public revenues in terms of economic efficiency * * * .

There is yet another argument favoring effluent fees—one that involves savings in certain transaction costs. A system of marketable emission permits requires an initial distribution of the permits. However, if this initial distribution is based on the grandfathering principle or some other mechanism that does not reflect the relative marginal abatement costs of the different sources, a series of transfers (purchases and sales) of permits will be required if the least-cost allocation is to be attained. The incentives for such transfers exist: Buyers who can reduce emissions only at a higher real cost will be willing to pay more than the reservation price of sellers. But there may well be significant search costs and elements of strategic behavior that impede the transfers of emissions entitlements that are necessary to achieve the least-cost outcome. In contrast, under a system of fees, no such transfers of permits are needed—each source simply responds directly to the incentive provided by the fee. It may thus prove easier in certain circumstances to attain the least-cost allocation of waste emissions under a set of fees than under a system of marketable permits.

### Notes and Questions

1. The Clean Air Act's nonattainment "offset" program, *see* pages 497-505, *supra*, and its acid rain program, *see* pages 339-45 and 582-586, *supra*, each have the effect of establishing marketable pollution rights. How were these rights initially distributed? Who paid for them?

2. Might it be that a system *mixing* fees and marketable rights might be more effective than either system standing alone? A strong argument can be made for combining techniques:

> [W]e have to discard the assumption that the question is "Which one of the available policy approaches should we use?" In fact, there is much to be gained by constructing a mixed strategy which can realize some of the advantages of more than one scheme simultaneously. For example, if we have effluent standards, using effluent fees in addition would serve to provide a floor under the marginal waste control costs incurred by each waste source. If costs turn out to be low, sources will clean up more than the standard to avoid the fees. At the same time, the standards provide some insurance against high levels of damage. Indeed, it is difficult to see why some fees should not be used almost everywhere

that standards are employed to provide additional incentives for current cleanup and for the development of new technology * * * .

Marc J. Roberts, *Environmental Protection: The Complexities of Real Policy Choice*, in Swainson, ed., Managing the Water Environment 198 (1976).

## G. THE LIMITS OF ECONOMIC INCENTIVES

## WILLIAM PEDERSEN, THE LIMITS OF MARKET-BASED APPROACHES TO ENVIRONMENTAL PROTECTION

24 Envtl. L. Rep. 10173 (1994)

Market-based approaches to protecting the environment based on buying and selling "pollution rights" have long been special favorites of the academic community. According to a growing body of literature, a much wider use of this approach could solve the problems of ineffectiveness, inefficiency, and rigidity that characterize our current system of environmental protection. * * *

[These suggestions] set out an important—indeed, essential—perspective. But they often underestimate the many different forms in which environmental problems arise. Those forms are too varied to yield to any single approach. Sometimes only one or two sources cause a pollution problem. Sometimes it is caused by many small sources like cars or dry cleaners. Sometimes it is caused by patterns of land use that allow pollutants to flow readily into a body of water. Sometimes the pollution discharges from different sources in an area vary significantly in toxicity. And often environmental protection involves deciding whether the risks from current or future use of certain chemicals is acceptable, and how to react if it is not, or setting the acceptable level of cleanup for a hazardous waste site, or determining where and how much to protect natural beauty or endangered species.

This Dialogue argues that applying market-based approaches to these problems is always difficult—often too difficult to be worth the effort—and sometimes conceptually impossible. For these reasons, market-based approaches yield significant benefits only in special circumstances that are only sometimes present.

More fundamentally, "pollution trading" is only a method of implementing policy. Whether an activity can be controlled by this method tells us literally nothing about whether it was worth controlling in the first place. The current enthusiasm for market-based approaches has considerable potential for obscuring that more basic issue, by hiding from us the variety of the problems we must address, and the choices we must make, to create a coherent environmental policy.

Although emissions trading approaches have much to offer us, for these reasons they cannot substitute for an informed debate on the goals of environmental policy and on what we must control to reach those goals.[4] And once we have chosen those goals, there is no automatic reason to believe that tradable emissions rights will be the regulatory mechanism best suited to reach them.

Any "pollution trading" approach requires the creation of a new form of property, namely, the rights that are traded. It also requires a system of market rules for trading them. For example, to establish a system of "discharge rights" for a river basin, the regulatory agency would have to decide which dischargers would be forbidden to discharge without holding such rights, what pollutants or combinations of pollutants the rights would cover, how many rights each discharger would receive, when and how the government could amend the rights, what the rules for trading rights would be, and how such trades would be recorded. Such markets take a considerable legal and political investment to establish, and a smaller but continuing investment to police. In addition, the market will not work unless sources can measure the exact quantity of their discharges. Only such precise measurement can tell them the extent to which their rights exceed their emissions—thus allowing them to sell rights to others—or the extent to which their emissions exceed their rights—thus requiring the purchase of more rights to cover the excess. In many cases, the same emissions will have significantly different impacts in different places. When that is true, the market must either adjust its trading rules to compensate (thus making trading more complicated), or accept a certain oversimplification of the environmental problem it purports to address. For pollution-trading systems to be worth establishing, the gains from trading must outweigh all these costs.

These conditions are far more demanding than is often realized. Due to them, pollution trading is best suited to broad environmental problems where the same emissions have about the same effect everywhere, where the "pollutant" being traded is relatively easy to measure, and where the market is restricted to a limited number of large sources that can bear the transaction costs. In those cases, our current system has already proved very open to pollution trading. * * *

In general, pollution-trading approaches do not work well when there are only one or two sources in an area, since then the trading possibilities are limited. Nor do they work well when the emissions from different types of sources are themselves different, since that can lead

---

[4] Trading pollution rights is not the only form of market-based (or somewhat market-based) environmental regulation discussed in the literature. *See, e.g.,* Robert W. Hahn & Robert N. Stavins, *Incentives for Environmental Protection: Integrating Theory and Practice,* 82 Am. Econ. Rev. 464 (1992). However, it is by far the most developed, both in publicity and in practice. The most potent single alternative—imposing a tax on pollution—has thus far failed to be adopted widely. In addition, because the impact of a tax on pollution is hard to predict in advance, and because the government must also decide how to use the revenues collected, a tax raises policy and program design issues even more complicated than those that attend emissions trading.

to different environmental effects. If emissions are hard to measure for any reason, or the amount of emissions per source is small, the difficulties of quantification may override the gains from trade. For example, it would probably be hard to design a market-based approach to controlling the use of wood stoves. Finally, environmental protection problems that involve acceptable risk or land use decisions are unsuited to market-based approaches by their essential nature. A review of our actual experience will show how frequently these barriers to market-based approaches are encountered.

## AIR POLLUTION

Despite many past successes, dramatic growth in emissions trading to control air pollutants appears unlikely. Even under our current system of technology-based individual controls, monitoring costs can amount to a considerable fraction of total compliance expenses. Yet under this system, monitoring need only determine whether a given emission level is or is not being met. For emissions trading to work, a source must define its exact emission level, not just whether it is under or over a regulatory standard. The first of these tasks is often technically more difficult than the second. Accordingly, a full pollution-trading approach could require markedly more elaborate quantification, data tracking, and accounting systems than we now employ. Moreover, over half of the emissions of many air pollutants now come from small sources and motor vehicles. There is no way to impose the monitoring costs of an emissions trading system directly on such sources. Although trading systems that use surrogate limits can be established, they, too, are expensive to design and implement. Finally, under the 1990 Clean Air Act Amendments, almost 200 air pollutants are now regulated as "hazardous." Trading will become literally impossible if the trading system must separately address emissions and emissions changes for each of these 200 substances.

With a regulatory problem defined in this manner, how often will the effort to establish a detailed new trading mechanism be worth it? As trading rules become more complicated, and the average size of sources to be controlled becomes smaller, the benefits of emissions trading will probably decline.

## WATER POLLUTION

Even more than with air, changes in water quality are sensitive to the location of a pollutant discharge. Also, the sources of water pollution tend to be small or unconventional—such as construction sites, plowed or fertilized fields, paved roads or parking lots. For that reason, protection of water quality can often require some form of land use control. That in turn must have a large regulatory component.

To take a realistic example, totally protecting water quality in a given stream might require that 80 percent of the bank should remain bordered by trees to a depth of at least 100 feet. Undoubtedly, economists could devise a mechanism for trading development rights in the remaining 20 percent. However, that misses an important point. It is deciding whether and how to restrict development of the 80 percent, not trading development rights in the 20 percent, which raises the central political and public policy issue.

### TOXIC CHEMICALS

Finally, much of our environmental regulatory effort is devoted to evaluating chemicals, pesticides, drugs, or food additives to determine whether they are safe enough to be allowed to stay on or enter the market, and, if they are not completely safe, whether any restrictions should be imposed on their use. It is hard to see how market-based approaches could make more than a marginal contribution to such judgments. Similarly, no market-based approach can tell us the exact degree of purity to which a hazardous waste site should be cleaned up, or create an alternative to the soil excavation, soil treatment, and soil testing needed to accomplish that cleanup. * * *

Markets work best under simple trading rules. That gives those who design markets an incentive to oversimplify environmental problems to make their market mechanisms more workable. Market-based control approaches are probably more efficient than the alternatives. But we cannot assume that the gains from increased efficiency will always outweigh the losses from oversimplification. * * * [M]arket mechanisms will not set our goals for us and may even disguise their absence. They are also not universally adapted to even achieving the goals that we have set. They will certainly be a useful tool, but only one among many—including product clearance, land use planning, labeling, "command and control," and removing direct subsidies and tax preferences for environmentally damaging activities—that should all have their place in a rational system of environmental control.

# H. PUBLIC DISCLOSURE

The theme of this chapter is smarter regulation. We have explored various ways to force polluters to reduce their emissions: command-and-control regimes, counterproposals, regulatory negotiations, tradeoffs, emission fees, and marketable permits. One remaining and surprisingly effective technique might simply be to require periodic disclosure of each polluter's emissions in a form easily available to the public.

## 1. TOXIC RELEASE INVENTORY

## NOTE ON THE COMMUNITY RIGHT TO KNOW ACT TRI DATABASE

Congress enacted the Emergency Planning and Community Right-to-Know Act (EPCRTKA) in 1986. The statute requires annual reporting to the EPA by a limited number of facilities about their handling of certain toxic chemicals. The following description is taken from the Right to Know Network (RTK NET), a web site at which members of the public may freely access all collected data:

The Toxic Release Inventory (TRI) is a database of information about releases and transfers of toxic chemicals from manufacturing facilities. Facilities must report their releases of a toxic chemical to TRI if they fulfill four criteria:

1. They must be a manufacturing facility (primary SIC [Standard Industrial Classification] code in 20-39);

2. They must have the equivalent of 10 full-time workers;

3. They must either manufacture or process more than 25,000 lbs of the chemical or use more than 10,000 lbs during the year;

4. The chemical must be on the TRI list of 350 specific toxic chemicals or chemical categories.

Therefore, not all, or even most, pollution is reported in TRI. However, TRI does have certain advantages:

1. It is multi-media. Facilities must report the amounts they release to air, land, water, and underground separately, and must report how much they send off-site;

2. All quantities are reported in pounds. This is an advantage compared to databases like PCS, which often report releases as concentrations, or other databases which report releases by volume of waste. These measures are often impossible to convert into pounds;

3. It is congressionally mandated to be [publicly] available, by electronic and other means, to everyone. This means that it's relatively easy to obtain TRI data and that the data is well-known, becoming a national "yardstick" for measuring progress in pollution and waste generation.

The TRI data is reported by individual facilities, who send their reports to Federal EPA every year. These reports are filled out on a form called "Form R". EPA takes these forms and converts them into an electronic database. * * *

RTK NET/OMB Watch, TRI Search: About the Data, http://www.rtk. net/triabout.html (Jun. 14, 1999).

Users logging into the RTK NET site may search the entire multi-year TRI database in highly significant ways, such as by zip code, by name of facility, and by chemical. Output can be sorted and downloaded in several formats, including formats that are easily imported into spreadsheets and database programs such as Microsoft Access. This data may be highly useful to citizen groups, competitors, and regulators.[c]

For example, a quick search of the RTK NET site establishes that Proctor & Gamble Company of Iowa City, Iowa, reported releases in 1996 of the following amounts of various air pollutants: 910 pounds of ammonia; 740 pounds of formaldehyde; and 910 pounds of hydrochloric acid. The company also reported that 4,000 pounds of ammonia, 4,340 pounds of diethanolamine, 580 pounds of formaldehyde, and 1,750 pounds of zinc compounds were transferred through water discharges to the local publicly owned treatment works in 1996, and that 1,800 pounds of diethanolamine, 5 pounds of formaldehyde, and 220 pounds of zinc compounds were shipped off site to Heritage Environmental Services in Indianapolis, Indiana.

---

Read the following sections of the Emergency
Planning and Community Right to Know Act

☐ § 313(a)      ☐ § 313(b)(1)(A)      ☐ § 313(c)

☐ § 313(f)(1)      ☐ § 313(j)

---

## 2. EFFECTS OF THE TRI INVENTORY

Has establishment of the TRI database done any good? In 1987, the first year of its implementation, manufacturers reported that they had released or disposed of at least 22.5 billion pounds of hazardous substances. *See* Philip Shabecoff, *Industrial Pollution Called Startling*, N.Y. Times, Apr. 12, 1989, at A18, col. 5. Industry representatives and government officials were surprised by the large volume of chemicals being released to air, water, and land—quantities far greater than what the EPA had anticipated. *See id.* The numbers were especially startling, because the 1987 TRI database included only a small segment of American industry: manufacturing facilities falling within a limited number of Standard Industrial Classification codes that used more than 10,000 pounds or produced more than 75,000 pounds of the listed substances. More than 25 percent of the manufacturers required to report in 1987 had failed to do so, and many *non*manufacturing facilities, such as dry cleaning shops, were exempt from the reporting requirement. *Id.*

Environmental groups have used the TRI database to call public attention to polluters. For example, the Louisiana Environmental Action Network effectively branded an American Cyanamid facility "the single largest polluting plant in the state," an allegation that was repeated in the New Orleans *Times Picayune. See* Keith Schneider, *For Communi-*

---

[c] Another excellent web site for searching the TRI database, established by the Environmental Defense Fund, is http://www.scorecard.org (Jul. 19, 1999).

*ties, Knowledge of Polluters is Power*, N.Y. Times, Mar. 24, 1991, at 5, col. 1. American Cyanamid conceded that "there is much more public pressure for us to reduce discharges, and we are reducing them." *Id.*

The pressure of public disclosure has induced a number of the nation's largest manufacturing programs to create voluntary pollution reduction programs. For example, AT&T announced that "it would stop all emissions of the listed chemicals into the air by the turn of the century." *Id.* William K. Reilly, EPA Administrator, concluded that the TRI "is fast becoming one of the most powerful tools we have to reduce toxic emissions." John Holusha, *The Nation's Polluters—Who Emits What, and Where*, N.Y. Times, Oct. 13, 1991, at 10, col. 1. Deborah H. Sheiman of the Natural Resources Defense Council asserted that "the information-only approach has done more to reduce toxic air emissions than the Clean Air Act's 20-year old regulatory program." *Id.*

More recent data show that total on- and off-site releases of the listed toxic substances declined by 42.8 percent during the ten year period preceding 1997, but rose 2.2 percent in 1997. *See* Judith Jacobs, *TRI Releases Rise 2.2 Percent in 1997*, 30 [Curr. Dev.] Env. Rep. (BNA) 132 (1999).

## 3.  EXPANSION OF THE TRI INVENTORY

In 1994, EPA added 286 chemicals and chemical categories to the TRI list. *See* 59 Fed. Reg. 61432 (1994). Five chemicals were removed from that expanded list in 1998 pursuant to a court challenge. *See* 29 [Curr. Dev.] Env. Rep. (BNA) 35 (1998). Seven industrial sectors—metal mining, coal mining, electrical utilities that burn coal or oil, hazardous waste treatment and disposal facilities, chemical wholesale distributors, petroleum bulk stations and terminals, and solvent recovery services—were added to the TRI reporting rule in 1997. *See* 28 [Curr. Dev.] Env. Rep. (BNA) 2649 (1997). The utility, coal mining, and metal mining industries challenged that action in court, alleging that mining and utility operations do not "manufacture," "process," or "otherwise use" the TRI chemicals as required by EPCRTKA § 313. *See* 29 [Curr. Dev.] Env. Rep. (BNA) 36 (1998). The electric utility's industry's arguments were rejected in a U.S. District Court ruling denying summary judgment. *See Dayton Power & Light v. EPA*, No. 1:97CV03074 (D. D.C. 3/31/99); *Court Rejects Utilities' Central Argument, Upholds EPA Extension of TRI Requirements*, 29 [Curr. Dev.] Env. Rep. (BNA) 2423 (1999).

In late 1998, EPA announced that the focus of EPCRTKA enforcement will shift from those who fail to file annual Form R reports to companies that submit inaccurate data. "EPA enforcement and program officials are concerned about some of the 'strange numbers' that have been appearing on TRI reports." 29 [Curr. Dev.] Env. Rep. (BNA) 1354 (1998).

### 4. CALIFORNIA PROPOSITION 65

## JOHN FELTMAN, DISCLOSURE LAWS CAN REGULATE GENTLY

N.Y. Times, Oct. 3, 1993, at 9, col. 2

In 1987, California began to require warning labels on products containing any one of more than 300 toxic chemicals. Rather than post such a notice on its typewriter-correction fluid, however, the Gillette Company simply removed the toxins, added other ingredients and called the product "new and improved." Dow Chemical, Sara Lee and dozens of other companies did similar things.

Known as Proposition 65, the statute does not outlaw toxins or otherwise regulate company conduct. It doesn't tap taxpayers to fund a big, regulatory bureaucracy, either. It simply requires companies to tell the public if their products contain certain substances. But despite this very light touch, Proposition 65 and other "public disclosure" laws can have powerful results.

This kinder, gentler regulation is not new. The securities laws have long required companies to disclose financial information to investors, and cigarette packs have long been stamped with the Surgeon General's warning. * * *

Like Proposition 65, the TRI law has had a powerful impact on corporate behavior. Monsanto, for example, was a major air polluter when the TRI law took effect in 1987. But, to avoid public relations fallout, the company volunteered to cut its worldwide emissions of air pollution by 90 percent within five years. And it did.

In lauding TRI in May, Business Week identified the engine that drives all such disclosure laws. "When it comes to cutting output of the most dangerous chemicals," the magazine said, "the Government has found a far more effective weapon than the law: embarrassment." Protective of their reputations, Gillette, Monsanto and other companies often will change their practices when faced with the prospect of revealing them to consumers, employees, journalists and others.

Public-disclosure laws can have many uses. To boost employee safety, simply tell companies to disclose work-related deaths, injuries and illnesses. To promote greater job opportunities, simply have companies report how many women and minorities they employ, with titles and salaries. Product safety, waste production, recycling, energy conservation—all these corporate practices can be altered by disclosure rules.

Reformers and their opponents will still argue about whether any regulation—including disclosure—is proper in a particular case. But if regulation is chosen, disclosure is often the best method. With it, taxpayers save the cost of the bureaucracy that regulation often brings, the public gets more information to make purchasing and job decisions, and companies avoid the cost and coerciveness of traditional regulation.

It's time to increase our reliance on disclosure. It's too good a tool to sit in the shed.

---

In an analysis of California Proposition 65's warning requirement, Professor Clifford Rechtschaffen reaches the following conclusions:

> Proposition 65 has had mixed success in realizing its underlying statutory goals of providing individuals with sufficient information to make meaningful choices and reducing exposure to toxic chemicals. The statute has been largely ineffective in promoting informed choice because of sparse statutory guidance and inadequate implementing regulations for its warning provisions. The lack of adequate regulatory criteria has also contributed to overwarning by enabling businesses to provide vague and uninformative warnings that recipients will likely ignore. However, in the consumer marketplace, where substitute chemicals are available, Proposition 65 has encouraged significant product reformulation. The Act has also helped to reduce toxic air emissions and other environmental exposures, the result of increased public scrutiny of its processes and concern about negative publicity. Its weakest impact has been in the workplace, where it largely has been subsumed by existing worker hazard communication programs.

Clifford Rechtschaffen, *The Warning Game: Evaluating Warnings Under California's Proposition 65*, 23 Ecol. L.Q. 303, 306-07 (1996).

# Chapter Eleven

## CLEAN WATER ACT

### A. WATER POLLUTION

We have now examined one federal statutory scheme—the Clean Air Act—in depth, and have explored some alternatives to traditional command and control regulation. In this chapter, we will engage in a less intensive analysis of the Clean Water Act. We start with a background reading on the general nature of the water pollution problem as perceived in 1970. We then consider a more recent assessment of water pollution in the United States.

### COUNCIL ON ENVIRONMENTAL QUALITY, FIRST ANNUAL REPORT
#### 30-32, 35-37 (1970)

Several basic biological, chemical, and physical processes affect the quality of water. Organic wastes decompose by bacterial action. Bacteria attack wastes dumped into rivers and lakes, using up oxygen in the process. Organic wastes are measured in units of biochemical oxygen demand (BOD), or chemical oxygen demand (COD), both measures of the amount of oxygen needed to decompose them. The COD measure is more inclusive than BOD, but BOD is much more commonly used. Fish and other aquatic life need oxygen. If the waste loads are so great that large amounts of oxygen are spent in their decomposition, certain types of fish can no longer live in that body of water. A pollution-resistant, lower order of fish, such as carp, replace the original fish population. The amount of oxygen in a water body is therefore one of the best measures of its ecological health.

If all the oxygen is used, an anaerobic (without air) decomposition process is set in motion with a different mixture of bacteria. Rather than releasing carbon dioxide in the decomposition process, anaerobic decomposition releases methane or hydrogen sulfide. In these highly polluted situations, the river turns dark, and odors—often overwhelming—penetrate the environment.

Heated water discharged into lakes and rivers often harms aquatic life. Heat accelerates biological and chemical processes, which reduce the ability of a body of water to retain dissolved oxygen and other dissolved gases. Increases in temperature often disrupt the reproduction cycles of fish. By hastening biological processes, heat accelerates the growth of aquatic plants—often algae. Finally, the temperature level determines the types of fish and other aquatic life that can live in any particular body of water. Taken together, these effects of excess heat operate to change the ecology of an area—sometimes drastically and rapidly.

One of the most serious water pollution problems is eutrophication—the "dying of lakes." All lakes go through a natural cycle of eutrophication, but normally it takes thousands of years. In the first stage—the oligotrophic—lakes are deep and have little biological life. Lake Superior is a good example. Over time, nutrients and sediments are added; the lake becomes more biologically productive and shallower. This stage—the mesotrophic—has been reached by Lake Ontario. As the nutrients continue to be added, large algal blooms grow, fish populations change, and the lake begins to take on undesirable characteristics. Lake Erie is now in this eutrophic stage. Over time, the lake becomes a swamp and finally a land area.

People greatly accelerate this process of eutrophication when they add nutrients to the water—detergents, fertilizers, and human wastes. They have done this in Lake Erie and countless other lakes. Human actions can, in decades, cause changes that would have taken nature thousands of years.

Although water pollution comes from many sources, the major ones are industrial, municipal, and agricultural. * * * The more than 300,000 water-using factories in the United States discharge three to four times as much oxygen-demanding wastes as all the sewered population of the United States. Moreover, many of the wastes discharged by industry are toxic. * * *

Municipal waste treatment plants handle more than just domestic wastes from homes and apartments. On a nationwide average, about 55 percent of the wastes processed by municipal treatment plants comes from homes and commercial establishments and about 45 percent from industries. Less than one-third of the Nation's population is served by a system of sewers and an adequate treatment plant. About one-third is not served by a sewer system at all. About 5 percent is served by sewers which discharge their wastes without any treatment. And the remaining 32 percent have sewers but inadequate treatment plants. Of the total sewered population, about 60 percent have adequate treatment systems. The greatest municipal waste problems exist in the areas with the heaviest concentrations of population, particularly the Northeast. * * *

Wastes from feedlots are a key source of agricultural pollution. The increasing number of animals and modern methods of raising them contribute to the worsening pollution of waters by animal wastes. Beef cattle, poultry, and swine feeding operations, along with dairy farms, are the major sources of actual or potential water pollution from animal wastes. * * *

Fertilizers contain nitrogen and phosphorus, two primary nutrients that nourish algae in water. Nitrates are the bigger problem since, unlike phosphates, which stick to soil, nitrates are very susceptible to runoff from rain. Also, nitrates leach into ground water. High nitrate concentrations in water cause infant methemoglobinemia or "blue baby." The use of chemical fertilizers has increased rapidly in the United States over the last decade and is expected to continue to rise, although at somewhat slower rates. In some areas, particularly in the West, water leached from irrigated lands has caused serious water pollution. In the Western United States, salt content in many rivers exceeds the levels considered acceptable for most types of crops.

# EPA OFFICE OF WATER,
# ENVIRONMENTAL INDICATORS OF
# WATER QUALITY IN THE UNITED STATES
## 1-16 (1996)

Water resources in the United States take many forms—running freely as rivers and streams; washing against coastlines and into estuaries; pooling as lakes, reservoirs, and wetlands; and moving under the land as ground water. We use these waters for many different purposes, including drinking, swimming, fishing, agriculture, and industry. Water resources are affected by many activities, both natural, such as rain, and human, such as water withdrawal and urbanization. * * *

There are 3.5 million miles of *rivers and streams* in the country. About one-third of these flow all the time, and two-thirds flow only periodically and are dry during a portion of the year. * * * Rivers and streams supply water for drinking, agriculture, industrial processes, and irrigation and support aquatic habitats, fishing, and recreation. Rivers and streams are impacted by pollution discharged directly into the water, as well as by pollution generated by activities occurring on land, which rainwater or snowmelt carries into these waterways in the form of runoff.

There are 41 million acres of *lakes and reservoirs* in the country. Lakes and reservoirs support the same uses as rivers and streams and are affected by the same types of pollution. These impacts, however, can be more severe because lakes and reservoirs do not have the natural flushing process characteristic of flowing streams and rivers.

*Estuaries* are coastal waters where the tides mix fresh river water with ocean salt water. For example, the Chesapeake Bay is a large estuary that receives freshwater flow from several rivers in Virginia and Maryland and connects with the Atlantic Ocean. There are many other smaller estuaries all along the coastline of the United States in total, over 34,000 square miles of estuaries. Estuaries are noted for their unique aquatic habitats, as well as for the fishing, shellfishing, and other recreational and economic opportunities they provide. Estuaries are in increasing danger of pollution considering that almost half the U.S. population now lives in coastal areas, many on estuaries. * * *

Because *ground water* flows beneath the earth's surface, it is hard to map the aquifers in which it resides or to know the overall quality of ground water in the United States. * * * Ground water flows are usually slower than surface waters and are replenished by interaction with streams, rivers, and wetlands and by precipitation that seeps through the soil. Ground water also can replenish other water-bodies by maintaining base flow to streams, rivers, and wetlands. Ground water provides almost one-fourth of all water used in the country, serving agricultural, industrial, and drinking water needs. Waste disposal, contaminated runoff, and polluted surface waters can degrade ground water quality.

*Wetlands* include swamps, marshes, tundra, bogs, and other areas that are saturated with water for varying periods of time. Under normal circumstances, these areas support plants specifically adapted to saturated conditions. Seeping water from wetlands can recharge ground water supplies. Unaltered wetlands in a floodplain can reduce flooding. The natural water filtration and sediment control capabilities of wetlands help maintain surface and ground water quality. More than 200 million acres of wetlands existed in the lower 48 states during colonial times. Less than half remain today, however, largely due to conversion to agricultural, urban, or suburban land. Wetland water quality can be impacted by many of the same sources that affect other surface water resources. * * *

### ENVIRONMENTAL INDICATORS

Understanding the condition of our nation's water resources, identifying what causes problems, and determining how to solve these problems are essential but difficult undertakings. The natural water cycle itself is intricate, and the addition of human activities increases this complexity. Consequently, answering the basic question, "How clean and safe is our water?" is not easy.

One way to present the condition of our water resources and the impacts of related human activities is to develop understandable measures, or *indicators*, that singly or in combination provide information on water quality. * * * Indicators can present information on status or trends in the state of the environment, can measure pressures or stressors that degrade environmental quality, and can evaluate society's responses * * * .

This report describes the indicators EPA and its partners have chosen to measure progress toward water quality objectives. * * * [The] report concentrates on the actual condition of our water resources. Thus, the indicators presented are predominantly state of the environment and pressure indicators. * * *

### FISH CONSUMPTION ADVISORIES

States [and some tribes] issue fish consumption advisories to alert anglers of risks associated with eating fish from rivers and lakes that are contaminated by chemical pollutants. * * * States and tribes report that 14 percent of total lake acres and 4 percent of total river miles have one or more fish consumption advisories. * * *

### SHELLFISH GROWING WATER CLASSIFICATIONS

[T]he *National Shellfish Register of Classified Estuarine Waters* * * * reports the classifications of all coastal and estuarine shellfish growing waters. * * * In 1990, there were 17 million acres of classified shellfish growing waters in U.S. coastal areas, with 63 percent approved for shellfish harvest—a 6 percent decline from 1985. Of the other 37 percent, 9 percent were conditionally approved for harvest, 3 percent were classified as restricted, and 25 percent were classified as prohibited. * * *

### BIOLOGICAL INTEGRITY

Assessing a waterbody for healthy biological communities is a complex process, and the science to do so is newer than that used in chemical monitoring. * * * The extent of biological integrity is determined by comparing the monitored site against a "reference site" that exhibits the desired characteristics. * * *

States were able to assess only 9 percent of their rivers for biological integrity; of those, 50 percent were found to have healthy aquatic communities. [The EPA] assessed 50 percent of the Nation's estuaries * * * and found that 74 percent of estuaries have healthy aquatic communities. Methods for biological monitoring of lakes are under development; consequently, there are not enough data yet to confidently report the number of lakes that support health aquatic life. * * *

### DESIGNATED USES

The Clean Water Act requires states and, if authorized, Native American tribes to adopt water quality standards that include uses they designate for their waterbodies or waterbody segments. These *designated uses* reflect the way we want to use our waterbodies and include such things as supplying clean drinking water, providing fish and shellfish safe for human consumption, allowing safe swimming and other forms of recreation, and supporting healthy aquatic life. * * *

[O]f the rivers and lakes assessed and reported on for [1994], 87 percent of the lake acres and 83 percent of the river miles that supply drinking water systems support this use [assuming conventional treatments of disinfection and filtration]. * * *

Currently, 77 percent or more of all river miles, lake acres, and estuarine square miles that the states and tribes have assessed are safe for all forms of recreation. * * * Approximately 70 percent of the Nation's assessed river miles, lake acres, and estuarine square miles can support the designated aquatic life use. * * *

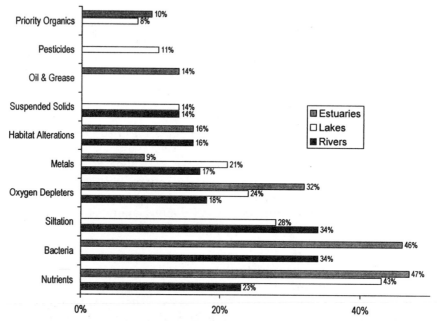

**Figure 11-1.** Leading stressors causing water quality impairment
Source: EPA Office of Water, Environmental Indicators of
Water Quality in the United States (1996), Figure 9a

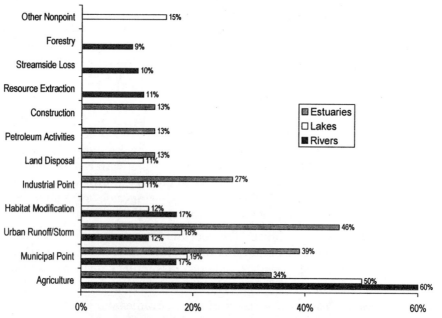

**Figure 11-2.** Leading sources of water quality impairment
Source: EPA Office of Water, Environmental Indicators of
Water Quality in the United States (1996), Figure 9b

LEADING POLLUTANTS AND SOURCES

[**Figure 11-1** and **Figure 11-2**] show the leading stressors and sources of impairment in assessed rivers, streams, lakes, reservoirs, and estuaries reported by states in 1994. * * * [The figures] include only those [affected waters] that have been assessed by states and tribes and identified as impaired. * * *

EPA and its partners have chosen to track a few of the many constituents that have significant effects on our surface waters. * * * [**Figure 11-3**] presents the change in concentration levels of six constituents, including dissolved oxygen, dissolved solids, nitrate, total phosphorus, fecal coliform, and suspended sediments. * * * Increases in the concentration level of dissolved oxygen, which is necessary for fish and aquatic plant life, indicate an improvement in ambient water quality. In contrast, increases in the concentration level of all of the other constituents reflect a decrease in ambient water quality.

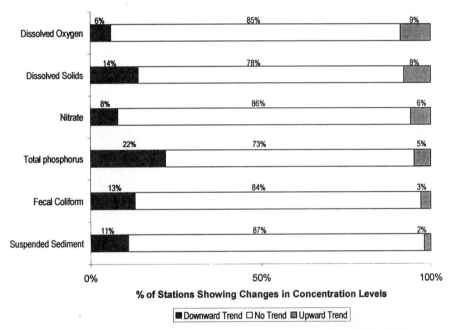

**% of Stations Showing Changes in Concentration Levels**

■ Downward Trend □ No Trend ▨ Upward Trend

**Figure 11-3.** Trends in river and stream water quality 1980-1989
Source: EPA Office of Water, Environmental Indicators of
Water Quality in the United States (1996), Indicator 12

## B. CLEAN WATER ACT OVERVIEW

In the air pollution context, we saw that today's Clean Air Act was inaugurated in 1970 amendments to a then-existing statute. Similarly, today's Clean Water Act took shape in 1972 amendments to a then-existing statute: the Federal Water Pollution Control Act. Like the Clean Air Act, the water statute was extensively amended in 1977. The Act was further amended by the Water Quality Act of 1987—a bill overwhelmingly enacted over a veto by then-President Reagan. Although some writers still refer laboriously to "the Federal Water Pollution Control Act, as amended," most attorneys now call the amended statute the Clean Water Act. The following reading provides a preliminary overview of the Clean Water Act's structure.

# WILLIAM H. RODGERS, JR.,
# 2 ENVIRONMENTAL LAW: AIR AND WATER
## §§ 4.1-4.2 (1986)

The Clean Water Act as we now know it is shaped * * * by legislative endeavors of earlier times, notably prior versions of the Federal Water Pollution Control Act, which made its first appearance in 1948, and the Rivers and Harbors Appropriations Act of 1899, commonly known as the Refuse Act. These two statutory roots are schizophrenic in conception, one espousing the water quality standards approach, the other stressing effluent limitations. (A water quality standard is a legal expression of the amount of pollutants allowed in a defined watercourse; an effluent standard describes the amount of pollutants that can be released legally by a specific source). The two concepts coexisted for several decades, mutually oblivious of one another, until Congress struck the balance mostly (but not entirely) in favor of control at the source in the 1972 Amendments.

After its initial appearance in 1948, the Federal Water Pollution Control Act was amended five times prior to the major revisions of 1972. * * * Striking a balance between the costs of control and human health needs was a problem from the beginning. * * * In 1965 came the major step of providing for the establishment of water quality standards applicable to interstate waters. Under a procedure not unlike that now governing the preparation of state implementation plans under the Clean Air Act, either the state or, in the event of state inaction, the Secretary of Interior, could promulgate water quality criteria and a plan for implementation and enforcement. * * *

The mandate of the 1965 Act was implemented by the gradual adoption of water quality standards. By 1972, states had adopted and obtained federal approval for their interstate standards, with a few exceptions. This "zoning" of both interstate and intrastate waters remains a significant legal tool.

While water quality standards evolved slowly under the auspices of the Federal Water Pollution Control Act, effluent standards were the preferred approach under a nineteenth century statute * * *. Section 13 of the Rivers and Harbors Act * * * flatly prohibits the discharging from a ship or shore installation into navigable waters of the United States "any refuse matter of any kind or description whatever other than that flowing from streets and sewers and passing therefrom in a liquid state." * * * A proviso states that the Secretary of the Army "may permit the deposit of any material above mentioned in navigable waters, within limits to be defined under conditions to be prescribed by him." Violations are enjoinable, and may be punished criminally. * * *

The water quality standards brought into being by the Federal Water Pollution Control Act and the effluent standards fixed by the Refuse Act Permit Program should be recognized as reflecting fundamentally conflicting regulatory philosophies. They offer, in substance, a repetition of the air pollution debate between the advocates of emission standards and the samplers of ambient air. Fundamentally, the competing schools disagree on whether uses that pollute water are just another economic activity or a form of moral turpitude. * * *

The water quality standards view of water pollution has many implications. It assumes a free use of water for waste disposal up to a point of "unreasonableness," however legally defined. It presupposes that the enforcement authority has the burden of proving that discharges harm marine resources or deter other water uses. * * * It insists that enforcement is a particularly local concern because the unique characteristics of the receiving water, the economics of the discharging plant, and even the prevailing political tolerance level are relevant to decisions to compel treatment or process change. Early versions of the Federal Water Pollution Control Act adhered closely to these premises.

The "no discharge" prohibitions of the Rivers and Harbors Act look the other way. They focus on the source—not the size, flow, and use of the receiving body of water. Pollution dilution is not part of the lexicon. The concept is absolutist. Moralism runs high. Rationalization about "reasonable" amounts of pollution is not easily reconciled with a statute declaring it a crime to dump "refuse of any kind or description whatever" into navigable waters. * * *

The 1972 Amendments represented a victory for the absolutists but not necessarily a defeat for the relativists. A compromise was struck, with the effluent standards assuming the dominant role and the water quality standards serving an important interstitial function. * * *

---

Read the following sections of the Clean Water Act

☐ § 101(a)(1)    ☐ § 301(a)    ☐ § 402(a)(1)    ☐ § 402(a)(2)

☐ § 402(b)*    ☐ § 402(d)(1)    ☐ § 402(d)(2)    ☐ § 502(6)

☐ § 502(7)    ☐ § 502(12)    ☐ § 502(14)    ☐ § 502(19)

*Omit the many subparts of § 402(b), which set forth a list of conditions similar to the items required for an acceptable SIP under CAA § 110(a)(2).

---

## C. NPDES PERMITS

The backbone of the Clean Water Act is the "National Pollutant Discharge Elimination System" [NPDES] permit program of § 402(a). Pause for a moment and consider how odd it is to use the phrase "discharge *elimination*." But in 1972, the words purported to mean what they said. *See* § 101(a)(1).

The threshold question is: who must obtain an NPDES Permit? One can only answer this question by taking a convoluted trip through several sections of the Act. Section 301(a) starts with the basic declaration that "the discharge of any pollutant by any person shall be unlawful." Section 402(a)(1) then indicates that an NPDES Permit must be obtained by any person who wishes to "discharge a pollutant." Does this mean that any person whose conduct "pollutes" a waterway must obtain such a permit?

Surprisingly, the answer is no. Section 502(12) has a peculiar definition of the term "discharge of a pollutant." Most important for our purposes is § 502(12)(A): "any addition of any pollutant to *navigable waters from any point source*" (emphasis supplied). Accordingly, no NPDES permit will be required unless three conditions are met: (1) the discharge must be from a point source; (2) it must be to navigable waters; and (3) it must involve the addition of a pollutant. We will explore the meaning of "navigable waters" and "addition of a pollutant" shortly, but for now, let's focus on the "point source" limitation. Consider the following questions, assuming in all cases that the receiving waters are unquestionably "navigable" within the meaning of the Act.

### Questions

1.   Farmer Smith owns a large cattle feedlot, housing 3,000 head of cattle. (A "feedlot" is a confined area used for the feeding and production of animals; the animals are penned up in such dense numbers that food must be provided where they stand.) Animal wastes are carried by rainwater from Farmer Smith's feedlot across gently sloping fields until they eventually wind up in the Scum River, located 3/4 mile away. Does Farmer Smith need an NPDES permit? Why or why not? *See* § 502(14).

2.   Farmer Jones owns 320 acres of rich farmland. She applies copious quantities of fertilizers and herbicides to increase the yield of her various crops. The farmland borders directly on the Scum River. Fertilizers and herbicides are periodically washed into the river by rainfall; indeed, that is one reason why the application rates for these products are quite high on Farmer Jones' land. Does Farmer Jones need an NPDES permit? Why or why not?

3.   Farmer Wilson owns 700 acres of farmland in an area of the country where rainfall is scarce. His operation involves heavy irrigation techniques. All irrigation water is eventually trapped in a series of "irrigation return" pipes, which collect the water not taken up by the crops. The irrigation return flow, heavily laced with fertilizers, herbicides, and salts, is directed by a series of pipes to one large discharge pipe, which returns the water to its original source—the Green River. Does Farmer Wilson need an NPDES permit? What if the water discharged through the pipe were merely rainwater—not irrigation water?

4.   The MegaWorld Shopping Center includes acres of asphalt-covered parking facilities. Rain runoff is collected throughout the parking lots and

diverted through pipes to the Moon River. Must the proprietors of the Shopping Center obtain an NPDES permit? Why or why not?

5. Atlas Metals Corporation operates a large metal finishing factory. All metal shavings and other plant wastes are discharged directly through floor drains to the municipal sewer system, where they are eventually transported to the Municipal Sewage Treatment Plant. After treatment, the Sewage Treatment Plant discharges effluent to the Wild River. This effluent contains heavy concentrations of lead, nickel, copper, and other metals from Atlas Metals, which have "passed through" the sewage treatment system. Must Atlas Metals obtain an NPDES permit? *See* § 307(b)(1).

## 1. POINT AND NONPOINT SOURCES

The following readings underscore the difference between "point sources" (requiring NPDES permits) and "nonpoint sources." The decision that a source is a "point source" is an important one, because the Act clearly contemplates that all point sources (other than a limited list of such sources exempted from the permit requirement) must engage in at least some treatment of the effluent to obtain a permit. *See* § 402(a).

# WILLIAM H. RODGERS, JR., 2 ENVIRONMENTAL LAW: AIR AND WATER
### §§ 4.9 (1986)

A nonpoint source, undefined but often used in the Act, "should be understood as any source of water pollution or pollutants not associated with a discrete conveyance. For simplicity, the universe of the causes of water pollution should be considered as covered fully by the categories of point and nonpoint sources." * * * Although information on the contributions to pollution loadings is skimpy, various estimates suggest "that nonpoint sources account for up to 99 percent of suspended solids and usually between 50 to 90 percent of other conventional pollutants." Even for toxics, the best estimates assign up to 50 percent of the problem to nonpoint sources.

Nonpoint source pollution is primarily responsible for the wholesale violation of water quality standards found in virtually all states. As a problem, it is "ranked first in 26 states and second in 13 others. Forty states reported that nonpoint sources need to be controlled if water quality is to continue to improve." The enormity of the challenge of nonpoint sources brings several responses. One is resignation and futility * * * .

The futility response was quick to assert itself in early litigation over the meaning of point source. EPA officials were concerned that the definition of "point source" was so broad the agency "may be forced to establish standards and issue permits for every pipe or ditch through which run-off is discharged into navigable waters, even where monitoring, measurement, and control techniques necessary to make this system of regulation work may not exist." To alleviate this administrative specter, EPA regulations excluded from the permit requirements a number of difficult-to-control point sources along with most discharges from agricultural and silvicultural activities without regard to whether they fell within the "point source" definition. This administrative exception to the Act was given short shrift by Judge Flannery, who decided that the permit program covers each "point source" as defined by Congress, not only major point sources, easily controlled point sources, or point sources in the traditional sense. *Natural Resources Defense Council v. Train*, 396 F.Supp. 1393 (D. D.C. 1975), *aff'd* 568 F.2d 1369 (D.C. Cir. 1977). The ruling imposed an enormous administrative burden on the EPA, requiring issuance of perhaps as many as 100,000 additional permits. * * * On appeal, the U.S. Court of Appeals for the District of Columbia essentially agreed, holding that administrative pleas of infeasibility were to be accommodated "by allowing general or area permits and by tolerating nonnumerical and descriptive obligations in those permits." * * *

It is evident that a source escaping the broad definition of "point source" is immune from important features of the Act, notably § 402 creating the National Pollutant Discharge Elimination System. * * * [T]he no-discharge policy and its implementing mechanism, the permit program, are directed only at point sources. Nonpoint sources, if covered at all, would be reached by the Rivers and Harbors Act of 1899, and other federal and state laws.

## U.S. v. PLAZA HEALTH LABORATORIES

3 F.3d 643 (2d Cir. 1993), *cert. denied*, 114 S.Ct. 2764 (1994)

Before OAKES, KEARSE, and PRATT, CIRCUIT JUDGES.

GEORGE C. PRATT, Circuit Judge

Defendant Geronimo Villegas appeals from a judgment * * * convicting him of two counts of knowingly discharging pollutants into the Hudson River in violation of the Clean Water Act ("CWA"). * * * Villegas was co-owner and vice president of Plaza Health Laboratories, Inc., a blood testing laboratory in Brooklyn, New York. On at least two occasions between April and September 1988, Villegas loaded containers of numerous vials of human blood generated from his business into his personal car, and drove to his residence * * * in Edgewater, New Jersey. Once at his condominium complex, Villegas removed the containers from his car and carried them to the edge of the Hudson River. On one occasion he carried two containers of the vials to the bulkhead that separates his condominium complex from the river, and placed them at low tide within a crevice in the bulkhead that was below the high water line.

On May 26, 1988, a group of eighth graders on a field trip * * * discovered numerous glass vials containing human blood along the shore. Some of the vials had washed up on the shore; many were still in the water. Some were cracked, although most remained sealed with stoppers in solid plastic containers or ziplock bags. Fortunately, no one was injured. That afternoon, New York City workers recovered approximately 70 vials from the area. * * * Ten of the retrieved vials contained blood infected with the hepatitis B virus. All of the vials recovered were eventually traced to Plaza Health Laboratories.

Based upon the May 1988 discovery of vials, Plaza Health Laboratories and Villegas were indicted on May 16, 1989, on two counts each of violating §§ 309(c)(2) and (3) of the Clean Water Act. * * * Counts II and IV of the superseding indictment charged Villegas with knowingly discharging pollutants from a "point source" without a permit. * * * [T]he jury found Villegas guilty on [both] counts. Renewing a motion made at trial, Villegas moved for a judgment of acquittal on all counts * * * . The district judge denied the motion * * * rejecting arguments that the act did not envision a human being as a "point source." * * *

Villegas contends that one element of the CWA crime, knowingly discharging pollutants from a "point source," was not established in his case. He argues that the definition of "point source," CWA § 502(14), does not include discharges that result from the individual acts of human beings. * * *

Reading § 301(a), the basic prohibition, and § 402(a)(1), the permit section, together, we can identify the basic rule, our rhumb line to clean waters, that, absent a permit, "the discharge of any pollutant by any person" is unlawful. CWA § 301(a). We must then adjust our rhumb line by reference to two key definitions—"pollutant" and "discharge." * * * "Discharge" * * * is "any addition of any pollutant to navigable waters from any point source * * * ." As applied to the facts of this case, then, the defendant "added" a "pollutant" (human blood in glass vials) to "navigable waters" (the Hudson River), and he did so without a permit. The issue, therefore, is whether his conduct constituted a "discharge," and that in turn depends on whether the addition of the blood to the Hudson River waters was "from any point source." * * *

During and after Villegas's trial, Judge Korman labored over how to define "point source" in this case. At one point he observed that the image of a human being is not "conjured up" by Congress's definition of "point source." Ultimately, he never defined the "point source" element but he did charge the jury:

> Removing pollutants from a container, and a vehicle is a container, parked next to a navigable body of water and physically throwing the pollutant into the water constitutes a discharge from a point source. * * *

As the parties have presented the issue to us in their briefs and at oral argument, the question is "whether a human being can be a point source." * * * [T]he problem [is] highlighted by the district court's analytical struggle to find somewhere in the Villegas transaction a "discernible, confined and discrete conveyance." Simply put, that problem is that this statute was never designed to address the random, individual polluter like Villegas. * * *

Human beings are not among the enumerated items that may be a "point source." Although by its terms the definition of "point source" is nonexclusive, the words used to define the term and the examples given ("pipe, ditch, channel, tunnel, conduit, well, discrete fissure," etc.) evoke images of physical structures and instrumentalities that systematically act as a means of conveying pollutants from an industrial source to navigable waterways. * * * Had Congress intended to punish any human being who polluted navigational waters, it could readily have said: "any person who places pollutants in navigable waters without a permit is guilty of a crime."

The Clean Water Act generally targets industrial and municipal sources of pollutants, as is evident from a perusal of its many sections. Consistent with this focus, the term "point source" is used throughout the statute, but invariably in sentences referencing industrial or municipal discharges. * * * As the statute stands today, the term "point source" is comprehensible only if it is held to the context of industrial and municipal discharges. * * * The legislative history of the CWA, while providing little insight into the meaning of "point source," confirms the act's focus on industrial polluters. * * *

We find no suggestion either in the act itself or in the history of its passage that Congress intended the CWA to impose criminal liability on an individual for the myriad, random acts of human waste disposal, for example, a passerby who flings a candy wrapper into the Hudson River, or a urinating swimmer. Discussions during the passage of the 1972 amendments indicate that Congress had bigger fish to fry. * * *

In sum, although Congress had the ability to so provide, § 502(14) of the CWA does not expressly recognize a human being as a "point source"; nor does the act make structural sense when one incorporates a human being into that definition. The legislative history of the act adds no light to the muddy depths of this issue, and cases urging a broad interpretation of the definition in the civil penalty context do not persuade us to do so here, where Congress has imposed heavy criminal sanctions. * * * We accordingly conclude that the term "point source" as applied to a human being is at best ambiguous.

In criminal prosecutions the rule of lenity requires that ambiguities in the statute be resolved in the defendant's favor. * * * [W]e conclude that the criminal provisions of the CWA did not clearly proscribe Villegas's conduct and did not accord him fair warning of the sanctions the law placed on that conduct. Under the rule of lenity, therefore, the prosecutions against him must be dismissed. * * *

OAKES, Circuit Judge, dissenting:

I begin with the obvious, in hopes that it will illuminate the less obvious: the classic point source is something like a pipe. This is, at least in part, because pipes and similar conduits are needed to carry large quantities of waste water, which represents a large proportion of the point source pollution problem. Thus, devices designed to convey large quantities of waste water from a factory or municipal sewage treatment facility are readily classified as point sources. Because not all pollutants are liquids, however, the statute and the cases make clear that means of conveying solid wastes to be dumped in navigable waters are also point sources. *See, e.g.*, CWA § 502(14) ("rolling stock," or railroad cars, listed as an example of a point source); *Avoyelles Sportsmen's League, Inc. v. Marsh*, 715 F.2d 897, 922 (5th Cir. 1983) (backhoes and bulldozers used to gather fill and deposit it on wetlands are point sources).

What I take from this look at classic point sources is that, at the least, an organized means of channeling and conveying industrial waste in quantity to navigable waters is a "discernible, confined and discrete conveyance." The case law is in accord * * * . Nonetheless, the term "point source" sets significant definitional limits on the reach of the Clean Water Act. Fifty percent or more of all water pollution is thought to come from nonpoint sources. S.Rep. 99-50, 99th Cong., 1st Sess. 8 (1985); William F. Pedersen, Jr., Turning the Tide on Water Quality, 15 Ecol. L.Q. 69, n.10 (1988). So, to further refine the definition of "point source," I consider what it is that the Act does not cover: nonpoint source discharges.

Nonpoint source pollution is, generally, runoff: salt from roads, agricultural chemicals from farmlands, oil from parking lots, and other substances washed by rain, in diffuse patterns, over the land and into navigable waters. The sources are many, difficult to identify and difficult to control. Indeed, an effort to greatly reduce nonpoint source pollution could require radical changes in land use patterns which Congress evidently was unwilling to mandate without further study. * * * Congress chose to regulate first that which could easily be regulated: direct discharges by identifiable parties, or point sources.

This rationale for regulating point and nonpoint sources differently—that point sources may readily be controlled and are easily attributable to a particular source, while nonpoint sources are more difficult to control without radical change, and less easily attributable, once they reach water, to any particular responsible party—helps define what fits within each category. * * *

While Villegas' activities were not prototypical point source discharges—in part because he was disposing of waste that could have been disposed of on land, and so did not need a permit or a pipe—they much more closely resembled a point source discharge than a nonpoint source discharge. First, Villegas and his lab were perfectly capable of avoiding discharging their waste into water: they were, in Professor Rodgers' terms, a "controllable" source.

Furthermore, the discharge was directly into water, and came from an identifiable point, Villegas. Villegas did not dispose of the materials on land, where they could be washed into water as nonpoint source pollution. \* \* \* I do not think it is necessary to determine whether it was Mr. Villegas himself who was the point source, or whether it was his car, the vials, or the bulkhead: in a sense, the entire stream of Mr. Villegas' activity functioned as a "discrete conveyance" or point source. The point is that the source of the pollution was clear, and would have been easy to control. Indeed, Villegas was well aware that there were methods of controlling the discharge (and that the materials were too dangerous for casual disposal): his laboratory had hired a professional medical waste handler. He simply chose not to use an appropriate waste disposal mechanism.

Villegas' method may have been an unusual one for a corporate officer, but it would undermine the statute—which, after all, sets as its goal the elimination of discharges, CWA § 301(a)—to regard as "ambiguous" a Congressional failure to list an unusual method of disposing of waste. I doubt that Congress would have regarded an army of men and women throwing industrial waste from trucks into a stream as exempt from the statute. \* \* \* I cannot see that one man throwing one day's worth of medical waste into the ocean differs (and indeed, with this type of pollution, it might be that only a few days' violations could be proven even if the laboratory regularly relied on Villegas to dispose of its waste by throwing it into the ocean). A different reading would encourage corporations perfectly capable of abiding by the Clean Water Act's requirements to ask their employees to stand between the company trucks and the sea, thereby transforming point source pollution (dumping from trucks) into nonpoint source pollution (dumping by hand). Such a method is controllable, easily identifiable, and inexcusable. To call it nonpoint source pollution is to read a technical exception into a statute which attempts to define in broad terms an activity which may be conducted in many different ways. \* \* \*

Having resorted to the language and structure, legislative history and motivating policies of the [CWA], I think it plain enough that Congress intended the statute to bar corporate officers from disposing of corporate waste into navigable waters by hand as well as by pipe. Further, I would note that this is not the sort of activity that Villegas could honestly have believed violated no statute, whether promulgated by federal, state, or local authorities. Thus, this is not a case in which the defendant had no fair warning that his actions were illegal. \* \* \*

# CONCERNED AREA RESIDENTS
## v. SOUTHVIEW FARM

### 34 F.3d 114 (2d Cir. 1994)

Before: OAKES and MINER, Circuit Judges, and CARTER, Senior District Judge.

OAKES, Senior Circuit Judge:

This is a citizen's suit under the Clean Water Act \* \* \*. The suit arises on account of the liquid manure spreading operations of a large dairy farm in western New York. * * * [T]he case proceeded to jury trial. * * * Following a jury verdict in plaintiffs' favor on five CWA violations and the state law trespass claim, the United States District Court for the Western District of New York, David Larimer, Judge, granted judgment to the defendants as a matter of law on the five CWA violations. * * * The court left standing the verdict and damages of $4,101 on the trespass count. * * *

The appeal by plaintiffs involves only the five CWA violations and raises anew the question what is a "point source" within the meaning of CWA § 502(14), a question this court touched upon in *United States v. Plaza Health Labs* * * *. The appeal also concerns whether the liquid manure spreading operations fell within the "agricultural stormwater discharges" exception to point source discharges under the Act. CWA § 502(14).

We now hold that the liquid manure spreading operations are a point source within the meaning of CWA section 502(14) because the farm itself falls within the definition of a concentrated animal feeding operation ("CAFO") and is not subject to the agricultural exemption.

Plaintiffs, who refer to themselves collectively as Concerned Area Residents for the Environment ("CARE"), are a group of land owners who live near Southview Farms, a dairy farm in the town of Castile, in Wyoming County, New York. Defendants are the farm itself, and Richard H. Popp, an individual. Southview Farm is one of the largest dairy farms in the State of New York. It employs twenty-eight full-time and nine part-time employees. As of 1992, it owned 1,100 crop acres and had an animal population of 1,290 head of mature cows with over 900 head of young cattle, heifers and calves, making a total of 2,200 animals.

Unlike old-fashioned dairy farms, Southview's operations do not involve pasturing the cows. Instead, the cows remain in their barns except during the three times per day milking procedure. Also unlike old-fashioned dairy farms where the accumulated manure was spread by a manure spreader, Southview's rather enormous manure operations are largely performed through the use of storage lagoons and liquid cow manure. The storage lagoons number five on the main farm property ("A" Farm). One four-acre manure storage lagoon has a capacity of approximately six-to-eight million gallons of liquid cow manure. * * *

Insofar as application of the manure as fertilizer to the land is concerned, there is a center pivot irrigation system for spreading liquid manure over the fields. The diameter of the circle of this irrigation system can be modified to conform to the field on which the application is being made. A series of pipes connects the pivot to the liquid manure storage lagoons. The pivot is self-propelled with the height of the arc from the manure spray being somewhere between 12 and 30 feet. * * *

It is significant to note, as previously stated, that the cows are not put out to pasture. The fields to which the manure is applied, as above indicated, are used for crops. The United States appears as amicus curiae in support of the appellants on the basis that, because the Southview operations involve more than 700 cattle, it is a facility which is defined in the regulations under the Act as a CAFO, and therefore one type of "point source" under the Act, thereby requiring a permit for discharges which was not obtained in this instance. As we have stated, the Act defines the term "point source" as including "any * * * concentrated animal feeding operation." CWA § 502(14). In this connection, the district court concluded that, as a matter of law, Southview was not a CAFO because crops are grown on a portion of the farm. The United States contends that Southview is a CAFO as a matter of law because crops are not grown in the feed lot in which the milking cows are confined. * * *

The July 13 violation, found by the jury but overturned by the district court, as we have said, occurred on field 104 on the Wyant property which shares the boundary line with Letchworth State Park. Field 104 contains a slew or swale which tends to collect liquid manure spread by Southview's tankers and conveys it through a pipe in a stonewall and through the stonewall itself into a ditch which runs for some length on the Southview property before it reaches the boundary of the state park.

On July 13, 1989, appellants Kirk Bly and Philip Karcheski observed the manure collecting in the slew or swale and flowing into the ditch which in turn flowed off of the Southview property into Letchworth State Park property, and, in turn, joined a stream which ultimately flowed into the Genesee River. * * *

The district court held and appellees contend that the July 13 discharge was not a point source discharge because the liquid simply and quite naturally flowed to and through the lowest areas of the field, and that the pollutants reached the stream that flows into the Genesee "in too diffuse a manner to create a point source discharge." The district court also suggested that the pollutants were not "collected" by human activity but in fact the opposite occurred in that the manure was dispersed over the ground. * * *

We believe that the swale coupled with the pipe under the stonewall leading into the ditch that leads into the stream was in and of itself a point source. As this court has previously noted, the definition of a point source is to be broadly interpreted. * * * Here, the liquid manure was collected and channelized through the ditch or depression in the swale of field 104 and thence into the ditch leading to the stream on the boundary of the Southview property as it adjoins Letchworth State Park. Nothing in *Plaza Health* is to the contrary. There the court simply refused to treat a human being as a "point source" under the criminal provisions of the Act by virtue of the rule of lenity. * * *

Moreover, we agree with the appellants that, alternatively, the manure spreading vehicles themselves were point sources. The collection of liquid manure into tankers and their discharge on fields from which the manure directly flows into navigable waters are point source discharges under the case law. * * * We agree with appellants that, while the statute does include an exception for "agricultural stormwater discharges," there can be no escape from liability for agricultural pollution simply because it occurs on rainy days. * * * We think the real issue is not whether the discharges occurred during rainfall or were mixed with rain water run-off, but rather, whether the discharges were the result of precipitation. * * *

Karcheski testified that, "after a rain[ ] and manure had been applied on the field, [the manure] was literally running off everywhere up and down those field-type areas." * * * We think the jury could properly find that the run-off was primarily caused by the over-saturation of the fields rather than the rain and that sufficient quantities of manure were present so that the run-off could not be classified as "stormwater." * * *

In short, we conclude with the United States as amicus, that Southview has an animal feeding lot operation with a tremendous number of cattle in a concentrated feeding facility in which no vegetation is grown; that operation in and of itself is a point source within the Clean Water Act and not subject to any agricultural exemption thereto.

## 2. NAVIGABLE WATERS

Once we have determined that a given source is a "point source," we must still decide whether its discharge is to "navigable waters" within the meaning of the Act; if not, no NPDES permit is required. CWA § 502(7) contains a rather peculiar definition of "navigable waters," which seems to strip any meaning from the word "navigable": "'navigable waters' means the waters of the United States, including the territorial seas." EPA has built on this definition in its regulations by defining "waters of the United States" in the following manner.

# EPA, NPDES DEFINITIONS AND GENERAL PROGRAM REQUIREMENTS
### 40 C.F.R. § 122.2 (1999)

"Waters of the United States or Waters of the U.S." means:

(a) All waters which are currently used, were used in the past, or may be susceptible to use in interstate or foreign commerce, including all waters which are subject to the ebb and flow of the tide;

(b) All interstate waters, including interstate "wetlands;"

(c) All other waters such as intrastate lakes, rivers, streams (including intermittent streams), mudflats, sandflats, "wetlands," sloughs, prairie potholes, wet meadows, playa lakes, or natural ponds the use, degradation, or destruction of which would affect or could affect interstate or foreign commerce including any such waters:

    (1) Which are or could be used by interstate or foreign travelers for recreational or other purposes;

    (2) From which fish or shellfish are or could be taken and sold in interstate or foreign commerce; or

(3) Which are used or could be used for industrial purposes by industries in interstate commerce;

(d) All impoundments of waters otherwise defined as waters of the United States under this definition;

(e) Tributaries of waters identified in paragraphs (a)-(d) of this definition;

(f) The territorial sea; and

(g) "Wetlands" adjacent to waters (other than waters that are themselves wetlands) identified in paragraphs (a)-(f) of this definition.

Waste treatment systems, including treatment ponds or lagoons designed to meet the requirements of CWA (other than cooling ponds as defined in 40 CFR 423.11(m) which also meet the criteria of this definition) are not waters of the United States.

### *Questions*

The City of Aurora, Minnesota, is located on the Iron Range and has a population of 2,500. The city's water supply consists of an abandoned open pit mine (the St. James Pit) which has filled up with rainwater, creating a moderate-sized "lake." The Aurora drinking water treatment plant filters the pit water to remove suspended solids, particularly iron particles, which would impair the quality of the finished tap water. Every two days, the treatment plant must unclog the sand filters by "backwashing"—sending finished water backwards through the sand filters to remove the solids which have accumulated on the filters and flush them away. The backwash water is discharged through a pipe into the St. James Pit. This backwash water has very high concentrations of total suspended solids (primarily iron). You should assume, for purposes of this question, that this backwash constitutes the "discharge of a pollutant" within the meaning of the Act. (Discharges that are high in total suspended solids may interfere with aquatic life.) The city could treat this backwash water by installing a 28,000 gallon holding tank or basin, at a cost of $10,000 to $20,000. The real question is whether the receiving waters—the St. James Pit—qualify as "navigable waters" within the meaning of § 502(7). There are no known outlets from the Pit. It is never used for boating, although teenagers have been known to swim in it on occasion. No one catches fish from the Pit and distributes them in interstate commerce. However, the Bide-a-Wee Motel in downtown Aurora has 13 units and out-of-state residents unquestionably stay in that motel on occasion and drink water that has been drawn from the St. James Pit.

1. Must an NPDES permit be obtained for this backwashing activity? *See* 40 C.F.R. § 122.2(c)(1), *supra.*

2. Would your answer be different if you were considering the discharge of cyanide into the St. James Pit by an adjacent company, which manufactures widgets sold only in *intra*state commerce? It is clear, is it not, that the question of whether the St. James Pit is a "navigable water" cannot be made to turn on the nature of the pollutant?

# NOTE ON NAVIGABLE WATERS

We have seen that CWA §§ 301(a), 402(a) and 502(12) effectively prohibit the "discharge of any pollutant" into "navigable waters" from a "point source" without a permit, and that the phrase "navigable waters" is defined by § 502(7) to mean "waters of the United States * * * ." We have also examined the EPA's broad definition in 40 C.F.R. § 122.2 of "waters of the United States"—which uses the interstate commerce power to reach intrastate bodies of water having a connection with interstate commerce.

The statutory phrases "navigable waters" and "waters of the United States" have also been read so broadly that there need not necessarily be any water. The court in *U.S. v. Phelps Dodge Corp.*, 391 F. Supp. 1181 (D. Ariz. 1975), explained:

> For the purposes of this Act to be effectively carried into realistic achievement, the scope of its control must extend to all pollutants which are discharged into *any waterway*, including normally dry arroyos, where any water which might flow therein could reasonably end up in any body of water, to which or in which there is some public interest, including underground waters.

> The intention of Congress was to eliminate or to reduce as much as possible *all water pollution* throughout the United States both surface and underground. * * *

> Thus a legal definition of "navigable waters" or "waters of the United States" within the scope of the Act includes any waterway within the United States also including normally dry arroyos through which water may flow, where such water will ultimately end up in public waters such as a river or stream, tributary to a river or stream, lake, reservoir, bay, gulf, sea or ocean either within or adjacent to the United States.

391 F. Supp. at 1187.

"Navigable waters" has been interpreted broadly in another Clean Water Act context, involving "dredge and fill" permits. The Act requires a § 404 permit (as opposed to an NPDES permit) from the Corps of Engineers to discharge dredged or fill material into navigable water. The § 404 wetlands program has been enormously controversial, with landowners detesting its interference with their property rights. *See generally* William H. Rodgers, Jr., Environmental Law § 4.6 (2d ed. 1994). The Corps of Engineers has defined "navigable waters," for § 404 purposes, to include "wetlands * * * the use, degradation or destruction of which" could adversely affect interstate or foreign commerce. 33 C.F.R. § 328.3(a)(3) (1999).

In *U.S. v. Riverside Bayview Homes*, 474 U.S. 121 (1985), the Supreme Court upheld the Corps' assertion that 80 acres of low-lying marshy land near the shore of an inland lake was subject to the § 404 permit requirement, even though the property was *not* subject to frequent flooding by adjacent navigable waters (the lake), and even though the source of the saturation on the disputed lands was groundwater. In reversing the Sixth Circuit's more narrow interpretation and upholding the Corps' construction of the statute, the Court said:

> On a purely linguistic level, it may appear unreasonable to classify "lands," wet or otherwise, as "waters." Such a simplistic response, however, does justice neither to the problem faced by the Corps in defining the scope of its authority under § 404(a) nor to the realities of the problem of water pollution that the Clean Water Act was intended to combat. In determining the limits of its power to regulate discharges under the Act, the Corps must necessarily choose some point at which water ends and land begins. Our common experience tells us that this is often no easy task: the transition from water to solid ground is not necessarily or even typically an abrupt one. Rather, between open waters and dry land may lie shallows, marshes, mudflats, swamps, bogs— in short, a huge array of areas that are not wholly aquatic but nevertheless fall far short of being dry land. Where on this continuum to find the limit of "waters" is far from obvious. * * *

474 U.S. at 132.

The result of the foregoing interpretations is that the EPA, the Corps of Engineers, and the courts will sometimes find navigable waters to exist, even where there is neither navigability nor water.

## 3. ADDITION OF A POLLUTANT

Even where there is a "point source" sending effluent to a "navigable water," no NPDES permit will be needed unless there is a "discharge of [a] pollutant." *See* §§ 301(a), 402(a)(1). Section 502(6) defines "pollutant," § 502(19) defines "pollution," and § 502(12) defines "discharge of a pollutant" to mean "any *addition* of any pollutant to navigable waters from any point source" (emphasis added). Consider the following questions.

### *Questions*

1.   Whamo Widget Co. draws its process water from the Plum River. The *influent* (the raw water coming in), has certain background levels of metals. The effluent, which is not treated, has precisely the same level of metals; in other words, these background contaminants pass right through the plant—no extra substances are added to the water. Must Whamo Widget obtain an NPDES permit? Why or why not? *See* § 502(12).

2.   Gigantic Gizmo Co. operates a facility adjacent to the Whamo Widget facility on the Plum River; it uses the same contaminated influent as process water. However, the process of making gizmos requires this company to purify the intake water by removing the metals. Through a technological process, the metal contaminants are diverted to a much more concentrated stream—for every 1,000 gallons coming into the plant, 999 pure gallons go to the gizmo assembly line, and one gallon of highly contaminated spin-off goes to a sump. Gigantic Gizmo decides to send both the purified process water and the sump residue back to the

Plum River. Does the Company's conduct involve "pollution," within the meaning of CWA § 502(19)? Must the Company obtain an NPDES permit? Does it make any difference whether it mixes the contaminants and the purified water prior to discharge? Why or why not?

3. The Minneapolis Drinking Water Treatment Plant provides finished drinking water for approximately one-half million people. Thousands of gallons of raw water are drawn up each minute through large intake structures located on the Mississippi River. This raw water contains sand and other suspended solids, which are collected in large settling basins in the intake structure. Periodically, the plant "backwashes" up to 800 tons of collected sand, returning it to the river. Does the backwash qualify as the "discharge of a pollutant"? Does it matter that the Army Corps of Engineers engages in a continuous dredging program to keep the Mississippi channel sufficiently deep to permit the passage of barges and other river-going vessels?

4. Would it matter, in the preceding paragraph, if the only reasonable alternative to the current sand backwashing activity were to pump the sand up a steep cliff to a land disposal site? Suppose it would cost the facility $10,000 per year to pump the waste sand up the hill, and it costs $1,000 per year for the Corps of Engineers to dredge the sand out of the river channel. Do these relative costs affect your judgment about whether the facility is engaging in a "discharge of a pollutant?" Would your judgment be affected if the relative costs were reversed?

## D. FEDERAL-STATE RELATIONS

## WILLIAM H. RODGERS, JR., 2 ENVIRONMENTAL LAW: AIR AND WATER

### § 4.26 (1986)

The NPDES program anticipated initial federal administration and a gradual turnover of authority to states demonstrating a capacity to administer their own programs, subject theoretically to a withdrawal of approval if a state's program fell short of legal requirements. Approval of state water pollution permit programs, not unlike approval of the implementation plans under the Clean Air Act, is dependent upon a demonstration of "adequate authority" in several respects, including the power to issue permits and to enforce them. * * * [T]he NPDES program in short order became largely state-administered and state-defined. * * *

The procedures for withdrawal of state programs would be suitable for the Nuremburg trials, and will be invoked only upon epochal occasions. A withdrawal of authority, or even the suggestion of it, is so demeaning and disruptive as to be eagerly avoided by both governments that are attuned to the necessities of coexistence. * * *

The dignity of any delegation is linked closely to the degree of supervision * * *. That EPA retains significant control over individual

NPDES permit decisions is confirmed by the requirement that the states transmit for review copies of applications and proposed permits and by the invitation to EPA to disapprove in writing the issuance of any permit as being outside the guidelines and requirements of the Act. § 402(d)(2). * * * The extensive procedural drumbeating that must attend a veto makes the action look like a withdrawal of program approval, and therefore something to be shunned. * * *

The counterpart of the federal veto power is found in § 401(a)(1). This section requires applicants for any *federal* license or permit who wish to pursue activities that may pollute to secure a certification from the state that the discharge "will comply" with applicable effluent limitations and water quality standards. * * * These certification requirements * * * add "muscle to the no-preemption pretensions of § 510."

### Questions

1.　You represent a company that is unquestionably discharging pollutants from a point source into a navigable water. The company does not yet have an NPDES permit. Obviously, the company must apply for such a permit immediately. Where is such an application to be filed? What information must be included in the application? Why?

2.　Suppose the EPA issues a permit that is silent on one or more pollutants in your client's discharge. Is your client's continued discharging of such unnamed pollutants lawful under the Clean Water Act? Why or why not? Should it make a difference if one or more of those pollutants was never disclosed in your client's permit application?

3.　How does the permit issuing authority go about the process of selecting effluent limitation numbers for things like $BOD_5$, TSS, pH, and the like? Does this method of selecting effluent limitation values make sense? Why or why not?

## E. PERMIT CONDITIONS

The most important aspect of the NPDES permit program consists of the *obligations* imposed on permittees, in the form of conditions set forth in the permits. The study of these conditions is a complicated undertaking. The effluent limitations, in particular, are highly varied and complicated.

## 1. TECHNOLOGY-BASED EFFLUENT LIMITATIONS

The Clean Water Act is a mass of contradictions, but the core of the NPDES permit program consists of the requirement that various *technology-based* standards—"best practicable treatment" (BPT), "best available treatment" (BAT), and the like—be met by industrial and municipal point source dischargers by specified deadlines. Note how different this is from the Clean Air Act, which has as its core nationally promulgated ambient air quality standards that must be attained by whatever means necessary. To be sure, the Clean Air Act regime does include technology-based standards as well—such as the new auto emission limitations and the new source performance standards—but they are designed primarily to assist in achieving the ambient air standards.

Professors Menell and Stewart point out a fundamental difference between the "technology-forcing" aspects of the Clean Water Act and those of the Clean Air Act :

> In many instances, workable air pollution control technology * * * is not available in a purely engineering sense. By contrast, engineering *is* presently available to turn all point source discharges of water pollution into distilled drinking water, achieving the [CWA's] stated goal of zero discharge. However, the costs of installing the requisite engineering would be enormous—trillions of dollars. In the absence of controlling federal ambient standards * * * EPA must somehow weigh the costs and benefits of different levels of control in establishing effluent limitations.

Peter S. Menell & Richard B. Stewart, Environmental Law and Policy (1994). Given this observation, the name of the game in setting effluent limitations under the Clean Water Act is economics: what will it cost? The statute gives very poor guidance about how the EPA is to factor costs into the various BPT, BAT, and other technology-based standards.

The establishment of technology-based standards requires extensive knowledge of technological options. EPA divided industrial point source dischargers into almost 500 different subcategories and sought to learn intricate details about the manufacturing operations and control technologies for hundreds industrial processes. Because it did not have sufficient resources to do this on its own, the agency hired consulting firms, including—because of their expertise—firms closely associated with the industry being studied. Often the effluent limitations resulting from this mechanism were not promulgated within the statutory deadlines and could not withstand judicial scrutiny in any event. The difficulties mirrored those encountered in *Portland Cement Association v. Ruckelshaus, see* page 350, *supra*, but were even greater, because the Clean Water Act standards apply not only to *new* sources (as was the case in *Portland Cement*), but also to *existing* sources.

Does the Clean Water Act really intend that uniform national effluent limitations should be met by all industrial dischargers in a given source category, even if the discharge of less-thoroughly controlled effluents by a specific factory would impose no harm on the receiving waters? If so, the Act seems to be ordering treatment for treatment's sake. Professors Stewart and Krier suggest that "the economic waste generated by the use of uniform effluent limitations * * * certainly run[s] into many billions of dollars." Richard B. Stewart & James E. Krier, Environmental Law and Policy 517 (2d ed. 1978). Consider the following case.

# WEYERHAEUSER CO. v. COSTLE

### 590 F.2d 1011 (D.C. Cir. 1978)

Before McGOWAN, TAMM, and RICHEY. * * *

McGOWAN, Circuit Judge:

Under the aegis of the [CWA] * * * the Environmental Protection Agency has embarked upon a step-by-step process of issuing effluent limitations for each industry that discharges pollutants into the waters of the United States. By these consolidated petitions, members of one such industry, American pulp and paper makers, challenge the validity of EPA regulations limiting the 1977-83 effluent discharges of many pulp, paper, and paperboard mills. * * * We are satisfied that EPA properly construed and rationally exercised the authority delegated to it by Congress and that, with one exception, it did so according to the appropriate procedures. Accordingly, we uphold the resulting effluent limitations in all but one instance. * * *

According to section 301(b), the first set of regulations must limit discharges between July 2, 1977 and July 1, 1983, inclusive, to levels characteristic of point sources utilizing "BPCTCA," i.e., the "best practicable control technology currently available." § 301(b)(1)(A). The second set applies thereafter and is defined in terms of the more restricted levels of discharges from point sources using "BATEA," i.e., the "best available technology economically achievable." § 301(b)(2)(A). * * *

The regulations at issue in this case are the result of a rulemaking process developed by the Agency over the past six years for promulgating industry-wide effluent limitations * * *. The procedures for these regulations began in early 1973 when EPA divided the American pulp and paper industry into two segments for purposes of establishing 1977 and 1983 effluent limitations. In "Phase I" of its rulemaking effort for the industry, it proposed, received several tiers of comments on, and promulgated 1977 and 1983 limitations for the "unbleached" segment of the industry, which produces unbleached pulp and paper. * * * This Court reviewed and upheld those regulations in full in 1976 * * *.

Promulgation of "Phase II" regulations for the apparently larger, "bleached" segment of the paper industry did not proceed with the same dispatch as in Phase I. * * *

Some of the paper mills that must meet the effluent limitations under review discharge their effluents into the Pacific Ocean. Petitioners contend that the ocean can dilute or naturally treat effluent, and that EPA must take this capacity of the ocean ("receiving water capacity") into account in a variety of ways.[40] They urge what they term "common

---

[40] Some petitioners contend that EPA should have taken receiving water capacity into account in setting pollutant parameters. They argue that the Agency should not have considered BOD as such a parameter because the ocean has so much dissolved oxygen that wastes with high BOD have negligible impact and that it should not have considered pH as a parameter because ocean salts buffer waste acidity.

sense," i.e., that because the amounts of pollutant involved are small in comparison to bodies of water as vast as Puget Sound or the Pacific Ocean, they should not have to spend heavily on treatment equipment, or to increase their energy requirements and sludge levels, in order to treat wastes that the ocean could dilute or absorb.

EPA's secondary response to this claim was that pollution is far from harmless, even when disposed of in the largest bodies of water. As congressional testimony indicated, the Great Lakes, Puget Sound, and even areas of the Atlantic Ocean have been seriously injured by water pollution. Even if the ocean can handle ordinary wastes, ocean life may be vulnerable to toxic compounds that typically accompany those wastes. In the main, however, EPA simply asserted that the issue of receiving water capacity could not be raised in setting effluent limitations because Congress had ruled it out. We have examined the previous legislation in this area, and the 1972 Act's wording, legislative history, and policies, as underscored by its 1977 amendments. These sources, which were thoroughly analyzed in a recent opinion of the administrator of the Agency, fully support EPA's construction of the Act. They make clear that based on long experience, and aware of the limits of technological knowledge and administrative flexibility, Congress made the deliberate decision to rule out arguments based on receiving water capacity. * * *

[B]y eliminating the issue of the capacity of particular bodies of receiving water, Congress made nationwide uniformity in effluent regulation possible. Congress considered uniformity vital to free the states from the temptation of relaxing local limitations in order to woo or keep industrial facilities. In addition, national uniformity made pollution clean-up possible without engaging in the divisive task of favoring some regions of the country over others. * * *

More fundamentally, the new approach implemented changing views as to the relative rights of the public and of industrial polluters. Hitherto, the right of the polluter was pre-eminent, unless the damage caused by pollution could be proven. Henceforth, the right of the public to a clean environment would be pre-eminent, unless pollution treatment was impractical or unachievable. * * *

The Act was passed with an expectation of "mid-course corrections" * * * and in 1977 Congress amended the Act, although generally holding to the same tack set five years earlier. * * * Notably, during those five years, representatives of the paper industry had appeared before Congress and urged it to change the Act and to incorporate receiving water capacity as a consideration. * * * Nonetheless, Congress was satisfied with this element of the statutory scheme. * * * [I]t resolved in the recent amendments to continue regulating discharges into all receiving waters alike.

Our experience with litigation under the Act, and particularly with this case, emphasizes the weight of Congress' policies. Even without receiving water capacity as an issue to delay it, EPA was late in promulgating these regulations. * * * Historically, the paper industry itself, and particularly the sulfite process sector, avoided the impact of regulation because of the difficulty of proving that its discharges adversely affected receiving water. * * *

Under the new statutory scheme, Congress clearly intended us to avoid such problems of proof so that a set of regulations with enforceable impact is possible. The dangers of ignoring this congressional mandate are clearly revealed by the one experiment in the Act with allowing consideration of receiving water capacity. As we have noted, thermal pollution regulation is the only area where the 1972 Act explicitly allowed receiving water capacity to continue as an issue. In reviewing the results of that experiment during consideration of the recent amendments to the Act, Congress found that the water capacity issue had led to a regulatory breakdown. "Heat has thus become an unregulated pollutant, clearly not the intent of the Congress. * * * That limited exemption has been turned into a gaping loophole." S.Rep. No. 370, 95th Cong., 1st Sess. 8, Reprinted in (1977) U.S. Code Cong. & Admin. News, pp. 4326, 4334. Given the clarity of Congress' desire not to allow the receiving water capacity loophole to engulf its overall regulatory efforts in this area, we affirm the Agency's refusal to consider water quality in setting its limitations.

**Table 11-1**
Technology-Based Effluent Limitations
and Compliance Deadlines

| Source | 1972 Act | 1977 Amendments | 1987 Amendments |
|---|---|---|---|
| Industrial Facilities | BPT by 1977<br><br>BAT by 1983 | For toxics BAT by 1984 or within 3 years<br><br>For conventional pollutants BCT by 1984 | BAT as soon as possible, within 3 years and no later than 3/3/89 |
| | | *1981 Amendments* | |
| POTWs | Secondary treatment by 1977<br><br>Advanced treatment by 1983 | Secondary treatment by 1988<br><br>Advanced treatment requirement eliminated | |

Source: Adapted from R. Percival, et al., Environmental Regulation: Law, Science, and Policy 881 (1992) and from Z. Plater, et al., Environmental Law and Policy: Nature, Law, and Society 285 (Supp. 1994)

## 2.  VARIETIES OF DISCHARGERS AND STANDARDS

In trying to sort out the Clean Water Act's confusing varieties of effluent limitations, it will help to bear two things in mind. First, the Act clearly distinguishes *industrial* sources from *municipal* sources; different limitations are to be established for these two types of sources. The municipal sources that the Act has in mind are Publicly Owned Treatment Works (POTWs), which handle domestic sewage as well as the wastes of those industries that discharge to the public system.

Second, you should recognize that the Act contains a series of commands for ever-tightening controls; the basic model of the Act is seen in the requirement that industries treat their wastes with BPT technology by 1977 and with BATEA technology by 1983. Unfortunately, this rather simple dichotomy blossomed in the 1977 Amendments to a confusing array of technology-based standards. **Table 11-1** depicts the most significant of the Clean Water Act's technology-based effluent limitation requirements and their deadlines.

## 3. INDUSTRIAL POINT SOURCE EFFLUENT LIMITATIONS

Because POTW dischargers pose unique problems that must be addressed separately, we begin our examination of the effluent limitations by considering *industrial* dischargers. Some of the points discussed in the following readings (such as intake pollutant credits, upsets, bypasses, and permit stability) are also relevant to POTW sources.

It is important to understand that effluent limitations are hammered out at a national level for each point source category and subcategory. For example, 40 C.F.R. Part 425 sets forth the effluent limitations (or "guidelines") for the leather tanning and finishing point source category, which is itself broken down into nine subcategories, based on the type of processing involved (e.g., the "hair pulp, chrome tan, retan-wet finish subcategory"). *See* 4 [Federal Regulations] Env. Rep. (BNA) 135:0581-588 (1987). These regulations specify maximum daily (and monthly average) discharge rates for $BOD_5$, TSS (total suspended solids), oil and grease, total chromium—expressed in kilograms per thousand kilograms of raw material—and pH. The task of any specific permit writer is, theoretically, to find the correct source category and subcategory in the EPA regulations and crank the pre-established values into the permit.

## WILLIAM H. RODGERS, JR., 2 ENVIRONMENTAL LAW: AIR AND WATER

§§ 4.28-4.29 (1986)

As originally constructed in 1972, the Act envisaged two giant technological steps in five year increments (BPT by 1977, BATEA by 1983) closing in on the no-discharge goal of 1985. * * *

### BPT AND FUNDAMENTALLY DIFFERENT FACTORS "VARIANCES"

As a general matter, the 1977 "best practicable" and the 1984/87 "best available" effluent limitations for existing industrial sources are defined by regulation prior to the issuance of a permit to an individual source. This means that claims of economic or technological infeasibility usually have no place in a permit proceeding since they involve a challenge to the underlying regulations. * * * [T]he Supreme Court made clear in *EPA v. National Crushed Stone Ass'n.*, 449 U.S. 64, 76 (1980), that the statute did not anticipate an escape from the BPT limitations for individual dischargers unable to afford the cost of control. * * *

The opinion in *National Crushed Stone Ass'n* approves an administrative variance if the discharger demonstrates "that the 'factors relating to the equipment or facilities involved, the process applied, or other such factors relating to such discharger are fundamentally different from the factors considered in the establishment of the guidelines.'" This sort of provision has been for the most part favorably received in the courts of appeals, and is easily defended. Rather than a variance, an acknowledgment of circumstances "fundamentally different" is better viewed as a declaration of inapplicability * * * [of] standards [to] a facility of a different species from the one considered [in rulemaking]. * * * [I]t is evident that the permit issuer is without authority to excuse technological controls because of depressed conditions within a particular geographical region or because receiving water conditions render the required controls superfluous or wasteful. * * *

Any judgment about whether a particular facility is "fundamentally different" from the one the rulemaker had in mind requires a messy reference back to determine the scope of the initial decision. The discharger has the burden of proving that its facility is "fundamentally different," and it is not enough to show some unique features or that a facility like yours won a variance somewhere else. * * *

### EXCURSIONS, UPSETS, AND BYPASSES

[There has been] debate over whether the permits (and the regulations controlling the permit provisions) must include some allowance for normal system failure. Usually included on a list of breakdowns are *excursions*, a bureaucratic euphemism denoting "small" violations of one kind or another; *upsets* where temporary noncompliance is beyond the control of the operator; and *bypasses* that include intentional diversions of waste streams for maintenance or more dire emergencies. Putting aside the countless nice differences between good excuses and bad ones (fires, floods, strikes, power failures, unexpected inflows, variations in feedstock, sabotage, homicide of the operators, etc.), the question boils down to whether the permits may require a perfection of performance unknown in the annals of human technology. * * * [A] permit that brooks no nonsense in this context can be described as preventing infinitesimal pollution at extraordinary cost. * * *

[I]t deserves emphasis that issues of extraordinary or improbable performance can be accommodated (or ignored) across the spectrum of pollution regulation. The ambient air standards often are written to forgive one formal violation, not to mention short term "excursions" that can be washed out by averaging exercises. In rulemakings, EPA often must decide whether to consider or put aside arguably "unrepresentative" performance data from plants in the throes of an upset or at least a very bad day. * * * Monitoring and enforcement policies invariably involve averaging exercises where violations here and there (from upsets and bypasses) are submerged in big picture analyses.

TECHNOLOGY TRANSFER: ACHIEVABILITY

For purposes of regulating industrial sources * * * the "best technology" performance standards can be described as progressing up four steps of a ladder, "with BPT as an initial standard for industry, BCT a smidgen tougher, BATEA tougher yet, and the new source standards [NSPS] the toughest of all." The EPA rulemakings on these subjects have been thoroughly tested in the courts, so we are dealing in many respects with a mature body of law. * * *

[T]he 1977 BPT standard normally "is based on the average performances of the best existing plants." * * * "[I]f pollution is to be diminished, limitations based on BPT must forbid the level of effluent produced by the most pollution-prone segment of the industry, that segment not measuring up to 'the average of the best existing performance.' So understood, the statute contemplated regulations that would require a substantial number of point sources with the poorest performances either to conform to BPT standards or to cease production." *EPA v. National Crushed Stone Ass'n*, 449 U.S. 64, 76 (1980). * * *

Under the 1983 (now 1984/87) "best available" standard, the Administrator clearly must push for the adoption of technology not in routine use and often not in use at all. * * * If industry performance was a factor at all, it was only the "best performer" that represented the "minimum" demands of the 1983 (now 1984/87) standard. The agency, indeed, may look beyond the "best performer" and beyond a pilot plant to "technologies that have not been applied as long as the record demonstrates that there is a reasonable basis to believe that the technology will be available by [1984/87]." Another "basic difference" between the 1977 and 1984/87 standards is that the more stringent of the two requires that "the total plant" be considered, not only "the control techniques used at the actual discharge of the point source." Thus, the 1984/87 "best available" standard is more demanding because it depends less on actual use, relies more on predictions and guesses about developments or transfers of technology, and imposes a stronger obligation to look beyond end-of-the-pipe controls and to consider more profound revisions in plant processes. * * *

## 4.　CREDIT FOR POLLUTED INTAKE WATER

# WILLIAM H. RODGERS, JR., 2 ENVIRONMENTAL LAW: AIR AND WATER

### § 4.30 (1986)

EPA's general NPDES regulations allow dischargers some "credit" to "the extent that pollutants in the intake water which are limited in the permit are not removed by the treatment technology employed by the discharger." The idea, simply put, is to excuse the discharger from the faults of the world outside. * * *

The puzzling ambiguities of this issue are scarcely touched by the reported judicial decisions. In statutory terms, pass-through pollutants certainly can yield "pollution" as the term is understood, so long as some people somewhere are responsible for it. *See* § 502(19). The requirement that a point source contribute an "addition" of a pollutant to the water is satisfied if the point source "itself physically introduces a pollutant into water from the outside world." On this reading, it would appear that a source discharging pollutants drawn from its intake waters would be functionally indistinguishable from the municipal sewage treatment plants that are routinely held accountable for toxics slipped into their effluent by uninvited and unwelcome suppliers.

Nor, indeed, would universal sympathy be extended to claims that polluted intake water is something "beyond the control" of the discharger. Economists would remind us, no doubt, that process water is just another input for the manufacturer, and you pay for what you get. There is industrial grade sulfuric acid on the market that may go begging for buyers because it is contaminated with heavy metals or other toxics that quickly would become big problems for the user. It might be said that the buyer (or taker) of bad water, like the user of low-grade acid or dirty coal, has made a production decision sufficient to invite cleanup responsibilities. * * * But none of this is fully responsive to the intuitive appeal of arguments that intake water quality should be excluded from the account of the discharger. * * * Yet even the hardest case—say, the drawing of a process water from the muddy Mississippi—does not appear to sustain a legal exemption for polluted intake waters. The act of returning the sediments where they came from would appear to be sufficient human intervention to give rise to "pollution" * * *. It is by no means clear, of course, that EPA's intake water provisions will be seen in this light or defended in this manner.

## 5.  PERMIT APPLICATION DISCLOSURES AND "NO-STANDARD" STANDARDS

# WILLIAM H. RODGERS, JR.,
# 2 ENVIRONMENTAL LAW: AIR AND WATER

### § 4.30 (1986)

At one time EPA considered requiring all applicants for NPDES permits "to characterize the amount and nature of *all* pollutants in each waste stream as completely as currently available analytical methodologies allow." Another possibility is to require information on only *specified* pollutants, which cuts down on knowledge but with obvious savings in analytical laboratory analyses. The EPA has chosen the latter approach * * *.

Whatever the approach adopted, it is evident that a gap appears between that which is reported and that which is discharged. Some constituents of the effluent could be known if looked for, some could be looked for if known, and some would be unknown even if looked for. In short, knowledge of effluent characteristics runs up against the familiar barriers of economic and technical feasibility.

The more interesting question is the extent to which approximate information in an application can buy an *immunity* in the permit. The answer seems to be that the immunity extends to the extent of the application *disclosures* and no further. Section 402(a) of the Act authorizes EPA to issue "a permit for the discharge of any pollutant, or combination of pollutants, notwithstanding" the generic prohibition against all discharges in § 301(a).

There is nothing in Section 402(a) to suggest that pollutants not named, or those undiscovered or unknown, are approved by the mere issuance of the permit. * * * It is thus a reasonably safe bet that the discharge of any pollutant not specifically permitted is unlawful.

May the permit issuer opt for a no-standard standard [a provision authorizing the discharge of a pollutant without placing any limits on its concentration or volume] and thus endorse a practice that would be a criminal offense but for this official nod? The answer appears to be "yes," although it is clear that the permit-approved discharges must meet the "applicable requirements" of several sections of the Act. This calls for, among other things, compatibility with state water quality standards and compliance with the various "best technology" tests. * * * More than a little process attention would have to be invested to convince a court that a no-standard standard, call it a full-discharge standard, is compatible with the no-discharge goals of the Act.

### Notes and Questions

The Second Circuit concluded in *Atlantic States Legal Foundation v. Eastman Kodak Co.*, 12 F.3d 353 (2d Cir. 1993), *cert. denied*, 115 S.Ct. 62 (1994), that the discharge of pollutants not listed in the permit is not unlawful under the CWA. Eastman Kodak had described estimated discharges of 164 substances in its permit application, and the permit established specific effluent limitations for approximately 25 pollutants. The citizen group plaintiff alleged that Kodak had discharged approximately 300,000 pounds of unpermitted pollutants in each of the last four years, including many substances listed as toxic chemicals in § 313(c) of the Emergency Planning and Community Right-to-Know Act. The Court of Appeals affirmed the district court's conclusion that "neither the CWA nor the federal regulations implementing it prohibit the discharge of pollutants not specifically assigned effluent limitations in an NPDES * * * permit." *Id.* at 356. Is this a sensible reading of §§ 301(a) and 402(a)? Why or why not?

## 6.  PERMIT STABILITY AND DURATION

# WILLIAM H. RODGERS, JR.,
## 2 ENVIRONMENTAL LAW: AIR AND WATER
### § 4.30 (1986)

The question of the scope of immunity provided by a permit is addressed in § 402(k) of the Act, which states that "compliance with a permit issued pursuant to this section shall be deemed compliance, for purposes of §§ 309 and 505, with §§ 301, 302, 306, 307, and 403, except any standard imposed under § 307 for a toxic pollutant injurious to human health." The purpose of the provision, according to the 1972 House Report, "is to assure that the mere promulgation of any effluent limitation or other limitation, a standard, or a thermal discharge regulation, by itself will not subject a person holding a valid permit to prosecution. However, once such requirement is actually made a condition of the permit, then the permittee will be held to comply with the terms thereof." * * * [I]n *Inland Steel Co. v. EPA*, 574 F.2d 367 (7th Cir. 1978), * * * [t]he Court upheld the inclusion of a provision in Inland's permit, called a *reopener clause*, that incorporates on an ongoing basis all toxic effluent standards that may roll off the administrative assembly-line during the life of the permit. * * *

The NPDES permits "are for fixed terms not exceeding five years." In practice, hundreds of permits have expired, and have not actively been caught up again in the process of reconsideration and reissuance. EPA handles this problem of eroding deadlines by the simple expedient of allowing an expired permit to "continue in force" so long as the permittee has submitted a "timely" and "complete" application for a new permit. Obviously, this approach is born of administrative desperation, although few would be willing to quarrel with the good faith of the plea that resources would be taxed impossibly to meet the deadlines. * * * Nor, indeed, is the applicant to be faulted; what can be done other than stand in line with your papers in order, at the Motor Vehicle Bureau or the EPA? * * *

## 7.  POTW POLLUTION CONTROL

We have now examined a number of issues unique to industrial NPDES dischargers, as well as some issues common to industrial and municipal (POTW) dischargers. The next series of readings addresses issues that are unique to POTWs. We start by considering the nature of POTW releases and the CWA standards provided for these effluents.

# WILLIAM H. RODGERS, JR.,
## 2 ENVIRONMENTAL LAW: AIR AND WATER
### § 4.31 (1986)

Publicly owned treatment works (POTWs) are very much the soft underbelly of the federal point source cleanup program. The municipal treatment plants look bad whatever the standard of success—compliance records, pollution loads, responsibility for water quality ills. * * * The failure of municipal treatment plant performance is old news in the Congress, with confirmatory studies now standard issue.

The reasons for poor municipal performance are hashed over habitually, with inadequate funding, incompetent management, and compassionate enforcement often mentioned. It is true, moreover, that the municipal pollution enemy is strangely "us," and this common responsibility brings an air of resignation to the whole affair, so that shared guilt is not guilt at all. More than a few bond issue voting turndowns stand behind slowed and failed cleanup campaigns. Responsible public officials, directly or more distantly in the background of POTW plant disappointments, also have at their disposal a variety of official and unofficial immunities unavailable to private polluters. * * *

The municipalities long have had a receptive ear in the Congress, and this has kept the national political body reasonably attentive to the comfort of the cities. * * * In brief outline, the cleanup obligation for the POTW falls well short of maniacal environmentalism: the federal taxpayer foots the bill for most of the cost; standards were set soft, and stayed soft; important variances were freely recognized in the 1977 Amendments and again in 1981; disparities between industrial and municipal plant performance were evened out legislatively not by tightening up the municipal obligations but by relaxing those of industry, through the means of the conventional pollutant provisions. * * *

### POTW STANDARDS

The Odyssey of the standards for municipal plants * * * is easily summarized: in 1972 Congress placed the POTWs on a track parallel to industry, requiring a stage one jump in performance ("*secondary treatment*" by July 1, 1977), to be followed by a second step comparable to the BATEA for industry ("best practicable waste treatment over the life of the works" by July 1, 1983).

EPA found it difficult to conform to this geometrical vision and did much in the intervening years to make the two standards indistinguishable. Congress belatedly endorsed this view in 1981, abandoning the "second turn of the screw" for the POTWs, and making possible a stretching out of the time for compliance with the "secondary treatment" standard until July 1, 1988. *See* Pub. L. 97-117, Dec. 29, 1981, *repealing* CWA § 301(b)(2)(B).

The phase two "best practicable" standard for POTWs still survives, not as an effluent standard but as a measure of how the plants are to be built under the funding provisions of the Act. * * * By retaining the stringent standard as a measure of construction * * * it might be said that the rules now require that plants be built better than they perform. This sounds flippant, but it may fortuitously express the institutional problem that the plants never seem to redeem the expectation of the designers. * * *

EPA defines "*secondary treatment*" by numerical values "for three conventional water quality parameters—biochemical oxygen demand (BOD), suspended solids, and acidity (pH). Some curious 'special' considerations are acknowledged for treatment works afflicted by flows from combined sewers (transporting both storm and sanitary sewage) or by contributions from industries who escaped with softer control regimes for key parameters. These sources are to be handled on a 'case-by-case' basis." * * *

As in any geometrical system, it is reasonable to expect something to be better than "secondary" if the occasion calls for it. This takes us to the level of "tertiary or so-called advanced secondary treatment techniques [that] can be used to remove nutrients like nitrogen and phosphorus; these techniques can be used to provide further reduction of suspended solids and biochemical oxygen demand." These higher technologies may be forced upon the unwilling if necessary to achieve applicable water quality standards, although the proof requirements are formidable. The carrot approach allows EPA to pay 85 percent of the cost of any treatment works using innovative or alternative technologies (100% in the case of failure). § 202(a)(2), (3). * * *

### COMBINED SEWER OVERFLOWS

In the rush for secondary treatment and beyond, an important first step is often neglected. It is called *primary treatment*, that presumes the waste stream will take a trip through a treatment plant where some of the grease, scum, junk, and settleable solids may be removed. Absent such a courtesy stop, waste streams that include flows from households result in discharges of raw sewage, a practice not recommended despite its widespread recurrence at municipal systems across the country.

The principal culprits in this drama were the engineering and construction choices to combine sanitary and storm sewers in the initial wave of sewer-building undertaken by the major cities in the early part of the twentieth century. Combined sewers are designed to transport both storm water and sanitary sewage. They thus bring to the treatment plant not only concentrated flows of domestic sewage but enormous and variable volumes of parasite waters, represented mostly by rainfall and street runoff. In particular, the "first flush" of a rainstorm may dump on the treatment plant huge volumes of accumulated solids. The result, too often, is that the treatment and transport systems are overwhelmed, defended by ad hoc "bypass" policies, a euphemism meaning the combined flows (containing raw sewage) are discharged to waterways without treatment. In the worst of times, "residents may find their basements, streets, and waterways flooded with raw sewage. This flooding causes millions of dollars of damage each year—and untold pollution, inconvenience, and disgust."

As one might expect, combined sewer overflows are subject to continuing attention under the grants program. The more interesting legal issue is how these overflow points are to be treated in the NPDES permits. The EPA policy has wandered about, as befitting a truly intractable problem with no clearly recommended outcome. The agency's "secondary treatment" regulations state, quite frankly, that treatment works receiving combined flows during wet weather may not be capable of meeting percentage removal requirements and that controls, if any, should be determined on a case-by-case basis. EPA also has made clear that its NPDES policy aims to "minimize discharge of pollutants * * * from combined sewer overflows," if this can be called a policy. Elsewhere, it has been said that overflow points will not be governed by separate effluent standards but will be adjudged by reference to whether they cause violations of the water quality standards.

As a strictly legal matter, it appears inescapable that the combined sewer overflow points, or bypasses, are "point sources" subject to the "secondary treatment" or "best practicable" effluent limitations otherwise applicable to publicly owned treatment plants. * * *

The dimensions of combined sewer overflows (together with stormwater discharges) are little appreciated. An NPDES permit for a major POTW may identify as many as fifty or sixty point sources, with the serious effluent limitations imposed on one or two principal outfalls at the treatment plant. Even major bypass points at the plant, used to protect the system from excessive flows during wet weather, may not be constrained seriously by the applicable permits. * * *

The evolutionary response of any system rigorously restricted at a few points and loosely supervised at others is entirely predictable: Do shoplifters squeeze through the checkout counter? * * * Will the raw sewage dutifully turn itself in at the treatment plant? Surely plant operators who are graded on their performance at outfall A are not to be maligned for shunting part of their problem off at diversion point B. * * * [R]aw sewage overflows, like the "fugitive" emissions of air pollution law, resist the single point source legal model embraced by contemporary pollution laws. They add the final irony to a picture of a shining new technology resting proudly at the end of a porous delivery system that spills and leaks on the way to the treatment plant.

### SEPARATE STORM SEWERS

A related but distinctive issue is the question of the standards that apply to runoff from separate storm sewers. A separate storm sewer means a conveyance primarily used for carrying storm water runoff in urban areas. In the past, these sources have not been considered serious problems, or at least problems about which anything could be done, although this assessment is subject to revision in light of the recognition that some of these discharges can be high in toxics. EPA's original decision to exempt storm sewers from the NPDES program was invalidated in the courts. The agency's response was to publish proposed regulations authorizing the owner or operator of a separate storm sewer to discharge, subject only to a reminder that conditions might be imposed later or a regular NPDES permit required. This was accompanied by a frank acknowledgment that "EPA has no reason to believe that effluent limitations guidelines for separate storm sewers will be forthcoming in the foreseeable future." Presently, separate storm sewers are technically subject to the NPDES program but can be covered by general permits. For the most part, this means a free ride, with the burden on the regulators to revise the *status quo*.

Storm sewers are a subject where comprehensive rationality fails at both extremes. Requiring control at every culvert is the stuff of comic filler. In many theoretical and practical respects, street runoff is a nonpoint source pollution problem that accidentally comes together at a discrete conveyance often not clearly controlled by an identifiable party. Storm water that is free of industrial and municipal waste may still appear on the agenda, but somewhat below the more prominent categories of raw sewage overflows. * * * The situation seems to be the classical no-win, with society caught somewhere between overregulation and underregulation, facing only high costs and poor choices in designing a scheme to distinguish between the two. * * *

### SEWER MORATORIA

Another important issue of municipal plant operation is the extent to which an NPDES permit may include no-growth or slow-growth provisions. Section 402(h) of the Act makes clear that the permitting authority, in the event an NPDES permit condition is violated, "may proceed in a court of competent jurisdiction to restrict or prohibit the introduction of any pollutant into [the] treatment works by a source not utilizing [the] treatment works prior to the finding that [the] condition was violated." * * * That inflow is as important as capacity is evident to anyone who has tried to put twelve pounds of sugar in a ten pound bag. But it is not so easy, of course, to justify the imposition of inflow restrictions by a federal agency charged with fashioning discharge conditions for a single sewage treatment plant. * * *

The EPA General Counsel ruled initially that a permit may not contain a hookup ban, reasoning that a moratorium on connections may be imposed only by a court and then only after a permit violation has occurred. This conclusion has been repudiated by one Court of Appeals, *Montgomery Environmental Coalition v. Costle*, 646 F.2d 568, 587-88 (D.C. Cir. 1980), but implicitly endorsed by another that has stated the case forcefully for a policy of extreme deference to local choices. *See Cape May Green, Inc. v. Warren*, 698 F.2d 179 (3d Cir. 1983) (invalidating a grant condition limiting hookups to a federally financed sewage treatment plant). Obviously, use of the permit decisions to enforce land use restrictions with economic reverberations throughout the community is another version of nonattainment or no significant deterioration, with all the political trappings those fighting words entail. * * * The objection of federal administrative insouciance is overcome if sewer moratoria are imposed by state or local officials, which happens with some regularity. * * *

## F. INDIRECT DISCHARGERS

The role of the POTW introduces an element to water pollution analysis that is not encountered in the air pollution context; we do not have centrally-located, government-operated air cleaning services, but municipal sewage treatment plants do offer centralized, publicly-funded wastewater cleanup services. Given the onerous obligations of the NPDES permit program, it is inevitable that an industrial source may seek to avoid the NPDES program entirely by discharging its wastes to the local POTW.

If the POTW can successfully treat the industrial effluent, there are frequently economies of scale to the centralized treatment facility. All too often, however, the POTW cannot handle the influent of these "indirect dischargers" and, even worse, may be damaged by the materials:

> For instance, a small silver plating shop that drained its tanks into the sanitary sewer would send a slug of cyanide solution through the sewage treatment plant that would kill the bacteria [used to treat ordinary sewage] and cause a large amount of raw human sewage to be dumped into a stream. A porcelain enamel plant might flush salts of heavy metals down the common drain, where they would pass untouched through a plant designed to treat human waste.

Frank J. Trelease, Cases and Materials on Water Law 581 (3d ed. 1979).

The EPA is supposed to issue *pretreatment standards* under § 307(b)(2), requiring indirect dischargers to remove from their waste streams toxic and other harmful substances that cannot be properly handled by the POTW. The following reading addresses the unique problems posed by such indirect dischargers and the solution of the pretreatment standards.

## OLIVER A. HOUCK, ENDING THE WAR: A STRATEGY TO SAVE AMERICA'S COASTAL ZONE

### 47 Md. L. Rev. 358, 383-88 (1988)

Over one trillion gallons of wastewater containing RCRA hazardous wastes are discharged annually into municipal sewers by some 160,000 industrial facilities. Without any treatment at industrial facilities, these discharges would contain at least 160,000 metric tons of hazardous components—including 62,000 metric tons of priority metals, roughly 40,000 metric tons of priority organic chemicals, and at least 64,000 metric tons of non-priority organic chemicals.

The preceding discussion notwithstanding, it is a fair bet that we will continue to live with the illogic of first putting human wastes into our water and then building ever more expensive plants to take them out. Were human wastes all that these plants had to treat, one could still clutch at a straw of hope. We might not improve things, but with enough money, we could hold our own. Unfortunately, we have instead designed a system (if it can be called that) that discharges industrial wastes and toxics in staggering amounts into POTWs, which, in turn, pass them on in staggering amounts to our coastal estuaries. The system, called 'industrial pretreatment,' may be the most unworkable aspect of an already troubled clean water program.

Pretreatment is one of those efficiency-based concepts that sounds plausible in a course in 'Economics and the Environment.' It is unnecessary to require industry to remove wastes and sewage that the local municipal plant is going to be treating anyway. Efficiencies of scale should allow industries to discharge their wastes into municipal systems with a credit for the municipal treatment. Congress, which bought this argument from the start, has directed the EPA to develop separate 'pretreatment' standards for industrial discharges into POTWs. The standards are of two types: (1) 'categorical' standards for a limited number of industries and for a somewhat larger number of toxics; and (2) general standards that, in essence, prohibit the introduction of substances that would harm the POTW system itself. The standards are implemented not by the EPA or the states, but by participating POTWs themselves. The federal standards have been a nightmare to develop. Local implementation is approaching, even at this late date, a state of chaos.

The EPA has labored at length on pretreatment standards. Fifteen years after the passage of the CWA, with litigation at every turn, the Agency has finally promulgated for twenty-seven industries categorical standards which regulate (but, of course, do not prohibit) the discharge of one hundred twenty-six toxic substances. The first shortcoming is obvious: any unlisted industries and toxics, which include a wide range of nasty substances, are essentially uncovered. Also, after considerable trial and error, as well as judicial review, the EPA has promulgated its 'prohibited' standards designed to prevent 'interference' with POTW systems. The basic shortcoming of this approach is that a POTW will rarely be able to locate the sources of 'interference' (i.e., who is putting what into its system and causing what impact). The POTW system is treated, in effect, as a receiving basin. Abatement of these effects is subject to the same kind of 'I'm not the one who is causing the problem' arguments and difficulties of proof that plagued the pre-1972 efforts at water pollution control.

Notwithstanding the difficulties with the standards noted above, their implementation presents an even larger problem. First, only major POTWs, which are defined as POTWs with a daily flow of more than five million gallons and others with significant industrial inputs, are required to have pretreatment programs. Thus, of the more than 15,000 POTWs in the United States only about 1,500 have pretreatment programs, which receive an estimated 82 percent of the total industrial wastewater entering POTWs. The remaining 18 percent escape the program and any pretreatment at all. Adding to this loophole is the fact that implementation of the program is left to the local POTW, whose responsibility it is to identify the industries that are discharging wastewater into its system, to permit those discharges, and to monitor compliance. Needless to say, even if the purpose of a national discharge program were to offset the political pressures placed on states to relax their programs, those same pressures are even more formidable at the local level, producing a wide variety of standards and levels of compliance among the local municipal systems. The only federal monitoring requirements for categorical industries and their discharges to local systems are a semi-annual report on these discharges and notification of any additional loads that would interfere with the POTW. The EPA guidance manual also recommends random sampling of industrial effluent and on-site inspections, but these recommendations are not mandatory.

At the end of the treatment process, the POTWs are left with a mountain of sludge that has been rendered useless, indeed hazardous, by the introduction of industrial wastes. These contaminants prevent the most obvious and beneficial uses of sewage sludges, while creating considerable pressure for other disposal methods such as incineration and ocean dumping that produce additional environmental hazards. Of course, those toxics that are not 'treated' and retained in the sludge are passed through to the receiving waters which turn out to be, in large part, the Nation's estuaries. No less than 37 percent of the toxics entering our Nation's waters and estuaries pass from industries through POTWs.

Virtually every review of the pretreatment program has rated it a failure. A 1980 Oversight Subcommittee report to the House Public Works Committee concluded that 'after eight years of trying, EPA has been almost totally unsuccessful in implementing this requirement of the law.' The hearings left the subcommittee 'with considerable doubt' about the workability of the program. A 1982 report by the General Accounting Office found the program 'undefined,' resulting in 'costly, inequitable and/or redundant treatment that may not address toxic pollution problems' and would 'drain * * * scarce Federal, State and local pollution control resources.' A 1987 Office of Technology Assessment report identified major, continuing shortcomings with the pretreatment program, none of them susceptible to any easy solution.

These findings speak for themselves. In 1987 Congress struck a glancing blow at the pretreatment program from the opposite end—the sludges. The EPA now must identify the toxics present in sewage sludge and specify numerical limits for them. The burden apparently will remain on the POTW, however, to work a reduction in toxic inputs from the sources. I wish them well. I am not holding my breath.

There comes a time in The Emperor's New Clothes when a village boy points out that the emperor, in fact, is not wearing any clothes at all. * * * [I]t is difficult for us to take a fresh look at pretreatment and municipal treatment as a whole. Even the staunchest defender of the municipal treatment program, however, has to blanch at the introduction of industrial pollution into its municipal sewer systems. Even the most vigorous defender of federalism has to blush at a program that turns the responsibility for regulating nearly half of the toxic pollution discharged in this country over to 15,000 disparate, local POTWs. Notwithstanding the notions of 'efficiency' that motivated this program, it has produced one set of categorical standards for those industries that discharge into POTWs, another set for those that do not, and an entirely new bureaucracy to implement and enforce these standards. In the name of 'efficiency' we have doubled the number of pollution standards, multiplied the number of regulatory agencies by about a hundredfold, and managed, in the end, to so poison our sewage sludges that they have become, in reality, hazardous wastes.

As was once said of the American involvement in Vietnam, it is time to declare this program a victory and get out.

### Questions

1.   Company A has asked your assistance in assuring Clean Water Act compliance at a proposed new industrial facility. Management tells you that contaminated wastewater could be discharged directly to an adjacent river or, alternatively, could be routed to the local municipal wastewater treatment plant or POTW. What Clean Water Act pollution control regimes would apply to each of these alternatives? What are the advantages and disadvantages of each approach?

2.   Assume that your client lives downstream from a municipality's wastewater treatment plant or POTW. The POTW, which is subject to its own NPDES permit, handles influent from numerous industrial facilities. The river flowing in front of your client's property is badly polluted due to POTW effluent, but the ultimate source of the scum, foul smells, and other pollutants is a mystery. How would you go about seeking relief for your client? What difficulties do you anticipate in eliminating the pollution? Would your case be any easier if the upstream polluter were a direct industrial discharger? Why or why not?

# G. WATER QUALITY STANDARDS

Our preoccupation with effluent limitations should not cause you to overlook the fact that there is, theoretically, a "backstop" mechanism for preventing the destruction of waterways by large numbers of dischargers—each of whom meets the applicable limitations—who collectively turn the waterways into open sewers. *Ambient* standards are the *starting* place under the Clean Air Act; under the Clean Water Act, they provide a sort of "safety net."

---

Read the following sections of the Clean Water Act

☐ § 303(d)(1)(A)     ☐ § 303(d)(1)(C)

---

## 1. WATER QUALITY STANDARDS AND DESIGNATED USES

# WILLIAM H. RODGERS, JR., 2 ENVIRONMENTAL LAW: AIR AND WATER

### § 4.16 (1986)

While the water quality standards are an integral part of the Clean Water Act, the standards themselves for the most part are written, enforced, and construed by state authorities. * * * The terms *water quality criteria* and *water quality standards* often are used synonymously, and they are in this text. Water quality criteria can be defined as ambient water standards, or legal expressions of permissible amounts of pollutants allowed in a defined water segment. This formulation typically appears in one or both of two forms: quantitative and descriptive. Examples of quantitative criteria are: not less than 5 parts per million of dissolved oxygen or more than 500 micrograms per liter of dissolved solids or more than 200 fecal coliform per 100 milliliters of water. Examples of descriptive criteria are: surface waters must be "free from floating debris, scum and other floating materials attributable to municipal, industrial or other discharges or agricultural practices in amounts sufficient to be unsightly or deleterious." Or: "toxic substances shall not be present in such quantities as to cause the waters to be toxic to human, animal, plant, or aquatic life."

*Designated uses* are accomplished by assigning segments of water to certain classes and defining the classes by reference to use. Thus, Class A waters must be suitable for recreation, and Class B waters suitable "for the growth and propagation of fish, other aquatic and semi-aquatic life both marine and freshwater * * * ." And, in past days, Class D waters could be used for "transportation of sewage or industrial wastes, or both without nuisance." Many states have classifications for high quality waters of "exceptional recreational or ecological significance" that, potentially at least, are starkly use restrictive under one version or another of nondegradation.

A conspicuous feature of state water quality standards is their comprehensiveness: for the most part, they reach everywhere and define everything. * * *

The water quality standards, given their historical plan-of-enforcement features, are strongly suggestive of the state implementation plans under the Clean Air Act. But, unlike the SIPs that "are subject to a regime of constant change," the standards appear as a much more durable body of law. They are, in the first place, usually printed and disseminated in a form that approximates a statement of what the rules actually are. A comparison of standards among states discloses * * * very strong similarities in format, language, standards, and narrative descriptions. Indeed, a comparison of the numerical standards with turn-of-the-century standards used for one purpose or another, including enforcement, disclose[s] no startling differences. * * * [This] suggests that the standards, at least in some particulars, are frozen in time, or marooned in some legal backwater.

One * * * reason perhaps for the consensus features of the water quality standards is that they were justified as study and planning, not as enforcement tools. * * * Many indicators, not the least of which is the absence of a functional nonattainment program, suggest that water quality standards impose nowhere near the constraints on public and private choice as air quality standards.

Another interpretation is that the serene era of the water quality standards is coming to a close, to be replaced by a period of flux and conflict more closely resembling the struggles attending the Clean Air Act SIPs. * * * For reasons not entirely clear, the standards themselves may be emerging from the backwaters to the forefront of water pollution policy.

## 2. TOTAL MAXIMUM DAILY LOADS

### OLIVER A. HOUCK, TMDLs: THE RESURRECTION OF WATER QUALITY STANDARDS-BASED REGULATION UNDER THE CLEAN WATER ACT

27 Envtl. L. Rep. 10329 (1997)

The Clean Water Act (CWA) is changing course, again. Originally predicated on state programs to achieve water quality standards, the Act was overhauled in 1972 to require technology standards for point source dischargers, an approach that would go on to revolutionize environmental law. For the past 25 years, the U.S. Environmental Protection Agency (EPA) and its state counterparts have labored to adopt, apply and enforce technology-based limits on water dischargers, supplemented by additional standards for toxic pollutants and by massive funding for municipal waste treatment systems. By any measure, the technology approach has produced significant results. Industrial pollution has plummeted; municipal loadings have dropped, despite the doubling and more of the populations they serve. Water quality standards, meanwhile, lay buried in the books, largely forgotten, taken for dead.

In the 1990s, water quality standards regulation has returned to the Clean Water Act and its players like the appearance of Banquo's ghost. Driven forward by environmental litigation, the Act's vestigial requirements for upgrading polluted waters by the application of standards have sprung out of the courtroom to catch EPA and the states by surprise. More than 20 such lawsuits were pending at the time of this Article. Several had led to judgments ordering accelerated schedules for the inventory of polluted water segments and the development of cleanup plans. Many others were working their way toward settlement and consent decrees. EPA was issuing guidance and memoranda on water quality regulation as fast as they could be prepared. The Agency also convened a Federal Advisory Committee Act panel of state agencies, dischargers, and environmentalists in an attempt to reach a consensus on goals and timetables for the coming years.

It will take years, for the news coming out of these cases and the resulting inventories of the nation's waters is sobering. States that were listing a handful of polluted water bodies are now listing several hundred. Idaho went from 32 listed waters to 960, and climbing. Following the inventories come the cleanup plans for each waterway. EPA wants neither job. A few states seem ready to take up the challenge. Others are throwing up their hands and looking to Congress for relief. Environmentalists are spurring the action forward. Nonpoint sources, largely responsible for the pollution now being identified and largely immune to date from the requirements of the Clean Water Act, are openly nervous about facing tangible abatement requirements. Municipal and industrial sources are unhappy with the prospect of getting tagged with nonpoint sources' share. From all of these groups and more, EPA is seeking an accommodation.

At the bottom of these developments is an approach to pollution control—regulating dischargers by their impact on receiving water quality—that never really worked in the first place and is back for another try. One could have legitimate doubts about it this time as well. It is no small irony that the reason the Clean Water Act retained this approach, and directed its use for the upgrade of polluted waters, is that both the states and pollution dischargers insisted on it. Adamantly. In a very real sense, this is the ghost they wanted. * * *

WATER QUALITY STANDARDS REGULATION AND TMDLS

It is, perhaps, the oldest argument in environmental law. Assuming there is a consensus that some attention should be paid to the environment, there is no consensus on why, and, therefore, by whom and how. The root question is whether we are protecting the environment or managing it for our use. The question rose early to the national level in water pollution control.

The theory of water quality standards-based regulation rests squarely on human use. Water is meant to be used, as is any other natural resource, and one legitimate function is the assimilation of wastes. Decisions about water use should be made by people who use it, local communities, industries, and authorities. * * * This was the nation's first strategy for pollution control * * * . It was elegant, straightforward, and logical. Unfortunately, it did not work very well.

By 1972, with reports on deteriorating water quality from every quarter, the nation was ready for a new strategy of pollution control. There was a new ethical premise, that water should simply be clean. There was a new political view, that pollution was a national problem and required federal intervention. And there was a new mechanism, technology standards. Retained in the Act, however, were the vestiges of a water quality standards-based program, codified in § 303. While the initial provisions of § 303 amplified on the process of establishing state water quality standards, § 303(d) added a prescription for using these standards to upgrade waters that remained polluted after the application of technology-based requirements. It has become a battleground.

# WILLIAM H. RODGERS, JR.,
# 2 ENVIRONMENTAL LAW: AIR AND WATER
### § 4.18 (1986)

In one respect, the pollution load assignment provisions of § 303(d) are a monument to the ambitions of rational decisionmaking. Like the nonattainment or PSD provisions under the Clean Air Act, what is anticipated is a theoretically simple and complete allocation of available capacity. All that is necessary is to define the universe of discharges of a pollutant (say 100 X) that would preserve desired uses in a given watercourse. Write off the capacity used up by nature (say 30 X), leaving another 70 X to carve up according to the allocation scheme desired (e.g., lottery, market, first-come/first-served, merit). Full allocation means no-growth, and no new entrants, unless they buy their way in or are the coincidental beneficiaries of retirements elsewhere.

In another respect § 303(d) represents an acutely political judgment keeping the banner of water quality in evidence despite the temporary ascendancy of technology-based controls. It was included in the Act at the insistence of the House conferees and reflects the historical water quality standards assumption that assimilation of wastes is a fit and proper function of a watercourse. In a sense, § 303(d) represents contingent planning by the Congress for the day when the no-discharge objective is abandoned in favor of basin level allocations of assimilative capacity.

In its full technical splendor, § 303(d) is supposed to come into play if the technology-based effluent limitations are deemed too lax to assure compliance with existing water quality standards. It is triggered by each state identifying waters within its boundaries for which the 1977 effluent limitations of § 301(b)(1) ("best practicable" control technology for industries and secondary treatment for existing sewage treatment plants) are not "stringent enough to implement any water quality standard applicable to such waters." These waters so identified are called *water quality limited segments*. The provision envisages a six-step procedure for tightening controls on individual sources: (1) identification of the problem waters by the state; (2) priority ranking of these waters by the state; (3) the state establishes the "total maximum daily load" of pollutants for those segments, in accordance with the priority ranking, "at a level necessary to implement the applicable water quality standards with seasonal variations and a margin of safety which takes into account any lack of knowledge concerning the relationship between effluent limitations and water quality"; (4) the state submits to the Administrator for his approval the waters identified and the loads established; (5) within thirty days the Administrator approves or disapproves the identification and load assignment; and (6) upon approval, the state incorporates the load allocations into its § 303(e) plan or, upon disapproval, the Administrator establishes loads as "he determines necessary to implement the water quality standards" and then the state incorporates them into the § 303(e) plan. The plan itself must include both total maximum daily loads and compliance schedules for individual dischargers. The permits are supposed to reflect the same loads and compliance schedules. * * *

With the help of a little hindsight, it was not unpredictable that the delicate house of cards erected by § 303(d) would come tumbling down.

## OLIVER A. HOUCK, TMDLs, ARE WE THERE YET? THE LONG ROAD TOWARD WATER QUALITY-BASED REGULATION UNDER THE CLEAN WATER ACT

27 Envtl. L. Rep. 10391 (1997)

Following the passage of the Federal Water Pollution Control Act Amendments of 1972, EPA was fully occupied, indeed overwhelmed, in promulgating technology standards for point sources under the Clean Water Act and defending them in court. The Agency had little inclination, and indeed saw little reason, to implement the "safety net" features of § 303(d) before the technology requirements were in place. After all, water quality upgrading was only required when polluted waters could not be brought up to standard through best available technology requirements. And these requirements were many years away. * * *

As for moving forward to identify polluted water bodies and establishing load limits on their own initiative, there is no evidence in the decade following the 1972 Amendments that the states were going to take this bull by the horns.

EPA took § 303(d) by the horns very gently. The section's obligations were to be triggered by EPA's formal identification of *pollutants* appropriate for water quality analysis and total maximum daily loads (TMDLs). Once these pollutants were identified, the drill began: states had 180 days to submit their lists of water quality limited segments (WQLSs), priorities for cleanup, and TMDLs. In October 1973, rather promptly considering its many duties under the new Act, EPA published a *proposed* notice of a two-volume set of pollutants appropriate for the § 303(d) process. Then, nothing happened. The identification languished. * * * Lawsuits in the late 1970s attempted to challenge the absence of TMDLs on the Colorado River and on waters in South Dakota and failed for want of a predicate: EPA hadn't started the clock. * * *

In 1978 * * * the Agency was brought up short by [a] court order requiring it to publish a final identification of TMDL pollutants. Regrettably, from EPA's perspective, the § 303(d) process would now be set in motion. * * *

EPA's regulations delayed, soft-pedaled, and understated the § 303(d) requirements to a remarkable degree. Seizing on the statutory language that the states' "first submissions" of polluted waters and TMDLs were due in 180 days, EPA asked states to identify "one or more" water quality limited stream segments, and one or more TMDLs, in those first six months. * * * In short, one TMDL submission would suffice. When the second one was due was anyone's guess, as was what would constitute a TMDL. The stage was set for inaction.

Inaction occurred. A few states submitted a few lists. Most states submitted nothing at all. The question became: what then? EPA's answer * * * was: nothing. * * *

*The author then describes a series of cases in the 1980s and early 1990s in which various citizen plaintiffs sought to force the EPA to identify WQLSs and TMDLs in states that had totally failed to fulfill their § 303(d) obligations and other states that had submitted no more than token designations covering a tiny fraction of their polluted waterways. These lawsuits culminated in 1996 decisions in Washington and Georgia excoriating the Agency for endless foot dragging. The federal district court in Georgia, noting that it would take more than 100 years for that state to prepare TMDLs for the 340 WQLSs on its list, ordered Georgia to complete all TMDLs within five years.*

### SCIENTIFIC UNCERTAINTY

The Achilles' heel of water quality standards-based regulation has always been the difficulty of ascribing and quantifying environmental effects for particular discharge sources. There is always another possible source, or another possible reason, that the fish in Lake Pontchartrain are dying. There is always an arguable threshold level for pollutants that may not harm fish, or for oxygen levels below 5 milligrams per liter. And when we come to more complex biological impacts such as the fate and effects of nutrients, particularly those effects hundreds of miles downstream, we are beyond any pretense of precise mathematics for cause and effect decisions. The question is whether we are also, for these same reasons, beyond the reach of law.

We should not be. Section 303(d) itself speaks directly to the issue in requiring a margin of safety in its TMDLs in order to accommodate the uncertainty of its underlying science. Other major provisions of the Clean Water Act—and the Clean Air Act, hazardous waste laws, and wildlife and endangered species laws as well—require similar, "best guess" judgments when we are at the far edge of science and decisions need to be made. * * *

This said, legal challenges are already rising over the degree of science necessary to support load calculations and their allocations to particular sources. As these challenges mount, it will be important first to distinguish between the allocations and the calculations themselves. Allocation of loadings to particular sources in the TMDL process is entirely political, as it is in the analogous state implementation plan process of the Clean Air Act; the mix of reductions from point and nonpoint sources a state may choose to meet its ambient standards is a matter for the state to legislate, negotiate, or otherwise determine. As for the underlying calculations, it is reasonable that they be rationally derived from the best available data; it is unrealistic to require more. Indeed, it would be fatal. * * *

If * * * courts begin to require the hypertechnical, isolated, cause-and-effect kinds of proof that are emerging from cases in hazardous waste regulation and toxic torts, TMDLs will never get off the ground. Science, in this area of the law, will never deliver precision. * * *

### NONPOINT SOURCES

The big enchilada. * * * [N]onpoint source pollution has become the dominant water quality problem in the United States, dwarfing all other sources by volume and, in conventional contaminants, by far the leading cause of nonattainment for rivers, lakes, and estuaries alike. It is no secret to any observer of the Clean Water Act that the primary reason for this mushrooming problem is the fact that while other sources have been abated through required controls and their enforcement, no comparable controls or enforcement have been applied to agriculture, silviculture, and the rest of the nonpoint world. Enter, now, TMDLs, with the potential for specific, quantified load allocations (i.e., reductions) from nonpoint sources. The nonpoint world quakes. And reacts.

From the outset of * * * agricultural interests made their view clear that § 303(d) does not apply to nonpoint sources. * * * [W]hile [§ 303(d)] is entirely silent as to whether it applies to only point, only to nonpoint, or to both point and nonpoint sources, the members of the House Public Works Committee, where this section was born, were well aware that nonpoint sources contributed significantly to the failure to attain water quality standards, and that the most logical reading of the process they arrived at is to read nonpoint sources as included. Indeed, in both the context of that time and the present, TMDLs for point sources alone make no pollution control sense at all. * * *

At this juncture, the only safe observation from the fact and scale of nonpoint source pollution and its effect on achieving water quality standards is that, unless TMDLs include quantified restrictions on nonpoint sources, they are wasting everyone's time. * * *

## 3. WASTE LOAD ALLOCATION

Once total maximum daily loads (TMDLs) have been established for water quality limited—i.e., polluted—segments (WQLSs), those loads must be allocated among the many sources which dump the pertinent pollutant into the affected waterbody. The process of rationing out these TMDLs among the various dischargers is called a *waste load allocation*.

# DONALD W. STEVER,
# WASTE LOAD ALLOCATION

in 2 Law of Environmental Protection
12-13 to 12-14 (Sheldon M. Novick, ed. 1998)

The difficulties inherent in translating an ambient standard into effluent limitations applicable to individual dischargers are compounded where there is more than one discharger putting pollutants into one receiving water body. Obviously, the state agency could not allocated all of the available "use," in the pollution sense, to a single user. It therefore had the task of allocating the waste load among competing users. In the simple case, where there were only two dischargers of essentially the same amounts of a pollutant who were equally able to reduce their effluent, waste load allocation could be accomplished.

There were, however, few simple cases. Often there were dozens or tens of discharge points within a short stretch of river, the dischargers having different technical and economic capabilities of pollutant reduction. And, of course, the situation would differ over time, with older dischargers leaving and new dischargers coming onto the receiving water. Some state agencies developed elaborate waste load allocation formulas, which they employed rigidly and inequitably, and which were little more than hocus pocus in their origin. A discharger could spend significant sums of money to meet the water quality standards, only to be faced with a request to reduce its load even more to accommodate a new industry.

The political difficulties inherent in such a scheme are obvious. Given a choice between placing a sometimes intolerable additional burden on existing dischargers or saying "no" to a new industry and its local economic benefits, the state agencies would be pressured to go along with a third alternative: reclassifying the stream segment to downgrade it. In short, waste load allocation was shown again and again to be impossible.

### Questions

1. What are the similarities between the waste load allocation process and the drafting of state implementation plans under the Clean Air Act? What are the differences?

2. What standards guide the state authorities in rationing out TMDLs between the various point and nonpoint sources contributing to a WQLS? Technological capabilities? Marginal control costs? Something else?

3. How might new sources be blended into "nonattainment" WQLS?

## 4. EPA-PROMULGATED WATER QUALITY BASED EFFLUENT LIMITATIONS

### WILLIAM H. RODGERS, JR., 2 ENVIRONMENTAL LAW: AIR AND WATER
§ 4.18 (1986)
SECTION 302

The load allocation authority of § 303(d) must be viewed independently of the *Administrator's* power to establish "water quality related effluent limitations" under § 302. The latter provision authorizes additional controls above and beyond the 1983/1987 "best available technology" limitations, not just the 1977 "best practicable" limitations addressed in § 303(d). Section 302 controls are a possibility if the Administrator determines that discharges "from a point source or group of point sources * * * would interfere with the attainment or maintenance" of the swimmable/fishable water goals. In such a case the Administrator can establish "effluent limitations (including alternative effluent control strategies)" that "can reasonably be expected to contribute to the attainment or maintenance of such water quality." This last turn of the screw is hedged closely by notice and hearing requirements affording an opportunity to probe economic or social costs of additional limitations. An affected source can defeat the proposals by showing that regardless of the state of the art "there is no reasonable relationship between the economic and social costs and the benefits to be obtained." * * *

Taken literally, § 302 is a no-nonsense prescription for a final showdown. The "effluent limitations" that can be imposed are by definition better than the best since they are incremental improvements on the 1983/87 standards that are quite stringent themselves. The "alternative control strategies" that might be imposed can only be described as drastic. These include, according to the Senate Report, "the transportation of effluents to other less affected waters or the control of in-plant processes." Another obvious option, well known at common law, is the shutdown, the threat of which explains the strict technological, social, and economic inquiries under § 302. * * *

In 1977 [this author] ventured to say that "§ 302 has remained moribund for several years but appears to have a future." The same statement can be made now but with growing doubts. * * * It may well be that § 302 has been stranded by the flow of events. * * * [I]t would not be the first time a carefully crafted statutory seed fell on soil too barren to sustain it.

## H. TOXIC WATER POLLUTION

The EPA's promulgation of technology-based limitations for inclusion in NPDES permits has addressed a relatively small handful of conventional and nonconventional (but nontoxic) pollutants, such as

BOD$_5$ (biochemical oxygen demand), TSS (total suspended solids), oil and grease, certain metal compounds, pH, phenols, heat, and some organic compounds. *See* Donald W. Stever, Effluent Guidelines, in 2 Law of Environmental Protection 12-71 (Sheldon M. Novick, ed. 1998). Large numbers of toxic pollutants are conspicuously absent from this list.

## OLIVER A. HOUCK, THE REGULATION OF TOXIC POLLUTANTS UNDER THE CLEAN WATER ACT

21 Envtl. L. Rep. 10528 (1991)

The Clean Water Act prohibits the discharge of toxics "in toxic amounts." [CWA § 101(a)(3)] Therein lies its flaw. It presumes that we are able to determine what "toxic amounts" are, and to act on that knowledge in the rare event we can make the call. Neither assumption is correct. In fact, after 19 years of struggle, the most effective abatement of toxic pollution has been achieved through technology standards that are not predicated on toxicity at all.

We are now engaged in a renewed effort to address toxic pollution through a variety of Clean Water Act provisions. What was intended to be the Act's major thrust, health-based standards, tripped over its own presumptions and has produced nothing since 1976. What emerged as the Act's major thrust, technology-based standards, produced mixed results and has, for the moment, run its course. A third approach, based on receiving water quality standards, returns us to the state-by-state, discharge-by-discharge analyses that defeated water pollution control efforts prior to 1972 and threaten to do so again. A related approach, based on "hot spots" of toxic pollution, insists that it all be done more quickly. Yet another program, based on whole-effluent testing, has the virtue of relative simplicity * * * and the limitations of relative simplicity. A final program, which for the moment exhausts the possibilities for new means of regulation, requires field testing of receiving waters and their biota.

The one silver lining in the "multiple warhead" nature of the Clean Water Act's approaches to toxic pollution is that there is at least the possibility that if one provision misses, another could well land. With the exception of the Act's health-based standards, these provisions are complementary to each other, and mandatory. By their very cumulation, they have also had the effect of encouraging industry to reduce toxic discharges if only to avoid the burden of compliance, and the specter of an occasional, unwelcome new requirement. Perhaps it is inevitable in a free-market economy that pollution control operate so indirectly; certainly the desire to avoid the procedures of the National Environmental Policy Act and the Resources Conservation and Recovery Act has stimulated reductions in environmental impacts and waste production. Still, something recoils at the idea of reducing toxic pollution by the sheer weight of the approval process. One longs for a better way. * * *

[W]here the intentional discharge of toxic compounds into public waterways is concerned, it is in everyone's interest to end the indirection and to set up a schedule for their elimination. * * *

The success of technology-based standards in abating toxic water pollution depends largely upon one's predisposition to enjoy the donut or regret the hole. Beyond doubt, technology standards have begun to force large reductions in the discharge of more than 100 highly toxic compounds in 24 major categories of industry. Also beyond doubt, however, a greater number of individual industries remain unregulated than regulated, and a growing list of toxics have escaped scrutiny and standards. There is every indication, further, that despite the incessant prodding of Congress and generally strong encouragement from the courts, EPA's technology-based program topped out somewhere between best practicable technology (BPT) and best available technology (BAT) and has since lost its momentum. Absent strong redirection from Congress or the courts, BAT is unlikely to achieve its intended goal. * * *

The objective of the Clean Water Act was to eliminate pollution discharge. Twenty years later, for even the most toxic compounds known to man, we do not have a discharge elimination program. Instead, we have six separate programs for regulating toxic discharges increasingly based on concepts of determining "acceptable" risk that characterized, and largely defeated, water pollution control efforts prior to 1972. For similar reasons, health-based standards failed long ago. Technology standards will move forward again only over EPA's unwilling body. State water quality standards are proving—once again—to be scientifically uncertain, politically manipulatable, infinitely litigable, and so variable as to encourage the flight of industry to the most permissive locations. Whatever Congress intended by abating toxic pollution in "toxic amounts," the debate over what toxic amounts are could continue—with vigorous, and even informed, disagreement—for the life of the democracy. It is time to move on.

One path is the way we have already chosen, only more so. Congress could turn up the heat on the existing programs by establishing deadlines for new EPA technology standards. It could, further, establish federal water quality criteria for toxic pollutants and a single, federal methodology for their application, reducing the variation in state standards and permit limits. The prognosis for these efforts is intensified warfare, with EPA thrust, unhappily, back into the lines. Against whole categories of industries unwilling to comply and still able to litigate each standard and permit level, the prognosis is also for grudging reductions at high transaction costs, over decades.

The alternative is to end the agony and fix a timetable for the elimination of toxic discharges. Indeed, Congress should fix several timetables, based on relative risk. Science may not be able to set absolute risk numbers, but it can identify categories of greater and lesser risk. Industry can obtain adequate lead time for the necessary process changes. Economists can identify incentives that will encourage industry to arrive on or ahead of schedule. And the engineers can, at last, design for the inevitable. To the extent that certain industries are participating willingly and even aggressively in voluntary pollution prevention and toxic reduction programs, a mandate this firm should only strengthen their hand, and lessen their competitive disadvantage. The critical elements of this alternative are that the mandate, lists, and schedules be made congressional, and therefore beyond litigation, and that they be made firm, When it finally becomes time to make batteries without PCBs, paint without lead, and refrigerants without CFCs, industry finds the way. At which point, ambient levels of these toxins drop precipitously.

We will never, of course, by these means or any other, see zero discharge. The exceptions to even the most stringent prohibitions have ways of bending the rule, and nonpoint and other contributions of toxics to the nation's waters are at present, less manageable. But in this life we manage what we can. We can abate point source toxic discharges with certainty, with fairness to industries wherever located, with adequate lead time and with incentives for those who have the will to arrive ahead of schedule. Or we can regulate toxic pollution . . . forever.

### Questions

1.  How does the toxic water pollution regime of the Clean Water Act differ from the hazardous air pollution control program of the Clean Water Act? Should the Clean Air Act approach be tried in the Clean Water Act setting? Why or why not?

2.  What solution to the toxic water pollution problem does Professor Houck recommend? Why? Do you suppose that he would recommend a similar approach to hazardous air pollution? Why or why not?

# Chapter Twelve

## HAZARDOUS AND
## TOXIC MATERIALS

---

### A. INTRODUCTION

This chapter is devoted to an exploration of the hazardous and toxic materials problems. While it is terribly simplistic to break these problems down into only two components, it is helpful to think of two broad categories of toxics problems. First, each of us is exposed to a large variety of chemicals intentionally placed into the stream of commerce in connection with consumer goods. To the extent that toxic chemicals assault us in this way, we are frequently not talking about toxic wastes at all; for want of a better term, we might refer to this crudely as the problem of "toxic *products*." Second, thousands of tons of toxic wastes are placed into the biosphere each year. Whether these wastes are unwanted by-products of industry or consumer goods that we no longer value, these are toxic chemicals that we are trying to discard. This second problem is usually referred to as the problem of "hazardous *wastes*."

Obviously, these two problems are intimately related. At the national level, they are now addressed by a bewildering collage of statutes. To make matters even more confusing, each statute has its own peculiar label (and definition) for overlapping fragments of the total universe of toxic products/hazardous wastes. Such materials are referred to under various statutes, as "hazardous substances," "toxic water pollutants," "hazardous air pollutants," "hazardous materials," "hazardous wastes," "toxic substances," and "regulated substances." Discerning the content of these labels is extremely important, because the statutes impose widely varying obligations on the handlers of each category of materials. The definitions are so complex and the obligations so pervasive, that we can only scratch the surface in this introductory environmental law text.

In our study of the hazardous and toxic materials problem, we will focus on the Resource Conservation and Recovery Act of 1976 (RCRA) and the Comprehensive Environmental Response, Compensation and Liability Act (CERCLA)—federal statutes primarily addressed to the problem of hazardous *wastes*. You should be aware, however, that other statutes address toxic issues. One of the most important statutes ignored by this text is the Toxic Substances Control Act of 1976 (TSCA).

## B. CRAZY QUILT COVERAGE

The federal government has enacted enough statutes and regulations on the hazardous/toxic materials problem to choke a horse. Before examining the two major statutes—RCRA and CERCLA—we begin with a perceptive reading on the significance of pollutant *definition*. Professor Dernbach does an excellent job of depicting what he calls the crazy quilt coverage of the federal statutory schemes.

## JOHN C. DERNBACH, THE UNFOCUSED REGULATION OF TOXIC AND HAZARDOUS POLLUTANTS

21 Harv. Envtl. L. Rev. 1-5, 7, 14-17, 26, 55-57 (1997).

Environmental regulation of manufacturing is at a turning point. The legal structure that has been in place for the past quarter of a century, with its permitting, enforcement, standard setting, and other regulatory apparatus, has unquestionably improved human health and the environment. Many say that the system is costly and inefficient, however, and urge that much or all of it be replaced or abandoned. Others look at the remaining and often ill-distributed costs of pollution itself and argue for strengthening regulation. * * *

The debate about *how* to regulate, however, has all but ignored the most fundamental question of all—*what* to regulate. The choice of which pollutants to regulate profoundly affects the environment, human health, and the economy. Manufacturing facilities emit thousands of different pollutants. Decision makers have not aimed to control all of these pollutants, perceiving such a goal as too expensive and technically complex. Instead, the major environmental and occupational health programs each regulate a list of toxic or hazardous pollutants. However, the lists of the various programs differ extraordinarily from one another. As a result, factories emit partially or wholly unregulated pollutants, creating potentially significant risks to human health and the environment and bolstering the argument for greater regulation. Yet the differences among the lists are also a major underlying reason for costliness and inefficiency in the current regulatory structure. * * *

All * * * aspects of environmental and occupational health protection programs depend on the decision about what to control. If a pollutant is regulated, it is "inside" the general regulatory program, and facilities, government agencies, consultants, and the public give it serious attention. If a pollutant is unregulated altogether or is unregulated under a particular statute, it is "outside" the system and most often is ignored.

The decision of which chemicals to manage provides a foundation for five federal statutes that regulate routine releases of toxic and hazardous pollutants from and within industrial facilities. Three statutes directly limit releases of such pollutants into various media of the environment. The Clean Water Act controls discharges of toxic and nonconventional pollutants into surface waters; the Resource Conservation and Recovery Act ("RCRA") controls the transportation, storage, and disposal on land of hazardous wastes; and the Clean Air Act controls the release of hazardous air pollutants into the ambient or outdoor air. A fourth statute, the Occupational Safety and Health Act ("OSH Act"), limits the concentration of toxic substances in the air inside the workplace. Finally, the Emergency Planning and Community Right-to-Know Act ("EPCRA") requires manufacturers to report publicly their releases of toxic chemicals to water, land, outdoor air, and other media and to report their off-site transfers of these chemicals. Although EPCRA does not impose restrictions on the type or concentration of pollutants that may be released, the public reporting of these releases has led to their reduction. * * *

Each of these statutes centers on a list that specifies which pollutants are subject to regulation. * * * To a degree, the list approach has worked. * * * [T]he laws have caused a major decline in improper hazardous waste management and a considerable reduction in releases to surface water of toxic and nonconventional water pollutants.

But there is a hidden problem with regulation by list. The strategy leaves gaps in what is regulated. The list names used by the various statutes—toxic chemicals, toxic materials, toxic and nonconventional water pollutants, hazardous waste, and hazardous air pollutants—sound comparable and nonspecialists use them interchangeably. Although lawyers recognize that the terms have different legal meanings, they tend to see formulation and use of the lists as best left to toxicologists, chemists, and engineers. The contents of each list, however, dramatically vary from that of the others. * * *

The sheer scale of differences in coverage is evident from an analysis of the statutory programs and the lists of toxic or hazardous pollutants on which they are based. * * *

A total of 1134 pollutants are regulated as toxic or hazardous under at least one of the five statutes:

| | |
|---|---|
| Regulated under all five | 49 |
| Regulated under at least four | 119 |
| Regulated under three or more | 210 |
| Regulated under two or more | 371 |
| Regulated under only one | 768 |

Each list excludes pollutants that are on all four of the others, and each list includes pollutants that are not on any of the others. * * *

When more than two lists are compared, the extent of the inconsistency increases substantially. [**Figure 12–1**] shows the relationship among pollutants on the Clean Air Act, Clean Water Act, and RCRA lists. * * *

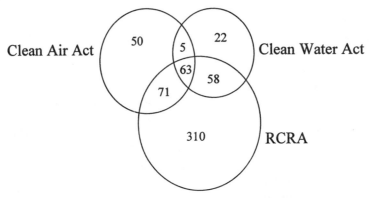

**Figure 12-1.** Comparison of CAA, CWA, and RCRA Lists
Source: Adapted from 21 Harv. Envtl. L. Rev. 1, 17 (1997), Figure 2

The regulation of listed pollutants varies substantially from program to program. Some require permits, some do not. Four of the five programs are administered by EPA and one is administered by OSHA; the two agencies have different missions and constituencies. The stringency of the five programs varies considerably. The detailed "cradle-to-grave" controls adopted under RCRA probably make compliance with that program more complex and difficult than any other. Thus, different types of regulation occur even with pollutants that all five statutes recognize as hazardous or toxic. * * *

### INCENTIVE FOR CROSS-MEDIA TRANSFERS

As practicing attorneys know well, industries affected by environmental and occupational health laws can comply with those laws in two basic ways. They can engage in a regulated activity and follow the prescribed requirements, or they can make the law inapplicable to them by not engaging in the regulated activity. If a law requires a permit for facilities constructed in a wetland, for example, a company might avoid the permitting requirement by constructing the facility elsewhere. This kind of avoidance behavior is common among regulated industries and, if properly directed, can benefit human health and the environment.

Inconsistent listing of toxic and hazardous pollutants, however, encourages a harmful type of avoidance behavior—moving pollutants to media where they are not regulated. The single-media control programs work by limiting the release of the listed pollutants into a particular medium. These limits impose costs on the facility. Because the facility's managers seek to minimize costs, they will ordinarily release or transfer pollutants in the least expensive manner that is technically feasible. Pollutants can be released to air or water, disposed of on land, or sent to a publicly owned treatment works. Process engineers can often select the medium into which waste or residue will be discharged. If a pollutant is not regulated in a particular medium, the cost of releasing it there is likely to be minimal. Inconsistent lists encourage industrial process engineers to design and operate manufacturing and pollution control systems so that toxic and hazardous pollutants are discharged into media where they are not regulated.

The phenomenon of cross-media transfers in environmental regulation is well known but not well understood. Many of the hazardous wastes that are discharged into publicly owned treatment works as part of industrial waste water volatilize into the air during treatment, creating air pollution. The most widely used means of controlling workplace exposure to chemicals is probably by venting them to the outdoor air. In fact, Congress has recognized that unregulated media invite the transfer of pollutants. When Congress passed RCRA, for example, it was aware that the Clean Air Act and the Clean Water Act were leading many companies to dispose of their wastes on land instead. RCRA, Congress thought, would close that loophole.

If the pollutants regulated under each of these statutes as toxic or hazardous were essentially the same—an assumption that is easy to make because of the similarity of their names—that conclusion might be appropriate. The assumption is wrong, of course. As a result, the statutory programs often have the effect of controlling pollutants in a particular medium by increasing them in media where they are not regulated. * * *

## C. ORIGINS OF RCRA SUBTITLE C

One cannot understand the stunning complexity of the current state of our hazardous waste laws without a rudimentary grasp of the history leading to their adoption. Accordingly, the following series of readings is designed to place the 105-page RCRA and 95-page CERCLA statutes in context.

### 1. SOLID WASTE DISPOSAL ACT

To begin with, one of the most curious things about this topic is our naïve failure to recognize in the early 1970s that hazardous wastes pose environmental problems separate and distinct from the air and water pollution concerns addressed by the Clean Water and Clean Air Acts. The following brief reading notes this peculiar phenomenon.

## WOROBEC, AN ANALYSIS OF THE RESOURCE CONSERVATION AND RECOVERY ACT

11 [Curr. Dev.] Env. Rep. (BNA) 634 (1980)

RCRA had its beginnings in 1965 with passage of the Solid Waste Disposal Act. As open dumps smoldered in cities across the United States (as recently as 1972, 47 percent of the fires in Washington, D.C. involved open dumps), the Department of Health, Education, and Welfare hoped to see authority over air pollution caused by burning dumps transferred to the Department of Housing and Urban Development. Although the legislation did not turn out exactly as envisioned—HEW still had to deal with open dumps and the resulting air pollution—Congress did provide for a small program to assist state and local governments interested in improving municipal waste disposal.

The Solid Waste Disposal Act was helping localities turn their dumps into covered sanitary landfills which not only looked better but also smelled better and cut down on the air pollution * * * .

In 1970, however, as Earth Day supporters were preparing for the first of their annual demonstrations, Congress amended the 1965 Act and produced the first Resource Conservation and Recovery Act. * * *

Thomas F. Williams, deputy director of the EPA Office of Public Awareness, explained the situation well during a January 30, 1980, speech to the Baltimore Environmental Center, Inc. * * *

> That is the way it was. If what the Federal Government does is a reflection of what active public opinions wants—and I believe it usually is—not many people gave a damn about waste, hazardous or otherwise.

In 1975, however, Congress began holding hearings to update the 1970 waste recovery law and included in the new law, the Resource Conservation and Recovery Act, a mandate for strictly controlling hazardous wastes.

## 2.  RCRA SUBTITLE C

Prior to 1976, there was no federal hazardous waste statute of any kind. Subtitle C of the Resource Conservation and Recovery Act (RCRA), enacted in that year, set forth the congressional directive that a "cradle-to-grave" regulatory program should be established for the handling of hazardous waste. As originally enacted, Subtitle C was surprisingly short; it provided no more than the outline of a remarkable new program to be developed by the EPA. Because virtually none of the statutory provisions was self-executing, the statute itself affected almost no one and no waste materials. Indeed, there was no such thing as a "hazardous waste" under federal law until the EPA promulgated regulations defining such materials in November of 1980. The following reading summarizes the limited direction given by the 1976 Congress to the agency.

## EPA ISSUES RCRA'S "CRADLE-TO-GRAVE" HAZARDOUS WASTE RULES

### 10 Envtl. L. Rep. 10130 (1980)

Section 3001 of the Subtitle C program requires EPA (1) to develop "criteria for identifying the characteristics of hazardous waste" and for listing hazardous waste and (2) to identify the characteristics of hazardous waste and list wastes on the basis of those characteristics. Under § 3002, generators of hazardous waste must comply with certain recordkeeping, labeling, packaging, reporting, and manifest system requirements [to be developed by the agency]. Transporters of hazardous waste must follow § 3003's requirements, which mandate that they may carry only waste that is properly labeled and must comply with the manifest system and the requirements of the Hazardous Materials Transportation Act. The standards of § 3004 [to be developed by the EPA] apply to owners and operators of hazardous waste treatment, storage, and disposal facilities and cover (1) recordkeeping, (2) compliance with the manifest system, (3) treatment, storage, and disposal of waste, (4) location, design, and construction of facilities, (5) contingency plans, (6) maintenance, and (7) financial responsibility. The permit program outlined in § 3005 of RCRA establishes the information required on the permit application, states when permits will be granted or revoked, and provides for a period of interim status during which a permit applicant will be treated as having been issued one until final action has been taken. Section 3006 calls for federal approval of state programs that are determined by the Administrator to be equivalent to the federal program, consistent with the programs in force in neighboring states, and adequately enforceable.

### 3. LOVE CANAL

Between the 1976 enactment of RCRA Subtitle C and the 1980 promulgation of its implementing regulations, America woke up to the hazardous waste problem. As noted in the following reading, the alarm clock was Love Canal.

## WOROBEC, AN ANALYSIS OF THE RESOURCE CONSERVATION AND RECOVERY ACT

11 [Curr. Dev.] Env. Rep. (BNA) 634 (1980)

In August 1978, President Carter declared a state of emergency in an area of Niagara Falls, New York, where more than 82 different long-buried chemicals were seeping into basements, burning children, and causing an alarming increase in spontaneous abortions and birth defects. Thirty-seven families were evacuated immediately, a nearby school was closed, and barbed wire fencing was strung around the heart of the working class neighborhood, now known around the world as Love Canal.

The canal was basically an uncompleted half-mile long waterway dug around the turn of the century by William T. Love. Beginning in the 1930s, the trench, with its clay lined bottom, was used as an industrial dump. In 1947, the land where the trench was located was purchased by Hooker Chemical and Plastics Corporation and until 1953 was used as a depository for an estimated 352 million pounds of industrial wastes. In 1953, under threat of condemnation, Hooker sold the site to the Niagara Falls Board of Education. The education department constructed a neighborhood school on the site and sold the unneeded portion to a developer who constructed several hundred tract homes there.

Life proceeded normally for the residents near Love Canal until 1976, when heavier than normal rains over a period of years raised the water table and sent the long-buried chemicals bubbling into basements and playgrounds. In August 1978, after two years of study—during which EPA identified 82 chemicals seeping from the site—the first disaster declaration was made and the first 37 families were moved from their homes on Love Canal.

In the two years since the tragedy of Love Canal surfaced, the number of families evacuated has climbed to over 1,000; cleanup and relocation costs have exceeded $30 million; and pending court suits and damage claims have escalated into the billions of dollars and are growing daily. During subsequent investigations, Congress discovered that Love Canal, while the best known of the hazardous waste sites, probably was not unique. In fact, it is only one of an estimated 50,000 hazardous waste disposal sites where more than 750,000 waste generators deposit or have deposited the more than 57 million tons of hazardous waste produced in the United States each year. And, according to EPA, only 10 percent of that waste is disposed of in such a way as to prevent future Love Canals.

The effects of years of indifference to hazardous waste disposal had exploded into the country's consciousness and the canal became a rallying cry for congressmen and environmental groups. Congressional hearings were held. The General Accounting Office issued reports. The State of Illinois and various environmental groups filed suit to force EPA to issue rules under RCRA * * * . Other Love Canals began to surface, with sites in California, Long Island, Kentucky, New Jersey, Maine, Massachusetts, Tennessee, and Michigan bringing the seriousness of the hazardous waste problem into national prominence.

"I believe that it is probably the first or second most serious environmental problem in the country," James Moorman, assistant attorney general for land and natural resources, told a House subcommittee in May 1979. "We do not know where the millions of tons of stuff is going," Moorman continued. "In my view, it is simply a wide open situation, like the wild west was in the 1870s, for toxic disposal. "The public is basically unprotected, there just are not any lawmen out there, state or federal, policing this subject."

In October 1978, barely three months after the situation at Love Canal gained national attention, the House Interstate and Foreign Commerce Committee's Oversight and Investigations Subcommittee began what would be 13 days of hearings on hazardous waste. After compiling 1,800 pages of testimony, the subcommittee in October 1979 issue a scathing report which criticized industry and government alike. "The subcommittee is very concerned over the failure of the Environmental Protection Agency, industry, and the Congress to meet the challenge presented by hazardous waste disposal," Bob Eckhardt (D-Tex.), chairman of the subcommittee, said in transmitting the report to the full committee. "EPA has failed to meet statutory deadlines for regulations on disposal of hazardous wastes; has failed to determine the location of all hazardous waste sites; and has not taken vigorous enforcement actions," Eckhardt said.

The subcommittee also attacked industry for "laxity, not infrequently to the point of criminal negligence, in soiling the land and adulterating the waters with its toxins." And it chastised itself for "lethargy in legislating controls and appropriating funds for their enforcement." "Our country presently lacks an adequate program to determine where these * * * sites are; to clean up unsafe active and inactive sites, and to provide sufficient facilities for the safe disposal of hazardous wastes in the future," the subcommittee report said. "Proper disposal of hazardous materials is the exception, rather than the rule. Even extraordinary effort, commenced immediately, cannot achieve adequate protection for the American public for years to come."

At the time of the hearings, most of the rules implementing RCRA had not even been proposed. In fact, not until December 18, 1978, did EPA *propose* standards for listing hazardous wastes and standards for generators of those wastes. Although the Act set out an elaborate system for controlling hazardous wastes from generation through disposal, only rules under two sections of the law had been proposed before the hearings began. Section 3003 rules, providing for transporter standards, had been proposed April 28, 1978. * * * Rules under § 3010, the notification of hazardous waste activities portion of the Act, were proposed July 11, 1978.

But even after proposal, the rules came in for some heavy congressional criticism. The Oversight and Investigations Subcommittee noted that the proposals would not require testing for four of the eight hazardous waste characteristics in the Act, would use toxicity testing procedures that do not adequately simulate real world conditions, and would fail to list a number of known carcinogens as hazardous. Further, it reported that the proposed rules would "wrongfully exempt" some generators of highly dangerous hazardous wastes based on the quantity to be disposed, would "not adequately regulate" the use of recycled wastes, would not be flexible enough to permit the continued use of important, small, single-waste or special-purpose facilities, and would allow migration of wastes from sites and stop monitoring long before the end of the wastes' toxicity. The proposals also would require insufficient monitoring for leachate and groundwater contamination and would permit the granting of interim permits to sites that are far below the minimum safety levels, the subcommittee said. * * * The mood of Congress definitely had shifted toward a tougher stance on hazardous waste.

Congress, however, was not the only governmental body preparing reports on hazardous waste. In a move that has become even more controversial with the passage of time, the General Accounting Office on December 19, 1978, released a report recommending that a self-sustaining national trust fund be established to pay for cleaning up abandoned hazardous waste sites. The first of two GAO reports on administration of RCRA, the fund recommendation shocked industry and made public debate and controversy over the recently proposed hazardous waste rules even more heated. The report said money should be available to pay claims resulting from disposal operations, to clean up resulting damages, and to prevent further contamination. The fund would be supported by fees assessed on disposal of hazardous wastes, but in developing the fee schedule, "an effort should be made to reflect the degree and duration of risk posed by specific wastes," the GAO reported noted. Inadequate disposal practices in the past have caused harm to humans and the environment many years after sites have closed, the report said. In many cases, site ownership was transferred or relinquished, making legal liability and responsibility difficult to establish and causing clean-up costs and remedial costs to be passed on to taxpayers. A federal fund is needed to address the liability problem the report stressed.

EPA agreed with GAO, saying it intended to propose legislation creating a federally administered trust fund to protect the public from damages occurring after hazardous waste disposal facilities are closed. The fund would be for damage claims and remedial actions, up to a specified amount, for sites with disposal permits under RCRA. Thus, the superfund, probably the most controversial outcome of RCRA, was conceived. It, like RCRA, would experience a slow birth with committee action in Congress still incomplete in mid 1980.

Meanwhile, several environmental groups and the State of Illinois filed suit to force EPA to issue final hazardous waste rules under RCRA. * * * In explaining the delay, Costle noted that the agency has received 1,200 sets of comments on the proposed RCRA regulations, comments constituting a stack seven feet high. The agency must "read, digest, analyze, and respond to every major point made by every commentator in that entire record," he said. "So to achieve effective regulation of hazardous waste we must take the time to do our homework."

EPA, indeed, did have a stack of comments to consider * * * most of them negative. Industry comments asked for an easing of the proposed rules. Environmental groups, on the other hand, protested that many wastes were excluded, and also criticized the agency's inability to move against hazardous wastes sooner. * * * This volume of comments did little to help EPA issue the RCRA rules before the December 31 [1979, court-ordered] deadline. In Costle's words, "These comments are designed to stake out territory on which industry lawyers can subsequently sue, seeking court-ordered stays and remands of promulgated regulations. In other words, these comments are a minefield with the potential of blowing our hazardous waste regulatory program right out of the water * * * . If we do not take such care, industry lawyers can, in the courts, undo everything we have been trying to achieve."

Several groups, however, did not see it this way. Incensed at the delay, the same groups that filed suit to force issuance of the hazardous waste rules dashed back into court to demand a hearing on the latest development. Calling the delay "inexcusable," the environmental groups asked the court "to help to get to the bottom of the problem apparently plaguing EPA and put the agency back on a realistic but specific implementation schedule" for these "most critical regulations."

The agency, however, apparently "got to the bottom" of the problem and on February 26, 1980, issued some of the regulations, for §§ 3002, 3003, and 3010 of RCRA, in final form. Costle called the regulations the cornerstone of the hazardous waste management program under RCRA. "We are issuing three regulations which will give us a national roadmap of where waste is and where it is going. * * *"

Finally, on May 5, the agency announced adoption of the final rules for § 3001 and 3004 of the Act. * * * The 750,000 estimated hazardous waste generators thus became subject * * * to the regulations under RCRA—generally conceded to be the most complex and voluminous ever promulgated by the Government * * * .

The agency also put 400,000 notification and reporting forms in the mail requiring generators and transporters of hazardous wastes, along with those who treat, store, or dispose of such wastes to register with the agency before August 18, 1980. The agency cautioned, however, that receipt or nonreceipt of the notification forms neither exempts nor requires a recipient to file a notification. Each firm or individual is responsible for determining whether reporting is required the agency stressed.

## D. THE MANIFEST SYSTEM

We will eventually examine the obligations of generators and transporters but, at this point, you must be at least minimally aware of the *manifest system* of RCRA. The following brief reading summarizes its features.

## EPA ISSUES RCRA'S "CRADLE-TO-GRAVE" HAZARDOUS WASTE RULES

10 Envtl. L. Rep. 10130, 10131-32 (1980)

Generators of waste deemed hazardous must, as a first step, notify EPA and receive an identification number from the Agency. Should the generator choose to send the waste off-site for storage, treatment, or disposal, it must prepare a manifest form that will accompany the waste from "cradle-to-grave." The manifest contains information identifying the nature and the quantity of the waste as well as the generator. The regulation also requires that the waste be packaged and labeled in accordance with the Department of Transportation's hazardous materials regulations. Wastes kept on-site are not subject to the manifest requirement but must be handled in accordance with other standards.

The manifest system is one of the key components in EPA's regulatory program. It is designed to prevent any dumping or loss of wastes during the crucial stage when they are at large in the environment. The manifest system also serves to delineate lines of accountability among the participants in the process.

Each person in the chain of custody of the waste, principally generators, transporters, and owners/operators of storage, treatment, or disposal facilities, must sign and keep one copy of the manifest. In addition, facility owners/operators at the end of the chain must send a copy of the manifest back to the generator. If the generator does not receive this copy within 45 days, it must attempt to trace the shipment and notify EPA in an "exception report."

Transporters are subject to a separate set of regulatory requirements. They must also obtain an EPA identification number, comply with the manifest system in delivering all designated waste to the facility, and follow the Department of Transportation's requirements for reporting spills of hazardous materials.

Although the generator and transporter regulations did not arouse controversy, the Agency did make several significant changes from the proposed version. Rather than allowing a generator to designate on the manifest any number of facilities to receive the waste, as was originally proposed, the final regulations require that the generator designate only one permitted facility and one alternative. EPA justified the change, which greatly tightens the controls on the waste shipments, on the basis of congressional intent to encourage generators to take responsibility for the ultimate disposition of their wastes and not simply pass the buck to transporters. This revision limits the discretion of the transporter and makes clear the duty of the generator to choose and be answerable to EPA for the disposal site of the waste. * * *

# E. RCRA "HAZARDOUS WASTES"[1]

Subtitle C is the hazardous waste portion of RCRA. It is difficult to craft an introductory study of the Subtitle C program that is not so superficial as to be essentially useless. The statutory and regulatory scheme is as complex in its own way as the Clean Air Act program that has served as the primary focus of study in this text. The following readings have been pulled together in an effort to give an honest flavor of the Subtitle C program—including a number of its complexities—without burying you in its minutiae.

---

[1] This section has been adapted from John-Mark Stensvaag, Hazardous Waste Law and Practice (1995).

## 1. IMPORTANCE OF THE HAZARDOUS WASTE DEFINITION

We will spend considerable effort in addressing the RCRA Subtitle C program's hazardous waste *definition*. This may seem odd. Nevertheless, as Professor Dernbach demonstrates at page 656, *supra*, the selection of *what* to regulate in any environmental control program profoundly affects the environment, human health, and the economy. Moreover, for the vast majority of potentially regulated entities throughout the United States, there is no more important environmental compliance question than this: "Do my materials fall within the RCRA Subtitle C regulatory system?"

RCRA Subtitle C is the only federal statutory program regulating the category of materials that has been formally designated as "hazardous waste." The program is staggering in its bulk, complexity, and significance. The law of hazardous waste established by and pursuant to RCRA Subtitle C permeates American society, imposing dozens of obligations on hundreds of thousands of actors handling thousands of materials. Entities regulated by Subtitle C include tens of thousands of actors who have never previously been subject to environmental regulation. Thousands of them are no doubt still ignorant of their status as regulated entities. These regulated entities are responsible for complying with an intimidating list of obligations, for which the stakes of noncompliance are extraordinarily high, including personal criminal penalties and massive potential civil liabilities.

Most regulated entities cannot possibly comply with their Subtitle C obligations without the assistance of legal counsel. Yet, as the universe of regulated actors has continued to expand, it has become increasingly clear that not every actor regulated under Subtitle C can obtain the services of the nation's excellent but small cadre of hazardous waste law specialists. Unless the contents and principles of the Subtitle C program are made accessible to a much wider audience of legal counsel for potentially regulated entities, the program will be doomed to failure. Notwithstanding the grand scope of RCRA Subtitle C, the program cannot successfully alter the conduct of persons who do not and cannot understand it.

## 2. SUBTITLE C PROBLEM-SOLVING ROAD MAP

Almost all Subtitle C problems may be solved by addressing three questions in the following order:

1. Is the material under consideration a *hazardous waste*?

2. If so, does the person handling the material fall within one or more of the categories of *actors* subject to Subtitle C regulation?

3. If so, with what *obligations* must the regulated actor comply in handling the hazardous waste?

In connection with the first analytical issue—is the material a hazardous waste?—readers are urged to consult **Figure 12-2** and **Figure 12-3**, set forth later in this chapter. These diagrams are carefully crafted maps for determining whether a material is a solid and a hazardous waste. The questions in each figure are addressed sequentially, starting with Question 1 and proceeding to the last question in each diagram. Readers who develop a familiarity with the figures will discover that they represent powerful tools for conducting environmental audits at potentially regulated facilities.

Because the potentially massive requirements of RCRA Subtitle C apply only to "hazardous wastes," the definition of that term has profound consequences. Ideally, the hazardous waste definition should include only substances for which Subtitle C regulation is appropriate. It should also be as precise as possible, so that potentially regulated entities and enforcement authorities can confidently and accurately ascertain the status of any given substance.

In light of the significant consequences of the hazardous waste definition, one might assume that Congress would play a major role in shaping it. In fact, however, the congressional contribution to defining hazardous waste has consisted of four modest facets. First, Congress has provided a narrative statutory hazardous waste definition—RCRA § 1004(5)—so broad and flexible that it cannot meaningfully delineate the outer bounds of the hazardous waste category. Second, Congress has established various steps that the EPA must follow in defining hazardous waste and in modifying the definition. Third, Congress has described and listed several substances that either cannot be hazardous wastes or that must remain exempt from Subtitle C regulation. Finally, in the 1984 RCRA amendments, Congress directed the EPA to consider certain expansions of the hazardous waste definition.

Beyond this limited statutory guidance, Congress has delegated the task of crafting a workable definition of hazardous waste to the EPA. Not surprisingly, that task remains unfinished more than two decades after RCRA's enactment. Nevertheless, the basic ingredients of the definition are in place and may be found in 40 C.F.R. Part 261, *Identification and Listing of Hazardous Waste*. These regulations are the essential starting place for any potentially regulated actor who needs to determine whether his or her substances are hazardous wastes.

Hazardous wastes are presently defined through a series of analytical steps. First, a substance must be a "*solid* waste," or it cannot be a hazardous waste. The Subtitle C definition of solid waste is one of the most complicated aspects of the hazardous waste definition. Second, a substance that is a solid waste will be a hazardous waste only if it:

1. Has been *listed* as a hazardous waste by EPA regulations;

2. Is a *mixture* containing a *listed* hazardous waste;

3. Is a solid waste *derived from* the treatment, storage, or disposal of a *listed* hazardous waste; or

4. Exhibits a hazardous waste *characteristic* defined by EPA regulations.

Even then, a substance will not be a hazardous waste if it falls within certain exclusions. Finally, hazardous wastes of certain types, or managed under certain conditions, are given special, somewhat pampered status by the regulations; such wastes are subject to special provisions, rather than the full range of Subtitle C requirements.

## 3. SIGNIFICANCE OF SOLID WASTE DEFINITION

The definition of *solid* waste may seem to be a peculiar place to begin the analysis in describing the universe of hazardous wastes regulated under RCRA. Nevertheless, the statute provides that "hazardous wastes" are a subset of "solid wastes." No matter how harmful a substance may be, it cannot be a hazardous waste—and therefore cannot be regulated under Subtitle C—unless it is a solid waste (or combination of solid wastes), within the meaning of RCRA. Because solid waste status is a fundamental prerequisite to regulation under Subtitle C, defining solid waste is the critical first step in defining hazardous waste. This first step has important regulatory consequences under Subtitle C: *every person who generates a solid waste has an obligation to determine whether that substance is a hazardous waste.*

## 4. NEED TO DISTINGUISH WASTES FROM NON-WASTES

Simply as a matter of language, the solid waste definition has two basic components: (1) a substance must be solid; and (2) it must be a waste. The statute provides reasonably clear—if somewhat surprising—guidance on what is meant by "solid." Yet, even though the RCRA Subtitle C and D programs provide only for the regulation of solid and hazardous "*wastes*," Congress failed to provide meaningful guidance on the distinction between wastes and other materials. Accordingly, one of the most difficult tasks facing the EPA in fashioning the first round of hazardous waste regulations was the need to distinguish wastes from non-waste materials.

To a layperson, it might seem that a dictionary definition should suffice: something is a waste if it is a byproduct or consumed product that is or has become worthless or useless. Such a definition would presumably acknowledge that worth and usefulness are in the eye of the beholder. Substances rejected as useless by one person may be useful resources to another person; materials that have no worth under certain circumstances and market conditions may have value under other circumstances or market conditions. Under such an approach, the status of a material as waste would hinge on the intentions of human beings.

**Figure 12-2. Regulatory Solid Waste Definition**
Source: John-Mark Stensvaag, Hazardous Waste Law and Practice (1995), Figure 3

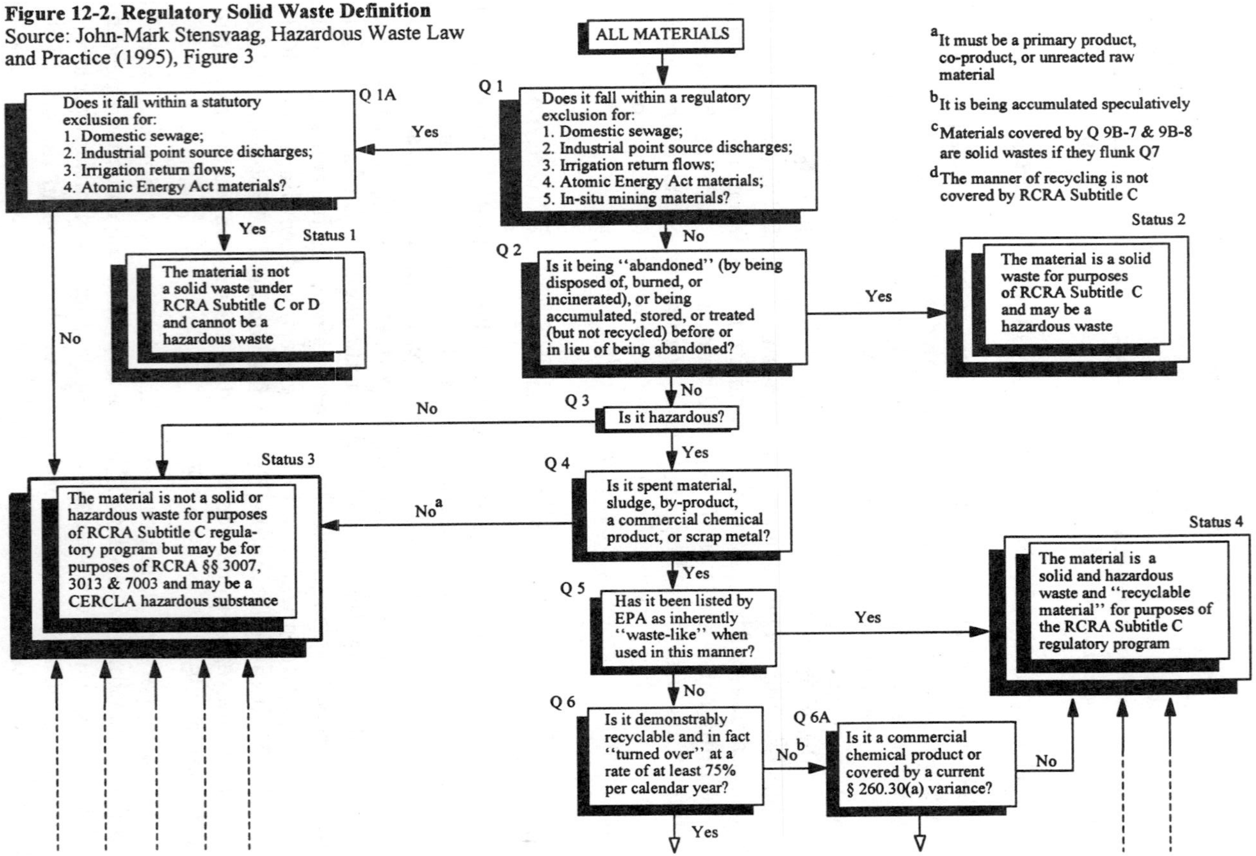

a It must be a primary product, co-product, or unreacted raw material

b It is being accumulated speculatively

c Materials covered by Q 9B-7 & 9B-8 are solid wastes if they flunk Q7

d The manner of recycling is not covered by RCRA Subtitle C

ALL MATERIALS

Q 1 Does it fall within a regulatory exclusion for:
1. Domestic sewage;
2. Industrial point source discharges;
3. Irrigation return flows;
4. Atomic Energy Act materials;
5. In-situ mining materials?

Q 1A Does it fall within a statutory exclusion for:
1. Domestic sewage;
2. Industrial point source discharges;
3. Irrigation return flows;
4. Atomic Energy Act materials?

Yes

Status 1 The material is not a solid waste under RCRA Subtitle C or D and cannot be a hazardous waste

Q 2 Is it being "abandoned" (by being disposed of, burned, or incinerated), or being accumulated, stored, or treated (but not recycled) before or in lieu of being abandoned?

Yes

Status 2 The material is a solid waste for purposes of RCRA Subtitle C and may be a hazardous waste

Q 3 Is it hazardous?

Q 4 Is it spent material, sludge, by-product, a commercial chemical product, or scrap metal?

Q 5 Has it been listed by EPA as inherently "waste-like" when used in this manner?

Yes

Status 4 The material is a solid and hazardous waste and "recyclable material" for purposes of the RCRA Subtitle C regulatory program

Q 6 Is it demonstrably recyclable and in fact "turned over" at a rate of at least 75% per calendar year?

Q 6A Is it a commercial chemical product or covered by a current § 260.30(a) variance?

Status 3 The material is not a solid or hazardous waste for purposes of RCRA Subtitle C regulatory program but may be for purposes of RCRA §§ 3007, 3013 & 7003 and may be a CERCLA hazardous substance

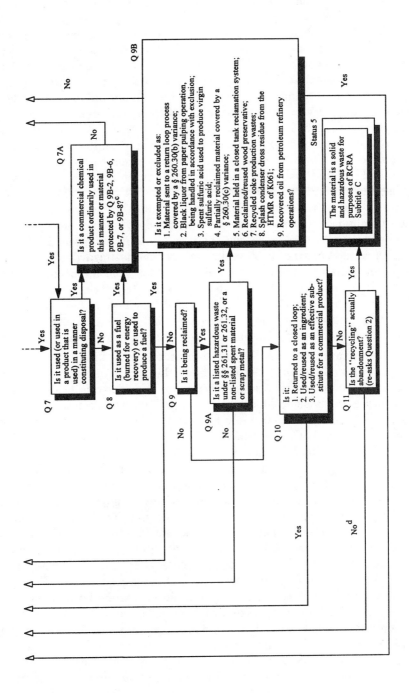

Despite the common sense nature of this dictionary approach, it is hard to imagine a worse definition of waste for RCRA purposes than one hinging on the subjective intentions of the person handling a material at any given moment. Actors wishing to avoid the regulatory controls of RCRA would simply declare that the materials were not worthless or useless—that they *intended* to use, reuse, recycle, or reclaim all or a portion of the materials. Such an ability to opt out of the regulatory system would destroy the efficacy of RCRA. First, unscrupulous actors might declare in bad faith that they intended to recycle their materials, even when they had no such intent. Materials handled by such actors would be in RCRA's hazardous waste management system only in the rare and isolated instances in which enforcement authorities were able to establish—usually after the fact—the bad faith of the claimed intent. Massive quantities of hazardous wastes would probably escape regulation through the inevitable loophole created by such a definition. Second, even if all actors disclosed their true intentions in good faith, materials would constantly move in and out of the hazardous waste system, depending on the intention of the person *then* handling the materials. The cradle-to-grave manifest system of Subtitle C could not effectively regulate materials having such chameleon-like status. The foregoing considerations led EPA to reject a definition of waste based on subjective intent, notwithstanding the ordinary use of that term.

Even apart from the difficulties inherent in linking the waste definition to human intent, the EPA had additional reasons for believing that it would be unwise and impractical to exclude from the solid waste category materials destined for recycling. First, the accumulation, storage, and transport of genuinely recyclable materials may pose many of the same dangers that Subtitle C was designed to minimize. The propensity of a hazardous material to explode, catch fire, or leak into the environment during storage and transport is the same, whether or not it is destined for recycling. Under changing market conditions, especially given the marginal economic nature of many recycling decisions, unmanifested hazardous recyclable materials may fail to reach their intended destination and disappear into the environment. Second, the "uses" of many hazardous materials that ostensibly remove them from the waste category often consist of activities that are similar—in terms of hazard—to the disposal or treatment of hazardous wastes. For example, although the placement of contaminated waste oil on land surfaces for purposes of dust suppression constitutes a use of the substance, the activity is in many ways the functional equivalent of landfilling. Such "use constituting disposal" presents an even greater health hazard by some pathways (for example, inhalation or skin contact) than its fully regulated disposal counterpart. Similarly, the burning of contaminated waste oil for the purpose of energy recovery in a school boiler is a use that may pose an equal or greater air pollution hazard than the regulated treatment process of incineration. Moreover, if such uses removed a material from Subtitle C regulation, the users of the hazardous materials would frequently be unaware of the hazard; their ignorance would intensify the risk. EPA was not speculating when it articulated these two fundamental similarities between the handling of wastes and recyclable materials. It could point to numerous damage incidents involving materials destined for recycling, recycling operations, and facilities that accumulated materials with the claimed intention of recycling them.

For the foregoing reasons, the EPA concluded that solid and hazardous wastes under Subtitle C could not be defined by reference to the ordinary meaning of the term waste. On the other hand, the Agency recognized that a broader definition would also have drawbacks. There is nothing phony about the notion that hazardous byproducts can be recycled in beneficial ways, and that such recycling is often preferable to disposal. Some manufacturing byproducts have such valuable properties that—as long as demand for such properties exceeds supply—they are more like products or commodities than wastes. For example, spent pickle liquor from steel finishing operations is commonly used to precipitate phosphorus and condition sludge at wastewater treatment plants, substituting for the equally hazardous commercial chemical, ferric chloride. Other byproducts may be used as raw materials for manufacturing or construction operations. Even when process streams or manufacturing residues are not directly useable as products or raw materials, valuable chemicals may sometimes be reclaimed; these chemicals may then be used as products or raw materials or reused in the original manufacturing process. A broad definition of "waste" would inevitably tend to bring many of these recyclable substances into the RCRA hazardous waste management system.

The prospect of regulating recyclable substances as hazardous wastes under RCRA Subtitle C presented a new set of problems. One concern was that a broad definition of waste could lead to EPA regulations intruding deeply into business management decisions at manufacturing facilities. The greater concern, however, was that a broad definition of hazardous waste might discourage the desirable handling and recycling of recyclable materials, in ironic contradiction to the resource conservation and recovery emphasis of the statute's title. The mere affixing of the hazardous waste label to recyclable substances might cause people to shun the handling of such substances and to oppose the siting of manufacturing and recycling facilities. Although the EPA asserted that the inclusion of recyclable substances in the hazardous waste management system should legitimate, rather than stigmatize, well-operated recycling facilities, the Agency acknowledged that it would be unwise to "place the hazardous waste stigma on recovered products without good cause." Moreover, because of the marginal economic incentives associated with many recycling decisions, the additional costs of Subtitle C regulation might make it unprofitable to continue present recycling practices. This would be especially true where regulated recycled material competed with nonregulated substances.

In dealing with these considerations, the EPA had to grapple with two related issues. First, the Agency had to decide whether to include recyclable substances within the categories of RCRA wastes—solid or hazardous; this decision focused on what *substances* were to be included in the RCRA program. Second, the Agency had to decide whether to regulate recycling and associated activities; this decision focused on what *conduct* was to be regulated under the statute. While the two decisions involved many of the same factors, the EPA concluded that they called for somewhat different approaches. The result of its conclusion is that the regulatory definition of solid waste includes recyclable materials, but much conduct involving such materials is given special, deferential treatment under the regulations.

By the time the EPA promulgated its first regulatory definition of solid waste on May 19, 1980, it had made two significant policy judgments: (1) that the definition would include recyclable materials; and (2) that the distinction between waste and non-waste status would not hinge on whether a generator or other handler intended to discard a substance. These critical decisions did not end the definitional task, but only made the drafting problem more difficult. The application of RCRA Subtitle C permitting, manifesting, and other requirements to raw materials, products, and manufacturing intermediates—no matter how hazardous—would have exceeded the congressional command to regulate *wastes*, and would have created a regulatory nightmare.

## 5. REGULATORY SOLID WASTE DEFINITION

The regulatory solid waste definition is as complex as anything in the law of hazardous waste. When the EPA adopted the definition in 1985, the Agency realized its complicated nature. Nevertheless, EPA's tortured effort to deal with the problem of recyclable materials had lasted almost a decade. During that time, the Agency had considered and tried several alternative approaches. Potentially regulated entities, watching the ebb and flow of the various proposals, had found it "exceedingly difficult to plan present and future business decisions while riding a regulatory roller coaster." The choice for complexity was, therefore, an experienced and, presumably, carefully considered judgment.

The most fundamental attribute of the regulatory solid waste definition is that one cannot determine the status of many materials without knowing both what the material is and how the material is being used or otherwise handled. It is this double-barreled approach to categorizing materials that accounts for the regulation's intricacy.

The regulatory solid waste definition is depicted in **Figure 12-2**. Each "Question" and "Status" depicted in **Figure 12-2** poses difficult issues of statutory and regulatory interpretation. Only those materials falling within **Figure 12-2**, Statuses 2, 4, or 5, are solid wastes for purposes of RCRA Subtitle C. **Figure 12-2** can be a powerful tool for interpreting and applying the regulatory solid waste definition, as long as one adheres to the following rule: any given question on the diagram is irrelevant to ascertaining the status of a material unless the answers to previous questions in the analytical chain have led to that question. It is imperative that one follow the diagram's sequence of questions.

---

Read the following sections of CERCLA

☐ § 101(10)(A)      ☐ § 101(10)(H)      ☐ § 101(10)(J)

☐ § 101(14)      ☐ § 107(j)

---

### Notes and Questions

1. Examine **Figure 12-2**. Will materials in an industrial point source discharge ever fall within the RCRA Subtitle C regulatory system? Why or why not? Note that the industrial point source discharge exclusion from RCRA solid waste status has both a statutory and regulatory basis. What do you suppose is the logic behind this exclusion? Does that logic make sense? Might the exclusion lead industrial facilities to alter their operations? *See* Professor Dernbach's view at page 658, *supra*.

2. Are industrial point source discharges subject to the CERCLA liability scheme? *See* CERCLA §§ 101(10)(A) and 107(j). Are POTW releases? *See* CERCLA § 101(10)(J). Does CERCLA cover releases of toxic and hazardous pollutants to the air? *See* CERCLA § 101(10)(H).

3. Evaluate the accuracy of the following argument: the failure of the Clean Water Act to regulate numerous toxic and hazardous pollutants, as illustrated by the *Eastman Kodak* opinion (described at page 633, *supra*), is okay because toxic and hazardous pollutants are regulated under RCRA Subtitle C and CERCLA.

4. The RCRA statute excludes from Subtitle C solid waste status "solid or dissolved material in domestic sewage." RCRA § 1004(27). That statutory exclusion for "pure domestic sewage" is depicted in **Figure 12-2**, Question 1A-1. The EPA's regulations exclude from Subtitle C solid waste status not only domestic sewage but also "[a]ny mixture of domestic sewage and other wastes that passes through a sewer system to a publicly-owned treatment works for treatment." 40 C.F.R. § 261.4(a)(1). This regulatory "mixed sewage" exclusion is depicted in **Figure 12-2**, Question 1-1. Because the statutory and regulatory domestic sewage exclusions are *not* coterminous, the RCRA Subtitle C definition has been effectively *bifurcated* into regulatory and statutory components. Assume that Company A's industrial wastes have been mixed with domestic sewage heading toward treatment in a POTW. The industrial wastes cannot be RCRA Subtitle C hazardous wastes, given the regulatory mixed sewage exclusion. Are Company A's industrial wastes nevertheless "hazardous substances," within the meaning of CERCLA? *See* CERCLA § 101(14). Pay special attention to the fine print in CERCLA § 101(14)(C).

5. Any material not culled out prior to **Figure 12-2**, Question 6, is accumulated *speculatively*—and therefore potentially a solid waste, notwithstanding its holder's plans for recycling—unless

the person accumulating it can show that the material is potentially recyclable and has a feasible means of being recycled; and that—during the calendar year (commencing on January 1)—the amount of material that is recycled, or transferred to different site for recycling, equals at least 75 percent by weight or volume of that material accumulated at the beginning of the period. * * *

40 C.F.R. § 261.1(c)(8). Assume that Company B has held—since the beginning of this calendar year—1,000 tons of a hazardous sludge that it intends to recycle. Must Company B actually recycle any of this material by next January 1 to avoid turning all of it into a Subtitle C solid waste? Why or why not?

## 6.  EVOLUTION OF THE HAZARDOUS WASTE DEFINITION

As we have seen, the starting point for the hazardous waste definition is the definition of *solid waste*: nothing can be a hazardous waste unless it is a solid waste. We have also seen that only materials falling within **Figure 12-2**, Statuses 2, 4, or 5, are solid wastes for purposes of RCRA Subtitle C. Which of these materials are also *hazardous wastes* subject to Subtitle C regulation? The answer to this question depends on the current regulatory definition of hazardous waste, depicted in **Figure 12-3**.

Before turning to **Figure 12-3**, however, it is important to understand the process through which the hazardous waste definition has evolved. **Figure 12-3** represents only the last of three sequentially developed components of the hazardous waste definition: (1) the *statutory* definition; (2) the regulatory *criteria* for fleshing out the definition; and (3) the *regulatory* definition.

The statutory language set forth in § 1004(5) of the 1976 enactment provided only the barest outline of a hazardous waste definition. Congress recognized that the definitional task was incomplete and, accordingly, established a two-step administrative process for fleshing out the meaning of hazardous waste. First, it directed EPA to "develop and promulgate *criteria* for identifying the characteristics of hazardous waste, and for listing hazardous waste." Second, it directed the Agency to "promulgate regulations identifying the characteristics of hazardous waste, and listing particular hazardous wastes * * * which shall be subjected to the provisions of this [Subtitle C] * * * based on the criteria." This two-step process was followed by the EPA.

The current hazardous waste definition evolved, therefore, through three hierarchical levels: from the general (statutory definition), to the specific (criteria), to the concrete (current regulatory definition). Theoretically, each level mandates certain attributes for and establishes certain limits on subsequent levels in the hierarchy. Such controls on the EPA's rulemaking powers are typical of federal pollution statutes and familiar to environmental lawyers.

The significance of these limits should not be exaggerated, but neither should the limits be overlooked. The regulatory criteria are vulnerable to attack if they violate the statutory language directing their establishment, if they seek to reach materials not covered by the statutory definition, or if they fail to include materials falling within the statutory definition. Similarly, the characteristics and lists promulgated in the regulatory hazardous waste definition are vulnerable to attack if they seek to embrace materials not covered by the statutory definition or by valid criteria, or if they fail to cover materials falling within the statutory definition or the criteria. Thus, the statutory definition and the regulatory criteria are not historical anachronisms that can be ignored: the legitimacy of the regulatory hazardous waste definition (**Figure 12-3**) must be tested by measurement against the higher authority of the regulatory criteria, and the legitimacy of the criteria is, in turn, dependent on their compliance with the statute.

## 7.  STATUTORY HAZARDOUS WASTE DEFINITION

The statute, RCRA § 1004(5), provides that the term "hazardous waste"

> means a solid waste, or combination of solid wastes, which because of its quantity, concentration, or physical, chemical, or infectious characteristics may—
>
> (A) cause, or significantly contribute to an increase in mortality or an increase in serious irreversible, or incapacitating reversible, illness; or
>
> (B) pose a substantial present or potential hazard to human health or the environment when improperly treated, stored, transported, or disposed of, or otherwise managed.

This definition is so broadly worded that potentially regulated entities cannot reasonably be expected to interpret and apply it; rather, the statutory language is intended as a mere starting place for administrative action.

Two fundamental attributes of the statutory hazardous waste definition dominate the RCRA Subtitle C program. First, drafters of the statute unmistakably envisioned that all solid wastes would be divided into two categories: hazardous wastes and nonhazardous wastes. The initial mandate to divide all solid wastes into two, and only two, categories virtually guarantees an extraordinary degree of aggregation or lumping. Consider, for example, one rapidly degradable material that is explosive when heated in relatively large quantities and a different, highly persistent and mobile material that is carcinogenic when ingested in minute concentrations. If the EPA were to conclude that each material required regulation under RCRA Subtitle C, it would have no choice but to call each of them a hazardous waste. The statute effectively mandates that a single label be attached to a wide spectrum of substances posing varying degrees of quite different types of harm.

To be sure, nothing in the statute precludes differentiating between types or degrees of hazard or risk for purposes of various *regulatory* requirements. Indeed, the two-pronged nature of the statutory definition itself suggests that hazardous wastes may be further broken down into subcategories. The EPA has gradually taken this approach, promulgating unique regulatory requirements for different kinds of hazardous wastes posing distinct types of risks and harms. This pragmatic flexibility has helped greatly to diminish calls by industry for a "degree of hazard" approach to defining hazardous wastes. But the fact remains that all materials regulated under RCRA Subtitle C share a common label—hazardous waste—and a common stigma associated with that label.

A second crucial attribute of the statutory hazardous waste definition is the inclusion of solid wastes that pose substantial hazards "when *improperly* * * * managed." The choice of this language is understandable; Congress had heard a litany of past damage incidents and had presumably concluded that damage is frequently caused by the mismanagement of materials that might pose little or no hazard if properly handled. Nevertheless, the "hazardous when improperly managed" notion—particularly when coupled with the congressional decision to include a wide range of management activities—implies an extraordinarily broad universe of hazardous wastes. Wastes that are routinely handled without incident by at least some potentially regulated entities, for example, would be included if harmfully mismanaged by others. The statute did limit its coverage to materials that pose *substantial* hazards when mismanaged—a phrase that would justify the exclusion of "broken glass in a schoolyard." However, the qualifying phrase "substantial" is notoriously devoid of content.

## 8. CRITERIA FOR IDENTIFYING AND LISTING HAZARDOUS WASTES

For the first four years following the enactment of RCRA, no material was a hazardous waste for purposes of Subtitle C regulation. The statutory definition was not self-implementing, but merely set the stage for two rulemaking steps by the EPA. First, the Agency was instructed to promulgate "criteria for identifying the characteristics of hazardous waste, and for listing hazardous waste." We refer to these as the *criteria*. Second, the Agency was directed to promulgate "regulations identifying the characteristics of hazardous waste, and listing particular hazardous wastes," which regulations were to be "based on the criteria." We refer to these regulations as the "regulatory hazardous waste *definition*."

The best way to understand the role of the criteria is to recognize that they guide the EPA *Administrator* in deciding whether the EPA should list or delist hazardous wastes, and in deciding whether the EPA should identify a particular hazardous waste characteristic. The criteria are not designed to directly guide any potentially regulated entity in determining whether its wastes are hazardous. Unfortunately, because the hazardous waste *characteristics* and the *criteria* both specify attributes that may cause a solid waste to be a hazardous waste, it is easy to confuse the two concepts. The characteristics may—and frequently do—lead the Administrator to list a material as a hazardous waste, but they are also designed to be directly consulted by persons who generate solid wastes; indeed, one of the primary obligations of solid waste generators is the duty to determine whether their solid wastes exhibit any of the hazardous waste characteristics. There is no similar obligation to determine whether solid wastes meet the hazardous waste criteria. Indeed, solid wastes which meet one or more of the criteria are *not* hazardous wastes unless they have been listed (or contain a listed waste) or exhibit one or more of the identified hazardous waste characteristics.

## 9.  CHARACTERISTICS CRITERIA

The statute directs EPA to develop "criteria for identifying the characteristics of hazardous waste, *and* for listing hazardous waste." The Agency took this directive literally and promulgated two sets of criteria: one to guide the EPA in identifying characteristics or properties that will result in hazardous waste status, and one to guide the Agency in determining which wastes to list. For convenience, we refer to these as the "characteristics criteria" and the "listing criteria." Because the listing criteria build on the characteristics criteria, we will focus on the latter. (For a brief discussion of the listing criteria—particularly the Appendix VIII constituents—*see* page 693, *infra*).

Before examining the criteria themselves, it is necessary to understand the notion of hazardous waste characteristics. There are two ways in which a solid waste may be a hazardous waste under the current regulatory definition. First, a solid waste may be *listed* by the EPA, or may contain or be derived from a listed hazardous waste. Second, a solid waste that is not listed may exhibit one of several *characteristics* identified by the Agency. It is the generator's obligation to determine whether his or her solid waste is a hazardous waste because of its inclusion on one of several lists or because the material exhibits a characteristic. Obviously, it should be a relatively simple matter to consult the hazardous waste lists, but ascertaining hazardousness due to characteristics can be more difficult. The generator must determine whether his or her solid waste exhibits a characteristic either by applying specified testing methods to the waste or by exercising judgment based on knowledge of the material or the process used to produce it.

To understand the ensuing discussion of the "measurability criteria" and the "listing preference," you should know that the EPA ultimately selected only four "characteristics" for hazardous wastes: ignitability, corrosivity, reactivity, and a narrow attribute called "toxicity." *See* page 684, *infra*. If a solid waste does not exhibit one of these characteristics (e.g., if it is "merely" a carcinogen), it will not be a hazardous waste unless the EPA has affirmatively listed the material.

The characteristics *criteria* are designed to assist the Agency in deciding which characteristics will result in hazardous waste status or—to use the statutory language—to assist in "identifying" the hazardous waste characteristics. Those criteria presently provide:

(a) The Administrator shall identify and define a characteristic of hazardous waste in Subpart C [of Part 261] only upon determining that:

(1) A solid waste that exhibits the characteristic may:

(i) Cause, or significantly contribute to, an increase in mortality or an increase in serious irreversible, or incapacitating reversible illness; or

(ii) Pose a substantial present or potential hazard to human health or the environment when it is improperly treated, stored, transported, disposed of or otherwise managed; *and*

(2) The characteristic can be:

(i) Measured by an available standardized test method which is reasonably within the capability of generators of solid waste or private sector laboratories that are available to serve generators of solid waste; or

(ii) Reasonably detected by generators of solid waste through their knowledge of their waste.

40 C.F.R. 26.10 (1986) (emphasis added).

Careful examination of these criteria reveals that they actually consist of two subgroups: (1) *statutory effects* criteria and (2) *measurability* criteria. The first subgroup of criteria merely recites verbatim the heart of the statutory hazardous waste definition; it provides, in effect, that any characteristic that may cause or significantly contribute to any of the statutory effects, is a *candidate* for identification as a hazardous waste characteristic. Because the statute sets forth two alternative groups of effects, there are two statutory effects criteria, and they are stated in the alternative: only one need be met. If the characteristics criteria consisted only of this first subgroup, they would add nothing to the statutory hazardous waste definition; indeed, the universe of solid wastes brought into the Subtitle C system because they exhibit hazardous waste characteristics would be identical to the ill-defined universe described by the statutory hazardous waste definition.

The criteria provide further, however, that the EPA *cannot* identify as a hazardous waste characteristic any characteristic that *only* meets one of the statutory effects criteria. The Administrator is forbidden from identifying such a candidate characteristic as a hazardous waste characteristic unless it also meets at least one of the two measurability criteria: it must be capable of being reasonably measured or detected by generators. As we will see, the measurability criteria have resulted in a considerable narrowing of the field of characteristics ultimately identified by the EPA. In the process, the criteria have revealed a great deal about the Agency's approach to defining hazardous wastes.

## 10. MEASURABILITY CRITERIA

Why did the EPA profoundly limit the range of identifiable hazardous waste characteristics by adopting the measurability criteria? After all, if a characteristic causes or contributes to one of the statutorily enumerated effects (such as an increase in mortality), one can make a reasonable argument that the EPA has no choice but to provide that any solid waste exhibiting that characteristic is a hazardous waste.

The wording of the measurability criteria suggests two reasons for their adoption. First, because the primary responsibility for determining whether solid wastes exhibit hazardous waste characteristics rests with generators, the Agency cannot demand unreasonable or impossible testing. If hazardous waste characteristics were not measurable by test methods that were "reasonably within the capability of generators * * * or private sector laboratories * * * available to serve generators," the obligations imposed on solid waste generators by Subtitle C would be unfairly onerous and costly, and the Subtitle C program would be unworkable.

This first rationale for the measurability criteria focuses on the testing capabilities of the solid waste generating community. If the limited testing capabilities of generators were the only reason for failing to identify a candidate characteristic that admittedly caused or contributed to the statutory effects, the Agency should presumably seek to make measuring tools more widely available; indeed, the phased introduction of such a characteristic into the hazardous waste system, with adequate warning, might inspire market forces to create less costly, more widely available testing capabilities. Certainly, it would be more appropriate for the Agency to provide resources and technical expertise to foster the growth of that testing capability, rather than to continually eschew identifying unquestionably hazardous characteristics.

Second, the wording of the criteria suggests an additional, more subtle rationale for requiring measurability: the possibility that testing for some characteristics—even concededly hazardous ones—is so unreliable that affirmative results, ostensibly finding the presence of the characteristics, cannot be trusted. For example, the EPA might conclude that a relatively simple, widely available, and inexpensive test for the characteristic of carcinogenicity erroneously finds the characteristic in a substantial percentage of tests, even though the characteristic is not actually present. Assuming that there were no other, more reliable tests for the presence of carcinogenicity, that characteristic would flunk the measurability criteria—not because of onerous or impossible measurement burdens on the generating community, but because carcinogenicity would not be a characteristic that "can be [m]easured."

Each of the two foregoing reasons for rejecting admittedly hazardous candidate characteristics is fully consistent with the wording of the measurability criteria. So viewed, the measurability criteria embody EPA's judgment that the Agency ought not identify a characteristic if *generators* cannot reasonably be expected to test for or otherwise detect the presence of the characteristic and—a fortiori—ought not identify a characteristic if *no* one can consistently and accurately measure or detect the presence of the characteristic. In accordance with this view of the measurability criteria, the preamble explains that the available test protocols for measuring many of the rejected candidate characteristics were "either insufficiently developed or too complex and too highly dependent on the use of skilled personnel and special equipment," and that the Agency was unable to "suitably define and construct" new testing protocols." Such explanations are fully consistent with the wording of the measurability criteria and the two rationales discussed above.

Additional preamble explanations for rejecting candidate characteristics indicate, however, that considerably more is going on—under the guise of flunking the measurability criteria—than the wording of those criteria would suggest. In fact, EPA may have relied on the measurability criteria to weed out characteristics that are actually being rejected for a fundamentally different reason than the inadequate testing capabilities of generators and the EPA. The preamble to the final criteria discloses this deeper rationale most plainly:

> Additionally, given the current state of the knowledge concerning such properties, EPA did not feel that it could define with any confidence the *numerical threshold level* at which wastes exhibiting these characteristics would present a substantial hazard. Furthermore, it questioned whether these tests sufficiently took into account the multiple factors which bore on the question of the hazardousness of such wastes.

45 Fed. Reg. 33,065, 33,105 (1980 (emphasis added).

At first glance, this explanation would seem to demonstrate a misapplication of the measurability criteria. There is nothing in those criteria—or in the statutory effects criteria—requiring that the EPA be able to establish "numerical threshold levels" for a characteristic, or that tests to determine the presence or absence of a characteristic take into account factors rendering the characteristic hazardous. Instead, the criteria require only that readily available testing methods can accurately measure or detect the presence of the characteristic.

The most striking example of this apparent misuse of the measurability criteria is the candidate characteristic of radioactivity. The EPA did not deny—nor could it—that the characteristic of radioactivity may cause or contribute to the harmful consequences set forth by the statutory effects criteria. Accordingly, the failure to identify radioactivity as a hazardous characteristic could be justified only under the measurability criteria. Yet, it would be preposterous for the Agency to assert that the characteristic of radioactivity cannot be "measured by an available standardized test method which is reasonably within the capability of generators * * * or private sector laboratories." No matter how mysterious radioactivity may seem to a layperson, the presence of this characteristic in a solid waste material should be readily and cheaply detectable. How, then, could the EPA purport to rely on the measurability criteria in failing to identify radioactivity as a hazardous waste characteristic?

The failure to identify radioactivity can be explained as an implementation of the measurability criteria, but to do so requires a radical rethinking about the nature of "characteristics." Because of our ordinary commitment to Aristotelian logic, we tend to think of characteristics in terms of two, rigid, true-false categories; in any given material, a characteristic is either present or it is absent. Thus, a solid waste is either radioactive or nonradioactive, corrosive or noncorrosive, and so on. So viewed, a characteristic is an unquantified physical or chemical property. In fact, however, virtually no characteristics can be defined in this way under RCRA; the use of unquantified properties cannot work because they are vastly overinclusive. Defining corrosivity as the mere presence of that attribute, for example, might include common softdrinks; similarly, defining radioactivity as the mere presence of unstable atoms would include virtually all solid wastes.

There is another way to view the concept of a characteristic, and that is in terms of a *quantified* property. Under this approach, a material does not exhibit the characteristic of radioactivity, for example, unless it emits a certain level of radiation or contains a certain quantum of radioactive material; similarly, a material does not exhibit the characteristic of corrosivity, unless its pH falls within a certain range, or it corrodes metal at a specified minimum rate.

Once we rethink the concept of characteristics, a new theme or reason for the current characteristics criteria emerges: the EPA is unwilling to identify and define a characteristic if the Agency cannot set legally defensible quantifications for the characteristic. Although this rationale does not show up in the technical wording of the criteria, it may explain the Agency's rejection of some candidate characteristics. Thus, in at least some cases, the *generator*'s inability to measure or detect the presence of a candidate characteristic may be no more than a surrogate justification in place of the real cause of inaction—the *Agency*'s inability to define or establish a *quantification* for the characteristic.

The foregoing discussion assumes that the EPA acted in good faith in identifying the four hazardous waste characteristics and rejecting all other candidate characteristics. At least one EPA employee involved in that process has alleged that the measurability criteria were after-the-fact rationalizations, invented to justify a curtailment of the characteristics actually motivated by an improper desire to reduce inflation. The superior EPA official accused of this motivation has called the allegation "a despicable lie."

The measurability criteria thus represent three distinct grounds for rejecting candidate characteristics: (1) the lack of accessible, inexpensive testing protocols for use by solid waste generators; (2) the unreliability of testing methods; and (3) the Agency's inability to define or establish defensible quantifications for the characteristics. The Agency's conclusions that each rejected candidate characteristic flunked the criteria on one or more of these grounds have been so controversial that Congress amended RCRA in 1984 to direct the identification of additional characteristics.

## 11. REJECTED CANDIDATE CHARACTERISTICS

The most obvious and immediate consequence of the measurability criteria was that the EPA decided to identify only four hazardous waste characteristics: ignitability, corrosivity, reactivity, and a peculiarly narrow property denoted "extraction procedure" (EP) toxicity. By the time of the formal 1978 proposal of the hazardous waste regulation, the measurability criteria had caused the Agency to reject the Subtitle C identification of four additional candidate characteristics (characteristics known to qualify for identification under the statutory effects criteria): radioactivity, infectiousness, phytotoxicity (toxicity to plants), and teratogenicity/mutagenicity.

Originally, the decision to reject most of these candidate characteristics was meant to be only temporary. Simultaneously with its 1978 proposal to limit the initially identified characteristics to the present four, the Agency issued an advance notice of proposed rulemaking which, if promulgated, would have expanded the characteristics to include radioactivity, "unnatural genetic activity" (including mutagenicity, carcinogenicity, and teratogenicity), bioaccumulation potential, organic toxicity to humans, aquatic species toxicity, and terrestrial plant toxicity (phytotoxicity). By the time of final promulgation of the hazardous waste characteristics in 1980, the EPA had abandoned any plans to add to the original four characteristics—again, in reliance on the measurability criteria.

## 12. THE LISTING PREFERENCE

It is important to understand that, from the EPA's point of view, the decision to reject various candidate characteristics did not mean that wastes exhibiting such characteristics would remain outside the Subtitle C system. Instead, the rejection of the characteristics represented a change in the EPA's philosophy. In 1978, the Agency envisioned a definitional scheme eventually involving at least ten hazardous waste characteristics—properties which *generators* would be required to detect or rule out in solid wastes. Under its then-existing regulatory strategy, listing would have played "a largely supplementary function."

When the EPA chose in 1980 to identify only four characteristics, it declared that it was "relying on the listing mechanism to bring wastes exhibiting the [rejected] properties into the system." The Agency stressed that "[t]he criteria for *listing* toxic wastes are intended by EPA to identify *all* those wastes which are toxic, carcinogenic, mutagenic, teratogenic, phytotoxic, or toxic to aquatic species." We refer to this new Agency policy as the "*listing preference.*"

The EPA's shift from reliance on the characteristics to a preference for the listing process in defining hazardous wastes was and still remains highly controversial. Critics have asserted that the listing preference: (1) resulted from a misapplication of the criteria—particularly the measurability criteria; (2) has vastly reduced the universe of regulated hazardous wastes; and (3) assures that the universe will remain small, because of its inappropriate allocation of obligations between the generating community and the EPA.

Critics contend first that the Agency arrived at the listing preference only after misapplying its own criteria for identifying hazardous waste characteristics. Oversight subcommittees in both houses of Congress were unconvinced by the EPA's assertion that the measurability criteria required rejection of candidate characteristics. The House subcommittee urged the EPA to require testing for four rejected characteristics:

> Even though there may be no simple, well-accepted tests that identify all wastes which are oncogenic, mutagenic, teratogenic, or bioaccumulate, there are currently tests which yield useful information regarding such characteristics. In fact, EPA presently employs some of these tests for screening under the [Toxic Substances Control Act]. * * * If the requirement [of testing] would impose an undue burden on small companies, then we would recommend that companies that produce the same waste share the cost of testing or that Federal funds be used to share in the burden.

The Senate subcommittee was equally dubious that the rejected characteristics had flunked the measurability criteria:

> EPA's explanation for failing to use characteristics to identify toxic, radioactive, infectious, phytotoxic, teratogenic and mutagenic substances under the proposed regulations for § 3001—that of not having reliable test protocols for these characteristics—is not consistent with the Agency's use of test protocols.

Given the wording of the measurability criteria, it is not surprising that the congressional subcommittees disagreed with the Agency's application of the criteria to specific candidate characteristics. However, neither subcommittee grappled with the more fundamental problem facing the Agency in connection with at least some of the rejected characteristics: assuming that application of a test protocol would "yield useful information," how could the EPA effectively quantify or define the characteristic in a rational, defensible way?

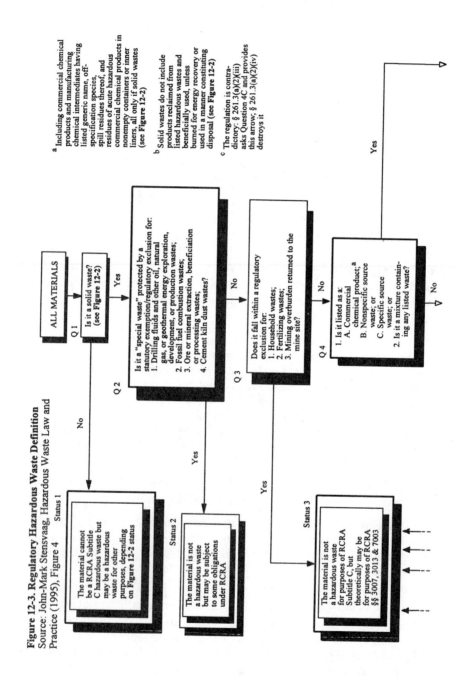

**Figure 12-3. Regulatory Hazardous Waste Definition**
Source: John-Mark Stensvaag, Hazardous Waste Law and
Practice (1995), Figure 4

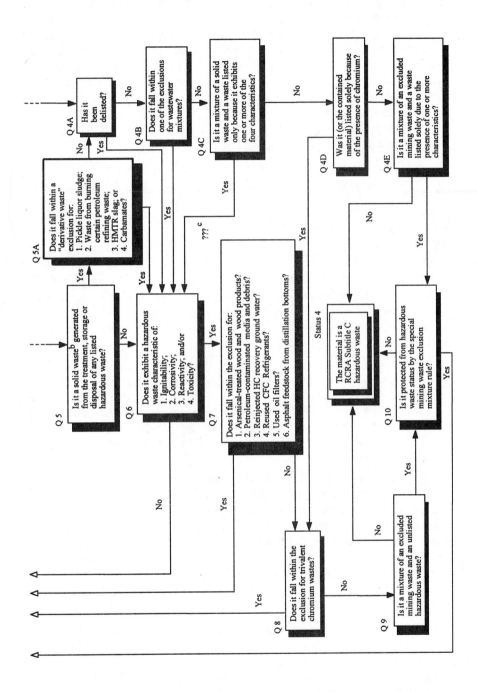

The difficulty of quantifying or defining some of the candidate characteristics may have been underestimated by the Agency's critics. It is true that an excessive preoccupation by the EPA with demonstrable threshold values would be inconsistent with congressional intent; the statutory definition provides, after all, that solid wastes which *may* cause or contribute to the enumerated effects are hazardous wastes. Nevertheless, society would not benefit from a regulatory regime in which vast quantities of nonhazardous solid waste flooded the Subtitle C system because of a poorly articulated, ill-defined effort to assure that no hazardous wastes escaped the regulatory net.

Second, even assuming that the EPA had correctly applied its measurability criteria to the rejected candidate characteristics, opponents of the listing preference criticized its most immediate consequence: a significant shrinkage in the universe of hazardous wastes first envisioned by the Agency. Many decried the resulting gap in RCRA coverage. The Senate oversight subcommittee concluded that nearly two-thirds of the nation's annual hazardous waste production would escape regulation because of the Agency's change in policy. One unhappy EPA employee, who had been involved in the Agency's rejection of the candidate characteristics, graphically disputed the EPA's suggestion that the hazardous waste lists adequately substituted for an identification of the characteristics:

> When the order was given to remove the characteristics as a way of defining a hazardous waste, if I can draw an analogy, it's like stripping off a wall-to-wall carpet from a floor; and, having done that, the Agency noticed that the floor was very bare, there were very few things regulated. So, to cover up the bareness, a few scatter rugs were thrown around. And these appendices [hazardous waste *lists*] * * * are those scatter rugs.

The third and most significant criticism of the listing preference has to do with its long-term implications for the hazardous waste definition. Congress intended that the definition of hazardous waste would change through time and, presumably, that the universe of hazardous wastes regulated under RCRA Subtitle C would expand. Because of the listing preference, however, the universe has been essentially static. One reason for this steady state is that the listing preference reallocated the obligation to determine the hazardousness of many solid wastes from generators to the Agency.

The preamble concedes that this reallocation of responsibility may retard the process of defining hazardous wastes: "One negative aspect of this change is that it shifts to the EPA the primary burden for identifying, analyzing and evaluating these wastes with the result that it may take longer to achieve full regulatory coverage." Critics have been more blunt, noting that the Agency's listing preference has led the EPA to assume "a massive burden in analyzing and evaluating the characteristics of thousands of wastes for which it feels it is not yet possible to define testing protocols sufficiently standardized for use by generators."

Given the size of its staff and budget, the Agency cannot possibly test hundreds of thousands of solid wastes for the presence of the rejected characteristics; instead, it must rely on literature searches and information gleaned from contractors hired to examine the solid wastes of specific industries. Particularly at a time of reduced Agency budgets, EPA's resources may be unequal to the task associated with its listing preference.

The burden imposed on the Agency is exacerbated by the EPA's failure to place *any burden* on the generating community in connection with the rejected candidate characteristics. Because of the frequently misleading logic of the measurability criteria—the notion that generators are not capable of testing for the presence of the rejected characteristics—there is no requirement that generators even *disclose* to the EPA that their solid wastes exhibit such characteristics.

For these reasons, the universe of solid wastes exhibiting the rejected characteristics that eventually winds up on the hazardous waste *lists* appears to be the product of almost random, fortuitous events, requiring no input from the solid waste generators. At a minimum, it seems likely that many solid wastes exhibiting the rejected candidate characteristics have not been listed by the Agency, in part because the EPA does not and cannot be expected to know of the existence or properties of solid wastes that have not been brought within the Subtitle C system.

The Agency insists, however, that this negative aspect of the listing preference—the shifting of burdens from generators to the Agency—is effectively balanced by a positive attribute of the approach: listing, according to the EPA, is a more "precise instrument" for making determinations of "marginal hazard" than the more crude identification of characteristics.

As the preamble notes, when a solid waste is found to be a hazardous waste because it flunks a test for one of the characteristics, the generator has no opportunity to rebut the assignment of the material to hazardous waste status. By contrast, "the listing mechanism allows for a more individualized consideration of hazard and * * * the delisting procedure affords generators an opportunity to demonstrate, through reliance on the specified factors, that their waste is not in fact hazardous." Because of this difference in consequences, the EPA has said that it is reluctant to define *characteristics* in ways that might be overinclusive, but does not feel the same reluctance and can be bold in *listing* wastes.

At the core of the Agency's defense of the listing preference is the implied assertion that *more* carcinogens, for example, will be regulated under Subtitle C through listing—because the Agency will list such materials broadly, without fear of overinclusion—than would be regulated had the EPA defined carcinogenicity as a characteristic—because the characteristic would have been defined so narrowly as to reach a smaller universe of potential carcinogens. The congressional oversight committees were highly skeptical of this claim.

In any event, Congress became convinced, by the time it enacted the Hazardous and Solid Waste Amendments of 1984 (HWSA), that the four identified characteristics were insufficient. The amendments provide that the Administrator "*shall* promulgate regulations * * * identifying *additional characteristics* of hazardous waste," within two years. Interestingly, Congress did not order the EPA to alter—or even reconsider—the *criteria* for identifying characteristics.

## 13. REGULATORY HAZARDOUS WASTE DEFINITION

The criteria for listing and identifying hazardous wastes are fundamental prerequisites to defining hazardous wastes, but they are not the definition itself. As we have previously noted, the criteria are not designed to guide any potentially regulated entity directly in determining whether its wastes are hazardous but, rather, to guide the Administrator in determining which wastes to list and which characteristics to identify. Thus, the criteria need not be consulted in the process of ascertaining which solid wastes are hazardous wastes. Instead, one ascertains the hazardous waste status of a material by consulting the regulatory hazardous waste definition.

The regulatory hazardous waste definition is depicted in **Figure 12-3**. Only those materials falling within **Figure 12-3**, Status 4 are hazardous wastes for purposes of RCRA Subtitle C. As with **Figure 12-2** (the regulatory *solid* waste definition), **Figure 12-3** can be a powerful tool for interpreting and applying the definition, as long as one follows the diagram's sequence of questions. For example, a negative answer to Question 6 does not justify the conclusion that a material is not a hazardous waste, unless the material has also avoided all preceding pitfalls; such pitfalls might include, for example, affirmative answers to Questions 4 or 5.

## 14. THE FOUR CHARACTERISTICS

The preceding reading suggests that the RCRA Subtitle C program can be understood most readily by dividing it into three overarching topics that confront potentially regulated entities: (1) the universe of regulated materials (hazardous wastes); (2) the universe of regulated actors (generators, transporters, and owners/operators of treatment, storage, and disposal facilities); and (3) the obligations of the numerous actors who handle various subsets of hazardous waste. You have now been introduced, in a limited way, to the universe of regulated materials and to some of the policy decisions that were made by the EPA in defining that universe.

Bear in mind that the EPA has *listed* specific substances as hazardous wastes. That list (actually, a set of four lists) is set forth in 40 C.F.R. 261.31-.33. Although the list was intended to successfully nab nasty materials that would otherwise escape hazardous waste status because of the agency's narrow approach to defining characteristics, Congress blasted the EPA for failing to reach even the most notorious hazardous substances. For example, a House subcommittee report issued in late 1982 concluded that the dioxin contamination leading to the abandoned ghost town of Times Beach, Missouri, could recur under RCRA, because only a small number of dioxin production processes or product uses were covered by the RCRA regulations, and most dioxin wastes were not listed as hazardous wastes under the rules. *See* 13 [Curr. Dev.] Env. Rep. (BNA) 1173 (1982). The report further noted that most dioxin wastes did not meet one of the four characteristics of hazardous waste. There is nothing surprising about this, because the characteristics are so limited.

A moment's reflection will disclose the narrowness of the first three characteristics. "Ignitability" refers to a material's propensity to cause fires during routine handling or to severely exacerbate the dangers of a fire once started. *See* 1 Cooke, *et al.*, Law of Hazardous Waste 2-59 (1987). The "corrosivity" characteristic embraces wastes with high (alkaline) or low (acidic) pH, or with the propensity to corrode steel. *Id.* at 2-60. "Reactivity" is the capability to explode or undergo violent chemical change. *Id.* at 2-61. We can sleep better at night knowing that generators of ignitable, corrosive, and reactive wastes must comply with the manifest system and ship their wastes only to approved hazardous waste facilities. But the average American citizen probably would scarcely articulate these properties when trying to describe the meaning of "hazardous waste." Instead, he or she would almost certainly stress the capacity of a chemical to make people sick: to cause cancer, birth defects, and other adverse human reactions. Obviously, the subject of hazardous wastes embraces something far more profound than the materials that fire departments have dealt with over the centuries.

Because of the limited scope of these first three characteristics, the wastes that we are uniquely and newly concerned about today will escape the Subtitle C regulatory system unless they are grabbed by the final two mechanisms: the toxicity characteristic—formerly known as the extraction procedure (or EP) toxicity characteristic—or EPA's hazardous waste lists. The lists are woefully incomplete. Can we rely on the toxicity characteristic? The following reading underscores the narrow scope of the EP toxicity characteristic, which was augmented and given a modified name in May 1990 as the "Toxicity Characteristic" or TC. The modification altered the leaching test and added 25 organic chemicals to the 14 substances flagged by the test.

## EPA ISSUES RCRA'S "CRADLE-TO-GRAVE" HAZARDOUS WASTE RULES

10 Envtl. L. Rep. 10130, 10132 (1980)

Of the four characteristics, only the toxicity standard attracted controversy or underwent significant alterations between the proposed and final regulations. As the only test used to assess toxicity, the Agency developed an "extraction procedure (EP)." The test attempts to duplicate leaching of toxic substances from landfills toward ground water, one of the most prevalent ways that toxic substances contaminate the environment. Specifically, the EP is intended to identify wastes likely to leach hazardous concentrations of toxic constituents into the ground water through improper management. A sample extract is analyzed to determine whether it contains a specific quantity of any of the toxic contaminants listed in the Safe Drinking Water Act's national primary interim drinking water standards. If the extract does contain such a quantity, the waste is then labeled as hazardous. The proposed regulations provided that a substance would be considered hazardous if a sample extract contained 10 times the Safe Drinking Water Act's (SDWA's) standard for a given toxicant. Many commenters, however, asserted that the multiplication factor was too conservative in that it failed to take account of natural filtration and absorption as chemicals leach through soil. In the final regulations the Agency recanted and set the multiplier at 100 times the SDWA levels.

The EP possesses significant defects. Even EPA admits that the procedure itself is crude and leads to inconsistent results. Another shortcoming is that the Safe Drinking Water Act sets standards for only 14 toxic substances. * * *

### Notes and Questions

1. Suppose that Company C generates a new, dangerous, chemical, as a byproduct of an innovative technique for manufacturing a valuable consumer good. Company C discards it by dumping it in open pits on the company's land, so the byproduct material is undeniably a solid waste within the meaning of RCRA Subtitle C. *See* **Figure 12-2**, Question 2. Do you suppose that the waste material is a *listed* hazardous waste? Why or why not? If the material is not a listed hazardous waste, what attributes might cause it to fall within the regulatory hazardous waste definition of **Figure 12-3**?

2. One might expect that American industry generates new types of wastes all the time. These wastes will remain unlisted unless and until the EPA chooses to move against them. Such waste materials will therefore be hazardous only if they exhibit ignitability, corrosivity, reactivity, or TC toxicity. The Toxicity Characteristic (TC) is measured by simulating groundwater leaching in a laboratory procedure and then testing the leachate for concentrations exceeding specified cutoff values of 14 Safe Drinking Water Act pollutants and 25 organics (such as benzene, chloroform, and pentachlorophenol). *See* 40 C.F.R. § 261.24 & Part 261, Appendix II.

3. The EPA's failure to promulgate a hazardous waste characteristic of infectiousness led to considerable hand wringing when medical debris, such as needles, syringes, blood bags, bandages, and vials, began washing up on public shorelines in Connecticut, New Jersey, and New York, in the summer of 1988. Congress echoed public sentiment that medical waste on the nation's beaches is "repugnant, intolerable, and unacceptable," enacting

the Medical Waste Tracking Act of 1988. *See* Pub. L. No. 100-582, 102 Stat. 2950 (1988).

## 15. APPENDIX VIII CONSTITUENTS

Although we will not cover in this text the many *listing* criteria—the regulations setting forth the touchstones that the EPA will use to list hazardous wastes—you should know that one of the several listing criteria (the "toxic waste listing criterion") allows the EPA to list (as hazardous wastes) any substance containing a harmful "constituent" chemical; the list of several hundred constituent chemicals is set forth in 40 C.F.R. Part 261, Appendix VIII. Wastes containing an *Appendix VIII constituent* are not automatically hazardous wastes; they will become hazardous wastes only if affirmatively listed by the EPA in a rulemaking proceeding.

It is helpful to emphasize what the Appendix VIII constituents are *not*. The Appendix VIII constituents are not hazardous waste characteristics. Indeed, they lack two fundamental attributes of the characteristics. First, unlike the characteristics—which, if present, automatically result in hazardous waste status—the presence in a solid waste of one or more Appendix VIII constituents never results in hazardous waste status unless the Agency undertakes the affirmative step of listing the waste. Thus, a solid waste is not a hazardous waste merely because it contains an Appendix VIII constituent. Second, also unlike the characteristics, a generator or other solid waste handler is not required to test for or otherwise determine the presence of the Appendix VIII constituents. Indeed, there is no obligation of any kind to report to the Agency that one's solid waste contains an Appendix VIII constituent.

The Agency has not promulgated a precise standard (or criterion) telling it how to go about *selecting* the Appendix VIII constituents. However, the associated toxic waste listing criterion declares that: "Substances will be listed on Appendix VIII only if they have been shown in scientific studies to have toxic, carcinogenic, mutagenic or teratogenic effects on humans or other life forms." These effects are ones which would have been addressed by several of the rejected candidate *characteristics*; the appearance of the effects, instead, as bases for selection of Appendix VIII *constituents* is one manifestation of the EPA's listing preference.

The EPA's selection of Appendix VIII constituents represents only the first of three steps in the hazardous waste listing process pursuant to the "toxic waste listing criterion." A solid waste containing an Appendix VIII constituent will be a hazardous waste only if two additional steps are taken: (2) the waste must be identified as a candidate for listing; and (3) the waste must not be found to be nonhazardous, when evaluated pursuant to the factors set forth in the toxic waste listing criterion. The second and third steps, like the first, are undertaken by the Agency, not by the generators.

Because the Agency bears these responsibilities, a solid waste containing an Appendix VIII constituent will not be a candidate for listing—much less a listed hazardous waste—unless the Agency *recognizes* that the waste contains such a constituent and identifies it as a potential hazardous waste. The EPA can only take this step when it has information about the constituents of a solid waste. One might think that the EPA would require the potentially regulated community to come forward with such information—at least where readily available. Surprisingly, the EPA has not done so. No matter how obvious it may be to a generator that a solid waste contains one or more of the Appendix VIII constituents, there is no obligation to notify the EPA of that fact. Instead, the Agency relies on contract studies, damage reports, and other, more indirect, means to secure information about solid waste constituents.

Environmental advocates have criticized the Agency for shouldering the burden of identifying Appendix VIII constituent-bearing wastes, and for failing to establish more aggressive mechanisms for developing waste constituent information. These critics make a valid point: the task of identifying all solid wastes containing Appendix VIII constituents—without the assistance of mandatory waste constituent reports from the generating community—is so massive that thousands of such wastes may remain unidentified and unregulated.

A solid waste is not a hazardous waste merely because the EPA (1) has selected Appendix VIII constituents and (2) has recognized that the waste contains one or more such constituents. The third and final step in the hazardous waste listing process pursuant to the "toxic waste listing criterion" is an evaluation of the waste pursuant to certain enumerated factors. Through this evaluation process, EPA has the discretion not to list a solid waste even though it contains an Appendix VIII constituent.

Environmentalists have questioned why there should be any discretion to refuse to list a solid waste which contains an Appendix VIII constituent. In effect these advocates would use the Appendix VIII constituents in the same manner as the EPA uses the hazardous waste characteristics: any solid waste containing an Appendix VIII constituent would be a hazardous waste without the need for further identification of the waste by the Agency and without any additional listing formality.

The following exchange, occurring during a Senate oversight hearing, illustrates this view and the Agency's response. "C-56" is hexachlorocyclopentadiene, an Appendix VIII constituent.

SEN. LEVIN: Is the chemical C-56 a chemical known to be hazardous to human health? * * *

MR. [THOMAS] JORLING [EPA]: * * * We are regulating waste. Very rarely do we have under regulation discrete, identifiable chemicals. It's usually a mixed glop, or often a mixed glop. So that what we have done is issued lists which refer to "process wastes." * * * Many times, chemicals such as some that have been alleged to have been omitted by the Agency, are included in those process wastes, and therefore they are included. * * *

SEN. LEVIN: Well, let's go back to C-56. If C-56 were spilled on the highway, would it have been covered under your proposed reg[ulations]?

MR. JORLING: If it was C-56 that was included in the wastewater from scrub water from chlorination [of] cyclopentadiene in production of chlordane, yes.[a] Now the question that you're really asking is: How many other places does C-56 get manufactured? And that's what our Agency is trying to analyze now to determine whether all C-56 is included—all waste C-56. We are doing that, Senator.

SEN. LEVIN: Why don't you simply say that if C-56 appears in waste that that waste will be considered hazardous? * * * Say it's in a waste which isn't listed. Isn't it just as hazardous as if it's in a waste which is listed?

MR. JORLING: Yes. The question is: Is that a real-world possibility?

SEN. LEVIN: The real question is whether it's a hazardous waste.

MR. JORLING: No. Our question is: Is C-56 moving through the society in ways other than those which we are covering in our regulation? * * *

SEN. LEVIN: * * * Is it true that waste material that contains some C-56, as well as other substances, and which is not hazardous in any other respect other than the fact that it has some C-56 in it, would not be identified as "hazardous" under the proposed regulations, since C-56 is not included in the [EP] toxicity characteristic?

MR. JORLING: Senator, obviously that question was very craftily put together, and the answer is "yes."

*Oversight of Hazardous Waste Management and RCRA: Hearings Before the Subcomm. on Oversight of Government Management of the Senate Comm. on Governmental Affairs,* 96th Cong., 1st Sess. 466-70 (1979).

Despite the unpopularity of the EPA's approach to listing hazardous wastes pursuant to the toxic waste listing criterion, the Agency's refusal to automatically list each and every solid waste containing an Appendix VIII constituent—or to treat such constituents as characteristics—is understandable. Some wastes might contain such dilute concentrations of Appendix VIII constituents, or may retain those constituents in such an immobilized form, that they do not meet the statutory hazardous waste definition. At a minimum, the automatic listing procedure suggested by environmental advocates would seem to require the articulation of de minimis cut-off levels for Appendix VIII constituent concentrations to avoid swamping the Subtitle C regulatory program with solid wastes containing only trace contaminations of such chemicals.

---

[a] *Ed.*—the reference is to a specifically listed hazardous waste.

Nonetheless, the Agency might have achieved more satisfying results if it had created a genuine—rather than a pro forma—presumption of hazardousness by providing that all solid wastes containing more than specified de minimis concentrations of Appendix VIII constituents are hazardous wastes *until delisted*. ("Delisting" is a formal process—widely used under RCRA Subtitle C—whereby a regulated entity may petition to have a listed waste removed from the hazardous waste list.) Such an approach would have had two valuable consequences. First, it would have minimized the risk that significant hazardous wastes would remain unregulated, by replacing the current policy of avoiding false positives with a policy of avoiding false negatives. Wastes of unknown hazard potential would have been regulated immediately, without the need for identification by the Agency, while information on their hazard was developed. Second, such an approach would have shifted much of the information-gathering burden from the EPA to the regulated community, providing an incentive to obtain empirical data with respect to such factors as mobility, persistence, and degradability factors that might justify delisting. Obviously, such an approach would not be workable without devoting substantial resources to the handling of delisting petitions.

## 16. ENUMERATED FORM PRINCIPLE AND MERE INGREDIENT COROLLARY

One of the major weaknesses of the hazardous waste lists is that they cover only materials that are in a specified or *enumerated form*; wastes taking a nonenumerated form, but containing essentially the same harmful chemical components are not covered by the list. For example, many commonly traded commercial chemical products (such as copper cyanide, toxaphene, and fluorine) are specified on the list and are hazardous wastes when they occur in certain enumerated forms; other substances that happen to *contain* these chemicals are not hazardous wastes, because they are in a nonenumerated form. We call this the *enumerated form principle* and the *mere ingredient corollary*. The following congressional testimony by a former EPA employee illustrates how the agency's "listing preference" (discussed at page 685, *supra*), coupled with the enumerated form principle and mere ingredient corollary, may leave dangerous waste materials outside the RCRA Subtitle C program. The participants are referring to hexachlorocyclopentadiene (C-56), a substance that has been listed as a hazardous waste by the EPA. (C-56 is also an Appendix VIII constituent, because the EPA sometimes lists the *commercial chemical product* form of a chemical that also shows up on the Appendix VIII constituent list. However, in the following discussion, the participants are referring to the *listed* hazardous waste, C-56).

MR. [WILLIAM] SANJOUR: [I]f a manufacturer took the C-56 he manufactured [one enumerated form] and threw it away, that would be covered by [the hazardous waste list]. But, of course, people don't throw pure C-56 away. They make it and they sell it.

If an off-spec batch [another enumerated form] of C-56 were thrown away, that would be covered by the regulations, too, and that is in fact a real problem.

If a C-56 spill [yet another enumerated form] were to happen, that would be covered by [the lists], and that's a real problem.

However, the fact that a waste *contains* C-56, that fact in and of itself does not make a waste "hazardous," no matter how much C-56 it contains. * * * [I]t's *not* regulated, for example, if it occurs in a byproduct, which is more often the case; if it occurs in the waste water treatment sludge, which is a very prominent case; if it occurs, let's say, in floor sweepings or equipment cleaning, any of those occurrences no matter how high the level, it wouldn't be a "hazardous waste."

SEN. LEVIN: Isn't it possible that the waste from the manufacture of C-56 would have at least one of the identified *characteristics*? And, if so, how can you say for certain that such a waste would not be covered?

MR. SANJOUR: Well, that's sort of like playing Russian roulette. You're saying that if a waste containing C-56 were hazardous for some *other* reason, then it would be a hazardous waste. If it were hazardous because it was flammable, if you were fortunate enough to have the waste flammable, then it would be a hazardous waste. Or, if it exploded, it would be a hazardous waste.

But, once again, it wouldn't be a hazardous waste *because* it contained the C-56. Now, granted, there are some wastes which contain C-56, and may be corrosive, and would be hazardous waste because they're corrosive; but again, not because they *contain* C-56.

SEN. LEVIN: Can you imagine wastes which contain C-56 which do not contain one of the covered characteristics?

MR. SANJOUR: Sure. *I imagine most of them don't.* In fact, because C-56 is a fire retardant, it's not going to burn, for one thing.

*Oversight of Hazardous Waste Management and RCRA: Hearings Before the Subcomm. on Oversight of Government Management of the Senate Comm. on Governmental Affairs,* 96th Cong., 1st Sess. 383-84 (1979) (emphasis added).

### Notes and Questions

1.  The EPA's lists of chemical substances traded in commerce specify that such "commercial chemical products" are hazardous wastes when discarded only if they are in certain enumerated forms, including

> the commercially pure grade of the chemical, any technical grades of the chemical which are produced or marketed, and all formulations in which the chemical is the sole active ingredient.

40 C.F.R. § 261.33(d), Comment.

2.  Your client, a garden shop, proposes to dispose of several cartons of an old, unsold product called "Acme Spider Spray." The label on each can says the following:

Active ingredients by wt.

*2-(1-Methylethoxy)phenyl methylcarbamate....... 1.0%

Petroleum distillate............................................. 82.3%

Inert ingredients ...................................... 16.7%

How would you go about determining whether these materials are RCRA Subtitle C hazardous wastes? Could the materials be a listed hazardous waste, given their commercial chemical product status? Why or why not?

3.  Assume that EPA discovers an abandoned dump site that is leaching high concentrations of copper cyanide, endangering a nearby drinking water supply. Copper cyanide is a listed commercial chemical product hazardous waste. Is the copper cyanide leachate a "hazardous substance" within the meaning of CERCLA? *See* CERCLA §§ 101(14) and 101(14)(C). Why or why not?

## F. RCRA ACTORS AND OBLIGATIONS

You have now been introduced to the threshold issue under RCRA: (1) what materials are hazardous wastes, subject to Subtitle C regulation? Two additional issues arise in virtually every RCRA context: (2) what actors are subject to RCRA regulation; and (3) what are their obligations?

### 1. OVERVIEW OF RCRA ACTORS AND OBLIGATIONS

## JOHN-MARK STENSVAAG, HAZARDOUS WASTE LAW: AN ESSENTIAL INTRODUCTION FOR THE NON-SPECIALIST

17 Vanderbilt Lawyer 16-23 (1987)

We * * * live in an extraordinarily regulated society when it comes to environmental matters. * * * In particular, a revolution has taken place * * * in hazardous waste law. * * *

The thesis of this essay, in addressing those of you who are non-specialists, is that this revolution has probably affected one or more of your clients. There is a unique danger that many such clients remain unaware of their new obligations and potential liabilities. Why do I say that this danger is unique? If you have clients who directly discharge wastes to water or to the air, surely they recognized years ago that they were altering the environment and that they might be subject to environmental regulatory programs; the Clean Air Act and the Clean Water Act did not sneak up on many people. But clients who deliver their solid wastes to businesses engaged in the trade of hauling it away have historically assumed that the obligations to comply with environmental laws rest with the haulers, rather than with themselves. This assumption is now wrong. It is extremely dangerous for clients to continue to operate in accordance with this obsolete and erroneous assumption.

## HAZARDOUS WASTE AUDIT

It is perhaps most helpful to approach the topic of hazardous waste law from the standpoint of an environmental audit. An environmental audit is one of the most valuable services that an environmental attorney can perform for her business client. The attorney approaches the firm's operations with a massive checklist of statutory, regulatory, and permit obligations, and painstakingly examines the firm's activities to assure that the client is in compliance with all environmental laws. This essay is designed to assist those of you who are non-specialists in conducting an analogous study of your clients—what we might call a hazardous waste law audit—by laying out for you various categories of regulated and otherwise affected entities and inviting you to consider whether you perform legal services for any such entities. Rather than focusing on what the law does, our focus will be on who is affected. It may be easiest to first list these categories of regulated and affected entities and then return to discuss each one in turn. This list is necessarily an oversimplification of the law—but it should be adequate to serve as an initial checklist for the non-specialist.

There are seven categories of regulated and otherwise affected entities on this simplified checklist:

1. Generators

2. Transporters

3. Owners or Operators of Facilities:

    a. Treatment, Storage, and Disposal Facilities (TSDFs)

    b. CERCLA Facilities or Vessels

4. Persons Acquiring the Assets of Any of the Foregoing

5. Insurers of Any of the Foregoing

6. Creditors of Any of the Foregoing

7. Victims

There are hundreds of thousands—perhaps even millions—of individuals and firms that fall into one or more of these categories. The purpose of our audit is to help you determine if any of them are your clients. Unless your clients have separate environmental counsel, your failure to recognize their presence in one or more of these categories may mean that your clients are without legal counsel on hazardous waste law issues.

## GENERATORS

Consider, first, the generator category. Most of this essay will be addressed to this category of actors. A generator is anyone who produces a hazardous waste. One of the most complicated aspects in all of hazardous waste law is the definition of "hazardous waste." * * * The ascertainment of hazardous waste status is so treacherous that no non-specialist should render advice on the issue without a thorough study of the regulations. Most importantly, you should not assume that your client's waste materials are nonhazardous, based on your preconceptions of what a hazardous waste looks like. The universe of hazardous wastes regulated under RCRA Subtitle C is much more vast than the handful of wastes that unsophisticated clients are likely to associate with the label "hazardous"; it is not limited to dioxin-contaminated oil and other highly visible targets. For example, any waste that is ignitable under RCRA test protocols is a hazardous waste.

### Small-Quantity Generators

Prior to September 22, 1986, the EPA divided all hazardous waste generators into two categories: (1) "small-quantity" generators and (2) all other generators (a category having no official label, but which I will refer to for convenience as "large-quantity" generators). Small-quantity generators were those that generated less than 1,000 kilograms (or 2,220 pounds) per month of nonacute hazardous wastes. Under most circumstances, the wastes of small-quantity generators were exempt from regulation under RCRA Subtitle C. Accordingly, a generator could produce more than 12 tons (or the equivalent of sixty 55-gallon drums) of hazardous waste per year without having to comply with meaningful regulation.

Because this small-quantity generator cut-off number was so high, the vast majority of large-quantity generators are in the manufacturing sector and recognized long ago their obligations under RCRA. I will assume that the non-specialist has no large-quantity generators for clients, except in instances in which those clients already have separate environmental counsel to assist them in Subtitle C compliance. My focus in addressing the non-specialist, therefore, will be on the small-quantity generator.

The vast majority of these small-quantity generators have been unaware of their obligations under RCRA, due to the safe harbor of the small-quantity generator exemption. Since September 22, 1986, however, amended regulations have effectively repealed the small-quantity generator exemption for all generators of more than 100 kilograms per month of hazardous waste, subjecting such actors and their wastes to the full panoply of Subtitle C regulation. This means that actors who generate more than 220 pounds (approximately one-half drum) of hazardous waste per month must now comply with detailed requirements previously applicable only to larger operations. Moreover, even actors who generate less than 100 kilograms of hazardous waste per month are entitled to a small-quantity generator exemption only if they comply with certain conditions—conditions that may frequently be violated in the absence of expert legal advice. * * *

Who are these formerly exempt small-quantity generators that * * * may remain unaware of their RCRA obligations? It is here, perhaps, that this audit may begin to home in on some of your clients. Various EPA studies and congressional hearings have indicated that there are hundreds of thousands of generators producing hazardous wastes in amounts of less than 1,000 kilograms per month. Contrary to what you might expect, the vast majority of small-quantity generators are not manufacturers, but are rather in the service sector of our economy. Consider the following partial list of small-quantity generators: painters, plumbers, electricians, gasoline service stations, auto repair shops, dry cleaners, schools, barber and beauty shops, local transportation systems (taxicabs and buses), municipal police departments, drinking water treatment plants, janitorial services, trucking companies, pharmacies, hospitals, publishers and printers, food processors, farmers, builders, car washes, airlines, electroplaters, metal fabricators, furniture builders, spinners, weavers, and retail stores (including the obvious hardware stores and garden stores but also department and specialty stores).

Perhaps you recognize some of your clients on this list. If so, and if you are a non-specialist in these matters, the time has come to confront the demands that hazardous waste law makes on your clients. Failure to confront those demands and to comply with RCRA Subtitle C obligations may lead to grief that is all out of proportion to the burdens of compliance.

### NONEXEMPT GENERATOR OBLIGATIONS

The EPA's generator standards apply to all generators of more than 100 kilograms (approximately one-half drum) of nonacute hazardous waste per month. We may call these actors "nonexempt generators." The nonexempt generator standards require determination of which solid wastes are hazardous wastes, notification to the EPA, acquisition of a unique generator identification number, proper labeling and packaging of hazardous wastes, the manifesting of hazardous waste shipments, delivery of such shipments only to transporters with EPA identification numbers, the selection of a destination facility that is authorized to receive the particular hazardous waste being shipped, the obligation to assure that shipments arrive at the facility designated by the generator, and periodic reporting to the EPA.

Most of these obligations kicked in for the first time on September 22, 1986, for generators of between 100 and 1,000 kilograms of hazardous waste per month. Because the EPA estimates that there are at least 100,000 such newly regulated entities, widespread noncompliance with the law is virtually certain to occur.

### CONDITIONALLY EXEMPT SMALL-QUANTITY GENERATORS

The September 22 regulations preserve an exemption for a subcategory of actors who were formerly embraced in the small-quantity generator category: those who have generated less than 100 kilograms of nonacute hazardous wastes in any given month. (Generators may be chameleons—in and out of the system from month-to-month, if their output occasionally exceeds 100 kilograms.) This exemption is conditional and does *not* dispense with three primary obligations.

First, a conditionally-exempt small-quantity generator has the same obligations as any generator to determine which of its solid wastes are, in fact, hazardous wastes. This includes the obligation to consult the EPA's lists of hazardous wastes, as well as the obligation to test the wastes for the four hazardous characteristics, unless the generator can confidently conclude, without such tests, that none of the hazardous characteristics is present.

Second, a conditionally-exempt small-quantity generator is required by law to ensure that any hazardous wastes are delivered only to facilities set forth in the regulations; essentially, these are authorized hazardous waste facilities, authorized solid waste disposal facilities, or legitimate recycling operations. I am not aware of any litigation on this, yet, but it is inconceivable to me that a small-quantity generator has complied with this second obligation by merely placing its hazardous wastes into a dumpster and paying a basically unknown, unidentified hauler to take it away to an unknown destination. Yet, I would be amazed if thousands of small-quantity generators are not continuing to do precisely that.

Third, a small-quantity generator must not store its hazardous wastes on site in amounts or for time periods exceeding the maximum storage limits in federal regulations. * * * The basic storage limits work as follows. If a conditionally-exempt small-quantity generator accumulates at any time through on-site storage more than 1,000 kilograms of nonacute hazardous waste, that generator is no longer exempt, and becomes subject to the full panoply of regulations applied to large-quantity generators. This loss of exempt status is triggered by the on-site accumulation of approximately five 55-gallon drums. * * * Given this relatively small storage trigger, it seems highly likely that thousands of small-quantity generators who assume that they are exempt from federal regulation are, in fact, subject to the full scope of the EPA's generator standards.

STORAGE FACILITY TRAP

All generators of more than 100 kilograms of hazardous waste in any calendar month face an additional danger under RCRA Subtitle C: if hazardous wastes are accumulated on-site for more than a specified number of days (90, 180, or 270, depending on certain conditions), the generator becomes the operator of a *storage facility*. This status carries with it obligations that almost defy description. Such a hapless generator must apply for a full-blown storage facility permit, and becomes subject to design requirements, operating requirements, monitoring requirements, planning requirements (including a closure plan), reporting requirements, financial responsibility requirements, employee training requirements, and recordkeeping requirements. This ton of bricks may be brought down upon its head solely because the generator accumulated slightly more than one-half drum of hazardous waste on site for a six-month period.

### STAKES OF NONCOMPLIANCE

The foregoing remarks about the new obligations of formerly exempt small-quantity generators should impress on you that these obligations are extremely easy to violate. In fact, it is quite likely that there are thousands of small-quantity generators who are in violation of the law. One need only consult the list of sanctions under RCRA to realize why you and your clients care about violations of the regulatory program, regardless of whether they may be characterized as technical infractions. Of greatest concern, no doubt, are the criminal sanctions—sanctions that may be applied to individuals (including directors, officers, and attorneys) in corporate settings. It is true that these criminal sanctions apply only to one who acts "knowingly." But the civil penalties—which do not require knowing violations—can be as high as $25,000 per violation per day.

Now, perhaps, even once you realize the possibility of noncompliance, you may conclude that there is safety in numbers—that the government will never prosecute on the basis of violations that are so widespread. Such a conclusion is risky, because hazardous wastes—even wastes from a small-quantity generator, may readily surface in a dangerous manner that becomes a local or even national cause célèbre. If hazardous wastes from a small print shop or hardware store endanger drinking water supplies or injure children playing in a field, the new Wyatt Earps charged with cleaning up the Wild West may relentlessly pursue the generators, no matter how small their operations may be. I, for one, would not want to wager that they will rule out criminal sanctions to make whatever example is deemed necessary.

### THE CERCLA PITFALL

Even if we assume, however, that "technical" violations of RCRA by small-quantity generators will go undetected or unpunished under that statute, there is a far greater potential risk to generators of all sizes under a separate federal statute: CERCLA, more commonly known as the superfund. CERCLA does not use the precise term "generator," but it does contain liability provisions directed at what RCRA calls the generator. The basic notion of CERCLA is that the federal government is authorized to respond to "releases" (very broadly defined) of "hazardous substances" (a term that includes all RCRA hazardous wastes and more). The federal government may spend money from a trust fund to clean up the site of a hazardous substance release, and may then turn around and sue a raft of "potentially responsible persons" for reimbursement of its costs. Generators of hazardous wastes are potentially responsible persons under CERCLA. Thus, if a client delivers hazardous wastes to a hauler, and those wastes wind up in a hazardous substance release site, the client may be sued for cleanup costs, as well as damages to natural resources owned by federal and state governments.

Now, one of the most striking things about CERCLA is that Congress clearly intended this liability to apply to generators who shipped wastes long before the statute was enacted. Of course, if you have a client who is in that category, such a client is already in a pickle and may need the help of an environmental specialist if sued by the fund. But CERCLA also has a prospective bite to it that is easily overlooked: the present management of a client's hazardous wastes may lead to CERCLA liability weeks, months, and even years from now. Moreover, unlike RCRA, CERCLA has never made special allowances for small-quantity generators; they are just as vulnerable to liability as any other generator. * * * Small-quantity generators who have sent their wastes to mere solid waste disposal facilities or—even worse—to facilities that they know nothing about, will be * * * vulnerable in the future to CERCLA liability * * * .

The liabilities that may be imposed on generators under CERCLA may be truly staggering. Once groundwater is endangered by hazardous waste disposal, it is not at all uncommon to hear quotations running into the millions of dollars for cleanup costs. And, with slight variations, court after court has agreed with the EPA's claim that CERCLA liability is joint and several; this means that a single generator which has contributed wastes to a hazardous substance release site may be liable for the full costs of cleanup, even though hundreds of other generators contributed wastes to the same site. To be sure, it is theoretically possible that a small contributor to a CERCLA site may be able to escape joint and several liability by proving—at trial—its individual contribution to the site and the damages uniquely caused by its wastes, but this is obviously a difficult burden of proof to shoulder. Most importantly, a generator has little hope of carrying this burden in a convincing manner unless it has taken its RCRA obligations seriously by: (1) identifying its hazardous wastes; (2) ensuring that its wastes were sent only to proper facilities under RCRA; and (3) carefully documenting these activities, as well as quantities shipped and destinations.

If the non-specialist were to learn only a single point from this essay, it should be this: a client need not be a large generator to get sucked into the maelstrom of a CERCLA lawsuit for reimbursement of cleanup costs, and may be dragged in on the basis of activities conducted today and tomorrow, as well as prior to the enactment of CERCLA.

No client in its right mind wants to be named as a defendant in a CERCLA lawsuit. One cannot improve on the metaphor offered by Randy Mott:

> [D]efendants must realize that they enter these cases almost like a frightened passenger in the back seat of a runaway car. Moreover, the only people in the front seat are the government and the media, and they have no interest in the brake pedal.

Randy Mott, *Defense Tactics for the Hazardous Waste "Responsible Party,"* 1 Envtl. Forum 5, 8 (1983).

If you do have a client who is named as a potentially responsible party in such a suit, you must either refer that client to a specialist or decide that you wish to become that specialist. If a client is important enough to your practice, the shortage of qualified experts may force you to adopt the latter course. It is not uncommon for the EPA to send out pre-litigation notices to dozens of potentially responsible parties in connection with a single site. Given the conflicts of interests between the various parties, it may be difficult to secure the assistance of skilled legal counsel. This will be especially true for the small-quantity generator, because the largest generators typically have the clout to retain the most experienced attorneys.

These, then, are some of the considerations that you should bear in mind as you reflect on the obligations and potential liabilities of this first category of possible clients in our hazardous waste audit exercise. The regulatory burdens on these generators are substantial, and the potential liabilities in the event of noncompliance or careless operation may be enormous.

## TRANSPORTERS

The second category of entities on our potential client list consists of transporters. Clients who are engaged in transportation services are obviously easier to spot than those who are hazardous waste generators, so we need not linger long on this category. However, four things should be emphasized in our little audit. The first three points have to do with obligations and liabilities of clients who transport wastes; the last, and perhaps most startling point, has to do with obligations and liabilities of transporters who are not in the business of hauling wastes at all.

### SOLID WASTE HAULERS

Consider, at the outset, transporters who are in the solid (but not hazardous) waste hauling business. To distinguish such actors from hazardous waste transporters, we may refer to them as "haulers." Even though these actors may seem immune to RCRA Subtitle C regulation, there are three unavoidable danger areas.

First, solid waste haulers violate RCRA if they accept hazardous wastes from nonexempt generators. This is so, because any hauler who carries hazardous wastes for nonexempt generators is a "transporter" within the meaning of RCRA Subtitle C and must comply with numerous regulatory requirements under that statute. Those requirements center primarily on the manifest system. If a nonexempt generator identifies itself as such to a solid waste hauler, the hauler will obviously be alerted to its RCRA obligations. Because it is a violation of RCRA for such a generator to deliver its wastes to a hauler who has not obtained an EPA identification number or to deliver its wastes without a manifest, one would think that there will be no unwitting transporters of regulated hazardous wastes. In fact, however, the statute recognizes that a nonexempt generator might violate the law by failing to use the manifest system and by failing to identify its wastes as hazardous. In that event, it is unlawful for the hauler to accept the unmanifested waste. Thus, there is an independent duty on solid waste haulers to assure that they are not handling the hazardous wastes of nonexempt generators. To use a familiar example, a municipality that provides a trash collection service for its residents almost certainly does not intend to enter the hazardous waste business and, therefore, does not register with the EPA as a hazardous waste transporter. Such a municipality violates RCRA if it accepts hazardous wastes from a nonexempt generator without a manifest. The same is true for private solid waste haulers who do not intend to engage in hazardous waste management. I would be amazed if such violations were not occurring on a regular basis throughout the country, especially given the likelihood that chameleons—generators that switch between exempt and nonexempt status from month-to-month—are either mistakenly or intentionally failing to disclose the occasionally nonexempt status of their hazardous wastes. It is wholly unrealistic to expect solid waste haulers to sort out the truth in dealing with small-quantity generator wastes, but the regulations currently demand such vigilance.

Second, solid waste haulers will frequently (and lawfully) be given hazardous wastes by conditionally exempt small-quantity generators, without being informed that the wastes are hazardous. This means that the hauler's employees will be regularly exposed to and occasionally injured by unmanifested hazardous wastes—wastes about which the hauler is unaware. It also means that the hauler will routinely deliver unidentified hazardous wastes to its normal solid waste disposal or treatment destination. While there are no RCRA Subtitle C obligations on the solid waste hauler to discover what these conditionally exempt small-quantity generator wastes are or to warn employees and disposal sites of their presence, such inadvertent hazardous waste haulers face uncertain liabilities under common law and other statutes whenever persons are damaged by incidents involving undisclosed hazardous wastes.

Third, even though a solid waste hauler whose only hazardous wastes are those of conditionally exempt small-quantity generators need not register as a hazardous waste transporter under RCRA, such a client is still a "transporter" of *hazardous substances* within the meaning of CERCLA. If such a transporter releases a reportable quantity of a hazardous substance to the environment (for example, in a spill), it is required by CERCLA to notify the National Response Center immediately of the release. Moreover, if the hauler of such hazardous substances selects the disposal site—as is virtually always the case for routine, solid waste collection businesses—then such a transporter is potentially liable under CERCLA for cleanup costs associated with problems that may later crop up at the disposal site. Such liability would appear to be joint and several. This is an extraordinary and often overlooked facet of the new regulatory system. In many cases, ordinary solid waste haulers (such as municipal systems) may become the unwitting victims of EPA's conditional small-quantity generator exemption; they are doomed to haul undisclosed quantities of undisclosed hazardous wastes, only to be eventually clobbered with liability for cleaning up disposal sites.

### NONWASTE CARRIERS

The final point about the transporter category has to do with clients who are even less likely to be aware of their obligations. Spills during the transportation of *nonwaste* materials (i.e., commercial products) may *create* hazardous wastes—consisting of the spilled product, the contaminated soil, and any contaminated cleanup materials. Thus, barge companies, trucking lines, railroads, and airlines engaged in the business of carrying commercial products may become accidental generators of hazardous wastes subject to the RCRA regulations.

Moreover, CERCLA defines hazardous substances so broadly that spills of many commercial substances during transportation trigger the notification requirements of CERCLA, as well as potential liability for government cleanup costs at spill sites. To be sure, carriers of hazardous materials—including nonwaste products—have been regulated for years by the Department of Transportation's hazardous materials regulations, but RCRA and CERCLA add totally new obligations and liabilities to such carriers. Moreover, DOT regulations formerly applied only to interstate carriers; the new hazardous waste regime includes wholly intrastate carriers.

### FACILITY OWNERS/OPERATORS

The third category of potential clients in our hazardous waste audit consists of owners and operators of "facilities." I have broken this category down into two different types of facilities. The first subcategory consists of "treatment, storage, or disposal facilities" (TSDFs) under RCRA. These are the entities that need full-blown, formal permits under RCRA to continue operations. Without going into the complex details of interim status and permitting procedure, it should be enough of a warning to point out that, if one of your clients owns or operates such a facility and has not applied for a permit under RCRA, it may be easier for a camel to pass through the eye of a needle than to obtain the legal right to continue operations at that facility pending issuance of a permit—a process that is projected to take years. Technically, under the RCRA statute, any such facility is operating unlawfully and there is no quick way to render it lawful. The possibility of a shutdown order—for example, at the behest of a citizen suit—is very real.

Given this serious consequence of non-compliance, how likely is it that you may have clients who own or operate RCRA facilities but have failed to recognize that fact? Unfortunately, it is quite possible that this has occurred. First, inadvertent facility status is possible because of the regulatory provisions limiting the storage of hazardous wastes. As we have seen, it is easy for a conditionally exempt small-quantity generator to be converted into a nonexempt generator by the mere passage of time, coupled with the accumulation of wastes. And the mere accumulation of hazardous waste for more than a specified number of days by a nonexempt generator converts the site into a "storage" facility under the RCRA regulations. Such unintentional establishment of a storage facility must be occurring at numerous sites. Second, "storage" and "treatment" are defined so broadly in RCRA and in the regulations that almost any lagoon, waste pile, surface impoundment, tank, or basin containing a hazardous waste qualifies as a facility. For example, the EPA has taken the position that any treatment facility involved in the purification of wastewater prior to discharge under a National Pollutant Discharge Elimination System (NPDES) permit may be a RCRA treatment facility and may require a separate permit under RCRA. These issues are extremely complex, and will often require assistance from an environmental specialist.

The second type of facility on our audit list refers to facilities as defined in CERCLA. Even if a client does not own or operate a TSDF under RCRA, the definition of facility in CERCLA is much broader, and embraces "any * * * structure * * * [including rail cars and aircraft] or any site or area where a hazardous substance has been * * * placed or otherwise come to be located * * * ." This means that clients who own or operate sites or structures associated with hazardous substance releases may be held liable, under certain circumstances, for reimbursement of government cleanup costs under CERCLA.

Perhaps the most important aspect of this facility business for the non-specialist is that—regardless of the type of facility being discussed—the various statutes impose obligations and liabilities on the "*owner or operator*." This means, for example, that clients who merely own land associated with hazardous waste storage, treatment or disposal, or associated with hazardous substance releases may face serious obligations and liabilities that are totally new to such passive investors. Clients who knowingly lease land to hazardous waste management ventures are obviously fully on the hook. But the liabilities and obligations may be more subtly acquired. For example, a standard technique of criminal elements in the hazardous waste field has been to rent an empty warehouse, fill it with leaking drums of unmarked hazardous wastes, and disappear. The same may be done by leasing other types of facilities, such as semi-trailers or railroad boxcars. Both CERCLA and RCRA create obligations and impose liabilities on the owners of these facilities. While one might assume that "innocent" owners would not suffer liability or punitive sanctions under these statutes, I see no such charity in the statutes; they clearly envision that, in many cases, the owner will be held fully responsible for the consequences of such activities.

These first three categories of potential clients are the most obvious ones to be concerned about as you conduct your own personal hazardous waste audit. They are the ones directly regulated by and directly liable under the new federal hazardous waste laws. For completeness, however, it seems to me essential that the non-specialist recognize the ramifications of these laws on three other categories of potential clients: persons engaged in acquisitions, insurers, and creditors.

## PARTIES TO ACQUISITIONS

Consider, first, persons acquiring (or planning to acquire) the assets of clients in the first three categories. I am not an expert in the law of successor liability. Moreover, I have no experience with the various acquisition and financing schemes that are the bread and butter practice of many attorneys. I do know, however, that the types of liabilities established by CERCLA are designed to be extraordinarily long-lived and tenacious. For example, CERCLA includes in its list of potentially responsible persons, the *present* owner and operator of a facility (i.e., site); the separate provision in the statutory list of potentially responsible parties for entities that owned or operated the site *at the time of the hazardous substance release* creates a strong inference that Congress, at least, envisioned some type of successor liability. There are serious problems, under CERCLA, of imputed ownership liability—the unintended acquisition of ownership liability—through merger, asset acquisition, business acquisition, or the old doctrine of piercing the corporate veil. The non-specialist must realize that deals involving any seller in the first three of our categories pose the risk that the purchasing client may be buying massive hidden liabilities. (Certainly, such a transaction is the ultimate occasion for insisting on an environmental audit.)

At the same time, attorneys representing sellers in such transactions should be wary of broad, generalized warranties. One environmental law specialist discovered to his horror upon joining a large law firm that it had included a boiler-plate warranty in such transactions for years, to the effect that the selling company was in compliance with "all environmental regulations." Such a warranty is reckless, because it is virtually impossible for anyone to comply with *all* environmental regulations. Persons who sign such warranties are playing Russian roulette.

## INSURERS

The fifth category of potential clients in our audit embraces insurers of all entities falling within categories one through four. Companies that insure manufacturing operations have usually had some inkling of what they were getting into. Under CERCLA, however, even such insurers have suffered a rude awakening. Because it is becoming increasingly clear that the retrospective liabilities under that statute may be enormous, potentially responsible parties are dredging out insurance policies—sometimes more than a decade old—in attempts to pass on the costs. Whether insurers on old policies will be required to indemnify CERCLA defendants for sums paid to the federal cleanup fund will hinge on the wording of such policies and how they are interpreted. It is doubtful that insurers of manufacturing operations are unaware of the many ramifications of the new hazardous waste laws; it is their business to understand those ramifications.

What some of your insurance company clients may overlook, however, are the many less-obvious insured parties falling into our categories one through four. As we have seen, there are potentially hundreds of thousands of legal clients who fall into these categories and do not realize it—from small-quantity generators to solid waste haulers and commercial product carriers, and from passive investors to purchasers of businesses and assets. Each of these clients is also a potential insured under one or more insurance policies. If insurance underwriters fail to recognize the new obligations and potential liabilities of these entities, they may eventually be required to indemnify such insureds in connection with unanticipated risks.

### CREDITORS

I have included the sixth category of potential clients—creditors (and potential creditors) of entities in categories one through five—merely to underscore for you the immense magnitude of the potential liabilities for any regulated entity under the new hazardous waste law regime. Lending institutions must be aware of these potential liabilities if they are to adequately assess the risks involved in loan transactions. Loans to these entities will often be occasions calling for environmental audits.

### VICTIMS

Finally, I have included for obvious reasons the possibility that you may have clients who are victims of improper (or supposedly proper) hazardous waste management practices. I do not mean to slight such clients and such legal practice by placing it at the bottom of the list. The purpose of our audit, however, has been to try to assist you in recognizing the hazardous waste legal problems of your clients that might otherwise be overlooked.

## 2. GENERATOR AND TRANSPORTER OBLIGATIONS

You have now been introduced to the various actors under RCRA—generators, transporters, and owners/operators of treatment, storage, and disposal facilities (TSDFs)—and have been given a brief glimpse at their obligations. The following readings contain brief descriptions of the various obligations under RCRA Subtitle C.

## SHELDON M. NOVICK & DONALD W. STEVER, THE REGULATION OF HAZARDOUS WASTE

in 3 Law of Environmental Protection
13-55, 13-58 to 13-59 (Sheldon M. Novick, ed. 1998)

Generators' principal obligation is to see that wastes are sent to permitted facilities for storage, or ultimate treatment and disposal, and that the government is notified of any other disposal or release. This responsibility is discharged by arranging for proper management and by documenting the arrangement with a "manifest," a shipping document that must accompany the waste until it reaches the designated destination. Proprietors of treatment, storage, or disposal facilities who receive properly documented wastes must return a copy of the manifest to the generator, who in turn must keep records and report any failure to receive this evidence of proper disposal.

To help EPA and the states keep track of millions of manifests, every generator must obtain an identification number. EPA also assigns numbers to all designated wastes; as the manifest now uses a single form in every state, the movement of hazardous wastes around the country is slowly being documented. * * *

EPA requires that transporters obtain identification numbers (which are in no sense permits), carry generator's manifests with every load of hazardous waste, identify the wastes they are carrying, and deliver the manifests along with the wastes. * * *

## 3.  TSDF OWNER/OPERATOR OBLIGATIONS

## SHELDON M. NOVICK & DONALD W. STEVER, THE REGULATION OF HAZARDOUS WASTE

### in 3 Law of Environmental Protection 13-59 to 13-60, 13-69 to 13-71, 13-76 to 13-77 (Sheldon M. Novick, ed. 1998)

No one may treat, store, or dispose of hazardous waste except in accordance with a permit; while only owners or operators must have permits, employees and any others who manage the wastes also may be individually subject to both civil and criminal penalties for violations. * * *

[O]wners and operators of hazardous waste management facilities * * * must apply to a state agency or EPA for a permit, and * * * may not operate their facility if the permit is denied. * * *

Individual facility permits will contain general requirements, categorical requirements established for that class of facility, and in most cases, facility-specific requirements negotiated with the permit-issuing agency. The general and categorical requirements are described in detail in [40 C.F.R.] Part 264 * * * .

All designs must meet some minimum performance standards. These are common sense requirements, and are stated in general terms. Incompatible wastes which might react or explode when brought together must be physically separated, and facility units must be designed and located in a way that protects them from earthquakes and floods, that prevents emergencies, and allows response action to be taken when emergencies of any kind do occur. * * *

The general operating requirements are extensive and detailed. The facility must of course comply with the manifest system; there are several operating procedures designed to support this system.

First, the facility operator must test each new waste received (and each waste received from a new generator), and must note any discrepancies between its test and the information on the manifest. * * * The permit holder must return to the generator a notice that the facility has a permit, and that the waste has been accepted * * * . The facility must maintain records of these documents and must make regular activity reports to EPA or a state agency.

The notice and recordkeeping requirements are at the heart of the whole regulatory scheme: The permit holder's records and notices allow the government to enforce the requirement that wastes be channeled to permitted facilities. * * *

Owner/operators are to provide either corporate guarantees or * * * mechanisms for insuring liabilities during the facility's active life and to provide several mechanisms to ensure that the cost of compliance with the closure and postclosure requirements will be met throughout the regulated death of the entity. * * * Permitted facilities' financial assurances must include the cost of corrective actions to clean up releases * * * .

All disposal facilities must comply with closure and postclosure requirements; storage facilities such as waste piles and surface impoundments, from which wastes are intended to be removed upon closure, need comply only with the closure requirements. * * * The closure and postclosure provisions involve a public proceeding, and the application of long-term maintenance and security obligations.

After the 1984 HSWA amendments, many facilities were unable or unwilling to meet the new provisions, to certify compliance with groundwater monitoring, and to meet financial responsibility requirements. As of January 1988, 956 of the 1,451 land disposal facilities were required to close. * * *

The duration of the postclosure period established by EPA is thirty years following completion of closure * * * . The third-year benchmark is more or less arbitrary, since experience, particularly with landfills, has demonstrated that the possibility of release of waste may exist for a long time beyond that point. EPA's adoption of the thirty-year period was a compromise, albeit a controversial one. * * *

## G.  LAND DISPOSAL

Recall Barry Commoner's reformulation of the law of conservation of matter at page 21, *supra*: "everything must go somewhere." The RCRA Subtitle C program has tried to grapple with this principle by formulating obligations for two types of TSDFs that represent the "grave" of the cradle-to-grave system: land disposal facilities and incinerators. In particular, the following readings explain the EPA's great difficulty in devising standards for land disposal facilities, the congressional reaction to this difficulty, and the inexorable move toward the increasing incineration of hazardous wastes.

The first outside reading in the series is a portion of a *preamble* published by the EPA in connection with proposed land disposal standards in 1981. We have not adequately explored the role of preambles in environmental law, so a slight digression about where to *find* federal environmental law is in order. This digression may be the most valuable information that you pick up in your environmental law course.

## 1.   RESEARCHING FEDERAL ENVIRONMENTAL LAW

In his splendid essay, excerpted at page 9, *supra*, Professor Elliott warns that "[t]he reality of environmental law practice today takes place deep down in the interpretative pyramid, not in the statutes and regulations at its apex." E. Donald Elliott, *The Last Great Clean Air Act Book?*, 5 Envtl. Lawyer 321 (1998). An attorney gets deep down into that pyramid by using simple research techniques that are all too often poorly understood by young lawyers. The following illustration explains those techniques.

If you turn to RCRA § 3004 in West Group's *Selected Environmental Law Statutes*—denoted by the acronym "SWDA" for the Solid Waste Disposal Act predecessor to the 1976 RCRA amendments—you will see that RCRA § 3004 sets forth, in great detail, congressional directives that the EPA promulgate regulations establishing standards applicable to owners and operators of TSDFs. The official U.S. Code citation for this statutory provision—clearly denoted in the statutory pamphlet—is 42 U.S.C. § 6924. If you then go to the Westlaw™ "CFR" database and search for "42 /5 6924" you will retrieve all portions of the *Code of Federal Regulations* in which the EPA has implemented this portion of the RCRA statute: 40 C.F.R. Parts 264, 270, and 273. The precise words of the regulations will be found in those provisions.

But the careful environmental law researcher does not stop with the words of any given federal regulation. The attorney must dig deeper into the meaning of those words by consulting the documents published in the *Federal Register* when the regulations were originally proposed and ultimately adopted by the agency. It is easy to find all underlying documents for any given regulation, because Westlaw displays the original source of every C.F.R. provision. For example, the source documents for 40 C.F.R. Part 264 on July 22, 1999, were displayed in Westlaw as: 45 FR 33221, May 19, 1980; 51 FR 25472, July 14, 1986; 52 FR 25946, July 9, 1987; 52 FR 44320, Nov. 18, 1987; 52 FR 45798, Dec. 1, 1987; 52 FR 46963, Dec. 10, 1987. Each of these underlying source documents can be accessed electronically or in hard copy.

These *Federal Register* references are extremely important. The *Federal Register* is published every weekday and contains the text of proposed regulations, adopted regulations, and other administrative matters. All federal environmental regulations appearing in the *Code of Federal Regulations* were originally published in the *Federal Register*. Most importantly, the *Federal Register* notices accompanying the publication of proposed and final agency rules almost always include *preambles*—narrative discussions by the agency going into considerable detail about the meaning and purpose of the regulations. Preambles accompanying *proposed* rules set forth the statutory bases for the rules and the agency's reasons for selecting the proposed regulatory language; preambles accompanying *final* rules contain similar discussions and also include detailed responses to comments submitted by the public on the proposed rules. It is not at all unusual for federal environmental regulations to be accompanied by several hundred pages of narrative preambles. These preambles are a gold mine of "regulatory history": they clarify the regulations far better than any other source. If you decide to practice environmental law, you should get in the habit of researching federal environmental issues by going from the statutes to the regulations to the preambles. You will be surprised at the effectiveness and the speed of this research technique.

The following reading is one example of the importance of the preambles. The speaker, as is always the case in EPA preambles, is the Administrator of the EPA. The preamble was issued in connection with a "reproposal" of standards for hazardous waste land disposal facilities—the EPA found the task of specifying land disposal standards so difficult that several rounds of proposals were necessary before issuance of the final regulations.

## 2. FUTILITY OF LAND DISPOSAL SAFEGUARDS

### EPA, REPROPOSAL OF PERMITTING STANDARDS APPLICABLE TO OWNERS, OPERATORS OF HAZARDOUS WASTE LAND FACILITIES

46 Fed. Reg. 11,126, 11,128-29 (1981)

Many hazardous wastes placed in land disposal facilities will not degrade to a point where they are no longer hazardous, or will do so only very slowly. Toxic heavy metals, for example, will not degrade although, in certain cases, their ionic stage may be altered to make them more or less toxic (e.g., converting the hexavalent form of chromium to the trivalent). Toxic organic constituents may degrade in the anaerobic condition of a landfill, but this degradation is usually slow (taking anywhere from a few years to 100 years or more) and may not be complete, leaving toxic degradation products. Moreover, current scientific knowledge about the degradation of hazardous wastes placed in land disposal facilities is imperfect. For these two reasons, it is necessary to assume, at this time at least, that hazardous wastes and hazardous constituents placed in a land disposal facility will remain hazardous for very long periods of time and therefore will remain a potential hazard to human health and the environment for very long periods of time.

There is good theoretical and empirical evidence that the hazardous constituents which are placed in land disposal facilities very likely will migrate from the facility into the broader environment. This may occur several years, even many decades, after placement of the waste in the facility, but data and scientific prediction indicate that, in most cases, even with the application of best available land disposal technology, it will occur eventually.

Natural water, from precipitation or from other sources (e.g., groundwater) will inevitably infiltrate into the facility unless a water-tight containment system (e.g., landfill cover) is constructed and perpetually maintained to prevent such intrusion. In addition, there inevitably will be liquids within the wastes placed in the facility (this is particularly true for surface impoundments but also will be true for [a] landfill even with the prohibition of disposal of bulk and containerized liquid wastes). Once in the facility, such water or liquid generates leachate, principally by solubilizing hazardous constituents in the waste. Such leachate inevitably leaks out of the facility and migrates into the underlying soils and groundwater, unless a containment system (e.g., a landfill or surface impoundment liner and/or leachate collection system) is constructed and perpetually maintained. * * *

Although it is technically possible to design and construct a land disposal containment system consisting of an impermeable liner and cover and a leachate collection system to interrupt this process, EPA seriously questioned whether such systems can be maintained and made to operate effectively and efficiently for long periods of time, or perpetually where this is required. Natural materials such as very low permeability clay soils are not impermeable. They possess some degree of permeability that allows infiltrating water or exfiltrating leachate to slowly but inevitably migrate through the material. Manmade impermeable materials that might be used for liners or covers (e.g. membrane liners or other materials) are subject to eventual deterioration, and although this might not occur for 10, 20 or more years, it eventually occurs and, when it does, leachate will migrate out of the facility. * * *

Consequently, the regulation of hazardous waste land disposal must proceed from the assumption that migration of hazardous wastes and their constituents and by-products from a land disposal facility will inevitably occur.

## 3. LAND DISPOSAL RESTRICTIONS

You can imagine how valuable the preceding document would be in a lawsuit brought by concerned citizens seeking to enjoin the permitting of a hazardous waste land disposal facility in their community. The following reading explains how the EPA and Congress have dealt with land disposal since 1982.

# SHELDON M. NOVICK & DONALD W. STEVER, THE REGULATION OF HAZARDOUS WASTE

in 3 Law of Environmental Protection 13-84 to 13-85,
13-87 to 13-90, 13-92 to 13-93 (Sheldon M. Novick, ed. 1998)

[A]fter several false starts, the Agency decided to accept an approach which provided for continuing land disposal of most hazardous wastes, which Congress very bluntly rejected in 1984.

The central issue is the leaking of liquids from landfills. Hazardous constituents in wastes stay pretty much where they are put, so long as they remain solid. If a landfill is thought of as a source of pollution, most of its emissions are liquids that seep or leak out of the landfill.

To prevent pollution from a landfill, therefore, one keeps liquids—rainfall, liquid wastes, surface water or groundwater—from entering in the first place, or from leaking out, once they are in. EPA began by setting up a system of controls on liquids placed in landfills and performance standards for the landfills themselves, which relied heavily on the notion of a liner and leachate collection system that would capture the leaks, and a monitoring system to detect failures in the liner.

By 1984, there was some evidence, and a lot of feeling, that EPA's regulations would delay but would not prevent the eventual seepage of hazardous wastes out of most landfills. * * *

In the 1984 Hazardous and Solid Waste Act Amendments, Congress addressed these questions in some detail. It greatly tightened the rules for disposal of liquids in landfills; set more stringent performance requirements for the landfills themselves to prevent leaking; and finally, acknowledging that these measures were at best temporary, created a staged ban on continued landfilling of most hazardous substances. * * *

## LAND DISPOSAL RESTRICTIONS

In 1984 * * * Congress prohibited land disposal of hazardous wastes on a schedule which automatically takes effect unless EPA adopts regulations granting one of the narrow statutory variances or extensions.

There are two escape routes from the land disposal ban. First, the wastes may be treated before disposal. If the hazardous wastes are first treated by the best available and demonstrated treatment technology [BDAT], the residue remaining after treatment may be disposed of on land.

The second escape from the ban is an exemption procedure. On petition, EPA may allow continued land disposal of a hazardous waste if the Administrator finds that the prohibition is *not* required to protect human health and the environment. To make such a finding the Administrator must first determine

To a reasonable degree of certainty, that there will be no migration of hazardous constituents from the disposal unit * * * for as long as the wastes remain hazardous. [RCRA § 3004(d)(1)]

The schedule for implementing the land disposal prohibition for wastes which do not escape through either route is set out in some detail in the statute * * * .

### ABORTED REGULATORY FRAMEWORK

On January 14, 1986, the Agency proposed a regulatory framework implementing the new land disposal restrictions. The proposal was not a success. * * *

The Agency had devised a "screening model" to use in making [the] two related [BDAT treatment and "no migration" exemption] determinations. The screening model was an effort to set risk-based groundwater quality standards. The model would predict the concentration of hazardous chemicals that would migrate through groundwater under usual conditions, if a land disposal facility failed to contain it. When wastes were so dilute or immobile that the model predicted no significant risk from migration of the wastes, EPA proposed to allow land disposal. If wastes passed the screening model they would be eligible for exemption, and if they did not, treatment would have to achieve the screening-model levels, if adequate technology were available.

EPA also proposed to allow land disposal of wastes treated by the best available, demonstrated technology, even when the criteria of its screening model would not be met; the environmental quality standards implicit in the screening model were only a goal to be achieved by advancing technology, but which never need be exceeded. * * *

This proposal brought down a rain of fiery criticism. First, several members of Congress objected; the statute plainly required a prohibition of land disposal except where the Agency found there would be "no migration" from the site. EPA had converted this to a risk-based environmental quality standard in the proposed rules, while the statute seemed to require a flat prohibition. Second, the Agency had proposed not to require even available treatment when the screening model showed it would not be needed to meet the risk-based standards.

On November 7, 1986, one day before the statute's first "hammer" provisions would have taken effect, EPA published its final regulations, and abandoned the screening model for the time being. Instead, the regulation allowed exemptions only where a petition could show that there would be "no migration" of land disposed wastes. The Agency said that it expected to grant few exemptions.

Treatment standards are based on the technology found to be demonstrated and available, and treatment is required, regardless of the degree of risk which remains. However, treatment technology which causes risks greater than those of land disposal are not considered "available."

EPA abandoned its risk-based approach only grudgingly, and announced that it would consider using the screening model at another stage in the hazardous waste regulation program—perhaps in the process of listing wastes as hazardous. * * *

### SCHEDULE OF RESTRICTIONS

The statute sets up categories of wastes [such as solvents, dioxin-contaminated wastes, and so forth] and for each category sets a date on which the land-disposal prohibition becomes effective. EPA's regulations establishing treatment standards for each category of wastes must be effective on the same date. * * * The regulations [were] promulgated in thirds. The first third of the land ban rules were promulgated in August 1988 and the second third were promulgated in June 1989. The last third of the land ban rules were issued June 1, 1990. * * *

### TREATMENT STANDARDS

Wastes treated with the best demonstrated, available treatment technology (BDAT) are exempt from the land disposal prohibition. [*See* RCRA § 3004(m)] BDAT standards are technology-based performance standards, similar in some ways to BAT standards for toxic discharges under the Clean Water Act. The Agency has authority, however, to specify actual treatment methods rather than performance standards. * * * Standards for BDAT are promulgated by EPA at [40 C.F.R. Part 268, Subpart D] * * * .

## 4.  LAND DISPOSAL STANDARDS

The foregoing reading explains the congressional approach to gradually banning the land disposal of hazardous wastes. Land disposal has not ceased, of course. Wastes treated with BDAT and wastes qualifying for the "no migration" exemption may be land disposed. What standards must land disposal facilities meet in connection with these materials? The answer is provided by the EPA's land disposal permitting standards. The standards described in the following reading are still in effect, with minor modifications.

## SUSAN BROMM, EPA'S NEW LAND DISPOSAL STANDARDS

12 Envtl. L. Rep. 15027 (1982)

On July 26, 1982, the EPA promulgated the long awaited hazardous waste land disposal standards. Publication of these regulations, which apply to hazardous waste landfills, surface impoundments, waste piles, and land treatment facilities, completes the core hazardous waste management regulatory program under Subtitle C * * * . The new regulations, which form the basis for granting permits to new and existing hazardous waste land disposal facilities, rely on a two-pronged approach for protection of human health and the environment. They establish a performance-oriented *groundwater protection standard*, implemented through groundwater monitoring and, if contamination is detected, corrective action. In addition, they describe performance-based *design and operating standards* aimed at preventing the release of waste and waste constituents during the facility's operating life and post-closure care period. * * *

Under the two-pronged approach of the new regulations, facilities are subject to both the groundwater protection requirements and a set of design and operating requirements, specific to the type of facility (i.e., landfill, waste pile, surface impoundment, or land treatment). In defining which waste management *components* are subject to the groundwater protection requirements, EPA uses the term "*regulated unit.*" A unit is contiguous area of land on or in which waste is piled. Examples of units include a single surface impoundment or a single waste pile. A "regulated unit" is any unit that receives hazardous waste after January 26, 1983 (the effective date of the regulations). All regulated units are subject to the groundwater protection provisions unless they have been constructed with a double liner system incorporating a leak detection system between the liners. The underlying rationale for this exemption is that the facility's design, coupled with an alternative monitoring system (i.e., the leak detection system) for detecting breaches in the uppermost liner, provide an acceptable substitute for groundwater monitoring. If a leak is detected, the uppermost liner must be repaired or replaced or, alternatively, the facility must begin complying with the groundwater protection requirements. Also exempt from the groundwater protection requirements are facilities located in areas with deep, tight soils (e.g., clay) that will prevent the migration of leachate to groundwater for at least 30 years after closure.

### GROUNDWATER PROTECTION STANDARD

The heart of the groundwater protection requirements is the assumption that significant leachate plumes reaching groundwater can and will be detected and removed through corrective action (e.g., counter pumping). * * * Although there is limited experience with corrective action to remove contamination from groundwater, this is likely to be a very expensive undertaking and should provide an economic incentive for owners and operators to employ designs and operating practices that minimize the chance that corrective action will be necessary.

The groundwater protection program is comprised of three phases—detection monitoring, compliance monitoring, and the corrective action program. New facilities and existing facilities at which no groundwater contamination has been detected during the interim status period will initially begin in the *detection monitoring* phase. During the phase, owners and operators are required to conduct a groundwater monitoring program typically using a small number of *surrogate* monitoring parameters capable of detecting broad classes of organic and inorganic hazardous constituents. Monitoring is to be conducted in the uppermost groundwater aquifer at the waste management area boundary. This monitoring must continue throughout the facility's operating life and the post-closure care period (normally 30 years after closure). If no statistically significant contamination (over pre-established background levels) is detected during this period, the owner or operator has fulfilled his permit responsibilities and may cease monitoring.

If detection monitoring indicates that leachate has reached groundwater, the second phase of the program, *compliance monitoring*, is triggered. Once leachate is detected, the owner or operator must analyze groundwater for *specific* hazardous constituents that are known to be in the waste at the facility and determine their concentrations. Appropriate hazardous constituents must be *selected* from a list of * * * constituents promulgated by the Agency * * * . The information on hazardous constituent concentrations must be submitted to the Agency within 90 days of detection, along with a *permit modification application* to begin the compliance monitoring program. EPA will then (after a public hearing) modify the permit to include a groundwater protection *standard*. This standard identifies the hazardous constituents for which monitoring must be conducted and the *allowable concentration limits* for these constituents. For the 14 hazardous constituents covered * * * under the Safe Drinking Water Act, the allowable concentration limits are those which have been specified as the maximum concentration limits for drinking water, or background concentrations (i.e., the concentrations already present in groundwater in the aquifer which has not been affected by a regulated unit), whichever is higher. For all other hazardous constituents, the concentration must not exceed background levels. However, the owner or operator has the opportunity to demonstrate that a concentration above background will not adversely affect human health and the environment. If a successful demonstration can be made for some or all hazardous constituents, the groundwater protection standard written into the permit will incorporate these alternate concentration limits. * * *

Compliance monitoring begins when leachate is detected and must continue for a number of years equal to the entire opening life of the facility. Thus, if a facility with an operating life of 20 years detects contamination in the 15th year of operation, compliance monitoring begins in the 15th year and continues for an additional 20 years. If the concentration limits established in the permit are not exceeded during this period, compliance monitoring ceases. However, should the specified concentration limits be exceeded at any time during the compliance monitoring phase, a *corrective action program* must be instituted.

If compliance monitoring indicates an excessive concentration of hazardous constituents, the owner or operator must immediately notify EPA and within six months submit an *application for a permit modification* for a corrective action program. This application must explain what actions the owner/operator proposes in order to return groundwater quality to within the acceptable concentration limits established in the compliance monitoring phase. The application must also include a groundwater monitoring scheme to verify the results of corrective action. Corrective action must continue until groundwater quality at the waste management boundary is again within the limits established in the groundwater protection standard for the unit.

Existing facilities at which contamination has been discovered prior to permit issuance * * * do not begin with detection monitoring but rather enter directly into the compliance monitoring phase, or, in some cases, the corrective action program. At such facilities, concentration limits will be established as part of the original permit and demonstrations for alternate concentration limits may be made as part of the original permit application. If concentrations exceed these established limits, corrective action must begin immediately.

Corrective action requirements are described in terms of the performance to be achieved, namely returning the concentration of hazardous constituents in the groundwater to within established concentration limits by removing the hazardous constituents or treating them in place. The regulations do not specify what type of corrective action must be undertaken, leaving this open for a case-by-case determination. * * *

Previously promulgated RCRA regulations require owners and operators of land disposal facilities to establish *financial assurances* (e.g., trust funds or bonds) for purposes of *closure* and *post-closure* activities. No similar requirements have been promulgated for the purpose of assuring that adequate resources are available for conducting corrective action, if it becomes necessary. However, establishing reasonable, yet adequate, financial assurance requirements is extremely difficult because of the uncertainties involved in predicting if or when corrective action will be necessary at a particular site. The Agency does, in the preamble to the land disposal rules, request comments on the issue of financial assurances for corrective action.

### DESIGN AND OPERATING STANDARDS

While the groundwater protection measures are *curative* in nature, the design and operating requirements are aimed at *preventing* groundwater contamination. As mentioned previously, new landfills, surface impoundments, and waste piles are required to have liner systems; existing portions of these facilities are not. Liner systems must be designed to prevent any migration of wastes out of the facility into adjacent subsurface soil or groundwater or surface water during the facility's operating life and closure period.

At *storage* facilities, migration of waste into the liner is acceptable, because storage facilities, by definition, will remove all wastes and contaminated liners at closure. This standard permits the use of single clay liners at waste piles and storage surface impoundments. *Disposal* facility liners, on the other hand, must be designed to prevent migration of wastes into the liner as well as the subsurface soil. In effect, this rules out the use of clay liners at disposal facilities. EPA states in the preamble that, to its knowledge, only synthetic liners will meet this standard.

Both new and existing surface impoundments and landfills must place a final *cap* on the facility at closure to minimize the infiltration of precipitation and run-on. This in turn is intended to minimize the generation of leachate after closure.

New landfills and waste piles are required to have leachate collection and removal systems to remove leachate generated during the operation of the facility and, in the case of landfills, during the post-closure care period. * * *

### IMPLEMENTATION

In a separate Federal Register notice, also published on July 26, 1982, EPA announced that states could immediately begin applying for the final phase of state authorization. Once a state receives final authorization, it takes over the principal role of issuing permits and enforcing permit conditions.

## H. INCINERATION

We have now examined RCRA's approach to the land disposal of hazardous wastes, including the growing pressure exerted by Congress to greatly curtail or eliminate this activity. The move away from land disposal is understandable; if the EPA is correct in its assumption that all landfills inevitably leak, each such facility represents a potential legacy of groundwater pollution.

Incineration—a process aimed at destroying most or all hazardous properties in waste materials—might present an attractive alternative to land disposal. Such an approach requires no long-term commitment to land and no post-closure monitoring of groundwater; it raises no specter of a perpetual threat to the public health. After all (goes the assumption), once burned, the wastes are destroyed.

The very wording of the RCRA statute suggests that incineration is the way to go. RCRA § 1004(34) defines *treatment* to include "any method, technique, or process * * * designed to change the physical, chemical, or biological character or composition of any hazardous waste * * * so as to render such waste nonhazardous * * * or reduced in volume." By contrast, RCRA § 1004(3) defines *disposal* to include "the * * * placing of any * * * hazardous waste into or on any land or water * * *." Given these definitions, landfilling is disposal, while incineration is treatment. Because disposal is bad, and treatment is good, it follows that incineration should automatically be preferred over landfilling.

Is this seductive logic misleading? Shouldn't each treatment option be skeptically examined with the same rigor applied to land disposal? In another context (incineration of municipal wastes), the Natural Resources Defense Council has expressed concern about an "incinerator stampede." *See* 17 [Curr. Dev.] Env. Rep. (BNA) 1570 (1987). Might the incineration of hazardous wastes be a matter requiring greater caution?

The following readings explore the EPA's incinerator standards and note some issues involved in hazardous waste incineration.

## 1. INCINERATOR STANDARDS

### SHELDON M. NOVICK & DONALD W. STEVER, THE REGULATION OF HAZARDOUS WASTE

in 3 Law of Environmental Protection
13-99 (Sheldon M. Novick, ed. 1998)

[Thermal treatment] includes incineration, open burning, detonation, and other thermal treatment. When wastes are hazardous solely because of ignitability or reactivity, burning or detonation leave no hazardous residue. * * *

By far the most common method of thermal treatment is incineration. High-temperature incineration is the most favored method for managing many of the wastes banned from land disposal, including solvents, dioxins, and PCBs. High-temperature incinerators tend to be temperamental and difficult to monitor, and EPA's initial incinerator performance standards were the subject of significant pulling and tugging over the questions of what destruction and removal efficiency [DRE] was economically or technologically feasible.

EPA's initial incinerator performance standards, issued in the waning days of the Carter administration, required 99.99 percent destruction and removal efficiency. The Agency repealed the initial standards on June 25, 1982, replacing them with less stringent standards. Congress legislatively overruled EPA's 1982 regulation in 1984. Section 3004(o)(1)(B) establishes as statutory incinerator performance standards the EPA regulations "in effect on June 24, 1982." * * * It is not clear that the pre-1982 requirements are as stringent as the best technology available [today] however. * * *

### EPA, STANDARDS FOR OWNERS AND OPERATORS OF HAZARDOUS WASTE INCINERATORS

40 C.F.R. Part 264, Subpart O (1998)

**§ 264.341 Waste analysis.**

(a) As a portion of the trial burn plan * * * or with * * * the permit application, the owner or operator must have included an analysis of the waste feed * * * .

(b) Throughout normal operation the owner or operator must conduct sufficient waste analysis to verify that the waste feed to the incinerator is within the physical and composition limits specified in his permit * * * .

## § 264.342 Principal organic hazardous constituents (POHCs).

(a) Principal Organic Hazardous Constituents (POHCs) in the waste feed must be treated to the extent required by the performance standard of § 264.343.

(b) (1) One or more POHCs will be specified in the facility's permit * * * for each waste feed to be burned. This specification will be based on the degree of difficulty of incineration of the organic constituents in the waste and on their concentration or mass in the waste feed, considering the results of waste analyses and trial burns or alternative data submitted with * * * the facility's permit application. Organic constituents which represent the greatest degree of difficulty of incineration will be those most likely to be designated as POHCs. Constituents are more likely to be designated as POHCs if they are present in large quantities or concentrations in the waste. * * *

## § 264.343 Performance standards.

An incinerator burning hazardous waste must be designed, constructed, and maintained so that, when operated in accordance with operating requirements specified under § 264.345, it will meet the following performance standards:

(a) (1) * * * an incinerator burning hazardous waste must achieve a destruction and removal efficiency (DRE) of 99.99% for each principal organic hazardous constituent (POHC) designated * * * in its permit for each waste feed. * * *

(2) * * * An incinerator burning [certain dioxin-contaminated] hazardous wastes * * * must achieve a DRE of 99.9999% for each POHC designated * * * in its permit.

(b) An incinerator burning hazardous waste and producing stack emissions of more than 1.8 kilograms per hour (4 pounds per hour) of hydrogen chloride (HCl) must control HCl emissions such that the rate of emission is no greater than the larger of either 1.8 kilograms per hour or 1% of the HCl in the stack gas prior to entering any pollution control equipment.

(c) An incinerator burning hazardous waste must not emit particulate matter in excess of 180 milligrams per dry standard cubic meter * * * when corrected for the amount of oxygen in the stack gas * * * .

(d) For purposes of permit enforcement, compliance with the operating requirements specified in the permit * * * will be regarded as compliance with this section. * * *

## § 264.344 Hazardous waste incinerator permits.

(a) The owner or operator of a hazardous waste incinerator may burn only wastes specified in his permit and only under operating conditions specified for those wastes * * *

(b) Other hazardous wastes may be burned only after operating conditions have been specified in a new permit or a permit modification * * * .

### § 264.345 Operating requirements.

(a) An incinerator must be operated in accordance with operating requirements specified in the permit. These will be specified on a case-by-case
basis as those demonstrated * * * to be sufficient to comply with the performance standards of § 264.343.

(b) Each set of operating requirements will specify the composition of the
waste feed (including acceptable variations * * * ). For each such waste
feed, the permit will specify acceptable operating limits including the
following conditions:

(1) Carbon monoxide (CO) levels in the stack exhaust gas;

(2) Waste feed rate;

(3) Combustion temperature;

(4) An appropriate indicator of combustion gas velocity; * * * and

(6) Such other operating requirements as are necessary * * * .

(e) An incinerator must be operated with a functioning system to automatically cut off waste feed to the incinerator when operating conditions deviate from limits established under paragraph (a) of this section.

(f) An incinerator must cease operation when changes in waste feed, incinerator design, or operating conditions exceed limits designated in its
permit. * * *

### § 264.347 Monitoring and inspections.

(a) The owner or operator must conduct, as a minimum, the following monitoring while incinerating hazardous waste:

(1) Combustion temperature, waste feed rate, and the indicator of combustion gas velocity specified in the permit must be monitored on a
continuous basis.

(2) CO must be monitored on a continuous basis at a point in the incinerator downstream of the combustion zone and prior to release to the
atmosphere.

(3) Upon request by the Regional Administrator, sampling and analysis
of the waste and exhaust emissions must be conducted to verify that
the operating requirements established in the permit achieve the
performance standards of § 264.343. * * *

### *Notes and Questions*

1.   The owner or operator of an incinerator seeking to obtain a RCRA permit must undertake a *trial burn* to establish the ability of the incineration
and air pollution control equipment to comply with the performance standards of 40 C.F.R. § 264.343. Because the trial burn is itself a potentially
dangerous undertaking, it cannot be conducted without a trial burn permit.
During the trial burn, the owner/operator checks to see that all performance standards are met, including the requirement of a 99.99% (or, for dioxin wastes, 99.9999%) DRE for enumerated "principal organic hazardous
constituents" or POHCs. The POHCs are specified by the EPA in the trial
burn permit, based on what dangerous constituents from 40 C.F.R. Part

261, Appendix VIII are likely to be in the waste materials to be incinerated by the facility. (For an explanation of the Appendix VIII constituents, *see* page 693, *supra*.) If the trial burn establishes that the performance standards can be met by the facility, it can apply for and obtain a RCRA permit. Because the selection of POHCs and the demonstration of adequacy are limited to the specific wastes tested in the trial burn exercise (the "waste feed"), the RCRA permit is only good for the wastes specified in the permit; if the permittee wishes to incinerate other wastes, it must begin the whole process again with another trial burn permit application.

2. The performance standards of 40 C.F.R. § 264.343 set forth minimum DREs for each POHC designated in the permit and specify limitations for HCl and particulate emissions. Must the owner or operator monitor compliance with these DRE values during the routine, ongoing operation of the incineration facility? Why or why not?

3. Once the permit has been issued, the regulation provides that compliance with the *operating* requirements specified in the permit "will be regarded as compliance with" the *performance* standards. *See* 40 C.F.R. § 264.343(d). What does this mean? Does this approach to curbing hazardous air emissions from hazardous waste incinerators surprise you? Recall the observation at page 723, *supra*, that "[h]igh-temperature incinerators tend to be temperamental and difficult to monitor."

## NOTE ON RCRA INCINERATOR STANDARDS

Putting aside the use of operating standards as surrogates for the direct measurement of performance standard compliance, the incinerator standards are startlingly crude. First, they are technology based. Because they are not designed to achieve any ambient air quality goals, they will result in widely varying ambient air quality, depending on atmospheric conditions.

Second, the RCRA incinerator standards are oblivious to adjacent populations and emission facilities; the same standards apply, whether an incinerator is located in an isolated desert or in the heart of Manhattan and whether an incinerator is the only one in the vicinity or adjacent to other hazardous pollutant emission sources.

Third, the amounts of hazardous air emissions being released in compliance with the RCRA incinerator standards are not trivial. A 1982 report concluded that incinerators operating at the required 99.99 percent combustion efficiency nevertheless emitted 4,000 tons of potentially hazardous emissions. *See* page 728, *infra*.

Fourth, because the RCRA incinerator standards are comprised solely of percentage reduction commands, they do not take into account varying throughput. If 10,000 tons of POHCs in hazardous wastes are incinerated, one ton of organic hazardous constituents may be emitted; the total quantity of POHCs released could be 100 times higher if one million tons were incinerated.

Finally, all hazardous emissions are lumped by the RCRA incinerator standards into three categories: POHCs, gaseous hydrogen chlorides, and particulates.

What *would* thorough, *health*-based incinerators standards look like, and what problems might be encountered in setting them? The mind-boggling complexity of the task should be evident by recalling the standard setting case study in Chapter 8, *supra*. A careful consideration of the many issues addressed in that chapter might suggest that the present RCRA incinerator standards are disturbingly simplistic.

The stampede to incineration is seductive, because the resulting pollution of the biosphere is more dispersed and less visible than the nasty groundwater pollution that has led to land disposal bans. Stated another way, hazardous waste incineration is unlikely to lead to the creation of new Superfund sites. Nevertheless, might not the dispersion of hazardous materials associated with incineration be a significant drawback, rather than an advantage? Might the concentration of hazardous materials associated with land disposal be an advantage, after all? If we do not approach this issue more thoughtfully, atmospheric dispersion of hazardous waste incineration residues may become the environmental issue of the 2000s.

Constant exposure of the public to low levels of environmental pollutants may bring about health effects that we do not foresee (and, indeed, that we may not see even while they are occurring). As one congressional study noted (drawing on the example of thalidomide, a drug that induced horrible birth defects in the offspring of ingesting mothers in the 1950s), "[i]f the malformation induced by thalidomide were a mental retardation of 10% of the IQ, instead of a highly characteristic and unusual deformation of the limbs, in an equal number of subjects, we would be unaware of it to this day." Subcomm. on the Environment and the Atmosphere of the House Comm. on Science and Technology, *Effects of Chronic Exposure to Low-Level Pollutants in the Environment*, 94th Cong., 1st Sess. CRS-153 (1975).

## 2. BOILERS AND FURNACES

The next three readings address an issue closely related to hazardous waste incineration: the burning of hazardous wastes as "fuel" in *non*regulated facilities.

# UNREGULATED BOILERS ESTIMATED TO EMIT TONS OF HAZARDOUS EMISSIONS

### 13 [Curr. Dev.] Env. Rep. (BNA) 629 (1982)

Approximately 1.2 million tons of potentially hazardous emissions are released annually from unregulated boilers that burn hazardous waste at a 97 percent combustion efficiency, compared to the 4,000 tons emitted from incinerators regulated at a 99.99 percent combustion efficiency under [RCRA], according to a new report prepared by Fred C. Hart Associates, Inc. As a result, 147 million people, representing 68 percent of the U.S. population, are exposed to potentially hazardous emissions, according to the study * * * .

The situation arises, according to the report, because a "loophole" in the RCRA hazardous waste regulations leaves hazardous waste substantially unregulated if burned in industrial or commercial boilers to recover usable energy. * * * Industry has a strong incentive to burn waste in boilers because the practice eliminates the need to comply with RCRA requirements, and saves about $2 for each gallon of fuel oil replaced by waste as fuel, the report maintained. It cited a recent EPA study that estimates that about 20 million tons of the approximately 40 million tons of hazardous waste generated annually are currently burned as fuel in boilers.

Approximately two million industrial and commercial boilers exist in the United States, according to the Hart report. Destruction efficiencies are as high as 99.99 percent in large, well-maintained, carefully operated boilers, it said. However, they can vary from 97 percent to 99.9 percent, a situation more likely to be found in the field, and can be 95 percent for some small boilers, it stated. A far greater number of people are exposed to higher concentrations of hazardous air pollutants from all boilers compared to all incinerators, the report said. * * *

Waste combustion should be prohibited in boilers smaller than 25 million British thermal units per hour, the report urged, which would eliminate boilers unsuitable for burning hazardous waste and would reduce the number of facilities to be regulated from two million to 34,000. Larger boilers should be issued permits under RCRA and required to meet the incinerator standards, the report said, adding that a system of class permits should be used for boilers that can burn particular wastes safely.

## WIDESPREAD UNCONTROLLED BURNING OF WASTE SAID TAKING PLACE AT INDUSTRIAL FACILITIES

17 [Curr. Dev.] Env. Rep. (BNA) 2086 (1987)

The amount of hazardous waste burned in uncontrolled, non-incinerator devices at certain types of industrial facilities has shown a "disturbing increase" recently, according to the Hazardous Waste Treatment Council. David R. Case, general counsel for the waste treatment industry group, told BNA * * * that the EPA appears to be ignoring or even encouraging such practices to compensate for a perceived shortage of hazardous waste incineration capacity in the United States.

The council said * * * that EPA and several states are allowing mining and smelting operations and industrial furnaces to burn hazardous waste without the same environmental safeguards that are required of commercial waste incinerators under RCRA. According to the council, some of these facilities claim to be exempt from RCRA control because they are "recycling" hazardous wastes although they perform the same function as permitted commercial incinerators, accept the same wastes, and actively solicit for incineration business. * * *

Richard C. Fortuna, executive director of the treatment council, told EPA in a * * * letter that the growth of uncontrolled burning practices by such "exemption enterprises" may be exacerbating environmental threats. These facilities meet virtually none of the incineration standards designed to protect health and the environment, he said. * * * Case added that the council believes that the agency should promptly impose RCRA regulations governing incineration of hazardous waste in industrial boilers and furnaces, which he said were years overdue.

EPA in November 1985 issued final rules severely restricting incineration of hazardous waste as fuel in *non*-industrial facilities, such as residential or institutional boilers. The agency has not yet issued rules governing such practices at industrial facilities * * * . Dwight Hlustick, a staff member in the combustion section of EPA's Waste Treatment Branch, told BNA * * * that the agency soon will propose RCRA regulations for industrial boilers and furnaces that burn hazardous waste.

# STANDARDS FOR BOILERS, INDUSTRIAL FURNACES HIT BY ENVIRONMENTALISTS, TREATMENT COUNCIL

### 22 [Curr. Dev.] Env. Rep. (BNA) 252 (1991)

The long-running controversy over controls on hazardous waste burned in boilers and industrial furnaces was reignited * * * by a lawsuit filed by environmentalists and the hazardous waste management industry (*Citizens for a Safe Environment v. EPA*, CA DC, No. 91-1240, 5/22/91). The suit challenged new [boiler and industrial furnace (BIF)] rules on hazardous waste incineration issued in April by the EPA * * * . EPA had issued those rules in response to a previous lawsuit by the Environmental Defense Fund.

The rules were designed to close a loophole that allowed companies other than hazardous waste incinerators to burn nearly 2 million tons per year of hazardous waste for energy and material recovery and claim an exemption from permit requirements available to recyclers. The new rules require previously unregulated boilers and furnaces that burn hazardous waste to obtain permits under the Resource Conservation and Recovery Act.

Approximately 1,000 unregulated boilers and industrial furnaces in the United States are burning 20 times more hazardous waste than incinerators that have obtained permits under RCRA, the Hazardous Waste Treatment Council said. Jackie Warren, an attorney with the Natural Resources Defense Council, said EPA's new regulations were not tough enough to correct the situation. "Local citizens and the national environmental organizations are very concerned, and EPA's inadequate standards do not respond to those concerns," she said. * * *

---

Most challenges to the EPA's BIF rules were upheld in *Complex Horsehead Resource Development Co. v. Browner*, 16 F.3d 1246 (D.C. Cir. 1994), although certain portions related to air emission controls were remanded for further notice and comment.

# I. WASTE MANAGEMENT CHOICES

You have now been exposed to most features of the RCRA Subtitle C program. Even if everything worked perfectly, the enactment and implementation of RCRA Subtitle C would not eliminate the need to make difficult policy choices. One such choice is presented in the following problem.

### Problem

Two weeks ago, a fire destroyed a warehouse owned by Ridz-Em Pesticide Company. Hundreds of pounds of deadly pesticides were partially consumed by the blaze; fire fighters noticed that birds flying over the site dropped like bricks when they encountered the fumes. The site is now heavily contaminated with pesticide residues, which were carried by water (used to extinguish the blaze) out to the surrounding soil.

The state pollution control agency is considering two proposals to dispose of these contaminated soils. The first proposal would be to scoop the contaminated soil into four large dump trucks and haul it to a hazardous waste landfill located 1,000 miles away in another state. (This is the closest authorized hazardous waste landfill.) The cost of this disposal method would be $150,000. The second proposal stems from an offer by the local utility company, Hawkeye Power. The power company has offered to incinerate the contaminated soil by feeding it slowly into its huge coal-fired electric generating plant; the soil would be dumped on the company's coal pile and gradually fed into the "furnace" with the coal. The experts at the state agency are convinced that the pesticides would be rendered harmless by this method; they have carefully calculated the minimum temperature in the furnace (1300° F) and the "dwell time" during which the pesticides would experience this temperature (30 seconds), to arrive at their conclusion that the incineration would be fully effective. The cost of this disposal method would be $10,000 (the cost of trucking the soil to the plant), because the utility company has offered its services free of charge.

The people who live down-wind of the utility stack (somewhere between 50,000 and 100,000 people, depending on the direction of the plume) are outraged at this second proposal. They do not trust anyone who assures them that the plume would be harmless. The people who live along the 1,000 mile stretch to the landfill are none too happy with the first proposal (at least those who have heard of it), and the people who live adjacent to the hazardous waste landfill are positively furious at the continued dumping of out-of-state toxics in their back yards.

How should this hazardous waste be "managed"?

# J. CRIMINAL EVASION

Notwithstanding the difficult nature of the policy choices that remain, our underlying assumption is surely that the world is a safer place, now that the basic Subtitle C program is in place. However, there are disturbing indications, fleshed out in the next readings, that the enormous efforts expended in the RCRA process may sometimes things worse. Far worse.

## ORGANIZED CRIME AND HAZARDOUS WASTE DISPOSAL: HEARINGS

Before the Subcomm. on Oversight and Investigations of the House
Comm. on Interstate and Foreign Commerce, 96th Cong., 2nd Sess.
5, 7-14, 16-17, 21-24, 28, 31-35, 41-42, 62-64, 69-70, 72, 76-78, 87, 89 (1980)

### Testimony Of Harold Kaufman

Mr. MAGUIRE. At this point I would like to request that all cameras be turned off. Both still and moving camera photography will be prohibited during the entrance and exit of our next witness. Our first witness this morning is Mr. Harold Kaufman.

Mr. Kaufman is currently in the Federal witness protection program. He was a confidential FBI informant for 2 years. He is knowledgeable about the solid and chemical waste disposal industries. He telephoned my office last week to make contact with this investigation, and this committee, and expressed an interest in providing us with testimony. * * *

Mr. GORE. Is the garbage collection industry in New York, where you began, controlled by organized crime?

Mr. KAUFMAN. Yes, it is, to my knowledge.

Mr. GORE. Now, that industry operates with a system of what you refer to as property rights?

Mr. KAUFMAN. Yes.

Mr. GORE. Can you briefly explain how the concept of property rights works, first of all, in the garbage business.

Mr. KAUFMAN. In order to do that I have to retrogress just 1 minute.

The price of a stop in New York City, right now—a stop is where a truck stops and picks up the garbage; the terminology is a stop, that's what they call a customer. A stop right now in New York goes for 25 to 35 to 1, which means 35 gross monthly payments for one stop. That's for a packer. For a rolloff, it's going from 40 to 45 to 50 to 1. This means for 50 months you don't make a nickel. You have to have a protection that nobody's going to come in there for that 50 months 'cause everybody picks up garbage the same way. There is no great technology about picking up garbage, especially in New York. So, how are you going to protect it? You protect it by the fact that you have property rights, that no other garbageman is going to go in and take that stop.

Mr. GORE. So if a company has the right to pick up the garbage at a particular stop, that right stays with that company? What happens if another company comes and tries to sign a contract with the person that's trying to dispose of the garbage and offers to charge them less money?

Mr. KAUFMAN. In New York, you have five, no four associations right now. First of all they are brought before the association. This is the first step in what I call the semiofficial grievance procedure. He is told to get out of there because it is not his stop. Second, it happens very seldom in New York. It's been going on—you know stops have been there for oh, I'd say for the last 15 to 20 years, they haven't really had any bad problems in the city by people taking each other's stops. So it doesn't happen that often. When it does, they first, they try to do it by economic punishment. In other words, everybody goes out and tries to take this fellow's stops.

Second, they'll do it by fear and intimidation. He knows, he knows there is a punishment coming because organized crime controls it. There's been beatings, there's been killings in New York, just like in New Jersey. This is the final culmination if they have to be taught a lesson.

Mr. GORE. Do you personally know of any murders that resulted from the encroachment by one company on the property rights of another company?

Mr. KAUFMAN. Yes, I do.

Mr. GORE. Can you tell us of those instances?

Mr. KAUFMAN. Yes, I can. There was Fred Dinardi, Custom Disposal; he was killed in New York by the Blue Angel. There was San Felice—Gabe, I think his first name was—but San Felice was his last name, Sano Carting; he was killed in New Jersey. * * *

Mr. GORE. * * * Now, at what point did companies picking up garbage begin to get into the toxic waste disposal business?

Mr. KAUFMAN. To my knowledge, again, it could have been before, you know, the illegal dumping, but to my knowledge, it's when the manifest system came out is when they found out the profit motive. * * *

Mr. KAUFMAN. The larger companies, the du Ponts, the Allied Chemical, and people like this, knew what toxic waste was. When the manifest system in New Jersey came out, you were asking people that were paying a dollar a yard to throw this stuff in the nearest landfill, all of a sudden, with the stroke of a pen, this stuff became toxic waste, $20 a yard. This was the problem in New Jersey, primarily, in my opinion, the fact that they never explained that the middle company had the problem. It's not the big company.

You take an Allied, and du Pont, they have 50 chemists working for them, or 100 chemists, but you take this printing ink industry in New Jersey, they had nobody. This was just ordinary garbage to them for many years. I don't want to get specific into companies, but the wholesale printing industry, which is a strong industry in New Jersey—you have to clean the machines with toxic waste, this is toxic, the stuff that is used to clean the machines. It's toxic ink, according to the manifest system. This same guy had to pay $20 a yard to get rid of the stuff the day before for a dollar. * * *

Mr. KAUFMAN. * * * See, like everything else, the idea was fantastic, cradle to grave. We're going to watch every piece of toxic waste in the State of New Jersey. That's—it was in every paper, it was in every headline. * * *

Mr. GORE. Did there come a time when you went to a company called Duane Marine?

Mr. KAUFMAN. Yes.

Mr. GORE. When was that?

Mr. KAUFMAN. Early 1978, I think.

Mr. GORE. And this was a chemical waste disposal facility, is that right?

Mr. KAUFMAN. Well, that is what is was called. It never disposed of anything, but you can call it that.

Mr. GORE. You offered a front to companies that wanted to pretend they were disposing of toxic waste.

Mr. KAUFMAN. No, that wasn't true. That wasn't true.

Mr. GORE. Well, explain it to me in your own words.

Mr. KAUFMAN. You're blaming the companies; 99 percent of these companies in good faith thought that Duane Marine had the facility.

Mr. GORE. I see.

Mr. KAUFMAN. Because the State licensed us. We were the first ones licensed. Duane Marine. Second, when the manifest system was explained to all the industry where they had a big meeting at this motel, I forgot what motel it was, and Duane Marine was on the first manifest that explained the manifest system. In other words, they were telling these industrial people who in good faith wanted to follow the law, if they wanted to cheat, they wouldn't have brought the stuff to us, because we were charging a lot of money. * * *

Mr. GORE. And there is an informal agreement that no one goes after the property rights that a company has on toxic waste?

Mr. KAUFMAN. It is not in writing, but it is not informal; you better not.

Mr. GORE. What would happen if you would encroach on that?

Mr. KAUFMAN. You get your legs broke; you get shot. * * *

See I don't blame the companies that brought waste to Duane Marine, because every one of them knew that we had a facility, we made out the manifest and everything else. I blame the licensing system, and I blame the fact that nobody followed through.

Mr. GORE. So, in effect, the people disposing of hazardous chemical waste in New Jersey are paying in many instances a kind of tax to organized crime?

Mr. KAUFMAN. If it is in concert with solid waste. * * * [A]ny company that does primarily solid waste, that got into the toxic field, understands property rights. They have to. Because they do so much more money right now in solid waste in New Jersey than in toxic. * * *

Mr. MAGUIRE. So, organized crime, as far as you understand the situation, is presently in control of solid waste and the likelihood is that the same schemes are being set up for toxic waste.

Mr. KAUFMAN. Congressman Maguire, when they set up the manifest system in New Jersey, the way you got a hazardous waste license to haul was the simplest way in the world. You sent the State of New Jersey $50, they sent you a sticker, for everyone that you had on the PUC. They made every garbageman in New Jersey that wanted to be, or is, because I got a lot of them their licenses, they made them hazardous waste haulers. Nobody checked out if they were qualified, did they know what they were doing, did they know what toxic waste was. There's where your danger is, through the haulers. I can't speak about all the facilities in New Jersey, because I don't know them.

Mr. MAGUIRE. But Duane Marine was a fraud?

Mr. KAUFMAN. Duane Marine was a complete fraud. He had no facility at all, he had no way at all of disposing. * * *

Mr. MAGUIRE. Mr. Gore.

Mr. GORE. Let me just conclude, Mr. Chairman, by saying that we saw organized crime infiltrate the toxic waste disposal business in New Jersey when the manifest system was put into effect. It then became very difficult for the run-of-the-mill midnight dumper to go out and dump it somewhere without some kind of front or cover. Organized crime was well able to provide that kind of cover. As the Nation institutes a regulatory system similar to the one New Jersey put into effect 2 years ago, we ought to take steps to make certain that organized crime does not expand its foothold in this new industry.

In your opinion, what is the best way to prevent organized crime from expanding its role here?

Mr. KAUFMAN. First of all, you've got to fund this thing where they have more inspectors, but if you're not going to do this, if Congress is not going to fund them where they have more inspectors, all right like they're crying now they haven't got enough, you've got to have priorities. There is toxic waste and there is toxic waste. Don't force the middleman, the middle company who wants to be honest into the midnight dumpers' hands because it is economically impossible for this man to comply with this. You're talking about a horrendous expense as this technology gets stronger, the price is going sky high. It's getting higher every day. A hundred dollars for a 55-gallon drum is not even unheard of anymore. I remember when we were charging $20 for the same thing. As the technology gets bigger, the price is going to get bigger. He doesn't know this is really going to hurt anything, the water, or anything else * * * .

Mr. RINALDO. * * * [C]ould you give us your opinion as to how the licensing system in the State of New Jersey could be improved in order to at least stem the infiltration of organized crime in this business? * * *

Mr. KAUFMAN. First of all, when you license a hauler, let's check on who the hauler is. The hauler starts it out. Forget about the generator. Let's not blame the people that are really trying to follow the manifest. See, in my opinion, these companies operate in good faith, in good faith—otherwise they wouldn't have called the people, they would have thrown it in the nearest dump. These people were trying to follow your law. You made that law saying this has to be done through a manifest system and they were trying to follow it, which is expensive for them.

You are telling, one, that the hauler is authorized to transport this. This hauler has no training in toxic waste. He was a garbageman. You are telling him to take the toxic waste. First of all, he doesn't know what toxic waste is. If there is an accident, if the thing blows up, never did they check the drivers to see if they were trained? Did the drivers understand emergency procedures? All you needed was $50 and you got yourself a sticker that you could transport hazardous waste. * * *

I have been going to landfills for 6 years. I have never seen anybody climb in that truck and look what was in it. Once in a while a State inspector will look at a rolloff truck because it's easy, but once that thing turns around you are not going to stick your head in there, and it's so easy to mix garbage with toxic waste it isn't even funny. Unless the thing has a horrendous odor, or it's really loose, and then, well again, I guess I can't say it.

**Testimony of John Albert, North Brunswick, N.J.**

Mr. ALBERT. My name is John Albert of North Brunswick, N.J. I would like to read one thing before we get started.

I have been subpoenaed to testify here today and will testify concerning the many lies and fatuations of Harold Kaufman as much as I am able to, at such time it doesn't affect the prosecution pending against me now.

Mr. ALBERT. When you say toxic waste business, was I in it, I was a hauler for National Starch, I took the drums from National Starch to a facility. That was my extent in the chemical business. I applied for a license to go into a facility. You say I told you I was in the chemical waste business. I was a hauler. I never ever had a facility license.

Mr. GORE. What facility did you take the waste to?

[Witness confers with counsel.]

Mr. ALBERT. This matter involves one of my pending cases and I have to take the fifth on it.

Mr. GORE. Very well.

Mr. ALBERT. Before I answer the question, I sat here for the last 20 minutes and listened to Mr. Kaufman testify before you people. I heard you people thank him for coming here and doing what he could to help the taxpayers and everyone.

I have to be a little bewildered when I look at you people, intelligent people, when a man can sit here and tell you that the company of Duane Marine was a fraudulent company.

This man drove a car that was owned by Duane Marine; he took a salary from Duane Marine; he had a charge account for Duane Marine. This man was part of that fraud, if it was a fraud.

This man knows Duane Marine had permits to dispose of solid waste. * * *

All of a sudden this man becomes religious. He comes in front of you people and tells you this and tells you that and that he is sacrificing his life for justice. This man is a whore, in plain English. You people can think what you want; this man was an officer of that company. He knew the inner works of the company. He signed checks for that fraudulent company. He was out getting work for that company.

When I sit here for 15 minutes, 20 minutes, and hear that man go through what he went through and you people thank him from the bottom of your heart for being so cooperative, to want to help justice, I got to get a little sick. I hate to tell you that; I have to get a little sick. Knowing where the man came from—the man has a criminal record. The man has been in jail. He done everything that has been done and all of a sudden he is snow white. He comes before you people and he is going to resolve all your problems.

### Testimony of Detective Sergeant Dirk Ottens and Detective Sergeant Jack Penney, New Jersey State Police

Mr. GORE. [L]arge profit margins make it attractive to organized crime and the disposal methods which are outside the law are more profitable if people are willing to use those methods. Is that also correct?

Mr. OTTENS. That is correct. Some of those methods have been explained to you. We also have a couple of examples of that if you so desire.

Mr. GORE. Yes, if you could give them quickly.

Mr. OTTENS. Of course we point out the midnight dumper which is highly publicized in that a tank truck is pulled up to a sewer and the contents disposed of in a sewer. We also note that during rainy weather, a tank truck would travel a major highway such as the New Jersey Turnpike and open the valves at the lower portion of the tank and continue to drive until the tank is completely empty.

We also note the use of roll-offs. The average capacity is 20 cubic yards. We have heard Mr. Kaufman discuss placing toxic or hazardous waste material into the roll-offs with solid waste or garbage. This is done by lining the roll-off with plastic, putting sand at the base of it in the corners and putting absorbent-type solid waste material into the roll-off, and then emptying drums of liquid hazardous waste material into that roll-off.

We, through sources, believe that approximately 60 drums containing hazardous or liquid waste can be disposed of in one container. This container is then hoisted on a chassis truck utilized to transport it and taken to a sanitary landfill where it is disposed of as solid waste or garbage.

Mr. GORE. Highly poisonous garbage?

Mr. OTTENS. Yes sir. * * *

Mr. GORE. Is there also an interrelationship between fuel oil companies and the disposal of chemical waste?

Mr. PENNEY. Yes sir, we received information this is another area of illegal disposal of flammable toxics. The methodology is such that the toxics, solvents of PCB's are mixed with recycled waste oil. For example with 6,000 gallons of fuel, you can mix about 10 percent of PCB with that matter and 30 percent with the flammable solvents. The result being, you have a lowering of the flash point and the Btu. You have an increase in the consumption which in turn would increase the cost to the consumer. We have received information that this adulterated fuel is being used in various large industries, school systems, and public utility companies.

Mr. GORE. Hospitals as well?

Mr. PENNEY. Yes, sir.

Mr. FLORIO. * * * How is it that one can leave someplace with a truckload of something, put on a manifest that you are going to take it to a certain spot, and then turn on one's valves as one goes down the New Jersey Turnpike, have it spread all over the New Jersey Turnpike and not be caught up short somewhere?

How does the system not operate so that we can account for that missing material that is dumped along the New Jersey Turnpike or wherever?

Mr. OTTENS. Well, if you have a prearrangement with the facility for a percentage, small cash flow to the facility, the facility can sign off that they have received it. * * *

---

Then-Representative Al Gore summed up the conclusion of the investigating panel: "Anyone who thinks that the problem of illegal disposal has been magically solved now that the regulations have been passed is crazy." *The Tennessean*, Dec. 16, 1980.

## K. ALTERNATIVE APPROACHES

When the RCRA Subtitle C cradle-to-grave manifest program was first put into place, it all seemed so sensible. Now, however, it appears that the consequences may parallel the hackneyed motto of gun control opponents: "When guns are outlawed, only criminals will have guns." Perhaps the root cause of the problem is that Subtitle C has created the wrong incentive: to evade onerous compliance costs by engaging in illegal behavior and even turning to organized crime. Is there a better way? Consider the following reading which serves, in part, as a bridge to the study of CERCLA.

### NOTE, ALLOCATING THE COSTS OF HAZARDOUS WASTE DISPOSAL

94 Harv. L. Rev. 584, 585-86, 589-91, 596-99, 601-03 (1981)

Several types of costs are associated with hazardous chemical wastes. *Avoidance costs* are the costs of proper disposal. Remedial costs of removal and cleanup following improper disposal can be termed *abatement costs. Compensation costs* are the measure of the injuries— immediate and latent—that occur between improper disposal of wastes and their cleanup or loss of toxicity through chemical degradation. The processes of controlling and allocating the costs of hazardous wastes involve *transaction costs*. Transaction costs include both governmental administrative costs, generally borne by the public, and costs, such as the cost of acquiring information needed to meet a burden of proof, usually borne by participants in a reallocation proceeding.

The relative magnitudes of these different types of costs vary considerably, but the estimated costs associated with the hazardous waste dump at the Love Canal in Niagara Falls, New York reveal a typical pattern: avoidance costs of $4 million, abatement costs of $125 million,[12] and compensation costs suggested by the more than $2.5 billion in claims for personal injury. These figures suggest that proper disposal is the cheapest method for dealing with hazardous wastes. The prevalence of improperly disposed hazardous wastes indicates that, from the point of view of disposers, the out-of-pocket cost of improper disposal plus anticipated liability for future costs has historically been considerably less than avoidance costs.

Allocations of hazardous waste disposal costs among potential cost bearers should attempt to achieve the broad objective of advancing welfare by minimizing the aggregate costs of avoidance, abatement, and compensation and the transaction costs of effecting the allocation. Deterring improper disposal is one strategy for allocating appropriate resources to avoidance and thereby reducing costs. * * *

As devices for deterring improper disposal, actions for compensation are of dubious value. The extremely long time that must elapse between the act of improper disposal and the reallocation of compensation costs is probably the most important reason. This inheres in the physical processes that give rise to hazardous waste-related injuries * * * . When a firm disposes of its wastes it will have little information and perhaps still less concern about the costs that it may bear decades later.

Tort litigation also fails as an effective procedure for spreading hazardous waste-related costs. From the victim's perspective, the extremely high transaction costs are the most serious obstacle to cost spreading. A major source of these costs is meeting the burden of proof—establishing a causal connection between the release of a chemical toxin and personal injury. * * *

As deterrents to improper disposal, public suits for abatement may prove more effective than private actions for compensation. Abatement suits can be initiated at the time of improper storage or disposal, creating the possibility of much more rapid cost reallocation to the responsible firm, though delays preceding the discovery of improper disposal are still likely. The very existence of a hazardous waste prosecution unit in the Justice Department and the publicity surrounding the suits it has initiated may do much to encourage proper disposal. * * *

The effectiveness of public suits for abatement in controlling the costs of hazardous wastes has yet to be determined. Suits of this type

---

[12] * * * EPA Administrator Douglas M. Costle has estimated that abatement costs associated with three hazardous waste incidents were between 20 and 60 times greater than avoidance costs would have been, and in some cases might be higher. * * * *See also* 45 Fed. Reg. 33,071 (1980) (EPA estimates society is spending $1,800 per ton for cleanup of wastes at the Love Canal whereas proper disposal of similar waste costs an average of $80 per ton).

are potentially far more valuable deterrents of improper disposal than actions for compensation. * * * Public subsidy of hazardous waste disposal costs has occasionally been used when sufficiently prompt action by responsible firms appeared unlikely. Such case-by-case legislation is, however, too cumbersome. A growing number of state statutes as well as the CERCLA have therefore established funds to shoulder abatement and, under some funds, compensation costs stemming from hazardous wastes.

The state funds and, in large part, the federal fund are financed by fees imposed on firms in some way related to hazardous waste production. Since the payments are not related to the firms' disposal policies these fees will not deter improper disposal.[63] Significant deterrence under fund statutes may come from provisions for litigation by the fund against firms responsible for toxic releases. * * *

Litigation by a fund could be a more effective deterrent than private actions for compensation * * * since a fund could be empowered to consolidate a large number of subrogated claims and thereby gain the cost advantages of a class action. A fund seeking recovery on many subrogated claims of individual injury might also ease the burden of proof problem by employing statistical methods of proof.

A fund may more effectively undertake abatement and spread compensation costs than litigation since procedures for disbursing fund monies are more streamlined than equivalent processes in the courts. Unlike public officials bringing suits for abatement, fund administrators can make unilateral decisions for abatement expenditures.

### AN ALTERNATIVE: "FREE" DISPOSAL

Funds could be structured to act prospectively, by encouraging proper disposal from the beginning. Since improper disposal results from the unwillingness of firms to incur the costs of proper disposal, a possible solution to the problem lies in separating the decision to allocate monies needed for proper disposal from the day-to-day decisions on how a firm is to dispose of its wastes.

If proper disposal were, on the margin, costless, firms would have no incentive to dispose of wastes improperly. Such an approach would involve the mandatory licensing of all waste generators and the imposition of flat fees roughly related to a firm's size, but not closely tied to the exact volume of wastes it generated. These fees would be used to

---

[63] The fact that fees may fall if many disposers individually decide to dispose of wastes properly provides only the most tenuous incentive for proper disposal. If fees are assessed on waste generators in proportion to the volume of wastes they generate, imposing the fees may in fact encourage *improper* disposal as a means of concealing the full amount of wastes produced. Fees imposed at licensed dump sites according to the volumes of wastes received will simply aggravate the apparent cost advantage of improper disposal. * * * If payment of fees is coupled with a statutory limitation of waste generator or disposer liability * * * the incentive for proper disposal is further weakened. Imposition of industry wide fees in the context of hazardous wastes is thus no more than a revenue-raising measure.

underwrite a "free" hazardous waste collection, transportation, and disposal system. Existing transporters and disposers would be eligible to participate in this system upon satisfying government safety standards. Upon joining the system they would offer their services without charge to all generators and would be compensated from a fund created by the generator fees. Regulation of the final disposal processes would still be required, but there would be no need to police closely the transfers of wastes as is necessary in traditional regulatory approaches.

A "free" disposal system is the logical extension of fund operation when the goal of minimizing the aggregate social cost of waste disposal is paramount. Although by externalizing costs from individual firms to the industry as a whole the system would eliminate incentives to lower the volume of hazardous wastes generated, it should eliminate the high, external costs of improper disposal.

### STATUTORY REGULATION

Regulatory systems can deter improper disposal in a manner that avoids many of the problems intrinsic to retrospective cost reallocation through litigation. If, for example, fines are prescribed as a penalty for improper disposal, an economic incentive for firms to incur necessary avoidance costs can be created without any need to assess the costs stemming from specific instances of improper disposal. The penalties can be imposed quickly since they depend on the act of disposal and not on often slow-to-develop injury to persons or property. Regulatory schemes also avoid having to rely on the diffuse, ad hoc decisionmaking that undermines deterrence through litigation for compensation or abatement.

The most important argument against regulation as an approach to deterrence is that the transaction costs of enforcement may be very large in comparison with the benefits achieved. Because of the strong economic incentive for improper disposal, effective implementation of the federal regulatory scheme may require very close governmental supervision. The EPA will have to police approximately 67,000 firms that collectively generate enormous volumes of hazardous wastes. Not only will the complexity of the operations involved and the extent of supervision needed produce large transaction costs, but they may also result in a large amount of "leakage" from the regulatory system. The fundamental weakness of the regulations is their reliance on circuitous, costly, and perhaps inaccurate tracking of wastes as they pass from firm to firm simply to ensure expenditures needed for proper disposal. A more direct means to the same end would be to extend hazardous waste funds to establish a "free" disposal system.

### Questions

Should society provide free hazardous waste disposal at publicly operated facilities? Wouldn't that end the problem of improper disposal? Do you see any drawbacks to such an approach?

_____

The underlying assumption of the preceding reading is that the goal of the nation's hazardous waste policy should be "proper disposal." We close out our consideration of RCRA by examining a student work taking issue with this assumption.

The following note was written at a time when federal policy favored landfilling of hazardous wastes. Ask yourself whether the author would change her views given our new emphasis on waste "treatment" (particularly incineration), following the 1984 enactment of the HSWA. Is her objection merely to the landfill mentality, or is it an objection to something deeper in the RCRA Subtitle C program—something that still dominates our national policy?

## NOTE, PUTTING IT DOWN: HAZARDOUS-WASTE MANAGEMENT IN THE THROWAWAY CULTURE

### 2 U.C.L.A. J. Envtl. L & Policy 115, 134-44 (1981)

This paper * * * attempts to put across one main point: as with everyday garbage, America's idea of dealing with the hazardous waste problem is to bury it and forget it. Currently, thanks to the RCRA and its offspring, we are burying the problem more securely and with more ceremony than [ever] before. * * * [T]his aspect of the situation should not be getting the priority it now does. Instead, we should give priority to determining ways to cut the output of hazardous waste. * * *

[F]or governments, both the problem and the implied solution are still easy to state: How can we best put it down?[95] * * * This section isolates three types of attempts—definition-redefinition, action versus activity, and divert and inter—engaged in by various levels of government to facilitate the put-down process in light of the hazardous waste problem's many dimensions.

#### DEFINITION-REDEFINITION

[M]uch of the scope-setting language used by governments in defining the hazardous waste problem is extremely astute and sensitive politically. Two examples from RCRA's background highlight this careful choice of words. The ultimate example may be in the name Congress gave to its dealings with hazardous waste, i.e., "management." It is hard to imagine a word with stronger, clearer connotations that the problem is in capable hands and, more specifically, that government has the problem under control. Given these connotations, one might predict that questions about the government program of hazardous

_____

[95] Here is a statement typical of the government problem view: "The failure to _properly_ dispose of hazardous waste is costing the public millions and the cost of cleanup is far more expensive than _proper_ disposal in the first place." _Subcomm. on Interstate and Foreign Commerce, Hazardous Waste Disposal Report_, 96th Cong., 1st Sess. 5 (1979) (emphasis added).

waste management would tend to relate to program adequacy rather than to government competency to program at all. One might also suspect that questions of adequacy are more easily answerable, in a statistical form familiar to citizens, than questions of competency.

A pair of popular phrases, associated with Subtitle C and often seen in scholarly articles and public relations pamphlets alike, provides another example of the way the federal government defined its solution to the hazardous waste problem. Read together, they conjure up a neat picture of the aims of hazardous waste management: "closing the circle of Federal environmental protection" by tracking hazardous wastes from "cradle to grave." Closer inspection of these terms reveals their usefulness. "Closing the circle" bespeaks getting a job done right * * * . [I]t also symbolizes something many of us associated with nature and the natural, i.e., complete cycles. "Cradle to grave" coverage implies that hazardous waste lives and dies the way people do, and that if we put a marker where it is buried and remember it occasionally on holidays as we do the dearly departed, we have paid our respects to the dead. Never mind that hazardous waste does not cycle nor stay "dead" just because it is buried. * * *

### ACTION VERSUS ACTIVITY

Because the hazardous-waste problem is a very lively issue today, it behooves government officials to demonstrate their true concern by engaging in lots of activity in the area. * * *

There is certainly no paucity of legislative activity relating to hazardous waste. "Everyone wants to be a pioneer in the hazardous waste area," noted one California administrator. At that time there were about 40 different bills before the California legislature. * * *

The yo-yo effect of government activity showed up recently at the federal level when regulatory reform hit the Reagan administration. According to the President's Task Force on Regulatory Relief, no hazardous waste regulations will be immune from review on cost-benefit analysis principles. * * * Whatever else this increased activity will bring, it will not inspire definitive action to ensure that "final final" hazardous waste management regulations issue by early 1982. In the meantime, compliance with regulations by generators is even less probable given that no one, even within EPA, completely understands the whole hazardous waste regulatory system. Multiply the resulting confusion by the fact that many generators are currently expected to comply with a set of state regulations as well as EPA, and the product is more confusion and less likelihood of protection for human health the environment.

In short, government officials are discovering, to their mounting frustration, that much ado about hazardous waste does not necessarily equal a program of action to put hazardous waste down. One state environmental official plainly expressed his own feelings about the futility of activity for activity's sake: "We may have to dig it all up, put it in

Baggies, and bury it in the same hole." Jasen, *Health Hazard*, Wall St. J., May 22, 1979, at 1, col. 6.

### DIVERT AND INTER

[G]overnments are gearing up to play "divert and inter" with the hazardous waste problem. The object of this game is to divert public attention from the perceived inadequacies of government programs and then to bury the problem.

Governments can play diversion in a variety of ways. One all-time favorite strategy, employed with gusto under RCRA's resource conservation provisions, is selective or token enforcement. * * *

For those who find ridiculous the EPA slogan "citizens and governments working together hold the key to the solution of hazardous waste problems," the prospect of forced siting on a regional basis, perhaps on government land, looms ominously. With regional, forced siting, it would be just too easy for the hazardous waste problem to slip back into the twilight zone—out of sight, out of mind.

### CONCLUSION

We might as well face it: government does not know how to solve the hazardous waste problem; in fact, government is currently having trouble covering it up. And before we lull ourselves into believing that technology to change waste from hazardous to innocuous is waiting just around the corner, we should remember that the federal government is putting its money into putting it down. * * *

This paper has suggested that ordinary people tend to think about hazardous waste in one way and government officials in another. Ordinary people think about hazardous waste as they read about it in the news magazine—as a bringer of horrible mutation, a symbol of what we neglected to do in the past, as a crisis and an aberration. When the news media stop talking about hazardous waste or people tire of reading about it, they forget about it. This is dangerous. On the other hand, government officials tend to think about hazardous waste as a *management* problem, i.e., managing people and programs to reach a predetermined end: hazardous waste tucked snugly into the ground where government can forget about it and plunge ahead to solve other problems. This is also dangerous.

We cannot make hazardous waste go away by forgetting it or hiding it in the ground. Nor can we solve the hazardous waste problem by shifting from one agency or one disposal site to another, or by making it impossible to put waste down. What we have already, we [must] keep essentially forever, unless and until we learn to undo the technology which made it hazardous. * * *

The effects of hazardous waste may be surer or more severe than those of ordinary garbage, but this does not mean that the sources of hazardous wastes are bizarre. Everyday products such as plastics, medicines, paints, oil and gasoline, metals, leather, and textiles generate hazardous waste streams. The more of these products we buy, the more hazardous waste we will get. The more we ignore this fact, the more hazardous waste government will force into the ground for us.

We owe it to our own survival and that of all living things to produce less hazardous waste. * * * [I]f government continues to focus exclusively on disposal, the hazardous waste problem will overcome us later if not sooner. Therefore, government must refocus its approach to include production and conservation, rather than engaging in pointless redefinition. But government cannot change us. We must refocus our attention by recognizing what we are advocating when we consume mass quantities of hazardous waste generating products, only to throw them out and demand more—and change this behavior. * * * We must mark the last days of the throwaway age.

## L. CERCLA

If RCRA Subtitle C worked according to its design, hazardous wastes generated, "managed," and disposed of today should cause no difficulties in the future. However, even as the EPA was putting the finishing touches on its initial RCRA regulations in 1980, Congress realized that the hazardous waste problem had a separate facet: the legacy of hazardous materials that have been handled "improperly" in the past. The "Superfund" program of the Comprehensive Environmental Response, Compensation and Liability Act (CERCLA) was initially adopted to deal with this separate facet. CERCLA, as amended by the 1986 Superfund Amendments and Reauthorization Act (SARA), is now 95 dense pages long.

The quantity of interpretive law generated by the CERCLA statute is frightening. In the nine years from 1990-1998, the federal courts handed down 2,392 published opinions on CERCLA, representing an average of 5 decisions per week. It is hard to imagine a human being who could keep up with this flow of rulings. To make matters worse, a leading practitioner warns that additional significant information about CERCLA must be found in "internal agency guidances, records of decisions, administrative orders on consent, consent decrees, government contracts, and private agreements among potentially responsible parties." Alfred R. Light, CERCLA Law and Procedure 5 (1991).

Given this massive body of Superfund law, we must be realistic about what we can accomplish in an introductory environmental law course. The key to unraveling CERCLA is to break it down into its essential components. In doing so, we run the risk of oversimplification, but strict attention to all technical curlicues would impede rather than enhance initial understanding.

## 1. FOUR THINGS CERCLA DOES

The CERCLA statute does four things. First, it defines triggers that—when pulled—kick each of the other three components into action. The triggers are worded in slightly different ways in different contexts, but a single, common trigger is central to almost all aspects of CERCLA: *the release or threatened release of a hazardous substance into the environment.* The consequences of finding that this trigger has been pulled are so significant that the precise meaning and application of the triggering language is frequently disputed. What is meant by "hazardous substance," by "release," by "environment"? Has the triggering event occurred at a particular site under a specific fact pattern?

Second, CERCLA empowers and obligates the EPA to undertake certain steps once the appropriate trigger or triggers have been pulled. (Technically, many CERCLA clauses direct the "President" to do this or that, but these powers have been delegated by the President to the EPA.) A great deal of the statute consists of detailed directions to the Agency, empowering the EPA to do things that it could not otherwise do: enter land, issue administrative orders, and—most importantly— spend money on cleanup activities and sue for recovery of those cleanup costs. Battles frequently arise over whether the EPA has exceeded its statutory powers—especially when potentially responsible parties seek to deny liability. But the detailed statutory provisions do more than merely empower the Agency to do things; they also obligate the Agency to do certain things, and to do those things in accordance with statutory criteria or standards and statutory timetables. Disputes arise over whether the EPA has fulfilled its many obligations in accordance with the standards that Congress has articulated in the Act.

Third, CERCLA imposes obligations and liabilities on certain actors once the appropriate trigger or triggers have been pulled. Under certain circumstances, individuals and entities may be obligated to provide notification of hazardous substance releases. They may also be obligated to clean up hazardous substance releases or reimburse the Superfund or other actors who have engaged in cleanup activities. The costs of CERCLA cleanup activities may be so staggering that potentially responsible parties sometimes face the prospect of bankruptcy if they fail to avoid or limit liability.

Finally, CERCLA grants to private actors who have undertaken cleanup efforts the right to seek reimbursement or contribution from others individuals or entities under certain conditions. The situations and conditions justifying such reimbursement or contribution may, of course, be contested by a defendant, giving rise to yet more disputes.

## 2.  THE CORE CERCLA TRIGGER

---

Read the following sections of CERCLA

☐ § 101(8)          ☐ § 101(14)          ☐ § 101(22)

☐ § 104(a)(1) [first sentence only]

---

# ALFRED R. LIGHT, CERCLA
# LAW AND PROCEDURE

### 67-68 (1992)

The principal CERCLA cause of action does not accrue, as one might have speculated, from the illicit disposal of a hazardous substance. Even where criminally illicit disposal has occurred, CERCLA cleanup liability might not exist. Section 103 provides for civil and criminal penalties for failure to report certain releases of hazardous substances into the environment. Section 104 requires persons to provide information and allow access to property where government has "a reasonable basis to believe that there may be a release or threat of release of a hazardous substance or pollutant or contaminant." For cleanup liability, however, sections 106 and 107 control, and they require more than a reasonable belief. The threshold for cleanup liability under section 107 is that there be a "release, or a threatened release which causes the incurrence of response costs, of a hazardous substance * * * ."

# SHELDON M. NOVICK & DONALD
# W. STEVER, SUPERFUND

### in 3 Law of Environmental Protection
### 13-134 to 13-138 (Sheldon M. Novick, ed. 1998)

CERCLA authorizes EPA to respond in certain situations in which some environmental harm has occurred or is imminent. These situations are characterized as actual or threatened "releases." The definition of "releases" is complex, and the authority conferred is very broad.

There are two elements in a release which establish response authority: Some designated substance must be present, and there must be a release or a threat of a release of that substance to the environment.

Most substances designated as toxic pollutants or hazardous wastes under other environmental protection statutes are collectively called "hazardous substances" under CERCLA. CERCLA authorizes EPA to respond to any release or threat of release of any hazardous substance. EPA may also fill gaps in generic designations under other statutes by responding to imminently hazardous releases or threatened releases of "pollutants or contaminants" which have not been previously designated as toxic or hazardous.

While the government's response authority is very broad, private party responsibility and liability may be somewhat more limited, depending on the substances released. * * *

A release is an escape into the outdoor environment by any route. "Release" authorizing a response is not qualified by any modifiers—any release, no matter how slight, beyond some implied *de minimis* amount, is apparently sufficient to trigger EPA's authority.

There may be some implied limit on EPA's authority to incur costs or impose liabilities in connection with a trivial release, but the mere presence of a release of a hazardous substance undoubtedly gives the Agency authority to investigate and to decide whether response action is needed. * * *

EPA was require to publish uniform guidelines for its exercise of response authority under CERCLA and other statutes, and it has done so in very general terms, enumerating the very general criteria in the National Contingency Plan. EPA considers the population at risk, the potential routes of exposure, the valuable natural resources which maybe threatened, and other common sense factors, including the likelihood that another agency of government will handle the situation.

Beyond this recital of general criteria, neither EPA regulations nor case law cast much light on the degree of risk that releases must pose. * * * There are few reported decisions construing EPA's response authority under CERCLA's section 104 imminent hazard response language, but similar language is used in section 106, specifying the conditions under which the Agency may seek injunctive relief; under that provision * * * it has been held that only the risk of injury, and not the injury itself, must be "imminent."

## 3.  EPA'S RESPONSE POWERS AND OBLIGATIONS

### SHELDON M. NOVICK & DONALD W. STEVER, SUPERFUND

in 3 Law of Environmental Protection
13-125 to 13-128 (Sheldon M. Novick, ed. 1998)

EPA may respond to "releases," including substantial threats of release, of hazardous substances, pollutants, or contaminants. Responses may be of two kinds, "removal" actions—which are limited and temporary measures—or "remedial actions," which are long-term or permanent measures. When EPA receives a notice or report of a release, it assesses the situation and then chooses the appropriate response. Unlike most other environmental protection programs, state governments and private parties play only a limited role in the response program. EPA designs site-specific responses, and either carries them out directly, or allows (or requires) other persons to carry them out under EPA supervision. * * *

CERCLA establishes a revolving trust fund, primarily funded by taxes on petrochemical feedstocks, crude oil, and general corporate income. Additional amounts may come from general revenues.[78] EPA may draw on this fund to finance its response activities, including the Agency's necessary overhead. * * * EPA must then see that the fund is replenished by the persons liable for response costs—informally called

---

[78] The Superfund was first financed entirely by the tax on chemicals. The initial authorization of $1.5 billion was increased to $8.5 billion in 1986, and additional taxes and appropriations from general revenue were authorized.

"responsible parties." If responsible parties decline to reimburse the fund voluntarily, EPA is authorized to bring suit.

Other units of government and private persons are authorized or required to carry out responses themselves under some conditions; in these cases, their response costs also may be reimbursed by the fund, or directly by responsible parties. * * *

The procedures for the response program are set out in the National Contingency Plan (NCP) [40 C.F.R. Part 300] * * *.

EPA's responses are triggered by reports and notices from the states, from private parties, and occasionally from its own investigations. An important part of the program, therefore, is the requirement that persons with knowledge of a release give notice to the government. Notices are required for past and present releases to air, water, soil, or groundwater, and there are criminal penalties for failure to give the required notices. * * *

These [notices and] reports are assembled in the Comprehensive Environmental Response, Compensation and Liability Information System (CERCLIS) which, by 1992, listed more than 35,000 sites.

Sites listed in CERCLIS receive a preliminary assessment; this is usually done by an On-Scene Coordinator (OSC), an EPA staff person assigned to a regional office. The preliminary assessment includes a review of the statutory requirements for a federal response, as well as more practical questions, such as a determination if someone else is already making a proper response. The preliminary assessment is a determination whether the federal government has jurisdiction, and whether there is an "imminent and substantial danger" which triggers EPA enforcement authority. The OSC has broad discretion to find that jurisdiction and authority exist, guided only by the criteria given in the National Contingency Plan.

The OSC's decision is documented and reviewed, when time allows, by several layers of managers in regional offices and EPA headquarters, but his or her judgment is usually accepted. * * *

If the preliminary assessment shows federal jurisdiction, the next step is usually to inspect the site carefully, and then to decide whether removal or remedial action is appropriate. * * * [S]ome imminent and substantial danger must exist if the response is to go beyond monitoring and assessment to actual cleanup. * * *

After the inspection, EPA regional staff prepare a "scoping" study, and using this study will decide whether to seek funding for a prompt removal action, or to recommend consideration of longer-term remedial action. In many situations of imminent danger, either removal or remedial action may be appropriate, and the Agency may decide for reasons of general policy to shift releases into one or the other program. Policies vary from time to time, as the Agency's bias shifts from rapid, unfettered removals, to more elaborate and permanent remedies.

If the release is treated as a removal, the OSC will take charge and will coordinate the actions of EPA contractors, and state and local agencies at the site. If the Agency decides the release requires the more elaborate, long-term treatment of remedial action, it will begin the elaborate process of ranking the site for the National Priority List * * * . Of course, the two are not incompatible; the OSC may decide that emergency action is needed while the site is being evaluated for longer-term cleanup.

Remedial actions are elaborate, long-term affairs, and are centrally managed. Operations on the site are directed by a Remedial Program Manager, who takes over from the OSC. This is likely to be a contractor supervised by EPA staff.

For Fund-financed responses, the cleanup work itself may be done by another EPA contractor, by a state or local government agency under a cooperative agreement with EPA, or by a private party. When private parties do the cleanup, EPA usually insists on their signing an administrative order, or judicial decree, on consent. Potentially responsible parties who have no present connection with a site, and who therefore may feel that EPA could not require them to perform a cleanup, nevertheless may sign orders on consent so as to be allowed to do the cleanup themselves. * * *

## DONALD W. STEVER, THE LAW OF CHEMICAL REGULATION AND HAZARDOUS WASTE

### 6-81 to 6-85, 6-87 to 6-90, 6-92, 6-102 to 6-103, 6-106 to 6-107 (1995)

Determining where CERCLA funds should be spent necessarily requires the government to identify where the problem sites are located and which sites need addressing first. CERCLA provides a three-step process of identification and prioritization. First, Section 102(a) required EPA to issue regulations that specify the substances it believes will present a "substantial danger" to the public health or welfare, or the environment, and to establish the quantities of release sufficient to warrant government attention ("reportable quantities"). EPA's reportable quantity regulation, 40 C.F.R Part 302, lists those substances for which EPA has established reportable quantities.

[Second], * * * [r]eleases of the substances in excess of those quantities within a twenty-four-hour period must be reported to the National Response Center. * * *

The third aspect of site targeting is the National Priorities List (NPL) required to be developed by EPA under Section 105(a)(8) of CERCLA. The priorities list serves two functions. Since 105(a)(8)(B) requires the states to establish their own priority lists and submit them to EPA, an additional method for identifying abandoned sites is provided. The list also forms the basis for ordering the priority of federal expenditures. * * *

## THE NATIONAL PRIORITIES LIST

EPA's implementation of the Section 105(a)(8)(A) obligation was to develop a mathematical model and associated input criteria and worksheets, which the Agency called the Hazard Ranking System. The HRS is published as Appendix A to 40 C.F.R. Part 300, and is designed to be employed primarily by state field personnel.

The HRS * * * produces a single risk value reflecting exposure potential and substance dangerousness. It tends to produce the highest scores when the scorer indicates that relatively toxic contaminants are in an exposure pathway that will contaminate drinking water. * * * EPA decisions to place a site on the NPL are reviewed by courts under an arbitrary and capricious standard. Significant deference is shown to these decisions, however, because of the highly technical issues involved and because the NPL represents only a rough list of priorities. * * *

No CERCLA funds may be spend for *remedial* work on sites not on the National Priorities List. Thus, inclusion of a site on the NPL constitutes a prerequisite to federally funded remedial action. This conclusion grows out of the requirement of Section 104(a)(1) that federal action be "consistent with" the National Contingency Plan, of which the NPL is a part. Since expenditure of remedial funds on an unlisted site would deprive a listed site, and hence one deemed to need priority treatment, of those funds, such expenditure would, almost by definition, be inconsistent with the NCP. Thus, as new problems are uncovered, EPA expands the NPL. * * *

Listing a site on the NPL also triggers the potential liability of the site owner, generators, and other responsible private parties under Section 107 for response costs or natural resource damages. Following publication of the initial NPL, several such entities sought judicial review of the EPA "action" of listing the site, in which they attempted to challenge the legality or rationality of the specific employment of the HRS. In the few reported decisions, the trial judge dismissed the complaint, ruling that the NPL was a regulation and, accordingly, exclusive jurisdiction over preenforcement review lies with the District of Columbia Circuit under Section 113(a).

A site owner may mount a challenge to the NCP, as applied to its site, by petitioning the D.C. Circuit for review of its site's NPL listing. In the context of such action, the litigant may raise a number of generic challenges to the HRS methodology. The court has typically upheld EPA's application of the HRS on all issues. EPA may apply the HRS with such imprecision, however, that its actions become arbitrary or capricious or not in accordance with law. In such cases, the D.C. Circuit can order a site deleted from the NPL. * * *

Section 104 requires that federal response actions be "consistent with" the National Contingency Plan, and Section 107(a)(4)(A) allows the government to compel private reimbursement of removal and remedial costs "not inconsistent with" the NCP. The NCP is thus the operational centerpiece of the government's hazardous waste cleanup program. * * *

EXTENT OF REMEDY

EPA initially chose to address the obligation to develop "methods and criteria for determining the appropriate extent of removal, remedy and other measures * * * " in vague, general language in the NCP. * * *

This approach effectively left the extent of remedy (also known as a "level of clean-up") decisions to field operating personnel on a case-by-case basis. It also avoided for EPA the necessity of setting acceptable levels of contaminant residue in the groundwater for all * * * listed hazardous substances.

Unfortunately, EPA's approach fostered significant disputes in virtually all CERCLA cases between potentially responsible parties and the government over just how clean the site had to be to satisfy CERCLA's mandate. The difference between a benchmark at the limit of detection for a given constituent and, say, 10 ppm in the groundwater [could] determine whether the cleanup cost of the site is in the millions or the tens of millions of dollars, an issue of obvious concern to PRPs. * * *

Easily the most significant change in the CERCLA program wrought by the 1986 [SARA] amendments was the adoption of Section 121, which imposes detailed remedial standards on the CERCLA-funded or CERCLA-ordered remedial actions and is generally believed to have increased the cost of the average remedy by at least three times. The Section 121 standards * * * represent a rejection of risk assessment-based remedial choices.

Section 121(b) sets forth "general rules" to be followed in all CERCLA remedial actions. These include a requirement favoring remedial options that reduce volume, toxicity, or mobility (that is, treatment/incineration remedies). Off-site transportation for disposal that does not involve treatment is not favored where "practicable treatment technologies are available." * * * Choice of a remedy that fails to meet this criterion requires detailed explanation. * * *

CERCLA Section 113(h) bars pre-enforcement judicial review of the merits of any remedial action chosen by EPA. This is true even if there are allegations that the government-selected remedy would irreparably harm human health or the environment. * * *

***Notes and Questions***

1. Suppose you learn that the EPA is about to list a superfund site on the National Priorities List, labeling it with your unique last name? To avoid embarrassment and notoriety, you ask the EPA to please pick another name. The bureaucrats insist on their choice. Is there anything you can do? *See D'Imperio v. United States*, 575 F.Supp. 248 (D. N.J. 1983), in which the District Court concluded that jurisdiction to review all aspects of the NPL

lies exclusively in the D.C. Circuit but that, in any event, the Agency's decision to refer to sites on the NPL by the owners' names is not arbitrary and capricious.

2. Why might local communities wish to challenge listings on the National Priorities List? Is it possible, do you suppose, that NPL listings and remedial actions (including decisions about where to ship contaminated cleanup residues) might involve discrimination against communities having large poor and minority group populations? *See* the discussion of environmental justice at pages 110-22, *supra*.

## 4. REPORTING OBLIGATIONS

---

Read the following section of CERCLA

☐ § 103(a)          ☐ § 103(b)

---

## DONALD W. STEVER, THE LAW OF CHEMICAL REGULATION AND HAZARDOUS WASTE

### 6-83 (1995)

Section 103(a) of CERCLA * * * requires "any person in charge" of a vessel or * * * facility to notify the National Response Center in the event of release (other than a federally permitted release) of a hazardous substance in an amount equal to or greater than the reportable quantity. Section 103(b) provides criminal penalties for failure to make notification or knowingly submitting a false or misleading report, and a grant of limited immunity from use of the information submitted in a criminal prosecution. Although this limited immunity, quasi-exclusionary rule was obviously intended to encourage complete reporting, it may in the long run have the unintended result of impeding criminal prosecution of willful actions under other environmental statutes. A willful discharge of a toxic water pollutant in amounts that grossly exceed the source's NPDES permit, for example, is a violation of the Clean Water Act. It is also not a "federally permitted release" and is accordingly subject to reporting. If the willful discharger promptly notifies the National Response Center or EPA, pursuant to the Section 103(a) obligation, use of the evidence in a prosecution for the willful discharge under the Clean Water Act will be barred.

## 5. LIABILITIES AND RESPONSIBLE PARTIES

---

Read the following sections of CERCLA

☐ § 101(9)          ☐ § 107(a)

---

# SHELDON M. NOVICK & DONALD W. STEVER, SUPERFUND

in 3 Law of Environmental Protection
13-143 to 13-149 (Sheldon M. Novick, ed. 1998)

One of the principal purposes of CERCLA is to fix liability for cleanup of abandoned facilities, both to fund the cleanup and to discourage the creation of further releases. This liability is fixed on "responsible parties," the class of persons liable for the costs of response actions taken by others, and for damages to natural resources, when hazardous substances are released or there is a substantial threat of their release. CERCLA provides a revolving fund for government responses; the fund is to be replenished by recoveries from responsible parties. * * * Responsible parties may also be subject to injunctions to compel assistance in responses, even at facilities to which they have no present connection.

Whether or not responsible parties may be compelled to participate in a cleanup, however, EPA will offer them an opportunity to comment before carrying out its own response, and their interest in the outcome may prompt involvement at an early stage. Responsible parties therefore are not usually passive recipients of liability, but are collaborators in the response program, sometimes over their own objections, and sometimes over EPA's objections. This adds a dimension of difficulty and conflict to an already complex program. * * *

EPA's authority is tied to "releases," wherever they may be. The liability of private parties, however, is established through their connection with the "vessels" or "facilities" at which the releases of hazardous substances may occur. * * *

CERCLA deals primarily with onshore spills, and for these purposes the statute defines "facility" somewhat laboriously [quoting CERCLA § 101(9)]. * * * [I]t is plain that a facility is simply any ascertainable location, including vehicles in motion. * * *

Responsible parties and their liability are defined in section 107. The generic term "responsible parties" is not used in this section but in section 104(a)(2), which defines EPA's response authority; the practice of referring to the parties listed in section 107 as "responsible parties" is, however, universal. Since liability is disputed, and some limited defenses are available, it is also common to refer to "potentially responsible parties," or PRPs, and this term is used in section 122, added in 1986.

"Owners and operators" of facilities are potentially responsible parties if they were owner or operators at the time of disposal of a hazardous substance at the facility, or if they are owners or operators at the time of the response, regardless of when the waste was disposed.

"Owner or operator" is defined as a single phrase in a series of somewhat circular enumerations: * * * "any person owning or operating [a] facility." It includes common carriers transporting hazardous substances. In the case of an abandoned facility, the phrase includes the owners and operators immediately before abandonment; it excludes mortgagees and other holders of security interests who have not foreclosed.[170] * * * States and municipalities may be PRPs as operators under CERCLA. * * *

Innocent purchasers of land on which releases are later found are responsible parties, but they may have a defense to liability if they had no reason to know of the contamination. The provisions creating the "innocent landowner" defense also strip landowners of any defense under CERCLA if they knowingly transfer property containing hazardous [substances] without notifying the purchaser. * * *

EPA will look first to owners and operators for assistance in response actions, but they are rarely major business enterprises; many Superfund sites are abandoned dumps. The government therefore often must look to the original generators of the wastes which are being cleaned up. * * * CERCLA ratified the government's litigation theory that generators of waste could be held liable for the waste's ultimate disposition. * * *

CERCLA does not use the term "generator," however; it provides liability for "any person" who arranges for transportation of hazardous substances to a facility, or who arranges for the treatment or disposal of hazardous substances at a facility where there is a response. * * * The generator may be liable even if the generator did not choose the disposal site and took reasonable steps to ensure safe disposal. * * *

CERCLA very bluntly discourages generators from disposing of hazardous wastes on land. Other "federally permitted releases" are excused from liability; most permitted discharges into sewer systems or into the air are excluded from the definition of releases that may create liability. But disposal of wastes at a RCRA permitted landfill is not a defense to CERCLA liability (unless the release which causes the response was expressly permitted in the facility's RCRA permit, which is unlikely). If EPA later determines that a permitted landfill is a hazard, a generator who sent wastes there may be liable for part of the cleanup, even if the generator was without fault and the landfill was properly permitted. There is an exception, however, for persons who are carrying out Superfund cleanups approved by EPA. Such persons may take wastes from a Superfund response site to a land disposal facility, if the facility is operating in compliance with RCRA, and if EPA has properly selected the off-site disposal remedy.

The net of liability for responsible parties is cast a little wider and also includes persons who accept hazardous substances from a generator and then determine the substance's disposition. It was formerly a common practice for truckers or disposal companies simply to receive

---

[170] But a mortgagee who forecloses becomes a responsible party. * * *

wastes, with nothing said about the site for disposal. Transporters who choose the site of disposal under such arrangements are also responsible parties.

Recent decisions have cast an even wider net on liability. Corporate officers may be held personally liable under CERCLA if they could have prevented or significantly abated a hazardous [substance] discharge. Successor companies can be held liable under CERCLA according to federal common law principles. A secured creditor is liable under CER-CLA if its involvement with the management of the facility is sufficiently broad to support the inference that it could affect hazardous [substance] disposal decisions. * * *

## 6.  NATURE OF LIABILITY

### ALFRED R. LIGHT, CERCLA LAW AND PROCEDURE

122-26 (1992)

[C]ourts have interpreted CERCLA to impose strict and potentially joint and several liability without the need for proof of causation. * * *

Except for the requirement that the release or threat of release must cause the plaintiff to incur response costs, section 107 contains no language setting forth any causation or nexus standard for liability under the statute. * * * The hazardous substance released at the site need not have belonged to the person held liable for disposal or treatment of any waste at the site.[377] * * *

Some confusion surrounds the role of causation under CERCLA, despite the judicial consensus that CERCLA does not require the plaintiff to prove proximate cause. Some cases view the matter as shifting the burden of proof to the defendant to disprove causation. * * * [A] generator might avoid liability by tracing its own wastes to show that they are not implicated in the threat, without any requirement to show the alternative source of the release.

Neither is a transporter liable if wastes accepted for transport do not get into the site in question. In *E.I. DuPont deNemours & Co. v. Star Trucking* [No. 89-C-7147, U.S. Dist. LEXIS 16,048 (N.D. Ill. Nov. 26, 1990)], DuPont arranged for disposal of its wastes with Star Trucking. EPA pursued the alleged generator, DuPont, which without litigation entered into a consent order to remedy the site. DuPont then sued Star Trucking for contribution. On a motion for summary judgment, Star Trucking was dismissed on the grounds that it had not transported any of DuPont's wastes that had ended up at the site. Ironically, evi-

---

[377] * * * A generator that has sent its waste to a site is said to be liable because there need be only release or threat of release of "a hazardous substance," not the generator's substance. *See United States v. South Carolina Recycling and Disposal, Inc.*, 653 F. Supp. 984 (D. S.C. 1984).

dence also tended to show that none of DuPont's wastes ended up at the site. DuPont apparently settled improvidently. * * *

Professor Prosser's hornbook states that the key consideration in deciding whether joint and several liability is appropriate is "of the feasibility and practical convenience of splitting up the total harm into separate parts. * * * Where a factual basis can be found for some rough practical apportionment * * * it is likely that the apportionment will be made." The Restatement position is that damages for harm are to be apportioned where "(a) there are distinct harms, or (b) there is a reasonable basis for determining the contribution of each cause to a single harm."

In the seminal district court case on this issue, *United States v. Chem-Dyne Corp.* [572 F. Supp. 802 (S.D. Ohio 1983)], the court held, based on * * * legislative history, that CERCLA incorporates the Restatement approach to joint and several liability as the applicable uniform federal common law standard under the statute. Other district courts during the same period adopted a more favorable standard to the defendants than the Restatement. For example, the court in *United States v. A & F Materials Co.* [578 F. Supp. 1249 (S.D. Ill. 1984)], read CERCLA's legislative history to require courts to apportion liability even though "a small contributor would not be able to prove his contribution." * * *

The [1986] SARA amendments did not modify the language of section 107 regarding the joint and several liability issue, but the legislative history is replete with congressional endorsements of the *Chem-Dyne* approach to the issue. Throughout the reauthorization process, however, there are also numerous indications that Congress assumed that demonstrably insubstantial contributors would not be held liable for all costs under the doctrine of joint and several liability. * * *

## 7. RECOVERABLE COSTS

## RICHARD H. MAYS, CERCLA LITIGATION, ENFORCEMENT, AND COMPLIANCE

§§ 7.07, 7.16 (1993)

### RESPONSE COSTS

Section 107(a)(4)(A) provides that the four classes of responsible parties described in the preceding sections shall be liable for, among other damages, all costs of removal or remedial action incurred by the United States, a state, or an Indian tribe, which are not inconsistent with the National Contingency Plan (NCP). There are two key issues in this subsection: first, what costs are included in removal and remedial costs, and second, what does "not inconsistent with" mean?

Some of the costs of removal and remedial actions that may be recovered are obvious, while others are not. A good starting point to determine whether a cost is recoverable is in the definition of the words "removal" and "remedial" actions contained in CERCLA § 101(23) and (24), respectively. * * *

Several courts have held that a broad definition of "response costs" is appropriate to fulfill the purposes of CERCLA, and that both direct costs and indirect costs may be recovered * * * .

Many courts have addressed whether attorney fees and related litigation expenses are recoverable, and there is a considerable split of opinions on the subject. * * *

A number of costs incurred as a direct or indirect result of contamination of a facility by hazardous substances have been held not to be recoverable in a CERCLA cost recovery action because they are not within the definition of "response" costs. Those costs include: (1) "business losses" related to suspension of business pending completion of response actions; [and] (2) diminution in property value and lost income.

NATURAL RESOURCE DAMAGES

Natural resource damage claims are addressed in CERCLA § 107(f).[b] They have, for some time, been a source of speculation * * * . Because of the amorphous nature of natural resource damage claims, and the sheer number of natural resources that may be involved in a claim, the damages assessed for them may make removal and remedial costs pale by comparison.

Relatively few claims have been asserted for natural resource damages to date. One reason for this is the delay experienced by the federal government in promulgating regulations for assessment of natural resource damage, and in the remanding by the * * * D.C. Circuit of some of those regulations for further development. * * * However * * * the potential number of cases, and the damage amounts, could be very large. States and Indian tribes in particular may view natural resource damage claims as a means of recovering large sums of money for restoration of contaminated resources. * * *

## 8. DEFENSES

Read the following sections of CERCLA

☐ § 107(b)          ☐ § 107(j)          ☐ § 101(10)

☐ § 101(35)(A)     ☐ § 101(35)(B)

---

[b] *Ed.*—Given the wording of § 107(f)(1), only the U.S. government or a state or a Native American tribe may recover natural resource damages. *See* Alfred R. Light, CERCLA Law and Procedure 90 (1992).

*Questions*

1.   Company E stores valuable chemical substances in large, above-ground tanks on its property. These chemicals have been listed as CERCLA hazardous substances; reportable quantities have been established for them in 40 C.F.R Part 302. The tanks are surrounded by an 8-foot chain link fence. On a night when the Chicago Cubs win the World Series, six delirious fans climb over the fence and open several of the tank values, causing the hazardous substances to flow over Company E's ground to adjacent properties and to a nearby river. Will Company E be liable for response costs under CERCLA? Why or why not?

2.   Assume the fact pattern described in the preceding paragraph. The EPA asserts that Company E should have: (1) installed locks on all tank valves; (2) added several layers of barbed wire to the protective chain link fence; and (3) built up a protective berm (a raised bank of soil) around each tank, to collect escaping chemicals and prevent their further migration. Does the Company's failure to undertake one or more of these protective measures preclude its defense to CERCLA liability? How many of these steps should be necessary to preserve the "third-party" defense? What if Company E had installed locks, but the vandals were easily able to break the locks with an ordinary hammer?

3.   Assume that Company E, whose operations are described in the two preceding paragraphs, has taken all precautions urged by the EPA, including the installation of kryptonite locks, barbed wire, and suitable berms. Disgruntled employees of Company E break into the property during their off-hours, force open the locks, cut swaths through the berms, and open the valves. Will Company E be liable for response costs under CERCLA? Why or why not? What if the employees were not disgruntled, but just Cubs fans doing their thing?

4.   Company F, a small family-owned corporation, has gradually during a fifty-year period created a contaminated mess at a facility where it overhauls and repairs outboard motors. The site is highly polluted with numerous CERCLA hazardous substances. Sensing that the Feds are about to move in, Company F sells the site and all of its corporate assets to the family patriarch, a geezer who is not long for this world, and promptly dissolves. The family patriarch dies, and the facility is bequeathed to his two grandchildren, who have never participated in ownership or operation of the site. The EPA has concluded that it will cost $10 million to clean up the facility which—when decontaminated—will be worth $5 million because it is in a prime real estate location. Will the grandchildren be liable for response costs under CERCLA? Why or why not?

# RICHARD H. MAYS, CERCLA LITIGATION, ENFORCEMENT, AND COMPLIANCE

## §§ 7.08, 7.11-7.12 (1993)

It is probably an overstatement to say that the three defenses listed in § 107(b) are the *only* defenses available to a responsible party, even in a cost recovery suit by the government. For example, § 107(a)(4)(A) provides that responsible parties are liable for costs of removal or remedial action incurred by the government "not inconsistent with the national contingency plan." This convoluted language has been held to shift the burden of proof to the defendants to show that response costs sought by the government in a cost recovery action were not consistent with the NCP, and the responsible parties must show that the government's actions were arbitrary and capricious. While the responsible party may assert such a defense, the practical effect of it is more likely to be a limitation on the amount of recoverable costs, rather than an absolute defense. * * *

Certain other defenses or exemptions from liability, such as the exemption for * * * federally permitted releases * * * are also available to a PRP under certain circumstances * * * .

### THIRD PARTY DEFENSE

The "third party" defense of § 107(b)(3) is, by far, the most useful to PRPs. Essentially, it provides that a PRP may not be liable for a release or threat of release of hazardous substances, and damages resulting therefrom, that are caused solely by the act or omission of a third party who is neither an agent or employee of the PRP, nor in a direct or indirect contractual relationship with the PRP. In addition, the PRP must also establish (1) that it exercised due care with respect to the hazardous substances concerned, and (2) that it took all precautions against foreseeable acts or omissions of any such third party, and the consequences of such acts or omissions. In other words, the owner or operator of the facility at which the hazardous substances are located must anticipate ways in which third parties may cause releases of hazardous substances to occur at the facility and take all reasonable precautions to protect the substances from the potential for releases in general, and the foreseeable acts of third parties in particular.

The "third party" defense frequently involves two major points of controversy. One frequent issue is that the third party's acts or omissions must be the *sole* cause of the release or threat of the release, and not merely a contributing factor * * * .

Second, there must not be any contractual relationship between the parties. While courts have been very strict in interpreting the "sole cause" requirement, they have been somewhat more liberal in determining the kind of contractual relationship that will deny a party the use of the "third party" defense. Lessors have attempted without success to raise the defense against claims arising out of releases caused by lessees at leased facilities due to the existence of a contract between them regarding the use of the property. An owner of a landfill has been held unable to claim the "third party" defense on the basis that some of its employees acted outside the scope of their employment and allowed unauthorized disposal of hazardous substances in the landfill. However, several cases have held that the mere existence of some contracts between the PRP claiming the "third party" defense and the third party who allegedly caused the release will not prevent the PRP from claiming the defense. The courts have held that the acts or omissions causing the release must be undertaken in connection with the contractual relationship in order to bar the use of the "third party" defense.

### INNOCENT LANDOWNER DEFENSE

Perhaps the most common use of the § 107(b)(3) "third party" defense is the variation referred to as the "innocent landowner" defense, and it is the most important defense as far as transactions are concerned. * * *

[C]urrent owners or operators of a facility are among the four classes of parties responsible for remediation, or the costs thereof, of the facility. Frequently, the contamination will have been placed on the facility by previous owners or operators, and the current owner or operator may not have been aware of the contamination at the time of acquisition. Under these circumstances, the question arises as to whether a deed, contract of sale, or other instrument of conveyance is a "contractual relationship" that will deny the current owner or operator the use of the "third party" defense.

A "contractual relationship" is defined by CERCLA § 101(35) * * * [to include] "land contracts * * * ." Therefore, an owner or operator of contaminated property would, without more, be unable to claim the "third party" defense * * * .

However, the same definition does go on to state an exception to that liability where the current owner or operator can establish the following conditions:

1. The real property was acquired by the PRP claiming the defense after the disposal or placement of hazardous substances on the property; and

2. At the time the PRP claiming the defense acquired the property, it did not know, and had no reason to know, of the presence of hazardous substances on the property; or

3. If the PRP claiming the defense is a government entity, it acquired the property by escheat, or through any other involuntary transfer, or through the exercise of eminent domain; or

4. The PRP claiming the defense acquired the property by inheritance or bequest.

In addition, in each case, the PRP claiming the defense must also satisfy the requirements of CERCLA § 107(b)(3) that the PRP exercise due care with respect to the hazardous substances, taking into consideration their characteristics, and that it also take precautions against foreseeable acts or omissions of any third parties and the consequences that could result from such acts.

In most cases, the condition for use of the "innocent landowner" defense that the PRP did not know, and had no reason to know, of the presence of hazardous substances on the property will be the most controversial. Section 101(35)(B) provides a standard for judging whether a

PRP had reason to know of the presence of hazardous substances on the property at the time of acquisition. The PRP

> * * * must have undertaken, at the time of acquisition, *all appropriate inquiry* into the previous ownership and uses of the property *consistent with good commercial or customary practice* in an effort to minimize liability. (Emphasis added)

In determining whether PRPs meet that test, § 101(35)(B) goes on to state that a court shall take into account the following factors:

1. Any specialized knowledge or experience on the part of the PRP

2. The relationship of the purchase price to the value of the property if contaminated

3. Commonly known or reasonably ascertainable information about the property

4. The obviousness of the presence or likely presence of contamination on the property

5. The ability to detect such contamination by appropriate inspection.

Section 101(35)(B) implies, and the legislative history supports the proposition, that persons who regularly engage in real estate transactions, and who may thereby be sophisticated property purchasers, are to be held to a higher standard than infrequent purchasers. The legislative history establishes a three-tier system: commercial transactions are to be held to the highest standard; private transactions are to be given more leniency; and inheritances and bequests are to be treated most leniently. * * *

With the notoriety that CERCLA has received and will continue to receive in real estate, financial and corporate transactions in the United States, the standard of care consistent with good commercial or customary practice (as required to be exercised by prospective purchasers of facilities in order to qualify for the "innocent landowner" defense) is constantly rising. Persons who purchase or otherwise acquire commercial or industrial property without having conducted an environmental assessment of that property will undoubtedly have a difficult time sustaining the "innocent landowner" defense, especially if those persons frequently deal in the real estate market.

The specific actions that one must take in any acquisition of property are not defined by CERCLA, and indeed may vary from case to case, depending on what may be determined from a general review of the condition of the property, its past use, history of ownership, and location. However, a procedure has been developed that appears to have become generally accepted common practice and procedure. That procedure, known as a "Phase I" environmental audit, involves the (1) review of the record of title for a reasonable period of time (depending on the length of property use); (2) review of aerial photographs taken periodically over time showing uses of the property; (3) review of federal, state, and local environmental agency records to determine whether there are any records of the presence or release of hazardous substances on the property, or liens for environmental cleanup; and (4) a physical inspection of the property and surrounding property to determine any manifestations of hazardous substances actually on, or that migrate onto, the property. * * *

## 9. SETTLEMENT

Many Superfund sites involve a large number of potentially responsible parties in different categories—generators, facility owners and operators, transporters, and the like. Should any given PRP settle, when faced with EPA demands to clean up the site or cough up money for response costs? The answer to this question is frequently complicated and sometimes counterintuitive. The following excerpt deals with just one of several settlement impediments perceptively explored by Professor Organ. The entire article is well worth reading.

## JEROME M. ORGAN, SUPERFUND AND THE SETTLEMENT DECISION: REFLECTIONS ON THE RELATIONSHIP BETWEEN EQUITY AND EFFICIENCY

62 Geo. Wash. L. Rev. 1043, 1044-45, 1058, 1061-68, 1092-97 (1994)

Unfortunately, a substantial number of judicial decisions interpreting CERCLA's liability language, taken in conjunction with the EPA's approach to implementing CERCLA, effectively penalize potentially responsible parties (PRPs) that settle with the EPA (settling PRPs) and reward PRPs that do not settle with the EPA (recalcitrant PRPs). Because these judicial interpretations discourage PRPs from settling with the EPA, they result in delays in cleanups and excessive transaction costs. * * * [T]o facilitate greater progress in cleanups and to minimize excessive costs, Congress should amend CERCLA to account for the disincentives to settlement that these judicial interpretations have created. * * *

To facilitate the negotiation and execution of RD/RA [Remedial Design/Remedial Action] Consent Decrees, CERCLA directs the EPA to compile a list of PRPs for a given site and to notify the PRPs of the opportunity for negotiations. * * *

Given CERCLA's liability system, the negotiation process for allocating liability begins with some effort to estimate how a court would allocate liability at trial. The process focuses PRPs on three questions. First, which parties involved with the site clearly have liability under CERCLA, and which parties may have a defense to liability? Second, how might a court allocate liability for response costs among the PRPs? Third, what are the response costs—the damages—for which PRPs will be liable? * * *

[M]any * * * PRPs may have questions about their liability either because of uncertainties regarding the breadth of the categories of liable parties, or because of uncertainties regarding the evidentiary foundation connecting the PRP to the site. Even when no disputes exist regarding liability, however, the relative lack of court decisions allocating liability among various PRPs, such as owner/operator PRPs and generator PRPs, and the factual specificity of these cases, has meant that PRPs engaged in allocation negotiations frequently are left to their own understandings of the appropriate weight to be given to various factors in developing an allocation formula. The inevitable disputes over the appropriate weight to be given to each of the equitable factors are complicated further by the fact that the universe of information on which to base allocation decisions is frequently incomplete, of suspect credibility, or both. Accordingly, the allocation process is often a "rough justice" process that culminates, if at all, when all PRPs are equally unhappy with the result.

Not surprisingly, when a PRP believes its allocated share is unfair (because the allocation formula failed to account appropriately for its arguments regarding defenses to liability, divisibility of harm, apportionment factors, or other evidentiary issues), the PRP may have an incentive to litigate its liability rather than to settle with the EPA on an RD/RA Consent Decree, particularly where the estimated response costs are relatively high. * * *

PRPs face four different liability risks when deciding whether to enter into an RD/RA Consent Decree. These include: (1) liability pursuant to a [CERCLA § 106(a)] unilateral administrative order (UAO) requiring performance of the selected remedy; (2) liability pursuant to a [§ 107] cost recovery action brought by the EPA to recover response costs it incurred in investigating the site and performing the selected remedy; (3) liability as a settling PRP through participation in an RD/RA Consent Decree; and (4) liability as a recalcitrant PRP subject to cost recovery actions brought by settling PRPs to recover response costs incurred in investigating or remediating the site or by the EPA to recover unreimbursed response costs.

Under the first two types of liability, PRPs face joint and several liability to the EPA if the PRPs fail to reach a settlement with the EPA on an RD/RA Consent Decree. PRPs might find these first two options unappealing for several reasons. First, under either option, the PRP faces the prospect of joint and several liability without any assurance regarding the number of other PRPs that will be asked to share the burden as recipients of a UAO or as defendants in a cost recovery action. Second, Congress has created a strong incentive to comply with a UAO, providing for the assessment of penalties and treble damages against PRPs that fail to comply with a UAO without reasonable grounds. Third, if the EPA implements the remedy, the EPA's response costs [may] far exceed the estimated cost * * * . Fourth, with either a UAO or a cost recovery action, PRPs face significant transaction costs in resolving their liability with the EPA and with other PRPs.

Congress had no incentive to make either of the first two options very attractive, because it wanted to encourage PRPs to elect the third form of liability exposure—that incurred when PRPs voluntarily agree to perform the selected remedy pursuant to an RD/RA Consent Decree. To facilitate the PRPs' voluntary involvement in the remediation process, Congress not only threatened PRPs with the "stick" of strict, joint and several liability for failing to settle with the EPA, it also offered settling PRPs the "carrot" of an RD/RA Consent Decree that would enable PRPs to define their liability to some extent, to receive the benefits of a covenant not to sue from the EPA, and to enjoy protection from contribution actions by recalcitrant PRPs concerning matters covered in the Consent Decree.

In theory, this "stick and carrot" approach should work, assuming the PRPs' only choice is either executing the Consent Decree or facing strict, joint and several liability (either as a recipient of a UAO or as a defendant in an EPA cost recovery action). The focus on these two choices, however, incorrectly assumes that PRPs will act in a monolithic fashion. In reality, the decisions of some PRPs to settle with the EPA and to execute an RD/RA Consent Decree impact the decisions of other PRPs to refrain from settling with the EPA.

Accordingly, to the extent that a PRP perceives that a critical mass of PRPs likely will agree to execute the RD/RA Consent Decree, it can anticipate reasonably that it no longer will face the risk of joint and several liability associated with a UAO or an EPA cost recovery action if it fails to execute the RD/RA Consent Decree. As a consequence, the PRP can focus on comparing the obligation it would assume under the RD/RA Consent Decree and Participation Agreement with the potential liability it would have as a recalcitrant PRP in a subsequent private cost recovery action or contribution action.

Comparing the probable liability exposure of settling PRPs with the probable liability exposure of recalcitrant PRPs requires an understanding of the liability that settling PRPs assume and the extent to which the settling PRPs can recover from recalcitrant PRPs. Because the EPA has used its equitable allocation tools infrequently, it generally has required that settling PRPs perform 100 percent of the selected remedy, pay nearly 100 percent of the EPA's past response costs and future oversight costs, and obligate themselves to perform any additional work that may be required in the future. Because the universe of settling PRPs almost always constitutes a subset of all PRPs at a site, the settling PRPs generally assume a disproportionate share of response costs associated with a site. Moreover, settling PRPs have the added burden of transaction costs required to recover from recalcitrant PRPs. In contrast, by shifting the responsibility for virtually all response costs onto the shoulders of the settling PRPs, the EPA leaves recalcitrant PRPs with little reason to be concerned about facing joint and several liability to the EPA. * * *

ILLUSTRATIONS

Assume that in the Record of Decision [ROD] for Superfund Site A, the EPA has chosen a remedy with an estimated cost of $20,000,000. Thus, the total site response cost at the time the PRPs need to decide whether to execute the RD/RA Consent Decree is estimated at $20,000,000. Further assume that there are twenty PRPs involved at the site, that each PRP would be deemed to have a five-percent share of liability equal to $1,000,000 (five percent or one twentieth of $20,000,000) and that three of the PRPs are essentially judgment proof. Accordingly, "orphan shares" constitute fifteen percent, or approximately $3,000,000, of the total estimated response costs. * * *

Were all the solvent PRPs to join in executing the Consent Decree, each PRP's share of liability would increase from one twentieth or five percent ($1,000,000) to one seventeenth or 5.88% ($1,176,000) to account for the orphan shares. For our analysis, however, we will assume that two solvent PRPs choose to become recalcitrant PRPs. Thus, each share of liability for the fifteen remaining settling PRPs would increase from one seventeenth or 5.88% ($1,176,000) to one fifteenth or 6.67% ($1,334,000) to account for both the orphan shares and the shares of the recalcitrant PRPs. What happens when the settling PRPs sue the recalcitrant PRPs (including the orphan PRPs)? Four possible scenarios suggest themselves based on the cases discussed above.

a. *Settling PRPs May Pursue Contribution Claims Based on a Theory of "Legal Contribution"*

In a joint and several liability system with legal contribution, a tortfeasor satisfying more than the tortfeasor's share of liability has a right to seek contribution from other tortfeasors, but only for each tortfeasor's own equitable share. Such a system imposes the risk associated with orphan shares on the tortfeasor that initially assumes more than its fair share.

Because legal contribution provides that recalcitrant PRPs face only several liability—liability for their own equitable shares—on the settling PRPs' response cost claim, in our example, each recalcitrant PRP would be liable for $1,000,000 (one twentieth (calculated over the universe of all PRPs) or 5% each of the $20,000,000 in response costs). As a consequence, each settling PRP would be liable for $1,200,000 (one fifteenth (calculated over the universe of settling PRPs) or 6.67% of the $18,000,000 balance of response costs ($20,000,000 - $2,000,000)). Accordingly, the characterization of the settling PRPs' claims as legal contribution claims under section 9613 would leave the settling PRPs "holding the bag" for all orphan shares, at an additional cost of $200,000 per settling PRP when compared to recalcitrant PRPs.

b. *Settling PRPs May Pursue Contribution Claims Based on a Theory of "Equitable Contribution"*

In a joint and several liability system with equitable contribution, a tortfeasor satisfying more than its share of liability has a right to seek contribution from other tortfeasors, not only for each tortfeasor's equitable share of liability, but also for its apportioned share of liability attributable to orphan shares. Such a system assures that orphan share liability gets distributed over all solvent tortfeasors. The Restatement (Second) of Torts and the Uniform Comparative Fault Act (UCFA) incorporate equitable contribution by defining a party's equitable share of liability among only the universe of solvent parties to the action.

Although recalcitrant PRPs face only several liability (as opposed to joint and several liability) under equitable contribution, because equitable contribution provides that each recalcitrant PRP's equitable share includes its proportionate share of liability attributable to orphan shares, each recalcitrant PRP and settling PRP in our example would be liable for approximately $1,176,470 (one seventeenth (calculated over the universe of solvent PRPs) or 5.88% each of $20,000,000). Accordingly, the characterization of the settling PRPs' claims as equitable contribution claims under section 9613 results in all solvent PRPs, settling PRPs and recalcitrant PRPs alike, sharing (pursuant to each PRP's equitable share of liability) in the distribution of liability for orphan shares.

c. *Settling PRPs May Pursue a Cost Recovery Claim in Which Recalcitrant PRPs Face Joint and Several Liability Based on* Peck Iron & Metal

Although * * * the court [in *Chesapeake & Potomac Telephone Co. v. Peck Iron & Metal Co.*, 814 F. Supp. 1269 (E.D. Va. 1992)], explicitly held that recalcitrant PRPs faced joint and several liability with respect to cost recovery claims under section [107], the court made it clear that recalcitrant PRPs were jointly and severally liable only with respect to the recalcitrant PRPs' share of liability. Specifically, the court provided that the plaintiff "will be liable—by itself—for its share of response costs and whatever portion of the 'orphan shares' the Court decides to allot to it at the contribution phase of this case. The defendants will be jointly and severally liable only for the non-[plaintiff] share of liability."

Applying this formula to our example, the settling PRPs' initial share of liability would be seventy-five percent (five percent times fifteen settling PRPs) and the recalcitrant PRPs' initial share of liability would be ten percent (five percent times two recalcitrant PRPs). Assuming liability for orphan shares were distributed on a proportional basis, the settling PRPs would take on overall liability of 88.235% (75/85ths), while the recalcitrant PRPs would take on overall liability of 11.765% (10/85ths). Thus, each settling PRP would have liability of $1,176,470 (a 5.88% share of liability (one fifteenth of 88.235%) times response costs of $20,000,000). Each recalcitrant PRP's share of liability likewise would be $1,176,470 (a 5.88% share of liability (one half of 11.765%) times response costs of $20,000,000).

Although this approach appears to result in the same distribution of liability for orphan shares as the equitable contribution approach, this approach differs from the equitable contribution approach because the recalcitrant PRPs would be jointly and severally liable for the $2,352,940 total attributable to recalcitrant PRPs, which would not be true under the equitable contribution approach. Thus, settling PRPs would appear to be able to seek recovery of this entire amount from either recalcitrant PRP, placing on that recalcitrant PRP the risk associated with inability to recover from the other recalcitrant PRP.

d. *Settling PRPs May Pursue a Cost Recovery Claim in Which Recalcitrant PRPs Face Joint and Several Liability for All Liability Not Attributable to Settling PRPs*

Although no court expressly has held that recalcitrant PRPs face joint and several liability for all response costs not attributable to settling PRPs, the language some courts have used allows an inference that they would apply joint and several liability in this manner. Applying this formula to our example, each settling PRP's share of liability would be limited to $1,000,000 (five percent of $20,000,000 in response costs), while each recalcitrant PRP would face joint and several liability for $5,000,000 ($20,000,000 in response costs, less the $15,000,000 in response costs attributable to the fifteen settling PRPs). Accordingly, this approach to joint and several liability would impose the risk associated with orphan shares entirely on recalcitrant PRPs.

### ANALYSIS OF ILLUSTRATIONS

The real question raised by this discussion concerns the allocation of liability for orphan shares. The question PRPs need to ask when considering settling with the EPA on an RD/RA Consent Decree is whether they ultimately will be able to find other PRPs with whom to share the burden of orphan shares that they will be accepting under the RD/RA Consent Decree. * * *

Although some courts essentially have applied "equitable contribution" by distributing orphan share liability over all solvent PRPs, no court has held expressly that recalcitrant PRPs face joint and several liability for all liability not attributable to settling PRPs, and many courts have used language suggesting that recalcitrant PRPs may face only several liability, in which they may not face liability for orphan shares. Accordingly, it should not be surprising that some PRPs perceive refraining from settling with the EPA on an RD/RA Consent Decree as an economically more attractive option than absorbing the disproportionate liability associated with settling with the EPA on an RD/RA Consent Decree.

### RECOMMENDATIONS FOR REFORM

Congress's goals in enacting CERCLA would be served better if all PRPs knew that, at a minimum, recalcitrant PRPs would share in the liability associated with orphan shares. Congress could make it clear to courts that recalcitrant PRPs should share in the risk, or possibly bear the entire risk, attributable to orphan shares by expressly providing that recalcitrant PRPs face joint and several liability with respect to settling PRPs' cost recovery claims under section [107] or contribution claims under section [113]. This is highly unlikely, however, given that Congress purposefully refrained from expressly adopting joint and several liability in CERCLA and in SARA. Congress can accomplish much the same purpose, however, by amending section [113(f)(1)] to give courts more explicit instruction regarding the application of the equitable factors in a cost recovery action or contribution action, clarifying that courts should distribute orphan share liability over all solvent recalcitrant PRPs and settling PRPs, so that settling PRPs are not left "holding the bag." * * *

## 10. CERCLA BLUES

### PAUL STANTON KIBEL, THE PALL CAST BY SUPERFUND'S SUPER MESS

Legal Times, Nov. 14, 1994, at 26

Although many explanations have been given as to why, the Congress that will officially adjourn later this year failed to rewrite [CERCLA]. There is widespread agreement that CERCLA * * * has proven to be one of the most controversial and least effective laws in recent memory.

Since its passage in 1980, more money has been spent on * * * litigation than on hazardous-waste removal and treatment. Less than 10 percent of the sites identified on the [NPL] have undergone cleanup. Superfund litigation has provided sustenance not only for the private sector, but also for the public sector as well. Nearly half the EPA's lawyers focus exclusively on hazardous waste liability issues. This has led some to suggest that a more appropriate name for CERCLA would be ELFEA, the Environmental Lawyers Full-Employment Act.

While the excessive litigation and basic ineffectiveness of the law are troubling enough, Superfund has given rise to perhaps an even more threatening consequence. More than any other law, it has managed to turn the business community against the very concept of environmental protection. In the private sector, the term environmental law has now become virtually synonymous with Superfund liability and litigation.

For those of us who work in the non-CERCLA areas of environmental law, areas that are fairly implemented, well-conceived, and effective, this backlash has become a serious obstacle. It has tainted the entire practice of environmental law and undermined public support for policies that seek to promote responsible resource use and sustainable development.

At both the federal and state levels, scores of laws have managed to further protection of the environment without drawing the full wrath of the private sector. True enough, these laws have imposed restrictions and costs on the business community that affect short-term profits. These restrictions and costs, however, have been structured so that they can be reasonably anticipated and thus factored into business-management decisions.

At the federal level, consider the Clean Air Act and the Clean Water Act. To preserve the environmental quality of our air and water, the federal government establishes total emission and discharge levels for particular waterways and air regions. Businesses wishing to release dangerous substances into the air or water must apply to the EPA for a permit. These permits are conditioned so that they ensure that total emission and discharge levels are not exceeded. Businesses that fail to obtain necessary permits, fail to maintain accurate records of daily discharges, or violate the terms of an issued permit are subject to severe fines and immediate shutdown.

At the state level, consider the California Forest Practices Act. To ensure sustainable yield and protection of the environment, private parties desiring to log on private land must prepare and submit a timber harvest plan, or THP, to the California Department of Forestry. The plan is then approved, modified, or rejected. To ensure that agency decision-making is based on the environmental criteria set forth in the law, THP approvals are subject to judicial review. Businesses or individuals who fail to follow these procedures are subject to severe fines, injunctions, and possible jail time.

Although these laws may not be welcomed by the private sector, they are accepted. While there may be ongoing debate concerning particular aspects of implementation, there is no call for repeal. This acceptance is due to two factors.

First, the restrictions and costs are set forth clearly and can therefore be integrated into business planning. Second, and perhaps more important, however, the laws have proven effective. Air and water quality have in fact improved considerably since the Clean Air Act and the Clean Water Act were passed. Forest management on private lands in California has improved since the Forest Practices Act was adopted. These undisputed results have perhaps been the most persuasive argument in favor of these federal and state laws.

In environmental law, the Clean Air Act, the Clean Water Act, and the California Forest Practices Act are the rule, not the exception. At the federal level, the list of fair and effective environmental legislation includes the National Environmental Policy Act, the National Forest Management Act, and the Toxic Substances Control Act. In California, it includes the California Environmental Quality Act, the California Coastal Act, and the Safe Drinking Water and Toxic Enforcement Act. Hundreds of such laws can be found in states all across the country. This body of legislation evidences that environmental protection need not be, and by and large is not, erratic or draconian.

Superfund is the exception. While its aims are worthy, CERCLA is an ill-conceived law that is both unfair and ineffective. As James Strock, California's secretary for environmental protection, recently commented, "The day is coming when Americans will ask why so much money has gone to pay for lawsuits under Superfund. At present, there is no good answer, and some may conclude, wrongly if not tragically, that the same is true for the entire enterprise of environmental protection."

Superfund's defenders have countered such criticism by pointing out that the law could work if there wasn't so much litigation. As Charles De Saillan, a senior attorney with the EPA's Office of Enforcement in Washington, D.C., observed, the law's ineffectiveness and high transaction costs are a result of "parties' decision to litigate rather than to settle CERCLA liability." Yet Mr. De Saillan seems to be confusing causes with consequences. The decision to litigate is not the cause of Superfund's ineffectiveness; rather it is the inevitable consequence of an arbitrary and poorly designed liability scheme.

If Superfund is not reformed to provide for more uniform, equitable, and effective implementation, the damage will be great. The legal profession will suffer, as the public witnesses environmental lawyers reaping the monetary harvest of a dysfunctional legal regime. The environment, and those of us who maintain that the law can be used to improve environmental protection, will suffer as well. In the interests of the legal profession, environmental law and the environment, this rotten apple must be removed.

# Chapter Thirteen

# NATIONAL ENVIRONMENTAL POLICY ACT

## A. INTRODUCTION

The final federal environmental statute that we will examine in this book—the National Environmental Policy Act (NEPA)—is quite different from any that we have yet encountered. Even though we turn to it last, it was actually the first to be enacted, in 1969.

Read the following sections of NEPA

☐ § 2        ☐ § 101        ☐ § 102        ☐ § 105

## B. THE JUDICIAL ENFORCEMENT PRINCIPLE

## CALVERT CLIFFS' COORDINATING COMMITTEE v. U.S. ATOMIC ENERGY COMMISSION

449 F.2d 1109 (D.C. Cir. 1971)

Before WRIGHT, TAMM and ROBINSON, Circuit Judges

J. SKELLY WRIGHT, Circuit Judge:

These cases are only the beginning of what promises to become a flood of new litigation—litigation seeking judicial assistance in protecting our natural environment. Several recently enacted statutes attest to the commitment of the Government to control, at long last, the destructive engine of material "progress." But it remains to be seen whether the promise of this legislation will become a reality. Therein lies the judicial role. In these cases, we must for the first time interpret the broadest and perhaps most important of the recent statutes: the National Environmental Policy Act of 1969 (NEPA). We must assess claims that one of the agencies charged with its administration has failed to live up to the congressional mandate. Our duty, in short, is to see that important legislative purposes, heralded in the halls of Congress, are not lost or misdirected in the vast hallways of the federal bureaucracy.

NEPA, like so much other reform legislation of the last 40 years, is cast in terms of a general mandate and broad delegation of authority to new and old administrative agencies. It takes the major step of requiring all federal agencies to consider values of environmental preservation in their spheres of activity, and it prescribes certain procedural measures to ensure that those values are in fact fully respected. Petitioners argue that rules recently adopted by the Atomic Energy Commission to govern consideration of environmental matters fail to satisfy the rigor demanded by NEPA. The Commission, on the other hand, contends that the vagueness of the NEPA mandate and delegation leaves much room for discretion and that the rules challenged by petitioners fall well within the broad scope of the Act. We find the policies embodied in NEPA to be a good deal clearer and more demanding than does the Commission. We conclude that the Commission's procedural rules do not comply with the congressional policy. Hence we remand these cases for further rule making.

We begin our analysis with an examination of NEPA's structure and approach and of the Atomic Energy Commission rules which are said to conflict with the requirements of the Act. The relevant portion of NEPA is Title I, consisting of five sections. Section 101 sets forth the Act's basic substantive policy: that the federal government "use all practicable means and measures" to protect environmental values. Congress did not establish environmental protection as an exclusive goal; rather, it desired a reordering of priorities, so that environmental costs and benefits will assume their proper place along with other considerations. In Section 101(b), imposing an explicit duty on federal officials, the Act provides that "it is the continuing responsibility of the Federal Government to use all practicable means, consistent with other essential considerations of national policy," to avoid environmental degradation, preserve "historic, cultural, and natural" resources, and promote "the widest range of beneficial uses of the environment without * * * undesirable and unintended consequences."

Thus the general substantive policy of the Act is a flexible one. It leaves room for a responsible exercise of discretion and may not require particular substantive results in particular problematic instances. However, the Act also contains very important "procedural" provisions—provisions which are designed to see that all federal agencies do in fact exercise the substantive discretion given them. These provisions are not highly flexible. Indeed, they establish a strict standard of compliance.

NEPA, first of all, makes environmental protection a part of the mandate of every federal agency and department. The Atomic Energy

Commission, for example, had continually asserted, prior to NEPA, that it had no statutory authority to concern itself with the adverse environmental effects of its actions.[4] Now, however, its hands are no longer tied. It is not only permitted, but compelled, to take environmental values into account. Perhaps the greatest importance of NEPA is to require the Atomic Energy Commission and other agencies to *consider* environmental issues just as they consider other matters within their mandates. This compulsion is most plainly stated in Section 102. There, "Congress authorizes and directs that, to the fullest extent possible: (1) the policies, regulations, and public laws of the United States shall be interpreted and administered in accordance with the policies set forth in this Act * * *" Congress also "authorizes and directs" that "(2) all agencies of the Federal Government shall" follow certain rigorous procedures in considering environmental values. Senator Jackson, NEPA's principal sponsor, stated that "[n]o agency will [now] be able to maintain that it has no mandate or no requirement to consider the environmental consequences of its actions." He characterized the requirements of Section 102 as "action-forcing" and stated that "[o]therwise, these lofty declarations [in Section 101] are nothing more than that."

The sort of consideration of environmental values which NEPA compels is clarified in Section 102(2)(A) and (B). In general, all agencies must use a "systematic, interdisciplinary approach" to environmental planning and evaluation "in decisionmaking which may have an impact on man's environment." In order to include all possible environmental factors in the decisional equation, agencies must "identify and develop methods and procedures * * * which will insure that presently unquantified environmental amenities and values may be given appropriate consideration in decisionmaking along with economic and technical considerations." "Environmental amenities" will often be in conflict with "economic and technical considerations." To "consider" the former "along with" the latter must involve a balancing process. In some instances environmental costs may outweigh economic and technical benefits and in other instances they may not. But NEPA mandates a rather finely tuned and "systematic" balancing analysis in each instance.

To ensure that the balancing analysis is carried out and given full effect, Section 102(2)(C) requires that responsible officials of all agencies prepare a "detailed statement" covering the impact of particular actions on the environment, the environmental costs which might be avoided, and alternative measures which might alter the cost benefit equation. The apparent purpose of the "detailed statement" is to aid in the agencies' own decision making process and to advise other interested agencies and the public of the environmental consequences of

---

[4] Before the enactment of NEPA, the Commission * * * argued that it could not consider [nonradiological] environmental impacts. Its position was upheld in *State of New Hampshire v. Atomic Energy Commission*, 406 F.2d 170 (1st Cir.), *cert. denied*, 395 U.S. 962 (1969).

planned federal action. Beyond the "detailed statement," Section 102(2)(D) requires all agencies specifically to "study, develop, and describe appropriate alternatives to recommended courses of action in any proposal which involves unresolved conflicts concerning alternative uses of available resources." This requirement, like the "detailed statement" requirement, seeks to ensure that each agency decision maker has before him and takes into proper account all possible approaches to a particular project (including total abandonment of the project) which would alter the environmental impact and the cost-benefit balance. Only in that fashion is it likely that the most intelligent, optimally beneficial decision will ultimately be made. Moreover, by compelling a formal "detailed statement" and a description of alternatives, NEPA provides evidence that the mandated decision making process has in fact taken place and, most importantly, allows those removed from the initial process to evaluate and balance the factors on their own.

Of course, all of these Section 102 duties are qualified by the phrase "to the fullest extent possible." We must stress as forcefully as possible that this language does not provide an escape hatch for footdragging agencies; it does not make NEPA's procedural requirements somehow "discretionary." Congress did not intend the Act to be such a paper tiger. Indeed, the requirement of environmental consideration "to the fullest extent possible" sets a high standard for the agencies, a standard which must be rigorously enforced by the reviewing courts.

Unlike the substantive duties of Section 101(b), which require agencies to "use all practicable means consistent with other essential considerations," the procedural duties of Section 102 must be fulfilled to the "fullest extent possible." This contrast, in itself, is revealing. * * *

Thus the Section 102 duties are not inherently flexible. They must be complied with to the fullest extent, unless there is a clear conflict of *statutory* authority. Considerations of administrative difficulty, delay or economic cost will not suffice to strip the section of its fundamental importance.

We conclude, then, that Section 102 of NEPA mandates a particular sort of careful and informed decisionmaking process and creates judicially enforceable duties. The reviewing courts probably cannot reverse a substantive decision on its merits, under Section 101, unless it be shown that the actual balance of costs and benefits that was struck was arbitrary or clearly gave insufficient weight to environmental values. But if the decision was reached procedurally without individualized consideration and balancing of environmental factors—conducted fully and in good faith—it is the responsibility of the courts to reverse. As one District Court has said of Section 102 requirements: "It is hard to imagine a clearer or stronger mandate to the Courts."

In the cases before us now, we do not have to review a particular decision by the Atomic Energy Commission granting a construction permit or an operating license. Rather, we must review the Commission's recently promulgated rules which govern consideration of environmental values in all such individual decisions. The rules were devised strictly in order to comply with the NEPA procedural requirements—but petitioners argue that they fall far short of the congressional mandate. * * *

The [petitioners] attack four * * * specific parts of the rules which, they say, violate the requirements of Section 102 of NEPA. Each of these parts in some way limits full consideration and individualized balancing of environmental values in the Commission's decision making process.

(1) Although environmental factors must be considered by the agency's regulatory staff under the rules, such factors need not be considered by the hearing board conducting an independent review of staff recommendations, unless affirmatively raised by outside parties or staff members.

(2) Another part of the procedural rules prohibits any such party from raising nonradiological environmental issues at any hearing if the notice for that hearing appeared in the Federal Register before March 4, 1971.

(3) Moreover, the hearing board is prohibited from conducting an independent evaluation and balancing of certain environmental factors if other responsible agencies have already certified that their own environmental standards are satisfied by the proposed federal action.

(4) Finally, the Commission's rules provide that when a construction permit for a facility has been issued before NEPA compliance was required and when an operating license has yet to be issued, the agency will not formally consider environmental factors or require modifications in the proposed facility until the time of the issuance of the operating license. * * *

The question here is whether the Commission is correct in thinking that its NEPA responsibilities may "be carried out in toto outside the hearing process"—whether it is enough that environmental data and evaluations merely "accompany" an application through the review process, but receive no consideration whatever from the hearing board.

We believe that the Commission's crabbed interpretation of NEPA makes a mockery of the Act. What possible purpose could there be in the Section 102(2)(C) requirement (that the "detailed statement" accompany proposals through agency review processes) if "accompany" means no more than physical proximity—mandating no more than the physical act of passing certain folders and papers, unopened, to reviewing officials along with other folders and papers? What possible purpose could there be in requiring the "detailed statement" to be before hearing boards, if the boards are free to ignore entirely the contents of the statement? NEPA was meant to do more than regulate the flow of papers in the federal bureaucracy. The word "accompany" in Section 102(2)(C) must not be read so narrowly as to make the Act ludicrous. It must, rather, be read to indicate a congressional intent that environmental factors, as compiled in the "detailed statement," be *considered* through agency review processes. * * *

NEPA requires that agencies consider the environmental impact of their actions "to the fullest extent possible." The Act is addressed to agencies as a whole, not only to their professional staffs. Compliance to the "fullest" possible extent would seem to demand that environmental issues be considered at every important stage in the decision making process concerning a particular action—at every stage where an overall balancing of environmental and nonenvironmental factors is appropriate and where alterations might be made in the proposed action to minimize environmental costs. * * * The Commission's hearing boards automatically consider nonenvironmental factors, even though they have been previously studied by the staff. Clearly, the review process is an appropriate stage at which to balance conflicting factors against one another. And, just as clearly, it provides an important opportunity to reject or significantly modify the staff's recommended action. Environmental factors, therefore, should not be singled out and excluded, at this stage, from the proper balance of values envisioned by NEPA. * * *

Congress passed the final version of NEPA in late 1969, and the Act went into full effect on January 1, 1970. Yet the Atomic Energy Commission's rules prohibit any consideration of environmental issues by its hearing boards at proceedings officially noticed before March 4, 1971. This is 14 months after the effective date of NEPA. And the hearings affected may go on for as much as a year longer until final action is taken. The result is that major federal actions having a significant environmental impact may be taken by the Commission, without full NEPA compliance, more than two years after the Act's effective date. In view of the importance of environmental consideration during the agency review process * * * such a time lag is shocking.

The Commission explained that its very long time lag was intended "to provide an orderly period of transition in the conduct of the Commission's regulatory proceedings and to avoid unreasonable delays in the construction and operation of nuclear power plants urgently needed to meet the national requirements for electric power." * * *

In the end, the Commission's long delay seems based upon what it believes to be a pressing national power crisis. Inclusion of environmental issues in pre-March 4, 1971 hearings might have held up the licensing of some power plants for a time. But the very purpose of NEPA was to tell federal agencies that environmental protection is as much a part of their responsibility as is protection and promotion of the industries they regulate. Whether or not the spectre of a national power crisis is as real as the Commission apparently believes, it must not be used to create a blackout of environmental consideration in the agency review process. NEPA compels a case-by-case examination and balancing of discrete factors. Perhaps there may be cases in which the need for rapid licensing of a particular facility would justify a strict time limit on a hearing board's review of environmental issues; but a blanket banning of such issues until March 4, 1971, is impermissible under NEPA.

The sweep of NEPA is extraordinarily broad, compelling consideration of any and all types of environmental impact of federal action. However, the Atomic Energy Commission's rules specifically exclude from full consideration a wide variety of environmental issues. First, they provide that no party may raise and the Commission may not independently examine any problem of water quality—perhaps the most significant impact of nuclear power plants. Rather, the Commission indicates that it will defer totally to water quality standards devised and administered by state agencies and approved by the federal government under the Federal Water Pollution Control Act. Secondly, the rules provide for similar abdication of NEPA authority to the standards of other agencies * * *

The most the Commission will do is include a condition in all construction permits and operating licenses requiring compliance with the water quality or other standards set by such agencies. The upshot is that the NEPA procedures, viewed by the Commission as superfluous, will wither away in disuse, applied only to those environmental issues wholly unregulated by any other federal, state or regional body.

We believe the Commission's rule is in fundamental conflict with the basic purpose of the Act. NEPA mandates a case-by-case balancing judgment on the part of federal agencies. In each individual case, the particular economic and technical benefits of planned action must be assessed and then weighed against the environmental costs; alternatives must be considered which would affect the balance of values. * * * The magnitude of possible benefits and possible costs may lie anywhere on a broad spectrum. Much will depend on the particular magnitudes involved in particular cases. In some cases, the benefits will be great enough to justify a certain quantum of environmental costs; in other cases, they will not be so great and the proposed action may have to be abandoned or significantly altered so as to bring the benefits and costs into a proper balance. The point of the individualized balancing analysis is to ensure that, with possible alterations, the optimally beneficial action is finally taken.

Certification by another agency that its own environmental standards are satisfied involves an entirely different kind of judgment. Such agencies, without overall responsibility for the particular federal action in question, attend only to one aspect of the problem: the magnitude of certain environmental costs. They simply determine whether those costs exceed an allowable amount. Their certification does not mean that they found no environmental damage whatever. In fact, there may be significant environmental damage (e.g., water pollution), but not quite enough to violate applicable (e.g., water quality) standards. Certifying agencies do not attempt to weigh that damage against the opposing benefits. Thus the balancing analysis remains to be done. It may be that the environmental costs, though passing prescribed standards, are nonetheless great enough to outweigh the particular economic and technical benefits involved in the planned action. The only agency in a position to make such a judgment is the agency with overall responsibility for the proposed federal action—the agency to which NEPA is specifically directed.

The Atomic Energy Commission, abdicating entirely to other agencies' certifications, neglects the mandated balancing analysis. Concerned members of the public are thereby precluded from raising a wide range of environmental issues in order to affect particular Commission decisions. And the special purpose of NEPA is subverted.

Arguing before this court, the Commission has made much of the special environmental expertise of the agencies which set environmental standards. NEPA did not overlook this consideration. Indeed, the Act is quite explicit in describing the attention which is to be given to the views and standards of other agencies * * * [quoting § 102(2)(C)].

Thus the Congress was surely cognizant of federal, state and local agencies "authorized to develop and enforce environmental standards." But it provided, in Section 102(2)(C), only for full consultation. It most certainly did not authorize a total abdication to those agencies. Nor did it grant a license to disregard the main body of NEPA obligations. * * *

Petitioners' final attack is on the Commission's rules governing a particular set of nuclear facilities: those for which construction permits were granted without consideration of environmental issues, but for which operating licenses have yet to be issued. These facilities, still in varying stages of construction, include the one of most immediate concern to one of the petitioners: the Calvert Cliffs nuclear power plant on Chesapeake Bay in Maryland. * * *

[T]he Commission has, as a blanket policy, refused to consider the possibility of temporarily halting construction in particular cases pending a full study of a facility's environmental impact. It has also refused to weigh the pros and cons of "backfitting" for particular facilities (alteration of already constructed portions of the facilities in order to incorporate new technological developments designed to protect the environment). Thus reports and statements will be produced, but nothing will be done with them. Once again, the Commission seems to believe that the mere drafting and filing of papers is enough to satisfy NEPA. * * *

[W]e conclude that the Commission must go farther than it has in its present rules. It must consider action, as well as file reports and papers, at the pre-operating license stage. As the Commission candidly admits, such consideration does not amount to a retroactive application of NEPA. Although the projects in question may have been commenced and initially approved before January 1, 1970, the Act clearly applies to them since they must still pass muster before going into full operation. All we demand is that the environmental review be as full and fruitful as possible.

We hold that, in the four respects detailed above, the Commission must revise its rules governing consideration of environmental issues. We do not impose a harsh burden on the Commission. For we require only an exercise of substantive discretion which will protect the environment "to the fullest extent possible." No less is required if the grand congressional purposes underlying NEPA are to become a reality. * * *

### Questions

1. What action was being challenged by the petitioners in *Calvert Cliffs*? Is this the type of lawsuit you envision when you think of NEPA and environmental impact statement litigation? Why or why not?

2. Why had the Atomic Energy Commission undertaken the action challenged in *Calvert Cliffs*? Does your answer help to explain the agency's attitude about its responsibilities?

3. Scarcely any American has failed to hear about environmental impact statements. Where, in the statute, does NEPA require the preparation of such documents?

4. What, according to the statute, is to be done with an environmental impact statement, once it has been prepared? How had the Atomic Energy Commission interpreted this statutory language? What did the court conclude about the agency's interpretation?

5. Judge Wright suggests a bifurcation of judicial review into two circumstances: (a) highly deferential (or nonexistent) judicial review of the "substantive" commands of NEPA § 101; and (b) more rigorous judicial review of the "procedural" commands of NEPA § 102. Does this distinction make sense? Does anything in the statute suggest that either or both of these commands are susceptible to judicial review?

## C. NEPA REGULATIONS

The regulations at issue in the *Calvert Cliffs* case had been promulgated by the Atomic Energy Commission in accordance with the statutory directive that each agency "identify and develop methods and procedures" to carry out the mandates of NEPA. *See* NEPA § 102(2)(B). Even though each federal agency is charged with this obligation, it makes sense to entrust one coordinating agency with the task of promulgating generic implementing regulations. That task has been given by Presidential Executive Order to the Council on Environmental Quality (CEQ). The CEQ issued formal regulations in 1977. The regulations of each federal agency are now properly understood to *supplement* the CEQ regulations; accordingly, they must conform to the CEQ's requirements.

# CEQ, NEPA REGULATIONS

### 40 C.F.R. Parts 1500-1508 (1998)

## § 1500.3 Mandate.

Parts 1500 through 1508 of this title provide regulations applicable to and binding on all Federal agencies for implementing the procedural provisions of [NEPA] * * * . These regulations * * * are not confined to § 102(2)(C) (environmental impact statements). The regulations apply to the whole of section 102(2). * * * It is the Council's intention that judicial review of agency compliance with these regulations not occur before an agency has filed the final environmental impact statement, or has made a final finding of no significant impact (when such a finding will result in action affecting the environment), or takes action that will result in irreparable injury. Furthermore, it is the Council's intention that any trivial violation of these regulations not give rise to any independent cause of action. * * *

## § 1501.4 Whether to prepare an environmental impact statement.

In determining whether to prepare an environmental impact statement the Federal agency shall:

(a) Determine under its procedures supplementing these regulations * * * whether the proposal is one which:

    (1) Normally requires an environmental impact statement, or

    (2) Normally does not require either an environmental impact statement or an environmental assessment (categorical exclusion).

(b) If the proposed action is not covered by paragraph (a) of this section, prepare an environmental assessment * * * .

(c) Based on the environmental assessment make its determination whether to prepare an environmental impact statement.

(d) Commence the scoping process * * * if the agency will prepare an environmental impact statement.

(e) Prepare a finding of no significant impact * * * if the agency determines on the basis of the environmental assessment not to prepare a statement. * * *

## § 1501.7 Scoping.

There shall be an early and open process for determining the scope of issues to be addressed and for identifying the significant issues related to a proposed action. This process shall be termed scoping. * * *

## § 1502.1 Purpose.

The primary purpose of an environmental impact statement is to serve as an action-forcing device to insure that the policies and goals defined in the Act are infused into the ongoing programs and actions of the Federal Government. It shall provide full and fair discussion of significant environmental impacts and shall inform decisionmakers and the public of the reasonable alternatives which would avoid or minimize adverse impacts or enhance the quality of the human environment. Agencies shall focus on significant environmental issues and alternatives and shall reduce paperwork and the accumulation of extraneous background data. Statements shall be concise, clear, and to the point, and shall be supported by evidence that the agency has made the necessary environmental analyses. An environmental impact statement is more than a disclosure document. It shall be used by Federal officials in conjunction with other relevant material to plan actions and make decisions.

## § 1502.2 Implementation.

To achieve the purposes set forth in § 1502.1 agencies shall prepare environmental impact statements in the following manner:

(a) Environmental impact statements shall be analytic rather than encyclopedic.

(b) Impacts shall be discussed in proportion to their significance. There shall be only brief discussion of other than significant issues. As in a finding of no significant impact, there should be only enough discussion to show why more study is not warranted.

(c) Environmental impact statements shall be kept concise and shall be no longer than absolutely necessary to comply with NEPA and with these regulations. * * *

(e) The range of alternatives discussed in environmental impact statements shall encompass those to be considered by the ultimate agency decisionmaker.

(f) Agencies shall not commit resources prejudicing selection of alternatives before making a final decision * * * .

(g) Environmental impact statements shall serve as the means of assessing the environmental impact of proposed agency actions, rather than justifying decisions already made.

## § 1505.2 Record of decision in cases requiring environmental impact statements.

At the time of its decision (§ 1506.10) or, if appropriate, its recommendation to Congress, each agency shall prepare a concise public record of decision. * * *

## § 1506.1 Limitations on actions during NEPA process.

(a) Until an agency issues a record of decision * * * no action concerning the proposal shall be taken which would:

(1) Have an adverse environmental impact; or

(2) Limit the choice of reasonable alternatives. * * *

## § 1508.14 Human Environment.

"Human Environment" shall be interpreted comprehensively to include the natural and physical environment and the relationship of people with that environment. * * * This means that economic or social effects are not intended by themselves to require preparation of an environmental impact statement. When an environmental impact statement is prepared and economic or social and natural or physical environmental effects are interrelated, then the environmental impact statement will discuss all of these effects on the human environment. * * *

## § 1508.18 Major Federal action.

"Major Federal action" includes actions with effects that may be major and which are potentially subject to Federal control and responsibility. Major reinforces but does not have a meaning independent of significantly * * * .

# D. ENFORCING NEPA THROUGH LITIGATION

## DANIEL R. MANDELKER, NEPA LAW AND LITIGATION
### §§ 3.01, 3.02, 4.01, 4.05, 4.06 & 4.10 (2d ed. 1998)

Judicial review has become the principal means through which NEPA's environmental decision-making responsibilities are enforced. Yet NEPA does not provide expressly for judicial review, and provisions in the Administrative Procedure Act which apparently provide a basis for the judicial review of agency decisions have been held not to be an independent source of federal court jurisdiction. The federal courts have held, nevertheless, that judicial review of agency decisions under NEPA is implied. Neither is judicial review under NEPA precluded by the Administrative Procedure Act provision stating that judicial review is not available when an agency decision is "committed to agency discretion." * * *

### NEPA PROCEDURE

NEPA does not elaborate the details of the environmental review process, which is more fully specified by the Council on Environmental Quality (CEQ) regulations. * * * [40 C.F.R. § 1500.1 *et seq.*]

CEQ regulations require the following environmental review process:

1. [Each] agency applies its regulations on "categorical exclusions" to determine whether its action "normally requires" or "normally does not require" an impact statement. The implication is that the agency need not prepare an impact statement if the action falls within a categorical exclusion. If the action does not fall within a categorical exclusion the agency may decide to prepare an impact statement.

2. If the action is not covered by a categorical exclusion, the agency prepares an environmental assessment. An environmental assessment is a document which briefly provides "evidence or analysis" on which the agency determines whether to prepare an impact statement.

3. If the agency decides not to prepare an impact statement it prepares a finding of no significant impact (FONSI) * * * based on the environmental assessment. The environmental review process terminates if the agency makes this finding.

4. The agency may also rely on the environmental assessment as the basis for a decision to prepare an environmental impact statement.

5. If the agency decides to prepare an impact statement, it prepares a draft impact statement followed by a final impact statement and a supplemental impact statement if necessary. The agency must circulate its draft and final impact statements to federal, state and local agencies with environmental expertise and to the public. The agency must also respond to any comments made on the impact statement.

6. The environmental review process concludes when the agency has responded to all comments and considers the impact statement adequate.

### NATURE AND TIMING OF JUDICIAL REVIEW

CEQ regulations state CEQ's intention that judicial review of agency compliance with its regulations should not occur before an agency has filed a final finding of no significance or a final impact statement. Judicial review normally occurs at these stages. The decision not to file an impact statement is know as the "threshold" decision under NEPA. The threshold decision is judicially reviewable. When the courts review an impact statement they consider whether it is "adequate" under NEPA's statutory requirements.

Agency decision making under NEPA is technically an "adjudication" as that term is defined by the Administrative Procedure Act (APA). [That] Act defines an adjudication as an agency decision that produces an "order," and defines an order as a "final disposition" other than a rule making. Despite this definition, agency decision making under NEPA is not formal adjudication that requires formal notice and hearing procedures. * * * [A]gency decision making under NEPA is characterized as informal agency adjudication or decision making. * * *

The time period required for agency decision making creates dilemmas for NEPA plaintiffs. Agency actions, such as federal and federally funded projects, often taken a substantial period of time to complete. The agency usually proceeds through a series of stages. Early consideration of the project is followed by project planning or by a federal funding commitment. Projection execution may come much later. The duty to prepare an impact statement may not attach until the project is well along. This circumstance creates a dilemma for plaintiffs. If they sue too early in the decision-making process they may face claims that their action is not ripe or that they have not exhausted administrative remedies. If they sue too late, a court may find their action moot or may bar it because of laches. The courts are sometimes, but not always, sensitive to this dilemma. * * *

NEPA is enforceable against federal agencies through a private right of action. Judicial review of a federal agency's compliance with NEPA is implied, and courts that hold against an agency can provide prospective relief, usually through an injunction. The courts do not award damages in NEPA cases. * * *

## STANDING

Standing to sue is critical in NEPA cases. Plaintiffs in NEPA cases are usually environmental organizations or other third parties who did not participate in the agency action that is the subject of the litigation. Unless a court is willing to grant these plaintiffs standing to sue, an agency action under NEPA will go unchallenged.

Standing doctrine has its origins in Article II, § 2 of the Constitution, which limits the federal judicial power to "cases and controversies." * * *

A party claiming standard must assert some actual or threatened injury from the defendant's claimed illegal conduct. This is the "injury-in-fact" requirement. He must also show that the injury was caused by the defendant's action, and can be redressed by a favorable legal decree. These are the "causation" and "redressability" requirements. * * *

Standing to sue under NEPA has not usually been troublesome. The Supreme Court liberalized the injury-in-fact requirement as it applies in NEPA litigation by allowing standing based on environmental injury, and lower federal courts applied this decision liberally. * * *

## BONDS

The Federal Rules of Civil Procedure require "the giving of security by the applicant [for a preliminary injunction], for the payment of such costs and damages as may be incurred or suffered by any party who is found to have been wrongfully enjoined or restrained." [FRCP 65(c)] Whether and in what amount a bond should be required lies in the discretion of the district court judge, although the exercise of discretion may be reviewable on appeal. The injunction bond allows the district court to grant a preliminary injunction the preserves the status quo in the case, yet protects the defendant against any damage it should suffer should the court later decide that a permanent injunction is not warranted.

Despite the language of the rule, which emphasizes the "costs and damages" that may be incurred by defendants, the NEPA cases have usually not required a bond at all or a nominal bond of one dollar. These cases have adopted a "NEPA exception" to the bond requirement. They note the important public interests in the enforcement of NEPA, the congressional policy that private organizations are to cooperate in its enforcement, and the deterrence to litigation that would result if substantial bonds were required. * * *

A few NEPA cases have required substantial bonds. These cases adopt a more traditional "balancing of the equities" approach. They may consider whether harm will occur from the delay, the agency's commitment to the project, and whether the plaintiff is a private entity rather than an environmental organization. * * *

PRELIMINARY INJUNCTION

Plaintiffs in NEPA cases usually ask for a preliminary injunction in district court to enjoin all or some of the activities of the government defendant until it has complied with the statute. The decision to grant or deny a preliminary injunction lies in the discretion of the district court although it is appealable and may be reversed by a court of appeals. Whether a district court will grant a preliminary injunction requires the usual "balancing of the equities" and depends on the circumstances of each case. * * *

Although not always stated absolutely, a number of courts adopted an exception for NEPA cases to the traditional balancing rules * * * . The NEPA exception is in doubt because of recent Supreme Court cases holding that injunctions are not available per se in environmental litigation, although some lower federal courts have continued to recognize the exception. * * *

A 1982 Supreme Court decision, *Weinberger v. Romero-Barcelo*, [456 U.S. 305 (1982)], has influenced some lower federal courts to reject the NEPA exception to the preliminary injunction rules and to apply the standard equitable tests. In *Weinberger*, the plaintiffs sued to enjoin the Navy from discharging ordinance into waters surrounding an island off the Puerto Rico coast. The Navy had not applied for the necessary permit under the Clean Water Act. The district court ordered the Navy to apply for the permit but did not enjoin its operations pending consideration of the permit application.

The Supreme Court held that this order was correct. It restated the traditional equitable rules for an injunction, held that a federal judge is not "mechanically obligated" to grant an injunction for every violation of law, and reminded lower federal courts that injunctions were to be granted only when necessary to protect against irremediable injury.

The application of *Weinberger* to NEPA is not clear. The district court did not allow the statutory violation to continue, as it ordered the Navy to apply for a permit. NEPA does not require a permit. An injunction is the only means available to prevent a statutory violation. Nor does NEPA, unlike the Clean Water Act, provide for any other sanctions for statutory violations. * * *

Despite these statutory differences, some lower federal courts read *Weinberger* to require application of the traditional preliminary injunction rules in NEPA cases and rejection of a NEPA exception. * * *

# E. THE ARCHEOLOGY
# OF NEPA LITIGATION

It is no secret that NEPA—particularly its environmental impact statement requirement—has been widely litigated. Two commentators found that NEPA litigation comprises "a substantial portion (approximately 70 percent in 1980) of the environmental litigation against the

United States." Nicholas C. Yost & James W. Rubin, The National Environmental Policy Act in 2 Law of Environmental Protection 9-38 (Sheldon M. Novick, ed. 1998). An April 1999 search in the ALLFEDS database of Westlaw™ found 2,697 cases containing the phrase "environmental impact statement."

Although it is always dangerous to generalize about such a large population of cases, NEPA litigation seems to have passed through three historical phases. In the first phase—the era of the missing environmental impact statement—environmental plaintiffs won case after case, because the stubborn refusal of many agencies to comply with their straightforward statutory obligation to prepare impact statements was so obviously improper.

In the second phase—the era of the inadequate statement—agencies wised up a bit, conceding that an impact statement was needed, but then trying to get by with poorly written documents. Environmental plaintiffs had a high success ratio in these cases as well, because judges could see that the agencies were faking it.

In the third phase—the era of allegedly wrong decisions—agencies got so adept at putting together slick, boiler-plated, air-tight impact statements that plaintiffs could no longer successfully fault them for failing to prepare adequate statements. As a result, plaintiffs were forced to urge reviewing courts to consider the merits of the underlying project or proposal, claiming that the agency had made the wrong decision in choosing to plow ahead with its original (or somewhat modified) plans. As we will see, this third phase was brought to a screeching halt by the United States Supreme Court. Accordingly, modern plaintiffs are limited to the arguments of phases one and two.

## 1. FAILURE TO PREPARE AN IMPACT STATEMENT

Plaintiffs did not, of course, win all phase one cases—cases in which they challenged an agency's failure to prepare an environmental impact statement. Occasionally, courts would agree with an agency's determination that an impact statement was not required under the Act. The two primary justifications for such a conclusion are that the challenged action: (1) will not significantly affect the quality of the human environment; or (2) is not federal.

## HANLY v. KLEINDIENST

### 471 F.2d 823 (2d Cir. 1972)

Before FRIENDLY, Chief Judge, and MANSFIELD and TIMBERS, Circuit Judges.

MANSFIELD, Circuit Judge:

This case, which presents serious questions as to the interpretation of [NEPA], the language of which has been characterized as "opaque" and "woefully ambiguous," is here on appeal for the second time. Following the district court's denial for the second time of a preliminary injunction against construction of a jail and other facilities known as the Metropolitan Correction Center ("MCC") we are called upon to decide whether a redetermination by the General Services Administration ("GSA") that the MCC is not a facility "significantly affecting the quality of the human environment," made pursuant to this Court's decision remanding the case after the earlier appeal * * * satisfies the requirements of NEPA and thus renders it unnecessary for GSA to follow the procedure prescribed by § 102(2)(C) of NEPA, which requires a formal, detailed environmental impact statement. In view of the failure of the GSA, upon redetermination, to make findings with respect to certain relevant factors and to furnish an opportunity to appellants to submit relevant evidence, the case is again remanded. * * *

Appellants are members of groups residing or having their businesses in an area of lower Manhattan called "The Manhattan Civic Center" which comprises not only various court-houses, government buildings and businesses, but also residential housing, including cooperative apartments in two buildings close to the MCC and various similar apartments and tenements in nearby Chinatown. GSA * * * is engaged in the construction of an Annex to the United States Courthouse, Foley Square, Manhattan, located on a site to the east of the Courthouse and immediately to the south of Chinatown and the aforementioned two cooperative apartments. The Annex will consist of two buildings, each approximately 12 stories high, which will have a total of 345,601 gross square feet of space * * * . One will be an office building for the staffs of the United States Attorney and the United States Marshal, presently located in the severely overcrowded main Courthouse building, and the other will be the MCC.

The MCC will serve, under the jurisdiction of the Bureau of Prisons, Department of Justice, as the detention center for approximately 449 persons awaiting trial or convicted of short term federal offenses. It will replace the present drastically overcrowded and inadequate facility on West Street, Manhattan, and will be large enough to provide space not only for incarceration but for diagnostic services, and medical, recreational and administrative facilities. * * *

In February 1972, appellants sought injunctive relief against construction of the MCC on the ground that GSA had failed to comply with the mandates of NEPA * * * .

Upon appeal this Court [ruled in *Hanly I*] that the GSA's threshold determination [with respect to the MCC], which had been set forth in a short memorandum entitled "Environmental Statement" * * * was too meager to satisfy NEPA's requirements. That statement confined itself to a brief evaluation of the availability of utilities, the adequacy of mass transportation, the removal of trash, the absence of a relocation problem and the intention to comply with existing zoning regulations. In remanding the case this Court * * * concluded that * * * the agency was required to give attention to other factors that might affect [the] human environment in the area, including the possibility of riots and disturbances in the jail which might expose neighbors to additional noise, the dangers of crime to which neighbors might be exposed as the consequence of housing an out-patient treatment center in the building, possible traffic and parking problems that might be increased by trucks delivering food and supplies and by vans taking prisoners to and from the Eastern District and New Jersey District Courts, and the need for parking space for prison personnel and accommodations for visitors, including lawyers or members of the family. [The Supreme Court denied *certiorari* in *Hanly I* at 409 U.S. 990 (1972).]

[W]e believe that the appropriate criterion in the present [*Hanly II*] case is the "arbitrary, capricious" standard established by the Administrative Procedure Act, since the meaning of the term "significantly" as used in § 102(2)(C) of NEPA can be isolated as a question of law. * * *

Upon attempting, according to the foregoing standard, to interpret the amorphous term "significantly," as it is used in § 102(2)(C), we are faced with the fact that almost every major federal action, no matter how limited in scope, has some adverse effect on the human environment. It is equally clear that an action which is environmentally important to one neighbor may be of no consequence to another. Congress could have decided that every major federal action must therefore be the subject of a detailed impact statement prepared according to the procedure prescribed by § 102(2)(C). By adding the word "significantly," however, it demonstrated that before the agency in charge triggered that procedure, it should conclude that a greater environmental impact would result than from "any major federal action." * * *

Although the existing environment of the area which is the site of a major federal action constitutes one criterion to be considered, it must be recognized that even a slight increase in adverse conditions that form an existing environmental milieu may sometimes threaten harm that is significant. One more factory polluting air and water in an area zoned for industrial use may represent the straw that breaks the back of the environmental camel. Hence the absolute, as well as comparative, effects of a major federal action must be considered. * * *

The [Environmental] Assessment makes clear that the MCC will not produce any unusual or excessive amounts of smoke, dirt, obnoxious odors, solid waste, or other forms of pollution. The utilities required to heat and air-condition the building are readily available and the MCC is designed to incorporate energy-saving features, so that no excessive power demands are posed. The GSA further represents that the building will conform to all local codes, use and zoning, and attaches a letter from the New York City Office of Lower Manhattan Development dated August 4, 1971, indicating approval of the Annex, which includes the MCC. * * *

Appellants offer little or no evidence to contradict the detailed facts found by the GSA. For the most part their opposition is based upon a psychological distaste for having a jail located so close to residential apartments, which is understandable enough. It is doubtful whether psychological and sociological effects upon neighbors constitute the type of factors that may be considered in making such a determination since they do not lend themselves to measurement. However we need not decide that issue because these apartments were constructed within two or three blocks of another existing jail, The Manhattan House of Detention for Men, which is much larger than the proposed MCC and houses approximately 1,200 prisoners. Furthermore the area in which the MCC is located has at all times been zoned by the City of New York as a commercial district designed to provide for a wide range of uses, *specifically including "Prisons."*

Despite the GSA's scrupulous efforts the appellants do present one or two factual issues that merit further consideration and findings by the GSA. One bears on the possibility that the MCC will substantially increase the risk of crime in the immediate area, a relevant factor as to which the Assessment fails to make an outright finding despite the direction to do so in *Hanly I.* Appellants urge that the Community Treatment Program and the program for observation and study of non-resident out-patients will endanger the health and safety of the immediate area by exposing neighbors and passersby to drug addicts visiting the MCC for drug maintenance and to drug pushers and hangers-on who would inevitably frequent the vicinity of a drug maintenance center. If the MCC were to be used as a drug treatment center, the potential increase in crime might tip the scales in favor of a mandatory detailed impact statement. The Government has assured us by postargument letter addressed to the Court that:

> "Neither the anticipated nonresident pre-sentence study program nor any program to be conducted within the Metropolitan Correction Center will include drug maintenance."

While we do not question the Government's good faith, a finding in the matter by GSA is essential, since the Assessment is ambiguous as to the scope of the non-resident out-patient observation program and makes no finding on the subject of whether the MCC will increase the risk of crime in the community. * * *

Notwithstanding the absence of statutory or administrative provisions on the subject, this Court has already held in *Hanly I* at 647 that federal agencies must "affirmatively develop a reviewable environmental record * * * even for purposes of a threshold section 102(2)(C) determination." We now go further and hold that before a preliminary or threshold determination of significance is made the responsible agency must give notice to the public of the proposed major federal action and an opportunity to submit relevant facts which might bear upon the agency's threshold decision. We do not suggest that a full-fledged formal hearing must be provided before each such determination is made, although it should be apparent that in many cases such a hearing would be advisable for reasons already indicated. The necessity for a hearing will depend greatly upon the circumstances surrounding the particular proposed action and upon the likelihood that a hearing will be more effective than other methods in developing relevant information and an understanding of the proposed action. The precise procedural steps to be adopted are better left to the agency, which should be in a better position than the court to determine whether solution of the problems faced with respect to a specific major federal action can better be achieved through a hearing or by informal acceptance of relevant data.

In view of the Assessment's failure to make findings with respect to the possible existence of a drug maintenance program at the MCC, the increased risk of crime that might result from the operation of the MCC, and the fact that appellants have challenged certain findings of fact, we remand the case for the purpose of requiring the GSA to make a further investigation of these issues, with directions to accept from appellants and other concerned citizens such further evidence as they may proffer within a reasonable period, to make supplemental findings with respect to these issues, and to redetermine whether the MCC "significantly affects the quality of the human environment". * * *

FRIENDLY, Chief Judge (dissenting):

The learned opinion of my brother Mansfield gives these plaintiffs, and environmental advocates in future cases, both too little and too much. It gives too little because it raises the floor of what constitutes "major Federal actions significantly affecting the quality of the human environment" * * * higher than I believe Congress intended. It gives too much because it requires that before making a threshold determination that no impact statement is demanded, the agency must go through procedures which I think are needed only when an impact statement must be made. The upshot is that a threshold determination that a proposal does not constitute major Federal action significantly affecting the quality of the human environment becomes a kind of mini-impact statement. The preparation of such a statement under the conditions laid down by the majority is unduly burdensome when the action is truly minor or insignificant. On the other hand, there is a danger that if the threshold determination is this elaborate, it may come to replace the impact statement in the grey area between actions which, though "major" in a monetary sense, are obviously insignificant (such as the construction of the proposed office building) and actions that are obviously significant (such as the construction of an atomic power plant). We would better serve the purposes of Congress by keeping the threshold low enough to insure that impact statements are prepared for actions in this grey area and thus to permit the determination that no statement is required to be made quite informally in cases of true insignificance.

While I agree that determination of the meaning of "significant" is a question of law, one must add immediately that to make this determination on the basis of the dictionary would be impossible. Although all words may be "chameleons, which reflect the color of their environment," * * * "significant" has that quality more than most. It covers a spectrum ranging from "not trivial" through "appreciable" to "important" and even "momentous." If the right meaning is at the lower end of the spectrum, the construction of the MCC comes within it; per contra if the meaning is at the higher end.

The scheme of the National Environmental Policy Act argues for giving "significant" a reading which places it toward the lower end of the spectrum. * * *

It is not readily conceivable that Congress meant to allow agencies to avoid [NEPA's EIS] requirement by reading "significant" to mean only "important," "momentous," or the like. One of the purposes of the impact statement is to insure that the relevant environmental data are before the agency and considered by it prior to the decision to commit Federal resources to the project; the statute must not be construed so as to allow the agency to make its decision in a doubtful case without the relevant data or a detailed study of it. This is particularly clear because of the absence from the statute of any procedural requirement upon an agency in making the threshold determination that an impact statement is not demanded, although the majority has managed to contrive one. What Congress was trying to say was, "You don't need to make an impact statement, with the consequent expense and delay, when there is no sensible reason for making one." I thus agree with Judge J. Skelly Wright's view that "a statement is required whenever the action *arguably* will have an adverse environmental impact," * * * with the qualification, doubtless intended, that the matter must be *fairly* arguable. * * *

I thus reach the question whether, with the term so narrowed, the GSA's refusal to prepare an impact statement for the MCC can be supported. Accepting the majority's standard of review, I would think that, even with the fuller assessment here before us, the GSA could not reasonably conclude that the MCC does not entail potentially significant environmental effects. I see no ground for the majority's doubt "whether psychological and sociological effects upon neighbors constitute the type of factors that may be considered in making such a determination [of significant environmental effect] since they do not lend themselves to measurement." The statute speaks of "the overall welfare and development of man," [§ 101(a)] and makes it the responsibility of Federal agencies to "use all practicable means * * * to * * * assure for all Americans safe, healthful, productive, and esthetically and culturally pleasing surroundings." [§ 101(b)] Moreover, [§ 102(2)(B)] directs that "presently unquantified environmental amenities and values * * * be given appropriate consideration in decisionmaking along with economic and technical considerations." * * *

I do not mean anything said in this opinion to imply that GSA will be unable to conclude in an impact statement that construction of the MCC is justified. Furthermore, as I have suggested in another case, "Once it is determined in any particular instance that there has been good faith compliance with those procedures [of NEPA], we seriously question whether much remains for a reviewing court." * * *

The energies my brothers would require GSA to devote to still a third assessment designed to show that an impact statement is not needed would better be devoted to making one.

I would reverse and direct the issuance of an injunction until a reasonable period after the making of an impact statement.

### Notes and Questions

1.   The Supreme Court denied *certiorari* in *Hanly v. Kleindienst* for a second time, *see* 412 U.S. 908 (1973). Following remand, the district court denied (for a third time), the plaintiffs' request for an injunction, and the appeals court affirmed in *Hanly III. See* 484 F.2d 448 (2d Cir. 1973). The Supreme Court once more denied certiorari. *See* 416 U.S. 936 (1974). Accordingly, the opponents of the MCC's construction ultimately lost their NEPA suit.

2.   The GSA's determination—based on an environmental assessment— that it would not prepare an environmental impact statement on the MCC project is called a FONSI (finding of no significant impact). The Second Circuit had reviewed this FONSI once in *Hanly I* (remanding the case for further consideration) and remanded it a second time in the *Hanly II* decision. The second remand seems to have been due primarily to the court's concern about the possible effects of drug addicts on the neighborhood, if the MCC eventually included a "drug maintenance" program in which addicts would be treated with chemical substitutes such as methadone. Government counsel assured the court by postargument letter that "[no] program to be conducted within the Metropolitan Correction Center will include drug maintenance." *See* page 789, *supra*. Nevertheless, the court insisted that "a finding in the matter by GSA is essential." *See id.* Why did the court insist on a formal finding? Would a formal finding in the FONSI bind the agency, so that it would be precluded from establishing a drug maintenance program in the MCC facility? Would a formal finding to that effect in a full blown environmental impact statement be binding? Should it be? How might such a finding be enforced?

3.   In *Noe v. MARTA*, 485 F. Supp. 501 (N.D. Ga. 1980), *aff'd* 644 F.2d 434 (5th Cir.), *cert. denied* 454 U.S. 1126 (1981), the court dismissed an action brought by a bookstore owner who complained that the actual noise levels resulting from the Metropolitan Atlanta Rapid Transit Authority's operations were significantly higher than those predicted by the associated environmental impact statement. The district judge concluded: "the court can find no duty on the part of MARTA or the construction companies to abide by the environmental impact statement." *Id.* at 504. The court continued:

The twin goals of requiring agency decision-makers to consider during the planning stage the environmental consequences of a proposed project and of informing the public about the environmental consequences of a proposed project have been met in this case. The environmental impact statement for the MARTA construction project has been approved. * * * The plaintiff has not pointed to any section of the National Environmental Protection Act which would require the defendants to abide by the particulars of the environmental impact statement. We refuse to imply both a duty and a cause of action. * * * Accordingly, the Secretary of Transportation owes no statutory duty to plaintiff. Noe has failed * * * to state a claim for which relief can be granted.

*Id.* The Fifth Circuit declared: "Because we agree with the District Court that the National Environmental Policy Act (NEPA) does not give rise to a private cause of action for failing to adhere to the [EIS] required by NEPA, we affirm the judgment of the District Court." 644 F.2d at 436. Do these rulings make sense? What message do they send to the agency representatives who prepare environmental impact statements?

4. Assume that the GSA in the *Hanly* litigation makes a formal representation in an environmental assessment (or in an environmental impact statement) that a drug maintenance program will not be included in the proposed MCC facility. After constructing the facility, the GSA promptly introduces a drug maintenance program. Does *Noe v. MARTA* foreclose suit by the original *Hanly* plaintiffs? Are the cases distinguishable?

5. In *NRDC v. Grant*, 341 F. Supp. 356, 366-67 (E.D. N.C. 1972), the court stated that an action is "major" within the meaning of NEPA if it "requires substantial planning, time, resources, or expenditure." Does this interpretation of the statute make sense? Is it consistent with the CEQ regulations, set forth at pages 780-782, *supra*?

# SCOTTSDALE MALL v.
# STATE OF INDIANA

549 F.2d 484 (7th Cir. 1977)

WILLIAM J. CAMPBELL, Senior District Judge.

Defendants-Appellees State of Indiana and The Indiana State Highway Commission withdrew a state highway project from a federal-aid highway program * * * and claim a right to proceed with state funds in the final stages and construction of the project. By electing to withdraw the project from federal funding consideration, defendants have avoided compliance with the environmental impact statement requirements which are made necessary for "major federal actions" by [NEPA] * * * . We are called upon to determine whether the project in this case is a "major federal action," and whether the state may avoid the requirements of NEPA by withdrawing the project from federal programming.

Plaintiff, an Ohio partnership, owns a shopping center through which defendants were about to construct a highway. The district court granted a preliminary injunction against defendants on the ground that there had been no compliance with federal environmental statutes. Following a trial on the merits, the district court dissolved the preliminary injunction and entered judgment in favor of defendants. We vacate that judgment and remand.

The facts are not in dispute. The project which is the focal point of the controversy in this case is a proposed development of a 28-mile-long by-pass around the South Bend-Elkhart metropolitan area in Northern Indiana. As the result of a study initiated more than twenty years ago by defendant Highway Commission, a four-lane limited access highway was conceived to alleviate traffic congestion * * * .

The by-pass project was programmed to be constructed as a federal project in four segments. One segment, from the western terminus on U.S. 20 to a point on U.S. 31 south of the City of South Bend, already has been constructed with an expenditure of approximately 6.7 million dollars in federal funds. This segment appears to occupy roughly one-fourth of the total mileage of the project. The remainder of the project, approximately 20 miles in length, was planned to be constructed as a federally funded program in three segments since 1966 or 1967. The First Segment was planned to run due east from the eastern terminus of the segment which had already been constructed to a point on State Road 331, a distance of 3.8 miles. It is the construction of this First Segment which gives rise to the controversy in this case.

In 1968 plaintiff purchased the site of the present Scottsdale Mall, a shopping center complex in South Bend. The district court found that, as presently planned, the 3.8 mile First Segment of the by-pass would bisect plaintiff's property, which is located near the western terminus of the proposed First Segment. Construction of the segment would permanently remove 599 parking spaces from the shopping center, and would render inoperative the expansion potential which is part of the inherent design of the shopping center. As the district court further found, the location for the corridor of the First Segment as well as the remaining segments was established in 1967 after considerable discussion regarding the general location of the proposed by-pass. At the time of acquiring the site of the shopping center, plaintiff knew that the by-pass corridor would bisect its property.

On December 5, 1974, the Highway Commission advised the plaintiff that it intended to proceed with the First Segment as originally proposed. As of that date, substantial steps had been taken under the Federal-Aid Highway Act to construct the remaining segments with the assistance of federal funds. Plaintiff then instituted this action, seeking to enjoin the State of Indiana and its Highway Commission from proceeding with the plans to construct the First Segment on the grounds that the selection of the route as proposed by the State of Indiana was arbitrary and capricious, and that the State had not filed an Environmental Impact Statement (EIS) as required by federal law. The district court granted the preliminary injunction on January 20, 1975. The defendants then decided to construct the First Segment and remaining segments without federal assistance and took steps to "de-program" this project from further federal consideration.

Our review of the record reveals a project with an extensive history of federal-state involvement. Since as early as 1966, the three remaining segments of the by-pass were scheduled, programmed, and worked upon as a federal project. * * * Location hearings were conducted as required by federal law. * * * [T]he Department of Transportation * * * approved the design plans for the First Segment. Between August, 1971, and February, 1975, defendants received $162,000 in federal money for purposes of completing preliminary engineering studies on the project. The record shows that the preliminary engineering stage was virtually completed, and that the state was about to commence right of way acquisition with federal funds when the plaintiff instituted this action.

In 1973, the Highway Commission requested authority to proceed with land acquisition for the First Segment. When the federal authorities advised that an EIS was required, the Highway Commission advised the Department of Transportation that it intended to withdraw its application for federal funding of the First Segment. The Department of Transportation then informed the Highway Commission that all three remaining segments were, for EIS purposes, considered one project, and that, even though the state had withdrawn its application for federal funds as to the First Segment, an EIS would be required for all remaining segments of the by-pass. Indiana's compliance with this requirement and the Department of Transportation's actions with respect thereto are less than exemplary. The State submitted a final EIS for approval to the Secretary of the Department of Transportation for the remaining two segments. The State then supplemented that EIS with an EIS as to the First Segment. Although the supplement was procedurally and may have been substantively deficient, the Secretary approved the submission. When plaintiff questioned the adequacy of the EIS, the Secretary, in January, 1975, responded by withdrawing its approval of the EIS and requiring another single EIS to be prepared for all three remaining segments of the by-pass.

In early 1975, approximately 185 million dollars were made available to finance Indiana highway projects. All of these funds had to be committed to specific projects by July 1, 1975. By that date, Indiana had committed all of the federal funds to projects other than the by-pass, and shortly thereafter took steps to "de-program" the remaining two segments of the by-pass from federal funding consideration. The State indicated on brief and during oral argument that the federal monies previously received for preliminary engineering study were "refunded" to the federal government. We note that the net amount of funds received by Indiana was not reduced by the "refund". In fact, the record indicates that Indiana made an accounting transfer of the money, apply the amounts received for the by-pass to other projects. * * *

In determining that Indiana had properly withdrawn the by-pass project from federal funding such that the project no longer could be considered a " major federal action" requiring an EIS, the district court noted: " (Highway Commission's) decision not to comply with the eligibility procedures necessary to maintain (its) option to receive federal highway funds cannot have the paradoxical effect of producing federal involvement." In this regard, the district court found that federal participation in the by-pass project was limited to the initial programming stage. We think the district court erred in this finding. Our review of the record indicates federal participation in the programming, location, design, preliminary engineering, and right of way acquisition stages. Hence, we have no difficulty in concluding on the basis of the record before us that the entire by-pass project is a "major federal action" * * * and that an EIS is required for the remaining three segments.

Inasmuch as the State of Indiana contends that under the circumstances of this case it may withdraw the project from federal funding participation, we are squarely faced with the troublesome question of whether by doing so at this late stage of the project, it is also relieved of its obligation to comply with NEPA. * * *

[W]e are convinced that there is a point in the on-going federal-state relationship under Federal-Aid Highway Act programming at which the requirements of NEPA must be met. Under the facts and circumstances of this case, Indiana's seeking and receiving federal approval at various stages of the project and receiving preliminary financial benefits so imbued the highway project with a federal character that, notwithstanding the state's withdrawal of the project from federal funding consideration, compliance with federal environmental statutes was necessary. Were we to hold otherwise, we would give little, if any, effect to the Congressional directive so cogently expressed by the phrase "to the fullest extent possible."

In the instant case, the record shows federal involvement up to and including right of way acquisition. The precise point at which a federally programmed state highway project becomes irrevocably federal in character for NEPA purposes is a decision we deem unnecessary to make since, for purposes of this case, we find the by-pass project sufficiently federal in character to require compliance with NEPA. We do not consider Indiana's act of withdrawal a crucial fact in the determination of whether or not the provisions of NEPA are applicable to the project in this case. Rather, we look to the history of federal-state involvement to determine if the project is a "major federal action" requiring NEPA compliance.

The State of Indiana has urged that preliminary federal-state dealings and its compliance with applicable federal statutes and regulations only present a possibility of federal funding, and by complying with federal requirements and receiving federal approval at various stages, the state preserves its option to seek federal funds for a project. * * * We reject these contentions. If Indiana had not long ago sought federal funding for the by-pass project, had not programmed the project for federal assistance, sought and received federal approval of the location and design stages, received federal funds for preliminary engineering studies, and had not begun right-of-way acquisition, but rather had proceeded with these various phases of the project on its own, the result in this case might have been different. * * *

Accordingly, the judgment of the district court is vacated and the case is remanded to the district court for further proceedings not inconsistent with this opinion.

### Notes and Questions

1. Other plaintiffs have not been so successful in combating the argument that a seemingly federal project is insufficiently federal to trigger application of NEPA. For example, in *City of Boston v. Volpe*, 464 F.2d 254 (1st Cir. 1974), the Massachusetts Port Authority (Port Authority) received the general approval of the Federal Aviation Administration (FAA) to construct an expansion to Boston's Logan Airport, and the FAA allocated $1.1 million for construction. Even though the Port Authority had commenced construction of a project that would allegedly generate unacceptable noise and interfere with the Boston Redevlopment Authority's efforts to rehabilitate an adjacent area, the court rejected the plaintiffs argument that the Port Authority's conduct had become "federal" action:

> What has happened, in brief, is that a state authority, fully empowered to raise and spend funds for airports, has "requested" a federal grant, * * * the federal agency has made a "tentative allocation" of funds for the project * * * and the authority has then submitted a formal application * * * .

> [T]he airport aid scheme contemplates, so far as the statute is concerned, a single decision to fund or not to fund a project. * * * [T]he federal defendants have promulgated a regulation authorizing the making of a tentative allocation of funds * * * which they interpret to be "preliminary and tentative in nature," fundamentally an administrative device for budgetary and program planning. Their interpretation is of course entitled to great weight, especially since the phrase "tentative allocation" is in this context their own. * * *

> It may well be urged that too little sanction remains, if a state project is allowed to wreak damage on the environment. To the extent to which the sanction is less here than under other federal programs, that is attributable to the nature of airport aid. A state may, after all, proceed with construction wholly independently of the federal government.

> Where the state authority does rely on the expectation of federal aid, it goes ahead with construction prior to approval only at great risk to the prospects for funding, since the options of the federal agency become increasingly limited to bald approval or rejection with no opportunity for modification.

While it is perhaps true that a state or other non-federal entity might have the funds to finance any specific project, it is straining credulity to suggest that such an entity would remain indifferent to the leverage of federal funding. Perhaps it would make a calculated judgment to proceed with an environmentally questionable project if a sufficiently high state priority were assigned to it, and non-federal funds were available; or, conversely, it might proceed cavalierly if the project were indisputably likely to receive a favorable impact statement.

But in most cases a state or community would be sensitive to its environmental obligations, not only to avoid jeopardizing its chances of obtaining assistance for the specific project, but also to avoid a negative report on future projects associated with the same facility. For, as we have noted, the federal agencies cannot close their eyes to ill-advised actions of the past as they assess a project in the present.

We therefore hold that the district court did not err in ruling that Boston is unlikely to prevail on the merits of its request for an injunction against the Port Authority. * * *

*Id.* at 258-60.

2.   In *College Gardens Civic Association v. U. S. Department of Transportation*, 522 F.Supp. 377 (D. Md. 1981), the court held that various roadway projects in and around city of Rockville, Maryland, were not required to be treated as single project for purposes of the National Environmental Policy Act, and therefore federal funding for .2-mile stretch of roadway project did not provide any basis for applying provisions of the Act to any of the other projects. Should state and local authorities be allowed to "segment" projects in ways which make only the controversial portions "nonfederal"? Won't they simply shift federal monies to the noncontroversial portions of the project?

3.   Projects may be segmented not only to avoid a finding of federal action but also to avoid a finding of significant impact. In *State of Minnesota v. U.S. Nuclear Regulatory Commission*, 602 F.2d 412 (D.C. Cir. 1979), petitioner argued that the Nuclear Regulatory Commission (NRC) had improperly segmented its consideration of the environmental impacts associated with the proposed expansion of spent nuclear fuel onsite storage capacity at a nuclear generating plant. Because the requested expansion would accommodate the spent fuel assemblies produced at the generating plant for no more than a few years and because industry had no long-term solution for dealing with ever mounting quantities of spent fuel assemblies, petitioner claimed that future requests for further expansion were inevitable and that the true environmental impacts of the proposed action could not be properly assessed without considering inevitable future expansions. The court rejected this argument: "[Petitioner] has not pointed to any consequence of future expansion that could not be adequately considered at the time of any requests for further expansion." *Id.* at 416 n.5. Accordingly, the court left undisturbed the NRC's refusal to prepare an environmental impact statement.

## 2.  INADEQUATE IMPACT STATEMENTS

# CHELSEA NEIGHBORHOOD ASSOCIATIONS v. UNITED STATES POSTAL SERVICE

### 516 F.2d 378 (2d Cir. 1975)

Before FRIENDLY and FEINBERG, Circuit Judges, and LASKER, District Judge.

FEINBERG, Circuit Judge:

The United States Postal Service (the Service) appeals from a decision of the United States District Court for the Southern District of New York, Robert J. Ward, J., enjoining it "from entering into any contract for, or proceeding in any way with, the construction of the U. S. Postal Service Vehicle Maintenance Facility" in the Chelsea neighborhood of Manhattan "pending final determination of this action or alternatively, pending * * * (the district) court's determination that there has been compliance with NEPA * * * ." The preliminary injunction was granted upon the motion of plaintiffs, a group of Chelsea neighborhood associations and individuals residing in the area. We affirm the order of the district court.

In 1968, the then Post Office Department acquired a square-block site next to the Morgan Station postal facility in New York City. Subsequently, it was proposed that the ground levels be used for a Vehicle Maintenance Facility (VMF) and the air space be granted to New York City for public housing. An apartment complex was to be built on the roof of the VMF. This was agreed upon in 1972, and the New York District Army Corps of Engineers [prepared] an Environmental Impact Statement (EIS) for the project. * * *

Plaintiffs characterize the VMF as a huge garage with space for over 900 vehicles. Its concrete walls would rise directly from the sidewalk for approximately 80 feet, on top of which would be a flat platform with housing extending upward from there. Noting that approximately 2,200 truck movements in and out of the VMF are anticipated daily, plaintiffs contend that the impact of the garage would devastate their community. The Service points out that many of the trucks would travel to and from the adjacent Morgan Station in any event; the Service also minimizes the impact of the VMF, asserting that it is not located in the Chelsea residential area, but rather on the border between Chelsea and a commercial district. According to the Service, the VMF will actually act as a buffer against further commercial encroachment and help stabilize the area. Nevertheless, plaintiffs clearly do not want the VMF in or near Chelsea. In July 1974, they requested the Service in writing to abandon the VMF and convey the site to the City for strictly residential purposes. Plaintiffs suggested that another site, the Yale Express garage located ten blocks away, be considered. The Service rejected the demand and this action followed. Plaintiffs sought to enjoin the project until the provisions of [NEPA] had been fully complied with, and asked for a mandate directing the Service to reconsider the VMF in light of the availability of the Yale Express garage. Thereafter, the Service solicited and obtained bids for construction of the VMF alone. Upon plaintiffs' motion, Judge Ward granted a preliminary injunction, finding that the Service was subject to NEPA, and that the EIS already prepared was inadequate. * * *

The adequacy of an EIS can only be considered in light of its purpose. "The primary purpose of the impact statement is to compel federal agencies to give serious weight to environmental factors in making discretionary choices." * * * NEPA, in effect, requires a broadly defined cost-benefit analysis of major federal activities. It seeks to insure that more than economic costs alone are considered. * * *

The EIS is a sizeable document whose very bulk is impressive. Unfortunately for the Service, however, Judge Ward was not sufficiently impressed with its substance, finding it lacking in three respects. These were the failure of the EIS to discuss sufficiently (1) the impact of the proposed housing; (2) the possibility that no housing would ever be erected; and (3) alternatives to the proposed construction.

Turning to the first of these alleged inadequacies, the judge found that one shortcoming of the EIS lay in using the housing portion of the project as a virtue, while ignoring many of its associated disadvantages. There is no doubt that the air-rights housing was a chief "selling point" for the entire project. * * *

Yet the EIS does not contain a comprehensive analysis of the environmental impact of the housing. There is brief mention of possible overcrowding at a local elementary school, the need for future expansion of local health services, and the effect on park usage. But the report does not treat the effect of the housing with anywhere near the thoroughness accorded the VMF. For example, the VMF will require closing 29th Street for most of the day and diversion of traffic onto adjacent streets. The EIS states that tightened parking enforcement on those streets will help keep the extra volume of traffic flowing. But the statement does not consider where those parked cars will go; nor does it discuss what will be done with the automobiles of the residents of the proposed 860 apartments in the air-rights housing or the automobiles of the 1,500 drivers and employees of the VMF. The required support services for the housing are not adequately discussed. Garbage collection is disposed of by a single paragraph stating, in effect, that it will all be trucked away. What will be the expected noise and air pollution contribution from those trucks is not adequately discussed.

A possibly more serious shortcoming of the housing analysis lies in the social, not physical, sciences. What effect will living at the top of an 80-foot plateau have on the residents of the air-rights housing? Will there be an emotional as well as physical isolation from the community? Will that isolation exacerbate the predicted rise in crime due to the increase in population density? That an EIS must consider these human factors is well established. * * * The EIS gives scant attention to these serious questions. It acknowledges that "project size, height and design and the incidence of crime" are all related. EIS at III-31. But the only response is to suggest that "[project] design should reflect this emerging body of research to the extent practicable." * * * This is not enough. We do not know whether informed social scientists would conclude that the top of the VMF would likely become a human jungle, unsafe at night and unappealing during the day. The question must be faced, however, by those who plan the project.

In short, we agree with Judge Ward that the impact of the housing was not accorded the "full consideration" required by NEPA. * * * The Service argues that since the housing portion of the project is speculative it cannot be required to assess the unknowable or to postpone the VMF indefinitely. We agree that the Service can only do the possible, but the total number of apartment units have been approximated and an evaluation of probable environmental impact need not await final detailed design.

The Service also contends that any inadequacy in the EIS treatment of housing is irrelevant because the entire project was, in effect, "segmented" by Congress into two parts—a VMF to be built by the Service and housing to be built by New York City. Since some other agency will construct the apartments, the Service asserts that a housing EIS is not its responsibility. But segmentation is not really the issue now before us. It is correct that the Service will not build the housing portion of this project, but even so, the Service cannot ignore it. If the potential impact of the housing is not considered before the VMF is constructed, it will be too late to reassess the project as a whole no matter what is shown by a later EIS for the housing prepared by another agency. * * *

This brings us to the failure of the EIS to disclose that the housing might never be built at all, the second defect found by Judge Ward. While the impact of the VMF alone was analyzed, the treatment of the VMF without housing was in some instances perfunctory compared with the analysis of the VMF with housing. This defect in itself may well be easily remedied. More significant, however, is the failure to assess the importance and impact of the VMF by itself. The lack is fatal to the EIS for it is at least possible that without the housing the "Assessment of Trade Offs" would result in a decision not to proceed with the project at all. * * *

Finally, Judge Ward found the EIS inadequate in its discussion of alternatives, holding that treatment of the "No Action" and "Scatter Site" possibilities was "conclusory and uninformative." * * * [T]he Service argues that since studies over the past decade all agree on the need for a consolidated VMF, certain alternatives could be rejected in the EIS without detailed analysis. But these studies were not made part of the EIS and so invocation of them cannot alone "permit a reasoned choice of alternatives." * * * Without a more detailed analysis of the rejected alternatives the community and other agencies will have no way of checking on the validity of the Service's conclusions. * * * If, as the Service contends, there are studies conclusively showing the need for a consolidated VMF and rejecting various alternatives, it should be a simple matter to include in a revised EIS the supporting data from these studies.

Plaintiffs also argue strenuously that the EIS is defective because it does not deal with the suggested alternative location of the Yale Express garage. * * * The Service contends that it was not required to consider that site because its availability was not known until after the EIS was completed. The district judge never reached this issue. Since the EIS must be revised in any event, the Yale Express location should be considered as one of the possible alternatives to the Chelsea VMF.

In sum, we agree with the district court that the Service has failed to meet the requirements of NEPA in making "a careful and informed decision," and we affirm the injunction of the district court. * * *

### Questions

Professors Stewart and Krier ask the following about the *Hanly II* (*see* page 786, *supra*), and *Chelsea Neighborhood* cases:

Do not both decisions call into question the value of mandating an island of federal planning in a sea of local indifference to planning? Might the Postal Service VMF be the best-planned building in New York? Or does the weaker efficacy of local political checks on federal activities justify this approach?

Richard B. Stewart & James E. Krier, Environmental Law and Policy 775-76 (2d ed. 1978).

## DANIEL R. MANDELKER, NEPA LAW AND LITIGATION

§§ 10.05 (2d ed. 1998)

Judicial review of the adequacy of an impact statement is known as procedural judicial review. * * *

The standard of judicial review that courts apply to impact statements is not entirely clear. For agency decisions on whether to prepare an impact statement, the Supreme Court adopted the arbitrary and capricious standard of judicial review authorized by the Administrative Procedure Act in *Marsh v. Oregon Natural Resources Council* [490 U.S. 360 (1989)]. The Court has not yet decided whether this standard applies to the judicial review of impact statement adequacy.

Some circuits have followed *Marsh* and apply the arbitrary and capricious standard to the review of impact statements. Other circuits continue to review impact statement adequacy by applying [a] "reason-ableness" standard * * * .

### Notes and Questions

1. In two 1989 cases—*Robertson v. Methow Valley Citizens Council*, 490 U.S. 332 (1989) (involving a permit for a major downhill ski resort in a National Forest), and *Marsh v. Oregon Natural Resources Council*, 490 U.S. 360 (1989) (involving construction of a dam)—environmentalists asserted that NEPA required inclusion of a "worst case" analysis and a "mitigation plan" in environmental impact statements. The Supreme Court rejected these claims, effectively concluding that the impact statements in each case were adequate.

2. Federal agencies routinely engaging in major federal actions significantly affecting the quality of the human environment (such as the Department of Transportation) presumably have employees whose sole function is to grind out environmental impact statements on highway interchanges, airport expansions, and the like. Once the contents of an "adequate" impact statement have been hammered out through numerous court rulings, does it seem likely that these officials will have learned how to crank out sufficiently adequate statements to withstand judicial scrutiny? Do you imagine that each new highway project impact statement is prepared from scratch, or you do suspect that vast portions of each new statement are simply cannibalized from predecessor documents? Do your answers to these questions suggest that opponents of such projects will find it increasingly difficult (if not futile) to attack the adequacy of the agency's impact statements?

## 3. WRONG DECISIONS

Environmental advocates faced with agency cutting and pasting of ever more bullet-proof impact statements eventually turned to their only remaining argument: courts should be free to reverse agency decisions to go ahead with projects in cases in which the environmental harms and mitigation alternatives catalogued in the impact statement cried out for a contrary decision. Although some lower courts accepted this theory, such an approach—often called "substantive review" of NEPA decision making—was dead on arrival at the United States Supreme Court.

## STRYCKER'S BAY NEIGHBORHOOD COUNCIL v. KARLEN

### 444 U.S. 223 (1980)

PER CURIAM

The protracted nature of this litigation is perhaps best illustrated by the identity of the original federal defendant, "George Romney, Secretary of the Department of Housing and Urban Development." At the center of this dispute is the site of a proposed low-income housing project to be constructed on Manhattan's Upper West Side. In 1962, the New York City Planning Commission (Commission), acting in conjunction with the United States Department of Housing and Urban Development (HUD), began formulating a plan for the renewal of 20 square blocks known as the "West Side Urban Renewal Area" (WSURA) through a joint effort on the part of private parties and various government agencies. As originally written, the plan called for a mix of 70% middle-income housing and 30% low-income housing and designated the site at issue here as the location of one of the middle-income projects. In 1969, after substantial progress toward completion of the plan, local agencies in New York determined that the number of low-income units proposed for WSURA would be insufficient to satisfy an increased need for such units. In response to this shortage the Commission amended the plan to designate the site as the future location of a high-rise building containing 160 units of low-income housing. HUD approved this amendment in December 1972.

Meanwhile, in October 1971, the Trinity Episcopal School Corp. (Trinity), which has participated in the plan by building a combination school and middle-income housing development at a nearby location, sued in the United States District Court for the Southern District of New York to enjoin the Commission and HUD from constructing low-income housing on the site. The present respondents, Roland N. Karlen, Alvin C. Hudgins, and the Committee of Neighbors to Insure a Normal Urban Environment (CONTINUE), intervened as plaintiffs, while petitioner Strycker's Bay Neighborhood Council, Inc., intervened as a defendant.

The District Court entered judgment in favor of petitioners. See *Trinity Episcopal School Corp. v. Romney*, 387 F.Supp. 1044 (1974). It concluded, *inter alia*, that petitioners had not violated [NEPA] * * * .

On respondent's appeal, the Second Circuit affirmed all but the District Court's treatment of the NEPA claim. See *Trinity Episcopal School Corp. v. Romney*, 523 F.2d 88 (1975). While the Court of Appeals agreed with the District Court that HUD was not required to prepare a full-scale environmental impact statement under Section 102(2)(C) of NEPA * * * it held that HUD had not complied with Section 102(2)(E), which requires an agency to "study, develop, and describe appropriate alternatives to recommended courses of action in any proposal which involves unresolved conflicts concerning alternative uses of available resources." * * * According to the Court of Appeals, any consideration by HUD of alternatives to placing low-income housing on the site "was either highly limited or nonexistent." * * * Citing the "background of urban environmental factors" behind HUD's decision, the Court of Appeals remanded the case, requiring HUD to prepare a "statement of possible alternatives, the consequences thereof and the facts and reasons for and against * * * ."

On remand, HUD prepared a lengthy report entitled Special Environmental Clearance (1977). * * * The last portion of the report incorporated a study wherein the Commission evaluated nine alternative locations for the project and found none of them acceptable. While HUD's report conceded that this study may not have considered all possible alternatives, it credited the Commission's conclusion that any relocation of the units would entail an unacceptable delay of two years or more. According to HUD, "[m]easured against the environmental costs associated with the minimum two-year delay, the benefits seem insufficient to justify a mandated substitution of sites." * * * After soliciting the parties' comments on HUD's report, the District Court again entered judgment in favor of petitioners. * * *

On appeal, the Second Circuit vacated and remanded again. * * * The appellate court focused upon that part of HUD's report where the agency considered and rejected alternative sites, and in particular upon HUD's reliance on the delay such a relocation would entail. The Court of Appeals purported to recognize that its role in reviewing HUD's decision was defined by the Administrative Procedure Act (APA), 5 U.S.C. Section 706(2)(A), which provides that agency actions should be set aside if found to be "arbitrary, capricious, an abuse of discretion, or otherwise not in accordance with law * * * ." Additionally, however, the Court of Appeals looked to "[t]he provisions of NEPA" for "the substantive standards necessary to review the merits of agency decisions * * * ." 590 F.2d at 43. The Court of Appeals conceded that HUD had "given 'consideration' to alternatives" to redesignating the site. *Id.* at 44. Nevertheless, the court believed that "'consideration' is not an end in itself." *Id.* Concentrating on HUD's finding that development of an alternative location would entail an unacceptable delay, the appellate court held that such delay could not be "an overriding factor" in HUD's decision to proceed with the development. *Id.* According to the court, when HUD considers such projects, "environmental factors, such as crowding low-income housing into a concentrated area, should be given determinative weight." *Id.* The Court of Appeals therefore remanded the case to the District Court, instructing HUD to attack the shortage of low-income housing in a manner that would avoid the "concentration" of such housing on Site 30. *Id.* at 45. * * *

*Vermont Yankee* cuts sharply against the Court of Appeals' conclusion that an agency, in selecting a course of action, must elevate environmental concerns over other appropriate considerations. On the contrary, once an agency has made a decision subject to NEPA's procedural requirements, the only role for a court is to insure that the agency has considered the environmental consequences; it cannot "interject itself within the area of discretion of the executive as to the choice of the action to be taken."[2] * * *

---

[2] If we could agree with the dissent that the Court of Appeals held that HUD had acted "arbitrarily" in redesignating the site for low-income housing, we might also agree that plenary review is warranted. But the District Court expressly concluded that HUD had not acted arbitrarily or capriciously and our reading of the opinion of the Court of Appeals satisfies us that it did not overturn that finding. Instead, the

In the present litigation there is no doubt that HUD considered the environmental consequences of its decision to redesignate the proposed site for low-income housing. NEPA requires no more. The petitions for certiorari are granted, and the judgment of the Court of Appeals is therefore reversed.

MR. JUSTICE MARSHALL, dissenting.

The issue raised by these cases is far more difficult than the *per curiam* opinion suggests. The Court of Appeals held that the Secretary of Housing and Urban Development (HUD) had acted arbitrarily in concluding that prevention of a delay in the construction process justified the selection of a housing site which could produce adverse social environmental effects, including racial and economic concentration. Today the majority responds that "once an agency has made a decision subject to NEPA's procedural requirements, the only role for a court is to insure that the agency has considered the environmental consequences," and that in this case "there is no doubt that HUD considered the environmental consequences of its decision to redesignate the proposed site for low-income housing. NEPA requires no more." The majority finds support for this conclusion in the closing paragraph of our decision in *Vermont Yankee Nuclear Power Corp. v. NRDC*, 435 U.S. 519, 558 (1978).

*Vermont Yankee* does not stand for the broad proposition that the majority advances today. The relevant passage in that opinion was meant to be only a "further observation of some relevance to this case," *id.* at 557. That "observation" was a response to this Court's perception that the Court of Appeals in that case was attempting "under the guise of judicial review of agency action" to assert its own policy judgment as to the desirability of developing nuclear energy as an energy source for this Nation, a judgment which is properly left to Congress. * * * The Court of appeals had remanded the case to the agency because of "a single alleged oversight on a peripheral issue, urged by parties who never fully cooperated or indeed raised the issue below." It was in this context that the Court remarked that "NEPA does set forth significant substantive goals for the Nation, but its mandate to the agencies is *essentially* procedural." *Id.* (emphasis supplied). Accordingly, "[a]dministrative decisions should be set aside in this context, as in every other, only for substantial procedural *or substantive* reasons as mandated by statute," *id.* (emphasis supplied). Thus *Vermont Yankee* does not stand for the proposition that a court reviewing agency action under NEPA is limited solely to the factual issue of whether the agency "considered" environmental consequences. The agency's decision must still be set aside if it is "arbitrary, capricious, an abuse of discretion, or otherwise not in accordance with law," 5 U.S.C. Section 706(2)(A), and the re-

---

appellate court required HUD to elevate environmental concerns over other, admittedly legitimate considerations. Neither NEPA nor the APA provides any support for such a reordering of priorities by a reviewing court.

viewing court must still insure that the agency "has taken a 'hard look' at environmental consequences," *Kleppe v. Sierra Club*, 427 U.S. 390, 410, n. 21 (1976).

In the present case, the Court of Appeals did not "substitute its judgment for that of the agency as to the environmental consequences of its actions," *id.*, for HUD in its Special Environmental Clearance Report acknowledged the adverse environmental consequences of its proposed action: "the choice of Site 30 for development as a 100 percent low-income project has raised valid questions about the potential social environmental impacts involved." These valid questions arise from the fact that 68% of all public housing units would be sited on only one crosstown axis in this area of New York City. As the Court of Appeals observed, the resulting high concentration of low-income housing would hardly further racial and economic integration. The environmental "impact * * * on social fabric and community structures" was given a B rating in the report, indicating that from this perspective the project is "questionable" and ameliorative measures are "mandated." The report lists 10 ameliorative measures necessary to make the project acceptable. The report also discusses two alternatives, Sites 9 and 41, both of which are the appropriate size for the project and require "only minimal" amounts of relocation and clearance. Concerning Site 9 the report explicitly concludes that "[f]rom the standpoint of social environmental impact, this location would be superior to Site 30 for the development of low-rent public housing." The sole reason for rejecting the environmentally superior site was the fact that if the location were shifted to Site 9, there would be a proposed delay of two years in the construction of the housing.

The issue before the Court of Appeals, therefore, was whether HUD was free under NEPA to reject an alternative acknowledged to be environmentally preferable solely on the ground that any change in sites would cause delay. This was hardly a "peripheral issue" in the case. Whether NEPA, which sets forth "significant substantive goals," *Vermont Yankee Nuclear Power Corp. v. NRDC, supra*, 435 U.S. at 558, permits a projected two-year time difference to be controlling over environmental superiority is by no means clear. Resolution of the issue, however, is certainly within the normal scope of review of agency action to determine if it is arbitrary, capricious, or an abuse of discretion.* The question whether HUD can make delay the paramount concern over environmental superiority is essentially a restatement of the question whether HUD in considering the environmental consequences of its proposed action gave those consequences a "hard look," which is exactly the proper question for the reviewing court to ask. *Kleppe v. Sierra Club, supra*, 427 U.S., at 410, n. 21 * * * .

---

* The Secretary concedes that if an agency gave little or no weight to environmental values its decision might be arbitrary or capricious. Pet. for Cert. in No. 79-184, p. 15, n. 16.

The issue of whether the Secretary's decision was arbitrary or capricious is sufficiently difficult and important to merit plenary consideration in this Court. Further, I do not subscribe to the Court's apparent suggestion that *Vermont Yankee* limits the reviewing court to the essentially mindless task of determining whether an agency "considered" environmental factors even if that agency may have effectively decided to ignore those factors in reaching its conclusion. Indeed, I cannot believe that the Court would adhere to that position in a different factual setting. Our cases establish that the arbitrary-or-capricious standard prescribes a "searching and careful" judicial inquiry designed to ensure that the agency has not exercised its discretion in an unreasonable manner. *Citizens To Preserve Overton Park, Inc. v. Volpe,* 401 U.S. 402, 416 (1971). Believing that today's summary reversal represents a departure from that principle, I respectfully dissent.

It is apparent to me that this is not the type of case for a summary disposition. We should at least have a plenary hearing.

### Questions

1. Were the courts in *Strycker's Bay* reviewing the appropriateness of an agency's decision in light of an environmental impact statement? Or had the agency prepared a somewhat different document? Does the distinction matter?

2. Under what circumstances does NEPA § 102(2)(E) take effect? What does it require?

3. Suppose the United States Department of Energy (DOE) proposes to undertake a synthetic fuels project in the far West. A full-blown environmental impact statement on the project concludes that, in exchange for 10,000 gallons of gasoline per day, the Colorado River would be converted into a stinking sewer, with waters unfit for human use. The impact statement further concludes that, for an expenditure of $100,000, harm to the river could be avoided. On the basis of this impact statement, DOE declares that it has fully "considered" the matter and has chosen to go ahead with the project as originally conceived. Can a reviewing court do anything under NEPA to halt or modify the project? Why or why not?

## BALTIMORE GAS & ELECTRIC CO. v. NATURAL RESOURCES DEFENSE COUNCIL

### 462 U.S. 87 (1983)

JUSTICE O'CONNOR delivered the opinion of the Court.

Section 102(2)(C) of * * * NEPA requires federal agencies to consider the environmental impact of any major federal action. As part of its generic rulemaking proceedings to evaluate the environmental effects of the nuclear fuel cycle for nuclear powerplants, the Nuclear Regulatory Commission (Commission) decided that licensing boards should assume, for purposes of NEPA, that the permanent storage of certain nuclear wastes would have no significant environmental impact and thus should not affect the decision whether to license a particular nuclear powerplant. We conclude that the Commission complied with NEPA and that its decision is not arbitrary or capricious within the meaning of Section 10(e) of the Administrative Procedure Act (APA, 5 U.S.C. Section 706).

The environmental impact of operating a light-water nuclear powerplant includes the effect of offsite activities necessary to provide fuel for the plant ("front end" activities), and of offsite activities necessary to dispose of the highly toxic and long-lived nuclear wastes generated by the plant ("back end" activities). The dispute in these cases concerns the Commission's adoption of a series of generic rules to evaluate the environmental effects of a nuclear power plant's fuel cycle. At the heart of each rule is Table S-3, a numerical compilation of the estimated resources used and effluents released by fuel cycle activities supporting a year's operation of a typical light-water reactor. * * *

In *Vermont Yankee Nuclear Power Corp. v. Natural Resources Defense Council, Inc.*, 435 U.S. 519 (1978), this Court unanimously reversed the Court of Appeal's decision that the Commission had used inadequate procedures, finding that the Commission had done all that was required by NEPA and the APA and determining that courts generally lack the authority to impose "hybrid" procedures greater than those contemplated by the governing statutes. We remanded for review of whether the original rule was adequately supported by the administrative record, specifically stating that the court was free to agree or disagree with Judge Tamm's conclusion that the rule pertaining to the "back end" of the fuel cycle was arbitrary and capricious within the meaning of Section 10(e) of the APA * * * .

The controlling statute at issue here is NEPA. NEPA has twin aims. First, it "places upon an agency the obligation to consider every significant aspect of the environmental impact of a proposed action." * * * Second, it ensures that the agency will inform the public that it has indeed considered environmental concerns in its decision-making process. * * * Congress in enacting NEPA, however, did not require agencies to elevate environmental concerns over other appropriate considerations. See *Strycker's Bay Neighborhood Council v. Karlen*, 444 U.S. 223, 227 (1980) (*per curiam*). Rather, it required only that the agency take a "hard look" at the environmental consequences before taking a major action. See *Kleppe v. Sierra Club*, 427 U.S. 390, 410, n. 21 (1976). The role of the courts is simply to ensure that the agency has adequately considered and disclosed the environmental impact of its actions and that its decision is not arbitrary or capricious. See generally *Citizens to Preserve Overton Park, Inc. v. Volpe*, 401 U.S. 402, 415-417 (1971).

In its Table S-3 rule here, the Commission has determined that the probabilities favor the zero-release assumption, because the Nation is likely to develop methods to store the wastes with no leakage to the environment. * * *

It is clear that the Commission, in making this determination, has made the careful consideration and disclosure required by NEPA. The sheer volume of proceedings before the Commission is impressive.

Of far greater importance, the Commission's Statement of Consideration announcing the final Table S–3 rule shows that it has digested this mass of material and disclosed all substantial risks. 44 Fed. Reg. 45367–45369 (1979). * * *

Congress did not enact NEPA, of course, so that an agency would contemplate the environmental impact of an action as an abstract exercise. Rather, Congress intended that the "hard look" be incorporated as part of the agency's process of deciding whether to pursue a particular federal action. It was on this ground that the Court of Appeals faulted the Commission's action, for failing to allow the uncertainties potentially to "tip the balance" in a particular licensing decision. As a general proposition, we can agree with the Court of Appeals' determination that an agency must allow all significant environmental risks to be factored into the decision whether to undertake a proposed action. We think, however, that the Court of Appeals erred in concluding that the Commission had not complied with this standard. * * *

The Court of Appeals recognized that the Commission has discretion to evaluate generically the environmental effects of the fuel cycle and require that these values be "plugged into" individual licensing decisions. The court concluded that the Commission nevertheless violated NEPA by failing to factor the uncertainty surrounding long-term storage into Table S–3 and precluding individual licensing decisionmakers from considering it.

The Commission's decision to affix a zero value to the environmental impact of long-term storage would violate NEPA, however, only if the Commission acted arbitrarily and capriciously in deciding generically that the uncertainty was insufficient to affect any individual licensing decision. * * *

In sum, we think that the zero-release assumption—a policy judgment concerning one line in a conservative Table designed for the limited purpose of individual licensing decisions—is within the bounds of reasoned decisionmaking.

It is not our task to determine what decision we, as Commissioners, would have reached. Our only task is to determine whether the Commission has considered the relevant factors and articulated a rational connection between the facts found and the choice made. * * * Under this standard, we think the Commission's zero-release assumption, within the context of Table S–3 as a whole, was not arbitrary and capricious.

*Notes and Questions*

1.   Recall the observation of Professor William Rodgers, Jr., that "[i]n a series of * * * decisions in the 1970s and '80s, the high court slowly squeezed the life out of" NEPA—a statute "commonly regarded as being the most significant environmental law on the planet." *See* pages 12-13, *supra.* "The cases brought to the Supreme Court were tactically and serially aligned to produce a law that became all process and no substance." *Id.* at 13.

2.   As if the corpse were not already dead, the Supreme Court throttled it once more in a unanimous opinion in *Robertson v. Methow Valley Citizens Council*, 490 U.S. 332 (1989):

> The sweeping policy goals announced in § 101 of NEPA are * * * realized through a set of "action-forcing" procedures * * * . Although these procedures are almost certain to affect the agency's substantive decision, it is now well settled that NEPA itself does not mandate particular results, but simply prescribes the necessary process. *See Strycker's Bay* * * * . If the adverse environmental effects of the proposed action are adequately identified and evaluated, the agency is not constrained by NEPA from deciding that other values outweigh the environmental costs. * * * Other statutes may impose substantive environmental obligations on federal agencies, but NEPA merely prohibits uninformed—rather than unwise—agency action.

*Id.* at 350-51.

3.   Judge Wright concluded in *Calvert Cliffs*, *supra* page 775, that the NEPA scheme would be futile if the statutory requirement—that the impact statement *accompany* proposals through agency review processes—meant no more than physical proximity. Do *Strycker's Bay* and *Robertson* require much more than that? How satisfactory is a regime in which agencies hell-bent on developmental projects need do no more than "consider" the environmental consequences of their actions?

## F.  PROPOSALS FOR LEGISLATION

NEPA requires environmental impact statements not only for "major Federal actions" but also for "proposals for *legislation* * * * significantly affecting the quality of the human environment." NEPA § 102(2)(C) (emphasis added). An early district court decision concluded that this requirement could not be enforced in an action by private parties, because it was designed solely for the benefit of Congress. *See Wingfield v. OMB*, 9 ERC 1961 (D. D.C. 1977). The Supreme Court confronted the "proposals for legislation" language in the following case.

## ANDRUS v. SIERRA CLUB

442 U.S. 347 (1979)

MR. JUSTICE BRENNAN delivered the opinion of the Court.

The question for decision is whether Section 102(2)(C) of the National Environmental Policy Act of 1979 (NEPA) * * * requires federal agencies to prepare environmental impact statements (EISs) to accompany appropriation requests. We hold that it does not. * * *

In 1974 respondents, three organizations with interests in the preservation of the environment, brought suit in Federal District Court for the District of Columbia alleging that Section 102(2)(C) requires federal agencies to prepare environmental impact statements to accompany their appropriation requests. Respondents named as defendants the Secretary of the Interior and the Director of the Office of Management and Budget (OMB), and alleged that proposed curtailments in the budget of the National Wildlife Refuge Systems (NWRS) * * * would "cut back significantly the operations, maintenance, and staffing of units within the System." * * * Respondents alleged that the proposed budget curtailments would significantly affect the quality of the human environment, and hence should have been accompanied by an EIS prepared by both the Fish and Wildlife Service and by the Office of Management and Budget.

The District Court agreed with respondents' contentions. Relying on provisions of the then applicable CEQ guidelines, and on the Department of the Interior's Manual, the District Court held that "appropriation requests are 'proposals for legislation' within the meaning of NEPA," and also that "annual proposals for financing the Refuge System are major federal actions which clearly have a significant effect on the environment." * * *

The District Court granted respondents' motion for summary judgment, and provided declaratory and injunctive relief. It stated that the Department of the Interior and OMB were required "to prepare, consider, and disseminate environmental impact statements on annual proposals for financing the National Wildlife Refuge System * * * .

The Court of Appeals for the District of Columbia Circuit modified the holding of the District Court. The Court of Appeals was apprehensive because "[a] rule requiring preparation of an EIS on the annual budget request for virtually every ongoing program would trivialize NEPA" * * * . Therefore the Court of Appeals concluded that Section 102(2)(C) required the preparation of an EIS only when an appropriation request accompanies a "proposal for taking new action which significantly changes the status quo," or when "the request for budget approval and appropriations is one that ushers in a considered programmatic course following a programmatic review." * * *

Section 102(2)(C) would thus have no application to "a routine request for budget approval and appropriations for continuance and management of an ongoing program." * * * The Court of Appeals held, however, that there was no need for injunctive relief because the Fish and Wildlife Service had completed during the pendency of the appeal a "Programmatic EIS" that adequately evaluated the environmental consequences for the NWRS of various budgetary alternatives. * * * We granted certiorari * * * and we now reverse.

NEPA requires EISs to be included in recommendations or reports on both "proposals for legislation * * * significantly affecting the quality of the human environment" and "proposals for * * * major Federal actions significantly affecting the quality of the human environment." * * * Petitioners argue, however, that the requirements of Section 102(2)(C) have no application to the budget process. The contrary holding of the Court of Appeals rests on two alternative interpretations of Section 102(2)(C). The first is that appropriation requests which are the result of "an agency's painstaking review of an ongoing program" * * * are "proposals for legislation" within the meaning of Section 102(2)(C). The second is that appropriation requests which are the reflection of "new" agency initiatives constituting "major Federal actions" under NEPA, are themselves "proposals for * * * major Federal actions" for purposes of Section 102(2)(C). We hold that neither interpretation is correct.

We note initially that NEPA makes no distinction between "proposals for legislation" that are the result of "painstaking review," and those that are merely "routine." When Congress has thus spoken "in the plainest of words," * * * we will ordinarily decline to fracture the clear language of a statute, even for the purpose of fashioning from the resulting fragments rule that "accords with 'common sense and the public weal." * * * Therefore either all appropriation requests constitute "proposals for legislation," or none does.

There is no direct evidence in the legislative history of NEPA that enlightens whether Congress intended the phrase "proposals for legislation" to include requests for appropriations. At the time of the Court of Appeals' decision, however, CEQ guidelines provided that Section 102(2)(C) applied to "[r]ecommendations or favorable reports relating to legislation including requests for appropriations." 40 CFR Section 1500.5(a)(1) (1977). At that time CEQ's guidelines were advisory in nature, and were for the purpose of assisting federal agencies in complying with NEPA. *Id.* at Section 1500.1(a).

In 1977, however, President Carter, in order to create a single set of uniform, mandatory regulations, ordered CEQ, "after consultation with affected agencies," to "[i]ssue regulations to Federal agencies for the implementation of the procedural provisions" of NEPA. Executive Order No. 11991 * * * . The President ordered the heads of federal agencies to "comply with the regulations issued by the Council * * * ." CEQ has since issued these regulations, 43 Fed. Reg. 55978-56007 (1978), and they reverse CEQ's prior interpretation of Section 101(2)(C). The regulations provide specifically that "[l]egislation includes a bill or legislative proposal to Congress * * * but does *not* include requests for appropriations." 43 Fed. Reg. 56004 (to be codified, at 40 CFR Section 1508.17). (Emphasis supplied.) CEQ explained this reversal by noting that, on the basis of "traditional concepts relating to appropriations and the budget cycle, considerations of timing and confidentiality, and other factors, * * * the Council in its experience found that preparation of EISs is ill-suited to the budget preparation process." *Id.* at 55989.

CEQ's interpretation of NEPA is entitled to substantial deference. * * * The Council was created by NEPA, and charged in that statute with the responsibility "to review and appraise various programs and activities of the Federal Government in the light of the policy set forth in this Act * * * and to make recommendations to the President with respect thereto." [NEPA Section 204(3)]

It is true that in the past we have been somewhat less inclined to defer to "administrative guidelines" when they have "conflicted with earlier pronouncements of the agency." * * * But CEQ's reversal of interpretation occurred during the detailed and comprehensive process, ordered by the President, of transforming advisory guidelines into mandatory regulations applicable to all federal agencies. * * * A mandatory requirement that every federal agency submit EISs with its appropriation requests raises wholly different and more serious issues "of fair and prudent administration," * * * than does nonbinding advice. This is particularly true in light of the Court of Appeal's correct observation that "[a] rule requiring preparation of an EIS on the annual budget request for virtually every ongoing program would trivialize NEPA." * * * The Court of Appeals accurately noted that such an interpretation of NEPA would be a *"reductio ad absurdum* * * * . It would be absurd to require an EIS on every decision on the management of federal land, such as fluctuation in the number of forest fire spotters." * * * Even respondents do not now contend that NEPA should be construed so that all appropriation requests constitute "proposals for legislation." * * *

CEQ's interpretation of the phrase "proposals for legislation" is consistent with the traditional distinction which Congress has drawn between "legislation" and "appropriation." The rules of both Houses "prohibit 'legislation' from being added to an appropriation bill." * * *

The distinction is maintained to assure that program and financial matters are considered independently of one another. This division of labor is intended to enable the Appropriations Committees to concentrate on financial issues and to prevent them from trespassing on substantive legislation.

The Court of Appeal's alternative interpretation of NEPA is that appropriation requests constitute "proposals for * * * major Federal actions." But this interpretation distorts the language of the Act, since appropriation requests do not "propose" federal actions at all; they instead fund actions already proposed. * * *

Even if changes in agency programs occur *because* of budgetary decisions, an EIS at the appropriation stage would only be repetitive. For example, respondents allege in their complaint that OMB required the Fish and Wildlife Service to decrease its appropriation request for the NWRS, and that this decrease would alter the operation of the NWRS in a manner that significantly affect the quality of the human environment. * * * But since the Fish and Wildlife Service could respond to OMB's budgetary curtailments in a variety of ways * * * it is impossible to predict whether or how any particular budget cut will in fact significantly affect the quality of human environment. OMB's determination to cut the Service's Budget is not a programmatic proposal, and therefore requiring OMB to include an EIS in its budgetary cuts would be premature. * * * And since an EIS must be prepared if any of the revisions the Fish and Wildlife Service proposes in its ongoing programs in response to OMB's budget cuts would significantly affect the quality of the human environment, requiring the Fish and Wildlife Service to include an EIS with its revised appropriation request would merely be redundant. Moreover, this redundancy would have the deleterious effect of circumventing and eliminating the careful distinction Congress has maintained between appropriation and legislation. It would flood House and Senate Appropriations Committees with EISs focused on the policy issues raised by underlying authorization legislation, thereby dismantling the "division of labor" so deliberately created by congressional rules.

We conclude therefore, for the reasons given above, that appropriation requests constitute neither "proposals for legislation" nor "proposals for * * * major Federal actions," and that therefore the procedural requirements of Section 102(2)(C) have no application to such requests. The judgment of the Court of Appeals is reversed.

### Notes and Questions

1. The Supreme Court's *Andrus* opinion does not deny—nor could it—that NEPA calls for an impact statement in connection with "proposals for legislation." Can this portion of NEPA be meaningfully enforced? Who may sue? Who may be sued?

2. Suppose a federal agency is required to prepare an impact statement in connection with a bona fide proposal for legislation. Could the agency evade the statute by having a private party—such as the National Manufacturer's Association—propose the legislation? Could a court enjoin the President or a cabinet officer (such as the Secretary of State) from transmitting to Congress a proposal for legislation without an accompanying impact statement? Could a court enjoin Congress from considering such a proposal for legislation? Could a court enjoin a cabinet officer from proposing legislation to the President without an accompanying impact statement? Do your answers to these questions lead you to believe that NEPA's command for impact statements in connection with proposals for legislation may be unenforceable as a practical matter?

3. In *Public Citizen v. Office of the U.S. Trade Representative*, 822 F. Supp. 21 (D. D.C.), *rev'd*, 5 F.3d 549 (D.C. Cir. 1993), *cert. denied*, 510 U.S. 1041 (1994), environmental groups brought an action against the Office of the United States Trade Representative (USTR) for failing to prepare an environmental impact statement on a proposal for legislation that would implement the North American Free Trade Agreement (NAFTA). Plaintiffs

alleged that NAFTA could have a significant impact on the environment, increasing air and water pollution in Canada, the United States, and Mexico. At the time of the lawsuit, the USTR had initialed the final text of NAFTA and the President had signed but not yet submitted it to Congress. Under "fast-track" procedures applicable to the NAFTA approval process, Congress had 90 days following the President's submission of the legislation in which to either adopt or reject NAFTA. District Judge Richey, concluding that "the plain language of the NEPA makes it a foregone conclusion that the [USTR] must prepare an EIS on the NAFTA," ordered the USTR to prepare an EIS "with all deliberate speed." 822 F. Supp. at 29-30. The D.C. Circuit reversed, finding that "NAFTA does not constitute 'final agency action' within the meaning of the APA [Administrative Procedure Act]." 5 F.3d at 551. The plaintiffs had sued too soon, according to the D.C. Circuit, because—notwithstanding the USTR's role in negotiating and finalizing NAFTA—the agreement would have no effect on Public Citizen's members "unless and until the President submits it to Congress." *Id.* Concluding that NAFTA must be left in the "hands of the political branches," the appellate court stated that the "judiciary has no role to play." *Id.* at 553. A perceptive analyst correctly notes the significance of the *Public Citizen* ruling:

> [T]he [D.C. Circuit] summarized its holding that the "'final agency action' challenged in this case is the submission of NAFTA to Congress by the President * * * [and] the President's actions are not 'agency action' and thus cannot be reviewed under the APA." [5 F.3d at 553] * * *
>
> There is no reason to believe that when Congress included the "final agency action" requirement of the APA it intended a procedure that first looked for the final action and then asked whether an agency performed such action. If Congress had intended this, it would be virtually impossible for plaintiffs to challenge agency compliance with statutes because nonagency action is often required to institute the agency's proposal. The circuit court in *Public Citizen* believed that it sufficiently allayed these fears * * * by limiting [its] application to those situations in which the President takes the "final step." [5 F.3d at 552] * * * [T]his distinction based on who submits the final proposal to Congress, an agency or the President, is unfounded in the legislative history of the APA. Nevertheless, according to *Public Citizen*, the former is subject to judicial review while the latter is not. * * *
>
> [A] strict importation of [the APA's finality requirement] into NEPA cases, where there is both agency and presidential action, acts essentially as a judicial repeal of NEPA's EIS requirement on legislative proposals. Without the power of the courts looming over agencies, there is no reason to believe that they will comply with NEPA. Indeed, because Article II grants the President constitutional power to submit legislation to Congress on behalf of the Executive Branch, all executive agencies could avoid the statutorily required EIS by submitting their proposals through the President. This sort of collusion between the administrative agencies and the President usurps legislative power by ignoring the purpose of a congressional statute. * * *
>
> An agency's failure to adhere to NEPA's EIS requirement should constitute a "final agency" action, thus allowing courts jurisdiction under

the APA. Contrary holdings, which extend a strict * * * articulation of "finality" to NEPA cases * * * renders NEPA's EIS requirement for legislative proposals unenforceable and moot. * * *

*Public Citizen* sounds the death knell of NEPA's environmental impact statement requirement on legislative proposals. * * *

Silvia L. Serpe, *Reviewability of Environmental Impact Statements on Legislative Proposals after* Franklin v. Massachusetts, 80 Cornell L. Rev. 413, 445 n.211, 446-47, 414-15, 449 (1995).

# G. NEPA BLUES

## SENATORS, WITNESS DISAGREE ON EFFECT OF NEPA ON STATUTORY ROLE OF AGENCIES

2 [Curr. Dev.] Env. Rep. (BNA) 1354 (1972)

Senators and the chairman of the Administrative Conference of the United States disagreed over whether [NEPA] modifies the statutory role of administrative agencies. In NEPA oversight hearings * * * by the Senate Public Works and Interior Committees, Roger C. Cramton, Chairman of the Administrative Conference, said that NEPA does not alter the promotional mission of line agencies. As an example, he said that the statutory mandates of the Atomic Energy Commission to promote the peaceful use of atomic energy or the Federal High Administration to use the highway trust fund to build highways could not be questioned by the agencies in [a] NEPA review.

Senator Howard H. Baker, Jr. (R-Tenn.), presiding over the hearings said that if Mr. Cramton's testimony were correct, then selection of the lead agency could predetermine the outcome of the NEPA review and make consideration of alternatives under NEPA meaningless. Senator James L. Buckley said that he shared Mr. Baker's puzzlement and that he could not conceive of NEPA having a purpose other than changing the ultimate result of agency determinations.

Mr. Cramton responded that "we were fooling ourselves" to think that the Civil Aeronautics Board would stop promoting local air transportation in favor of railroads. He added that there was virtue in letting the specific statutory authority of the agencies control over the general requirements of NEPA. He added that if Congress tells an agency to promote a certain activity, that agency is acting illegally if it does not promote that activity. He also said that whether or not NEPA authorizes the agencies to examine the basic premises of their statutory mandates, as a practical matter, the agencies will take their basic statutory authority more seriously than NEPA.

Mr. Cramton said that to change priorities, it must be done by Congress and not by the agencies. "In areas such as transportation and energy, where national policy is confused in content and diffused in administration, the President and Congress will need to rethink fundamental questions and examine a broad range of alternatives," he said.

Mr. Baker said that what was at stake was the integrity of the NEPA requirement to consider alternatives.

## JOSEPH L. SAX, THE (UNHAPPY) TRUTH ABOUT NEPA

### 26 Okla. L. Rev. 239, 240, 245, 248 (1973)

Most regulatory laws fail because the people who write and enforce them seem oblivious to the one matter they should most care about— the behavioral realities that govern the institutions sought to be regulated. The field of administrative law, whose domain this is, seems hopelessly out of touch. Ignoring the real forces that drive institutional beasts hither and thither, it blandly sermonizes about how things ought to be. The following excerpt from a recent court decision illustrates my point. We must, the court opined,

> [E]nsure that the administrative process itself will confine and control the exercise of discretion. Courts should require administrative officers to articulate the standards and principles that govern their discretionary decisions in as much detail as possible. * * * [D]ecisions should more often be supported with findings of fact and reasoned opinions. When administrators provide a framework for principled decision-making, the result will * * * enhanc[e] the integrity of the administrative process. * * * [*Environmental Defense Fund v. Ruckelshaus*, 439 F.2d 584, 598 (D.C. Cir. 1971).]

I cannot imagine a more dubious example of wishful thinking. I know of no solid evidence to support the belief that requiring articulation, detailed findings or reasoned opinions enhances the integrity or propriety of the administrative decisions. I think the emphasis on the redemptive quality of procedural reform is about nine parts myth and one part coconut oil. * * *

The [NEPA] statute arose out of a concern that many agencies had been insufficiently sensitive to the environmental costs of their programs; NEPA's obvious, if unstated, assumption was that by requiring the agencies to explore, consider, and publicly describe the adverse environmental effects of their programs, those programs would undergo revision in favor of less environmentally damaging activities.

How, exactly, was this to come about? Neither the statute nor its history makes this clear, but there are a number of likely hypotheses upon which it is fair to assume that the draftsmen of the law operated:

1.  To the extent that agencies had simply not been alerted to environmental problems, NEPA might serve as a sort of road sign warning of dangers ahead.

2.  Insofar as NEPA required a study and report, it would require new, environmentally knowledgeable staff and consultants; per-

sons whose own professional perspectives might help revise traditional agency perspectives.

3. To the extent that NEPA statements would be made public, they would alert other interested persons or agencies who could bring their weight to bear in encouraging agencies to modify their actions.

4. Because NEPA articulates a congressional policy, it may induce the agency to shift its emphasis to accord with perceived new congressional goals.

5. Because the NEPA statement will reveal important data, the force of fact will itself induce modifications in traditional agency patterns of behavior. * * *

[Professor Sax then analyzes NEPA's impact on airport expansion decisions. He asserts that a 1970 study by a distinguished multidisciplinary team at the Kennedy International Airport concluded that various alternatives to airport expansion would provide much more effective (and often cheaper) ways to cope with airport congestion and noise. These alternatives included modified landing fees, consolidated flight schedules, improved air traffic control systems, vertical short take off and landing aircraft, and high speed trains.]

These are just some of the dramatic findings and conclusions of the Kennedy Airport Study. Yet this study has seemingly disappeared from the face of the earth for all one could tell by reading environmental impact statements prepared by American airports. Not only has it seemed not to have the slightest effect on the planning of airport officials, who quite uniformly go forward with recommendations for new runways, but I see no trace of it in the issues that are discussed in the statements. The typical impact statement identifies only three possibilities: build the proposed new runway; build a new airport elsewhere; or adopt what is usually called, "the do-nothing alternative."

If there is an example of a more perfect failure of the idea of the NEPA than the "disappearance" of the Kennedy Airport model environmental impact statement, I would be hard pressed to identify it. * * * Why do airport authorities behave this way; why does the real intent of NEPA seem to have so little effect on them; why has the hope for environmentally innovative thinking about problems like airport expansion been thus far so dismal a failure? * * *

*Professor Sax then identifies several factors leading to failure: (1) airport authorities opt for the solutions over which they have personal control, because they are driven by the need to "do something," and many alternatives are beyond their powers; (2) agencies favor solutions in which the financing is the most certain, and Congress keeps pouring money into runway expansions; (3) interest groups favoring airport expansions are frequently far more powerful than the isolated groups of negatively affected property owners.*

Is the situation hopeless? No. Conduct can be modified as long as we understand the forces that impel it. We must begin by rooting out legal sentimentality and revising our legal structure to reflect behavioral realities. Here are five basic rules of the game as I see them[:]

1. Don't expect hired experts to undermine their employers.

2. Don't expect people to believe legislative declarations of policy. The practical working rule is that what the legislature will fund is what the legislature's policy is.

3. Don't expect agencies to abandon their traditional friends.

4. Expect agencies to back up their subordinates and professional colleagues.

5. Expect agencies to go for the least risky option (where risk means chance of failing to perform their mission).

These rules tell us that it is nearly certain that airport authorities will continue recommending and building new runways as the solution to their noise and congestion problems, whether or not there is a NEPA and whether or not courts require them to file elaborate, multi-volume impact statements.

If we want them to change their behavior, we must give them signals that will register. If, for example, we really want them to choose between new runways and flight consolidation, we must make it as easy for them to effectuate one solution as the other. If we want a choice to be made between investment in engine retrofit and new runways, we must make money as freely available for one purpose as the other.

If we want the interest of people who live near the airports to get as much consideration as the interests of contractors who build airports, we must assure each equivalent degrees of political and economic power. We can make these adjustments, for example, by direct money subsidies, by the grant of enforceable legal rights, or even by extensive public opinion campaigns.

If we want the fullest data to be presented, we must ensure that the data gatherers have no incentives that bind them regularly to any particular client group. Obviously NEPA is now producing exactly the opposite development.

Until we are ready to face these hard realities, we can expect laws like NEPA to produce little except fodder for law review writers and contracts for that newest of growth industries, environmental consulting.

### Notes and Questions

1. Is the foregoing argument by Professor Sax too cynical? NEPA admirers insist that its most effective consequences may be little noticed but subtle (or "soft") improvements. For example, they assert that many federal agency employees care about environmental protection; NEPA provides them with substantial leverage in championing their views. Fans of NEPA also point out that various environmentally sensitive agencies are part of

the NEPA commenting process; their concerns become part of the administrative record of the agency pondering an environmental impact statement and may provide credible ammunition to opponents of the underlying project. These scholars believe that the second and third of the "draftsmen's hypotheses" mocked by Professor Sax, *see* page 818, *supra*, are legitimate.

2. NEPA supporters point out that institutional change takes time:

> One value of NEPA * * * is that it has been the spur for the creation of an institutional infrastructure in every agency, concerned with the environment. The worst Forest Service proposals of today pale compared with the drive for clear cutting and managed forests of the '60s. Every Forest Service, BLM, BuRec, and even DOT office in the country has people whose jobs begin and end with environmental regulation and concerns. For reasons of self preservation, as well as for more altruistic motives, they are concerned with the perpetuation of environmental protection. There is a long way to go, but the EIS process * * * does result in every agency having a cadre of people more or less concerned about the environment, within its walls. That can never be a bad thing. It is a good step in a long range move to a different way of doing business.

E-Mail Message of Professor Constance K. Lundberg (Jul. 28, 1995).

3. Thirteen years after his skewering of NEPA, Professor Sax seems to have expressed a change of heart:

> NEPA, and its requirement of an environmental impact statement open to public view and comment, ventilated the planning processes of federal agencies in a way that had never occurred before. The citizen, once only a nosy intruder, became a legitimate participant. My own recent study of the behavior of federal land management agencies persuades me that legitimating public participation, and demanding openness in planning and decisionmaking, has been indispensable to a permanent and powerful increase in environmental protection, and that the presence of citizen-initiated litigation is a major factor that keeps public agencies from slackening in their resolve to see that environmental laws are enforced. * * *
>
> I now recognize that I underestimated the influence of NEPA's "soft law" elements. * * *

Joseph L. Sax, *Environmental Law: More Than Just a Passing Fad*, 19 U. Mich. J.L. Ref. 797, 803-04 & n.28 (1986).

4. Professor Sax was the driving force behind the Michigan Environmental Protection Act (MEPA), described at page 224, *supra*. Which regime—NEPA or MEPA—offers the greatest hope for influencing the environmentally destructive conduct of agencies and private actors? Which statutory scheme offers the most powerful judicial remedies? Why?

## H. THE FUTURE OF NEPA

Our final reading brings us full circle to the materials in Chapter 2, calling for fundamental change. Think back on all that you have read: the rich and varied, the eloquent and dull, the technical and not so technical materials that you have struggled to master. It is time to ask—not only what is the future of NEPA—but what is the future of environmental law?

## STEPHANIE POLLACK, REIMAGINING NEPA: CHOICES FOR ENVIRONMENTALISTS

9 Harv. Envtl. L. Rev. 359, 359-63, 366-76,
379-85, 387-93, 395, 401, 404-18 (1985)

In the five years since the end of "the environmental decade" of the 1970's, the environmental movement has developed two apparently divergent strategies for shaping future directions. On the one hand, the fear and reality of toxic pollutants has brought environmental problems home to a broad spectrum of people, enhancing opportunities for grassroots organizing. On the other hand, the increasing technical sophistication required for environmental litigation and lobbying has led some environmental groups to reduce outreach efforts in favor of increasing internal expertise.

These conflicting strategies recreate a tension that has always existed in the environmental movement. Environmental degradation can be viewed as a problem solvable by expert, scientific management of natural resources, and simultaneously as an issue requiring ongoing, participatory, value-based debate. This debate between what I will call the "technocratic" and "grassroots" approaches, however, embodies only a limited spectrum of imagination about environmentalism. A third, "deep ecology" perspective criticizes both approaches and treats environmental degradation as a symptom of deeper societal problems, solvable only by massive changes in current values and institutions.

By articulating the assumptions underlying all three visions of environmentalism, I hope to free the current debate from its tendency to oscillate between polar versions of technocratic and grassroots perspectives. Once liberated, environmentalists can more easily debate a broader range of assumptions about the nature of environmentalism and subsequently begin to generate more imaginative answers to the question of how best to address environmental problems. * * *

The conventional debate over the efficacy of NEPA and EISs has become stereotyped and sterile because the protagonists tend to argue from relatively fixed positions, which do no more than replicate the tension between technocratic and grassroots perspectives. By introducing the idea of deep ecology into this debate, I hope to expand the scope of the discussions and clarify all three visions of environmentalism. Rather than trying to resolve the conventional NEPA debate, this article seeks to evaluate the statute and its interpretations more critically.

### WHY WORRY?

In 1980, environmentalists celebrated the tenth anniversary of Earth Day and the signing of NEPA—and mourned the election of Ronald Reagan. In the intervening five years environmentalists have debated the future of the environmental movement. Much of this debate assumes that the movement must, should, or will move in one of two directions: toward increased grassroots participation or toward increased technocratic professionalism.

Grassroots activists note that as a "reborn" environmental movement focuses increasingly on toxics contamination, its emphasis necessarily shifts to "local organizing around local threats," and environmental concern is born in a wider array of people. In the words of * * * David Sive, "[t]he movement is changing as part of a shifting emphasis toward where we live and work, as distinguished from where we vacation." Since the Love Canal disaster, dozens of local environmental groups of sprung up to battle toxics exposure. Legal services lawyer Robin Alexander told the *New York Times* that "[t]here is a tremendous potential for uniting people around the health and safety issue." The future of the environmental movement, according to the grassroots view, lies in tapping that potential.

Ironically, on the same day that the *New York Times* article appeared, the *Boston Globe* reported that, in the words of the Wilderness Society's Patricia Hedge,

> [t]he [environmental] revolution is over. Movements do not go on forever, and we are now entering a new stage of environmental protection. The question is whether the organization will be run by well-paid, skillful professionals or whether we will cling to the bleeding hearts concept. If we continue with the latter, I believe we are doomed.

Other commentators concur. The Sierra Club's Brock Evans, for example, concedes that "[f]rom now on, our movement will need fewer rabble-rousers like me, and more technicians." * * *

The debate between these opposing visions is often couched in language of imminence and necessity. Patricia Hedge's statement is one example; another comes from former EPA Administrator Douglas Costle, who argues that the shift "from the ragged squad of citizens' militia to the disciplined platoons of lawyers, scientists, and civil servants * * * is part of the natural maturing process of any successful public movement."

Both forces see their position's triumph as inevitable because of the changing nature of environmental problems. For grassroots advocates, the driving force is the spread of toxics contamination. For technocrats, there must be "[a]n increased emphasis on technical expertise, especially the language of economics, as the debate shifts from general environmental mandates to questions of 'how' and 'at what cost.'"

This article seeks to dispel the false sense of necessity in the current debate over the future of the environmental movement. Environmentalism will not necessarily become more grassroots or more technocratic—indeed there is no guarantee that it will continue as a movement at all. The direction environmentalism will take in the 1980's and beyond will be the product of conscious choices by environmentalists and others.

For these choices to be made wisely, however, those choosing must rid themselves of any disabling sense of necessity. * * *

This article uses NEPA as an interpretive frame for examining the broader tensions and debates within environmentalism. This statutory frame was chosen to provide environmentalists with a concrete forum in which to make choices for the future. NEPA, like any other element of environmentalism, does not force people to choose either technocratic or grassroots solutions. The development of NEPA doctrine to date does not preclude environmentalists from adapting deep ecology principles to the law or from creating hybrid interpretations based on all three strains of environmentalism. Choices remain to be made. * * *

One purpose of focusing on NEPA, then, is to assess the Act's contribution to the reality or perception that the environmental movement is moving toward professionalism and away from grassroots efforts. Sally Fairfax protested early on that NEPA was a disaster for the environmental movement because it shifted efforts toward analyzing documents. Environmental activist and former environmental bureaucrat Dave Forman has complained about "commenting on dreary Environmental Impact Statements." More important, he warns that as environmentalists become "less part of a cause and more part of a profession," they become indistinguishable from those they are ostensibly fighting. By opening environmentalists' eyes to the broader possibilities embodied in NEPA, this article seeks to allay such fears. * * *

As part of the focusing process, the article singles out three issues and accompanying NEPA doctrines that adequately reflect the most important differences among the [perspectives]. First, NEPA doctrine about the range of alternatives that must be discussed in Environmental Impact Statements illustrates the differing views concerning the nature and significance of environmental problems. Second, doctrinal debates over whether EISs are subject to substantive or only procedural judicial review embody differing notions about the allocation of decisionmaking authority among citizens, agencies, and courts. Finally, questions about the role of science and technology in environmental destruction and management are raised by NEPA's doctrines governing submission and consideration of public comments.

### TECHNOCRATIC ENVIRONMENTALISM

*Plaintiffs refuse to accept the verdict of those best qualified to resolve such matters * * * . Congress has wisely left these technical matters to the technicians.*

J. Sax, Defending the Environment: A Handbook for Citizen Action ix (1970) (quoting a government lawyer seeking dismissal of citizen-initiated lawsuits).

One vision of environmentalism is "technocratic," a word which evokes both a scientific bent and a belief in top-down, hierarchical decisionmaking. Technocratic environmentalists see environmental problems from an anthropocentric point of view, and see those problems as largely the result of economic, market failures that are amenable to technological solutions. They view NEPA as necessary to promote internal reform of administrative agencies—especially improvement of the science they use—without reallocating decisionmaking authority away from the experts with whom it belongs. The Supreme Court and many lower courts subscribe to technocratic environmental thinking and therefore tend to interpret NEPA narrowly and with great deference to agency expertise. * * *

Technocratic environmentalists see themselves as carefully preserving and managing natural resources, in accordance with the needs of humankind, present and future. It is an anthropocentric approach, sometimes traced in origin to the Biblical injunction to "be fruitful and multiply and replenish the earth and subdue it." * * *

In the late nineteenth and early twentieth centuries, technocratic environmentalism was divided into two movements. These movements have been labeled preservation and conservation.

The preservation movement was the political edge of a romantic back-to-nature movement. Its chief spokesperson, naturalist John Muir, advocated "righteous management" and national parks. * * * Although Muir also presaged the deep ecology movement, his preservation movement was quite elitist, backed by newly moneyed aristocrats and based on a vision of nature as an amenity for people—actually certain people—to preserve and enjoy. By 1908, Muir's Sierra Club had been joined by six other national preservation organizations.

The contemporaneous conservation movement took a utilitarian approach to federal land policy. The movement "was basically an elite scientific movement geared toward the efficient use of resources to guarantee sustained economic well-being." The leading proponents of "scientific conservation" were Ivy League-trained scientists such as John Wesley Powell and Gifford Pinchot. These conservationists believed that land and other natural resources should be used wisely to benefit humankind, not preserved untouched indefinitely. * * *

For the technocrat, "environmental problems are perceived as incidental to the normal operations of the technoeconomic system." Environmentalism is a conservative ideology and "a 'safe' issue—unlikely to upset or even challenge the existing political and economic structures within the United States." A clean environment is simply one economic goal to be balanced against other economic goals, such as high employment and business profitability.

William Baxter has summarized the technocrats' view of environmental problems: "To assert that there is a pollution problem or an environmental problem is to assert, at least implicitly, that one or more resources is not being used so as to maximize human satisfaction. * * * [E]nvironmental problems are economic problems. * * *"

Technocrats undertake the difficult task of finding the level of environmental degradation at which the costs of further abatement begin to exceed the benefits. Some environmental commodities, such as wilderness, have no market value and so "shadow" prices must be calculated. Experts also must make decisions lacking full information about the health and other costs of environmental degradation and clean-up.

Despite these difficulties, technocrats believe that "proper application of [the] right technique will in time yield solutions to any problem." In their view, the role of NEPA is narrow: ensuring that agencies conduct proper scientific and economic analysis. * * *

The technocrats' view of the market-oriented nature of environmental problems and the need for experts to solve them is reflected in doctrines governing judicial review of the adequacy of an EIS's discussion of alternatives. Technocratic courts tend to take a narrow, formalist approach to the statutory requirement that agencies consider alternatives to planned actions. The position, taken to an extreme, is that "Congress did not order agencies, explicitly or implicitly, to compare alternatives, to evaluate alternatives according to a cost-benefit scale, or even to choose the best alternative assuming it could be recognized; Congress mandated only that agencies should *consider* alternative solutions."

In reviewing an agency's consideration of alternatives, courts apply a "rule of reason," which requires only that an agency consider all "reasonable" alternatives to a proposed action. * * *

So applied, the "rule of reason" permits agencies to define the range of reasonable alternatives. Agencies can create "threshold tests" that bar some suggested alternatives. In some instances, agencies need only consider those alternatives that achieve the same statutory objective as the proposed action. * * * For example, in preparing an EIS for constructing a freeway, an agency did not have to consider a "no action" alternative because that alternative did not fulfill the goal of building a highway. * * *

According to the technocrats, decisionmaking authority not allocated to legislatures and property owners should rest with experts in agencies, not with citizens. * * *

NEPA addresses many of the concerns of the technocrats regarding the ability of agencies to handle decisionmaking authority. Technocrats view NEPA as an extraordinarily effective administrative reform statute. * * * Technocrats believe that NEPA's EIS requirements have fulfilled their purpose and "stimulated increases in the mobilization of expertise" in many agencies. * * *

Technocratic environmentalists are optimistic about the prospects for solving environmental problems using science and technology. * * *

NEPA has contributed to the creation of a new kind of environmental science and a new class of ecological professionals; it has thus ensured a continuing high quality of science in agency decisionmaking. * * *

For the technocratic environmentalist, NEPA envisions only a narrow role for the public. * * *

Some judicial interpretations of the public comments requirements have accepted the technocratic view that an EIS is primarily an informational document for the benefit of agency decisionmaking, not the public. * * *

For the technocrat, a major problem with the NEPA commenting process is that the general public does not provide meaningful information. Many comments simply express support or opposition. Emotionalism often distorts even these citizen views. One court felt compelled to remind some NEPA litigants that their "emotional environmentalism must be tempered with rational realism."

### GRASSROOTS ENVIRONMENTALISM

*Simply put, the fact is that the citizen does not need a bureaucratic middleman to identify, prosecute, and vindicate his interest in environmental quality. He is perfectly capable of fighting his own battles—if only he is given the tools with which to do the job.*

J. Sax, Defending the Environment at 56.

The grassroots strain of environmentalism substitutes a bottom-up, value-oriented approach for the top-down, expertise orientation of technocratic environmentalism. Grassroots environmentalists see environmental problems as political and value-based, believe that citizens are entitled to share in federal agencies' decisionmaking authority, and worry that science and technology are part of the environmental problem. They view NEPA as an important symbol of the environmental movement and use the Act and the courts to channel public concerns on both science and values into environmental decisionmaking.

The history of the grassroots strain of environmentalism usually begins in the 1960's. An important milestone was the publication in 1962 of Rachel Carson's *Silent Spring*, which alerted people that environmental problems affected their health. In 1969, public concern for the environment was galvanized by a string of ecological disasters: the Santa Barbara oil spill, DDT contamination of salmon in Wisconsin and Minnesota, and a fire on Cleveland's Cuyahoga River. That same year controversies erupted over the Alaska pipeline, a Walt Disney development in Mineral King Valley, and the SST aircraft. These events were swiftly followed by the signing of NEPA on January 1, 1970, and then Earth Day in April, celebrated at 1500 college campuses.

The grassroots environmental movement was only one of the many public responses to rapid social change in the 1960's, along with the antiwar and civil rights movements. Some people undoubtedly turned to environmentalism out of frustration, feeling unable to bring about real change in Vietnam war policies or civil rights.

The spread of such feelings of powerlessness has contributed to the breadth of the grassroots environmental movement. From the beginning of the movement, people felt that anyone could do something about pollution. The imagery of environmentalism in the early 1970's is of housewives and businessmen together barring the ways of bulldozers poised to begin dam or highway construction. * * *

Grassroots environmentalists view environmental problems as social or political, rather than market-oriented, scientific, or technical. As a result they believe that individuals can and should have more control over environmental decisionmaking. Grassroots activists combine their desire to reform the environmental decisionmaking done by agencies with a suspicion that technology is more a cause of environmental problems than a cure. These positions lead grassroots environmentalists to use the NEPA process widely; in court they advocate consideration of broader ranges of alternatives in EISs, substantive judicial review of agencies' final decisions, and more attention to public comments on EISs. * * *

This value-orientation has two implications for grassroots environmentalism. First, people's opinions and values must count in environmental decisionmaking. Second, solutions to environmental problems may require changes in values. Michael McCloskey, then Sierra Club executive director, has pointed out that "[a] revolution is truly needed— in our values, outlook and economic organization. For the crisis of our environment stems from a legacy of economic and technical premises which have been pursued in the absence of ecological knowledge." * * *

Grassroots environmentalists have made NEPA's two alternatives requirements the linchpin of their efforts to force agencies to acknowledge the complex political and social nature of environmental problems. The Act both requires agencies to consider alternatives in EISs and to study, develop, and describe alternatives to proposed actions that do *not* require an EIS. * * *

The EIS process allows grassroots activists to instruct agencies as to which alternatives deserve study. * * *

Grassroots environmentalists are striving to end people's feelings of powerlessness and inability to participate effectively in the decisions that affect their daily lives. Ideally they seek to redistribute power from experts in the public and private sectors to individual citizens, by expanding direct, participatory democracy. In practice part of their strategy must involve use of the courts, which are more open than other societal institutions to claims of right by individuals. Because litigation does not necessarily promote widespread participation and because it shifts power to courts, however, it can only be one part of a grassroots environmental strategy.

Grassroots environmentalists take individual responsibility for improving the environment. They focus on the individual as ultimate decisionmaker as highlighted in NEPA, which notes that "each person has a responsibility to contribute to the preservation and enhancement of the environment." Grassroots environmentalists thus value participatory democracy highly. They believe that *who* makes environmental decisions strongly controls *what* gets decided, and so insist on participating in the decisionmaking process themselves. In fact, grassroots environmentalists assert that "organized grass-roots citizen action is the most effective way to get local environmental problems addressed."

Individual participation is so important to grassroots environmentalists that they seek to extend it into areas where expert decisionmaking has been the accepted norm. * * *

With respect to governmental decisionmaking in particular, grassroots environmentalists do not accept current levels of citizen involvement as sufficient. Direct democracy may be needed rather than representative democracy, especially because the government itself is viewed as part of the environmental problem. * * *

This grassroots mistrust of experts and agencies leads such environmentalists to use NEPA to exert external pressure on agencies. Like the technocrat, the grassroots environmentalist wants to improve the way agencies make decisions, but unlike the technocrat, the grassroots environmentalist believes that this goal can be accomplished only through external pressure, primarily litigation. In the grassroots view, NEPA as a purely internal reform device can never effectively correct the problem of agency ties to concentrated and powerful economic interests in the private sector. Grassroots environmentalists are concerned about such agency capture * * * .

The goal of grassroots activists has been to obtain judicial review of an agency's decision to proceed with a project after preparing an EIS. As one commentator states the ideal standard, "courts should judge the project itself on the basis of that information [amassed] to determine whether the project contravenes the goals and policies of NEPA liberally construed." Grassroots environmentalists fear that a law interpreted to focus only on the procedures followed in compiling EISs will do nothing to change agencies' decisions. * * *

Grassroots environmentalists' efforts to persuade courts to review agency decisions based on information in EISs have occurred in two phases. Many of the early NEPA cases framed the issue as whether NEPA allows "substantive" or only "procedural" review. More recently, litigators have tried to give meaning to the arbitrary and capricious standard of review used by many courts. * * *

Despite all their work to secure judicial review of EISs, grassroots environmentalists recognize that NEPA litigation alone cannot achieve desired substantive changes in agency decisions. Although such litigation can delay projects, and thus give grassroots activists time to organize lobbying or other campaigns, grassroots activists seek more than just delay. As environmental litigators have realized these problems with NEPA, they have shifted their attention to "substantive" laws regulating air and water pollution. Some grassroots lawyers who had aggressively used NEPA to challenge water resource projects gave up when they realized that their suits would neither permanently halt projects nor change agency attitudes. Thus, Tom Cochran has said that "[w]ith respect to NEPA, I must conclude that we have already gained almost all of the public interest victories that are to be gained under that statute." * * *

### DEEP ECOLOGY

*Integrity is wholeness,*
*the greatest beauty is*
*Organic wholeness, the wholeness*
*of life and things, the*
*divine beauty of the*
*universe. Love that,*
*Not man apart from that * * ***

R. Jeffers, *The Answer*, in The Selected Poetry of Robinson Jeffers 594 (1959)

Deep or deconstructionist ecologists treat environmental problems as symptoms of a much deeper problem in the relationship between people and nature. This "deep" perspective leads such environmentalists to question the very premises of modern society and call for major transformations in value and forms of social organization. Although the deep perspective on environmental problems is complex, the ethic of this perspective was summarized by Aldo Leopold in 1949: "A thing is right when it tends to preserve the integrity, stability, and beauty of the biotic community. It is wrong when it tends otherwise." * * *

Perhaps the overall philosophy of the deep ecologists is best summarized by Peter Heinegg's observation that "[e]cology leads to revolution." Deep ecologists espouse a comprehensive world view embodying "a new metaphysics, epistemology, cosmology, and environmental ethics of person/planet." * * *

To the deep ecologist, environmental problems are significant both in themselves and as indicators of fundamental problems underlying all of Western society. Timothy O'Riordan has written that "[e]nvironmentalism challenges certain features of almost every aspect of the so-called western democratic (capitalist) culture—its motives, its aspirations, its institutions, its performance, and some of its achievements." Environmental problems viewed in this manner are so significant yet intractable in the current institutional setting that revolutionary change is needed. California poet Gary Snyder thus believes that "you can't be serious about the environment without being a revolutionary. You have to be willing to restructure society."

The concept of interdependence lies at the heart of the deep ecologists' understanding of environmental problems. Barry Commoner's first law of ecology is that "Everything is Connected to Everything Else." * * *

In this view, a person is simply one * * * part of nature. Deep ecologists reject anthropocentrism, a philosophy holding that things are valuable only insofar as they further human interests. Anthropocentrism dictates a managerial approach to nature, which "ignores the value of other beings within natural ecosystems." As a result, "the public goods of nature increasingly are despoiled for a relative handful of individual consumers at the expense of all human, animal and plant life that once lived, lives now or might live in the future * * * ."

Even if it were legitimate for people to manage nature, the deep ecologists' rejection of anthropocentrism leads to a humility about undertaking such a project. Aldo Leopold realized that implicit in the view of the human as conqueror of the natural community is the assumption "that the conqueror knows, *ex cathedra*, just what makes the community tick, and just what and who is valuable, and what and who is worthless, in community life. It always turns out that he knows neither, and this is why his conquests eventually defeat themselves." Barry Commoner makes a similar point in his third law of ecology—Nature Knows Best—which, he admits, "appears to contradict a deeply held idea about the unique competence of human beings." As another commentator reminds us, "[n]o matter how great our laws, technologies, or armies, we can't make the sun rise every morning nor the rain dance on the goldenback ferns."

For the deep ecologists, one of the most damaging legacies of the anthropocentric view of nature is the institution of private property. * * * Deep ecologists view capitalism and the private ownership of property as among the most important sources of environmental problems and exploitative relationships.

In turn, one of the harmful side effects of capitalism and private property is humankind's resulting acquisitiveness, which is manifested in a desire for unchecked economic growth. * * *

Deep ecologists "question the sacred assumption that economic growth is always an unmixed blessing." Rather than quantity, they would focus on quality: "The quality [of] human existence and human welfare should be measured not only by quantity of products."

Some of these concerns are at times reflected in NEPA doctrine. NEPA formally commits the United States to a policy of environmental harmony. * * *

Commentators have gone far beyond courts in seeing NEPA's deep ecology potential. For example, Daniel Dreyfus and Helen Ingram see the statute as embodying a revolution in values in its acknowledgment that "valuable economic opportunity might in some instances be foregone in order to achieve an environmental goal." * * *

Deep ecologists argue that allocating decisionmaking authority in part involves creating new institutions to absorb and direct that authority. They view existing decisionmaking institutions as merely "compounds of accident, fortuitous circumstance, and the cumulation of triviality, while their primary function is to maintain confidence in the existing social order." Under this view, the current social order becomes historically contingent rather than an empirical necessity. Such environmentalists thus focus on reimagining institutional structures.

The act of reimagining itself reallocates decisionmaking authority, because current institutions do not empower anyone to imagine or effect significant change. * * *

Deep ecologists believe that some power should devolve to the level of the bioregion. A bioregion can be defined as "a part of the earth's surface whose rough boundaries are determined by nature rather than human dictates, distinguishable from other areas by attributes of flora, fauna, water, climate, soils, and land forms, and the human settlements and cultures those attributes have given rise to." Deep ecologists would turn such bioregions into "fully empowered, politically autonomous, economically self-sufficient social units in which bioregional citizens understand, and control, the decisions that affect their lives."

One perceived advantage of a bioregion as a unit of governance is that, by definition, all life within the bioregion is an interdependent community. As one author notes, people have always existed in community—all deep ecology does is extend that community to include soils, waters, plants, and animals. This emphasis on interconnectedness also extends deep ecology beyond traditional environmental concerns, for it highlights that "[e]xploitation of natural resources will not cease till exploitation of human beings ends." * * *

For the deep ecologist, the current conceptions of science and technology are institutions desperately in need of revision. Science is "a cold and insensitive instrument whose work is devoid of or even antagonistic to social and humanistic value." Technology is linked to elitist expertise, central state authority, and anti-democratic institutions. Nothing inherent in either institution, however, suggests that the institutions of science and technology cannot change radically. As E.F. Schumacher has written, "science and engineering produce 'know-how'; but 'know-how' is nothing by itself; it is a means without an end, a mere potentiality, an unfinished sentence." * * *

Economics, one of the technocrats' favorite disciplines, fares little better in the eyes of these environmentalists. For E.F. Schumacher, cost/benefit analysis "constitutes but an elaborate method of moving from preconceived notions to foregoing conclusions." * * *

Deep ecologists also fear that technology is currently substituted for participatory decisionmaking. Thus Andre Gorz warns that decisionmakers often impose important social policies under the pretense that they are only making a technology choice. * * * As Tim Luke writes, "the problem is not in *how* the technological regime functions but rather in *who* controls, manages, and benefits from its operations."

Given who is currently in control, deep ecologists believe there is now "[a] runaway technology, whose only law is profit." * * *

For the deep ecologist, any new version of science and technology must also divorce itself from the anthropocentric approach to nature that currently infects those institutions. As Laurence Tribe argues, the anthropocentric perspective affects the content of values and distorts perception. E.F. Schumacher mocks the person who talks "of a battle with nature, forgetting that, if he won the battle, he would find himself on the losing side."

The deep ecologists' view that technical expertise and values are inseparable changes the meaning of using NEPA to improve the "science" behind agency decisions. The ecologists' version of improved science would integrate expertise and ethics, reason and morality, and would require more participation. Deep ecologists might, for example, have scientists and citizens work together to produce review documents that do not separate technical issues from value questions. Their goal for such a process would be to narrow the gap between scientist and layperson, eventually eliminating "false" expertise.

CLOSING OBSERVATIONS

*After all the juggling with economic figures is done, there is still life to be lived.*

H. Skolimowski, Eco-Philosophy: Designing New Tactics for Living vii (1981). * * *

Despite Aldo Leopold's belief to the contrary, it is hard to know which approach to environmentalism is "right" for any person or in any situation. As one commentator explains, "[e]nvironmentalism does not offer a clear-cut alternative to our present discomforting existence; instead it points out a number of paradoxes and a struggle to find the middle way between equally tempting, but diverging, system states." What environmentalism does offer each of us is a range of choices, each leading to a different future. * * *

Technocratic variants of environmentalism have little to do with people's everyday lives. If environmental groups move toward professionalism, their experts may increasingly disable lay-people from helping solve the environmental problems that more and more people are experiencing every day. * * *

While grassroots and deep ecology both stress the importance of touching everyday lives, they differ as to whose life is being affected, and consequently who should be empowered to make decisions. While the grassroots focus remains firmly on individuals as the decisionmakers, deep ecologists realize that individuals must govern as members of communities that include both humans and non-human nature. The ecologists' focus on the person-in-community creates the hope that "a sense of collective happiness can infuse individual self-interest so that belief in the communal good will overcome a fear of personal sacrifice."

The expression of hope is not unique to deep ecologists: optimism is the hallmark of all forms of environmentalism. Technocrats are optimistic that environmental problems can be solved by experts, grassroots activists are hopeful about people's ability to participate effectively in decisions affecting their daily lives, and deep ecologists optimistically believe that major societal change is possible when people act in community. Environmentalism is not, as has sometimes been said, end-of-the-world naysaying. Environmentalists "are not ecological doomsayers. They beckon us to alternative paths that carry the prospect of hope, not despair; life, not death."

For me, such environmental optimism is justified by my belief in the existence of alternative futures and faith in people's ability to choose intelligently and freely among them. Ecological limitations on our planet do not impose limits on our imagination. Thus, Kenneth Boulding writes

> [w]e know something about the limits to growth. What do we know about the limits to love? The limits to community? The limits to benevolence? * * * The limits to dedication? The limits to freedom? The limits to justice? The answer is very little. We hope that these limits are a long way from where we are now.

Fear does play an important part in arousing environmental concerns in people, but there is nothing inconsistent about an optimism born of fear. For "if we choose to be plagued by big nightmares, we are entitled to offset them with equally big daydreams." * * *

NEPA can play an important role in the struggle for the future of the earth—and for the future of the environmental movement. Environmentalism is and should be many things to many people. Technocratic expertise, grassroots participation, and deep ecological imagining all have a role to play. For those, including myself, who share the deeper concerns of the grassroots environmentalists and deep ecologists, however, the current mix of these elements needs to be altered. No collection of experts and computers can replace the insight, passion, and optimism that people can bring to the fight for our environment. The time has come to rework the discourse of NEPA and environmental law to ensure that environmental beliefs can play a role in people's daily lives and to help them solve their problems as members of a community of people and nature. In giving this direction to environmental optimism, we begin to reimagine environmental law.

# Index

References are to page numbers.

References are to page numbers.

ISBN 0-314-21147-0

9 780314 211477

00006

90000